LEGAL NURSE CONSULTING
PRINCIPLES
and PRACTICE
Second Edition

LEGAL NURSE CONSULTING
PRINCIPLES
and PRACTICE
Second Edition

Edited by

Patricia W. Iyer, MSN, RN, LNCC

Associate Editors:

Marguerite Barbacci, BSN, RN, MPH, RNC, LNCC
Deborah Dlugose, BA, BS, RN, CCRN, CRNA
Betty Joos, MEd, BSN, RN
Barbara J. Levin, BSN, RN, ONC, LNCC
Joan K. Magnusson, BSN, RN, LNCC
Ann M. Peterson, EdD, MSN, RN, CS, LNCC
Nancy Wilson-Soga, BS, MS, RN
Mona Yudkoff, BSN, MA, RN, MPH, CRRN, CCM, CLCP

 **AMERICAN ASSOCIATION OF
LEGAL NURSE CONSULTANTS**

CRC PRESS

Boca Raton   London   New York   Washington, D.C.

Library of Congress Cataloging-in-Publication Data

Legal nurse consulting : principles and practice / American Association of Legal Nurse
Consultants ; edited by Patricia W. Iyer.—2nd ed.
    p. cm.
    Includes bibliographical references and index.
    ISBN 0-8493-1418-6 (alk. paper)
    1. Nursing consultants—Legal status, laws, etc.—United States. 2. Nursing—Law and
legislation—United States. I. Iyer, Patricia W. II. American Association of Legal Nurse
Consultants.

KF2915.N8 L35 2002
344.73'0414—dc21   2002073730

This book contains information obtained from authentic and highly regarded sources. Reprinted material is quoted with permission, and sources are indicated. A wide variety of references are listed. Reasonable efforts have been made to publish reliable data and information, but the authors and the publisher cannot assume responsibility for the validity of all materials or for the consequences of their use.

This publication is designed to provide accurate and authoritative information in regard to the subject matter covered. It is sold with the understanding that neither the author nor the publisher is engaged in rendering legal, accounting, or other professional service. If legal advice or other expert assistance is required, the services of a competent professional should be sought.

The views expressed in this publication are strictly those of the authors and do not necessarily represent official positions of the American Association of Legal Nurse Consultants.

Trademark Notice: Product or corporate names may be trademarks or registered trademarks, and are used only for identification and explanation, without intent to infringe.

Visit the CRC Press Web site at www.crcpress.com

No claim to original U.S. Government works
International Standard Book Number 0-8493-1418-6
Library of Congress Card Number 2002073730
Printed in the United States of America   2 3 4 5 6 7 8 9 0
Printed on acid-free paper

Acknowledgments

This edition is the culmination of the efforts of dozens of people. The original authors as well as the new ones who joined the team for this edition deserve tremendous credit for giving up hours of time and sharing expertise to participate in this effort. The time-consuming and often difficult process of writing affected all involved in this text. The enthusiastic contributions of our authors are a credit to our profession.

The reviewers provided us with excellent feedback and helped shape the completed work. We appreciated their timely advice.

The associate editors were my bedrock. All poured their hearts into the project and successfully worked their way through the maze of this project. They readily responded to my requests and offered guidance to help this edition take shape.

The staff of AALNC provided unstinting support to us as we worked through issues and requested updates on information so we could stay on track.

I am grateful to the support staff of my business who assumed the responsibility for helping me ensure that all of the chapters were appropriately formatted for the publisher.

Finally, I am thankful that Julie Brewer Pike, the editor of the first edition, had the courage to take this project on initially. Now that I have been in her shoes, my appreciation of what she experienced has dramatically increased. Building on her solid foundation has made the work of this edition much easier.

Patricia Iyer, MSN, RN, LNCC
Editor

Preface

The first edition of this text in 1998 was a culmination of years of effort to establish standards and define the core curriculum of legal nurse consulting. The first edition guided the development of the certification examination administered by the American Legal Nurse Consultant Certification Board (ALNCCB), leading to the granting of the LNCC credential to experienced legal nurse consultants who have demonstrated a mastery of this practice area. Students in legal nurse consulting curriculums and independent learners eagerly purchased the text. The material presented in the first edition was used as the entry way to this exciting field.

Legal nurse consulting and the American Association of Legal Nurse Consultants have continued to expand since the publication of the first edition of this text. The publication of this second edition represents more than a year of intense effort.

The process began with an analysis of the first edition. The structure was evaluated to identify redundancy of material, determine if the chapters were logically placed into sections, and identify new chapters that were needed to expand the scope of the publication. This analysis resulted in the reorganization of the chapters, elimination of four chapters, and condensing of five chapters into two.

This new edition includes 15 new chapters. Each of these chapters highlights important aspects of legal nurse consulting practice.

- Chapter 7: Entry into Specialty Practice of Legal Nurse Consulting
- Chapter 9: Certification
- Chapter 11: Nursing Theory: Applications to Legal Nurse Consulting
- Chapter 13: Elements of Triage: Effective Case Screening of Medical Malpractice Claims
- Chapter 14: Nursing Home Litigation
- Chapter 15: Principles of Evaluating Personal Injury Cases
- Chapter 16: Common Mechanisms of Injury in Personal Injury Cases
- Chapter 20: ERISA and HMO Litigation
- Chapter 22: The Legal Nurse Consultant as a Case Manager
- Chapter 33: Report Preparation

- Chapter 34: Locating and Working with Expert Witnesses
- Chapter 40: The Role of the Legal Nurse Consultant in Preparation of Technical Demonstrative Evidence
- Chapter 44: Successful Marketing for the Legal Nurse Consultant
- Chapter 45: Growing a Business
- Chapter 46: Business Practices and Ethics

In addition to development of new chapters, each of the other 31 chapters was examined by the original or replacement author for relevance and currency. Changes were made as needed to update examples and content to reflect the current state of legal nurse consulting practice. Chapters were made uniform with the inclusion of objectives and test questions to help the reader focus on key concepts and test understanding of the material. A comprehensive glossary was compiled from terms provided by the authors. Each chapter was reviewed by the editor, associate editors and a peer reviewer, who are all legal nurse consultants. The authors were given helpful suggestions for additions and changes.

Each of the associate editors maintained an active role throughout this project. Responsible for between 4–10 chapters each, they worked with the original or replacement authors, recruited reviewers, ensured that the publisher's formatting guidelines were adhered to and that permissions to reprint material were obtained. Most importantly, they encouraged the authors and helped them accomplish the goal of completing the chapters.

It has been a privilege to have been an associate editor of the first edition and editor of the second edition. I had the enjoyable role of recruiting the talented and dedicated associate editors, reading and editing each chapter, and steering the project to keep it on target. This work represents the collective wisdom of a large group of experienced legal nurse consultants. We are proud to offer it to you.

Patricia Iyer, MSN, RN, LNCC
Editor

About the Editors

Editor

Patricia W. Iyer, MSN, RN, LNCC

Patricia Iyer received her diploma in nursing from Muhlenberg Hospital School of Nursing in Plainfield, New Jersey and her Bachelor of Science in Nursing and a Master of Science in Nursing from the University of Pennsylvania in Philadelphia. She entered the field of legal nurse consulting as a medical surgical expert witness in 1987. In 1989, she established Med League Support Services, Inc., an independent legal nurse consulting practice located in Flemington, New Jersey. Prior to her involvement with this edition, she was an associate editor of the first edition. Her experience as an author and editor began in 1980. She has co-authored or edited 11 textbooks written for nurses or attorneys, including *Medical Legal Aspects of Pain and Suffering* (2003), *Nursing Malpractice*, Second Edition (2001), and *Nursing Home Litigation, Investigation and Case Preparation* (1999), all published by Lawyers and Judges Publishing Company. Ms. Iyer is a frequent lecturer to attorneys, paralegals, nurses, and legal nurse consultants. She has served as president of the Philadelphia chapter of the American Association of Legal Nurse Consultants (AALNC) and on the national board of AALNC in the role of secretary, director-at-large, president-elect, president, and past president, with her term as past president being completed in April 2004.

Associate Editors

Marguerite Barbacci, BSN, RN, MPH, RNC, LNCC

Marguerite Barbacci received a Bachelor of Science in Nursing from The University of Akron and a Master of Public Health from The Johns Hopkins University School of Public Health. Her clinical career has included maternal-infant nursing, in which she is certified. She worked in clinical research for 8 years prior to making the transition to legal nurse consulting. Ms. Barbacci's research focus was infectious diseases, with a specialty in sexually transmitted diseases and AIDS. Ms. Barbacci has been an LNC since 1991. She has worked in-house for both plaintiff and defense firms and as an independent LNC for 2 years, consulting on Medicare fraud, medical malpractice, products liability, and personal injury cases for both plaintiff and defense. For the past 7 years, Ms. Barbacci has been a staff LNC at a legal nurse consulting firm. She has been a member of AALNC since 1991 and was among the first group of LNCs to achieve certification in 1998. She served on the AALNC National Conference Program Committee and the AALNC National Board of Directors as a director-at-large. As a founding member of the Greater Baltimore Area chapter of AALNC, she served in the offices of director-at-large, secretary, and president.

Deborah Dlugose, BA, BS, RN, CCRN, CRNA

Deborah Dlugose is President of Wright Professional Associates, Inc. She blends a quarter century of clinical expertise with her background in communications. She is nationally recognized as a speaker, writer, and editor in nurse anesthesia, critical-care nursing, and legal nurse consultant practice. Ms. Dlugose was an associate editor for the first edition of this text as well. She maintains an active clinical practice in nurse anesthesia along with her commitments to nursing education and literature.

Betty Joos, MEd, BSN, RN

Betty Joos received her Bachelor of Science in Nursing from the Medical College of Virginia and her Master in Education with a minor in nursing from the University of Florida. Her nursing career includes pulmonary and emergency clinical areas as well as a college nursing educator. Her legal nurse consulting career began at a law firm in the late 1980s and continued to independent practice in the early 1990s. In the ensuing years, she maintained her independent practice, consulted with schools and universities in setting up LNC programs, taught legal nurse consulting, and co-authored *Marketing for the Legal Nurse Consultant*. Ms. Joos served on the national board of AALNC in 1991–1992 and was on the editorial board of the AALNC newsletter, *Network*, and the *Journal of Legal Nurse Consulting* from 1991 until 1998. She has served as president of the Atlanta AALNC chapter and remains active with that group. Her current practice focuses on defense of medical malpractice and personal injury cases.

Barbara J. Levin, BSN, RN, ONC, LNCC

Barbara Levin of Hingham, Massachusetts obtained her Bachelor of Science in Nursing from Boston University School of Nursing. Ms. Levin is an independent legal nurse consultant who is currently serving as the AALNC director-at-large and is past president of the Rhode Island chapter of AALNC. She also served as the National Conference Chair in 2000 in Boulder, Colorado. In addition to being an associate editor for this book, she co-authored Chapter 39, "Alternative Dispute Resolution: Settlement, Arbitration, Mediation." Ms. Levin has testified at deposition, trial, and court mediations/arbitrations as an expert witness and fact witness. Currently, she is participating on the Malpractice Tribunals for the state of Massachusetts. Ms. Levin works at Massachusetts General Hospital in the orthopaedic/trauma unit, where she has implemented an in-service teaching program that focuses on clinical diagnosis and treatment. Her clinical expertise includes orthopaedics, trauma, and medical surgical. Her clinical experiences also include medical and cardiac intensive care, telemetry, and spinal cord injury. Speaking engagements have included various organizations such as the National Association of Orthopaedic Nurses, American Association of Legal Nurse Consultants, bar associations, and nursing programs.

Joan K. Magnusson, BSN, RN, LNCC

Joan Magnusson is a nurse consultant with the law firm of McMillen, Reinhart and Voght, P.A., in Orlando, Florida, practicing primarily in the areas of medical malpractice and personal injury for the past 15 years. Joan received her diploma in nursing from Orange Memorial Hospital School of Nursing and her Bachelor of Science in Nursing from Florida Southern College, graduating summa cum laude. Her clinical background includes experience in perioperative nursing, staff development and nursing education, and infection control and epidemiology. She is licensed in Florida as a Health Care Risk Manager. She is on the adjunct faculty of University of Central Florida, Department of Continuing Education. She is a charter member of the AALNC. She served on the national board of directors for 5 years and was the AALNC president in 1995–1996. She is also the founding president of the Greater Orlando chapter and continues to participate in chapter activities. Joan was the primary author of the Standards of Practice and Professional Performance for Legal Nurse Consultants. She served as the first chairperson of the American Legal Nurse Consultant Certification Board (ALNCCB) from 1997 to 2000.

Ann M. Peterson, EdD, MSN, RN, CS, LNCC

Ann Peterson, president of Ann M. Peterson & Associates, received a diploma in nursing from Boston City Hospital School of Nursing, a Bachelor of Arts in Psychology, a Master of Science in Nursing, and a Doctorate in Higher Education Administration. Dr. Peterson is an experienced legal nurse consultant working with both defense and plaintiff attorneys on medical malpractice, nursing negligence, personal injury, and criminal cases. She has a background in health care administration and advanced clinical practice, has held an academic appointment as an assistant professor on the graduate level, and has multiple publications to her credit. She is a current member of AALNC and the past president of the Rhode Island chapter of AALNC. Dr. Peterson has also served on the Massachusetts Nurses Association (MNA) Congress on Nursing Practice and Blue Ribbon Commission on Health Policy and Legislation, and is a panel member of the Massachusetts Medical Malpractice Tribunal.

Nancy Wilson-Soga, BS, MS, RN

Nancy Wilson-Soga has maintained an independent legal nurse consulting practice since 1990. Her specialty focuses in the area of alternative dispute resolution as well as personal injury and mental health issues. She was trained by the New York State Office of Court Administration in conflict resolution and is a mediator both in the private sector and court appointed. She served on the Commission of Quality Care for the state of New York as a Surrogate Decision-Making panel member. Ms. Wilson-Soga is a faculty member at a college and is coordinator of the Legal Nurse Consulting Program. She instructs in the legal studies and psychology departments. Ms. Wilson-Soga received her Bachelor of Science from Cameron University in Oklahoma, majoring in psychology, and her Master of Science in Clinical Counseling from Long Island University, and has been practicing nursing for over 16 years. She is a charter member of the Morristown, New Jersey chapter of the AALNC, holding executive board positions of secretary and director-at-large, and was president for the year 2002. Ms. Wilson-Soga volunteers as a mental health counselor to assist those unable to obtain care due to financial hardships; she also provided assistance in crisis management to rescue/relief workers during the tragedy of September 11, 2001.

Mona Yudkoff, BSN, MA, RN, MPH, CRRN, CCM, CLCP

Mona Yudkoff has been the owner of Mona Yudkoff Rehab Consultants since 1989. The company offers private case management services for catastrophically injured clients and provides life care plans for both plaintiff and defense law firms. She has authored chapters on life care planning in two textbooks and is a frequent lecturer on aspects of life care planning at national professional meetings. Ms. Yudkoff was a founding member of the Philadelphia chapter of AALNC and served as the treasurer and president of that chapter. She has a Bachelor of Science in Nursing from the University of Pennsylvania, a Masters in Public Health from Hebrew University in Jerusalem, and is certified as a rehabilitation nurse (CRRN), case manager (CCM), and life care planner (CLCP). Ms. Yudkoff serves as a consultant at Children's Seashore House, a pediatric rehabilitation hospital, and Bancroft NeuroHealth, a residential facility for persons with brain injuries and developmental delays.

Contributors

Tonia Dandry Aiken, JD, RN
President–Nurse Attorney
Resource Group, Inc.
New Orleans, Louisiana

Julie C. Anderson, JD, MSN, RN
Sheehy, Scrpe and Ware PC
Houston, Texas

Kathleen Woods Araiza, BA, RN
North Bethesda, Maryland

Gretchen Aumman, PhD, BSN, RN
Houston, Texas

Mary T. Baldwin, MRA, BSN, RN, PHN, CCM, CRRN
(deceased)
San Diego, California

Marguerite Barbacci, BSN, RN, MPH, RNC, LNCC
Manns Choice, Pennsylvania

Patricia A. Jenkins-Barnard, RN
Newtown, Pennsylvania

Susan Barnes, MSHCA, MSN, RN
CEO, Legal Nurse Consultant
Sue Barnes Medical Consulting
  Services, Inc.
Phoenix, Arizona

Jane Barone, BS, RN, LNCC
Short Hills, New Jersey

Jenny Beerman, RN, LNCC
Beerman & Associates
Kansas City, Missouri

Adrienne Randle Bond, JD, BA
Hughes, Watters & Askanase, LLP
Houston, Texas

Judith Bragdon, MN, RN
Silver Spring, Maryland

Lorraine E. Buchanan, MSN, RN, CRRN
President, Independent Allied Health
  Consultants, Inc.
Blue Bell, Pennsylvania

Roxanne Bush, MHSA, BSN, BA, RN
R&G Medical Consultants, Inc.
Anthem, Arizona

Elena A. Capella, MPA, RN, LNCC, CPHQ
Catholic Healthcare West
Santa Cruz, California

Doreen Casuto, BSN, RN, MRA, CRRN, CCM, CLCP, F-ABDA
Rehabilitation Care Coordination
San Diego, California

Karen Cepero, MSN, RN, CCRN, CEN, CS
Director, Cardio-Pulmonary Services
Jersey City Medical Center
Jersey City, New Jersey

Tracey Chovanec, BSN, RN
Dushman, Friedman & Franks, PC
Fort Worth, Texas

Jan Smith Clary, BSN, RN, LNCC
Clary Medical Legal Consulting
Greenwell Springs, Louisiana

April Clemens, MSN, RN
Venice, California

Margo Reed Conklin, MSN, RN, LNCC
Conklin Legal Nurse Consulting
Kingstowne, Virginia

Patricia Costantini, MEd, RN, LNCC
Rehabilitation Consultant
Costantini Rehab Incorporated
Pittsburgh, Pennsylvania

Maureen A. Cregan, RN
Reed Smith LLP
Philadelphia, Pennsylvania

Eileen Croke, EdD, MSN, RN, LNCC
Brea, California

Colleen D'Amico, BS, RN
Preferred LiNC LLC
Watertown, Connecticut

Deborah D. D'Andrea, BSN, BA, RN
Medical Legal Consulting Associates
Chicago, Illinois

Cynthia Dangerfield, RN, CPN
Jacksonville, Florida

Doug Davis, BSN, RN, DABFN
Arlington, Texas

Shirley Cantwell Davis, BSN, RN, LNCC
Davis & Associates
Atlanta, Georgia

Nathan Dean, MEd, CRC, CDMS
Vocational Consultants, Inc.
Phoenix, Arizona

Deborah Dlugose, BA, BS, RN, CCRN, CRNA
Wright Professional Associates, PC
Oldsmar, Florida

Kevin Dubose, JD
Hogan Dubose & Townsend
Houston, Texas

Elizabeth Edel, MN, RN
Houston, Texas

Nancy R. Ellington, BS, RN
Medical Review & Analysis, Inc.
Jacksonville, Florida

Lucille Evangelista, BS, RN
Succasunna, New Jersey

Diana Faugno, BSN, RN, CPN, FAAFS
Director, Forensic Health Services
Palomar Pomerado Health
Escondido, California

Janet G. Foster, MSN, RN, CCRN
Adjunct Faculty
College of Nursing, Houston Baptist University
Houston, Texas

Karen Fox, BSN, RN LNCC
Medical Resource Network, Inc.
Portland, Oregon

Gail N. Friend, JD, RN
Friend & Associates, LLP
Houston, Texas

Patricia A. Fyler, BS, RN, CEN
Fyler Associates
Brea, California

Margery Garbin, PhD, RN
President, C-Net
Jersey City, New Jersey

Adella Toepel Getsch, BSN, RN, LNCC
Robins, Kaplan, Miller & Ciresi
Minneapolis, Minnesota

Agnes Grogan, BSN, RN
V/G Associates
Ontario, California

Kathy Gudgell, JD, RN
Healthcare Law Consultants
Lexington, Kentucky

Julianne Hernandez, MPH, BSN, RN
Key Largo, Florida

Jill D. Holmes, MSN, FNP, RNCS
Nurse Practitioner
Senior Biohavioral Health Unit at
  Thornton Hall
La Jolla, California

Patricia W. Iyer, MSN, RN, LNCC
President, Med League Support
  Services, Inc.
Flemington, New Jersey

Rosanna Janes, BSN, RN
Luce, Forward, Hamilton & Scripps, LLP
San Diego, California

Geraldine B. Johnson, BSN, RN, LNCC
Medical Review & Analysis, Inc.
Jacksonville, Florida

Betty Joos, MEd, BSN, RN
Betty Joos RN & Associates
Sautee, Georgia

Patricia Karalow, BA, RN, LNCC
Prescott, Arizona

Betsy Isherwood Katz, BSN, RN, LNCC
Williams & Trine
Boulder, Colorado

Bruce Kehoe, JD
Wilson Kehoe & Winingham
Indianapolis, Indiana

Patricia Ann Steed King, RN
Duluth, Georgia

Arlene King Klepatsky, JD, BSN, BA, RN
Faculty, California State University
Castro Valley, California

Janet Kremser, BS, RN, C-SN, CDON/LTC
Windhorst, Gaudry, Ranson & Higgins
Gretna, Louisiana

Jo Anne Kuc, BSN, RN, LNCC
Midwest Medical Legal Resources, Inc.
St. John, Indiana

Mary Lanz, RN, LNCC
Tempe, Arizona

Barbara J. Levin, BSN, RN, ONC, LNCC
Massachusetts General Hospital
  Orthopaedic Trauma Unit
Hingham, Massachusetts

Pamela M. Linville, RN, CCRC, CPBT
President, MedResearch, Inc.
Louisville, Kentucky

Barbara Loecker, MSEd, BSN, RN
Medical Litigation Resources
Olathe, Kansas

Melanie Eve Longenhagen, MBA, MSN, RN, CCM
Southampton, Pennsylvania

Mary Lubin, BS, MA, RNC, NHA
Skilled Nursing Facility Consultant
San Leandro, California

Joan K. Magnusson, BSN, RN, LNCC
McMillen, Reinhart and Voght, PA
Orlando, Florida

Susan H. Mahley, BSN, MSN, RNC, C-WHNP
Assistant Professor of Nursing
Research College of Nursing
Kansas City, Missouri

Kathleen Martin, MSN, MPA, CCRN, CS
Director of Nursing
Jersey City Medical Center
Jersey City, New Jersey

Joseph R. McMahon III, JD
Metairie, Louisiana

Thomas B. Méndez, MSN, RN, ANP
Assistant Vice President
Medical Research Consultants
Houston, Texas

Joan E. Miller, MS, RN, CRRN, CCM, LNCC
Owner, Miller Medical Consulting
  Services, Inc.
Phoenix, Arizona

Phyllis ZaiKaner Miller, RN
Robins, Kaplan, Miller & Ciresi
Minneapolis, Minnesota

Renee Miller, MSN, RN
Fayetteville, Georgia

Barbara Noble, BSN, RN
Cantey & Hanger, LLP
Fort Worth, Texas

Regina Noonan, MSN, RN, LNCC
San Diego, California

Rosie Oldham, BS, RN, LNCC
President/CEO, R&G Medical
  Consultants
Peoria, Arizona

Maureen Jane Orr, BS, RN, LNCC, CIRS, CCM
AIG Health Care Management Services,
  Inc.
Plantation, Florida

Melanie Osley, MBA, RN, CPHRM
Bolton, Connecticut

Valerie V. Parisi, RN, CCM, CRRN
President, ValPar Consultants
Doylestown, Pennsylvania

Marva J. Petty, MSN, RN
Vancouver, Washington

Julie B. Pike, MN, RN, LNCC, CPHRM
Risk Management Specialist
Kansas City, Kansas

Patricia L. Pippen, BSN, RN, LNCC, OCN
Dallas, Texas

Jennifer L. Rangel, JD
Locke Liddell and Sapp LLP
Austin, Texas

Patricia Raya, BS, RNC
PAR Enterprises
Princeton, New Jersey

Sherri Reed, BSN, RN, LNCC
Wilson Kehoe & Winingham
Indianapolis, Indiana

Judy Ringholz, BSN, RN
McFall, Sherwood & Sheehy
Houston, Texas

Paula Schenck, BSN, RN
Sidley & Austin
Glen Ellyn, Illinois

Suzanne D. Schutze, MS, RN
Austin, Texas

William J. Scott, Esq.
Jacksonville, Florida

Nancy Wilson-Soga, BS, MS, RN
Warren County Community College
Long Valley, New Jersey

Kathleen Spiegel, MSN, RN
Risk Management Consultant
Medical Inter-Insurance Exchange
 (MIIX)
Pittsburgh, Pennsylvania

Therese A. Steinhardt, MSN, RN
Warren County Department of
 Health
Belvidere, New Jersey

Barbara Stilwell, MSN, RN
Brown & Kelly
Buffalo, New York

Brett Storm, Esq.
(deceased)
Houston, Texas

**Sheila Webster, BSN, RN, C-HROB,
 RNC, LNCC**
Webster Medical Consulting, Inc.
Glen Ellyn, Illinois

Karen L. Wetther, BSN, RN
Medical Legal Resources
Carlsbad, California

Renee Wilson, BSN, MS, RN
Vice President, Medical Research
 Consultants
Houston, Texas

Paula Windler, MS, RN, LNCC
R&G Consultants, Inc.
Chandler, Arizona

**Doreen James Wise, EdD, MSN, RN,
 C-P/MH**
President, Medical Research
 Consultants, Inc.
Houston, Texas

**Mona Yudkoff, BSN, MA, RN, MPH,
 CRRN, CCM, CLCP**
President, Mona Yudkoff Rehab
 Consultants
Bala Cynwyd, Pennsylvania

Elizabeth K. Zorn, BSN, RN
Faraci & Lange
Rochester, New York

Reviewers

Dolores Austin, JD, RN
Medical Legal Consulting
Kingston, Washington

Jeannie Autry, BS, RN, LNCC
LNC Connection, Inc.
Mesquite, Texas

Susan Bernstein, BSN, RN
George Hartz, Lundeen and Fulmer
Longwood, Florida

Nancy Blevins, BSN, RN, LNCC
San Diego, California

Debra Blyth, JD, BA, RN
Everett, Massachusetts

Linda A. Bowers, BSN, RN, LNCC
North Carolina Health and Human
  Services
Division of Facility Services
Asheville, North Carolina

**Susan Brandlin-Marks, BSN, RN,
  LNCC, CPHQ**
Creative Education Unlimited
Los Angeles, California

Rosemarie Braz, BS, RNC, LNCC
Braz and Lovelace
Casper, Wyoming

**Elizabeth Peggy Camp, MPH, RN,
  LNCC**
Beaufort, South Carolina

**Cynthia L. Chalu, MSN, ARNP,
  LNCC**
Independent Nurse Consultant
Clearwater, Florida

Mindy Cohen, MSN, RN
President, Mindy Cohen & Associates
Nursing and Medical/Legal
  Consultation
Villanova, Pennsylvania

**Margo Reed Conklin, MSN, RN,
  LNCC**
Conklin Legal Nurse Consulting
Kingstowne, Virginia

Nancy Cooke, BS, RN
AIGCS
Blue Bell, Pennsylvania

Pamela Curren, BSN, RN, LNCC
Curren Consultants, Inc.
Longwood, Florida

**Shirley Cantwell Davis, BSN, RN,
  LNCC**
Davis & Associates
Atlanta, Georgia

Sondra Fandray, BS, RN, LNCC
Dickie McCamey & Chilcote
Pittsburgh, Pennsylvania

Janet G. Foster, MSN, RN, CCRN
The Woodlands, Texas

Patricia A. Fyler, BS, RN, CEN
Fyler Associates
Brea, California

Sharon Gentile, RN
Gentile & Company, Inc.
Baltimore, Maryland

Susan Glover, RN, AD, LNCC
Kitch, Drutchas, Wagner & Valitut
Detroit, Michigan

Betty Joos, MEd, BSN, RN
Sautee-Nacoochee, Georgia

Jennifer L. Kalapaca, BSN, RN
Medical Analyst
Dickerson, Maryland

**Lynda Kopishke, BSN, MSN, RN,
RNC, LNCC, CCRN, CCM, CLCP**
Newark, Delaware

**Barbara J. Levin, BSN, RN, ONC,
LNCC**
Hingham, Massachusetts

Diane Littlepage, JD, RN
Glen Burnie, Maryland

Linda Love, RN, LNCC
Cypress, Texas

Elaine Noren, BS, RN, LNCC
Warwick, Rhode Island

Margaret A. Oakes, BSN, RN, CPC
Special Claims Investigator
Claims Administration Corporation
Frederick, Maryland

Michael Patton, JD
Buxmont Medical-Legal Consulting
Warrington, Pennsylvania

Julie B. Pike, MS, RN, LNCC, CPHRM
Risk Management Specialist
Kansas City, Kansas

Elizabeth Riggs, PhD, RN, CNM
Lawrenceville, Georgia

Gary B. Schweon, MS, RN
Director Administration & Special
   Projects
Beth Israel Deaconess Medical Center
Boston, Massachusetts

Mary Ann Shea, JD, BS, RN
St. Louis, Missouri

Lorraine Shoaf, RN, LNCC
Shoaf & Associates, Inc.
Salt Lake City, Utah

**Serita Mendelson Stevens, MA, BSN,
RN**
Valley Village, California

**Nadine Neville-Turpin, BSN, RN,
LNCC**
President, Lighthouse Medical-Legal
   Consulting, Inc.
Cumming, Georgia

Claudette Varanko, BS, RN
VG Associates
Westminister, California

Marlene Vermeer, BAN, RN
Office of Marlene R. Vermeer, RN
Irvine, California

Susan V. White, PhD, RN
Florida Hospital Association
Orlando, Florida

Paula Windler, MS, RN, LNCC
R&G Consultants, Inc.
Chandler, Arizona

Contents

SECTION III: LEGAL PRACTICE AREAS

SECTION IV: ROLES OF THE LEGAL NURSE CONSULTANT

SECTION V: RESPONSIBILITIES OF THE LEGAL NURSE CONSULTANT

SECTION VI: THE LEGAL NURSE CONSULTANT AS EXPERT WITNESS

SECTION VII: MEDIATION, SETTLEMENT, AND TRIAL

SECTION VIII: BUSINESS PRINCIPLES

LEGAL THEORY

I

Chapter 1

The Law, Standards of Care, and Liability Issues

Tonia Dandry Aiken, JD, RN

CONTENTS

0-8493-1418-6/03/$0.00+$1.50
© 2003 by AALNC

Objectives

- To discuss the definition of "law"
- To discuss the types of law
- To define the elements of negligence
- To discuss quasi-intentional and intentional torts
- To define "standard of care"
- To discuss sources of standards of care
- To discuss standards of professional performance
- To define the steps in a trial process
- To define common areas of liability in the health care arena
- To discuss the implications of a malpractice claim on a health care provider's license
- To discuss common documents/materials requested and used to pursue or defend claims

Introduction

In today's legal environment, the legal nurse consultant (LNC) must be knowledgeable in many aspects of law, nursing, and medicine, as well as the social influences controlling and affecting patient care, legal claims, and litigation. It is extremely important that the LNC be well read on such topics as managed care, case management, health care administrative concerns and issues, advanced practice issues, and health care policy. These are the legal "hot" buttons that are being "pressed" in today's judicial arena.

Over the centuries, the law has evolved into a quagmire of rules, statutes, regulations, case law, codes, and opinions that, in many instances, will vary from state court to state court, state court to federal court, and jurisdiction to jurisdiction. Laws are used to control and guide people and entities in relationships, unions, and interactions. They are also used to resolve conflicts involving people, corporations, countries, and states. Laws have evolved through the ages and have resulted in major changes in the way people live and work.

Sources of Laws

The word "law" originates from the Anglo-Saxon term "lagu," meaning "that which is fixed." There are several sources of laws that affect individuals, society, and the medical arena. Sources of laws include constitutional law, statutory law, administrative law, and common law.

Constitutional Law

Constitutional law is a compilation of laws, principles, and amendments that are used to govern and guide federal and state governments, corporations, society, and individuals. The constitutional laws and amendments guarantee individuals certain rights, such as the right to privacy, freedom of speech, and equal protection (see Appendix 1.1). The U.S. Constitution grants certain powers to the federal government and agencies. The Constitution is the supreme law of the land and takes precedent over state and local laws. Constitutional law is the highest form of law in the United States. If not addressed in federal law, then the issue is "given" to the state government. In some instances laws are codified at both the state and federal levels for different circumstances.

An example of a federal act that affects health care providers is the Omnibus Budget Reconciliation Act (OBRA). Enacted in 1987, OBRA regulates the manner in which nursing homes deliver care, monitor quality of care, supply staff, train assistants, and protect the patient's rights. See Chapter 14, Nursing Home Litigation, for more information about OBRA.

Federal and state governments have the constitutional authority to develop and create laws. In addition to creating laws, they also have the ability to enforce the laws that have been established.

Statutory Law

Statutory laws are laws enacted by federal, state, and local legislative bodies. Many health care providers, special interest groups, legal groups, and attorneys are involved in lobbying for certain bills or amendments to pass, promote, or protect their specific interests. An example of statutory law in many states is the law outlining the statute of limitations for filing a medical malpractice, wrongful death, or personal injury claim. Other statutory laws relate to the reporting of elder and child abuse and communicable diseases.

Administrative Law

Administrative laws originate from administrative agencies that are under the arm of the executive branch of the government. For example, state boards of nursing are state administrative agencies. These agencies promulgate rules and regulations to guide nursing practice in the state and to enforce the nurse practice acts. Such nursing board regulations are considered administrative laws that are legally binding. The state boards for health care professionals conduct investigations and hearings to ensure enforcement of the practice acts. Health care professionals can have their licenses limited, revoked, suspended, or probated. They can also receive formal or informal reprimands and fines if it is determined that they have violated the practice act.

The following are examples of violations that can affect a health care provider's license. Check the specific practice act for the acts considered violations in a particular profession or locality.

1. Practicing while using a license or diploma illegally obtained, illegally signed, or unlawfully issued
2. Practicing when the license has been revoked or suspended
3. Aiding or abetting a felon
4. Practicing when the license has lapsed due to failure to renew
5. Misappropriating narcotics
6. Failing to follow the diversionary or recovering health care provider program
7. Failing to exercise appropriate judgment and skills
8. Falsifying documents
9. Aiding unlicensed practice
10. Abusing drugs or alcohol
11. Failing to intervene and follow orders
12. Delegating care improperly
13. Diverting patient medications
14. Failing to disclose prior arrests or criminal convictions
15. Presenting an illegal prescription

It is important for any LNC working on a matter involving nursing practice, medical practice, or the practice of any health care provider to have access to the statutes that regulate that practice.

Another example of administrative law is an attorney general's opinion. The attorney general provides an opinion regarding a specific interpretation of the law that cannot be found in a statute or regulation. The opinion is based on statutory and common law principles.

Common Law

Common law was developed in England on a case-by-case basis when the king decided in his "divine right." Common law is used by all states and the federal courts except for Louisiana. Louisiana is the only state that has adopted the Napoleonic Code, developed from a compilation of French, Spanish, and Roman civil law. The Civil Code is a compilation of rules and regulations authorized by the legislature.

Common law derives from the judiciary branch of government. It is based on judicial decisions. Court cases that are resolved through the judicial process act as a data bank for those seeking information in various types of cases, whether personal injury, medical malpractice, workers' compensation, admiralty, bankruptcy, or domestic issues. Attorneys search for cases similar to the ones that they are evaluating, mediating, arbitrating, settling, or trying. The case information provides valuable insight into the value of the case, damages and injuries suffered, experts used, and the "mind-set" of the judge or jury on deciding for or against the plaintiff and awarding damages.

Common law interprets disputed legal issues, statutes, and regulations and is created by the various courts. Research can be done to determine the value of a case and the decisions made regarding various legal issues.

Legal doctrines affecting cases include *res judicata*, *stare decisis*, and *res ipsa loquitur*. For example, the doctrine of *res judicata* ("a thing or matter settled by judgment") prevents the same parties from trying a case based on the same issues.

Intentional Torts

Intentional torts include assault, battery, invasion of privacy, false imprisonment, trespass to land, and intentional infliction of emotional distress. Assault is an intentional act that causes fear or apprehension that a person will be touched in an injurious or offensive manner. Battery is the actual unpermitted touching. Medical battery is the unpermitted touching of a patient associated with the lack of informed consent to perform the procedure or treatments. For example, a surgeon has an informed consent to amputate the right foot because of gangrene but actually amputates the left foot. In such a case, the patient may file a tort claim based on medical negligence along with an intentional tort claim of medical battery for amputation of the wrong foot.

Other intentional torts include the following:

1. Invasion of privacy occurs when a person's privacy right has been violated through public disclosure. Disclosure is such that a reasonable person would object to such an intrusion or disclosure. For example, the use of photographs (taken before and after plastic surgery) for an advertisement, without the patient's consent, is an example of an unauthorized disclosure. An important act that focuses on protection of the patient is the Health Insurance Portability and Accountability Act of 1996 (HIPAA). This act establishes privacy and security standards to protect a patient's health care information. In December 2000, the Department of Health and Human Services issued final regulations governing privacy of this information under HIPAA.[1]
2. False imprisonment is another intentional tort that is defined as the unlawful intentional confinement of a person through physical, chemical, or emotional "restraints" so that the person is conscious of being confined and harmed by it. Areas of health care where there are more likely to be claims include emergency room and psychiatric facilities. Documentation is the key to protection.
3. Trespass to land can be both an intentional tort and a negligent act that occurs when a person refuses to leave a place, places something on the property, or causes another person to enter that property. For example, a visitor absolutely refuses to leave the hospital after visiting hours and is asked to leave by facility personnel.
4. Intentional infliction of emotional distress is the intentional invasion of the patient or person's peace of mind by the defendant's behavior.

Example 1.5: Wal-Mart and one of its loss-prevention investigations were found liable by a Texas jury for intentional infliction of emotional distress. The jury awarded $13 million for malicious prosecution. A 31-year-old mother was arrested on shoplifting charges. Wal-Mart allegedly gave the police a surveillance tape that they claimed they did not receive. The defendant's mailman stated that he had seen her on the day of the alleged shoplifting 200 miles from the store where it took place.[2]

Standards of Care

Law has numerous rules, regulations, and cases that provide guidance to those affected, whether it is in the civil or criminal arena. When professionals are the

The doctrine of *stare decisis* ("to stand by things decided") applies to previously tried cases with similar fact patterns. The doctrine of *res ipsa loquitur* ("the thing speaks for itself") is another doctrine commonly used in operating room cases where "things" have been left in the abdomen or other cavities. The doctrine shifts the burden of proof to the defense, which must disprove the elements of negligence.

Types of Law

The LNC may encounter practice issues involving civil law, criminal law, contract law, and tort law.

Civil Law

Civil law is law that applies to the rights of individuals or entities, whereas criminal law deals with offenses against the general public. With civil law the remedies for a person or entity involve money or compensation, or perhaps "specific performance" may be required of the defendant to make the plaintiff "whole again." If a defendant has breached a contract, the court may order the completion of the work or reimbursement of money.

Criminal Law

Criminal law is created to provide guidance and protection to those injured by offenses against society. The criminal justice system has been created to deter, punish, and rehabilitate persons who perform criminal acts. Criminal conduct can include forgery, burglary, murder, assault, battery, theft, rape, and false imprisonment. A criminal action by an individual is considered a criminal act against society even if it is directed solely at an individual. For example, with a charge of assault and battery, the criminal justice system is designed so that the offense is seen and viewed as an act against society as a whole. In a criminal action, the level of proof required is "beyond a reasonable doubt," which must be 51% or more. In a medical malpractice claim (civil tort law), the proof is met by a "preponderance of the evidence."

Example 1.1: If, for example, a person is practicing medicine without a license, is that considered a civil or criminal offense? (This is a criminal offense because it is viewed as an offense against the general public and society.)

Example 1.2: If the state statute requires that child or elder abuse be reported and a nurse or physician refuses to report the abuse, is this considered a civil or criminal action? (Criminal)

Example 1.3: If a patient receives too much of a medication because the nurse fails to properly administer the correct dose, causing respiratory arrest and brain damage, is this considered a criminal or civil matter? (Civil)

Contract Law

Contract law involves agreements between parties, individuals, and entities. The three requirements for a contract include offer, acceptance, and consideration. A contract can be in oral or written form, depending on the subject matter and the reason for the contract. However, it is advantageous to have a written contract specifically outlining details of the agreement, along with the consideration agreed upon by parties, in case there is a dispute that later arises. Today, health care providers are faced with many opportunities for employee/employer contracts and for other types of contracts with health maintenance organizations, suppliers, and facilities. Litigation evolves around allegations of failure to perform or a breach of contractual duties.

Tort Law

Basics of Tort Law

Tort law is an area of civil law that encompasses negligence, personal injury, and medical malpractice claims. A tort is a wrongful act that is committed by someone or an entity that causes injury to another person or property. Tort law remedies attempt to make someone whole again, usually with compensation in the form of a monetary award. This is in contrast to criminal law, which usually imprisons and fines the defendant. See Chapter 12, Evaluating Professional Negligence Cases, for more information.

Negligence is a failure to act as an ordinary prudent person or "reasonable man" would do under similar circumstances. Four elements of negligence must be proved in order for there to be a viable medical malpractice claim:

1. A duty must be owed to the patient. This duty usually occurs when the health care provider accepts responsibility for the care and treatment of that patient.
2. There is a breach of duty or standard of care by the professional. The standard of care for the specialty and treatment must be determined to see if there has been an act of omission or commission that has caused damage to the patient.
3. Proximate cause or causal connection must be evident between the breach of duty and the harm or damages that have occurred to the patient/plaintiff.
4. Damages or injuries must be suffered by the plaintiff. Damages or injuries can take the form of any of the following, including, but not limited to, loss of love and affection; loss of nurturance; pain and suffering; mental anguish; emotional distress; loss of chance of survival; disfigurement; past, present, and future medical expenses; past, present, and future loss of wages; premature death; and loss of enjoyment of life.

Example 1.4: A jury returned a verdict against defendants for $10,232,523. The plaintiffs filed a medical malpractice action against the hospital and physician to recover for damages allegedly suffered by their daughter, who was severely brain-damaged. Allegations of breaches of the standard included:

1. Failure to adequately treat
2. Discharging a mother from a hospital when she was leaking amniotic fluid prior to delivery

The mother called the physician with complaints of chills, cramping, and diarrhea. She later returned to the hospital in active labor. The infant was born severely distressed, limp, and nonresponsive. The infant was diagnosed with staph aureus sepsis and severe prenatal asphyxia.

Professional negligence is different from ordinary negligence because professionals are held to certain standards of care dictated by the profession. Ordinary negligence is conduct that involves undue risk of harm to someone.[1] For example, a nursing assistant sees water on the floor in the patient's room but fails to clean the floor. The patient falls and breaks a hip, requiring an additional surgery, along with medical expenses.

Examples of professional negligence that resulted because health care providers breached acceptable standards of care include failure to:

1. Detect signs and symptoms of gastrointestinal bleeding, resulting in hemorrhaging and death
2. Timely diagnose and treat cancer, resulting in loss of chance of survival and an untimely death
3. Provide a patient with a safe environment, resulting in the patient's molestation
4. Properly position the patient in surgery, resulting in a paralyzed limb
5. Prescribe the recommended medication, resulting in further patient injury
6. Properly monitor restrained patients, resulting in asphyxia, brain damage, or death
7. Timely perform a cesarean section, resulting in fetal death or brain injury
8. Check properly and administer the correct medication, resulting in death
9. Properly evaluate a limb in a cast, resulting in an infection and osteomyelitis
10. Perform a procedure timely and properly, resulting in a retained foreign body (e.g., lap pad, hemostat, cotton ball, needle)

Quasi-Intentional Torts

A "quasi-intentional" tort is another type of tort that involves speech (oral or written). The claim focuses on protection of an individual's interest in privacy, the person's reputation, and freedom from legal action that is unfounded. In contrast to the malpractice cases based on negligence, quasi-intentional and intentional torts are not based on the negligence theory. These torts are intentional, in that the person or entity is reasonably certain that harm will result from his actions.

For example, defamation (libel—written defamation and slander—oral defamation) is a quasi-intentional tort. It is the false communication of information to a third party that in some way causes harm to the person (e.g., economic loss, loss of esteem/reputation in the community). Truth is a defense in such a claim. Breach of confidentiality is another quasi-intentional tort. Health care providers must be especially cautious in "common areas" where such breaches can occur. For example, a health care provider talks about the HIV results of Patient Smith in the elevator. Smith's neighbor hears this information and "spreads the news" that the patient is HIV-positive. Suit may be brought against the facility and health care provider for breach of confidentiality of the patient's medical condition.

subject of focus of a claim or lawsuit, the LNC must determine the appropriate professional standards of care that apply to the situation.

"Standard of care" is a term used to designate what is accepted as "reasonable" under the circumstances. It is a "measuring scale." In a malpractice claim, LNCs must determine what the standard of care was at the time of the alleged act or omission that caused damage to the plaintiff. The standard of care is that degree of skill, care, and judgment used by an ordinary prudent health care provider under similar circumstances. The standard of care may encompass more than one "reasonable" action in a given situation.

When a plaintiff seeks the advice of an attorney regarding a possible medical or nursing negligence claim, the first documents that must be obtained are the medical records. The attorney or LNC can then review the care and treatment rendered to the patient by examining the records. Routinely, a timeline or chronology of events is done so that it is easier to put things in perspective. Medical records are read "across the board," meaning that the records are read day by day. In other words, all tests, treatments, medications, and care given are put in chronological sequence for each day.

A chronology of events can be based on a minute-by-minute evaluation of the record or day-by-day evaluation, depending on the allegations of the specific acts of medical negligence. If the LNC is dealing with a product liability case or toxic tort, the standards applicable to the specific set of circumstances must be determined to see if breaches occurred. Product liability claims involve cases where medical products such as defective hip implants, medications, breast implants, and birth-control devices have caused damage or injuries to a patient.

Experts

In most jurisdictions, an expert witness in the same field of practice as the defendant is required to testify to what is the standard of care and whether or not the standard was breached. In addition, an expert witness provides the necessary testimony on proximate cause and damages. If the records must be sent to an expert, then the records should be organized in a binder with individual sections noted (e.g., Dr. Smith's record). In the author's opinion, each page should be numbered, if it has not been numbered by the facility. A copy of the complaint or petition for damages should be included, if it has been filed. A table of contents indicating what records are being sent to the expert must be included. A duplicate set should be maintained for the attorney so that the expert can talk to the attorney and refer to pertinent pages, information, or entries.

In the letter to the expert, the attorney or LNC usually requests an objective medical or nursing opinion on whether or not liability exists on the part of the defendant based on the appropriate standards of care. The expert may be asked to provide cites, references, and copies of the appropriate supporting documents for the standards of care. A written report may be required, but the expert should be instructed to call first to discuss his or her findings prior to writing a report. Note that a nursing expert witness should not testify about medical causation.

Example 1.6: In *Flanagan v. Labe*, the Superior Court of Pennsylvania held that a nursing expert was not competent to testify on medical causation. Also, the state law forbade nurses from formulating medical diagnoses. The plaintiff presented a nursing expert to prove that the nurse's failure to treat properly led to the development of progressively worsening subcutaneous emphysema. The court would not allow the nurse expert to testify to a "reasonable degree of medical certainty" regarding causation. The nursing expert, however, testified as to the breaches of the standard by the nurse, who should have provided reasonable nursing care to a patient who had complaints of pain and breathing problems.

Sources for Standards

If the LNC or expert is requested to obtain the standards of care for a case (e.g., skin care for a diabetic patient), numerous sources can be found. For example, the American Nurses Association has standards of care manuals for nurses in all aspects of nursing (e.g., neurosurgical, perioperative, and school nursing; see Appendix 1.2). National professional organizations also have standards of practice pertinent to their areas. See Appendix 1.3 for a list of many of the national nursing specialty organizations.

Statutes and regulations also provide standards for how health care providers practice. For example, in most states, health care providers are required by law to report child and elder abuse. If they are not reported, fines and penalties can be imposed.

Authoritative textbooks are also used as standards. Many times the authors of these textbooks are also retained as experts by the parties. It is presumed that the textbooks have the most current information on the conditions, treatments, and standards in a particular field of medicine or nursing, although some experts say that by the time a textbook is published, the information is outdated.

The state practice acts are also used as standards of care. For example, the act may state that a nurse may not render a diagnosis because this would be considered practicing medicine.

State practice guidelines are also used as standards. Boards determine whether certain treatment, actions, and functions can be performed and delegated.

Facility and unit policies and procedures may also establish standards of care for the health care provider. Many times, health care providers are informed that there are policies and procedures, but fail to take the time to review and understand them. Policies and procedures are commonly used in negligence claims.

In the following case, the actions of the resident were evaluated in comparison to the standard of care as defined by the hospital and the medical literature:

Example 1.7: A resident in internal medicine became a defendant in a lawsuit after he decided to intubate a 22-year-old woman who was combative and refusing oxygen. After being given several medications, she was intubated and then arrested. Ventricular fibrillation was diagnosed and cardiopulmonary resuscitation begun. Although the resident considered this intubation elective, the anesthesiologist considered it an urgent to impending code or emergency intubation. The plaintiffs alleged that the intubation could and should have been delayed in order to preoxygenate the patient and place monitors for assessment or respiratory and cardiac status. The plaintiffs further alleged that the resident had failed to conduct the cardiac arrest resuscitation of the patient in accordance with hospital protocols and standards set by the American Heart Association. The patient suffered severe hypoxia, permanent brain damage, and neurocortical death, and was left in a persistent vegetative state. The case was settled for $1,750,000. Should the two minor children live their expected life terms, the yield from the settlement structure will be $8,566,343.[3]

Policies and procedures are commonly used to establish the standard of care. Examples include the following:

1. Pressure ulcer claims: Policies and procedures maintaining skin integrity of a diabetic patient
2. Heating pad burn claims: Policies and procedures on monitoring and documentation of the skin condition at specific intervals (e.g., to prevent burns) to show that the patient was not monitored properly and in a timely fashion
3. Fall claims: Policies and procedures on fall risk assessments
4. Failure to timely detect cancer claims: Policies and procedures on diagnostic studies to be done when signs or symptoms of cancer are exhibited

In the above examples, the policies and procedures are usually requested by plaintiff's counsel in a Request for Production of Things and Documents. These requests for production of documents and things can be requested by the plaintiff or defendant for items from the other party that pertain to the issues of the lawsuit and that may lead to discoverable information. A subpoena *duces tecum* may also be issued by the court to obtain the necessary documents. It is served on an entity or person who is in control of specific documents and other materials relevant to facts in issue. See Figure 1.1 for a sample subpoena.

Equipment manuals are also used to establish the standard of care. For example, an intravenous infusion set requires a special filter to be used to prevent an air embolism. If the nurse fails to set up the system properly by omitting the filter, a breach has occurred. It is important that the LNC request personnel files to see whether the staff have received instructions and education on equipment that is the focus of the lawsuit, either before or after the malpractice claim has been made. The attorney and LNC must also decide whether there is the possibility of a medical product liability claim against the manufacturer of the equipment. It may be determined that the medical product is defective in design, use, or material.

Job descriptions can also be used as standards of care. For example, an operating room nurse is required to do three counts in a surgical procedure. If the nurse fails to do the required number of counts for whatever reason, a breach may be alleged because the nurse failed to perform the requirements of her job, resulting in injury to the patient (e.g., lap pad left in the abdomen that caused sepsis).

Critical pathways or guidelines are not mandatory. If a critical guideline is treated as a standard of care, then it must be followed.

Administrative code regulations, both state and federal, play an important role in certain health care settings (e.g., home health and nursing homes). Such regulations establish standards to be met.

Court decisions and administrative rulings are also used as standards. Case law may set out certain guidelines and standards involving malpractice, personal injury, contract, and other areas of laws. A review of case law should be done to determine how the courts have decided on such issues. This generally is not a duty for the LNC but usually falls to the attorney or paralegal.

The Joint Commission on Accreditation of Healthcare Organizations (JCAHO) also sets out standards for health care professionals.

CIVIL DISTRICT COURT FOR THE PARISH OF JONES
STATE OF _____

SUBPOENA

No. _____   DIVISION _____   Docket No. _____

BRETT AIKN VS. ALEXES BEAM

TO: _____

    CLERK, CIVIL DISTRICT COURT - Please issue a subpoena to the above party as directed below.

SUBPOENA REQUEST

[   ] **YOU ARE COMMANDED** to appear in the Civil District Court, Parish of Jones, in Division

"_____," 421 Ratcliff Ave., New Algiers, LA 99999, on the _____ day of _____, 2002, at _____o'clock ___.m., to testify the truth according to your knowledge, in a controversy pending herein between the parties above named; and hereof you are not to fail under the penalty of the law. By order of the Court.

DEPOSITION SUBPOENA REQUEST

[   ] **YOU ARE COMMANDED** to appear at the place, date and time specified below to testify at the taking of a deposition in the above case.

PLACE OF DEPOSITION   DATE AND TIME

REQUEST FOR WRIT OF SUBPOENA DUCES TECUM

[   ] **YOU ARE COMMANDED** to produce and permit inspection and copying of the following documents or objects for the _____trial, _____deposition, or _____hearing (state type) _____at the place, date and time specified below (list documents or objects) pursuant to the provisions of article 9999 et seq. of the Code of Civil Procedure.

PLACE   DATE AND TIME

Issued at the request of and fees and costs guaranteed by undersigned.

ATTORNEY _____ Attorney's signature _____

ATTORNEY'S NAME & BAR NO. _____

ADDRESS & _____

TELEPHONE NUMBER _____

File original and two copies with Clerk, fourth copy for Attorney's File

Figure 1.1   Sample Subpoena

RETURN FOR PERSONAL SERVICE	RETURN FOR DOMICILIARY SERVICE
On the _____ day of _____, 2002, served a copy of the within _____ on _____ in person _____	On the _____ day of _____, 2002, served a copy of the within _____ on _____ by leaving same at _____ domiciled or usual place of abode _____ in the hands of a person of suitable age and discretion, residing therein as a member of _____ domiciliary establishment, whose name and other facts connected with his service I learned by interrogating the said _____ _____ being absent from _____ domicile at time of said service.
_____ ENTERED _____ PAPER RETURN _____ SERIAL NO. DEPUTY PARISH	Return same day _____ Deputy Sheriff of Jones Parish _____

Figure 1.1   Sample Subpoena (*Continued*)

Standards of Professional Performance

Standards of professional performance are described in terms of competency, not reasonable care. Technological advancements provide new and better aids and equipment to treat patients. The criteria to measure compliance with the use of such new technology will also change. Criteria to determine the standards of practice are being developed by the specialty areas of medicine and nursing. Standards may be used for different reasons, as evidence for or against a plaintiff or defendant in medical malpractice cases, disciplinary actions, custody matters, workers' compensation claims, commitment proceedings, and personal injury claims.

Liability of Health Care Providers

Liability requires that the party or person responsible for injuries or damages be held accountable. Legal accountability requires that the health care provider be held responsible for the action taken when providing care and treatment to patients. Vicarious liability occurs when the law, in certain limited instances, imposes liability on a principal for the acts or omissions of an agent. Ostensible authority is a doctrine of law whereby a hospital is liable for the negligence of an independent contractor if the patient has a rational basis to believe that the independent contractor is a hospital employee, for example, a physician in the emergency department.

Diagnostic Errors

Allegations of diagnostic errors are common in medical negligence claims. Some of the reasons for errors include physician's expertise, knowledge base, and experience with the medical problems presented. Errors can also arise from inaccuracies in diagnostic studies or the interpretations of the studies, and diseases that have atypical presentations.

LNCs should review the records to determine whether the physicians utilized any of the following strategies in assessing the patient.

1. A careful history is important. Is communicating with the patient difficult because of a language barrier? Other factors to be considered are the patient's mental status, or his inability to understand the physician's questions. A red flag should go up as a potential area for liability if this is a factor.
2. Careful physical exams can demonstrate evidence of the presence or absence of a disease entity or medical condition.
3. Diagnostic tests have limits. The clinical picture may warrant additional testing, even with a previous negative finding: Could the additional testing have discovered that the patient had a subdural hematoma or embolism?
4. Did the physician consider all working diagnoses so that all possible tests and evaluations could be done?

Example 1.8: A 37-year-old mother of two minor children was seen by a physician 19 times between January 1995 and April 1998. She reported seeing blood in her stools. The physician diagnosed her as having a small hemorrhoid. Subsequently the patient reported having rectal pressure, abdominal pain, blood in her stool, and constipation. The physician again diagnosed her as having a hemorrhoid. When seen by a different physician covering the practice, the patient complained again of the same symptoms. She was referred to a gastroenterologist, who performed a colonoscopy, removed polyps, and informed her that they were cancerous. The patient was diagnosed with metastatic colon cancer and died one month after the colonoscopy. The case was settled for $1,800,000.[4]

Treatment Issues

Treatment issues occur in hospitals, long-term care facilities, and home health settings. Treatment issues involve a wide variety of potential breaches. For example, these may involve failure to:

1. Treat in a timely fashion
2. Treat properly
3. Perform the treatment
4. Use equipment properly
5. Treat in a timely way when signs and symptoms of a deteriorating condition are evident

Example 1.9: A 42-year-old diabetic sustained an injury to his right foot. Home care was provided, consisting of wound care, administration of IV antibiotics, and teaching. The plaintiff alleged that the defendant home care agency had failed to treat the foot injury. This resulted in a transmetatarsal amputation of a portion of the plaintiff's right foot. The infection did not get better. The plaintiff claimed that the nurses should have contacted the physician to relay that the patient should have been taking Cipro. The plaintiff's treating podiatrist was seeing him while the defendant home care agency was involved with the plaintiff. The defendant contended that at the time of discharge from the hospital, the amputation was inevitable when the defendant undertook the care of the plaintiff. Prior to trial, the plaintiff settled with the podiatrist for $250,000 policy limits. The jury returned a defense verdict for the home care agency.[5]

Communication Issues

Communication is crucial today because of all the different "players" involved in the care and treatment of the patient. Communication lines must be open between the health care provider and:

1. The patient
2. Other health care providers
3. Social services
4. Administration
5. Risk management
6. The case manager
7. The insurer

With managed care and case management, communication lines must be open and direct. Otherwise, the patient may suffer injuries, and facilities and insurers may be sued and held liable for damages. Common types of communication failure allegations include failure to:

1. Communicate
2. Communicate in a timely fashion
3. Document communication with patient, patient's family, and other health care providers
4. Communicate the appropriate information
5. Act based on the communication received
6. Inform the patient of test results

Example 1.10: In a claim for loss of chance of survival, the plaintiff must establish by a preponderance of the evidence that the patient had a chance for survival (not that he would have survived but for the defendant's negligence) and that the chance was lost due to the defendant's negligence.

The court held that the physician and hospital failed to inform the patient that she had an abnormal chest x-ray even though evidence showed that her lung cancer was untreatable when the x-ray was taken. The plaintiff could have had more time to live a normal life before becoming so ill.[6]

Monitoring

Monitoring a patient involves all levels of health care providers from physicians to nursing assistants. Policies and procedures that set out monitoring responsibilities are important sections in the facility's policy and procedure manuals. Monitoring breaches include failure to:

1. Properly monitor the care, treatment, and condition of the patient
2. Monitor in a timely fashion
3. Report deviations (changes in the patient's status when monitoring) to the appropriate person
4. Document monitoring
5. Use the proper equipment to monitor the patient
6. Properly instruct and teach the patient about monitoring her condition (e.g., sugar level to determine insulin needed)
7. Use the equipment properly when monitoring a patient (e.g., turning off the alarm button on an infusion pump or telemetry monitor)
8. Monitor and check equipment and use of equipment

Example 1.11: In a survival action and wrongful death claim, the parents sued for malpractice when their infant was delivered by cesarean section and suffered asphyxia causing severe brain damage, kidney failure, other complications, and ultimately death. Allegations of breaches of the standard of care included:

1. Inadequate care
2. Administration of Pitocin after a previous test showed fetal distress
3. Delay in performing an emergency cesarean section

The negligence was found to be the cause of the baby's injuries. The award was $3,000,000, but was reduced to $500,000 as imposed by the statutory cap. Special damages of $41,833.73 were awarded.[7]

Supervision

Supervisory issues have always been an area of great interest, whether they involve the physician in an operating room or a clinical instructor with a student. The common areas of potential liability vary. For instance, with unlicensed assistant personnel, there is great concern over the issue of who is actually supervising the patient.

Supervisory liability focuses on the failure to supervise properly and delegate properly. For example, if a supervisor knows that the staff does not possess the knowledge, experience, and expertise to perform a delegated task, but delegates it anyway, legal liability may result if the patient is injured.

Additionally, if the supervisor fails to supervise properly or gives the incorrect instructions, liability may occur. For example, a nurse asks a supervisor to show her how to z-track because she has forgotten. The supervisor uses her forearm, because she is in a hurry, and demonstrates. The nurse enters the patient's room and z-tracks on the forearm, causing severe necrosis and disfigurement. Both the supervisor and nurse may be held liable for their breaches.

Supervisory breaches include failure to:

1. Supervise properly
2. Delegate properly
3. Properly evaluate the health care provider rendering treatment
4. Educate properly and "check off" that the staff has demonstrated the required skills
5. Document that the staff has been oriented, evaluated, and trained
6. Use good judgment

Medication

Medication errors are high on the list of potential areas of legal exposure. Errors can be acts of omission or acts of commission. Breaches involving medication may include such things as failure to:

1. Administer the correct drug
2. Administer medication in a timely fashion
3. Administer the drug properly using the correct route
4. Give the medication to the correct patient
5. Check intravenous sites (e.g., for infiltration or infection)
6. Administer any drug
7. Administer the correct dosage
8. Confirm or clarify a medication order
9. Detect signs and symptoms of drug toxicity
10. Order or request an order for drug levels
11. Recognize adverse reactions and side effects
12. Recognize and check the chart for drug allergies, resulting in administration of the wrong drug and a potentially dangerous reaction
13. Document the injection site
14. Use the proper size needle for the specific drug administered and the required site
15. Use aseptic technique

Example 1.12: A 93-year-old man went to the emergency department for treatment of a bowel blockage. A physician directed one of the nurses to administer 15 mg of Demerol intravenously to the plaintiff. The nurse allegedly programmed the IV pump incorrectly, resulting in delivery of 70 to 90 mg of Demerol. After the patient went into respiratory arrest, he was successfully resuscitated, but suffered extensive hypoxic brain damage, resulting in a diminished IQ, and now requires care 24 hours a day. The jury returned a verdict of $863,180.[8]

Falls

Patient falls are extremely common problems and the reason for numerous lawsuits. Geriatric patients, medical-surgical patients, and pediatric patients are all potential fall victims. Patients with the following conditions are more susceptible to falls than others:

1. Heavily sedated patients
2. Patients with mobility problems
3. Patients with mental conditions (e.g., Alzheimer's, dementia, organic brain syndrome)
4. Patients who wake up to go to the bathroom or get out of bed for some other reason
5. Patients on numerous medications that when combined may cause problems with drowsiness, balance, coherence
6. Patients who have fallen before
7. Noncompliant patients

Sometimes it is difficult to predict which patient will fall. Falls can result in injuries that range from minor bruising to subdural hematomas and death. Documentation of what was found at the time of the fall must be examined by the LNC.

1. Was there an order for side rails?
2. Did the health care providers follow hospital policies and procedures?
3. Was the patient properly managed and treated after the fall? Were there any protocols for monitoring?
4. What injuries did the patient suffer?
5. Did the fall exacerbate a preexisting condition or cause a new injury?
6. Was the policy and procedure with regard to notifying the physician and family followed?
7. Were sitters, bed alarms, or more frequent monitoring warranted?
8. If the patient fell, was an incident report written?
9. What were the conditions of the surroundings (e.g., the floor where the fall took place)?

All of the above should be considered by LNCs when working on a fall claim whether it is for a plaintiff or a defendant. Also, LNCs should talk to the risk manager and interview those involved in the fall if they are working with the defendant. Obtaining an independent medical exam should be considered if the damages claimed are not consistent with documented damages.

Example 1.13: A wheelchair-bound patient claimed to have fallen from his wheelchair while he was a passenger in the defendant's ambulance. He suffered from diabetes, renal failure, peripheral vascular disease, and legal blindness and was being transported from a dialysis center. He contended that the driver made a sharp turn, causing him to fall from his wheelchair and strike his head. He contended that the vehicle was not equipped with a seat belt, and the driver claimed that the patient had refused to wear the belt. The plaintiff sustained a hematoma to the scalp, which resulted in gangrene, and removal of half of his scalp to halt the gangrene spread. The action settled for $825,000.[9]

Restraints

Restraints can cause circulatory damage or nerve damage, brain damage, and death. It is important that the policies and procedures be requested or subpoenaed to determine whether they were followed. For example:

1. Was the patient properly monitored and in a timely way?
2. Was the patient abandoned for a period of time wherein he suffered injuries?
3. Were all the alternatives to restraints used?
4. Were body system checks done (e.g., neurological, respiratory, circulatory)?

Documentation must be evaluated carefully along with an analysis of policies and procedures.

If the health care professional makes an error in judgment, he is not liable for negligence. Two factors must be present for an action to be called an error in judgment:

1. The health care provider's care must have conformed to the current professional standards of care.
2. The health care provider must possess knowledge and skills similar to those of an average member of the profession.

The Lawsuit

Prelitigation Panels for Malpractice Claims

Once a lawsuit is instituted, based on a breach of the standard of care, several steps are involved in the trial process. In some states, a statutory provision requires the plaintiff to go through a prelitigation or medical review panel process. The panel members may consist of health care providers, lawyers, and judges, depending on the state. Documents and materials are submitted to the panel members, who then determine whether malpractice occurred.

Arguments for prelitigation panels include a decreased number of frivolous lawsuits filed. Attorneys can drop cases that the panel has determined have little or no merit. Those opposing the use of prelitigation panels argue that they simply delay the plaintiff from entering the judicial arena and add to the costs of pursuing and defending a case. However, the panel opinion sometimes facilitates settlement.

The Procedural Process

Initiation of a Lawsuit

1. The client interview should be detailed, and all the necessary documents should be requested or obtained at a later date.
2. Review and evaluation of pertinent medical/physician records and other documents can be done in the law firm or by an outside expert.
3. Determine whether any breaches (acts and omissions) have caused damages to the plaintiff by identifying the standards of care.
4. Determine the damages (e.g., lost wages, medical expenses, pain and suffering, loss of chance of survival, disfigurement, loss of society, loss of consortium, loss of love and affection, emotional distress, mental anguish, and diminution of the enjoyment of life).

5. The attorney will file the necessary documents to institute the prelitigation panel process if applicable.
6. The attorney will file the Petition for Damages or Complaint in the appropriate court after the panel process; if there is no prelitigation process, this is the first step in the lawsuit. See Figure 1.2 for a sample complaint.
7. There will be an answer by the defendant, who will allege defenses to the allegations or denials. (If not answered in a timely way, possible entering of a default judgment by the court.)
8. There may be filing of a Motion to Dismiss the matter.
9. There may be possible filing of counterclaims.
10. There may be possible filing of amended and supplemental pleadings by either party (e.g., additional defendant added).[1]

Discovery Stage

Discovery Tools

Discovery tools are used to learn about pertinent facts surrounding the circumstances of the claim. "Tools" include interrogatories, Request for Production of Things and Documents, and admission of facts and depositions. (These tools are described in detail below.) Potential sources of information that will aid the LNC in gathering facts about the case include:

1. Ambulance run reports
2. Emergency department records
3. Emergency department logs
4. Coroner's report
5. Death certificate
6. X-ray department
7. Code logs
8. Switchboard operator's log
9. Nursing supervisor shift reports
10. Laboratory logs
11. Fetal monitor strips
12. EKG strips
13. Telemetry strips
14. Holter monitor strips
15. Patient census sheets
16. Long-distance phone bills to show calls to physicians or patients
17. Employee time cards
18. Medication wastage records
19. Surveys for long-term care facilities (to determine whether cited for deficiencies)
20. Laboratory computer tapes and records
21. Employee personnel files
22. Police report
23. Insurance policies
24. Medical records

STATE OF _____

IN RE: MEDICAL REVIEW PANEL

NUMBER:

MADELINE OURSO, WIFE OF, INDIVIDUALLY AND
ON BEHALF OF THE ESTATE OF FRANCIS OURSO

VERSUS

CITY MEDICAL CENTER, ABC HOSPITAL,
ANDREA ALI, M.D., and KYLE WAYNE, M.D.

COMPLAINT: REQUEST FOR MEDICAL REVIEW PANEL

The complaint of Madeline Ourso, wife of, individually and on behalf of the estate of Francis Ourso, persons of the full age of majority and residents of the Parish of Rabine, State of _____ and proper plaintiff's beneficiary under Louisiana Civil Code Article 2315.1 and 2315.2, with respect represent that:

I. Made defendant herein is City Medical Center, which upon information and belief is duly licensed and authorized to do business as a healthcare facility in the Parish of Rabine, State of _____, and at all material times herein rendered care to the deceased, Francis Ourso.

II. Made defendant herein is ABC Hospital, which upon information and belief is duly licensed and authorized to do business as a healthcare facility in the Parish of Rabine, State of _____, and at all material times herein rendered care to the deceased, Francis Ourso.

III. Made defendant, Andrea Ali, M.D., which upon information and belief is a physician, duly licensed and authorized to and practicing in the State of _____ who rendered care and treatment to Francis Ourso.

IV. Made defendant, Kyle Wayne, M.D., which upon information and belief is a physician, duly licensed and authorized to and practicing in the State of _____ who rendered care and treatment to Francis Ourso.

V. The above defendants are jointly, severally and in solido liable unto Petitioners for damages sustained by Madeline and Francis Ourso.

VI. On or about January 1, 2000, Mr. Ourso sought the services of physicians at the City Medical Center. From January, 2000, until his death on December 17, 2001, he was treated by Dr. Ali and Dr. Wayne. Throughout this time period he had complaints consistent with cancer.

VII. In January of 2001, Mr. Ourso was hospitalized at ABC Hospital for several weeks. Cancer was not diagnosed.

VIII. He was also seen at ABC Hospital numerous times for complaints consistent with cancer, e.g., weight loss, rectal bleeding and anemia.

IX. On or about December 17, 2001, Mr. Ourso expired. The cause of death according to the Death Certificate was 1. Cardiorespiratory arrest due to or as a consequence of 2. Metastatic adenocarcinoma.

Figure 1.2   Sample Complaint

X. City Medical Center and ABC Hospital are liable unto petitioners under the doctrine of respondeat superior for the acts and/or omissions of their agents and/or independent contractors, and/or employees, including but not limited to:

1. Failure to perform the appropriate and timely diagnostic tests to determine the cause of Mr. Ourso's complaints;
2. Failure to properly assess and evaluate patient's serious medical condition;
3. Failure to timely diagnose cancer;
4. Failure to timely treat cancer;
5. Failure to timely refer to an appropriate specialist;
6. Failure to recognize signs and symptoms of cancer; and
7. Any and all other acts of negligence that may be proven at the trial of this matter.

XI. Andrea Ali, M.D., and Kyle Wayne, M.D., are liable unto your petitioners for acts and/or omissions including but not limited to:

1. Failure to perform the appropriate and timely diagnostic tests to determine the cause of Mr. Ourso's complaints;
2. Failure to properly assess and evaluate patient's serious medical condition;
3. Failure to timely diagnose cancer;
4. Failure to timely treat cancer;
5. Failure to timely refer to an appropriate specialist;
6. Failure to recognize signs and symptoms of cancer; and
7. Any and all other acts of negligence that may be proven at the trial of this matter.

XII. As a result of defendants' acts and/or omissions, Mr. Ourso has sustained severe pain and suffering, emotional distress, mental anguish, lost wages, diminution of the enjoyment of life, loss of life expectancy, loss of chance of survival, premature death and any other damages to be proven at the trial of this matter.

XIII. As a result of the acts and/or omissions of defendants, Mrs. Ourso has sustained emotional distress, mental anguish, funeral expenses, medical expenses, loss of consortium and any other damages to be proven at the trial of this matter.

XIV. Petitioners demand damages as are reasonable in the premises in accordance with the law; however, they reserve their right to demand a specific dollar amount and prove a specific dollar amount at the trial of this matter.

XV. Petitioners are entitled to and demand that a Medical Review Panel be convened in this matter to determine the negligence of the defendants herein above named. In the event that defendant is not entitled or is not a participant in the state's Patient's Compensation Fund, then Petitioners request to be notified of that fact so that additional filings may be taken.

XVI. Petitioners allege that Rev. Stat. Ann., et seq. is unconstitutional in whole or in part and that by filing this request for a Medical Review Panel as is required, Petitioners do not concede the validity of the statute.

XVII. Wherefore, Petitioners pray that defendants be served with a copy of this complaint and that a Medical Review Panel be convened in this matter to determine the negligence of the defendants and that after due proceedings that there be a decision that defendants violated applicable standards of care and for all general and equitable relief.

Respectfully submitted,

_____

Alexes E. Nekia
123 Sunvalley Road, Suite 200
New Algiers, LA 70355
(903) 999–9999
(903) 999–9998 (fax)

Figure 1.2   Sample Complaint (*Continued*)

25. Pharmacy bills
26. Physical therapy records/bills
27. Client's uninsured policy (if applicable)
28. Psychiatric records
29. Lost wages information
30. Other bills (e.g., traction units, cervical collars)
31. X-ray diagnostic studies that show injuries (e.g., MRI, CT scan)
32. Toxicology screens (if drugs/alcohol suspected)

Interrogatories

Interrogatories are written questions/requests sent to a party in a suit that are answered under oath and used to "discover" information. For example:

1. Please list all places of employment, position, duties, years employed at the facility, and reasons for leaving.
2. Please list the names and addresses of any parties listed on your witness list who are or were employees of Aken Hospital.
3. Please list any and all exhibits that will be used in the trial of this matter.

See Figure 1.3 for a sample interrogatory request.

Request for Production of Things and Documents

The Request for Production of Things and Documents is another discovery tool used to elicit information from the opposing party. This written tool is used to obtain medical records, hospital policies and procedures, personnel records, and other documents or things that may aid in proving that the standard of care was or was not breached. An example of such a request is: "Please provide any and all documents, materials, policies, procedures, guidelines, and standards used by the nursing staff at James Hospital from 2000–2001 regarding skin care to be administered to diabetic patients."

Admission of Facts

Admission of Facts is a written discovery tool used to streamline information received in a case. For example:

1. Do you admit or deny that Patient Alexes Johnanthony was a patient in your practice?
2. Do you admit or deny that signs and symptoms of gastrointestinal bleeding can be abdominal guarding, hypotension, and/or tachycardia?
3. Do you admit or deny that Ms. Johnanthony had signs and symptoms of a gastrointestinal bleeding?

29TH JUDICIAL DISTRICT COURT FOR THE PARISH OF SUN
STATE OF _____

NO: 501–235   DIVISION "O"

ELIZABETH CHAUVIN, WIFE OF, INDIVIDUALLY AND
ON BEHALF OF THE ESTATE OF JOE CHAUVIN

VERSUS

BRETT MACON, M.D.

FILED: _____   _____
                                                        DEPUTY CLERK

INTERROGATORIES AND
REQUEST FOR PRODUCTION OF DOCUMENTS

TO: BRETT MACON, M.D.
    Through his attorney of record,
    Alexes E. Nekia
    123 Sunvalley Road, Suite 200
    New Orleans, LA 70113
    (903) 999–9999
    (903) 999–9988 (fax)

Petitioner, Elizabeth Chauvin, appearing through her undersigned counsel of record, requests that the defendant answer the following interrogatories, under oath, within fifteen (15) days from the date of service thereof, pursuant to the provisions of Article 1491 of the Louisiana Code of Civil Procedure.

INTERROGATORY NO. 1:

Please list the following information for Dr. Brett Macon:

1) Have you retained an expert to act on your behalf in any matter pertaining to this action? If so, for each expert state:
   a. Name, office address and telephone number.
   b. Occupation and specialty.
   c. Brief description of testimony and/or opinion to be given.

INTERROGATORY NO. 2:

Please list all fact witnesses that you will call at the trial of this matter:

   a. Fact witness's name, address, and telephone number.
   b. Scope of facts to which the witness is expected to testify.

INTERROGATORY NO. 3:

Is there any person who has knowledge or information concerning the case whose name and address are not listed in the preceding interrogatories? If so, for each such person state:

   a. His name, address and telephone number.
   b. The address of the place where he is employed, occupation and job title.
   c. What information or knowledge concerning this case does the person possess?

Figure 1.3   Sample Interrogatories and Request for Production

INTERROGATORY NO. 4:

Please list the following information for Dr. Brett Macon:

1) Were you associated, or in partnership, with any other medical practitioner at the time of the occurrences complained of in this action? If so, state:
   a. The name, address, specialty and qualifications of each person with whom you were associated or in partnership.
   b. The nature of your business relationship to each such person.
   c. The nature of your professional relationship with Smith Medical Center at the time of the alleged incident.
   d. The number of years of experience you have in your specialty.
   e. A description of the services the defendant has been employed to perform.
   f. Whether defendant has ever been a party in any other lawsuit and, if so, the name of the suit, kind of suit involved, the name of the court and the date of filing, as well as the disposition of the suit.

REQUEST FOR PRODUCTION OF DOCUMENTS

REQUEST NO. 1:

Please list the following information regarding Dr. Brett Macon:

   a. A copy of Dr. Macon's resume/curriculum vitae.
   b. Board certificates, specialties and dates received and rectified
   c. Educational background.
   d. Employment history.
   e. Publications and/or medical presentations (title, publisher and date published and/or written).
   f. Any and all agreements, contracts or other documents pertaining to Dr. Macon with Smith Medical Center at the time of the alleged incident.

REQUEST NO. 2:

Have you ever written, or contributed to, any medical or nursing textbook or professional journal? If so, for each state:

   a. Title, publisher and date of publication.

Respectfully submitted,

_____

Alexes E. Nekia
123 Sunvalley Road, Suite 200
New Algiers, LA 70355
(903) 999–9999
(903) 999–9988 (fax)

CERTIFICATE OF SERVICE

I hereby certify that a copy of the foregoing has been forwarded to counsel of record by depositing copy of same in the U.S. mail, postage prepaid and properly addressed, this _____ day of _____, 2002.

Alexes E. Nekia

Figure 1.3 Sample Interrogatories and Request for Production (*Continued*)

Depositions

A deposition is a structured interview in which the person being interviewed (the deponent) is placed under oath and asked questions about issues of the lawsuit. Depositions are held to:

- Discover all available information about the allegations and circumstances surrounding the lawsuit
- Evaluate the demeanor and the credibility of the witness and parties to the lawsuit
- Determine the availability of insurance coverage
- Assist attorneys in assessing the strengths or weaknesses of their cases and their opponents' cases
- Determine the existence of pertinent documents
- Preserve the testimony of a witness who may be unavailable at the time of trial (e.g., the witness may be out of town or may be dead as a result of a failure to timely diagnose cancer)
- Refresh the witness's memory or impeach a witness's credibility during the trial

Depositions require preparation and education. Nurses are deposed for many reasons. For example, a nurse may be a defendant (the person sued), a fact or material witness who may have knowledge about facts surrounding allegations and circumstances in the lawsuit, an expert witness (a person who may be able to prove liability or damages), or a holder of important documents (e.g., an emergency room supervisor who has the emergency room log for patients).

The expert witness, fact witness, or defendant who is being deposed should appear professional, confident, organized, knowledgeable, honest, and credible. The witness should:

- Review the pertinent documents
- Prepare for the deposition
- Have the medical records available at all times
- Refer to the medical records when needed to answer questions
- Tell the truth
- Dress professionally
- Answer the question asked
- Listen to each specific question and ask for clarification if needed
- Ask for a break if tired, confused, aggravated, or upset
- Wait before answering the question to give the attorney the opportunity to make the proper objection
- Reserve the right to read and sign the deposition (Rules may vary from state to state as to what changes and additions can be made in a deposition.)
- Ask to see the documents that opposing counsel is referring to prior to answering the questions
- Speak clearly and slowly and answer verbally
- Listen to the specific objections made by the attorney
- Ask the opposing counsel to break up a compound question
- Ask the opposing counsel for clarification of unclear or complex questions

- Be cautious about hypothetical situations that may not have the exact facts of the case at issue
- Give short and concise answers

A witness must also avoid displaying hostility, anger, sarcasm; volunteering information; or making assumptions.[10] More information on how to answer questions in a deposition is found in Chapter 38.

Trial Process

Once it has been determined that a breach of the standard that caused damages has occurred, or that the party has a basis to sue, then the lawsuit is filed in the appropriate jurisdiction and venue. Most lawsuits proceed in the following order:

1. Prelitigation conferences may be held.
2. Settlements may be proposed.
3. Mediation or arbitration may be done to avoid trial.
4. Trial of lawsuit.
5. Selection of the jury if it is a jury trial; voir dire questioning of potential jurors.
6. Opening statements by plaintiff and defendant.
7. Plaintiff presents his case.
8. Motion for directed verdict against plaintiff.
9. Defendant presents his case.
10. Rebuttal.
11. Closing statements by plaintiff and defendant.
12. Jury instructions.
13. Jury deliberations.
14. Verdict.
15. Appeal (optional).[1]

See Chapters 41 and 42 for more information about preparing for and assisting at trials.

Conclusion

LNCs are in an excellent position to review, evaluate, and analyze potential liability and damage claims. Medical negligence claims, personal injury, workers' compensation, product liability, toxic torts, and automobile cases are all areas of law to which LNCs can apply their skills to assist the attorney in pursuing or defending the claims.

References

1. Aiken, T.D., Ed., *Legal and Ethical Issues in Health Occupations*, W.B. Saunders, Philadelphia, 2001.

  2. *Aquilera-Sanchez v. Wal-Mart Stores, Inc.,* No. 95–61 (Starr Co. Tex. Dist. Ct.); *The National Law Journal,* October 18, 2001; In Touch…with LTLA, October 26, 2001.
  3. Laska, L., Ed., Failure to pre-oxygenate patient, *Medical Malpractice Verdicts, Settlements and Experts,* January 2002, 3.
  4. Laska, L., Ed., Failure to diagnose bowel cancer leads to death, *Medical Malpractice Verdicts, Settlements and Experts,* January 2002, 13.
  5. Laska, L., Ed. Failure to provide adequate home nursing wound care for diabetic patient leads to partial amputation of foot, *Medical Malpractice Verdicts, Settlements and Experts,* January 2002, 20.
  6. *Hebert v. Parker,* 796 So. 2d 19 (La. Ct. App. 2001).
  7. *Conerly v. State of Louisiana,* 690 So. 2d 980 (La. Ct. App. 1997).
  8. Laska, L., Ed. Nurse administers near-lethal dose of Demerol in emergency room, *Medical Malpractice Verdicts, Settlements and Experts,* January 2002, 21.
  9. Laska, L., Ed. Ambulette driver fails to seat belt wheelchair-bound patient, *Medical Malpractice Verdicts, Settlements and Experts,* January 2002, 22.
 10. Aiken, T., Depositions: what you need to know, *Journal of Legal Nurse Consulting,* 6(4), 1995.

Additional Reading

Aiken, T.D., Ed., *Legal, Ethical and Political Issues in Nursing,* F.A. Davis, Philadelphia, 1994; 2nd ed., 2002.
Guido, G., *Legal Issues in Nursing,* 2nd ed., Appleton Lange, Stamford, CT, 1997.
Iyer, P., Ed., *Nursing Malpractice,* 2nd ed., Lawyers and Judges Publishing Company, Tucson, AZ, 2001.
O'Keefe, M., *Nursing Practice and the Law,* F.A. Davis, Philadelphia, 2001.

Test Questions

1. The four elements of negligence include all of the following EXCEPT:
   A. Breach of the standard
   B. Damages
   C. Duty owed
   D. Proximate malpractice

2. Which of the following statements about battery is true?
   A. It is a quasi-irregular tort.
   B. It is unpermitted touching.
   C. It is based on the *stare decisis* theory.
   D. It is only a criminal offense.

3. All of the following are intentional torts, EXCEPT:
   A. Battery
   B. Defamation
   C. Assault
   D. False imprisonment

4. Which of the following statements about the standard of care is true?
   A. It is based on the highest level of care at the time.
   B. It is used only in cases involving malpractice.
   C. It is based on the current standards for when the suit is filed.
   D. It is used to designate what is reasonable under the circumstances.

5. Which of the following statements about the standard of care is true?
   A. It is determined only by the experts.
   B. It includes authoritative texts and consensus opinions.
   C. It includes statutes and policies.
   D. It is found in the medical records.

Answers: 1. D, 2. B, 3. B, 4. D, 5. C

Appendix 1.1
U.S. Constitutional Amendments 1 to 10 and 14

1. Congress shall make no law respecting an establishment of religion, or prohibiting the free exercise thereof; of abridging the freedom of speech, or of the press; or the right of the people peaceably to assemble, and to petition the Government for a redress of grievances.
2. A well-regulated Militia, being necessary to the security of a free State, the right of the people to keep and bear Arms, shall not be infringed.
3. No soldier shall, in time of peace, be quartered in any house, without the consent of the owner, nor in time of war, but in a manner to be prescribed by law.

4. The right of the people to be secure in their persons, houses, papers, and effects, against unreasonable searches and seizures, shall not be violated, and no Warrants shall issue, but upon proper cause, supported by Oath or affirmation, and particularly describing the place to be searched, and the persons or things to be seized.

5. No persons shall be held to answer for a capital, or otherwise infamous crime, unless a presentment or indictment of a Grand Jury, except in cases arising in the land or naval forces, or in the Militia, when in actual service in time of War or public danger, nor shall any persons be subject for the same offense twice put in jeopardy of life or limb, nor shall be compelled in any criminal case to be a witness against himself, nor be deprived of life, liberty, or property, without due process of law; nor shall private property be taken for public use, without just compensation.

6. In all criminal prosecutions, the accused shall enjoy the right to a speedy and public trial by an impartial jury of the State and district wherein the crime shall have been committed, which district shall have been previously ascertained by law, and to be informed of the nature and cause of the accusations; to be confronted with the witnesses against him; to have compulsory process for obtaining witnesses in his favor, and to have the Assistance of counsel for his defense.

7. In Suits at common law, where the value in controversy shall exceed twenty dollars, the right of trial by jury shall be preserved, and no fact tried by a jury, shall be otherwise reexamined in any Court of the U.S. than according to the rules of the common law.

8. Excessive bail shall not be required, nor excessive fines imposed, nor cruel and unusual punishments inflicted.

9. The enumeration in the Constitution, of certain rights, shall not be constructed to deny or disparage others retained by the people.

10. The powers not delegated to the U.S. by the Constitution, nor prohibited by it to the States, are reserved to the States respectively, or to the people.

14. Section I. All persons born or naturalized in the U.S., and subject to the jurisdiction thereof, are citizens of the U.S. and the State wherein they reside. No State shall make or enforce any law that shall abridge the privileges of immunities of citizens of the U.S.; nor shall any State deprive any person of life, liberty, or property, without due process of law; nor deny to any persons within its jurisdiction the equal protection of the laws.

Appendix 1.2
ANA Nursing Standards

Scope and Standards for Nurse Administrators
Scope and Standards of Advanced Practice Registered Nursing
Scope and Standards of College Health Nursing Practice
Scope and Standards of Diabetes Nursing
Scope and Standards of Forensic Nursing Practice
Scope and Standards of Home Health Nursing Practice
Scope and Standards of Nursing Informatics Practice

Scope and Standards of Nursing Practice in Correctional Facilities
Scope and Standards of Parish Nursing Practice
Scope and Standards of Pediatric Oncology Nursing
Scope and Standards of Practice for Nursing Professional Development
Scope and Standards of Professional School Nursing Practice
Scope and Standards of Psychiatric–Mental Health Nursing Practice
Scope and Standards of Public Health Nursing Practice
Standards and Scope of Gerontological Nursing Practice
Standards of Addiction Nursing Practice with Selected Diagnoses and Criteria
Standards of Clinical Nursing Practice (2nd Edition)
Standards of Clinical Practice and Scope of Practice for the Acute Care Nurse
    Practitioner
Statement on the Scope and Standards for the Nurse Who Specializes in Devel-
    opment Disabilities and/or Mental Retardation
Statement on the Scope and Standards of Genetics Clinical Nursing Practice
Statement on the Scope and Standards of Oncology Nursing Practice
Statement on the Scope and Standards of Otorhinolaryngology Clinical Nursing
Statement on the Scope and Standards of Pediatric Clinical Nursing Practice
Statement on the Scope and Standards of Psychiatric–Mental Health

Appendix 1.3
National Nursing Specialty Organizations

Academy of Medical-Surgical Nurses (AMSN)
American Academy of Ambulatory Care Nursing (AAACN)
American Association of Critical-Care Nurses (AACN)
American Association of Diabetes Educators (AADE)
American Association of Legal Nurse Consultants (AALNC)
American Association of Neuroscience Nurses (AANN)
American Association of Nurse Anesthetists (AANA)
American Association of Nurse Life Care Planners (AANLCP)
American Association of Occupational Health Nurses (AAOHN)
American Association of Spinal Cord Injury Nurses (AASCIN)
American College of Nurse-Midwives (ACNM)
American Holistic Nurses Association (AHNA)
American Long-Term Sub-Acute Nurses Association
American Nephrology Nurses Association (ANNA)
American Nursing Informatics
American Organization of Nurse Executives
American Psychiatric Nurses' Association (APNA)
American Radiological Nurses Association
American Society for Long-Term Care Nurses
American Society of Ophthalmic Registered Nurses, Inc. (ASORN)
American Society for Pain Management Nurses
American Society for Peri Anesthesia Nurses
American Society of Plastic and Reconstructive Surgical Nurses, Inc. (ASPRSN)
American Society of Post Anesthesia Nurses (ASPAN)

American Urological Association Allied, Inc. (AUAA)
Association of Nurses in AIDS Care
Association of Operating Room Nurses, Inc. (AORN)
Association of Pediatric Oncology Nurses (APON)
Association of Peri Operative Registered Nurses
Association for Practitioners in Infection Control (APIC)
Association for Professionals in Infection Control and Epidemiology, Inc.
Association of Rehabilitation Nurses (ARN)
Association of Women's Health, Obstetric, and Neonatal Nurses (AWHONN)
Case Management Society of America
Dermatology Nurses' Association (DNA)
Emergency Nurses' Association (ENA)
Endocrine Nurses Society
Home Healthcare Nurses Association
Hospice and Palliative Nurses Association
International Nurses Society on Addictions
International Society of Nurses in Genetics, Inc. (ISONG)
International Transplant Nurses Society
Intravenous Nurses Society, Inc. (INS)
League of Intravenous Therapy Education
National Association of Clinical Nurse Specialists
National Association of Hispanic Nurses
National Association of Neonatal Nurses
National Association of Nurse Massage Therapists (NANMT)
National Association of Nurse Practitioners in Reproductive Health (NANPRH)
National Association of Orthopaedic Nurses
National Association of Pediatric Nurse Associations and Practitioners (NAPNAP)
National Association of School Nurses, Inc. (NASN)
National Black Nurses Association, Inc.
National Council of State Boards of Nursing
National Federation of Licensed Practical Nurses
National Federation for Specialty Nursing Organization
National Flight Nurses Association (NFNA)
National Gerontological Nurses Association
National League for Nursing (NLN)
National Nurses Society on Addictions (NNSA)
National Nursing Staff Development Organization
National Organization for Associate Degree Nursing
National Student Nurses Association
Oncology Nursing Society (ONS)
Sigma Theta Tau International Honor Society of Nursing
Society of Gastroenterology Nurses and Associates, Inc. (SGNA)
Society of Otorhinolaryngology and Head-Neck Nurses, Inc. (SOHN)
Society for Urologic Nurses and Associates
Society for Vascular Nursing
Transcultural Nursing Society
Wound, Ostomy, and Continence Nurses Society

Chapter 2

Access to Medical Records

Kathy Gudgell, JD, RN

CONTENTS

Objectives

At the conclusion of this chapter, the legal nurse consultant will be able to:

- Identify the sources of law governing the content and preservation of medical records
- Explain the reasons for the confidentiality of the medical record
- Discuss the appropriate times for disclosure
- Describe the process for accessing medical/health records, agency records, and other pertinent records
- Delineate the rules of evidence for introducing medical records at trial

Introduction

Legal nurse consultants (LNCs) spend many hours reviewing, analyzing, and preparing medical records for litigation. This task often includes identifying and obtaining records that are missing. In order to know what is missing, LNCs must first know what is supposed to be in the record and why. They must then know whether a record is obtainable and how to obtain it. Lastly, LNCs should be aware of some basic rules of evidence controlling the admissibility of the record in a court of law in order to ensure that the record meets these requirements.

Medical Records

Standards/Regulations Governing the Content of the Medical Record

What the medical record must contain is dictated by federal, state, and local regulations; accrediting organizations; licensing agencies; institutional policy; and the professional standards of the practitioner who enters data in the record. The statutory requirements most often reflect the standards of health information management required by one of the largest accrediting bodies in the United States, the Joint Commission on Accreditation of Healthcare Organizations (JCAHO).[1,2]

Joint Commission on Accreditation of Healthcare Organizations

JCAHO is a private, nonprofit organization that was founded in 1951 in order to provide a minimum level of quality in the medical care setting. The Commission publishes annual manuals for different health care settings, with a fairly universal requirement for all settings that the medical record contain "sufficient information to identify the patient, support the diagnosis, justify the treatment, document the course and results, and promote continuity of care among health care providers."[2]

The hospital record generally consists of two categories of information — administrative data and clinical data. The administrative data contain:

1. An admission/discharge sheet with basic identification information
2. The primary and secondary diagnoses, the final diagnosis, and the major procedures that were performed during the hospital stay

3. Conditions of admission to which the patient has consented in order to receive basic care
4. Consent forms for release of information/special consents for operative procedures

Clinical data include:

1. History and physical (H&P) — A concise summary of past medical problems, familial history, social and personal data, as well as the present illness or chief complaint that led to the hospitalization. This summary, along with the physical exam described below, should be completed within 24 hours of admission and be readily available if the patient undergoes a surgical procedure. The physical examination should include a review of systems (ROS) assessment followed by the physician's impression/conclusions and a plan of care.
2. Physician's order sheets — All orders must be written, dated, and authenticated or confirmed by authors that entries are correct, usually accomplished by the signature of the author. Verbal orders are acceptable only in emergency situations and must be signed and dated by the physician at the earliest possible time. Fax orders and authentication by computer key may be acceptable in some states.
3. Physician progress notes — Notes should be entered daily or with any change in the patient's condition or according to hospital policy.
4. Diagnostic studies/special reports.
5. Surgical reports — Includes preanesthesia and postanesthesia assessment.
6. Discharge summary report — The attending physician should summarize the major events that occurred during the hospitalization along with a discharge plan. The summary should be completed within 30 days of transfer. A transfer note must accompany a patient who is transferred to another facility.
7. Nurses' notes/data — Initial assessment must include an assessment of pain, the identification of possible abuse victims, discharge planning, and an assessment of the patient's nutritional status and functional status. A plan of care must be instituted and reassessment should occur at regular intervals according to hospital policy.
8. Evidence of known advance directives.
9. Medication administration record — Must include every medication ordered, prescribed, and administered. The reason that an ordered medication or dosage is not given should be identified.
10. Consult reports.
11. Records of donation and receipt of transplant or implants.
12. Discharge instructions to the patient or family.
13. Autopsy results.
14. Rehabilitation services documentation.
15. Restraint/seclusion documentation with appropriate justification for use.[2]

According to JCAHO guidelines, the long-term care facility record should contain similar data and documentation as the hospital record: orders, physician notes, nursing data, assessments, reassessments, medication/treatment documentation, and discharge summaries. JCAHO standards also specifically require documentation concerning the provision of certain services. The response of the resident to the activities program and to nutritional services must be documented quarterly. Standards also require documentation concerning the resident's response to rehabilitative and social services treatment. JCAHO prefers that data definitions and methods for collecting data are uniform. The long-term care facility generally satisfies this requirement by implementing a Minimum Data Set (MDS) form that standardizes definitions, codes, classifications, and terms.[3] The JCAHO evaluation of a long-term facility focuses on how the facility improves outcomes by respecting residents' rights, how it maximizes coordination of care within the continuum of care, how it assesses the residents' needs and their response to care, and how it provides care and educates the residents. Other performance areas that long-term care facilities must address are the leader's role in coordinating services, the management of the environment, the management of human resources, and infection control.[3]

Federal

Federal regulations regarding the content of the medical record apply to those institutions participating in federal reimbursement programs. These regulations are issued by the certifying governmental agency, the Centers for Medicare and Medicaid Services (formerly known as the Health Care Financing Administration [HCFA]), and are published in the Code of Federal Regulations (CFR). Generally, the federal requirements coincide with those of JCAHO. They too require that the record include information to justify admission and continued hospitalization, support the diagnosis, and describe the patient's progress and response to medications and services.[4] Like JCAHO, the federal agency has published specific regulations for different health care settings.

State

State regulations governing the content of the medical record vary greatly. Some states have promulgated a very detailed regulatory scheme that is based on JCAHO guidelines and federal Conditions of Participation rules, while others have only general requirements that would allow the institution to form its own guidelines as long as they conform to other controlling regulations.[5] For those states with more comprehensive regulations, the regulations will most likely be found in the state's administrative code rather than the statutes. Again, there will usually be specific regulations for different health care facilities, such as an underlying universal requirement that the record "contain sufficient information to identify the patient clearly, to justify the diagnosis and treatment and to document the results accurately."[6]

Institutional

Institutional policies may further define the content of the facility's records. If institutional policies are more stringent than JCAHO or federal guidelines, the institution can be held to the higher standard by the JCAHO. The institution should strive to be consistent with whatever policy it has implemented.

Most institutional policies dictate only the actions of employees. Although physicians are usually not hospital employees, some courts have found that an institution has a duty to monitor the nonemployee physician's compliance with federal record-keeping regulations. If the physician is not in compliance with these regulations, his privileges to use the facility may be revoked or suspended.

Professional Standards

The American Medical Association (AMA) has collaborated with the Centers for Medicare and Medicaid Services (CMS) in an attempt to propose documentation guidelines that would satisfy CMS requirements for justification of approving payments for procedures, care, and medications. In order to avoid charges of fraud or abuse of billing practices, the AMA recommends that the physician's record be complete, legible, and compliant with general practices of accurate medical record keeping. The AMA further recommends that each encounter with the patient include the reason for the encounter; relevant history; physical examination findings; prior diagnostic test results; assessment, clinical impression, or diagnosis; plan for care; and date and legible identity of the observer. Appropriate health risk factors should be identified. The patient's progress and response to treatment, as well as changes in the treatment plan and revisions in the diagnosis, should be documented.[7]

The standards of nonphysician health care professionals may require certain information to be timely recorded. The Standards of Clinical Nursing Practice published in 1998 by the American Nursing Association require that an assessment be "documented in a retrievable form," and a diagnosis be "documented in a manner that facilitates the determination of expected outcomes and plan of care." Other required recordings include measurable outcomes, the plan of care, interventions, and revisions of care.[8]

Retention of Records

Once the record is in existence, the holder or "custodian" of the record has the responsibility to safeguard the record and the information therein. The specific question that will be addressed in this section is the length of time that the record must be preserved. As with the content of medical records, retention of medical records is controlled by JCAHO recommendations; federal, state, and local regulations; institutional policies; and professional organizational standards. Other factors such as space available and cost of storage may also influence a health care facility's retention of records policy.

According to JCAHO, the "hospital determines how long medical record information is retained, based on law and regulation and the information use for patient care, legal, research, and educational purposes."[2] Federal law requires that institutions participating in federal reimbursement programs preserve records for a minimum of five years.[9]

As expected, state regulations vary. Some states mandate extensive retention policies that address requirements for various health care providers, while other states do not address the issue.[12] Most states require a 5- to 10-year retention period. In some states, there may be special rules that apply to the records of deceased patients that would allow destruction of the record earlier than the mandated period. Some rules mandate preservation of the whole record for a certain number of years and then permanent preservation of only specific parts thereafter.[10]

In the absence of specific state requirements, the American Health Information Management Association (AHIMA) recommends that health care providers retain records for 10 years after the most recent encounter. AHIMA further recommends that diagnostic images be retained for 5 years; that fetal heart monitor records be retained for 10 years after the infant reaches the age of majority; and that registers of births, deaths, and surgical procedures be retained permanently.[10]

The state record-keeping requirements and individual institutional policies are or should be heavily influenced by the state statute of limitations that controls tort and contract actions. A state may require that a medical malpractice case be commenced within 5 years of the date of injury. In that state, the record retention period would most likely be at least five years.[11] Many states observe the "discovery" rule in determining the statute of limitations for tort actions. This generally means that the statute of limitations is not triggered until the patient has discovered an injury that was caused by someone's negligence.[12] In these jurisdictions, many years can elapse between the actual discovery of the negligence and when the cause of action commences. Once the statute of limitations is triggered by discovery of the negligence, the plaintiff/complainant must bring the action within the time period specified by the statute of limitations for that jurisdiction or lose the ability to bring the action forever. It would be prudent for a facility in a jurisdiction that follows the discovery rule to retain records indefinitely.[13]

Similarly, rules for the retention of records of minors are influenced by the statute of limitations for tortious actions against minors. Since a legal action can be commenced up to 1 or 2 years after the minor turns 18 in most states, the records of minors should be retained at least this long. Some states mandate that minor records must be kept until the age of majority plus 3 years. For those states following the discovery rule (see above), indefinite retention of records may be necessary.

The mission of the facility may have an impact on an institution's record retention policies. Educational and research facilities may have special needs for long-term preservation of records as they may wish to perform retrospective reviews or monitor long-term effects of drug trials. For these reasons, this type of facility may choose to retain records for 75 years or for an indefinite period.[11] Businesses that keep exposure records as mandated by the Occupational Safety and Health Administration (OSHA) must retain the exposure record for 30 years. Medical records mandated by OSHA must be kept by the business for the duration of employment plus 30 years.

The custodian has the added duty to preserve the record in good order. Microfilming or computer storage is generally acceptable, although the process of conversion from a written record to a different form of record keeping must be reliable in order to ensure the integrity of the record. If and when a document is destroyed, AHIMA recommends that a record should be made of the name of the patient, the date of destruction and the records destroyed, inclusive dates covered, a statement that the records were destroyed in the normal course of business, and the signatures of the persons witnessing the destruction.[14] The shredding or incineration or other method of destruction should obliterate all information contained within the document. Many facilities microfiche records to reduce the amount of storage space that is needed. The process of microfiching eliminates the paper copy of the medical record, and thwarts the ability to perform a chemical analysis of the record to detect tampering.

Confidentiality/Privacy/Privilege

Patients reveal many details of their private and personal life to their physician. This disclosure of private information is expected and encouraged so that a physician is in possession of all pertinent information needed to make a diagnosis and treat the patient appropriately. In turn, it is the ethical duty of the physician to maintain the details of the patient's illness, and communications arising thereof, in confidence. This confidentiality between physician and patient has been an accepted practice since the time of Hippocrates, who said:

> Whatsoever things I see or hear concerning the life of men, in my attendance on the sick or even apart therefrom, which ought not be noised abroad, I will keep silence thereon, counting such things to be as sacred secrets.

This tradition to maintain confidential communications between physician and patient has been extended to the information contained within the written record. The right to confidentiality or protection from the unauthorized release of information stems from the right to privacy that the U.S. Supreme Court has determined is guaranteed by the U.S. Constitution.

In the past, a patchwork of state laws and federal laws (Privacy Act of 1974, Americans with Disabilities Act) has attempted to protect the confidentiality of medical records. Most recently, final regulations controlling the implementation of the Health Insurance Portability and Accountability Act of 1996 (HIPAA) that took effect in April 2001 will greatly impact disclosure of personal medical record information.

HIPAA was enacted as a health care reform measure designed to "ensure health insurance portability, reduce health care fraud and abuse, guarantee security and privacy of health information, and enforce standards for health information."[15] HIPAA requires that individually identifiable information that is transmitted or stored electronically be safeguarded from unauthorized disclosure. Uniform national transaction standards must be used to transmit data. This has required many facilities to initiate new information system policies and procedures.

HIPAA applies directly to health care providers, health care clearinghouses, and health plans. HIPAA also applies indirectly to any business partner of the health care provider, clearinghouse, or plan. Any service that is outsourced to a nondirect facility subjects that facility to compliance with HIPAA. Failure to comply with the security requirements of HIPAA can lead to civil and criminal penalties.[15, 16]

HIPAA preempts state laws controlling confidentiality unless the state law mandates a stricter regulation than HIPAA. The act "sets a national 'floor' of privacy standards that protect all Americans, but in some states individuals enjoy additional protection." Disclosure of protected information must be limited to the minimum necessary and cannot be used by employers to make personnel decisions or by financial institutions.[16]

An evidentiary rule that goes hand in hand with confidential communications between physician and patient is the concept of "privileged" communication between certain professionals and other individuals. Most states recognize communications between physician/patient and psychotherapist/patient as beyond the reach of discovery. The patient is the one who holds the privilege, which means that the professional may not reveal the details of the communication unless the patient permits the professional to do so. Some exceptions to this rule of disclosure are discussed below.

In order for the communication to be privileged, however, it must have occurred in a confidential setting. Describing one's signs and symptoms to one's physician on the golf course in front of other players destroys the privilege. The relationship must also be one that society seeks to foster, and confidentiality must be necessary to maintaining a full and satisfactory relationship between the parties. Lastly, the injury that would result to the relationship by disclosure must be greater than the benefit gained in litigation.[12]

If the above conditions are met, a physician/patient communication is considered privileged and immune to discovery. This privilege may extend to the physicians' office staff if they are functioning as agents of the physician. No specific statutory privilege addresses communications between the nurse and the patient.

Access by the Patient

It is now acknowledged that ownership of the physical medical record, including x-rays and all other reports, resides in the facility or the health care practitioner who made the record, subject to the patient's interest to the information contained therein. In the past, the custodian has argued that the subject of the information did not have the right of access to the record. In response, many states conferred a statutory right of access to the patients. Other state courts recognized a common law right to access.[5]

HIPAA now provides for universal access by a patient to review and copy his medical records. Under HIPAA, the patient can also request that corrections/amendments be made to the record and request restrictions on the uses and disclosures of the information. The patient can request a history of disclosures that have been made to third parties.[17]

OSHA mandates that an employee have access to his record of exposure to toxic substances and any relevant medical records held by the employer. If no exposure record exists, the employee has the right to review records of other employees with similar job duties without the other employees' permission. Access to medical records of other employees with similar job duties requires specific written consent from the other employee.[18]

The right to request the records of a minor patient resides in the parent or the legal guardian (HIPAA uses the term "personal representative"). In the case of divorced parents, the custodial parent is the one with the right to access for a minor child. For a deceased patient, the administrator of the estate may request medical records.[19]

Access is defined as reasonable access. The patient or the patient's representative may review the record in the medical records department of a health care facility under supervision at a time that is convenient for the facility, usually during business hours. If a notarized request identifying the specific records that the patient desires is sent to the facility, the institution has the responsibility to reproduce the record in a timely fashion. The facility cannot refuse to reproduce the record despite nonpayment of other outstanding bills. Most states allow the facility to charge a reasonable fee for the copying services. This fee has been customarily $1/page, but this may vary from state to state.[20]

When a potential plaintiff requests a copy of his record from a health care practitioner, the copy may be an uncertified copy unless a certified copy is requested. A certified copy of the record meets the criteria for admissibility as evidence in a court of law (see evidence section below). To certify the records, the custodian of the record swears by affidavit that the copy of the medical records is a true and accurate copy, that the record was made and kept in the usual course of business at the time the medical treatment was provided, and that it was made by persons having knowledge of the information set forth in the records. Certification does not guarantee that the record is complete; it guarantees only that it is an accurate copy of the record held by the facility. The health care provider may charge an additional expense for certification of the record.

Access by Third Parties without the Patient's Express Consent

Information may be released to a third party when the actions of the patient have implied consent or waiver. It is generally assumed when a spouse, family member, or significant other is present during a discussion of the patient's medical condition that the health care practitioner may speak freely concerning private information. If there are questions concerning which family members should have access to information at a later date, the health care practitioner should consult with the patient. The health care practitioner must be especially careful in the release of information concerning substance abuse even to close family members.

In some states, the filing of a lawsuit that brings the plaintiff's physical or mental condition into issue acts as a waiver for express consent to examine the relevant portions of the individual's medical records. Consent of a patient to store information in a clinical data repository may be construed by some state courts as a waiver of the physician/patient privilege, making those records no longer confidential.[21]

Access to information regarding nonparties to a lawsuit that would be used to prove recurring negligence or some other issue may or may not be allowed. If the identity of the other patients can be redacted from the record and the litigant can show good cause, the court may allow discovery of such information.[12] In criminal cases, patient records are generally obtainable when investigating charges of Medicaid fraud or when the patient is a victim of a crime.[22]

Access to sensitive information such as HIV results or information indicating a diagnosis of AIDS may be denied to nonauthorized individuals. In some states, a request for "all" medical records does not include the release of information about sexually transmitted diseases. Rather, a very specific request outlining the exact information that the patient is willing to release must be included. The same specific request may also be necessary for some genetic screening and testing information.[21]

Two other areas of very sensitive information are sperm donor and adoption records. In both instances, strict confidentiality laws were designed partially to protect the identity of the natural parents. Access to both types of records has undergone major changes in the last 20 years. Although the federal courts have upheld the constitutionality of the older statutes that refuse to break the seal of secrecy of donor/adoption records, many states have changed those restrictive laws to allow disclosure of relevant medical information to the child or child's representative. However, the disclosure is, most often, not automatic and falls within the discretion of a governing body or the court that will release the information only upon the showing of good cause.[11]

Mandatory Disclosure

Some types of confidential medical record information must be disclosed. The specific nonvoluntary reporting requirements may vary from state to state, but every state has mandated the reporting of suspected child abuse. Different contagious diseases are also reportable in different states. All states require the reporting of AIDS. Some states allow the health care practitioner to disclose a patient's HIV status to the patient's partner, although it may not create a duty to do so.[11]

Other mandatory disclosures include:

1. The reporting of births and deaths, certain wounds, accidents, and/or other violently incurred injuries
2. Fatalities due to blood transfusions and certain medical devices
3. Workers' compensation claims, seizures, and certain congenital diseases, such as the inborn error of metabolism phenylketonuria
4. Induced termination of pregnancy
5. Occupational diseases

Most states have Open Records Acts that make medical records at a state hospital available to the general public except for an exemption protecting the confidentiality of the records. The Freedom of Information Act (FOIA) is the federal counterpart to the states' Open Records Acts. Like the Privacy Act, however, it applies only to true federal agencies and not to those agencies merely receiving federal funds. The FOIA also exempts disclosure of medical records if it would "constitute a clearly unwarranted invasion of personal privacy."[12] Other business records from public institutions, though, including minutes of meetings of Board meetings, are subject to disclosure under the state or federal Open Records law.[13]

In a famous California case, *Tarasoff v. Regents of University of California*, the court imposed a duty on health care practitioners to warn third parties of a credible threat against them.[48] In this case, a patient informed his psychiatrist of his intent to harm a third person, the patient's ex-girlfriend. Considering himself bound by confidentiality, the psychiatrist did not reveal the danger to the girlfriend. The girl was attacked by the patient and died on her front lawn. In litigation brought by the victim's parents, the court found that the psychiatrist not only had been released from the bonds of confidentiality, but had a duty to warn the third party of the impending danger. The patient was deported to his native country.

Computerized Records

Not all record-keeping guidelines have kept pace with computer technology. For example, some states still require that records be written or signed in ink. This requirement is clearly inconsistent with computerized records and calls into question the legality of the computerized record in that state. The trend toward computerized records, however, is clear. Many private health care facilities are in the process of implementing or have implemented some form of medical record computerization. Several hospitals have converted to an electronic medical record, which has allowed increased accessibility for health care practitioners and improved reliability in documentation.[23]

The growing acceptance of computer technology and the new requirements of HIPAA have revolutionized the management of information. The health care practitioner/facility must adjust to the new problems caused by the integration of computerized data. New challenges include maintaining restricted access to confidential records and the risk of loss or destruction of computerized data. Standardized electronic transactions of information approved by HIPAA and unique identifiers for providers, health plans, and employers will be required. HIPAA has proposed a unique identifier for the individual receiving services, but the "patient identifier" is on hold until and unless privacy legislation permitting the establishment of the individual identifier is passed.[15]

Transmission of identifiable individual data may be protected by various technical features, such as passwords; procedural approaches, such as security training and periodic risk assessments; physical safeguards, such as restricting access to terminals; and personnel safeguards, such as hiring and educating staff who can abide by confidentiality requirements.[24]

There should be a well-designed user identification system. Properly designed audit trails that are adequately monitored enhance accountability.[25] Encryption of the data and digitalized signatures may be used to ensure that data has not been altered during transmission. Dial-back modems that check the identity of the person calling for access is one method to authenticate a request for data. Backup programs and virus detection programs will protect the computerized data from destruction or loss.

Whatever system is instituted, it should balance the right of privacy and the need for quick access to the data.[26] The method of generating computer records must also be trustworthy enough to meet the evidentiary rules for admission of the medical record into evidence during litigation (see below). If the facility modifies or updates its software package, its previous database must remain intact and accessible by the newer program so that older records are not lost by changes in technology.

Nondiscoverable Information

Other than sensitive health care information cited above that cannot be released without express authorization, various administrative or monitoring records pertaining to patient care may be sought in a medical malpractice action. These include credentialing surveys, infection control committee reports, departmental logs, risk management data, utilization review reports, peer review records, and incident reports. This type of data is generally discoverable unless protected by a state statute.[11]

Discoverable information refers to materials, documents, or witnesses that must be made available to the opposing party in a lawsuit. Discoverable information is not always admissible in court, however. The judge or other trier of fact makes the final decision about information that is relevant and probative enough to be admitted as evidence.[11] For example, photographs of victims involved in a fatal motor vehicle accident may be available and discoverable to both sides. The photographs may be extremely graphic and serve only to produce an emotional response in the viewer. Unless the party who would like to introduce the photographs at trial can show that the photographs are needed to prove an issue that is in contention, the judge will generally rule that the photographs are inadmissible because they are not probative. In other words, they do not support or defend an issue in the case.[27]

Peer Review

Medical staff of health care facilities are generally charged with the responsibility to ensure the quality of patient care and to oversee the ethical and professional practices of staff members. Part of this responsibility is carried out by peer review, which entails the evaluation of "professional performance, ethical behavior, quality of care, utilization patterns, or selected aspects of the performance" of the medical staff and other health care professionals.[28]

In order to promote open and frank discussion during peer review evaluations, many states have mandated that communications revealed during these conferences are privileged and immune to discovery.[29] This means that participants cannot be sued for statements made during an evaluation conference that might otherwise be considered defamatory, nor will the record of the meeting be made available for a patient pursuing a legal action against the subject of the peer review.

There is a high degree of variability among the states as to what, if any, information is protected. Some states have extended the privilege to all professional committees including Quality Assurance,[1] while other states have narrowed the peer review privilege.[13] The extent of undiscoverable items may be restricted to the notes/minutes/reports made by the committee itself, whereas recommendations made by the committee concerning the continuing or revocation of staff privileges based on a finding of the board may be discoverable.[29] Similarly, any statement made by the subject of the peer review may be discoverable in a subsequent action related to the subject matter reviewed at the meeting.[1]

Incident Reports

An incident report is a report of an unusual event "not consistent within the routine operation of the hospital or the routine care of a particular patient... it may be an accident or a situation which could result in an accident."[30] If the incident report is filed as part of the medical record, it may be discoverable and admissible into court under the business records exception to the hearsay rule (see below).

If the incident report is directed to the legal department of the facility, it may be nondiscoverable as the facility can argue that the report was made in anticipation of litigation. Documents that are prepared with "an eye toward litigation" are considered the attorney's work product, which is generally not discoverable. If the incident report can be characterized as part of the peer review process, statutory immunity to discovery may apply.[1]

Using the Legal Process to Obtain Access to Medical Records

It may be necessary to involve the legal process in obtaining records if one of the parties refuses to allow the other party access to the documents in his possession. If a party refuses to disclose medical records, the statute of limitations may be tolled based on the theory of fraudulent concealment.[31] Fraudulent concealment is the hiding of an essential fact that the opposing party has a right to know. The health care practitioner/facility cannot protect itself from a lawsuit by failing to produce records within the usual statutory time frame as the start of the statute of limitations time period may not be triggered until or when the plaintiff discovers that the defendant is purposefully concealing material information. The tolling of the statute of limitations with fraudulent concealment is similar to the tolling of the statute of limitations under the discovery rule discussed above. In some states, the statute of limitations is not triggered until the plaintiff discovers or should have discovered that he suffered an injury due to a tortious act.

The statute of limitations refers to the time period after which a lawsuit can no longer be pursued. In most instances, the legislature sets the time frame according to the cause of action (personal injury or contract or medical malpractice suit). For example, a state may mandate a 2-year statute of limitations for a contract case but only a 1-year statute of limitations for a wrongful death case.

After a lawsuit is filed, whether in federal or state court, the parties begin investigating the facts/issues of the case through formal discovery processes. One method of discovery is the request for production of documents. If the document is not produced, the party seeking the document can file a motion with the court to compel production. If the motion is granted, the opposing party must produce the document or face the possibility of sanctions, including a charge of contempt of court.[32]

Another method of discovery is the subpoena, which would require attendance of a party or witness to court or to a deposition. This may be accompanied by a subpoena *duces tecum*, which requires that certain documents be brought to the deposition.[33] If the witness at trial or deposition is asked to reveal privileged or confidential information, the witness should consult his attorney before responding. The attorney may file a motion for a protective order asking the court to allow the witness to refuse to answer. In the case of substance abuse records, under federal law, a court order must accompany the subpoena finding that disclosure of this confidential information "is more important than the purpose for which Congress mandated confidentiality" before disclosure should occur.[12]

Spoliation of Medical Records

Spoliation of evidence refers to "any action including destruction, alteration, or concealment of records, which deprives the court or parties to a dispute of evidence."[34] Discovery in the American legal process relies heavily on the voluntary compliance of the parties to produce documents and other evidence that are in the files/possession of one of the parties. Failure to preserve and produce evidence is one of the worst forms of discovery misconduct and can lead to severe consequences, including punitive damages (which are not covered by insurance policies).

One of the legal consequences of loss or destruction of a medical record is a jury instruction that can adversely affect the defendant's position at trial, whether the loss was intentional or negligent. The jury may be instructed that they can infer that the evidence that was destroyed was unfavorable to the person who was responsible for its safekeeping. Discovery sanctions, including the entry of a default judgment, can be imposed against the party that destroyed or withheld evidence. Alternatively, the health care facility/practitioner may face professional disciplinary actions or criminal penalties.[34,35]

In the first case of its kind, a licensed practical nurse (LPN) working in a Pennsylvania nursing home was prosecuted for a violation of HIPAA. The LPN received a verbal order to reduce a resident's anticoagulant medication. A short time thereafter, the LPN realized that she had failed to transcribe the order. She then falsified the resident's medical record to indicate that the physician order had been implemented correctly. This falsification of the record formed the basis for criminal charges. The HIPAA law was used, which precludes making "false statements" involving a federal health care benefit program (Medicare/Medicaid programs). This provision criminalizes the falsification of a medical record in support of a bill for services. The penalties for such false statements are a maximum term of 5 years' imprisonment and a $25,000 fine.[36] The resident in this case was admitted to the hospital and died 10 days later. The LPN was sentenced to 10–16 months in federal prison and agreed to surrender her nursing license.[37]

Some states have allowed a separate cause of action based on the tort of intentional spoliation of evidence that would allow a lawsuit to proceed against the person who destroyed or lost evidence. The courts that have recognized the tort require the presence of a legal duty to preserve the evidence that is relevant to the lawsuit, the existence of a causal relationship between the evidence destruction and the inability to prove the lawsuit, and damages. A minority of courts have recognized the tort of negligent spoliation of evidence with similar criteria.[38]

Controversy exists about the most effective method of improving compliance with the discovery process in regard to the production and preservation of documents, especially crucial in a case involving medical issues. Some litigators suspect that spoliation of evidence is a pervasive problem with the need for severe punitive measures in order to prevent it.[35] However, if the loss or destruction of evidence is unintentional and not essential to the proving of the plaintiff's case, the court is less likely to impose extensive punitive measures.[35,38]

Health Care Practitioner Information That Must Be Requested by the Health Care Facility

National Practitioner Data Bank

In 1990, a national data bank called the National Practitioner Data Bank (NPDB) was created pursuant to the 1986 Health Care Quality Improvement Act. The NPDB established reporting requirements from health care entities to the NPDB whenever an adverse licensure or professional review action or a payment occurred as a result of a medical malpractice action. According to JCAHO, a practitioner must apply for clinical privileges at a health care facility every 2 years. Each time that an application is made, the facility must request information from the NPDB regarding that practitioner. "Knowledge of an adverse action is imputed to the hospital whether the hospital makes the inquiry or not."[39]

The NPDB will disclose information of the adverse action or payment of a claim only to those health care groups that qualify under the law. There is one instance whereby the information will be disclosed to an attorney. If an attorney has filed suit against an institution and requests information from the NPDB concerning a defendant party, the NPDB will release the information "only upon submission of evidence that the hospital failed to request information from the Data Bank as required by 60.10(a), and may be used solely with respect to litigation resulting from the action or claim against the hospital."[39]

Health Care Integrity and Protection Data Bank

As part of HIPAA's attempt to combat fraud and abuse, the Secretary of Health and Human Services was directed to create the Health Care Integrity and Protection Data Bank (HIPDB),[40] a data bank similar to the NPDB (see above). Health plans and licensing/enforcing federal and state agencies are required to report certain final adverse actions taken against health care practitioners, including nurses, providers, and suppliers. The same entities who must report to the bank are the only agencies that are allowed access to the bank, although legislation has been introduced to expand HIPDB access.[1] The HIPDB is meant to be a "nationwide flagging system" to alert users that a comprehensive review of the practitioner's, provider's, or supplier's past actions may be prudent.[38] An integrated service has been made available for a user to query both the NPDB and the HIPDB at a single site on the Internet, http://www.npdb-hipdb.com.

JCAHO: Sentinel Event and Tell-All Standard

Sentinel Event

A sentinel event is an unexpected occurrence that according to JCAHO "signals the need for immediate investigation and response."[2] If a sentinel event occurs, a facility is expected to perform a root cause analysis and formulate an action plan that "identifies the strategies that the organization intends to implement to reduce the risk of similar events occurring in the future."[2]

A sentinel event is defined by JCAHO as any unexpected occurrence involving death or serious physical or psychological injury, or the risk thereof. Examples of sentinel events include a suicide in a setting where the patient is receiving 24-hour care, an infant abduction or discharge to the wrong family, a hemolytic transfusion reaction related to mismatched blood products, rape, and surgery on the wrong patient or wrong body part.[2] Since January 1995, JCAHO has been informed of 1,447 sentinel events (as of October 23, 2001). The majority of the sentinel events has involved the general hospital arena (62.4%). The three most commonly reported events were patient suicide (16.9%), perioperative complications (12.4%), and medication error (11.6%).[41]

The root cause analysis is an internal investigation that should focus on the system rather than the individual. Once the facility is aware of the event, a credible and thorough analysis with an action plan must be performed within 45 days. Although the JCAHO standards state that the facility is encouraged to report the event to JCAHO and it is not required to do so, failure to report the event can carry serious consequences. If JCAHO becomes aware of the event by some means other than self-report, the facility will be required to submit the root cause analysis.[2]

In order to protect the patient's confidentiality when a root cause report is submitted to JCAHO, the organization has advised organizations to not provide patient or caregiver identities when reporting sentinel events. Submitting the report to JCAHO may allow discovery of the report should a medical malpractice claim arise from the underlying event. In order to limit legal exposure as a result of sending the root cause analysis documents to JCAHO, the organization has agreed to allow the review of the documents with return of the documents on the same day, or review of the documents on-site, or the review of the root cause analysis process on-site.[1]

Tell-All Standard

In November 1999, the Institute of Medicine (IOM) reported that between 44,000 and 98,000 people died in the hospital each year as a result of medical errors.[42] Besides medication errors, the reported errors included diagnostic problems, equipment failure, nosocomial and postsurgical wound infections, blood transfusion errors, and misinterpretations of orders.[43] In response to the IOM's reports, JCAHO proposed new patient safety standards that went into effect on July 1, 2001. Included in the revised standards is a mandate that patients be informed about all outcomes of care. According to JCAHO, the intent of the new standard is that the practitioner or his designee "clearly explains the outcome of any treatments or procedures to the patient and when appropriate, the family, whenever those outcomes differ significantly from the anticipated outcomes."[44]

Initial reactions to the impact of these standards have been mixed. Some health care professionals fear that informing patients and families that medical errors have occurred will bring an increase in medical malpractice lawsuits. Others believe that the health care professionals have always had ethical obligations to be truthful about errors. When patients believe that they are being lied to about the cause of an error, they are more likely to seek the help of an attorney. See Chapter 10, Ethical Theory and the Practice of the Legal Nurse Consultant, and

Chapter 27, The Legal Nurse Consultant's Role in Health Care Risk Management, for more information.

Evidentiary Rules

Introduction

Just as there are federal and state rules of civil and criminal procedure controlling the process of a legal action, there are federal and state rules controlling what information and witnesses can be used in the courtroom. Since state rules vary, the emphasis in this discussion will be on the Federal Rules of Evidence (FRE).

Hearsay Rule

Part of the trier of fact's job in the courtroom, whether the trier of fact is a judge or jury, is to evaluate the witness's perception, memory, and narration of events. The court system attempts to promote these three factors by requiring the witness to take an oath and testify in the personal presence of the judge or jury, but, most importantly, by subjecting the witness to cross-examination.[27]

The right to cross-examine adverse witnesses has been considered so vital to the legal process that the FRE does not allow statements into evidence that are offered to prove the truth of the matter asserted unless the declarant is present at trial. This is the hearsay rule of evidence. In many instances, however, the court has found the out-of-court statement to be so reliable and trustworthy that cross-examination of the declarant who made the statement is not necessary to test its truthfulness. These instances have been incorporated into the FRE as exceptions to the Hearsay Rule.

Business records fall into the category of reliable and trustworthy evidence that is admissible whether the declarant is available or not when it meets the requirements of FRE 803(6):

A memorandum, report, record, or data compilation, in any form, of acts, events, conditions, opinions, or diagnoses, made at or near the time by, or from information transmitted by, a person with knowledge, if kept in the course of a regularly conducted business activity, and if it was the regular practice of that business activity to make the memorandum, report, record, or data compilation, all as shown by the testimony of the custodian or other qualified witness, unless the source of information or the method or circumstances of preparation indicate lack of trustworthiness.

According to the rule, the three indicators of reliability of business records are that (1) they were made as a part of a regularly conducted business, (2) they were made close in time to the event, and (3) the events were observed and recorded by a person with knowledge or transmitted to the recorder by a person with knowledge.[45]

Medical records usually fall into the category of business records as they are made by persons under a "business duty" to record accurate information to assist in the diagnosing and treating of patients (the ordinary course of business for health care practitioner/facility). The information is further authenticated by the responsible individual with a signature. The record is made close in time to the event so that the record is not skewed by lapses in memory. It is made by persons with firsthand knowledge or by those with information transmitted by persons with firsthand knowledge, again ensuring accuracy.

If the record can be contested on any one of these grounds, it may not be accepted as a reliable enough piece of evidence to allow admission under the business rule exception to hearsay. Computerized printouts will generally qualify as a business record as FRE 803(6) is fairly broad in its description of what a record is (report, memorandum, or "data compilation"). However, if a computerized record does not provide an acceptable legal signature, it may be contested. If there are not safeguards in place within the computerized system to protect against modifications without erasing the original entry, the accuracy and reliability of the record can be contested.[46] Another problem with the computerized record is the inability to determine whether the record is complete or not, a necessary requirement to be admissible under another evidentiary rule.[47]

In order to prove to the court that the medical record is reliable and trustworthy, it must be introduced at trial in such a way that it fulfills the requirements of FRE 803(6). A witness must be able to identify the record and verify that it was made at or near the time of the event by a person with knowledge in the regular course of business. In the case of computer records, the witness should also be familiar with the safeguards that were/are in place to protect the reliability and accuracy of the record, including ways that the data are gathered, stored, and retrieved.[27] The FRE no longer requires that the custodian of the record be the one through whom the evidence is introduced as long as the witness is qualified to testify how the record was made. Many state rules of evidence are consistent with the federal business records exception to hearsay.[47]

There are other grounds upon which the medical record can be contested to prevent admission of the document into evidence. There may be instances in the record whereby the statement that is recorded is hearsay — the "double hearsay" problem (FRE 805). For example, the health care practitioner may have recorded statements concerning the immediate cause of injury or assertions about fault. Unless those statements fall within an exception to the hearsay rule, they cannot be admitted into evidence to prove the cause of injury or fault. Most often, however, the admission of medical records is not an issue at trial as the parties will generally resolve any disputes concerning the medical records at pretrial conference.

Public Records Exception (Federal Rule of Evidence 803[8])

The public records exception is another exception to the Hearsay Rule that is very similar to the business records exception. Like the business records exception, its reliability for accurateness depends on the recording of data by persons with firsthand knowledge under a duty to make the report. For example, an accident report is a public record made by a police officer who has a duty to record the details of the accident. In a personal injury case, the accident report would be admissible under the public records exception to hearsay. In a medical malpractice suit, the public records exception would generally apply only to records made by public offices or agencies and so would be useful only concerning records of public health care facilities.

Best Evidence Rule ("Original Document Rule" [Federal Rule of Evidence 1001])

The original document rule requires the proponent to offer the original of a document, photograph, or recording in evidence if the proponent seeks to prove its contents and the contents are directly in issue, unless production is excused under the terms of the rule. The original document rule is a "rule of preference," with numerous qualifications. The original document need not be produced when it is lost or destroyed, if it cannot be obtained by judicial process, or if the original is in the control of the opponent. The rule applies when the facts contained in the document are directly in issue in the case and the facts do not exist independent of the document.

In most other cases, "a duplicate is admissible to the same extent as an original unless (1) a genuine question is raised as to the authenticity of the original or (2) in the circumstances it would be unfair to admit the duplicate in lieu of the original" (FRE 1003). The authenticity requirement is met when there is sufficient evidence "to support a finding that the matter in question is what the proponent claims."[27]

Federal Rule of Evidence 1006

Medical records are often voluminous. FRE 1006 allows the preparation of summaries of writings, recordings, or photographs that cannot conveniently be examined by the court, as long as the originals are available. The parties must have notice of the use of summaries at trial and an opportunity to compare the summaries to the record for accuracy. The federal rule, however, does not specifically state that the summary must be made available to the opposing party at pretrial conference, although it has been argued that "the framers of the Rule clearly contemplated a pretrial resolution of any issues that may be raised concerning the use of summaries."[27] Some states do require exchange of proposed summaries prior to trial. More information about the use of the nurse to prepare and testify about such summaries is provided in Chapter 36, The Expert Fact Witness: Noneconomic Damages Testimony.

Exhibits

A summary is essentially an example of an exhibit as it is an aid in the presentation of the case to the trier of fact. An exhibit can be "anything, other than testimony, that can be perceived by the senses and be presented in the courtroom."[47] There are some restrictions as to the information that will be acceptable for admission. The exhibit cannot be so prejudicial or inflammatory that it outweighs its probative effect.[27] This determination is made by the judge.

There is also a particular sequence of questions/actions that must be followed in order to meet the foundation requirements for admissibility. These requirements are that the witness is competent to introduce the evidence, and that the evidence is relevant and authenticated. The exhibit must also reasonably depict the place/ device it represents and, in some courts, be helpful in the witness's explanation of the events to the trier of fact. See Chapter 40, The Role of the LNC in Preparation of Technical Demonstrative Evidence, for more information.

Summary

A complete and comprehensible medical record can be a decisive piece of evidence in a case that involves medical issues. The LNC is in a unique position to assist an attorney in gathering, organizing, and reviewing the medical information contained in the record. Familiarity with the standards and rules that pertain to medical records will give the LNC a better understanding of what records should contain, why and when they are confidential, how to obtain them, how long they should be available, and how/why they can be used at trial.

References

1. Carroll, R., *Risk Management Handbook for Health Care Organizations*, 3rd ed., Jossey-Bass, San Francisco, 2001, 874.
2. Joint Commission on Accreditation of Healthcare Organizations, *2001 Hospital Accreditation Standards*, Oakbrook Terrace, IL, 2000.
3. Joint Commission on Accreditation of Healthcare Organizations, *2000–2001 Comprehensive Accreditation Manual for Long Term Care*, Oakbrook Terrace, IL, 2000.
4. 42 Code of Federal Regulations 482.24(c) (1994).
5. Murer, C., Murer, M., and Lyndean, B., *The Complete Legal Guide to Healthcare Records Management*, McGraw-Hill, New York, 2001.
6. Kansas Hospital Regulations, 28–34; 9a(d)(5) (1993).
7. American Medical Association, *Federal Fraud Enforcement Policy Statement*, Office of the General Counsel, Division of Health Law, Oak Brook, IL, 1998.
8. American Nurses Association, *Standards of Clinical Nursing Practice*, Washington, D.C., 1998.
9. 42 Code of Federal Regulations 482.24(b) (1994).
10. American Health Information Management Association, *Practice Brief: Retention of Health Information*, June 1999.
11. Roach, W., *Medical Records and the Law*, 3rd ed., Aspen Publishers, Inc., Gaithersburg, MD, 1998.
12. Hirsch, H., Disclosure about patients, in *Legal Medicine*, C.V. Mosby, St. Louis, 1995, 312–342.
13. Kingsolver, J., *Kentucky Health Law*, University of Kentucky, Lexington, 2001.
14. American Health Information Management Association, *Practice Brief: Destruction of Patient Health Information*, January 1996.
15. Maddox, P., Update on the health information portability and accountability act: HIPAA, *Nursing Economic$*, 18(6), 312, 2000.

16. U.S. Department of Health and Human Services, HHS Fact Sheet: Protecting the Privacy of Patients' Health Information Summary of the Final Regulations, December 2000.
17. U.S. Department of Health and Human Services, HHS Fact Sheet: Protecting the Privacy of Patients' Health Information, May 2001.
18. Occupational Safety and Health Administration, *Access to Medical and Exposure Records*, U.S. Department of Labor, 1993, 1–18.
19. Release of patient medical records, *KMA Journal*, 93, 297–300, July 1995.
20. Stearns, P., Access to and cost of reproduction of patient medical records, *Journal of Legal Medicine*, 21(1), 2000.
21. Gosfield, A., *Health Law Handbook*, Clark, Boardman, Callaghan, Deerfield, IL, 1996, 145–173.
22. Pozgar, G., *Legal Aspects of Health Care Administration*, Aspen Publications, Gaithersburg, MD, 1996.
23. Fletcher, R.L., Dayhoff, R., Wu, Ch., Graves, A., and Jones, R., Computerized medical records in the Department of Veterans Affairs, *Cancer*, 91(8), 1603–1606, 2001.
24. Lawrence, L., Safeguarding the confidentiality of automated medical information, *Journal on Quality Improvement*, 20(11), 639, 1994.
25. Institute of Medicine, *The Computer-Based Patient Record*, National Academy Press, Washington, D.C., 1997.
26. Murphy, G., Hanken, M., and Waters, K., *Electronic Health Records: Changing the Vision*, W.B. Saunders, Philadelphia, 1999.
27. *Federal Rules of Evidence*, West Publishing Co., St. Paul, MN, 1992.
28. Cronan, C., Credentialing and peer review, in *Kentucky Health Law*, University of Kentucky, Lexington, 1995.
29. Neil, B., Medical records committees: should they tell us what they know? *Trial Diplomacy Journal*, 17, 11–15, 1994.
30. Hirsch, H., Medical records, in *Legal Medicine*, C.V. Mosby, St. Louis, 1995, 297–311.
31. Feutz-Harter, S., *Nursing and the Law*, 5th ed., PESI, Eau Claire, WI, 1993, 73–84.
32. Lobe, T., *Medical Malpractice: A Physician's Guide*, McGraw-Hill, New York, 1995.
33. Mulvey, T., Subpoenas, *Journal of Legal Nurse Consulting*, 6(2), 12–13, 1995.
34. Gilbert, J., Whitworth, R., Ollanik, S., and Hare, F., Evidence destruction — legal consequences of spoliation of records, *Legal Medicine*, 181–200, 1994.
35. Adamski, K., A funny thing happened on the way to the courtroom: spoliation of evidence in Illinois, *J. Marshall Law Review*, 32, 325, 2000.
36. Martin, R., Falsification of medical records, *Advance for Nurses, Greater Philadelphia*, June 4, 2001, 44.
37. Miller, R., Former nurse to serve time for falsifying patient's chart, *Express Times*, November 2001.
38. Judge, J., Reconsidering spoliation: common-sense alternatives to the spoliation tort, *Wisconsin Law Review*, No. 2, 441, 2001.
39. 45 Code of Federal Regulations 60.11(5) (1994).
40. U.S. Department of Health and Human Services, Health Resources & Services Administration (HRSA), *Fact Sheet on the Healthcare Integrity and Protection Data Bank*, August 2000.
41. Joint Commission on Accreditation of Healthcare Organizations, *Sentinel Event Statistics*. 2001.
42. Lovern, E., JCAHO's new tell-all standards require that patients know about below-par care, *Modern Healthcare*, 31(1), 2, 2001.
43. Agency for Healthcare Research and Quality, *Medical Errors: The Scope of the Problem*, Fact Sheet, Publication No. AHRG 00-P037, Rockville, MD, 2000.
44. Joint Commission on Accreditation of Healthcare Organizations, *Revisions to Joint Commission Standards*, Oakbrook Terrace, IL, 2001.

45. Egan, T., Admission of business records into evidence: using the business records exception and other techniques, *Defense Law Journal*, 42, 677, 1993.
46. Waller, A., Computerized records: legal and security issues, in *Health Care Facility, Records: Confidentiality, Computerization and Security*, Loyola University, Chicago, 1995, 47–72.
47. Mauet, T., *Trial Techniques*, Little, Brown, Boston, 1996, 139–213.
48. *Tarasoff v. Regents of University of California*, 17 Cal. 3d 425, 551 P.2d 334, 131 Cal. Rptr. 14 (1976).

Additional Reading

Am. Jur. Trials, 36, 695, Obtaining, Organizing and Abstracting Medical Records for Use in a Lawsuit.
Antoine, M., Protecting peer review and hospital committee records, in *Health Care Facility Records: Confidentiality, Computerization and Security*, Loyola University, Chicago, 1995, 27–46.
Hirsch, H., Medical records: everything you always wanted to know, *Medical Trial Technique Quarterly*, 40, 285–326, 1994.
Huffman, E., *Health Information Management*, Physicians Record Company, Berwyn, IL, 1994.
Jessen, J., Electronic evidence discovery opens new doors in litigation, *Medical Malpractice: Law & Strategy*, 11, 1–2, 1994.
Minor, B., The impact of information technology on medical records privacy, *Medical Trial Technique Quarterly*, 87–105, Summer 1996.
Nolfi, E., *Basic Legal Research*, Macmillan/McGraw-Hill, New York, 1993.
Scott, R., *Legal Aspects of Documenting Patient Care*, 2nd ed., Aspen Publishers, Gaithersburg, MD, 2000.

Test Questions

1. The statute of limitations is
   A. The time beyond which a lawsuit can no longer be pursued
   B. Consistent for different causes of actions
   C. Tolled when a health care practitioner moves to a different state
   D. The limit of damages that can be awarded in a particular jurisdiction

2. An institution should maintain a pediatric medical record
   A. For 5 years
   B. For 10 years
   C. Until the patient reaches the age of majority
   D. Until the patient reaches the age of majority plus the controlling jurisdictional time period for pursuing a medical malpractice action

3. To obtain a client's medical record
   A. A request for certification must accompany the request.
   B. A dated, notarized request for the record must be made.
   C. Payment must accompany the request.
   D. The client must request the record in person.

4. Spoliation of the records
   A. Results in a summary judgment for the plaintiff
   B. Includes destruction of records from natural disasters
   C. Can result in civil and criminal charges against the health care practitioner
   D. Includes late entries that are inconsistent with earlier entries

5. A root cause analysis report
   A. Is prepared by JCAHO and must be implemented within 45 days by the health care facility
   B. Must include an action plan that focuses on corrective action concerning the individual's behavior
   C. Is automatically discoverable should the incident be the subject of litigation
   D. Stems from an internal investigation regarding the flaws within the system that contributed to a sentinel event

Answers: 1. A, 2. D, 3. B, 4. C, 5. D

Chapter 3

Discovery and Disclosure

Julianne Hernandez, MPH, BSN, RN, Barbara Noble, BSN, RN, Barbara Stilwell, MSN, RN, and Mary Lanz, RN, LNCC

CONTENTS

0-8493-1418-6/03/$0.00+$1.50
© 2003 by AALNC

Objectives

Upon completion of this chapter, the reader will be able to:

- List five discovery tools used in litigation
- Give one example of nondiscoverable (i.e., privileged) information
- List two advantages and two disadvantages of interrogatories
- List three purposes of depositions
- Identify three specific ways in which the legal nurse consultant may assist in deposition preparation

Introduction

The legal nurse consultant (LNC) makes a strong contribution to the litigation process by identifying and refining the medical issues and theoretical underpinnings of the case. While this remains the focus of the LNC's work, frequently LNCs find themselves in unfamiliar territory during the legal process. The meshing of medicine and law requires some basic understanding of legal terminology and processes. In the same way that neophyte nurses once painstakingly gained familiarity with anatomy, physiology, and pharmacology, becoming knowledgeable about the legal process is essential to cross over to the legal arena. Though not lawyers, LNCs are dealing with the law, which is organized very differently from medicine. A basic knowledge of the legal process will build the LNC's confidence in the role, delineate the boundaries of the medical/legal process, and help the LNC more effectively communicate with the attorney/client.

Rules of Civil Procedure

The entire litigation process is regulated by detailed instructions known as the rules of civil procedure. These rules are an invaluable resource to the LNC, describing exactly how to get around the game board of litigation, from serving the initial complaint to final determination of the matter. Although this chapter will refer to the Federal Rules of Civil Procedure (FRCP), the rules have been adopted either totally or in part by most states. In addition, states have their own rules that are directly derived from the federal rules. The rules are available on the Internet and are the LNC's new toolbox. It is best to assume nothing. It is imperative to refer to the rules of civil procedure of the state as needed. Specifically, the FRCP tell the parties how to:

- File a lawsuit
- Complete pretrial preparations
- Conduct themselves during a trial
- Obtain a final binding judgment[1]

The purpose of this chapter is to provide general background about the discovery portion of litigation. The courts and legislatures have created various pretrial tools allowing each adversary to discover certain nonprivileged information about the other party's position in the dispute.

Complaint

Pursuant to FRCP 3, civil action commences with the filing of a complaint with the court, the plaintiff's initial pleading.[2] A complaint's purpose is to inform the defendant and the court of the basis for the plaintiff's claim.[1] Pursuant to FRCP 8, the complaint need only contain a short, plain statement of the claim upon which relief is sought, indication of the type of relief requested, and justification that the court has jurisdiction to hear the case.[3] However, FRCP 12(e) clarifies that the complaint cannot be so vague that the party cannot reasonably respond.[4] A sample complaint is provided as Appendix 3.1.

When a defendant has been served with a complaint, the Federal Rules require that the defendant respond. The defendant can file an answer, citing the defenses to the claim, or may file a motion to dismiss the claim. A motion is a request to the court for a ruling on a particular issue. FRCP 12(b) lists seven defenses known as motions to dismiss:[1,5]

1. Lack of jurisdiction over the person
2. Lack of jurisdiction over the subject matter
3. Improper venue
4. Insufficiency of process
5. Insufficiency of service of process
6. Failure to state a claim upon which relief can be granted
7. Failure to join a necessary party

If the defendant doesn't file a motion to dismiss, or if the court denies the motion, then the defendant must file an answer.

Discovery

After the complaint has been served and the defendant has responded, each side may still have only a very sketchy view of its opponent's position.[1] The goal of discovery is to:

- Narrow the issues in the case, both legal and factual
- Ascertain the opposing party's allegations
- Obtain relevant information at the least cost to the clients
- Preserve testimony of witnesses unable to testify at trial
- Eliminate the element of surprise in litigation[6]

The discovery process facilitates and encourages settlements of litigation prior to trial. During the discovery process, each party learns the strengths and weaknesses of the other's position. FRCP 26(b)(1) establishes the guidelines for discovery within the federal court system.[7] Parties may obtain discovery regarding any matter not privileged that is relevant to the subject matter involved in the pending action, whether it relates to the claim or defense of the party seeking discovery, or to the claim or defense of any other party. This includes the existence, description, nature, custody, condition, and location of any books, documents, or other tangible things, and the identity and location of persons having knowledge of any discoverable matter. It is not grounds for objection that the information sought will be inadmissible at the trial if the information sought appears reasonably calculated to lead to the discovery of admissible evidence. For example, an injured party's previous work history and income tax forms would be admissible. In contrast, an expert witness's income tax forms may be considered inadmissible in some states, but the percentage of income derived from testimony may be admissible.

The LNC must be aware that if communication is privileged, the subject matter may not be learned through the discovery process. The most common form of privilege is attorney/client privilege, preventing any third party from obtaining information about the subject matters discussed by attorney and client. Documents containing privileged information should be clearly identified as "attorney work product," thereby making such documents exempt from discovery. Discretion must be used when posting information on listservs or disclosing any information to others about the case. Careless handling of case information, written or verbal, could well lead to the inadvertent sharing of privileged case information with the opposing side.

Generally, there are five discovery tools:

1. Written interrogatories
2. Requests for production of documents, things, and inspections
3. Requests for admission
4. Physical and mental examinations
5. Depositions

Written Interrogatories

Interrogatories are sets of written questions that one party submits to another and that must be answered in writing and under oath (see Appendices 3.2 through 3.5 for an example). FRCP 33(a) provides, "Any party may serve upon another party written interrogatories to be answered by the party served," meaning that only a plaintiff, defendant, or additional party is required to answer interrogatories.[8] Interrogatories may relate to any matter not privileged that is relevant to the subject matter of the litigation. This is a relatively inexpensive discovery tool, but the answers are only as good as the questions asked. Answers to interrogatories are not spontaneous responses and do not provide the examining party with the same flexibility as a deposition might. In a deposition, the questioner has the capacity to ask follow-up questions and to probe the witness further for responses. Also, as mentioned above, interrogatories may be directed only to the parties in the case and not third persons, and are more limited than depositions.[1,6] The Certificate of Service, shown in Appendix 3.3, is signed by the attorney. It is a formal declaration stating to whom a document, with or without attachments, was served. The Certificate of Service should always itemize what documents are being served, should there ever be a future question or dispute.

The Jurat Sheet, shown in Appendix 3.5, is a notarized affirmation by the plaintiff that he has read the attached document and finds all the answers to the interrogatories to be true and correct. Before executing the Jurat Sheet, the client should review the final draft responses. Occasionally, attorneys will find out in the deposition of the plaintiff or defendant that the attorney or paralegal wrote the answers to the interrogatories without input from the person who signed the affirmation, or that the person who signed the affirmation did not read the answers. This casts doubt on the credibility of the answers.

It is important to carefully review the original complaint for the allegations made. By doing so, the LNC will be able to prepare a list of further information needed to determine the liability aspects of the case, the damages, and an evaluation of the opponent's position. The LNC must know all pertinent medical facts. Often the LNC working in a law firm also assists in preparing and answering interrogatories. There are resources available to assist in this process. For example, the state rules of civil procedure offer a forms section, setting forth standard interrogatory questions for medical malpractice and other areas of litigation. A standard set of interrogatories may be used when a case involves product liability and a large number of plaintiffs. For example, all people claiming injury from defective orthopaedic appliances may be asked to complete a standard set of interrogatories specific to the issues in the case. If the case involves a unique situation, for example, a nuclear power plant spill, it may be more difficult to determine specific questions that should be asked in interrogatories.

An excellent resource is *American Jurisprudence Proof of Facts* (AmJurPOF). This publication describes in detail each aspect of any legal topic and provides background information. For example, an attorney may not be very familiar with hospital-acquired infections. An AmJurPOF section on hospital-acquired infections would include causes, complications, treatment, control measures, accreditation standards, specific liabilities, collateral references, sample testimony of plaintiff and plaintiff's expert, and case illustrations.

Occasionally in reviewing interrogatories, the LNC will find that the other side has attempted to use the wrong set of interrogatories. For example, a set of interrogatories more appropriate to a slip and fall may be supplied in a medical malpractice case. The LNC's suggestions for specific interrogatories related to the facts of the case may be invaluable.

Both parties can learn from preliminary information gathered by interrogatories about the opponent's position and expert witnesses to be called at trial. The LNC will learn from additional sources that records still need to be requested. The LNC working with the plaintiff's attorney will look for information supportive of the plaintiff's case. Working on the defendant's case involves seeking weak areas in the plaintiff's case, including facts that will limit damages.

Each state has laws regarding the length of time that a party has to answer the opposing party's discovery request. Various deadlines are statutory, while others are imposed by the court through scheduling orders. Answers must be produced within the stated time frame. For example, FRCP 33 states that answers must be served to opposing counsel within 30 days after service of interrogatories, 45 days if the interrogatories are served along with the original complaint.[8] Some states include an additional 5 days for mailing. Toward this end, it is important for the LNC to develop good rapport with the client and to stress the need for timeliness in response. The LNC should review questions and requests with the client and assist in drafting answers. The completed draft should be submitted to the attorney for final review.

Requests for Production

The request for production is a formal written request for copies of relevant, nonprivileged documents, including:

- Medical records
- Personnel records
- Policies and procedures
- Incident reports
- Income tax returns
- Medical bills
- Treating physician reports
- Copies of nonprivileged correspondence
- Photographs
- Any and all documents that the opposing party intends to introduce into evidence or use at time of trial
- Copies of bills
- Contracts and special medical equipment
- Plane fares related to treatment
- Any other documentation of damages claimed in the lawsuit

The LNC should review the responses to interrogatories to identify additional documents that should be requested. A request to produce can be sent with the initial complaint or at any time during the litigation. The deadlines for responding to interrogatories also apply to requests for production that are governed by FRCP 34.[9] These requests are limited to documents and things that are in the possession, custody, or control of the party upon whom the request is served. Anything not within the party's control or possession need not be produced. If the LNC needs to examine an original medical record, the request for production should specify "a reasonable time, place, or manner for doing this and the opposing party should reply that the review will be permitted, and when, or state a basis for the objection to this request" (see Appendix 3.6, Defendant's Request for Production).

Review of Interrogatories and Request for Production

Litigation can grow complicated with the exchange of requests for documents, x-rays, and medical records. Therefore, it is essential for the LNC to develop a method of tracking both what is being produced and what is being received. Checklist/production tables serve this purpose (see Figure 3.1).

The division of labor varies in law firms. Thus, in some instances, the LNC may determine what needs to be requested and reviews documents that have been received, but the paralegal or secretary sends out the actual requests. There is one caveat: when several individuals are working on a file and responsibilities are delegated, important deadlines can be missed. The smart LNC will maintain a personal tickler file to absolutely ensure follow-up on important issues that could fall through the cracks when, say, someone is on vacation. For example, a tickler date may represent a reminder to notify opposing counsel that documents from them are still pending. The dates of these reminders can be recorded on the checklist/production table tool. It is important to actually receive each and every thing that has been requested, avoiding surprises at the time of trial. If one side resists producing documents, such as a hospital's refusal to produce incident reports, policies, etc., the requesting attorney may need to file a Motion to Compel with the court. The judge may elect to review the documents in question to determine whether they are relevant and have to be produced.

When producing records to opposing counsel, the LNC should count the number of pages being sent and record on the checklist/production table who is and should be getting a copy of the documents. Later, when another party or the same party requests the materials, there will be a simple record in place to show who got what and when. If the requesting party asks for documents a second time, this simple but valuable tracking list will verify the date of the previous request and date that the documents were mailed out in response. Perception of the LNC's legal team's competence versus less-than-stellar competence of the adversary is important. Any competitive edge is valuable during the adversarial litigation process.

The LNC must carefully review the opposing party's answers and summarize those answers. The medical records are analyzed and information placed into a concise format that is easy for the attorney to understand. Usually a narrative of medical issues and facts is valuable for the attorney's use and for potential experts to review. These summaries will be discoverable. The LNC should provide a chronology of all that happened to the plaintiff, identified by date and time. One way to summarize the data and to present them is in a flow sheet format as shown in Figure 3.2 or in a summary as shown in Appendix 3.7. It is helpful to include the specialty of all treating physicians, to offer normal ranges for any laboratory testing done and described, to define medical terms and abbreviations, and to define and give rationale for prescribing all medications. Another approach is to create a calendar showing the medical treatment as in Figure 3.3. In this example, a calendar is useful in that it reveals to the attorney the number and frequency of prescriptions issued to the plaintiff, by whom they were issued, and where they were filled.

The LNC's job is to relate the facts of the case in a format easily understandable to the attorney. Always remember the "ABC's" of writing: accuracy, brevity, and clarity. The LNC should be as concise as possible when writing summaries. The attorney will not appreciate an encyclopedia of each and every lab test done on the client during a 20-day hospitalization. Rather than list 50 tests that were done and found to be normal, it is better to say simply what is relevant. For example:

"The daily CBC (complete blood count) and electrolytes were normal from 1/2/99–1/15/99. The 3/3/99 laboratory results showed marked elevation in the CPK (creatine phosphokinase) level of 1536. (Normal values are 5–70. This test measures tissue damage.) The WBC (white blood count) was 25,000. (Normal values are 5,000–10,000.) This value is elevated in the presence of infection and severe trauma."

No matter how much the LNC knows, his or her value in the litigation process is jeopardized by an inability to clearly and concisely communicate with the attorney. Please refer to Chapter 30, Legal Writing, where this important topic is discussed in greater detail.

Requests for Admissions

Requests for Admissions are written requests by one party asking another party to acknowledge the truth of certain facts or the authenticity of certain materials.

Doe v. General Hospital et al.

	Hospital Record, 7/1/97 Admission	Income Tax Returns, '93–'97	Complete x-ray Copies, 23 Films	Dr. X Treating Records '97 through Current	Pending from Defendant
Atty. Smith (defendant hospital)		Produced 1/5/99		Produced 2/1/99	Pending insurance info, employment contract
Atty. Jones (Dr. P, radiologist)	Produced 2/1/99	Produced 1/5/99		Produced 2/1/99	Pending copy of insurance policy, verification of PA name
Atty. Green (Dr. N, surgeon)	Produced 3/1/99	Produced 3/1/99	Produced 3/1/99	All (except Dr. N's and Dr. L's) produced 3/1/99	
Atty. McKay (Dr. L, surgeon)	Produced 2/1/99	Produced 1/5/99	Produced 3/1/99	All (except Dr. N's and Dr. L's) produced 2/1/99	Pending CV; 2nd request sent 3/6/99

Figure 3.1 Production Table

Medical History Chronology — Mary Owens
Re: Owens v. Smith et al.

Date	Physician/ Place	Diagnosis	Diagnostic Exams	Observations/Procedures	Treatment
6/19/31				Date of birth in Choctaw, OK	
6/13/76	George Gaynor/ The Oaks Hospital	1. Rule out cardiac disease or coronary insufficiency 2. Possible degenerative disk disease with radicular pain to the left upper extremity 3. Rule out polycythemia	Stress test: Abnormal findings; Gallbladder x-rays: normal except for a small sliding hiatus hernia; Chest x-ray: showed interstitial fibrosis and some degenerative changes to C5–6 of the cervical spine	She had a high blood count and a complaint of chest pain; she also complained of neck pain and numbness to the left upper arm along with some radicular pain down the left trapezius; bone marrow studies showed the borderline polycythemia to be due to pulmonary fibrosis; she was seen by a cardiologist	Persantine (vasodilator), Aspirin, physical therapy to include cervical traction and hot packs, Inderal (antiarrhythmics), Valium, Febridyne #3 (analgesic with codeine)
6/20/76– 6/22/76	D.G. Richards/ City Hospital		Coronary angiogram: exam was essentially normal with no mitral valve prolapse or undue thickening of the left ventricle	45-year-old female with a 1.5-year history of intermittent discomfort in the left inframammary area radiating to the left arm; recent treadmill test at The Oaks was positive; blood pressure 130/60, pulse 100; exam revealed a positive left thoracic outlet syndrome with minimal costochondral tenderness on the left; based on testing, it was felt that her discomfort was due to left thoracic outlet syndrome	Low-fat diet, Ascriptin (Maalox-coated aspirin), Persantine

Figure 3.2   Medical History Chronology

Date	Provider/Location	Diagnosis	Notes	Treatment
6/24/76	George Gaynor/Office		Weight: 142.5 lbs; patient had a negative coronary arteriogram, but does have thoracic outlet syndrome; has numbness of the left hand; also has diminished sensation to pain in L4–5	Motrin, Robaxin
8/11/76	George Gaynor/Office		Still has burning of the left scapular area between the medial border and spine	Injection of Aristocort into two trigger points
8/18/76	George Gaynor/Office		Weight: 144 lbs; patient in constant pain	Injection into right mid thoracic/paraspinal region
8/27/76	George Gaynor/Office	Possible cervical disk rupture	Weight: 142 lbs; she may be a little bit improved, but she still has pain; there was no improvement from the injection; will admit into the hospital	
8/31/76–9/2/76	George Gaynor/Medical Plaza Hospital	Herniated nucleus pulposus at C6–7 of the cervical spine; Cervical myelogram: showed an extradural defect at C6–7 with bilateral widening of the nerve root	Chief complaint: neck pain radiating down the left upper extremity into the left upper chest area; exam showed tenderness and limitation of range of neck motion due to pain; deep tendon reflexes are normal; her blood chemistry did show an elevated blood sugar, but this was not felt to be significant	Motrin (mild analgesic), Robaxin (musculoskeletal relaxant)
9/17/76	George Gaynor Office		Weight: 144 lbs; patient still having trouble; return as needed	

Figure 3.2 Medical History Chronology (*Continued*)

| 9/13/90–10/12/90 | George Gaynor/Medical Plaza Hospital | Recurrent herniated lumbar disk, L4–5 with degenerative disk | MRI of lumbar spine: large herniated pulposus at L4–5 which is centered slightly to the left of midline; post-op changes at this level from prior laminectomy; Lumbar spine x-ray: status post laminectomy at L5–S1 and interbody fusion at L4–5; no spondylolysis or spondylolisthesis is noted | Surgery: Assisted by Dr. Ralph Dodge, Drs. Miller and Christensen performed a posterior L4–5 re-exploration with L4 & L5 nerve root decompression, with reexploration, removal of large central recurrent L4–5 disk, with discectomy and posterior lumbar interbody fusion; prognosis is guarded due to the discovery of a great deal of scar tissue at the L4–5 nerve root and surrounding epidural sac | Baclofen, Flexeril, Anaprox |
| | | | CT scan of lumbar spine: status post inner body fusion at L4–5 with minimal protrusion of the bone plug into the spinal canal; massive epidural fibrosis surrounding the thecal sac and nerve roots at L4–5; Blood chemistry: Glucose 165 (high with normal levels 66–110), Sodium 130 (low with normal levels 135–145), Potassium 3.0 (low with normal levels 3.5–5.0), LDH 350 (high with normal levels 83–200) | Hospital course: Postoperatively, she had weakness of the left leg and weakness of dorsiflexion of the left foot | |

Figure 3.2   Medical History Chronology (*Continued*)

			Current meds: Baclofen (skeletal muscle relaxant), Anaprox (nonsteroidal, anti-inflammatory agent), Vicodin (analgesic)
10/24/90	Thomas Miller/ Office		She is improving; good majority of her left leg pain is resolving and her foot strength is improving; she still does not have much dorsiflexion (ability to move toes upward toward head) of her toes, but her anterior tibialis muscle group is better; she is wearing a back brace; overall, things seem to be improving; to return in 2 weeks	
11/15/90	Thomas Miller/ Office		She has had more back pain; this may be related to her activities; she has some slight residual discomfort in the lateral calf, but most of her pain is in the back and right hip; this should resolve with time; she continues to cut down on the Vicodin; to return in 2 weeks when she sees Dr. Christensen	

Figure 3.2 Medical History Chronology (*Continued*)

Date	Provider/Location		Current meds:
11/26/90	Thomas Miller/ Office	She still has "a great deal" of back pain along with pain in the right hip and groin; however, she has been increasing her activities and she is finding things somewhat easier to do; she was on Percodan before her surgery and now she is down to 3 Vicodin a day; she reports that upon rising in the morning she has bilateral leg cramping and numbness that improves during the day; he wants her to get down from 2 pills to 1 a day. She can dorsiflex her foot; discussed with the patient and her daughter the need for surgery and her overall limitations; she has a good disposition and seems to be accepting things in stride; to return in January	Current meds: Flexeril (musculoskeletal relaxant), Anaprox, Vicodin, Baclofen
1/7/91	Thomas Miller/ Office	She seems to be doing well; her leg and foot weakness have improved almost back to normal and she has been having less leg pain — the pain is tolerable; she still takes Vicodin 3–4 tablets/ day; told to stop taking the Baclofen	Current meds: Vicodin, Flexeril, Baclofen, Anaprox

Note: See Figure 25.1 in *Legal Nurse Consulting: Principles and Practice,* Bogart, J., Ed., CRC Press, Boca Raton, FL, 1997.

Figure 3.2 Medical History Chronology (*Continued*)

Sunday	Monday	Tuesday	Wednesday	Thursday	Friday	Saturday
	1	2	3 Percocet #60 Filled at Brown's Pharmacy in Miami	4	5	6
7	8	9	10	11 Percocet #60 Filled at Brown's Pharmacy in Miami	12	13
14	15 Percocet #60 Filled at Brown's Pharmacy in Miami	16 Valium 10 mg as needed 4 times daily for anxiety — Rx Dr. Jones	17 Valium 10 mg #60 Filled at Brown's Pharmacy in Miami	18	19	20
21	22	23	24	25	26 Percocet #60 Valium 10 mg #60 Filled at Brown's Pharmacy in Miami	27
28	29	30 Valium 10 mg #60 Filled at Brown's Pharmacy in Miami				

Figure 3.3   Calendar Method of Organizing Data

The party served must file a written answer or objection within 30 days, or such time as the individual state allows. The answer must admit parts that are true, deny any other parts specifically, or detail a reason why the party can neither truthfully admit nor deny the matter. If the party upon whom the admissions are served fails to respond, the requests are admitted as written. Requests for Admission are used most often to narrow issues of fact or law that are essential to one's case. They also provide one way to establish the authenticity of documents provided during discovery. For example, a Request for Admissions could ask a defendant physician to affirm or deny that he is board-certified in thoracic surgery, and that he has performed at least 200 coronary bypass procedures. If the defendant does not answer the Request for Admissions, the statements are accepted as written (i.e., the defendant is board-certified in thoracic surgery and has performed at least 200 coronary bypass procedures).

Physical and Mental Examinations

An adverse party may require a physical or mental examination of a person by an "impartial" doctor when that physical or mental condition is at issue in a lawsuit.[6] In practice, physical and mental examination is usually limited to personal injury or paternity suits. If there is no agreement between the parties as to medical examinations, a compulsory exam is available when (1) the mental or physical condition, including the blood group of a person, is in controversy; and (2) the requesting party demonstrates that there is "good cause" for ordering such an examination. The party requesting the exam can select the doctor to conduct it. The role of the LNC in this case can be to assist the attorney in selecting said physician, make arrangements for the actual examination, and attend the exam as an observer. Please refer to Chapter 29, Defense Medical Examinations, which discusses this topic in detail.

Depositions

A deposition is the oral examination of any person a party believes has relevant information. Deposition testimony is like trial testimony in that the entire process is conducted under oath and recorded by a court reporter. The deposition provides the opportunity to question the party and further evaluate the strength of the case. It is also an opportunity to evaluate the impression that a witness will make on a jury. The principal purposes of deposition are to:

- Identify the opposition's issues and opinions
- Explore issues likely to arise at trial
- Preserve testimony if the witness is unavailable at the time of trial
- Identify other sources of relevant evidence
- Provide material for summary judgment motion and impeachment of witnesses at trial
- Identify and explain documentary and physical evidence
- Identify what witnesses do not know
- Obtain admissions
- Evaluate the credibility and experience of an expert witness

The LNC has a strong role before the actual deposition of witnesses. Before any oral deposition, the attorney and LNC should review answers to previous interrogatories, all documents produced, and any other information obtained relating to the lawsuit. This review makes it possible to identify people whose depositions should be taken, and areas and wording of questions to be pursued at deposition.

To prepare the attorney for the medical malpractice deposition of defendants, the LNC must identify the applicable standards of care and the failure of each deponent to meet the standard. It will simplify the task to list specifically each standard and how it was breached, indicating what supportive documentation appears in the medical records (see Appendix 3.8). It is helpful to make a copy of the medical record and sequentially number-stamp or use clear, numbered labels to number the pages. By using this working copy, the attorney can access the exact location of the referred information. The attorney needs to quickly locate the source of information with page numbers from that medical record.

The LNC should also prepare deposition questions for the attorney in all areas relating to medical issues. A review of interrogatories and medical records identifies areas that need clarification (see Appendix 3.9). In this example, a nurse deponent documented in the nurse's notes that the patient was "uncooperative" but did not relate the behavior to its apparent cause — poor oxygenation. The attorney would need to explore this area further. The LNC is able to educate the attorney regarding types of safety features of the relevant monitoring equipment etc.

Preparation is key to winning lawsuits, and the LNC soon realizes that depositions are extremely important in evaluating the strength or weakness of the opponent's case. Prior to each deposition, the LNC must gather as much information about the deponent as possible. If the deposition of a medical expert will be taken, the attorney needs all related information. A review of a copy of that expert's curriculum vitae helps the LNC identify board certification in the appropriate areas and prior practice experience. The relevant medical board can provide a copy of the expert's complete licensure file. The medical board also has information whether or not the deponent has ever been subject to formal disciplinary action against his or her license. Some of this information is now available on the Internet at the professional regulatory agency's site, such as the Board of Nursing or Board of Medical Examiners. Competency of the deponent is at issue, and if the deponent has had problems in the past, it will strengthen the opposition's case. Copies of all such investigative files should be available for use during deposition.

It is important to determine whether the testifying expert has ever been a defendant in a medical malpractice case. A request for searches of the applicable civil trial record in the state in which the individual practices medicine should be made. If any cases are found in the search, a request for a copy of the complaint and docket sheet to determine any relevant allegations is appropriate. If the expert has testified in previous cases, copies of previous deposition testimony are useful; contradicting testimony in the current deposition will lessen the credibility of that witness. Both plaintiff and defense attorneys can now access transcripts from services that collect deposition transcripts supplied by other attorneys who have deposed the witness. The LNC must perform an exhaustive literature search to find everything the expert has written in regard to the specific issue in contest. Computerized medical literature searches help to do this quickly. It is also important to get hard copies of relevant journal articles, book chapters, and textbooks. The LNC should summarize each article, pointing out areas of inconsistency with the opposition's point of view in the particular case. An expert testifying in contrast to articles may lessen the expert's credibility. Intense preparation for deposition prevents surprises. One must not overlook the importance of a deposition. It is the one possible time to require a nonparty to appear for questioning or to produce documents.

Subpoenas

The LNC needs to understand the purpose and use of subpoenas. A subpoena is a tool requiring a witness or a nonparty to appear or to produce documents. Subpoenas preserve one's rights at the time of trial by allowing the assessment of costs to anyone not complying. More important, subpoenas have the force and effect of a court order and are strictly interpreted in accordance with the language in which they are written. Accuracy in wording is crucial. If the individual is not named correctly, the person does not need to comply with the subpoena. During the trial phase of litigation, a subpoena to appear is a command from the court and must not be ignored. Without a subpoena, there is no recourse if the witness fails to appear. During the discovery phase, the subpoena makes it possible to retrieve documents from third parties. There is one caveat: a subpoena *duces tecum* (to appear accompanied by certain documents or things) and subpoenas for deposition are not required for a party to the lawsuit, but are required for nonparties.

In summary, the discovery phase of litigation is key to the outcome of any case. LNCs are unique members of the law team because of their superior knowledge about the medical aspects of complex litigation. The LNC contributes greatly to each phase of discovery and assists in defining and redefining the issues of the case.

References

1. Schultze, E.H., Jung, P.M., and Adams, R.P., *Introduction to the American Legal System,* Pearson Publishing, Dallas, 1994.
2. Fed.R. Civ.P. 3.
3. Fed.R. Civ.P. 8.
4. Fed.R. Civ.P. 12(e).
5. Fed.R. Civ.P. 12(b).
6. Weinstein, M.I., Ed., *Introduction to Civil Litigation,* 3rd ed., Delmar Publishing, Albany, 1993.
7. Fed.R. Civ.P. 26(b) (1).
8. Fed.R. Civ.P. 33(a).
9. Fed.R. Civ.P. 34.
10. Garner, B.A. and Black, H.L., Eds., *Black's Law Dictionary,* 7th ed., West Publishing, St. Paul, 1999.

Additional Reading

Statsky, W.P. and Werner, R.J., Jr., *Case Analysis and Fundamentals of Legal Writing,* 4th ed., West Publishing, St. Paul, 1995.
Strunk, W., Jr. and White, E.B., *The Elements of Style,* 3rd ed., Macmillan, New York, 1979.

Test Questions

1. All of the following are limitations of interrogatories as a discovery tool
   EXCEPT:
   A. They are expensive to use.
   B. Answers are not spontaneous responses.
   C. They can be served only to parties in the litigation.
   D. The answers are often vague.

2. All of the following are uses of depositions EXCEPT:
   A. To identify the opposition's issues and opinions
   B. To identify the applicable standards of care in the case
   C. To explore issues likely to arise at trial
   D. To determine what type of witness the deponent will make

3. All of the following information can easily be obtained when researching
   a defense expert's background EXCEPT:
   A. Curriculum vitae
   B. Complete licensure file
   C. Complete list of the expert's publications
   D. Income tax returns

4. All of the following apply to subpoenas EXCEPT:
   A. They may be served to parties or nonparties in the litigation.
   B. They are loosely interpreted in accordance with the language in which
      they are written.
   C. They have the force and effect of a court order.
   D. They make it possible to obtain documents from third parties.

5. All of the following are discoverable documents EXCEPT:
   A. Hospital policies and procedures
   B. Attorney's notes from client conference
   C. Plane fare receipts relating to treatments
   D. Operation manuals for medical equipment

Answers: 1. A, 2. B, 3. D, 4. B, 5. B

Appendix 3.1
Complaint for Damages

IN THE CIRCUIT COURT OF THE
900TH JUDICIAL CIRCUIT IN
AND FOR HAPPY COUNTY, FLORIDA

CASE NO.

JOHN Q. SMITH and SALLY SMITH, his wife,

Plaintiffs,

vs.

CITY HOSPITAL, INC.; SID
SIDNEY, M.D.; SIDNEY & JONES, M.D., P.A.,

Defendants.
Florida Bar No. 111111

COMPLAINT FOR DAMAGES

The plaintiffs, JOHN Q. SMITH and SALLY SMITH (collectively hereinafter the "plaintiffs"), sue the defendants, CITY HOSPITAL, INC., SID SIDNEY, M.D., AND SIDNEY & JONES, M.D., P.A. (collectively hereinafter the "defendants"), and allege as follows:

1. This is a medical negligence case in which the damages at issue are more than Fifteen Thousand Dollars ($15,000.00) exclusive of costs, interest, and attorneys' fees.
2. The plaintiffs JOHN Q. SMITH and SALLY SMITH are individuals residing in Happy County, Florida.
3. The defendant CITY HOSPITAL (hereinafter the "defendant HOSPITAL") is a corporation licensed and doing business in Happy County, Florida.
4. The defendant SIDNEY was, at all times material hereto, acting within the course and scope of his employment with SIDNEY & JONES, M.D., P.A.
5. All the acts described below took place in Happy County, Florida.
6. The plaintiffs have complied with all common law and statutory conditions precedent to the bringing of this action.
7. Undersigned counsel for the plaintiffs hereby certify that a reasonable investigation has been undertaken in connection with this case and said investigation has given rise to a good faith belief that grounds exist for an action against each named defendant.

THE FACTS

8. The defendant doctor was a member of the medical staff of the defendant HOSPITAL.
9. JOHN Q. SMITH was referred to the defendant SIDNEY for a mass in his left thigh. The defendant SIDNEY did not perform a biopsy of the mass.

The defendant SIDNEY performed an excision of the mass at the defendant HOSPITAL on January 1, 1999. The hospital pathologist reported that the mass was benign. A later review of the slides showed the mass to be a grade 3 squamous epithelioma.

10. The patient was never referred to an oncologist or returned to surgery after findings were learned.

11. JOHN Q. SMITH has now suffered a recurrence of his disease by metastasis.

COUNT I — THE HOSPITAL — VICARIOUS LIABILITY FOR ACTS OF ITS EMPLOYEES AND AGENTS

12. Plaintiffs reallege all the allegations contained in paragraphs (1) through (11) and further allege as follows:

13. The actions of the employees and agents of the defendant HOSPITAL were negligent in their care and treatment of JOHN Q. SMITH by failing to identify malignant cells in JOHN Q. SMITH's mass.

14. The actions of the defendant HOSPITAL described above were below applicable standards of care for accredited hospitals in Happy County, Florida and similar medical communities and were below the standard of care set forth in § 766.102, Fla. Stat. (1999) (i.e., below that level of care, skill, and treatment that in light of all relevant circumstances was considered appropriate by reasonably careful hospitals in similar communities having the same facilities).

15. As a direct and proximate result of the negligence described in this Count, the plaintiffs JOHN Q. SMITH and SALLY SMITH suffered the injuries described below.

COUNT II — DEFENDANT SIDNEY

16. Plaintiffs reallege all the allegations contained in paragraphs (1) through (11) and further allege as follows:

17. In his management of JOHN Q. SMITH, the defendant SIDNEY was negligent in his care and treatment in the following respects:

   A. By failing to determine the nature of JOHN Q. SMITH's lesion prior to removing the same;

   B. By failing to refer JOHN Q. SMITH to a surgical oncologist for evaluation;

   C. By failing to return the patient to surgery to obtain clear tissue margins after learning the true pathological findings of the mass.

18. The actions of the defendant SIDNEY described in paragraph (17) above were negligent and below applicable standards of care for physicians practicing the specialty of orthopedics in Happy County, Florida and similar medical communities and were below the standard of care set forth in § 766.102, Fla. Stat. (1999) (i.e., below that level of care, skill, and treatment that in light of all relevant circumstances was considered appropriate by reasonably careful physicians in similar communities having the same facilities).

19. As a direct and proximate result of the negligence described in this Count, the plaintiffs JOHN Q. SMITH and SALLY SMITH suffered the injuries described below.

COUNT III — THE DEFENDANT SIDNEY & JONES, M.D., P.A.

20. The plaintiffs reallege all the allegations contained in paragraphs (1) through (11) and further allege as follows:
21. The defendant SIDNEY & JONES, M.D., P.A. is liable to the plaintiffs for injuries sustained as a result of the negligence of the defendant SIDNEY in that, while treating the plaintiff JOHN Q. SMITH, the defendant SIDNEY was acting within the course and scope of his employment and agency with the defendant SIDNEY & JONES, M.D., P.A.
22. As a direct and proximate result of the negligence described in this Count, the plaintiffs JOHN Q. SMITH and SALLY SMITH suffered the injuries described below.

DAMAGES

23. As a direct and proximate result of the above-described negligence, JOHN Q. SMITH has suffered recurrence of his disease by metastasis and has suffered the following additional damages: bodily injury, pain and suffering, disability, disfigurement, mental anguish, loss of capacity for the enjoyment of life, aggravation of an existing disease or defect, expenses for hospitalization and medical and nursing care, past lost earnings, and loss of ability to earn money in the future.
24. As a direct and proximate result of the injury, SALLY SMITH has been caused to suffer the loss of her husband's consortium, services, love, affection, society, and attention. The losses are either permanent or continuing.

WHEREFORE, the plaintiffs JOHN Q. SMITH and SALLY SMITH demand judgment against the defendants CITY HOSPITAL, INC., SID SIDNEY, AND SIDNEY & JONES, M.D., P.A. in excess of Fifteen Thousand Dollars ($15,000.00), plus costs, and all other relief deemed just and proper under the circumstances, and request trial by jury of all issues triable as of right by jury.

Dated this 20th day of February, 2002.

Respectfully submitted,

BROWN AND JONES ATTORNEYS, INC.

Attorneys for Plaintiffs
15 Trendel Place
Talver, Florida 11111
Telephone: 411–411–0911
By _____
Carla Ridge, Esq.

Appendix 3.2
Defendant's First Set of Interrogatories to Plaintiff

NO. 96-1234-Z

JOHN PLAINTIFF	•	IN THE DISTRICT COURT OF
VS.	•	HARRIS COUNTY, TEXAS
DAVID DEFENDANT, M.D.	•	007TH JUDICIAL DISTRICT

TO: Plaintiff, John Plaintiff, by and through his attorney of record, R.E. Ryan, RYAN, WILSON & GOLDSMITH, P.A., 555 N. 23rd, Houston, Texas 77001

Pursuant to Rule 168 of the Texas Rules of Civil Procedure, the Defendant, _____, serves the attached interrogatories upon you, the answers to which shall be made under oath separately and fully in writing within thirty (30) days after the service of such interrogatories and shall be given to the undersigned counsel of record. To the extent possible, each interrogatory should be answered in the space following it. The answers should be signed under oath in the space following the last interrogatory. The Defendant also requests that the Plaintiff continue to supplement the answers to the interrogatories as provided by Rule 168. The original of the interrogatories is being forwarded to the above attorney as required by the Texas Rules of Civil Procedure.

Respectfully submitted,
SMITH DEFENSE FIRM

By: _____
Walter Smith
SBN 01010101

Address
Houston, Texas 77001
(713) 555–5555
(713) 555–5555 FAX
Attorneys for Defendant
David Defendant, M.D.

Appendix 3.3
Certificate of Service

I hereby certify that I have caused a true and correct copy of the foregoing instrument to be served upon opposing counsel of record herein, by certified mail, return receipt requested, or by hand-delivery, and upon all other counsel of record herein, by regular mail, on this _____ day of _____, 20_.

_____
Walter Smith

Appendix 3.4
Defendant's Interrogatory Questions to Plaintiff

Defendant's First Set of Interrogatories to Plaintiff

1. Please state your name, date of birth, place of birth, current address, social security number, driver's license number, date of each marriage, and the name and age of each dependent child.
2. State what education you have had, including the names and addresses of the schools you have attended, and list all diplomas and degrees you have received.
3. Please state specifically the nature of any damage and injuries suffered by you that you allege to have been caused by this Defendant.
4. Have you recovered from the damages and injuries you allege to have been caused by this Defendant in this lawsuit? If not, what complaints do you still have?
5. If you have been hospitalized for any reason since the date of the incident made the basis of this suit, please state:
   A. The name and address of the hospital
   B. The date of admission and date of discharge
   C. The total hospital charges
6. For each of the doctors you have seen for any reason related to the incident made the basis of this suit, please give:
   A. The name and address of the doctor
   B. The date you saw the doctor
   C. What the doctor charged you
   D. The diagnosis of your injuries, damages, or complaints as related to you by the doctor
7. If any doctor has told you that you will need to undergo a surgical procedure or other treatment as a result of the injuries and damages that you allege were caused by this Defendant, please state:
   A. The name and address of each doctor
   B. The date such doctor told you that you needed surgery or other treatment
   C. The type of surgical procedure or other treatment such doctor said you would need to undergo
   D. The approximate cost of such surgery or other treatment
8. Has any doctor been critical of the care given to you by this Defendant? (This excludes consulting experts, whose opinions are privileged by the Texas Rules of Civil Procedure or are protected by the attorney/client privilege.) If so, please state:
   A. The name and address of each doctor
   B. The date and place such statements were made
   C. The names and addresses of all persons who heard said statements
   D. The substance of such statements
9. Has anyone ever told you that this Defendant or anyone else caused the injuries or complaints made the basis of this suit? If so, please state:
   A. Specifically, what was said about who caused said injuries
   B. The date these statements were made

        C. The names and current addresses of all witnesses who heard such statements

        D. The names and current addresses of all persons making such statements

10. Please state the following information regarding your employment history for 10 years prior to the date of the incident made the basis of this suit:

    A. The name and address of each employer for whom you worked, and the name of your immediate supervisor

    B. The period of time you worked for each employer and the reason each employment terminated

    C. What you earned per hour in each employment and your average weekly wage in each employment

    D. The nature of your duties in each employment

11. Please furnish the following information with respect to your work history since the date of the incident made the basis of this suit:

    A. The name and address of each employer for whom you have worked and the name of your immediate supervisor

    B. The approximate period of time that you worked for each employer and details concerning the reason that such employment was terminated

    C. Your average weekly wage for each employment period

    D. The nature of your employment for each employer and the duties that you performed

    E. Whether any complaints have been made to you by any employer regarding the manner in which you performed your job; if so, please describe these complaints

12. Have you missed any time from work as a result of any injuries or damage allegedly caused by this Defendant? If so, please state how much time you have lost from work and how much in wages, if any, you have lost as a result of the incident made the basis of this suit.

13. Provide a complete chronological medical history for the last 10 years, listing all hospital admissions (include name and address of hospital or medical care facility), physicians who have treated you (include name, address, and telephone number for each), medications prescribed for you, the conditions you were treated for, and the treatment you received.

14. State whether you have ever had or now have any unusual physical or mental condition or ailment, such as diabetes, a heart condition, arthritis, etc., and if so, describe them in detail and state whether you have ever received medical treatment for these conditions.

15. State whether you have ever been convicted of or pleaded guilty to any felony offense or misdemeanor involving moral turpitude, and whether you have ever been confined in any jail or prison. State whether you are presently on probation in connection with any conviction, and if so, state the name and location of your probation officer.

16. State the amount of taxable income that you reported for the preceding 5 years. If you will do so without a Motion to Produce, attach to your answers to these interrogatories a copy of your income tax return for each of the aforesaid years.

17. State whether you have ever had a claim for workers' compensation or any other type of claim or lawsuit for personal injury against any person,

firm, or corporation and the details surrounding such claims or lawsuits, including the part of your body alleged to have been injured.

18. Please state the name, current business address and business telephone number, and area of specialty of any expert witness that you may call to testify at the time of trial of this cause. Also, please state each expert's mental impressions and opinions.

19. Please state the specific text of each report, factual observation, and opinion that each expert identified in response to the preceding interrogatory has made regarding this lawsuit. In the alternative, please attach true and complete copies of each expert's reports.

20. State in detail the treatment, alleged complications arising from the treatment, lack of treatment, omissions, and all negligent acts that you contend were committed or omitted during this Defendant's course of treatment that contributed to any injuries or damages claimed by you. Include the date and time of treatment when describing acts or omissions, and include *which* agent or representative committed such act or omission.

21. What expenses or monetary losses, other than lost wages and medical expenses, do you attribute to injuries and damage that you allege to have been caused by this Defendant?

22. Please state the names, addresses, and telephone numbers of all persons with knowledge of relevant facts concerning Plaintiff's claims against this Defendant, the treatment in question, Plaintiff's alleged damages, or any other aspect of this suit.

23. Please list the name, address, and telephone number of each pharmacy where you obtained medications for two years prior to the incident giving rise to this lawsuit and to the present. Please include your prescription numbers and medications obtained.

24. Please state the name, current and last known address, current and last known employer, and home telephone number of all eyewitnesses to the treatment made the basis of this lawsuit.

25. Please state whether there are any Medicare/Medicaid liens, or whether any Plaintiff herein receives Medicare/Medicaid benefits related to the care and treatment made the subject of this lawsuit.

Appendix 3.5
Jurat Sheet

THE STATE OF TEXAS
COUNTY OF HARRIS

BEFORE ME, the undersigned authority, on this day personally appeared JOHN PLAINTIFF, known to me to be the person whose name is subscribed to the above and foregoing instrument, who, after being by me duly sworn, upon oath stated that he has read the foregoing instrument and knows the contents thereof, and states that the answers are true and correct.

_____

JOHN PLAINTIFF

SUBSCRIBED AND SWORN TO BEFORE ME, the undersigned authority, on this the _____ day of _____, 2002 to certify which witness my hand and seal of office.

_____
Notary Public in and for
The State of Texas

My Commission Expires:

_____

Appendix 3.6
Request for Production

CASE NO. 96–1234-Z

JOHN PLAINTIFF   IN THE DISTRICT COURT

       VS.   007TH JUDICIAL DISTRICT

DAVID DEFENDANT, M.D.   HARRIS COUNTY, TEXAS

REQUEST FOR PRODUCTION

TO: Plaintiff, JOHN PLAINTIFF, by and through his attorney of record, BADIE, TURK AND TENNEY P. C., 5555 N 33rd, Houston, Texas 77001

Pursuant to T.R.C.P. 167, Defendant DAVID DEFENDANT, M.D., requests that the following documents and tangible things be produced for inspection and copying at the offices of the undersigned within thirty-three days from receipt of this request.

1. Plaintiff's federal income tax returns for the past five years, including W-2 forms, if any lost wages or diminished earnings capacity is claimed in this suit.
2. All doctor, hospital, medication, and all other medical bills and expenses that are claimed in this suit.
3. The names, addresses, and phone numbers of all expert witnesses whom Plaintiff may call to testify in this case.
4. All reports, correspondence, or writing of any kind from all expert witnesses whom Plaintiff may call to testify in this case.
5. All statements, as defined by T.R.C.P. 166b(2)(g), made by this Defendant or any of his agents or employees.

6. All recordings of any expert witness in this case whom Plaintiff may call to testify in this case.
7. All correspondence or writings from Defendant to Plaintiff or members of Plaintiff's family.
8. All medical, doctor, or hospital records related to Plaintiff's alleged injuries in Plaintiff's possession or constructive possession (please sign and return with your responses to these Requests the attached medical authorization).
9. Any and all documentation of any damages claimed in this lawsuit.
10. Any and all documents or written materials that you contend were authored by, published by, produced by, manufactured by, or made by this Defendant that are in any way relevant to the above-styled lawsuit, including but not limited to documents that Plaintiff intends to introduce into evidence at the time of trial.
11. Any and all photographs taken of Plaintiff's alleged damages or injuries.
12. Any and all documents that Plaintiff intends to introduce into evidence or use at the time of trial for any purpose. This is an ongoing request requiring supplementation pursuant to the Ohio Rules of Civil Procedure.
13. All statements, as defined by T.R.C.P. 166b(2)(g), made by any witness with knowledge of relevant facts concerning the incident or treatment made the basis of this suit.
14. Any and all pharmacy records of Plaintiff regarding medications obtained in the five years prior to the incident made the basis of this lawsuit and to the present time, including but not limited to records indicating the name of the medication, the name and location of the pharmacy filling each prescription, the date on which each prescription or medication was received, and the name of the physician prescribing such medication.
15. All documents and other tangible items provided to any expert witness whom Plaintiff may call to testify at the trial of this cause or whose work product forms a basis, in whole or in part, of the mental impressions and opinions of a testifying expert.

WHEREFORE, PREMISES CONSIDERED, Defendant, DAVID DEFENDANT, M.D., prays that the above items be produced at the time and place as requested.

Respectfully submitted,

WESTER DEFENSE FIRM

By:_____
Robert Wester
SBN: 01010101
1234 Main Street
Houston, Texas 77001
(XXX) 555–5555
FAX: (XXX) 555–5555
ATTORNEYS FOR DEFENDANT
DAVID DEFENDANT, M.D.

CERTIFICATE OF SERVICE

I hereby certify that a true and correct copy of the above and foregoing document has been forwarded to Plaintiff's counsel of record by certified mail, return receipt requested, on this _____ day of _____, 2002.

_____

Robert Wester

MEDICAL AUTHORIZATION

TO WHOM IT MAY CONCERN:

This will authorize you to allow Ann Russ, or her agents or representatives, to inspect the originals of any and all medical records on JOHN PLAINTIFF that are in your possession or subject to your control, to allow copies to be made of such records, and to discuss JOHN PLAINTIFF'S medical care and treatment with you, PROVIDED:

1. Information obtained by this authorization is for use in the pending litigation, and shall not be disseminated for any other purpose.
2. You are specifically and expressly authorized to accept a copy of this authorization as though it were an original.
3. You are specifically and expressly released from any liability that would otherwise arise from the release of this information.

Also, a copy of this release may be used as an original.

_____

JOHN PLAINTIFF

S.S. No. _____

GIVEN UNDER MY HAND AND SEAL OF OFFICE, this _____ day of _____, 2002

_____

NOTARY PUBLIC IN AND FOR THE STATE OF HAWAII

_____

Printed name of notary and expiration date of commission

Appendix 3.7
Medical Record Summary

JANE JONES
RE: JONES VS. SMITH, et al.

REGIONAL MEDICAL CENTER, JUNE 22–28, 2000

ADMITTING DIAGNOSIS: Severe dysmenorrhea, rule out endometriosis

ATTENDING PHYSICIAN: Dr. Ken Smith

Time	Documentation	Care Provider
June 22, 2000		
6:30 a.m.	44-year-old obese Caucasian female ambulatory to room 13 with male friend; states allergy to sulfa, Demerol, and synthetic plastics	Nurse's notes
6:50 a.m.	EKG done; to x-ray via wheelchair; error; states she had x-ray on 6/21/00	Nurse's notes
7:00 a.m.	To OR via stretcher with OR staff	Nurse's notes
7:45 a.m.	Height: 5'6"; weight: 270 lbs.	Anesthesia record
7:50 a.m.	Arrival in OR	Operating room record
8:10 a.m.	Incision	Operating room record
	Pre-Op diagnosis: Severe dysmenorrhea, rule out endometriosis; during the laparoscopy, dense adhesions were noted between the rectosigmoid and the posterior uterus; the uterus was densely adherent to the bladder; there was no readily discernible plane of dissection between the left ovary and the rectosigmoid and the pelvic side wall; there was brisk bleeding noted and it was decided at this point that exploratory laparotomy was indicated; the patient's significant other was notified of the findings and the need to proceed with an exploratory laparotomy; there was a very hard mass at the rectosigmoid, which was densely adherent to the pelvic side wall and posterior lateral aspect of the uterus on the left; Dr. Smith performed a total abdominal hysterectomy and he removed the fallopian tubes and ovaries; Dr. Al Miller performed a resection of the rectosigmoid colon followed by reanastomosis	Operative report
	Post-Op Diagnosis (per Dr. Smith): severe pelvic adhesive disease, diverticulitis and pending pathology; post-op diagnosis (per Dr. Miller): mass in pelvic colon, probably inflammatory, but cannot exclude malignancy	

11:10 a.m.	Admitted to diagnostic laparoscopy this morning to rule out endometriosis; the patient has severe dysmenorrhea that is progressive and becoming quite incapacitating; the patient requested surgical intervention. She underwent a diagnostic laparoscopy; however, because of severe adhesions surrounding rectosigmoid and left ovary, pelvic side wall and posterior-lateral aspect of uterus, the _____ _____ was not possible and an adequate plane of dissection was not obtained; there was brisk bleeding noted, as such then it was decided to proceed into an exploratory laparotomy; the patient's significant other was apprised of the findings and then of management; in light of patient's symptoms and the severity of the adhesions and a palpable mass in colon, it was decided to proceed with total abdominal hysterectomy and bilateral salpingo-oophorectomy and intraoperative surgery consult; Dr. Miller consented and proceeded with bowel resection and secondary reanastomosis; the patient tolerated this procedure well. Estimated blood loss 600 cc	Dr. Smith progress note
11:15 a.m.	Closure	Operating room record
11:30 a.m.	To the recovery room	Operating room record
11:30 a.m.	(Uneventful period)	Recovery room
8:00 p.m.	Patient resting well; vital signs stable; afebrile; abdominal incision dressing in place; no vaginal bleeding; draining adequately; continue present therapy	Dr. Smith progress note
June 23, 2000		
7:18 p.m.	Complains of being thirsty, no flatus, no bowel movement; vital signs: blood pressure 118/70; afebrile; chest clear; heart — regular rhythm and rate; abdomen obese, soft, appropriately tender; no bowel sounds; abdomen binder in place; scant vaginal discharge; extremities nontender and negative Homan's sign; pathology: endometriosis, adenomyosis, diverticulitis; labs: CBC, BUN, and creatinine WNL; white blood cell count 10.2 (nl 5000–10,000), hemoglobin 12.2, hematocrit 34.7, sodium 139, potassium 3.9, chloride 99, carbon dioxide 27, glucose 133, BUN 7.0, creatinine 0.8; assessment: status post total abdominal hysterectomy and bilateral salpingo-oophorectomy; stable today; awaiting return of bowel functions; plan: (1) continue present management, (2) ambulate, (3) continue nothing by mouth, (4) pathology discussed with patient	Dr. Smith progress note
7:40 p.m.	Doing well — explained the colon pathology; patient states she was diagnosed to have diverticulitis some years ago in Austin, Texas	Dr. Miller progress note

Appendix 3.8
Standard of Care and Failure to Meet Standard of Care

Nurse X cared for Patient A (diagnosed with pneumonia) on the day shift of 1/1/01. The following are the issues concerning her care and treatment of Patient A.

1. Failed to Appreciate the Deterioration in the Patient's Condition

At 8:00 a.m., Nurse X documented that the patient was cooperative, but very anxious and restless (p. 14). [Note: the page number corresponds to the page of the number-stamped record.]

Additionally, Nurse X documented that he "managed to dislodge his IV" and was later seen manipulating his IV. This agitated behavior, which was a change from Patient A's normal behavior, could indicate poor oxygenation, but was not recognized as such by the nurse. No pulse oximetry readings were obtained/documented; no blood gases done secondary to the above.

2. Failed to Report Significant Patient Information to the Physician

Nurse X failed to report Patient A's agitated behavior to the physician and also did not report an oxygen saturation (O_2 sat) of 60% on room air, documented at 7:20 a.m. (p. 20). This reading was significant and should have been linked to the patient's agitated behavior as a sign of hypoxemia.

3. Failed to Protect the Patient's Safety

Nurse X failed to adequately observe Patient A. He was found by the respiratory therapist on room air — mask off — on 1/1/01 at 9:20 a.m. with a resulting O_2 sat of 64. He was also manipulating his IV. This was a confused patient who should have been closely observed to ensure that his oxygen mask remained on to adequate oxygenation. He needed protection from injuring himself.

Nurse X also did not ensure that the pulse oximeter alarms remained set. Had the alarms been set, she or another staff member would have been alerted when the O_2 sat dropped below the upper alarm limit.

4. Failed to Ensure That Physician's Orders Were Executed

Nurse X failed to ensure that continuous pulse ox was done, as had been ordered by Dr. Y (p. 30). She failed to ensure that oxygen saturations were maintained at 90%, as had been ordered on 1/1/01 by Dr. Z (p. 33). No oxygen saturations were documented during her shift.

Additionally, she failed to execute a PRN order for arterial blood gases (ABGs), written by Dr. Z on 11/23 and 11/24. ABGs should have been done when the pulse ox was found to be 60% on room air.

In view of the order to keep oxygen saturations at 90%, she should have verified the pulse oximeter alarm setting to ensure that the O_2 sat did not drop without an alarm sounding.

Appendix 3.9
Sample Deposition Questions Prepared by LNC for Attorney Consideration

On 1/1/01, Nurse X found Patient A (with a diagnosis of pneumonia) cooperative, but very anxious and restless. Questions:

1. What was the staffing pattern that day? What was the normal assignment? How many patients was she responsible for? Was that a burdensome assignment? If you have not already established the proximity of Patient A's room/bed in relation to the nurses' station, find out where it was located.
2. What could cause anxiety and restlessness in a patient with pneumonia? (Poor oxygenation.)
3. Nurse X charted that "wife was at bedside, critical of the care given him." Nurse's perception of being criticized can affect care rendered. Explore this issue with the witness.
4. At 9:20 a.m., respiratory therapist B found Patient A on room air and his PO_2 was 64. Dr. Y had ordered continuous pulse ox. Was that being done? At what settings were the alarms? Was the alarm on? Did it go off? Was the alarm sound volume high enough? Did the nurses ignore the alarms?
5. Was this nurse aware of that low PO_2 on room air? Was she aware then that the patient was in danger of taking off his mask and becoming hypoxic? Why were blood gases not done at that time? There are no oxygen saturations charted during that shift, nor any blood gases drawn. Ask if that meets the standard of care in a patient whose PO_2 was 64 on room air and who had an order to check blood gases every morning and PRN.
6. What is her understanding of the term "PRN" in terms of blood gases? What are the indications to draw blood gases?
7. Ask her to describe signs and symptoms of hypoxia. At 9:30 a.m., Nurse X charted "patient managed to dislodge IV." That sounds judgmental. Patient A's behavior, "anxious, restless, picking at the sheets," is a *classic sign* of hypoxia. She misses it altogether. At 1:00 p.m., she writes another note, "patient seen manipulating IV."

Chapter 4

Informed Consent

Julie C. Anderson, JD, MSN, RN

CONTENTS

0-8493-1418-6/03/$0.00+$1.50
© 2003 by AALNC

Objectives

- To define and describe the legal concept of the duty to obtain informed consent
- To state the majority rule for the standard used to measure whether a physician or health care provider has the legal obligation to obtain informed consent
- To state who must obtain informed consent
- To list four situations where informed consent must be obtained
- To describe the elements that a patient/plaintiff must prove in order to prevail on an informed consent theory
- To identify the resources in a jurisdiction for locating the law on informed consent
- To identify two potential areas of expansion of the theory of informed consent

Definitions and Terminology

Informed Consent

Informed consent is a communication process that involves disclosure of information by health care professionals to a competent patient who is presumed to have the capacity to understand it and a decision by that patient based on the information received. This is usually thought of in the context of a patient's decision whether to consent to or refuse a proposed treatment, such as a surgical procedure or medical therapy.

Duty

Duty in this context arises out of the relationship between a patient and a health care provider, wherein the provider has a responsibility to make reasonable disclosure to the patient of the risks incidental to medical diagnosis and treatment. This is based on the patient's right to determine what shall be done to his own body.

Reasonable Person

The hypothetical "reasonable person" is a means by which to measure a duty to be performed objectively. The reasonable person with respect to informed consent law is a hypothetical objective person in the same or similar circumstances as the patient/plaintiff. The measurement is whether or not this hypothetical objective person would be influenced in his decision-making process by disclosure of risks in the same or similar circumstances.

Inherent Risk

Inherent risk is one of the factors considered in determining how much information must be disclosed. This is a risk of a complication that is existent in and inseparable from the procedure contemplated. For example, bleeding or hemorrhage is a possible complication of every surgical procedure and is an inherent risk. Other examples of inherent risks include brain damage or death during anesthesia; allergic or sensitivity reactions to blood transfusions, contrast media, or drugs such as antibiotics; and swelling, pain, tenderness, or bleeding at the puncture site of blood vessel perforation for invasive procedures, such as radiographic studies or cardiac catheterization, that use contrast media.

Something that is done to correct a complication that has occurred is not considered an inherent risk. An example of this is intervention necessary to correct a condition or complication that occurred as a result of a procedure or treatment, such as surgical reexploration to locate and repair bleeding vessels within the abdomen after abdominal surgery.

Material Risk

Materiality of the risk is the other factor that is considered in determining how much information must be disclosed. Materiality involves the relative importance to the patient of the specific risk at issue, or whether or not knowledge of the risk could influence the patient's decision to consent. This becomes a balancing test, whereby the court will consider factors, such as remoteness of the risk, the probability of the risk occurring, and the severity of the risk. Even a statistically remote risk may be considered material if its severity is such that a patient could consider it in his decision to undergo the proposed therapy or reject it.

An illustrative case involved a patient who developed tardive dyskinesia while on psychotherapeutic medications. The expert who testified at trial stated that the statistical risk of this side effect was "small to extremely small," but the court held that the incidence of occurrence, along with evidence of the seriousness of the condition, its permanence, its presentation, the lack of known cures, and its overall effect on the body, was sufficient evidence that the risk was material enough to influence a reasonable person.[1]

Standards

Standards are the measuring sticks by which compliance with a duty is measured. There are essentially three standards or tests by which to measure a health care provider's fulfillment of the obligation to disclose risks inherent in contemplated medical procedures to the patient. The standard used depends on the particular jurisdiction.

1. Subjective test — This standard considers what inherent risks the patient/ plaintiff believes were material to his decision to undergo treatment and should have been disclosed. Only a few jurisdictions use this particular standard because of inherent difficulties in objective proof.
2. Objective standard — This standard considers what inherent risks a reasonable patient in similar circumstances to the patient/plaintiff would have believed were material and thus should have been disclosed. Also known as the "reasonable person" rule, this is the majority rule in the United States.

3. Professional standard — This test considers what risks a reasonable medical practitioner of the same school and same or similar community and circumstances would have disclosed to the patient.

Scope of the Duty

Overview

The consent process is the opportunity for the health care professional responsible for a patient's medical care to provide the patient with information with which to make a decision regarding diagnostic tests, medical treatment, or surgical intervention. The information should be patient-specific, based upon salient medical history information and an understanding of the patient's desired outcomes of the test or treatment. Although the laws of the 50 states differ to some extent, the basic elements share a common core:

■ An assessment of the patient's needs
■ An explanation of the proposed test or treatment
■ A discussion of the relative risks and benefits of the test or treatment
■ A description of alternative treatment options and the risks and benefits attendant to those options
■ Any expectations relevant to those options
■ The potential consequences if the patient chooses to forgo treatment altogether

Corollaries to these common core elements include the right of the patient to ask questions and receive understandable answers, freedom from coercion or undue influence in an attempt to obtain treatment authorization, and sufficient time to weigh the information provided before making a decision.

Discussion of remote risks should also be a part of informed consent communications. Indeed, this aspect may take on even greater importance with the recent addition by the Joint Commission on the Accreditation of Healthcare Organizations (JCAHO) of standard RI.1.2.2. This standard requires health care providers to inform patients and their families about outcomes, including unanticipated outcomes.[2] An "unanticipated outcome" is a result that differs significantly from what was anticipated to be the result of a treatment or procedure, and the fear of many health care providers is that such disclosure will inevitably be seen as an admission of negligence or fault, leading to a lawsuit. However, there is a major difference for all concerned in discussing what is categorized as an "unanticipated" risk as compared to what was known as a potential outcome, however remote. When a patient is informed in advance about risk potential, the fact that it has come to fruition no longer renders the outcome unexpected, and the resultant discussion about a less than desirable outcome may have decreased potential for legal ramifications.

Obviously, health care professionals strive to involve patients in their own care, and to that extent share information at many different levels. However, certain types of care give rise to a legal duty to share information, and that is where informed consent law comes in. The questions become when is it necessary, who has the duty, and to whom is the duty owed?

When Must Informed Consent Be Obtained?

It is necessary to obtain informed consent whenever a patient is faced with alternative treatment choices and needs information to make an informed decision. The more common situations are those where the patient is presented with a choice involving surgery, anesthesia, blood transfusions, diagnostic invasive procedures such as cardiac catheterization or intravenous pyelogram, radiation treatment for conditions such as cancer or leukemia, or chemotherapy for certain disease states. Other situations that call for informed consent to be obtained from the patient before embarking on the proposed treatment plan include experimental treatments or studies, sterilization, or certain immunizations. Additionally, federal law requires that patients who are to be transferred (or who have refused recommended transfer) to another facility for health care treatment under emergency circumstances must be informed of the risks and benefits of transfer as opposed to staying in the original facility.[3] These are all situations that require written documentation of consent. An informed consent issue that does not necessarily require formal written documentation is the prescription of medications; this issue is commonly litigated when a prescribed medication results in an untoward side effect to the patient, and the patient claims that he would have been influenced not to take the medication if the side effect had been disclosed.

Who Performs the Duty?

The Patient's Personal or Attending Physician

Traditionally, the treating physician has the responsibility to explain to patients the alternatives, risks, and benefits to any proposed treatment plan or option. However, medical treatment and surgical procedures often require the involvement of additional health care personnel. In some jurisdictions, such as Texas and Washington, the duty has been expanded by statute to include "health care provider." Such statutory language usually includes nurses, hospitals, dentists, podiatrists, pharmacists, and nursing homes as well as physicians. Whether or not this broader language will be held to mean that every entity and every individual has equal informed consent obligations will depend on case law construing such language in the particular jurisdiction. Practically speaking, however, such a construction would present an undue burden and an administrative nightmare for the various medical and health care personnel. Current case law in those jurisdictions continues to hold the physician primarily responsible.

One exception to the general rule that the physician is responsible for obtaining informed consent is patient transfer pursuant to the federal antidumping statute discussed above. This law specifically mandates that the hospital, not the physician, take reasonable steps to obtain a patient's informed consent both for transfer under emergency conditions and for refusal of transfer if transfer is deemed medically appropriate.[3]

Primary or Referring Physician versus Specialist or Consultant

The vast majority of jurisdictions are quite clear that the responsibility to obtain informed consent rests with the patient's own attending physician. However, if someone other than the attending physician, such as a specialist or consultant, actually performs a specific treatment or surgery, it then becomes that person's duty to inform the patient of the risks. For example, the anesthesiologist must discuss with the patient possible anesthetic complications during a planned surgery, and the gastroenterologist consulted by the attending physician must discuss risks and hazards of the endoscopy procedure he proposes.

Courts have generally been reluctant to impose upon a referring physician a duty to obtain informed consent for a procedure that is to be performed by a specialist who presumably is most familiar with the procedure and its risks and alternatives. However, several jurisdictions have held that a physician who actually prescribes the specific diagnostic procedures to be performed by another physician could be held liable for failure to obtain the patient's informed consent.[4] These courts reason that the patient's personal physician bears primary responsibility for all phases of treatment, including procedures performed by specialists to assist in the patient's diagnosis. However, this is not the general rule.

Who Can Give Consent?

The Patient or Authorized Agent

There is a legal presumption that any person who has reached the age of majority (usually 18 years) is competent and may make decisions about medical care. For informed consent, competence refers to decision-making capacity, or the patient's ability to engage in rational decision-making, rather than the patient's clinical condition.

Many people have executed health care directives that authorize another person, usually a spouse or significant other, to make health care decisions when and if the person becomes incapacitated and unable to do so (see section on treatment decisions). Sometimes a person will have a legal guardian, in which case that person is authorized to give or withhold consent to treatment for the patient. However, health care providers who communicate medical information to a third person who is not authorized by the patient to make health care decisions for the patient expose themselves to liability for breach of statutory privileges, invasion of privacy, or breach of contract.

Minors

In the case of minors, parents must give consent. If parents are unavailable in a given situation, certain others, usually next of kin in a hierarchical fashion, may be authorized under the jurisdiction's Family Code. Sometimes minors can consent independently. For example, some Family Codes provide that a minor need not have parental consent in order to obtain treatment for venereal disease, drug addiction, or pregnancy. In addition, emancipated minors (e.g., minors who are married or have been legally adjudicated as emancipated) can consent to treatment without parental participation. What constitutes an emancipated minor differs from state to state, and each state's Family Code should be consulted for those laws.

Mentally Incompetent Persons

Finally, the Family Codes or the Mental Health Codes of a particular state may contain provisions allowing procedures to be performed without the usual consent, when the patient is mentally incompetent or committed to a mental institution and cannot give informed consent because of that mental condition. In Texas, this exception allows for the performance of surgery or other treatment in these circumstances under the advice and consent of three licensed physicians, without consent of the patient's guardian.[5]

Exceptions to the Duty

In certain situations when it is not possible or feasible to obtain informed consent, the duty is suspended.

No Need for Treatment

When a physician determines that a patient is not in need of medical treatment, the physician is not required to inform the patient of possible risks and benefits of nontreatment. Courts have held that the informed consent doctrine cannot be extended to require disclosure of the risks of a recommendation of nontreatment, when the physician, in the exercise of his best judgment, believes no treatment is necessary. This has been litigated in the context of alleged failure to diagnose certain conditions, where the patient/plaintiff alleges that the physician should have performed further testing.[6]

Emergency Situations

Consent is implied when a patient, who is unconscious or otherwise unable to give express consent, needs immediate treatment necessary to save his life, and the harm from failure to treat is imminent and outweighs the harm threatened by the proposed treatment. In such cases, the rule is suspended and the physician is not held liable for failing to obtain informed consent, even if complications occur that would be considered both inherent and material. In this context, the rule requiring parental consent for a minor is suspended, if the minor needs emergency treatment and the parents are not available to give consent.

Therapeutic Privilege

This is a rare exception that allows a physician to withhold information that he reasonably believes could hinder treatment or prove harmful to the patient. Also called "not medically feasible," the concept has been employed in an attempt by the defendant physician to justify nondisclosure on the basis that it is in the best interests of the patient not to do so. For example, in the above case involving the psychotherapeutic drug that resulted in the side effect of tardive dyskinesia,[1] the doctor argued that the patient's schizophrenia rendered him unable to have the reactions of a reasonable person that justified nondisclosure of the risk. The court disagreed, holding that the patient's right to disclosure was not negated just because his doctor did not believe that his patient was reasonable. Situations that fall under this category are extremely rare.

Practical Considerations

Documentary Requirements

Informed consent, as a process resulting from dialogue between the patient and the physician or health care provider, does not refer simply to a signature at the bottom of a form. A form is the document reflecting the consent process, but it does not replace the dialogue between the patient and the health care provider. In all cases where informed consent is required, it should be documented that such consent was in fact obtained by the person who had the duty to obtain it. Sometimes oral disclosure will be sufficient, but the proof becomes problematic if the only witnesses to the conversation were the doctor and the patient.

Executed consent forms should be a part of the patient's permanent medical record. Consent forms can be general, such as the broad form that a patient signs consenting to medical care and the release of certain information on admission to a hospital, or specific, such as the consent form for the administration of blood or blood products. The forms must be signed by the patient or authorized agent and witnessed, usually by a nurse or other person who must ascertain that the patient has in fact had a discussion with the physician and has given informed consent based on that discussion. If a patient does not speak English, a translator must be involved in the process, and should also sign the consent form. If no form is required or used in a particular facility, narrative chart notes by the health care provider should suffice.

The Health Code of a jurisdiction should be consulted for the applicable law in that state. In some jurisdictions, specific language is required by statute for certain forms. In Texas, for example, the legislature has determined what constitutes the inherent and material risks for a large number of procedures, and these risks, specified in List A, must be disclosed by the health care professional.[7] List A procedures require full disclosure of risks by the physician or health care provider to the patient or person authorized to consent for the patient. If this form is used for disclosure of risks, it is admissible in court and creates a rebuttable presumption that the health care provider has complied with the statutory standard and is not negligent. Two examples from List A are below:

1. Cholecystectomy with or without common bile duct exploration:
   a. Pancreatitis
   b. Injury to the tube between the liver and the bowel
   c. Retained stones in the tube between the liver and the bowel
   d. Narrowing or obstruction of the tube between the liver and the bowel
   e. Injury to the bowel and/or intestinal obstruction
2. Myelography:
   a. Chronic pain
   b. Transient headache, nausea, vomiting

c. Numbness

d. Impaired muscle function

List B procedures require no disclosure. Examples include local anesthesia, hemorrhoidectomy, myringotomy, needle biopsy or aspiration, lumbar puncture, many invasive radiological procedures, and others. When a procedure is performed that does not fall in either List A or List B, the extent of disclosure is governed by the common law.

Proof in Court

Informed consent as a theory of liability on which the plaintiff tries to obtain a money judgment is most frequently combined with a medical negligence theory rather than being the sole theory in a claim. The elements of the plaintiff's case in an informed consent action are the same as in general medical negligence: duty, breach of duty, and proximate cause of the injury.

Under the majority rule, plaintiffs asserting informed consent claims must prove (1) that the complication or condition in question was a risk inherent in the procedure performed, (2) that a reasonable person fully informed of all inherent risks would not have consented to the treatment in question, and (3) that the patient/plaintiff was in fact injured by the occurrence of this complication or condition about which he was not informed. The nexus between the failure to disclose a particular risk and the later occurrence of that complication must be shown in order for the patient/plaintiff to prevail in the lawsuit.

Generally, expert medical testimony is necessary to prove the plaintiff's case in a negligence action based on informed consent (and to defend a physician's actions in this regard). The expert must testify regarding the inherency of the risk complained of and all other facts concerning the risk that show that knowledge of the risk could influence a reasonable person in making a decision to consent to the procedure.

Viability of the Cause of Action

Practically speaking, an informed consent claim is often difficult to sell to a jury, especially if the procedure or treatment in question is lifesaving, curative, or necessary for a serious medical condition. When lack of informed consent is raised as an issue in a medical malpractice case, it is often difficult to prove what occurred during the informed consent discussion. There are frequently discrepancies between the physician's and patient's versions of the information transmitted during this conversation. Often it becomes a swearing match between patient and physician whether or not discussion of risks was actually held, even if there is documentation. Some physicians specifically document the conversation in physician progress notes as well as on an informed consent form. (This may occur more often when the physician is getting consent for high-risk surgical procedures.) In cases where the defendant physician or health care provider has proven compliance with a statutory or common law duty, and a properly executed consent form is part of the record, the patient/plaintiff must resort to claiming that the scope of the disclosure was inadequate, or that the validity of the consent is in question. In that regard, the patient may claim that he did not have the capacity to give consent, or that he did not sign the form. Contract defenses such as fraud, mutual mistake, accident, and undue influence are typically employed in such situations.

On the other hand, the reasonable person standard increases the difficulty of a physician's obtaining summary judgment, because the defendant must counter the argument that knowledge of a particular risk of injury could influence a reasonable person in making a treatment decision. This is typically a question of fact for the jury rather than a question of law for the court. (Summary judgment is the process by which a court decides, based on evidence presented by the defendant doctor, that there is no genuine issue of material fact for a jury to consider, and dismisses the case against the defendant as a matter of law.)

Resources

A variety of resources in every jurisdiction can be consulted to determine the law and to research the issue.

External Sources

These sources include institutional and individual licensing provisions, accreditation standards, and federal and state statutes and regulations. The state hospital licensing laws and the medical, dental, podiatric, chiropractic, and nurse practice acts of each state are excellent sources, and should be consulted at the outset. While there is no universal federal law specific to informed consent in general, the previously mentioned federal antidumping statute speaks to the specific issue of patient transfers and the consent required therein. Also, because of Medicare or Medicaid requirements for those entities receiving federal funds as providers, a health care facility may be indirectly affected in this area. Federal courts will follow state law when faced with this issue in a federal lawsuit. State statutes and regulations that might address informed consent issues include tort reform laws and statutes regulating the insurance industry. Besides statutes addressing informed consent requirements, JCAHO requires a hospital or health care facility to have a policy on informed consent, developed by the medical staff and governing body of the hospital and consistent with any legal requirements. For the facility to be accredited, every patient medical record must contain evidence of informed consent for any procedures and treatments that are covered by such policy. See the *Accreditation Manual for Hospitals*, published by JCAHO, for the exact language in a given year. Finally, legal literature, such as law review articles and legal practice guides, can be consulted for guidance on the applicable law.

Internal Sources

These resources include hospital policies and procedures; individual job descriptions; and hospital documents, such as contracts, that might identify or define certain responsibilities with respect to informed consent. Medical staff bylaws, rules, and regulations are required to address the issue. Local custom (practices within other hospitals in the community) may also be informative for the purposes of comparison.

Areas for Potential Expansion of the Doctrine

The informed consent doctrine as it currently exists has been the subject of extreme criticism. This mainly focuses on concerns about the doctrine in the clinical setting, and the incongruity between the doctrine and actual medical practice. The legal doctrine focuses on the physician's disclosure of information rather than the patient's comprehension, which may not accurately reflect the realities of factors that contribute to the patient's overall experience and basic understanding. In addition, a more systemic problem may be the legal system's ignorance of the realities of medical practice, and the assumption that medical practice will adjust to the dictates of informed consent law. Following is a discussion of several areas of expansion or suggested reform to traditional informed consent doctrine.

Disclosure of Provider-Risk Statistics

In recent years, proponents of an expanded informed consent doctrine have urged a shift in focus aimed at increasing patients' rights to participate in their health care management. One fertile area is the idea of requiring physicians to disclose their own statistical information to their patients as part of the informed consent conversation. It is argued that provider-risk information, which is essentially physician-specific statistics regarding lawsuits, complication rates, and the like, is much more likely to impact a patient's decision and ultimate welfare than more general procedure-specific information. Wisconsin has opened the door to this new liability theory.[8] A patient who became a paraplegic following surgery by her physician alleged that the surgeon had not told her that his complication rate for the particular procedure that he had recommended to her was significantly higher than that of more experienced surgeons. She argued that he had had a duty to disclose this information to her, and that, had he done so, she would not have agreed to allow him to perform the procedure. The Wisconsin Supreme Court agreed with her, noting that this type of physician-specific risk information could be a more significant factor in a patient's decision to undergo a procedure than information on general risks.

Proponents of this expanded theory of liability argue that the patient's proof of causation would be simplified, in that it would be easier to offer quantifiable objective evidence to support the subjective component of the traditional informed consent case. One mechanism to access such provider-risk information is already in existence. The National Practitioner Data Bank (NPDB) was created by federal law[9] a decade ago to address the issue of incompetent physicians who simply move from location to location to avoid having their poor reputations follow them. The NPDB currently stores litigation and professional disciplinary information on individual physicians and makes this information available to hospitals, health maintenance organizations (HMOs), and other medical employers. Access to this information could be expanded to include lawyers or even the general public, according to proponents of the theory. Critics of the theory, which thus far has not taken hold in other jurisdictions, argue that it would wreak havoc with the health care system by prematurely ending the careers of younger, less experienced physicians and encouraging providers to falsify reports to improve their statistics.

Disclosure of Noncovered Alternative Treatments

Current informed consent law does not clearly require the disclosure of treatment alternatives or provide guidance to the content of such disclosure. With the widespread development of "managed care" organizational systems, health care cost containment measures have given physicians both explicit and implicit incentives to withhold information regarding noncovered treatment options. This directly conflicts with the informed consent doctrine's principal purpose of requiring physician disclosure in order to give patients the right to make informed medical decisions regarding their own bodies.

Explicit measures in a managed care contract that could influence a physician to withhold certain disclosures include preapproval limitations, thus preventing the physician from discussing proposed treatment prior to obtaining plan approval. Also, antidisparagement clauses in the plan may explicitly prohibit physicians from making statements that could undermine public confidence in the plan. Finally, confidentiality clauses in plans that require physicians to maintain confidentiality of proprietary information, such as clinical practice guidelines and payment structure, could inhibit frank discussions of treatment alternatives.

Implicit incentives in managed care include "termination without cause" provisions and measures, such as structuring the financial incentives of a plan, so that physicians internalize the structure and impose their own restrictions on patient interactions.

Several theories have arisen that could impact these limitations. First is to extend the duty for physicians to include disclosure of information regarding financial incentives to perform certain types of care. For example, if a physician were involved in research that might result in economic gain for the physician, it could be argued that such activity might affect the physician's professional judgment and therefore should be disclosed to the patient for consideration as a factor in any treatment decision.

Second is a creative use of the Employee Retirement Income Security Act (ERISA). ERISA has a preemption clause that has often worked in favor of HMO defendants who use it as an affirmative defense to preclude jury trials and limit patients' recovery to benefits denied the patients. However, because of ERISA's incorporation of the trust concept of a fiduciary, its use may also provide a viable cause of action for patients alleging a failure to disclose information on noncovered treatment alternatives.

Finally, fiduciary requirements under state law could also be used in a similar manner, when a benefit plan conceals the existence of financial incentives and policies that might affect physician judgment. Such cases are few to date, and they mainly reflect opinions that have arisen very early in the litigation process, such that the ultimate fate of this type of argument in a trial court is unknown (see Chapter 20, ERISA and HMO Litigation, for more information).

Renegotiation of Informed Consent with Laboring and Birthing Patients

Traditional informed consent doctrine reflects that women are to some degree unable to make rational decisions during labor and delivery, and that labor and birth should be treated as processes that simply happen without choice or decision. Wisconsin disagrees with the traditional view. The Wisconsin Supreme Court held that a physician violated the informed consent statute of that state when he refused to perform a cesarean section after his laboring patient withdrew her prior consent for a vaginal delivery and requested the cesarean section.[10] The baby was ultimately born by c-section but had cerebral palsy. The court's language in this case frames informed consent as a dialogue that is both ongoing and highly dependent on context, and expands the doctrine beyond its previous boundaries toward a more patient-centered approach. Such an approach involves both benefits and risks in the context of informed consent.

Clearly, this case reflects shifts in cultural views of both physicians and laboring women. Benefits include giving the laboring woman a measure of power and autonomy that she did not previously enjoy, and inspiring a greater amount of trust between a patient who requests and her doctor who agrees to renegotiate informed consent during the course of labor. On the other side of the coin, the case fails to give physicians any guidelines about where the duty to renegotiate informed consent ends. This view also increases the risk of suit and liability that could cause doctors to hesitate in taking medically necessary steps in a timely fashion and to be more distracted and less able to respond to emergency situations.

Conclusion

The law of informed consent is fairly straightforward, being based on negligence principles. Variations among jurisdictions in the standards for proof of the elements are not extreme, and can easily be found by consulting the appropriate authorities. However, the law is evolving, based on difficulties in application that are inherent in the law itself.

References

1. *Barclay v. Campbell*, 704 S.W.2d 8 (Tex. 1986).
2. Joint Commission for Accreditation of Healthcare Organizations, *2002 Accreditation Manual for Hospitals*, Oakbrook Terrace, IL, 2001.
3. *See* 42 U.S.C. §1395dd (West Supp. 1996), known as the "antidumping" statute.
4. *See Bowers v. Talmage*, 159 So. 2d 888 (Fla. Dist. Ct. App. 1963); *Prooth v. Wallsh*, 432 N.Y.S.2d 663 (Sup. Ct. 1980); *Berkey v. Anderson*, 1 Cal. App. 3d 790, 82 Cal. Rptr. 67 (1969); *Jacobs v. Painter*, 530 A.2d 231 (Me. 1987).
5. *See* Tex. Health & Safety Code §551.041 (Vernon 2001), but these laws will vary from state to state. Refer to each state's Mental Health statutes.
6. *Scalere v. Stenson*, 211 Cal. App. 3d 1446, 260 Cal. Rptr. 152 (1989).
7. Tex. Rev. Civ. Stat. Ann. Art. 4590i (Vernon 2001).
8. *Johnson v. Kokemoor*, 545 N.W.2d 495 (Wis. 1996).
9. 42. U.S.C. §11101 *et seq.* (West 2001), known as the Health Care Quality Improvement Act.
10. *Schreiber v. Physicians Insurance Co. of Wisconsin*, 588 N.W.2d 26 (Wis. 1999).

Test Questions

1. The duty to obtain informed consent prior to a medical procedure is the responsibility of
   A. The attending physician
   B. The nurse obtaining the patient's signature on the consent form
   C. The physician who is to perform the medical procedure
   D. The patient

2. Most jurisdictions follow which rule for measuring whether or not a health care provider has met the obligation for obtaining informed consent?
   A. The reasonable professional standard
   B. The reasonable person standard
   C. The subjective patient standard
   D. The rational expectations standard

3. A physician must obtain the patient's informed consent for all of the following EXCEPT:
   A. Administration of blood or blood products
   B. An elective cholecystectomy
   C. Voluntary sterilization
   D. Transfer to another hospital at the patient's request

4. In order to prove a case, a plaintiff relying on an informed consent theory must present testimony showing all of the following EXCEPT:
   A. The condition about which the plaintiff is complaining is an inherent risk attendant to the procedure that the plaintiff underwent.
   B. The plaintiff in fact developed a condition defined as a risk of the procedure.
   C. The plaintiff would not have consented to the procedure had he been fully informed of the risk.

5. A new development in the area of informed consent law is
   A. A decision requiring the inclusion of provider-risk statistical information as part of the informed consent discussion between a physician and patient
   B. Reducing the paperwork needed for informed consent
   C. Requiring a witness to the explanation of risk
   D. Providing a written list of risks to the patient

Answers: 1. C, 2. B, 3. D, 4. C, 5. A

Chapter 5

Treatment Decisions

Jennifer L. Rangel, JD, Gail N. Friend, JD, RN, and Brett Storm, Esq.

CONTENTS

0-8493-1418-6/03/$0.00+$1.50
© 2003 by AALNC

Objectives

At the conclusion of this chapter, the legal nurse consultant will be able to:

- Understand medical or health care powers of attorney
- Describe the process for a terminally ill patient to refuse medical care
- Identify the different types of legal documents granting a family member or other surrogate decision-maker the right to make health care decisions for a patient
- Delineate a hospital's duties and obligations to provide a screening examination and emergency stabilizing treatment to a patient presenting to the hospital and requesting emergency care
- List potential causes of action that might be alleged if a patient is given medical care over his express refusal

Origin and History of the Right to Refuse Medical Treatment

> Every human being of adult years and sound mind has a right to determine what shall be done with his own body.
>
> *Schloendorff v. Society of New York Hosp.*, 105 N.E. 92, 93
> (N.Y. 1914)

Justice Cardozo's statement in 1914 has been quoted by numerous courts in determining a person's right to make the treatment decisions affecting his own person. As discussed in the preceding chapter, every patient has the "right" to give informed consent before medical treatment is rendered. The corollary to this is the "right" of a patient to refuse medical treatment, even lifesaving medical treatment. The law in the U.S. is generally settled regarding a competent patient's ability to refuse treatment. However, many issues arise in regard to the rights of an incompetent patient.

The right to refuse medical treatment did not reach center stage in the courts until recently. The majority of the law concerning this issue has been created in the last 10 years. The reason for this recent abundance of court and legislative interest is the advances in medical technology that make it possible for the life of a patient on the brink of death to be sustained by machines and artificial means. Patients may not desire that their lives be extended if the quality of life has dissipated. Consequently, the legislatures and the courts must carve out guidelines for the termination of life-sustaining medical treatment when patients or their legal representatives refuse to consent to the treatment or seek withdrawal of current treatment.

The U.S. Supreme Court recognizes that a person has a constitutionally protected liberty interest in refusing unwanted medical treatment. In *Cruzan v. Missouri Department of Health*, the Supreme Court held that this liberty interest arises from the Fourteenth Amendment to the U.S. Constitution. An individual's liberty interest in the refusal of medical treatment must be balanced against a state's interests in preserving life, preventing suicide, protecting the integrity of the medical profession, and protecting innocent third parties. This "right" to refuse medical treatment is not absolute. However, the courts generally hold that a competent person's interest in refusal outweighs the state's interests. The balancing test customarily becomes a serious obstacle only when a patient is incompetent.

In addition to the U.S. Constitution, the common law in the states has been found to guarantee the right to refuse treatment. This means that courts have held that the case law in individual states grants patients this right. The common law right flows from the Informed Consent Doctrine that requires a patient's informed consent before treatment is rendered. For example, in 1989, the Illinois Supreme Court held that Illinois common law provides a person the right to reject medical treatment. The court in *In re Estate of Longeway* determined that this right encompassed all treatment including life-sustaining treatment, such as artificial hydration and nutrition.

Other state courts have relied on their own constitutions or state statutes in concluding that a person has the right to decline medical care. In the wake of suits brought by patients and their families or guardians, state legislatures have enacted various statutes to address the mechanics of refusal of treatment. Courts may find that these statutes enunciate such a right. For example, the Illinois Living Will Act expressly states that "the legislature finds that persons have a fundamental right to control the decisions relating to the rendering of their own medical care, including the right to have death delaying procedures withheld or withdrawn in instances of a terminal condition." Further, many state courts have held that their state constitutions create a privacy right that encompasses the right to refuse treatment. Consequently, many state constitutions are stronger than the U.S. Constitution in providing a basis for the right to refuse treatment as opposed to merely establishing a liberty interest.

Categories of Refusal

Refusal of medical treatment can include refusal of a specific medical procedure like surgery, refusal of medications, or refusal of artificial treatment such as a respirator or nutrition and hydration through a tube. Refusal might also take the form of a "do not resuscitate" (DNR) order. This is a physician's order that a patient is not to be resuscitated by any means if his heart should stop or he stops breathing spontaneously. Thus, cardiopulmonary resuscitation (CPR) should not be administered.

All states empower parents to consent to medical treatment for their minor child. Along with this responsibility comes the right to refuse treatment for their child. However, when a parent refuses to consent to lifesaving treatment for a child, the state may intervene to save the child's life. In most states, the state agency responsible for protecting children may petition a court to take temporary guardianship of a child for the purpose of consenting to treatment. This frequently occurs in cases where a parent refuses medical treatment for religious reasons. The parent's right to refuse medical treatment for a child may be limited by the state. In such a situation, the state's interest in preserving the child's life outweighs the parent's rights because the child is too young to legally express what his wishes would be.

A Competent Patient's Right to Refuse

The law has principally determined that a competent patient has the "right" to refuse any medical treatment. This right is recognized regardless of the potential outcome of the refusal. In acknowledging this prerogative, courts have upheld an individual's right to refuse blood transfusions, resuscitation, and artificial life-sustaining measures (e.g., hydration and nutrition) intravenously or through a nasogastric or other tube. A competent person's right to reject medical treatment has been challenged by physicians and hospitals, but the patient's wishes usually prevail.

In *Bouvia v. Superior Court of Los Angeles County*, a California appellate court held that a competent patient had the right to refuse life-sustaining medical treatment and that the state and her physicians must abide by her refusal. In this case, Elizabeth Bouvia was a 28-year-old woman who suffered from severe cerebral palsy and, as a result, was a quadriplegic. Ms. Bouvia was in severe pain, bedridden, and completely immobile except for the ability to move a few fingers on one hand and to make some slight head and facial movements. Ms. Bouvia, who was mentally competent and college-educated, expressed her desire to die and requested the removal of the nasogastric tube supplying her with hydration and nutrition. She dictated her wishes regarding removal of the tube to her assistant, who wrote them down, and she then signed the paper with an "X" made by holding a pen in her mouth.

The court held that Ms. Bouvia had the right to control her own medical treatment, and the court required the withdrawal of the nasogastric tube. The right to have life-support equipment disconnected is not limited to terminally ill patients or patients in a persistent vegetative state. After stating that it was immaterial that the removal of the tube might hasten Ms. Bouvia's death, the court commented: "Being competent she has the right to live out the remainder of her natural life in dignity and peace." According to this court, Ms. Bouvia's right to decide for herself what treatment she received outweighed any state interests in preserving her life. Most courts, although not employing language as strong as the language used by the California court, hold that a competent patient has a right to refuse medical treatment that must be respected by the state.

So strong is the recognition of and respect for a patient's right to refuse medical treatment that some courts have held that even in emergency situations, consent for treatment must be obtained from the patient or a legally authorized representative, if at all possible. In *Shine v. Vega*, a physician administered treatment to an asthmatic patient, even though the patient had explicitly refused such treatment. The physician and hospital argued that the situation was an emergency and that it was not necessary to obtain patient consent. The Massachusetts Supreme Judicial Court rejected this argument. The court recognized the "emergency exception" to the patient consent requirement but held that the exception applied only if the patient was incapable of consenting (for instance, if the patient were unconscious) and time and circumstances did not permit the hospital to obtain consent from a family member. Absent those conditions, a physician must obtain consent for treatment, even in an emergency situation.

Religious Motivation for Refusal of Lifesaving Treatment

The right to refuse medical treatment is further strengthened when the patient refuses on the basis of religion. The most well-known cases involve patients who are Jehovah's Witnesses and refuse the administration of all blood products because of their religion, even when such treatment is necessary to save or extend their lives. The courts customarily respect an individual's First Amendment right to freedom of religion even if the exercise of this right places the individual's life in jeopardy. Regardless, hospitals and physicians are trained to save lives and tend to feel an overwhelming obligation to at least attempt to administer the lifesaving treatment. For this reason and to avoid potential liability from failure to provide medical care, the health care providers of an individual refusing treatment often seek court guidance when dealing with this issue.

In *Fosmire v. Nicoleau*, the New York Court of Appeals held that a competent adult has a right to refuse a blood transfusion. The patient lost a substantial amount of blood following a cesarean section to deliver her child. She refused the transfusions because she was a Jehovah's Witness. The hospital sought a court order to administer the transfusion. The court signed an order, without notice to the patient or her family, granting authorization for the hospital to administer blood products to the patient to save her life. The patient appealed the decision even though she had already received two transfusions. The appellate court vacated the court order and held that the court should never have granted permission for the transfusion to occur because the patient had the right to refuse even lifesaving treatment and the state's interests do not override this right.

Despite the body of law to the contrary, many lower-level state courts continue to order blood transfusions over the patient's strong objections in order to save the individual's life. As illustrated above, the orders that have been appealed were usually overruled by the courts that held that the patient's refusal must be respected. However, in most cases, the damage has already been done. For example, a U.S. district court in Connecticut granted permission to a hospital to administer blood to a patient who refused the transfusion on the ground that the treatment was against his Jehovah's Witness religion. In *United States v. George*, the transfusion was administered immediately following the court's order and the patient had no time to appeal the ruling. An appeal could potentially nullify the court's order but could not undo the transfusion. The main purpose of an appeal is to protect the patient against future transfusions.

Some courts have taken an even broader view of the appeals process. In *In re Duran*, the Pennsylvania Superior Court rationalized that even though the patient who was the subject of the appeal had died, the appeal was nevertheless important in light of the interests of numerous other Jehovah's Witnesses who might be in similar situations. In that case, a woman underwent a liver transplant after which she needed a blood transfusion to save her life. However, the woman was a Jehovah's Witness and had executed a durable power of attorney, indicating her refusal of a blood transfusion, even if it were necessary to save her life. Notwithstanding the durable power of attorney, the woman's husband petitioned the lower court to appoint him as an emergency guardian for the purpose of consenting to a blood transfusion for his wife. The court granted the husband's petition, but the woman died before the case was appealed. However, the superior court sustained the appeal in light of the fact that similar issues regarding refusal of lifesaving treatment would likely arise in other cases given the large number of Jehovah's Witnesses residing in the U.S. In this case, even though the appeal was no longer relevant with respect to the patient for whom the appeal was originated, it was still allowed to proceed in light of the interests of others who may face similar issues.

A few courts have considered limiting an individual's right to refuse when the individual has minor children. In a Massachusetts Supreme Court case, a competent adult was hospitalized for a bleeding ulcer and her physicians believed that a blood transfusion was necessary to save her life. In *Norwood Hospital v. Munoz*, the patient, a Jehovah's Witness, refused the transfusion on religious grounds. The hospital sought a court order to administer the transfusion in order to protect the patient's child from abandonment by his mother. The court held that the state's interest did not override the individual's right to refuse medical treatment absent compelling evidence that the child would be abandoned if the mother died and only the father was left to raise the child. In this case, there was no evidence that the father with the support of his family could not raise the child. It would be very rare that compelling evidence would exist on this issue. The majority of the states hold that an individual with a minor child has the same right to refuse medical treatment as any other competent adult.

However, if the patient is a minor, the right of the minor and his parents to refuse is not nearly so absolute. Because a minor lacks the capacity to consent or refuse medical treatment, this right advances to the minor's parents. Generally, a parent has the right to make medical decisions for a minor child. Nevertheless, this right is not unconditional. If a parent's refusal of treatment endangers the child and amounts to neglect, virtually all states allow a temporary guardian to be appointed or the state to intervene in order to consent to the treatment. The courts reason that such patients lack the capacity to decide what their beliefs are for themselves and, thus, should not lose their life based on the parent's beliefs. In *HCA, Inc. v. Miller*, a Texas intermediate appellate court held that while parents do have the statutory right to refuse life-sustaining treatment for their minor child who is terminally ill, this right does not exist when the minor child is not terminally ill. Consequently, because in *Miller* the child was not terminally ill, the hospital was not obligated to follow the parents' wishes to withhold urgently needed life-sustaining treatment from the minor child and was not liable in tort for providing life-sustaining treatment without the parents' consent.

The issue becomes more complicated when the minor is mature. The Illinois Supreme Court held that a 17-year-old was a mature minor and had the right to refuse medical treatment. In the case of *In re E.G.*, the minor suffered from leukemia and needed blood transfusions to extend her life. The state filed a petition seeking an order stating that the minor was neglected because her parents would not consent to the transfusion and appointing a guardian to consent. The juvenile court granted the order, but the family appealed and the appellate court and Supreme Court vacated the order. The Illinois Supreme Court determined that if the evidence is clear and convincing that a minor is mature enough to appreciate the consequences of her actions, the minor has the same right as an adult to refuse medical treatment. This right has generally been conferred only on minors of the ages of 16 and 17 on a case-by-case basis. A hospital faced with a minor's refusal of medical treatment would be wise to seek state intervention and court guidance.

The courts have also grappled with a pregnant patient's right to refuse lifesaving treatment that will affect the birth/life of the unborn child. An Illinois appellate court determined that a competent adult patient has the right to refuse treatment regardless of pregnancy. In the case of *In re Baby Boy Doe*, a pregnant woman's fetus was diagnosed as receiving insufficient oxygen in the womb, and her physicians recommended an immediate cesarean section or induced labor. The patient refused both treatments on the basis of her religion. She had complete faith in God's healing powers and chose to await natural childbirth. The physicians and hospital contacted the state's attorney, who petitioned a court to appoint the hospital as custodian of the fetus for immediate delivery. The court denied the petition and upheld the patient's right to refuse treatment. This decision was affirmed by the appellate court, holding that the potential impact on the fetus from the patient's refusal was legally irrelevant. This was because under Illinois law, a fetus has no rights separate from the mother while *in utero*. In this case, no harm resulted from the patient's refusal as she delivered a healthy baby naturally. Nonetheless, positive results such as these do not always occur.

The holding in *In re Baby Boy Doe* has subsequently been followed by another Illinois appellate court. In *In re Fetus Brown*, a woman refused a blood transfusion on the basis of her religion even though the hospital determined that a transfusion was necessary to save her life and that of her unborn baby. The hospital administrator won a trial court petition to be appointed temporary custodian of the fetus in order to consent to the blood transfusion for the benefit of the fetus. The woman appealed this determination. The appellate court held that a blood transfusion was an invasive procedure affecting the bodily integrity of an individual. Furthermore, the court determined that the state's interest in the viable fetus did not outweigh the woman's right to make competent treatment decisions. Consequently, following *In re Baby Boy Doe*, the appellate court held that the woman was entitled to refuse the blood transfusion, notwithstanding the effect on the fetus, and that the lower court had erred in allowing the hospital administrator to consent to the blood transfusion as temporary custodian of the fetus.

In contrast to Illinois, a minority of courts has limited the rights of a pregnant woman in regard to refusal of medical treatment. In 1981, the Georgia Supreme Court affirmed a court order authorizing the performance of a cesarean section and the administration of any necessary blood transfusions to a pregnant patient refusing the treatment on the basis of her religion. The patient and her husband believed that the Lord had healed her body and that whatever happened would be the Lord's will. In *Jefferson v. Griffin Spalding County Hospital Authority*, the patient was in her 34th week of pregnancy and due to deliver any time. Her physicians discovered that she suffered from complete placenta previa and that therefore the child could not survive natural childbirth. The mother had only a 50% chance of surviving childbirth. According to the doctors, a cesarean was necessary to save both the mother and the fetus. Due to the viability of the child and the nearness of the patient's due date, the court granted temporary custody of the fetus to the Department of Human Resources with the authority to make all medical decisions. The court ordered the patient to submit to a sonogram and, if the sonogram showed placenta previa, to submit to a cesarean. The Georgia Supreme Court upheld this order, finding that the fetus had the right to the state's protection. This decision is in the minority as most states do not recognize the rights of a fetus, especially as superior to the mother's right to refuse treatment. However, many states have established that CPR may not be withheld from a pregnant woman regardless of her wishes.

Consequently, the law is relatively settled that a competent adult has the right to refuse medical treatment on the basis of religion. In most states, this right extends to a pregnant woman irrespective of the refusal's effect on the fetus. The only absolute limitation on this right is if the patient is a minor, in which case the state will normally appoint a temporary guardian to consent to the treatment in order to protect the child's life.

The Right of an Incompetent Person to Refuse Medical Treatment

In general, the courts realize that the right to refuse medical treatment extends to incompetent patients. In *Brophy v. New England Sinai Hospital, Inc.*, the Massachusetts Supreme Judicial Court reasoned that incompetent patients as well as competent individuals must have this right because the "value of human dignity extends to both." Nevertheless, the issues concerning an individual's right to refuse medical treatment become further complicated when the individual is incompetent. A few examples of incompetent patients are persons who are minors, in comas, mentally deteriorated, or mentally ill. Pursuant to law, such persons cannot legally consent to medical treatment or make decisions for themselves. A surrogate decision-maker, usually a parent, a spouse, another family member, or an appointed guardian, makes decisions for the patient. However, the law limits a surrogate decision maker's right to refuse lifesaving or life-sustaining medical treatment for an incompetent individual. The courts and legislatures fear abuse if surrogates are allowed the unrestricted right to withdraw or refuse treatment. In response to these concerns, a number of methods have been developed by states to determine the legality of a surrogate's refusal of treatment.

A Person Is Incompetent but Made Desires Known When Competent

The individual states provide varying methods through which a competent person may memorialize his desires regarding medical treatment if the person becomes incompetent in the future. In order to encourage individuals to execute such directives, the Federal Patient Self-Determination Act requires hospitals, nursing homes, hospices, home health agencies, and other specified entities to provide written information to each individual receiving medical care regarding the individual's rights under state law to make decisions regarding medical treatment. This includes the right to accept or refuse treatment and to execute advance directives. The health care provider must document in the patient's medical record whether or not the patient has executed an advance directive. In addition, the health care provider must ensure compliance with the requirements of state law regarding executed directives.

Do-Not-Resuscitate Orders

The National Conference of Commissioners on Uniform State Laws proposed the Uniform Rights of the Terminally Ill Act. This act established uniform provisions regarding powers of attorney for health care, living wills, and other directives. Most states have adopted at least portions of this act. This section discusses three specific types of directives and the statutory guidelines for each. These directives include DNR orders, living wills, and durable powers of attorney for health care.

A patient's consent to administer emergency care, including CPR, is generally presumed in an emergency medical situation. Due to the urgency of the patient's condition, health care professionals are compelled to initiate emergency care without inquiring into the patient's wishes. The majority of the states have enacted legislation authorizing and prescribing guidelines for the use of DNR orders. A DNR order is a statement that resuscitation methods should not be attempted on a patient if the need arises. Such orders are different from written directives because they are executed by a physician with the patient's or his representative's consent when the physician believes that a situation requiring resuscitation is anticipated. Ordinarily, the patient has already been diagnosed with a terminal condition or is in a persistent vegetative state when the order is issued. In contrast, written directives are executed by the patient, when he is competent, in antici-pation of the need to make important medical decisions should the patient become incompetent. Most written directives expressly consent to a DNR order when the circumstances support its issuance.

Most statutes regulating the use of DNR orders specifically apply to medical emergencies that occur either in a health care facility, such as a hospital or nursing home, or outside of a facility, such as in a patient's home. Many states authorize the use of a DNR identification device that the patient wears so that the emergency medical technicians will be aware of and honor the DNR order. Although the statutes generally allow for the issuance of DNR orders for competent and incompetent patients, a few states' legislatures require that DNR orders be issued only upon a competent patient's consent. The statutes also vary in regard to who may consent for an incompetent patient, whether witnesses are required, and whether the patient must have a terminal condition. A limited number of statutes expressly require that the patient's condition be terminal. Other states' statutes are silent on this issue apparently relying on the physicians to issue DNR orders only in appropriate circumstances. Even though the laws vary slightly on the specific requirements for issuing a DNR order, the state statutes have the same general purpose. Following is a sampling of the specific requirements in a few states in order to provide an overview of the law in this area.

Georgia has enacted a statute providing that an adult competent patient with decision-making capacity may consent to a DNR order and its implementation at a later time. This consent may be oral or written. A physician may issue the DNR order after the patient has provided consent. If the patient is incompetent, an authorized surrogate decision-maker may consent based upon what the patient would have wanted under the circumstances. In addition, the parent of a minor patient may consent. However, if the physician determines that the minor is of sufficient maturity to understand the nature and effect of a DNR order, the order will not be valid unless the minor patient's consent is obtained as well. If the patient is incompetent and no authorized decision-maker exists, the attending physician may issue an order, provided that a second physician concurs in writing in the patient's medical record that the order is appropriate; an ethics committee or similar panel concurs in the physician's opinion; and the patient is receiving inpatient or outpatient treatment or is a resident of a health care facility other than a home health agency or hospice.

Similarly, the Texas statute that governs out-of-hospital DNR orders states that a competent person may execute a written DNR order at any time directing health care professionals to withhold CPR and other designated life-sustaining treatments. The order must be honored in any out-of-hospital setting that includes, but is not limited to, hospital outpatient or emergency departments, physicians' offices, the patient's home, a nursing home, and an assisted living facility. The order must be signed by the attending physician, the patient in the presence of two witnesses, and the two witnesses. The fact that an order exists should be noted in the patient's medical record. A standard form for out-of-hospital DNR orders has been prescribed by the Texas statute. In addition, Texas allows for the issuance of a DNR order by nonwritten communication. In this situation, a competent adult patient must consent in the presence of the attending physician and two witnesses. The order must be signed by the witnesses and the doctor, and the issuance of the order must be noted in the patient's medical record.

The Texas statute also provides for issuance of an out-of-hospital DNR order when the patient is incompetent and cannot provide consent. If the patient is a minor, the patient's parents, legal guardian, or managing conservator may consent. If an adult patient is incompetent but previously issued a Directive to Physicians, the physician may rely on the directive to issue a DNR order. For adult incompetent patients without a living will, the patient's legal guardian, proxy, or agent designated by a medical power of attorney may consent to the issuance of the DNR order. If the adult does not have an agent, proxy, or guardian, the attending physician and at least one qualified relative may execute the DNR order. A "qualified relative" means a person in the following order of priority: (1) the patient's spouse, (2) the patient's reasonably available children, (3) the patient's parents, and (4) the patient's nearest living relative. The decision to consent to a DNR order for an incompetent patient must, if possible, be based on knowledge of what the person would desire. The order must be executed in the presence of at least two witnesses. If no qualified relative is available, the attending physician with the concurrence of another physician who is not involved in the patient's care or who is a member of the ethics or medical committee may institute the order. A relative wishing to challenge a decision made under these provisions must apply for temporary guardianship under the Texas Probate Code.

In California, a succinct statute establishes only that a DNR order must be a written document signed by the patient or a legally recognized surrogate decision-maker and a physician. In contrast, Kansas has enacted a statute requiring that DNR orders be issued by a physician only upon the consent of the patient. Further, the order must be in writing, signed by the patient or another at the patient's express direction, and dated and signed in the presence of a witness. New York's statute requires the consent of an adult with capacity. If the patient is in the hospital, consent may be expressed orally in the presence of a physician associated with the hospital and another witness. A patient may also express consent in writing, dated and signed in the presence of two witnesses. If the physician determines in writing that to a reasonable degree of medical certainty a discussion of resuscitation would cause the patient to suffer immediate and severe injury, he may issue an order without consent after receiving the written concurrence of another physician, ascertaining the wishes of the patient to the extent possible, listing the reasons for not consulting the patient in the medical records, and obtaining the consent of the patient's agent or a surrogate decision-maker.

The majority of the statutes provide immunity for health care professionals acting in good faith in reliance upon a DNR order. Professionals either providing or withholding CPR pursuant to a DNR statute are protected from civil, criminal, and professional liability. This means that disciplinary action may not be taken by a licensing board and that the professionals may not be sued by the patient or his family. In addition, the state may not criminally prosecute a professional. This immunity generally applies if the professional withholds resuscitation pursuant to a DNR order or provides resuscitation because he is reasonably unaware of the order or believes it to be revoked.

When a statute requires that a witness sign the DNR order to verify that the patient or another qualified person consented to the order, the witness generally must fulfill certain requirements. Texas law serves as a basic example of these requirements. In Texas, each witness must be a competent adult and at least one of the witnesses may not be:

- Designated by the declarant to make a treatment decision
- Related by blood or marriage to the patient
- Entitled to any part of the declarant's estate pursuant to a will or by operation of law
- An attending physician
- An employee of the attending physician
- An employee of the health care facility in which the declarant is a patient (if the employee is providing direct patient care to the patient or is an officer, director, partner, or business office employee of the health care facility)
- A person who has a claim against any part of the patient's estate after the patient's death

Most states attach similar limitations to who may serve as a witness. As illustrated, the statutes regulating DNR orders vary only minimally from state to state. Nevertheless, nurses should consult the statute in the state in which they practice.

Living Wills

Living wills, another type of directive, are recognized and respected by health care professionals in most states. Also known as advance directives to physicians, living wills must adhere to specific statutory guidelines in order to be honored in many jurisdictions. Traditionally, the statutes governing living wills are called Natural Death Acts. More recently, these statutes have been called Advance Directive Acts or Health Care Decisions Acts. A living will is generally defined as a written expression by a competent adult of his desires regarding life-sustaining treatment in the event of a terminal illness or injury. Because the statutory guidelines regarding living wills vary among the states, a sampling of state statutes will be discussed in this section. These statutes generally provide that a directive does not apply when the patient is pregnant.

In Texas, the Advance Directive Act declares that a competent adult may execute a written directive at any time, provided that the directive is signed in the presence of two witnesses who also sign the directive. The declarant must notify his attending physician of the existence of the directive, and it should be included in the patient's medical record. If the patient is unable to communicate, another person may notify the physician. Customarily, the directive provides that the declarant does not wish for life-sustaining procedures to be used to artificially prolong the patient's life if in the future the declarant develops a terminal or irreversible condition as certified by the attending physician. An irreversible condition is defined as a condition, injury, or illness that:

- May be treated but is never cured or eliminated
- Leaves a person unable to care for or make decisions for himself
- Is fatal without life-sustaining treatment provided in accordance with the prevailing standard of medical care

Moreover, a terminal condition is an incurable condition caused by injury, disease, or illness that according to reasonable medical judgment will produce death within six months even with available life-sustaining treatment provided in accordance with the prevailing standard of medical care. A patient who has been admitted to a program under which the person receives hospice services provided by a home and community support services agency is presumed to have a terminal condition. Once this certification is made, the patient becomes "qualified" under the directive. In addition, the directive may name a proxy whom the declarant authorizes to make treatment decisions if the declarant becomes incompetent. The directive may be revoked by the declarant at any time, and the patient's current communicated desires always outweigh the force of the directive. For example, if the patient has executed a living will, but requests life-sustaining procedures after being certified as having a terminal condition, the current wishes must be respected.

If a qualified patient becomes incompetent or otherwise mentally or physically incapable of communication, the attending physician will make treatment decisions in conjunction with the person designated by the patient in the directive and based upon the patient's directions. If no person was designated by the directive to make decisions for the patient, the attending physician must comply with the directive unless the physician believes that the directive does not reflect the patient's present desire. The term "incompetent" means lacking the ability, based on reasonable medical judgment, to understand and appreciate the nature and consequences of a treatment decision. This includes the significant benefits and harms of and reasonable alternatives to a proposed treatment decision.

Pursuant to the Texas statute, a competent, qualified adult may execute a directive orally if it is issued in the presence of the attending physician and two witnesses. The witnesses must meet the requirements set out above under "Do-Not-Resuscitate Orders." The physician must make the existence of the directive and the names of the witnesses an entry in the declarant's medical record. In addition, a directive may be executed on the behalf of a minor, under the age of 18, by the patient's adult spouse or, if none, the parent or legal guardian.

A hospital or provider may refuse to comply with a directive and may provide life-sustaining treatment until a reasonable opportunity has been given for the transfer of the patient to another physician or health care facility that is willing to follow the directive. A provider who promptly notifies the patient of his refusal to follow the directive and cooperates with a transfer of the patient is not civilly, criminally, or administratively liable for his refusal. However, a physician's refusal to honor an advance directive must be reviewed by an ethics or medical committee of the hospital. The patient shall receive life-sustaining treatment during the review, and the patient or the person responsible for making health care decisions for the patient must be informed of the committee review process at least 48 hours before the meeting at which the patient's directive will be discussed unless the time period is waived by mutual consent. The patient or his decision-maker is entitled to attend the meeting and receive a written explanation of the committee's decision. The written decision must also be included in the patient's medical record. If the physician, patient, or patient's decision-maker does not agree with the committee's decision, the physician must make a reasonable effort to transfer the patient to a physician who is willing to comply with the directive. The hospital's personnel must assist in arranging the transfer to another physician, an alternative care setting within the facility, or another facility.

If the patient is requesting life-sustaining treatment that the attending physician and the committee have decided is inappropriate, the patient must be given available life-sustaining treatment pending transfer. The patient is responsible for any costs incurred in the transfer to another facility. Texas law further provides that the physician and hospital are not obligated to provide life-sustaining treatment after the tenth day following the date on which the committee's decision is provided to the patient or his decision-maker. The only exception to this is that the appropriate district or county court, at the request of the patient or his decision-maker, must extend the time period if it determines by a preponderance of the evidence that there is a reasonable expectation that a physician or facility that will honor the directive will be located if the extension of time is granted. This provision is extremely important because it allows a provider to discontinue inappropriate life-sustaining treatment against the family's wishes if the above requirements are met. This is intended to avoid the provision of expensive life-sustaining treatment to a patient for years on end when no likelihood of recovery exists. It should be noted that this section does not require a nursing facility or home health agency to provide treatment beyond its capabilities. For example, if a nursing facility is not capable of providing care for a ventilator-dependent patient, this statute does not require the facility to obtain that capability to accommodate a particular patient.

The Texas Advance Directive Act states that a physician, health care facility, or health professional that causes or participates in the withholding or withdrawal of a life-sustaining procedure in accordance with a patient's directive and the statute is not civilly, criminally, or professionally liable as a result of that action unless he failed to exercise reasonable care when applying the patient's directive. In addition, a provider cannot be held civilly or criminally liable for failing to act in accordance with a directive if the provider had no knowledge of the directive. Nevertheless, a physician or health care professional is subject to review and disciplinary action by the appropriate licensing board for *failing* to follow a directive in violation of the statute. Thus, a nurse would not be subject to a civil suit, criminal charges, or an action by the licensing board for unprofessional conduct if the nurse acted pursuant to a living will that met the requirements of the statute. A professional is potentially liable only if he is proven to have acted negligently. For example, if a valid living will exists but there is a later dated physician's progress note stating that the patient has revoked the living will, the nurse may be negligent if the nurse fails to read the note and as a consequence the patient is not resuscitated.

In Texas, a directive is not honored until the patient is certified as having a terminal or irreversible condition. Illinois has enacted an analogous statute. A directive executed pursuant to the Illinois Living Will Act may be given effect only when the patient has a terminal condition defined as "an incurable and irreversible condition which is such that death is imminent and the application of death delaying procedures serves only to prolong the dying process." Arguably, a directive will not be followed if a patient is in a persistent unconscious state but is expected to live for years and is not in a terminal condition. Nevertheless, Illinois courts have construed the definition of "terminal" to include persons in a persistent unconscious state if death would be imminent upon withdrawal of the life-sustaining treatment. The guidelines for executing a directive and immunities provided for following a directive are identical to the Texas statutory requirements.

In contrast, California's Health Care Decisions Act provides that a directive may be given effect when the primary physician determines that the patient has a terminal condition, the patient is in a persistent unconscious state, or the likely risks and burdens of treatment would outweigh the expected benefits. The California statute is virtually identical to the Texas statute in the requirements for the execution of the directive. The directive becomes operative when it is communicated to the attending physician. However, a living will has no force in California if it was executed while the patient was admitted to a skilled nursing facility unless one of the witnesses was a patient advocate or ombudsman designated by the state's Department of Aging.

As with the Texas law, a provider honoring a directive or acting in accordance with reasonable medical standards is immune from civil, criminal, or professional liability. A physician or other provider may presume that a declaration is valid in the absence of contrary knowledge. Regardless of these immunities, California has enacted strict penalties for failure to comply with the Health Care Decisions Act. A number of other states have adopted this approach. Under this section of the statute, a physician or provider who is unwilling to comply with the directive must transfer the individual to another physician or health care provider who will honor the directive. Failure to do so subjects the physician or provider to civil liability and possibly to criminal charges. In addition, a physician who willfully fails to record a determination that a patient has a terminal condition or is in a permanent unconscious state or the terms of the directive in the patient's medical record faces civil liability and possible criminal charges. An individual who willfully conceals, defaces, or obliterates another person's directive without the declarant's consent; falsifies a revocation; or coerces or fraudulently induces an individual to execute a directive faces civil liability and possible criminal charges. Also, a person who requires or prohibits a directive as a condition of providing insurance or receiving health care services may be subject to civil liability and possible criminal charges.

In addition to civil liability, California provides an even more severe penalty for an individual who falsifies or forges another person's directive or willfully conceals personal knowledge of a revocation with the intent to cause the withholding or withdrawal of life support. Such conduct constitutes unlawful homicide if life-sustaining treatment is withheld or withdrawn and death hastened as a direct result.

The Illinois Living Will Act also imposes a series of penalties for violating the statute. The Illinois penalties are not as severe as the California penalties but still serve to protect patients from the desires of others overriding their wishes regarding life-sustaining treatments. The willful concealing, obliterating, defacing, or damaging of another's directive or the falsifying of a revocation creates civil liability. This means that the patient or his representative may bring a civil suit against the wrongdoer. Further, a physician who willfully fails to notify the health care facility or fails to comply with the statute is guilty of unprofessional conduct under the Illinois Medical Practice Act. If a physician willfully fails to record the determination of a terminal condition in the medical record, without giving notice to the patient or the patient's representative of the physician's refusal to follow the directive so that the patient could have been transferred, that physician is also guilty of violating the Medical Practice Act. The Living Will Act provides that a physician who records a determination in the medical record is presumed to be acting in good faith unless it is proven that the physician violated the standard of reasonable medical care. In addition, the statute provides that requiring or prohibiting the execution of a directive is a misdemeanor. Illinois also has a provision similar to California's regarding criminal homicide, calling such a crime involuntary manslaughter.

As illustrated, most state laws involving living wills follow the same basic rules regarding the execution and use of directives. The states vary mainly on the determination of when a patient has a qualifying condition allowing for the use of the directive. Some states require the patient to be certified as having a terminal condition, while other states also allow directives to be utilized when a patient is in a persistent vegetative state. Some states, such as Alabama, provide that living wills may be used when a patient is in a permanent unconscious state, which is generally equated with a persistent vegetative state. Many states enforce serious penalties against providers and other persons who refuse to comply with a directive, prevent the use of a valid directive, or knowingly cause an invalid or revoked directive to be followed, causing a patient's death. All the statutes provide immunity from civil, criminal, and professional prosecution for following the statutes and a directive in good faith.

Furthermore, a health care provider may also be protected from liability under the common law for failing to follow a directive if the provider had no knowledge of the directive. In *Allore v. Flower Hospital*, a patient with asbestosis had executed a living will directing that no life-sustaining treatment be administered to him if he suffered from a terminal condition or was in a permanently unconscious state. The patient was admitted to the hospital with severe respiratory difficulties. Although the patient's primary physician was aware of the directive, he did not communicate this information to a nurse who reported the patient's condition to a specialist or to the specialist who ordered intubation and ventilation, which had the effect of prolonging the patient's life. The patient subsequently died, and his wife sued for battery on the grounds that in light of the directive, the intubation and ventilation were given without her husband's consent. The court rejected this claim, holding that because the situation was an emergency and because the patient had declined to the point where he could not indicate his consent for or refusal of the treatment, the principles regarding implied consent in emergency cases applied. While a directive could normally override the implied consent in emergency situations, it did not in this case because the specialist and nurse did not know of the directive's existence. Consequently, they were not liable for battery in failing to follow the directive, which resulted in life-sustaining treatment being provided to the patient.

The court in *Allore* also held that the patient's wife could not receive damages for the prolongation of her husband's life because such a "harm" is one for which courts have repeatedly refused to compensate. Because Ohio did not recognize a cause of action for the prolongation of life, the patient's wife was left with only a battery claim for harm caused directly by the treatment to which the patient did not consent. The Ohio court's holding raises an interesting issue, which may vary depending upon state law, regarding the type of claims that can be brought for the administering of life-sustaining treatment in contravention of a directive.

Durable Health Care Powers of Attorney

A durable health care power of attorney or medical power of attorney is a document executed by a declarant that delegates to an agent the authority to make health care decisions if the declarant becomes incompetent or incapable of communication. Many states have enacted legislation creating rules for the execution and use of a durable power of attorney for health care. However, some states rely on older established statutes regulating general powers of attorney. Following is a representative sample of the durable power of attorney for health care statutes.

Within the medical power of attorney section of the Texas Advance Directive Act, the Texas legislature provides that a competent adult may execute a document appointing an agent to make health care decisions for the person if the person becomes incompetent. The principal (the person executing the document) may not designate as an agent his health care or residential care provider or an employee of the provider unless the employee is a relative. The power of attorney must be signed by the principal in the presence of two witnesses. The witnesses must meet the same requirements as set out above in the "Do-Not-Resuscitate Orders" section of this chapter. If the principal is physically unable to sign, another person may sign for the principal in the principal's presence and at the principal's express direction. The power of attorney may designate an alternative agent should the first designee be incapable of acting as an agent. The power of attorney is not effective unless the principal asserts and signs that the principal has received and understood the contents of a statutorily prescribed statement disclosing the effect and requirements of a power of attorney. The document is effective indefinitely but may be revoked at any time. If the power of attorney contains an expiration date and on that date the principal is incompetent, the medical power of attorney continues to be effective until the principal becomes competent, unless it is revoked.

A designated agent may exercise decision-making authority only if the principal's attending physician certifies in the medical record that, based upon the physician's reasonable medical judgment, the principal is incompetent. The agent must make health care decisions in consultation with the attending physician and according to the agent's knowledge of the principal's wishes, including religious or moral beliefs. If the principal's wishes are not known, the agent must base his decision on the principal's best interests. The physician does not have a duty to verify that the agent's decision is consistent with the principal's wishes or beliefs.

The statute specifically provides that a health or residential care provider that knows of the existence of a medical power of attorney must follow the directive to the extent that it is consistent with the desires of the principal and the statute. As with other directives, if the physician refuses to comply with the agent's decision, the physician must inform the agent, who may select another physician. If this occurs, the procedures discussed in the "Living Wills" section above regarding the role of the ethics or medical committee must be followed if the agent's directive concerns providing withholding or withdrawing life-sustaining treatment. It should be noted that the statute does not authorize a health or residential care provider to act in a manner contrary to a physician's order. An agent may request, review, receive, authorize the release of, or consent to the disclosure of the principal's medical information. An agent may not, under any circumstances, consent to voluntary inpatient mental health services, convulsive treatment, psychosurgery, abortion, or the omission of comfort care for the principal.

Even though the agent becomes the decision-maker, the attending physician must make a reasonable effort to inform the principal of any proposed treatment or of any proposal to withdraw or withhold treatment. Treatment may not be given or withheld if the principal objects, regardless of whether a medical power of attorney is in effect or the patient is competent at that time. If a petition for appointment of a guardian is filed or a guardian is appointed, the guardian may file a motion asking the probate court to determine whether or not to suspend or revoke the power of attorney. The court must consider the preference of the principal as expressed in the power of attorney. A health care provider, residential care provider, managed care organization, or insurer may not discriminate against a person because the person has or does not have a medical power of attorney.

Pursuant to the Texas statute, an agent is not criminally or civilly liable for a health care decision made in good faith under the terms of the power of attorney and the statute. In addition, a physician or other health care provider is not subject to criminal, civil, or professional liability for an act or omission if done in good faith pursuant to the power of attorney and the statute and does not constitute a failure to exercise reasonable care in the provision of health care services. A provider is not liable for failure to comply with a durable power of attorney if the provider was not provided a copy of it or had no knowledge of the directive. Providers are also not liable if they act as directed by a power of attorney that has expired or been revoked without their knowledge. The existence of a power of attorney does not alter the liability for health care costs. The patient and any responsible party remain liable for treatment costs. A near relative of the principal, a guardian, social worker, physician, clergyman, or another responsible adult directly interested in the principal may bring an action to request that the power of attorney be revoked because at the time it was signed the principal was not of sound mind to make a health care decision or was under duress, fraud, or undue influence.

The majority of the state statutes regarding durable health care powers of attorney are comparable to the Texas statute. The powers of attorney for health care section of the California Health Care Decisions Act is virtually identical to the Texas section and varies in only a few minor areas. For example, in California the power of attorney may be either signed by two witnesses or acknowledged before a notary public. The witnesses must attest that the principal is personally known to them or that the principal's identity was proven by convincing evidence. Convincing evidence means that the witness has no knowledge that would lead a reasonable person to believe that the principal is not who he claims to be. The agent may rely on a valid identification card or driver's license, a passport, or a similar document containing a photograph and description of the principal. This must be signed by the principal, with an identifying number, and must be issued within the last 5 years. California places a penalty that Texas does not on any person who alters or forges a power of attorney for health care or willfully conceals or withholds knowledge of a revocation intending to cause the with-holding or withdrawal of life-sustaining health care. If these acts or omissions directly cause such treatment to be withheld, thus hastening the death of the principal, that person may be prosecuted for unlawful homicide.

The Illinois Power of Attorney for Health Care Act is in harmony with the Texas act. However, Illinois places a duty on the agent to notify the health care provider of the existence of the power of attorney or its revocation if the patient is unable to or fails to do so. Illinois places the same penalty as California on a person whose acts or omissions cause the withholding or withdrawal of life-sustaining treatment. Illinois labels this as involuntary manslaughter. Additionally, the Illinois Act provides that a person is civilly liable if he willfully conceals, cancels, falsifies, forges, or alters a power of attorney or an amendment to revocation without the principal's consent. A person is civilly liable and commits a Class A misdemeanor if he requires or prevents the execution of a power of attorney as a condition of ensuring or providing any type of health care services. Illinois allows for nonstatutory health care powers of attorney to be recognized provided that they are executed by the principal, designate the agent and the agent's powers, and designate that the agent is not a person prohibited from being named as an agent, such as the principal's health care provider. A nonstat-utory power of attorney need not be witnessed to be valid.

These statutes illustrate the various attempts by the states to provide a means for individuals to make health care decisions or appoint another to do so if the person becomes incompetent and is ill or injured. The state statutes are generally similar, but nurses should become familiar with the specific provisions applying to the state in which they consult.

A Person Is Incompetent and Failed To Provide Prior Written Directions

The majority of states that have confronted the issue of the withdrawal or withholding of life-sustaining medical treatment in the absence of a directive have done so through the courts and not the legislatures. The rules produced by the courts tend to be more restraining than if the state legislatures were to enunciate guidelines. Without legislative guidance, the courts tend to examine each case on its own facts and are reluctant to set forth any broad guidelines. In spite of strong urging by the highest courts in many states, the state legislatures have rarely responded by passing relevant statutes.

The Forms of Substitute Decision-Making

This section discusses the various standards set out by the courts in order to illustrate the differences and similarities. The highest courts in approximately half of the states have decided cases regarding surrogate decision-makers along with a handful of federal courts, including the U.S. Supreme Court. In general, the courts adopt one of two basic theories in deciding these cases. The courts employ either the surrogate-decision-making standard or the best-interests-of-the-patient standard.

The Legal Standard of Surrogate Decision-Making

Courts that utilize the surrogate-decision-making standard require that the surrogate make the treatment decision based on evidence of the patient's desires and beliefs. In some states, this is a very rigorous test that very few cases meet and generally requires the surrogate to apply to a court for permission to withdraw or withhold treatment. A few states have developed differing standards depending on whether the patient has a terminal condition or is in a persistent vegetative state. The tests are typically stricter for coma patients as opposed to terminally ill patients. A cross section of the court decisions regarding withholding or withdrawing life-sustaining medical treatment is set forth below.

In *Cruzan v. Director, Missouri Department of Health*, the U.S. Supreme Court approved the Missouri Supreme Court's test regarding the withdrawal of life-sustaining treatment from a patient in a persistent vegetative state. In this case, the family of Nancy Cruzan, a 30-year-old victim of an automobile accident, petitioned the court to allow Ms. Cruzan's health care providers to remove the feeding tube providing her with nutrition. The case progressed to the Missouri Supreme Court, and the court denied the family's plea, holding that the family had failed to present clear and convincing evidence that Ms. Cruzan would have wanted the feeding tube withdrawn. The U.S. Supreme Court affirmed the Missouri decision determining that the state's interest in preserving life was strong enough to allow it to require clear and convincing evidence of the patient's wishes before withdrawing life-sustaining treatment. Although the court affirmed the Missouri Supreme Court, other states are not required to adopt this stringent standard of proof. The U.S. Supreme Court merely held that it is permissible for a state to do so.

The New Jersey Supreme Court has developed separate tests for the withdrawal or withholding of life-sustaining medical treatment depending upon the condition of the patient. In one of the earliest cases decided regarding this issue, *In the Matter of Karen Quilan*, the court established guidelines for patients in persistent vegetative states. The court reiterated and expanded on the *In the Matter of Karen Quinlan* decision in *In the Matter of Nancy Ellen Jobes*. The *Jobes* case involved a 31-year-old patient who had degenerated into a persistent vegetative state as a result of an automobile accident. The court determined that although evidence of Ms. Jobes's wishes was presented, this evidence was not clear and convincing. The court relied on the *Quinlan* test.

In order for treatment to be withheld or withdrawn, the patient's family must consider the patient's personal value system; prior statements about and reactions to medical issues; the patient's personality; and religious, ethical, and philosophical values in order to determine what course of medical treatment the patient would choose. The patient's close family members' substituted judgment will be relied upon unless the health care professionals are uncertain about whether or not family members are protecting the patient's interests. If the professionals are concerned, treatment should not be terminated absent the appointment of a guardian by a court. Generally, judicial review of the family's decision is not required. However, the family must obtain statements from two independent physicians knowledgeable in neurology attesting that the patient is in a persistent vegetative state and without a reasonable chance of recovery. The patient's attending physician must also submit a similar statement. However, if the patient is in a hospital setting, the prognosis committee's review should be substituted for the statements of two independent physicians.

In 1985, the New Jersey Supreme Court created guidelines for the withdrawal of life-sustaining medical treatment from a terminally ill elderly patient in a nursing home. In *In the Matter of Conroy*, the patient suffered from organic brain syndrome, arteriosclerotic heart disease, hypertension, and diabetes mellitus. She could not speak, was unable to move from a semifetal position, was incontinent, and was limited in her ability to swallow. However, Ms. Conroy exhibited some level of consciousness and was not comatose.

The court determined that life-sustaining treatment could be withheld only if a specific procedure was followed. First, the patient must have been determined to be incompetent by a court and a guardian must have been appointed. A person who believes that withholding or withdrawing life-sustaining treatment would realize the patient's wishes or be in the patient's best interests must notify the Office of the Ombudsman. The ombudsman should investigate the situation and report to the Commissioner of Human Services and any other agency that regulates the facility. The attending physician and nurses should furnish evidence concerning the patient's condition. Two unaffiliated physicians should be appointed by the ombudsman to confirm the patient's diagnosis and prognosis. Treatment may then be withheld or withdrawn if the guardian, physicians, and ombudsman concur that one of the following tests has been met. In order to meet the *subjective test*, evidence must be presented to clearly show that the patient would have refused treatment under the circumstances involved if able to choose for herself. This evidence may be drawn from, but not limited to:

1. A living will
2. An oral directive to a family member, friend, or health care provider
3. Statements made by the patient regarding medical treatment administered to others
4. The patient's religious beliefs
5. Consistent patterns of conduct in prior medical decisions

In addition, medical evidence regarding the patient's condition, treatment, and prognosis is an essential prerequisite. This evidence must establish that the patient is elderly, is incompetent, resides in a nursing home, has severe and permanent mental and physical impairments, and has a life expectancy of approximately 1 year or less. Treatment may also be withheld if one of two *best interest tests* is met. These tests will be discussed in detail in the next section.

The Illinois Supreme Court has developed a slightly different test for withdrawal of treatment. The court initially determined that a patient must be terminally ill and in a persistent vegetative state or in an irreversible coma before artificial sustenance may be withdrawn. In *In re Estate of Longeway*, the court required the patient's attending physician and two other consulting physicians to concur in this diagnosis. If this factor is met, the patient's guardian or family must utilize the substituted judgment test to determine what decision the patient would make if competent. The decision-maker may rely on relevant statements made by the patient while competent and the patient's personal value system, religious beliefs, ethical beliefs, life goals, attitudes toward sickness, and any other relevant information regarding the patient. In addition, a court must review this evidence, and if the evidence is clear and convincing, the court may order that the treatment be withdrawn or withheld.

In a later decision, *In re Greenspan*, the Illinois Supreme Court provided some slight latitude in the definition of "terminal illness." The court determined that a patient was in a terminal condition when death would be imminent if the life-sustaining procedure were not being provided. Pursuant to this broader definition, virtually any patient in a persistent vegetative state who requires a feeding tube for nutrition is in a terminal condition because without food and water, the patient will die within a short period of time. However, the Illinois decisions continue to allow the withdrawal of treatment only if the patient is comatose. An incompetent patient with a terminal illness who has some level of consciousness could not have treatment withheld or withdrawn. The remainder of the guidelines established in *Longeway* are still in effect.

The highest court in Massachusetts also allowed the removal of a feeding tube from a patient in a persistent vegetative state pursuant to substituted decision-making. In *Brophy v. New England Sinai Hospital, Inc.*, the family provided evidence regarding the patient's prior statements about life-sustaining treatment, his religious beliefs, the impact on the patient's family, the probability of adverse side effects, and his prognosis with and without treatment. However, the court upheld the right of the health care facility to refuse to withdraw the treatment. The family was allowed to transfer the patient to a facility that would comply with their decision to discontinue treatment. Similarly, in *Guardianship of Jane Doe*, the court utilized the substituted judgment test in analyzing the removal of a feeding tube from an incompetent, mentally retarded adult in a persistent vegetative state. The court enunciated a procedure for such cases in which a judge must hold a hearing to identify the choice that the patient would have made if competent. The lack of evidence of prior statements regarding medical treatment does not bar the use of the substituted judgment test because the court may additionally look to the factors discussed in *Brophy*.

The Arizona Supreme Court has established simpler guidelines for the withdrawal or withholding of life-sustaining treatment from an incompetent patient. In *Rasmussen v. Fleming*, the court held that judicial intervention is not necessary unless the interested parties conflict regarding the decision. In situations where the parties concur, the family and guardian should conduct substituted decision-making. If no reliable evidence of the patient's wishes exists, the best interests test should be conducted.

The Pennsylvania Supreme Court adopted the substituted judgment standard in determining whether to allow the withdrawal of a gastronomy tube from a 43-year-old patient in a persistent vegetative state. In *In re Fiori*, the patient had been in this state since the age of 24. His mother, who was also his legal guardian, petitioned the court to allow the tube to be removed. The court determined that life-sustaining treatment for a patient in a persistent vegetative state with no chance of recovery could be terminated even though the patient had never expressed any opinions regarding termination of treatment. This is provided that a close family member utilizes the substituted judgment test and two qualified physicians certify that the patient is in a persistent vegetative state without reasonable possibility of recovery. Court involvement is not necessary unless a dispute exists or no close family member exists. In this case, a guardian should be appointed and court direction must be sought before treatment is terminated.

Although most states rely on court decisions regarding surrogate decision-making, Texas provides a unique provision in its Advance Directive Act regarding the withdrawal or withholding of life-sustaining treatment when a patient has not executed a living will but is incompetent or otherwise incapable of communication. The Texas Advance Directive Act allows the attending physician and the patient's legal guardian or an agent under a medical power of attorney to make treatment decisions, including the withdrawal or withholding of life-sustaining treatment from the patient. If the patient does not have a legal guardian or designated agent, the physician and one person from the following categories of persons in the order listed below may make treatment decisions: (1) the patient's spouse, (2) the patient's reasonably available adult children, (3) the patient's parents, or (4) the patient's nearest living relatives. The decision must be based on what the patient would desire, if known, and must be documented in the patient's medical record and signed by the physician. In the unfortunate event that none of the persons listed above are available to assist in making treatment decisions, a treatment decision by the patient's attending physician must be concurred with by another physician who is not involved in the patient's care or who is a representative of an ethics or medical committee of the hospital. It should be noted that the mere fact that a patient has not executed a directive does not mean and should not create a presumption that the patient does not want treatment withheld or withdrawn. If any of the persons listed above (who can make treatment decisions when no legal guardian or agent under a medical power of attorney exists) wish to challenge a treatment decision made under the provision allowing for decisions to be made when no directive has been executed, that person must apply for temporary guardianship under Section 875 of the Texas Probate Code.

These cases and statutes illustrate the broad interpretations of the substituted judgment standard that has been adopted in various states. Some states require court intervention whenever a decision to withdraw or withhold life-sustaining treatment from an incompetent patient is made, while other states allow intervention by a judge only in a dispute between the interested parties. The states employing this standard also differ on the burden of proof applicable to the determination. A few states require clear and convincing evidence of the patient's desires. This is a much higher burden than the one used in most civil suits, although it does not rise to the level of a criminal trial, which requires proof beyond a reasonable doubt.

The Legal Standard of Best Interests of the Patient

The standard of best interests of the patient is an easier burden for families to meet. Under this test, the decision maker must decide not what the patient would have wanted, but what is best for the patient. This involves consideration of the patient's suffering, prognosis, the invasiveness of the treatment, and the patient's quality of life. Although the majority of states have not adopted this standard and rely solely on the substituted judgment test, a growing minority of states are utilizing the best interests standard in situations in which no evidence of the patient's intent exists.

The Washington Supreme Court adopted the best interests standard in determining whether or not artificial nutrition could be withdrawn from a patient with Batten's disease. In *In the Matter of the Guardianship of Barbara Grant*, Ms. Grant was 22 years old and in an almost vegetative state due to a terminal genetic degenerative condition of the central nervous system. Her parents sought an order from the court providing that certain life-sustaining treatments not be initiated should they be indicated, including CPR, the use of an artificial respirator, and the insertion of a nasogastric tube. Ms. Grant resided in a state-operated school with a policy to use all measures necessary to sustain an individual's life. However, the attorney general agreed to follow the parents' wishes if the court agreed.

In response to the Grants' petition, the court established a standard for withholding life-sustaining treatment from an incompetent patient. First, the attending physician and two other qualified physicians must determine with reasonable medical judgment that the patient is in an advanced stage of a terminal and incurable illness and is suffering severe and permanent mental and physical deterioration. The patient's legal guardian, if one has been appointed or, if not, the patient's family must then determine that if the patient were competent, she would choose to refuse treatment. If this is not possible, the family must decide that withholding treatment would be in the patient's best interests. Neither any members of the patient's family nor the physicians and health care facility may object to the decision. In determining the patient's best interests, the guardian or family should examine evidence regarding the patient's:

- Present level of physical, sensory, emotional, and cognitive functioning
- Degree of physical pain from the medical condition, treatment, and termination of treatment
- Degree of humiliation, dependence, and loss of dignity
- Life expectancy and prognosis
- Treatment options, including the risks, side effects, and benefits of each

Under these circumstances, court intervention is not required.

Similarly, the Wisconsin Supreme Court utilized the best interests standard for a persistent vegetative patient with a history of schizophrenia. In the decision, *In re Guardianship of L.W.*, the court pronounced guidelines for allowing a guardian to consent to the withdrawal of life-sustaining treatment when a patient was never competent, or whose conduct when competent was not sufficient to allow the use of the substituted judgment standard. In order to terminate treatment, the attending physician and two independent neurologists must conclude that the patient is in a persistent vegetative state with no reasonable chance of recovery, and the guardian must determine in good faith that the withdrawal of treatment is in the patient's best interests. The guardian must look to certain factors in determining the best interests of the patient. The factors given by the court are the same as those enunciated by the Washington Supreme Court in the *Grant* case. In addition, if a health care facility has a bioethics committee, it should also be consulted. Court involvement is not necessary without a dispute among the interested parties. The Wisconsin Supreme Court has limited this decision to persons in a persistent vegetative state in *Matter of Edna M.F.* and refused to extend the reach of this case to a person with an irreversible or incurable condition.

In the *Conroy* case discussed above, the New Jersey Supreme Court allowed treatment to be withdrawn from an elderly nursing-home patient with a life expectancy of less than 1 year if the substituted-decision-making or one of two best interests tests were demonstrated. Pursuant to the first best interests test, some trustworthy evidence must exist that the patient would have refused treatment. In addition, the decision-maker must be satisfied that the burdens of the patient's continued life with the treatment outweigh the benefits. In other words, the patient's suffering with the treatment must greatly exceed any physical pleasure, emotional enjoyment, or intellectual satisfaction that the patient still derives from life. Under the second test, treatment may be withheld absent evidence of the patient's wishes if the net burdens of the patient's life with the treatment clearly outweigh the benefits that the patient derives from life. To meet this test, the administering or continuing of life-sustaining treatment must reach the level of being inhumane. The mere fact that a patient's prognosis is poor or his functioning is limited is insufficient to meet this last test. In either of the best interests tests, the patient's family must also concur in the decision to withdraw or withhold treatment.

Similarly, in the *Rasmussen* case that was discussed in the previous section, the Arizona Supreme Court held that the best interests test should be adopted whenever the substituted judgment test is inapplicable, such as when patients were never competent or no evidence of their wishes exists. The court provided that, in the best interests test, the decision-maker evaluates the patient's suffering, preservation or restoration of functioning, and quality and extent of sustained life.

In regard to minors, the Illinois Supreme Court, in *Curran v. Bosze*, utilized a best interests analysis in holding that the testing of minor twins' bone marrow to determine their suitability as donors should not be ordered when one parent, the primary caretaker and sole custodian, refused consent and the other parent consented. In this case, although the parents had never married, they had entered into an agreed order stating that the mother had the sole care, custody, and control of the children. However, in matters relating to health, the mother was required to consult and confer with the father. Another of the father's children, the twins' half-sibling, suffered from acute undifferentiated leukemia and needed a bone marrow transplant. The father requested that the twins be tested to determine whether they were compatible donors. However, the mother refused to consent to the test and harvesting procedure. The court determined that the procedure was not in the twins' best interest. The court emphasized three factors in determining a child's best interest:

1. The parent who consents on behalf of the child must be informed of the risks and benefits inherent in the procedure
2. There must be emotional support available to the child from the child's primary caretakers
3. There must be an existing, close relationship between the donor and the recipient

In *Curran*, the court stated that no close relationship existed between the children, especially since the twins did not know that the patient was related. Further, the mother would not be able to support the twins fully during the procedure because of her opposition to the donation.

These cases illustrate that a few states have adopted the best interests standards when the patient's wishes could not be ascertained. Most of the states adopting this standard do not require court involvement and allow the family or guardian and the physicians to make the decision after considering a number of relevant factors.

Active Euthanasia or Assisted Suicide

When a physician or other person assists a terminally ill patient in ending his life, this is termed assisted suicide or euthanasia. The most well-known method of assisted suicide is the prescription of drugs that will effectively and painlessly terminate the patient's life. Although the majority of states prohibit any act that assists another to die, some health care providers strongly believe that a patient has the right to die with dignity and end intolerable suffering. As a result, these health care providers occasionally violate these statutes privately. In a high-profile, unprecedented case, a Michigan jury convicted Dr. Jack Kevorkian of second-degree murder and delivery of a controlled substance for his performance of an assisted suicide in 1998. However, the public has a growing support for assisted suicide — a few states have attempted to enact statutes legalizing physician-assisted suicide under specific guidelines, and several state statutes prohibiting assisted suicide have been tested in the courts.

State Statutes That Prohibit Assisted Suicide

Although no state currently prohibits suicide or attempted suicide, 39 states have statutes prohibiting assisted suicide, six states (Alabama, Idaho, Massachusetts, Nevada, Vermont, and West Virginia) prohibit assisted suicide through their common law, and four states (North Carolina, Ohio, Utah, and Wyoming) have neither statutory nor common law prohibiting assisted suicide.

In two recent federal appellate cases, the Washington and New York state statutes prohibiting assisted suicide faced constitutional challenges. In the end, the Supreme Court declared the statutes valid. In *Compassion in Dying v. Washington*, a group of physicians, seriously ill patients, and a nonprofit organization (Compassion in Dying) asked the courts to declare the Washington law unconstitutional. The Ninth Circuit, sitting *en banc,* held that a terminally ill person has a right to die. Specifically, the court determined that a person with a terminal condition has a liberty interest in determining the time and manner of one's death pursuant to the Due Process Clause of the Fourteenth Amendment. On appeal and referred to as *Washington v. Glucksberg*, the U.S. Supreme Court reversed the Ninth Circuit decision and stated that Washington's state statute prohibiting a person from "knowingly [causing] or [aiding] another person to attempt suicide" rationally related to legitimate government interests and did not violate the Due Process Clause of the Fourteenth Amendment.

In the majority opinion, Justice Rehnquist stated that the holding "permits the debate [about the morality, legality, and practicality of physician-assisted suicide] to continue...." The Court limited the applicability of its decision to a physician providing a patient with the means to commit suicide when the patient commits the suicidal act. The Court reserved its ruling on situations in which a patient could not self-administer the lethal dose of medications prescribed by the physician.

Shortly after the Ninth Circuit's decision in *Compassion in Dying v. Washington*, the U.S. Court of Appeals for the Second Circuit held that New York's state statute prohibiting assisted suicide was also unconstitutional. However, in *Quill v. Vacco*, the court relied on the Equal Protection Clause of the U.S. Constitution, stating that competent terminally ill patients were treated differently, instead of following the Ninth Circuit's reasoning that relied on the Due Process Clause. The Second

Circuit noted that competent adults with terminal conditions on life support have a right to withdraw treatment and utilize their physician and a surrogate decision-maker to assist. The court pointed out that this, in effect, hastened death and could be equated to suicide. However, a competent terminally ill adult not on life support was prohibited, by law, from gaining assistance from a physician or other person to hasten death. According to the Second Circuit, this violated the Equal Protection Clause of the Constitution because the differentiation between terminally ill patients was not rationally related to a valid state interest.

In *Quill v. Vacco*, the U.S. Supreme Court similarly reversed the Second Circuit decision. While acknowledging that the line between refusing lifesaving medical treatment and assisted suicide might appear unclear, the Court insisted that the distinction bears a rational relationship to legitimate governmental interests.

Prior to both the Ninth and Second Circuit considerations regarding assisted suicide statutes, but in further support of the U.S. Supreme Court's eventual resolution of the cases, the Michigan Supreme Court decided a similar case. The court held that the Michigan statute prohibiting assisted suicide had been validly enacted and did not violate either the state's constitution or the U.S. Constitution. In *Michigan v. Kevorkian*, the Michigan Supreme Court decided that no right to commit suicide existed and that as a consequence, a person has no right to assist others in committing suicide. According to the court, a person has only a right to withdraw or withhold life-sustaining treatment and not a general right to die. The U.S. Supreme Court has denied a petition for *certiorari* in this case, and therefore, the Michigan Supreme Court opinion defines the law in Michigan.

Similar to the Michigan Supreme Court, the Alaska Supreme Court upheld that state's statutory prohibition against assisted suicide in *Sampson v. Alaska*. The Alaska statute defined assisted suicide as criminal manslaughter and made no exception for physicians who assist their patients to die. The supreme court held that while a ban on physician-assisted suicide may impinge upon some degree of privacy and liberty interests guaranteed by the Alaska constitution, such interference was valid in light of the countervailing consequences that could arise from allowing assisted suicide. The court expressed concern that if such a practice were permitted, undue influence could be exerted on vulnerable persons to consent to assisted suicide. The court also concluded that no clear distinctions could be drawn to ascertain what persons should be allowed to consent to physician-assisted suicide. For similar reasons, the supreme court concluded that the statutory ban on assisted suicide did not violate any equal protection guarantees.

In spite of the numerous state statutes prohibiting physician-assisted suicide, there are few reported cases of a criminal conviction against a physician. As one of the most widely publicized figures in the debate, Dr. Kevorkian was convicted for his part in assisting a patient's suicide. Though Oakland County prosecutors dismissed charges brought under Michigan's 1998 law banning assisted suicide, the jury convicted Dr. Kevorkian of other charges — second-degree murder and delivery of a controlled substance. In other cases, physicians have not been criminally convicted. For example, a grand jury refused to indict a physician who intentionally prescribed barbiturates to a patient for the patient to use to end her life. The physician was arrested after admitting his actions in an article in the *New England Journal of Medicine*.

Despite the lack of prosecution under existing statutes, one state has enacted strong legislation prohibiting such assistance. On August 5, 1996, Rhode Island enacted legislation making it a felony for an individual or licensed health care professional to provide the physical means by which another person can commit or attempt to commit suicide. A health care professional includes a physician, nurse, nurse anesthetist, podiatrist, physician assistant, pharmacist, and dentist. This statute excepts from prosecution the legal withdrawal or withholding of life support and the prescription or administration of medications or procedures to relieve a patient's discomfort even if it hastens death. This is one of the few statutes that is specific to physician-assisted suicide.

State Statutes That Legalize Assisted Suicide

At this time, five states have held referenda on proposals to permit physicians to assist terminally ill, competent adults to commit suicide. The proposals in Washington and California failed, probably due to the fact that the measures contained few safeguards. Nevertheless, these votes were very close, and a more protective proposal could potentially be passed in the future. Soon after Dr. Jack Kevorkian's negatively publicized crusade, voters in Michigan rejected, more convincingly, a similar 1998 proposal. However, the most recent referendum failed by only a 3% margin in Maine. Overall, nationwide public-opinion polls have indicated growing support for physician-assisted suicide in proper circumstances.

In another state election in Oregon, the proposal passed. The Oregon Death with Dignity Act contains numerous guidelines designed to protect patients when assisted suicide is chosen. In 1995, a federal district judge entered an injunction preventing the statute from taking effect. In *Lee v. Oregon*, the judge ruled the statute unconstitutional because it fails to ensure that only competent adults with terminal conditions will choose assisted suicide. According to the court, the statute contains no procedures for determining that the patient is competent to make such a decision and is not under the influence of any other person. The attending physician makes the determination whether or not the patient is qualified to decide to die. However, the injunction was overturned on appeal to the Ninth Circuit, which held that the opponents in the suit lacked jurisdictional standing. The U.S. Supreme Court declined to hear the case. The statute took effect by late 1997 and has since been followed and only slightly amended. In 1998, 16 patients took lethal medications prescribed under the Oregon law. In 1999 and 2000, 27 people took the prescribed medication. Studies have revealed that education level stands as the only distinguishable difference between those who died of similar underlying diseases naturally and those who have chosen physician-assisted suicide. Those choosing assisted suicide have generally held college or post-baccalaureate degrees.

Over the past few years, the federal government has made several moves to support state control of assisted suicide laws. As a way of diverting national debate and ensuring that states set their own assisted suicide policies, Congress passed the Assisted Suicide Funding Restriction Act of 1997, which prohibits the use of federal funds to subsidize physician-assisted suicide. In 1998, U.S. Attorney General Janet Reno issued a decision clarifying that state law controls physician-assisted suicide and that the Controlled Substance Act does not affect physician-assisted suicides. The Pain Relief Act, introduced in 1999, was an effort by members of the U.S. House to regulate assisted suicide on a national level. The Act, which failed to get through the U.S. Senate, would have banned the use of federally regulated drugs for assisted suicide and prevented the U.S. Attorney General from recognizing any state law permitting assisted suicide or euthanasia, including Oregon's Death with Dignity Act. However, since the legislature chose not to pass the Pain Relief Act, state control of assisted suicide remains.

A Health Care Provider's Potential Liability Resulting from the Right to Refuse Treatment

Health care providers are placed in a precarious position when faced with a patient who is refusing medical care. Although the statutes and the courts attempt to protect providers, failure to respect a patient's right to refuse medical treatment may give rise to a civil suit by the patient for damages. In addition, withholding or withdrawing treatment pursuant to a patient's alleged wishes can also lead to liability if the family disagrees or claims that the patient did not want treatment withdrawn. Court intervention prior to withholding treatment might not always protect a provider either. Nevertheless, if a health care provider is in doubt as to the proper course of action, involving the court is a prudent step. This area of the law is just beginning to develop, and cases are still relatively rare in many states. However, a few intrepid courts have found liability against providers.

Wrongful Life

A cause of action for wrongful life has not been recognized by the majority of states. In the minority of states that have recognized this action, the action has arisen because of the birth of a child. For instance, a mother may have an amniocentesis to determine the health of her fetus. She is informed by her physician that the results are normal, but the child is born with birth defects. A wrongful life cause of action is brought on behalf of the child against the doctor, and it will normally allege that the doctor has negligently given the child life. In this situation, the child's parents, in some jurisdictions, have a claim for wrongful birth, asserting that they would have aborted the fetus if they had known of the serious birth defects. Another cause of action, wrongful pregnancy, may be alleged when a pregnancy occurs, despite a person's undergoing a medical procedure for sterilization.

A cause of action similar to wrongful life may theoretically be used when a person on life support is kept alive against his wishes. A claim by a person on life support will differ from a child's claim because life is only being extended and not given as in the case of a child. However, both the patient on life support and the child complain because they are alive. Courts generally have not favored this action, possibly due to the disturbing ethical problems it raises in valuing life. For example, the Ohio Supreme Court recently held in *Anderson v. St. Francis-St. George Hosp., Inc.*, that "there is not [a] cause of action for wrongful living." As noted by the concurring opinion, the furthering of life cannot be considered a damage under the confines of present negligence law. The Indiana Court of Appeals made a similar decision, declining to create a tort of "wrongful prolongation of life" because the court said that existing Indiana law adequately protects those who do not want to be kept alive by invasive means.

Wrongful Death

In contrast, most states recognize wrongful death as a viable cause of action. In these states, the cause of action usually arises statutorily (i.e., it is created by the state legislature rather than by the state courts). Generally, these actions are allowed to be brought when a person has died because of the tortious or criminal act of another person or entity. For instance, in *Beverly Enterprises-Florida v. Spilman*, the Florida District Court of Appeals found that Beverly had caused Mr. Spilman's death by allowing him to contract fatal infections. The court reasoned that Mr. Spilman was a person covered by the Florida wrongful death statute and that Mr. Spilman's injury had occurred because Beverly tortiously deprived Mr. Spilman of his rights as a nursing home resident.

For purposes of this chapter, a wrongful death action may arise when a patient is not competent to consent to withdrawal of treatment or an unqualified person consents to withdrawal of the patient's life support. For example, a patient's family may sue for wrongful death if a patient does not consent to a DNR order, but a perceived spouse or common law spouse consents to no resuscitation. If the patient's children prove that the person who ordered no resuscitation was not a spouse, the children have a potential claim for wrongful death. These cases all have a common characteristic in that the person bringing suit alleges that the patient has not legally refused treatment. A potential wrongful death action may occur each time life support to a patient is withdrawn not in accordance with the statutes that govern its removal. As seen, state statutes regarding withdrawal of life support differ. In these areas, determination of whether a wrongful action has occurred must begin with an analysis of the statutes and case law that specify when it is legal to remove life-sustaining devices.

Violation of Right of Bodily Self-Determination

A recent case in Connecticut has created a new potential cause of action against providers who fail to respect a patient's refusal of treatment. In *Stamford Hospital v. Vega*, Ms. Vega was admitted to the hospital for the birth of her child. After delivering a healthy baby, Ms. Vega began to hemorrhage. She was a Jehovah's Witness and had signed a form refusing all transfusions. The doctors tried a number of alternatives, but realized that a blood transfusion was necessary. Both Ms. Vega and her husband continued to refuse the transfusion. The hospital sought an injunction from a court allowing a transfusion to be administered. After holding an emergency hearing, the court ordered the transfusion. After receiving transfusions, Ms. Vega recovered and was discharged. She then initiated an appeal of the court's order authorizing the transfusions.

The Connecticut Supreme Court held that the case was not moot even though Ms. Vega had already received the transfusion of which she was complaining. The court reasoned that the issue was one that would arise in the future when other Jehovah's Witnesses refused blood transfusions and that the court should resolve the issue now. According to the court, Ms. Vega's common law right of bodily self-determination had been violated by the court's injunction and the administration of the transfusions. Pursuant to the court's opinion, the hospital had no right or obligation to administer unwanted medical care to a patient who competently declined the care after having been fully informed of the consequences of her decision. The court held that both the hospital and trial court were obligated to respect Ms. Vega's choice to refuse a blood transfusion. The case was then remanded by the Connecticut Supreme Court to the trial court for judgment to be rendered for Ms. Vega. This is an important case to be aware of because it unequivocally states that the hospital should not have questioned Ms. Vega's refusal.

Battery

When medical treatment is rendered to a person without informed consent, a court may hold that a battery was committed. A battery is an unwelcome touching. This cause of action has generally been applied when a person consents to a medical procedure, such as surgery, but the physician failed to provide the patient with all the necessary facts for the patient to make an informed decision regarding the treatment. Although this claim has been infrequently made in the context of an expressed refusal of treatment that was not respected by a provider, it is a potential area on which a patient may rely in bringing suit against a hospital or other health care provider.

Violation of Due Process

If the hospital is managed by a governmental unit such as a county, a municipal district, or the state, a patient could potentially bring suit against the facility for violation of due process. In this type of claim, the patient alleges that the facility failed to provide notice and a hearing prior to obtaining a court order and administering medical treatment in spite of the patient's express refusal. This type of suit has customarily been brought when a patient refuses treatment that his physician believes is necessary to save his life.

For example, in *Novak v. Cobb County Kennestone Hospital Authority*, a 16-year-old Jehovah's Witness patient and his mother refused a blood transfusion. The hospital petitioned the court for the appointment of a guardian *ad litem* for the patient. The court considered the petition and appointed a guardian without notice to either the patient or his mother. The following day, due to the patient's deteriorating condition, the court held an emergency hearing at the hospital. Although the physicians and the guardian attended and testified, neither the patient nor his mother was given notice. At the conclusion of the hearing, the court ordered the transfusion, which was then promptly administered. The patient and his mother brought suit against the hospital for violating their due process. The U.S. Court of Appeals for the Eleventh Circuit dismissed the patient's claims, holding that the court had independently held a hearing and ordered the transfusion. The court has judicial immunity and cannot be held liable for its order. The hospital could be held liable only if the patient proved that the hospital and the physicians had conspired with the judge to administer the transfusion. This is a relatively high burden that few patients could prove. If the hospital had acted without a court order in administering the transfusion, the patient's claims may have been successful.

Violation of Federal Constitutional Rights

Even if a hospital is not managed by a governmental entity, the hospital and physicians may be liable for violating a patient's constitutional right to freedom of religion. If the health care providers act pursuant to a court's order, they are acting under the color of state law. In *McKenzie v. Doctors' Hospital of Hollywood, Inc.*, a U.S. district court in Florida held that a patient had jurisdiction to assert this claim. The patient was hospitalized, and her physicians recommended a blood transfusion. When the patient and her husband refused on the basis of their religion, the hospital obtained a court order authorizing the transfusion. Upon learning of the order, the patient left the hospital and sought treatment elsewhere. The court dismissed the patient's claims, holding that because the patient left the hospital of her own free will without receiving the transfusion, the hospital had not prevented the patient from executing her constitutional rights. Although this claim has not been actively pursued by injured patients, it is a potential claim that may be brought by persons refusing medical treatment on the basis of religion.

Refusal of Family to Pay Further Medical Costs

In *Grace Plaza of Great Neck, Inc. v. Elbaum*, a patient's family refused to pay the patient's future medical costs due to the long-term facility's refusal to remove the patient's feeding tube. The patient's husband successfully petitioned the court to allow removal of the feeding tube. However, due to the facility's continued refusal, the husband was forced to remove the patient from the facility. He refused to pay for the patient's treatment from the time of the facility's first refusal of his request to withdraw artificial nutrition before he had sought court authorization. The facility brought suit against the husband to recover the past-due costs of the patient's care. The court determined that the husband was required to pay for the services because the facility had not acted in bad faith in refusing to withdraw treatment. Pursuant to the court's opinion, a facility that is uncertain about the discontinuance of treatment is within its rights to refuse to terminate the care until the issue has been legally determined.

This is one of the first cases regarding who must pay for treatment that the patient and the family have decided should be withdrawn. Although the outcome in this case protected the facility, health care providers should be aware of this potential cause of action because it may become a more familiar argument due to the expense of life-sustaining treatment and in cases where life-sustaining treatment is extended without cause.

Emergency Medical Treatment and Active Labor Act

While the majority of this chapter has been devoted to analyzing a patient's right to refuse treatment, the converse issue, namely, a patient's right to receive emergency medical treatment, is also important. To that end, nurses and other health care providers should be aware of federal and state laws governing this issue.

The most significant law regarding a patient's right to receive treatment for an emergency medical condition is the federal Emergency Medical Treatment and

Active Labor Act (EMTALA). The U.S. Congress passed this law in 1985 because of growing concerns that indigent patients were being denied treatment at hospital emergency rooms. EMTALA ensures that all individuals who go to hospitals for evaluation and treatment of a possible emergency medical condition will receive a statutorily defined minimum level of care, regardless of wealth, race, socioeconomic status, or ability to pay.

The EMTALA statute itself contains specific provisions for examining and treating individuals with emergency conditions. Furthermore, additional clarification and guidance is provided by federal regulations that were implemented in conjunction with the statute. EMTALA requires a Medicare-certified hospital with an emergency department to provide to any person who presents to the emergency department and requests treatment an appropriate medical screening examination to determine whether an emergency medical condition exists. If one is found to exist, the hospital must provide stabilizing treatment or an appropriate transfer to another medical facility for further evaluation and treatment.

EMTALA applies only to hospitals that satisfy two criteria: (1) the hospital receives Medicare funds, and (2) the hospital provides emergency treatment services. It does not matter whether a hospital operates a formal emergency department. As long as the hospital provides services to treat emergency conditions, it will be subject to EMTALA. A hospital subject to EMTALA must comply with certain statutory and regulatory requirements. Furthermore, physicians who practice within that hospital are also subject to specific obligations.

A hospital must provide a medical screening to any individual who comes onto hospital property seeking treatment for a possible emergency medical condition. An individual does not have to come to the actual emergency department at a hospital in order to trigger that hospital's EMTALA obligations. It is sufficient that the individual comes onto hospital property, which includes the entire hospital campus (up to 250 yards away from the main building) as well as areas that are more than 250 yards away or off the main hospital campus, but that are determined to be departments of the main hospital.

The medical screening that the hospital must provide is not satisfied by conducting a triage of the individual. What is required in the medical screening depends upon the patient's symptoms and can range from simple to complex. However, the hospital must provide the same screening examination to all patients who have the same symptoms. The hospital must not delay the medical screening in order to obtain payment or insurance information from the individual. However, if it is clear that inquiries about payment and insurance will not delay the screening examination, the hospital may obtain such information before beginning the screening.

One significant issue that arises in the screening context is the hospital's liability for failing to detect an emergency medical condition by screening. In numerous cases, plaintiffs have attempted to argue that the hospital's failure to detect an emergency condition through the screening should be actionable under EMTALA. However, the courts have been almost unanimous in rejecting under EMTALA claims that a medical screening was inadequate to detect an emergency condition, so long as the screening is consistent with the screening given to all patients with the same symptoms. The complete absence of any screening examination would give rise to an EMTALA claim, as would a hospital's rendering a screening examination that was less than the usual screening that the hospital would provide for patients with similar symptoms.

Failure of the screening to detect an emergency condition, when there is no indication that the screening was less than that usually given to patients with the same or similar symptoms, is a separate issue that is to be addressed under state malpractice laws. For instance, in *Vickers v. Nash General Hospital, Incorporated*, the hospital provided a medical screening to a patient who had been in an altercation. The doctor at the hospital diagnosed the patient as simply having a head laceration and treated the patient by suturing the laceration. The patient later died from a skull fracture that had not been detected by the medical screening. The administrator of the patient's estate sued the hospital, contending that EMTALA provided a cause of action for failure to conduct a more extensive examination that arguably would have detected the skull fracture. The court rejected this argument, stating that under EMTALA the hospital is obligated to provide a screening commensurate with what the hospital perceives the patient's condition to be. Whether the hospital was negligent in not realizing that a more extensive screening examination was called for is an issue for state malpractice law, not EMTALA.

If it is determined through the screening that the patient does not actually have an emergency medical condition, the hospital has no other obligations under EMTALA with regard to that patient, and the hospital may discharge or transfer the patient. If it is determined that the patient does have an emergency condition, the hospital must either stabilize the patient or effectuate an appropriate transfer to another hospital. With regard to stabilization, the hospital must offer treatment to the patient and explain the risks and benefits of such treatment to the patient or the patient's legally authorized representative. If the patient refuses the stabilizing treatment, the hospital must attempt to obtain the patient's written informed refusal. If such attempts are unsuccessful, the hospital must document the steps it took to obtain the refusal. On the other hand, if the patient does not refuse treatment and the hospital engages in stabilizing treatment, it must do so within the capabilities of the staff and facilities available at the hospital. Stabilizing a patient does not require that the medical condition be finally resolved; it requires only that the emergency nature of the condition be treated. However, if the medical condition is not entirely resolved, the hospital must determine whether the patient is stable for transfer to another hospital or stable for discharge, whichever is applicable.

A patient is stable for transfer if the treating physician determines, within reasonable clinical confidence, that the patient will suffer no material deterioration during transport between the hospitals and that the receiving hospital has the capability to care for the patient's condition. In contrast, a patient is considered stable for discharge if, within reasonable clinical confidence, it is determined that the patient is at a point where any additional care and treatment can be reasonably provided to the patient as an outpatient or as an inpatient at a later time. When the patient is discharged, the hospital must provide discharge instructions and a plan for appropriate follow-up care.

If the emergency nature of the patient's condition has not been stabilized, the hospital may not discharge the patient unless he requests it. The hospital can also transfer the patient only if he requests the transfer or the treating physician certifies that the benefits of a transfer outweigh the risks. Prior to the transfer, the transferring hospital must provide medical treatment to the patient within its capacity in order to minimize the risks to the individual's health. Another element of an appropriate transfer is that the receiving hospital has available space and qualified personnel to treat the patient and agrees to accept the transfer. The transferring hospital must send all available medical records to the receiving hospital at the time of the transfer and must send any records available later, such as lab results, as soon as practicable. Further, the transfer must be effected through qualified personnel and transportation equipment that are medically appropriate and necessary. It is the responsibility of the transferring physician to determine the mode of transportation, what personnel should accompany the patient in addition to paramedics (if indicated), and the equipment that should be utilized during the transfer or be available during the transfer. If the patient refuses the transfer, the hospital must document the refusal and obtain that patient's written refusal of transfer. If the patient is unwilling to sign a written refusal, the hospital must document its attempts to obtain the written refusal.

In addition to the above duties, the hospital must also maintain a central log on each individual who comes to the emergency department seeking assistance and whether the person refused treatment, was refused treatment, was transferred, was admitted and treated, was stabilized and transferred, or was discharged. The hospital must maintain a list of on-call physicians, including specialists and subspecialists, who are available to provide further examination and stabilizing treatment to a patient determined to have an emergency medical condition. The hospital must also be able to receive the transfer from another hospital of a patient with an emergency condition. Every specialty or subspecialty provided by the hospital on a routine basis must be included on the list even if the service is provided only intermittently.

Like the hospital itself, these on-call physicians at the hospital also have certain obligations under EMTALA. A physician who is on call and who is called by the hospital must come to the hospital to examine the patient within a reasonable period of time and cannot request that the patient be referred to the physician's office. The hospital is responsible for implementing policies requiring that on-call physicians arrive within a reasonable period of time. If a physician cannot be available for call when he is scheduled, the physician is responsible for securing a qualified alternative and for communicating this information to the hospital. With regard to transfers from another hospital, if a physician is not on call and receives a transfer request, he may refuse the transfer. However, if the physician refuses the transfer, he must still inform the party seeking the transfer that the party should call the hospital directly to see whether the hospital is willing to accept the transfer. In the case of a physician who accepts a transfer, his acceptance of a transfer does not qualify as the hospital's acceptance. The hospital itself must also accept the transfer. A physician who accepts a transfer must still tell the party seeking the transfer to call the hospital admissions department to see whether the hospital will also accept the transfer.

In addition to all of the above, there are also separate requirements when an individual comes to a hospital's department rather than to the main hospital to seek treatment for an emergency condition. Numerous factors are involved in determining whether a facility is a department of a hospital, the consideration of which is beyond the scope of this book. Essentially, a department of a hospital is a facility that is under the ownership and administrative and financial control of the main hospital. A department is not on the main hospital campus, but operates under the main hospital's license and provider number. It is an extension of the main hospital located away from the main campus. If an individual comes to a hospital's department for treatment, the EMTALA obligation extends to the hospital and its capabilities as a whole. However, at least initially, evaluation will be provided by the department to which the patient presents.

As a general rule, there should be a mechanism for direct contact between the department and the main hospital. EMTALA does not require a department to be staffed with additional personnel solely to handle medical emergencies. However, if the department routinely has physicians, registered nurses, or licensed practical nurses on hand, the department will need to ensure that such individuals are trained in protocols for handling emergency cases. Furthermore, the main hospital may need to dispatch practitioners from the main hospital to the department in order to provide screening and stabilization and transfer, if needed.

Depending on the facilities, a department may begin the screening and then transfer the patient to the main campus to complete the screening and, if necessary, provide stabilization and transfer to another hospital. If, due to the patient's condition, there is insufficient time to transport the patient to the main hospital, or if the main hospital lacks the specialized facilities needed, the department may transfer the patient to another hospital instead. In this case, the department must follow the EMTALA transfer requirements.

Conclusion

Nurses and other health care providers should familiarize themselves with the law in the state in which they practice. The issues of refusal of medical treatment and right to die have gained national attention and support in recent years, yielding an onslaught of litigation. To protect themselves, providers must follow the statutory and court guidance in their state in order to respect a patient's right to refuse treatment. Many potential causes of action exist that patients or their families may utilize to bring suit against providers who do not adhere to these state guidelines. In addition to the right to refuse treatment, patients also are entitled to receive treatment for emergency medical conditions at any hospital that provides treatment for medical emergencies. Health care providers at such hospitals must also be cognizant of the duties imposed upon them for the treatment of emergency conditions, particularly under the federal EMTALA law.

References

Allore v. Flower Hospital, 699 N.E.2d 560 (Ohio Ct. App. 1987).
Anderson v. St. Francis-St. George Hosp., Inc., 77 Ohio St. 3d 82 (1996).
Assisted Suicide Funding Restriction Act, 42 U.S.C. §§14401–14402 (1999).
Beverly Enterprises-Florida v. Spilman, 661 So. 2d 867 (Fla. Dist. Ct. App. 1995).
Bouvia v. Superior Court of Los Angeles County, 225 Cal. Rptr. 297, 305 (Ct. App. 1986).
Brophy v. New England Sinai Hosp., Inc., 497 N.E.2d 626, 638 (Mass. 1986).
Cal. Prob. Code §§4652–4805 (2001).
Compassion in Dying v. Washington, 79 F.3d 790 (9th Cir. 1997).
Cruzan v. Director, Missouri Department of Health, 497 U.S. 261 (1990).
Curran v. Bosze, 566 N.E.2d 1319 (Ill. 1990).
First Healthcare Corp. v. Hamilton, 740 So. 2d 1189 (Fla. Dist. Ct. App. 1999).
Fosmire v. Nicoleau, 75 N.Y.2d 218 (1990).

Ga. Code. Ann. §31-39-4 (2000).

Grace Plaza of Great Neck, Inc. v. Elbaum, 82 N.Y.2d 10 (1993).

HCA, Inc. v. Miller, 36 S.W.3d 187 (Texas. App. – Houston [14th Dist.] 2000).

755 Ill. Comp. Stat. 45/4 (2001).

Illinois Living Will Act, 755 Ill. Comp. Stat. 35/1–8 (2001).

Illinois Medical Practice Act, 225 Ill. Comp. Stat. 60 (2001).

In re Baby Boy Doe, 632 N.E.2d 326 (Ill. App. Ct. 1994).

In re Estate of Longeway, 549 N.E.2d 292 (Ill. 1989).

In re Duran, 769 A.2d 497 (Pa. Super. Ct. 2001).

In re Fetus Brown, 689 N.E.2d 397 (Ill. App. Ct. 1997).

In re Guardianship of Jane Doe, 411 Mass. 512, cert. denied *sub nom. Doe v. Gross*, 502 U.S. 950 (1992).

In re Guardianship of L.W., 482 N.W.2d 60, 71 (Wis. 1992).

In re Peter, 529 A.2d 419 (N.J. 1987).

In the Matter of Conroy, 98 N.J. 321 (1985).

In the Matter of Karen Quinlan, 70 N.J. 10 (1975), cert. denied *sub nom. Garger v. New Jersey*, 429 U.S. 922 (1976).

In the Matter of Nancy Ellen Jobes, 108 N.J. 394 (1987).

Indiana Taylor v. Munice Medical Investors LP, No. 18A02–9904-CV-265 (Ind. Ct. App. Apr. 20, 2000).

Jefferson v. Griffin Spalding County Hospital Authority, 274 S.E.2d 457 (Ga. 1981).

Kan. Stat. Ann. §65 (2001).

Knight v. Beverly Health Care Bay Manor Healthcare Center, — So. 2d —, 2001 WL 996048 (Ala. 2001).

Lee v. Oregon, 107 F.3d 1382 (9th Cir. 1997).

Matter of Edna M.F., 563 N.W.2d 485 (Wis. 1997).

Michigan v. Kevorkian, 447 Mich. 436 (1994), cert. denied, 514 U.S. 1083 (1995).

N.Y.C. L.S. §§2960–2979 (2001).

Norwood Hosp. v. Munoz, 564 N.E.2d 1017 (Mass. 1991).

Novak v. Cobb County Kennestone Hosp. Auth., 74 F.3d 1173 (11th Cir. 1996).

Oregon Death With Dignity Act, Or. Rev. Stat. §§127.005–127.897 (1999).

Pain Relief Promotion Act, H.R. 2260, 106th Cong. (1999).

Quill v. Vacco, 521 U.S. 793 (1997).

Rasmussen v. Fleming, 741 P.2d 674, 685 (Ariz. 1987).

Sampson v. Alaska, 31 P.3d 88 (Alaska 2001).

Schloendorff v. Society of New York Hosp., 105 N.E. 92, 93 (N.Y. 1914).

Shine v. Vega, 429 Mass. 456, 709 N.E.2d 58 (Mass. 1999).

Stamford Hosp. v. Vega, 236 Conn. 646 (1996).

Tex. Health & Safety Code Ann. §§166.032–166.044 (Vernon, 2002).

Tex. Health & Safety Code Ann. §§166.082–166.089 (Vernon, 2002).

Tex. Health & Safety Code Ann. §§166.153–166.165 (Vernon, 2002).

Washington v. Glucksberg, 521 U.S. 702 (1997).

Test Questions

1. A do-not-resuscitate (DNR) order is
   A. Executed by a patient, when competent, in anticipation of the need to make important medical decisions when the patient becomes incompetent
   B. Executed by a physician, with consent, when the physician anticipates a situation requiring resuscitation
   C. Executed by a representative, when the patient is incompetent, in anticipation of the need to make future medical decisions
   D. Executed by an attending physician when the need for resuscitation develops

2. A minor's role in refusing medical treatment includes
   A. The absolute right to refuse care
   B. A right to refuse care that varies depending on age and maturity
   C. No right to refuse care
   D. Any rights that the minor's parents allow the minor

3. A durable health care power of attorney is
   A. A document that a physician provides and executes for a patient who may need serious medical care
   B. A document that an attorney executes while his client is incompetent in order for the attorney to gain decision-making authority
   C. A document executed by a competent patient delegating the authority to make health care decisions to an agent if the patient becomes incompetent or unable to communicate
   D. A document executed by a close family member claiming the authority to make health care and estate decisions if the patient becomes terminally ill

4. A person who refuses medical care for religious reasons
   A. Can refuse treatment in all states
   B. Has his rights most strongly protected by federal law and the United States Constitution
   C. Must petition the court and receive treatment if the court does not answer quickly enough
   D. Is guaranteed the right to refuse treatment in some states

5. In 1997, the Supreme Court rulings in *Washington v. Glucksberg* and *Quill v. Vacco*
   A. Upheld the constitutionality of state statutes that prohibited assisted suicide
   B. Struck down two state statutes that detailed living wills and DNR orders
   C. Upheld the constitutionality of state statutes that allowed assisted suicide
   D. Struck down state statutes that would have legalized euthanasia

Answers: 1. B, 2. B, 3. C, 4. D, 5. A

PROFESSION OF LEGAL NURSE CONSULTING

Chapter 6

The History and Evolution of Legal Nurse Consulting

Joan K. Magnusson, BSN, RN, LNCC,
Betty Joos, MEd, BSN, RN,
Julie B. Pike, MN, RN, LNCC, CPHRM,
Rosanna Janes, BSN, RN, and
Jenny Beerman, RN, LNCC

CONTENTS

0-8493-1418-6/03/$0.00+$1.50
© 2003 by AALNC

Objective

- To recognize the role of the American Association of Legal Nurse Consultants in developing the nursing specialty practice of legal nurse consulting

Early Legal Nurse Consultant Practice

It is difficult to determine when nurses gained recognition as legal nurse consultants (LNCs), since attorneys have sought nurses to answer questions for many years regarding medical-legal matters. Nurses have been recognized as consultants to attorneys and have been compensated for their expertise and contribution since the early 1970s. Nurses' earliest and most common experiences in the legal arena have been as expert witnesses in nursing malpractice cases. As the courts began to recognize that nurses, rather than physicians, should define and evaluate the standard of nursing practice, nurses were sought to review cases and offer opinion testimony about nursing care. During the 1980s, nursing malpractice litigation expanded along with medical malpractice. Nurses became more interested and educated about the legal issues impacting health care. The role of the expert nurse witness came to be recognized as an essential professional function. It was clear to both nurses and attorneys that nurses were uniquely qualified to aid attorneys in their medical-legal practices.

During the same period, attorneys were searching for resources to help them understand medical records, medical literature, hospital policies and procedures, and medical testimony. Nurse consultants came to be valued as cost-effective alternatives to physician consultants, who were often unavailable as a result of practice demands. Law firms began to employ nurses for their expertise. Attorneys began to value their input on a broader scope, not just medical and nursing negligence cases, but personal injury and criminal cases as well. Since then, the scope of practice of LNCs has considerably broadened from these areas. Many of those areas are discussed in this chapter.

Formation of the Association

During the 1980s, nurses in California, Arizona, and Georgia, who were practicing as consultants to attorneys, formed local professional groups. Their goals were to educate the legal profession about the effectiveness of the nurse consultant as liaison between the legal and medical communities, and to provide a network for members to share expertise. Leaders from these three groups became the driving force for founding the national association. On July 29, 1989, a steering committee composed of these leaders met in San Diego and founded the American Association of Legal Nurse Consultants (AALNC).

The national steering committee was replaced as the decision-making body of AALNC when the first board of directors was elected in March 1990. AALNC's mission of promoting the professional advancement of registered nurses practicing in a consulting capacity in the legal field was inaugurated.

Major Contributions

Establishment of Chapters

While AALNC offered national membership benefits to nurses licensed in any state of the U.S., it was through the establishment of chartered chapters that AALNC fostered membership growth, networking, and education at the local level. Within 10 years, chapter activity went from the three original local groups to chapters in more than 45 cities in 31 states. The number of chapters continues to increase each year.

Continuing Education

The first annual AALNC educational conference was held in Phoenix, AZ, in 1990. Since then, this annual conference has become the major networking and educational opportunity for LNCs. The conference offers cutting-edge topics and high-profile speakers as well as sessions for the less experienced LNC. It also includes the AALNC annual business meeting and provides for transition of the new board members.

AALNC also offers other regional conferences as well as educational materials in written, audio, and video format designed to assist nurses at all levels of expertise in legal nurse consulting practice. More information may be obtained by visiting the association's Web site at http://www.aalnc.org.

Publications

Network News

From its inception AALNC has provided a newsletter to its members called the *Network News*. This communication tool is used to inform members of association activities.

Journal of Legal Nurse Consulting

In January 1995, AALNC issued the first edition of the *Journal of Legal Nurse Consulting*, which is the official publication of AALNC. It is a refereed journal providing articles of interest to nurses in the legal nurse consulting specialty and is considered one of the most valued benefits of membership.

Legal Nurse Consulting: Principles and Practice

The first edition of *Legal Nurse Consulting: Principles and Practice*[1] was published in 1997 as AALNC's effort to provide a core curriculum for LNCs. It became the primary resource text for nurses who wished to learn more about the specialty practice. It also paved the way toward AALNC's goals of developing a certification program for LNCs. This second edition is a continuation of the effort to provide nurses with a reference regarding the practice of legal nurse consulting.

AALNC also publishes a variety of other professional resources available for sale to beginning and advanced LNCs to assist them in establishing and growing their businesses or practices. These materials are designed to give realistic and practical information to enhance the practitioner's knowledge and skills. Materials are available in various forms of media, depending on the source and content.

Standards and Guidelines

The Code of Ethics for Legal Nurse Consultants with Interpretative Discussion

The Code of Ethics for Legal Nurse Consultants with Interpretive Discussion[2] was adopted in April 1992 (see Appendix 6.1). The code provides the guidelines for professional performance and conduct for practice and affirms the values and practices of the American Nurses Association (ANA) and the American Bar Association (ABA). More information on the interpretation and application of these ethical standards may be found in Chapter 10, Ethical Theory and the Practice of the Legal Nurse Consultant.

Scope of Practice for the Legal Nurse Consultant

In an effort to develop a scope of practice and standards of practice, AALNC conducted a role delineation study in 1992. The survey document contained 108 questions divided into categories dealing with: biographical data; professional activities; medical review, analysis, and research; document preparation; client/ expert liaison activities; and specialized activities as an expert witness or life-care planner. Following the analysis of the data provided by this survey of member LNCs, AALNC published the first edition of the Scope of Practice for the Legal Nurse Consultant[3] in January 1994.

Scope and Standards of Practice for the Legal Nurse Consultant

In 1995, questions arose regarding inconsistencies in AALNC's philosophy regarding the professional identity of LNCs. The AALNC Board of Directors discussed whether the practice of legal nurse consulting should be considered a profession in its own right, a specialty practice of nursing, or a specialty practice of law.

A review of AALNC's bylaws, scope of practice, and code of ethics reinforced the board's conviction that the nursing profession was the basis for the practice of legal nurse consulting. While these documents acknowledged the need for acquiring certain knowledge and skills from the legal profession, it was clear that LNCs did not practice law.

With this focus in mind, AALNC finalized its efforts to develop standards of practice using a model promoted by the ANA and used by many other nursing specialties. Minor revisions were made to the 1994 Scope of Practice to be consistent with AALNC's position, and the document became part of the Scope and Standards of Practice for the Legal Nurse Consultant,[4] published in October 1995 (see Appendix 6.2). Details on the application of the standards of practice may be found in Chapter 8, Professionalism, Standards of Practice, and Standards of Professional Performance.

Professional Relationships

National Federation of Specialty Nursing Organizations

In January 1994, AALNC applied for membership in the National Federation of Specialty Nursing Organizations (NFSNO), to strengthen AALNC's relationship with other nursing specialty organizations and to validate its identity as a professional nursing association. At that time, NFSNO consisted of more than 40 nursing organizations representing more than 400,000 nurses. On July 21, 1994, AALNC was seated as an affiliate member of NFSNO at its annual meeting.

Nursing Organization Liaison Forum

In November 1996, representatives of AALNC's board audited the Nursing Organization Liaison Forum (NOLF) meeting in Washington, D.C. At that time, NOLF provided a forum for interaction among national nursing organizations to increase unity in the nursing profession. In December 1996, AALNC became a regular participant in NOLF.

Nursing Organizations Alliance

By 2001, NOLF and NFSNO, noting that both organizations were designed to achieve identical goals, merged to form one organization, the Nursing Organizations Alliance (NOA), of which AALNC is a member. Delegates from member associations meet regularly to address issues of mutual concern across nursing specialties. Through educational efforts, the leadership of the NOA work to improve the role of nursing specialties. Through legislative efforts the alliance gives input to health care legislation.

Position Statements

Role of the Legal Nurse Consultant as Distinct from the Role of the Paralegal and Legal Assistant

In 1999, AALNC published the statement on the Role of the Legal Nurse Consultant as Distinct from the Role of the Paralegal and Legal Assistant.[5] The position addressed the distinctions between the nursing specialty practice of legal nurse consulting and the practice of the paralegal and legal assistant as defined by the ABA (see Appendix 6.3). This position was taken in an effort to clarify that nurses do not need to obtain education through programs approved by the ABA in order to be LNCs, since those programs' primary focus is legal education. Rather than focus on the shared or separate "tasks" of either entity, nurses should be reminded that the primary role of an LNC is to evaluate, analyze, and render informed opinions on the delivery of health care and the resulting outcomes. In 1984, the

National Association of Legal Assistants defined the terms "paralegal" and "legal assistant" as "persons who assist attorneys in the delivery of legal services. Through formal education, training and experience, legal assistants have knowledge and expertise regarding the legal system and substantive and procedural law which qualify them to do work of a legal nature under the supervision of an attorney."[6] Chapter 7, Entry into Specialty Practice of Legal Nurse Consulting, provides additional information on this topic.

Education and Certification in Legal Nurse Consulting

AALNC's second position statement, Education and Certification in Legal Nurse Consulting,[7] was published in the summer of 2000, in an effort to clarify the association's position on the preferred model for an educational program in preparation for entry into the specialty practice (see Appendix 6.4). The position paper clearly states AALNC's position on the use of professional credentials as initials following one's name. AALNC supports the practice initiated by the ANA of listing the initials of one's credentials in the following order: highest educational degree and highest nursing degree if different, then one's governmental license, followed by any professional certifications. In support of specialty nursing certification, AALNC recognizes the American Legal Nurse Consultant Certification Board's Legal Nurse Consultant Certified (LNCC®) as the credential for LNCs. One may find more information on certification in Chapters 7, Entry into Specialty Practice of Legal Nurse Consulting, and 9, Certification.

Summary

This chapter focuses on the development of the specialty practice of legal nurse consulting through the efforts of the members and staff of AALNC. Considering the relative newness of this specialty of nursing, the association has moved quickly to become the organization known as the representative voice for nurses in this field. AALNC will continue to strengthen the advancement of the specialty practice through communication with organizations, such as NOA, ANA, ABA, and the American Board of Nursing Specialists, and by offering education and networking opportunities for nurses in the specialty. More information about the activities and materials listed in this chapter is available from AALNC. One is encouraged to use the association's Web site as a resource for more information about membership, certification, educational materials, and offerings.

References

1. Bogart, J.B., Ed., *Legal Nurse Consulting: Principles and Practices*, CRC Press, Boca Raton, FL, 1998.
2. American Association of Legal Nurse Consultants, *Code of Ethics for Legal Nurse Consultants with Interpretive Discussion*, AALNC, Glenview, IL, 1992.
3. American Association of Legal Nurse Consultants, *Scope of Practice for the Legal Nurse Consultant*, AALNC, Glenview, IL, 1994.

4. American Association of Legal Nurse Consultants, *Scope and Standards of Practice for the Legal Nurse Consultant,* AALNC, Glenview, IL, 1995, 2002.
5. American Association of Legal Nurse Consultants, *Role of the Legal Nurse Consultant as Distinct from the Role of the Paralegal and Legal Assistant,* AALNC, Glenview, IL, 1999.
6. National Association of Legal Assistants, *What Is a Paralegal, Background and Definition,* National Association of Legal Assistants, Tulsa, OK, 1984.
7. American Association of Legal Nurse Consultants, *Education and Certification in Legal Nurse Consulting,* AALNC, Glenview, IL, 2000.

Appendix 6.1
Code of Ethics and Conduct of the American Association of Legal Nurse Consultants

Code of Ethics and Conduct with Interpretive Discussion

Preamble

The Code of Ethics of the American Association of Legal Nurse Consultants is based on belief about the nature of individuals and society. The Code of Professional and Ethical Conduct provides guidelines to its members for professional performance and behavior. The success of any professional organization is the competence and integrity of its members. Our goal to those we serve is that they be assured of our accountability.

We recognize a responsibility to other professional organizations with which we are aligned, particularly, the American Nurses Association and the American Bar Association. We accept and abide by the principles of their Codes of Ethics and Conduct.

By our support of the Code of Ethics of the American Association of Legal Nurse Consultants, we affirm that the rights and trust placed in us will not be violated.

I. The legal nurse consultant does not discriminate against any person based on race, creed, color, age, sex, national origin, social status, or disability and does not let personal attitudes interfere with professional performance.

Individual differences do not influence professional performance and practice. These factors are understood, considered, and respected when performing activities.

II. The legal nurse consultant performs as a consultant or an expert with the highest degree of integrity.

Integrity refers to uprightness, honesty, and sincerity. The legal nurse consultant directs those attributes to the requirements of the profession. Integrity is a personal and sacred trust and the standard against which the legal nurse consultant must ultimately test all decisions. Honest errors and differences of opinion may occur, but deceit, poor judgment, or lack of principles must not be tolerated.

III. The legal nurse consultant uses informed judgment, objectivity, and individual competence as criteria when accepting assignments.

The legal nurse consultant does not purport to be competent in matters in which he/she has limited knowledge or experience. Only services which meet high personal and professional standards are offered or performed.

IV. The legal nurse consultant maintains standards of personal conduct that reflect honorably upon the profession.

The legal nurse consultant abides by all federal and state laws. The legal nurse consultant who knowingly becomes involved in unethical or illegal activities negates professional responsibility for personal interest or personal gain. Such activities jeopardize the public confidence and trust in the nursing profession.

V. The legal nurse consultant provides professional services with objectivity.

The legal nurse consultant provides services free of personal prejudice and conflict of interest. The legal nurse consultant reflects on all current assignments and commitments before accepting assignments, making decisions, rendering opinions, or providing recommendations. Personal prejudices and conflicts of interest must be recognized, as they may interfere with objectivity and adversely affect performance.

VI. The legal nurse consultant protects client privacy and confidentiality.

The legal nurse consultant uses confidential materials with discretion. The legal nurse consultant respects and protects the privacy of the client. The legal nurse consultant does not use any client information for personal gain.

VII. The legal nurse consultant is accountable for responsibilities accepted and actions performed.

VIII. The legal nurse consultant maintains professional nursing competence.

The legal nurse consultant is a Registered Nurse and maintains an active nursing license. The legal nurse consultant is knowledgeable about the current scope of nursing practice and understands the standards of the profession. The legal nurse consultant does not practice law.

Conclusion

Each individual's personal commitment to the Code of Professional and Ethical Conduct of the American Association of Legal Nurse Consultants is the ultimate regulator of his/her behavior. By adopting this Code of Ethics, we affirm to those with whom we serve that they have the right to expect us to abide by this code.

As members of the American Association of Legal Nurse Consultants, we pledge to demonstrate to the public this commitment of integrity and professional excellence.

Appendix 6.2
Scope and Standards for the Legal Nurse Consulting Practice

Introduction

AALNC was founded in 1989 as the professional association of registered nurses who practice in a consulting capacity in the legal field. The association's purpose is to promote the professional advancement of legal nurse consultants and to provide a resource for information relating to legal aspects of nursing and healthcare law.

In October 1990, AALNC began to formulate the scope of practice for the legal nurse consultant (LNC) and to develop standards of practice and professional performance. Because this was a newly identified field for registered nurses, a role delineation study was conducted first. Based on the results of that study, the scope of practice was created and was adopted in January 1994. This document emphasized the knowledge and skills that are unique to nursing and that are useful in the critical analysis of healthcare issues involved in various legal processes. The current edition of the Scope of Practice for Legal Nurse Consultants, revised in 1995, is contained in this publication.

The first draft of standards was completed in October 1994. In January 1995, in order to further legal nurse consulting as a functional specialty of nursing practice, AALNC made a commitment to use the framework for standards promulgated by the American Nurses Association (ANA) in 1991. This framework was the result of a collaborative effort by ANA and numerous specialty nursing organizations to provide a consistent format that would clarify and strengthen Nursing's ability to articulate professional standards. AALNC supports this effort by using the framework as a model for standards applicable to its specialty practice.

The standards are authoritative statements by which the profession describes the responsibilities for which its practitioners are accountable. Standards of Clinical Nursing Practice (ANA, 1991) describes a competent level of practice demonstrated by the nursing process and includes assessment, diagnosis, outcome identification, planning, implementation, and evaluation (ANA, 1991). These six elements are found in Section I of the Standards of Legal Nurse Consulting Practice. For the purposes of legal nurse consulting, the concept of diagnosis is interpreted to mean those opinions or conclusions formulated by the nurse in his or her analysis of the data to identify healthcare issues that are relevant to the outcome of legal claims or cases.

The standards of professional performance in Section II describe a competent level of professional conduct common to all nurses and include activities related to quality of services rendered, performance appraisal, education, collegiality, ethics, collaboration, research, and resource utilization (ANA, 1991). Key indicators that define the expectations associated with legal nurse consulting accompany the standards in this section. All LNCs are expected to engage in those professional role activities that are appropriate to their education, experience and practice settings.

The glossary of terms clarifies the application of terms commonly used in the nursing profession as well as some commonly used in the legal profession. The reader is advised to review the glossary before reading the standards.

The publication of this scope and standards for legal nurse consultants establishes a basis for core curriculum development. They may be used to guide the development of job descriptions, performance appraisals, peer review, quality assurance systems, organizational structures, educational offerings, and certification activities.

To serve the consumer of healthcare and legal services, the nursing specialty of legal nurse consulting must continue to develop practice guidelines to enhance the identification of advanced practice in the field. In addition, standards and guidelines must be evaluated on an ongoing basis and revised as necessary. The dynamic nature of the healthcare environment, tort reform, and the growing body of nursing and health sciences research will directly influence the practice of legal nurse consulting.

Acknowledgments

AALNC recognizes the foresight and dedication of the ad hoc AALNC Standards Committee who, through the development, institution, and analysis of the 1992 role delineation study, developed the framework for the scope of practice and the initial concepts of the standards. We acknowledge the contributions of those committee members as well as others who participated in the completion of this document.

Scope of Practice for the Legal Nurse Consultant

Introduction

The legal nurse consultant is a licensed registered nurse who performs a critical analysis of healthcare facts and issues and their outcomes for the legal profession, healthcare professions, and others, as appropriate. With a strong educational and experiential background, the legal nurse consultant is qualified to assess adherence to standards of healthcare practice as it applies to the nursing and healthcare professions.

This Scope of Practice for the Legal Nurse Consultant has been developed from data gathered by the American Association of Legal Nurse Consultants. The results reflect the diversity of practice settings of and services performed by legal nurse consultants nationwide. The American Association of Legal Nurse Consultants acknowledges the *American Association of Legal Nurse Consultants Code of Ethics* for legal nurse consultants, which provides the guidelines for professional performance and conduct for practice and affirms the values and practices of the American Nurses Association and the American Bar Association.

Practice Environment

The legal nurse consultant practices the art and science of his or her nursing specialty in a variety of settings, including law forms, government offices, insurance companies, hospital risk management departments, and as self-employed practitioners. The legal nurse consultant is a liaison between the legal and healthcare communities and provides consultation and education to legal, healthcare, and appropriate other professionals in areas such as personal injury, product liability, medical malpractice, workers' compensation, toxic torts, risk management, medical professional licensure investigation, and criminal law.

Role of the Legal Nurse Consultant

The primary role of the legal nurse consultant is to evaluate, analyze, and render informed opinions on the delivery of healthcare and the resulting outcomes. While the practice of each legal nurse consultant varies with respective practice opportunities and experience levels, certain commonalities prevail. Parameters of the practice may include, but are not limited to:

1. Facilitating communications and thus strategizing with the legal professional for successful resolutions between parties involved in healthcare-related litigation or other medical-legal or healthcare-legal matters.
2. Educating attorneys and/or others involved in the legal process regarding the healthcare facts and issues of a case or a claim.
3. Researching and integrating healthcare and nursing literature as it relates to the healthcare facts and issues of a case or a claim.
4. Reviewing, summarizing, and analyzing medical records and other pertinent healthcare and legal documents and comparing and correlating them to the allegations.
5. Assessing issues of damages and causation relative to liability within the legal process.
6. Identifying, locating, evaluating, and conferring with expert witnesses.
7. Interviewing witnesses and parties pertinent to the healthcare issues in collaboration with legal professionals.
8. Drafting legal documentations in medically related cases under the supervision of an attorney.
9. Developing collaborative case strategies with those practicing within the legal system.
10. Providing support during discovery, depositions, trial, and other legal proceedings.
11. Supporting the process of adjudication of legal claims.

Summary

This document identifies the legal nurse consultant as a specialist unique in the profession of nursing and as someone whose practice is of value in the legal field. The intent of this document is to conceptualize the legal nurse consultant's practice as it exists today; it is limited only by the depth and breadth to which the nursing specialty has currently developed. It is anticipated that future studies will indicate expanded roles and practice environments for the legal nurse consultant.

Section I: Standards of Practice

The legal nurse consultant has the knowledge and capability sufficient to conduct his or her practice in accordance with each of the standards set forth below.

Standard 1. Assessment

The legal nurse consultant collects data to support the systematic assessment of healthcare issues related to a case or claim.

Standard 2. Analysis and Issue Identification

The legal nurse consultant analyzes collected data to identify the healthcare issues related to a case or claim.

Standard 3: Outcome Identification

The legal nurse consultant identifies the desired outcome of his or her work product as related to the healthcare issues of a case or claim.

Standard 4. Planning

The legal nurse consultant formulates a plan of action to achieve the desired outcome.

Standard 5. Implementation

The legal nurse consultant implements the plan of action.

Standard 6. Evaluation

The legal nurse consultant evaluates the effectiveness of the plan of action in achieving the desired outcome.

Section II: Standards of Professional Performance

Standard 1. Quality of Practice

The legal nurse consultant (LNC) evaluates the quality and effectiveness of his or her practice.

Key Indicators

1. The LNC participates in quality of practice activities as appropriate to the individual's role, education, and practice environment.
2. The LNC uses the results of quality of practice activities to initiate changes in practice.

Standard 2. Performance Appraisal

The legal nurse consultant evaluates his or her own performance in relation to professional practice standards and relevant statutes and regulations.

Key Indicators

1. The LNC engages in performance appraisal, identifying areas of strength as well as areas for professional practice development.
2. The LNC seeks constructive feedback regarding his or her own practice.
3. The LNC takes action to achieve goals identified during performance appraisal.
4. The LNC participates in peer review, as appropriate.

Standard 3. Education

The legal nurse consultant acquires and maintains current knowledge in nursing and healthcare issues.

Key Indicators

1. The LNC participates in ongoing educational activities pertaining to the health sciences and the law relevant to his or her practice areas.
2. The LNC seeks experiences necessary to maintain current licensure as a professional registered nurse.
3. The LNC seeks the knowledge and the skills that are appropriate to the LNC's practice setting.

Standard 4. Collegiality

The legal nurse consultant contributes to the professional development of peers, colleagues, and others.

Key Indicators

1. The LNC shares knowledge and skills with colleagues and others.
2. The LNC provides peers with constructive feedback regarding their practice.
3. The LNC contributes to an environment that is conducive to the education of nurses entering the field of legal nurse consulting.
4. The LNC contributes to an environment that is conducive to the health science education of legal team members, as appropriate.
5. The LNC contributes to an environment that is conducive to the education of healthcare professionals regarding legal issues applicable to the health sciences.

Standard 5. Ethics

The legal nurse consultant's decisions and actions are determined in an ethical manner.

Key Indicators

1. The LNC's practice is guided by the ANA's Code for Nurses with Interpretive Statements (1985) and the AALNC Code of Ethics.

2. The LNC's practice affirms the values, standards, and practices of the profession of nursing.
3. The LNC maintains confidentiality commensurate with the attorney-client privilege.
4. The LNC practices in a nonjudgmental and nondiscriminatory manner.
5. The LNC evaluates all cases and clients for potential conflicts of interest and declines when conflicts are evident.
6. The LNC seeks available resources to help formulate ethical decisions.
7. The LNC who testifies as an expert witness confines testimony to his or her area of expertise.

Standard 6. Collaboration

The legal nurse consultant may collaborate with legal professionals, healthcare professionals, and others involved in the legal process.

Key Indicators

1. The LNC consults with legal professionals, healthcare professionals, and others, as appropriate.
2. The LNC makes referrals as needed.

Standard 7. Research

The legal nurse consultant recognizes research as a methodology to further the legal nurse consultant's practice.

Key Indicators

1. The LNC takes action substantiated by research as appropriate to his or her role, education, and practice environment.
2. The LNC participates in research activities as appropriate to his or her role, education, and practice environment.

Standard 8. Resource Management

The legal nurse consultant considers factors related to ethics, effectiveness, and cost in planning and delivering client service.

Key Indicators

1. The LNC selects expert assistance based on the needs of the case or the claim.
2. The LNC assigns tasks based on the knowledge and skill of the selected provider.

3. The LNC assists legal professionals and others in identifying and securing appropriate services available to address healthcare issues pertaining to the case or the claim.

Glossary

Analysis: Judgment following investigation and study of healthcare issues related to a case or a claim in the legal process that results in identification of relevant issues.

Assessment: A systematic, dynamic process by which the legal nurse consultant through interaction with legal professionals, healthcare professionals, and appropriate others collects and interprets data about the healthcare issues of a case or claim.

Attorney-Client Privilege: An evidentiary rule that confidential communications in the course of professional employment between an attorney or the attorney's representative and the client may not be divulged by the attorney or his representative without the consent of the client.

Case: A general term for an actual or potential action, cause, or suit at law or equity; a question contested before a court of justice.

Claim: An actual or potential demand for compensation or retribution.

Client: One who employs, uses, or contracts the services of the legal nurse consultant and may be, for example, an attorney, claims manager, or a company, agency, or institution involved in the investigation or processing of a case or claim.

Confidentiality: State or quality of being confidential; reliance on another to keep secrets; relationship of trust.

Evaluation: Process of determining the progress of legal professionals, healthcare professionals, and appropriate others toward the attainment of desired outcomes and the effectiveness of practices.

Health Care Issue: A matter that pertains to one or more of the following: a professional's, institution's, or organization's responsibility to provide for another's physical and psychological well-being; adherence to standards, guidelines, or policies, and the provision of reasonable healthcare; disputes that arise from the relationship between adherence to established standards, accepted guidelines, or validated scientific or technological knowledge and the claimant's outcomes; and the evaluation and assessment of a claimant's damages.

Health Care Providers: Individuals with special expertise who provide healthcare services or assistance to clients. They may include nurses, physicians, psychologists, social workers, nutritionists or dietitians, and various therapists. Providers also may include service organizations and vendors.

Implementation: May include any or all of these activities: intervening, delegating, and coordinating. Legal professionals, healthcare professionals, and others, as appropriate, may be designated to implement the steps, components, and interventions identified in the plan of action.

Key Indicator: A measure, gauge, or sign that there is compliance with and achievement of a standard.

Plan: Comprehensive outline of actions to attain the expected or desired outcome.

Standard: Authoritative statement enunciated and promulgated by the profession by which the quality of practice, conduct, and education can be judged.

Standards of Practice: Authoritative statements that describe a competent level of legal nurse consulting demonstrated through assessment, analysis and issue identification, outcome identification, planning, implementation, and evaluation.

Standards of Professional Performance: Authoritative statements that describe a competent level of behavior in the professional role, including activities related to quality of practice, performance appraisal, education, collegiality, ethics, collaboration, and resource management.

Work Product: The expression of opinions, conclusions, and materials developed at the request of the client that will assist the client in carrying the case or claim to completion.

References for Appendix 6.2

American Nurses Association, *Code for Nurses with Interpretive Statement*, Washington, D.C., 1985.

American Nurses Association, *Standards of Clinical Nursing Practice*, Washington, D.C., 1991.

Appendix 6.3
The Role of the Legal Nurse Consultant as Distinct from the Role of the Paralegal and Legal Assistant

The American Association of Legal Nurse Consultants (AALNC) has defined legal nurse consulting as a specialty practice of the nursing profession. AALNC does not recognize legal nurse consultants (LNCs) as a special category of paralegals.

Attorneys and others in the legal arena consult with psychologists and engineers, for example, because of their expertise in their respective professions; similarly, they consult with LNCs because of their expertise in nursing and healthcare. Many LNCs have bachelor's and advanced degrees in nursing and other health-related fields. Some LNCs practice as independent consultants; others are employed by law firms, insurance companies, and other institutions in a wide variety of roles.

While many legal nurse consultants have acquired knowledge of the legal system through such experience as consulting with attorneys and attending seminars, legal education is not prerequisite to the practice of legal nurse consulting. (In contrast, legal education is frequently a requirement for paralegals.) Professional nursing education and healthcare experience make LNCs unique and valuable partners in legal processes.

The AALNC *Code of Ethics and Conduct*,[1] *Scope of Practice for the Legal Nurse Consultant*,[2] and *Standards of Legal Nurse Consulting Practice and Professional Performance*[3] describe the specialty of legal nurse consulting. The primary role of the legal nurse consultant is to evaluate, analyze, and render informed opinions on the delivery of healthcare and the resulting outcomes. The following list of activities helps to distinguish the practice of legal nurse consulting:

- Facilitating communications and thus strategizing with the legal professional for successful resolutions between parties involved in healthcare-related litigation or other medical-legal or healthcare-legal matters.
- Educating attorneys and/or others involved in the legal process regarding the healthcare facts and issues of a case or a claim.
- Researching and integrating healthcare and nursing literature, guidelines, standards, and regulations as related to the healthcare facts and issues of a case or claim.
- Reviewing, summarizing, and analyzing medical records and other pertinent healthcare and legal documents and comparing and correlating them to the allegations.
- Assessing issues of damages and causation relative to liability with the legal process.
- Identifying, locating, evaluating, and conferring with expert witnesses.
- Interviewing witnesses and parties pertinent to the healthcare issues in collaboration with legal professionals.
- Drafting legal documents in medically-related cases under the supervision of an attorney.
- Developing collaborative case strategies with those practicing within the legal system.
- Providing support during discovery, depositions, trial, and other legal proceedings.
- Testifying at depositions, hearings, arbitrations, or trials as expert healthcare witnesses.
- Supporting the process of adjudication of legal claims.
- Contacting and conferring with vendors to develop demonstrative evidence or to collect costs of healthcare services, supplies, or equipment.
- Supervising and educating other nurses in the practice of legal nurse consulting.

Confusion about roles arises because in some settings LNCs do some of the same work that legal assistants and paralegals do, particularly in small law offices where they are the only staff available to assist the attorneys.

Legal education programs offered for nurses by legal assistant or paralegal education programs also cause confusion about roles. To the extent that legal education is provided to nurses by legal assistant or paralegal education programs, it should be considered separate from the education of paralegals and legal assistants because of the differences in their practice in the legal arena.

In March 1998, the Standing Committee on Legal Assistants of the American Bar Association (ABA) decided that "…legal nurses and legal nurse consultants fall squarely within the ABA definition of 'paralegal/legal assistant'…"[4] In contrast, AALNC recognizes a clear distinction between the roles of the legal nurse consultant and the paralegal.

The ABA also determined that "…the educational programs designed to train [legal nurses and legal nurse consultants] are paralegal programs or program options…" and as such are required to meet ABA guidelines and to be approved by the ABA if offered by an institution with an approved program.[5] AALNC does not support required ABA approval of legal nurse consulting education programs.

AALNC has defined legal nurse consulting as a specialty practice of nursing. AALNC's position, therefore, is that legal nurse consulting education should be developed and presented as specialty nursing curricula by nurse educators in partnership with legal educators.

References for Appendix 6.3

1. American Association of Legal Nurse Consultants, *Code of Ethics and Conduct of the American Association of Legal Nurse Consultants,* Glenview, IL, 1992.
2. American Association of Legal Nurse Consultants, *AALNC Scope of Practice for the Legal Nurse Consultant,* Glenview, IL, 1995.
3. American Association of Legal Nurse Consultants, *Standards of Legal Nurse Consulting Practice and Professional Performance*, Glenview, IL, 1995.
4. American Bar Association Standing Committee on Legal Assistants, More on legal nurse programs, *SCOLA Update*, Chicago, IL, Winter 1999.
5. American Bar Association Standing Committee on Legal Assistants, More on legal nurse programs, *SCOLA Update*, Chicago, IL, Winter 1999.

Appendix 6.4
AALNC Position Statement on Education and Certification in Legal Nurse Consulting

AALNC has defined legal nurse consulting as the specialty practice of the profession of nursing in which Registered Nurses apply their nursing education and clinical expertise to the medically related issues of the litigation process. The primary role of the legal nurse consultant is to evaluate, analyze, and render informed opinions about the delivery of healthcare and the resulting outcomes.[1]

The practice of legal nurse consulting predates any specialty organization, training program, or certification. While many legal nurse consultants have acquired knowledge of the legal system through such experience as consulting with attorneys and attending seminars, legal or paralegal education is not prerequisite to the practice of legal nurse consulting. In the early days of the specialty, nurses became legal nurse consultants (LNCs) without the benefit of formal education, relying on their nursing expertise and informal guidance or "on the job training" from attorneys. Then as now, nurses entered the specialty with a variety of educational backgrounds and practical experiences in nursing. The nurses who founded the American Association of Legal Nurse Consultants in 1989 were already practicing as LNCs when they came together to share their experience and to promote the specialty by forming a professional association.

Education

Today, numerous educational opportunities are available to nurses who wish to become LNCs. While formal training in legal nurse consulting is not required to practice, some nurses may benefit from a structured introduction to the specialty. AALNC believes that the individual nurse is best able to determine what, if any, program will meet his/her needs and goals.

While AALNC does not recommend or endorse particular programs, the following criteria should be considered in assessing credible, useful, legal nurse consulting education:

1. Institution. Legal nurse consulting education is offered by universities, colleges, community colleges, for-profit businesses, and not-for-profit organizations. In assessing the value of these programs, the reputation and accreditation of the sponsoring institution should be considered.
2. Program. Legal nurse consulting education programs may be found in various colleges or departments including the School of Nursing, the College of Health Sciences, the Office of Continuing Education, and the Paralegal Department, among others. To the extent that legal education is provided to nurses by legal assistant or paralegal education programs, it should be considered separate from the education of paralegals and legal assistants because of the differences in their practice in the legal arena. The primary focus of legal nurse consulting education should be to build on nursing education and clinical experience and to prepare nurses to function in the legal arena. In evaluating a particular program, its mission and purpose should be compared to this standard.
3. Program directors and instructors. AALNC maintains the position that legal nurse consulting education programs should be developed and presented as specialty nursing curricula by nurse educators in partnership with legal educators. The qualifications of the program directors and instructors should be considered when evaluating a program. In general, programs developed and taught by experienced nurse educators who are practicing LNCs are preferred.
4. Curriculum. AALNC recommends *Legal Nurse Consulting: Principles and Practices* as the core curriculum of legal nurse consulting education. Courses of study based on this curriculum vary in length from one day to two years. Nurses are encouraged to choose a course of study that meets personal needs and professional goals.

Certification

Most LNC education programs offer a certificate that testifies to the completion of a course of study and, in some cases, to passing an examination on the course material. Some graduates of LNC certificate programs chose to include letters such as "LNC" after their names, along with their educational degrees and professional credentials. AALNC does not endorse this practice. It is customary to list such certificates in the education section of a resume or curriculum vitae.

These certificate programs should not be confused with the certification programs offered by nursing certification boards, which are commonly affiliated with professional nursing associations. Certification is a process that recognizes an individual's qualifications and demonstrated knowledge in a specialty. In 1997, AALNC established the American Legal Nurse Consultant Certification Board (ALNCCB) to administer the Legal Nurse Consultant Certified (LNCC®) program. The LNCC certification program is accredited by the American Board of Nursing Specialties (ABNS).

The purpose of the LNCC program is to promote a level of expertise and professionalism in legal nurse consulting. Legal nurse consultants must meet the eligibility requirements, which include consulting experience, and achieve a passing score on a multiple-choice examination to earn the LNCC designation. As with many clinical nursing certification programs, the LNCC credential is designed for those who have demonstrated experience and knowledge in the specialty.[2] Certification is an appropriate goal for those who are committed to a professional legal nurse consulting practice.

AALNC supports the practice initiated by the American Nurses Association of listing one's credentials in the following order: highest educational degree, highest nursing degree if different, licensure, and professional certifications. "LNCC" is the only legal nurse consulting credential recognized by AALNC and ABNS.

References for Appendix 6.4

1. Refer to the AALNC Position Statement on The Role of the Legal Nurse Consultant as distinct from the role of the paralegal and legal assistant.
2. The LNCC credential can be compared to recognized nursing credentials such as RNC; CCRN; CEN; CPN; and CRRN.

Chapter 7

Entry into Specialty Practice of Legal Nurse Consulting

Therese A. Steinhardt, MSN, RN

CONTENTS

Objectives

- To define the qualities and traits of a legal nurse consultant
- To compare entrepreneurial skills with intrapreneurial skills
- To demonstrate goal-setting through the nursing process
- To enhance communication skills
- To describe educational options
- To identify time management skills

Introduction

This chapter is designed to provide an overview of the qualities and traits that set the role of legal nurse consultant (LNC) apart from other specialties of nursing. It also discusses the impact of personal and professional changes for a career shift from clinical areas of nursing to legal nurse consulting. Many of the terms and issues discussed represent values familiar to a professional nurse. Since the days of Florence Nightingale, the technology of nursing science has evolved to a higher level of practice for the professional nurse. This has the potential for greater risk of error. Combined with the litigious mind-set of our society, the technology of nursing science has increased the need for competent practitioners to act as liaisons between the fields of law and health care. Logically it follows that nurses must be the authority for nurses (i.e., expert witnesses) in matters that evaluate the practice of nursing. This chapter will identify types of education that can prepare the LNC and skills that will assist the novice and assure the advanced practitioner of a successful career as an LNC.

Qualities and Traits

The three words that are comprised in the acronym "LNC" are self-defining: "legal," referring to the law; "nurse," a professional health care provider; and "consultant," a person who offers advice. What is special about the combination of these words is the union of two independent fields, law and nursing. Each represents years of required formal education from accredited facilities and professional licensure. Each has established standards of practice, a scope of practice defining parameters of professionalism, and a code of ethics. Each in its professional capacity offers advice, guidance, and information to those who seek help. However, lawyers do not practice nursing and nurses do not practice law. This distinction between the two professions has been the impetus for the unique services that nurse consultants bring to the legal arena.

Above all, LNCs are nurses. As resolved in 1995 by the board of directors of the American Association of Legal Nurse Consultants (AALNC), the professional foundation of legal nurse consulting is nursing.[1] It is this basic foundation of nurse education and experience in a field of nursing that provides the structure for the growth of the specialty of legal nurse consulting. The number-one requirement for an LNC is to be a registered nurse; the product that is provided to those seeking assistance is nursing knowledge. The lawyer benefits from the ability of LNCs to integrate their nursing knowledge with the challenges of criminal and civil litigation.

An LNC will always be a nurse first. The LNC's area of consultation will depend on experience that has been gained in a field of nursing, as well as personal motivation and entrepreneurial skills. For nurses, organizational skills and professionalism are integrated within the fundamentals of training and education that prepare graduates for a variety of opportunities upon completion of basic nursing education. The development of nursing expertise that combines on-the-job learning with formal education is essential preparation for those interested in becoming an LNC. Being a nurse is only the beginning of preparing for the role of an LNC. Specific qualities and traits need to be in place to ensure success as an independent practitioner or an in-house LNC.

Personal attributes and business acumen are parts of an identifying lifestyle of professional nurses, workers, moms, dads, family members, and friends. Attributes such as dependability, efficiency, and a positive attitude are reflected in these lifestyles, both professionally and personally. So too are good judgment, wisdom, expertise, and intelligence about nursing knowledge, marketing, accounting, and a multitude of other business skills that may need to be used differently as an LNC. To succeed, LNCs must be reliable and competent, as practicing nurses must be, which is demonstrated by showing up for work or meetings on time and being prepared to do any job efficiently and accurately.

Successful entry into the specialty practice of legal nurse consulting, whether as an independent LNC or as an employee in a new setting, from a hospital to a law office, or from a doctor's office to an insurance office, will require change. This change will also be impacted by choices made from both a personal and a business perspective. Some may be brilliant and successful choices; others may be errors in judgments that only wishing can erase. A distinctly human trait is that of making a choice, not merely responding to an instinct or a Skinnerian response. As Warner states, "It is amazing that some people are unaware that their future is controlled in large part by this sum of choices — internal and external — and, furthermore, by the degree of control that they exercise over those choices."[2]

It is important to keep a positive attitude, be confident in making choices, and believe in a successful outcome. Nursing knowledge, strong work performance, and dependability are attributes basic to quality performance. Other qualities and traits are also needed, and these are described below.

Autonomy

Being willing to exercise the freedom to make choices is a stepping-stone quality to beginning the new and exciting role as an LNC. The independence of working for oneself brings with it the need to be self-sufficient, and an ability to set rules and follow them without the support of a work force or staff with whom to confer. There is a sense of empowerment that comes from control over the right to choose assignments, hours of work, fees, and expenses. This liberation also comes with the need to initially plan well on how to be emancipated from the traditional role of employee within a structured organization. With determination, a nurse can succeed as an independent LNC. Autonomy also provides the opportunity to choose to work as an in-house consultant in the type of legal setting that has the most appeal and best matches the consultant's experience.

Drive

Drive or determination, as a quality to building a successful practice, requires a certain amount of ambition, energy, and effort in preparing for a specialty practice such as legal nurse consulting. This ambition is grounded in goal-oriented plan-ning, a characteristic that every nurse uses in reaching an objective. One will need to investigate what necessary attributes are in place and what deficits need to be addressed to improve the chances for success. Aspiring LNCs should determine whether they are self-disciplined enough to be able to work indepen-dently. Some independent consultants are uncomfortable with the lack of structure in working from a home office. It may take a regular routine to provide the daily discipline needed to work without someone looking over the nurse's shoulder. This effort is rewarded in the long run by adding proficiency and competence to the list of resources that the legal nurse provides a lawyer-client. The motivation or incentive for joining the specialty of legal nurse consulting is a necessary trait that may spur one to action, but it cannot be fueled impulsively. Enthusiasm, as a quality, can be the driving force behind a great idea, such as being independently employed as an LNC. Industry or hard work is the trait that supports this quality. Others are diligence and the thoroughness to see a task to completion with attentiveness to details.

Initiative

Initiative is an intrinsic quality of an experienced nurse. Some of the traits that one can expect to use are the ability to be clever, inventive, handy, and imagi-native. Having the knack to know when to be creative or to follow a traditional style requires a certain aptitude for farsightedness and forethought. Productivity and creativity as traits of a successful LNC are demonstrated by good organization, competence, and vision. Inspiration and ingenuity support these qualities.

Analytical Skills

To succeed in this profession, an LNC needs to be analytical. Analysis of medical records and other information often focuses on critical details related to injuries, timing of events, and completeness of information. The analytical LNC spots the missing record, the sequence of events that seems to be out of order, and the deviations from the standard of care on the part of the health care provider. The role of the LNC often involves the ability to collect and synthesize data in an effort to reconstruct a series of events or determine what should have been done for a patient. Attorneys rely on the knowledge base of the LNC, coupled with the ability to place data into a framework that will help the attorney understand the medical information.

Attention to Detail

A keen sense of what is and is not essential is another trait important to a conscientious LNC. Being detail-oriented is more than just dotting all the *i*'s and crossing all the *t*'s. A detail-oriented nurse makes sure that all records are in order, all data are collected, and all filing is completed accurately. Detail-oriented nurses can work through the minutiae of lengthy documents with an eye for the smallest items of importance. The ability to review each element for its potential significance to a case is a valuable service that a detail-oriented nurse can provide a client.

Communication Skills

It is important to be an active listener in order to show empathy and be assiduous when a client relates details of a case. Concentrating on facts and at the same time perceiving body language that may or may not be contradictory are basic active listening skills honed by most nurses through years of clinical practice. Being able to systematically and logically list data in a specific manner may not be innate. The ability to accurately yet succinctly document what is heard and observed requires practice and is crucial in discriminating between critical information and pointless items. Decisive writing skills that provide a plethora of information in a succinct manner will be needed to record data. Finally, much of what an LNC generates and reviews is in the form of written documentation; the ability to proofread will be needed to correct or amend communications between parties. Fine-tuning a document without modifying the content is another essential skill for LNCs to master. Written and oral communications skills can be improved through several types of educational formats discussed later in this chapter.

Self-Awareness

Self-awareness is another attribute that is often overlooked when investigating the possibility of changing specialties and nursing roles. A change in professional roles is a good time to take stock of personal assets that may have an impact on professional life. According to Tamparo and Lindh, "The value in self-analysis is the fact that it helps us determine who we are as seen by self and by others."[3] Taking time to do a self-analysis in preparing to change from one career to another might help to identify necessary changes. This can be done by making a list of negative and positive characteristics about oneself. Which list is longer? Which was the easiest to complete? What does the list say about feelings of self-worth? Not surprisingly, a positive attitude is revealed in a longer positive list. If the negative list is longer, one should use one of the items identified as a strength to change the negative list into a shorter one in order to increase feelings of self-esteem. Often overlooked in self-appraisal are daily accomplishments and habitual tasks that not only are taken for granted, but also absorb time and energy. One should take credit for what gets done in a given amount of time, for substituting options when the original plan falls through but the job gets done, and for using creative alternatives no matter how effortless they seemed.

Quality/Trait	Descriptor
Autonomous	Free to make own choices
Motivated	Intrinsically driven
Industrious	Likes hard work
Productive	Gets the job done
Creative	Originator of ideas
Driven	Progresses with momentum
Detail-oriented	Attentive to particulars
Analytical	Logical
Rational	Reasonable
Methodical	Disciplined
Systematic	Orderly
Critical	Judicious in evaluation
Diagnostic	Able to determine fact
Investigative	Observant

Figure 7.1   List of Qualities and Traits That Would Benefit a Nurse Interested in Entry into the Specialty of Legal Nurse Consulting

There are many self-help books that identify methods for improving and changing personal and professional attitudes. Using role models and mentors are two other helpful ways to improve self-image and gain confidence in abilities. One should observe and ask questions of those who are practicing in an area of interest. This might require contacting an LNC and asking to shadow a case in progress. If the goal is simply to tutor the novice, mentoring can be time-consuming and costly to the experienced LNC who must maintain an established business. Contractual agreements can be made with a more experienced LNC in a local area to provide an opportunity to "learn on the job" as a subcontracted independent LNC. This method can provide experience and guidance for the novice, but protect clientele of the established LNC practice. (See Chapter 43, Starting a Business: Legal and Business Principles, and Chapter 45, Growing a Business, for more information.) The great comedienne Lucille Ball once said, "One of the things I learned the hard way was that it doesn't pay to get discouraged. Keeping busy and making optimism a way of life can restore your faith in yourself."[2]

A list of qualities and traits that benefit the LNC for an entry-level position can be found in Figure 7.1. The qualities and traits listed above, including resources such as mentors and self-help books, are provided as examples of answers to common questions about entry into the specialty practice of legal nurse consulting. Possessing these qualities does not ensure a smooth transition or capability, but it is a beginning.

Intrapreneurial and Entrepreneurial Skills

Puetz and Shinn[4] use Pinchot's[5] definition of intrapreneurship to describe an employee as one "who is innovative, creative, and willing to take risks in the work setting by forging ahead with a new product, idea, or process." Writing for the American Nurses Association, Manion advanced that definition for nurses as "one who creates innovation within the health care organization through the introduction of a new product, a different service, or simply a new way of doing something."[6] In a subsequent article, she identifies many of the same qualities and traits for nurse intrapreneurs that this chapter acknowledges as important attributes of a successful LNC, including being inquisitive, a visionary, and a good salesperson.[7]

By comparison, Wilson identifies an entrepreneur as "a person who organizes and manages an enterprise, especially a business, usually with considerable initiative and risk."[8] The difference between an entrepreneur and an intrapreneur is whether the skills are used independently as a self-employed consultant or as an employee. In either scenario, the successful nurse needs the ability to plan well, problem-solve, and be accountable. The nurse working as an employee can be as creative in developing the legal nurse consulting role for an employer, as the independent LNC in establishing a practice for different clientele, such as attorneys, insurance firms, or pharmaceutical companies. What these authors have confirmed is that nurses must present a professional image of leadership when leading is required, or of competent team players when collaboration is necessary.

In an entry-level position as an LNC, it is necessary not only to provide nursing knowledge as a product, but to have communication, problem-solving, and networking skills as well as political savvy. An intrapreneur may need to fit within an organization that can be challenging to get ideas acknowledged. Enthusiasm may need to be channeled in an innovative manner in order to reach the boss with the recommendation. As an entrepreneur, the independent LNC is the boss, so the challenge may be to overcome the fear of taking risks in a new market. Whatever the challenge, as an experienced nurse, the most useful tool is a familiar one — the nursing process. In the next section of this chapter, the nursing process is used to demonstrate how to prepare for an entry-level move into legal nurse consulting.

The Nursing Process as a Tool for Success

A good way to investigate legal nurse consulting is with the nursing process steps of assessing, diagnosing, planning, implementing, and evaluating. Each step in this variation of the problem-solving format of the nursing process can guide the novice in making a career-change decision. For the experienced consultant, these steps can assist in reevaluating progress and roles as an independent or in-house consultant.

Collect, Assess, Analyze, and Interpret the Information

As a first step, an assessment of the work and responsibilities of the LNC, as either the in-house or independent consultant, can be accomplished by researching journals and interviewing others already involved in the practice of legal nurse consulting. Additional insights can be gained by joining the AALNC, attending professional conferences sponsored through the association, and attending chapter meetings to discover issues addressed by the specialty practice of legal nurse consulting. Information can be gleaned from accessing AALNC's Web site, http://www.aalnc.org, which offers a plethora of information about services, products, and other helpful links. Many pamphlets, such as "Getting Started in Legal Nurse Consulting," are available through the Web site. Analyze what needs to be adjusted to ensure successful outcomes before developing a plan of action. As data are gathered, analyzed, and interpreted, the next step in the process will begin to take shape.

Diagnosis: Identification of Issues and Outcomes

This step provides an opportunity to list the results hoped for at the end of the process. Once data have been collected and pros and cons compared, the skills and requirements needed to be successful can be listed as strong or weak areas, such as knowledge deficits related to business structures. This step permits the LNC to identify issues that require immediate attention, such as the need to set up a business structure and consider marketing strategies.

When considering options, it is helpful to be as objective as possible in listing individual skills and unique qualities. The collection of information and analysis of data may identify issues and outcomes that deal with being a self-starter, organizer, or self-motivated worker, whether self-employed or employed in an office. Other issues may deal with family, personal relationships, and budgeting needed to develop an independent practice. This is the step where the advantages and disadvantages of options can be identified. Once the task of identifying issues and outcomes has been completed, the next step is to outline a plan that will be most helpful in reaching the desired goal most efficiently and effectively.

Planning

One should develop the plan in a step-by-step manner that allows for flexibility. Identifying short-term and long-term goals should be part of planning. Short-term goals can be designed to be achieved within the time frame of a long-term goal. The plan may include learning how to write a business financial and marketing plan for an independent practice. This step may take several weeks to complete. It may require a few days to update a resume or curriculum vitae. The plan may also require attending classes to upgrade communication skills. This is a good time for the LNC to write out the steps to success, if these were not identified earlier. A written plan provides a ready review of progress, allows for a visual reminder of what comes next, provides organization, and offers a mental boost when items are completed and crossed off the list of "to dos." Time frames can be adjusted with a written plan. The plan should be written in straightforward terms that are measurable and timely. It is important to avoid vague generalizations such as "furnish office." It is better to list needed items specifically and set a budget and a date for ordering them.

If the plan requires the development of a financial business plan to present to a financial institution for start-up capital as an independent consultant, it is wise to investigate professional sources that offer guidelines for completing this task. The United States Small Business Administration (SBA), found in all states, the District of Columbia, the Virgin Islands, and Puerto Rico, can be accessed on line at http://www.sba.gov. The SBA offices offer financing, training, and advocacy for people interested in starting their own enterprises. In addition, SBA works with thousands of lending, educational, and training institutions nationwide that can also provide information and guidance.

Planning requires being able to predict the consequences of actions. During planning it may be helpful to continue brainstorming. A difficult part of completing a plan is knowing when it is done. With a comprehensive plan in place, the next step in reaching a successful outcome, the implementation of the plan, can begin.

Implementation

The action part of problem-solving and decision-making is much easier to accomplish if the previous steps have provided a sound foundation. An important part of implementing a plan is to document progress. Keeping records is a skill with which nurses have a great deal of experience. Record-keeping can be accomplished quickly and easily with several different software packages available. One should remember to back up data in case of system failures. Data to be recorded may include such items as inventory of equipment and supplies, purchase price of these items, replacement of items, warranty items, and their dates of expiration and renewal. Financial records may include loans, leases, salaries, professional fees, assets, and expenditures for maintaining the business and tax information. Maintaining marketing records as to what form of advertisement netted the most response from potential clients and what was not as effective can be of benefit later when evaluating the impact of this phase. Time management records, indicating the length of time from onset to completion of a task, can be beneficial in adjusting the way in which a task is organized and completed.

Evaluation

Once the plan is implemented, it is important to evaluate progress at regular intervals. A review of each step can be made succinctly if a comprehensive business journal identifying the process from data collection to implementation has been maintained. Any area that presented specific challenges can be identified and adjustments made. The success of any outcome will be contingent on the foundation prepared in initiating this process. Some steps may appear to overlap from identifying issues and outcomes to planning and implementing actions taken. Evaluation takes place throughout the steps of the nursing process as outcomes are identified, plans are designed, and implementation begins. Questions such as, "Have all resources been included?" and "Have all data been collected?" are evaluations of the information-gathering process. The final evaluation occurs when the consequences of the plan are reviewed during the evaluation step.

Nursing Process Steps	Strategies
1. Assessment	Research and investigate all resources
2. Diagnosis	Diagnose and predict
3. Planning	Map the strategy
4. Implementation	Put it into action. Document, document, document
5. Evaluation	Consequences and regeneration

Figure 7.2 The Nursing Process Steps

During the planning stage of the process, progress can be evaluated by answering the question, "How are things going?" During the evaluation step review, questions include how the process started, what was learned, and what might need to be kept or done differently next time. Elizabeth Kubler-Ross believed that "we are solely responsible for our choices, and we have to accept the consequences of every deed, word and thought throughout our lifetime."[2]

There are likely to be some unexpected disappointments and challenges as well as successes. When Gordon Moore, founder and CEO of Intel, retired at 72, he said that he never feared failure because he thought of it as a form of success. It meant that he had discovered something to be eliminated. In her article "The Failure of Success," Kuc cites that "failing at something does not mean that we are failures."[9] Mary Pickford, a silent-screen star, once said, "This thing we call failure is not the falling down, but the staying down."[2]

In Figure 7.2, the nursing process steps are shown with a brief description of what each step comprises. As a strategy for entry into the specialty of legal nurse consulting, the nursing process is a practical tool.

The use of the nursing process can be adapted for solving a myriad of challenges faced by an LNC. However, this tool like any other is only as good as the person preparing it. The very minimum skill that an LNC will need in using the nursing process is a solid background in communication skills. The ability to send and receive messages is expedited today with the use of computers, palm assistant devices, fax machines, copy machines, and the telephone, wireless or otherwise. How the message is designed may depend on how it will be sent as much as what needs to be said. Knowing how to write a business report, business letter, legal report, medical report, and office memo are important skills. The next section of this chapter will highlight some issues of communication that may be helpful to an entry-level LNC.

Communication Skills: The Five Cs

LNCs need to meet with other professionals, clients, and litigants who depend on effective communication skills to introduce issues, define positions, and present documents for litigation. Wilkes and Crosswait[10] describe what they call the 5 Cs of successful communication: (1) complete, (2) clear, (3) concise, (4) cohesive, and (5) courteous elements of a message. Effective communication skills are a cornerstone of successful consulting. Communication requires understanding the message being forwarded and feedback received as sender and

The 5 Cs	The message component should provide:
1. C = complete	all the necessary information
2. C = clear	unimpeded and well-enunciated words
3. C = concise	succinct and directly delivered content
4. C = cohesive	rational and organized ideas
5. C = courteous	expected politeness

Figure 7.3   The Five Cs of Communication

receiver interchange information. When what is said does not agree with how it is said, the message is distorted and communication may be altered. Misunderstandings in medical and legal documents can have catastrophic outcomes. When speaking face to face, words are accentuated with facial expressions, gestures, and body language. These associated means of communication, known as *kinesics*, add significantly to the message. In written communication, where these nonverbal elements are lacking, care must be taken to convey their meaning. Today much of our communication takes place electronically. Words must carry the message without the benefit of a smile or frown, inflections in a voice or the tone of a sentence, or eye contact. To increase the success of a message being heard and understood, it is necessary to use the 5 Cs of communication.

A *complete* message requires that all the pertinent information needed to convey the intent of the message be included but eliminates the superfluous. A *clear* message uses language that avoids jargon and technical terms that the listener may not know. This includes spelling words correctly, using the correct word or phrase while avoiding colloquial expressions, writing legibly, or speaking with a minimal accent. A *concise* message gets to the point and eliminates unnecessary information. This means that the messages must stick to the point. If more than one important point must be included, make a list of the pertinent information to follow each point. A *cohesive* message flows in a reasonable and likely fashion rather than skipping from issue to issue. Hopping from one point to another can confuse the listener and interfere with a logical response. Changing the subject, shifting the focus, or lecturing are barriers to a cohesive message. Finally, a message, even one in debate, can be *courteous*; otherwise, the listener may become defensive and the message received will be misinterpreted. A courteous message includes polite expressions, such as a "thank you," "respectfully yours," or "please." Figure 7.3 describes concisely how the 5 Cs benefit message construction.

Employing effective business techniques in communicating with clients and other professionals is a skill that can be learned. The rules of the 5 Cs, along with good listening techniques, are methods that help the LNC practice good communication skills. The use of barriers to communication, such as contradicting, criticizing, belittling, or moralizing, may impede the continuation of dialogue with a client.

The next section describes educational options available to a nurse interested in entering the specialty of legal nurse consulting or an experienced legal nurse consultant who may be interested in upgrading current skills.

Types of Education

An entry-level LNC position does not require additional education in a formal program. However, the evaluation of the nursing process may lead to the conclusion that additional education may be helpful beyond the expertise gained as a nurse. Training in specific areas, such as communication skills, legal terminology, medical research, and writing methods, coupled with a fundamental understanding of the law and the basics of the management of a law or business office, can be reassuring for the novice. There are several ways to increase knowledge of these areas and improve a resume or credentials, which may widen employment opportunities. AALNC believes that the nurse is best able to determine what, if any, program will meet these needs, but as of now, does not recommend or endorse particular programs. AALNC's Web site provides educational materials for continuing education.

Formal education is provided by proprietary schools; for-profit businesses; and nonprofit businesses, universities, four-year colleges, and community colleges. This education is offered through traditional on-campus programs, telecourses, and distance courses that are both print-based and on line. Proprietary schools offer certificates or diplomas, which may include continuing education units. Colleges offer certificates, an associate degree, or a baccalaureate degree. Some college programs also provide continuing education units. In evaluating the merit of any program, the reputation and accreditation of the sponsoring institution should be considered, as well as the cost and length of the program, the convenience of the location or on-line accessibility, and the type of text materials required. Other important aspects of the program to consider are whether it offers a student placement externship in a law firm before completion of the program, and what percentage of graduates are being hired by attorneys or businesses in the area.

Although legal education is provided to nurses by legal assistant or paralegal education programs, it must be stressed that the education of paralegals and legal assistants is different from the needs of the nurse in practice in the legal arena. "Paralegal" and "legal assistant" are terms that are sometimes used interchangeably in different parts of the country. According to the ABA definition adopted by the ABA House of Delegates in August 1997, a legal assistant or paralegal is "a person qualified by education, training or work experience…employed by an attorney…who performs specifically delegated substantive legal work for which a lawyer is responsible." By contrast, the legal nurse consultant is "distinct from the paralegal or legal assistant" because the legal nurse consultant "brings specialized education and clinical expertise to the medically related issues of the litigation process."[11] As a result of experience, education, and focus, an LNC should not be referred to as a paralegal or legal assistant.

The primary focus of legal nurse consulting education must be to build on nursing education, clinical experience, and the function of the nurse in the legal arena. In evaluating a particular program, its mission and purpose should be compared to the standard presented in the position statement forwarded by the AALNC on the role of the LNC.[12] AALNC maintains the position that legal nurse consulting education programs must be developed and presented as specialty nursing curricula by nurse educators in partnership with legal educators. The qualifications of the program directors and instructors should be considered when evaluating a program. In general, programs developed and taught by experienced nurse educators who are practicing LNCs are preferred.

As a proprietary provider of education, AALNC offers pamphlets, home study materials based on actual cases, video and audio tapes from providers, and conferences, seminars, and the AALNC-sponsored professional legal nurse consulting course. These methods offer a unique way to increase both skills and knowledge base in legal nurse consulting depending on the novice's level of need. AALNC recommends the publication *Legal Nurse Consulting: Principles and Practice* as the core curriculum for legal nurse consulting education. Courses based on this curriculum vary in length from one day to several weeks. Nurses are encouraged to choose a course that meets their personal requirements and professional goals.

It is important to remember that nursing education is the basic educational requirement for preparation as an LNC, but employment as an in-house LNC may provide experience on the job under the guidance of an attorney or another LNC. As an independent LNC, joining and participating in the national organization and local AALNC chapter will afford both the novice and seasoned practitioner the opportunity to remain current with legal nurse consulting practice.

How To Succeed with Time Management Skills

As a fundamental organizational skill, time management is a building block of success for the LNC whether employee or independent. Knowing how much time a task will need and allotting enough time for completion of the task is a necessity for success and preventing job stress. The expression "time is money" refers to the cost of wasting time on tasks that are repeated unnecessarily, are done inefficiently, or do not need to be done at all. Our predecessors had fewer electronic devices to help them in their daily lives, but completed many tasks. Yet today's nurses remain "overworked" or "overwhelmed."

How can time spent be accounted for? The first task in answering this question is to collect data. The LNC should start with a time log for a week or two, documenting how time is being spent, being as precise as possible, and including descriptions of methodology of the task. Consultants' fees are paid in billable hours. It is necessary to develop an efficient and exact method to keep records of time spent on these hours. Other tasks that require time and energy must be included in the log. Eventually, each task can be prioritized to consume as little of the remaining work hours as necessary. A review of this log can indicate time that is not used in the wisest manner.

An example of time consumption that can be restructured is mail-sorting. The experts[13] recommend that mail should be opened near a wastebasket, so the mail can be discarded immediately if it is disposable. Some junk mail can be discarded without opening it. Mail should be either attended to at that time or designated for action. This allows for handling each piece only once and avoids clutter on desks or piles of mail accumulating on tables and counters.

Another important aspect of time management is maintaining organized files. The lesson learned from handling the mail is applied to managing files. Deciding what data are kept and what are superfluous uses the same process as sorting the mail. One should make a choice the first time the document is handled as to whether it will be kept or discarded, then act on that choice and move on to the next item. Many software packages, such as Microsoft Excel, provide systems for entering data expediently. Computerized filing also eliminates paper usage and handling, and reduces misfiling of material. As a bonus, computerized filing can save the expense of buying paper that ends up being shredded or tossed when files get purged.

There are many challenges for the "pack rat" who hoards everything or the procrastinator who cannot decide what to do with an item. Clutter is a waste of time from two perspectives. First, it ends up being handled more than once, which is usually not necessary and definitely a waste of time. Second, searching through a pile of items that are in no particular order wastes time.

As projects are accepted or a task arises, one should set up a tickler file that allows for adjustments in scheduling weekly or monthly to provide a way to break large assignments into smaller segments. Completion of each part increases momentum to finish by offering the tangible reward of seeing goals achieved.

Development of a simple system that works best may take time, but is worth the effort in the long run if it provides organization. This may be a modification of a professional system or an individual invention gleaned from the log. Once the LNC is organized with a system in place, one may keep control by regular maintenance checks. The LNC may redo the log from time to time to track time spent on various projects or tasks. It is easier to maintain a good system than to have to start over again.[4] This can also be applied to keeping an index of journals and books on the library shelf, which can be filed alphabetically by author or subject. The important issue is to pick something that is comfortable and easy to maintain. The less complex the system is, the more apt it is to be maintained.

Summary

This chapter examined the qualities and traits of the nurse interested in the specialty of legal nurse consulting from an entry-level position. Descriptions of entrepreneurial and intrapreneurial skills were introduced. Methods of preparation and requirements for entering the field were discussed and included descriptions of the nursing process as a tool to reach objectives. Formal programs or on-the-job training options, communication skills, and factors that impact success from personality, time management, and goal-setting were described.

References

1. Bogart, J., Ed., *Legal Nurse Consulting: Principles and Practice*, CRC Press, Boca Raton, FL, 1998, 198.
2. Warner, C., *A Treasury of Women's Quotes*, Prentice-Hall, Englewood Cliffs, NJ, 1992.
3. Tamparo, C.T. and Lindh, W.Q., *Therapeutic Communications for Health Professionals*, 2nd ed., Delmar Division of Thomson Learning, Canada, 2000, 11.
4. Puetz, B. and Shinn, L., *The Nurse Consultant's Handbook*, Springer Publishers, New York, 1997.

5. Pinchot, G., *Intrapreneuring*, Harper & Row, New York, 1985.
6. Manion, J., *Change from Within: Nurse Intrapreneurs as Health Care Innovators*, American Nurses Association, Kansas City, 1990, 2.
7. Manion, J., How to innovate from within, *American Journal of Nursing*, 94, 38, 1994.
8. Wilson, L., *Stop Selling and Start Partnering*, Oliver Wight Publications, Inc., Essex Junction, VT, 1994, 143.
9. Kuc, J., The Failure of Success, *Journal of Legal Nurse Consulting*, 11(4), 23, 2000.
10. Wilkes, M. and Crosswait, C.B., *Professional Development: The Dynamics of Success*, Harcourt Brace Jovanovich Inc., San Diego, 1991.
11. American Association of Legal Nurse Consultants, What Is a Legal Nurse Consultant?, brochure, Glenview, IL, 1995.
12. American Association of Legal Nurse Consultants, Education and Certification in Legal Nurse Consulting, http//www.aalnc.org, Glenview, IL, 2000.
13. DeVoe, D., Learn to balance projects and daily tasks, *InfoWorld*, 20, 49 (Farmingham, December 7), 132, 1998.

Test Questions

1. One who organizes, manages, and assumes the risks of a business or enterprise is known as
   A. An intrapreneur
   B. An entrepreneur
   C. A manager
   D. An employee

2. In the 5 Cs of communication, a message that does not include unnecessary information is
   A. Coherent
   B. Complete
   C. Concise
   D. Courteous

3. A quality that requires a certain amount of energy, ambition, and effort for success is
   A. Autonomy
   B. Creativity
   C. Self-analysis
   D. Drive

4. During which step of the nursing process would the LNC develop actions to achieve the desired outcome?
   A. Planning
   B. Implementation
   C. Evaluation
   D. Assessment

5. What type of education does a nurse need to enter the specialty of legal nurse consulting?
   A. Two-year degree in law
   B. Baccalaureate degree in legal assisting
   C. Degree or diploma in nursing
   D. Certification of completion from a proprietary school

Answers: 1. B, 2. C, 3. D, 4. A, 5. C

Chapter 8

Professionalism, Standards of Practice, and Standards of Professional Performance

Joan Magnusson, BSN, RN, LNCC,
Julie B. Pike, MN, RN, LNCC, CPHRM, and
Maureen Jane Orr, BS, RN, LNCC, CIRS, CCM

CONTENTS

Objectives

- To identify the key elements that define a profession relative to nursing practice
- To discuss the relationship of the specialty practice of legal nurse consulting to the profession of nursing
- To define the nursing process as it applies to legal nurse consulting
- To define the Standards of Professional Performance as they apply to legal nurse consulting
- To explain by example how the legal nurse consultant can apply the Standards of Practice to a typical case
- To explain by example how the legal nurse consultant can apply the Standards of Professional Performance to consulting in the legal arena

Introduction

How we define ourselves as a specialized area of nursing practice is the heart of what distinguishes legal nurse consultants (LNCs) from other nursing professionals. In order for attorneys, judges and juries, risk managers, insurance adjusters, health care providers, and the public to understand who we are and what we do, we must clearly define our practice and clarify our similarities and differences with other nursing specialties. We also are obligated as professionals to define and ensure our ethics and quality of practice. In practice, our actions must meet criteria that can be measured. Standards provide that basis for practice accountability. The Standards of Practice and Professional Performance were written by the American Association of Legal Nurse Consultants (AALNC) to meet these professional goals.

This chapter is designed to provide an overview of the broad scope of the Standards of Practice and Professional Performance for legal nurse consulting. Because the standards are based on the American Nurses Association (ANA) model of standards and the nursing process, many of the terms in this chapter will be familiar to nurses who have been in active clinical practice. Utilization of the nursing process occurs as second nature to the experienced nurse. With care and thought, that same process is adapted and applied by LNCs to all aspects of their work.

Definition of a Professional

Everyone remembers the nursery rhyme, "A butcher, a baker, a candlestick maker." One may recall jobs such as babysitter, waiter, salesperson, etc. There are many occupations, but not all are considered professions.

Endeavors have been made to define a profession by identifying various common characteristics. Five attributes generally accepted as essential for an "occupation" to attain recognition as a profession are:

- A high status granted by society because of altruistic motivation and commitment to serve society

- A systematic, unique body of theory, obtained through a university-based education with practical experience to master the knowledge base
- An authority to define the profession and autonomy in its practice
- A code of ethics
- A professional culture that embodies certain values and norms[1–4]

Whether or not nursing qualifies as a true profession has been debated for decades. The discussion itself has promoted recognition of inconsistencies and movement toward solutions, most notably in the areas of educational preparation and control over professional practice. Nursing continues to evolve toward full attainment of these attributes, but it is generally accepted as a profession.

One of the concepts used to define a profession is that its services are vital to the health and viability of a society. It is generally accepted that nurses provide a valued service based on altruistic motivation. The public assumes that the title of "nurse" carries with it a certain level of expertise and commitment, and accepts nurses as providing essential services desired and needed by society. This assumption, in part, sets the legal precedent of professional "duty." Many of the changes in health care delivery may further validate nursing as a profession because of its increasing responsibility and authority in public health maintenance as well as illness management.

While the nursing profession may accept various levels of education as entry into practice, a commonality is the knowledge base of health sciences and the nursing process coupled with a minimum level of experience necessary to prepare one for licensure and practice. The continued application of this theory in practice supports the premise of a profession. It is the one common bond that all nurses share.

The concept of autonomy in practice has also been an area of challenge for nursing as well as for many other professions. It is probably true that no single health care professional, with the complexities in providing health care today, can claim absolute autonomy. Changes in the health care system have actually propelled nurses into more autonomous roles (nurse practitioners, clinical specialists, and case managers) as cost-effective providers of health care services.

Professionals have codes of ethics to help regulate their relationships with clients as well as each other. The ANA developed a formal written Code for Nurses in 1985, which was revised to its current version in 2001.[5] Formal codes of ethics are usually based on a set of values and norms that represent the philosophy and practice of the profession.

Professionals have strong values pertaining to their occupational identity. This identity impacts on all aspects of the professional's attitude and behavior toward work and lifestyle. The values established by the profession become the rules of expected behavior among the members of the profession, with expectations of loyalty and adherence.

In examining the role of the nurse as an LNC, one must remember that direct patient care is no longer the defining parameter of what makes a nurse a nurse. How nurses apply health science education and expertise to the ultimate benefactor of the service is the defining parameter. Using a broad application of the nursing process, nursing education and practice experience, and professional ethics and standards to benefit the health care system and the patients it serves more aptly defines the scope of the practice of nursing.

Nursing in the legal arena seeks to identify and right a wrong, prevent future untoward events, and manage or mitigate injuries resulting from such events. LNCs provide direct and indirect services to that end for patients and the health care system within the legal environment. For example, whether an LNC is working on the plaintiff or defense side of a professional negligence case, the goal is defense of the standard of care. The standard of care directly affects patient care and is defined by the legal as well as the health care practice arena.

Legal Nurse Consulting as a Specialty Practice of Nursing

The AALNC Board of Directors resolved in 1995 that first and foremost, the professional foundation of legal nurse consulting is nursing. By applying that foundation in a consulting capacity in the legal arena, AALNC defined a new specialty practice of nursing. The LNC is valued in the legal arena for one's health care education and experience, rather than knowledge of the law. One may apply this special expertise in legal environments that did not previously have the benefit of the nurse's services. In so doing, the quality of the application of the law to health-care-related cases, issues, projects, or practices has been improved. Clients may be patients, attorneys, insurance companies, hospitals, government agencies, or a variety of others. Although knowledge of the law enriches the LNC's contribution, the client depends on the LNC's health care knowledge. The ultimate beneficiary of the LNC's work is the quality of health care.

A duty of any profession is to promulgate standards by which the quality of practice of its members can be assessed. As in other nursing specialties, AALNC published the Scope of Practice and Standards of Practice and Professional Performance, found in Appendix 8.2, to meet its professional responsibility to its clients and society.

Standards of practice provide common ground for basic practice accountability.[6] They are authoritative statements by which the profession describes the responsibilities for which its practitioners are accountable. The Standards of Practice for Legal Nurse Consulting are based on the ANA model and incorporate the nursing process with adjustments for the context of legal nurse consulting practice (see Figure 8.1).[7]

The Nursing Process as It Applies to Legal Nurse Consulting

The nursing process consists of actions that are logical, interdependent, sequential, but cyclic: *assessment, diagnosis, planning, implementation, evaluation.*[8] This is a basic problem-solving process or approach to any assignment. Nursing diagnoses are derived from an analysis of the assessment data. All of these actions require critical thinking, the use of clinical experience, and health science education.

In adapting the nursing process to the practice of legal nurse consulting, the following actions are identified: *assessment, analysis and issue identification, outcome identification, planning, implementation, evaluation.* The concept of nursing diagnosis is interpreted to mean those opinions formulated by the LNC from analysis of the data to determine health care issues important to resolution of legal claims or cases. Those opinions are called issue identification. The

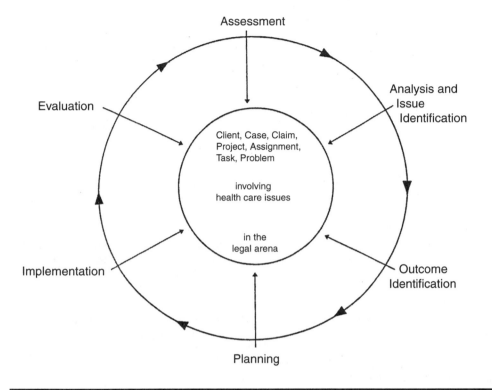

Figure 8.1 Standards of Practice for LNCs

anticipated or hoped-for outcomes of the process are then identified and listed. Planning, implementation, and evaluation of the plan of action follow. (See Table 8.1 for comparison of clinical nursing standards and LNC practice standards.)

The purpose of using the nursing process is to provide the LNC with a framework or consistent problem-solving approach for meeting the needs of the particular case, client, task, or role. This framework also gives the LNC the skills to work with various colleagues in the legal realm so that a successful outcome can be achieved. It also provides the means of measuring how well standards are met by practitioners.

While the Standards of Practice spell out how LNCs problem-solve and manage tasks, the Standards of Professional Performance constitute the guidelines for the LNC's professional behavior. Adherence to these guidelines will bring a consistency to the practice, so the person engaging the services of an LNC is assured quality of practice.

Incorporation of the AALNC Standards of Practice and Standards of Professional Performance into one's practice aids in the development of a consistently high standard of practice and job satisfaction, as well as peace of mind that all aspects of an assignment are covered from every possible angle. Meeting the needs of the client generates goodwill and additional work. Having a plan of action to guide the LNC through every assignment results in significant savings of time and energy and ensures a consistent quality product.

The LNC works with a client to obtain the information necessary to make an assessment. After analysis of the case, the issues are discussed jointly. The client

Table 8.1   Comparison of ANA Standards of Clinical Nursing Practice and the AALNC Standards of Practice

Clinical Nursing Standards	*LNC Practice Standards*
Standard I: Assessment	
The nurse collects patient health data	The LNC collects data to support the systematic assessment of health care issues related to a case or claim
Standard II: Analysis and Nursing Diagnosis	
The nurse analyzes the assessment data and makes a nursing diagnosis	The LNC analyzes data to identify the health care issues related to a case or claim
Standard III: Outcome Identification	
The nurse identifies expected outcomes that are individualized to the patient	The LNC identifies the desired outcome of the work product as it relates to the health care issues of a case or claim
Standard IV: Planning	
The nurse develops a plan of care that prescribes interventions to attain expected outcomes	The LNC formulates a plan of action to achieve the desired outcome
Standard V: Implementation	
The nurse implements the interventions identified in the plan of care	The LNC implements the plan of action
Standard VI: Evaluation	
The nurse evaluates the patient's progress toward the attainment of expected outcomes and alters the plan accordingly	The LNC evaluates the effectiveness of the plan of action in achieving the desired effect and alters the plan accordingly

often assists with issue identification and outcome identification. Implementation of the plan often occurs in partnership, and evaluation is an ongoing process.

Summary

A plan of action needs thoughtful preparation and a consistent guideline in order to aid professionals in their work. These standards can be adapted and used as such a guide for the LNC. Purposeful thought should be applied to any case or assignment. The steps of assessment, analysis and issue identification, outcome identification, planning, implementation, and evaluation will assist LNCs in achieving the best possible outcome of their work.

   Application of the Standards of Legal Nurse Consulting Practice and Standards of Professional Performance creates a foundation for the practice. This is illustrated in the examples found in Appendices 8.1 and 8.2. LNCs may build on that sound foundation in their own practice based on their individual education, experience, and enthusiasm.

References

1. Quinn, C.A. and Smith, M.D., *The Professional Commitment: Issues and Ethics in Nursing*, W.B. Saunders, Philadelphia, 1987.
2. Chaska, N.L., *The Nursing Profession. Turning Points*, C.V. Mosby, St. Louis, 1990.
3. Oermann, M.H., *Professional Nursing Practice. A Conceptual Approach*, J.B. Lippincott, Philadelphia, 1991.
4. Moloney, M.M., *Professionalization of Nursing. Current Issues and Trends*, 2nd ed., J.B. Lippincott, Philadelphia, 1992.
5. American Nurses Association, *Code of Ethics for Nurses with Interpretive Statements*, Washington, D.C., American Nurses Publishing, 2001.
6. Litwack, K., *Core Curriculum for Post Anesthesia Nursing Practice*, 3rd ed., W.B. Saunders, Philadelphia, 1996, 8–14.
7. American Nurses Association, *Standards of Clinical Practice*, Kansas City, MO, American Nurses Association, 1991.
8. Iyer, P., Taptich, B., and Bernocchi-Losey, D., *Nursing Process and Nursing Diagnosis*, 3rd ed., W.B. Saunders, Philadelphia, 1995, 1–33.
9. American Association of Legal Nurse Consultants, *Code of Ethics and Conduct*, American Association of Legal Nurse Consultants, Glenview, IL, 1992.

Test Questions

1. After reviewing the witness testimony, the LNC determines that the dep-
    osition questions for the defendant should be revised to explore the
    anesthesia standards of care. This is known as
    A. Analysis and issue identification
    B. Outcome identification
    C. Planning
    D. Evaluation

2. After analyzing the data in the records and literature, the LNC determines
    that a medical expert will opine that the anesthesiologist fell below the
    standard of care. This is known as
    A. Analysis and issue identification
    B. Outcome identification
    C. Implementation
    D. Planning

3. The best way for independent LNCs to evaluate the quality of their work is to
    A. Show their work product to other LNCs at the local chapter meeting
       and solicit feedback.
    B. Keep track of how many cases each client sends.
    C. Compare the amount of income made this year from LNC activities to
       that made last year.
    D. Solicit a discussion with the client after the work is submitted and the
       case is resolved to determine whether the materials provided had a
       positive impact on the resolution.

4. In order to meet the standard of professional performance by contributing
    to the professional development of peers, colleagues, and others, a begin-
    ning LNC would be expected to
    A. Actively participate in an LNC class group assignment involving case
       review.
    B. Teach a class on how to evaluate the credibility of a testifying expert.
    C. Accept an assignment from a law firm involving evaluating the nursing
       negligence of a nurse colleague with whom the LNC has worked in
       the past.
    D. Offer advice on an LNC listserv about complex mass tort cases.

5. The LNC who was hired to provide expert witness testimony on the nursing
    standard of care of a resident in a long-term care facility should refuse to
    testify on all the following issues, EXCEPT:
    A. The federal and state laws and guidelines that define residents' rights
       in long-term care facilities
    B. The potential differential diagnoses and actual cause of death of the
       resident involved in the claim
    C. The care rendered by the nurses in the emergency department where
       the resident was taken

D. The risks and known complications of the emergency surgery that the
resident underwent

Answers: 1. D, 2. B, 3. D, 4. A, 5. B

Appendix 8.1
Application of the Standards of Practice for the Legal Nurse Consultant

The following are four examples of activities pertaining to the Standards of Practice.
It is important to emphasize that legal nurse consulting is not merely a group of
isolated activities, but rather a process. Properties of the process are listed in
Table 8.2. Examples are by no means comprehensive. Not all activities will be
undertaken in all assignments. Certain activities may be listed under different
headings, depending on assignment or points in time in case progress. Preparation
of a chronology, for instance, may be part of assessment in one case, and
implementation in another. The examples are meant to give the reader further
explanation of how the Standards of Practice can be applied in various situations.

Example 8.1

The family of a resident of a long-term care facility who died unexpectedly after
undergoing multiple surgeries notified the facility that they are considering filing
suit. The LNC has been engaged by an attorney client to evaluate the claim for
merit. (The attorney in this instance could represent either the family or the facility.)

Assessment: Data Collection as Basis for Further Activities

> The LNC reviews medical records from the hospital where the surgeries
> were performed, the nursing home facility, and the hospital where the
> patient was taken prior to her death.
> The LNC requests and reviews a copy of the death certificate and autopsy
> report to determine the cause of death.
> The LNC reviews the literature pertaining to the applicable state regulations
> for medical care rendered in a long-term care facility.

Table 8.2　Properties of the Nursing Process for Legal Nurse Consulting

1. Purposeful	Goal-oriented
2. Systematic	Uses an organizational approach to achieve a purpose or solve a problem
3. Dynamic	Involves continuous change and adaptation
4. Cyclic	Steps are sequential, interdependent, and recurrent
5. Interactive	Based on a reciprocal relationship between LNC and client
6. Flexible	Can be adapted to any LNC field; phases are used sequentially and cyclically

The LNC obtains and reviews medical literature regarding the indications for, risks of, and known complications of the surgeries.

The LNC prepares a timeline summary (chronology) of the hospital and nursing home care from the records obtained.

The LNC attends the attorney's interviews of the decedent's family members to gain more information regarding the decedent's condition and inter-action with the health care providers prior to death.

Analysis and Issue Identification: Analysis of the Data to Determine the Health Care Issues Related to the Claim

Based on the timeline summary and the state's requirements for documen-tation, the LNC determines that a portion of the records pertaining to the care in the nursing home is missing.

Based on the information from the hospital records, autopsy report, and medical research information, the LNC determines that the decedent's cause of death was *not* an expected or known risk of the surgical procedures.

Based on a comparison of interviews with family members and analysis of the timeline of events, the LNC identifies long periods of time lacking patient assessment by nursing personnel and a delay in getting appro-priate treatment.

The LNC determines that based on current information available, the decedent's death may have been due to lack of appropriate care in the nursing home.

Outcome Identification: Results Hoped for Related to Analysis and Issue Identification

The LNC determines that the missing records may contain information to support (or refute) the alleged negligence and should be obtained if they exist.

The LNC determines that an RN [registered nurse] experienced in the care of patients in long-term care facilities would be an appropriate expert to render an opinion on the standard of care.

Planning: Plan of Action to Achieve the Desired Outcome

The LNC recommends that the client request additional records and forward them to the LNC for review.

The LNC recommends that the client retain nursing standard of care experts to review the case and render opinions.

Implementation: Actions Taken to Implement the Plan

The client requests the missing records and informs the LNC that the facility responded that no such records exist.

The LNC interviews three nursing experts in long-term care, verifying qualifications and clinical experience, availability, testimony experience, and fees.

The LNC consults with the client regarding which expert he or she recommends based on the above criteria.

The LNC organizes material to be sent to the expert and sends a memo to the client concerning when to expect a response from the reviewer.

Evaluation: Determine Effectiveness of Plan in Achieving Desired Outcome

The LNC and the client review the response of the expert to determine whether the issues initially identified were correct.

Based on the expert's opinion, the client determines that the case has merit.

The LNC and the client revise the plan of action to begin pursuit or defense of the claim.

Example 8.2

The LNC working as risk manager is notified of the occurrence of a wrong site surgery.

Assessment: Data Collection as Basis for Further Activities

The RM [risk manager] obtains a letter of direction from legal counsel to investigate under attorney/client privilege.

The RM interviews nurses, surgical techs, and physicians involved in the patient's care.

The RM reviews the medical record documentation and secures the original record for safekeeping.

The RM reviews the policy on surgical site identification.

The RM reviews the JCAHO [Joint Commission on Accreditation of Health-care Organizations] standards and Sentinel Event Alerts on surgical site identification.

Analysis and Issue Identification: Analysis of the Data to Determine the Health Care Issues Related to the Claim

The RM determines the incident to be a sentinel event in need of a root cause analysis.

The RM determines the incident to be a potential lawsuit or claim.

The RM determines that the incident should undergo both physician and nurse peer review processes.

The RM determines that appropriate and ongoing communication with patient and family regarding the incident is necessary.

Outcome Identification: Results Hoped for Related to Analysis and Issue Identification

The RM identifies a need for changes in hospital procedures and practices to prevent a reoccurrence.

The RM determines, based on the current communications with the surgeon and patient and family, that the claim may be resolved to the satisfaction of the claimant and hospital prior to a lawsuit being filed.

The RM believes that the process through appropriate peer review committees will result in improvement in practice of providers.

Planning: Plan of Action to Achieve the Desired Outcome

The RM identifies appropriate participants for a working meeting to conduct a root cause analysis.

The RM arranges for copies of medical records to be sent to counsel and the insurance representative.

The RM arranges meetings with defense counsel to review case and schedule interviews with the employees involved.

The RM discusses patient and family communications with the surgeon and nurse manager to determine appropriate persons to provide ongoing information.

Implementation: Actions Taken to Implement the Plan

The RM prepares a packet of information for the root cause analysis team meetings and facilitates the process.

The RM ensures the implementation of practice and process changes developed in team meetings.

The RM ensures completion of quality assurance monitoring of practice and process changes.

The RM reports a summary of the case and root cause analysis to quality committees, hospital board of directors, JCAHO, and state licensing boards, depending on laws and guidelines.

The RM works with the attorney and insurance adjuster to arrive at a fair and equitable resolution with patient and family.

Evaluation: Determine Effectiveness of Plan in Achieving Desired Outcome

The RM follows up with surgeon, surgery department staff, and manager for evaluation of the root cause analysis process.

The RM evaluates case preparation and the settlement with defense counsel.

The RM reports the outcome to the hospital board of directors and answers any questions.

The RM responds to JCAHO in the event of an on-site survey.

Example 8.3

The LNC working as an investigator for the state licensing board receives a case involving an allegation of sexual misconduct by a psychologist.

Assessment: Data Collection as Basis for Further Activities

The LNC reviews the allegations and pertinent state statutes.

The LNC searches in-house database and reviews files of two similar previous complaints.

Analysis and Issue Identification: Analysis of the Data to Determine the Health Care Issues Related to the Claim

The LNC determines that the case is a high priority due to seriousness of the charge and previous similar complaints.

The LNC determines that confidentiality is especially critical to all parties due to the nature of the allegations.

Based on the sensitivity of the case, the LNC determines that experts will be needed to testify for the state if probable cause is found.

Outcome Identification: Results Hoped for Related to Analysis and Issue Identification

The LNC determines that the director of investigations should be immediately notified that this is the third complaint regarding this health care provider so that the appropriate board can decide whether immediate temporary action is necessary.

The LNC determines that a completed report should be submitted to the director of investigations within 30 days.

Planning: Plan of Action to Achieve the Desired Outcome

The LNC asks for case reassignment of two other new cases in order to concentrate on the immediacy of this complaint.

The LNC identifies the involved parties and witnesses that he or she needs to interview: accused, accuser, and office personnel.

The LNC prepares a list of the accuser's medical records and psychological reports that need to be obtained and reviewed.

The LNC reviews resources to identify which medical experts would be appropriate to conduct a review and give an opinion on the conduct of the accused.

Implementation: Actions Taken to Implement the Plan

The LNC transfers one pending case to another investigator, and places the other on hold per supervisor direction.

The LNC immediately schedules appointments and conducts interviews with the accused, office personnel, and the individual making the accusation.

The LNC reviews and summarizes findings in the accuser's medical records.

The LNC locates and retains an expert psychologist, organizes and submits materials for review, interviews expert, and summarizes expert's opinions.

The LNC submits a summary report to the director concluding that the evidence supports the allegations, and makes recommendations for further action.

Evaluation: Determine Effectiveness of Plan in Achieving Desired Outcome

The LNC notes that the expert psychologist's opinion has confirmed that the behavior of the accused constitutes misconduct.

The LNC follows up with the director to learn whether the recommendations for disposition of the case were followed.

In anticipation of a hearing, the LNC determines whether further information or evidence is needed to support the complaint.

Example 8.4

The LNC who is skilled in life care planning is hired by a plaintiff attorney to determine the long-term damages for the adolescent victim of a drunk-driving moving vehicle accident. The teenager suffered a significant closed head injury.

Assessment: Data Collection as Basis for Further Activities

The LNC reviews the medical records pertaining to treatment of injuries due to the accident.

The LNC requests the adolescent's prior medical records to identify any preexisting physical or mental condition.

The LNC reviews the adolescent's school records and testing for the years preceding and following the accident.

The LNC evaluates the teenager and family in their home.

Analysis and Issue Identification: Analysis of the Data to Determine the Health Care Issues Related to the Claim

The LNC determines that the teenager's grades have gone from above average to below average in school.

The LNC determines that the teenager will require long-term cognitive and physical rehabilitation.

Outcome Identification: Results Hoped for Related to Analysis and Issue Identification

The LNC will be able to develop and document a long-term plan of care, detailing costs of care, with the goal of returning the child to the optimum level of function considering the injury.

The plan and costs for care and services will be accepted by the defendants in settlement or by jury at trial.

A video of the child's rehabilitation would favorably impress the defendants at settlement or a jury if the case goes to trial.

Planning: Plan of Action to Achieve the Desired Outcome

The LNC will set appointments to interview current caregivers, therapists, and neuropsychologist.

The LNC will set appointments to interview the adolescent's teachers.

The LNC recommends to the attorney that a rehabilitation video be produced.

Implementation: Actions Taken to Implement the Plan

The LNC solicits recommendations for future care from current caregivers, therapists, and neuropsychologist.

Based on multiple sources of information, the LNC writes the plan of care and obtains and calculates costs for all care and services.

With attorney approval, the LNC facilitates the videotape production of the child's daily rehabilitation program with the videographer and the various rehabilitation caregivers.

Evaluation: Determine Effectiveness of Plan in Achieving Desired Outcome

The LNC seeks feedback from the attorney regarding the plan data and costs of care report.

The LNC is able to successfully defend the life care plan in deposition.

The life care plan is used to support the demand for settlement and facilitates a resolution prior to trial.

The defense attorney who deposed the LNC calls the LNC 3 months later requesting review of a life care plan submitted to his firm in another case.

Appendix 8.2
Standards of Professional Performance as It Applies to Legal Nurse Consulting

Standard I: Quality of Practice

The LNC evaluates the quality and effectiveness of his or her practice as an LNC.

Key Indicators

1. The LNC participates in quality of practice activities as appropriate to the individual's role, education, and practice environment. Examples:
   A. The LNC develops a job description for his or her role in a law firm using the AALNC Standards of Practice for Legal Nurse Consultants.
   B. The LNC collects data on the volume, type, and results of the activities performed for each of his or her clients.
   C. The LNC reviews various software programs used to organize medical information for case chronologies.
   D. The LNC develops policies and procedures for LNCs working in an insurance claim department to provide consistency in the method of data collection and report writing.
2. The LNC uses the results of quality of practice activities to initiate changes in the practice. Examples:
   A. The LNC recommends revision of the firm's current LNC job description to include activities identified in the AALNC Standards of Practice not previously utilized.
   B. Based on an analysis of client activity, the independent LNC sets meetings with those clients who show a decline in use of their services to discuss what services may be improved.
   C. The LNC purchases a new computer software program that will allow more flexibility in preparation of individualized chronologies and reports.
   D. Based on implementation of new policies and procedures, the LNC makes recommendations for changes to facilitate processing of insurance claims.

Standard II: Performance Appraisal

The LNC evaluates his or her own performance in relation to professional practice standards and relevant statutes and regulations.

Key Indicators

1. The LNC engages in performance appraisal, identifying areas of strength as well as areas for professional development. Examples:
   A. The LNC who has developed a business with five employees establishes a review board of one attorney and one LNC to meet with her on a quarterly basis to review the business plan, progress of the business, and the goals and direction for the future.
   B. The LNC employed by a law firm meets on a regular basis with the employer or senior LNC for performance appraisal.
   C. The independent LNC establishes a mentoring relationship with another LNC who works in a similar setting to assist in quality of performance evaluation without breaching client confidentiality.
   D. The LNC in any setting reviews and reflects candidly on personal performance and plans to attend continuing education for self-improvement.
2. The LNC seeks constructive feedback regarding his or her own practice. Examples:
   A. The LNC conducts an annual survey of clients to determine how well the work product and selected experts met the goals of the client.
   B. The LNC serving as an expert witness seeks feedback from the client to determine how style of presentation of information to the jury could be improved.
   C. The LNC asks a co-worker LNC to review a life-care plan for accuracy and completeness before it is submitted to the client.
   D. The LNC working for an insurance company reviews the potential questions for deposition that have been developed with the supervisor prior to a meeting with the defense attorney.
   E. The LNC as Risk Manager meets monthly to review all cases, claims and other work with the Vice President of Medical Affairs and solicits suggestions for improvements in management.
3. The LNC takes action to achieve goals identified during performance appraisal. Examples:
   A. Based on client survey results, the LNC revises the format used to submit summary reports so that the LNC's conclusions are more easily identified.
   B. The LNC discontinues recommending medical experts who were not able to meet client deadlines and searches for new qualified experts to replace them.
   C. The LNC providing expert witness testimony plans for more preparation time with the client prior to trial in the future.
   D. The LNC elaborates on the potential complications and their expenses in the life-care plan to better provide the information the client is seeking.
4. The LNC participates in peer review, as appropriate. Example: The LNC volunteers to be a member of the quality assurance team for a national insurance company. Responsibilities include evaluation of reports generated by LNCs and generation of recommendations for improvement.

Standard III: Education

The LNC acquires and maintains current knowledge in nursing and health care issues.

Key Indicators

1. The LNC participates in ongoing educational activities pertaining to the health sciences and the law relevant to his or her practice areas. Examples:
   A. The LNC working primarily with environmental and toxic tort claims attends university courses pertaining to public health.
   B. The LNC working in the area of insurance management attends seminars on workers' compensation law and case management.
   C. The LNC attends professional continuing education programs pertaining to clinical nursing and medical practice most relevant to his or her LNC practice.
   D. The LNC reads professional health care and law journals applicable to his or her LNC practice.
2. The LNC seeks experiences necessary to maintain current licensure as a professional registered nurse. Examples:
   A. The LNC seeks information regarding the requirements to maintain licensure in each state in which he or she is licensed and obtains all necessary knowledge and skills.
   B. The LNC keeps accurate records for the maintenance of his or her license and renews it prior to expiration.
3. The LNC seeks the knowledge and the skills that are appropriate to the LNC's practice. Examples:
   A. The LNC who works for a plaintiff's medical malpractice firm attends a seminar offered by the American Trial Lawyers Association (ATLA) on the latest issues in medical malpractice litigation.
   B. The LNC participates in an AALNC chapter educational workshop on performing on-line medical research.
   C. The LNC attends the annual AALNC educational conference and selects concurrent sessions useful to his or her subspecialty.
   D. The LNC reads the *Journal of Legal Nurse Consulting* and other similar publications.

Standard IV: Collegiality

The LNC contributes to the professional development of peers, colleagues, and others.

Key Indicators

1. The LNC shares knowledge and skills with colleagues and others. Examples:
   A. The LNC obtains medical information regarding a new federal requirement for long-term care facilities and takes a copy of it to the local chapter meeting.

    B. The LNC participates in roundtable discussions at the annual AALNC Networking Luncheon on selected topics pertaining to development and organization of work product information.

    C. The LNC acts as a mentor to a less experienced LNC just hired by the employer law firm.

    D. The LNC presents an educational program at a local or national AALNC conference.

    E. The LNC submits an article to the *Journal of Legal Nurse Consulting*.

2. The LNC provides peers with constructive feedback regarding their practices. Examples:

    A. The LNC answers questions posed by a subcontracting LNC regarding the clarity and accuracy of work product.

    B. The LNC reviews the marketing plan of a colleague and suggests ways to increase visibility among clients.

    C. The LNC evaluates billing procedures for a less-experienced colleague and advises changes to improve fee collections.

3. The LNC contributes to an environment that is conducive to the education of nurses entering the field of legal nurse consulting. Examples:

    A. The LNC welcomes interested nurses who attend the local chapter meetings and encourages them to join AALNC.

    B. The LNC writes an article on legal nurse consulting for another nursing publication.

    C. The LNC gives a presentation to the local college LNC program on the role of the LNC as Risk Manager.

    D. The LNC encourages nurses who are inquiring about the specialty practice to obtain AALNC's written, audio, and video materials published for this purpose.

4. The LNC contributes to an environment that is conducive to the health science education of legal team members, as appropriate. Examples:

    A. The LNC determines the legal team members lack information about the appropriate use of CPR in a case in which CPR was used inappropriately. The LNC arranges for an educator to come to the firm to teach the staff about the latest techniques of when, where, why, and how to use CPR.

    B. The LNC presents a program on medical terminology for the legal secretaries and paralegals at his or her firm.

    C. The LNC collects medical literature on shoulder dystocia, with accompanying illustrations, and presents it to the attorney client to assist in the evaluation of a case.

    D. The LNC obtains a Groshong catheter and demonstrates its use to the attorney in a case of professional malpractice in which a home health nurse allegedly misused it, causing a severe infection.

5. The LNC contributes to an environment that is conducive to the education of health care professionals regarding legal issues applicable to the health sciences. Examples:

    A. The LNC participates in an educational program for home health nurses on the most common areas of liability in their clinical practice.

    B. The LNC coordinates seminars for medical groups on risk management activities for their practices to minimize medical malpractice claims.

C. The LNC assists in the preparation of a nurse who will be giving testimony as a defense witness in deposition.

D. The LNC researches the current standard of care for primary VBAC and presents the information with an assessment of legal risks to the Obstetrics Department and hospital administration.

Standard V: Ethics

The LNC's decisions and actions are determined in an ethical manner.

Key Indicators

1. The LNC's practice is guided by the ANA Code for Nurses with Interpretive Statements (2001)[5] and the AALNC Code of Ethics.[9]
2. The LNC's practice affirms the values, standards, and practices of the profession of nursing. Examples:
    A. The LNC bases opinions and recommendations on the published theory and practices of the health sciences, as well as his or her own knowledge gained through clinical experience.
    B. The LNC acting as expert nurse witness provides an objective opinion regardless of whether engaged by the defense or plaintiff attorney.
3. The LNC maintains confidentiality commensurate with the attorney/client privilege. Examples:
    A. The LNC adheres to ethics of confidentiality by refraining from discussing any issues pertaining to the merits of a case with anyone except the client who engaged him or her, the client's employees, or the party whom the client represents.
    B. The LNC providing expert witness testimony clarifies with the client when the LNC's communications and opinions may become discoverable and prepares written reports only on the request of the client.
4. The LNC practices in a nonjudgmental and nondiscriminatory manner. Examples:
    A. The LNC avoids using defamatory language in writing or when talking about the persons involved in any case.
    B. The LNC acting as expert nurse witness remains objective in his or her analysis of the health care issues in a claim and does not alter testimony solely to satisfy the needs or goals of the client.
5. The LNC evaluates all cases and clients for conflicts of interest and declines when conflicts are evident. Examples:
    A. The LNC begins the review of a hospital claim and recognizes that one of the potential defendants is a personal friend. The LNC notifies the client, declines the case, and recommends the services of another LNC with commensurate expertise.
    B. The LNC in independent practice keeps accurate records of all cases he or she has reviewed or is working on for attorneys. The LNC cross-checks each new file for conflicts of interest before accepting a case.

C. The LNC has been asked to review a claim in anticipation of providing expert witness testimony. The nursing care in question was rendered at a facility that is part of the same hospital chain employing the expert. The LNC declines the case on the premise that it is a conflict to testify in a case involving one's employer.

D. An attorney who does a high volume of personal injury claims and potentially could be a good source of revenue for the independent LNC asks the LNC to review a backlog of several potential claims and prepare a summary of each claim. However, the attorney will only pay for a maximum of 1 hour on each claim, regardless of the amount of medical information reviewed. The LNC declines to accept the assignment on the basis that an adequate and valid review cannot be made with those restrictions.

6. The LNC seeks available resources to help formulate ethical decisions. In each of the examples given in all of the previous key indicators, the LNC could use the following resources to assist him or her in making an ethical decision: The ANA Code for Nurses,[5] the AALNC Code of Ethics,[9] the applicable state's Bar Association Rules of Ethics, the ABA's Code of Ethics, members of the AALNC Board of Directors, members of the chapter leadership and experienced colleagues.

7. The LNC who testifies as an expert witness confines testimony to his or her area of expertise. Examples:

A. An LNC is testifying as an expert witness based on her experience as head nurse in a pulmonary unit of a large teaching hospital. Prior to that experience, she taught aerobics part-time. The opposing counsel asks her questions about exercise, obesity, and nutrition. She declines to speak about those issues from an expert point of view, as her primary purpose in the case is to testify about the nursing responsibilities in observing blood gas levels in a patient with chronic obstructive pulmonary disease.

B. An LNC working in a perinatal setting is asked to review the standard of care rendered by the nurses at the delivery of a baby with severe shoulder dystocia. The attorney asks the LNC to give an opinion on the cause of the child's brain injury. The LNC limits his testimony to the nursing care issues and defers causation issues to the perinatologist expert.

Standard VI: Collaboration

The LNC may collaborate with legal professionals, health care professionals, and others involved in the legal process.

Key Indicators

1. The LNC consults with legal professionals, health care professionals, and others as appropriate. Examples:

    A. The LNC confers with a toxicologist and a pulmonologist about the medical consequences of inhalation of toxic fumes in a case of inhalation of a combination of burned chemicals.

    B. The LNC obtains information regarding whom the client represents in the claim and what access the LNC will have in gaining information from the party or providing information to the party.

    C. The LNC discusses the issues pertaining to standards of care, injuries, and causal relationships with the expert witness reviewing the claim to assist the client in evaluating the merits of a claim.

    D. The LNC consults with an IV therapy nurse specialist to inquire about standards of care for central lines.

2. The LNC makes referrals as needed. Examples:

    A. An obstetrical case has been assigned to the LNC with primary expertise in mental health. He feels reasonably sure that he can obtain the necessary information for the attorney on the case, but it will involve days of research and hours of billable time. Instead, he refers the case to an LNC whom he knows has the background in obstetrics and the research material at her fingertips. Not only is time and money saved for the client, but also the credibility of the LNC will be enhanced.

    B. The LNC working as Risk Manager in a small hospital setting is presented with a surgical case that is a sentinel event in which the patient died in the OR. A root cause analysis was done and changes in hospital practices were made to prevent a reoccurrence. The anesthesiologist and surgeon's management is to be peer reviewed. The Risk Manager recommends to the small surgical department that the case be sent outside for an objective review. She locates and contracts with an appropriate anesthesiologist and surgeon in a nearby community, prepares the records and the engagement letter and presents the reviews to the Department of Surgery for consideration and action as indicated.

Standard VII: Research

The LNC recognizes research as a methodology to further the LNC's practice.

Key Indicators

1. The LNC takes action substantiated by research as appropriate to his or her role, education, and practice environment. Examples:

    A. The LNC has a strong background in oncology and nursing home administration. He or she is working in-house for a large firm that is involved in obtaining patents for new pharmaceuticals. The work entails development of spreadsheets that detail the results of the physicians' clinical trials. The LNC's expertise enables him or her to interpret the data and inform the attorneys of the implications of the results.

    B. The LNC has over 12 years experience providing services to law firms who handle medical malpractice insurance defense. He or she also has a degree in journalism and is published in several nursing journals.

The LNC offers to participate as an item writer for the association's certification program.
2. The LNC participates in research activities as appropriate to his or her role, education, and practice environment. Examples:
   A. The LNC develops a database of claims activity for his or her insurance company employee in order to identify trends in the successful resolution of claims for the company.
   B. The LNC completes and returns a practice analysis survey questionnaire developed by his or her professional association's certification program.
   C. The LNC in risk management conducts a survey study to determine the reasons critical care nurses are sued and, based on results, develops risk management activities targeted to reduce the risks for the facility.

Standard VIII: Resource Management

The LNC considers factors related to ethics, effectiveness, and cost in planning and delivering client service.

Key Indicators

1. The LNC selects expert assistance based on the needs of the case or claim. Examples:
   A. The LNC has been asked to assist on a case in which a patient developed paralysis after an anterior thoracic diskectomy. A review of the surgical reports indicates that the team of physicians included an anesthesiologist, an orthopedic surgeon, and a thoracic surgeon. After numerous inquiries, however, the LNC determined that one physician was a vascular surgeon instead of a thoracic surgeon. In searching for expert physicians to assist in the case, the LNC located an expert orthopedic surgeon who then assisted her in locating a vascular surgeon and an anesthesiologist. Background information was then obtained and confirmed on all the experts, including confirmation of education, board certification, and publications.
   B. The LNC as Risk Manager receives a call from a nearby hospital reporting a possible EMTALA (Emergency Medical Treatment and Labor Act) violation by the Risk Manager's hospital. The Risk Manager's investigation includes a review of the medical record, and interviews with the ER physician, nursing staff involved in the transfer of the patient to the other hospital, ER Medical Director, and Nurse Manager. After determining the hospital may not have complied with a key element of the law, the Risk Manager arranges a phone conference with the hospital's compliance attorney and CEO to present the case, assess liability and decide whether to self report to the Center for Medicare and Medicaid Services (CMS; formerly HCFA).
2. The LNC assigns tasks based on the knowledge and skill of the selected provider. Examples:
   A. The LNC working in-house for an insurance defense firm supervises their national team of LNCs. A case has arrived on her desk that demands

a response in 3 days and involves an incident in a pediatric intensive care unit. The LNC locates a consultant who has recent pediatric ICU experience and who also works well under the pressures of a deadline.

B. The LNC is responsible for obtaining an illustration of a surgical procedure to be used as demonstrative evidence at trial. The LNC selects a company with an in-house medical illustrator who has proven ability to make visually complex subjects simple and understandable for the jury, to produce the product.

C. The LNC receives a large stack of medical records, which need to be organized, paginated, and indexed for use as a trial exhibit. The LNC assigns the task to a legal assistant with experience in organizing large volumes of documents for trial.

3. The LNC assists legal professionals and others in identifying and securing appropriate services available to address health care issues pertaining to the case or claim. Examples:

A. There has been a leakage of nitrous oxide from an overturned railroad car in a large metropolitan area. There are 2000 claimants. The LNC has been requested by the insurance company to assist in locating expert physicians who can assist in defending the multiple claims. Potential side effects of exposure to the chemicals are researched and the LNC determines that medical experts should include toxicologists, pulmonary specialists, gastroenterologists, neurologists, dentists, and ophthalmologists. Experts are contacted and assigned to the appropriate cases.

B. The LNC is working on a catastrophic brain injury case with the workers' compensation attorney. The LNC reviews the life care plan and conducts a survey to locate a suitable rehabilitation facility that will meet the injured person's needs.

Chapter 9

Certification

Sheila Webster, BSN, RN, C-HROB, RNC, LNCC, and
Margery Garbin, PhD, RN

CONTENTS

0-8493-1418-6/03/$0.00+$1.50
© 2003 by AALNC

Objectives

- To identify at least two of the purposes or goals of specialty nursing certification
- To distinguish between specialty certification and certificates of achievement
- To identify credentials that should be used as part of the professional nurse's title
- To describe how the Legal Nurse Consultant Certified (LNCC®) meets the accepted standards for specialty nursing certification

Introduction

The founding members of the American Association of Legal Nurse Consultants (AALNC) have been credited for their long-range vision for the association and for the specialty of legal nurse consulting. Though their roles may be taken for granted, some very basic decisions had to be made by our founders before the association could move forward. There were several turning points in AALNC's past that left indelible marks on the current certification program offered by the American Legal Nurse Consultant Certification Board (ALNCCB®).

One key issue was to define who legal nurse consultants are. Are they legal assistants? Do they need additional training beyond their nursing education and experience? Are they paralegals, or are they a distinct group of professionals, separate from both nursing and legal assistants?[1]

Defining Legal Nurse Consultant Practice

The early members of AALNC ultimately agreed that the legal nurse consultant (LNC) was hired or retained for his or her knowledge and experience as a nurse. Additional education in legal nurse consulting could be formal or informal if the nurse so desired, but it was not a requirement of practice. The basis for legal nurse consulting was — and still is — the application of nursing knowledge and the nursing process to analysis of health care and safety issues when those issues also involve the legal system.

The importance of the AALNC consensus should not be underestimated. Because AALNC acknowledged that legal nurse consulting is a specialty of nursing, the following points were defined:

- The Scope of Practice for the Legal Nurse Consultant and Standards of Legal Nurse Consulting Practice and Standards of Professional Performance are based on widely accepted standards of care and ethics for all nurses.
- Control has been retained over legal nurse consulting practice.
- The certification program is modeled on the high standards of other respected nursing specialty certification programs.
- The specialty is open to all licensed registered nurses.

- Additional formalized training is not required for entry into the specialty.
- Legal nurse consulting is not advanced practice nursing; recent legislation has not affected LNCs by requiring master's level education in the specialty or mandatory certification for licensure to practice.

Certification Conundrums

Nurses who are new to legal nurse consulting frequently express confusion about certificates, certifications, and continuing education offered by non-AALNC sources of LNC education. There are two primary reasons for their confusion, both of which have been addressed in AALNC's first two position statements.

Role of the LNC versus Role of the Legal Assistant

Before the term "legal nurse consultant" gained widespread use, nurses working in law firms were often referred to as "nurse paralegals." (Use of this title is discouraged by AALNC.) In 1998, the Standing Committee on Legal Assistants of the American Bar Association (ABA) suggested that LNCs "fall squarely within the ABA definition of 'paralegal/legal assistant'." The ABA's committee took the position that any educational programs designed to train LNCs were, therefore, paralegal programs that must adhere to ABA guidelines for paralegal education. This includes approval of the educational offering by the ABA if offered by an institution with an approved program.[2]

In response, the AALNC published its first position paper in April 1999, The AALNC Position Statement on the Role of the Legal Nurse Consultant as Distinct From the Role of the Paralegal and Legal Assistant.[2] In the position statement, the association reaffirmed that legal nurse consulting is a specialty practice of nursing and that nurses are not paralegals or legal assistants, but are professionals consulted for their expertise in health care. Although legal professionals may require that legal assistants or paralegals obtain education and certification in ABA-approved paralegal programs, the ABA has no jurisdiction over regulating the practice of nurses. To review the position statement in its entirety, see Chapter 6, Appendix 6.3.

Defining LNC Education and Certification

The second source of confusion about certification is a more persistent problem. Despite the fact that educational preparation for LNC practice is voluntary, a lucrative market developed for seminars and courses about legal nurse consulting. Today there are many options for nurses who want to learn about the specialty before deciding whether it is a good fit for them. See Chapter 6, Appendix 6.4, AALNC Position Statement on Education and Certification in Legal Nurse Consulting,[3] for information about how nurses can best determine whether these resources meet their needs.

Nurses looking for nontraditional alternatives in nursing practice often learn about legal nurse consulting via advertisements by well-marketed businesses that offer LNC training. Perhaps as a way to set their educational programs apart from the increasing number of competitors, providers of LNC education began offering certificates or "certification" in legal nurse consulting.

As more nurses were exposed to advertisements offering certificates or certification, the AALNC received an increasing number of queries from nurses wanting to know how to earn a certificate so they could become LNCs. The AALNC Position Statement on Education and Certification in Legal Nurse Consulting was published to correct the widespread misperception that formal education and certification were required for entry into the specialty. The statement also emphasized that certification should be reserved to acknowledge the skills of the experienced practitioner, as is true of other nursing certifications.

Some of the LNC educational programs have encouraged nurses to use various initials (e.g., "LNC") as part of their title. The AALNC position statement explained the position of the American Nurses Association (ANA) on proper use of credentials as part of the nursing professional's title:

AALNC supports the practice initiated by the American Nurses Association of listing one's credentials in the following order: highest educational degree, highest nursing degree if different, licensure, and professional certifications.[3]

The initials "LNC" denote practice in the specialty, not an earned credential. Using "LNC" in this manner (e.g., Nancy Smith, BSN, RN, LNC) is comparable to an intensive care unit nurse signing her name Nancy Smith, BSN, RN, ICU. The nurse's specialty area of practice is not a credential to be used as part of one's title. Similarly, ANA does not approve of listing certificates as a credential. This would lead to titles like Nancy Smith, MSN, RN, CPR, ACLS.

Certification in a Nursing Specialty

Professional certification in nursing is widely used to recognize a higher level of nursing skill and expertise within a specialty than is expected from nurses with the minimal qualifications required for entry into the practice setting. Standards for nursing professional certification programs vary, but three minimum components are generally required:

1. Licensure as a nurse
2. Eligibility criteria, which include experience in the specialty, such as clinical experience or a specified number of work hours using skills and knowledge unique to the specialty
3. Identification and testing of a specialized body of knowledge that is distinctly different from the general practice of nursing

In both medicine and nursing, there is widespread recognition that the professional organization representing practitioners in the specialty is best qualified to set criteria for the certification programs.[4] The content of the examination is usually based on a "practice analysis" of critical skills and concepts needed to be proficient in the specialty, as identified by nurses practicing in the specialty.

In legal nurse consulting, the only certification that currently meets (and exceeds) those minimum requirements is the Legal Nurse Consultant Certified, designated as LNCC®. LNCC is comparable to other recognized specialty credentials, such as CCRN, RN-C, and RNC, to name a few. Since LNCC meets the definition of a credential, LNCC becomes part of the professional title, as in Nancy Smith, MPH, BSN, RN, LNCC. The LNCC is the only credential in legal nurse consulting that is recognized by AALNC, as well as the 39 member boards of the American Board of Nursing Specialties, Sigma Theta Tau International, and ANA.

Nurses in all specialties should discourage the use of unrecognized credentials. If professional certification is to be meaningful to the public and have any value for certified nurses in any specialty practice, nurses must be vigilant about promoting the public's perception that professional certification is granted only to those nurses with demonstrated experience and knowledge in the specialty.

The American Board of Nursing Specialties: Using the Goal of Accreditation to Plan the Certification Program

Early in AALNC's research process, one of the goals for the development of the certification program for LNCs was to meet the standards necessary for accreditation.[1,4] The early certification committees identified the American Board of Nursing Specialties (ABNS) as the accreditation body most able to give the certification program the credibility they sought.

ABNS was incorporated in 1991 with support from the Macy Foundation. ABNS was formed with the original intention to be "the certifier of certifiers" for nursing specialties. As such, it sought to protect the public and consumers by setting and enforcing standards for certification. The ABNS mission is to provide assurance to the public that the nurse holding the credential from an accredited certification program possesses the knowledge, skills, and competency for quality practice in his or her particular specialty.[5] In order to achieve its mission, ABNS currently has 18 standards (Table 9.1), which must be met and documented before any nursing certification program can undergo a stringent peer review by the ABNS Accreditation Council.

Maxine E. Bernreuter, executive director of ABNS, summarized how accreditation validates that the goals of certification have been met: "Without third party accreditor recognition such as that conferred by ABNS, neither the consumer, the employer, nor certified nurses themselves can be assured of the quality of any certification."[5]

The American Legal Nurse Consultant Certification Board

ABNS standards call for a "certification board with organizational autonomy," which may continue a collaborative relationship with the nursing specialty organization. The justification for the requirement is as follows:

The certification board must be sufficiently independent from the specialty association to ensure integrity of the certification process, to maintain clear lines of accountability, and to prevent undue influence on the part of the vested interests.[6]

Autonomy

The American Legal Nurse Consultant Certification Board (ALNCCB®) was established in September 1997. The board is composed of experienced LNCs with proven leadership who come from a variety of legal nurse consulting work settings with a range of field experience. Geographic diversity is also considered. The ALNCCB bylaws call for terms of three years with a rotation mechanism so that two board members have terms ending each year, with the option to run for reelection for one additional term.

ALNCCB has independent responsibility for the certification program. It is the board that determines the eligibility criteria for the examination, audits applications for compliance with the criteria, sets fees, and sets maintenance criteria for renewal of certification. ALNCCB is charged with the responsibility of maintaining the examination so that it is valid, reliable, and legally defensible.

Necessary Expertise

ABNS standards have detailed requirements for maintaining statistical validity, reliability, and security of the certification examination. These can rarely be achieved in any nursing organization without help from experts in the testing field. After extensive investigation of companies offering testing services, the AALNC signed a contract with the Center for Nursing Education and Testing (C-NET®).

Beginning in October 1997, ALNCCB worked with the president and staff of C-NET to develop the certification program. These professional test developers, like health care professionals, also follow sets of standards. Standards for developing valid and reliable examinations, including certification and licensure examinations — the Standards for Educational and Psychological Testing (1999) — are published jointly by the American Educational Research Association, the American Psychological Association, and the National Council on Measurement in Education. Standard 14.4 states:

The content domain to be covered by the examination should be defined clearly and justified in terms of the importance of the content for credential-worthy performance in an occupation or profession.[7]

Table 9.1   ABNS Standards for Accreditation

#	ABNS Accreditation Standard	ALNCCB (Example of Documentation That Meets Criteria)
1	Definition and scope of nursing specialty	Scope of Practice for LNC, Standards of LNC Practice, AALNC Code of Ethics and Conduct
2	Research-based body of knowledge	*Journal of Legal Nurse Consulting, Legal Nurse Consulting: Principles and Practice*
3	Organizational autonomy (certification board)	ALNCCB policies, AALNC operating policies
4	Public representation	Public member position description
5	Eligibility criteria for test candidates	Application handbook for the LNCC examination
6	Test development (psychometrically sound)	Contract with C-NET (testing professionals), pilot-test statistical analysis
7	Validity	LNC practice analysis, blueprint, post-examination statistical analysis
8	Reliability	Postexamination statistical analysis
9	Elimination of bias/sensitive items	Nondiscrimination policy, postexamination statistical analysis
10	Test administration	C-NET contract, testing policy
11	Test security	C-NET contract, security/confidentiality agreements from board/item writers, staff
12	Passing scores (set using psychometrically sound methods)	Postexamination statistical analysis, equating procedure
13	Continued competency	Certification maintenance criteria
14	Communications (information for candidates and stakeholders)	Application handbook for the LNCC examination, ALNCCB section of AALNC Web site
15	Confidentiality	Confidentiality policy and procedure
16	Appeals	Appeals policy and procedure
17	Disciplinary action	Disciplinary action policy and procedure
18	Practice analysis	Survey of Legal Nurse Consulting Practice, 1998

Note: The ABNS list of 18 standards that must be met by nursing specialty certification programs in order to attain accreditation of the program. The last column shows just a small part of the background that was developed as required before the ALNCCB submitted its application and was granted accreditation for the LNCC° program in fall 1999. For a detailed description of the ABNS standards, go to the ABNS Web site, http://www.nursingcertification.org.

The same standard also specifies that the knowledge and skills addressed should be those necessary to protect the public. In general, the standard states that the knowledge and skills contained in a core curriculum designed to train people for the profession are relevant. Thus, *Legal Nurse Consulting: Principles and Practice*, developed by AALNC, is used as a primary resource for test development. In addition, ALNCCB adheres to guidelines of the Equal Employment Opportunity Commission to ensure validity of test content and fairness to all test-takers.

Determining What to Test

A practice analysis provides the primary basis for defining the content domain of a certification examination. The first role delineation survey performed by AALNC

Table 9.2 Weights of LNC Activities and Types of Cases, 1998

Weights for LNCC Blueprint Categories

Type of Case	% of Questions
A. Medical malpractice	30–35%
B. Personal injury	23–28%
C. Product liability/toxic tort	11–16%
D. Workers' compensation	10–15%
E. Risk management	5–8%
F. Life care planning	4–7%
G. Elder law	1–3%
H. Administrative health law	1–3%
I. Criminal/forensic	1–3%

LNC Activity

1. Collect and investigate health care records, research literature, standards, guidelines, laws, costs, etc. related to case, concerning issues of standards of care, causation and damages (16–21%)

2. Analyze data in the pertinent medical records, research, literature, standards, guidelines, laws, costs, etc. related to a case, concerning issues of standards of care, causation, and damages (16–21%)

3. Facilitate communication between clients (e.g., attorney, claims manager, agency) and parties, experts, witnesses, and vendors) (15–20%)

4. Draft materials considered attorney work product or to be used as evidence in health-care-related cases (14–18%)

5. Educate oneself and clients on the health sciences pertaining to issues in a case (8–11%)

6. Collaborate with clients to support case strategy during discovery or case management (10–14%)

7. Support the process of adjudication of cases (e.g., trial, settlement, arbitration, or mediation) (4–8%)

8. Testify as an expert opinion/fact witness (4–6%)

Note: The blueprint for the LNCC certification exam is a synthesis of the criticality of various LNC activities based on the types of cases and the percentage of time spent on critical activities as reported by practicing LNCs on the Survey of Legal Nurse Consulting (1998). The data for the blueprint is shown here in outline form.[9]

took place in 1992; a more extensive and updated practice analysis was needed by 1997. At the first meeting of the ALNCCB and C-NET, a survey was designed to determine the relative frequency and the importance (or criticality) of legal nurse consulting activities and knowledge, taken in part from the 1992 Role Delineation Survey, the AALNC Standards of Legal Nurse Consulting Practice (1995), *Legal Nurse Consulting: Principles and Practice* (1998), and membership data.[8] After multiple revisions, the Survey of Legal Nurse Consulting Practice was mailed to 1000 practicing LNCs in February 1998. C-NET analyzed the 221 usable surveys returned, and the final "blueprint" for the certification examination was adopted (Tables 9.2–9.3). The 200 questions found on any edition of the certification examination are matched to the blueprint specifications.[9]

Table 9.3 ALNCCB Certification Examination Blueprint, 1998

Ideal Distribution of 200 Test Items by Blueprint Categories

LNC Activity Type of Case	1 Investigate	2 Analyze	3 Communicate	4 Draft Documents	5 Educate	6 Strategize	7 Support Adjudication	8 Testify	Total
A. Medical malpractice	11	11	12	11	5	8	5	3	30–35% (60–70)
B. Personal injury	8	8	9	8	4	7	4	2	23–28% (46–56)
C. Product liability/toxic tort	4	4	5	4	2	4	2	0–1	11–16% (22–32)
D. Workers' compensation	4	4	4	4	2	4	2	0–1	10–15% (20–30)
E. Risk management	2	2	2	2	0–1	2	0–1	0–1	5–8% (10–16)
F. Life care planning	2	2	2	2	0–1	0–1	0–1	0–1	4–7% (8–14)
G. Criminal/forensic	0–1	0–1	0–1	0–1	0–1	0–1	0–1	0–1	1–3% (2–6)
H. Administrative health law	0–1	0–1	0–1	0–1	0–1	0–1	0–1	0–1	1–3% (2–6)
I. Elder law	0–1	0–1	0–1	0–1	0–1	0–1	0–1	0–1	1–3% (2–6)
Total	16–21% (32–42)	16–21% (32–42)	15–20% (30–40)	14–18% (28–36)	8–11% (16–22)	10–14% (20–28)	4–8% (8–16)	4–6% (8–12)	100% (200)

Note: Blueprint for the LNCC® Certification Examination was developed from the practice analysis: Survey of Legal Nurse Consulting Practice, 1998. The numbers and ranges show the number of items (test questions) for each type of case combined with an LNC activity for a valid 200-item test. The blueprint may change based on future practice analysis.[9]

The practice analysis will be repeated as the specialty changes, to ensure that the blueprint and the examination are valid measures of current practice in legal nurse consulting. Individual LNCs have the ability to influence the recognized scope of legal nurse consulting practice and the content of the certification examination by completing a practice analysis survey issued by AALNC or ALNCCB.

Writing the Examination

The initial examination questions, or "items," were developed by a group of 12 item writers who were selected from the AALNC membership. The group was selected from experienced LNCs in a wide range of practice settings from all regions of the country. All item writers were required to meet the eligibility requirements for the examination. Under the direction of C-NET, the item writers crafted 250 questions during 2 intense 4-day sessions.[8]

The original and current examination questions are designed to test the nurse's ability to apply legal nurse consulting knowledge in situations that simulate the actual practice. The majority of questions are in the form of case studies in which a passage describing a legal case is followed by several questions relating to the case.[9]

Each individual item is coded by the type of case and by one LNC activity. Currently, the categories under "type of case" that are assigned the highest percent of test questions are medical malpractice and personal injury. More than 50% of the questions on any version of the certification examination based on the 1998 survey of legal nurse consulting are likely to concern these two areas.[9] The percent of questions in these two categories will change if a future practice analysis demonstrates a shift in the percentage of LNCs working in these areas.

Validating the Test Items

Two pilot tests were developed using the 250 items written. The pilot tests were offered to all LNCs attending the 1998 AALNC National Education Conference in Dallas, TX. The pilot tests did not exclude LNCs who would not have met eligibility criteria, but a questionnaire included with the pilot tests revealed that most of the 217 LNCs who sat for the pilot tests would have met eligibility requirements. The superior performance by those who met eligibility requirements served as validation that the eligibility criteria did tend to identify those candidates who had reached the level of proficiency measured by the examination.[10]

The pilot tests and each certification examination given since then were subjected to postadministration statistical analysis by C-NET staff. Each item was reviewed to determine whether it was too easy or too difficult, and whether the item discriminated between high and low scorers. The items that did not meet psychometric standards were eliminated or revised by the ALNCCB members and C-NET before the items were pilot-tested on another certification examination. Any new or revised item is not scored until it can be proven to be a "good" question through statistical analysis.[9]

Mission Accomplished

Thanks to the efforts and support of the early certification committee members, the board members and staff of AALNC and ALNCCB, the C-NET testing professionals, the item writers, and the application auditors, the first Legal Nurse Consultant Certification Examination was offered on October 24, 1998. Of the 156 candidates, 126 (81%) passed and were awarded the LNCC credential.[11] The ALNCCB board members and the item writers, who were judged eligible to sit for the examination prior to being involved in the item writing, were awarded the LNCC with the caveat that they must pass the examination in 2003 during the first certification renewal cycle to retain the LNCC. The other 156 LNCCs will have the option to renew by meeting the renewal criteria, including options for continuing education hours or reexamination. The examination continues to be offered every April and October in various cities around the country, as well as at the AALNC annual education conferences.

Postadministration analysis has consistently found the examination to be psychometrically sound; it is "valid." In other words, the questions are directly related to the roles of experienced LNCs as identified by the practice analysis, and the majority of LNCs who meet eligibility criteria perform successfully on the examination.

The examination is "reliable" and consistent. Statistical analysis indicates high consistency of performance of individual candidates throughout the examination. Performance on individual items remains stable from one form of the examination to another, and overall performance on various editions of the examinations is similar. Test forms are statistically equated, so that equally qualified LNCs are neither penalized nor advantaged by sitting for an examination that is more difficult or easier than another edition.

Setting the LNCC Apart through Accreditation

Having built the examination to ABNS standards, ALNCCB determined that the sound psychometric results that had been achieved were the final data needed before making the application for accreditation to the ABNS. With the support of AALNC, ALNCCB was able to submit the extensive application for ABNS accreditation nearly a year earlier than planned. As a result, the ALNCCB program was awarded accreditation at the September 1999 ABNS meeting. The staff and volunteer members of AALNC and ALNCCB as well as the C-NET professionals, who were involved in creating a quality certification program, are credited with achieving this goal so early in the program's history.

Protecting the Value of LNCC

Nurses who achieve specialty certification want their credential to be meaningful to others. Indeed, the aim of nursing specialty certification and accreditation is to provide assurance to the public that the certification holder is proficient in the specialty practice at a level that exceeds the minimum requirements for entry into practice.

To that end, ALNCCB has taken a number of steps. Both "ALNCCB" and "LNCC" are now registered trademarks. No other organization may use "LNCC" to designate certification as an LNC. While it is not necessary to use the registered trademark symbol with the credential, its use may help distinguish the LNCC from the ever-evolving list of entry-level certificates.

ABNS accreditation indicates that the LNCC is comparable to other nursing specialty certifications with high standards and legally defensible programs. The ABNS accreditation standards meet or exceed standards held by other widely recognized professional nursing certifications, and include a stringent third-party peer review process of all applications submitted for accreditation.

Since the primary goal of nursing certification is to protect the public, ALNCCB also includes a "public member." The role of the public member is to represent the interests of consumers (i.e., the employers of LNCs and the clients they represent). The public member keeps ALNCCB grounded in its duty to the public at large, enhancing the value of the credential outside the nursing community.

ALNCCB (with C-NET) performs ongoing review of the examination and the individual items and writes new items as needed. The eligibility and renewal criteria are periodically reviewed and modified as necessary. The certification application booklets are revised to clarify the information or to add questions to the application that may improve the statistical review process. A practice test is available for purchase by LNCs who are interested in preparing for the exam.[9] Future practice analysis will identify changes in legal nurse consulting practice, and the examination blueprint and content will change accordingly.

Applications to sit for the examination and for maintenance (renewal) of certification are subject to audit by appointed members of the audit panel. A percentage of all applications are reviewed to confirm that eligibility or renewal criteria have been met. A policy is in place for appeals that is open to those who have been denied access to an examination, who have been denied renewal of certification, or who have had certification revoked.

Confidentiality of potential candidates is maintained, and candidate information cannot be used outside the intended purposes of the certification board. Security of the examination is strictly maintained. C-NET is required to safeguard all examination booklets, the item banks, and items still in the development stage in order to prevent the compromise of current and future examinations. Confidentiality regarding test content is a strict requirement for every member of ALNCCB, its staff, and contracted advisers. Test-takers are reminded that they should also maintain the confidentiality of the test content. All candidates are required to read and sign a confidentiality statement that appears on the first page of their test booklets.

Value Is as Value Does

Ultimately, the public should judge the value of the LNCC credential. In describing the purposes of nursing certification in patient care settings, Ann Cary, Director of the International Program of Research on the Certified Nurse Workforce, states:

> Ostensibly, [nursing certification] protects the public from unsafe and incompetent providers, gives consumers more choices in selecting health care providers, distinguishes among levels of care, and gives better trained providers a competitive advantage.[12]

This statement can easily be adapted to the LNC role, even though competent practice by LNCs does not generally involve direct patient care.

As in other nursing specialties, the process of proving the value of certification takes a great deal of time. In a study of the certified nursing work force from January 2001, it is reported that nurses hold more than 410,000 certifications in 134 specialties from 67 certifying organizations.[12] But the lack of research proving the link between certification and improved outcomes at the bedside or in non-patient-care practice settings has delayed broad-based recognition of the value of many nursing certifications. It is difficult to prove that any individual professional certification fulfills the purposes cited above, even though the achievement of those goals receives at least intuitive support.[13]

A specialty as small as legal nurse consulting is at a greater disadvantage in this regard. The LNC's employers and clients usually do not work with enough LNCs to make comparisons between those who have achieved the LNCC credential and those who have not. Consumers, including the LNCC employer's clients, may not even know of the LNCC's involvement in a case and have no way to judge the LNCC's impact on the case. The complexity of legal processes makes it difficult to measure any one individual's impact on case outcome.

LNCCs and LNCs must be willing to educate their employers and clients about the LNCC credential and about the great lengths to which AALNC and ALNCCB have gone to ensure that the credential is meaningful to them — the consumers of LNC services. Attorneys and other employers need to be made aware that accreditation by ABNS is evidence confirming that the LNCC credential meets the highest standards for nursing certification. The LNCC credential should be promoted as a reliable indicator of an experienced and knowledgeable LNC who ultimately will serve the best interests of the employer's clients. An essential part of the educational process is the demonstration by LNCCs' expertise and commitment to continual improvement through continuing education. However, direct education of consumers about the LNCC credential is needed to help them differentiate the LNCC from other less meaningful credentials.

LNCs are encouraged to aspire to LNCC certification. Meanwhile, adhering to the ANA's recommendations for listing credentials in one's professional title will help to prevent confusion about the LNCC credential. The AALNC recommends listing certificates and entry-level "certifications" in the education section of a resume or curriculum vitae, rather than adding initials to one's title that do not represent attainment of specialty nursing certification.[3]

One of the challenges facing the ALNCCB is how best to support the educational process of the public that benefits from services of LNCCs. As we go forward, ALNCCB will be relying on LNCCs to live up to the standards and ethics of legal nurse consulting practice as part of their commitment to quality practice of nursing in the specialty. LNCCs will demonstrate that "value is as value does."

References

1. Janes, R., Bogart, J., Magnusson, J., Joos, B., and Beerman, J., The history and evolution of legal nurse consulting, in *Legal Nurse Consulting: Principles and Practice*, Bogart, J.B., Ed., CRC Press, Boca Raton, FL, 1998, chap. 1.
2. American Association of Legal Nurse Consultants, *AALNC Position Statement on the Role of the Legal Nurse Consultant as Distinct from the Role of the Paralegal and Legal Assistant*, Glenview, IL, 1999.
3. American Association of Legal Nurse Consultants, *AALNC Position Statement on Education and Certification in Legal Nurse Consulting*, Glenview, IL, 2000.
4. Ehrlich, C.J., Certification development, *Journal of Legal Nurse Consulting*, 6, 6, 1995.
5. Bernreuter, M.E., The American Board of Nursing Specialties: nursing's gold standard, *JONA's Healthcare Law, Ethics, and Regulation*, 3, 5, 2001.
6. American Board of Nursing Specialties, *ABNS Standards: Organizational Autonomy*, San Antonio, TX, 2002.
7. American Education Research Association, American Psychological Association, and National Council on Measurement in Education, Standards for Educational and Psychological Testing, American Educational Research Association, Washington, D.C., 1999.
8. Magnusson, J., AALNC's certification exam approaches completion, *Journal of Legal Nurse Consulting*, 9, 26, 1998.
9. American Association of Legal Nurse Consultants, *Handbook for the LNCC Practice Test*, Glenview, IL, 2002.
10. American Association of Legal Nurse Consultants, ALNCCB completes certification examination pilot test, *Journal of Legal Nurse Consulting*, 9, 19, 1998.
11. American Association of Legal Nurse Consultants, October 1998 LNCC examination report, *Journal of Legal Nurse Consulting*, 10, 36, 1998.
12. Cary, A.H., Certified registered nurses: results of the study of the certified workforce, *American Journal of Nursing*, 101, 44, 2001.
13. Cary, A.H., Data driven policy: the case for certification research, *Policies, Politics, & Nursing Practice*, 1, 165, 2000.

Test Questions

1. Three of the following are eligibility requirements to sit for a certification examination in a nursing specialty. Which one is NOT required?
   A. Experience as a registered nurse
   B. Evidence of formal education in the specialty
   C. Current licensure as a registered nurse
   D. Current practice in the specialty

2. Which tool should be used to determine the test specifications (blueprint) of a nursing specialty exam?
   A. A core curriculum
   B. Accreditation standards
   C. A practice analysis
   D. Postexamination statistical analysis

3. Which of the following is an accepted credential that can be used as part of a registered nurse's title?
   A. NICU
   B. LNC
   C. LNCC
   D. ACLS

4. The *primary* goal for nursing certification is to
   A. Protect the consumers of nursing specialty service.
   B. Reward skilled nurse specialists.
   C. Differentiate placement on an employer's pay scale.
   D. Establish who may enter the specialty practice.

5. Accreditation of a specialty certification board by the American Board of Nursing Specialties provides assurance that the
   A. Educational programs in the specialty are of high quality.
   B. Bylaws of all specialty certification boards are uniform.
   C. Board of the specialty association maintains control of the certification board's decisions.
   D. Specialty certification program meets the highest standards.

Answers: 1. B, 2. C, 3. C, 4. A, 5. D

Chapter 10

Ethical Theory and the Practice of the Legal Nurse Consultant

Elena A. Capella, MPA, RN, LNCC, CPHQ, and
Gretchen Aumman, PhD, BSN, RN

CONTENTS

221

Objectives

- To discuss the ethical basis of nursing and legal nurse consulting
- To distinguish between two basic ethical positions
- To identify the primary principles underlying the ethical positions
- To discuss resources available to the legal nurse consultant regarding ethical issues in nursing
- To discuss the ethical foundations underlying legal nurse consulting
- To discuss some major ethical issues in legal nurse consulting

Introduction

The practice of legal nurse consulting bridges both health care and law, two fields that are characterized by complex issues and competing interests. Within this dynamic, legal nurse consultants (LNCs) direct a variety of activities to discover truth and arrive at equitable solutions. Whether LNCs work on behalf of plaintiffs or defendants, LNCs have a professional duty to support justice. It is in this context that LNCs consider different values, perspectives, and interests when evaluating cases and making professional decisions. Intrinsic to the understanding of these differences is a clear comprehension of the ethical principles that guide the involved parties.

This chapter presents a proactive approach to ethical reflection and decision-making. Ethics is best understood through the examination of everyday issues. This section presents several issues that LNCs are likely to encounter in their practices. In addition, the discussion includes an overview of prominent ethical principles and codes that are basic to medical, nursing, and LNC practice. As such, these principles supply the framework for thoughtful reflection on issues of clinical and legal ethics.

Solutions to ethical problems are not arrived at easily. LNCs come to the profession familiar with the ethical decision-making processes basic to nursing practice. The practice of legal nurse consulting requires LNCs to develop additional ethical perspectives that provide answers to questions specific to the practice of legal nurse consulting. The development of an ongoing, proactive process to understand ethical principles helps the LNC make decisions in a manner that is consistent with standards of the profession.

Definition of Ethics and Morals

Ethics is the inquiry into the principles of morality, particularly of right and wrong conduct.[1] Our thinking regarding what is right or wrong or good or bad is based on ethical principles that have roots in Western philosophical thought. The concept of ethics involves discussion of differences in what is meant by "good." In contrast, morality is seen as the set of standards of right and wrong that prevails in society.

Morality refers to the common societal conceptions of what is right and what is wrong. Our morality and morals are reflected in how we live, the decisions we make, and what we hold as valuable. Moral consensus in the United States is often arrived at through public discussions or hearings on topics such as abortion, health care, and gun control. When a society holds a strong view and deems that the documentation of that view is important, documentation often takes the form of a law, act, or code of laws. The laws of a society are a reflection of its moral stance on issues of special importance.

Basic Ethical Theories

Before an ethical problem can be resolved, it is necessary to understand the nature of conflict between ethical views. Ethical positions are derived from several types of ethical theories, two of which are consequence-based theories and duty-based theories. It is within these frameworks that health care professionals address specific issues, such as autonomy, confidentiality, and veracity.

Ethical theories serve several purposes: they provide a general overview of the conception of the good according to the theory, they delineate individual rights and duties held by the framework, and they set the ordering of priorities of the elements within the framework. Whether certain goals, duties, or rights are basic or subordinate to something else is an important element in the formulation of an ethical theory.

Theories provide a framework for ethical decision-making, but they do not provide specific direction. Specific direction is found through an exploration of the basic principles that emerge by considering how those ethical theories apply to a particular case. Although there are many important ethical principles, those addressed in this chapter are specific to nursing and to legal nurse consulting.

Consequence-Based Ethical Theory (Utilitarianism)

A consequence-based theory of ethics defines the rightness or wrongness of actions by the outcome of those actions. In this view no action is, in and of itself, inherently right or wrong. The outcome determines how the action is to be judged. A form of consequence-based ethical theory that is influential in Western thought is utilitarianism.[2] Articulated by Jeremy Bentham (1748–1832) and John Stuart Mill (1806–1873), the premise of utilitarianism is that the combined good of all those involved in a situation has greater importance than the good of a single individual. "The greatest good for the greatest number" is the common formulation of this premise. In this theoretical model, an action is right or wrong according to its usefulness in promoting the good of all concerned.

When presented with an ethical dilemma, the person reasoning through utilitarian arguments first must identify potential outcomes of actions. The criterion for action in the utilitarian framework is that it produces the greatest balance of good over harm for all concerned. The initial difficulty for the utilitarian is to decide how large to make the circle of people whose good should be taken into account. The number of people affected is a matter of judgment that will vary with each situation and potential action.

Example 10.1: An LNC may help an attorney who is handling a product liability case involving a large number of plaintiffs who were injured by a defective surgical implant. As the LNC and attorney discuss the strategic and ethical decisions that affect the handling of the case, they recognize that a particular decision may be best for a large number of plaintiffs, but adversely affect a few plaintiffs. The utilitarian perspective would require them to make decisions that would provide the greatest good for the greatest number.

The second problem for the utilitarian is deciding how to define "good" when tallying the amount that each potential action would produce. Any situation involving several individuals consists of several discrete individual concepts of good. Averaging those different concepts together to calculate the good of the group may override the interests of an individual. Continuation of life and the associated physical pain may represent a greater good for one individual, and a greater harm for another. For a general good to be conceptualized, it is necessary to regard harms and benefits as comparable for everyone. For example, it would be necessary to decide that a particular good, such as preservation of life, is the highest good for everyone. This definition of "good" is not consistent with benefits that are by nature personal and determined subjectively by each individual.

Utilitarianism is primarily concerned with raising the quality of life; it holds that persons are morally obligated to increase well-being and to decrease the amount of pain and suffering in the world.[2] These are significant goals for every health care practitioner, and considerations of utility are important in health care decision-making. Who can imagine discussing chemotherapy or surgical procedures without pondering the risks and benefits involved? Utilitarianism does not provide a complete and adequate moral philosophy. Other ethical viewpoints, based on conceptions of duty or obligation, have emerged in response to the inadequacies of utilitarianism.

Duty-Based Theory (Kantianism)

A duty-based theory of ethics defines the rightness or wrongness of actions in the principles that govern behavior. Such theories make some particular duty or set of duties the fundamental base of ethical decisions. The American Nurses Association (ANA) Code of Ethics for Nurses reflects the concept of duty-based ethics (see Appendix 10.1). This document defines the fundamental duties intrinsic to the role of the registered nurse. Professions, such as nursing, medicine, and the law, establish codes of ethics to highlight the important duties in the professional practice.

One major ethical viewpoint, known as Kantianism (Immanuel Kant, 1724–1804), holds that consequences do not make an action right or wrong. Rather, the moral rightness of a person's actions is dependent upon whether or not those actions uphold a principle, regardless of outcome.[2]

Example 10.2: An LNC may advise the attorney that a medical record provides a totally different description of how an accident occurred than relayed by the plaintiff during interview. If the attorney chooses to ignore the LNC's concern and litigates the case based on what the plaintiff says happened, the LNC has nonetheless fulfilled a professional and ethical duty-based obligation to advise the attorney.

Kantian theory proposes that nothing is good in and of itself except a "good will," which is the unique human capacity to act according to the concept of law or principles. In estimating the total worth of one's actions, Kantianism proposes that a "good will" takes precedence over all else.[3] Contained in a "good will" is the concept of duty. According to Kantianism, when persons act from a notion of duty, their actions have moral worth. For instance, health care providers have a duty to tell patients the truth when a medical error has been made. The fact that the health care provider tells the patient the truth does not necessarily mean that the action was morally worthy. According to Kantian theory, if the reason the health care provider tells the patient the truth is to prevent legal problems rather than to act out of a sense of duty, the action is not morally worthy. For the Kantian, actions have true moral worth only when they arise from recognition of a duty and a choice to perform that duty.

Kantian theory also holds that an absolute moral truth must be consistent and free from internal contradiction. In order for a rule of conduct to be a moral rule, it must hold true universally and in all situations. Kantianism also posits that in keeping with the idea that humans are rational beings, they should treat each other as ends in themselves, not as a mere means to an end.[4] Medical researchers, no matter how important their goals, may never use human beings in research without first obtaining valid informed consent.[5]

A duty-based framework of ethics such as Kantianism contains several appealing elements that are applicable to health care. First, Kantian ethics takes much of the "guesswork" out of moral decision-making in questions related to health. To act morally is to act on principle, regardless of the consequences or situational nuances. When health care providers tell patients the truth about a medical error they committed, they are acting in a manner that is consistent with Kantian theory.

Second, Kantian ethics recognizes that humans are intrinsically worthy of respect. Unlike consequentialist ethics, the Kantian mandate is to treat persons as ends in and of themselves and not as means to an end. In the health care setting, this serves to bring a much-needed humanism to care increasingly dominated by machines and technology.[6]

Third, the Kantian concept of duty implies that the moral obligation to act is based upon a respect for rights and recognition of responsibilities. Subscribing to this theory necessitates defining rights and responsibilities clearly and then acting on moral imperatives. Because each participant in the nurse/patient relationship has equal claims and duties, Kantian ethics imply mutuality in the relationship between patients and nurses that is not addressed in utilitarian frameworks.

Criticisms of Kantianism arise from several areas. First, there is no clear method to resolve conflicts of duties. For instance, suppose that a patient who has been injured by the negligent actions of a physician asks the nurse whether he should see an attorney. By advising the patient to forget about it, the nurse knows he can spare that patient emotional turmoil and pain. The nurse presumably has a duty to tell the truth as well as a duty to refrain from causing pain. Which obligation takes precedence over the other? Kantian theory is quite clear that duties are owed to beings who are rational and autonomous.[7] How does one resolve the question of who qualifies as a rational autonomous being? Where do children or senile adults fit in? How should nurses consider their duties to nonrational or nonautonomous persons? There is no compelling reason for certain actions to hold without exception.[8] In the Kantian view, truth-telling in nursing practice means that all patients should be told all the truth all the time. Clearly, this contradicts common sense and what nurses experience in their day-to-day practice. The rigidity of Kantian rule, which allows no exceptions, precludes it from being fully accepted as the basis for nursing practice. Despite its obvious shortcomings, Kantianism holds an appeal for nursing practice because it recognizes the humanity intrinsic to nursing practice and offers more than the utilitarian scale on which to balance risks and benefits.

Principles Underlying the Ethical Positions

Theories are meant to provide an underlying philosophy or way of thinking about the ultimate goals of ethical reasoning. Such theories are only minimally helpful in day-to-day situations, when one reasons through the difficult dilemmas that arise in health care practice. Each of the ethical theories has a foundation in a number of underlying principles. Of the many ethical principles, a few are presented in this chapter that apply to health care providers. These principles are: *respect for autonomy, beneficence and nonmaleficence, veracity,* and *justice.*

Autonomy

Autonomy is the right to self-determination and independence when individuals consider and act upon decisions that they believe serve their interests. A common ethical situation in LNC practice is when the nurse and the attorney disagree on the strategy that will provide the maximal benefit to the client (defendant or plaintiff).

The Kantian view holds autonomy as a primary ethical principle. Respect for a person's autonomy denotes an ethical position based on the individual claim to self-determination. In support of the individual's claim to self-determination, the LNC, concerned with acting in the client's interest, does not define that interest in any way contrary to the client's own definition. In this view, it is clients, not legal professionals, who determine what is in their best interest.

Respect for autonomy includes a recognition of limitations imposed by illness and the patient's need for assistance in a situation that may be both unfamiliar and frightening. The health care provider does not merely supply patients with the facts and then withdraw, leaving the decision in the patient's hands. In an obligation-based framework, the relationship between the health care provider and the patient is a partnership. It assumes that patients can be more fully and freely self-determining if they are actively assisted in that endeavor. The purpose of the partnership is for patients' own values to ultimately guide a decision that is consistent with their concept of health. This principle is applied in informed consent discussions, which may be an issue in a medical malpractice suit.

Beneficence and Nonmaleficence

Beneficence and nonmaleficence refer to the duties to protect the patient from harm and to provide treatment that promotes the good of the individual. Conflict occurs when a health care provider must do harm to a patient in order to provide benefit. A common example of this is performing surgery, which involves incising a patient's body in order to provide a benefit, such as removing a ruptured appendix.

Beneficence can at times lead to patient harm, such as in the case of paternalism and coercion. Paternalism is in effect when health care providers believe that they know what is in the patient's interests better than the patient does. It is rooted in beneficence and may be ethical, such as when a patient has an urgent need and is comatose. Unethical paternalism is when the health care provider uses some form of coercion to benefit a patient who does not regard the intended outcome as a benefit, or does not regard it as a great enough benefit to outweigh the suffering required.

Example 10.3: If a health care provider fails to obtain explicit consent or fails to provide the patient with adequate information on which to base consent, this represents coercion. Coercion may be an element in obtaining consent, particularly for experimental treatment.

Veracity

Veracity is the principle of telling the truth without deception. In general, it is believed that it is good for health care providers to tell the truth to their patients. There are situations where the principle of veracity conflicts with the principle of nonmaleficence.

Example 10.4: If a health care provider determines that telling a patient that he has cancer would result in the patient being harmed through psychological distress, then in keeping with consequence-based ethics, telling such a patient the truth would not be the right thing to do. Health care providers use consequence-based reasoning when deciding whether the benefits of a particular medical treatment outweigh the risks involved.

Justice

Justice is a principle of ethics that addresses the obligation to be fair to all persons. While there are several types of justice, including retributive (punishment) and procedural (the process of law), justice here is meant to be *distributive.* By this we mean that the distribution of a good, such as health care or legal assistance, will be performed as fairly as possible. Thus, good will not be distributed on the basis of race, sex, marital status, financial status, or even merit. The good of health care is distributed on the basis of need, which means that some people get more health care than others because their need is greater. Societal discourse related to the basic minimum health care that should be available to citizens in light of the burden to society is an example of an ethical dilemma related to justice.

Moral Authority of the Professions

A profession is an occupation that requires considerable training and specialized study. Professionals are generally called to their profession, and they hold a particular view or attitude toward the work in their domain. As individuals who experience a high level of dedication, they accept responsibility for the quality of their work. Through the social dimensions of their professions, they share their professional perspectives with peers in informal and formal settings. The formal setting of the professional organization offers the individual an opportunity to strengthen and enhance practice. It is the professional's dedication to practice that creates moral authority, a condition where society holds the professional in a position of high regard and accountable for professional practices.

There are three characteristics that distinguish the work of the professional from the work of the nonprofessional. The first of these characteristics is competence at a high level of expertise. A professional may not claim authority solely due to the ability to perform services. To claim the moral authority of a profession, the professional must demonstrate maximal competence, based on extensive education, experience, continued learning, and the mastery of principles distinct to that body of knowledge. A second characteristic of a profession is that it be of social value. Professionals claim to perform work that has significant value to the people within the society. Professional competence is linked to something that holds an important societal value, such as health, education, justice, or religion. Autonomy in their work is the third characteristic of professionals. The distinguishing feature between a profession and a craft, job, or other type of endeavor frequently hinges on the criterion of the practitioner's ability to control various aspects of the work, such as how the work is done, the goal of the endeavor, conditions of employment, and so forth. Professionals maintain their claim to autonomy through the development of specialized competence. In order to continue to claim professional autonomy, the professional has an obligation to pursue further training and education in the area of practice.

Nursing is a profession that involves caring for, treating, comforting, and protecting those who suffer. Nursing derives its moral worth from the nature of the work and the societal good that results from the work. As a profession, nursing has developed a code of ethics that holds nurses accountable for ethical decisions and behavior within nursing practice. The establishment of a code of ethics is an important method of defining the autonomous goals, distinct body of knowledge, and special competence in a profession that holds significant value in the society. The ANA Code of Ethics is the statement of such claims for nursing.

Legal nurse consulting is a subspecialty of nursing that derives much of its moral agency from knowledge of the ethical perspectives of the nursing profession. Because LNCs work within the framework of the legal system, they gain additional moral authority through an understanding and acceptance of legal professional ethics. The American Association of Legal Nurse Consultants (AALNC) code reflects ethical principles of the nursing and legal professions that pertain to the practice of legal nurse consulting. The AALNC Code of Ethics and Conduct with Interpretive Discussion may be found in Chapter 6, Appendix 6.1.

When individuals undertake professional practice, they make a commitment to uphold and support the values and obligations expressed in ethical codes. Accountability in individual practice is a hallmark of a professional and is the keystone of professional practice. Professionals are accountable for their practice, including the decisions and judgments they make regarding clients. The question then arises regarding how professionals can make responsible judgments in their practice, particularly in difficult cases, unusual circumstances, or emerging issues. The next section of the chapter provides more in-depth discussion of the AALNC Code of Ethics and Conduct.

The AALNC Code of Ethics: Application to Practice

Health care providers in clinical practice are commonly presented with ethical dilemmas involving clashes between trying to respect patient autonomy and their duty to provide a benefit to the patient. LNCs deal with the principle of justice as the underlying ethical foundations of their practice. The goal of a lawsuit is to discover the truth in a particular situation, and to arrive at a just and equitable solution. Legal cases often question the concept of justice in the form of a conflict between fairness to the individual and fairness to society. The AALNC Code guides LNC practice in a manner that is consistent with justice and its underlying ethical principles. An examination of the elements of the code reflects the values of the profession.

---

1. The legal nurse consultant does not discriminate against any person based on race, creed, color, age, sex, national origin, social status, or disability and does not let personal attitudes interfere with professional performance.

Whether LNCs work as independent contractors or as employees on behalf of plaintiffs or defendants, they have a duty to be fair and to support justice to all the clients involved in the case. Individual differences do not influence the LNC's professional performance and practice.

---

2. The legal nurse consultant performs as a consultant or an expert with the highest degree of integrity.

The principle of justice is served when a medical malpractice case is settled reasonably and fairly based on an objective and honest analysis by an LNC.[9] Justice is also served when people who have not been damaged by a company's product are prevented from collecting that to which they are not entitled. A primary responsibility of the LNC is to demonstrate professional integrity, moral soundness, and professional behavior by establishing an honest and forthright discussion of the facts of the case.

---

3. The legal nurse consultant uses informed judgment, objectivity, and individual competence as criteria when accepting assignments.

An ongoing dedication to maintaining excellence also supports the principle of justice. The LNC promotes excellence by providing high-quality expertise that does not mislead clients and harm their interests. An additional activity that supports excellence in practice is the regular attendance of continuing education programs, specific to legal nurse consulting and medicine, to keep up with advances in the professions.[10]

---

4. The legal nurse consultant maintains standards of conduct that reflect honorably upon the profession.

The moral authority of legal nurse consulting is based on an understanding that LNCs will abide by federal and state laws and practice with high ethical and legal standards that are free of personal interest or gain. In order to respect a client's autonomy, conflicts of interest that exist between the LNC's relationships with the client or the attorney must be revealed to the client. A *conflict of interest* refers to a situation where the legal nurse consultant has information that may potentially influence a case and cause harm, injury, or prejudice to the client. The information does not have to be privileged or include actual documented facts about the client. Once the client is notified, the client then retains the prerogative of staying with the firm/attorney or finding another one or the LNC withdraws from the case. It is a significant violation of both ethical and legal principles to fail to reveal a recognized conflict of interest. Even the appearance of a conflict of interest must be recognized and reported.

Conflicts of interest in the LNC's practice frequently result from personal or business relationships outside the legal environment or from legal matters at the LNC's former place of employment. They include situations such as the following:

- An LNC may change jobs and move from one firm that is handling a legal matter for a client to another firm that is handing the same matter on behalf of the opposition.
- The LNC may be related to or close friends with a party, client, or someone involved in a legal matter.
- An LNC may have knowledge of or relationships with others through business or other organizations that may lead to or be perceived as leading to a conflict of interest.
- An LNC expert witness may be asked to take a case from a plaintiff attorney who is suing another hospital in the same health care system that is employing the LNC.

An LNC must give serious consideration to issues of conflict of interest each time a new case comes in, particularly when an LNC moves from one firm to another. Once a conflict of interest has been identified, the LNC may continue to work in the firm, provided the client is informed of the conflict, the client consents to continued representation, and the firm creates an "ethical wall" around the LNC. In a particularly adversarial matter, the attorney may decide to obtain the opposing party's consent as well as the client's.

LNCs who are independent contractors are at greater risk for conflicts of interest than LNCs employed in attorneys' offices. The independent LNC must scrutinize each new case carefully for conflicts of interest before doing any substantive work on the case. Doing any work on a case that may represent a potential conflict of interest is unethical and may put the LNC at risk of legal action. The independent LNC must immediately report all potential or actual conflicts of interest to the referring attorney.

At times, attorneys ask LNCs or experts to work on a contingency fee basis. It is never appropriate for an LNC or expert to work on a contingency basis. Working on a contingency basis creates a conflict of interest that makes the process of rendering an objective opinion suspect. It is illegal for experts to work on a contingency basis in most states. Another billing practice that is unethical is not returning an unused portion of a retainer.

LNCs may find themselves in the position where they question the professional conduct of others. It is appropriate for the LNC to advise the proper authorities of any action that clearly demonstrates deceit, dishonesty, fraud, or misrepresentation by another LNC or by an expert witness. LNCs are required by their ethical code to maintain the highest standards of personal conduct that reflect honorably on the LNC and nursing professions.[11]

---

5. The legal nurse consultant provides professional services with objectivity.

Objectivity is the state of being free from bias, emotion, or prejudice that would influence decision-making. The LNC should strive to keep an objective frame of mind despite the presence of the "win at all costs" mentality that characterizes many legal situations. The desire to win can cloud the concept of justice and lead to outcomes that are unfair and unjust to the clients, the legal and medical systems, and society in general. While nurses are urged to become advocates for their clients, advocacy for any nurse, including the LNC, includes supporting the client's interests within the ethical boundaries of objectivity. Noonan describes the role of the LNC as "one who manages care interventions for clients in differing jurisdictions by bridging the paradigms of law and health care for the purposes of reducing conflict or producing change."[12] An LNC who advocates for his or her client must do so in a neutral manner that is fair to all those involved in the case. The role of the LNC is to give support to reasonable cases over unwarranted ones, even when the LNC works for an aggressive law firm.

LNCs who work as expert witnesses must be objective, honest, and fair in their reports and opinions. On occasion, LNCs will find themselves in a position where they must resist pressure from others working on the case who advocate changing or modifying opinions. If the expert reviews the case and has a helpful opinion, the expert may be retained to do further work on the case. The point of a lawsuit is to discover truth and redress injustice. These goals are met when the LNC gives honest and unbiased opinions that are consistent with the ethical standards of the profession. LNCs who hire and retain experts must also be scrupulous in their efforts to allow for honest differences of opinion and to retain experts who demonstrate appropriate ethical standards.

6. The legal nurse consultant protects client privacy and confidentiality.

Confidentiality refers to keeping private all information provided by the client or acquired from sources before, during, and after the course of the professional relationship.[13] In the LNC's practice, this includes information from or about the client obtained through the review of medical records.[14] Confidentiality requires that an LNC not use privileged information either to the advantage of the LNC or to the disadvantage of the client. Further, the principle of confidentiality also requires that an LNC not engage in any unnecessary or indiscreet communications concerning clients.

Example 10.5: A communication in the health care environment is the "elevator consult" that occurs frequently and repeatedly in hospitals in violation of the patient's confidentiality.[15] An LNC may not disclose any information regarding a client to anyone who is not directly involved in the evaluation of the case.

In the interest of maintaining confidentiality, LNCs operate within the legal guidelines of discovery. Medical summaries by LNCs are made available only to the attorney or firm that contracts with the LNC. While medical summaries by expert witnesses are produced for the court and reviewed by opposing counsel, medical summaries by LNCs who do not serve as expert witnesses are generally treated as a work product of the contracting attorney. As such, these medical summaries are considered part of the body of documents protected by attorney work product guidelines if they are handled in a manner that is consistent with such documents. Should an attorney share a medical summary with an expert witness, health care provider, or opposing counsel, the medical summary is not subject to the protections of attorney work product provisions. In one such case, the medical summary of an LNC was produced for opposing counsel and opposing counsel subpoenaed the LNC to testify.[16] The LNC was successful in obtaining a protective order from the court, partly based on the fact that the LNC had been placed in an "ethically precarious" position that was not justified. This case demonstrates confusion in the legal system regarding the discovery of work product produced by LNCs, particularly LNCs who do not act as expert witnesses in a case.

7. The legal nurse consultant is accountable for responsibilities accepted and actions performed.

Society holds a profession in a position of high regard when it has demonstrated accountability for professional practices. It is the responsibility of each LNC to be personally accountable for the practice.

---

8. The legal nurse consultant maintains professional nursing competence.

The development of specialized competence is the hallmark of LNC practice. This competence, although specialized, is rooted in nursing practice and requires the LNC to maintain an active nursing license and a current understanding of nursing practice.

Identifying and Handling Ethical Dilemmas in Legal Nurse Consulting

Ethical dilemmas in the profession of legal nurse consulting arise in the form of differences of opinion regarding the conduct of a case, such as performing the intake, review, billing, or opinion, and in matters such as working with or as an expert. The LNC can identify an ethical dilemma by the sense of unease or discomfort that the LNC experiences when dealing with the case or client. At such times, the LNC can gain insight into the ethical dilemmas associated with the case by reviewing the goals that are being addressed, and whether the goals are in keeping with LNC ethical directives. A review of the ANA Code of Ethics for Nurses and the AALNC code may be helpful in shedding light on the source of the LNC's moral discomfort. Additional help can be found in reviewing the codes for ethical behavior of related professions, such as the legal, paralegal, and business codes. Other sources for ethical problem-solving include discussing the issue, in confidence, with another LNC, or with a representative of the State Board of Nursing or State Bar.

As health professionals who work within the domains of health care and law, LNCs frequently deal with ethical issues. Sometimes the right ethical decision is clearly indicated after a simple review of the applicable codes, but more often than not, the process requires additional thought and consideration. LNCs benefit from the use of a systematic process for ethical decision-making that accounts for personal bias and the perspectives of others. The use of such a system gives the LNC an opportunity to define and explore ethical considerations in a manner that is consistent with ethical practice. A framework for a systematic analysis of ethical issues in the practice of legal nurse consulting is presented and summarized below. Gretchen Aumman[17] originally proposed the model in the first edition of *Legal Nurse Consulting: Principles and Practice*:

1. *Collect data and formulate a problem statement.* The LNC collects and reviews information relevant to the case or problem. From this collection of data, the LNC formulates a problem statement with a specific description of the ethical dilemma.
2. *Identify personal bias.* The LNC asks, "Whom do I most identify with in the situation?" The answer to the question gives the LNC insight into

personal bias. Once that sympathy is elucidated, the LNC is in the position to address whether or not the personal or professional biases involved hold undue sway over the situation or those involved.

3. *Define different points of view.* The LNC identifies all other points of view relevant to the problem. In this way, the LNC gathers information on different ethical perspectives pertinent to the case. The LNC may choose to obtain additional points of view from discreet consultation with appropriate individuals, such as legal, medical, or nursing personnel.

4. *Analyze ethical issues.* The LNC should evaluate all the issues in light of the ethical principles, rules of ethics, and codes of ethical behavior applicable to the case. The analysis is enhanced when conducted with the help of others, such as other LNCs or legal professionals. Input from other individuals familiar with legal issues is another way to reduce the influence of personal bias. All discussions are undertaken with gravity and in confidence.

5. *Decide and act.* In consultation with appropriate individuals, the LNC makes a decision regarding the appropriate actions. The LNC then acts on the decision in a manner that is consistent with ethical standards and authority.

LNCs support the principle of justice through the anticipation, thoughtful consideration, and implementation of solutions to resolve ethical dilemmas. This proactive approach requires LNCs to develop an ongoing familiarity with prevailing ethical principles in health care and law. When faced with an ethical dilemma, LNCs use a systematic method to reflect on the issues, identify bias, and make appropriate decisions that are consistent with the concept of justice. As professionals with experience in the health care and legal professions, LNCs are in a unique position to work toward issues of health care justice. The development of an awareness of and adherence to sound ethical principles enhance the LNC's ability to address these issues with a high level of professional integrity. Such work produces benefit to all parties, patients, health care providers, and in the long term, society as a whole.

References

1. Reich, W.T., Ed., *Encyclopedia of Bioethics*, Macmillan, New York, 1978.
2. Arras, J. and Rhoden, N., Eds., *Ethical Issues in Modern Medicine*, 3rd ed., Mayfield Publishing, Palo Alto, CA, 1990.
3. Macklin, R., Moral concerns and appeals to rights and duties, *Hastings Center Report*, 6, 31–38, 1976.
4. Beecher, H.J., Ethics and clinical research, *New England Journal of Medicine*, 274(24), 1354–1360, 1966.
5. Englehardt, H.T., Bioethics in pluralist societies, *Perspectives in Biology and Medicine*, 26(1), 65–78, 1982.
6. Bursztain, H.J. et al., The technological target: involving the patient in clinical choices, in *The Machine at the Bedside: Strategies for Using Technology in Patient Care*, Reiser, S.J. and Anabar, M., Eds., Cambridge University Press, New York, 1984, 177–191.
7. Katz, J., Respecting autonomy: the struggle over rights and capacities, in *The Silent World of Doctor and Patient*, Macmillan, New York, 1984.

8. Ramsey, P., The nature of medical ethics, in *The Teaching of Medical Ethics*, Veatch, R., Ed., The Hastings Center, Hastings-on-Hudson, NY, 1973, 123–129.
9. Hussey, T., Nursing ethics and codes of professional conduct, *Nursing Ethics*, 3(3), 250–258, 1996.
10. Aiken, T.D., What nurses need to know about legal, ethical, and political issues, *Revolution*, 4(2), 72–75, 1994.
11. Fiesta, J., Failing to act like a professional, *Nursing Management*, 25(7), 15–17, 1994.
12. Noonan, R., Enhancing our practice: a conceptual framework as a theoretical foundation for legal nurse consulting, *The Journal of Legal Nurse Consulting*, 11(2), 3–12, 2000.
13. Thomas, B., Duty of confidence, *Nursing Times*, 92(39), 53, 1996.
14. Simpson, R.L., Ethics and privacy in a technologically driven health care network, *Nursing Administration Quarterly*, 21(1), 81–84, 1996.
15. Warr, T., Breaking patient confidentiality, *Nursing N.Z.*, 2(8), 12, 1996.
16. Santos, C.P., Does the legal system recognize legal nurse consultants' standards of practice?, *The Journal of Legal Nurse Consulting*, 11(4), 1–11, 17, 2000.
17. Aumman, G., Ethics and the legal nurse consultant, in *Legal Nurse Consulting: Principles and Practice*, Bogart, J.B., Ed., CRC Press, Boca Raton, FL, 1998, 175–194.

Additional Reading

Aiken, T.D. and Catalano, J.T., *Legal Ethical and Political Issues in Nursing*, F.A. Davis, Philadelphia, 1994.
American Association of Legal Nurse Consultants, *Code of Ethics and Conduct*, Glenview, IL, 1995.
American Association of Legal Nurse Consultants, *Scope of Practice for the Legal Nurse Consultant*, Glenview, IL, 1995.
American Association of Legal Nurse Consultants, *Standards of Legal Nurse Consulting Practice*, Glenview, IL, 1995.
American College of Healthcare Executives, *Code of Ethics*, Chicago, IL, 1993.
American Nurses Association, *Code of Ethics for Nurses with Interpretive Statements*, American Nurses Publishing, Washington, D.C., 2001.
American Nurses Association, *Guidelines on Reporting Incompetent, Unethical, or Illegal Practices*, American Nurses Publishing, Washington, D.C., 1994.
Badaracco, J.L. and Webb, A., Business ethics: a view from the trenches, *California Management Review*, 37, 8–21, 1995.
Beauchamp, T.L. and Cuildress, J.F., *Principles of Biomedical Ethics*, Oxford University Press, New York, 1994.
Brody, H., The physician patient relationship, in *Medical Ethics*, Veatch, R.M., Ed., Jones & Bartlett, Boston, 1989, 75–79.
Brown, M.T., *Working Ethics*, Jossey-Bass, San Francisco, 1990.
Curtain, L.L., The nurse as advocate: a philosophical foundation for nursing, *Advances in Nursing Science*, 1(3), 1–10, 1979.
Davis, A.J. et al., *Ethical Dilemmas and Nursing Practice*, Appleton & Lange, Stamford, CT, 1997.
Garrett, T.M., Baillic, II.W., and Garrett, R.M., *Health Care Ethics: Principles and Problems*, 3rd ed., Prentice-Hall, Upper Saddle River, NJ, 1998.
Grover, S.L., Lying, deceit, and subterfuge: a model of dishonesty in the workplace, *Organizational Science*, 4(3), 478–495, 1993.
Hall, J., *Nursing Ethics and Law*, W.B. Saunders, Philadelphia, 1996.

Joint Commission on Accreditation of Healthcare Organizations, Patient rights and organizational ethics, in *Comprehensive Accreditation Manual for Hospitals: The Official Handbook*, Oakbrook Terrace, IL, 1997.

Kolhnke, M.F., The nurse as advocate, *American Journal of Nursing*, 80, 2038–2040, 1980.

Mill, J.S., *Utilitarianism*, Hackett, Indianapolis, IN, 1979 (originally published in 1861).

Murphy, J.G., *Kant: The Philosophy of Right*, Macmillan, London, 1970.

Rawls, J., *A Theory of Justice*, The Belknap Press of Harvard University Press, Cambridge, MA, 1971.

Rest, J.R., *Moral Development: Advances in Research and Theory*, Praeger, New York, 1986.

Silva, M.C., *Ethical Decision Making in Nursing Administration*, Appleton & Lange, Norwalk, CT, 1997.

Smart, J.J.C., *An Outline of a System of Utilitarian Ethics*, The University Press, Cambridge, MA, 1961.

Weston, A., *A Practical Companion to Ethics*, Oxford University Press, New York, 1997.

Wetlaufer, S., A question of character, *Harvard Business Review*, 77(5), 30–34, 37–38, 40–43, 1999.

Worthley, J.A., *The Ethics of the Ordinary in Healthcare: Concepts and Cases*, Health Administration Press, Chicago, IL, 1997.

Test Questions

1. Ethical theories serve several purposes. Which of the following is NOT a purpose of ethical theory?
   A. Provide a general overview of the concept held by the theory.
   B. Delineate individual rights held within the ethical framework.
   C. Set the ordering priorities of elements within the framework.
   D. Address the strengths and weaknesses of the ethical framework.

2. Of the following individuals, which one contributed most to the development of the theory of utilitarianism?
   A. John Stuart Mill
   B. Socrates
   C. Immanuel Kant
   D. Justice Earl Warren

3. Which of the following criticisms is NOT a common criticism of Kantian theory?
   A. It offers no method to resolve conflicts of duty.
   B. Calculating overall good is difficult to do.
   C. No ethical rule holds in all situations.
   D. There is no provision for beings who are not rational.

4. Self-determination is closely related to which of the following ethical principles?
   A. Confidentiality
   B. Justice
   C. Autonomy
   D. Objectivity

5. Which one of the following situations is LEAST likely to represent a conflict of interest for the LNC?
   A. The LNC has recently changed jobs and is now working for an attorney who has asked her to evaluate a case on behalf of the defendant. The LNC had previously evaluated the same case on behalf of the plaintiff.
   B. An independent LNC is asked to evaluate a case on behalf of the plaintiff. The LNC is a close friend of the plaintiff's mother.
   C. The LNC has read an extensive newspaper account that was critical of the plaintiff in a high-profile case. An attorney asks the LNC to evaluate the case on behalf of the plaintiff.
   D. The LNC is asked to serve as an expert on behalf of the defendant. The LNC is married to the attorney who is handling the case for the opposing firm.

Answers: 1. D, 2. A, 3. B, 4. C, 5. C

Appendix 10.1
American Nurses Association: Code of Ethics for Nurses

1. The nurse, in all professional relationships, practices with compassion and respect for the inherent dignity, worth, and uniqueness of every individual, unrestricted by considerations of social or economic status, personal attributes, or the nature of health problems.
2. The nurse's primary commitment is to the patient, whether an individual, family, group, or community.
3. The nurse promotes, advocates for, and strives to protect the health, safety, and rights of the patient.
4. The nurse is responsible and accountable for individual nursing practice and determines the appropriate delegation of tasks consistent with the nurse's obligation to provide optimum patient care.
5. The nurse owes the same duties to self as to others, including the responsibility to preserve integrity and safety, to maintain competence, and to continue personal and professional growth.
6. The nurse participates in establishing, maintaining, and improving health care environments and conditions of employment conducive to the provision of quality health care and consistent with the values of the profession through individual and collective action.
7. The nurse participates in the advancement of the profession through contributions to practice, education, administration, and knowledge development.
8. The nurse collaborates with other health professionals and the public in promoting community, national, and international efforts to meet health needs.
9. The profession of nursing, as represented by associations and their members, is responsible for articulating nursing values, for maintaining the integrity of the profession and its practice, and for shaping social policy.

Source: Reprinted from American Nurses Association, *Code of Ethics for Nurses with Interpretive Statements*, American Nurses Publishing, American Nurses Foundation/American Nurses Association, Washington, D.C., 2001. With permission.

Chapter 11

Nursing Theory: Applications to Legal Nurse Consulting

Regina Noonan, MSN, RN, LNCC

CONTENTS

Objectives

- To introduce the idea of a theoretical foundation for the practice of legal nurse consulting
- To differentiate the legal nurse consultant between the paralegal and legal assistant

- To explore advocacy as a component of legal nurse consulting practice
- To propose cross-jurisdictional advocacy as a foundation for legal nurse consulting practice
- To identify the attributes of a cross-jurisdictional advocate
- To exemplify legal nurse consulting cases in which cross-jurisdictional advocacy is utilized
- To encourage legal nurse consultants to practice within theoretical and conceptual frameworks to strengthen legal nurse consulting as a specialty nursing practice

Introduction

Legal nurse consulting continues to gain professional recognition in both the health care and legal environments. To further enhance the profession and maintain an alliance to the nursing profession, a conceptual framework has been proposed as a foundation for theory development. The conceptual framework is the author's viewpoint, and serves only as an introduction of one potential theoretical foundation for further theory development. The legal nurse consulting profession will benefit from theory development as it further distinguishes the specialty as a nursing domain and differentiates the practice from other roles in the legal environment. The chapter's purpose is to introduce the idea of nursing theory and the applications to legal nurse consulting practice.

Thoughts on Theory Development

Legal nurse consultants (LNCs) absorbed in the rigorous, daily tasks of legal nurse consulting might wonder why concepts and theory are necessary in legal nurse consulting, or how these could enhance their daily practice. After all, isn't theory development more appropriately a concern for university nursing professors? The answer to this would be "no." Theory development is not just for university nursing professors. A conceptual and theoretical model for practice is the foundation of all professions. Theory development would enhance legal nurse consulting practice, and establish legal nurse consulting as a specialty, grounded in both the nursing profession and the legal environment. This would differentiate LNCs from paralegals and legal assistants, who also work in the legal consulting domain.

LNCs are "doers and thinkers," and a conceptual framework as a theoretical foundation would provide guidance and direction to thought and a means to move away from a task and functional orientation. Meleis defined "functional orientation" as the "act of performing procedures rather than thinking, reflecting, and solving problems."[1] If LNCs were to continue to practice without a conceptual or theoretical framework, they would compromise the profession to a functional orientation and risk "intellectual subordination."[1] Just as early nursing education used the apprenticeship model of learning that led to practicing under the medical model, an apprenticeship model of legal nurse consulting could lead to practice in a paralegal model. A theoretical foundation for legal nurse consulting practice would strengthen the position statement of the American Association of Legal

Nurse Consultants (AALNC) on the Role of the Legal Nurse Consultant as Distinct from the Role of the Paralegal and Legal Assistant.[2]

Legal Nurse Consulting as a Specialty Nursing Practice

The individuals who helped to define the role of legal nurse consulting were the AALNC founding members, LNCs practicing in the 1970s and 1980s, and legal nurse consulting educators and independent entrepreneurs. These individuals combined clinical (experiential) expertise with forward vision to answer questions, such as "What are nursing (legal nurse consulting) goals?" and "What ought to be the aims of nursing (legal nurse consulting)?" Today, these answers represent our legal nurse consulting perspective.

From this perspective, legal nurse consulting domains were identified. These domains have been referred to by LNCs as practice environments[3] and practice areas.[4] Practice environments include law firms, insurance companies, managed care organizations, risk management departments, state and government agencies, and independent legal nurse consulting practices. Practice areas include medical malpractice, personal injury, product liability, toxic tort, workers' compensation, criminal law, employment law, administrative law, elder law, and health policy.

LNCs developed a core curriculum,[5] a policy statement on education and certification,[6] and have been recognized as representatives of a specialty practice of nursing by the American Board of Nursing Specialties (ABNS). Although not involved in direct patient care, legal nurse consulting is felt to have its nursing roots, from a caring perspective, in a broader application — the defense of the standard of care.[7] Defending the standard of care provides the framework for advocating for patients, clients, and health care systems.

An Advocacy Model

For the author's theory, an advocacy model was chosen as the legal nurse consulting conceptual framework. This was done as advocacy has historical significance to nursing. Advocacy is at the foundation of nursing and can be traced to Florence Nightingale. Since Nightingale's time, advocacy has been explained in different ways, including human advocacy,[8] models of existential advocacy,[9] self-advocacy models,[10] sociopolitical, moral, and ethical advocates,[11] legal advocates,[11-14] and Jezewski's[15,16] advocacy model of "culture broker."

As the domains of nurse advocacy evolved, the expectation for one nurse's ability to respond to all of these domains created a sense of being overwhelmed. Legal nurse consulting evolved to alleviate some of these anxieties. The legal, ethical, and political domains of nursing advocacy are legal nurse consulting paradigms. LNCs are nurses capable of advocacy from both legal and nursing advocacy perspectives.

A nursing advocacy theory as a foundation for legal nurse consulting practice would be consistent with both nursing and legal nurse consulting caring perspectives. The use of such a model to guide legal nurse consulting practice would constitute an advanced nursing methodology. Without guiding principles from conceptual and theoretical models, just as physician/patient and attorney/client

Figure 11.1   Process of Concept Derivation (From Walker, L.O. and Avant, K.C., *Strategies for Theory Construction in Nursing*, Prentice-Hall, Upper Saddle River, NJ, 1995. With permission.)

advocacy can be paternalistic, nursing advocacy, including legal nurse consulting advocacy, can be paternalistic. The nursing advocacy theory model most applicable to legal nurse consulting is Jezewski's advocacy model of "culture brokering,"[15,16] which is described below.

Theory Development

In this chapter, the concept of "cross-jurisdictional advocacy"[17] will be developed using Walker and Avant's[18] methods of concept derivation and concept analysis. Concept analysis is the method for examining attributes and characteristics of a concept as a foundation for theory development. Jezewski's culture brokering will be the nursing model through which cross-jurisdictional advocacy will be derived.

The terms "conceptual framework," "nursing model," and "theory" have been used interchangeably in nursing.[1,18] They are all conceptualizations of nursing reality. They are mental images of phenomena that help identify how experiences are similar by categorizing likeness. They define a specialty's body of knowledge, organize and integrate the knowledge, provide guidelines for practice, assist in decision-making, and justify a discipline to the public. In this chapter, cross-jurisdictional advocacy will be referred to as a conceptual model and framework, and a proposed theory — a middle range theory. Middle range theories differ from the grand theories of Rogers, Roy, Orem, et al. Middle range theories are more specific. They have the conceptual focus and mental image that reflect a discipline's values, but they are aimed at an aspect of reality that is more limited than grand theory, but not as concrete as practice theory.[1,19] Culture brokering has been identified in the nursing literature as a middle range theory.[19] Cross-jurisdictional advocacy is a proposed middle range theory that has been generated from the middle range theory of culture brokering.

Concept Derivation

Concept derivation is a process in which a previously defined concept from a parent field is transposed to a new field, then redefined as a new concept in the new field (see Figure 11.1). Concept derivation can occur only when there is meaningful analogy between two phenomena. Concept derivation is useful in that the established concept can give initial meaning to a new concept. The four-step process of concept derivation includes:

Figure 11.2 The Application of Concept Derivation for Cross-Jurisdictional Advocacy in Legal Nurse Consulting

1. Becoming familiar with the literature on one's topic (advocacy)
2. Searching other fields (legal nurse consulting) for new ways to look at the concept
3. Selecting a parent concept to use in the derivation process (culture brokering)
4. Redefining the new concept (cross-jurisdictional advocacy) in the new field[19]

Jezewski's[15,16,20,21] advocacy model of culture brokering in the field of nursing was transposed and redefined to the conceptual model of cross-jurisdictional advocacy in the field of legal nurse consulting (see Figure 11.2). Jezewski defined "culture brokering" as "the act of bridging, linking, or mediating between groups or persons of differing cultural backgrounds for the purpose of reducing conflict or producing change,"[16] and included constituents of networking, negotiation, mediation, intervention, innovation, and support.

As shown in Figure 11.3, Jezewski identified critical attributes reflecting her theoretical definition of culture brokering. Conflict in interaction was the antecedent to culture brokering, and conflict resolution was the primary consequence. These critical attributes, antecedents, and consequences are congruous with legal nurse consulting practice. The critical attributes of legal nurse consulting practice are not meant to be the list of functional tasks that LNCs perform.

The LNC's role involves bridging the differing cultures of the legal and health care world. The LNC assumes this role when there is conflict, which is generally litigious, and there is the need for resolution. The LNC acts as the go-between,

1. Intervening in conflict situations
2. Standing guard in critical junctures of interactions
3. Possessing role ambiguity
4. Functioning marginally in one or more systems
5. Encouraging potential for changing systems
6. Cultivating varied social relationships
7. Mediating between traditions
8. Innovating when traditions are inflexible
9. Facilitating communication by translation
10. Bridging value systems
11. Functioning as the go-between
12. Bringing people together through networking

Figure 11.3 Jezewski's[16] Defining Attributes of Culture Brokers

1. Intervening in conflict situations
2. Possessing role ambiguity
3. Functioning marginally in one or more systems
4. Functioning as a go-between
5. Bridging value systems
6. Mediating between traditions
7. Innovating when traditions are inflexible
8. Facilitating communication by translation
9. Educating members of differing jurisdictions to each other's paradigms
10. Strategizing to integrate health care and legal knowledge for case development
11. Bringing people together through networking
12. Encouraging activism as change agents

Figure 11.4   Defining Attributes of Cross-Jurisdictional Advocates

facilitating communication by translating terminology and cultural values, and bridging these value systems by facilitating client education in both systems. The LNC's specialized body of knowledge, not always familiar to health care and legal practitioners, can create role ambiguity. This ambiguity, although not ambiguous to the LNC, facilitates functioning marginally in both systems. Functioning marginally is a critical attribute of the LNC. Marginalization enables the LNC to be on the periphery of the different jurisdictions, yet have the power, knowledge, and resources to comfortably go back and forth across the boundaries and be effective at functioning at the core of the conflict. LNCs are advocates as they are facilitators, mediators, negotiators, liaisons, innovators, and change agents.

As shown in Figure 11.4, the defining attributes of cross-jurisdictional advocacy correspond with those of Jezewski's model of culture brokering. Education and case development are critical roles of the LNC. Additional defining attributes of the cross-jurisdictional advocate include educating members of differing jurisdictions to one another's paradigms and strategizing to integrate health care and legal knowledge for case development.

Concept Analysis

The concept of cross-jurisdictional advocacy was further developed with guidance from Walker and Avant's[18] method of concept analysis. The concept analysis involved:

- Selecting a concept
- Determining the aims or purposes of the analysis
- Identifying all uses of the concept
- Determining the defining attributes
- Constructing model cases

Concept derivation provided the foundation for the concept analysis. The term "cross-jurisdictional advocacy" did not appear in database searches of Cumulative Index for Nursing and Allied Health Literature (CINAHL), PsychINFO or LegalTrac major law reviews, or specialty and bar association journals. The term was initially identified on a Children's Center for Child Protection brochure, "Cross-Jurisdictional Child Advocacy," in the offices of the San Diego District Attorney's Family Protection Division.[22] According to Bellucco, victim support specialist for the San Diego City Attorney's office, the term was coined for a grant that supported a multidisciplinary advocacy program that was no longer in existence.[23] Cross-jurisdictional advocacy in legal nurse consulting integrates aspects of culture brokering, nursing, and nonlawyer legal advocacy.[24] LNCs interact in health care and legal jurisdictions both prior to and during involvement in court systems.

A theoretical definition of a cross-jurisdictional advocate is one who manages interventions for clients in differing jurisdictions by bridging the paradigms of law and health care for the purpose of reducing conflict or producing change. The concept of cross-jurisdictional advocacy will be developed further as exemplified in model cases. The constructed cases will operationalize cross-jurisdictional advocacy roles of LNCs in tort law (both plaintiff and defense), risk management, criminal justice, forensic nurse specialty, and government agency domains. A model case is an example of the concept that includes all the defining attributes of cross-jurisdictional advocacy.

Model Cases

Model Case 11.1: The LNC in Medical Malpractice Defense and Risk Management

The following is a case in which the LNC worked for the defense. The complaint alleged a failure to diagnose breast cancer. The LNC reviewed plaintiff's complaint and discovery responses having prerequisite knowledge that failure and delays in diagnosis of breast cancer are one of the leading causes of medical malpractice complaints.[25,26] The medical records were reviewed.

A 44-year-old female presented to her regular gynecologist (OB/GYN) with a lump in the breast. The OB/GYN palpated the lump. Axillary lymph nodes were negative. The gynecologist decided it was fibrocystic breast disease (FBD) and discharged the patient for follow-up in 1 year. The woman presented 2 years later. On examination the lump was larger. The gynecologist referred her for a screening mammogram. The screening mammogram was indeterminate. The diagnosis was FBD. Reassurance was provided, and she was discharged with instructions for follow-up in 6 months. In 6 months, the lump was larger and the axillary nodes were positive. A biopsy confirmed cancer. The diagnosis was T3, N2, M0, Stage IIIa malignant neoplasm of the breast.

Although the patient was noncompliant with the instruction to return in 1 year, the defense of contributory negligence was not a strong one, as there was negligence prior to this time. The LNC was hired by the defense. As there were limited defenses, this was difficult. The LNC's advocacy was as "truth-teller." The case was evaluated to determine whether there were duty, breach of duty, proximate cause, and damages. Duty was established because the OB/GYN was the patient's practitioner for 5 years. The breach of duty was the initial lack of referral for additional evaluation on palpation of the mass. The physician only rescheduled routine screening mammography although the appropriate standard was for diagnostic mammography or surgical evaluation.[27–30] The breach of duty was the proximate cause of the damages. The delay in diagnosis led to significant damages as the eventual diagnosis was metastatic cancer. The LNC had the case reviewed by an OB/GYN expert, who concurred that there was negligence. The case was settled.

The advocacy for the defendant was the recognition of the negligence and early settlement. The legal nurse consulting advocacy was consistent with cross-jurisdictional advocacy. There was conflict and resolution of conflict through case settlement. The LNC mediated between the legal and health care paradigms, strategized to integrate health care and legal knowledge for case development, educated the members of the legal jurisdiction (defendant and plaintiff attorney, and insurance carrier) to health care standards of care, and educated the health care jurisdiction (defendants and risk manager) to the legal framework of negligence.

In this particular case, the LNC provided additional advocacy for the defense as she pursued risk management research for the managed service organization (MSO), an additional defendant in the case. The short-term advocacy was for the defense. The long-term advocacy was for all clients, as the goals were for prevention of delays in diagnosis of breast cancer. A data collection tool was developed. Quantitative research by retrospective chart review was conducted. Newly diagnosed women with Stage III or higher breast cancer were identified. Their medical records were reviewed for adherence to breast cancer standards of care. The findings were presented to the MSO's health care practitioner population through the quality improvement department. The MSO's policies, procedures, and practice guidelines were revised. The LNC and the defense attorney presented an educational program to the health care providers. This extended advocacy illustrates additional advocacy opportunities for LNCs and risk managers.

LNCs may not be involved in risk management research or processes, but they can be advocates when reviewing and recommending revisions to defendants' policies and procedures during case development, and by offering educational programs on medical-legal issues. These interventions provide direct advocacy to defendants and indirect advocacy to potential plaintiffs and patient populations at large. Research has indicated that medical errors kill 44,000 to 98,000 people a year in the United States, exceeding the number of people who die annually from motor highway accidents, breast cancer, and AIDS.[31] Prevention of errors is a strong element of advocacy.

Model case 11.1 might have turned out differently if the defense attorney had utilized a legal assistant or paralegal, and not an LNC. The legal assistant or paralegal, without health care knowledge, may not have known the standards of breast health care, and not recognized the breach of duty. There would have been no cross-jurisdictional advocacy. There would also not have been any strategizing or integration of health care and legal knowledge for case development or education to the differing jurisdictions. The case would likely have progressed further through the discovery process with settlement discussions delayed until after depositions and after medical standard of care and causation expert reviews. This would not be advocacy for the plaintiff or defendant parties involved as the litigation process is time-consuming, adversarial, and stressful. In addition, the delay in resolution of conflict would not have been cost-effective.

Model Case 11.2: The LNC in Plaintiff Nursing Home Litigation

This is an example of a case in which an LNC worked for a plaintiff's attorney on a potential nursing home case. The family of the nursing home resident presented to the attorney with allegations of negligent care and treatment and elder abuse. The resident's family alleged that there had been negligent supervision during feedings, causing aspiration and subsequent death. The LNC screened the case for merit, as the allegations were typical of the injuries associated with negligence in nursing home cases.[32,33] A review of the nursing home records indicated that not only was there supportive documentation of negligent monitoring of the resident during feedings, but there were previous incidents of choking and observed swallowing deficits, without referral for speech therapy evaluation. In addition, there was documentation of significant weight loss and advanced pressure ulcers, which are additional injuries typical of nursing home negligence.[32,33] These findings were analyzed within the context of the federal Omnibus Budget Reconciliation Act (OBRA) regulations[34] and the California Code of Regulations[35] and confirmed as negligent.

There were problems with legal advocacy in this case. The last incident of alleged aspiration was actually diagnosed by the staff as suspect of a cerebral vascular accident (CVA). The resident was transferred to the emergency room (ER) of a nearby hospital where she died. A review of the ER records and death certificate documented the cause of death as CVA. This was confirmed on CT scan images of the brain. The negligent care and treatment received in the skilled nursing facility was not the proximate cause of the death. A lawsuit was not filed.

The LNC was unable to provide advocacy for the client for litigation, but was able to resolve conflict through cross-jurisdictional advocacy. As there was documentation of negligent care and treatment at the nursing home, the LNC referred the family to the Department of Health and Human Services (DHHS) and California Advocates for Nursing Home Reform (CANHR). DHHS conducts complaint site inspections regardless of whether the complainant is deceased. CANHR maintains a file of reported complaints on all skilled nursing facilities and resident care facilities for the elderly. These referrals, made by the LNC, provided advocacy for current residents of the nursing home as well as potential consumers, as both DHHS and CANHR records are available for public inspection.

Model case 11.2 would not have been a model case if an LNC were not involved in screening the case. Without the assistance of an LNC's health care knowledge, the plaintiff's legal assistant or paralegal would have recommended that the case proceed, or the attorney would have accepted the case and filed the complaint, based on the evidence of documentation of nursing home negligence. The records from the hospital ER may not have been retrieved and reviewed until after the case was in discovery.

Model Case 11.3: The LNC in Child Abuse Criminal Law

In this case, the LNC worked with a deputy district attorney (DDA) in the prosecution of a child abuse case. A 6-month-old baby boy was transferred to the hospital after sustaining traumatic head injury, bodily bruises, and fractures to numerous ribs. The district attorney's office received the complaint because the injuries were life-threatening and the father of the baby was thought to have inflicted the injuries. The LNC developed a document, "Severity Indicators," in which she educated the DDA about the extent of the injuries, including those that were residual damages. The defendant pleaded not guilty. The defense reported that the baby had been born premature with congenital heart disease. The defense claimed that the bodily bruises were from taking Inderal, which the baby was prescribed at birth, and that the fractured ribs had resulted from the defendant attempting to perform cardiopulmonary resuscitation (CPR). The defendant claimed that he was not knowledgeable about CPR and performed the procedure incorrectly, using two hands instead of two fingers, and therefore inflicting unintentional injury.

The LNC reviewed the child's birth records. The child had been born premature, which required a long stay in the neonatal intensive care unit (NICU). Prior to discharge, the parents received CPR education. The medical records documented that a CPR video was watched, that CPR instruction was given, and that there was return demonstration by the parents. The baby was 1 month of age at the time the CPR instruction was given, only 5 months prior to the assault.

In addition, a review of the medical research revealed that the injuries claimed as resulting from improper CPR technique were not consistent with the medical literature.[36–38] The research indicates that iatrogenic infant rib fractures from CPR are of low likelihood secondary to resistance to fractures from the elasticity of the normal infant's rib cage. In addition, the location of the baby's fractures did not fit the usual profile of CPR fractures. Anterior-posterior compression of CPR can result in lateral and bilateral rib fractures, whereas abusive injuries are typically unilateral and posterior. In this case, the child's fractures were at differing stages of healing, indicating multiple episodes of abuse.

The LNC retrieved and reviewed pediatric office and pharmacy records. The pediatric records showed that the Inderal had been discontinued at 4 months of age. A subsequent complete blood count indicated a normal platelet level. The pharmacy records showed that the amount of Inderal that was last dispensed would have been utilized by the time of the 4-month examination.

The defendant was found guilty at trial. The mother and child refused referral to the district attorney's on-site California Victim/Witness Assistance Program and were lost to follow-up. The LNC in this case functioned as a cross-jurisdictional advocate. The LNC functioned as the go-between, bridged systems, facilitated communication through translation, educated the members of the legal and health care jurisdictions to one another's paradigms, networked with experts, strategized to integrate health care and legal knowledge for case development, expanded traditional nursing domains into the judicial system, and shared this experience by publishing an article in a professional nursing journal.[17] Writing and publishing articles is an additional vehicle for legal nurse consulting advocacy. It shares knowledge with a number of practicing LNCs, who then utilize this knowledge to advocate on a variety of different levels for a variety of different clients.

Model case 11.3 could be considered not to be a model case because all the critical attributes of cross-jurisdictional advocacy were not exemplified for all the parties involved. There was conflict in advocacy because the child's mother did not want the father prosecuted. Thus, the mother of the child and the child were not networked into the district attorney's office Victim/Witness Advocacy Program.[39] The LNC was able to provide tertiary cross-jurisdictional advocacy in the criminal justice jurisdiction for the people of the state by assisting in the prosecution of the defendant; however, the LNC was unable to provide secondary cross-jurisdictional advocacy interventions for the mother and child as the referral for victim's advocacy services was rejected. There was no assurance that the hospital's nursing, social service, or discharge departments had provided adequate advocacy or home health referral follow-up.

In addition, by providing advocacy interventions for the people of the state and because the mother did not want her husband prosecuted, some may feel that there were moral conflicts. In this case, this LNC felt there was no moral conflict as she determined that the advocacy was for the child, who was incapable of advocating for himself. In cases of domestic violence, when women survivors of domestic violence recant, there is conflict in advocating both for the domestic violence survivor and for the people of the state through prosecution of the defendant.

Model Case 11.4: The LNC as Developmental Disabilities Forensic Nurse Specialist

McCarthy[40] shared an example of a model case in which a forensic nurse specialist acted as a cross-jurisdictional advocate. In April of 2001, McCarthy was a forensic nurse specialist in private practice specializing in the sexual health and safety of persons with developmental disabilities. She was asked to act in the role of LNC for an Assistant District Attorney (ADA) in a western Massachusetts jurisdiction. McCarthy's practice included forensic evaluation of persons with developmental disabilities, including communication challenges, for which sexual assault was suspected. McCarthy's protocol for adaptive interviewing, based on an intensive preparatory assessment of an individual's abilities and patterns of health, was employed in a multidisciplinary team interview approach involving members of diverse jurisdictions. These jurisdictions have at times included:

- Officers of local police departments
- Massachusetts state police officers of the State Police Detective Unit attached to the Massachusetts Disabled Persons' Protection Commission (SPDU of the DPPC)
- The Massachusetts state police officers attached to the offices of the district attorneys (who liaise with the SPDU of the DPPC)
- Investigators from the Massachusetts Department of Mental Health (DMH)
- The Massachusetts Department of Mental Retardation (DMR)
- The Massachusetts Rehabilitation Commission (MRC)
- Investigators employed by the DPPC
- The Victim's Witness Advocate
- The Guardians Ad Litem appointed by the court

- Caseworkers of protective agencies such as the Department of Social Services (DSS)
- The ADA prosecuting the case
- A clinician, a family member, or a personal care attendant, in instances where a communication ally was needed to interpret the vocalizations or signs or gestures of the individual

In the April 2001 case, the local police officers had conducted the initial interview immediately upon the presentation of the victim with developmental disabilities at the police station by her mother. The 30-year-old woman with Down syndrome had been on a brief shopping errand in her neighborhood when she encountered two men loitering near a store. She reported, upon her delayed return home with soil on her clothing, that she had had her money taken and had been "hurt" by the men. The young woman had significant speech challenges, but with the assistance of her mother as a communication ally had been able to relate the details of the assault and give descriptions of the two assailants to the two investigating police officers. The young woman was taken to the hospital to be checked for injuries and to have a rape kit done. McCarthy's role as an LNC in this case was one of a cross-jurisdictional advocate. She had been retained to work with both the ADA and the victim in the many instances where clear communication and comprehension were critical for preparation of the plaintiff's case for prosecution. Although the defendants had given incriminating statements and there was a preponderance of physical evidence, there was conflict related to the victim's possible difficulties in testifying and the hesitancy of the defendants to negotiate just pleas.

McCarthy advocated by strategizing to integrate health care and legal knowledge for preparation of the young woman for the courtroom experience. She did this by educating the diverse jurisdictions in the health care elements; educating on how to minimize posttraumatic stressors; and ensuring necessary supports for her involved family, roommate, supported living staff, and service agencies' clinicians. The advocacy role required role ambiguity, a blurring of responsibilities. As Hardy and Hardy[41] point out, such role ambiguity may be positive in that it may offer opportunities for creative possibilities.

The Victim Witness Advocate acted on recommendation of the LNC in scheduling and supporting the young woman's frequent advance visits to the courtroom, not only to familiarize her with the formal atmosphere and acclimate her to using a microphone, but also to see court officers functioning in proximity to participants for security. As a result, on the day that the first defendant entered a plea, the young woman was able to participate in the proceedings and take the stand and state her satisfaction with the outcome.

The LNC functioning as a forensic nurse specialist must function marginally in one or more systems, oftentimes as a go-between to bridge differing value systems. The advocacy is for the vulnerable population of persons with developmental disabilities. McCarthy encouraged activism as a change agent in presentations:

- To classes of graduate nurses in the master's of science: forensic nursing program at Fitchburg State College
- To members of the SPDU and the DPPC Investigation Unit
- To the investigators of the Massachusetts Department of Mental Retardation

- To the International Association of Forensic Nurses (IAFN) in an Advance Sexual Assault workshop
- To state associations for nurses in practice specialties of mental health and developmental disabilities.

According to McCarthy, the traditions of the many jurisdictions that are involved in the recognition/detection, reporting, and investigation and prosecution of sexual assault of persons with developmental disabilities are responding to her innovations in Massachusetts. A priority in her practice is work in primary prevention with individuals, families, and support persons to teach concepts of personal safety and appropriate sexual expression that are both healthy and respectful of the rights of others.

Model Case 11.5: The LNC in Personal Injury Compensation at the United States Department of Justice

This case involves an LNC who worked for the U.S. Department of Justice, Civil Division, in the Radiation Exposure Compensation Program.[42] The Radiation Exposure Compensation Program was initiated as an outcome of the Radiation Exposure Compensation Act of 1990 to serve as a "financial apology" for those individuals unknowingly exposed to ionizing radiation during U.S. nuclear weapons testing experiments. The claimants approved for compensation were those who were uranium miners (Navajo Nation), on-site participants (military, contractors), and "downwinders" (farmers, Native Americans living in four corners of United States) who had adverse health effects of cancer or nonmalignant disease of the lungs.

The role of the LNC in this program was as follows:

- A radiation exposure content expert
- A liaison between hospitals, state agencies, and federal agencies (i.e., National Cancer Institute, Indian Health Services, National Institute of Occupational Safety and Health, state tumor registries, and University of New Mexico)
- An outreach worker with the Navajo Nation
- A claimant and family advocate and educator
- An educator of the attorney
- A fraud investigator
- An eligibility determiner
- A statistician
- A health policy research activist

The LNC acted as a cross-jurisdictional advocate for more than 5,000 claimants by:

- Assisting claimants to resolve conflict (i.e., functioning as the go-between from claimants to attorneys to differing health care and federal jurisdictions)
- Facilitating communication and taking Navajo language classes, learning about the Navajo culture and values, and visiting the Navajo reservation
- Mediating the geographical barriers that prevented the Navajo Nation from seeking health care services

- Strategizing eligibility determination and integrating documentation from differing legal and health care jurisdictions
- Promoting networking for referrals for health services and eligibility determinants
- Being an activist in providing testimony for a presidential task force investigating the responsiveness of the compensation program

There are numerous additional model cases exemplifying the attributes of the cross-jurisdictional advocate in legal nurse consulting. Additional domains of LNCs as cross-jurisdictional advocates are:

- In product liability cases, including multidistrict and coordinated national counsel cases
- In health care fraud cases
- As corporate compliance officers
- In toxic tort and environmental litigation cases
- In the Vaccine Compensation Injury Program[43]
- In workers' compensation cases
- As criminal and death investigators
- As correctional care health specialists
- As psychiatric emergency response team (PERT) nurses[44]
- As health policy analysts

Implications for Legal Nurse Consulting Practice

LNCs can lose sight of the larger advocacy perspective of their practice when daily functional tasks, such as reviewing medical records, are overwhelming. This is similar to clinical nurses who find themselves caring for five chemotherapy patients in one shift. They can become consumed with administering chemotherapy, checking urine samples for specific gravity and pH, giving rescue factor, taking temperatures, transcribing doctors' orders, checking laboratory results, giving blood products, and holding emesis basins. The nurse advocacy perspective seems to get lost in the exhausting functional tasks. However, if the nurse operates from a conceptual framework, all the functional tasks become components of a larger advocacy model. Operationalizing advocacy, particularly during long periods of tedious and overwhelming functional tasks, can be a problem for LNCs, particularly when there is no advocacy model to begin with to guide legal nurse consulting practice. This chapter was developed to assist with that guidance. LNCs who practice within a cross-jurisdictional advocacy framework provide caring-based interventions that have roots in nursing advocacy models. This framework serves to maintain that LNCs are nurses and differentiates LNCs from paralegals and legal assistants.

Conclusions

Cross-jurisdictional advocacy has been proposed as the theoretical foundation for legal nurse consulting practice as it has roots in nursing advocacy models. The theoretical definition of a cross-jurisdictional advocate is an LNC who manages interventions for clients in differing jurisdictions by bridging the paradigms of law and health care for the purpose of reducing conflict and producing change. The author hopes that this introduction to the theory of cross-jurisdictional advocacy and its application to legal nurse consulting will precipitate further discussion of theoretical foundations of legal nurse consulting practice. As noted by Walker and Avant, "scientific thought grows through a self-correcting process…[as] the submission of one's ideas to the critique and analysis of one's colleagues leads to a phenomenon of revision, validation, and extension of a given theory [concept/model]."[18] The initiation of peer critique will stimulate a "think-tank" approach to refining legal nurse consulting theory and developing a legal nurse consulting epistemology.

Cross-jurisdictional advocacy has been proposed as a conceptual model, a framework, and a theoretical foundation for a middle range theory of legal nurse consulting practice. In order to substantiate this theory, research needs to be undertaken to generate and refine the conceptual framework, and substantiate that cross-jurisdictional advocacy is the means by which LNCs advocate for their clients. Research is the next logical step in the validation of legal nurse consulting as a profession and a specialty practice of nursing. From a research agenda, the profession of legal nurse consulting can be justified.

This introduction to the theory of cross-jurisdictional advocacy was also intended to remind LNCs of their nursing origins and prompt them to reconnect with the nursing aspect of legal nurse consulting. Individually internalizing advocacy perspectives and collectively practicing within a cross-jurisdictional advocacy model can do this.

References

1. Meleis, A.I., *Theoretical Nursing: Development and Progress*, Lippincott-Raven Publishers, Philadelphia, 1997.
2. American Association of Legal Nurse Consultants, AALNC position statement on the role of the legal nurse consultant as distinct from the role of the paralegal and legal assistant, *Journal of Legal Nurse Consulting*, 10(2), 32, 1999.
3. Barnes, S., Schenck, P., Spiegel, K., Holmes, J., Schutze, S., and Bragdon, J., The legal nurse consultant practice environment, in *Legal Nurse Consulting: Principles and Practice*, Bogart, J.B., Ed., CRC Press, Boca Raton, FL, 1998, chap. 10.
4. Barnes, S., Holmes, J., Toepel, A., Constantini, P., and Davis, D., The legal nurse consultant practice area, in *Legal Nurse Consulting: Principles and Practice*, Bogart, J.B., Ed., CRC Press, Boca Raton, FL, 1998, chap. 11.
5. American Association of Legal Nurse Consultants, *Legal Nurse Consulting Principles and Practice*, Bogart, J.B., Ed., CRC Press, Boca Raton, FL, 1998.
6. American Association of Legal Nurse Consultants, AALNC position statement on education and certification in legal nurse consulting, *Network News*, 2(2), 2000.
7. Orr, M.J., Bogart, J., and Magnusson, J., Professionalism and standards of practice and professional performance for legal nurse consulting practice, in *Legal Nurse Consulting: Principles and Practice*, Bogart, J.B., Ed., CRC Press, Boca Raton, 1998, chap. 13.
8. Curtin, L.L., The nurse as advocate: a philosophical foundation for nursing, *Advanced Nursing Science*, 1(3), 1, 1979.

9. Gadow, S., Existential advocacy: philosophical foundations of nursing, in *Ethics and Nursing: An Anthology*, Pence, T. and Cantrall, J., Eds., National League for Nursing, New York, 1980, 41.

10. Kohnke, M.F., The nurse as advocate, *American Journal of Nursing*, 80, 2038, 1980.

11. Copp, L.A., The nurse as advocate for vulnerable persons, *Journal of Advanced Nursing*, 11, 255, 1986.

12. Curtin, L.L., The nurse as advocate: a cantankerous critique, *Nurse Management*, 14, 9, 1983.

13. Weisz, A.N., Legal advocacy for domestic violence survivors: the power of an informative relationship, *Families in Society: The Journal of Contemporary Human Services*, 80(2), 138, 1999.

14. Winslow, G.R., From loyalty to advocacy: a new metaphor for nursing, *The Hastings Center Report*, 14, 32, 1984.

15. Jezewski, M.A., Culture brokering as a model for advocacy, *Nursing and Health Care*, 14(2), 78, 1993.

16. Jezewski, M.A., Evolution of a grounded theory: conflict resolution through culture brokering, *Advanced Nursing Science*, 17(3), 14, 1995.

17. Noonan, R.A., Cross-jurisdictional advocacy in family violence: the role of the advanced practice nurse in the judicial system, *Advanced Practice Nursing Quarterly*, 3(4), 61, 1998.

18. Walker, L.O. and Avant, K.C., *Strategies for Theory Construction in Nursing*, 3rd ed., Appleton & Lang, East Norwalk, CT, 1995.

19. Liehr, P. and Smith, M.J., Middle range theory: spinning research and practice to create knowledge for the new millennium, *Advanced Nursing Science*, 21(4), 81, 1999.

20. Jezewski, M.A., Culture brokering in migrant farm workers health care, *Western Journal of Nursing Research*, 12, 497, 1990.

21. Jezewski, M.A., Staying connected: the core of facilitating health care for homeless persons, *Public Health Nurse*, 12(3), 203, 1995.

22. Children's Center for Child Protection, Cross-Jurisdictional Child Advocacy, brochure, San Diego, CA, 1996.

23. Bellucco, E., personal communication, 1999.

24. Kritzer, H.M., *Legal Advocacy: Lawyers and Nonlawyers at Work*, The University of Michigan Press, Ann Arbor, MI, 1998.

25. Physician Insurers Association of America, *Breast Cancer Study*, Washington, D.C., 1990.

26. Physician Insurers Association of America, *Breast Cancer Study*, Washington, D.C., 1995.

27. American College of Obstetricians and Gynecologists, The role of the obstetrician-gynecologist in the diagnosis of breast disease, ACOG Committee Opinion 67, Washington, D.C., 1989.

28. American College of Obstetricians and Gynecologists, *ACOG Newsletter*, 38(10), 1994.

29. American College of Radiology, ACR standard for the performance of screening mammography (rev.), *ACR Standards*, Reston, VA, 1994.

30. American College of Radiology, ACR standard for diagnostic mammography and problem-solving breast evaluation, *ACR Standards*, Reston, VA, 1994.

31. Pear, R., Group asking U.S. for new vigilance in patient safety, *The Boca Raton Times*, November 30, 1999, A1, A18.

32. Iyer, P.W., Nursing liability issues, in *Nursing Home Litigation: Investigation and Case Preparation*, Iyer, P.W., Ed., Lawyers & Judges Publishing Co., Inc., Tucson, AZ, 1999, chap. 6.

33. Levin, S.M., Screening the nursing home case, in *Nursing Home Litigation: Investigation and Case Preparation*, Iyer, P.W., Ed., Lawyers & Judges Publishing Co., Inc., Tucson, AZ, 1999, chap. 9.
34. Health Care Financing Administration, OBRA Regulations and Survey Procedures for the Long Term Care Facility, HCFA Publication No. 7, Heaton Publications, Washington, D.C., 1999.
35. Title 22, California Code of Regulations, 1999, section 5.
36. Bush, C.M., Jones, J.S., Cohle, S.D., and Johnson, H., Pediatric injuries from cardiopulmonary resuscitation, *Annals of Emergency Medicine*, 28(1), 40, 1996.
37. Feldman, K.W. and Brewer, D.K., Child abuse, cardiopulmonary resuscitation, and rib fractures, *Pediatrics*, 73(3), 339, 1984.
38. Spevak, M.R., Kleinman, P.K., Belanger, P.L., Primack, C., and Richmond, J.M., Cardiopulmonary resuscitation and rib fractures in infants: a postmortem radiologic-pathologic study, *JAMA*, 272(8), 617, 1984.
39. Villmoare, E. and Benvenuti, J., *California Victims of Crime Handbook*, McGeorge School of Law, University of the Pacific, Sacramento, CA, 1988.
40. McCarthy, M., personal communication, 2001.
41. Hardy, M.E. and Hardy, W.L., Role stress and role strain, in *Role Theory: Perspectives for Health Care Professionals*, 2nd ed., Appleton & Lange, Norwalk, CT, 1988, 159.
42. Bragdon, J.L., The Legal Nurse Consultant at the U.S. Department of Justice, presented at American Association of Legal Nurse Consultants Symposium, San Diego, CA, April 17–20, 1996.
43. Ashley, B.Z., The National Childhood Vaccine Injury Act: What You Don't Know Could Hurt You, presented at American Association of Legal Nurse Consultants Symposium, Orlando, FL, May 3–6, 1995.
44. Lau, M., Program pairs health professionals with police [Healthcare Beat], *Nurseweek*, 11(19), 13, 1998.

Additional Reading

Kikuchi, J.F., Simmons, H., and Romyn, D., *Truth in Nursing Inquiry*, Sage Publications, Thousand Oaks, CA, 1996, 111–124.

Meleis, A.I., *Theoretical Nursing: Development and Progress*, Lippincott-Raven Publishers, Philadelphia, 1997.

Pence, T. and Cantrall, J., *Ethics and Nursing: An Anthology*, National League for Nursing, New York, 1980.

Walker, L.O. and Avant, K.C., *Strategies for Theory Construction in Nursing*, 3rd ed., Appleton & Lang, East Norwalk, CT, 1995.

Test Questions

1. Concept derivation and concept analysis are processes used to develop
   A. Theory
   B. LNCs
   C. Model cases
   D. Ethical frameworks

2. Which one of the following reasons is NOT important in theory development to the profession of legal nurse consulting?
   A. It provides an LNC with a task and functional orientation.
   B. It provides guidance and direction to thought and a foundation to the profession of legal nurse consulting.
   C. It distinguishes the specialty of legal nurse consulting as a nursing domain.
   D. It differentiates legal nurse consulting from other roles in the legal environment.

3. Which of the following is NOT a defining attribute of a cross-jurisdictional advocate?
   A. Educating members of differing jurisdictions to each other's paradigms
   B. Functioning marginally in one or more systems
   C. Reviewing medical records and preparing a chronology
   D. Intervening in conflict situations

4. LNCs who practice within a model of cross-jurisdictional advocacy share defining attributes with
   A. Paralegals
   B. Legal assistants
   C. Culture brokers
   D. Attorneys

5. Model cases are constructed to
   A. Provide a sequence in which to screen a plaintiff's case for merit.
   B. Identify the key elements of the tasks of legal nurse consulting.
   C. Exemplify defining attributes of a proposed concept.
   D. Define standards of care.

Answers: 1. A, 2. A, 3. C, 4. C, 5. C

LEGAL PRACTICE AREAS

Chapter 12

Evaluating Professional Negligence Cases

Renee Wilson, BSN, MS, RN, Doreen James Wise, EdD, MSN, RN,
Julie B. Pike, MN, RN, LNCC, CPHRM, and
Susan H. Mahley, BSN, MSN, RNC, C-WHNP

CONTENTS

Objectives

- To identify the key elements of professional negligence suits
- To describe and perform the steps in critically evaluating professional negligence cases for liability, causation, and damages

- To delineate the unique contribution of legal nurse consultants to professional negligence litigation, including developing case strategies
- To differentiate the unique properties of the selection/qualification process of expert witnesses for professional negligence litigation
- To address "other" issues that can affect the pursuit and outcome of professional negligence litigation

Introduction

Perhaps the most poignant litigation in which legal nurse consultants (LNCs) are involved, and that for which they are most specially qualified, is professional (i.e., medical or nursing) negligence. When a plaintiff believes that there has been an injury as a direct result of negligent health care, one avenue of recourse provided by law is the pursuit of litigation.

LNCs offer valuable informed assistance in the development of either the plaintiff or defense case, and may be found serving as law firm employees, independent consultants, and testifying expert witnesses. In-house LNCs may have more informational sources about the case available to them, along with more expanded duties, than the independent LNCs. The extensive education, analytical skills, and clinical experience of the seasoned LNC can contribute to business-like evaluation and informed assistance with professional negligence litigation. Such litigation is fraught with challenge; the LNC must perform a critical job in the face of powerful forces inherent in medical negligence work. The plaintiff may be profoundly injured, the family overwhelmed, and the amount of money at stake staggering.

Although shifting in some jurisdictions, in many communities there is the prevailing societal view attributing almost godlike properties to health care professionals. Correspondingly, health care professionals remain reluctant to participate in candid clinical peer evaluation, and juries can seem hesitant to penalize even disturbingly negligent care. Complicating matters further, some attorneys accept cases based solely on the "jury appeal" driven by the potential financial value of the plaintiff's injuries, even when there may have been no professional negligence. Unhappily, in such cases even an innocent defendant is forced to prepare and mount a costly defense. In other cases in which negligent care has been proven, some defense attorneys needlessly prolong litigation in order to maximize their hourly billing to the insurer client, or to exhaust the plaintiff's resources before the case is completed. These forces and others serve to make professional negligence a tumultuous, demanding arena of LNC practice.

The Key Elements

As always, the burden of proof is on the plaintiff. Thus, the LNC evaluating a plaintiff's action when consulting with either the plaintiff or defense attorney must appraise the case for four key attributes. If these particular qualities are not present, the plaintiff's attorney cannot "get to the jury" (i.e., meet requirements specified by law to bring or "prove" a plaintiff's action). Not uncommonly, the LNC's greatest contribution from either plaintiff or defense perspective is the sophisticated, dispassionate analysis of the events and outcomes in a medical misadventure for worthiness as a malpractice case.

Any professional negligence action must meet four demands, commonly known as the four Ds. The LNC can play a role in determining whether or not they are met. The criteria to be determined are:

1. Was there a *Duty* for the defendant to provide care to the plaintiff?
2. Was there a *Dereliction* of that duty (negligence)?
3. Are there *Damages*?
4. Are the damages *Due* to, or a *Direct* result of, the negligence of the provider (is there proximate cause)?

Is There a Duty?

Ordinarily, analysis of duty will be performed by the attorney, and is a matter of law. Although infrequently involved in this appraisal, the LNC may be asked to research the nature of the relationship between the plaintiff and possible defendant. Was there a duty on the part of the health care provider to perform certain functions for the patient? A classic case in point is *Lunsford v. Board of Nurse Examiners of the State of Texas*.[1] In this matter, a supplemental staffing nurse followed hospital policy and the staff doctor's input by referring an emergent patient with a myocardial infarct in progress to a public hospital some miles distant, rather than assessing and initiating treatment herself. The patient arrested and died en route. In its findings, the Board of Nurse Examiners opined that because she was practicing under an RN license, issued at the pleasure of the state's citizenry, Nurse Lunsford held a duty to serve the patient that transcended doctor's orders and hospital policy. She lost her license and the right to practice, although the physician did not. A civil appellate court upheld the finding on appeal.

Was There Negligence or a Breach in the Standard of Care?

Negligence is the failure to meet, or the departure from, the recognized standard of care (i.e., failing to do what a reasonably prudent health care provider possessing the same or similar knowledge and skills would do in the same or similar circumstances). This also applies to a provider "doing" something that the reasonably prudent provider "would not do" under the same or similar circumstances. It must be differentiated from a mistake, an error in judgment, or a bad outcome resulting from acceptable care. Malpractice "refers to any professional misconduct that encompasses an unreasonable lack of skill or unfaithfulness in carrying out professional or fiduciary duties."[2]

Because professional negligence litigation is more technical than the scope of common knowledge, the law requires in most circumstances that expert witnesses with special medical qualifications provide guidance to the judge or jury. The articulation of standards of care must be made through the testimony of a qualified testifying expert witness. The jury is provided access to enough technical information to render a more informed judgment. The public has become aware of such diverse opinions of experts from opposing sides during litigation. An example is that which has occurred in breast implant litigation. The *Daubert* principles provide guidance in determining reliability and relevance and help focus on principles and methodology utilized by the expert.[3]

Although rules of procedure vary by state, in general the best expert witness for either plaintiff or defense will have comparable education and experience to the expert on the opposing side, will have been practicing in a similar setting at the time of the incident in question, and also will be in current active practice. Having been duly qualified, the expert may articulate the standard of care relevant to the matter in question, based on that professional's education and clinical experience. After independent review of all facts and critique of care actually given and documented, the expert may then offer an opinion about whether the care in question met the standard or was indeed negligent (see Chapter 35, The Liability Nurse Expert Witness).

To further the effort, the LNC reviews the health care literature to determine standards of care published by professional and specialty organizations, certifying bodies, and recognized and relevant professional texts and journals. For example, the American Medical Association prints and distributes a compendium of sources of professional practice standards.[4] Also, boards of nursing publish practice acts and rules and regulations related to licensure as well as professional conduct and practice. The LNC studies the medical records, comparing and contrasting care documented with published standards, determining whether or not there was a breach of the standard of care in a given matter. The appraisal will help to educate the attorney and determine the case issues and worthiness. It will also facilitate exacting selection of properly qualified experts.

Based on federal or the individual state's rules of civil procedure, the LNC may search for and recommend appropriately qualified experts to the attorney (see Chapter 34, Locating and Working with Expert Witnesses). The LNC may coordinate the dispatch of records to the selected expert, then follow up to determine opinions and need for additional materials. In matters concerning nursing care, the independent, clinically active LNC may be approached to serve as the reviewing, and later testifying, expert. The LNC should be aware that if retained to screen a case for liability, any work product may become discoverable if the LNC is named as an expert witness. The scope of the assignment with any potential for being used as an expert should be defined at the beginning of the work on the product and billed accordingly.

In rare instances, the issue in question in a professional negligence suit is deemed to be within the arena of common knowledge, comprehension by a layperson, or common sense for the jury. Known as *res ipsa loquitur,* "the thing speaks for itself," in most states these cases require no expert testimony for proof of the liability issues. In fact, all the plaintiff must prove is that the instrument or object causing the damages was "in the exclusive control of the defendant, that the plaintiff did not voluntarily contribute to the result, and that the injury was the type that normally does not occur in the absence of negligent care."[2] Once the plaintiff has so proved, the burden falls to the defendant to disprove any such responsibility.

Example 12.1: After surgery, and a period of unexplained complications, a patient is determined to have a surgical instrument present in the operative site. Such a case can be litigated successfully without the testimony of a surgeon or nurse since it is evident that inadvertently leaving a foreign body is, by definition, negligent. Expert testimony might be helpful in determining the mechanism of injury (i.e., exactly what the object left behind has done to harm the patient).

Example 12.2: In *Beverly Enterprises-Virginia v. Nichols*, the decedent was an elderly patient with Alzheimer's disease who was prone to choke if not spoon-fed as ordered. In fact, when left to feed herself unattended, despite orders to the contrary, she choked and died. Her family successfully brought a wrongful death suit against the nursing home. When the nursing home appealed the case because the plaintiff had failed to provide expert witness testimony, the appellate court upheld the lower court's ruling. "The nursing home and its staff were aware of the patient's mental and physical condition...the fact that she was unable to feed herself and that she had two prior choking incidents. In spite of this knowledge, the nursing home's employee left a tray of food with the plaintiff and failed to provide assistance to her. Certainly, a jury does not need expert testimony to ascertain whether the defendant was negligent because its personnel failed to assist the patient under these circumstances."[5]

Are There Damages?

To meet the requirements for proof in potential malpractice cases, there must be evidence of injury sustained as a result of the negligence alleged. Medical damages (i.e., "actual loss or damage to the interests of the patient"[2]) can be financial, physical, or emotional in nature. As a general rule, the more observable, extensive, and comprehensible any damages are to a jury, the more "desirable" they are found by the plaintiff's attorney. Correspondingly, they seem more ominous to the defense attorney. Given the monetary costs of extensive care projected across a lifetime, and the value traditionally placed on youth in our culture, cases involving injury to an infant, child, or young person are also seen as greater financial threats to the defense and potentially more rewarding to the plaintiff. Current trends in litigation related to long-term care facilities involve damage awards not only for medical malpractice, but also for violation of patient's rights.

Documentation of damages is most often found in the medical records. For this reason collection, organization, and detailed assessment of complete medical records are critical to support or dispute damage claims. Another significant source of information about damages is the plaintiff and family. Collection of data regarding damages also may be accomplished in a variety of ways allowed for under rules of discovery. These include:

- Preliminary interview by the plaintiff's attorney considering taking the case
- Answers to requests for production and interrogatories from both sides
- Depositions of the plaintiff, family, and treating health care professionals
- Private investigation
- Independent examination of the plaintiff and family and evaluation of their living conditions

The product of such inquiry is documentation and detailed understanding of the nature and extent of the alleged damages.

Evaluation of damages is one of the strongest arenas for positive LNC contribution. The painstaking review, summary, and evaluation of all medical information are best accomplished by the LNC, usually in two phases: (1) early evaluation of the strength of the case, and (2) evaluation of damages as the case progresses.

Early Evaluation of the Strength of the Case

The LNC assisting a plaintiff's attorney may be asked to perform a preliminary review of the records for evidence of the claim's validity. This early review by an LNC assisting the plaintiff's attorneys can support responsible determination of whether suit should even be filed.

The business reality of medical malpractice litigation may mean that if there are no damages resulting from even grave acts of negligence, the plaintiff's attorney should not undertake the case. Plaintiff's attorneys may use the following five questions to gauge whether or not to accept a case:

- Do the damages justify contingency fee representation?
- Can the damages be proved to be due to negligent conduct?
- Can a board-certified, reputable health care provider provide clear and convincing evidence that the defendant breached the standard of care?
- Is the claim credible?
- Is the jury going to like the plaintiff? (Some individuals will not be viewed in a sympathetic light, no matter how valid their claims. Convicted felons, intravenous substance abusers, those that abuse welfare privileges, etc., may be viewed in an unsympathetic light. Other plaintiffs may have personal qualities that make them unlikable.)

These are questions that the LNC must also consider and address. There may be irrefutable negligence, but damages too small to warrant recommending that the attorney proceed with the case. Sometimes there is evidence of damages in the medical record of which the attorney is unaware.

Example 12.3: One LNC tells of reviewing a record involving a 33-year-old male alleging unnecessary gastrointestinal surgery, who had been too embarrassed to reveal the resulting sexual dysfunction to his attorney. In the medical records reviewed by the LNC there was an almost illegible reference made by the treating urologist to "problems with erections." The LNC obtained and summarized a complete copy of that doctor's records and found documentation of permanent sexual dysfunction with plans made for future penile implant. This revelation of the extent of damages helped the attorney decide to commit to the case.

Later Evaluation of Damages

Once suit has been filed and discovery is underway, the LNC working with either side will want to perform a more extensive damage assessment. As seen in the example above, detailed documentation found in the records of medical providers offers clues to the veracity and extent of the plaintiff's suffering. Typically, nursing notes are replete with such entries. Consistency is crucial to evaluate — does the plaintiff complaining of unremitting pain have a correspondingly curtailed lifestyle? If the answer is at all questionable, the attorney may even hire an investigator to secretly videotape the plaintiff in his normal daily routine. In one instance, an attorney taped his own would-be client, who was claiming unremitting back pain, as the "injured" man loaded a friend's furniture into a moving van. In another account, a nursing note stated that the "patient shuffles and stumbles when around staff, but was observed walking normally when she thought no one was watching!" Comparison and contrast of current level of function with the plaintiff's premal-practice activity also help to document the extent of change resulting from the negligence. All such damages must be directly caused by the acts of negligence.

Is There Proximate Cause?

In order to proceed successfully with professional negligence cases, the plaintiff must show that any damages claimed were directly caused by the acts of negligence of the defendants. Correspondingly, the defense challenge is to dispute and disprove such a proximately causal relationship. Legal causation varies from medical causation in that it "refers to a single causative factor and not necessarily the major cause or even the most immediate cause of the injury, as is the case with medical causation...." Legal causation "is frequently the most difficult and elusive concept for the jury to understand because of the many complex issues."[2] Legal causation involves *causation in fact* and *foreseeability*. The plaintiff must prove that the defendant's negligence was the cause in fact of injuries and that those damages were reasonably foreseeable. Causation in fact can be tested with the so-called "but for" test, in which a certain event, in this case an injury, is caused by, or happens only because of, the occurrence of another event, the negligence. The damage in question would not have taken place "but for" the negligent acts of the health care provider.

Example 12.4: Five hours following esophageal dilatation, a patient was found to have a gastric perforation. "But for" the negligently performed dilatation, there would have been no medical misadventure (i.e., the subsequent perforation). This meets the test for causation in fact.

Foreseeability implies that the damages must be the foreseeable result of substandard practice of the defendant health care provider. In the example above, perforation is a foreseeable and known risk of dilatation when the procedure is not properly performed.

Delay in diagnosis and treatment is a common precipitant for professional negligence actions. The key issue is determining whether or not an obvious delay makes a difference in the occurrence of a negative outcome. The LNC would review and carefully evaluate related literature for the necessary information. Failures to diagnose cancer cases possibly best exemplify this issue.

Example 12.5: A patient experienced a 15-month delay between the onset of symptoms and diagnosis of small bowel malignancy. The attorney dismissed the case after learning that this patient's prognosis more than likely would not have been improved by earlier diagnosis (i.e., there was no causation between the failure to diagnose in a timely manner and the patient's condition[6]).

In the above example the plaintiff's damages would have occurred even without the delay in treatment. Many jurisdictions "hold that in such a situation, a plaintiff cannot recover any damages unless he or she can prove that there was a greater than 50% chance of survival if the diagnosis had been made earlier and treatment had been more timely."[2]

Proximate cause is so essential to the outcome of any case that legal professionals may seek the independent review and opinion of a qualified causation expert even prior to that of a liability expert. Expert opinions regarding causation are required under any circumstances, and often necessitate retaining additional, more specialized health care professionals for the role. This is especially true in cases with extensive injury and in which the plaintiffs are deemed to have very strong "jury appeal," such as ministers, teachers, infants, young children, etc. To identify strong experts on causation, the LNC first will analyze the medical literature. By seeking medical experts in literature written and critiqued by credentialed medical professionals, one is more likely assured higher-quality opinion and compliance with the demands exerted by the *Daubert* decision. (The reader is advised to refer to the additional reading list at the end of this chapter for sources about *Daubert* principles.) No doubt the single most frustrating situation for a plaintiff's attorney is to be told by the consulting LNC or causation expert that while compelling evidence of negligence and tragic damage exist, there is no support for a causal relationship between the two because of an intervening cause. Perhaps no greater defense challenge exists than defending a professional who implemented the best care possible with an unavoidable tragic patient outcome. Starting case review with an opinion from a strong causation expert can anticipate and resolve either dilemma.

Exception to the Rule: Loss of Chance

Generally, proof of causation requires expert testimony stating that to a reasonable degree of medical certainty the health care provider's failure to meet the standard of care proximately caused the injuries alleged. The burden of proof is that more likely than not the negligence caused the injury. There must be a probability of greater than 50% that the injury occurred as a result of the defendant's negligent care. If this burden of proof is met, the plaintiff can recover monetary compensation for 100% of the injury even if there is as much as a 49% chance that the injury would have occurred anyway. This is the *all-or-nothing* concept of determining damages once the burden of proof for causation is met.

There are cases in which proof of causation falls below this greater than 50% benchmark. If the plaintiff is shown, for example, to have a 30 or 40% chance of survival (or of avoiding injury) absent the negligent acts, shouldn't that plaintiff be compensated for the *loss of chance* to survive or be healthy? In the classic example of the patient with undetected cancer above, the decedent's chances of survival might have been markedly reduced by the defendant's negligent oversight. The plaintiff alleged that although a cure was not probable even when symptoms first appeared, the doctor failed to detect, diagnose, and treat in a timely manner. The cancerous tumor was discovered too late to cure, and the patient's chances of survival were drastically reduced. Under the all-or-nothing rule, the patient would recover nothing unless earlier detection would have ensured a greater than 50% chance of 5-year survival.

In some courts, recovery can be made for a 50% or less chance of survival. This has been done through relaxation of the standard of proof of causation or by allowing a new cause of action for loss of chance. Plaintiffs before these courts can recover for damages based on the percentage of harm actually caused by the defendants, reflecting an actual value of the chance that was lost. If the negligence is shown, for example, to have reduced a patient's chance of survival from 45 to 25%, the negligent defendant is liable for 25% of the damages. In such cases, the plaintiff still must prove that there was a deviation from the standard of care, and that negligence caused the patient to lose substantial possibility of survival or of avoiding injury.

Example 12.6: A patient with a history of myocardial infarction, stroke, and unstable angina was admitted for a 5-vessel coronary bypass. During the postoperative days he had several occasions of respiratory problems, was transferred to a critical care unit for bronchoscopy and treatment, and then returned to the nursing unit. The patient's wife testified that her calls for nursing assistance on the first day there went unheeded for 1 hour and 15 minutes, during which time the patient stopped breathing. He suffered a respiratory arrest from which he died 2 days later. The nursing expert testified that the nurse's actions fell below the standard of appropriate care in many ways, including failing to note that the patient was at high risk for respiratory arrest and taking responsive precautions. Testimony by a physician panel member was that the patient should have been cared for in the critical care unit, and that because of the negligent care rendered by the floor nurses, the patient's chances of survival were lessened. "Accordingly, the Court adopted a 'loss of chance' doctrine," in *Ard v. East Jefferson General Hospital.*[7]

The LNC is advised to determine state law regarding loss of chance proof of causation. If the damages failed to be more likely than not attributable to the negligence, were they nonetheless related, but to a lesser degree? Did the negligence substantially increase the risk of harm or, alternatively, eliminate a substantial possibility to survive, recover, or avoid injury? The LNC must answer these questions by reviewing the medical literature to determine whether the medical community generally accepts the suggested intervention, and whether reliable medical studies or treatises confirm the likelihood of successful treatment.

One may then reason that by failing to institute proven treatment, the defendant was negligent, thereby increasing harm to the patient and causing the patient to lose a reasonable opportunity to recover.[2,8]

Another key role for the LNC is to carefully review the medical records and other discovery for signs of preexisting or intervening causes for the plaintiff's alleged damages.

Example 12.7: A plaintiff alleging development of "being unable to walk" as a result of back surgery had engaged the plaintiff attorney's interest in taking his case. On review of the medical records, the plaintiff was found by the LNC to have had spina bifida, a congenital defect, confining him to a wheelchair from birth. The limitations associated with this preexisting condition must be differentiated from any changes resulting from the alleged negligence.

Example 12.8: A plaintiff alleging AIDS by an HIV-infected transfusion was found to have been subsequently exposed to an HIV-positive sexual partner. This was an intervening and mitigating factor in the case.

Example 12.9: A plaintiff alleged that her deceased husband had contracted and succumbed to hepatitis C from an infected blood product given for emergent cranial hemorrhage. Initially doubtful about the case because hepatitis is a known risk of transfusion, the plaintiff's attorney became enthused about the case only through investigatory efforts of the LNC engaged to review the case. Thorough review of prior medical records yielded evidence of an earlier malpractice. Some months before the hemorrhage, the patient had received several anticoagulant drugs, but was never evaluated or followed for bleeding potential. The emergent hemorrhage was more likely than not the subsequent result. But for the earlier malpractice, there would have been no hemorrhage or the need for blood products. Legal causation, though not proximate in time, was convincingly demonstrated nonetheless, and the case resolved for the plaintiff.

Many states have abolished the doctrine of contributory negligence that completely bars a plaintiff's recovery if the damage is partly the plaintiff's own fault. Instead, comparative negligence has been adopted, which compares plaintiff and defendant in terms of blameworthiness. This reduces the plaintiff's recovery proportionally to his own degree of fault in causing the damage, rather than barring it completely. Once the LNC has reviewed the case for liability and causation, the next step in a plaintiff's practice is to prepare to file suit.

Filing a Professional Negligence Claim

If review of medical records and contrast with published standards and those articulated by expert witnesses reveals evidence of negligence, causation, and resulting damages, the plaintiff's attorney will likely "give notice" and file suit. It is most important to identify all potential defendants. The suit must be filed within the period of time allowed for such claims, known as the *statute of limitations*. It is the attorney's responsibility to determine when the plaintiff knew or should have known that malpractice occurred. Each state defines the time limit from this point on during which the plaintiff can file suit. It is often extremely difficult to extend the statute of limitations.

Once the attorney has determined that the statute of limitations has not "tolled" (ended), the attorney will "sign up" the plaintiff as a client of the firm. This involves reviewing the contract and determining how the costs of the suit will be paid (by either the plaintiff or the attorney). The attorney will explain the contingency fee structure applicable in that state.

With the agreement of the plaintiff, pleadings will be filed detailing the events, alleging negligence, and claiming damages suffered as a direct result of the breach of the standard of care. The defendant must "answer," usually through counsel. The defense attorney faced with a bona fide negligent defendant may advise the client to offer insurance policy limits to settle the matter early in the suit. This, of course, is the most elegant scenario when there has been negligence. Although money is at best an incomplete solace to any injured plaintiff, when offered in a timely manner and in keeping with the seriousness of injury, it can make the plaintiff's life more tolerable. However, this quiet acknowledgment of negligence and dignified resolution of the matter is a rare occurrence. In the late 1980s as part of the Health Care Quality Improvement Act, the National Practitioner Data Bank was created. This database collects, stores, and releases information on the nation's health care practitioners, including malpractice claims, settlements, and disciplinary actions. As a result, there may be some reluctance to settle prematurely.

The LNC may be a participant in the drafting of medically related portions of the pleadings, or reviewing and evaluating them for the attorney. Correspondingly, the LNC working with the defense attorneys may advise about the veracity and significance of the allegations, medically speaking. LNCs may be participant-advisers in negotiation and settlement proceedings, providing medical information and support to the attorney (see Chapter 39, Alternative Dispute Resolution: Settlement, Arbitration, and Mediation).

Once suit has been filed, a growing number of states require that a written report or affidavit attesting to the merit of each plaintiff's malpractice action be submitted to the court within a specified short time after filing. Although the states have various versions of this requirement, there are some commonalties. Ordinarily, such affidavits confirm that the filing attorney has obtained a written opinion by a legally qualified health care professional outlining each named defendant's professional negligence. The written opinion must state that the defendant failed to use such care as a reasonably prudent and careful health care provider would have done under similar circumstances, and that such failure to use reasonable care directly caused the damages claimed in the petition. The affidavit must cite the qualifications of the expert offering the opinion. In some states, such as Texas, the identity of the expert is revealed "in camera" (to the judge only). In others, it is never revealed and the "affiant," or author, of the affidavit never needs to testify. However, in ideal circumstances, the attorney seeks expert review and affidavits prior to filing suit. In the best possible case, the expert writing the report or affidavit also testifies as an expert witness.

In cases with nurse defendants, or defendants who employ nurses and cover them under *respondeat superior*, LNCs may be qualified to prepare and submit such affidavits, later testifying as an expert. In those states in which the author of the affidavit must have special knowledge, but is not necessarily required to testify, there is an even greater possible role for LNCs. It is incumbent on LNCs who are pursuing this role to research and comply with all state regulations. They must be sure of their eligibility to qualify in this role before signing an affidavit.

Selecting the Best Experts

Appraisal of medical experts for malpractice cases demands particular attention to detail. In addition to those qualities highlighted in references regarding experts within other chapters of this text, there are several additional considerations in this particular arena of medical litigation. Although specific traits are valued depending on the locale, the following qualities, while sometimes appearing mutually exclusive, are all of value in a testifying medical expert.

Qualities desirable in an expert follow:

- Well educated, clinically experienced, and board-certified in at least one field (Check to see whether there are any abnormalities [e.g., multiple attempts to pass the certifying exams].)
- Current active clinical practice and practice at the time of the incident
- Testimony balanced between plaintiff and defense
- Sophisticated presentation as an expert witness
- An experienced, unflappable teacher (An outstanding expert remembers that jurors often approach their service with the respect they accord church

attendance, and expect the level of mutual respect of attorneys and experts. The most appreciated expert establishes rapport with the jury and testifies steadfastly, respectfully, and in an unruffled manner even in the face of harrowing cross-examination.)

- No prior malpractice suits against the expert, or more realistically, if sued, suits in which the expert clinician prevailed
- No "skeletons" in one's personal closet (Some attorneys would include psychotherapy, arrest for drug abuse or driving under the influence of alcohol, prior professional negligence lawsuits, bankruptcy, discharge from employment, and unflattering news coverage [even if inaccurate] as truly serious occurrences. In fact, most such "skeletons" do not necessarily rule out expert service. It is in the best interest of the case if such items are revealed proactively to the attorney so that any "damage control" can be undertaken.)
- Consistent opinions in all public writings and testimony (Nothing is more embarrassing to the expert, nor more damaging to a case, than prior writings that contradict the expert's opinions in the case. Independent LNCs should offer to serve as a valuable member of the in-house legal team in reviewing in detail all public utterances of any expert.)
- Expert testimony as a minimal portion of total income (The strength of any clinical expert's opinion is drawn from clinical expertise. While an expert in another field may be able to make a career as an expert, the minute a medical professional leaves or dramatically reduces active practice, usefulness as an expert on medical negligence matters diminishes. A variation of this caution is an expert who demands an extraordinarily high hourly fee. Attorneys gravitate to the expert who has the same modest hourly fee for review and testimony or who donates fees to charity. It is advisable to avoid any expert who hints that the fee is based on the opinion, or opens by saying to the attorney, "What is it that you want me to say?")

While evaluation of the expert's credibility always is important, it is imperative when the case relies substantially on the expert's testimony.

Example 12.10: Beware of the case that is not substantially proven by the written record, but must rely heavily on testimony from plaintiff, defendant, or other fact witnesses. The opposition will offer contradicting testimony from their witnesses in rebuttal. In such a "swearing match," the believability of the witness becomes the key to success rather than only hard evidence.

The LNC can prove to be a valuable member of the legal team regarding how jurors might view potential experts. It is of considerable help for the experienced LNC to meet with critical witnesses in addition to the usual screening. To establish and cement credibility, the LNC can anticipate and ask, in a pretestimony setting, the same questions a juror would ask if allowed to do so. By listening and observing, making note of what is believable and what might be distrusted or discarded as false, the LNC can help to maximally qualify the expert for such cases. The LNC should also secure the expert's references, talking directly with a sample of attorneys with whom the expert has worked. Independent practice LNCs should discuss this important level of screening with their attorney client, especially if the attorney has no in-house staff to perform this function.

Other Issues

Defense Issues

Identifying the Indefensible Case

LNCs play a key role in cases for both plaintiff and defense. The LNC may help the defense attorney identify clearly indefensible cases. The following are examples of indefensible cases (examples courtesy of Patricia Iyer):

Example 12.11: A 26-year-old man was struck by a car when he was crossing a street. He was placed in a cervical collar by the rescue squad and sent to the emergency room. On admission he was moving his extremities. Despite the fact that a cervical x-ray showed prevertebral swelling, a CT scan of the cervical spine was not ordered. The patient was rushed to surgery to repair his fractured legs. The cervical collar was removed without an order. Upon awakening from anesthesia, the patient was unable to move his extremities. A CT scan of the cervical spine revealed a C1 fracture. The case settled on the eve of trial.

Example 12.12: An anesthesiologist decided to put an IV bag behind the shoulders of a young woman in order to elevate her body off the operating room table. He took the IV bag from the side of the autoclave where it was being stored. The recovery room nurse found a burn on the patient's back that perfectly matched the shape of an IV bag. The case settled.

Example 12.13: Following a hip replacement surgery, the patient's blood pressure began to drop in the postoperative hours. The slow decline, coupled with blood draining steadily into the Hemovac, did not alarm the nurse. The nurse caring for the patient did not see any reason why morphine should not be administered to the patient when her blood pressure was 80/45. The patient was found dead a few hours later. The hospital admitted liability and the case was tried to determine damages.

Example 12.14: An elderly woman was receiving physical therapy in her home. She protested when the physical therapist attempted to put her arm through range of motion. The therapist told her that she was being a baby. Excessive force was applied to the woman's arm. She developed a fractured humerus. The case settled.

Example 12.15: A 42-year-old, 250-pound man had a cervical discectomy. When the 120-pound aide came into his postoperative room to help him get out of bed, he protested, saying that it had taken 3 people to get him up that morning. She insisted that she could get him up by herself. He fell to the floor, landing on his back. Later that night, he complained to the nurse that his legs felt weak. She told him that he was complaining too much. When he asked for help getting up in bed, she said that she had a bad back and instructed him to pull himself up. He felt an "electric-like" sensation travel down his neck to his toes. As the hours wore on, he developed numbness, tingling, and weakness of his feet and legs. The nurse did not notify the neurosurgeon of these changes until the paralysis had ascended to the level of his nipples. Emergency surgery was unsuccessful in reversing his paralysis. The case settled after depositions were taken.

It is the responsibility of the defense attorney to determine whether this type of case should be settled early or after discovery has failed to provide any avenue of defense.

Supporting the Defendant Health Care Provider

LNCs assisting defense attorneys can provide support to defendants in the form of updates on the litigation progress and events, "reality testing" information, and encouragement for the confused and baffled defendant. Language used in documents stating allegations of negligence are routinely "boilerplated" on the plaintiff attorney's computer, and are not personal. The LNC can also provide accurate information to the attorney about the defendant's capacity to testify in his own behalf and pinpoint any inaccuracy to the plaintiff's allegations. The defendant's credentials, how well he will present to the jury, where and what he has published or presented verbally, and how this information will impact the jury's view of the case is important. It is also extremely helpful to teach the defendant how to present well in deposition and trial. As in any other arena for practice, there are skills and approaches that work best in those settings. Defensiveness or arrogance can be masks for the fear and anxiety that any defendant may feel; however, emphasizing the defendant's more humane traits can bring greater empathy and understanding from the jury. Additional information on how the LNC assists the defendant is found in Chapter 25.

Defense goals are to limit liability or mitigate damages. The LNC's duties are to:

- Pinpoint inaccuracies in the plaintiff's allegations
- Look for evidence to support those practices documented in the medical record
- Identify preexisting or concurrent conditions and causes for the plaintiff's symptoms other than the defendant's actions that would impact the case

Accusations of professional negligence can be devastating to health care providers. Such accusations often become turning points in their lives. Some settle their cases prematurely or even leave practice rather than run the risk of future long and grueling litigation experiences. Most health care providers are sincere, caring professionals who do not intentionally err. They may be disappointed or disillusioned by allegations of negligence from patients they sought to cure. They can be stunned to find that medical colleagues will testify against them, sometimes even when no negligence has taken place. Inevitably, they are shocked when treated callously or worse by the plaintiff's or their own insurer's attorneys. Valuable practitioners can be lost to medicine following vigorous pursuit of an invalid lawsuit.

Plaintiff Issues

Life as a litigant is usually a lonely and miserable one. Some discourage undertaking it in all but the most evident cases of medical negligence. As noted elsewhere,[9] the plaintiff in professional negligence cases becomes "fair game" for the defense attorney. By the time a negligence case is filed and then litigated to resolution, 3 to 5 years may have passed. Frequently, plaintiffs in catastrophic cases are financially, physically, and emotionally drained of all resources long before the process ends in some manner. Even plaintiffs whose previous lives had been balanced and joyful are usually enervated when it is finally time to go to trial. Their lives are routinely combed by the defense attorney seeking details that could potentially influence the case. A successful plaintiff's attorney will have conducted close inquiry before agreeing to represent them. Are they who and how they claim to be? Did they contribute themselves in any way to the negligence? Are there skeletons in their own closets that will emerge under close inspection? Has there been a history of drug abuse, psychiatric problems, etc.? As with experts, such skeletons rarely undo a plaintiff's meritorious case. However, they do need to be identified and proactively revealed by the plaintiff's attorney. Failing to do this homework can be disastrous during discovery. The diligent defense attorney surely will have done that same homework, revealing the findings as if the plaintiff had intended to deceive by withholding them.

Strategies need to be planned for coping with any unsavory qualities, or those with the potential to aggravate the anticipated prejudices of the jury. As part of the due diligence conducted for the would-be plaintiff, it is also important to point out the rigors of litigation. In high-stakes claims, any and all skeletons will be brought out with the worst possible spin placed on them. It is ethical to anticipate for the already stressed claimant that life is about to get much worse, at least for the duration of litigation, the outcome of which is uncertain at best. It is critical that the plaintiff understands the contract with the attorney and the fee arrangements. This not only is the ethical thing to do, but may help to prevent later lawsuits by claimants unhappy with the terms of settlement.

Once the decision is made to proceed despite the risks, the LNC can help evaluate the plaintiff and family's potential impact on the jury, and "teach" them how to best present their view of the case. As described above for defendants, there are skills associated with being a successful plaintiff. The attorney who works well with the client has a better chance to win the case. Not having one's client working in concert with the attorney's strategy has undermined more than one otherwise strong malpractice case.

LNCs working with plaintiff's attorneys can provide accurate information about the medical standard of care without being biased by the tragedy of the plaintiff's conditions. In this way, more responsible lawsuits are pursued. In addition, the strengths of the case can be emphasized and the weaker aspects of the case minimized.

It may be helpful for the LNC who is assisting with the development or defense of a professional negligence action to consult the checklist highlighted in the next section.

Legal Nurse Consultant Professional Negligence Checklist
Initial Evaluation

- Has any conflict of interest been ruled out? The law firm and expert or "behind the scenes" LNC must be certain that there is neither an outright conflict nor even the appearance of a conflict. Example: The independent LNC working with a plaintiff attorney on a case against the hospital in which the LNC practices clinically part time is a conflict of interest.
- Have all of the plaintiff's medical providers been identified?
- Are medical records complete? If not, create a list of others needed and see that they are obtained.

- Have all records been entirely reviewed? Has a chronological summary of critical medical events been prepared?
- Has a list of all of the plaintiff's medical providers been prepared, with each address, phone, and practice license number included? From this listing, have potentially culpable parties been identified with listing of negligent deviations (for a plaintiff's case), or has each alleged act of negligence been independently assessed? Are there any other potential defendants?
- Are all "four D's" met? Is there duty and negligence? Are there damages? Are the damages due to the negligence?
- Have medical-legal issues been identified? Has dispassionate assessment been made of both strengths and weaknesses of the case?
- What policies, procedures, and protocols are needed to fully assess the claims?
- Are there inconsistencies in the records? What are they? How do they impact the case?
- Are there preexisting conditions or concurrent illnesses that impact the alleged negligence?
- What type of experts may be necessary for liability and causation?
- Has medical literature been reviewed and have "learned treatises" been identified? Learned treatises consist of annotated review and critique of related professional literature, highlighted for support or possible disagreement with the medical-legal issues of the case. Be sure that they include, among others, publications written and cited as excellent by one's own and the opposition's expert witnesses.
- Has a glossary of medical terms relative to the case been prepared? Have appropriate anatomic drawings been prepared?
- Has frank discussion been held with the attorney? Is this a case that should quietly settle, or is there true reason to go to trial? What are the attorney's client's preferences? (These discussions may be appropriate at various points during the litigation process.)

Intermediate or Discovery Phase

- Have all medical aspects of pleadings been prepared (plaintiff) or answered (defense)? Have all medically related interrogatories been prepared and answered? During this phase, be certain to obtain all relevant internal policies and procedures from the defendant institution.
- Have potential expert witnesses been identified, conflicts ruled out, and curriculum vitae (CV) and current fee schedules obtained? Have background information and copies of relevant publications been critiqued? Are potentially applicable experts available during the time needed for review, deposition, or trial? Are they willing to go to trial? Have the LNC and/or attorney interviewed the expert by phone or face-to-face?
- Have expert reports been solicited in a timely fashion? Do they contain the proper elements (i.e., citation/refutation of all acts of negligence and causal relationship to damages)? Are reports complete enough to qualify the experts' testimony without being overfilled with information?

- Have the opposition's experts been thoroughly investigated? Have sample questions been prepared for the attorney's use in taking the opposition's witnesses' depositions? The LNC should comb through the opposition's expert's CV and publications for hints of inconsistency or unexplained breaks in service. Search *Science Citation Index* for other, possibly contradictory publications. Verify employment and references.

- Have one's own experts been prepared for "worst-case scenario" questions that they could be asked in deposition? Have background and all prior testimony of one's own experts been examined for possible vulnerabilities? If one's expert has testified numerous times, it is critical to be sure that testimony in similar cases is consistent. Beware of experts "for hire" who contradict themselves.

- Have medically related trial exhibits been proposed and critiqued by experts? Has all testimony by medical experts been carefully reviewed? Is testimony of own experts consistent and on point? Is there helpful/truly hurtful testimony from opposition's expert?

In conclusion, LNCs play a very responsible, informative role in plaintiff or defense preparation of professional negligence cases.

References

1. *Lunsford v. Board of Nurse Examiners for the State of Texas*, 648 S.W. 2d 391 (Tex. Civ. App. Austin, 1983).
2. Flamm, M.B., Physician as defendant in medical malpractice, in *Legal Medicine*, Sanbar, S.S. et al., Eds., C.V. Mosby, St. Louis, 2001, 84, 85, 90.
3. *Daubert v. Merrell Dow Pharmaceuticals, Inc.,* 509 U.S. 579, 113 S.Ct. 2786 (1993).
4. American Medical Association, *Guide to Professional Standards*, AMA, Chicago, 1997.
5. *Beverly Enterprises-Virginia v. Nichols*, 441 S.E. 2d 1-VA (1994), as noted in *The Regan Report on Nursing Law*, 34(12), 4, 1994.
6. Fink, S. and Chaudhuri, T.K., Medical characteristics of 61 unwarranted malpractice claims, *Southern Medical Journal*, 88(10), 1011–1019, 1995.
7. Nurses fail to respond: "Loss of chance" — death, Case in Point: *Ard v. East Jefferson General Hospital*, 636 So. 2d 1042, LA (1994), *The Regan Report on Nursing Law*, 35(3), 2, 1994.
8. Apfel, D., Loss of chance in obstetrical cases, *Trial*, May, 48–55, 1993.
9. Wise, D.J. and Green, S.E., Psychiatric nursing malpractice, in *Nursing Malpractice*, Iyer, P., Ed., Lawyers and Judges Publishing Company, Tucson, AZ, 1996.

Additional Reading

O'Keefe, M.E., *Nursing Practice and the Law: Avoiding Malpractice and Other Legal Risks*, F.A. Davis, Philadelphia, 2001.

Oldknow, P., *Daubert*, The scientific method, and the legal nurse consultant, *The Journal of Legal Nurse Consulting*, 12(4), 3–9, 2001.

Sanbar, S.S. et al., Eds., *Legal Medicine*, C.V. Mosby, St. Louis, 2001.

Test Questions

1. Any professional negligence case must include the following key elements:
   A. Duty, Breach of Duty, Damages
   B. Duty, Dereliction of Duty, Causation, Damages
   C. Dereliction, Causation, Breach of Duty, Standard of Care
   D. Duty, Breach of Duty, Proximate Cause

2. To be considered or heard, a malpractice claim must be filed
   A. In a state court
   B. In a federal court
   C. Within the statute of limitations
   D. Only if there is concrete evidence of negligence and damages

3. Experts in a professional negligence case should preferably possess the following qualities, EXCEPT:
   A. Similar education to the opposing counsel's chosen expert
   B. Clinical experience in a specialty similar to the opposing expert
   C. Publications and presentations on the topic
   D. Testimony only for plaintiff cases if being hired as a plaintiff's expert or only for defense if a defense expert

4. In preparation of a professional negligence case, the LNC will perform the following tasks, EXCEPT:
   A. Ensure that medical records are complete as much as possible.
   B. Prepare summary and chronology of information from medical records.
   C. Identify appropriate experts.
   D. "Sign up" the plaintiff as a client of the firm by explaining the contingency fee structure.

5. Key roles of the LNC in a professional negligence case, working for the defense, include all the following EXCEPT:
   A. Advise the client to settle for policy limits early in the suit.
   B. Screen and meet with critical defense witnesses.
   C. Talk with attorneys with whom the defense expert has worked.
   D. Obtain and review previous testimony and publications of all experts.

Answers: 1. B, 2. C, 3. D, 4. D, 5. A

Chapter 13

Elements of Triage: Effective Case Screening of Medical Malpractice Claims

Phyllis ZaiKaner Miller, RN, and
Marguerite Barbacci, BSN, RN, MPH, RNC, LNCC

CONTENTS

0-8493-1418-6/03/$0.00+$1.50
© 2003 by AALNC

Objectives

Upon completion of the chapter, the reader will be able to:

- Define the process of "triaging" medical malpractice cases under investigation
- Name at least five elements to consider when screening every medical malpractice case
- Define the three types of damages and give examples of each
- Explain the difference between negligence and "known complication"
- Name where jury instruction guides can be obtained for each state

Introduction

Legal nurse consultants (LNCs) pride themselves on producing excellent work product. Medical record summaries are created, research on assigned topics is completed, and experts to review and testify on a given topic are identified in the time frame requested. What many LNCs fail to recognize is how their work product fits into the larger picture of the investigation and litigation of a claim. Many LNCs wonder why they do not get repeat business from an attorney who just months before had told them that their work product was fine. This chapter will touch upon topics that are part of the larger picture of claims management, and describe how the LNC can assist the attorney in the successful pursuit of potential claims. Supporting an attorney in bringing a claim to a successful conclusion will often be more valuable than completion of singular assignments.

The following topics are "elements of triage" that should be addressed and evaluated each time a potential medical malpractice case is presented for investigation. The elements include:

- Liability
- Damage
- Causation
- Statute of limitations
- Contributory/comparative negligence
- Conflict of interest
- Economics
- The defendants
- The client
- Venue and jurisdiction
- Other considerations

Each item will be explained with an example given to illustrate the element. By using these elements as guidelines for recognizing (triaging) cases likely to be successful, LNCs can enhance their business practice focus from a task-oriented service to an analytical and substantive contribution highly regarded by the attorney. Summaries and other "assigned tasks" can be done by others who have some familiarity with medical terms, but only a registered nurse has the depth of knowledge and experience to evaluate the merits or problems of a potential case.

The ability to analyze case facts in the context of medical negligence sets LNCs apart from other individuals on the litigation team.

Medical malpractice is in large measure about medicine as well as law. The lawyer understands the law and the advocacy system. Blending the talents of the lawyer with an LNC who understands how the two systems fit together makes for a more successful endeavor for the attorney and increased business for the LNC.

When discussing a medical malpractice case with an attorney, inquire about the elements of triage. If the attorney has not revealed enough information about the case to know whether the elements were considered, the LNC should ask the attorney about the various elements. Complete information about the elements of the case will assist the LNC in producing a work product that will be truly helpful to the case. For example, if the LNC is familiar with the case facts and elements, it may be clear that an assignment of summarizing certain medical records would be nonproductive and not likely to contribute to the outcome of the claim. The LNC might be able to suggest to the attorney additional or alternative projects that would be more useful.

Trying to pursue a malpractice claim built on only one or two elements of professional negligence is like trying to build a car with just an engine or bake a cake with only flour; it is a losing proposition. Caveat emptor: After reviewing the elements of the case, it becomes apparent to the LNC that the lawyer may be trying to build a car with an engine and two doors. The lawyer believes the case has "great jury appeal." To be most helpful, the LNC should determine how best to approach the attorney with a clear discussion of the missing or difficult elements and an opinion to counter his exuberance. While the decision to proceed with or defer a potential claim ultimately rests with the attorney, giving the attorney advance warning of potential pitfalls likely to be encountered is a valuable service. If the LNC working for the plaintiff attorney does not recognize and point out issues with the potential to blindside the attorney, chances are that a smart defense lawyer or his LNC will. Although the information may not be what the attorney wanted to hear, he will be grateful as long as the basis for a "less than optimistic" outlook for the potential success of the claim is explained.

Medical malpractice laws are designed to protect patients' rights to pursue monetary compensation for injuries incurred as a result of negligence. The reality is that medical malpractice suits are difficult and costly to win. Theoretically, any person can attempt to seek compensation for an injury caused by negligence, regardless of its severity. Most attorneys will pursue cases only where damages are serious or permanent, which translates into significant monetary compensation.[1]

Almost without exception, attorneys representing plaintiffs in malpractice claims work on a contingency basis. This means that the attorney makes no money unless the claim settles or a verdict is reached and damages are awarded. The contingency fee is a percentage of the settlement or verdict. This fee pays the salaries of the attorney and other office staff plus overhead expenses. When working on a contingency basis, the attorney usually fronts the costs for all aspects of the litigation (e.g., record retrieval, consultant and expert services including the LNC, court reporter, etc.). Attorneys working on a contingency basis make nothing when a decision is made not to pursue a claim after an investigation has taken place. The attorney may invest a significant sum for expenses and have nothing to show for it.

Most malpractice cases take 3 to 5 years to resolve. The attorney working on contingency may subsidize a case for a long period of time before receiving any salary or reimbursement of expenses. While the attorney subsidizes the case over the course of a number of years, the cost of maintaining his practice continues. The prudent attorney will screen potential cases carefully before investing time and money. By employing the "elements of triage" when asked to work on a plaintiff claim, LNCs can assist the attorney in making an economically sound decision regarding the investigation and eventual pursuit of the claim. Use of the elements will help LNCs give the best possible advice to the attorney and add value to their professional services.

Elements of Triage

Before accepting an assignment or when asked to interview a new potential client, the LNC should ascertain as much information as possible about each of the elements. The information obtained early in the investigation of the case will help the LNC fine-tune the work product and assist the attorney in identifying weaknesses and potential defenses of the claim.

Liability

Liability is also known as negligence. The plaintiff should be engaged in a thorough discussion of what he feels the physician did wrong. Is the plaintiff's theory of liability something that will anger a jury or merely make them yawn? The investigation of liability should not be confined to the plaintiff's theory of negligence. Many times a thorough review of the records will reveal that what the plaintiff believes to be negligence is actually acceptable, while negligence causing the injuries that the plaintiff alleges may have occurred in different circumstances.[2]

Consider the following questions when reviewing the case facts: Has a health care provider acted outside the accepted standards of practice? Was something done or not done that any reasonable practitioner would have done or not done under the same circumstances? "Known or commonly occurring" complications do not typically constitute liability, while failure to recognize and appropriately treat complications may. An unusual complication may well suggest a breach of care. Using clinical judgment to choose one of many acceptable treatments, even if the choice does not have a good outcome for the patient, is not necessarily negligence.

Do not determine liability with the benefit of hindsight. In a case of "failure to diagnose," remember that the potential defendant did not know what the reviewer knows. A potential defendant's liability must be determined based on the information available to the defendant in that time and place and under the circumstances described.

If the initial evaluation of the case makes determining liability difficult, assume that liability exists. Proceed with the case review to determine whether the other elements of negligence are present. If other elements are present warranting the expert review phase, the medical expert identified can determine the existence of liability.

Damages

Damages are divided into three types: special, general, and punitive. Special damages are the out-of-pocket expenses incurred by the plaintiff as a result of the negligence. General damages are nonpecuniary damages recognized as compensable, but on which the law is unable to place a dollar amount. The most common example of general damages is "pain and suffering." General damages are sometimes referred to as "noneconomic" damages. Punitive damages, also known as exemplary damages, are damages exceeding the amount intended to make the plaintiff whole. Punitive damages are intended to punish the defendant, to set an example, and to deter future behavior considered "outrageous." Most jurisdictions determine whether punitive damages can or cannot be awarded and often set a cap on the amount that can be awarded.

The value of any claim is based on the perceived value of the plaintiff's damages. Thoroughly discuss with the plaintiff all potential damages from the alleged negligence. If there are no damages, there is no case, irrespective of the egregiousness of the conduct.[2]

Every injury has a theoretical value. The astute LNC will consider the full impact of any claimed injury and over time will get a feeling for how this translates into the monetary amount the attorney is considering. Ask the attorney what he thinks his case is worth. Imagine sitting on a jury and thinking, "How much should this person be awarded?" In assessing damages, determine every way in which the plaintiff's life has been changed as a result of the injury. Permanency of an injury and impairment in ability to work or engage in activities of daily living must all be considered in determining damages.[3] Has there been a death or an injury? Is the injury permanent and/or serious? Determine whether the plaintiff's life expectancy would have been reduced absent the negligence. Would the disease have progressed despite any intervention? Can the plaintiff be compensated for "loss of chance"?

Some jurisdictions recognize a theory of recovery in medical malpractice cases for a patient's loss of chance of survival or loss of chance of a better recovery. Under this theory, the compensable injury is the lost opportunity to achieve a better result, not the physical harm caused by the plaintiff's initial condition. This theory applies where the patient is suffering from a preexisting injury or illness that is aggravated by the alleged negligence of the health care provider to the extent that (1) the patient dies, when without negligence there might have been a substantial chance of survival, or (2) the patient had a chance of surviving his illness but for the delay in diagnosis. Because of the negligence, that chance has been lost. This is different from the claim that the patient had a more than likely expectation of cure that has now been lost due to negligence.[4]

In some states, a plaintiff must have a greater than 50% chance of survival at the time of the alleged negligence that caused the chance of survival to go below 50%. In this circumstance, there would be no claim for negligence that reduced the plaintiff's chance of survival from 49 to 0% or from 95 to 51%, but there would be a claim for negligence that reduced the chance of survival from 51 to 49%.[5]

When assessing damages, look carefully at the plaintiff's health history. Preexisting medical conditions (such as a diagnosis of cancer) or surgeries, medical bills, and disability that would have been encountered even with appropriate care are not elements of damage. Are the client's injuries severe enough to warrant further investigation? Can the injuries be seen on x-rays, electrocardiograms

(EKGs), magnetic resonance imaging, or other electronic imaging? If the injury is difficult to understand, presenting it to a jury and assigning a monetary value may prove difficult. Cases in which the primary injuries are soft-tissue injuries, mild head injuries, or mental distress can pose special problems because these injuries cannot be seen by the jurors.[4]

Causation

The issue of causation is the battleground in a great number of medical malpractice cases.[2] Negligence must be causally related to the injury claimed. The LNC must think carefully about the following questions and be comfortable with the answers. Did the negligence cause the damage? Did the negligence cause all or part of the plaintiff's problem? Was the negligence responsible for only part of the damages? If so, determine which part. Is there any reason why the result would have been the same absent the negligence? In death cases, would the plaintiff have died absent the negligence? If death was a possibility, even absent the negligence, be prepared to support this conclusion in discussions with the attorney. Damages proximately caused by the alleged negligence must be distinguished from those that the client would or did suffer irrespective of any negligence.[2]

Causation is typically the most difficult element of medical negligence to prove. The precise definition of cause for each state can be found in the jury instruction guides for the jurisdiction in question. The jury instruction guides state the precise language that a judge will read to the jury when instructing them about the information to consider when rendering a verdict. The information that the jury will be asked to consider is what the attorney will have to prove in court. Jury instruction guides can be found in a local law library or on the Internet.

During the course of a case investigation, the LNC should ask several times whether the alleged negligence caused the elements of damage being claimed. The relationship can sometimes become very fuzzy over the life of a claim. Fuzzy issues are hard to prove in court, may be vigorously and expensively defended, and usually represent difficult claims for the plaintiff to win. If the LNC can't explain the causation of a claim to the attorney, odds are that neither an insurance adjuster nor a jury will understand it either.

Statute of Limitations

Every state has a different statute of limitations (SOL) for medical malpractice claims. The SOL will be different for minors or when a mentally impaired individual is involved. Some states have a different SOL for death claims and another for discovery of the injury or negligence. Knowing the applicable SOL will give the attorney time to prepare or avoid a costly appeal on a case where the SOL has run. While it is ultimately the attorney's responsibility to determine with certainty the applicable SOL, the actual dates in the medical records will usually be the determining factor, not what the client may have told the attorney.

Be alert for the applicable dates in the record and alert the attorney as soon as possible if a potential problem or the SOL is near. A case to be pursued with a statute running should be made a high priority. If the attorney is overcommitted, it may be prudent to suggest that the case be turned down rather than risk having the statute run out while the file is the attorney's responsibility.

Contributory/Comparative Negligence

Some states recognize the doctrine of contributory negligence as a complete bar to a plaintiff's recovery. If the plaintiff did anything that could be perceived by a jury as having contributed to his own injury, even if the blame is only 1%, recovery is precluded. In states where the doctrine of comparative negligence is recognized, the jury can assign a percentage of fault to the plaintiff and deduct that amount from any award. In some jurisdictions, the verdict may be reduced to zero if the percentage of fault attributed to the plaintiff is 51% or more.

Be mindful of the actions and inactions of the plaintiff client. Because the distinct possibility exists that a plaintiff will walk away from the courthouse with nothing because of these doctrines, the attorney must consider the plaintiff's actions in determining the value of a case. Did the client do anything to incur or aggravate his own injury? Was the plaintiff compliant with the prescribed course of care? Did the plaintiff follow the health care provider's instructions, keep scheduled appointments, inform his provider of new symptoms or problems, etc.? Was the plaintiff harmed by medication that he continued to take after being instructed to discontinue the medicine?[2-3]

The following is an example of contributory negligence: A negligent health care provider misses a subtle finding that might indicate the presence of cervical cancer. The patient had not had a pap smear in 30 years. Who bears the most responsibility for the advanced stage of cancer when diagnosed? A jury could conclude that much of the fault lies with the patient/plaintiff and therefore fail to award damages based on the doctrine of contributory negligence.

Conflict of Interest

When assessing a potential claim, it is important to identify any possible conflicts of interest as early in the investigation as possible. While not exactly conforming to the legal definition of "conflict," most lawyers would decline to handle a claim against their personal physician, a physician neighbor/acquaintance, or a physician who was about to testify for them on behalf of another plaintiff. Often, large law firms will maintain a "conflict list," a list of physicians' names against whom the firm will not enter into litigation. If the attorney has such a list, the LNC should become familiar with it and refer to it when evaluating any potential case.

Economics

The attorney must evaluate whether the costs involved with litigating a case justify the potential outcome. Regardless of how strong the case is of liability, one simply cannot justify spending $30,000 to pursue a case that, if the plaintiff wins, is expected to return a jury verdict of $50,000. Very few medical malpractice cases worth less than $150,000 justify pursuit. The average medical malpractice case can cost between $25,000 and $100,000 in expenses to litigate.[2]

In a contingency practice, time is money. The more time the attorney spends, the more money he will need to recover from the contingency fee. Experts and consultants are expensive. If a potential case has low damages, but the projected number of expensive experts is high and analysis time-consuming, the attorney may well be looking at spending a dollar to recover a dime. This is not good business practice. If the potential for recovery is low, there is little reason for the attorney to accept the case. An injury resulting in a crooked fifth finger in an arthritic older man who cannot remember how he was injured is far different from the same injury in a concert pianist. A case requiring emergency medicine experts, an internist, a pulmonologist, and a surgeon to testify on liability and causation issues will be very expensive and need higher damages to justify the extra expenses to be incurred. If the case otherwise looks good, but the economics are shaky, the LNC should enter into a discussion with the attorney about the potential cost of the case.[4,6-8]

The issue of sovereign immunity needs to be factored into the equation. Certain institutions, providers, or governmental agencies have special protection and liability limits, such as a state or university-connected hospital. An act of the legislature in that state may even be required to exceed the damage limit. This is an important economic consideration. Cases that deal with issues such as vaccines or brain-damaged babies may be governed by a compensation fund set up by federal or state law. These compensation funds may also limit damages.

The Defendant

If the defendant is a sympathetic character, damages awarded by a jury may be unconsciously reduced. In medical malpractice cases, the qualifications and standing of the defendant in the medical community needs to be considered. With a highly regarded and well-respected defendant, the process of identifying medical experts willing to testify may be difficult. If the defendant's area of practice is highly specialized, the pool of potential testifying experts is small and would make the task of finding an expert next to impossible. Are multiple defendants from different jurisdictions involved? This scenario could lead to costs in excess of damages due to increased travel, need for multiple testifying experts, expanded discovery, and so on.

The Client

At the initial meeting, the attorney and LNC form impressions about the client. Is the client likable, articulate, and believable? Does the client evoke sympathy? What are the client's motives for bringing a lawsuit? The plaintiff must be evaluated by the attorney and LNC in terms of how he will appear to a jury under the facts of the case.[2]

Be wary of issues suggesting credibility problems. If the record says one thing and the plaintiff says another, the argument can rapidly disintegrate to a "he said/she said" contest. Such a contest is almost always won by the defendant physician or nurse.

The client whom the jury may perceive as untruthful because of his background is another cause for concern. History of a prior criminal conviction, general unsavory appearance, or a questionable job, such as a loan shark, may cause the juror to regard the plaintiff with suspicion and discount the estimated value of the case. Consider the plaintiff's background and habits. Representing convicted felons, wife beaters, drug addicts, or alcoholics is generally not a moneymaking proposition. In these cases, juries tend to sympathize with the physician and not the plaintiff. A jury will not likely be inclined to award large sums of money to a person with any of these questionable traits.[2,4,6-8]

A greedy client is easy to spot by attorneys and juries. Obtaining justice takes a backseat to the greedy client's interest in obtaining "suitcase money." A subset of greedy clients is plaintiffs who have filed many claims. Problems of credibility will occur if evidence of prior claims surfaces at trial. The attorney and LNC will need to determine whether credibility problems such as these can be overcome with the strength of the case.[2,4,6-8]

Finally, is the plaintiff the type of person who is likely to take an active role in the case? Will the plaintiff assist the attorney and litigation team with tasks, such as answering interrogatories, providing documents for production to the adversary, and attending defense medical examinations?[2]

Venue and Jurisdiction

Venue and jurisdiction may also affect the decision to investigate a case. In what court will the case be tried? If the county where the negligence occurred has never had a plaintiff verdict and only one hospital is in that locale, be careful and be sure. Because of demographics, certain areas are not conducive to suits against health care providers. Other areas may have the reputation of being plaintiff friendly. It is helpful to know the litigation climate of the possible venue at the onset of the investigation.[7] If multiple defendants are involved, the attorney must decide the jurisdiction in which to sue.

Other Considerations

Informed Consent

Claims involving only informed consent issues are generally not winners. The burden of proof is high and requires a plaintiff to prove that no reasonable person would have gone along with the treatment, medication, or surgery "if he had only been told" that whatever unfortunate thing has come to pass could possibly have happened. The plaintiff also has to prove through expert testimony that the standard of care required the particular risk to be disclosed. As a rule, physicians are not required to disclose every possible complication that can occur or every potential or rare side effect of every drug prescribed.

Cosmetic Surgery Cases

Cosmetic surgery cases with less than hoped-for results are difficult cases to litigate. The surgery is typically elective, and many jurors may feel that the plaintiff "should have left well enough alone." Cases involving abortion, body parts, and functions not typically discussed in public forums are also claims that the attorney would closely examine prior to pursuing an investigation.

Was the Case Previously Rejected for Investigation?

In deciding to pursue investigation of a case, it is important to discern whether other attorneys have investigated and turned down the case and the reasons behind the decision. Because a case has been rejected by one attorney doesn't necessarily preclude further investigation, but should alert the attorney to the possibility of potential problems with the case.

Cooperation of the Subsequent Treating Physician

It is often important to know whether the subsequent treating physician will cooperate with the prosecution of the case, especially where she is the only observant of a crucial object or event. For example, in a case involving an allegedly botched surgery, the observations of the subsequent surgeon are of crucial importance. She is the only ostensibly "neutral" person who has seen the site of the original surgery. Jurors are more likely to believe the observations of the treating physician over the opinions of hired experts.[2]

Illustration of Elements

The following examples set forth the facts as gleaned from the plaintiff and/or medical record, followed by the analysis of the claim.

The Disastrous Hysterectomy

A 47-year-old female had a long history of painful uterine fibroid tumors and very heavy periods. She was prescribed iron supplements, but still had trouble maintaining a normal hemoglobin level. Her condition was unmanageable; she wanted no additional children and opted for a hysterectomy. An abdominal approach for the hysterectomy was planned as her surgeon believed there were too many adhesions from prior cesarean sections and other abdominal surgeries. During the surgery, the surgeon injured a ureter while trying to free the uterine ligaments from dense adhesions. The injury to the ureter went unnoticed. The surgery was completed "without complication" as stated in the operative report. On postoperative day 3, the patient was distended and complaining of severe abdominal pain. An ileus was suspected. Laxatives were given and ambulation encouraged. On postoperative day 4, the patient was febrile and seemed sicker. An abdominal film was ordered and something beyond an ileus was seen. Additional testing was done and the severed ureter was discovered. The patient was returned to surgery and had a stent placed by percutaneous nephrostomy. The abdomen was irrigated and the urinoma cleaned out. Days later and still miserable, the patient was discharged. She was instructed to return 6 weeks later for the removal of the stent and tubing. Subsequent testing showed the ureter to be functioning well with adequate renal function.

Analysis: This case has problems with liability and economics. The injury to the ureter could easily be said to be an expected complication and not an act of negligence. Even the most careful surgeon could have caused this injury under these circumstances. The fact that the injury went unnoticed at the time of surgery may also not be negligent. The failure to diagnose the damaged ureter immediately when the patient did not recover as expected may also be within the standard of care. If looked at without the benefit of hindsight, an ileus is certainly more common and presents just about the same way for many postsurgical patients. Certainly the patient experienced a less than desirable outcome, but even prompt recognition in the surgical suite may well have led to the identical course of treatment, albeit a few days sooner. The economics of pursuing a claim based on a few days of misery in a patient who was going to be sick and recovering from surgery anyway do not make sense. The final summary: the patient incurred a known commonly occurring complication not related to an act of negligence and there were no permanent injuries.

The Missed Myocardial Infarction

A 62-year-old man presented to the emergency room of the local hospital with burning chest pain that had developed while he was at work on a construction site. The man is a bricklayer and had a history of previous episodes of similar chest pain. Upon arrival at the emergency room, the pain had subsided. His cholesterol level was found to be "a little high," but he claimed to be "eating better since he found out." He also stated that he "used to take blood pressure pills," but stopped taking them because it was ruining his "married life." An EKG was done and interpreted as showing only nonspecific changes. The man was discharged to home with a diagnosis of heartburn and symptomatic treatment prescribed. A few days later the pain returned, "worse than ever," and continued unabated. The man was taken to the emergency room by his wife. An acute myocardial infarction was diagnosed and angioplasty with placement of stents carried out. Five days later, the patient was discharged. Echocardiogram prior to discharge revealed an ejection fraction of 55%. A retrospective analysis of the EKG done at the first emergency room visit disclosed that the first EKG had been misread and had evidence of ischemia.

Analysis: This case has possible good liability, but has problems with damages and even possibly contributory negligence, making the economics very questionable. The EKG was misread and accepted standards of care likely required admission for treatment of the ischemia, evaluation of the extent of disease, possible angioplasty, or bypass and modification of risk factors at time of the initial emergency room visit. This case resulted in these exact sequence of events just a few days later than it should have occurred. The patient underwent an angioplasty with placement of stents. The small amount of damages incurred, based on the near normal ejection fraction, means that the patient will likely keep working. (No wage loss was caused by the negligence.) The plaintiff's failure to take his antihypertensive medication as directed may well have contributed to the extent of his cardiac disease. In summary, the clinical case had a good outcome. The plaintiff was permanently injured by neither the improper reading of the initial EKG nor his contributory negligence.

Delayed Diagnosis of Breast Cancer

A 35-year-old woman was recently diagnosed with breast cancer. She was told by her oncologist that the cancer should have been caught earlier. The patient was shown the missed lesion on a mammogram performed and read as normal 14 months prior to her diagnosis. The patient underwent a lumpectomy and subsequent chemotherapy and radiation.

On further questioning, the patient told the attorney that she had a copy of the pathology report and would fax it to the office. The pathology report described the following lesion: 2 cm in greatest dimension in the upper outer quadrant of the breast with clear margins. The pathology of the lesion was an infiltrating ductal carcinoma. The sentinel lymph node biopsy was positive with positive estrogen receptors. The patient's cancer was designated a Stage II.

Analysis: At face value, this case represents possible liability on the part of the radiologist for failing to properly interpret the mammogram. The much more difficult elements to prove in a case such as this are causation and damages. Being successful in this claim would require the plaintiff to prove to a reasonable degree of medical certainty that the delay of 14 months led to a progression of her cancer, and that in turn that interval caused her harm. In other words, except for the negligent delay in diagnosis, her outcome (treatment and prognosis) would have been different and better. In all cancer cases, the first thing the LNC should do is to look up the statistical survivability of the cancer at all stages and how the specific type of cancer diagnosed normally progresses.

Fortunately for the plaintiff, a Stage II breast cancer is very curable, and the plaintiff is still more likely to survive. In other words, even if it is proven that the plaintiff was a Stage I 14 months prior to her diagnosis (no lymph node involvement), progressing from a Stage I to Stage II did not change the likelihood that she would survive the cancer. The delay may have reduced the survival odds a bit, but she is still quite curable. If the attorney wanted to consider the damage to be the change from Stage I to Stage II, not all states recognize "loss of chance" claims. (In this case, loss of chance would be a downward change in the statistical survivability of the cancer.) Even a Stage I cancer would have required surgery and likely radiation. The only damage the plaintiff is likely to recover is the need for chemotherapy, which would come into play only with testimony that she would not have had positive lymph nodes 14 months prior to her diagnosis (i.e., absent the negligence). This claim would be very difficult to litigate with damages that are hard to prove despite the fact that there may be liability.

The Failed Back Surgery

Mr. Jones had a two-level lumbar fusion with placement of hardware, including two pedicle screws and autologous transplant of bone harvested from his iliac crest. After the surgery and weeks of therapy, Mr. Jones was no better. In fact, in some ways his condition was worse. It was determined that the spinal fusion did not take and was not solid. Mr. Jones required additional surgery to have the hardware removed and the fusion redone. He remained in daily pain and was unable to return to work for a period of several additional months. Mr. Jones and his wife were unable to pay the medical bills and went bankrupt. He was certain that his surgery had been done incorrectly or he would not have had the postoperative pain and suffering. Before the surgery, Mr. Jones' doctor assured him that he would be able to return to work 6 weeks after surgery. Mr. Jones said that his diagnosis now is failed back surgery and believed that if he had been told there was a chance that the surgery would not work, he never would have gone through with the spinal fusion and hardware placement.

Analysis: It would seem that this case is a good example of significant general and special damages in pain and suffering, medical bills, and lost wages. Unfortunately, failed fusions are not uncommon and are considered a risk of the procedure. Unless the plaintiff could prove that the fusion failed not by chance, but due to an act of negligence, there is no liability. On the informed consent issue, it is not likely that the attorney would be able to convince a jury that this man would have opted for the misery he was in before the surgery even if he had been told of a small chance that the surgery would not work.

Sinus Surgery

Marvin Goldstein, a 32-year-old man, went to see an otolaryngologist for sinus surgery. Under IV conscious sedation, the surgeon entered the sinus with a surgical instrument. Applying pressure on the instrument, the surgeon pierced the posterior wall of the sinus, the cribiform plate, and entered the brain. Noting bright red blood and grey brain tissue coming out of the area, the surgeon stopped the procedure. An emergency CT scan of the brain was arranged. The surgeon decided to operate on the opposite side's sinus while waiting for the CT scanner to be ready. The posterior wall of the sinus was also pierced, resulting in bleeding and removal of brain tissue.

The patient was transferred on an emergent basis to the hospital, where surgery confirmed the brain damage sustained during the sinus surgery. Following an acute care admission, the patient underwent rehabilitation. He was left incontinent, unable to think clearly, and emotionally impulsive.

Analysis: This case meets the test of a viable medical malpractice claim. The damages included cognitive losses, wage loss, and permanent disability. The liability issue was easy to establish since the surgeon used excessive force when performing the procedure. Brain damage from intrusion into the brain was not considered a known risk of the procedure. The surgeon used poor judgment in operating on the second sinus moments after entering the brain through the first sinus. There was no difficulty establishing that the standard of care was breached and resulted in the damages.

The plaintiff attorney learned that the otolaryngologist had repeated this same medical misadventure 3 months later with a second patient. Both suits settled.

Summary

Developing a quality work product often means doing more than was asked. For the LNC, this means expanding the business from a task-oriented practice to one built on solid analytical and investigative skills. It means going beyond producing a narrative record summary or literature review requested by the attorney to applying assessment skills in determining whether the plaintiff client will have jury appeal. Adding value to the LNC's service means that the LNC must explore the case facts fully to know what parts of the medical records are important, what information is necessary to highlight, and what facts can be glossed over.

It means tactfully pointing out to the attorney things in the record that give rise to real concerns about contributory negligence or causation or less than expected damages.

Many attorneys handling plaintiff claims are justifiably proud of their advocacy in the courtroom and believe that if they could "present their case in front of a jury," they would be able to make a great recovery. The attorney is and should be an advocate for the plaintiff's position. However, the LNC with unique knowledge and experience can often be most useful by playing the devil's advocate and reminding the attorney of the possible defenses he will face as the case moves forward. The LNC may be the member of the team that has to tell the lawyer that the client was less than forthcoming about the extent of his true injury and has recovered fully. The LNC may need to be the person to approach the attorney with the news that the plaintiff's renal failure is from Type I diabetes that he failed to mention and is unlikely to be related to negligence on the part of the doctor. The case where a long delay in the diagnosis of cancer ultimately did not change the client's prognosis may need to be brought to the attention of the attorney to avoid being blindsided by the fact that the plaintiff was a 26-year-old woman with three small children. It is not easy to remind an attorney that the child death case he is contemplating will require eight or ten out-of-state depositions and three or four expensive world-class experts to determine negligence and causation and could quite easily cost more to pursue than the value of such a claim in his jurisdiction.

Assuming this role takes assertiveness on the part of the LNC and may take some practice for the LNC to be comfortable. The LNC is uniquely qualified to fill this role and by doing so will elevate the profession of legal nurse consulting.

References

1. Findlaw.com Online Findlaw for the public, *Medical malpractice. Do you have a case and is it worth pursuing?*, 1, 2001.
2. Cardaro, T.C., Case Screening and Investigation of a Potential Medical Malpractice Claim, presented to the Maryland Trial Lawyers Association, Baltimore, MD, May 2000.
3. Cartwright, R.E., Evaluating a case, *Trial*, 62, September 1987.
4. Shandell, R.E. and Smith, P., *The Preparation and Trial of Medical Malpractice Cases*, rev. ed., Law Journal Press, New York, 1999, chap. 1.
5. *Fennell v. Southern Maryland Hospital*, 580 A.2d 206 (1990).
6. Mackauf, S.H., Medical-legal issues facing neurologists, *Neurologic Clinics*, 17, 345, 1999.
7. Egan, D.E., Finding diamonds in the rough, *Trial*, 37, December 2000.
8. Bartimus, J. and Eaton, C.J., Should you accept the case?, *Trial*, 50, May 1986.

Test Questions

1. All of the following are typically considered complications rather than the result of negligence EXCEPT:
   A. An infection in a surgical wound
   B. A stroke during a carotid endarterectomy
   C. Severe bleeding after lytic therapy for a heart attack
   D. Nerve injury from the stirrups following gynecological surgery

2. In a contingency fee claim, the attorney is paid
   A. A percentage of the settlement or verdict
   B. A percentage of the calculated value of all special damages
   C. Costs plus a percentage of the verdict or settlement
   D. A percentage of the calculated value of the time spent on the claim plus costs

3. Claims of informed consent require the plaintiff to prove that
   A. The doctor failed to inform him of a particular side effect of his medication.
   B. The complication suffered could happen to anyone.
   C. He would not have proceeded with the surgery or medication if this risk had been disclosed.
   D. Accepted standards of care required disclosure of the risk.

4. Contributory negligence might include all EXCEPT:
   A. Smoking
   B. Obesity
   C. Treated hypertension
   D. Missed clinic appointments

5. Special damages are defined as
   A. Nonpecuniary damages recognized as compensable, but on which the law is unable to place a dollar amount
   B. Out-of-pocket expenses incurred by the plaintiff as a result of negligence
   C. Exemplary damages awarded to punish the defendant and to deter future "outrageous" behavior

Answers: 1. D, 2. C, 3. D, 4. C, 5. B

Chapter 14

Nursing Home Litigation

Patricia W. Iyer, MSN, RN, LNCC, and
Mary Lubin, BS, MA, RNC, NHA

CONTENTS

0-8493-1418-6/03/$0.00+$1.50
© 2003 by AALNC

Objectives

- To identify reasons for an increase in nursing home litigation
- To identify common defenses for nursing home cases

Introduction

It is more likely than ever before that legal nurse consultants (LNCs) will play some role in the burgeoning field of nursing home litigation. This rapidly growing area of specialized medical and nursing malpractice has seemingly overnight changed the complexion of the nursing home industry. Cases involving elderly people, which a few short years ago would have been considered financially unrewarding to pursue, are now resulting in six- and seven-figure verdicts and settlements. This chapter will trace the history of nursing home cases, provide information about the outcomes of these types of cases, and explore the liability issues associated with the field. It will present information on how the standards of care are used to litigate and defend these cases, and define how the LNC participates in this area of litigation. It will conclude with examples of expert witness and consulting reports specific to nursing home cases.

History of Nursing Home Litigation

Care provided in nursing homes has come under increased scrutiny for at least a half century. Traditionally responsible for the care of elderly parents, women entered the workforce in accelerating numbers at the time of World War II and thereafter. The need for nursing homes multiplied with the loss of the traditional caretaking role. As the numbers of nursing homes increased, the awareness of the conditions within them resulted in efforts to set standards and make improvements. For-profit chains began to build nursing homes in addition to those run by the typical "mom and pop" model.

The 1980s were marked by disturbing reports about the number of elderly who were being restrained in nursing homes. Plaintiff attorneys became aware of instances during which elderly were strangled by restraints. The attorneys' focus on this issue spurred the nursing profession to begin to evaluate the harmful effects of restraints. Key nursing literature exposed the risks of restraints and stimulated an examination of policies, practices, and regulations regarding restraints. An image began to emerge of elderly people tied down and chemically restrained with sedatives. These individuals were warehoused and taken care of by staff with no preparation to address the needs of the long-term care resident. There was no systematic way to assess needs and assure the resident of basic rights.

In 1986, a report prepared by the Institute of Medicine addressed the quality of care concerns specific to the nursing home industry. This report, "Improving the Quality of Care in Nursing Homes," was based on data and the expertise of professionals. Many of these recommendations were incorporated into the Nursing Home Quality Reform Act, Omnibus Budget Reconciliation Act of 1987 (OBRA).[1] In order to ensure passage of this legislation, it was tacked onto an essential act needed to stabilize the economy. OBRA 87 put into place new requirements for resident assessment and rights, training for nursing assistants, and reduction and control of the use of psychotropic medications. Perhaps its most controversial requirement related to the reduction in the use of restraints.

The provisions of OBRA were published and open for public response and then phased in over time. OBRA's regulations are now part of the Code of Federal Regulations (CFR). Many states have patterned their regulations after the wording used in OBRA. The regulations have had a critical and sweeping impact on the quality of nursing care delivered in nursing homes. The threshold was set for staffing, preparation of certified nursing assistants, the initial admission assessment, resident rights, and a whole host of aspects that govern the care of people in long-term care facilities. Many small mom-and-pop nursing homes closed rather than to be forced to comply with the OBRA requirements. As surveyors from regulatory agencies became trained in the new standards, they were provided with a tool to monitor the quality of care during routine inspections and visits in response to complaints. Fines can be imposed for substandard care. The facility may be prohibited from accepting new residents for a period of time or it may be closed.

Reasons for Increase in Litigation

Societal trends have influenced the increased litigation in long-term care. Many of those in nursing homes today are the parents or grandparents of the baby boomer generation. The baby boomer generation is more likely than their parents to seek out and correct a wrong. Societal awareness of the needs of the elderly has been promoted by a variety of groups, both professional and consumer. The aging of our society has resulted in larger numbers of people living longer. There are approximately 19,000 nursing facilities in this country. With the aging of America, this number will continue to increase. Recent estimates suggest that approximately a third of all women and half of all men over the age of 75 in 2000 will spend some time in a nursing facility. As the aging population grows, more emphasis is being placed on quality health care and viable options for the elderly who need medical care in a long-term setting.

Despite the provisions of OBRA, substandard care still continues to be delivered within long-term care facilities, a concept which the public readily accepts. "The nursing home industry is one of the most heavily regulated in the country. Homes must agree to abide by complex federal and state laws to be licensed, certified, and paid."[2] Armed with a specific set of regulations that govern care, attorneys have increasingly become involved in lawsuits against nursing homes. In the 1990s, the numbers of cases began to increase. Prior to 1998, one of the authors (Iyer) often heard attorneys speak of the fact that nursing home cases were unattractive because they did not bring large verdicts, or there were Medicare liens on files, reducing the value of the case. It was thought that the case expenses would far outweigh any potential recovery. In 1998, a startlingly large verdict against a for-profit chain forever changed the belief that jurors would not award much money to an elderly resident who was going to die soon. In *Gregory v. Beverly Enterprises*, a California jury returned a verdict of $95 million against a facility for a fall that resulted in a broken hip and shoulder. The majority of the damages were punitive. Since that time, interest in nursing home litigation has dramatically increased. In Texas and Florida in particular, there have been several multimillion-dollar awards, some with punitive damages.

In the current climate, there is an increased need for attorneys and their LNCs to be competent in litigating nursing home cases. Plaintiff attorneys who can effectively screen meritorious cases and avoid nonmeritorious cases will be in the best position to manage their resources. Defense attorneys who recognize cases that should be settled without lengthy and expensive litigation will be instrumental in reducing the high costs of insurance. Efforts are underway or have been taken in several states to place a cap or other restrictions on the amount of money that can be awarded in a nursing home case. For example, some states, such as Florida, require the plaintiff attorney to prove that the deviations from the standard of care were the direct cause of the resident's death. The cost of medical malpractice insurance for nursing homes has increased in response to the increasingly large verdicts and settlements.

Trends in Settlements and Jury Verdicts

Whereas a nurse who is put on trial in a hospital case generally has the sympathy of the jury, the nurse who works in a nursing home has a disadvantage. A "guilty unless proven innocent" mentality affects this type of litigation. Public awareness about nursing home care has risen as a result of newspaper, magazine, and television coverage about the quality of care in nursing homes. The nursing home industry suffers from a general assumption in the jury pool that nursing homes are poorly staffed by overworked and underpaid nursing aides. This belief gives rise to a conclusion that nursing home residents receive little care. Many elderly people are fearful of the need to be put in a nursing home because of this concern. It is easy for many jurors to believe the claims of the plaintiff. These factors influence the process of identifying meritorious claims, settlement negotiations, and trial strategies.

In order to determine trends affecting settlements and verdicts, a national publication was analyzed. *Medical Malpractice Verdicts, Settlements and Experts*

2000	Percent of All Cases
Skin breakdown	37%
Sexual abuse	6%
Neglect	14%
Medication error	3%
Fractures	23%
Miscellaneous	6%
Wandering	6%
Choking	6%

2001	Percent of All Cases
Skin breakdown	35%
Choking	4%
Burns	2%
Wandering	4%
Sexual abuse	9%
Neglect	22%
Miscellaneous	9%
Medication errors	4%
Fractures	11%

	Range	Average
Skin breakdown	$70,000–$10,100,000	$1,827,567
Sexual abuse	$125,000–$8,000,000	$4,062,500
Neglect	$81,308–$5,100,000	$2,670,327
Medication error	$901,478	$901,478
Fractures	Confidential–$550,000	$220,270
Miscellaneous	Confidential–$446,000	$446,000
Wandering	$9,031–$300,000	$154,515
Choking	$45,000–$75,000	$60,000

	Range	Average
Skin breakdown	Confidential–$321,700,000	$38,697,777
Choking	$700,000–$763,333	$731,666
Burns	$650,000	$650,000
Wandering	$200,000–$698,785	$449,392
Sexual abuse	$175,000–$12,028,000	$4,738,250
Neglect	$125,000–$2,475,000	$691,653
Miscellaneous	$115,264–$298,000	$195,088
Medication errors	$91,040	$91,040
Fractures	$24,000–$623,544	$261,885

Figure 14.1 Outcomes of 2000 Cases (Based on 12 Months) and 2001 Cases (Based on 9 Months)

prints case information on a wide variety of medical malpractice cases. Information specific to nursing home litigation is summarized in Figure 14.1. The nursing home cases included in this sample were reported in issues published between January 2000 and September 2001. Note that of those cases that went to trial, the plaintiff attorney won far more often than did the defendant in both years.

The cases for 2000 and 2001 were further analyzed to identify the common areas of liability. These were divided into broad categories. A few explanatory notes about these categories follow.

1. The objects that the residents choked on included small objects, candy, meat, a restraint, and a latex glove.

2. The category of neglect was used to define cases involving failure to prevent, diagnose, and treat medical problems; dehydration; sepsis; and malnutrition.

3. The largest number of pressure ulcers on one person was cited as 20, in a case that settled for $500,000.[3] The case that resulted in the largest verdict (of $2.71 million in compensatory damages and $310 million in punitive damages) involved 16 pressure ulcers in Texas.[4]

4. Residents who wandered out of the facility fell and fractured hips or were hit by cars.

5. Fractures of the neck, pelvis, femur, and hip resulted from falls or being dropped by staff.

6. Sexual assault resulted from attacks by other residents, visitors, or teenage males. A case of a young mentally retarded woman who was raped resulted in a pregnancy, which was terminated, and an $8 million award.[5]

7. Medication errors resulted from overdoses of insulin and morphine, and overmedication with ibuprofen.

8. Examples of the miscellaneous category included a family who received $446,000 when they were not notified of the resident's death, battery, misplacement of a feeding tube, failure to carry out an order for continuous pulse oximetry, and a closed head injury after a fall.

Two facilities were closed as a result of the lawsuits that were filed:

Example 14.1: In a Texas case, the plaintiff was the guardian of mentally retarded twin daughters who were 29 years old. The daughters lived in a community-based group home, which was sold, and the living conditions allegedly deteriorated rapidly. Written promises were made to remedy the situation, but nothing was done. The plaintiff alleged that she lodged a formal complaint with the Texas Department of Human Services. The defendants responded by retaliating against her and attempting to discharge her daughters to a state school, which was a 6-hour drive away from the mother's home community. The mother alleged extensive damages of mental and emotional distress pertaining to excessive worry regarding the health and welfare of her daughters. In the course of the attempt to discharge the daughters, the defendants' attorneys asked if they could legally just transport the twins and abandon them at the front gate of the state school, thereby forcing the state facility to assume immediate care of the twins. A judge issued a temporary injunction forbidding discharge, and the state of Texas shut the home down. The jury found in the plaintiff's favor on every special issue and awarded $1,500,000 in actual damages, $600,000 in attorneys' fees, and $3,000,000 in punitive damages for a gross verdict award of $5,100,000. *Nancy Chesser v. Normal Life, Inc. and Normal Life of North Texas, Inc.*[6]

Example 14.2: A Washington state resident suffered from cerebral palsy and mental retardation. She was a lifelong assisted living resident. A visitor on the premises in a highly intoxicated state walked the resident to her room and returned an hour later to rape her. He is serving a 5-year prison term. The facility had a long history of inadequate staffing and negligent supervision of residents. The facility was permanently closed as a direct result of this incident. The plaintiff suffered from posttraumatic stress disorder, rape trauma syndrome, rape, emotional distress, agoraphobia, and ongoing nightmares and panic attacks.

The case settled for $175,000. *Jane Doe v. Westwood Manor Retirement Center and Mark Wheaton.*[7]

Punitive Damages

Four cases in this sample involved punitive damages. Usually not covered by insurance policies, punitive damages are designed to punish the defendant. Horowitz[8] notes that several situations may give rise to punitive damages:

- Fraudulent charting orders approved by management agents, such as the director of nursing or the administrator
- Knowingly being understaffed in order to increase profits
- Fraudulent Medicare and other billings
- Blatant failure to screen employees
- Repeated offenses with knowledge by managing agents

Other cases with the potential for granting of punitive damages include strangulations, rapes, wandering, and severe pressure ulcers. An example of the kind of case that resulted in punitive damages in the 2000–2001 sample is provided below.

Example 14.3: A Texas nursing home was sued for the care provided to a woman who developed multiple adverse changes in her physical status, which the plaintiffs alleged were the direct result of negligence. The resident developed malnutrition, dehydration, contractures, and 16 pressure ulcers (5 of which deteriorated to stage IV). The defendant failed to produce subpoenaed documents. The jury returned a unanimous plaintiff verdict, and awarded $2,710,000 for pain and suffering, impairment, disfigurement, and mental anguish of the decedent in the two and a half years of care before her death. They additionally awarded $310,000,000 in punitive damages. *Cecil Fuqua, as Executor of the Estate of Wyvonne Fuqua, Deceased, v. Horizon/CMS Healthcare Corporation f/k/a/Horizon Healthcare Corporation.*[9]

Common Liability Issues

All cases involving injury and death can be emotional. In many cases, before going to see the attorney, plaintiffs have undergone the emotionally draining experience of seeing their loved one become no longer self-sufficient. The family has been forced to recognize that the type of care needed cannot be provided by the family. If this experience is aggravated by what the family perceives as poor care, then guilt and anger may result. It is very important to separate out from the family's description of the facts the acts constituting negligence from acts that are unavoidable in the nursing home situation. The LNC working as a consultant can be invaluable in helping the attorney see through the emotion to determine whether the case has merit. By screening cases for merit, LNCs may provide a useful service to attorneys handling nursing home cases. This service may be performed by an in-house or independent LNC working for either the plaintiff or defense attorney. Knowledge of the common areas of liability assists the LNC in this process. The LNC can be instrumental in helping the attorney understand the liability and damages issues. Just because the patient fell and had a fracture does not mean that someone was negligent. This is true in nursing homes as it is elsewhere in the health care system. Keep in mind that when these nursing home cases began to be filed, there was a greater chance that the case would be settled than there is today. The defense attorneys have learned that they must vigorously defend the marginal or nonmeritorious cases.

Pressure Ulcers

When plaintiff attorneys receive phone calls from potential clients, certain red-flag issues capture their attention. Pressure ulcers that are stage III or IV; are infected; or cause sepsis, osteomyelitis, or gangrene are red-flag issues. It is hardly surprising that many nursing home litigation issues involve pressure ulcers (formerly called decubitus ulcers), since less than stringent control of any one of several factors can increase the risk of pressure ulcers. In general, most nurses work hard to prevent pressure ulcers from occurring, especially when caring for a nursing home's very frail and chronically ill residents. Many well-intentioned nurses and physicians use out-of-date information concerning preventive skin and tissue care. Some nursing homes do not have the appropriate equipment and supplies to prevent skin breakdown. The registered nurse in a nursing home seldom sees the skin condition of nursing home residents on a daily basis, since certified nursing assistants (CNAs) administer most of the bathing, positioning, and skin care. There is a continuing need for CNAs to be taught skin care and observation while performing these very basic nursing procedures. In addition, most laypeople are aware that many pressure ulcers are preventable and are repulsed by the sight of a pressure ulcer on their loved one's body. All of these factors often lead to litigation and are factors for the LNC to investigate when reviewing a case.

Example 14.4: A typical suit involving a pressure ulcer is reported in *Medical Malpractice Verdicts, Settlements and Experts*. In a case that resulted in a confidential settlement in Texas, the plaintiff maintained that the nursing home had failed to properly nourish and care for a 78-year-old man with Alzheimer's disease, resulting in two stage II pressure ulcers and one stage IV pressure ulcer, which were infected. The plaintiff alleged that the resident had not been fed dinner for months at a time and had lost over 40 pounds. As a result, he died. *Rafaela Aguilar et al. v. Benner Convalescent Center.*[10]

The LNC can find the applicable standards of care in the Agency for Health Care Policy and Research (AHCPR) guidelines, published in 1992 and 1994.[11–12] (AHCPR is now called Agency for Healthcare Research and Quality [AHRQ].) Maklebust and Sieggreen[13] have written a definitive text, *Pressure Ulcers: Guideline for Prevention and Nursing Management*. The book is based on the AHCPR Guidelines and can be used in conjunction with the guidelines in the evaluation of the care that the patient received. Further guidance on the standards of care based on the AHCPR Guidelines can be found in the Pressure Ulcer Therapy Companion published by the American Medical Directors Association.[14] Note, however, that the Federal Resident Assessment Protocol guidelines require the use of "back grading" the staging process in the minimum data set (MDS) assessment. Back grading refers to calling a healing stage IV ulcer a stage III and so on as it heals. Wound care specialists prefer to call the wound a healing stage IV. Back grading is required because the transmitted MDS is also used for reimbursement. (The MDS is described in depth later in the chapter.) If the nursing home uses current staging definitions, the staging of a healing pressure ulcer in the medical record may differ from the staging on the MDS.

Analysis of the medical record of the resident includes evaluation of the risk factors for the development of a pressure ulcer. Risk factors for pressure ulcers include:

- Chronic disease, such as diabetes, cancer, peripheral vascular disease, and coronary artery disease
- Incontinence
- Dehydration and malnutrition
- Immobility
- Immunosuppression
- Fractures
- History of steroid use
- Significant obesity or thinness
- Mental impairment, such as occurs in coma, altered level of consciousness, sedation, or confusion[15]

Review of the medical record includes analysis of the following factors:

- Weekly assessments of general skin condition
- Identification of the risk factors with discussion of the plan of care at team conferences
- Applicable nursing care plans
- Preventive measures taken to reduce the risk of pressure ulcers
- Correct use of the pressure ulcer classification system and skin assessment forms
- Notification of the nursing home resident's physician to obtain treatment orders
- Periodic (at least weekly) notations about the size, depth, locations of, and treatment rendered for the pressure ulcers
- Use of pressure-relieving devices (e.g., fluidized beds)
- Albumin and electrolyte measurements
- Weight loss analysis and monitoring
- Assessment of the need for positioning devices and turning schedules
- Implementation of dietary and topical therapy designed to heal the ulcer
- Photographs (if any) showing the progress of the ulcer (although there is a trend away from the use of photographs as they may make it easier for an attorney to prove negligence)

Pressure ulcer cases may be defended by attributing the changes to peripheral vascular disease, diabetes, and other circulatory diseases, particularly if the ulcer is on the foot. It is also argued that the preexisting conditions of the resident may have made the skin breakdown inevitable.[16] The medical record must be carefully evaluated to determine whether the ulcer developed in the nursing home or elsewhere.

Malnutrition and Dehydration

Many malpractice, neglect, and abuse matters include charges of malnutrition and dehydration. Severe malnutrition and dehydration are red-flag issues for plaintiff attorneys. In the past, little emphasis was placed on the need not only to provide for, but to aggressively pursue adequate nutritional and hydration levels in the residents. Due to the high incidence of malnutrition and dehydration among geriatric populations, recent focus on nutrition and hydration has been forced upon nursing homes by the federal and state survey process. Dehydration is designated as a "sentinel event," to be reported to the Department of Health, and significant unintended weight loss is considered serious. Nursing homes are expected to take immediate remedial action to improve the health of the resident. Often there are other additional factors in such cases, such as skin breakdown, failure to monitor diabetes, failure to monitor medications, and other assessment issues.

Example 14.5: A $540,000 settlement in California was the result of weight loss, dehydration, and a knee contracture. An 80-year-old woman with Alzheimer's disease was admitted and within 5 months lost 25% of her body weight, developed serious pressure ulcers, and had a knee contracture. The plaintiff alleged that the nursing home did not assist with feeding, hydration, and mobility. After transfer to another nursing home, she attained a complete recovery with the exception of the contracture. *Louisa Brandt v. Apple Valley Christian Center.*[17]

Review of the medical record includes analysis of the following documents:

- Intake and output records and activities of daily living (ADL) flowsheets indicating the percentage of the meal intake; reduced intake should be addressed in the care plan
- Weight sheets to determine whether a pattern of weight loss is evident
- Dietary notes to determine whether the dietician was making recommendations for changes in nutritional intake, and whether there was consideration of the need for insertion of a percutaneous endoscopic gastrostomy tube in a resident who was not eating
- Physician progress notes to determine whether the physician was aware of and addressing weight loss
- Emergency department records that indicate that the resident was received in a malnourished or dehydrated state
- Laboratory test results of low albumin and high sodium
- Speech and language swallowing evaluations

The LNC should be aware that some nursing homes are being directed to discard ADL flowsheets, with the argument that these documents are not a permanent part of the medical record. Many plaintiff attorneys take the position that this constitutes tampering with the medical record.[18]

A California research study published in 2000 was based on a concern that nutritional intake was not accurately recorded. This study showed that nursing home staff tends to significantly overestimate total food intake of nursing home residents. The accuracy of staff estimations of food intake is important because OBRA guidelines require an assessment to be conducted when a resident eats 75% or less of most meals. In this study, the nutritional intake of 56 residents was monitored for 3 meals a day, across 3 consecutive days, and using 3 methods. Trained research observers conducted independent observations during the 9 meals and recorded the total percentage of food and fluid intake. Photographs were taken of each resident's tray before and after each of the 9 meals. The percentages of intake were then compared to the corresponding percentages documented by nursing home staff in each resident's medical record. There was significant agreement between both the direct observations of the tray and the photographs. Nursing home staff documentation reflected a significant overestimation of 22% of the residents' total intake levels. The staff failed to identify the more than half (53%) of those residents whose intake levels were equal to or below 75% for most meals.[19]

An excellent reference to review is the article "A Recipe for Nutrition and Hydration."[20] Other sources include standard gerontological nursing and physiology texts. A guide to meeting federal requirements can be found in Survey Procedures for Long Term Care Facilities.[21]

Elder Abuse and Neglect

Little conjures up a more negative mental picture than the mention of elder abuse, mistreatment, and neglect. Congressional hearings in 2001 and 2002 focused on this subject. Physical or sexual abuse is a red-flag issue for plaintiff attorneys. Elder abuse can take the form of physical, sexual, financial, and emotional acts of exploitation. Often there is a combination of these factors. Since July 1999, nursing homes have been required to proactively prevent and protect residents from abuse, mistreatment, and neglect. This protection includes:

1. Having specific policies and procedures for abuse, mistreatment, and neglect prevention
2. Screening employees before hire
3. Offering ongoing educational programs for employees, residents, and families
4. Identifying, investigating, and reporting suspected or actual abuse, mistreatment, and neglect

Surveys for Medicare/Medicaid certification include a specific and rigorous requirement to survey for adherence to these regulations. In investigating a medical record, the LNC must look for evidence of all types of abuse. At times this involves study of the resident's business file as well as the medical record.

Much professional discussion has been centered on injury inflicted by an incompetent resident against another person. It is generally agreed that attack of an incompetent person directed toward a staff member is not abuse. Instead, the debate is whether or not the attack of one incompetent resident against another incompetent resident is abuse. The federal definition of "abuse" includes the phrase "the willful infliction." The latest interpretation is that although not abuse, such incidents are not only preventable, but reportable to the state licensing agency.

Example 14.6: A case involving abuse was reported in *Missouri Lawyers Weekly*. The nursing home settled for $1.5 million in a case where a newly admitted brain-damaged male resident with a history of violence and sexual preoccupation beat and raped a brain-damaged female resident. The plaintiff's position was that the nursing home did not prevent the attack, which would have been prevented if the nursing home had carefully determined whether the nursing home could properly care for this male resident.[22]

Reviewing a matter for abuse can be difficult and require painstaking attention to the details in documentation and the lack of complete documentation. Review of the medical record includes analysis of:

- Bruises that are inconsistent with the description of an incident
- Documentation of bruising, particularly without a specific documented incident or when inconsistent with the description of the incident
- Photographs of injuries
- Radiology reports for spiral fractures, particularly of the arm, which can occur when the wrist is grabbed and the resident's arm is twisted
- Mandatory reports submitted to the Department of Health

Example 14.7: The decedent was a 75-year-old patient at the defendant nursing home. She was bedridden, but was able to get up with assistance. Care included turning by the staff every 2 hours. While getting the decedent ready for her bath, the nurse noticed a bruise on the resident's left lower leg. The resident complained of pain with any movement. X-rays demonstrated spiral fractures of the tibia and fibula. The resident was transferred to a hospital, where she died 9 days later. The defendant nursing home refused to disclose to the decedent's family how her leg had been broken, but simply stated that the matter was under inquiry. How and when the leg was broken was never determined or disclosed. A settlement was reached for $60,000 cash and a deferred payment of $7,354 in five years. *Diana Hodgson, Special Admin. of the Estate of Doris Genita Serratt, Deceased, v. Medi-Homes, Inc.*[23]

Baumhover and Beall[24] provide step-by-step procedures in the assessment of and intervention in elder abuse, as does Burke.[25] For federal assessment procedures, consult Survey Procedures for Long Term Care Facilities.[21]

Falls and Fractures

Falls and fractures are a major cause of disability and death in the elderly. Two of a nursing home's biggest responsibilities are to maintain mobility and prevent falls. In the past, nursing homes used restraints and devices, such as side rails and chair trays, to limit mobility and reduce falls and resulting fractures. The fracture rate for most nursing homes was not reduced by the use of restraints and side rails. The effects of research and OBRA regulations have significantly reduced the use of chemical and physical restraints and devices and increased the mobility of residents. Moreover, facilities must now take an interdisciplinary approach to fall prevention and mobility preservation on an individual basis. The

Types of Falls	Characteristics	Preventive Measures
Anticipated physiological (78%)	History of previous fall; weak or impaired gait; use of mobility aid; incontinent; lack of judgment; disoriented/confused; impaired cognition; medications	Fall risk assessment tool interdisciplinary assessments; effective care plan; implemented care plan; periodic reassessments
Unanticipated physiological (8%)	Pathological fracture; seizures; drop attacks; orthostatic dizziness	Teach resident to rise slowly and recognize prodromal symptoms
Accidental (14%)	Environmental causes; slippery floors, spills; glare, poor lighting; faulty equipment; use of restraints; use of side rails	Effective safety and preventive maintenance programs; restraint reduction committee and program

Figure 14.2 Types of Fall Characteristics (Adapted from Morse, J.M., *Preventing Patient Falls*, Sage Publications, Thousand Oaks, CA, 1997.)

medical record should reflect this in its risk assessment documentation, MDS, resident assessment protocols (RAPs), care plan, and notes by nursing and the interdisciplinary team. The actions should be designed not only to prevent falls, but also to increase or maintain mobility. The standard for maintaining mobility is to have a restorative program in place. The LNC would look for this plan to be in place as part of the nursing care plan. The rehabilitation services department should periodically screen for the need for these services to ensure that the resident is not getting worse.

When the LNC is reviewing a medical record, it is important to identify the type of fall that has occurred. A fall can be defined as a rapid descent and relocation to a lower surface, including "slipping," persons found on the floor, and assisted falls. Falls can be classified as anticipated physiological, unanticipated physiological, or accidental falls.[26] It is important to define the type of fall documented in the medical record so that the planning and postfall actions of the nursing home can be evaluated by the LNC for appropriateness. See Figure 14.2 for definitions and characteristics of falls. Fall risk should be reassessed periodically and immediately after a fall.

Example 14.8: Failure to supervise the aides to follow the plan of care resulted in permanent neurological injury to a resident in Washington and a $900,000 settlement. A woman in her 70s was admitted to the nursing home for rehabilitation following surgery. There was an order to ambulate with the assistance of two aides. On one occasion, she was ambulated by one aide, fell and fractured an ankle, and suffered a spinal cord injury. The ankle was casted and she was placed in a cervical halo device. The halo device became dislodged during a bed transfer and she sustained permanent central nervous system damage. She then required 24-hour nursing care at home. *James and Helen Patenaude v. Providence Mother Joseph Care Center & Providence St. Peter Hospital.*[27]

Analysis of the medical record includes review of documentation such as:

- MDS and RAPs for determination of the risk for falls
- Nursing care plan for interventions that were defined to reduce the risk of falls, such as bed alarms, wanderguards, use of a toileting schedule, and placement of the mattress on the floor
- Interdisciplinary care planning committee meetings for evaluation of the effectiveness of the strategies in preventing falls and revision of interventions after a fall
- Nursing documentation for description of the events leading up to a fall, the resident's status after a fall, and evidence that the physician and family were notified of the fall
- Physician progress notes for an evaluation of the resident after a fall, if injury had occurred
- Revision of the medical plan of care based on the underlying reasons why the resident fell, such as effects of medication, hypotension, weakness, etc.
- Physician orders for transfer to an emergency department for further evaluation after a fall with injury, such as a fracture

"Careful review of the home's policies and procedures, its staffing and care plans, and its history of documented complaints and health department surveys, as well as a thorough investigation of the fall, may reveal a case of long-term substandard care that resulted in a debilitating injury to the resident."[28] A useful reference when determining standards of care for falls is Morse's *Preventing Patient Falls*[26] and the *Falls and Fall Risk, Clinical Practice Guidelines* published jointly by the American Health Care Association and the American Medical Directors Association.[29] Most falls do not result in injury to the resident. Fractures of the hip as a result of a fall are rare, but constitute a majority of the lawsuits filed involving falls. In some cases, a fall is not reported by the individuals involved at the time of the incident. For example, a nursing assistant who drops a resident may fear punishment and not tell the professionals about the incident. See Appendix 14.1 for an example of an expert witness report written concerning this type of incident. Indications that there was a delay in diagnosis of a fractured hip and that the resident was asked to walk on an undiagnosed fractured hip increase the value of the claim.

Wandering

Because most nursing homes are considered the home of the residents, access to and egress from nursing homes is usually not restricted. Yet nursing homes have many residents who are cognitively impaired and lack common judgment and must be protected from injury, elopement, and becoming lost. Wandering resulting in drowning or being hit by a car or other moving vehicle is a red-flag issue for the plaintiff attorney. Many types of alarm systems can alert the staff when a resident enters an area not designed for residents. Usually the resident identified as having a potential to escape wears a bracelet that triggers an alarm when the resident enters a dangerous area. The alarmed areas may include such dangerous places as elevators, windows, and stairways as well as kitchen, laundry, storage, and maintenance areas. Externally there is the danger of traffic, exposure, and becoming disoriented and unable to return. Many nurses working on units designated as Alzheimer's units are allowed to alarm, but not lock, the exits from the unit. Some residents are capable of learning the sequence of buttons on a keypad that must be pushed in order to open a door.

When reviewing a medical record involving an internal or external elopement, the LNC must determine whether the nursing home properly evaluated the risk of elopement, properly developed the care plan, and took preventive measures to prevent the escape. Further, if a resident eloped, were proper measures taken to care for him after the episode? Was the situation reviewed by the interdisciplinary team to prevent a reoccurrence by that resident as well as any other resident?

Example 14.9: In California, a $3,000,000 settlement was reached as a result of an 80-year-old female, who wandered from her board and care facility, fell and fractured her hip. The plaintiff claimed that the resident was known as a wandering risk but not supervised adequately and that the front door was not alarmed. The facility license, which was under potential suspension at the time of the wandering, was revoked after this incident. *Susan L. Perry, Executor of the Estate of Carmen M. Ramsey, Deceased v. Evelyn Tuazon and Mario Tuazon d/b/a Langdon du Soleil Gardens Board and Care.*[30]

Analysis of the medical record should include review of the following:

- Nursing care plan for evidence of identification of wandering behavior
- Interdisciplinary review team analysis of the strategies effective in reducing wandering, such as diversion, moving the resident to a room closer to the nurses' station, applying wanderguard devices, and implementing a regular toileting schedule
- Revision of the plan of care if the resident was successful in leaving the facility at least once before the incident that led to injury
- Social services notes in the event that the facility was unable to safeguard the resident (there should be evidence that the facility attempted to find an alternative location for the resident)

Specific sources for standards of care concerning wandering are difficult to find. Some gerontological nursing texts have given passing attention to the subject of wandering. Several sources of reading are found in the additional reading section at the end of this chapter. The best source may well be the expert's clinical experience in keeping residents safe.

General Sources of Standards of Care

As in all areas of nursing, the standards of care for the nursing home nurse can be found in the respective nursing practice acts of the state where the nurse practices. The nursing practice acts today follow the nursing process of assessment, diagnosis, planning, implementation, and evaluation. In addition, the American Nurses Association's Standards of Clinical Nursing Practice[31] and Scope and Standards of Gerontological Nursing Practice[32] set standards of care in the nursing home. For administrator involvement in the care of residents, there is also the Standards of Practice for Long-Term Care Administrators[33] adopted by the American College of Health Care Administrators. In some states, the nurse practice acts include the standards of licensed practical (vocational) nursing, and in other states, there is a separate licensed practical nursing act. Requirements for CNAs are found in OBRA and individual state regulations.

Nursing homes are licensed by the state in which they provide services. Each state issues regulations for the operation of the nursing homes. For nursing homes that provide Medicare- and/or Medicaid-reimbursed services, the OBRA regulations set standards for the operation of nursing homes. Note that these are not standards of care in the most stringent analysis, but the regulations are crafted in such a way that without meeting professional standards of care, a nursing home cannot meet the regulatory requirements. These standards can be obtained by requesting a copy of the CMS (Center for Medicare and Medicaid Service, formerly Health Care Financing Adminstration) state operation manual with interpretive guidelines for the surveyors. A nursing home's record of compliance with the OBRA and state regulations can be obtained from the local state agency that surveys nursing homes. The LNC should study these records for relevance to the matter at hand.

The LNC must also review the facility's own policies, procedures, and protocols to see whether those requirements have been met. Other sources of standards of care can be found in authoritative textbooks and professional journals as well as numerous Internet resources. Useful references to help evaluate direct care can be found in *Nursing Interventions Classification* (see McClosky and Bulachek[34]) and *Nursing Outcomes Classification.*[35] These references are linked to North America Nursing Diagnosis Association[36] nursing diagnoses as well as to each other. These three resources can help the LNC to evaluate the nursing process documented in a nursing home medical record. The most helpful Internet resource is the National Medical Library's PubMed, http://www.PubMed.gov. The Internet is a wealth of other information specific to a condition but must be evaluated for its source and validity.

Common Defenses

As it becomes increasingly costly to settle cases, the defense attorney's role focuses on minimizing losses and defending the cases deemed defensible. The LNC and attorney identify those cases that are defensible and contain elements of contributory negligence. The section that follows identifies some commonly used defenses.

In any medical malpractice case, the plaintiff has to prove that there was duty to the resident, a breach of that duty (deviation from the standard of care), damages, and a proximate link between the breaches and the injuries. Additionally, some medical malpractice cases are defended by attacking credibility or character of the resident or family. Nursing home cases are defended using any or a combination of these strategies. The section below expands on these defenses.

Spontaneous Fracture versus Traumatic Fracture

Spontaneous fractures are fractures that occur without the degree of trauma that would generally be accepted as being necessary to break a bone.[37] They are commonly associated with pathologic conditions that impair bone strength, such as cancer and Paget's disease. There have been few reports of spontaneous fractures of the shafts of long bones. Kane et al. studied all residents of 11 Wisconsin nursing homes with 1903 residents to develop the first prospective survey of long bone and spontaneous fractures incidence rates. Overall, long bone fracture incidence (commonly hip fractures) was 3.52 residents per 100 residents per year. The incidence of spontaneous fractures was 8.4 residents per 1000 residents per year. They occurred in residents who were less mobile and more likely to be bed-bound during turning or transferring. The location of the fracture was more likely to be below the hip. In the only recent study available, Martin-Hunyadi[38] reported on a French study of elderly patients in 30 nursing homes encompassing 3052 residents. They found the incidence of 1.3% with fractures of the femoral neck, tibia, or fibula and humerus. Fractures of the femoral shaft were associated with the highest mortality: 7 out of 13 patients died versus 2 out of 15 patients who had fractures of the femoral neck. Overall, 13 residents per 1000 residents per year had spontaneous fractures.

Determining the cause of fractures is often difficult and debated among orthopaedic and endocrinology experts. Most traumatic fractures resulting from falls in the elderly involve fractures of the wrist or hip. Pathological fractures are most often due to osteoporosis, hypoparathyroidism, or malignant metastases and are not often immediately recognized. In addition to fractures of long bones, pathological fractures commonly involve the vertebra. It is important for the LNC to determine the type and cause of the fracture and to help the attorney determine whether a fracture, even following a fall, was traumatic or pathologic in origin. As osteoporosis is a major factor in falls in the elderly, the LNC needs to look for evidence of osteoporosis in the medical record. Burke[25] discusses osteoporotic risk factors in the elderly. With a properly carried-out plan of care to prevent falls, a defense can be mounted in the case of fractures.

Deficient Documentation Did Not Cause Injuries

A defense attorney has a difficult case to present when the documentation is inadequate. Reasons the documentation can be deficient include: tampering with the medical record, documenting on the wrong medical records, and writing incorrect information. The LNC's analysis is essential to assist the defense attorney in these circumstances. The LNC working with a defense attorney must look for clues that the care was given. For example, the resident had a recorded temperature of "95.9°F" and acetaminophen was charted as given. There was a physician's order for acetaminophen for an oral temperature over 99.5°F. It can be inferred that the resident's temperature was documented incorrectly. The LNC must be alert to the deficiencies and inconsistencies in the medical record and be able to interpret their significance to the attorney.

Care is so ingrained into the culture of working in the nursing home that often care is given by a member of the team but not documented. This can occur for a variety of reasons. Perhaps the resident received care by staff not assigned to the resident's care, perhaps the caregiver did not think at the time that the situation was significant, or perhaps the caregiver forgot to document an observation. In this instance, the defense may try to portray the situation as a real life situation and that the care was given, but not documented for some very human reason.

The defense will often agree that the documentation should have been done, but the important thing is that the resident received the required care.

The Standard of Care Was Met but the Resident Was Injured Anyway

As is true of other health care facilities, it is often impossible to prevent certain injuries. The mere existence of an injury does not mean that the staff was negligent. Using falls as an example, defense experts note that cognitively intact residents may lose their balance, turn unexpectedly, or otherwise perform some action that results in a fall and injury. Cognitively impaired residents are more mobile as a result of lessening of the use of restraints and are more able to place themselves in situations where a fall may occur. Defense experts may argue that ambulatory cognitively impaired residents may fall and fracture bones without any evidence of negligence.

Natural Aging Process Caused Damages Rather Than Neglect

Although a facility may formulate a goal that a resident will not deteriorate while under its care, residents do age and die as part of the natural processes. A nursing home resident's preexisting conditions are often so debilitating that any injuries caused by abuse or neglect may be irrelevant to the resident's condition, life span, or quality of life. Separating the harm caused by the alleged neglect from these preexisting conditions involves a detailed examination of the resident's condition not only at the time of the neglect but also in the days, weeks, and months preceding it.[16] An LNC's skills can be quite helpful in this analysis. A nursing home that has accepted a resident with known preexisting conditions has, in effect, asserted that it can provide adequate care for that resident. If medical testimony can show that a preexisting condition would have eventually led to the resident's death, the plaintiff attorney must prove that the defendant's conduct lessened the ability to enjoy the life that remained or hastened the death. If it can be shown that the abuse or neglect accelerated death caused by a preexisting condition, the defendants are generally held accountable.[16]

The defense is charged with the need to establish that the processes that led to the resident's death were not set in motion by negligent care. For example, there is recent evidence that Alzheimer's disease is associated with weight loss as it progresses. This information may be used to refute a claim that weight loss was due to underfeeding. Laying the blame on the aging process rather than accepting the charge of negligent care was noted in a number of the cases that were reviewed in the sample of 2000–2001 cases described above. A representative case is described below.

Example 14.10: In a Florida case resulting in pressure ulcers, a gangrenous amputation stump, and sepsis, the defense argued that the resident was predisposed to skin breakdown despite proper skin care. The deterioration of her condition and decline in function were expected, they argued. The woman's death was asserted to have been from her medical conditions and their progression. This case resulted in a $930,000 settlement. *Estate of Louis Lark, by Carla Rowe, PR of the Estate v. Enterprise Care Facilities, Inc., d/b/a Katherine E. and Michael J. Franco Nursing and Rehabilitation Center, et al.*[39]

Family Would Make Extremely Unsympathetic Plaintiffs

From the perspective of the plaintiff attorney, the ideal plaintiffs are the close-knit family who made frequent visits to the nursing home to see the resident. Their altruistic motivation in filing a suit is to make sure that other residents are not affected by neglect, rather than to obtain a large award. The LNC may at times encounter documented evidence that the resident was never visited by family, or that there was friction between the resident and the family, or between the family and the facility's staff. These details should be shared with the attorney. Jurors may be reluctant to award money to a family they perceive as not caring about the resident while he was alive, but instead developing an interest only when financial incentives are provided. Similarly, evidence of hostility between the resident and family may influence the defense of a claim. In one case, nursing documentation stated that the spouse was hitting his wife during their visits. These entries were important in refuting an allegation that the nursing staff was striking the resident.

A common strategy used by defense attorneys is to ask the family why they did not remove the resident from the nursing home if they believed inadequate care was being delivered. The family may have trusted the staff in the facility or been promised that the care would get better. In some cases, the family did not know that pressure ulcers were developing, or feared retaliation against the resident if they complained.

Competent Resident/Guardian Refusing Care or Contributorily Negligent

Although ethical conflicts arise over this concept, a competent resident has the legal right to refuse care. Health care practitioners often find this difficult to accept. The LNC may find that the medical record contains detailed documentation concerning efforts to convince the resident to accept care. Competent family members with the responsibility of being legal guardians may also refuse care on behalf of the resident. This issue is addressed in the following Michigan case.

Example 14.11: The plaintiff's decedent was a widow in her 70s. Her son had guardianship because she was not eating properly and was mentally incompetent. The son took his mother to the emergency room where she was found to be malnourished. She was placed in the defendant nursing home where a number of consultations with health care professionals occurred. The decedent refused to eat. Her son declined to agree with medical advice to sign an authorization to allow his mother to have a feeding tube. She lost weight over a number of months and was finally transferred to a hospital where "no code" instructions were given. She died of pneumonia the same day she was sent to the hospital. The plaintiff alleged that the defendant had failed to give proper nourishment and care to the decedent, and that the plaintiff's decedent had died because of malnourishment. The defendant contended that the plaintiff's decedent had been appropriately cared for and that she had died of pneumonia, for which the plaintiff as her legal guardian had refused protective vaccination. The jury returned a defense verdict. *Estate of Norma Obery and Lee Garvin, PR v. DMC Nursing Homes, Inc.*[40]

The concept of contributory negligence permits the defense to shift part of or the entire burden of responsibility for the incident onto the plaintiff. For example, if the resident fell while trying to get to the bathroom, the home may say that he failed to use the call light and wait for help. An investigation may reveal that the home was so understaffed that call lights went unanswered. OBRA regulations require that residents be provided with proper assistive devices to protect them from harm. Issuing a warning to a demented person is not an adequate nursing intervention.[28]

Disputes Regarding Cause of Skin Breakdown

The LNC evaluating skin breakdown cases, particularly those that involve the feet, should carefully examine the documentation in the medical record. Both preexisting medical conditions, such as diabetes and peripheral vascular disease, and the location of the breakdown should be evaluated. Wounds on the heel are more likely to be due to unrelieved pressure than those on the tips of the toes, as may be seen in diabetes. The LNC should assist the attorney in understanding the causes of skin breakdown. In the following Florida case, the defendant alleged that the skin breakdown was not due to negligence.

Example 14.12: The plaintiff developed pressure ulcers on her feet during a stay in the defendant's nursing home. She alleged that the ulcers had not been properly diagnosed and treated. The defendant alleged that the ulcers were the result of peripheral vascular disease and were not due to any negligence in care. The defendant further alleged that the plaintiff's medical providers had not treated the plaintiff's skin problem adequately. The patient eventually required a below-the-knee amputation. The case was settled before trial for $700,000. *Ella White v. Enterprise Care Facilities, Inc., d/b/a Franco Nursing and Rehabilitation Center.*[41]

The LNC has an essential role in the evaluation of the medical record to determine when skin breakdown occurred. Scrutiny of the admission assessment completed by the nursing home staff will provide key information about the condition of the resident's skin. Flowsheets documenting skin breakdown by location, stage, and size are helpful in tracking changes in the resident's skin. Some facilities also take photographs. The transfer form completed at the time of transfer to the hospital, as well as the assessment completed at the hospital, also should be examined for data about the resident's skin. In the following Florida case, the defendants alleged that the skin breakdown had occurred prior to admission to their facility.

Example 14.13: Upon admission to the nursing home, the resident was free of pressure ulcers and her prognosis for rehabilitation was considered to be quite good. Within weeks of her admission, she lost weight, became dehydrated and malnourished, and developed multiple pressure ulcers on both heels and her sacrum. The plaintiff alleged that the nursing staff at the nursing home had failed to properly monitor the resident's condition, provide appropriate wound care, document the progression of the ulcer, and notify the resident's physician and family of the significant changes in her overall condition. The plaintiff alleged that the nursing staff had lied about the care they were allegedly providing, falsified records, and failed to document the significant medical changes as they developed. Ultimately, the resident's bones were exposed in her heels and sacrum. She died due to massive infection. The defendant nursing home contended that its staff had acted appropriately under the circumstances and that she was prone to developing pressure ulcers and developed them prior to her admission to the nursing home. The action settled for $1,100,000. *Maria Lourdes Townshend,*

Individually, and Maria Lourdes Townshend, as PR of the Estate of Berta Perez-Balladares, Deceased, v. Palms Convalescent Care, Inc., d/b/a The Plaza Nursing and Rehabilitation Center, Scott R. English, MD and Scott R. English, MD, PA.[42]

The Injuries Did Not Occur as Alleged by the Plaintiff

Raising questions about the nature of the injuries and their cause can be an essential and successful strategy for the defense. The LNC will be expected to comb through the medical record and evaluate alternative theories of the injuries. The defense theory can range from "It did not happen here," as shown in Appendix 14.2's defense expert witness report, to "It happened here but not the way the plaintiff says it happened." The "It did not happen here" defense was successfully used in this Texas case.

Example 14.14: The plaintiff alleged that the resident had fallen in the nursing home and broken his hip, which required surgical intervention of an open reduction with internal fixation. During this surgery, he suffered a stroke, leaving him unable to feed himself. His family declined a feeding tube and he died in a hospice 28 days later. The defendant argued that the resident had not sustained his fractured hip at its facility. And if he did, the nursing home was not negligent, because it had done everything to adequately protect him. The jury found no negligence. *Audrey Dobson v. Heritage Geriatric Housing Development, Inc., d/b/a Heritage Danforth Gardens.*[43]

Obtaining Medical Records

Review of the nursing home chart is often the first step in initiating a suit or responding to a suit. Under 42 CFR § 483.10, the nursing home is required to produce a medical record within 2 working days of a request. The plaintiff attorney may contact the governmental agency at the state level responsible for surveying facilities to initiate an investigation if the chart is not produced within 2 working days. The rationale behind the 2-day time limit is to prevent the nursing home from having time to alter the medical record.[18] The medical records authorization form used to request records should contain the following language:

If you are a Medicare or Medicaid-certified nursing home or long-term care facility, please be advised that this request is made pursuant to 42 CFR 483.10, which states in pertinent part: "The resident or his or her legal representative has the right (1) upon an oral or written request, to access all records pertaining to himself or herself, including the clinical records, within 24 hours (excluding weekends and holidays); and (2) after receipt of his or her records for inspection, to purchase at cost not to exceed the community standard, photocopies of the records or any portion of them upon request and two working days' advance notice to the facility."[2]

The medical record should be carefully scrutinized for evidence of alteration. It is increasingly difficult to "lose" medical records in the information age. Juries assume that a missing document is damaging. LNCs should always advise an attorney of suspected tampering. It is particularly important to look for documentation on flowsheets indicating that care was delivered in the nursing home after the resident was transferred out of the facility or died.

Suggestions for detecting tampering with the medical records include:

- Understand the chart based on common practice, facility policies, and state and federal regulations. Recognize that nurses' notes are documented frequently in the beginning of the admission, and then decrease in frequency unless the resident sustains an injury.
- Compare the medical records with the billing records.
- Compare the medication administration record with the nurses' notes.
- Look for obliteration of entries.
- Compare the observations of the nurses with those of the physician.
- Detect changes in style of note-writing (e.g., a longer note on the day of the incident).
- Correlate staffing sheets/timecards with the chart to detect documentation by any staff not present that day.
- Detect entries that are out of chronological order.
- Detect fraudulent addition for the purposes of covering up an incident. This can be detected through documents examiners' use of current technology: chemical analysis; ultraviolet and infrared examination; spectrophotometry; chromatography; and ink dating, which is an expensive process.
- Detect omitted documentation through interviews with former employees.

Analysis of Medical Records

Analysis of the medical record will depend in part on the issues of concern. A thorough review of all the pertinent clinical documentation will assist in the determination of whether the standards of care were followed.

Suggestions for reviewing the records include:

- Organize the medical records into sections, using tabs for each type of record.
- Look for indications that the resident was transferred to an emergency department or admitted to the hospital during the resident's stay at the home. Obtain these records.
- Evaluate the descriptions of the family, as reflected in the medical record.
- Look for noncompliance in the mentally competent resident.
- Note descriptions of the resident that may reveal antagonism between the resident and staff.
- Look for descriptions of an incident.
- Note finger-pointing or blaming of other staff members or professionals.
- Evaluate the facility's compliance with the standards of care.
- Determine whether the record contains evidence of sentinel events: dehydration, fecal impaction, and pressure ulcer development in a low-risk resident. These must be reported to the surveying agency.

Days Since Admission	Medicare-Covered Residents	Other Residents
5	X	
14	X	X
30	X	
60	X	
90	X	
Quarterly	N/A	X
Annually	N/A	X
Change of Condition	X	X
Discharge	X	X

Figure 14.3   Days Since Admission That the MDS Must Be Completed and Submitted for Medicare-Covered and Other Residents (From *Federal Register*, 63(91), 26267, 1998.)

Nursing Home Documentation Requirements

Nursing home medical records have some documentation requirements specific to nursing homes. Most notable are the requirements of the resident assessment instrument (RAI), which includes the MDS, RAPs, and resident care plan. This process applies to all residents in facilities that are certified for Medicare and Medicaid. The MDS must be electronically completed and transmitted to the state agency on specific dates depending on the resident's Medicare benefit status and length of stay in the facility (see Figure 14.3). A new MDS must be completed with a significant change in the resident's condition. The care plan must be revised with a significant change. A significant change must be documented in the progress notes.

Note that although most residents have Medicare benefits, the residents are not automatically "covered" by Medicare in a nursing home. Medicare coverage requires a 3-day acute hospitalization for the same diagnosis being treated in the nursing home and a daily Medicare-defined "skilled" service. There are further restrictions on receiving benefits. The benefit status of a resident may need to be defined in consultation with a Medicare expert.

The MDS data are used to calculate a resource utilization guide (RUG) score. The MDS and RUG score are transmitted electronically to state and federal fiscal intermediaries for reimbursement. CMS groups the MDS data according to resident needs and problems and makes the data available to facilities and state surveyors in the form of "quality indicators." The quality indicators are not found in the resident's medical record. Although not required to do so, some facilities retain them. It is often worth requesting this data for the time period involved in a matter.

Two important documents in the medical record that should be analyzed are the assessments and the resident care plan. Nursing assessments and care plans are the responsibility of a registered nurse. In fact, the MDS assessment requires the signature of the registered nurse assessment coordinator. Under the nurse practice acts, assessments and formulating the resident care plan are beyond the scope of practice for the licensed practical (vocational) nurse. Most of the nursing oversight is done by licensed practical nurses, and they often do "assessments" and make entries into care plans. When the LNC reviews assessments and care plans, one has to keep that fact in mind and determine:

1. Who made the assessment and care plan entry
2. The appropriateness of the assessment and the care plan entry
3. How the plan was carried out

Facilities that fail to properly assess their residents or to follow their resident care plan increase their liability. Moreover, the LNC should be alert to omissions in assessments and care plans that could contribute to the resident's injury or illness. The care plan must be evaluated to determine whether it was revised after a significant change in the resident's condition, or a pattern became evident. For example, the care plan should be modified after a fall to identify strategies designed to reduce the risk of subsequent falls.

Other documentation requirements may vary from state to state, but all documentation must meet acceptable standards of care. Physicians must visit their residents every 30 days or more often if indicated, participate in the interdisciplinary team actions, and maintain documentation that meets standards of care. Physicians' orders must be reviewed and signed every 30 days. A consulting pharmacist must review each resident's medication regimen every 30 days and make any indicated recommendations. There must be documentation by the licensed nurses periodically. In California, for example, licensed nurses must document a summary of care every week. Medications and treatments are documented when given. CNAs normally document ADL care on a shift-by-shift basis. Periodic assessments and documentation by members of the interdisciplinary team, including dietary, activities, and social services, must be in the medical record. There should be periodic screening for fall risks, mobility, ADL training, and swallowing evaluations by the rehabilitation services. The LNC should also look for indications that dental, audiology, podiatry, vision, and psychology services were available to the resident.

Documents That the Attorney Can Request

LNCs are instrumental in assisting the attorney to define needed information. There may be four separate policy and procedure manuals:

1. Administrative policies and procedures
2. Resident care policies
3. Personnel policies
4. Procedures and policies for the control of communicable diseases

The attorney may ask for the table of contents of each manual and then request pertinent policies. A logbook, journal, or daily diary is used in some facilities. In one case, the author (Iyer) came across an entry directing the staff to rewrite the medical record and to leave extra space for the night shift to chart. This case settled. Personnel files of caregivers should be requested, although the defense attorney may fight their production. Staffing pattern documents help determine the identity of CNAs and orderlies. Job descriptions of all involved personnel are useful. Nurse consultants, corporate nurse consultants, and quality assurance (QA) consultants should be identified. Reports from the QA committee can be requested, although they may be considered to be peer review and therefore protected in some states.

The LNC should be familiar with the government regulatory forms utilized by the enforcement agencies and ask the attorney to request those forms. Past surveys and complaints filed against the home may be requested. Daily census forms, acuity assessments, and forms reflecting the actual number of hours of care per resident can be helpful. LNCs should review inservice education schedules. They should also review brochures, advertisements, and other documents available to the public. Budgets, guidelines, expense restriction or limitations, and suggested operational cost or expense ceilings may be useful. Letters of complaint, letters of resignation, and family letters about a subject relative to the lawsuit may provide information. Reports of fines paid to the regulatory agency for repeated violations, specifically in relation to the lawsuit, are valuable. Incident and accident reports often provide additional descriptions of an incident.

The Joint Commission on Accreditation of Health Care Organizations (JCAHO, http://www.jcaho.org) grants accreditation to some nursing homes. These standards are more rigorous and do not constitute the standard of care for all nursing homes. Most nursing homes do not have JCAHO accreditation. If a nursing home does have JCAHO accreditation, an LNC should be familiar with these standards. The JCAHO patient safety standards require the nursing home to advise the resident and family of outcomes, including unexpected outcomes, which places the responsibility on the facility to inform the resident and family of accidents and injuries.

Knowledge of the Aging Process and Geriatric Nursing Care

The LNC reviewing nursing home medical records needs extensive knowledge of the aging process and the physiological and psychological changes that develop over time. It is critical that the LNC have a solid foundation in the process of aging or seek expert advice in aging. Competence in this area is imperative, since the LNC has a duty to help an attorney understand the difference between normal processes and bodily insult. This understanding may be the basis upon which the attorney makes a decision whether or not to proceed with a legal action.

There is no substitute for a clinically experienced geriatric nurse with current nursing home experience to review a nursing home medical record. If the LNC does not have those qualifications, the LNC must seek out such assistance. This is important because the elderly resident of a nursing home is usually in the chronic stage of several medical conditions. The clinical presentation of the chronic nature of the medical condition is very different from the acute stage as often seen in the acute care hospital. The nursing home nurse's duty is to maintain the chronically ill resident and recognize changes early in any exacerbation of the resident's conditions. The typical nursing home resident often does not exhibit the same symptoms as a younger person with the same bodily changes. Further, often the elderly person does not or cannot report symptoms and the geriatric nurse is better prepared to identify subtle changes.

The nursing home nurse is also responsible for the prevention or delay of decline and complications. Nowhere is this more important than in the prevention of pressure ulcers. The LNC reviewing nursing home medical records needs to thoroughly understand the difference between a wound caused by pressure, shear, and friction and a wound caused by impaired circulation and the treatment and care protocols for each. Many pressure ulcers can be prevented by good and knowledgeable nursing care. When a pressure ulcer occurs, each type and stage of wound should be thoroughly assessed, properly treated, and well documented. Often an enterostomal therapist needs to regularly review the healing and treatment process. Wounds and lesions caused by circulatory problems can sometimes be prevented by such procedures as special skin care, providing warmth and elevation of affected limbs, and keeping the skin dry. It is important to have the clinical experience to determine whether the pressure ulcer or circulatory lesion in question was avoidable and whether the appropriate treatment and care were given. In her article on pressure ulcers, Nelson[44] relates the difficulties and challenges in the care of pressure ulcers.

The LNC also needs to have a good clinical background and understanding of nursing home residents' medical conditions and the nursing management of those conditions. Specifically, the LNC needs to know about diabetes, especially Type II diabetes, and the complications experienced by the resident. Appendix 14.3 contains an example of an expert witness report involving diabetes. The LNC should be knowledgeable in the effects of hypertension, stroke, and heart disease and their impact on respiratory and renal function in the elderly. Dementia and cognitive impairment produce confusing behaviors and often obscure many symptoms and make medical record review difficult.

Understanding Staffing Requirements in Nursing Homes

Staffing in nursing homes varies widely. Nursing staffing includes a mix of registered nurses, licensed practical nurses, and CNAs. OBRA requires staffing adequate for the care of the facility's residents. The facility must provide services by sufficient numbers of personnel on a 24-hour basis to provide nursing care to all residents in accordance with resident care plans.[45] The regulations describe the requirement that the services of a registered nurse be used for at least 8 consecutive hours, 7 days a week and that a licensed nurse must be designated as charge nurse on each tour of duty. Nursing assistants must meet training and competency requirements.[46] Professional staff must be licensed, certified, or registered in accordance with state laws.[47] State regulations vary in regard to nursing staffing, and the requirements can usually be found in individual state nursing home regulations. Some states refer to staffing in nursing hours per patient day, and others use ratios. Other than nurses, a nursing home must have as a minimum a licensed administrator, a medical director, and sufficient professional and technical staff to meet residents' needs. When a nursing home does not have a particular professional on staff, such as a dietician or social worker, the nursing home must contract with one.

When reviewing the staffing patterns, the LNC needs to be aware of several factors besides the federal and state regulations. The type of nursing home and the services it provides give an indication of the staffing it requires. For example, the nursing home serving elderly persons who need mainly ADL management differs widely from one that specializes in rehabilitation or that provides only pediatric services. In many nursing homes where there are several units, residents may be placed by nursing needs, and the staffing needs on each unit may differ. When requesting staffing information, all these factors need to be included in the request.

Damages

Many plaintiff attorneys apply a threshold of damages before taking a nursing home malpractice case. The costs of litigating a claim have to be reimbursed by the potential return. Medicare and Medicaid liens that will be subtracted from a settlement or verdict have to be identified before the plaintiff attorney takes on a nursing home claim. Low-value cases include minor skin injuries, bruising, and minor and resolved psychological injuries, to name a few. In the following California case, the defense argued that the patient sustained limited damages and that other allegations made by the plaintiff were false.

Example 14.15: The plaintiff was admitted to a nursing home after a stroke. She developed a stage I pressure ulcer that resolved without progressing further. The plaintiff claimed that she was allowed to remain in her feces for extended periods of time and that she developed serious and significant pressure ulcers. She also alleged that the facility was plagued with a leaking roof and that her room was infested with vermin. The defendant argued that the patient was incontinent as a result of the stroke, and was seen by the nursing staff between 34 and 38 times per day. The pressure ulcer that she developed was resolved. The defense asserted that there were no vermin in her room and that the roof did not leak. The jury returned a defense verdict. *Cekimber Hobson, individually, and as Conservator of the Person and Estate of Autumn Brandon Hobson, Conservatee, v. Sharon Care Center and Summit Care Corporation.*[48]

This case reinforces the need to have significant injuries in order to make it worthwhile to pursue. The analysis of the medical record would be one way to count the number of times that the resident was seen each day, in addition to using testimony of the nursing staff.

Many nursing home negligence cases are cases of negligence that occurred over a long period of time versus a sudden, untoward event. The LNC can help the attorney understand the slow decline and provide helpful tools, such as chronologies (see Appendix 14.4 for an example) or charts of weight loss. Selection of photographs and preparation of demonstrative evidence to show injuries can help the attorney comprehend the issues more clearly.

If the resident entered the nursing home from his own home, the LNC will have to depend on the nursing home's initial evaluation to determine the status on admission. For example, in pressure ulcer cases, the documentation about the skin condition on admission to the nursing home or transfer back to the hospital is crucial. If the resident entered the nursing home from a hospital, the hospital's discharge summary will be available. Once a baseline is established, the resident's progress in the nursing home can be followed. Hospitalization records prepared before the nursing home placement will be valuable for identifying the resident's status before admission to the nursing home. Within this framework, the attorney and LNC can begin to determine whether the resident's physical or mental deterioration or injury resulted from the unavoidable processes of aging or from neglect.

Summary

LNCs have much to offer attorneys involved in litigating nursing home claims. A sound knowledge of clinical issues and an understanding of regulatory requirements help LNCs provide support in this rapidly growing and challenging area of litigation.

References

1. Omnibus Budget Reconciliation Act of 1987, The Nursing Home Reform Act, 42 CFR § 401 (1987).
2. James, S., Creative discovery in nursing home cases, *Trial*, 36, 98, 2000.
3. Laska, L., Ed., Florida nursing home patient develops multiple bed sores, *Medical Malpractice Verdicts, Settlements and Experts*, 29, August 2000.
4. Laska, L., Ed., Death of nursing home resident following development of pressure sores, contractures, and malnutrition, *Medical Malpractice Verdicts, Settlements and Experts*, 37, August 2001.
5. Laska, L., Ed., Sexual assault/rape, negligence, and abuse of a mentally retarded group home resident, *Medical Malpractice Verdicts, Settlements and Experts*, 38, October 2000.
6. Laska, L., Ed., Facility retaliates against mother after she files complaint with state of Texas regarding substandard care of her twin adult mentally retarded daughters, *Medical Malpractice Verdicts, Settlements and Experts*, 36, September 2000.
7. Laska, L., Ed., Failure to properly monitor mentally retarded cerebral palsy resident, *Medical Malpractice Verdicts, Settlements and Experts*, 39, August 2001.
8. Horowitz, S., Settlement strategies, in *Nursing Home Litigation: Pretrial Practice and Trials*, Krisztal, R., Ed., Lawyers and Judges Publishing Company, Tucson, AZ, 2001.
9. Laska, L., Ed., Death of nursing home resident following development of pressure sores, contractures and malnutrition, *Medical Malpractice Verdicts, Settlements and Experts*, 37, August 2001.
10. Laska, L., Ed., Alzheimer's nursing home patient dies from multiple decubitus ulcers' infection, *Medical Malpractice Verdicts, Settlements and Experts*, 38, April 2001.
11. Agency for Health Care Policy and Research, Clinical Practice Guideline, No. 3, Pressure Ulcers in Adults: Prediction and Prevention, U.S. Department of Health and Human Services, Rockville, MD, 1992.
12. Agency for Health Care Policy and Research, Clinical Practice Guideline, No. 15, Treatment of Pressure Ulcers, U.S. Department of Health and Human Services, Rockville, MD, 1994.
13. Maklebust, J. and Sieggreen, M., *Pressure Ulcers: Guidelines for Prevention and Nursing Management*, 2nd ed., Springhouse, Springhouse, PA, 1996.
14. American Medical Directors Association, *Pressure Ulcer Therapy Companion*, Columbus, MD, 1998.
15. Levine, J., The pressure sore case: a medical perspective, *Elder's Advisor*, 44, 2000.
16. Rhodes, J.T. and Castillo, J., Proving damages in nursing home cases, *Trial*, 41, August 2000.

17. Laska, L., Ed., Negligent care of resident — weight loss, pressure sores and contracture of eighty year old woman, *Medical Malpractice Verdicts, Settlements and Experts*, 36, February 2001.
18. Krisztal, R., Personal communication, October 24, 2001.
19. Simmons, S. and Reuben, D., Nutritional intake monitoring for nursing home residents, *Journal of the American Geriatrics Society*, 209–213, February 2000.
20. Wagner, L., A recipe for nutrition and hydration, *Provider*, 27(1), 20–28, 2001.
21. Department of Health and Human Services, Survey Procedures for Long Term Care Facilities, Health Care Financing Administration, Appendix P, State Operations Manual Provider Certification, Transmittal 10, 1999, 62–64.
22. Maniscalco, S.S., Woman raped in nursing home settles for $1.5 million, *Missouri Lawyers Weekly*, http://www.molawyersweekly.com/mofeat.cfm, October 15, 2001.
23. Laska, L., Ed., Woman dies after suffering unexplained broken leg in nursing home, *Medical Malpractice Verdicts, Settlements and Experts*, 32, June 2000.
24. Baumhover, L.A. and Beall, S.C., *Abuse, Neglect and Exploitation of Older Persons: Strategies for Assessment and Intervention*, Health Professions Press, Baltimore, MD, 1996.
25. Burke, S., Boning up on osteoporosis, *Nursing 2001*, 31(10), 36–42, 2001.
26. Morse, J.M., *Preventing Patient Falls*, Sage Publications, Thousand Oaks, CA, 1997.
27. Laska, L., Ed., Failure to have two attendants for walking patient results in fall and neurological injury for woman, *Medical Malpractice Verdicts, Settlements and Experts*, 30, August 2000.
28. Gray, G., Nursing home falls: not your average slip-and-fall case, *Trial*, 91, July 2000.
29. American Health Care Association and American Medical Directors Association, Falls and Fall Risk, Clinical Practice Guidelines, Columbia, MD, 1998.
30. Laska, L., Ed., Elderly patient wanders from facility and fractures hip, *Medical Malpractice Verdicts, Settlements and Experts*, 33, April 2000.
31. American Nurses Association, Standards of Clinical Nursing Practice, Washington, D.C., 1991.
32. American Nurses Association, Scope and Standards of Gerontological Nursing Practice, Washington, D.C., 1995.
33. American College of Health Care Administrators, Standards of Practice for Long-Term Care Administrators, Alexandria, VA, 1986.
34. McClosky, J.C. and Bulechek, G.M., Eds., *Nursing Interventions Classification (NIC)*, 3rd ed., C.V. Mosby, St. Louis, 2000.
35. Johnson, M. et al., Eds., *Nursing Outcome Classifications (NOC)*, 2nd ed., C.V. Mosby, St. Louis, 2000.
36. North America Nursing Diagnosis Association, Nursing Diagnosis: Definitions & Classification, 2001–2002, Philadelphia, PA, 2001.
37. Kane, R., Burns, E., and Goodwin, J., Minimal trauma fractures in older nursing home residents: the interaction of functional status, trauma, and site of fracture, *Journal of the American Geriatrics Society*, 43, 156–159, 1995.
38. Martin-Hunyadi, C., Clinical and prognostic aspects of spontaneous fractures in long term care units: a thirty-month prospective study, *Revue de Medecine Interne*, 21(9), 2000.
39. Laska, L., Ed., Woman declines over four months in nursing home, *Medical Malpractice Verdicts, Settlements and Experts*, 33, February 2000.
40. Laska, L., Ed., Wrongful death, *Medical Malpractice Verdicts, Settlements and Experts*, 39, October 2000.
41. Laska, L., Ed., Inadequate care of developing pressure sores results in below-the-knee amputation for woman, *Medical Malpractice Verdicts, Settlements and Experts*, 29, September 2001.

42. Laska, L., Ed., Decubitus ulcers develop during nursing home stay, *Medical Malpractice Verdicts, Settlements and Experts*, 39, March 2001.

43. Laska, L., Ed., Wrongful death of Alzheimer's patient following fall in which hip was broken in facility, *Medical Malpractice Verdicts, Settlements and Experts*, 37, May 2001.

44. Nelson, M., Pressure ulcer assessment and documentation: the beginning of a plan of care, *Journal of Legal Nurse Consulting*, 12(4), 22–25, 2001.

45. 42 CFR § 483.30.

46. 42 CFR § 483.75(e) and (f).

47. 42 CFR § 483.75(g).

48. Laska, L., Ed., Negligent care of resident blamed for stage one decubitus ulcer, *Medical Malpractice Verdicts, Settlements and Experts*, 39, December 2000.

Additional Reading

Algase, D.L., Wandering: a dementia-compromised behavior, *Journal of Gerontological Nursing*, 25(9), 10–7, 51, 1999.

American Health Lawyers Association, Fraud and Abuse: Do Current Laws Protect the Public Interest?, report on the 1999 Public Interest Colloquium, Washington, D.C., January 29–30, 1999.

Amo, M.F. and Rowe, N.L., Seven attributes of abuse prevention in long-term care, *Balance*, 4(3), 6–8, 10, 2000.

Archiable, N., Preventing serious injuries from falls, *Provider*, 26(9), Suppl. 8–9, 16, 2000.

Black, J., Preventing those other pressure ulcers, *Provider*, 26(12), 24–25, 2000.

Bong, M.R. et al., Hip fractures: a risky ordeal for the elderly, *Provider*, 27(10), 73–74, 2001.

Bradley, A.M. and Roach, J.L., Preserving mobility in people with dementia, *Provider*, 26(9), Suppl. 12–13, 2000.

DeLuca, J., Preventing abuse and neglect, *Provider*, 25(2), 42–44, 1999.

Edwards, D.J., Coping with the pressure of wound care, *Provider*, 26(9), 68–69, 2000.

Fox, S.C., Primum non nocere (first do no harm): nursing home litigation. I, *Journal of Legal Nurse Consulting*, 8(1), 5–9, 1997.

Fox, S.C., Primum non nocere (first do no harm): nursing home litigation. II, *Journal of Legal Nurse Consulting*, 8(4), 8–15, 1997.

Fox, S.C., Primum non nocere (first do no harm): nursing home litigation. III. Use of nursing home records in case evaluation, *Journal of Legal Nurse Consulting*, 9(4), 33–40, 1998.

Frolik, L.A., Nursing home liability because of resident wandering and elopement, *Health Care Law Monthly*, 15–18, October 2000.

Gray-Vickrey, P., Protecting the older adult, *Nursing Management*, 32(10), 36–40, 2001.

Harris, C., The road to documenting mobility, *Provider*, 26(9), Suppl. 4–5, 16, 2000.

Hawes, C. et al., The OBRA-87 nursing home regulations and implementation of the resident assessment instrument: effects on process quality, *Journal of American Geriatrics Society*, 45(8), 977, 1997.

Iyer, P., Ed., *Nursing Home Litigation: Investigation and Case Preparation*, Lawyers and Judges Publishing Company, Tucson, AZ, 1999.

Kayser-Jones, J., Improving the nutritional care of nursing home residents, *Provider*, 26(10), 56–59, 2000.

Ledford, L., Research-Based Protocol: Prevention of Falls, The University of Iowa Gerontological Nursing Interventions Research Center, University of Iowa, Iowa City, 1997.

Lee, S.K. and Turnbull, G.B., Wound care in a PPS environment, *Nursing Homes*, 50(3), 34–36, 2001.

Neufeld, R., A better idea for bed mobility, *Provider*, 26(9), Suppl. 10–11, 2000.

Nichols, J., Easing pain for mobility, *Provider*, 26(9), Suppl. 6–7, 16, 2000.

Peck, R.L., The "ins and outs" of wandering, *Nursing Homes*, 49(8), 55–56, 2000.

Stephen, S., Care planning for independence, *Provider*, 26(9), Suppl. 2–3, 16, 2000.

Weiss, H.P., Attorney General Reno calls for crack down of facilities providing poor care, *Balance*, 4(5), 4–5, 2000.

Zawadzki, D. and DeLuca, J., Turning a new leaf, *Provider*, 25(3), 59–61, 1999.

Test Questions

1. In 1986, an Institute of Medicine report addressed
   A. The need to reduce the number of nursing homes in the United States
   B. The preparation of a model for the operation of nursing homes
   C. The quality of care concerns about nursing homes
   D. Changes in the Code of Federal Regulations known as OBRA

2. The most common areas for nursing home liability are all of the following EXCEPT:
   A. Medication errors
   B. Pressure ulcers
   C. Fractures
   D. Sexual and physical abuse

3. Tampering with medical records can be inexpensively identified by all of the following EXCEPT:
   A. Comparing nursing notes with physician notes
   B. Looking for documentation that has occurred after the resident has been discharged
   C. Reviewing entries that are out of order
   D. Having a page analyzed by a documents examiner

4. In reviewing a case, the LNC needs access to expert geriatric knowledge and experience to
   A. Correctly interpret the care given.
   B. Accurately explain the needs of a resident based on chronic disease states.
   C. Explain the RAI process of the nursing home.
   D. Prepare to testify at trial.

5. Which of the following statements about nursing home documentation is NOT true?
   A. Much of the care is delivered and documented on flowsheets by CNAs.
   B. The MDS must be completed when there is a change in the resident's condition.
   C. Nurses' notes are written with the same frequency as they are in hospitals.
   D. Care plans must be written based on the problems identified by the MDS.

Answers: 1. C, 2. A, 3. D, 4. B, 5. C

Appendix 14.1
Expert Witness Report Involving a Dropped Resident

Date

Attorney
Law Firm
Address

Re: Mary G.*

Dear Attorney,

Thank you for forwarding materials related to this case. I have reviewed the following information:

- Transcription of a telephone message left by Administrator for Daughter
- Investigation of incident form
- Letter dated 9/30/99 by Official, Department of Health and Senior Services, to daughter
- Incident summary
- Admission to L. Nursing Home (7/19/97–2/7/99)
- Deposition transcript of Aide A and Aide B
- Written statements of Aide A and Aide B
- Deposition of RN 1
- Deposition of RN 2
- Written statement of LPN 3
- Deposition of LPN 3
- Deposition of RN 4
- Report of Dr. A for plaintiff
- Report of Dr. B for plaintiff
- Corporate lifting policy and accident reporting policy

Summary of Medical Events

Mrs. Mary G. was a 76-year-old resident of L. Nursing Home on 2/6/99. She was a heavy diabetic woman. Her daily care was performed by nursing assistants and her medications were administered by a registered nurse. On 2/6/99, she was assigned to the care of Aide A, a nursing aide. While Aide A was in the process of transferring Mrs. G. out of bed, she claims that Mrs. G. slipped partly to the floor. She maintains that the resident did not hit the floor (page 28 of her deposition). When Aide A called for help, a fellow aide, Aide B, came to help her. Together, she claims, they lifted her back to the wheelchair (page 28). Aide A claims to have told LPN 3 that the resident slid out of the chair (page 29).

Aide A claimed that she was asked by RN 2 to do an incident report (page 36) on 2/6/99 (page 35), but also testified that LPN 3 was the only nurse she

---

* Names have been changed.

reported the incident to (page 49). She claims to have told RN 2 that the patient did not slide to the floor (page 51).

Aide B testified that she would let the resident stand and hold onto the wheelchair and would help her turn to sit in the chair (page 68). According to Aide B, the resident was constantly sliding and was combative the day of the incident (page 71). Aide B testified that Aide A was holding onto the resident when she entered the room, but "Mary was still sliding" (page 72). She did not recollect any conversations with RN 2 about the incident (page 78).

On 2/7/99, Mrs. G. was found to have an externally rotated leg. An x-ray confirmed the presence of a fractured hip. She was ultimately transferred to the care of an orthopedist and admitted to Underlook Hospital. After surgery, she was discharged back to L. Nursing Home. She was subsequently transferred back to Underlook, where she died on 3/2/99.

Deposition Testimony

RN 1 was the unit coordinator at the time of the incident. She testified that there were "so many people that I fired there for not doing their job. It's not safe for the residents" (page 55). RN 1 testified that she was told by RN 2 that two nursing assistants dropped the resident to the floor (page 57). RN 1 testified that RN 2 stated that these two assistants did "not follow instruction and fooled around" (page 65). According to RN 1, the patient was heavy (page 76) and she had (in the past) observed a two-person transfer. RN 1 testified that the nursing care plan dated 10/23/98 specified that a Hoyer lift be used to transfer the resident because Mrs. G. was heavy, and "for safety-wise, it's better to use a Hoyer lift" (page 99).

RN 2 believed she was the nursing supervisor/senior clinical nurse for the 3–11 shift on the date in question (page 15). She testified that on 2/7/99, the resident told her that she had had a fall on 2/6 (page 19). She recalls speaking with Aide A that day (page 28) as well as Aide B (page 29). According to her, Aide B told her that the patient slid to the floor but did not fall (pages 30–31). In a phone call with LPN 3, who was off duty on 2/7, RN 2 learned that LPN 3 did not know how the resident had hurt her leg (page 45).

The written statement by LPN 3, who came in from home on 2/7/98 to write her statement, states that Mrs. G. complained of pain in her right foot. When confronted, Aide B stated that the patient's foot had been hurt when she was being transferred from the bed to the wheelchair.

The staff development instructor, RN 4, testified that transfers were "a minimum of two people" and could not recall cases where it would be only one person (page 29). She recalled teaching the aides to use a Hoyer lift when the patient was heavy (page 34).

Standard of Care

Aide A and Aide B deviated from the standard of care for nursing assistants in the care provided to Mrs. G. on 2/6/99. By the deposition transcripts, it is clear that Mrs. G. was a heavy woman. A patient with limited mobility who requires extensive assistance with activities of daily living is at risk for falls. The last quarterly review prior to the fall described "falls" as a potential problem. The interdisciplinary nursing care plan stated that a Hoyer lift should be used in the transfer of the patient. The Corporate Lifting Policy specifies that it is the responsibility of the staff to obtain assistance when a resident needs two or more people for lifting. At a minimum, two people should have been used to transfer the resident. The Corporate Lifting Policy, as well as the testimony of RN 4, establishes that aides are taught how to perform two-person lifts and to use the Hoyer lift during their orientation to the facility. Aide A deviated from the standard of care by not following the nursing care plan, not using the Hoyer lift, and not following the lifting policy and instead attempting to single-handedly transfer Mrs. G. from the bed to the wheelchair.

Aide A and Aide B deviated from the standard of care by not reporting the incident in detail. The minimizing of the incident, as evidenced by their testimony and the written statements, caused a delay in the evaluation of the resident. The Accident Reporting Policy, as well as the national standard of care, required the aides to report the incident to their direct supervisor. The reporting process permits the registered nurse to examine the patient and determine whether physician notification and further evaluation is needed. The details of the incident are then documented in the resident's medical record to alert subsequent staff to the problem and their requirement to observe for signs of injury. It is beyond the scope of the aide's background to make an accurate assessment of the resident for the purposes of determining whether an injury has occurred. The failure to report the incident contributed to the delay in diagnosis of the fractured hip.

Yours truly,

Expert Nurse, MSN, RN

Outcome: This case was settled.

Appendix 14.2
Defense Expert Witness Report Involving Disimpaction

Date

Attorney
Address
City, State

Re: Darlene Doan*

Dear Attorney,

Thank you for forwarding the medical records of this patient. I have reviewed this information:

- Office records of Dr. Martin
- Office records of Dr. Lincoln

---

* All names have been changed.

- Admission to General Medical Center (3/18/99–4/11/99)
- Admission to Royal Care Center (4/11/99–4/20/99)
- Office records of Dr. Visa
- Admission to General Medical Center (4/24/99–5/11/99)
- Admission to Kitterly Institute for Rehabilitation (5/11/99–5/27/99)
- Office records for Depths Medical Associates
- General Medical Center Same Day Surgery (7/28/99)
- General Medical Center Same Day Surgery (10/27/99)
- Admission to General Medical Center (11/26/99–12/2/99)
- Home Care Nursing Notes (4/20/99–4/24/99)
- Expert witness report of Marie Quinton
- Millie Baily's answers to interrogatories
- Dr. Kennedy's answers to interrogatories
- Dr. Karlson's answers to interrogatories
- Royal Care Center's answers to interrogatories
- Darlene Doan and Henry Doan's answers to interrogatories
- Insurance Company's answers to interrogatories
- Plaintiff's answers to Insurance Company's interrogatories
- Sandy Perry's answers to interrogatories
- Luci Appel's answers to interrogatories
- Elaine Quissel's answers to interrogatories
- The Kitterly Institute's answers to interrogatories
- Jose Manez's answers to interrogatories
- Deposition of Dr. Karlson
- Deposition of Elaine Quissel
- Deposition of Darlene Doan
- Deposition of Dr. Daniel Doan
- Deposition of Henry Doan
- Deposition of Sandy Perry
- Deposition of Luci Appel
- Deposition of Amy Bourdeux
- Deposition of Jose Manez
- Deposition of Dr. Kennedy
- Royal Care Center Department of Nursing Policy and Procedure Manual

Summary of Medical Facts

At the time Darlene Doan was admitted to General Medical Center on 3/18/99, she was a 62-year-old woman who had been injured in a car accident. She was taken to the operating room 3 times for stabilization of her leg fractures. During the postoperative period, she complained of pain and constipation. Her preexisting medical conditions included irritable bowel syndrome.

On 4/11/99, Mrs. Doan was transferred to Royal Care Center for extended recovery. According to the medical record, she had a bowel movement at least daily. On 4/12/99, the patient stated that she had taken milk of magnesia the night before but did not move her bowels. The nurse notified Dr. Kennedy, who ordered a Fleets enema. The patient had a soft bowel movement that night, and she was not impacted, so the Fleets enema was not given.

On 4/15/99, the patient refused an offer of a Fleets enema. She requested an enema on 4/16/99. On the day shift, Nurse Appel noted that Mrs. Doan was impacted. The Fleets enema was given with poor results. The nurse manually disimpacted the patient and gave her prune juice. At 6:30 p.m. the patient was manually disimpacted by A. Bourdeux, RN, with poor results and was encouraged to drink prune juice. Dr. Kennedy provided an order for a soapsuds enema, which was given that evening with poor results.

On 4/17/99, on the night shift, Nurse Perry disimpacted the patient. On the day shift, she had a huge amount of stool. The medical record contains no further mention of enemas or disimpaction. It is noted that the patient refused Metamucil (increases bulk of stool) for 7 of the 9 doses that were ordered, and refused Colace and Senokot (both stool softeners) on one occasion.

Mrs. Doan came under the care of Nurse Baily, RN, when she arrived home on 4/20/99. On 4/21/99, the patient passed a stool. Mrs. Doan continued to feel the need to pass stool and was unable to expel it even with "a gentle assist." She passed small hard-formed stool later that day. On 4/22/99, she passed a moderate amount of soft stool. On 4/22/99, stool was coming from her vagina. Arrangements were made to have her evaluated by Dr. Martin the following day. A colostomy was performed.

Standard of Care

Review of the Royal Care Center procedure for manual removal of a fecal impaction shows that the procedure is consistent with accepted methods of disimpaction. It states that manual removal of an impaction *may* be preceded by a retention enema (which requires a doctor's order). The use of an enema before a disimpaction is a matter of nursing judgment. The decision would be made based on a number of factors, including the medications the patient was taking, the effectiveness of previous enemas, the length of time since a bowel movement, the degree of the patient's discomfort, and the use of prune juice.

Nurse Appel's description of the disimpaction was consistent with the standard of care. She testified that she inserted her finger an inch into the patient, and gently performed the procedure. She stated that she stopped the procedure when the patient was screaming and that she did not see any blood on her gloves.

Nurse Bourdeux, who performed the second disimpaction, testified that she would determine whether the patient was impacted by applying lubricant and inserting a gloved finger into the patient's rectum. She described a procedure, which is consistent with the standard of care (using her index finger in a scooping motion to pull the feces down). She did not observe any blood on her gloves. When she was not able to remove stool, she followed the standard of care by notifying the physician. Nurse Bourdeux complied with the standard of care by offering the patient prune juice instead of milk of magnesia. Prune juice is a natural alternative to milk of magnesia, and is often effective in stimulating a bowel movement.

Nurse Perry's testimony regarding how she would perform a disimpaction is consistent with the standard of care. She testified that she would use lubricant as a step in the procedure of disimpaction, but would not necessarily document that since it was part of the procedure. She would insert a portion of a finger in order to disimpact the patient.

I note that the last nurse to disimpact the patient before the development of her fistula was Nurse Baily. I have not seen any deposition testimony or answers to interrogatories regarding her involvement with the patient.

It is my opinion, with a reasonable degree of nursing probability, that the nurses at Royal Care Center complied with the standard of care relating to the management of the patient's constipation. The testimony regarding the disimpactions, enemas, and communication with the physician was consistent with the standard of care.

Yours truly,

Expert Witness, MSN, RN, LNCC

Outcome: The defense won the case at trial.

Appendix 14.3
Plaintiff Expert Witness Report Involving Diabetes

Mary Brown, MS, RN
Legal Nurse Consultant
123 Main Street
Anywhere, USA
(111) 222–3333

DATE:	March 21, 2001
TO:	Robert Roe, Esquire
CAPTION:	Doe v. Moe Nursing Center
OUR FILE:	444-XA

Nursing Medical Record Review

At your request, I have reviewed the provided medical records of John Doe to ascertain whether or not the nursing care Mr. Doe received at Moe Nursing Center met established nursing standards of care. Mr. Doe was an 87-year-old retired plumber admitted to Moe Nursing Center on November 21, 2000, from Bluebird Nursing Home, where he had received rehabilitation therapy after a surgically repaired fracture of the left hip. On October 4, 2000, his physician at Bluebird Nursing Home had listed the following diagnoses:

1. Post open reduction and internal fixation (ORIF) of the left femur
2. Stable non-insulin-dependent diabetes mellitus
3. Abdominal aneurysm
4. Stable hypertension

Records from Bluebird Nursing Home also mentioned that the resident had a history of Alzheimer's disease.

The admitting physician's orders at Bluebird Nursing Home included:

1. 1800-calorie American Diabetes Association diet
2. Glipizide 10 mg twice a day (for diabetes)
3. Metformin HCl 500 mg three times a day (for diabetes)
4. Insulin twice a day, the dosage dependent on blood glucose reading
5. Benazepril HCl 20 mg daily (for high blood pressure)
6. Indapamide 2.5 mg daily (for high blood pressure, a diuretic)
7. Lortab 5, one or two tablets every four hours as needed for pain
8. Temazepam 15 mg at bedtime as needed for sleep

Mr. Doe received the medications as ordered up to the time of discharge from Bluebird Nursing Home. While at Bluebird Nursing Home, his blood glucose was measured four times a day and he was treated with a sliding-scale dosage of insulin as indicated. However, Mr. Doe did not progress as expected with his rehabilitation and was transferred on November 21, 2000, from Bluebird Nursing Home to Moe Nursing Center for long-term care. The physician's discharge summary dictated on November 20, 2000, does not address the care of his diabetes. On admission to Moe Nursing Center, the new attending physician listed the following diagnoses:

1. Status post ORIF of left hip
2. Diabetes mellitus, Type II
3. History of prostate surgery
4. Abdominal aortic aneurysm
5. Hypertension
6. Dementia of the Alzheimer's type

His orders included:

1. Aspirin 325 mg daily
2. Acetaminophen 325 mg, 2 tablets every 4 hours for pain or fever
3. Magnesium hydroxide 30 ml at bedtime as needed for constipation
4. "Blood sugar capillary glucose check @ 0630 and 1630 for one week"
5. No concentrated sweets diet

An admitting note by a nurse practitioner states that the diabetic medications were discontinued upon admission without noting the reasons. Laboratory tests were ordered for November 22, 2000 and November 26, 2000. The test on November 22 included a serum glucose report of 108 mg/dL, and on November 26, the serum glucose was 318 mg/dL. (The normal is 70–110 mg/dL.) The report of November 26 was faxed to the physician by a Moe Nursing Center nurse, but there is no indication of any discussion or consultation between the nurses and the physician relative to this report.

The blood glucose levels were measured twice a day at Moe Nursing Center for a week as ordered. The results were:

Date	0630	1630
11/21/00	—	45 mg/dL*
11/22/00	146	152
11/23/00	151	148
11/24/00	142	204**
11/25/00	101	36*
11/26/00	—	112
11/27/00	169	123
11/28/00	206**	

* Low enough to notify MD. No indication of
  action by any nurse.

**High enough to notify MD. No indication of
  action by any nurse.

While on the diabetic medications at Bluebird Nursing Home, the resident's glucose level ranged from 83–364 mg/dL.

The physician wrote on November 26 that the glucose readings were "120–160 mg/dL" and "cont. to monitor accu-ck bl. sug" (continue to monitor Accu-check sugar ["Accu-check" is the commercial name for the glucose-metering device]). There is no indication that the nurse, upon reviewing this note, attempted to correct the physician's estimation of the blood glucose, nor did the nurse continue the blood glucose testing as he ordered. Mr. Doe received a physical therapy evaluation, and a restorative program was established to make him as independent as possible. He sustained falls on November 24 and December 14 with no reported injury. The staff was concerned about his continual desire to smoke cigarettes, which caused him to smoke in inappropriate places and to attempt wandering in search of an area to smoke in.

On December 21, 2000, a nurse documented in the medical record, "Resident is more confused than last week," and "has become incontinent of B(owel) & B(ladder)." There is no plan for investigation of this change of condition.

On December 22, 2000 at 3:00 p.m., the resident was quoted as stating, "I feel different." The nursing assistant reported he had been "pocketing food" (i.e., holding food in the cheek), indicating swallowing difficulty, and the nurse noted that he was pale and weak on the left side. His vital signs were taken (temperature — 98.4°F, pulse — 90, respirations — 26, blood pressure — 142/82), and these were reported to the physician, Nurse T. Brown, RN, and the family. The physician ordered evaluations by the physical therapist and the speech therapist and a CAT scan of the head.

At 9:30 p.m. the nurse wrote in the medical record that the resident's weakness was increasing, he was unable to swallow, his hand grip was minimal, and there was difficulty moving both his legs. Vital signs were taken (temperature — 98.4°F, pulse — 80, respirations — 26, blood pressure — 148/82).

At 12:10 a.m. on December 23, 2000, the resident's respiratory rate and pulse had increased (R — 36, P — 90) and the respirations were shallow. Oxygen saturation was 90% (Normal = > 90%). Rhonchi were heard in both lungs. At 12:45 a.m., the nurse noted the admitting diagnosis of diabetes mellitus, Type II, and tested the blood glucose with a reading of 536 mg/dL. The physician was called and ordered 12 units of regular (fast-acting) insulin and to repeat blood glucose level at 7:00 a.m. The head of the bed was raised to 45° to facilitate breathing. The respiratory rate was 26 per minute at 2:15 a.m.

At 6:30 a.m. on December 23, the blood glucose was reported as 470 mg/dL, and the physician was notified and ordered 12 units of regular insulin. Mr. Doe was reportedly responsive to tactile and verbal stimuli.

At 8:00 a.m., Mr. Doe was unable to eat breakfast, responsive only to pain stimuli, his oxygen saturation had fallen to 79%, and respiratory therapy was called to evaluate the patient. His vital signs were taken (pulse — 100, respirations — 40, blood pressure — 100/52). The blood glucose was 517 mg/dL. The physician was again called at 8:10 a.m., and he ordered the resident transported to the nearest emergency room for evaluation. Community Ambulance was called.

At the time of transfer (not noted in the medical record) the oxygen saturation was 80% and the resident was unresponsive. The medical record at Community Medical Center notes an admission time of 10:18 a.m. on December 23, 2000. The family was notified of the transfer at 10:00 a.m.

Upon admission to Community Medical Center, the patient was in respiratory failure, hyperglycemic (excessive glucose in the blood), and hypernatremic (excessive sodium level in blood). He was started on life support until a discussion with his family determined that the patient had no wish to be on life support. Life support was withdrawn, and Mr. Doe was pronounced dead at approximately 6:00 p.m. on December 23, 2000.

Discussion

1. The Moe Nursing Center medical record does not include an interagency transfer form, which is used to transmit medical and nursing information from one institution to another. Thus the nursing staff at Moe Nursing Center had no information to plan continued care.

   The standard of care requires that there be written exchange of medical and nursing information upon discharge from one institution or level of care to another.

   NPA (Nurse Practice Act) 4962.212(2)(l); 42 CFR (Code of Federal Regulations) § 483.20(e); 42 CFR § 483.75(n); ANA (American Nurses Association) STND III(7)

2. There is no indication that on admission the nurse practitioner or the nurses assigned to care for Mr. Doe questioned the precipitous change in medication regimen with the physician.

   The standard of care requires a nurse to question unusual or erroneous orders.

   NPA 4962.220(1)(a), (b); NPA 632.0385; 42 CFR § 483.20(a); 42 CFR § 483.75(n); ANA STND I(1, 2); ANA STND IV(1, 2)

3. There is no minimum data set (MDS), a resident assessment tool, in the medical record as required of facilities participating in the Medicare and Medicaid programs. The MDS is the basis for the comprehensive resident assessment, development of the resident assessment protocols, and development of the patient care plan.

   This is a federal requirement.

   42 CFR § 483.20(b)

4.   The patient care plan states that the patient would be observed for signs of hypoglycemia or hyperglycemia. There is no indication that the physician was notified when the blood glucose serum levels were abnormal on 11/21/00, 11/24/00, 11/25/00, and 11/28/00, nor was he notified of the wide variations of values noted. There is no indication that the nurses brought to his attention the discrepancy in his note of 11/26/2000. There is no validation that the patient's blood glucose was monitored by the nurses after 11/28/00, although the patient care plan indicates that blood glucose testing would be done as necessary.

   The standard of care requires the nurse to constantly review and follow the care plan approved by the interdisciplinary team, to constantly reassess the patient's condition, and to update the care plan as necessary.

   NPA 4962.212(2)(e); 42 CFR § 483.20(b); ANA STND VII(1, 2, 4, 5, 6)

   The standard of care requires the nurse to recognize and report unusual findings and symptoms to the physician.

   NPA 4962.218(5); 42 CFR § 483.25; ANA STND VI(1, 2, 3)

5.   The low levels of blood glucose on 11/21/00 and 11/25/00 would suggest that the patient was severely hypoglycemic and the nurse should have (a) immediately given a high-glucose preparation like orange juice, (b) assessed the patient's condition, (c) promptly notified the physician, and (d) repeat the testing of the glucose level as necessary or as ordered by the physician. Note that (a) it is unusual for a patient with Type II diabetes who is not taking diabetic medication to have a low blood glucose and (b) many elderly diabetics do not demonstrate typical symptoms of hypoglycemia as early as younger persons. Blood glucose testing is often the only way to prevent severe consequences by intervening before symptoms become profound.

   The standard of care requires the nurse to recognize unusual responses to treatments and tests and to attempt to verify the results with appropriate professionals.

   NPA 4962.216(1)(d); 42 CFR § 483.20(c); ANA STND IV(3); ANA STND VI(1, 2, 3)

   The standard of care requires the nurse to recognize and take emergency actions as needed.

   NPA 4962.216(1)(f); 42 CFR § 483.75(n); ANA STND I(1); ANA STND V(1, 2)

6.   No assessment was made of the patient after a change of condition was noted on December 21 and December 22. Symptoms of hyperglycemia include drowsiness; confusion; weakness, which is often one-sided; shallow but rapid respirations; weak but increased pulse rate; hot and dry skin; increased urine output; dehydration (note the increased sodium level); and unconsciousness.

   The standard of care requires the nurse to continually assess the patient, recognize serious and life-threatening symptoms, and report the symptoms promptly to the physician.

   NPA 4962.216(1)(f); 42 CFR § 483.20(d)(3); ANA STND VI(1, 2, 3, 6)

   The standard of care requires ongoing assessment, especially after a change of condition.

   NPA 4962.212(2)(e); 42 CFR § 483.20(b)(4); ANA STND V(2)

7. There is an unexplained 2-hour delay in transferring the patient to the hospital on 12/23/00. It may be that 911 was not called but instead the ambulance service was called for routine service.

    The standard of care requires the nurse to continually assess patients, recognize serious and life-threatening symptoms, and take appropriate action.

    NPA 4962.216(1)(f); NPA 4962.218(6); 42 CFR § 483.75(n); ANA STND I(1); ANA STND V(1, 2)

Records Reviewed

- Bluebird Nursing Home Medical Record of John Doe
- Moe Nursing Center Medical Record of John Doe
- Community Medical Center Medical Record of John Doe
- C. Smith, MD's Medical Record of John Doe
- Death Certificate of John Doe

Sources Reviewed

OBRA (Omnibus Budget Reconciliation Act of 1987, as amended) and its Federal Guidelines.

Nurse Practice Act, Chapter xxx of the State Administrative Code.

American Nurses Association, Standards of Clinical Nursing Practice.

Edelman, Steven V. and Henry, Robert R., *Diagnosis and Management of Type II Diabetes*, 2nd ed., Professional Publications, Inc., 1998.

Tucker, Susan M. et al., *Patient Care Standards: Collaborative Practice Planning Guides*, 6th ed., C.V. Mosby, St. Louis, 1996, 472–487.

Outcome: This case was settled.

Appendix 14.4
Chronology Prepared by a Consultant Involving Aspiration

Date

Attorney
Firm
Address

Re: Estate of Mrs. W. v. Lily Pond Nursing Home*

Dear Attorney,

    I have reviewed the medical records of Mrs. W. The following is my summary. Numbers in parentheses refer to the page numbers in the medical record.

---

* All names have been changed.

1. Summary of Condition on Admission to Lily Pond Nursing Home (12/16/92)

Mrs. W. was a 91-year-old woman at the time she was admitted to Lily Pond Nursing Home. She was described as a widow who was transferred to the nursing home from West Nile Medical Center after being admitted to the hospital on 11/29/92 for dementia and urinary tract infection with septicemia (blood infection). On admission to the nursing home she was alert and pleasant. She fed herself and ate 100% of her meals. A Foley catheter was in her bladder at her request, which could be discontinued at the direction of Dr. K.

2. Summary of Stay in Nursing Home (12/16/92–1/4/94)

The physician notes for this period of time show that Mrs. W. was out of bed daily in a wheelchair. She was treated for a vaginal discharge and had osteoarthritis complaints.

She was confused and disoriented. In August 1993, she was complaining of headaches. On 12/29/93, the doctor noted that she was not eating and had lost a large amount of weight during the past month. She was to begin with a clear liquid diet. On 1/4/94, the doctor noted that she was running an intermittent fever and arrangements were made that she be admitted to the hospital. A note on 1/4/96 states that the resident was constantly losing weight. Her sponsor refused the idea of having nasogastric feedings.

3. West Nile Medical Center (1/4/94–1/14/94)

On 1/4/94, Mrs. W. was taken to West Nile Medical Center for treatment of pneumonia. The transfer form states that she required assistance with feeding and had refused to eat for the past 3 to 4 days, allowing liquid to run out of her mouth. She was returned to the nursing home on 1/14/94. Her diagnoses included acute respiratory infection, Alzheimer's disease, and osteoarthritis. A nasogastric tube was in place. The doctor's orders included turning every hour, oxygen, and tube feeding.

4. Lily Pond Nursing Home (1/14/94–4/30/96)

The nursing home doctor noted that upon return, Mrs. W. was unresponsive with clear lungs and intact skin. Her diagnoses were senile dementia, organic brain syndrome, and malnutrition. In February 1994, the doctor planned to give her progressive feedings until she could tolerate a soft diet. The tube feedings would then be stopped. Her condition was satisfactory, according to the doctor, for the next year. A stage II bedsore was present in April 1994.

The resident's sacral bedsore was healed by January 1995. The doctor noted in February 1995 that she was not malnourished. In March 1995, she was receiving nasogastric tube feedings. Her condition was described as stable or satisfactory until 12/13/95. On that date, the doctor noted that she had been having episodes of vaginal bleeding. A gynecological exam was to be obtained. By 12/20/95, the bleeding had stopped. Her appetite was poor. The doctor wrote "will continue to observe closely." Mrs. W.'s appetite was still poor in January 1996.

The multidisciplinary progress notes state on ?/28/96 (the month is cut off the page) that the resident had ulcerations on her right and left buttocks. She had contractures of her knees. Intermittent vaginal bleeding was mentioned again as an issue on 4/6/96. She was to be admitted to the hospital for evaluation of vaginal bleeding and a newly diagnosed mass in the left breast. Instead, a pelvic ultrasound and a pap smear were done in the emergency room of Local Community Hospital and the resident returned to the nursing home.

5. Local Community Hospital (4/30/96–5/7/96)

On 4/30/96, Mrs. W. was transferred to Local Community Hospital. She had ulcers on her coccyx (base of the spine) and left inner ankle and was incontinent of bowel and bladder. Her medical diagnoses/condition included hypotension (low blood pressure), an unresponsiveness to stimulus, and senility. She was receiving tube feeding through a nasogastric tube. Mrs. W. was returned to the nursing home on 5/7/96 with diagnoses of left lower lobe pneumonia, dehydration, new onset diabetes, dementia, iron deficiency anemia, malnutrition, coronary artery disease, and right bundle branch block (heart irregularity). She had a stage II pressure ulcer on her sacrum. She was to receive treatment from physical therapy and occupational therapy.

6. Lily Pond Nursing Home (5/7/96–5/15/97)

Mrs. W. was improved upon her return from the hospital. There was a stage II pressure ulcer on her sacrum and another on her left ankle. On 5/23/96, a care plan meeting was conducted due to an overall deterioration of the resident's status including a decline in her hearing. She was being fed with a syringe. An ulcer was present on her sacrum. She was dehydrated and had a new onset of diabetes with fingerstick blood sugars performed each day. Mrs. W. developed a fever during the evening of 7/12/96, but her temperature returned to normal the next day. As of August 1996, she was taking a regular pureed diet. She was put on antibiotics in September 1996. Antibiotics were given again in November 1996 for a respiratory infection. Mrs. W. continued to consume a regular pureed diet at that time.

Mrs. W. was consuming a regular pureed diet in February 1997. In March 1997, the doctor noted that she had some blood in her urine. Cultures were obtained and revealed a urinary tract infection. She remained stable the next few months. On 5/14/97, the doctor was called to see the resident because of a fecal impaction. She passed a large amount of blood, and it was noted that she had a large amount of soft stool in the rectum. Enemas were ordered. On 5/15/97, the doctor noted that her condition continued to deteriorate and her breathing was labored. Mrs. W.'s family wanted to have her hospitalized, so she was admitted to Local Community Hospital.

7. Local Community Hospital (5/15/97–5/27/97)

Mrs. W. was sent to the hospital on 5/15/97 with a diagnosis of congestive heart failure and was receiving oxygen. She was noted to have contractures and bladder and bowel incontinence. Mrs. W. returned to the nursing home 12 days later with diagnoses of *E. coli* urosepsis (urinary tract infection from a bowel organism), right upper lobe pneumonia with left lower lobe pneumonia, severe dehydration, end stage dementia, anorexia secondary to dementia requiring tube feeding, and resolved hypoalbuminemia (low albumin levels). There was a pressure ulcer on her right buttock, which was stage II. Duoderm was to be used on her right buttock.

8. Lily Pond Nursing Home (5/27/97–12/25/97)

A swallowing evaluation was performed on 6/6/97 and showed that the resident was unable to follow directions to swallow. Supplemental feedings were not recommended. On 6/12/97, the physician noted that the nasogastric tube feedings would be stopped for 4 hours to see if this would stimulate her to take food by mouth. On 6/21/97, the speech and language pathologist identified the resident as at risk for aspiration with even a small amount of oral intake and advised against oral intake (page 01593).

On 7/11/97, the doctor noted that an order for discontinuing the nasogastric feedings for 4 hours daily was being canceled because there was no change in her food intake. The nasogastric feedings were being resumed for 23 hours daily. In October 1997, Mrs. W. was allowed to take liquids by mouth along with the tube-feeding solution flowing through the nasogastric tube. On 12/11/97, the nurse noted that Mrs. W. was now able to eat pureed foods. The resident remained stable until 12/25/97. She was coughing with some respiratory difficulty and was sent to the hospital for evaluation, where she was diagnosed with probable pneumonia.

9. Local Community Hospital (12/25/97–1/12/98)

A lengthy admission occurred on 12/25/97 when the resident was sent to the hospital with rapid breathing and increased sputum production. At this time she was on a regular pureed diet. When she returned to the nursing home, her diagnoses included bilateral perihilar pneumonia (top of her lungs) with sepsis and hypotension, severe dehydration, end stage dementia, anorexia secondary to dementia, and hyponatremia (low sodium level) secondary to dehydration. Mrs. W. was to be treated by physical therapy. Other orders included resuming tube feedings, initiating physical therapy, and implementing a 2-hour turning schedule. A nasogastric tube was to be used for tube feeding.

10. Lily Pond Nursing Home (1/12/98–7/15/98)

When Mrs. W. returned to the nursing home, her diagnoses included senile dementia, diabetes, coronary artery disease, and anemia. She remained nonverbal. There were three water-filled blisters on her back, and her knees were contracted. A nasogastric tube was in her nose. A note by the dietician on 1/30/98 commented that the rate of 60 cc tube feeding/hour did not meet her caloric or protein needs. She was at 86% ideal body weight with an admission weight of 105 lb. Despite the fact that the rate did not change, her weight gradually rose. On 5/28/98, the quarterly assessment conference note stated that Mrs. W. was getting tube feeding. She weighed 114 lb. A note by the doctor on 7/2/98 states that she was stable.

11. Comments in Nurses' Notes Regarding Nasogastric Tube (January–July 1998)

When Mrs. W. returned from the hospital on 1/12/98, there was documentation to support that the correct placement of the nasogastric tube was checked by instilling air and checking for residual fluid in her stomach (auscultation). The head of the bed was elevated at 45 degrees. Some nurses simply documented that the tube was checked for placement and residual (fluid in her stomach), and others specified that they auscultated and aspirated. "Auscultation" means that air was forced into the tube with a syringe, while the nurse listened with a stethoscope over the stomach for the sounds of the air. "Aspirated" in this context indicates that the nurse put a syringe at the end of the tube and pulled back on the plunger to get feeding solution into the syringe. This is not to be confused with the term "aspiration/aspirated" when it is used to describe inhalation of fluid or food into the lungs.

On 2/5/98, the nasogastric tube was changed because it was clogged. After it was replaced, the nurse verified placement by auscultating (01729). On 2/17/98, the patient's tube was again clogged. When the tube was removed, the nurse noted a thick buildup of formula on the end of the tube (01735). On 2/18/98, a new tube was inserted (01736).

On 3/15/98, the nasogastric tube was clogged. The nurse noted that the resident poorly tolerated the change in tube with continuous coughing. She checked the placement, and the next nurse noted that the tube was functioning properly (01746).

On 3/26/98, the nurse noted a moderate amount of mucus in the patient's mouth and suctioned it out (01751).

At 5:05 p.m. on 4/9/98, the resident was found in bed and was turning a deep red purple color. There was a gurgling sound coming from her throat and clear vomit coming out of her mouth. She was suctioned and the head of the bed was elevated. Dr. Kilper was called. Her lungs sounded very congested. She had a nonproductive cough. Dr. Kilper ordered Lasix. She was suctioned two more times that shift. The nasogastric tube was removed at some point during this shift (01758). On 4/10/98, a new nasogastric tube was inserted and checked for placement. Feeding was resumed (01759). She was suctioned again on 4/15/98 when gurgling sounds were heard (01824). This occurred again on 4/17/98 (01825). She had scant secretions on 4/19/98 for which she was suctioned (01827). On 4/21/98, the resident was heard gurgling. She was suctioned three times (01827). The tube became dislodged on 4/22/98. It was reinserted on 4/23/98 (01828).

Mrs. W.'s head was bumped against the headboard on 5/19/98 when she was transferred back to bed. No areas of redness or swelling were seen. The family and physician were notified (01835).

On 6/1/98, a nurse noted that the nasogastric tube was secured to the bridge of Mrs. W.'s nose, but it extended out beyond the benchmark. The tube was checked and was dislodged. There was emesis of clear mucus with feeding (solution) on the bed. The tube was removed. There was slight congestion in the lungs. She was coughing at intervals and was suctioned once for white secretions. When Dr. Kilper was informed that the tube was out, the response was "OK, thank you." A new tube was inserted at 8:10 a.m. (01841) on 6/1/98. At this point the nursing notes begin incorporating a 24-hour nursing report form, which specifically documents about the enteral feedings. (This form had not previously been contained in the nursing notes section of the medical record.)

The nasogastric tube became dislodged again on 6/9/98 and it was replaced. The resident did some coughing after it was placed (01853). The tube came out on 6/18/98 when the resident was being transferred from the shower chair to the geri chair. The doctor was informed, and a new tube was inserted into her nose the same morning (01869). There were increased secretions and gurgling noted on 6/20/98, for which the resident was suctioned (01873). On 6/20/98, the resident was again suctioned for thick white mucous secretions (01875). A skin tear of Mrs. W.'s right third finger occurred on 6/23/98 when her hand was caught in a side rail (01879). Rales were noted in her lungs on 6/27/98. (This indicates fluid in the small airways of the lungs.)

On 6/29/98, at 12:40 a.m., the resident was coughing and sneezing and the tube was found to be dislodged. It was removed. At 5:30 a.m., when Dr. Kilper was informed that the tube was out, the response was "OK, leave it out and we will take care of it." The tube was replaced at 10:20 a.m. (01891).

On 7/6/98 the resident was coughing at intervals and suctioned for moderate thick white mucus (01905). On 7/7/98, the nurse heard "audible mucus" in the throat and suctioned the resident for a moderate amount of thick white mucus (01907). Mrs. W. was suctioned once on 7/8/98 for excessive mucus at 1:00 a.m. Her nasogastric tube was out at 10:00 a.m. on 7/8/98 and replaced by a nurse (01911). The tube was out at 10 p.m. on 7/9/98. The nurse attempted to reinsert it, but the resident was coughing and had a lot of oral secretions. She was suctioned. She had "some reported discomfort." On 7/10/98, the tube was noted "dislodged on rounds." She had no signs of distress and was breathing with ease, but coughed and was suctioned. The tube was reinserted without difficulty. This note states that Mrs. Gilbert, RN, and Ms. Williams were present (at the time of tube reinsertion). The pump was in use, and no residual was present (01915). (Note that this is the only chart entry that identifies who was present when the tube was put in.)

Documentation for the night shift of 7/12/98 states that the resident was coughing thick white mucus and was suctioned for thick white mucus. Her nasogastric tube was intact. The evening nurse documented that she was suctioned as needed (01919). On 7/13/98, the night nurse noted that her respirations were unlabored and she was suctioned one time for a moderate amount of thick white secretions. The day shift nurse suctioned her for a small amount of clear mucus. The evening nurse suctioned her as needed.

12. Summary of Events Surrounding the Aspiration

Time	Page Number	Entry
11:00 p.m. (7/14/98)– 7:00 a.m. (7/15/98)	01902/01962	Glucerna 60 cc/hour via nasogastric tube via Patrol pump 1440 cc–1440 cal per 24 hrs daily (initialed as running); flush nasogastric (NG) tube every shift and as needed with 240 cc water (initialed as done by KW)
2:15 a.m.	01922	The tube was flushed with 120 cc; there was no residual and placement was checked; the resident had a low tolerance for suctioning; the feeding tube bag was changed by MG

Time	Page Number	Entry
3:30 a.m.	01923	Have large amount of mucus; suctioned orally throughout shift; on initial rounds for NG tube out; *replaced by writer* (held feedings); tube feeding amount might need to be evaluated since she has so much secretion (M. Gilbert)
7:00 a.m.–3:00 p.m.	01902/01962	Glucerna 60 cc/hour via NG tube via Patrol pump 1440 cc–1440 cal per 24 hrs daily (initialed as not running); flush NG tube every shift and as needed with 240 cc water (initialed as done by SG)
9:00 a.m.	01902/01962	May-Vita Elixir administered per NG tube
11:00 a.m.	01922	Blood pressure 108/58
~12:00 noon	01938	Nurse's aide care plan indicates that patient got gastrostomy tube for lunch
1:00 p.m.	01902/01962	May-Vita Elixir administered per NG tube
3:00 p.m.–11:00 p.m.	01902/01962	Glucerna 60 cc/hour via nasogastric tube via Patrol pump 1440 cc–1440 cal. per 24 hrs daily (Initialed as not running); flush nasogastric tube every shift and as needed with 240 cc water (initialed as not done by SG)
3:40 p.m.	01923	Resident alert; skin cool; left side of chest congested; 102/46, pulse 112, 36 respirations, 102 degrees rectal temperature; notified Dr. Kilper; Lasix 20 mgs IM now ordered per Kilper; *tube feeding remains in progress per NG tube*; will continue to monitor; suction 2_ (S. Askew, RN)
3:40 p.m.	01922	Glucerna 474 was added; there was no residual and placement was checked; the resident had low tolerance for suctioning (SA [S. Ally])
3:40 p.m.	01922	Blood pressure 102/46, temperature 102 degrees rectal, pulse 112, respirations 36
4:30 p.m.	01923	Sponsor in house requesting for resident to be transferred to Local Community Hospital for evaluation; beeped Dr. Kilper 3×; no answer thus far; resident remains congested at this time (S. Ally)
4:45 p.m.	01923	Dr. Kilper beeped again; unsuccessful; will continue to try again (S. Jacobs, LPN)
5:00 p.m.	01923	Attempted to contact Dr. Kilper (beeped via telephone); continue to await return call (S. Jacobs, LPN)
5:20 p.m.	01923–01924	Sponsor telephoned facility; Dee Feingold stating that she had talked with Dr. Jackson and he would see her in the ER; there was no problem; writer telephoned E. Whitely, RN, and informed her that I was unable to get in touch with Dr. Kilper and sponsor requesting for resident to be transferred to hospital for evaluation; Whitely stated contact him one more time; if he doesn't respond go ahead and contact Dr. Jackson; attempted to contact Dr. Kilper (beeped again) via telephone; awaiting return call (S. Jacobs, LPN)
5:45 p.m.	01924	Writer telephoned Dr. Jackson at Seaside Clinic; informed him of resident status; order to send resident to Local Community Hospital ER for evaluation; contacted Dee Feingold, sponsor, at home; lady (who) answered the phone stated she wasn't there but would contact her in her car phone; writer stated, "OK, thank you"; writer in room with resident at this time; checked her fecal impaction, neg.; stool soft and abdomen nondistended; VS temp 102° rectal, pulse 112, respirations 34, BP 100/40; upon auscultation, upper lobe congestion and suction with thick clear secretions; also some wheezing heard upon breathing expirations; resident also coughing up thick clear secretions from mouth; unable to make needs known; will continue to assess and observe resident (S. Jacobs, LPN)

Time	Page Number	Entry
5:50 p.m.	01924	Contacted Stat Ambulance Service and informed of resident status; we will be right in (S. Jacobs, LPN)
5:55 p.m.	01924	Stat Ambulance in building with resident on stretcher; accompanied by one male and one female; resident remains congested and coughing at intervals (S. Jacobs, LPN)
6:00 p.m.	01924	Local Community Hospital ER telephone per writer; informed of resident's status and resident en route to hospital and stated, "Thanks for calling." (S. Jacobs, LPN)
6:15 p.m.	01924	Dr. Kilper in building informed of resident status, that resident was transferred to Local Community Hospital and Dr. Jackson called and stated, "He will be her doctor while she is in hospital"; Dr. Kilper stated, "OK." (S. Jacobs, LPN)
6:30 p.m.	01925	Contacted R. Whitely, RN, Supervisor, and M. Pool, Administrator; informed of resident transferred to hospital (S. Jacobs, LPN)
7:07 p.m.	Report found in Lakeshore Family HealthCare record, test done at Local Community Hospital.	Chest x-ray: Erect PA and lateral views show an NG tube is in place, but it apparently has catheterized the tracheobroncheal tree and the tip is in a right lower lobe bronchus; the heart size is within normal limits; there is some infiltrate in the right lower lobe; the left lung is clear; no mass is seen *Impression*: NG tube is in the right lower lobe bronchus; probable pneumonia in the right lower lobe Portable chest dated 7/15/98: AP view now shows that the NG tube has been replaced and the tube is now in the stomach; infiltrates persist in the right lower lobe; the left lung remains clear; heart size within normal limits *Impression*: Right lower lobe pneumonia unchanged; NG tube is now in satisfactory position
7:30 p.m.	01925	The nurse called from Local ER and stated that resident will be admitted to hospital with chest x-ray showing infiltration of the upper right lobe (S. Jacobs, LPN)
11:00 p.m.–7:00 a.m.	01938	Nurse's aide care plan — care is documented as having been given on the 11–7 shift

13. Local Community Hospital (7/15/98–7/25/98)

The transfer form states that Mrs. W.'s last hospital admission occurred on 7/15/98. She was congested in her upper lung lobes and had a temperature of 102°. She had been given a dose of Lasix at 3:40 p.m., "with relief."

A history and physical done by Dr. Evan Jackson dictated on 7/16/98 states that the patient was admitted for congestion associated with low-grade fever. She was moaning a little to touch. Her temperature on admission was 101°. Her lungs had mild left lower lobe inspiratory crackles and coarse right inspiratory crackles. She had contractures of her arms and legs. The chest x-ray had revealed a nasogastric tube in the right lower lobe bronchus and a pneumonia in the right lower lobe. The assessment was:

- Right lower lobe pneumonia probably secondary to improper placement of the nasogastric tube in the right lower lobe bronchus
- End stage dementia
- Type II diabetes mellitus

- Contractures at the knees particularly
- Mild peripheral vascular disease
- Probable coronary artery disease
- Mild anemia possibly secondary to anemia or chronic disease versus anemia associated with vaginal bleeding
- Prerenal azotemia probably secondary to mild dehydration (Must also consider blood in the stools; however, I doubt this at this time.)

The plan was to place the patient on antibiotics, start on tube feeding ("now that the feeding tube is in the proper location"), and monitor for exacerbation of congestive heart failure associated with the fluid administered by tube.

A chest x-ray dated 7/17/98 states that she had worsening pulmonary infiltrates, which might be due to pneumonia, but the radiologist could not rule out a component of congestive heart failure and pulmonary edema. There was no improvement in an x-ray done on 7/20/98. A chest x-ray done on 7/22/98 shows pulmonary edema superimposed on previously described infiltrates.

A certificate of death dated 7/25/98 states that the causes of death were aspiration pneumonia with a chemical pneumonitis and placement of nasogastric tube in right bronchus.

14. Missing Records

There arc no observation records for January 1998 and March–July 1998. The chart is missing nurses' notes and 24-hour nursing report for 7/14/98.

15. Liability Issues

The patient with a nasogastric feeding tube is at risk for aspiration. When the tube is inserted, the placement is to be checked. The ideal method to verify placement is to take a chest x-ray to ensure that the tip of the tube is in the stomach, which was not done at the facility following the insertion of the feeding tube. Although an x-ray is the safest method of verifying placement, it is less commonly done in nursing homes than hospitals. Inserting air in the stomach and listening with a stethoscope was no longer considered to be the standard of care as of 1993, according to Metheney, Minimizing Respiratory Complications of Nasoenteric Tube Feedings, State of the Science: *Heart and Lung*, 22, 213–223. Note that Davis, Arrington, Fields-Ryan, and Pruitt, Preventing Feeding-Associated Aspiration, *MEDSURG Nursing*, April 1995, stated that this method (listening for air with a stethoscope) was *unreliable* with small bore feeding tubes. This is because the air being injected through the tube may enter the lungs, and the nurse may be unable to differentiate between the air going into the lungs versus the stomach. Aftcr performing a chest x-ray to verify placement, the next safest method is to test the fluid for pH that comes out of the tube. Secretions in the lungs are alkaline with a pH of greater than 7.4. Secretions in the stomach arc acidic with a pH of less than 5.

If aspiration is suspected, the feeding should be stopped and the physician informed. Based on my analysis of the medical records, the exact time that the feeding was stopped cannot be confirmed, but occurred sometime after 3:40 p.m. Assuming that the feeding tube was inserted into the lungs at 3:30 a.m. on 7/15/98, the resident received at least 12 hours of feeding solution at 60 cc per hour. This totals 720 cc of fluid, plus 240 cc of water, on both the night shift and day shift, to total 480 cc in addition to the 720 cc of tube-feeding solution. This would have resulted in 1200 cc of feeding solution and 2 doses of May-Vita Elixir in her lung. The symptoms Mrs. W. displayed are consistent with aspiration.

There were warning signs that Mrs. W. was at risk for feeding-tube-associated aspiration. Her episode of turning purple on 4/9/98 may have been due to aspiration of feeding solution. One of the ways to detect this complication is to mix blue dye, also known as methylene blue, into the feeding solution, and then look for blue secretions coming from the lungs. If the nursing staff had suspected an aspiration, they could have contacted the nutrition department and this department could have formulated the tube feeding with methylene blue. This was not done at any point by the nursing home staff, despite several instances of gurgling and dislodgment of the feeding tube in June and July 1998. During the last weeks she was in the facility, the nurses were suctioning her on a more frequent basis, which may have been related to ill effects from episodes of aspiration small enough not to cause significant respiratory distress.

Coughing and sneezing can accidentally dislodge a nasogastric tube. The records show that the tube became dislodged 7 times in the last 6 weeks Mrs. W. was in the nursing home, on 6/1/98, 6/9/98, 6/29/98, 7/8/98, 7/9/98, 7/10/98, and 7/15/98. Aside from the risk of aspiration, long-term use of a nasogastric tube can cause erosion of the inside of the nose, back of the throat, and esophagus. The greater question is why the physician did not insert a PEG (percutaneous endoscopic gastrostomy) tube through Mrs. W.'s abdomen to prevent this known complication of nasogastric tube feeding. Although PEG tube insertion carries some risks, it is a far safer long-term feeding solution. Aspiration is still possible with this method, but it is much less likely. The medical record does not contain any indication that this option was discussed with Mrs. W.'s sponsor, who was her granddaughter.

Note that the documentation by M. Gilbert on the night shift of 7/15/98 includes a late entry or addition to her notes. The words "held feeding" were added after her entry was written.

Thank you for the opportunity to assist you with this case.

Yours truly,

Consultant, MSN, RN, LNCC

Outcome: This case was settled.

Chapter 15

Principles of Evaluating Personal Injury Cases

Arlene King Klepatsky, JD, BSN, BA, RN

CONTENTS

0-8493-1418-6/03/$0.00+$1.50
© 2003 by AALNC

Objectives

- To describe at least five roles of the legal nurse consultant in assisting the attorney in a personal injury case
- To define "comparative negligence" and describe how it may affect the plaintiff's monetary award
- To list three types of experts that may testify in a personal injury case
- To discuss the difference between special and general damages and the role of the legal nurse consultant in analyzing these damages

Introduction

Legal nurse consultants (LNCs) perform many important functions for attorneys. It is well known that the LNC is a valuable asset in medical malpractice litigation. Attorneys are also beginning to recognize the value of LNCs in personal injury (PI) litigation. In a medical malpractice case, a major function of the LNC is to determine the applicable standards of care. This is not the focus of the LNC with respect to a PI case. This chapter will describe the many functions that an LNC may perform in assisting the attorney in working up these interesting cases.

Most PI cases involve the analysis of medical records and other medical evidence. The LNC has a unique ability to make sense of those sometimes voluminous medical records, and to extract the medical evidence buried within them. The LNC transforms that stack (or those boxes) of records into meaningful, concise documents that assist the attorney in successfully resolving the case, whether through settlement or litigation. The LNC's research and well-reasoned insights assist the attorney in the legal decision-making that will best serve the attorney's client.

In order to identify and analyze the key issues in a PI case, the LNC must be familiar with what the attorney must prove (or disprove) to win the case. It is also helpful to have at least a basic understanding of various mechanisms of injury and biomechanics to enable the LNC to more accurately "picture" what happened. This allows the LNC to knowledgeably identify and evaluate the medical issues.

This chapter will provide a review of the elements that the plaintiff's attorney must prove in a PI negligence case. The author will include examples to illustrate how the LNC uses the medical records to extract information that the attorney will use to prove or disprove each of the elements (or defenses) of a negligence case.

Personal Injury Litigation

PI litigation serves a number of purposes in our legal system. For example, it:

- Provides a mechanism for awarding compensation to those who are injured as a result of the wrongful conduct of others (with the goal of making the injured party "whole" again)
- Provides an incentive to act safely in conduct that affects others
- Allocates accountability to the party with the most control over the conditions that cause risk of the injury
- Spreads the risk through the liability insurance system

PI litigation involves many different types of incidents leading to injury. Examples of such incidents include motor vehicle collisions and incidents involving other modes of transportation, such as airplanes, trains, and ships. PI cases also include premises liability involving falls, elevator and escalator accidents, and other dangerous conditions on property. There are also workplace injuries (often litigated in the state workers' compensation system), product liability cases (injuries due to defective products), injuries caused by animals or toxic substances, and other miscellaneous incidents. For example, in a recent case, a young boy contracted hepatitis after eating at a restaurant. There are even more recent cases of children choking to death on a certain type of gel candy. Almost any condition or situation leading to injury may be the subject of a PI lawsuit.

PI litigation involves the law of torts. A tort, which comes from the Latin word "torquere," meaning "to twist," is a civil wrong committed against a person, property, entity, or relationship. There are many different torts, each with its own set of elements and defenses. Some examples of torts include assault, battery, false imprisonment, negligence, strict liability (including products liability), intentional and negligent infliction of emotional distress, defamation, invasion of privacy, nuisance, and trespass.

Each tort has its own set of elements that must be proven to state a *cause of action* as well as its own set of defenses. The plaintiff's attorney must present sufficient evidence to satisfy the *burden of proof* for each one of the elements of the tort. The burden of proof in a torts case is the "preponderance of the evidence" standard. The preponderance of the evidence means that it is more probable than not. When just over 50% of the evidence is in favor of a party, that party has met the burden of proof by a preponderance of the evidence. (There are different burdens of proof to meet in other types of legal cases, such as criminal cases.)

Conversely, the defense attorney needs to present evidence to refute the plaintiff's claims regarding the elements of the cause of action (or at least one of the elements). The defense argues that the plaintiff has not met the burden of proof on any one or all of the elements. The defense attorney may also present evidence of one or more *affirmative defenses*. (These are defenses to the plaintiff's claim, such as comparative negligence, pled by the defendant.) The defense has the burden of proof when asserting the affirmative defenses. It is a function of the LNC to identify the medical facts in the records that may serve as evidence to prove the existence of the elements (when working for the plaintiff) and the defenses (when working for the defense). The LNC will also look for entries that

■ Failure to use reasonable care ...	Liability (Duty and Breach of Duty):
■ resulting in ...	Causation
■ harm.	Damages

Figure 15.1   Derivation of the Elements of Negligence

may favor the opposing party. The attorney needs to be aware of these entries as well in order to prepare an appropriate argument as early as possible.

The Tort of Negligence

PI litigation frequently involves the tort of *negligence*. As discussed above, the LNC must know the elements that the plaintiff's attorney must prove to state a cause of action for negligence. Negligence is the failure of a party to act as a reasonable person, under the same or similar circumstances, which causes harm. (Another way to say this is that negligence is the failure of a party to use reasonable care, which causes harm.) This definition, when broken down into its component parts, determines the elements of negligence. These elements are derived directly from the definition of "negligence" (see Figure 15.1). The attorney needs to know whether there is information in the medical records to support these required elements. The examples that follow under each of the elements of negligence should assist the new LNC in understanding this legal jargon.

Liability

Did the defendant (or prospective defendant) fail to use reasonable care under the circumstances? Is the defendant *liable* for the injury? If not, who is? Occasionally, evidence of liability can be found in the medical records.

Example 15.1: A young woman slipped and fell in a grocery store, straining her back and fracturing her elbow. The woman brought suit against the store, alleging that the floor was not maintained properly and was allowed to become too slippery. An LNC was contracted to summarize and analyze the medical records for the attorney representing the store's insurance carrier. The LNC quickly discovered that the emergency department records were missing. The LNC informed the attorney, who instructed the paralegal to order them. When they arrived, the LNC found a note by the triage nurse documenting the plaintiff's explanation for the fall. The woman had stated that she had recently purchased new sandals and that the soles were "unusually slippery." She told the nurse that she had previously slipped when wearing those shoes. The LNC has identified important information on the issue of liability. This piece of evidence suggests that the woman herself may have been liable, or at least partly liable, for the fall. (She was not using reasonable care in wearing those shoes that she knew were too slippery.) It suggests that the floor may not have been a causative factor in the slip and fall, and that the store may have used reasonable care in maintaining the floor. It also suggests a potential cross-claim against the manufacturer, distributor, and retailer of the shoes under a product liability theory.

Example 15.2: An elderly man was walking on a sidewalk in front of a parking lot entrance. He was on the way to his car after visiting his cardiologist. He claimed that he was hit by a full-sized pickup truck as it crossed the sidewalk to enter the parking lot. It knocked him violently to the ground. The man had preexisting, poorly controlled hypertension. His blood pressure was 205/110 en route to the hospital. The defense claimed that the truck had not hit the man, but that he had passed out in front of the truck due to his hypertensive state. There were no eyewitnesses to the accident. It was not clear from the medical records which scenario occurred. The only documented injuries were the injuries sustained from contact with the ground. The plaintiff's attorney began to worry and called her favorite LNC to review the records. The LNC knew that evidence of a point of contact would be of great help in proving that the truck had hit the plaintiff. On very careful examination, the LNC noticed a barely legible "scribble" in a handwritten admission note. The scribble, on closer examination with a magnifying glass, appeared at first to be one unintelligible word: "EcchyLSI." The translation was "ecchymosis left sacroiliac." There was a bruise on the left hip. This notation provided the critical evidence of a contact point by the truck. The author of the scribble verified its meaning. The plaintiff's accident reconstructionist determined that the bruise was anatomically located exactly where the truck would have made contact with the plaintiff. The LNC's thorough review of the medical records uncovered the critical evidence needed to help determine liability for the injuries.

Causation

Did the failure to use reasonable care cause the injury? Another way to say this is: Was the failure to use reasonable care a *substantial factor in causing* the injury?

Example 15.3: A 19-year-old man was driving on a highway at the speed limit. A pickup truck changed lanes safely in front of him. The driver of the pickup truck suddenly accelerated, causing his load of large logs (which were not covered or properly tied down) to fall onto the highway in front of the young driver. He was unable to avoid the bouncing logs. He ran into one and lost control of his vehicle, hitting the center divider at a high rate of speed. Though he was properly restrained, the young man suffered a fractured femur, as well as some other less serious injuries. In this example, there is little question that the failure to properly secure the load on the truck (i.e., the truck driver's failure to use reasonable care) was a substantial factor in bringing about the young man's fractured femur. Assuming that there were no mechanical problems with the young man's truck, it appears that there are no other factors to complicate the element of causation.

In contrast, sometimes other factors are involved, such as preexisting degenerative changes and congenital conditions. For example, in the case of "whiplash" injuries of the neck, degenerative changes are commonly seen in the cervical spine on radiological imaging studies performed after the incident. Depending on the seriousness of these changes, the defense might argue that the true cause of the ongoing symptoms is the degeneration and not the incident. The LNC will review the medical records prior to and after the incident. Sometimes the LNC will note that similar symptoms were present immediately prior to the incident. The author has reviewed cases in which a motor vehicle collision occurred on the way back from the chiropractic visit to treat the preexisting neck pain. But there are also cases in which, despite the degenerative changes noted on the imaging studies, the plaintiff was totally asymptomatic prior to the incident. In the latter case, though the degenerative changes were present, they were "silent" until the accident caused them to become symptomatic.

The LNC will see many cases in which the plaintiff has suffered multiple incidents of injury. In these cases, the LNC extracts the subjective complaints and the objective findings from the medical records before and after each of the incidents. This will help to unravel the tangled web of causation. It will assist the medical causation expert in determining which of the signs, symptoms, and impairments were caused by (1) preexisting conditions (such as injuries, illnesses, and congenital conditions), (2) the incident that is the subject of the case, and (3) subsequent incidents. Often the LNC will see a situation in which a plaintiff is making progress with a prior significant injury when another incident occurs. Often, the second incident aggravates the prior injury. In this situation, the plaintiff will not be able to recover damages from the defendant for the entire second injury, but will recover solely for the aggravation of the initial injury.

Often the LNC educates the attorney regarding pathophysiology that will make the causation quite clear. Following are some examples of how this process has had a direct impact on the outcome of the case.

Example 15.4: A 54-year-old woman was sitting in her disabled truck on the shoulder of the highway awaiting roadside assistance. The driver of a semi truck allegedly fell asleep and veered into the truck, causing it to roll down an embankment. It rolled over several times, and the woman was ejected. She suffered multiple injuries, including a flail chest and a head injury. She was nonresponsive at the scene. Paramedics arrived 25 minutes after the incident. Among other things, they intubated and oxygenated the woman and transported her to the nearest emergency department. Her oxygen saturation on arrival at the emergency department was 80%. A CT head scan revealed a very small subdural hematoma (SDH). The woman gradually regained consciousness and eventually recovered enough to leave the hospital, but was left with serious cognitive deficits. She was also irritable and was prone to outbursts of anger. Due to these deficits, she was unable to return to work. She sued the truck driver for causing her injuries, including the brain injury leading to the cognitive deficits and irritability. The neurology expert hired by the defense testified that the small SDH could not have caused the cognitive deficits suffered by the plaintiff. He stated that the SDH was too small and was not in a location that would cause such deficits. At this point in the case, the plaintiff's attorney called his LNC.

The LNC reviewed the records and performed some basic research regarding flail chest and head injuries. She concluded that there had likely been a period of prolonged hypoxia because of the flail chest and obtundation from the head injury, in addition to the long response time of the first responders. The LNC wondered whether there had been a hypoxic brain injury as opposed to traumatic brain injury. The attorney stated that he had considered that theory but that a medico-legal reference he had consulted indicated that an "oxygen level around

50" was usually required to prove hypoxic brain injury. He recalled that the plaintiff had an "oxygen level of 80," so he believed that the theory was not likely to be successful. The LNC educated the attorney regarding blood gases, including the difference between the pO_2 and the O_2 saturation. Using the hemoglobin/oxygen dissociation curve, the LNC explained to the attorney that an O_2 saturation of 80% coincides with a pO_2 of 50 mmHg. The LNC also explained that the pO_2 had likely been at an even lower level since the patient suffered from flail chest and loss of consciousness at the scene. Medical experts confirmed that the patient exhibited signs and symptoms consistent with a hypoxic brain injury. The attorney discussed this new information with the defense attorney. The case settled shortly thereafter.

Example 15.5: A 70-year-old man (with preexisting coronary artery disease) tripped over a cable stretched across an area in the parking lot of a restaurant. He was unable to see it because it was dark and the lighting was poor. As he fell, he struck his left shoulder on the side mirror of a car. He suffered extreme pain in the shoulder area. He was transported to the hospital where x-rays revealed numerous fractures, including fractures of the humerus and clavicle. The pain began to increase, and the area became extremely ecchymotic. During surgery, it was discovered that he had injured his brachial artery and it had developed a bleed. He underwent surgery to repair the fractures and the artery. He required blood replacement and fluid therapy. He was discharged from the hospital on the eighth postoperative day. At home, he tried to lie down to rest, but became very short of breath and was returned to the hospital by ambulance. A chest x-ray revealed severe pulmonary edema, and he was diagnosed with congestive heart failure (CHF). He was hospitalized for another 5 days. In a subsequent lawsuit against the restaurant, the defense attorneys asserted that the second hospitalization was in no way related to the trip-and-fall incident. After all, this was a plaintiff with preexisting heart disease and a history of CHF. Furthermore, the cardiac problems had occurred 8 days after the incident.

An LNC performed a chronology and analysis for the defense attorney in order to extract the medical facts. The LNC determined on analysis of the medical records that the intake and output totals (which had not been added up by the nurses) revealed an overall fluid excess of 4000 cc's at the time of discharge. This went undetected and untreated until he developed the signs and symptoms of CHF. The LNC informed the defense attorney about the massive fluid overload and explained the pathophysiology of CHF. (One can see that this is very similar to the patient teaching that nurses do in clinical practice.) The medical experts, of course, confirmed the LNC's theory. In the final analysis, the CHF was caused by the treatment required for the injury suffered in the trip-and-fall incident. The defense was liable. The defense attorney appreciated this information. She could now predict the plaintiff's theory. Also, the information helped her decide whether to settle the matter or take it to trial.

Damages

Evidence of damages (i.e., the harm suffered by the plaintiff) is documented in the billing records (special damages) and in the medical records (general damages).

Special Damages

Special damages are the quantifiable or "out-of-pocket" costs of medical care. (This includes both the care received up to the time the case is settled or litigated and the costs for predictable future care.) Some components of special damages may include:

- Medications and treatment supplies
- Office visits and hospitalizations
- Home care services
- Costs of travel to and from medical appointments
- Assistive devices and other medical equipment
- Modifications to the environment (such as ramps and safety bars)
- Costs of help with services to assist with necessary household functions (shopping, housecleaning, lawn cutting, and even snow removal when appropriate)

Other out-of-pocket expenses may be involved depending on the particular circumstances. Special damages also include wages lost as a result of the injury. Documentation of lost wages is demonstrated through payslips before and after the injury; employment records; and business records, such as profit and loss statements for the self-employed person.

To assist with the calculation of the damages, the LNC identifies and requests all billing records for medical care related to the incident. The LNC is especially well prepared for this task because the LNC understands the health care system. For example, the LNC knows that one visit to the emergency department will often yield separate bills from the ambulance company, the hospital, the emergency physician's group, the outside laboratory, and the radiologist. The LNC also knows that a surgical procedure may yield separate bills from the hospital or surgical center, the surgeon, the assistant surgeons, the anesthesiologist, and perhaps even a radiologist and an outside laboratory. Billings for office visits, such as doctor visits, chiropractic visits, and physical and other therapy visits, often arrive in the form of an organized, easy-to-understand ledger with a total at the bottom. Sometimes, health care providers keep separate ledgers for each incident. Be sure to request all ledgers for all care, rather than solely for the incident at issue. (This may uncover some additional helpful evidence.) The LNC generally prepares a list of what is missing, and these items will be obtained. When they arrive, the LNC creates a "medical specials list." The dates, service (or product), and costs are listed, and a total is calculated.

No discussion of special damages would be complete without mentioning the *collateral source rule*. This rule prevents the defendants from telling the jury that the plaintiff had health care insurance (including Medicare and Medicaid) that covered all or part of the damages. If the jury were told of this, the wrongdoers might escape liability and the loss would be borne by the private health insurance companies or by the government (in the case of Medicare or Medicaid). This sounds like the plaintiff could get a double recovery — having the bills paid and then obtaining the money from the lawsuit. This generally does not happen because the insurance companies and the government file a lien against any recovery for reimbursement of the costs of care needed as a result of the defendant's wrongful conduct. Plaintiff's attorneys often negotiate with the insurance companies regarding what they are willing to accept on the lien.

General Damages

General damages are not easily quantifiable, but a monetary figure is determined based on the severity of the damages and the impact on the plaintiff's life. General damages (also referred to as noneconomic damages) include:

- Pain and suffering (both physical and emotional)
- Loss of function
- Loss of enjoyment of life
- Inconvenience
- Fear (such as fear of driving) resulting from the incident
- Embarrassment
- Emotional pain of disfigurement

There may be other components as well. In medical malpractice cases, the recovery for general damages is limited. For example, in California, there has been a cap of $250,000 on this component of damages since 1975. But California has no such cap on general damages in PI cases at this point in time.

Sometimes, the LNC is asked to extract evidence of pain, suffering, loss of function, and other indications of general damages from the records. With this information along with the special damages, the attorney can determine the value of a case and plan settlement and litigation strategies. A pain and suffering summary may be used for presentation to the insurance company in the settlement package (perhaps even in the demand letter) or, if the case goes to trial, for presentation to the jury. The role of the LNC in preparing a pain and suffering summary is presented in Chapter 36, The Expert Fact Witness: Noneconomic Damages Testimony.

The LNC may also assist in the production of a "day in the life" video. This is used especially with catastrophically injured persons to show the insurance company and the jury what the plaintiff goes through in a typical day. This is often contrasted with a video of the plaintiff prior to the injury to illustrate how the incident has changed the plaintiff's life.

The LNC may also review the damages to identify issues (such as inconsistencies) regarding the claims. This is often performed for the defense, but the plaintiff's attorney benefits from recognizing such red flags as well. The plaintiff's attorney may have to make a decision regarding whether or not to take a case in the first place, or to decide whether or not to accept a particular offer of settlement from the insurance company. The attorney may want to explore reasonable explanations for such red-flag issues with the client. It is important for the attorney to know what he is "up against" in order to plan an appropriate litigation strategy.

The defense attorney uses evidence of inconsistencies to identify potential credibility problems. Also, the defense attorney is on the lookout for exaggeration and malingering. The LNC is able to analyze the records to identify issues regarding whether or not the plaintiff's claims "make sense" given the incident. (The medical causation experts can do further analysis on these issues spotted through the LNC's exquisitely detailed review.)

Example 15.6: A truck driver claims that his semi truck was rear-ended by a Honda Civic at a red light. The emergency room records document his statement of the facts and his complaints. The truck driver states that he was thrown into the steering wheel and injured his chest and neck. No areas of redness or bruising were noted on his chest during physical examination. No rib or sternal fractures were noted on the x-ray. The next day, he told his primary doctor that he had been thrown against the steering wheel and ended up on the floor of his cab. The next week, he told the consulting neurologist that he had been thrown against the steering wheel, then onto the floor, then out of the door of his cab and onto the roadway. Physical examination still had not revealed any bruises, abrasions, or lacerations. There were additional embellishments of the story in the records. The LNC listed each of the plaintiff's statements describing the accident. The progressive embellishment of the story as told to each successive health care provider was now glaringly obvious, and it hurt this plaintiff's credibility. The LNC made a chart listing each entry regarding the plaintiff's account of the accident. This was a concise presentation that revealed a striking pattern of progressive embellishment.

Example 15.7: In another case, a man fell off a ladder at work, injured his leg, and developed complex regional pain syndrome. The incident report said that the ladder was 4 ft high. As he retold the story, the ladder became as tall as 20 ft.

Other common inconsistencies that may be seen in the medical records of plaintiffs claiming personal injuries deal with seat belt use and loss of consciousness at the scene. The records of rescue and emergency personnel may include documentation regarding these factors based on direct observation. Subsequent medical records may contain conflicting information as the plaintiff changes the details of what happened. The astute LNC who detects these inconsistencies should share them with the attorney in detail. Another type of inconsistency arises when a plaintiff claims inability to return to work, but appears to be able to do other activities similar to those performed at work.

Example 15.8: The plaintiff, a mechanic, claimed to be unable to return to work after a motor vehicle collision. Surveillance videotapes (also known as "sub rosa" investigation) taken by an investigator for the defense showed the plaintiff effortlessly replacing the engine in his own vehicle and later playing a vigorous basketball game with some friends.

The plaintiff may be able to explain why he was able to do such activities on that day. He could have been having a good day, he may have taken pain medication and muscle relaxers, or he may have suffered pain before and after the activities. Yet these videotapes may be damaging when a plaintiff claims limited function but tapes show otherwise. The LNC may have access to these videotapes or the written surveillance report that describes the plaintiff's activities. The LNC may be able to compare these to what is documented in the medical records.

Punitive Damages

Punitive damages (also known as exemplary damages) may be awarded when a defendant's conduct is considered to be oppressive, malicious, or fraudulent. In

California, the word "despicable" is added. The burden of proof for proving the requirements for punitive damages is "clear and convincing." This is a higher standard of proof than is required for proving the elements of negligence. The amount awarded by the trier of fact is an amount likely to punish the defendant. The defendant may have to produce financial records to aid the determination of an amount that would adequately punish the defendant. (The medical records of the plaintiff are of no help with this component of damages, since the focus is on the conduct of the defendant.) The rules regarding punitive damages may differ from state to state.

Loss of Consortium

Loss of consortium is an independent claim that can be made. The spouse of an injured party may sue the defendant for loss of consortium. This involves the loss of love, comfort, companionship, affection, sexual relations, assistance in maintaining the household, and other components of the relationship. The loss of consortium must have been caused by the injuries suffered in the accident.

Payment of Damages

Most of the time, an insurance company pays the damages. Damages arising from motor vehicle collisions are paid by the liable party's insurance company. Damages arising from premises liability cases are paid by the property owner's insurance or from commercial general liability (business) policies. In addition, there may be excess coverage that covers losses above a certain amount. In exchange for the premiums collected, the insurance company promises both to defend and to indemnify (pay damages on behalf of) the insured. The defense attorney is chosen by the insurance company. The insurance company generally retains a measure of control over the litigation. It is the duty of the defendant to cooperate.

Uninsured/Underinsured Coverage

When a driver and passengers are injured by an uninsured or underinsured driver, damages may be paid by the driver's own insurance company. When the liable driver has no insurance, uninsured motorist coverage comes into play. When the liable driver has a policy limit that is not large enough to cover the proven damages, then the underinsured motorist coverage applies. (The amount of uninsured/underinsured coverage available may depend on the plaintiff's own policy limits.) Payments under uninsured and underinsured motorist coverage are not automatic. These cases are often litigated. The injured person often must prove the case with respect to liability, causation, and damages. In some states, these cases are litigated by binding arbitration as opposed to trial by jury.

Lack of Insurance

In a situation where no valid insurance coverage is found to apply to an incident, a liable party may have to pay damages from personal assets. However, occasionally the liable party is *judgment proof.* This means that there are no substantial assets to satisfy a judgment. Some attorneys prefer not to take a case when there is no valid insurance coverage. Very often, one of the initial inquiries by a plaintiff's attorney is regarding the existence and amount of an insurance policy.

Self-Insured Entities

Some large companies or other entities, such as universities, may decide to self-insure. In other words, they set aside funds to cover the costs of defense and indemnification. Sometimes entities that are self-insured purchase excess coverage. This is insurance coverage that applies once the value of a case reaches a certain amount.

No-Fault Insurance

Thirteen states have no-fault insurance for automobile accidents: Colorado, Florida, Hawaii, Kansas, Kentucky, Massachusetts, Michigan, Minnesota, New Jersey, New York, North Dakota, Pennsylvania, and Utah. In general, under a no-fault system, each party's own insurance covers the damages (up to policy limits) regardless of which party is at fault. This system was created in an attempt to avoid the costly litigation that took place in order to determine who was at fault in accidents. While special damages are covered under the no-fault system, an injured party may still sue for general (noneconomic) damages under certain circumstances as determined by state law and the insurance policy. In general, these cases involve the more serious accidents.[1] LNCs in the no-fault states may be able to assist in working up these cases.

Defenses to Negligence

Once a PI case is filed and served, the defendant asserts defenses by disputing the existence of any one of the elements of the cause of action, or by presenting evidence of an affirmative defense. This section will discuss just a few of the affirmative defenses to negligence, including comparative negligence, the seat belt defense, and assumption of risk.

Comparative Negligence

With this defense, the defendant alleges that it was the plaintiff who caused the injury. This may be a complete or a partial defense. The trier of fact (jury or arbitrator) may find the plaintiff 100% liable for the incident, may find the defendant 100% liable, or may allocate some fault to the defendant and some to the plaintiff. The rule varies from state to state, but in general, the plaintiff's award is decreased in proportion to the plaintiff's own negligence. This defense used to be known as contributory negligence when any negligence by the plaintiff completely barred any recovery. The doctrine of comparative negligence allows partial recovery by the plaintiff. For instance, in Example 15.1, a young woman slipped and fell in a grocery store. In the subsequent lawsuit, the defendant claimed that the woman had been negligent in wearing shoes that she knew were too slippery. If the jury were to find the plaintiff 40% liable for the injuries, the plaintiff would receive 60% of the award.

The LNC should be aware of the defense of comparative negligence and look for any facts that suggest that the plaintiff's conduct contributed to the incident. The LNC who reviewed the above case was aware of the significance of the statement given to the nurse regarding the shoes' being too slippery and brought it to the attorney's attention.

The Seat Belt Defense

The seat belt defense is one form of the comparative negligence defense. In motor vehicle cases, if the plaintiff was not wearing a seat belt, the defense wants to know what damages the plaintiff would have suffered had he been wearing one. This requires the opinion and testimony of an expert witness. The defense argues that it should not have to pay for any damages that occurred as a result of the failure to wear a seat belt.

Example 15.9: The plaintiff was an unrestrained passenger in a vehicle without airbags on the passenger side. The vehicle in which the plaintiff was riding was involved in a moderate-speed frontal collision. The plaintiff struck her head on the windshield and suffered a subdural hematoma. The defense hired a biomechanics expert, who testified that if the plaintiff had been wearing her seat belt, her head would not have come in contact with the windshield. In fact, her head would not have struck anything. The defense declined to pay for treatment and sequelae of the head injury since it was caused by the plaintiff's failure to buckle up.

Assumption of Risk

Assumption of risk is an interesting defense, though it is unlikely that the LNC will work on these cases. Plaintiff's attorneys are aware of this defense and decline to take cases in which the defense is likely to apply. This defense applies in cases involving recreational activities that cannot be made entirely safe without materially altering the activity. Some of these activities are skiing, golfing, water-skiing, river rafting, rock climbing, horseback riding, and martial arts. The defense of primary assumption of risk is based on the notion that these activities, by their nature, have inherent risks. The defendant has no duty to protect the plaintiff from the inherent risks of the activity. For example, the owner of a ski resort has no duty to remove trail markers because the markers are an inherent part of the sport of skiing. There is no negligence when a skier runs into such a marker (in states, such as California, that have this doctrine). The ski resort owner does have a duty to adequately maintain equipment, such as the tow cables. Injury from a broken tow cable is not an inherent part of the sport of skiing.

Experts in PI Cases

The experienced LNC is very familiar with medical experts. In PI cases, the attorney may need to work with many other types of experts to analyze and to testify regarding the issues of liability, causation, and damages. A very brief discussion

■ Mechanism of injury (e.g., forces and direction of impact, seat position, use of restraint devices, vehicle specifications)

■ Anatomy of the particular plaintiff (e.g., height, weight, congenital anomalies, position of plaintiff at impact — head, hands, arms, torso)

■ Data from radiology/imaging studies

■ Clinical data (past medical history, postincident medical care)

■ Surgical findings (if any)

Figure 15.2   Factors Considered by a Forensic Anatomist in Determining the Causation of Injury in a Personal Injury Case (Reprinted with permission of Dr. Lawrence Elson.)

of some of these experts will follow to illustrate the wide range of experts that attorneys use in presenting a PI case to the trier of fact.

Liability Experts and Causation Experts

A *forensic anatomist* may testify regarding causation of injury. Some of the factors considered by the forensic anatomist in reaching a conclusion regarding causation involve information contained in the medical record (see Figure 15.2). An LNC may extract and summarize these data from the medical records for this type of expert. (This author has summarized medical and other accident records for a forensic anatomist for well over a decade. The author knows of other similar experts who use LNCs to assist them with medical and other records.) In addition to rendering an opinion on the causation of injury, this type of expert may also be able to unravel disputed facts using forensic evidence. For example, this type of expert may be able to determine who was driving when this fact is in dispute. (When the driver and the passenger are both ejected, there may be an issue regarding who was driving. Also, there are cases in which each party denies that he was the driver.) A close look at the types of injuries suffered by the occupants provides clues. Usually, the driver suffers injuries that differ from those of the passengers due to contact with the steering wheel. In a side impact, the side of the body that the injuries are on may suggest who was driving.

Biomechanical/biomedical engineers analyze the effects of various forces on the human body. They apply engineering principles to the biological systems of the human body.

Accident reconstructionists calculate important data regarding the forces involved in a particular motor vehicle collision. These experts may perform inspections of the vehicles involved in the collision and of the collision scene. Using a computer program, the accident reconstructionist enters data regarding such facts as vehicle damage and certain details about the specific vehicles involved. In this way, the accident reconstructionist determines the "delta v" (the change in velocity) and the Gs (sometimes referred to as "G forces") on the occupants. The delta v and Gs are discussed in Chapter 16, Common Mechanisms of Injury in Personal

Injury Cases. The accident reconstructionist may also reenact the accident using similar vehicles and conditions or by creating a computerized reenactment.

Human factors engineers analyze the interactions of humans with their environment. This type of expert may be used when the possibility of human error is a factor in a case.

Physicians may also serve as causation experts in PI cases. For example, a neuropsychiatrist may be able to testify that a certain type of head injury was the cause of certain cognitive deficits or emotional changes. A neurosurgeon may be needed to testify that injury to the spinal cord at C2 caused the plaintiff's paralysis. A neuroradiologist may be hired to reinterpret diagnostic studies such as magnetic resonance imaging and CT scans.

Forensic pathologists render opinions regarding the cause of death. For example, a pathologist may be used to testify how a blunt head trauma caused intracranial bleeding leading to increased intracranial pressure, tentorial herniation, and brain death. The pathologist may also be able to determine which of many injuries actually caused the death. This can be important in PI cases.

Example 15.10: Some young men were riding in the open back of a pickup truck. They were being pursued by a law enforcement vehicle. The driver of the truck tried to evade the patrol car and took a turn at high speed. One of the occupants of the truck bed was thrown out onto the road, landing on his head. The patrol car came around the corner and ran over the victim's chest. The pathologist was asked to determine which injury caused the death.

Damages Experts

Vocational experts determine whether a plaintiff can perform specific job functions given the disabilities from an injury. They can determine the degree of impairment and disability. They may also determine the need for vocational rehabilitation if the person is not able to return to duties of his customary job.

Life care planning experts are often nurses with special knowledge and training in life care planning. The registered nurse may hold a certification in life care planning. A life care planner evaluates all the future needs of a severely injured plaintiff and determines the cost of those products and services. In addition to future medical care, the life care planner also considers the need for and costs of residential modifications, such as the addition of a ramp or the installation of safety bars. The life care planner then drafts a life care plan for use in calculating damages in the case. An economist is often used to factor in the cost of inflation. For more information on the life care planning expert, see Chapter 37, The Life Care Planning Expert.

Economists are used by attorneys to assist in calculating damages. The future value of the medical costs needs to be calculated, adjusting for inflation. Economists may also help to determine what a person's future income likely would have been if the person had not been injured. The economist knows what factors to consider in order to determine projected future income.

Life expectancy experts are actuaries, Ph.D.s, and occasionally medical doctors who render opinions regarding the plaintiff's life expectancy, taking into account many factors unique to that plaintiff. Predicted life expectancy is important when future damages are to be calculated for the rest of an injured person's life. As one would expect, the defense life expectancy expert often predicts a shorter life expectancy than a plaintiff's expert.

Following is a list of just some of the additional types of experts that may assist in a PI case:

- Bicycle experts
- Motorcycle experts
- Truck experts
- Road design experts
- Aviation experts
- Arborists (for falling-tree cases)
- Construction defect experts
- Safety engineers
- Mechanical engineers
- Slip-and-fall experts (can test floors for coefficient of friction value and perform slip tests)
- Toxicologists
- Electrical engineers
- Flammability experts
- Metallurgists
- Premises liability experts
- Failure analysis experts
- Forensic meteorologists
- Security experts
- Playground experts
- Amusement park experts

Wrongful Death Cases

Wrongful death statutes outline special rules for trying a case in which the injury results in death. In wrongful death cases, the damages are not based on the grief of the survivors, but on the loss of the benefits of the relationship, such as the economic support of the deceased person. In some states, there is no recovery for pain and suffering in a wrongful death case. Only certain heirs as outlined in the statute are able to sue under the wrongful death statute.

Roles of the LNC in PI Litigation

The LNC can assist the attorney (or insurance company) with PI cases by performing a variety of functions. The examples in the section on negligence law have suggested some of the functions that the LNC can perform. LNCs carry out the functions that they are competent to perform and that the attorney agrees upon. It may be up to the LNC to suggest to the attorney what specific functions may be helpful to the case. Often, attorneys are not accustomed to delegating functions to a nurse. A well-articulated suggestion, along with an example of how the function can be of help, may encourage the attorney to give it a try. This section will give LNCs some ideas about what they can do to assist the PI attorney.

Analyze the Medical Records

The LNC, whether on the plaintiff or defense side of the litigation, reviews the medical records to identify issues in the case, including the strengths and weaknesses and important evidence. (Recall Example 15.2, in which the LNC found an otherwise unintelligible scribble in the record. That scribble, when examined and interpreted by the LNC, provided a key piece of evidence for the plaintiff's case.)

The LNC's analysis of the medical records does not involve giving an expert opinion regarding accident biomechanics or causation of the plaintiff's injuries. This is beyond the expertise and scope of practice of the LNC. Instead, the LNC's analysis involves issue-spotting, identifying facts or statements that may suggest the liability of other parties, inconsistencies (or consistencies) of the plaintiff's complaints and findings, and the consistency between the mechanism of injury and the claimed and documented injuries. The LNC does not provide the definitive opinions regarding the latter, but does help to identify the issues that require further exploration by the appropriate causation and other experts.

The LNC is also very effective in identifying crucial missing records. The LNC is often the one who determines that the records of a specialist are missing, or that a report of a key diagnostic test is not included in the first set. An LNC working for the defense can be instrumental in identifying past medical providers and prior diagnostic tests. These records are often crucial to the defense case. The additional records can then be requested early, before there is any danger of encountering a discovery cutoff date.

Following are some examples of the kind of information that the LNC should be alert for in the medical records. These entries assist the LNC in (1) identifying issues in the PI case, and (2) identifying the strengths and weaknesses of a PI case:

- Consistencies or inconsistencies in the plaintiff's description of the accident and the symptoms and injuries claimed (see Example 15.6)
- The patient's perception of the cause of the symptoms/injuries

Example 15.11: The plaintiff filled out a questionnaire in which he attributes ongoing symptoms to a prior work injury.

- Any statement by the plaintiff, including statements on questionnaires, estimating the length of time the symptoms have been present (such as "back pain for many years")
- Facts or statements that suggest liability of another party (in a prior example, the plaintiff told the emergency department nurse that her new shoes seemed unusually slippery)
- Consistency or inconsistency between the mechanism of injury and the claimed injuries

Example 15.12: The plaintiff is involved in a low-speed rear-end collision and claims to have been thrown into the windshield.

- Consistencies or inconsistencies between the medical records and discovery documents such as depositions

Example 15.13: The plaintiff testified under oath in her deposition that she had never suffered neck problems prior to this accident. The LNC reviewed the medical records, which included insurance payment ledgers. She noted that the insurance company had paid for a cervical spine x-ray and a doctor's visit the year prior to the accident. The LNC requested those records. When they arrived, the records confirmed that the plaintiff had complained of neck pain to an orthopedic surgeon the year prior to the accident. The cervical spine x-ray showed some degenerative changes, including a disc bulge at the C5–6 level.

- Descriptions of the injury by the plaintiff that are unusually precise

Example 15.14: The plaintiff claimed that she had lost consciousness for 17 seconds.

- Facts that support or refute liability (see Example 15.2, in which the LNC found the scribble that, when deciphered, provided documentation of a contact point between the defendant's vehicle and the plaintiff's hip)
- Preexisting injuries or conditions (including congenital conditions, such as congenital spinal stenosis, and degenerative conditions, such as degenerative disc or joint disease)
- Other conditions that affect the current complaints

Example 15.15: The plaintiff complains of knee pain but is obese and has an elevated uric acid level.

- Preexisting injuries or symptoms similar to the current injuries or symptoms
- Delay in seeking treatment

Example 15.16: The plaintiff's first visit for medical care was a month after the incident.

- Gaps in treatment

Example 15.17: The plaintiff had been seeing the physician once a month, skipped three months, then returned to the once-a-month visits.

- Subsequent injuries, exacerbations, or "flare-ups"

Example 15.18: The plaintiff was in another motor vehicle collision after the one involved in the case the LNC is working on.

- Entries made by a health care provider that reflect doubts regarding the plaintiff's symptoms, such as references to psychosomatic, symptom magnification, functional overlay, secondary gain, and a lack of objective findings to explain the symptoms
- Compliance or noncompliance with medical regimen such as physical therapy, activity restrictions, or medications; frequent "no-shows"

Example 15.19: The plaintiff did not attend prescribed physical therapy for a shoulder injury and ultimately suffered a "frozen shoulder." This might have been prevented if the patient had attended the prescribed therapy.

- Activities seemingly inconsistent with claimed limitations

Example 15.20: Physical therapy notes state that the plaintiff is sore after moving a refrigerator last weekend.

- Limitations caused by pain, dysfunction

Example 15.21: The plaintiff can no longer work or do other activities that she used to do.

- Emotional responses to symptoms, to loss of function, or to the accident itself

Example 15.22: The plaintiff states that she has been afraid of driving on the freeway since the accident. She says that she cannot sleep, and when she is able to, she has nightmares.

- Changes in relationship with spouse due to pain, changes in function, or emotional responses to the incident (including changes in sexual function and relationship; irritability causing friction, arguments).
- Information regarding habits or activities that may affect the plaintiff's condition (plaintiff has a nonunion of a lumbar fusion and he is a smoker).
- Any information that suggests lack of credibility, substance abuse, or other illegal activities on the part of the plaintiff. The attorney needs to be aware of any negative information regarding the client, so that the attorney can decide how to handle the case in light of that information.

Example 15.23: A PI attorney in Hayward, CA, told the author how he successfully handled a case in which his client had many characteristics of the "unsavory" plaintiff. The plaintiff was an unkempt alcoholic and drug addict with a criminal record and ended up in jail for public drunkenness instead of arriving at the settlement conference for his case. In contrast, the defendant was a well-groomed, articulate businesswoman. The defendant had hit the plaintiff when he was crossing in a crosswalk while under the influence of alcohol. The plaintiff suffered a serious leg fracture. At trial when addressing the jury pool, the attorney's first words were: "Ladies and gentlemen, you won't like my client. I don't like my client. Do we all agree that this fact should not make a difference if he is entitled to recover for his injuries?" He made a similar statement about the defendant regarding how, in contrast, she was likable and how that should not make a difference if she were found liable for causing the plaintiff's injuries. In that way, the attorney defused the situation. The defendant was no longer able to use any of those "bad" facts against the plaintiff. Instead, they were immediately discussed and put into perspective by the plaintiff's own attorney. After both sides presented their case to the jury, the jury found in favor of the plaintiff and awarded a significant sum of money.[2]

Educate the Attorney

The LNC educates the attorney regarding medical conditions, anatomy, and physiology (see Example 15.4); injuries suffered by the plaintiff; and pronunciation of medical terminology. Sometimes attorneys are not sure how to pronounce certain medical words. It is very important for the attorney to know how to pronounce medical words correctly when discussing the case with opposing parties and medical experts, and during depositions and trials. This is a natural function for the LNC.

The LNC should be familiar with finding or creating appropriate teaching materials, articles, drawings, and diagrams to assist the attorney in understanding the medical information. Show the attorney an illustration of the anatomical area related to the case. In the case of a torn anterior cruciate ligament (ACL), the LNC would provide a good anatomical illustration of a normal knee with its anatomical components along with an illustration showing a torn ACL. These illustrations may be from books, Web sites, computer programs, and even companies that specialize in medical illustrations. Some illustrations are free, and some may be had for a fee.

Transform the Information in the Medical Records into a Format Useful to the Attorney

The LNC will organize the medical records sets. The most logical way to do this is to order the sets chronologically. Do not worry if there is some overlap of time periods. Once the sets are organized chronologically, the LNC creates a comprehensive chronology. This is the best way to understand and analyze the information in the medical records. To create the chronology, the LNC briefly summarizes every visit, procedure, diagnostic test, and all other entries in strict chronological order. Chapter 31, Medical Record Analysis, illustrates a format for the chronology. Once the chronology is completed, it is quite easy to draft a narrative summary using the chronology as a guide. Using the chronology and the narrative summary, the LNC can then identify missing records, key issues, and some of the case's strengths and weaknesses based on the documented medical facts. The LNC has decoded that amorphous stack of records in the moving box into a clear, easy-to-understand document.

Perform Searches of the Medical Literature

In medical malpractice cases, the LNC performs research of the medical literature regarding the standard of care, as well as causation and damages. In PI cases, the LNC performs research regarding the issues of causation and damages.

Example 15.24: An attorney contacted this author after a client came in claiming that he had suffered Guillain-Barré syndrome after a minor rear-end collision. His neck was sore, and then a month later, he developed the progressive paralysis of that disease process. He was sure that it had been caused by the collision. The attorney wanted to know whether the literature contained any cases of trauma-induced Guillain-Barré syndrome.

Example 15.25: Another example of causation research involved a case of pancreatitis that occurred soon after a major frontal collision. The author searched the literature for cases of pancreatitis related to trauma.

Literature research is also helpful on the issue of damages. For example, the author researched sequelae of splenectomy, so that the attorney could include those potential problems in the demand letter to the insurance company.

A search of the peer-reviewed medical literature can be performed using the free PubMed/MEDLINE online database (a service of the National Library of Medicine). Some subscription databases may be useful as well. For example, MD Consult, http://www.mdconsult.com, is a useful subscription site for researching some of the major medical textbooks in a variety of specialties, as well as patient educational handouts and practice guidelines. See Chapter 32, Literature Research, for more information.

Assist with Discovery

Discovery consists of various legal processes used to gather evidence to determine the facts of a case. The LNC assists with discovery in a variety of ways. The LNC identifies additional medical records that would be helpful in the case. Almost always, in reviewing a medical record, the LNC determines that other records should be obtained. Very often there are references to other physicians; other conditions; and prior procedures, hospitalizations, and diagnostic tests. The LNC should make a list of the additional medical records needed. Other documents beyond the medical records also may be helpful to a case. These include accident reports, employment records, academic records, and other records, depending on the facts of the case.

The LNC may also suggest questions that the attorney should ask through interrogatories or at deposition. In general, the LNC does not draft the actual questions to be presented to the party or witness, but informs the attorney regarding additional information that should be obtained. The attorney or paralegal will put the questions into the appropriate format.

Interview Clients

LNCs are well suited to interview clients who have been injured. Nurses are practiced in the communication skills needed to perform intake interviews, and know how to extract important information about the client's injuries and complaints. See Chapter 23, Legal Nurse Consultant Practice within a Law Firm, and Chapter 24, Communication with Plaintiff Clients, for more information.

Assist in Preparing Settlement Documents

The LNC may assist the attorney in drafting documents used for settlement negotiations. Prior to filing a lawsuit, the attorney often sends a *demand letter* to the insurance company. This letter sets out the liability of the tortfeasor (the person committing the tort) as well as the injuries suffered by the attorney's client. The LNC will review the medical records and extract, interpret, and summarize important information to persuade the insurance company to settle with the injured party. The LNC is also adept at suggesting exhibits from the medical records to illustrate the points made in the demand letter. The LNC may also list and calculate the medical care costs to date.

After the case is filed, the attorney will often put together a settlement package for the insurance company. This may be more complex than the demand letter. The LNC is able to assist the attorney in preparation of this package as well.

These settlement documents need to paint a picture of the injured client. The LNC's skill in extracting the key information from the medical records and in effectively communicating this information is helpful in effectively painting this picture. See Chapter 39, Alternative Dispute Resolution: Settlement, Arbitration, and Mediation for more information.

Attend Independent Medical Examinations

In a PI case, the state code of civil procedure provides for an examination by a physician of the defendant's choosing. This is called the independent medical examination (IME). Some states allow the plaintiff's attorney or a representative of the plaintiff's attorney to attend this examination. This is a perfect role for the LNC.

Depending on the discovery code of the state, an LNC may be allowed to audiotape the examination in addition to observing it and taking notes. The LNC then reviews the IME physician's report. The LNC will, if necessary, testify regarding what she observed. For example, the LNC may have documented that the client grimaced during the shoulder range-of-motion examination, but the physician reported that there was full range of motion without pain. The LNC can testify as to her observations. Also, the LNC can be called to testify (without being disclosed in advance) as an impeachment witness to refute the testimony of the IME physician. Generally, the LNC who is attending the IME is not the same LNC who is reviewing the other aspects of the case. The role of attorney's representative at the IME compromises the LNC's behind-the-scenes, nontestifying role. For more information on the IME, see Chapter 29, Defense Medical Examinations.

Testify as an Expert Fact Witness

Because of years of clinical experience, the LNC is well suited to the unique role of *expert fact witness*. The expert fact witness reviews the medical records and medical literature relevant to the case. The LNC then explains this factual material to the jury in "layperson's" terms. This LNC gives no opinion regarding the standard of care (which is not usually an issue in a PI case). This role of expert fact witness is one that will serve the attorney well in a PI case, especially when the medical records are voluminous or confusing. This role could also prove to be valuable to the defense attorney when there is a significant amount of past medical history that could weaken the plaintiff's claims of injury. For more information on this emerging role, see Chapter 36, The Expert Fact Witness: Noneconomic Damages Testimony.

Assist in Locating Expert Witnesses

Many LNCs find medical experts for attorneys. Occasionally, medical experts are needed to testify in PI cases, especially on the issues of causation and damages. The LNC who chooses to locate experts for attorneys for PI cases should begin compiling a database of non-medical experts, such as accident reconstructionists and biomechanical engineers (see "Experts in PI Cases" section above). The details regarding *Daubert* issues (issues regarding reliability of evidence and testimony) are beyond the scope of this chapter and are best left up to the attorney. The LNC should make it clear that the attorney retains the responsibility for ensuring that the chosen experts are providing opinions that are legally sound according to the laws of the particular jurisdiction. See Chapter 34, Locating and Working with Expert Witnesses, for more details.

Assist with Trial Preparations

The LNC can assist the attorney in preparing for trial in many ways. The LNC, as a trained patient educator, possesses the skills to assist the attorney in creating or obtaining the demonstrative evidence that will best illustrate the points of the case to the jury. The LNC may identify entries in the medical records that may be "blown up" for presentation to the jury. The LNC may suggest items, diagrams, or charts that would help to educate the jury about the case. For example, in one case, it was important to obtain an endotracheal tube to illustrate how the cuff is inflated and deflated and why the cuff is important. Because of the years of clinical experience, the LNC knows about such equipment and is able to teach how and why it is used. The LNC can assist a graphics artist in creating charts, diagrams, and timelines that can make information and associations clear. This type of demonstrative evidence assists the jury in understanding the theories of the case and in understanding the attorney's arguments.

The LNC may review the depositions of medical witnesses and suggest further questions to be asked during trial. In addition, the LNC will perform research on issues arising before or during trial. See Chapter 41, Trial Preparation, for more information.

Example 15.26: One attorney recently discovered that his LNC was valuable in assisting him in preparing his client for testimony at trial. This particular LNC was especially skilled in providing the emotional support that the client needed prior to going on the stand. The client later expressed how much he appreciated having the LNC there for support.

Beyond Legal Nurse Consulting: Additional Roles

There are additional roles that nurses may take on in the world of PI litigation. Some of these roles are beyond that of the LNC and require additional specialized expertise and experience. Life care planning (see Chapter 37), case management (see Chapter 22), and jury consulting are some of the additional roles that the LNC may explore.

Conclusion

The LNC can make a significant contribution to the PI attorney on either side of the litigation. This chapter has provided some suggestions on how to begin working up these very interesting cases.

References

1. Auto Insurance: The Basics, http://www.insurance.com/insurance_options/auto/auto_basics_no_fault_ins.asp, 2001.
2. Simons, R., personal communication, 2001.

Test Questions

1. Which of the choices below best completes the following sentence? Negligence is _____ .
   A. The intentional causing of harm
   B. The failure to use reasonable care that results in harm
   C. Relevant only in medical malpractice cases
   D. A crime

2. Roles of the LNC in assisting the attorney in working up a personal injury case include all of the following EXCEPT:
   A. Performing medical literature searches dealing with the mechanism of injury
   B. Educating the attorney regarding anatomy and physiology related to the areas of injury
   C. Testifying on the issue of injury causation
   D. Analyzing the medical records to identify information relevant to the strengths and weaknesses of the case and identifying potential issues

3. Which of the following statements is NOT true?
   A. The LNC informs the attorney regarding preexisting injuries and conditions of the plaintiff documented in the medical records.
   B. The LNC informs the attorney regarding noncompliant behavior on the part of the plaintiff documented or suggested by the medical records.
   C. The LNC informs the attorney regarding behavior by the plaintiff, as documented in the medical records, that may affect the plaintiff's credibility in the eyes of a jury.
   D. The LNC may ignore medical record entries made prior to the incident at issue.

4. Which of the following is an affirmative defense to a claim of negligence?
   A. Self-defense
   B. Failure to prove one of the elements of negligence
   C. Comparative negligence
   D. Lack of insurance covering the claim

5. Special damages include the following:
   A. Damages for pain and suffering
   B. An award designed to punish the defendant for malicious conduct
   C. Costs of medical care and lost wages
   D. Damages for loss of companionship

Answers: 1. B, 2. C, 3. D, 4. C, 5. C

Chapter 16

Common Mechanisms of Injury in Personal Injury Cases

Arlene King Klepatsky, JD, BSN, BA, RN

CONTENTS

0-8493-1418-6/03/$0.00+$1.50
© 2003 by AALNC

Objectives

- To describe the primary direction of movement of the vehicles' occupants in the following types of collisions: frontal, rear end, right lateral, and left lateral
- To discuss three restraint mechanisms in passenger vehicles
- To describe at least five factors that affect the severity of injury in a motor vehicle collision
- To discuss the significance of the delta v of the vehicles in a collision
- To describe and discuss three types of falls

Introduction

The legal nurse consultant (LNC) assisting the personal injury attorney will likely encounter two common types of cases: the motor vehicle collision and the fall cases. This chapter will discuss the various factors that are important in evaluating these types of cases.

Motor Vehicle Collision

One of the most common types of personal injury cases involves the motor vehicle collision. If the LNC has a basic knowledge of occupant kinematics (the movement of the occupants due to the impact), the LNC's ability to effectively analyze the medical records will be increased. Trauma nurses and other trauma providers are knowledgeable about mechanisms of injury in order to anticipate likely injuries. LNCs can also benefit from gaining basic knowledge regarding biomechanics and occupant kinematics of motor vehicle collisions. This knowledge will assist the LNC in being able to "picture" what happened and more accurately identify the issues in the medical records. The LNC can pursue this additional knowledge by attending conferences and courses by the Association for the Advancement of Automotive Medicine.

For complex and serious motor vehicle collisions, an accident reconstructionist should be on the case. The accident reconstructionist will analyze the factors in the collision and determine the load on the occupants. When an accident reconstructionist has evaluated a case, be sure to request a copy of the report. There may be an accident reconstructionist for each side in the litigation.

The LNC needs to know some of the basic terminology to be able to understand the accident reconstructionist's report. For example, the vehicle that runs into another vehicle (the striking vehicle) is called the *bullet vehicle*. The vehicle that gets run into (the struck vehicle) is called the *target vehicle*. The location of the impact is described using the numbers of a clock, with the car in the center of the clock facing toward the 12, and the other numbers surrounding the car (see Figure 16.1). A straight-on frontal collision is at 12 o'clock. A straight-on rear-end collision is at 6 o'clock. A collision into the passenger door is at 3 o'clock, and a collision into the driver's door is at 9 o'clock. There are, of course, all the oblique angles involving the other numbers of the clock face.

Parts of the car have names with which the LNC should become familiar. For example, the passenger compartment has support pillars that are referred to when

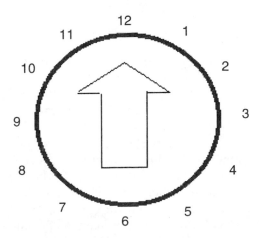

Figure 16.1   Labeling System: Location of Impact Forces on a Vehicle (The point of the arrow is the front of the vehicle.)

discussing motor vehicle collisions. The pillar at the front corner is called the *A-pillar*, the pillar between the front and back seats is called the *B-pillar*, and so on. For example, a report may state, "There was deformation of the A-pillar," or, "The driver hit his head on the B-pillar due to the deployment of the airbag." Familiarity with these terms allows the LNC to more accurately picture what the report is referring to. The LNC will also encounter terms such as *delta v* and *Gs*. These will be explained below in the next section.

Basic Occupant Kinematics

Kinematics deals with motion. Occupant kinematics deals with the movement of motor vehicle occupants due to a motor vehicle collision. A discussion of kinematics would not be complete without a brief discussion of Isaac Newton's Laws of Motion. These laws provide the scientific bases for many of the calculations and conclusions of the accident reconstructionist. There are three laws of motion as described by Newton:

Newton's First Law of Motion

An object in motion tends to stay in motion (at the same speed and direction) until acted upon by a force. Conversely, an object at rest tends to stay at rest until acted upon by a force. When a car is traveling at 30 mph, the occupant, who is not a part of the car, is also traveling at 30 mph. When the car hits a nonyielding wall head-on, the vehicle is stopped by the wall. The occupant continues to travel forward until stopped and/or slowed by something. The occupant continues the forward motion until stopped by the lap/shoulder belt and the airbag. (In the case of the unrestrained occupant, the objects that stop the occupant include the steering wheel, dashboard, windshield, and floor [often referred to as the "floor pan"].)

Newton's Second Law of Motion

Force (F) is the product of mass (m) and acceleration (a), or $F = ma$. This formula represents a number of relationships. It shows that when two objects with the same mass are being pushed, the one being pushed harder (that is, with greater force) will accelerate at a greater rate. Also, there is an inverse relationship between mass and acceleration. That means that the heavier the object is, the slower it will accelerate when a given force pushes it.

In terms of motor vehicle collisions, compare the acceleration of two different vehicles, both at a stop, and both hit by the same-sized car. If one of the vehicles is a massive semi truck and the other is a Volkswagen Bug, both hit in the rear by the same-sized car, the massive semi truck would accelerate slower than the Volkswagen Bug. The LNC knows this as a matter of common sense. Newton's second law expresses this relationship in terms of the laws of physics. In another example, a car at a stop is hit in the rear by a Volkswagen bug. The same car is later hit by a semi truck at the same speed as the Volkswagen hit it. Common sense (and Newton's second law) tells us that the second collision was of a greater force than the first one. (When acceleration remains constant, a collision by an object of greater mass causes a greater force.)

Newton's Third Law of Motion

For every action, there is an equal and opposite reaction. For example, the tires push on the road and the road pushes on the tires, each with the same amount of force.

Thinking in terms of Newton's first law of motion, one can predict which way an occupant will move in a collision. To make the analysis simple, a rule of thumb is that the occupant tends to move toward the direction of the impact. An occupant in a frontal collision will move toward the front of the vehicle. A rear-end collision causes the occupant to move toward the rear of the vehicle. A side collision (sometimes referred to as a "T-bone" collision) on the passenger side causes the occupant to move toward the passenger side door, and a collision on the driver's side causes the occupant to move toward the driver's side door. Of course, not all collisions involve forces that are so clear-cut. Sometimes a vehicle spins after impact and may hit other objects after the initial collision.

The LNC may see the terms "delta v" and "Gs" in the accident reconstructionist's report. The accident reconstructionist is responsible for calculating the "delta v" of the vehicles in the collision. The "delta v" is the change in velocity due to the impact. ("Delta" is a Greek letter depicted as a triangle and stands for "change." The "v" stands for velocity.) The delta v is the difference between the speed just prior to the impact and the speed immediately after the impact. A low-velocity motor vehicle collision is generally one with a delta v of approximately 10 mph or less, but the definition may differ from expert to expert.

Example 16.1: A car traveling at 30 mph hits a deer. The impact with the deer slows the vehicle to 28 mph. The delta v of the car is 2 mph. The deer is accelerated from 0 to 28 mph. The deer experienced a delta v of 28 mph. It is easy to see how the forces on the unfortunate deer are greater than the forces on the driver of the car. (The degree of injury suffered also depends on the time over which the delta v occurs. This will be discussed later.)

The accident reconstructionist also calculates the load on the occupant imposed by the acceleration or deceleration. This load is imposed on the occupant whenever there is a change in velocity. The unit of measurement of this acceleration/deceleration load is the "G." One G is the load experienced by a person or thing on the surface of the Earth. (This is referred to as the "force" of gravity, hence the "G.") A person on a roller coaster experiences more than 1 G. An occupant in a motor vehicle collision experiences more than 1 G. A jet pilot might experience 6 Gs in a turn, so the pilot who weighs 200 lb on the ground felt as though he weighed 1200 lb during the turn.[1] The greater the load on the occupant, the greater the potential for injury.

In some cases, the deceleration (or even acceleration) itself causes injury. These are generally called *deceleration injuries*. The change in velocity over a short period of time causes tears in structures such as the aorta and blood vessels in the brain.

Many factors of the collision interact to determine the severity (or lack of severity) of injury:

- The configuration of the impact (such as sideswipe versus head-on)
- The speed of the vehicles just prior to impact
- The delta v of the vehicles
- The time period over which the change in velocity occurs, expressed as the "delta t" (For example, an impact at 30 mph into an unyielding wall will cause greater injury than an impact at 30 mph into a water-filled, give-way barrier. Both collisions have the same overall delta v, but they occur over different time periods. The shorter the time period over which the change in velocity occurs, the greater the potential for injury.)
- Size and weight (mass) of the target vehicle
- Size and weight (mass) of the bullet vehicle
- Seating position of the occupant in the vehicle (e.g., driver, right front passenger, left rear passenger, etc.)
- Body position of occupant (e.g., looking straight ahead, head/torso turned, in a reclined position)
- Awareness of impending impact
- Use or lack of use of safety equipment (seat belts, airbags, head restraints)
- Proper/improper use of safety equipment
- Occupant status (age, size, gender, preexisting conditions)

Types of Motor Vehicle Collisions

The major types of motor vehicle collisions include the frontal collision, the rear-end collision, the side collision (including the sideswipe collision), and the rollover collision. It is important to look at the collision from the reference point of the injured party. For example, the traffic collision report (TCR) may label the accident as a rear-end collision. It is a rear-end collision with respect to the occupants of the target car (the car that is struck in the rear). It is a frontal collision with respect to the occupants of the bullet car (the car that struck the car in front of it). It is important for the LNC to be knowledgeable about the type of collision that the occupant has experienced because it affects the type of injuries that are suffered. In fact, Hyde states that, as a general rule, "each principal direction of force (collision direction) has its own, rather typical constellation of injuries and each location within a particular vehicle has a usual pattern of injuries."[2] He also states that the pattern of injuries will often indicate whether or not the occupant was wearing the seat belt restraints at the time of the collision.

Also keep in mind that in any one accident, an occupant may have experienced impacts from various directions depending on the sequence of events in the particular accident scenario.

Frontal Collisions

In frontal collisions, the force is at the front of the vehicle from the 10 o'clock position to the 2 o'clock position. Many crash tests are performed in which the vehicle hits a wall straight on, at the 12 o'clock position. Most actual frontal collisions are offset frontal collisions (i.e., at the 10 and 11 o'clock positions on the left and the 1 and 2 o'clock positions on the right). These offset frontal collisions have effects that differ from the straight-on frontal collision. The reason for the difference is that in an offset collision, the forces may be concentrated in a smaller area rather than spread out over the entire front of the vehicle.

The forces on the occupant in a frontal collision cause the occupant to travel toward the front of the car (or toward the direction of the force). As explained above, the car basically stops its forward motion, but the occupant, who is not a part of the car, keeps traveling forward at essentially the same speed until slowed or stopped. Hyde states that, in a 30 mph frontal collision into a barrier, the knees of the unrestrained driver are the first to make contact.[2] They will hit the dashboard at approximately 60 msec (.06 sec) into the collision, "causing the lower body to abruptly stop its forward motion and causing the upper torso to flex." The upper body then strikes the steering wheel at approximately 75 msec (.075 sec) into the collision. The head and neck flex further when the chest strikes the steering wheel and then contact (often passing into and through) the plane of the windshield, shattering the windshield at about 90 msec (.090 sec) into the collision. According to Hyde, the occupant in this hypothetical collision has experienced an average deceleration of 15 Gs.

Some frontal collision situations are worsened by crush of the vehicle, causing intrusion into the so-called "survival zone" of the passenger compartment. In severe frontal impacts, the engine block can intrude into the passenger compartment. Footwell intrusion by the engine block may cause injuries to the lower extremities. (When a vehicle is defective, there may be a product liability action against the vehicle manufacturer for lack of crashworthiness.)

In frontal collisions, the airbags are designed to deploy. In fact, the airbags are set to deploy only in frontal collisions and only when a collision is at a certain speed as determined by a sensor device. Some are set to deploy at around 10 mph. There will be further discussion regarding airbags later in the chapter.

Sometimes a frontal collision is referred to as a head-on collision. One might hear, "He hit the light pole head-on." A head-on collision may also mean that two vehicles ran into each other, both with their front ends. Such collisions often occur on roads with no physical divider between oncoming lanes.

Rear-End Collisions

The rear-end collision, of course, occurs when a vehicle is hit in the rear. It can also occur when a vehicle backs into an object. One type of rear-end collision occurs when the target vehicle is at a stop (perhaps stopped in traffic or waiting at a red light). When the vehicle is stopped, the occupant is also stopped. When hit in the rear, the car is pushed forward but the occupant stays in the same position until struck by the seat back and head restraint. The occupant appears to move backward into the seat and head restraint. Since the seat back is not rigid but padded, the occupant sinks back into the padding of the seat, allowing the occupant to slow down. (This is called the "ride-down.") If the collision forces are great enough, the neck will hyperextend (bend backward) unless it is stopped by a properly adjusted head restraint or high seat back. Then the neck will flex or hyperflex (bend forward) in a rebound motion, hence the term *whiplash*. As one may predict, neck injury is the most frequent allegation in rear-end collisions. Whether or not injury actually occurs depends on the many factors listed previously.

In some severe impacts, the load on the seat back of the front seats may be sufficient to break the seat back (and sometimes even the seat brackets). The occupant may then "ramp up" the seat back. The occupant may even continue moving out of the seat backwards as a projectile, and may even strike the C-pillar or the D-pillar of the vehicle and the ceiling of the passenger compartment.

In some older pickup trucks, if the occupant's neck hyperextends and there is no head restraint, the head may impact the window in the rear of the cab. In automobiles, rear seat passengers have actually been ejected through the rear window in the case of severe rear-end impacts.

Side (Lateral) Collisions

There are two types of side, or lateral, collisions. There is the sideswipe, in which the two impacting vehicles are almost parallel to each other and impact against each other. The second type is the side collision (sometimes called a "T-bone" collision). As one would expect, most side collisions occur at intersections. In a side impact occurring at the same side and location of the occupant, there is not much space between the bullet vehicle and the occupant. This causes a potential for injury. Many of the injuries due to a collision on the occupant's side are on the same side as the impact. For example, a side impact at the location of the driver will cause the driver to move toward the driver's door at the same time the bullet vehicle is colliding into the door. If the driver is injured, the driver (assuming that the driver is on the left side) will most likely have left-sided injuries. If the collision is of sufficient force, the driver will strike the driver's door with his left side. Same-side injuries may also occur as a result of objects protruding into the passenger compartment from that side, such as a tree, a light pole, or even the bullet vehicle itself. Opposite-side injuries can be caused by a loose object that has become a projectile in the collision, from an unrestrained right front or middle passenger, or even from a pet. Head injuries are common in side-impacts, even when the occupant is restrained. Newer vehicles are equipped with side-impact protection (i.e., side airbags). These may decrease the incidence of head injuries in side-impact collisions (see "Side Airbags" below).

Rollover Collisions

There are different types of rollover collisions. There is a rollover preceded by a collision, and there is the simple rollover without a collision.[2] Some of the major dangers of a rollover collision are ejection, usually through a side window, and impact of the head on the ceiling, which can cause severe head and neck injuries. According to Hyde, a rollover collision is the most common cause of ejection. Failure to use seat belts greatly increases the chances of serious injuries in a rollover collision. Seat belts are important in these collisions because they prevent ejection. The amount of roof crush can also be important in the causation of injuries in a rollover collision.

Interestingly, Hyde states that in his experience, the injuries from rollover collisions either are lethal or very severe (such as resulting in paralysis) or are trivial. In his experience, rollover collisions seem to leave little middle ground.

Crash tests show that certain models of sport-utility vehicles may be prone to rollover collisions when certain types of maneuvers, such as sudden steering corrections, are carried out. A good source of additional information is http://www.crashworthiness.com.

Chain-Reaction Collisions

Chain-reaction collisions involve multiple vehicles. One typical type of chain-reaction collision is the chain-reaction rear-end collision, in which a car is rear-ended and pushed into the car in front. These accidents may involve as few as three cars and may involve many cars, such as in cases of poor visibility in fog, smoke, or even wind-whipped sand. The occupants in the middle cars suffer at least two impacts, both frontal and rear-end impacts. In addition, the front car may receive more than one rear-end impact.

Injuries Suffered (and Alleged) in Motor Vehicle Collisions

In motor vehicle collisions, there is a wide range of potential injuries. There may be no injury at all in some collisions. Conversely, there may be devastating injuries, such as crush injuries or dismemberment. A motor vehicle collision actually involves three separate collisions. For example, in a frontal collision, the first collision occurs when the vehicle hits an object. The second collision occurs when the occupant's forward motion is stopped by the lap and shoulder belt (or other parts of the car if the occupant is unrestrained). The third collision occurs when the internal structures of the occupant are exposed to the forces (or load) caused by the collision. The forces on the organs, connective tissues, muscles, and bones may be tensile (stretching), shear, and compressive. If the strains on an organ exceed its tolerance, disruption occurs.[3] In major collisions, internal organs may be injured. Fractures of bones may result, especially involving the extremities, pelvis, skull, facial bones, ribs, spine, and sternum. Ligaments, tendons, and muscles may be disrupted. Injuries to joints can also occur in certain circumstances.

Head injuries, ranging from mild traumatic brain injuries to very severe head and brain injuries, can occur in motor vehicle collisions. These injuries are frequently the subject of litigation. Disruption of the temporomandibular joint is another common allegation in motor vehicle collision litigation. Scars from such accidents may also be the subject of litigation.

Neck and back injuries can occur (and are common allegations in motor vehicle collision litigation). These injuries involve soft tissue alone or may involve spinal fractures, disc injuries, and spinal cord injuries. The latter may cause paralysis and death.

One of the major issues of contention in motor vehicle collision cases is related to soft tissue injuries. For example, the plaintiff will claim that a disc was herniated, causing pressure on the spinal cord or nerve roots, but the defense will claim that the injuries were only to the soft tissues, such as the muscles and ligaments, and should resolve in a relatively short period of time. It may be helpful for the LNC to review vertebral and dermatomal anatomy. It is also helpful to be familiar with common tests that are performed in a physical examination related to the neck and back.

Some of the less obvious types of injuries from motor vehicle collisions include the deceleration injuries. With this mechanism of injury, the load caused by sudden deceleration (or acceleration) causes tears in structures such as the aorta and blood vessels of the brain.

Additionally, motor vehicle collisions may involve thermal injuries and injuries to the respiratory tract when a fire or explosion occurs as a result of the collision. Toxins may be inhaled from such burning substances as plastic. They also may be released and inhaled in a collision with a tanker truck carrying a toxic substance such as ammonia. Drowning or near drowning can occur when a vehicle becomes submerged in a body of water. When a car comes in contact at an intersection (or otherwise) with a semi truck, because of the respective heights, the top of the passenger vehicle can be sheared off, causing decapitation of the occupants. The author knows of a situation in which the occupants were aware of the impending impact and ducked. The top of the vehicle was sheared off, but the occupants survived with relatively minor injuries.

Injuries can also be caused by loose objects in the passenger compartment, or even by unrestrained passengers who become projectiles as a result of the collision forces. Objects on the road can also become airborne and penetrate the passenger compartment and occasionally the occupants as well. The author is aware of such a situation in which an object came through a windshield and decapitated the driver.

Restraint Devices

An important factor in motor vehicle collisions is what restraint devices were used and whether or not they were used correctly (see "The Seat Belt Defense" in Chapter 15). The following are the common restraint systems or devices used in motor vehicles.

Seat Belts

There are state laws mandating the use of seat belts. Seat belts do prevent injuries, especially in frontal and rollover collisions. One of the main functions of a seat belt is to prevent ejection (which has a high rate of mortality). Seat belts in most passenger vehicles are of the three-point type (lap and shoulder belt combination). In older vehicles and in many rear seats (where children should sit), there may be only a lap belt. Some vehicles have a passive shoulder restraint that automatically goes into place when the door is closed. Sometimes the occupant with a passive shoulder restraint fails to buckle the lap belt and ends up wearing only the shoulder belt.

Seat Belt Failure

There are some reports in the literature about seat belt latch failure. This can occur when the occupant thinks the belt is latched, but it is not. The literature also suggests that some seat belts can come unlatched with some forces. If this is suspected in a case the LNC is working on, an expert who has experience with seat belt issues should be consulted. Tests can be done to shed light on what actually happened. For example, the fabric of the belt can be examined to see what forces it has been exposed to. If the fabric has been subjected to the great stretch forces that the belt would sustain in a major frontal collision, this could be interpreted to mean that the occupant had the seat belt on in the collision and that the latch eventually failed. The latch mechanism would likely be tested as well, to see whether it would fail under certain stresses. In any case, the experts should be called in to gather data and reach conclusions based on that data.

Improper Use of Seat Belts

Sometimes seat belts are not worn properly. This improper use can contribute to injury by reducing seat belt effectiveness and by causing additional risks from the seat belt itself. Some cars have a passive shoulder harness that is supposed to be used with the lap belt (which is not passive). Sometimes the shoulder belt is used alone. In a frontal collision, when the shoulder belt alone is used, the occupant can "submarine" (i.e., slip under the belt) until the neck is caught by the belt. This has caused death from strangulation and from neck injury. When using the lap and shoulder belt combination, some people put the shoulder harness under the arm. This can also contribute to injuries, because it allows too much forward motion of the head and chest. A seat belt that is worn too loosely can contribute to injuries, again by allowing too much forward motion. This can also cause an occupant to "submarine" under the belt. A seat belt that is worn too high on the abdomen, instead of lower on the bony pelvis, can contribute to injuries because the force is transmitted over the soft abdominal area and can injure abdominal organs. In addition, seat belts are designed to protect the occupants when they are sitting upright. They may not provide protection from injury when the occupant is in the reclining position. In one case, a seat-belted woman lying down on the backseat of a car was thrown headfirst into the side panel of the car. She was rendered quadriplegic.

There are still some situations in which seat belts are not used at all, such as in some school buses. When seat belts have been installed, use by the occupants has not been consistent.

The Seat Belt Syndrome

Even with use of the lap and shoulder belt combination, often called the three-point restraint, injuries can occur from the seat belt itself. The constellation of injuries caused by seat belts is referred to as the "seat belt syndrome." Bruises left by the seat belts are referred to as the "seat belt sign."

The literature indicates that seat belts can cause a number of injuries, primarily with frontal and side impacts. The following are just some of the injuries that have been caused by seat belts:

- Abdominal organ injuries (spleen, liver, pancreas, kidneys, intestines)
- Thoracic and lumbar fractures

- Rib fractures
- Anterior lung herniation
- Shoulder girdle injuries

When the lap belt is worn alone, the occupant can suffer from what is referred to as the "lap belt complex." "Patients with chance-type fractures of the lumbar spine were more likely to be rear seat passengers and to be using a lap belt."[4] Hollow viscus injuries were also more common with the lap belt alone.

Airbags

The federal government mandated the installation of driver and passenger side airbags as of the 1999 automobile models.[5] Some models have had airbags since the early 1990s. Older cars may have airbags only on the driver's side or not at all. Airbags, along with seat belts, slow the occupant down in a frontal collision. Recall that the occupant in a frontal collision keeps moving forward at the speed of the vehicle, even though the vehicle has been stopped by the collision. The airbag and seat belt allow the occupant to slow down. In addition, airbags keep the head, face, and chest from hitting the steering wheel, the dashboard, and the windshield. The airbag has sensors that are programmed to deploy in frontal collisions at a certain force, usually equivalent to hitting a wall at 10 to 16 mph.[5] If the airbag has not deployed, there are a few possible reasons why it has not:

- It was not a frontal collision.
- The collision did not meet the threshold speed at which the airbag was set to deploy.
- The airbag was defective.
- The airbag was switched off. (In newer vehicles, the passenger side airbag can be switched off.)

A number of injuries can be caused by airbags. Children are especially at risk for airbag injuries. Injuries are more likely when the occupant fails to wear the seat belt, when the occupant sits too close, and when the occupant is small. The medical literature documents a number of injuries from airbags, including chemical burns of the face, upper extremities, and trunk (from the sodium azide propellant). These burns can be second-degree. Alkali keratitis can also occur. Other injuries include:

- Eye injuries, including a documented case of blindness from lens subluxation and traumatic mydriasis
- Hearing loss due to the loud noise of airbag deployment
- Diaphragmatic rupture
- Chest wall injuries
- Fractures of the hand, cervical vertebrae, and ribs
- Maxillofacial fractures

Some of the more unusual injuries include bilateral carotid artery dissection in a 39-year-old man, resulting in hemiplegia, and a case of fatal airway compromise caused by a retropharyngeal hematoma in an elderly woman in a minor collision. Children have died from head and spine injuries, including a case of atlanto-occipital dislocation. (The above is not an exhaustive list of the injuries caused by airbags.)

It is interesting to note that the airbag module cover can cause severe injuries if an occupant is in close proximity to it at the time of deployment. An article in the literature discusses three such injuries, ranging from traumatic avulsion of a thumb to subdural hematoma with subsequent cerebral edema and respiratory arrest.[6] It is important to be aware that the airbag module cover itself can cause serious, even fatal, traumatic injuries.

Side Airbags

Some new cars are equipped with side airbags that deploy in side impacts. These airbags are smaller than the frontal airbags. They serve as energy-absorbing buffers between the occupants and the same-side door. They also may prevent objects (such as trees, poles, and the hood of the bullet vehicle) from protruding into the occupant's space from the side. They are mounted in the side of the roof, the seat, or the door. Side airbags are designed to protect the head and even the chest in a side impact.[5]

Head Restraints

Most vehicles have adjustable head restraints or have high seat backs to support the head in a rear-end collision and prevent hyperextension. Some vehicles on the road still do not have head restraints in the rear seats. For the head restraint to be effective in preventing neck extension, it must be adjusted properly for the height of the occupant. In some pickup trucks without head restraints, the occupant's head may make contact with the passenger cab's rear window.

Infant Car Seats

States mandate the use of car seats for infants up to a certain age and weight. One of the main issues with infant car seats is that a great number of them are not properly installed. (The author has heard from a local California Highway Patrol officer that up to 80% of infant car seats are not properly installed.) Another issue involves whether or not the seat that is being used is approved for use in cars. Occasionally a seat designed only for carrying the child may be used as an infant car seat. When an infant is injured or killed in a collision, the infant car seat is inspected.

As nurses are aware, an infant car seat, especially a rear-facing one, is never to be placed in a front seat with an airbag. Such placement puts the infant at risk for death.

Child Booster Seats

States are beginning to mandate child booster seats up to a certain weight for children who are no longer required to sit in the infant car seats. Whether or not mandated, booster seats are recommended for children who are no longer in infant car seats. The booster seat elevates the child to fit the lap and shoulder belt combination properly. Without the seat-belt-positioning booster seat, the shoulder harness is at the neck level and the lap belt rides over the abdomen, both of which can cause severe injuries in a collision.

Motorcycle Accidents

In collisions involving motorcycles with other types of vehicles, there is a high likelihood of injury because of the lack of impact protection. Whether or not a helmet was worn is important in these accidents. According to Peitzman, cranial injuries account for 75% of the deaths of motorcycle riders.[3] This risk is significantly reduced when a helmet is worn. The speed of the motorcycle can be an important factor in the severity of the injuries. Spine, pelvis, and extremity injuries are common. Lower-extremity injuries are often open and severe. Motorcycle riders can also suffer a great deal of road rash unless they are wearing protective gear.

Pedestrian Accidents

Injuries from collisions involving pedestrians tend to be severe because of the lack of impact protection. In these collisions, there is a high risk of fatality because "all energy is absorbed by the unprotected pedestrian. Severity of injuries depends on vehicle speed and relative heights of pedestrians and front structures of the vehicle."[3] Adults are often struck in the lower extremity and knocked to the ground. In some collisions, either the pedestrian is thrown onto the hood of the car and then to the ground or the pedestrian can actually be pulled under the tires of the vehicle.[3]

Adults commonly suffer lower-extremity fractures, thoracic and abdominal injuries from impact with the vehicle, and upper-extremity and craniofacial injuries due to impact with the ground.[3] A common issue in these cases is the location where the pedestrian attempted to cross the street (i.e., in the crosswalk versus "jaywalking"). In Example 15.2, one of the issues was whether or not the vehicle actually hit the plaintiff versus the plaintiff's losing consciousness and falling to the ground in front of the vehicle. In that case, the documentation in the medical record regarding a point of impact between the pedestrian and the vehicle was crucial.

Children, because of their size, are more prone to being "run over." This, of course causes crush injuries. Common scenarios include a child darting into the street in front of a passing vehicle or a child who is behind a vehicle that backs up, often in the family's driveway. In the latter situation, the child cannot be seen by the driver.

Records of Rescue and Emergency Department Personnel

The medical records of the initial health care providers are critical in evaluating the injuries of the victim of a motor vehicle collision. Those responding to the scene and those transporting the plaintiff to the hospital document important facts relevant to the condition of the plaintiff shortly after the collision. These records often include documentation of the following important information:

- How the plaintiff exited the vehicle (such as by the door, window, or an extrication procedure in which the "Jaws of Life" were used and how long the extrication took)
- The plaintiff's level of consciousness at the scene (such as whether or not there was a period of loss of consciousness, or level of alertness and orientation)
- The plaintiff's activities at the scene (such as whether the plaintiff was ambulatory or stationary)
- The plaintiff's behavior at the scene
- The extent of vehicle deformation (such as a broken or "starred" windshield and other broken windows, a bent steering wheel or column, broken seats, and whether there was passenger compartment intrusion)
- Use of restraint devices (such as whether the plaintiff was in a seat belt and whether the belt or latch had broken, whether the airbag had deployed, whether an infant car seat was in place)
- Initial complaints (including areas and degree of pain, numbness, nausea and vomiting, blurred vision)
- The location and extent of objective signs of injury (bleeding, cuts, lacerations, abrasions, and other marks [e.g., redness and early bruising, deformation of an extremity or other area])
- Immobilization used during transport
- Initial vital signs and other physical examination findings
- Treatment provided at the scene and during transport
- Statements made by the plaintiff regarding the incident
- Diagrams of the location and types of injuries

Beyond the Medical Record: Additional Documents in Motor Vehicle Collisions

A number of documents are used in working up the motor vehicle collision. These will be briefly described below. They provide the LNC with important data about the motor vehicle collision. The LNC should request these documents from the attorney as early as possible in the case. In some cases, not all of these documents will exist. When there is no TCR, the LNC may need to rely on interrogatory responses and depositions of the parties to determine the details about the collision. Sometimes the attorney will provide a description of the accident in the cover letter to the LNC.

The Traffic Collision Report

Often referred to as the "police report," the TCR contains important information about the collision. It is filled out by the responding law enforcement officer, often the state highway patrol. The form differs from state to state. A typical TCR may include some or all of the following information:

- The date, time, and location of the collision
- Data about the drivers (name, address, age, date of birth, height, and weight [weight may not be accurate since it occasionally changes over time], and other identifying information
- A description or diagram of the scene
- Data about the vehicles (type, year, make, model)
- The extent and location of damage to the vehicles (including damage to the windshield, steering column or wheel, and seats)
- A drawing of the vehicles that indicates the location of damage
- The name of the registered owner of the vehicle (may be different from the driver)
- Whether or not there were any obvious mechanical defects of the vehicles
- The type of collision (head-on, sideswipe, rear-end, broadside, hit object, overturned)
- Involvement of other factors, including pedestrians, bicycles, animals
- The seating position of all the occupants
- Seat belt use at the time of the accident, the type of seat belt (lap and shoulder combination or lap belt alone), and whether or not seat belt failure or damage was noted
- Whether or not there was an airbag and whether or not it deployed
- Whether or not a child restraint system (infant car seat) was used and whether or not it was properly secured
- Whether or not a helmet was worn (when a bicycle, motorcycle, or scooter is involved)
- Whether or not the drivers were under the influence of alcohol or drugs (which may include herbs [e.g., Kava])
- The weather, roadway surface conditions, and lighting at the time of the collision
- In a collision involving a pedestrian, whether or not the pedestrian was crossing in the crosswalk
- Insurance companies covering the drivers and the policy numbers
- The statements of the drivers (and sometimes witnesses)
- A diagram of the collision
- Measurements of important distances, such as the length of skid marks (an indication of braking) or the distance of an ejected occupant from the vehicle
- A physical evidence diagram (this includes the location of debris and other physical evidence)
- The opinions and conclusions of the law enforcement officer, including an opinion regarding who or what was the cause of the collision
- A brief description of the complaints and the extent of injuries to the occupants
- Whether or not the occupants were transported to the hospital, by whom, and to which hospital
- A list of the citations issued and vehicle code sections that were violated
- The officer's recommendations for further handling (such as "Refer to District Attorney for possible criminal charges")
- An indication of whether or not photographs were taken as part of the accident investigation and occasionally an entry noting how many were taken

It is not unusual for the attorneys to attempt to challenge the officer's conclusions as stated in the TCR. Occasionally, the attorneys will cross-examine the reporting officer regarding his training, experience, and expertise in accident reconstruction. The attorney may have the accident reevaluated.

TCRs are not available in all cases. Sometimes parties do not call the police after an accident. Sometimes a TCR is not filled out by the law enforcement officer if the collision appears to be a "noninjury" or "property damage only" collision.

In "major" motor vehicle collisions, there may be additional investigative reports. For example, some states may have a *multidisciplinary accident investigation team* (MAIT) that may generate a report. The MAIT investigators have special training in the physics of collisions, accident reconstruction, occupant kinematics, and the use of equipment such as surveying equipment and computer-aided design software. The main purpose of the MAIT is to analyze causation factors in order to prevent future similar accidents.[7] Other states may have specialized investigation teams, similar to the MAIT, for use in major collisions.

Photographs

Color photographs or laser color copies of the photographs assist the LNC in understanding more about the collision. There may be photographs of the scene, of the vehicles from various angles (interior and exterior), and of specific relevant areas of the vehicle. Occasionally, there are photographs of the occupants' injuries. In major motor vehicle collisions, the law enforcement personnel may assign someone to take photographs as part of the investigation. This may be noted on the TCR. In less serious accidents, the insurance company or even the parties themselves take the photographs. Occasionally someone, perhaps even the media, has made a videotape of the scene, the vehicles, and the injured party. The photographs taken by newspaper reporters may be obtainable and helpful.

Repair Estimates/Damages Appraisals

Body shops prepare an estimate of what it would cost to repair a vehicle. The parties may obtain more than one estimate to see who offers the best prices. If the insurance company determines that the repair costs are greater than the worth of the vehicle, then the vehicle is considered "totaled."

The repair estimate form lists the areas of the vehicle that need to be replaced or repaired. Areas of damage may be listed that are not apparent from reviewing the photographs. When a TCR and photos do not exist, sometimes a quick look at the repair estimate helps the LNC determine which vehicle is which. For example, in a rear-end collision the repair estimate for the target vehicle will list parts such as the rear bumper as needing replacement. The repair estimate listing parts at the front of the vehicle would most likely be related to the bullet vehicle.

Transcripts of Recorded Statements

Frequently, the insurance company records a statement of the parties, usually over the telephone. These statements are transcribed and are available for review. The statements are often taken prior to the involvement of any attorneys in the case.

Accident Reconstructionist's Report

Occasionally, an accident reconstructionist's report is available. Be sure to request this if it is available. There may be one for each side of the litigation, so be aware of whether it is a report by the expert for the plaintiff or the report by the expert for the defense. These reports contain valuable information about how the accident occurred and the forces involved in the collision. Most likely the accident reconstructionist will calculate the delta v and the Gs. The report may also describe damage to the vehicles in detail. Much of this data may be gathered during a vehicle inspection by the expert. The accident reconstructionist may also visit the scene of a collision to make observations and take measurements, photographs, and even videotapes. Sometimes photographs and videotapes are taken from an elevated perspective to capture an aerial view of the scene (often using a tall crane known as a "cherry picker"). Accident reconstructionists may also obtain vehicles similar to the ones in the collision and attempt to re-create the accident. Computerized reenactments may also be created once the key factors are determined.

Potential Defendants in a Motor Vehicle Collision Case

It is fairly clear that the "other driver" is a defendant in a lawsuit regarding the collision. Additional defendants may include:

- The vehicle's owner (if different from the driver)
- The driver's employer (if the driver was driving as part of employment duties)
- The manufacturer of the vehicle
- The manufacturer of a component part of the vehicle (such as the tire manufacturer)
- A repair facility (if faulty repairs contributed to the collision)
- A government entity, depending on which one is responsible for design and maintenance of the road (city, county, state, or federal government)
- A company that may share responsibility for road design, maintenance, or repair

The "Black Box"

Recently, some models of vehicles have been equipped with a "black box." This device, similar to the ones that airliners use, records data about the vehicle and the accident. Facts, such as the speed at impact and the time it took the airbag to deploy, may be recorded.

Crash Test Information

Crash test information is available online at the following Web sites: the National Highway Traffic Safety Administration, http://www.nhtsa.org, and the Insurance Institute for Highway Safety, http://www.hwysafety.org. Both of these sites are extremely helpful for additional research regarding motor vehicle collision data.

Premises Liability: Falls

Another common mechanism of injuries in personal injury cases is the fall. There are different types of falls, each with its own characteristics and issues. Falls involve potential liability of the owner of the property on which the fall occurred. The owner is liable when there is improper maintenance, a dangerous condition, poor lighting, or failure to meet certain standards. Risk factors relative to a plaintiff's conduct involve running or walking too fast, inattention, and carrying large objects. The elderly and people with disabilities may be at increased risk of falling. Safety signs and cones should be used to warn people of hazards. A brief description of some types of falls and some of these issues will follow.

Slip and Fall

This type of fall occurs when a person's foot slips on the floor surface, causing loss of balance and often followed by a fall. A slip is caused by a slippery surface, often made worse by the wrong footwear.[8] In normal walking, there are two types of slips. The first type is where the forward foot slips and the person falls backward. The second type is when the rear foot slips backward and the person falls. The issues that often arise involve the coefficient of friction, or the degree of slipperiness, of the floor or other surface. On ice and on wet and oily surfaces, the coefficient of friction is low (.10). Excellent traction is at a coefficient of friction of .40 to .50 or more. "Slip resistant" is defined as a coefficient of friction (COF) of .50 "under most state laws, municipal ordinances and building codes."[9] Some sources state that a COF of .50 should be the minimally safe value for a walkway surface, dry or wet. The Americans with Disabilities Act requires level surfaces to have a COF of .60 and requires inclined surfaces to have a COF of .80.

Slip-and-fall experts can perform a "slip test" to determine the COF of a surface where a fall has occurred. The expert can use a number of different devices to perform this test. The expert may also reconstruct the circumstances of the fall to determine causation. In addition, the expert should know whether any standards apply in a given situation, such as in a particular type of workplace or public place.

In a slip-and-fall case, the plaintiff often alleges that the floor was too slippery, or was allowed to become slippery through poor maintenance. The defense often claims that the plaintiff was wearing footwear that caused or contributed to the fall (see Example 15.1). Another cause of falls is the presence of a foreign substance (e.g., liquid or food) on the floor. A common defense is that the defendant did not have notice of the spill prior to the fall, and that the spill did not exist long enough for it to have been discovered. In some cases, an accident or incident report will document the facts regarding the fall. (There is most likely no privilege to keep the parties from obtaining the report as there is with reports relating to patient incidents in the medical arena.) In some areas of the country, ice on walkways or sidewalks is a source of fall incidents. In some falls, there may be injuries associated with guarding with the upper extremities. A Colles fracture of the wrist may occur when a person tries to break his fall. The author has reviewed cases in which head injury was alleged from a slip and fall backward. It was alleged that the back of the head contacted the floor. Injuries to the head, back, joints, and extremities may occur. Other injuries may be suffered depending on the unique circumstances of each fall.

Trip and Fall

The trip and fall usually occurs when the victim's foot impacts or catches on an object or some type of protrusion on the ground. The foot is suddenly stopped. The upper body is thrown forward, causing a fall.[8] Common scenarios for the trip and fall include a person tripping over a loose piece of carpeting, on the edge of a mat, or on a raised section of sidewalk. According to Becker, as little as 3/8 of an inch rise in a walkway is enough for a person to stub his toe and fall. Parking lot barrier blocks also cause people to trip. See Example 15.5, in which there was a low rope-type barrier strung across the exit of the parking lot. Poor lighting compounded the problem, and the plaintiff tripped over the rope. He fell into an object, injuring his shoulder. As this example illustrates, poor lighting is a risk factor for trip and falls, as well as step and falls discussed below.

Step and Fall

The step and fall occurs when the front foot lands on a surface that is lower than expected. An example of this kind of fall is a when person unexpectedly steps off a curb in the dark. In this type of fall, the fall is usually forward.[8]

Fall Due to Loss of Consciousness and Other Conditions

As nurses well know, some falls occur because of a sudden loss of consciousness. In such a fall, there is often no attempt to break the fall with the hands. When there are injuries to the face, the possibility of loss of consciousness should be considered. Occasionally, people fall because they have lost their balance or have experienced vertigo related to various conditions. The LNC may need to explore the plaintiff's medical conditions, medications, or other conditions (such as electrical shock) that might offer an explanation for the fall.

Failure of Lower Extremity

Occasionally, a fall occurs due to some type of failure of the lower extremity. In persons with such conditions as advanced osteoporosis or bone metastasis, a pathologic fracture of a hip may occur, causing the fall. In patients with these conditions, the occurrence of a pathological fracture should be considered. (See Chapter 14, Nursing Home Litigation, for more details.) Falls can also occur when a joint, such as an unstable knee joint, suddenly dislocates. A turned ankle can also cause a fall.

Falls from a Height

The previously discussed falls are usually same-level falls (except for the step and fall). Falls from a height most commonly include falls from ladders and stepping stools, roofs, trees, vehicles, loading docks (often with a step backward), windows, and even beds. The greater the fall distance, the greater the likelihood of severe injury. The type of surface that is struck and the position on impact affect the injuries suffered in the fall. When the victim lands on his feet, the force is transmitted to the vertebrae and can cause a compression fracture in the lumbar spine area in addition to calcaneal fractures, lower-extremity and hip fractures, and vertical shear injuries of the pelvis, as well as fractures at any other segment of the spine.[3] This can result in spinal cord injuries from bone fragments. In children under 5 years of age, the head is the heaviest part of the body, and it tends to impact first. When the fall victim lands in an odd position, the injury constellation is less predictable. For example, the author has worked on a case in which a fall from a top bunk resulted in an atlanto-occipital dislocation with sudden death when the victim struck his head on a desk on the way to the ground. Other injuries that may be suffered, depending on the kinematics of the fall, include head injuries, wrist injuries, abdominal injuries, and thoracic visceral injuries, including a tear at the aortic root.[3]

Falls On or Down Stairs

When a fall on or down stairs occurs, the factors to be considered and investigated by experts include the height of the stair, the coefficient of friction of the surfaces (i.e., degree of slipperiness), and the slope of the staircase. Even a slight difference in the height of one of the stairs can cause a person to trip. According to Becker, all steps should have the same rise and depth with visible edges.[8] In addition, a person should have one hand free to use the handrail. Injuries can be severe because of the height involved, as well as the momentum from the fall down the stairs and the potential for a tumbling motion.

Other Types of Personal Injury Cases

Personal injury litigation also involves other types of cases not covered in this chapter. Injuries are caused by any number of different modalities. The LNC should use the basic principles of biomechanics and common sense in working up these cases.

The Process: Working Up a Personal Injury Case

The following steps illustrate one way to do a review. Generally, this is how the author proceeds.

Step One: The Initial Phone Call from the Attorney

The involvement of the LNC may begin with a phone call from the attorney. For the purposes of this example, the phone call is from a defense attorney who would like the LNC to "work up a large box of medical records." First, the LNC clarifies exactly what the attorney needs. The attorney replies that she has no idea what records are in the box and does not have the time to look at them. The case involves a 26-year-old man claiming severe injuries from a rear-end motor vehicle collision. It is set for a settlement conference in 3 weeks, and she wants to know what injuries are documented in the medical records. There is a discussion regarding fees. Then the LNC provides a rough time estimate for the attorney and the attorney approves the time. (Sometimes defense attorneys need to inform the insurance carrier of the proposed cost of the review and need to await approval.) The LNC clarifies exactly when the attorney needs to have the work completed. At some point in the conversation, the LNC discusses the necessary business items regarding any contract or retainer requirements that the LNC may have. The LNC agrees to work up the case by the deadline.

The LNC then requests copies of all the medical records that the attorney has on this plaintiff. (It is not a good idea to have the attorney's only copy of the records in case of loss in transit, or in case the attorney needs to refer to them for some reason.) Because the LNC knows that the following documents are helpful in motor vehicle collision cases, the following documents are requested:

- TCR
- Accident reconstruction reports
- Other written reports documenting the accident
- Copies of the photographs (usually laser color copies)
- Repair estimates on both (or all, as the case may be) vehicles
- Recorded statements (usually taken by an insurance company)
- Depositions of the parties, witnesses, treating health care providers, and experts
- Responses to interrogatories (the plaintiff's responses are often especially helpful)
- The summons and complaint

When the attorney asks why the LNC has requested these documents, the LNC should explain that having as much information as possible regarding the collision enhances the ability to identify the issues in the case. The LNC will be able to note important consistencies or inconsistencies in the medical records compared with the other documents.

Step Two: Organize the Records

Sometimes it feels overwhelming to see numerous stacks of records covering the LNC's desk (or spread out on the floor). The first thing to do is to put the records into a meaningful order. LNCs may develop their own methods, but the author will share her method. First read the cover letter to make sure the assignment is still the same as it was at the time of the prior discussion. Note any facts that the attorney may provide in the cover letter. Next, put the records in the following order and number them consecutively in pencil. (When these are the LNC's own copies, there is no problem in writing on them. Otherwise, use Post-Its.)

- TCR and any other accident reports
- Photographs or laser copies of photographs
- Repair estimates
- Accident reconstruction reports (there may be one from the plaintiff's expert and one from the defense expert)
- Transcript of the recorded statements taken by the insurance company
- Plaintiff's responses to interrogatories (and the defendant's if available)
- Transcripts of the plaintiff's and defendant's depositions

Next, organize the medical records sets into chronological order by the date of the earliest visit in the set. To do this, quickly flip through, scanning for the earliest visit date, and write it in pencil on the cover of the set. Put aside any exact duplicate sets. (Set these aside only when they are exact duplicates with the same copy service numbers, if used, and exactly the same pagination. Be sure that no nonduplicate pages are ignored.) Put the sets into chronological order starting with the one with the earliest visit. Continue numbering the sets from where you left off with the documents listed above. (The author does not take the sets apart. This seems to be too time consuming for the benefit that it yields, and it impairs the ability to identify the location of a document in terms of set and page number. It makes it easier to have a discussion with the attorney when the attorney has an identical set on the other end of the phone or desk.) Other LNCs may prefer to organize the medical records into categories, such as those found in a hospital admission, as well as organizing physician records into component parts, such as office notes, correspondence, diagnostic tests, copies of hospital records, reports from other health care providers, billing records, and miscellaneous (prescriptions, copies of insurance cards, back-to-work forms, and questionnaires).

Step Three: Beginning the Report: Summarize the Motor Vehicle Collision

Next, review and summarize the TCR (if one exists) to try to learn as much about the collision as possible. If there is no TCR, look for descriptions of the accident in the attorney's cover letter, the transcript of the recorded statement, responses to interrogatories, and deposition transcripts. Note the date of the collision, so that past medical history can be differentiated from postaccident medical care. Note the seating position of the plaintiff and what safety equipment was involved. Try to "picture" the collision as much as possible and try to get an idea of the forces involved. Look at any photographs of the vehicles to note the location of the damage. Review the repair estimates to see what areas of the vehicle were damaged and what areas of the vehicle needed to be replaced. (Sometimes the repair estimate shows that there was damage to a part of the vehicle that is not depicted in the photographs.) If there are accident reconstructionists' reports, review them to try to get an idea of the delta v of the vehicles and the Gs experienced by the plaintiff.

It is important to keep your report privileged as attorney work product. The LNC should write at the top of the first page, "Confidential: Attorney Work Product Privilege." Some LNCs include this statement as a header on every page.

Step Four: Prepare the Chronology

Now that the LNC has a "picture" of the collision, the LNC is ready to begin drafting the chronology. It is advisable to begin a written report with a listing of all the records reviewed. This way, it is clear that the LNC is basing the analysis only on the records actually reviewed. This can be important when another record that the LNC does not yet have changes the analysis.

Example 16.2: The plaintiff refused to have a procedure that the doctor had strongly recommended. In his report, the LNC discussed that the plaintiff had chosen not to follow the doctor's advice. But there was a record, one that the LNC did not yet have, documenting that the procedure was eventually performed. Anyone reviewing the LNC's report listing the documents received would realize that the LNC did not yet have the file documenting the procedure. Without the list of records reviewed, it might look as though the LNC had missed the fact that the procedure was performed.

If further records are sent to the LNC after the first report has been given to the attorney, then the LNC can write an addendum to the report. The LNC will begin the addendum with a listing of the additional records received.

The easiest way to generate the chronology is to use a table in a word processing or spreadsheet program with columns for the date of the visit, health care provider, and location in the records. The author usually uses the set number assigned in step two and the Bates stamp page number (e.g., Set 5, page 22) to pinpoint the exact location of the entry in the records. The Bates stamp is the stamped number added by the copy service or other person, usually located on the bottom right corner of each page. A summary of the visit (S.O.A.P. format works well here), diagnostic test, or procedure is entered in the wider column on the right (see Appendix 16.1). Another format that is useful lists the history, symptoms, examination, diagnosis, and plan.

It is important to record in great detail the entries of medical care immediately following the collision, with a focus on all the objective signs of injury. Note the location of bruises, abrasions, and lacerations, fractures, and all the complaints. As previously stated, the rescue personnel who respond to the scene often document important facts about the vehicle that are relevant to the plaintiff's condition (such as the amount of crush, whether the windshield is cracked, or whether the steering column or wheel was bent). If the plaintiff was hospitalized, be sure to note such facts as the amount of pain medication needed by the plaintiff. If there is no emergency care after the accident, pay particular attention to when the first visit occurred and to the complaints and objective signs of injuries documented at the first visit. Continue adding the rest of the visits, tests, and procedures to the chronology. Focus on any complaints and objective evidence of injuries, including any loss of function. Be sure to include the results of any diagnostic tests as well (as reported by the radiologist or the ordering health care provider).

The accident questionnaires or even the new patient questionnaires that some health care providers use often include important entries. It is useful to add these to the chronology as well. Regarding physical therapy visits, look for any entries that discuss any activities that the plaintiff has engaged in, as well as the compliance with and response to the therapy. (It is not unusual for physical therapy records to include entries such as, "The patient is sore after going skiing over the weekend," and "The patient was in another accident on Tuesday.")

Once the postaccident visits, diagnostic tests, and procedures are entered, add the entries relating to the care prior to the accident (i.e., the past medical history). (Some LNCs may prefer to record the past medical history first, but just be sure that the date of the accident is clear, so that one knows which care occurred prior to the accident and which occurred after it.)

The LNC should also define medical words with which the attorney is not likely to be familiar. The LNC may also need to state the indications for or the actions of medications (usually one word is sufficient) and briefly explain some of the diagnostic tests. A common way to add definitions or explanations in the text of a report is to enclose such comments in brackets. Be sure to clarify this for the attorney. For example, the LNC may write, "Dr. Jones prescribed coumadin [anticoagulant] and ordered a pro-time [coagulation study]." The level of detail depends on the issues in the case.

Step Five: Identify and Request Missing Records

This is the point at which it becomes obvious when records are missing. The orthopaedist may have documented that he referred his patient to the neurologist but the neurologist's records are not included. The health care providers may be referring to a particular diagnostic test that is not included with the records. The past medical history sections of history and physical reports may mention a previous procedure that is relevant to the case (such as a prior neck surgery in a neck injury case). It is advisable to notify the attorney in writing, perhaps via fax, of what records are missing.

Step Six: Prepare the Summary

Using the chronology as a guide, draft a concise summary so that the attorney can get a brief overview of what the records show.

Step Seven: Perform Any Needed Medical Literature Research

Occasionally, this is the point at which some research may be needed for clarification. For example, the LNC might want to do a search of the medical literature regarding injuries caused by airbags. See Chapter 32, Literature Research, for additional information.

Step Eight: Perform the Analysis

Now that the LNC knows what happened in the accident and knows the details in the medical records, the LNC will be able to spot issues as well as obvious strengths and weaknesses in the case. At this point it is not unusual for the case's issues, strengths, and weaknesses to practically "pop" into the LNC's mind. At this point, the analysis is usually quite easy. The author finds that it is not unusual to wake up in the middle of the night with an important thought about the case. The author advises the LNC to write these down because the thoughts may be gone in the morning. (See Chapter 31, Medical Record Analysis, for additional hints.)

Step Nine: Report Back to the Attorney

The LNC calls to make an appointment to submit and discuss the report in person. If this is not possible, the report can be mailed or e-mailed if approved by the attorney.

Conclusion

LNCs will enhance their practice by becoming proficient in working up these challenging but very interesting personal injury cases.

References

1. The National Technical Review Web site, FAQs, http://www.nationaltech.net/faq.html.
2. Hyde, A.S., *Crash Injuries: How and Why They Happen*, Hyde Associates, Inc., Key Biscayne, FL, 1992.
3. Peitzman, A.B. et al., *The Trauma Manual*, Lippincott, Williams & Wilkins, Philadelphia, 1998.
4. Anderson, P.A., The epidemiology of seatbelt-associated injuries, *Journal of Trauma*, 31(1), 60, 1991.
5. Insurance Institute for Highway Safety, Q & A: Airbags, http://www.hwysafety.org/safety_qanda/airbags/html, December 2000.
6. Smock, W.S., Airbag module cover injuries, *Journal of Trauma*, 38(4), 489, 1995.
7. California Highway Patrol Web site, http:// www.chp.ca.gov/html/mait.html, 2001.
8. Becker, W., Preventing injuries from slips, trips and falls, The National Ag Safety Database, University of Florida, http://www.cdc.gov/niosh/nasd/docs/as04200.html, 1992.
9. Miller, B.C., Slip resistance standards: sorting it all out, *Safety and Health*, March 1999.

Test Questions

1. Which of the following documents does not usually provide important information about what happened in a motor vehicle collision?
   A. The traffic collision report
   B. Vehicle damage estimates
   C. The accident reconstructionist's report
   D. An informed consent form

2. As a general rule, the occupants in a vehicle first move in which direction on impact in a rear-end collision?
   A. Toward the front of the vehicle, being pushed away from the point of impact.
   B. Toward the rear of the vehicle, toward the point of impact.
   C. It is not generally predictable how an occupant will move in a particular type of collision.
   D. Toward the driver's side of the vehicle.

3. Which of the following statements is NOT true about airbags?
   A. The airbag module cover can cause injury, especially when the occupant is in close proximity to it at the time of impact.
   B. Airbags are set to deploy only in certain types of accidents.
   C. Airbags enhance the safety of children of all ages.
   D. Some newer vehicles are equipped with side airbags.

4. Which of the following statements is NOT true about seat belts?
   A. When the passive shoulder restraint is used without the lap belt component, the occupant can submarine under the belt in a frontal collision.
   B. The lap belt portion of the seat belt should be worn high on the abdomen.
   C. The fabric of the seat belt can be forensically examined to determine whether it has been subjected to stretch forces from a collision.
   D. One major function of the lap belt/shoulder harness combination is to prevent ejection of the occupants.

5. Choose the phrase that makes the following statement false: The coefficient of friction _____ .
   A. Is most relevant in slip-and-fall cases
   B. Can be measured
   C. Should be at least a value of .50 for minimum safety, but some laws require even more slip-resistant surfaces
   D. Is most relevant in trip-and-fall cases

Answers: 1. D, 2. B, 3. C, 4. B, 5. D

Appendix 16.1
Sample Chronology Format

The chronology below has been created with the Table function of a word processing program. Highlight and click on three columns of the top row of the table icon in the toolbar, then move the column lines to the preferred location. (Place the cursor on the lines and drag them.) To add more rows, hit the Tab key. To insert (or add) rows, click on Table and then on Insert. This procedure works in both the Microsoft Word and WordPerfect programs.

Confidential: Attorney Work Product Privilege

Records of Jane Jackson
Date of birth: 12/1/48
Date of accident: 1/26/98
Age at time of accident: 49
Date of report: 9/6/2001

Records Reviewed

1. Traffic Collision Report, 8 pages, 1/26/98
2. Repair Estimate, XYZ Auto Body, 4 pages, 1/29/98 (plaintiff's vehicle)
3. Roger Smith, MD, 57 pages, Copy Cat Copy Service file # 4321
4. ABC Imaging Center, 6 pages, Copy Cat Copy Service file # 4322
5. ABC Community Hospital, 324 pages, DEF Copy Service, file # B2604–22
6. Donald Jones, MD, not Bate, stamped set, 16 pages, no copy service noted

Chronology of Medical Care

1/22/98 Set 3, p. 5	Roger Smith, MD (orthopedic surgeon)	**Orthopedic Surgery Office Visit** S: Plaintiff complains of continuing neck pain O: Range of motion of neck is markedly decreased; right arm strength is 4/5 all muscle groups, sensation decreased entire right arm A: Herniated disc at C 4–5 with symptoms of radiculopathy down right arm P: Discectomy at C 4–5 is advised; advise pre-op MRI
1/25/98 Set 6, p. 2	Donald Jones, MD ABC MRI	**Cervical Spine MRI** Impression: Posterior osteophytes at C 4–5; focal disc bulge at C 4–5
1/26/98 Set 1, pp. 1–6	Traffic collision report	**Motor Vehicle Collision** Date/time of accident: 1/26/98, 1632 Type of accident: Broadside on driver's side Driver: Jane Jackson, wearing lap and shoulder belt; head restraint was noted to be in the lowest position Vehicle driven by Jane Jackson, 1998 Honda Civic Other vehicle driven by Jay Smith, 1996 Cadillac Seville; Jay Smith transported to hospital with head laceration and loss of consciousness Plaintiff was transported to ABC Community Hospital by XYZ Ambulance Company with complaints of pain to neck, left arm, and head

1/26/98 Set 8, p. 3	XYZ Emergency Ambulance Services	**EMS Transport** Time of call: 14:02 Arrive on scene: 14:18 Departed scene: 14:25 Arrival at ABC General Hospital: 14:37 S: Pt found sitting on curb near crash scene; denies LOC (loss of consciousness); complains of pain to neck, left elbow, and head; oriented (he knows who he is, where he is, what day/time it is, and is aware of current circumstances) with "appropriate" behavior O: One-inch laceration above left eyebrow; reddened area on left elbow size of a quarter Driver's side window broken out; major damage to driver's door with about one foot of passenger compartment intrusion; pt states he exited through passenger side door (include vital signs, additional objective findings, treatments, and transport information)

It is helpful to include the specialties of the treating physicians. This can be determined by going to the American Medical Association's Web site, http://www.ama-assn.org.

Narrative Summary

In this section, give a brief narrative summary of medical care with emphasis on points relevant to the case. Include information about time off work, return to work, and work limitations if such information is noted in the medical records. Employment records can also be used to glean this information.

Analysis

In this section, note the issues raised by information in the medical records, including strengths and weaknesses of the plaintiff's case. For example, it would be important to note that Jane Jackson's records reveal a preexisting symptomatic herniated cervical disc.

Additional Records/Discovery

This is the section in which to list missing records and other documents that would be helpful to the case. Include as much identifying information as possible. For example, if the plaintiff's answers to interrogatories include the name and address of a treating physician, include the address in this section. If the address is not listed in any of the documents, it can usually be obtained by going to the American Medical Association's Web site.

Timeline

A timeline is helpful in complex cases because it shows, at a glance, the type and frequency of care. It is also helpful when timing is an issue in the case. The format of a timeline includes the date, followed by a brief description of the event. For example:

1/22/98: Office visit, orthopedic surgeon (R. Smith, MD), neck pain/ herniated cervical disc, surgery advised

1/25/98: Preoperative MRI of cervical spine

1/26/98: Motor vehicle collision

1/26/98: Transported to ABC ER via ambulance from the accident scene

1/30/98: Consultation with orthopedic surgeon (D. Jones, MD)

2/12/98: Physical therapy, initial evaluation (Physical Therapy Incorporated)

2/13/98: Returned to work part-time with restrictions

Chapter 17

Evaluating Product Liability Cases

Rosie Oldham, BS, RN, LNCC,
Paula Windler, MS, RN, LNCC,
Pamela M. Linville, RN, CCRC, CPBT,
Patricia L. Pippen, BSN, RN, LNCC, OCN, and
Shirley Cantwell Davis, BSN, RN, LNCC

CONTENTS

0-8493-1418-6/03/$0.00+$1.50
© 2003 by AALNC

Objectives

- To state the difference between the legal theories of strict liability and negligence in a product liability case
- To describe hypothetical instances of defective design and defective manufacturing of a medical product
- To discuss three criteria used to determine the adequacy of manufacturer warnings
- To formulate a request for an adverse drug reaction report or medical device report under the Freedom of Information Act
- To describe the informed consent process for pharmaceutical clinical trials
- To knowledgeably rule out professional medical negligence and establish clear causation in a medical product liability case
- To be able to research and maintain a current knowledge base of new drugs in product liability cases

Introduction

Few areas of litigation are as fascinating and complex for the lawyer and the legal nurse consultant (LNC) alike as pharmaceutical and medical devices product liability litigation. In order for LNCs to successfully work in product liability litigation involving drugs and devices, they must have a basic understanding of legal theories regarding strict liability and negligence as well as design defects, manufacturing defects, and failure to warn. LNCs must also be cognizant of the steps involved in Food and Drug Administration (FDA) approval of a new drug or device and the postmarketing processes. A good working knowledge of the standard of care practiced by health care practitioners who use prescription drugs and medical products is essential so that a differentiation can be made between a medical malpractice and a product liability matter. Additionally, the causal relationship between drugs and disease provides one of the most difficult challenges for the nurse consultant working on pharmaceutical litigation, as drug-induced damage may be highly obscure.

Theories of Liability

Product liability is a concept in the law holding a manufacturer strictly liable or responsible for the article placed on the market. Although the underlying legal theories of product liability stem from the common law, which is based on old English law and essentially handed down from generation to generation, common law comprises the principles of law that are generally recognized in the U.S. The definition of product liability can be found in the *Restatement (Second) of Torts* § 402A (1965):

> One who sells any product in a defective condition, unreasonably dangerous to the user or consumer or to his property, is subject to liability for physical harm thereby caused to the ultimate user or consumer, or his property, if:
>
> A. The seller is engaged in the business of selling such a product, and
> B. The product is expected to and does reach the user or consumer without substantial change in the condition in which it is sold.[1]

In other words, a manufacturer owes a duty to the public for the injuries caused by the product upon which the manufacturer made a profit. Within the realm of product liability law, three causes of action dominate: strict liability, negligence, and breach of contract. In practice, a plaintiff can allege negligence, strict liability, or both when failure to warn is alleged.

Strict Liability

Strict liability will almost always be a part of the plaintiff's cause of action. In strict liability, the plaintiff must prove that:

1. The defendant sold the product (this is especially true when there are several manufacturers of a generic drug or multiple retailers of a device as in breast implants)
2. The product was defective
3. The defect was the proximate cause of the plaintiff's injuries
4. The plaintiff has damages

Strict liability is responsibility to the user or consumer without a showing of fault or the need to show fault. The emphasis is product-oriented, focusing on the safety of the drug or device rather than on the reasonableness of the manufacturer's conduct. This places the responsibility for the safety of the drug or device on the pharmaceutical or medical device company. If the manufacturer produces a drug that harms a person, the manufacturer may be held strictly liable for the injury regardless of the fact that the medication may have been taken improperly or for an indication other than that for which the drug is approved.

Fundamental to a strict liability argument is proof by the plaintiff that the product was defective, that the defect existed when the product left the manufacturer's control, and that the defect caused the plaintiff's injury. In a strict liability analysis, it is assumed that the defendant knows the dangerous propensity of the product to potentially cause injury; under a negligence theory, the plaintiff must prove that the defendant knew or should have known of the danger. Thus, the plaintiff's burden is less onerous under a strict liability theory than under negligence. However, under strict liability the plaintiff must still establish proximate cause between the product defect and the harm suffered by the plaintiff.

Example 17.1: In 2001, the FDA was investigating reports of more than 50 patient deaths worldwide, including 4 in the United States, that may have been caused by certain dialyzers made by Baxter Healthcare Corporation. In mid-October 2001, Baxter notified all of its customers to stop using these dialyzers immediately and return any inventory. Preliminary tests have led Baxter to conclude that a perfluorohydrocarbon-based performance fluid used in a manufacturing step may have played a role in the deaths of these patients. Confirmatory tests are underway. Baxter reported that it had permanently ceased manufacturing these dialyzers.

When trying to prove that a product is defective or unreasonably dangerous, the LNC must remember that drugs and medical devices are designed and created with the inherent nature of causing side effects. In every case, drugs and devices used for medical purposes must be examined and analyzed from a risk/benefit ratio in order to assess whether or not they are unreasonably dangerous in the first place. It is important to examine the question whether the desired and foreseeable actions of the drug or device are sufficiently beneficial to justify the risks of adverse reactions.

Example 17.2: One of the known risks of artificial heart valves is thrombogenicity, or the risk of clot formation. Because the artificial heart valve is a foreign object and does not have the hemodynamics of a natural heart valve, thrombus formation will occur in a certain number of patients. Thrombosis is considered a reasonable risk for an artificial heart valve, and if thrombosis does occur, in most cases the valve would not be considered unreasonably dangerous or defective.

Another issue in drug and device product liability involves the *Restatement (Second) of Torts* Section 402A, Comment k, which deems some drugs as incapable of being made safe. Comment k does not seek to prevent all suits against drug manufacturers, but rather seeks to protect the manufacturer against liability for design defects.[2] Comment k thus provides a special defense for what are termed unavoidably unsafe products. These products cannot be redesigned or otherwise changed to remove some inherent danger, but the substantial benefits of the product justify the risks created by its unsafe features. Pharmaceuticals are considered a classic example of such products. Because their formulas are a fixed, scientific constant, they cannot be redesigned to eliminate the risks that must necessarily accompany their use. Therefore, some drugs and devices are neither defective nor unreasonably dangerous when properly designed and accompanied by proper directions and warnings. If the manufacturer has met these obligations, then strict liability cannot be imposed. However, if the warning accompanying the prescription drug or device is deemed inadequate, the manufacturer will not be able to rely on the Comment k defense.[3] Comment k is still being used, but *Restatement (Third) of Torts* Product Liability Section 6 may provide access to more claims due in part to direct advertising of prescription drugs to patients.

Example 17.3: A good example of an unavoidably unsafe drug is the broad-spectrum antibiotic chloramphenicol, which is of great value in the treatment of certain systemic infections. This drug has been linked to aplastic anemia in a small percentage of users. The manufacturer clearly denotes this association in all product labeling in order to provide adequate warning of this potentially fatal adverse reaction to the drug.

Vaccine Liability

In 1986, Congress passed the National Vaccine Injury Act (NVIA), partly in response to the overwhelming number of lawsuits claiming strict liability on the part of vaccine manufacturers for vaccine-related injuries.[4] Parties seeking compensation for injuries from vaccines must do so now under NVIA. The act created a "no-fault" compensation program that provides vaccine manufacturers with liability protection in order to let them continue to make their product without undue economic pressure from the threat of litigation. The act also enables children who have suffered vaccine hypersensitivity reactions easier access to compensation instead of going through the courts.

In 1995, the courts ruled that plaintiffs must prove not only that they experienced symptoms of an injury after receiving a vaccination, but that there were no symptoms of that injury prior to the vaccination.[5] Claimants who do not prove actual causation must show that the first symptoms or significant aggravation of the condition occurred within 3 days of the vaccination. Adverse effects are succinctly defined in NVIA. For instance, encephalopathy is specified as significant acquired abnormality, injury, or impairment of brain function. In 1997, a final rule was published, which in part provides for the "automatic" addition of future vaccines recommended by the Centers for Disease Control and Prevention (CDC) for routine administration to children. Under current statutory language, 8 years' retroactive coverage will be provided for those claiming injury or death resulting from a vaccine newly added to the National Vaccine Injury Compensation Program.

Example 17.4: The parents of a 4-month-old infant filed a compensation claim under NVIA for brain injuries allegedly occurring following a vaccination for diphtheria, pertussis, and tetanus. A pediatric neurologist found that the infant had seizures within 3 days of the vaccine. However, the neurologist also found that the infant had significant preexisting microcephaly and concluded that the seizures were not the first symptoms of brain injury. Thus, the claim was rejected under the rules of NVIA.

Negligence

Negligence is the failure to use due care. This term refers to conduct that falls below the standard established by law for the protection of others against unreasonable risk of harm. When negligence is alleged, the defendant's conduct is central to the liability question. To succeed, the plaintiff must establish the following:

1. *Duty* — The manufacturer must exercise the ordinary care, diligence, and prudence of a reasonable manufacturer under like and similar circumstances when manufacturing and distributing the product.
2. *Breach of that duty* — One must prove that the manufacturer did not exercise the ordinary care, diligence, and prudence that a reasonable manufacturer would have used in like or similar circumstances when manufacturing and distributing the product.
3. *Damages* — The plaintiff must have suffered actual physical harm. In some jurisdictions, the harm may encompass emotional injuries for a perceived or future physical harm.
4. *Proximate cause* — The harm must be proximately caused by or have flowed directly from the breach of the manufacturer's duty.

A drug company has a duty to act prudently, and a breach of this duty would include, for example, not performing a product recall after several unexplained deaths in the first 3 months after FDA approval of a new drug. FDA approval does not in and of itself provide an adequate defense for a manufacturer when negligence is alleged. Alternatively, a product manufacturer may have breached its duty to act prudently by employing someone who is not qualified to run the product clinical trials. Both of these are examples of a pharmaceutical or medical device manufacturer's failure to exercise ordinary care, diligence, or prudence, breaching its duty to the consumer or user of the product.

Example 17.5: In 1999, Bayer Corporation indicated that it had changed the Baycol prescribing information to include a contraindication with Lopid (gemfibrozil). Bayer Corporation indicated that the combined use of (Baycol) cerivastatin and gemfibrozil is contraindicated due to a risk for rhabdomyolysis, and concurrent use should not occur under any circumstances. The labeling changes did not go into the new *Physicians' Desk Reference* until November 2000. A letter dated May 21, 2001, was sent out to all health care providers regarding the warning, and potential problems and patients were to report to their physicians any muscle problems, malaise, or fever. Since Bayer Corporation knew of this problem, the alert letter should have been sent out prior to May 2001. Bayer Corporation indicated that it had made the revisions due to receiving reports of muscle weakness and rhabdomyolysis during the postmarketing period.

Warranty

Warranty is an assurance by the manufacturer, either express, which is an overt assurance, or implied, that the goods are merchantable and of average quality. A manufacturer implies a warranty of fitness by selling a product that the manufacturer contends is merchantable and reasonably fit for a particular purpose. For example, a prosthetic hip should not fracture after implantation. If it does fracture, a breach of warranty may exist because the prosthetic hip is not, by definition, merchantable or fit for the purpose for which it was sold. Warranty and breach of warranty are concepts used in both strict liability and negligence.

Important Concepts Used to Prove Liability in Product Liability Litigation

Three theories of recovery are used in product liability litigation, regardless of whether negligence or strict liability is alleged. These theories are defective design, defective manufacture, and failure to warn.

Defective Design

Defective design exists when a drug or device is not reasonably safe for its intended use or a use that can be reasonably anticipated. This may occur when a drug or device is formulated to specifications, but is not efficacious for the intended purpose or is a product with massive side effects. If the product's design is found to be defective, all the products manufactured using that same design are considered to be defective.

Example 17.6: In the silicone breast implant litigation, the plaintiffs have alleged defective design of silicone-gel breast implants, claiming increased risk for connective tissue disorders, immune system illnesses, and implant rupture due to the faulty design of the implants. The plaintiffs claim that the manufacturers knew or should have known that the defective design of the implants would cause them to leak or rupture, with consequent migration of silicone, and ultimately result in systemic effects. In June 1999, an independent committee of scientists concluded that although silicone breast implants may be responsible for localized problems, such as hardening or scarring of breast tissue, implants do not cause any major diseases (e.g., lupus or rheumatoid arthritis). The committee apparently did not conduct any new research, but only reviewed past information. A study published in 2001 referred to data suggesting an association between extracapsular silicone gel and fibromyalgia.

Defective Manufacture

Defective manufacture can be alleged if the product is defective as a result of the manner in which it is manufactured and the defect existed when the product left the manufacturer's control. Defective manufacture is usually alleged when there is a one-time mistake (e.g., when one batch of a drug is tainted such that the flawed product differs from the manufacturer's intended design and manufacturing).

Example 17.7: In August 1989, L-tryptophan, an essential amino acid defined by the FDA as a food supplement and popularly used as a natural sedative, was associated with an epidemic of eosinophilia myalgia syndrome (EMS). More than 1500 people were diagnosed with EMS, and 38 deaths were reported as being associated with the use of L-tryptophan. Studies proved that the disease was caused by ingestion of contaminated L-tryptophan manufactured by a Japanese company, Showa Denko K.K.[6]

Failure to Warn

The duty of the manufacturer to warn of the dangers associated with the use of a product is crucial in any drug or device case, whether the case encompasses strict liability, negligence, or both. The key issue when failure to warn is alleged is the adequacy of the product label. It is assumed that when a warning is given, the manufacturer may reasonably expect that it will be read and heeded. While that presumption operates to the benefit of the manufacturer, when an inadequate warning is found, the presumption operates to the benefit of the plaintiff as if there were no warning, and the product can be presumed to be defective.

Drug and device companies routinely warn of adverse reactions in the labeling and package inserts that accompany each bottle or single package of the product or device or, in the case of drugs, the *Physicians' Desk Reference*.[7] The FDA requires a labeling revision, supplementation to the package insert, and in some cases direct notification to the physicians prescribing the product as soon as there is reasonable evidence of an association between a newly recognized serious hazard and a drug or device. A causal relationship does not need to be proven.[8] The argument by a defendant drug company that it was not bound to provide a warning until the occurrence of the side effect was frequent and clearly defined will often be rejected by the courts.[9]

Learned Intermediary

In the case of prescription drugs and medical devices, the manufacturer's duty to warn goes to the physician rather than the patient, since the patient can obtain the product only through the physician. The learned intermediary stands between the manufacturer of a medical device or product and the person who uses the product. The physician acts as the "learned intermediary" with regard to the drug and is expected to convey to the patient the labeling information provided by the manufacturer. The plaintiff, as the patient and consumer, has to rely on the health care expertise of the physician to read and be cognizant of the warnings.

Example 17.8: Schering Corporation, which manufactures Garamycin (genta-mycin), cannot be expected to warn patients directly concerning the potential effects this drug can cause (e.g., nephrotoxicity and neurotoxicity). The burden falls on the "learned intermediary," the person with knowledge who prescribes the drug, to be informed and to monitor the patient for these potential problems. Schering Corporation has warned of these adverse reactions through such sources as the package insert and the *Physicians' Desk Reference*.[7]

By providing adequate information to the physician, the manufacturer in effect erects a barrier to liability. To the extent that the labeling information is inadequate, that barrier is weakened, and the manufacturer becomes more vulnerable.

Over-the-Counter Products

Conversely, a number of health care products are not dispensed by prescription. FDA Class II devices, which are available for purchase over the counter (OTC), must carry adequate warnings of potential hazards written in language that consumers can understand, since there is no learned intermediary when using these products.

Example 17.9: In March 1999, the FDA announced that a new regulation would be available for OTC medications. The regulation called for a standardized format that would improve the labeling on drugs Americans use most — nonprescription or OTC drugs. By clearly showing a drug's ingredients, dose, and warnings, the new labeling would make it easier for consumers to understand information about a drug's benefits, risks, and proper use. The FDA indicated that the new labeling would be in effect 2 years from the date of the announcement and that all OTC medications would have to adopt the new labeling within 6 years.

Conduct of the Manufacturer

Whether the cause of action is negligence or strict liability, there are criteria regarding warnings against which the conduct of a manufacturer will be judged.[10] These criteria focus primarily on three factors:

1. Knowledge of the risk
2. The nature and timing of the duty to warn
3. Language used to convey the warning

Knowledge of the Risk

The drug company may not be held liable for failure to warn of adverse effects unless the adverse effects were known or reasonably scientifically knowable at the time the product was distributed by the manufacturer. The manufacturer is held to the standard of an expert in the field and is charged with actual knowledge of adverse drug reactions arising from both its own research and knowledge of reported reactions from outside sources, such as the scientific literature.

Example 17.10: In 1990, Eli Lilly, the manufacturer of the antidepressant Prozac, should have been placed on notice when a letter to the editor appeared in the British journal *Lancet* regarding Prozac. The letter reported on five patients who had become suicidal after initiation of Prozac in their therapy for depression. The case report was unsubstantiated, lacking in detail, and not a scientific study; the article itself, despite being in a foreign journal, constituted a report of reactions associated with Eli Lilly's product. The company had knowledge or should have had knowledge of these adverse effects.

The Nature and Timing of the Duty to Warn

The determination whether the manufacturer acted reasonably regarding warnings depends on the company's knowledge of the risks associated with the product at the time the product was distributed to the plaintiff. The duty to warn does not expire when the product is placed on the market, but is continuous. This imposes an obligation on the manufacturer to seek out information regarding its product. If information becomes available indicating that a certain danger is associated with the use of the drug, then the manufacturer cannot disregard the information in drafting or altering its warning simply because the manufacturer feels the evidence is unconvincing. The onus is on the company to communicate and warn physicians regarding a new risk as soon as it is reasonably practical. The drug or device manufacturer is not allowed to wait until a statistically significant number of people have been injured or until a causal relationship has been established by epidemiological studies.

In previous cases, the courts have rejected the defendant manufacturer's argument that it was not bound to provide warnings until the occurrence of side effects was so frequent and the evidence of causation was so clear-cut that the manufacturer itself was convinced that the drug caused or contributed to such problems.[9] On this issue, the court's view agrees with the FDA regulations requiring a labeling revision as soon as there is reasonable evidence of an association of a serious hazard with a drug. A causal relationship need not have been proved.

Example 17.11: A case in point was a problematic defibrillator manufactured by Marquette Electronics, Inc. The defibrillator used a special battery pack, which was found to wear out prematurely, manifesting as a rapid loss of charge capacity after being removed from the battery charger. The FDA eventually initiated a Class I recall (complete recall) of the battery charger. However, FDA Medical Device Reports (MDRs) revealed that Marquette had been on notice of this problem for a significant period of time prior to recall. A Freedom of Information Act (FOIA) request (to obtain information on a certain drug or device) revealed a number of reports of the defibrillator's failure to work due to rapid loss of charge capacity in the batteries, causing death in some instances, for a substantial period of time prior to Marquette's warning to users of this association. The FOIA can be found in Title 5 of the United States Code, section 552. It was enacted in 1966 and provides that any person has the right to request access to federal agency records or information. Additional information can be found at the United States Department of Justice Web site, http://www.usdoj.gov/04foia/.

Language Used to Convey the Warning

The FDA regulates all prescription drug and medical device promotional activities that fall within the definition of labeling and advertising.[11] Once a determination has been made to include a warning in the drug or device labeling, it is incumbent upon the manufacturer to adequately convey the warning to the doctor. Product labeling includes written material both physically on the product and accompanying the product. Labeling has been widely interpreted to include the package insert, exhibits, brochures, product-detailing pieces, press releases, speeches by company officials, and other promotional materials (e.g., "Dear Doctor" letters) that are sent to medical providers with information regarding problems with different medications or devices.

The format and content of drug labeling is rigidly controlled by the federal regulations. Labeling must include indications, precautions, warnings, contraindications, and dosage, among other information. The product label is approved by the FDA during the drug approval process; the label is not a document arbitrarily designed by the drug manufacturer. All subsequent promotional materials must conform to the language in the approved labeling. The FDA labeling regulations impose a continuing obligation on the manufacturer, and new data must be incorporated in the label as it becomes available. The regulations permit the manufacturer in specified instances to change its labeling without prior authorization of the FDA. A failure to share new information could result in the drug's being improperly labeled or misbranded. This would constitute evidence for the plaintiff in a product liability suit.

The adequacy of the warning included in the labeling is measured not only by what is stated, but also by the manner in which it is stated.

Example 17.12: If Stevens-Johnson syndrome has been reported on multiple occasions with the use of a drug, then the manufacturer must not only warn of a cutaneous reaction, but use terminology to indicate the seriousness of the side effect, such as severe exfoliative dermatitis or toxic epidermal necrolysis.

A warning can be found inadequate if the facts are insufficient, the response unduly delayed, or the manner of the words reluctant or lacking in intensity. The warning must be expressed in a tone congruent with the nature of the risk.

Example 17.13: The court ruled against Ortho Pharmaceutical Corporation in a case involving birth control pills, declaring a warning of abnormal blood clotting inadequate. The court ruled that the absence of the word "stroke" unduly minimized the warning's impact.[12]

There are several important considerations in the review of warnings. Warnings must be conspicuous and prominent. Warnings can be considered ineffective and insufficient if they are printed in a body of other information of the same size and color. This means that it is incumbent upon the manufacturer to make the warnings conspicuous and prominent. As the result of litigation involving toxic shock syndrome associated with tampon use, the warnings are now usually printed on the top of the box or prominently located in a package insert placed on top of the product. In the *Physicians' Desk Reference*,[7] drugs with particularly dangerous side effects, such as agranulocytosis and teratogenesis, have special warnings, sometimes referred to as "black box warnings," with bold print and placement at the beginning of the labeling.

To be adequate, warnings must convey the risk of the danger associated with the use of the product. The question of adequacy depends upon the language used and the impression that such language might reasonably be calculated to make upon the physician or consumer. The wording used must be simple and straightforward. If a warning with reference to a particular side effect is labeled "rare," the physician might be more inclined to recommend the product than if the side effect were labeled as "common" or "occasional."

Warnings must also be unambiguous. The warnings can be inadequate because of the lack of clarity or narrowness. The risks and types of possible adverse reactions must be clear and straightforward. Over-promotion and such activities as direct consumer advertising may dilute the warnings or even render them insufficient.

Example 17.14: Excessive promotion of a certain aspect of a product occurred in the marketing of tampons in the early 1980s. Manufacturers were advertising super absorbency as the foremost marketing pitch without adequately warning about the association between super absorbency of these tampons and toxic shock syndrome. Consequently, the zealous advertisements of super absorbency were judged, in many instances, to render the warnings about toxic shock syndrome insufficient.

Furthermore, advertising claims can create such a high expectation of benefit in the consumer that any warnings of risks may be disregarded by the consumer.

Example 17.15: In the case of Oraflex, an antiarthritic drug marketed by Eli Lilly in 1982, the word "cure" actually appeared in some of the direct advertising to the public. This led some people to believe that the risk of taking the drug was outweighed by the fact that the drug would "cure" their arthritis symptoms.

A manufacturer has a duty to keep abreast of the current state of knowledge regarding their products as gained through research, medical literature, and adverse reaction reports. The subsequently acquired knowledge may necessitate a further duty to notify both physicians and potential consumers of this new information. Manufacturers have a duty to warn of all potential dangers either known or that should have been known in the exercise of reasonable care.

Example 17.16: A large verdict was returned in Georgia regarding the failure of Ortho Pharmaceutical to warn about the potential for teratogenicity of Ortho-Gynol Contraceptive Jelly. The plaintiff showed that substantial research proved a connection between spermicidal jelly and birth defects and that the manufacturer had failed to include this information in the warnings. The failure to change the warnings to reflect this knowledge meant that the warnings were inadequate, and the product was deemed defective.[13]

FDA Regulatory Process for Product Approval

The FDA was formulated under the auspices of the Food, Drug, and Cosmetic Act of 1938. This act was aimed at strengthening government regulation of medications and required that there be evidence of safety prior to the marketing of a new drug. This act introduced the use of prescriptions for the majority of drugs and established a regulatory agency, the FDA, to oversee the market and set the policies for the sale of new drugs.[14] Due to the grave adverse reactions associated with thalidomide, the Kefauver-Harris Amendments of 1962 to the Food, Drug, and Cosmetic Act imposed strict guidelines regarding drug safety and labeling and resulted in 7000 drugs' being removed from the market. Since that time, the FDA's role has been centered on identifying and communicating adverse reactions associated with pharmaceuticals and medical devices.[15]

Clinical Trials of Pharmaceuticals

The FDA controls the regulation of medical and pharmaceutical products in the U.S. The drug approval process is constructed to theoretically minimize the possibility that drug errors will make their way to consumers. Before approving a new drug for marketing, the FDA must ascertain the drug's safety and efficacy. This verification process requires the drug manufacturer to put the drug through a lengthy experimental protocol. The FDA approves a drug based on these premarketing evaluations, or clinical trials, performed by the drug company to determine the safety and effectiveness of the drug. Clinical trials are considered the gold standard of pharmaceutical research, but the results apply to only a small range of questions and cannot be applied to the general population. Clinical trials compare outcomes among two or more groups — one group is deliberately exposed to the new therapy, while the others receive standard or alternative treatment or a placebo. These trials are used to test the efficacy of new treatments.[16]

Prior to the submission of a new drug application (NDA) to the FDA, drug manufacturers undertake three phases of testing to demonstrate the safety and efficacy of a new drug. In Phase 1 trials, the drug is tested for the maximum tolerated dose. This research is typically carried out in a small number of healthy subjects using dose escalations and watching for side effects. Phase 2 trials evaluate the drug's safety and efficacy in the target population. This phase is typically done in small samples of 50 to 100. Phase 3 studies are randomized, blind, and, many times, placebo-controlled. Randomization is a mechanism of assigning the study patients to treatment arms, like tossing a coin or throwing dice. The chance of being put on the study drug is usually 50%. The study researcher is not allowed to choose who receives the study drug and who receives the comparison study therapies. Blinding the studies means that both the study participants and the investigators who carry out the protocol and collect the data do not know which study subjects are receiving the study drug. Both of these elements are used to prevent researcher bias when treating and evaluating the study patients.

The FDA closely regulates all three phases of the clinical trial process in cooperation with the drug manufacturer. Safety is maintained by giving the drug under controlled circumstances with careful monitoring by physician experts in the treatment of the particular disease under consideration. The experts give meticulous attention to reporting adverse consequences of all types.[17]

The results of all the clinical studies are submitted to the FDA for review. After sufficient research and review have been completed, the FDA grants an NDA and the drug can be manufactured. To contest the charges by consumers, drug manufacturers and special interest groups complained that the approval process was taking too long. Congress passed the Prescription Drug User Fee Act in 1992, requiring manufacturers to pay a fee to expedite approval time. The number of new drugs approved for use doubled from 26 in 1992 to 53 in 1996. At the same time, the average approval time for new drugs, which was 20.5 months in 1996, decreased to an amazing average of 10.8 months in 1997.[18] Since that time the FDA has continued to review the process and anticipated shortening the process even more. The agency was also looking at ways to improve the manufacturing and dispensing of new medications while at the same time ensuring the health and safety of Americans.

As a result of the FDA regulatory process, when the average drug is marketed, consumers have a reasonable expectation that serious adverse effects are unlikely to occur when the drug is used:

- For its approved indication
- At its recommended dose
- For limited periods
- In medically uncomplicated, nonpregnant young or middle-aged adults who are medically compliant

Because of limited sample sizes and duration of clinical trials, these studies often cannot detect or measure serious adverse effects that are infrequent or related to long-term use. Additionally, the effects of a new drug on a frail elderly patient with multiple illnesses may be difficult to predict even after the completion of the clinical trials.[19]

Example 17.17: Oraflex, the antiarthritic manufactured by Eli Lilly, had serious hepatotoxicity associated with its use, especially in the elderly. Since the clinical trials did not typically include persons over 65, the adverse reaction was not detected in the original studies and became apparent only after widespread use in elderly persons.

At present, the FDA has no authority to require clinical studies after a drug has been approved. Most postmarketing studies are voluntary on the part of the manufacturer. This may involve studies on special populations, such as the elderly or young children. In drug development, it is logistically impractical, prohibitively expensive, and ethically questionable to delay the marketing of an effective drug until every potential risk associated with its use is known. It is imperative for postmarketing surveillance to be done to learn additional information about the side effects and dangers of drugs, which sometimes become known only when the drug is given to larger numbers of people.

Example 17.18: A good example involves the drug Zomax, a nonsteroidal anti-inflammatory, which was also used as an analgesic. McNeil Pharmaceuticals warned in its package insert that as with other nonsteroidal anti-inflammatory drugs, anaphylactoid reactions have been reported, but it was not until the drug had been marketed for quite a period of time that it became apparent that many anaphylactoid reactions were occurring, and the drug was finally recalled by the manufacturer. This is a classic case of postmarketing surveillance identifying the true incidence of a dangerous side effect.

Another reason for postmarketing surveillance is that clinical trials, while adequate for regulatory purposes, may not be adequately designed to detect an adverse reaction in certain patient populations. The system has proved to be very effective for most drugs; however, a small number of drugs have been found to have latent effects, which were evident only after an extended period of time.

Informed Consent in Clinical Trials

Protection of human research subjects in the field of clinical trials has been a key issue since the reported abuses of human subjects in biomedical experiments, especially during World War II. Some of the significant guidelines regarding the safety of human subjects and proper research conduct that have been developed since the reported abuses include The Nuremberg Code (1949), The Belmont Report (1979), The Declaration of Helsinki (1964), and Good Clinical Practice (GCP) Guidelines. The Nuremberg Code encompasses the directives for human experimentation and voluntary consent. The Belmont Report summarizes the basic ethical principles and guidelines for research involving human subjects. The Declaration of Helsinki is an ethical principle to guide physicians and other medical personnel regarding human subject medical research. GCP Guidelines are used as standards for all aspects of clinical trials. The Code of Federal Regulations (Title 21 CFR, Part 50, Subpart B) explains the requirements, eight basic elements, and documentation of informed consent.[20]

Obtaining an informed consent that is voluntarily signed, dated, witnessed by an investigator or designee, and approved by the Institutional Review Board (IRB) from the human research subject is required by law for the subject's protection. It must be obtained before research procedures are performed. The informed consent can be obtained from the subject's legally authorized representative. The informed consent process involves providing the research subject with adequate and understandable study information, including possible risks, and sufficient time and opportunity for discussion (with the investigator or designee and others, such as family, when appropriate), including the opportunity to ask questions for comprehension. If the subject voluntarily chooses to participate, then he must sign the informed consent document. A copy of the document is part of the permanent medical record, and a copy is given to the subject.[21] Chapter 4, Informed Consent, discusses the informed consent process in greater detail.

Frequently found deficiencies or violations involve inadequate informed consent and failures of the health care facility's IRB.

Example 17.19: On June 2, 2001, a healthy 24-year-old female volunteer, in a university asthma study died during the study of acute respiratory distress and lung damage, as reported by the *Bureau of National Affairs, Inc. Health Law Reporter*. Investigators for the Office of Human Research Protection found several violations of research regulations involving the investigators and the university IRB, including inadequate IRB review of protocols and IRB's failure to properly monitor the study conduct. Findings included an inadequate informed consent (in which there were failures to explain possible risks and difficult-to-understand language). There was also failure to seek FDA approval for experimental use of hexamethonium (used in tablet form for hypertension in the 1940s and 1950s; FDA withdrew approval later) and failure to obtain published literature regarding the association of lung damage with hexamethonium. The university study involved inhalation of the drug for the purpose of observing a healthy study participant's lung reaction to the irritant in order to gain more understanding of the mechanisms of asthma. It had not been approved for human use as an inhalant. As a result, all studies at the university were halted for a period of time for an investigation of the university's standards regarding studies. The National Bioethics Advisory Commission recommended establishment of mandatory IRB accreditation to prevent similar future problems.[22–28]

Example 17.20: In early 2001, a proposed class action lawsuit was filed against a cancer research center. Approximately 80 out of 82 enrolled patients allegedly died from treatment complications; 20 deaths were attributable to study treatment. Inadequate informed consent regarding risk information was alleged. The site indicated that the risks were not known upon patient enrollment. Seven causes of action were cited involving failures of the investigator.[29,30]

Serious Adverse Event Reporting

During clinical trial conduct, serious adverse event occurrences (SAEs) are to be reported by the investigator to the sponsor group immediately. The pharmaceutical sponsor must notify the FDA and all participating study investigators in a written IND safety report. SAEs are defined in 21 CFR § 312.32 as:

1. Death
2. A life-threatening adverse drug experience
3. An occurrence that requires or prolongs inpatient hospitalization

4. A congenital anomaly/birth defect
5. A persistent or significant disability/incapacity
6. Important medical events that may jeopardize the patient and may require medical or surgical intervention to prevent one of the outcomes listed in this definition[31]

Current Trends in Pharmaceutical Trial Conduct

The current trend in pharmaceutical research conduct appears to be that pharmaceutical sponsors are increasingly requiring certification of either the clinical research coordinator, also known as the study coordinator, or the principal investigator by an appropriate certifying organization, prior to the approval of the investigator to conduct the trial. The purpose is to increase the likelihood of proper and ethical conduct of clinical trials.

Implications for the LNC

One of the first issues to be considered by the LNC in pharmaceutical liability case reviews is whether or not the patient was involved in a clinical trial with a study drug. If not, then other product liability issues would need to be evaluated, as described below. During medical record review of a case, the LNC may discover a reference to a study someplace within the medical records. This should be researched further for possible areas of liability.

If the patient was involved in a clinical trial of a study drug, the LNC should look for a clinical trial consent form document found within the medical records. If not found, the LNC should search for evidence within the medical records that the patient was involved in a clinical trial with a study drug: Is that consent form signed, dated, and witnessed? Is it signed by the patient or the patient's legal representative? The consent form would need to be closely evaluated for all the required elements as regulated by law. All study-related documents would need to be requested, reviewed, and evaluated for compliance with the FDA Code of Federal Regulations. The study documents include, but are not limited to, study patient source documents, informed consent, IRB documents, and the study protocol. The LNC should evaluate relevance of any changes in the patient's health status, or the occurrence of medical problems, termed adverse events, that were reported by the study subject or noted by study personnel.

Other areas to consider for review are possible protocol violations regarding enrollment of an ineligible subject and fraudulent activity of the investigator.

Example 17.21: In 1998, the U.S. District Court for the Central District of California sentenced a California physician to 15 months in prison for providing falsified data in the conduct of pharmaceutical clinical studies, as president and principal investigator of a research center. It was determined that his falsifications, which included fabricating nonexistent study patients, were motivated by greed.[32]

Medical Devices

Medical devices were not subject to extensive FDA regulation until 1976, when the Medical Device Amendments to the Food, Drug, and Cosmetic Act were passed. Before 1976, medical devices could be marketed without review by the FDA. Under the Medical Device Amendments, medical devices have been subject to the regulatory scheme that is similar to that utilized for pharmaceuticals. There are important differences.

The statutory definition of a medical device is all-encompassing. Essentially, any item promoted for a medical purpose that does not rely on chemical action to achieve its intended effect is considered to be a medical device. *In vitro* diagnostic tests are also regulated as medical devices. Unlike the regulation of new drugs, in which standards of safety and effectiveness are applied uniformly, the regulation of medical devices is based on risk. Securing FDA approval of a new medical device before marketing requires that the manufacturer provide reasonable assurance that the device is safe and effective when used for the purpose for which the approval is sought. Safety and effectiveness are assessed with specific reference to the uses for which the device is intended, as set forth in the labeling on the device. Safety is evaluated by weighing the probable benefits to health against the probable risks of injury. The risk/benefit ratio must be acceptable, but proof that the product will never cause harm or will always be effective is not required.

There are three different regulatory classes for medical devices. Only devices classified as "Class III" undergo the strict scrutiny of a premarketing approval (PMA) process. This class is reserved for devices deemed critical, such as heart valves, that are implanted within the body or whose failure would be life-threatening. Class II devices do not undergo the PMA process but are subject to special controls, which usually take the form of additional quality control requirements imposed during the manufacturing process. Manufacturers of devices classified as Class I need only comply with good manufacturing practices in the manufacture of such products. Most medical devices are not subject to FDA scrutiny, in sharp contrast to pharmaceuticals, all of which pass through the detailed approval process.[31]

FDA's Spontaneous Reporting System

In order to document adverse effects not readily or reliably uncovered by clinical trials, federal regulations require adverse drug reaction reporting to the FDA. The central focus of the regulations, which are directed to drug manufacturers, is the timely collection, analysis, and reporting of the adverse drug reaction data to the FDA. An adverse drug reaction is defined in the regulations as any adverse event associated with the use of a drug, whether or not it is considered drug-related. Regulations require that a manufacturer submit a report to the FDA within 15 days of learning of any serious event, death, or hospitalization. Compliance with these regulations will constitute important evidence for a manufacturer in the course of a product liability suit and may be a key element in avoiding liability.[31]

Once adverse events are known to occur in association with specific products, combination of products, or specific diseases, the drug may be taken off the market or recalled either at the request of the FDA or voluntarily by the pharmaceutical manufacturer. A few drugs have been taken off the market by their manufacturers after intense media attention based on anecdotal reporting. Examples of recent product recalls include Fen-Phen, Redux, Baycol, PPA (phenylpropanolamine), Propulsid, and Rezulin. Examples of medical devices recently taken off the market are the Sulzer hip implant, Ortho Summit Processor Instrument used for screening infectious diseases in human blood, and Baxter dialyzers.

The FDA's Spontaneous Reporting System of adverse drug reactions (ADRs) plays an important role in the litigation process. Physician reports, which are the mainstay of the system, are voluntarily made mainly to manufacturers, who are required by regulation to summarize and forward the data to the FDA in a timely manner. Some physicians report ADRs directly to the FDA, as do some pharmacists, patients, nurses, and others. Any death or hospitalization associated with the use of a vaccine must be reported directly to the FDA by a physician. This is the only type of product for which physicians are legally responsible to report an ADR. The burden of reporting ADRs for nonprescription drugs falls on the consumers.

Meeting the standard of the reasonably prudent manufacturer with respect to ADR reporting requires a considerably greater allocation of resources today than it did in the past. The obligation to analyze and categorize each ADR report to ensure timely and appropriate reporting falls, for the most part, on the manufacturer. The manufacturer is responsible for analyzing adverse reaction reports from multiple sources, including foreign and domestic reports, commercial marketing experiences, postmarketing clinical evaluations, postmarketing epidemiological surveillance studies, scientific and medical literature, and unpublished manuscripts.

While an efficient compilation of ADR reports is necessary to meet the regulatory requirements, these same documents may provide the plaintiff with important evidence regarding when the manufacturer became aware of the risk in question. A crucial element in the drug manufacturer's litigation control program is the establishment of procedures for timely internal investigations of ADR reports from the moment the data are first received. The drug company that is compliant with the regulations and has excellent documentation will have a better inherent defense in a product liability suit.

Since the manufacturer is responsible for keeping abreast of all written articles or letters to the editor reporting observed adverse effects of its product, the plaintiff should certainly address the issue regarding the length of time between the first reports in the medical literature and when the product label was changed to include an adverse reaction. The plaintiff can then follow the paper trail from the manufacturer, including, for example, the date on which a "Dear Doctor" letter was sent to notify prescribing physicians of reported serious side effects, as well as when the product-detailing literature changed to reflect the inclusion of the side effect. The Spontaneous Reporting System of the FDA is no guarantee of drug safety; it serves public health as an early warning system to monitor possible drug risk. In fact, it may be the most efficient and the only affordable method of detecting serious clinical events that occur less frequently than 1 in 10,000 drug exposures.

There are contributions and limitations to the adverse drug event reporting system. One contribution is that a "signal" is generated from the field of clinical use as to unacceptable, even rare, drug toxicities. The limitations are many, including reports laden with opinion, overreporting, misinterpretation, and underreporting. The most serious drawback to the system is the rate of underreporting. In several studies, a physician's perceived legal liability correlated with his unwillingness to report adverse reactions. The reporting may be biased and cluttered with events that are not attributable to the drug, causing false negatives and false positives in the system. Thus, the system must not be used for calculation of specific rates of adverse reactions. Only with proper epidemiological studies, where biases can be detected, can the true rates of adverse reactions and the nature of the causation of those reactions be appropriately determined.

In June 1993, the FDA instituted a new adverse event reporting system called MEDWatch, the FDA Medical Products Reporting Program, to ensure that health providers identify and report adverse events (see Appendices 17.1 and 17.2). The premise for emphasizing the health care provider's responsibility in reporting is that only by the reporting of events to the FDA or drug manufacturer can the FDA ensure the safety of drugs and biological and medical devices. Even the large clinical trials of a new drug may study only several thousand persons. If an adverse event occurs for 1 in 1000 users, these trials may miss identifying a potentially harmful side effect. Only when the drug is released to the mass market and hundreds of thousands are using the product will a large number of incidences of the potentially harmful side effect be detected. Additionally, when the drug is taken with other medications or OTC products, interactions may occur that were not previously identified in the limited study populations of the clinical trials.[33,34]

The MEDWatch system was developed to make it easier for health care provider, including doctors, nurses, and pharmacists, to report to the FDA serious events, which are defined as death, risk of death, hospitalization, significant disability, congenital anomaly, or events requiring intervention to prevent impairment or damage. Under this system the FDA should also be notified about medical device problems, such as defects, inaccurate or illegible product labels, package or product mix-ups, drug contamination, or drug stability problems. In the past, the notification of adverse reactions has resulted in critical FDA action on several occasions. It is hoped that MEDWatch will increase the ease of reporting, resulting in higher numbers of reports for the FDA to analyze. LNCs can review current and past information for medications and medical devices from MEDWatch by accessing the FDA Web site and selecting the link to MEDWatch, http://www.fda.gov.cder/.

Example 17.22: FDA examination of accumulated adverse drug reports from physicians led to the determination that *torsade de pointes* ventricular arrhythmias could occur when terfenadine (Seldane) was concomitantly taken with ketocon-azole, an antifungal agent, or erythromycin, an antibiotic. Also, in 1992, a box warning was added to all angiotensin-converting enzyme inhibitor labels as a result of accumulated adverse drug reports to alert physicians to use caution with these drugs in patients in their second and third trimesters of pregnancy.

The LNC's Role in Case Analysis

Rule Out Medical Negligence

The LNC has a large role in working on the pharmaceutical and medical device litigation team. The first and foremost responsibility of the nurse consultant when evaluating a medical product liability claim is to examine the standard of care practiced by the medical practitioner who prescribed the drug or medical device. If the health care practitioner has not prescribed the drug or used the device in accordance with the manufacturer's recommendations, common sense would dictate that the manufacturer might not be held liable for any injury that occurred as a result of the use. Findings of medical malpractice may shift liability in part or completely to the health care practitioner. Review of the plaintiff's medical records will be helpful in establishing clear causation and should be examined to confirm whether there is misdiagnosis, below-standard medical treatment, or inadequate follow-up by any of the health care providers. In previous years, drug manufacturers marketed almost exclusively to health care professionals. A large allocation of advertising dollars is now spent marketing to consumers. The ever-increasing number of prescriptions filled is proof that this type of marketing is successful. The downside of the equation is that less informed physicians coupled with greater pressure from patients who desire more control of their own health care equals a new arena of prescribing errors.

Develop the Plaintiff's Medical History

The LNC must also obtain and thoroughly review all the records pertaining to the plaintiff. This includes medical, mental health, employment, education, criminal, and military records. The LNC should be aware that it is sometimes difficult to recognize drug-induced illness in a person who has multiple coexisting illnesses, such that the appearance of a drug-induced symptom may be difficult to distinguish from the plaintiff's preexisting problems or conditions.

Example 17.23: For many years, Parlodel, manufactured by Bristol-Myers Squibb, was prescribed for lactation suppression in the postpartum period. Plaintiffs in recent litigation have alleged an unacceptably high incidence of hypertensive crises and cerebrovascular accidents (CVAs) in women who take this drug in the first 7 to 10 days postpartum. (In 1994, the FDA required Bristol-Myers to withdraw its labeling regarding use of lactation suppression.) It is essential that the LNC working on such a case elicit all information regarding risk for stroke. The patient may have a strong family history of hypertension, or she may have had pregnancy-induced hypertension or preeclampsia in the prenatal or postpartum period. Alternatively, she may be a smoker, may have had a postpartum clotting disorder, or may have had a preexisting aneurysm. Additionally, the LNC must be able to document the purchase and ingestion of the drug during the postpartum period and the medical history leading to the CVA.

It is imperative that the LNC fully delineate the plaintiff's pharmaceutical history. The history will identify possible drug–drug interactions, contraindications for prescribing the drug in question, prior use of the alleged drug or a drug in the same family without injury, or "physician-hopping" and obtaining multiple prescriptions resulting in overusage. Also, the LNC should not overlook references to alcohol in the review, as alcohol can potentiate or interact with some drugs.

In alleged negligence matters, the plaintiff is bound to the statute of limitations, or the period of time within which the plaintiff must initiate an action against the defendant. First, the LNC must know the statute of limitations for the product liability cases in the state where the matter has been filed. Second, the LNC must review the medical records, cross-checking the dates of the prescriptions, product use, or device implantation and failure against the date on which the suit was filed to ensure that it falls within the statute of limitations.

A sample product liability narrative report is found in Appendix 17.3. Each law firm may have specific requirements for the type of medical information placed in the format. The sample summary shows the relationship of medical facts, provides a condensed analysis of the medical facts of the case, highlights crucial medical information, references the medical records, identifies additional information needed, and recommends physician experts for the case. If the law firm requires a more detailed analysis of the medical records, a detailed chronology with analysis would be submitted.

Identify Possible Third-Party Counterclaims

A counterclaim is a separate cause of action that a defendant asserts against a third person or party. In the answer to the plaintiff's petition, defendants may allege a separate claim against the third party they believe is at fault in the matter. If an orthopedic surgeon purposefully bends a metallic plate to make it conform with the patient's spine and the plate subsequently fractures, the plate manufacturer may counterclaim for improper use of the device against the orthopedic surgeon, if he is not already a defendant in the case. The plate manufacturer would state in its counterclaim that any negligence found by the judge or jury occurred as a result of the orthopedic surgeon's actions.

Establish Clear Causation

It is also important that the LNC make the causal link between the injury and the drug or device therapy. The medication in question must be shown to be the active cause that sets in motion a chain of events that brings about a result without the intervention of any other source. The plaintiff's LNC should utilize the medical records to show that the drug given or device used caused the ensuing injury and should exclude other contributing events or conditions. Causation can be formulated by the "but for" rule, which states that one event is a cause of another when the second event would not have occurred but for the first event.

Example 17.24: A patient has been found to have heart rhythm abnormalities and died as a result. If the plaintiff can show that he was not taking any other drug but Propulsid (Janssen Pharmaceutica) and had no other history of cardiac arrhythmias, the plaintiff could easily prove that but for the consumption of Propulsid, no cardiac arrhythmia would have occurred and the patient would not have died.

The LNC may find it difficult to prove clearly that one drug caused the symptoms/illness alleged in the suit. This is even more challenging when the drug-induced illness mimics the very condition for which the medication is prescribed.

Example 17.25: Many antiarrhythmics, such as quinidine and Procainamide, have the well-known property of generating arrhythmias in certain doses in some patients. Instead of decreasing the frequency of cardiac irregularities, the drugs may actually make them worse. Another paradoxical side effect is akathisia, or restlessness and an inability to sit down or be still, associated with many antipsychotic drugs. As restless behavior is often a clinical symptom of psychoses, there may be a failure to recognize this adverse reaction as a drug event associated with antipsychotic medication.

Research for Discovery

The LNC must perform thorough medical literature searches concerning the product prior to and during discovery. Before beginning this task, the LNC must know about the complete circumstances of the use of the drug or device, including the indications for the product and patient outcome.

The LNC involved in pharmaceutical litigation will find that the drug or device label in the case will be the most-referred-to exhibit during the discovery and trial process. The LNC should be intimately familiar with this document and any changes made in it from year to year. Most important, the LNC should review the warnings for the year or time period in which the medication or device was prescribed. The LNC should review not only the package insert, but the language and content of the advertisements published by the drug company.

Since the early 1970s, the National Library of Medicine (NLM) has made searching the biomedical literature faster and easier by providing online information retrieval on the Medical Literature Analysis and Retrieval System (MEDLARS) family of databases. MEDLINE is the NLM premier database, having more than 7 million citations of biomedical articles. The LNC should execute a computer online search, using a service such as MEDLINE, ensuring that the drug and similar drugs are cross-searched with the resultant injury and similar injuries. For instance, instead of simply checking whether a particular suspect drug causes cardiomyopathy, the LNC should research the entire family of drugs and their association with cardiac effects, not just cardiomyopathy. Thorough research of the scientific literature has tremendous benefit to both case development and case strategy. The LNC must discover everything, both positive and negative, for a full understanding of the plaintiff's theories and defense positions in the case. A search engine may be useful in finding Web sites with references to specific drugs. Sometimes the LNC will be able to identify law firms seeking clients who have been allegedly injured by a product, consumer Web sites, and the manufacturer's Web site. All may contain useful information about the issues involved.

Research material can be crucial in establishing exactly what the manufacturer knew or should have known and when that knowledge was or should have been acquired. Additionally, pinpointing this information can be essential in determining when certain data were known by medical researchers and experts in the field. The literature can be used to establish "duty," as the manufacturer has a duty to keep up with current information about the product in the medical literature. All information should be indexed and catalogued for use during discovery.

Obtain Adverse Reaction and Medical Device Reports

As mentioned previously, adverse effects of drugs and devices are reported properly in the postmarketing surveillance period of a particular product or device. The MDRs and ADRs are requested by the FDA when an injury is linked to a medical product, drug, or device. Under the FOIA, every citizen is entitled to request this information from the FDA. LNCs may want to exercise their right under the FOIA and write to the FDA requesting information regarding ADRs or MDRs for a particular drug or device.

To make an FOIA request, write: Freedom of Information Staff, HFI-35, FDA, Room 12A-16, 5600 Fishers Lane, Rockville, MD 20857. FOIA searches can be fruitful, although it often takes a long time to receive a response. If the drug has not been approved and is still investigational, the FDA will not give out information regarding the drug, and the LNC will have to rely on medical literature and computer databases.

In response to an FOIA request, the LNC may receive a literal copy of the FDA's computerized tabulations of the various adverse reports for the requested drug or device. (Older data are not organized or computerized, but may be sent in an unorganized state.) Specific requests can be made for edited (confidential patient information removed) copies of the actual reports themselves. These reports are often impossible to validate, and the adverse effects can be a result of excessive doses or too frequent use of the drug. Through FOIA responses, some plaintiffs have identified extremely compelling reports of a drug's association with similar symptoms as those alleged in their claims. The LNC should remember that these reports do not represent cause and effect, and the plaintiff cannot prove his case with adverse reaction reports.

Identify Epidemiological Studies and Epidemiologists

The final outcome of a pharmaceutical product liability case can depend on the court's acceptance or rejection of epidemiology evidence. Epidemiology is the study of disease in people, and epidemiologists are educated specialists in the science of defining and explaining the various factors that determine the frequency and distribution of disease.[35] For example, epidemiological studies have been pivotal in identifying the causal relationship between smoking and lung cancer.

To provide meaningful conclusions, the epidemiology study must meet certain criteria of scientific method to avoid bias and error. The epidemiology expert can speak to the reliability of these studies and validate whether or not the study can demonstrate cause and effect. The data considered by the epidemiologist in a product liability lawsuit include epidemiology studies that show statistically significant evidence that the plaintiff is a member of the group that has been exposed to a drug or toxin at the required level and duration to cause an adverse effect. The epidemiology expert is able to show the interrelationship between scientific information, including laboratory, clinical, and experimental studies, and the plaintiff's alleged injuries. In any drug or device product liability case, the plaintiff has to prove that the product could cause the alleged injury and did cause the injury in the particular matter. Since the courts have recognized that epidemiology studies provide evidence on both sides of these issues, the LNC should ensure that the enlisted experts have knowledge of the strengths and weaknesses of the epidemiology data pertinent to the case.

Evaluate All the Evidence to Prove or Disprove the Legal Basis for the Plaintiff's Case

The LNC should review all the available data, including medical and other records concerning the plaintiff, medical literature, drug and device labeling, and adverse reaction and medical device reports, for clues as to the feasibility of the legal basis for the plaintiff's and the defendant's case. The LNC, in conjunction with the attorney, should analyze all the evidence that does or does not support a strict liability or negligence claim against the manufacturer. A checklist might include the following questions:

1. Did the defendant sell the product?
2. When and where was the product manufactured?
3. Did the product reach the user or consumer without substantial change from the condition in which it was sold?
4. When and where was the product consumed or used and for how long?
5. Was the device unreasonably dangerous at the time it was manufactured?
6. Is the product unreasonably unsafe based on the type of warnings given by the manufacturer?
7. Did the manufacturer exercise ordinary care in manufacturing and distributing the product?
8. Does the product have a design or manufacturing defect?
9. Did the defendant know of the danger of the defect in the product at the time it was manufactured or sold?
10. Was there a learned intermediary?
11. Did the learned intermediary use the product correctly?
12. Did the manufacturer adequately warn of the dangers associated with the use of the product in its labeling, package insert, and advertising?
13. When should the manufacturer reasonably have known of the risk of danger and warned of it?
14. Did the manufacturer act reasonably regarding the manner in which the warnings were formulated?
15. Did the manufacturer change its product warnings without undue delay when the information of new risks became available?
16. Is the language used to express the warnings adequate to convey the risk of danger associated with the use of the product?
17. Are the warnings conspicuous and prominent?
18. Are the warnings ambiguous?
19. Was the product excessively promoted?
20. Did the advertising falsely create high expectations on the part of the consumer such that the warnings were disregarded?
21. Have the warnings been changed since the time of the events alleged in the case?
22. What was the basis for the change in the warnings?
23. Have there been any FDA enforcement actions regarding the product? If so, did the manufacturer comply with the FDA enforcement rulings?

The answers to the above questions may not be readily apparent, especially to the plaintiff's LNC prior to filing a lawsuit, but the LNC should keep all of these questions in mind as the lawsuit proceeds since the answers will form the basis for the outcome of the litigation.

Obtain Medical Experts

An additional critical task for the LNC is obtaining qualified medical and technical experts who can explain to the jury not only the medical issues of the case, but also the issues surrounding design and manufacture of a product, development of warnings, epidemiological studies, and, perhaps, marketing. An attempt should be made to utilize experts who have done research, performed clinical trials, or written medical articles regarding the medication or device in question. A review of all generally available scientific literature may assist both in determining the elements of causation and in the identification of potential expert witnesses. The enlisted experts should be extremely familiar with the drug or device and its indications, adverse reactions, metabolism, and method of action. Experts must be able to demonstrate that their testimony has a reliable basis in the knowledge and experience of their own discipline. Experts should be able to cite literature to support their conclusions.

Example 17.26: The defense enlists one of the plaintiff's treating physicians as a defense expert to provide testimony that the plaintiff was diagnosed with the alleged symptoms before the drug in question was ever prescribed. However, on cross-examination by plaintiff's counsel regarding whether or not he utilizes or prescribes the suspect drug, the physician responds negatively. The fact that the expert does not use or prescribe the drug may have a devastating effect on the defense of the case.

Through a series of court rulings, the trial judge has been designated as the gatekeeper for determining the admissibility of expert evidence. The courts are to examine the basis of an expert's opinion to assess its scientific reliability before allowing the evidence to be presented before a jury. The trial judge's role as gatekeeper is to keep out unscientific and speculative testimony in favor of pertinent evidence based on scientifically valid principles. The U.S. Supreme Court has ruled that judges are advised to take into account whether or not expert testimony is based on published data contained in peer-reviewed journals.[36–38]

In *Kumho Tire Co. Ltd. v. Carmichael*, the U.S. Supreme Court expanded the application of the *Daubert* rule. The Court's ruling in *Kumho* determined that the criteria set forth in *Daubert* apply to nonscientific or applied science testimony, also.[39] Although all criteria may not specifically apply to an economist, actuary or accountant, as examples, the judge is still to ensure that testimony is reasonable, credible, and relevant, whatever the discipline. Together the rulings in *Daubert* and *Kumho* challenge "junk science" from entering the courtroom. In 2000, these standards on admission of expert testimony were incorporated into the Federal Rules of Evidence.[40–43] Although the Federal Rules of Evidence do not apply to state courts, the cases are often cited in state court decisions, and more states are electing to follow these guidelines. Either side has the option to challenge whether the named experts are qualified to testify and whether their opinions are based on published scientific data.

It is imperative for the LNC to locate medical experts who can substantiate and support the legal theories of the case. The medical expert's role is primarily that of educating the jury, rather than acting as an advocate for the client. The LNC has a pivotal role in ensuring that prospective experts have completely reviewed the entire records, medical and otherwise, in the matter prior to being designated; that they understand all the issues; and that they feel strongly about their opinions in the case.

Example 17.27: At trial, plaintiff's counsel enters into evidence multiple ADR reports received in response to an FOIA request regarding a toxic side effect not mentioned in the product labeling. The plaintiff would benefit substantially from placing an FDA regulatory expert on the witness stand who could testify that spontaneous reports of adverse experiences in association with pharmaceutical use represent the most potentially powerful signal for early detection of rare but unacceptable drug toxicities.

Conclusion

Due to the complexity of today's world, especially in advanced medical science, much of the current theories driving drug and device suits are based on case law. Although many lawsuits are unique and applying legal theories can be difficult, case law is increasingly important, with precedent-setting cases occurring daily.

When consulting on drug and device product liability matters, the LNC will be challenged to utilize both legal knowledge and medical expertise. The LNC must perform periodic research to remain current and knowledgeable regarding various drugs and devices that fall under the product liability statutes. A complete understanding of manufacturers' responsibilities and regulatory processes is essential to a thorough review of the case. The LNC has the opportunity to be a valuable asset to the litigation team once these are learned and employed in the consulting process.

References

1. *Restatement (Second) of Torts* §402A (1965).
2. *Restatement (Second) of Torts* §402A, cmt. k (1965).
3. MacNeill, M., Pharmaceutical product liability, in *Legal Medicine*, 3rd ed., Sanbar, S. et al., Eds., Mosby-Year Book, St. Louis, 1995, 170.
4. National Childhood Vaccine Injury Act, Pub. L. 99–660, 100 Stat. 3755.
5. *Shalala v. Whitecotton*, 514 U.S. 268 (1995).
6. Sloan, M., *DiRosa v. Showa Denko, Network*, 5, 6, 1994.
7. *Physicians' Desk Reference*, 55th ed., Medical Economics Company, Inc., Montvale, NJ, 2001.
8. Shulman, S. and Ulcickas, B., Update on ADR reporting regulations: products liability implications, *Journal of Clinical Research and Drug Development*, 3(2), 91, 1989.
9. *Wooderson v. Ortho Pharmaceutical Corp.*, 681 P.2d 1038, 1051 (Kan. 1984).
10. 21 U.S.C. §321 (1982).
11. 21 C.F.R. §§201.56, 201.57 (1988).
12. *MacDonald v. Ortho Pharmaceutical Corp.*, 475 N.E.2d 65, 71 (Mass. 1985).
13. *Wells v. Ortho Pharmaceutical Corp.*, 615 F. Supp 262 (N.D. Ga. 1985).
14. Food, Drug and Cosmetic Act of 1938, Ch. 675, Pub. L. 75–717, 52 Stat. 1040. Drug Amendments of 1962, 102, Pub. L. 87–871, 76 Stat. 781.
15. 21 U.S.C. §360c, d, e, & i (1982).
16. Inman, W.H.W., *Monitoring Drug Safety*, Lippincott, Philadelphia, 1980.

17. Avorn, J., Detection and prevention of drug-induced illness, *Journal of Clinical Research and Drug Development*, 3, 5, 1989.
18. Toxic rx: prescription for error, *MTI Review*, 3, 9, 1998.
19. Dukes, M. and Swartz, G., *Responsibility for Drug Induced Injury*, Elsevier Science Publishers, Amsterdam, 1988.
20. Code of Federal Regulations, Title 21, Part 50.25, U.S. Food and Drug Administration, U.S. Government Printing Office, Washington, D.C., 2000.
21. Code of Federal Regulations, Title 21, Part 50.20, Part 50.27, U.S. Food and Drug Administration, U.S. Government Printing Office, Washington, D.C., 2000.
22. Department of Health and Human Services, Office of Human Research Protection (determination letter), July 19, 2001, http://ohrp.osophs.dhhs.gov/detrm_letrs, retrieved January 28, 2002.
23. Medical research: bioethics group says its new standards could have prevented Hopkins study death, *BNA's Health Law Reporter*, Biomedical Ethics, Washington, D.C., September 20, 2001.
24. Medical research: temporary halt of Hopkins research shows need for human study accreditation, *BNA's Health Law Reporter*, lead report, Washington, D.C., 2001.
25. Medical research: Feds halt Johns Hopkins experiments, but new safeguards may allow resumption, *BNA's Health Care Daily Report*, News Executive Briefing, Washington, D.C., 2001.
26. MSNBC Staff and Wire Reports, Hopkins to resume federal clinical trials, http://www.msnbc.com, retrieved July 23, 2001.
27. Verango, D., U.S. suspends research aid to Johns Hopkins, *USA Today*, http://www.usatoday.com, retrieved July 20, 2001.
28. FDA Information Sheets for Institutional Review Boards and Clinical Investigators, U.S. Food and Drug Administration, 1995.
29. PharmSource Information Services, Inc., Class action suit against Fred Hutchinson Cancer Center sends shock waves through clinical trials community, *Clinical Trials Advisor*, 6, 2001, retrieved from http://www.clinicaltrialsadvisor.com.
30. Wilson, W. and Heath, D., Class-action suit filed against 'The Hutch,' *The Seattle Times*, March 27, 2001, http://www.seattletimes.com, retrieved February 9, 2002.
31. Code of Federal Regulations, Title 21, Part 312.32, U.S. Food and Drug Administration, U.S. Government Printing Office, 2000.
32. Nordenberg, T., Physician sentenced for doctoring drug data, *FDA Consumer*, 33(3), 35, 1999.
33. Kessler, D., Introducing MEDWatch: a new approach to reporting medication and device adverse effects and product problems, *Journal of the American Medical Association*, 269, 2765, 1993.
34. Kuc, J., A progress report on the FDA's MEDWatch, *Journal of Legal Nurse Consulting*, 6, 5, 1995.
35. Hallberg, M., The use of epidemiological studies and epidemiologists in proving or disproving causation, *Network*, 5(1), 19, 1995.
36. *Daubert v. Merrell Dow Pharmaceuticals, Inc.*, 509 U.S. 579 (1993).
37. Annas, G., Scientific evidence in the courtroom: the death of the *Frye* rule, *New England Journal of Medicine*, 330, 1018, 1994.
38. Oldknow, P.F., *Daubert*, the scientific method, and the legal nurse consultant, *Journal of Legal Nurse Consulting*, 12, 3, 2001.
39. *Kumho Tire Co., Ltd. v. Carmichael*, 526 U.S. 137, 1999.
40. FED. R. EVID. 702.
41. FED. R. EVID. 702, Supp., 2000.
42. FED. R. EVID. 703.
43. FED. R. EVID. 703, Supp., 2000.

Additional Reading

F-D-C Reports: Current information on the worldwide health care industry.

Federal Register and *Federal Register Abstracts*: Daily publication of the U.S. government providing notification of official agency actions, regulations, proposed rules, and legal notices, such as when the FDA requests that a drug company change its warning.

Health Devices Alert: Reports problems with diagnostic and therapeutic medical and implanted equipment.

Health Devices Sourcebook: Current information regarding diagnostics and therapeutic medical devices.

Pharmaceutical News Index: Current news about drugs and medical devices.

Additionally, the following recommended trade journals may provide beneficial information:

Devices and Diagnostics Letter (weekly) and *Clinica: World Medical Device & Diagnostic News* (weekly): updates on what is new in research and development, legislation, and recalls of drugs and devices.

Pharmaceutical Litigation Reporter (monthly): summaries of the latest verdicts in pharmaceutical litigation.

The following Web sites are recommended for additional information regarding product liability and are not meant to be inclusive of all possible Web sites:

http://classaction.findlaw.com/: Provides information from the FindLaw Class Action and Mass Tort Center.

http://ohrp.osophs.dhhs.gov/index.htm: Provides information from the Office for Human Research Protection.

http://ohsr.od.nih.gov/: Provides information from the Office of Human Subjects Research.

http://www.fda.gov: Provides information from the Food and Drug Administration regarding current drug and product liability, links to MEDWatch.

http://www.law.cornell.edu/topics/products_liability.html: Provides information regarding product liability from the Legal Information Institute.

http://www.productslaw.com: Provides pertinent and up-to-date information regarding product liability and gives links to relevant Web sites.

http://www.usdoj.gov/04foia: Provides information from the United States Department of Justice regarding the Freedom of Information Act.

Test Questions

1. The plaintiff must prove all of the following in a strict liability cause of action EXCEPT:
    A. The defendant sold the product that was defective.
    B. The product was the proximate cause of the plaintiff's injuries.
    C. The plaintiff has damages.
    D. The user made a mistake in the use of the product.

2. The drug manufacturer's duty to warn:
    A. Expires when the product is placed on the market.
    B. Obliges the manufacturer to seek out information regarding its product.
    C. Is not required until a causal relationship between the drug and adverse effect is proved.
    D. Can wait until a statistically significant number of people have been injured.

3. As a result of the Food and Drug Administration's regulatory process, when the average drug is marketed, consumers have a reasonable expectation that serious side effects are unlikely when the drug is used EXCEPT:
    A. For its approved indication
    B. Above the recommended dose
    C. For limited periods
    D. In medically uncomplicated, nonpregnant, compliant, young to middle-aged adults

4. The accuracy and reliability of the scientific evidence presented in the courtroom is the responsibility of the:
    A. Jury
    B. Attorneys representing each side
    C. Judge
    D. Product manufacturer

5. An informed consent form is signed and dated by the participant:
    A. Before any study procedures are performed
    B. At the end of the study
    C. Before the Institutional Review Board provides final approval
    D. When the study drug is administered

Answers: 1. D, 2. B, 3. B, 4. C, 5. A

Appendix 17.1
FDA MEDWatch Form for Voluntary Reporting of Adverse Events and Product Problems by Health Professionals

MED**W**ATCH
THE FDA MEDICAL PRODUCTS REPORTING PROGRAM

For VOLUNTARY reporting
by health professionals of adverse
events and product problems

Page ____ of ____

Form Approved: OMB No. 0910-0291 Expires:12/31/94
See OMB statement on reverse

FDA Use Only

Triage unit
sequence #

A. Patient information

1. Patient identifier	2. Age at time of event: or Date of birth:	3. Sex ☐ female ☐ male	4. Weight ____ lbs or ____ kgs

In confidence

B. Adverse event or product problem

1. ☐ Adverse event and/or ☐ Product problem (e.g., defects/malfunctions)

2. Outcomes attributed to adverse event (check all that apply)
- ☐ death ____ (mo/day/yr)
- ☐ life-threatening
- ☐ hospitalization – initial or prolonged
- ☐ disability
- ☐ congenital anomaly
- ☐ required intervention to prevent permanent impairment/damage
- ☐ other: ____

3. Date of event (mo/day/yr)	4. Date of this report (mo/day/yr)

5. Describe event or problem

6. Relevant tests/laboratory data, including dates

7. Other relevant history, including preexisting medical conditions (e.g., allergies, race, pregnancy, smoking and alcohol use, hepatic/renal dysfunction, etc.)

C. Suspect medication(s)

1. Name (give labeled strength & mfr/labeler, if known)
#1
#2

2. Dose, frequency & route used	3. Therapy dates (if unknown, give duration) from/to (or best estimate)
#1	#1
#2	#2

4. Diagnosis for use (indication)
#1
#2

5. Event abated after use stopped or dose reduced
#1 ☐ yes ☐ no ☐ doesn't apply
#2 ☐ yes ☐ no ☐ doesn't apply

6. Lot # (if known)	7. Exp. date (if known)
#1	#1
#2	#2

8. Event reappeared after reintroduction
#1 ☐ yes ☐ no ☐ doesn't apply
#2 ☐ yes ☐ no ☐ doesn't apply

9. NDC # (for product problems) –

10. Concomitant medical products and therapy dates (exclude treatment of event)

Suspect medical device

1. Brand name

2. Type of device

3. Manufacturer name & address

4. Operator of device
- ☐ health professional
- ☐ lay user/patient
- ☐ other: ____

5. Expiration date (mo/day/yr)

6.
model # ____
catalog # ____
serial # ____
lot # ____
other #

7. If implanted, give date (mo/day/yr)

8. If explanted, give date (mo/day/yr)

9. Device available for evaluation? (Do not send to FDA)
☐ yes ☐ no ☐ returned to manufacturer on ____ (mo/day/yr)

10. Concomitant medical products and therapy dates (exclude treatment of event)

E. Reporter (see confidentiality section on back)

1. Name, address & phone #

2. Health professional? ☐ yes ☐ no
3. Occupation
4. Also reported to
- ☐ manufacturer
- ☐ user facility
- ☐ distributor

5. If you do NOT want your identity disclosed to the manufacturer, place an " X " in this box. ☐

FDA Mail to: MEDWATCH
5600 Fishers Lane
Rockville, MD 20852-9787
or FAX to: 1-800-FDA-0178

FDA Form 3500 (6/93)   Submission of a report does not constitute an admission that medical personnel or the product caused or contributed to the event.

SAMPLE

ADVICE ABOUT VOLUNTARY REPORTING

Report experiences with:

- medications (drugs or biologics)
- medical devices (including in-vitro diagnostics)
- special nutritional products (dietary supplements, medical foods, infant formulas)
- other products regulated by FDA

Report SERIOUS adverse events. An event is serious when the patient outcome is:

- death
- life-threatening (real risk of dying)
- hospitalization (initial or prolonged)
- disability (significant, persistent or permanent)
- congenital anomaly
- required intervention to prevent permanent impairment or damage

Report even if:

- you're not certain the product caused the event
- you don't have all the details

Report product problems – quality, performance or safety concerns such as:

- suspected contamination
- questionable stability
- defective components
- poor packaging or labeling

How to report:

- just fill in the sections that apply to your report
- use section C for all products except medical devices
- attach additional blank pages if needed
- use a separate form for each patient
- report either to FDA or the manufacturer (or both)

Important numbers:

- 1-800-FDA-0178   to FAX report
- 1-800-FDA-7737   to report by modem
- 1-800-FDA-1088   for more information or to report quality problems
- 1-800-822-7967   for a VAERS form for vaccines

If your report involves a serious adverse event with a device and it occurred in a facility outside a doctor's office, that facility may be legally required to report to FDA and/or the manufacturer. Please notify the person in that facility who would handle such reporting.

Confidentiality: The patient's identity is held in strict confidence by FDA and protected to the fullest extent of the law. The reporter's identity may be shared with the manufacturer unless requested otherwise. However, FDA will not disclose the reporter's identity in response to a request from the public, pursuant to the Freedom of Information Act.

The public reporting burden for this collection of information has been estimated to average 30 minutes per response, including the time for reviewing instructions, searching existing data sources, gathering and maintaining the data needed, and completing and reviewing the collection of information. Send your comments regarding this burden estimate or any other aspect of this collection of information, including suggestions for reducing this burden to:

Reports Clearance Officer, PHS
Hubert H. Humphrey Building,
Room 721-B
200 Independence Avenue, S.W.
Washington, DC 20201
ATTN: PRA

and to:
Office of Management and
Budget
Paperwork Reduction Project
(0910-0230)
Washington, DC 20503

Please do NOT
return this form
to either of these
addresses.

FDA Form 3500-back   **Please Use Address Provided Below – Just Fold In Thirds, Tape and Mail**

**Department of
Health and Human Services**

Public Health Service
Food and Drug Administration
Rockville, MD 20857

Official Business
Penalty for Private Use $300

NO POSTAGE
NECESSARY
IF MAILED
IN THE
UNITED STATES
OR APO/FPO

BUSINESS REPLY MAIL
FIRST CLASS MAIL   PERMIT NO. 946   ROCKVILLE, MD

POSTAGE WILL BE PAID BY FOOD AND DRUG ADMINISTRATION

MED**W**ATCH
The FDA Medical Products Reporting Program
Food and Drug Administration
5600 Fishers Lane
Rockville, MD 20852-9787

Appendix 17.2
FDA MEDWatch Form for Mandatory Reporting of Adverse Events and Product Problems by User Facilities, Distributors, and Manufacturers

Form Approved: OMB No. 0910-0291 Expires: 12/31/04
See OMB statement on reverse

Mfr report #

UF/Dist report #

FDA Use Only

MEDWATCH
THE FDA MEDICAL PRODUCTS REPORTING PROGRAM

For use by user-facilities, distributors and manufacturers for MANDATORY reporting

Page _____ of _____

A. Patient information

1. Patient identifier   2. Age at time of event:

or _____

Date of birth:

In confidence

3. Sex
☐ female
☐ male

4. Weight
_____ lbs
or
_____ kgs

B. Adverse event or product problem

1. ☐ Adverse event   and/or   ☐ Product problem (e.g., defects/malfunctions)

2. Outcomes attributed to adverse event (check all that apply)
☐ death _____ (mo/day/yr)
☐ life-threatening
☐ hospitalization – initial or prolonged
☐ disability
☐ congenital anomaly
☐ required intervention to prevent permanent impairment/damage
☐ other: _____

3. Date of event (mo/day/yr)

4. Date of this report (mo/day/yr)

5. Describe event or problem

6. Relevant tests/laboratory data, including dates

7. Other relevant history, including preexisting medical conditions (e.g., allergies, race, pregnancy, smoking and alcohol use, hepatic/renal dysfunction, etc.)

C. Suspect medication(s)

1. Name (give labeled strength & mfr/labeler, if known)
#1 _____
#2 _____

2. Dose, frequency & route used
#1
#2

3. Therapy dates (if unknown, give duration) from/to (or best estimate)
#1
#2

4. Diagnosis for use (indication)
#1
#2

5. Event abated after use stopped or dose reduced
#1 ☐ yes ☐ no ☐ doesn't apply
#2 ☐ yes ☐ no ☐ doesn't apply

6. Lot # (if known)
#1
#2

7. Exp. date (if known)
#1

8. Event reappeared after reintroduction
#1 ☐ yes ☐ no ☐ doesn't apply
#2 ☐ yes ☐ no ☐ doesn't apply

9. NDC # – for product problems only (if known)

10. Concomitant medical products and therapy dates (exclude treatment of event)

D. Suspect medical device

1. Brand name

2. Type of device

3. Manufacturer name & address

4. Operator of device
☐ health professional
☐ lay user/patient
☐ other: _____

5. Expiration date (mo/day/yr)

6. model # _____

7. If implanted, give date (mo/day/yr)

catalog # _____

serial # _____

8. If explanted, give date (mo/day/yr)

lot # _____

other # _____

9. Device available for evaluation?   (Do not send to FDA)
☐ yes ☐ no ☐ returned to manufacturer on _____ (mo/day/yr)

10. Concomitant medical products and therapy dates (exclude treatment of event)

E. Initial reporter

1. Name, address & phone #

2. Health professional?
☐ yes ☐ no

3. Occupation

4. Initial reporter also sent report to FDA
☐ yes ☐ no ☐ unk

FDA

Submission of a report does not constitute an admission that medical personnel, user facility, distributor, manufacturer or product caused or contributed to the event.

FDA Form 3500A (6/93)

SAMPLE

Medication and Device Experience Report
(continued)

Refer to guidelines for specific instructions

Submission of a report does not constitute an admission that medical personnel, user facility, distributor, manufacturer or product caused or contributed to the event.

Page ____ of ____

U.S. DEPARTMENT OF HEALTH AND HUMAN SERVICES
Public Health Service • Food and Drug Administration

FDA Use Only

F. For use by user facility/distributor–devices only

1. Check one
☐ user facility   ☐ distributor

2. UF/Dist report number

3. User facility or distributor name/address

4. Contact person

5. Phone Number

6. Date user facility or distributor became aware of event (mo/day/yr)

7. Type of report
☐ initial
☐ follow-up # ____

8. Date of this report (mo/day/yr)

9. Approximate age of device

10. Event problem codes (refer to coding manual)
patient code ____ – ____ – ____
device code ____ – ____ – ____

11. Report sent to FDA?
☐ yes ____ (mo/day/yr)
☐ no

12. Location where event occurred
☐ hospital
☐ home
☐ nursing home
☐ outpatient treatment facility
☐ outpatient diagnostic facility
☐ ambulatory surgical facility
☐ other: ____ specify

13. Report sent to manufacturer?
☐ yes ____ (mo/day/yr)
☐ no

14. Manufacturer name/address

G. All manufacturers

1. Contact office – name/address (& mfring site for devices)

2. Phone number

3. Report source (check all that apply)
☐ foreign
☐ study
☐ literature
☐ consumer
☐ health professional
☐ user facility
☐ company representative
☐ distributor
☐ other: ____

4. Date received by manufacturer (mo/day/yr)

5.
(A)NDA # ____
IND # ____
PLA # ____
pre-1938 ☐ yes
OTC product ☐ yes

6. If IND, protocol #

7. Type of report (check all that apply)
☐ 5-day   ☐ 15-day
☐ 10-day ☐ periodic
☐ Initial ☐ follow-up # ____

8. Adverse event term(s)

9. Mfr. report number

H. Device manufacturers only

1. Type of reportable event
☐ death
☐ serious injury
☐ malfunction (see guidelines)
☐ other: ____

2. If follow-up, what type?
☐ correction
☐ additional information
☐ response to FDA request
☐ device evaluation

3. Device evaluated by mfr?
☐ not returned to mfr.
☐ yes ☐ evaluation summary attached
☐ no (attach page to explain why not) or provide code:

4. Device manufacture date (mo/yr)

5. Labeled for single use?
☐ yes   ☐ no

6. Evaluation codes (refer to coding manual)
method ____ – ____ ____ – ____
results ____ – ____ ____ – ____
conclusions ____ – ____ ____ – ____

7. If remedial action initiated,
☐ recall
☐ notification
☐ inspection
☐ replace
☐ patient monitoring
☐ relabeling
☐ modification/adjustment
☐ other: ____

8. Usage of device
☐ initial use of device
☐ reuse
☐ unknown

9. If action reported to FDA under 21 USC 360i(f), list correction/removal reporting number:

10. ☐ Additional manufacturer narrative   and/or   **11.** ☐ Corrected data

SAMPLE

The public reporting burden for this collection of information has been estimated to average one-hour per response, including the time for reviewing instructions, searching existing data sources, gathering and maintaining the data needed, and completing and reviewing the collection of information. Send your comments regarding this burden estimate or any other aspect of this collection of information, including suggestions for reducing this burden to:

Reports Clearance Officer, PHS
Hubert H. Humphrey Building, Room 721-B
200 Independence Avenue, S.W.
Washington, DC 20201
ATTN: PRA

and to:
Office of Management and Budget
Paperwork Reduction Project (0910-0291)
Washington, DC 20503

Please do NOT return this form to either of these addresses.

FDA Form 3500A - back

Appendix 17.3
Sample Format for Product Liability Narrative Report
(R&G Medical Consultants)

Date

<u>Privileged and Confidential — Attorney Work Product</u>

Firm Name:
Attorney:
Address:
City/State/Zip:

Subject: (Name) Case Number if available
            DOB:
            SS#:
            DOD: (if applicable)
            State (e.g., Texas)

            (Introductory paragraph here)

Case Impressions:

    1.

    2.

    3.

        A. Family History

        B. Other pertinent history

          1)

Preexposure Medical History:

Preexposure Medications:

Summary based on the pharmacy and medical records provided.

Date	Physician	Medication Prescribed	Medication Dispensed

History of Exposure:

Summary based on the pharmacy and medical records provided.

Date	Physician	Medication Prescribed	Medication Dispensed

Total Amount of <Medication> :

Please note that the information provided is based on records available at the time of review.

Records reviewed were: PROVIDERS

Please obtain the following additional records: PROVIDERS

An in-depth medical chronology would provide you with greater detail in this case. Thank you for allowing our firm to assist you with this most unfortunate case.

LNC name & credentials

Chapter 18

Case Analysis: Evaluating Toxic Tort Cases

Jan Smith Clary, BSN, RN, LNCC,
Marva J. Petty, MSN, RN, April Clemens, MSN, RN, and
Kathleen Woods Araiza, BA, RN

CONTENTS

0-8493-1418-6/03/$0.00+$1.50
© 2003 by AALNC

Objectives

- To define the concept of a toxic tort
- To describe the relationship between a claimant's risk factors and exposure history
- To describe the importance of a complete review of medical, educational, social, and occupational records in the preparation of a toxic tort case
- To identify the types of experts that may be required in preparing the toxic tort case
- To identify resources for researching chemical substances

Introduction

Toxic torts are civil actions asserting a demand for recovery of damages where there was an exposure to a chemical substance, emission, or product that allegedly resulted in physical and psychological harm. During the last two decades, the world news has been inundated with stories of toxic tort cases involving thousands of plaintiffs, many of whom allege repeated exposures to one or more toxic substances. Even the occasional news watcher is aware of the Chernobyl radiation leak, complaints of groundwater contamination resulting in spontaneous abortion and birth defects, and asbestos litigation that can last for years. Events such as these have raised public awareness of individual and collective vulnerability to toxic substance exposures in the home, workplace, and global environment.

Toxic tort cases have their origin in product liability litigation, and much of the case law is still found there. A toxic tort case shares many of the properties of other tort cases: negligence theories; causation issues; insurance coverage issues; and the determination of fraudulent, possibly even criminal, behavior of involved parties.

In a toxic tort case, the plaintiff must prove that an injury occurred as the result of an exposure to substances or products. The plaintiff's discovery involves the development of both medical causation issues and scientific proof that the alleged injury or injuries occurred as the result of exposure to the substances or products. Conversely, the defense will attempt to disprove plaintiff's theories. The defense will develop strategies related to the following:

- The exposure was insufficient to result in the alleged damages.
- The substance or product did not cause the alleged injury.
- The alleged condition was incorrectly diagnosed.
- There are other causes for the alleged injury (e.g., familial disorder, preexisting condition, and other unrelated exposures).

The legal nurse consultant (LNC) assisting in a toxic tort case may experience significant anxiety when confronted with reviewing and summarizing voluminous medical records in addition to performing extensive literature searches, analyzing stacks of scientific papers, and deciphering a maze of federal regulations. The key to preparing the case lies in careful strategic planning and maintaining the information in an organized fashion as it is received.

Generally, toxic tort cases center on efforts to prove or disprove the relative safety of one or more chemical substances or products. These cases offer the LNC an exciting opportunity to combine nursing and medical knowledge with research, pure science, and regulatory law. During the preparation of such a case, the LNC may have an opportunity to work with experts in toxicology, industrial hygiene, occupational health, neuropsychology, pulmonology, and other medical specialties.

This chapter is not intended to be an exhaustive work regarding toxic tort litigation, but rather is a general framework for the LNC preparing a toxic tort case for the plaintiff or defense attorney.

Toxic Tort Cases: A Complex Subject

Whether the LNC is working from a plaintiff or defense standpoint, similar procedures will be followed in developing the case. The first step is the identification of the type of case. It is not uncommon for a toxic tort case to involve multiple plaintiffs and multiple defendants, each with their attendant attorneys, experts, and consultants. The plaintiffs may allege single or multiple exposures to single or multiple toxic substances.

These types of cases are usually extremely complex, and where possible, the LNC should participate in the early planning processes for managing the case. Without adequate planning and budgeting for file management, data acquisition, and document storage, it becomes nearly impossible to manage the thousands, and even millions, of pages of depositions, opinions, scholarly papers, and medical records that will accrue throughout the life of a case.

Not all toxic tort cases are complex. A single-claimant case may involve an individual exposed to one or more substances in a single (acute) exposure or over a long period of time (chronic). Multilitigant cases typically involve many individuals with similar exposure, but with medical claims differing in type and severity. In some cases involving multiple litigants, attempts may be made for the court to certify a *class action* suit. Class action suits involve multiplaintiff litigation; certain standards established by the court must be met in order for the class to be certified as a class action. Often a representative, or bellwether group, is selected to represent the class.

Learning the Language of the Toxic Tort Case

The LNC must first learn the basic language of this specialized area of litigation before tackling a toxic tort case. This language deals with how the exposure occurred, how it is measured, the acronyms of measurement, and the acronyms for the regulatory agencies. Appendix 18.1 lists and defines the basic terms used in describing how an exposure is measured.[1]

Often in the early stages of a case, only a portion of the chemicals or compounds is identified. The discovery process will reveal whether the plaintiff was exposed to a single chemical, a chemical compound, or numerous chemicals and compounds. Recalling previous chemistry courses, the LNC will be reminded that there is an important distinction between a single element and a combination of elements resulting in a compound.

The plaintiffs may allege that injury occurred as the result of synergistic effect between two chemicals in a compound. Such an effect can render two relatively "harmless" chemicals more potent and able to cause dramatic afflictions that the individual chemicals are not known to produce alone. The LNC should work with designated consultants to determine the validity of any such assertion.

Measuring Exposure

The most important determination to be made during the preparation of the case is the confirmation that an exposure occurred. Exposure is measured in terms of the *route* or means of exposure. Discovery will reveal facts whether the plaintiff sustained an exposure by inhalation, oral ingestion, or cutaneous absorption, including ophthalmic exposure.

Once the type of exposure is known, one must look carefully at the *duration* of the exposure. How long was the plaintiff exposed? Various advisory panels and regulatory agencies (see Appendix 18.2) set forth guidelines for safe exposure time to many chemicals and compounds. The LNC will find that most of the experts in the toxic tort cases have a formal association with these advisory bodies.

Not only must one know the duration of the exposure in understanding the event and alleged injuries, one must also know the *frequency* of the exposure. Did the individual experience a single sustained exposure, also known as an acute exposure, or was it an exposure that occurred repeatedly during the day, over the course of weeks or years, or intermittently over an extended period of time, producing a chronic exposure?

When the information regarding the route, frequency, and duration of exposure has been obtained, the LNC can work with toxicologists and industrial hygienists to estimate the dose of the exposure. The process used to quantify the relationship between the level of exposure and increased risk of adverse effects is termed the *dose-response*.[2] It is important to determine whether the plaintiff experienced a sustained or repeated exposure and whether the amount ingested, inhaled, or absorbed was at a minimum or maximum dose.

The Mechanics of Chemical Exposure

In preparing toxic tort cases, consideration must be given to how the exposure actually occurred. The vast majority of toxic tort cases involve inhalation exposure. Many chemicals are absorbed through the lungs. Inhalation exposures are not only limited to gaseous chemicals, such as chlorine, solvents, and isocyanates, but also include particulate matter such as fiberglass, asbestos, animal dander, silica dust, bacterial pathogens, and viral pathogens. Inhalation exposures can occur in the home, workplace, or global environment. Noxious fumes from carpets, glues, and paints are typically found in the home. Environmental exposure cases include tobacco cases, surface and groundwater contamination cases, and *sick-building syndrome*. The term "sick building syndrome" is used to describe the cluster of symptoms found to occur in office environments, particularly in sealed buildings with centrally controlled mechanical ventilation.[3]

In the past few years, it has become evident that inhaled pollutants do not result only in respiratory-related effects. Cardiovascular and systemic effects also occur, especially in persons with preexisting conditions. In some instances, these nonrespiratory health effects may be more important than the respiratory effects.[4] As an example, the solvent benzene, which is found in gasoline, paint removers, and many commercial solvents, is easily inhaled but causes little damage to the respiratory system when inhaled at low doses, even over a long period of time. However, chronic exposure even at low doses can result in hematopoietic system injury. Prior to 1963, it is estimated that several hundred cases of fatal aplastic anemia resulted from chronic benzene exposure.[5]

Inhalation exposures are also alleged to be associated with changes to the immune and nervous systems. It is important to realize that the practice of immunology is relatively new. Many diagnostic immunology tests, which determine *dysfunction* of the immune system, are experimental and may be performed in nonstandard laboratories. Such tests may be considered outside the mainstream of general medical practice, and the LNC should seek reputable professionals, as experts and information sources concerning these tests.

Toxic tort cases involving immune system dysfunction typically include complaints of allergies, hay fever, hives, and asthma. Autoimmune disease has been alleged as a response to a variety of drugs, vaccines, and bacterial toxins. These disorders must be looked at carefully for determination of idiopathic autoimmune diseases such as lupus and scleroderma. While certain immunodeficiencies are congenital, others are acquired, such as radiation sickness and radiation-related cancers. Others occur as the result of exposure to environmental toxins, such as pesticides, nuclear waste, and groundwater contaminants.

Ingestion exposures may occur anywhere. The plaintiff may have accidentally swallowed solvents or other substances in the workplace or at home, or may have ingested unwashed fruits or vegetables contaminated with pesticides or fertilizers. Even handling food or other items with unwashed hands may transmit undesirable substances via ingestion. It may be difficult to quantify the dose of an ingested substance. A toxicologist or pharmacologist may be required to use simulation to calculate how much chemical was ingested and metabolized or excreted unchanged.

Cutaneous exposure results from direct skin contact with a substance. Because of the protective function of the skin, cutaneous exposures may often be limited to local reactions such as irritation, pruritus, and urticaria. The popular press has recently carried stories relating to the purported increase in generalized reactions to dermal exposure to substances such as newsprint, latex, detergents, and other substances commonly found in the home and work environments. Since a chemical may enter the body via skin, hair follicles, sweat glands, and sebaceous glands, particular attention should be paid to determining the preexposure condition of the skin. Was more chemical absorbed because of rashes, cuts, or other skin breaks?

Product Labeling Information

Strict interpretation of exposure guidelines presents other challenges for both the plaintiffs and the defendants. Issues of accurate labeling, storage, proper use of protective equipment and clothing, and the proper disposal of the chemical substance must be examined.

Proper labeling and safe use guidelines are important in cases of chemical exposure. The material safety data sheet (MSDS) describes what is in a compound, any health hazards, fire hazards, first aid, optimal use, storage, and disposal. MSDS forms are found in the home and workplace. Anyone changing a toner cartridge in a printer or copier will find an MSDS in the box. In the workplace, MSDS forms may be found in or on the packaging container. Because the MSDS of a product may change over the years, all the MSDS forms for the relevant time periods are likely to become exhibits in the litigation. The MSDS can also provide a quick reference for delineating changes in exposure guidelines over a period of time.

In 1989, the Occupational Safety and Health Administration (OSHA) set permissible exposure limits (PELs) for nearly 500 hazardous chemicals in the United States. The American Conference of Governmental Industrial Hygienists (ACGIH) is an association composed of occupational health professionals employed by government and educational institutions. The Threshold Limit Value Committee and Ventilation Committee of the ACGIH publish guidelines annually, which are used worldwide. In some cases, the ACGIH exposure limits are lower than the OSHA PELs. When a case involves a workplace exposure, it is important to determine which exposure limits the workplace relied on at the time of the alleged exposure.

The LNC's Role in the Toxic Tort Case

Establishing the Presence or Absence of Causation

Causation requires a relationship between the exposure and the alleged adverse outcome. Generally, plaintiffs have the burden of showing by a "preponderance of the evidence" that the exposure resulted in the injury.[2] However, proving that a toxic substance caused a physical injury is not easy. This requires proving scientific causation. Scientific causation is established using statistical methods to determine a high-confidence or statistically significant relationship between exposure and illness. The illness or injury must be substantiated in the medical and social records, and the substance at issue must be proved to cause the alleged injury. Of utmost importance is careful evaluation for the presence of unrelated disease or other pathological processes.

One of the problems in proving injury includes a long period of time between exposure and illness (latency period). If the plaintiff has developed a disease, such as cancer, it can be very difficult to prove that the exposure caused the disease. A long latency period gives rise to increased probability of exposure to multiple deleterious or toxic substances, complicating the causation issue. In regard to low-level toxic substance exposures, the "scientific" evidence is generally very limited. Epidemiological studies may show a statistical association between the exposure and increased rates of disease. Unfortunately, there may not be any existing studies, and it can be extremely expensive to perform them.[2]

At toxic levels, all chemicals attack a target organ or organ system. For example, benzene, a well-known solvent, is known to be linked to specific types of leukemia; it is not known to be associated with colon cancer. Through the use of the timelines and comparative charts, the defense team could easily demonstrate the lack of causal link between the alleged exposure (e.g., benzene) and the symptom cluster (e.g., colon cancer symptomatology).

The LNC must be mindful of the alleged specifics of the exposure during the initial review of medical records. LNCs working for either the plaintiff or defense team are likely to follow the same process in their goal of advancing the client's case. Both will be establishing the extent of the injury and trying to prove or disprove the causal link between exposure and injury.

The LNC working for the defense team may or may not be able to visit the worksite or other location where the alleged exposure occurred. If such a site visit is not possible, the LNC reviews the materials produced during discovery for references to the presence or absence of the client's product at the site. The manufacturer's defense team will want to show that their product cannot be traced to the plaintiff's alleged exposure. If it is established that the product was available in the workplace at the time of exposure, the defense team will try to prove that the product was not actually in use in an area where the plaintiff could experience an exposure, that the substance was not properly stored and maintained by the plaintiff, or that it was not used in accordance with suggested and required guidelines.

The defense may try to show that claimed injuries were not caused by the client's product, or that any alleged injuries are not consistent with those known to be caused by the subject product. Finally, the defense position in mitigating damages may be to show the plaintiff's contributory negligence by failing to seek timely treatment, failure to use available safety equipment, or misusing the product.

The LNC working with the plaintiff team may have unlimited access to the injured party. The plaintiff must prove product tracing and plaintiff exposure. The team will try to prove that despite the plaintiff's appropriate storage and care in the use of the defendant's product, their client sustained a measurable exposure to that product resulting in injury to person and property.

Example 18.1: A high school student assisted his friend one weekend at a full-service gas station. One week later, he presented to the doctor with fatigue, fever, bone pain, and multiple bruises. A bone marrow study confirmed the diagnosis of acute myelomonocytic leukemia. Knowing that the young man had worked with gasoline, a diagnosis of benzene-related exposure was made and he filed suit. The literature reveals that acute myelomonocytic leukemia can be linked to chronic benzene exposure (latent period of 5–15 years.) The LNC advises the attorney that in the absence of the temporal relationship described in the literature, it would be unlikely for a young man with a single exposure to a small amount of benzene to develop leukemia, particularly this quickly.

Reviewing and Analyzing the Records

Social Records

The importance of obtaining a complete set of medical records, along with other information about the plaintiff (e.g., school records, occupational records), cannot be overemphasized. Detailed information about the plaintiff is the crux of establishing the validity of the injury. Close examination of the relationship among the exposure, claimed injury, and preexisting medical condition is essential. The complete social and medical records should provide the necessary information.

The social history can be obtained from school records and occupational records. Records from childhood may describe congenital problems, debilitating childhood illnesses, or traumatic events that affected the plaintiff. Neurological or IQ testing may confirm that the plaintiff has a reduced earning capacity based on limited intellectual and learning abilities. The plaintiff's occupational records may yield valuable information about other sources of exposure and other risk factors for disease that are not the responsibility of the defendant.

The litigation of workplace exposure cases depends heavily on a thorough employment history. For example, did the plaintiff ever work in a shipyard or in an environment where there was asbestos? Does the plaintiff currently work in an environment where other substances or conditions might adversely affect him? Was the alleged exposure in an enclosed area or outdoors? Ventilation and atmospheric dispersion will impact an inhalation exposure case and need to be thoroughly investigated. A former mechanic may have been exposed to airborne concentrations of chlorinated fluorocarbons, cleaned machine parts in other solvents, and inhaled endless amounts of lead- and benzene-laden exhaust, yet his claim may arise out of his current employment in a film laboratory. Which chemical or compound caused his illness?

Obviously, exhaustive deposition questioning must be used to obtain a complete history of chemical exposures sustained over a plaintiff's lifetime. Occupational health records may contain some of this information. These same records are likely to include preemployment physical examinations, regular medical screenings, laboratory results, and employee attendance records. Efforts should be made to determine whether each place of employment was in compliance with state and federal laws designed to assist workers in protecting themselves from such hazards. These laws are known as the "right-to-know" legislation.

Lifestyle habits of the plaintiff and others who live with him are also important. Is the claimant living with a smoker or doing laundry for someone whose clothing may be contaminated with pathogens or carcinogenic chemicals? Does the plaintiff pursue hobbies that involve exposure to chemicals? Avid gardeners may be exposed to pesticides, fungicides, and rodenticides, in addition to organic and inorganic fertilizers. Crafters may be exposed to solvent-laden paints and glues, phenols, ketones, and other dangerous substances. Does the plaintiff spend long periods of time in a manicure salon inhaling noxious chemicals used in preparing and painting fingernails? Does the plaintiff use "harmless" household chemicals to keep the bathroom sparkling clean? Furniture polish, bleach, ammonia, spot removers, and pine cleaners are solvents known to produce a variety of transient symptoms.

Example 18.2: A 58-year-old man presents to an attorney inquiring about filing suit against his employer. He points to a rash around his face, neck, and chest and says that he works in a warehouse "around a lot of chemicals." He believes that as the result of his exposure, he has become sensitive to the sun and burns easily. The LNC is asked to review the medical aspects of the case.

The LNC takes an extensive history from the client, attempting to obtain a complete list of exposures that might have been sustained at the workplace and at home. Eventually, the claimant brings in a list of the chemicals and a notebook full of MSDS forms from his workplace. Upon research, the LNC learns that most of the chemicals are inert liquids and not used by the plaintiff. The potential plaintiff's doctor has confirmed a diagnosis of contact dermatitis and attributes the cause to the chemicals in the work environment. Since a workplace exposure has been ruled out, the LNC must look to the social history. She visits the claimant's home, making an extensive list of products in use there. The client shows her his bathroom, and she sees many bottles of aftershave cologne. When she begins to make a list of the product names, the claimant tells her that he no longer uses those products as they irritate the pruritic areas on his face and neck.

Research reveals that a number of the claimant's aftershave products contain musk ambrette and two preservatives, methylparaben and Quaternium-15. The literature reports that musk ambrette is known to cause not only contact dermatitis, but also photosensitivity. The LNC also learns that members of the paraben family are the most commonly used preservatives in cosmetics and generally considered to be among the safest. Quaternium-15 has been identified as an antibacterial preservative belonging to a family of formaldehyde-releasing chemicals. Further research reveals that combining preservatives can cause sensitivity, characterized by localized dermatitis, to develop. The would-be plaintiff is advised that he does not have a good exposure case against his employer and any product manufacturer of the workplace chemicals.

It is easy and dangerous to overlook other sources of exposure. Because everyone is exposed to chemicals and substances every day, most individuals do not consciously consider the variety of daily exposures to which they are subject. Both the defense and plaintiff teams must construct questions and deposition outlines that will prompt the individual to confront these alternative exposures.

Medical Records

All parties must obtain the medical records as soon as possible from the plaintiff's health care providers. Individuals are often unprepared for the degree of invasion of their privacy when entering litigation. Many are embarrassed about certain medical treatments, including treatment for sexually transmitted disease, plastic surgery, psychiatric treatment, and alcohol or chemical dependency, and may conveniently "forget" or even refuse to identify the relevant providers. Other plaintiffs may simply be poor historians and genuinely unable to remember all of their health care providers. Records of payments by the plaintiff's insurers to providers may reveal the otherwise unidentified providers.

Plaintiffs often allege neurological or central nervous system (CNS) injury in toxic tort cases. In no other area of the case preparation is the LNC likely to face more challenges than in the evaluation of the medical and social records for preexisting and concurrent psychoemotional disorders. Neurological or CNS complaints are often subjective, vague, and difficult to measure or disprove. Some neuropsychological testing is poorly standardized, and results are directly related to the effort put forth by the test subject. Some tests are sensitive to the subject's efforts to falsify present physical and mental conditions.

The LNC should work with expert neurologists, neuropsychologists, neuropsychiatrists, and others skilled in measuring cognitive function when evaluating claims of toxic encephalopathy, organic brain syndrome, and convulsions. Claimed injuries to the peripheral nervous system may include allegations of neuropathy and sensorimotor dysfunction.

The medical record establishes the plaintiff's preexisting health status, defines the existence and extent of the injury, describes the treatment rendered, and often gives a prognosis for recovery. This information not only provides an outline, but also provides a focus to the case as it develops.

The LNC compares postexposure complaints with preexisting problems to determine whether or not there is a relationship between the two. Pathological processes are dynamic in nature, sometimes resulting in a "natural" and progressive decline in health. Such declines may be completely unrelated to the exposure, although the plaintiff may allege that his condition developed or worsened as the result of the exposure. Such allegations require the defense to prove either that the underlying disease did not worsen or that the pathology is simply the product of age. The defense may also seek to prove that the plaintiff sought medical care because he thought he was affected or because he was anticipating litigation. If it is determined that an exposure caused an exacerbation of a preexisting condition, such an injury is usually compensable.

As the LNC develops chronologies, summaries, and timelines concerning the facts of the case, information will be added from the literature that describes symptoms known to be associated with a particular substance. With those additions made, one can readily compare the plaintiff's symptoms with those known to be associated with exposure. Further comparison can be made between the preexisting ailments and the postexposure complaints.

Chronologies are essential to the LNC, who must assimilate and explain the medical and scientific elements of the case to the attorney. When the financial, personnel, and equipment resources are available, computerized databases are recommended for cataloguing specific information about the plaintiff's symptom history, such as when each symptom appeared, what events were related to the symptom, what precipitants were identified, and what treatment was given. This information can be used to create a sophisticated timeline to show the presence or absence of causal links between exposure and injury. Summaries should document the date of each contact with health care providers, the complaint, physical findings, diagnosis, treatment, diagnostic test results, and anecdotal information entered by the health care provider. In addition, it is advantageous to paginate the medical records and cite the pages in the summary. Keep in mind that all charts, chronologies, and demonstrative evidence should be user-friendly for the nonmedical professionals, such as attorneys, insurance adjusters, and workers' compensation panels.

Evaluating the Corporate Defendant's History

Plaintiffs aren't alone in having to reveal personal information about themselves during the course of discovery. When the defendant is a corporate entity, it will have to reveal corporate practices and how those practices may or may not relate to the allegations made against it. The LNC may be asked to evaluate "in-house working papers" or other documents prepared by the client during the research, development, manufacturing, and marketing of the product in question. These papers are likely to include both *in vivo* and *in vitro* studies conducted with cellular, animal, and human subjects. These internal documents are generally considered to be proprietary and should be handled as confidential material.

Since the relative safety of the subject product is important to the case, the defense must demonstrate that it was properly labeled and packaged with instructions for safe use. The LNC may be asked to compare MSDS inserts with their contemporaneous package labeling and any other packaging information in an effort to evaluate claims of proper labeling. Litigants in the past have tried to show that internal corporate studies were fraudulent, leading to misrepresentation to the governing body and the public.

Despite organization, diligence, and persistence, it may be difficult for the plaintiff to prevail in attempts to prove that a corporate defendant showed reckless disregard and conspired to defraud the public regarding the safety of the product. This is not to say that litigants are not successful in proving these claims. In many instances, when it can be demonstrated that a corporate entity has committed a civil wrong, executive and supervisory staff not only may be found civilly liable, but may face criminal charges as well.

Identifying and Working with Experts

The LNC may participate in the selection of experts for preparation of the case. It should be noted that these complex cases tend to require specialized experts, such as epidemiologists, toxicologists, industrial hygienists, safety engineers, and physicians practicing in such specialty areas as occupational medicine, neurology, oncology, immunology, and pulmonology.

Epidemiologists evaluate causal links based on observations of the relationships between a disease entity and its presence in the general population. Like other scientists and researchers, epidemiologists must have a well-defined research hypothesis, a well-defined and adequate cohort, high-quality data, analysis of attributable actions, and minimal bias or skew in the data.

Like the epidemiologist, the toxicologist also contributes significantly to the case. The toxicologist may be the best expert to describe or refute the soundness of methods used in evaluating or testing a chemical substance. The toxicologist evaluates "poisonous" materials and their effects on living organisms. This is known as the "dose-response effect." A chemical considered "harmless," "safe," or "non-toxic" in small doses can be toxic in higher doses. For example, two aspirin can relieve pain, but a full bottle is lethal. Simply put, "the dose is the poison."

Because the toxicologist must evaluate dose-response when assessing any chemical substance at issue, the discovery process must obtain the most accurate possible data regarding the exposure and the environment in which the exposure occurred.

Various medical experts may be called on to evaluate the medical and psychosocial data in a toxic tort case. Neuropsychologists and other cognitive experts may offer testimony about any changes or lack of changes in cognition or perception in the postexposure plaintiff. Early school records may become important as the only objective baseline data available that delineate the subject's ability to process cognitive and sensory information.

The search for the experts may be pursued through the writings found in the literature search and through various professional organizations, such as the ACGIH, the American Institute of Chemists, and other organizations like the National Environmental Law Center. Appropriate experts may include practitioners, researchers, and academicians from universities, the National Institutes of Health, the Environmental Protection Agency, the Food and Drug Administration, the Centers for Disease Control, and other research facilities. The appropriate experts must be identified for trial testimony. In researching possible experts, the LNC must consider whether the candidates could be deemed biased if a defendant company funded any of their research.

The LNC is often the person on the litigation team who interacts directly with the experts as the case develops. The attorney must be able to rely on the LNC to summarize the findings of the various experts, to assess the expert's suitability as a witness, and to determine the relevance of the expert's testimony. Moreover, as the liaison between the experts and the attorney, the LNC is in the best position to coordinate the efforts of the various experts, often preventing costly overlap of research and testimony.

Reviewing the Literature

Along with collecting data about the plaintiffs and the defendants, both sides will perform literature searches. Gathering factual data in an effort to support toxico-logical and medical findings and conclusions is required to substantiate or refute claims. In some instances, the LNC will perform this task for the experts. At other times, the attorney may prefer to have the experts perform their own searches for purposes of strategy. When experts perform their own searches, they will be free of any accusation that conclusions were drawn and opinions formed on the basis of another's bias in how the literature searches were conducted.

Ideally, the LNC will have access to a library with such basics as references on occupational health, toxicology, chemistry, and medicine. The Internet is a valuable tool for locating specialized online databases and for providing access to the various regulatory and advisory agencies.

The authoritative literature discusses and describes the illnesses and symptoms known to be caused by the product at issue. Detailed information may be found about signs and symptoms of illness as the result of acute and chronic exposures in humans and animals. In the area of solvent toxicity, for example, Sweden has conducted long-term studies of individuals exposed to various solvents. These studies address findings ranging from serious illness to subtle changes seen only at the cellular level.

As in other areas of legal nurse consulting, attention must be paid to gathering data relevant to the time frame of the case. In addition, the literature search should also include the most current information. Where possible, it is suggested that research specialists and librarians familiar with scientific databases be consulted in conducting searches of widely accepted and peer reviewed literature.

Often, the toxic tort case requires a jury to sit through tedious testimony regarding biochemistry, pharmacology, toxicology, and physics — subjects they may be unable to understand. As a result, attorneys may present as evidence "studies" with jury appeal that were not conducted by proper scientific method. These "studies" may have had inadequate numbers in their study population, may not have been subject to peer review, or may have been published in the popular literature rather than in scholarly journals. In some venues, courts have been very generous in allowing spurious findings to be accepted into evidence in the toxic tort case, believing that because the subject matter is complex, it is better to allow all literature and expert testimony. New case law severely limits the ability to include such material as evidence. Standards established as the result of *Daubert v. Merrell Dow Pharmaceuticals* (1993) have resulted in the trial judge's role as gatekeeper. In this role, the judge evaluates the basis of the methodology, reliability, and relevance of expert opinions. If the judge determines that the expert opinions are not based on valid scientific methodology, the expert opinions are not admitted as evidence in the courtroom. Although *Daubert* standards are not utilized in all courts, they are becoming more widely recognized. The LNC should understand how these standards are interpreted and applied to medical evidence. Equipped with the awareness of *Daubert* standards, the LNC will be able to better analyze the medical records, medical expert reports, and medical literature.[6]

The literature search may include obtaining journal articles and abstracts published in foreign journals. The LNC who overlooks or disregards materials simply because they are in another language may be missing articles published by distinguished researchers from well-respected institutions. Articles published in a foreign language may have English abstracts that will provide a clue to the articles' usefulness. Certified translators may be used to provide authentic translations. The LNC may be asked to obtain a translator and should be aware that translators can be costly.

Ultimately, the literature search will yield such diverse items as doctoral dissertations, medical journal articles, textbook reference materials, regulatory position papers, and even "letters to the editor," making anecdotal reports of findings. From this eclectic assembly, each side will find relevant materials to prove its own and dispel the opposition's causation theories.

Summary

It is insufficient for a litigant to merely profess that he is ill as the result of chemical exposure. The plaintiff's trial team must prove that the client sustained a sufficient period of exposure to a substance at a dose high enough to cause the alleged harm. The defense team will attempt to prove otherwise.

Undoubtedly, work experience in specialty areas of nursing may assist LNCs in preparing the toxic tort case. Experience in occupational health or in pulmonology may be helpful. For other types of cases, nurses who are knowledgeable about immunology, neurology, or oncology may find it easier to master the reading material. There is no requirement that LNCs be experts in occupational medicine or other specialty areas in order to assist in preparing these cases. The real requirements include a willingness to use one's nursing and general science backgrounds in preparing cases with objectivity and careful analysis. Whether LNCs are working for attorneys or consulting firms, they must possess the ability to review and analyze information from a variety of sources. LNCs must be able to work with experts and act as liaisons between the experts and the attorneys in order to bring a powerful, proficient multidisciplinary team approach to this novel area of litigation.

References

1. Gots, R.E., *Seven Steps to Toxic Tort Analysis and Defense*, The Defense Research Institute, Chicago, 1991.

2. Gaba, J.M., *Environmental Law*, 2nd ed., West Group, St. Paul, MN, 2001, 48, 196.
3. Fauci, A.S. and Braunwald, E., *Harrison's Principles of Internal Medicine*, 14th ed., McGraw-Hill, New York, 1998, 2522.
4. Yeates, D.B. and Mauderly, J.L., Inhaled environmental/occupational irritants and allergens: mechanisms of cardiovascular and systemic responses, *Environmental Health Perspectives*, 109, 4, 2001.
5. Baselt, R.C., *Disposition of Toxic Drugs and Chemicals in Man*, 5th ed., Chemical Toxicology Institute, Foster City, CA, 2000, 79.
6. Oldknow, P.F., The scientific method, and the legal nurse consultant, *Journal of Legal Nurse Consulting*, 12, 4, 2001.

Additional Reading

Adams, R.M., *Occupational Skin Disease*, 3rd ed., W.B. Saunders, Philadelphia, 1999.
Bass, R. and Vamvakas, S., The Toxicology Expert: What Is Required?, *Toxicology Letters*, 112–113, 383–389, March 15, 2000.
Food and Drug Administration, An FDA Overview: Protecting Consumers, Protecting Public Health, http://www.fda.gov/oc/opacom/fda101/sld001html, April 2000.
Lewis, R.J., *Sax's Dangerous Properties of Industrial Materials*, 10th ed., John Wiley & Sons, New York, 2000.
McElhaney, R. and Beare, P.G., Expert witness/legal consultant: the importance of data collection, clinical nurse specialist, *The Journal for Advanced Nursing Practice*, 12, 3, 1998.
Occupational Health and Safety Administration, Permissible Exposure Limits, http://www.osha-slc.gov/SLTC/pel/index.html, 2001.
Patnaik, P., *Comprehensive Guide to the Hazardous Properties of Chemical Substances*, 2nd ed., John Wiley & Sons, New York, 1999.
The American Conference of Governmental Industrial Hygienists, Threshold Limit Values for Chemical Substances and Physical Agents and Biological Exposure Indices, The Conference, 1996.

Test Questions

1. All of the following agencies or advisory bodies have informational resources on chemical exposures EXCEPT:
   A. Natural Resources Conservation Service
   B. Environmental Protection Agency
   C. American Conference of Governmental Industrial Hygienists
   D. Occupational Safety and Health Administration

2. You are working for the plaintiff's attorney in an environmental exposure case and are asked to obtain information about the health of the plaintiff's neighbors. Why?
   A. The plaintiff and his attorney care about those around the plaintiff and want to be assured that they are healthy.
   B. If the neighbors are sick all the time, the plaintiff's case will look better to the jury. If many of the neighbors have a variety of symptoms, it will prove that the chemical in the groundwater has made everyone sick.
   C. The attorney wants to prove that his client's illness is part of a cohort of individuals who have been made ill by the exposure. Similar symptoms in the neighbors may strengthen the claim.
   D. This a great opportunity for the plaintiff to find out more about his neighbors.

3. Mrs. Jones has alleged that since she had breast implants, she has developed a tendency to develop rashes and rhinitis. You review the medical and social records. All of the following are items of importance in your review, EXCEPT:
   A. Mrs. Jones has had saline implants for 10 years. She has her hair colored every 4 weeks at the same salon where she has her nails done.
   B. Mrs. Jones has 8 children, 6 of whom are being treated for eczema and multiple food allergies.
   C. Mrs. Jones had silicone implants until one of them broke and was replaced with saline.
   D. Mr. Jones' sister has lupus.

4. A worker had a single, acute exposure to formaldehyde and claims that as a result he has elevated liver enzymes. He has approached a plaintiff attorney regarding the merits of his claim. You are asked to do a literature search and compare it against the medical record. You find that the worker has had intermittent liver enzyme elevations over the last few years. The employer's occupational health clinic notes make a reference to his being referred to a chemical dependency treatment program. Your first step is
   A. To advise the plaintiff attorney not to accept the case because the plaintiff is an alcoholic.
   B. To consult the databases for information on liver injury as the result of exposure to formaldehyde.
   C. To ask what the route of exposure was before starting the reviews.
   D. To request the plaintiff's childhood medical records.

5. The defense attorney has asked you to assist in an alleged ammonia (inhalation) exposure case. The plaintiff, a 30-year-old female, works for the defendant janitorial service and states that the use of household concentration ammonia products over the past year has resulted in her progressive development of emotional problems, clumsiness, incoordination, fatigue, paresthesias, and urinary incontinence. All of the following information is critical and will be beneficial in the mitigation of this case EXCEPT:
   A. The plaintiff's family physician referred her to a neurologist two years ago for a multiple sclerosis workup.
   B. Inhalation of household ammonia products causes few effects unless they are in large quantities.
   C. The plaintiff had mononucleosis as a teenager.
   D. The plaintiff's condition has rapidly deteriorated since the birth of her baby 4 months ago.

Answers: 1. A, 2. C, 3. D, 4. C, 5. C

Appendix 18.1
Measuring Exposure

TLV   Threshold limit value — Also known as TWA (time weighted average). The daily exposure that a worker can sustain to airborne concentrations 8 hours per day, 40 hours per week without adverse effect. These exposures may be described in parts per million (ppm) or billion (ppb), or in the case of dermal exposure, in milligrams per cubic meter (mg/m³).

PEL   Permissible exposure limit — Similar to TLV/TWA.

STEL Short-term exposure limit — A short exposure added to the TLV/TWA. STEL exposures may not exceed 15 minutes more than 4 times daily, with each exposure separated by at least 60 minutes. Workers must not suffer irritation, chronic tissue damage, or inability for self-rescue.

IDLH Immediately dangerous to life and health — The maximum concentration from which one could escape within 30 minutes without experiencing irreversible health effect or impairing self-rescue.

MSDS Material safety data sheet — Form included with shipment of products containing chemical substances. The MSDS lists the chemical ingredients, their Chemical Abstracts Service registry identification information, and information related to exposure and handling. Manufacturers and vendors are legally required to include this with each shipment of product.

PPE   Personal protective equipment — Includes protective garments, masks, goggles, and respirators worn to protect the individual from exposure to chemicals and pathogens.

Appendix 18.2
Advisory and Regulatory Agencies

ACGIH   American Conference of Governmental Industrial Hygienists
         http://www.acgih.org/
AIHA   American Industrial Hygiene Association
         http://www.aiha.org/
EPA   Environmental Protection Agency
         http://www.epa.gov/
OSHA   Occupational Safety and Health Administration
         http://www.osha.gov/
NAS   National Academy of Sciences
         http://www.nas.edu/
NRC   National Research Council (not to be confused with the Nuclear Regulatory Council)
         http://www.nas.edu/nrc/
NIOSH   National Institute for Occupational Safety and Health
         http://www.cdc.gov/niosh/homepage.html
SOT   Society of Toxicology
         http://www.toxicology.org/

Appendix 18.3
Toxic Tort Treasures

1. Obtain all medical records, mental health records, school records, and employment records. (Special authorizations may be required for sensitive information [e.g., HIV status]. Separate authorizations are also required for mental health records.)
2. Obtain missing records (e.g., billing records indicate that an office visit occurred, yet office records for that date are missing; EMS run sheet, lab results).
3. Prepare a list of additional health care providers mentioned in the records, so that the attorney can obtain these records.
4. Review past medical history carefully. For example, a plaintiff states that leukopenia was first diagnosed following the exposure in question. With careful review of the records, the LNC learns that a hematologist was consulted 6 years prior to the incident in question for leukopenia. The plaintiff failed to share this history with the attorney or current physicians.
5. Family medical history (e.g., asthma) should not be ignored. The defense team will address genetic influences vs. exposure.
6. Note current medications listed in the health care providers' records. Often, you may see a current medication not previously mentioned. Who prescribed this medication? This may lead to identification of yet another treating health care provider.
7. In preparing the chronological summary, you may become aware of time lapses in which there are no medical records. Question this! Why are there

large time gaps? Did the plaintiff live elsewhere during this period? Was the plaintiff healthy and not in need of medical care?

8. Pharmacy records provide another source of identification of additional treating physicians.

9. Note conflicts in the records. Sometimes the plaintiff is simply a poor historian, or will carefully select what he shares with a particular health care provider. This will become evident to the prudent LNC in preparing the chronological summary. Often it is clear that a particular physician may not have been made aware of some previous events, such as motor vehicle accident resulting in neck and back injuries. For example, a neurologist diagnosed a plaintiff with neuropathies and related them to the alleged toxic exposure. The physician was unaware of the plaintiff's history of neuropathies related to a motor vehicle accident.

10. Question the existence of other lawsuits. The plaintiff may be alleging the same injuries in more than one case.

11. Note the absence of a physician's physical examination or appropriate diagnostic tests. For example, the plaintiff's alleged symptoms included watery eyes, stuffy nose, congestion, wheezing, and shortness of breath as a result of the exposure in question. The plaintiff stated that his symptoms began immediately following the incident and continued for several months. Although the treating physician saw the plaintiff within 2 hours of the alleged exposure, the physician failed to document any physical findings. One week later, the plaintiff was seen by his physician on follow-up. Again, no physical exam was documented. Because there were no documented physical findings, it is not clear whether diagnostic tests should have been ordered. Question this lack of documentation. Is this treating physician a hired gun?

12. Finally, be suspicious and be inquisitive!

Appendix 18.4
Medical Records Summary Excerpt

Many different formats may be used in summarizing medical records. Below, you will find one example of a medical records summary entry:

02/10/01 — OFFICE NOTE — JOHN DOE, M.D., DERMATOLOGIST:

(pp. 0001–0003)
    RE: Referral from Dr. Smith — Rash on hands and forearms.

- Patient was seen by Dr. Smith yesterday on advice from her attorney, Mr. Sharp.
- Patient states that she sustained a formaldehyde exposure while washing her husband's work clothes on one occasion 2 months ago.
- Current complaints: Itchy rash to bilateral hands and forearms that began 2 months ago. Denies history of allergies or rashes. Denies any other complaints at this time.

- Current medications: None
- Physical exam: BP 142/88 P 82 R 20 T 98.7°; No acute distress; HEENT (head, eyes, ears, nose & throat): WNL (within normal limits); Heart: RRR (regular rate and rhythm); Lungs: clear; Abdomen: soft, nondistended, audible BS x 4 (bowel sounds in all four quadrants of abdomen); Extremities: erythematous (red) lesions to both hands and forearms; Lower extremities WNL.
- Impression: Contact dermatitis
- Recommendations: Betamethasone cream (steroid cream) to affected areas. Benadryl prn itching (antihistamine as needed for itching). Follow-up in 1 week.

Author's Note: Prior records clearly show that this patient has a long-standing history of allergies and skin rashes. However, she denied this history when asked by Dr. Doe. See Dr. Jones' records 06/02/99 for detailed dermatology history.

Chapter 19

Evaluating Forensics Cases

Doug Davis, BSN, RN, DABFN,
Diana Faugno, BSN, RN, CPN, FAAFS,
Joseph R. McMahon III, JD, and Patricia Ann Steed King, RN

CONTENTS

Objectives

- To provide an overview of specific areas of criminal law, procedure, and evidence

- To review the basic constitutional protections afforded to those accused of criminal offenses in connection with the collection and admission of evidence
- To address the admissibility of scientific evidence in criminal proceedings
- To discuss how the burden of proof for a criminal case differs from that for a civil case
- To describe the roles and responsibilities of law enforcement, the prosecuting attorney's office, and the medical examiner or coroner in the investigation of a criminal case
- To identify three ways in which the legal nurse consultant can assist the attorney in the prosecution or defense of a criminal case
- To describe how the processes of evaluation, assessment, and implementation are ongoing in a criminal case and why this is important

Introduction

Criminal law is a field that, by itself, is extremely broad and continues to grow broader with each passing legislative session or appellate decision. The practice of criminal law encompasses the application of law, procedure, and evidence. The information in this chapter will provide the legal nurse consultant (LNC) with the basic concepts of criminal law and the criminal justice system as they relate to the analysis of criminal cases.

There are inherent differences between civil and criminal cases. Civil cases involve wrongs that are personal in nature, such as property, contracts, and torts. Civil actions are considered private matters between individual parties.[1] Criminal cases involve wrongs against society. A crime is defined as any act that is forbidden by law, or as the omission of an act required by law. Criminal law is statutory and will vary from municipality to municipality. Crimes are generally divided into misdemeanors and felonies. Legislatures enact criminal codes that distinguish between the two basic types of crimes.[2] Generally, a misdemeanor is a crime punishable by imprisonment of up to 1 year, and a felony is a crime punishable by imprisonment of more than 1 year or death. The same act may give rise to both civil and criminal causes of action. For example, O.J. Simpson was prosecuted under both criminal and civil law after he was accused of murdering his wife. Although the law applying to criminal and civil cases is different, the basic concept of determining the truth based on evidence is common to both.

Criminal Law

Criminal law is the body of law by which all human conduct is judged. Although laws that make conduct criminal vary widely from community to community, state to state, and country to country, each system of laws is based upon the social mores and values of the society that establishes them. Laws are the enactment of social, political, and moral viewpoints of a society.

Unlike the consequences under civil law, rarely are criminal consequences attached to negligent acts. Although some jurisdictions have enacted statutes that penalize the consequences of a negligent act, these damages are more commonly than not addressed in the civil courts of our country where monetary damages are at issue. In the rare incidences where criminal law considers the effects of negligence, wanton disregard of human safety is a general issue that must be considered, and prosecutorial discretion has great flexibility.

Although each of us is familiar with a variety of terms used within the context of criminal law and evidence from entertainment and the media, our understanding of the topic is generally flawed by inaccuracies inherent in the media. For instance, many of us have heard the television prosecutor argue that the murder was premeditated; in most jurisdictions, there is no requirement that the prosecutor prove that a killing was premeditated to support a conviction for murder. Several of the everyday inaccuracies in criminal law will be addressed while exploring criminal law, procedure, and evidence in this chapter.

Violations of criminal law generally require some level of intent to commit the crime charged. General criminal intent is present whenever there is specific intent and also when the circumstances indicate that the offender, in the ordinary course of human experience, must have expected the prescribed criminal consequences as reasonably certain to result from his act or failure to act. In a general intent crime, the criminal intent necessary to sustain a conviction is shown by the very doing of the acts that have been declared criminal. Specific criminal intent is that state of mind that exists when the circumstances indicate that the offender actively desired the prescribed criminal consequences to follow his act or failure to act.

An example of a general intent crime is simple possession of narcotics. The prosecutor in Louisiana who seeks to convict a defendant of simple possession of narcotics must prove that the defendant possessed a narcotic substance that has been classified as illegal.

An example of a specific intent crime under the common law is burglary. Burglary requires the breaking and entering into a dwelling of another, but in addition to the general intent to commit the trespass, it must also be established that the defendant acted with intent to commit a felony within the premises. The prosecutor is required to establish that the offender had "specific intent" to commit a felony in addition to the breaking and entering in order to secure the conviction.

In Louisiana, the law defines "second-degree murder" as the killing of a human being when the offender has the specific intent to kill or cause great bodily harm. In order to successfully prove the elements of this crime and obtain a conviction, the prosecutor must prove to the jury that the defendant killed the victim and that the defendant possessed the specific intent to kill or inflict great bodily harm upon the person of the victim. If the prosecutor is unable to prove that specific intent existed, the jury should not find the defendant guilty of second-degree murder.

Because criminal law statutes differ from state to state, the LNC must be familiar with the statutes that are specific to the jurisdiction in which the case is being tried.

Criminal Procedure

The prosecutor is required to prove the level of intent along with each and every element of the crime to support a conviction for any crime, whether it is a felony or misdemeanor. The criminal defense attorney is not required to prove anything in a criminal prosecution, whereas the defense attorney in a civil trial has an equal and opposite responsibility to present evidence supporting the defense position. The Fifth Amendment to the U.S. Constitution grants the accused the right to be silent and not to testify against or incriminate himself. Specifically, the amendment provides, "No person...shall be compelled in any criminal case to be a witness against himself." The prosecution bears the entire burden of proof. After the prosecution has presented its case, the accused may present witnesses on his behalf or rest upon the presumption that a person is innocent until proved guilty. If a defendant elects to present a defense in a criminal case, his counsel will generally seek to disprove the facts presented by the prosecution that support the elements of the crime, or the attorney will attempt to create doubt in the mind of the judge or jury. For example, a person charged with the crime may present alibi witnesses who place the person in a different location at the time of the offense or may attack the reliability of evidence used by the prosecution.

The prosecution in a criminal case bears the burden of proof. Just as in a civil case, the party bringing the action is required to prove the case. Civil and criminal cases differ in the standard by which they are to be judged. Civil cases are generally judged by the preponderance of the evidence standard. This standard requires the finder of fact to listen to the evidence and render a verdict based upon a finding of which side presented the best evidence to support its position. In criminal law, the prosecutor is required to prove his case beyond a reasonable doubt in the eyes of the trier of fact. This standard has been defined several times by numerous scholars and practicing members of the criminal bar across the country. While no two will agree about the definition of "reasonable doubt," suffice it to say that it is generally agreed that reasonable doubt is doubt based on reason and common sense. The trier of fact is called upon to listen to the evidence as presented by the prosecution or defense to determine whether the facts as presented are logical, credible, and worthy of belief. If so, the facts should be used as a basis for reaching a verdict. If they are not logical, credible, and worthy of belief, then they should be used to reach the opposite verdict.

Should the prosecution fail to prove the allegations beyond a reasonable doubt in the eyes of the trier of fact and an acquittal or "not guilty" verdict is rendered, the prosecution may not subject the accused to another trial. The Fifth Amendment to the U.S. Constitution further provides, "Nor shall any person be subject for the same offense to be twice put in jeopardy of life or limb." This provision, commonly referred to as *double jeopardy*, is more far-reaching than the amendment or its name implies. Not only is the prosecution barred from bringing an action for the same offense against an accused who has been acquitted, it is also barred from pursuing criminal charges against an accused for crimes that require proof of the same elements. For example, although an accused may be charged with theft and possession/receiving stolen things, the accused may be neither tried nor convicted of both offenses in most jurisdictions under double jeopardy.

The Sixth Amendment to the U.S. Constitution provides that in addition to the right to a speedy trial, an accused has the right to confront his accusers and to be represented by counsel. This amendment allows the accused to take advantage of the subpoena power of the court to require witnesses to appear and to testify. It also secures competent counsel for an accused to assist in his defense. The test for determining whether or not counsel was competent was outlined in *Strickland v. Washington*.[3] In order to prove ineffective assistance of counsel, the defendant must show that counsel's performance was deficient and that this deficiency prejudiced the outcome of the trial. To show that counsel was deficient, the defendant must demonstrate that counsel failed to meet the level of competency normally demanded of attorneys in criminal cases. The U.S. Supreme Court has held that the benchmark for judging a charge of ineffectiveness is whether the attorney's conduct so undermined the proper functioning of the adversarial process that the trial cannot be considered to have produced a just result (*U.S. v. Cronic*).[4] Decisions of counsel regarding trial strategy are generally not considered as the basis for an ineffective-assistance-of-counsel claim under the Sixth Amendment and the holding of *Strickland v. Washington*.

Evidence

In criminal law, prosecutors and defense counsel rely on three types of evidence: testimonial evidence, physical evidence, and scientific evidence. Within each of these three types of evidence, there is direct and indirect evidence. Before discussing the three types of evidence, direct and indirect evidence should be defined. Direct evidence is evidence that, taken alone, is designed to establish a fact or element. For example, a witness can testify that he observed a defendant point a gun at a convenience store clerk and demand money, or a videotape could be introduced showing a robbery that took place. This would serve as direct evidence that an armed robbery had occurred. Indirect evidence is competent evidence that establishes a fact or element by reference. This evidence, although competent, must be viewed by the trier of fact to eliminate all other reasonable explanations.

For example, as the trial progressed, evidence was presented that revealed that a search of the defendant's residence had uncovered a handgun similar to that described by the clerk. Although this is competent evidence and should be considered by the jury, it does not conclusively establish that the defendant committed the armed robbery. Equally true is the following example: When the jurors walked into the courtroom, it was a sunny spring day. During the trial, a man wearing a wet raincoat and carrying a wet umbrella walks into the courtroom. This is indirect evidence that it may be raining outside. If there are no other reasonable explanations or evidence presented, indirect evidence can be used to establish that it is or has been raining.

Whether LNCs work for the defense or prosecution, they play a significant role in reviewing and analyzing the evidence to ensure that proper evidence collection protocols are followed as it relates to the medical issues of the case.

Testimonial Evidence

Testimonial evidence is best defined as that evidence presented through the words of victims, witnesses, and parties to a criminal case. This evidence amounts to the words of those who were present when a crime was committed, those who investigated the crime after it took place, or those who dispute the accused's involvement. Although a defendant is not required to testify at trial, the words of a defendant prior to trial may be used against him. In *Miranda v. Arizona*,[5] the court held that before the state may introduce into evidence what purports to be a confession or statement of a defendant, it must first affirmatively show that the statement was freely and voluntarily given and was not made under the influence of fear, duress, menaces, threats, inducements, or promises. In addition, if the statement was made during custodial interrogation, the state must prove that the accused was advised of his Miranda rights and intelligently and voluntarily waived those rights. It is not sufficient for the words to be read to an accused; officers and prosecutors looking to use the accused's words against him must prove to the court that the accused understood the rights as explained and voluntarily waived the rights.

Physical Evidence

Physical evidence consists of objects or tangible items that are used to demonstrate or establish facts or elements of the crime charged. Physical evidence generally consists of drugs, money, guns, photographs, or other objects found or discovered in conjunction with the investigation of the crime. Objects that are taken from the person or control of a defendant are subject to constitutional protections. The Fourth Amendment to the U.S. Constitution provides that:

> The right of the people to be secure in their persons, houses, papers, and effects, against unreasonable searches and seizures, shall not be violated, and no Warrants shall issue, but upon probable cause, supported by Oath or affirmation, and particularly describing the place to be searched, and the persons or things to be seized.

This amendment seeks to protect individuals against unreasonable search and seizure. The prosecution is required to prove that seizure of items from an accused was done in a manner so as to enforce the constitutional protections granted to the defendant. Property that is abandoned by a defendant is not constitutionally protected. Therefore, the subject who flees from the police while discarding narcotics does not enjoy constitutional protections over the narcotics; however, officers must meet constitutional safeguards when serving search warrants or taking property from an accused person. These safeguards include those provided by the amendment. A police officer must provide to the court by affidavit or oath sufficient facts to establish probable cause for the issuance of the search warrant. Probable cause exists when the facts and circumstances within the officer's knowledge and of which the officer has reasonably trustworthy information are sufficient to cause a person of reasonable caution to believe that an offense has been or is being committed.

Evidence may also be seized by officers without the necessity of a warrant under certain jurisprudentially approved circumstances. For instance, officers may seize evidence from the person of an accused when the search is performed incidental to a lawful arrest. Property may be seized from a vehicle when that vehicle is being impounded. Evidence may be seized when it is in the plain view of an officer. For example, a police officer walking through a neighborhood observes a marijuana plant growing in the front room of a home. The officer may seize the plant as evidence. Equally true, an officer conducting a traffic stop who observes a weapon or narcotics on the floorboard of the stopped vehicle may seize the evidence. The officer may not shuffle through the vehicle to uncover the contraband or place it in plain view. These are a few examples of issues common to the constitutional questions involved in searches and seizures by law enforcement officers. This area of the law is extremely broad and cannot be completely covered here.

Scientific Evidence

Scientific evidence is that field of expertise in which physical objects and technology merge to establish facts or elements or to disprove facts or elements. Scientific evidence includes fingerprint analysis; ballistics; blood testing; and DNA testing in blood, saliva, and semen.

Admissibility of Scientific Evidence

The Federal Rules of Evidence provide the basis for most rules of evidence that have been adopted by individual states and that determine the admissibility of scientific evidence. Federal Rule of Evidence 702 provides:

> **If scientific, technical, or other specialized knowledge will assist the trier of fact to understand the evidence or to determine a fact in issue, a witness qualified as an expert by knowledge, skill, experience, training, or education may testify thereto in the form of an opinion or otherwise.**

Subsumed in the requirements of Rule 702 is the premise that expert testimony must be reliable to be admissible (*State v. Cressey*).[6] A U.S. Supreme Court case, *Daubert v. Merrell Dow Pharmaceuticals, Inc.*,[7] set forth a means for determining reliability of expert scientific testimony and answered many questions as to proper standards for admissibility of expert testimony. The standard for admissibility of evidence in criminal cases is equally applicable to civil litigation and should not be thought of as a separate or distinct standard.

In *Daubert*, the Court was concerned with determining the admissibility of new techniques as the basis for expert scientific testimony. Formerly, the test for admissibility of expert scientific testimony was based on a short, citation-free 1928 decision of the District of Columbia Court of Appeals, *Frye v. United States*.[8] In *Frye*, the rule for admissibility of expert testimony was delineated as requiring "general acceptance" of a technique in its respective scientific field before the technique would be considered admissible. Finding that "a rigid 'general acceptance' requirement would be at odds with 'the liberal thrust of the Federal Rules,'" the Court in *Daubert* concluded that *Frye*'s "austere standard, absent from and incompatible with (this liberal thrust), should not be applied in federal trials."

The Court replaced *Frye* with a new standard that requires the trial court to act in a gatekeeping function to "ensure that any and all scientific testimony or evidence admitted is not only relevant, but reliable." This requirement stems from a belief that the rules on expert testimony serve to relax "the usual requirement of first-hand knowledge" to ensure reliability on the part of a witness. This relaxation is justified so long as "the expert's opinion has a reliable basis in the knowledge and experience of his discipline."

The reliability of expert testimony is to be ensured by a requirement that there be "a valid scientific connection to the pertinent inquiry as a precondition to admissibility." This connection is to be examined in light of "a preliminary assessment" by the trial court "of whether the reasoning or methodology underlying the testimony is scientifically valid and of whether the reasoning or methodology properly can be applied to the facts in issue." The Court went on to make some suggestions as to how a court could fulfill its gatekeeping role. These involve whether or not the technique had been subjected to peer review and/or publication, the "known or potential rate of error," the existence of "standards controlling the technique's operation," the technique's "refutability," or, more simply put, testability, and finally, an incorporation of the *Frye* general acceptance in the scientific community as only a factor in the analysis.

The Court also stated that other rules of evidence govern this testimony, mainly Federal Rule of Evidence 403's balancing test that will exclude probative evidence if outweighed by its potential for unfair prejudice. The Court noted the possibility that the expert's testimony can be quite misleading and prejudicial if this gatekeeping role is not properly satisfied, requiring a flexible approach and a careful evaluation of the methodology surrounding the testimony and its conclusions. Conjectures that are probably wrong are of little use. However, in the process of reaching a quick, final, and binding legal judgment, they are often of great consequence regarding a particular set of past events. In practice, a gatekeeping role for the judge, no matter how flexible, inevitably on occasion will prevent the jury from learning of authentic insights and innovations. That, nevertheless, is the balance struck by rules of evidence designed not for the exhaustive search for cosmic understanding but for the particularized resolution of legal disputes.

This raises the question of the admissibility of the latest scientific evidence, such as DNA testing, to be commonly used in criminal law and civil law. Both federal and state courts have found that, in general, DNA profiling is a reliable technique and is admissible, for example, in *United States v. Jackboots*,[9] *Hayes v. State*,[10] *Commonwealth v. Rodgers*,[11] *Trimboli v. State*,[12] and *Caldwell v. State*.[13] Courts have agreed that the principles of DNA profiling and restriction fragment length polymorphism analysis are both relevant and reliable and thus are admissible.

In DNA analysis, as with any type of scientific evidence, it is of utmost importance that the party wishing to introduce such evidence be able to show a *chain of custody*. The "chain of custody" relates to the handling of evidence from the time of retrieval up to testing and until presentation before the trier of fact. The chain of custody is a requirement for admissibility, because it substantiates reliability of the evidence by seeking to prevent altering of or tampering with evidence. Although different methods are used from jurisdiction to jurisdiction to protect the chain of custody for different types of evidence, the most common method used for medical evidence is to place the evidence in sealed containers.

The containers are sealed with tape upon which identification information is written. As the evidence travels from one individual or agency to another, records are kept of the date, time, and person who handled the evidence. At trial, these persons are called to testify as to when and how they received the evidence, and what they did with it while it was in their possession. This procedure is necessary to illustrate to the court that the evidence is reliable and has not been tampered with or altered in any way.

Last, when attempting to present scientific evidence, the presenter is required to prove that the witness is qualified to render an expert opinion in the field for which the witness has been called. This requires the party calling the witness to show that the witness has knowledge, experience, and training that is sufficient to support his statements and conclusions. Generally, courts will look to the educational background, work experience, and training of a potential witness when considering allowing him to testify as an expert. Additionally, the court will consider whether or not the potential expert has published any materials on the topic and whether or not the witness has been qualified or refused qualification in any other court. Only after a witness has been qualified as an expert will the court allow a witness to render opinion evidence; otherwise, witnesses are limited to factual testimony only.

The effect of scientific evidence on a criminal case can best be illustrated by the following example. In a rape case, there are generally only two defenses available to defense counsel. The first is consent of the victim. This is tantamount to the defendant's admitting to engaging in sexual intercourse with the victim, but denying that it was against the victim's will. The second defense is one of faulty identification. In a trial where the first defense was employed, the prosecution would seek to introduce evidence to show that the sex act was not consensual. This evidence would include the victim's testimony, photographs of the victim's physical appearance shortly after the incident, and medical evidence of bruising or tearing. Scientific evidence is not especially useful in this situation because of the defendant's admission of engaging in sexual intercourse with the victim. Scientific evidence, in particular DNA testing, becomes especially relevant under the second defense. When an accused claims incorrect identification, the case hinges upon the prosecution's ability to establish that the victim's identification is not incorrect. If the physician who examines the victim shortly after the rape is able to locate semen or other bodily fluids, DNA can be used to link the accused to the crime. The availability of DNA testing has resulted in convictions of sex offenders who in the past would have escaped conviction.

Investigation

Criminal investigation is a complex profession. With the advances in forensic science, criminal investigations require the cooperative efforts of professionals from many different disciplines within the criminal justice system. Law enforcement, forensic scientists, pathologists, and attorneys must work together in the investigation and solution of criminal acts. In reviewing criminal cases, the LNC becomes a medical investigator whose main responsibility is to provide the defense or prosecution with medical expertise as to the medico-legal aspects of the case.

Law enforcement officers take the leading role in criminal investigations. In order to be successful, investigators must have the education and experience to recognize, collect, and use evidence in criminal investigations. The most important aspect of any criminal case is the crime scene. The primary goal in crime scene assessment is to detect all traces that indicate that a crime has been committed and establish any association between the crime and victim, or victim and perpetrator. The crime scene is the place from which much physical evidence is obtained and, in the majority of cases, is the key to the solution of a crime. The crime scene provides the investigator with a starting point, a beginning of the investigation to determine the identities of the suspect and victim and to piece together the circumstances of what happened during the crime.

All physical evidence collected at the crime scene will be carefully processed, documented, and placed in the proper custody until such time as it is utilized in the legal process. Any physical evidence that may be introduced in court must be identified, described, and maintained in proper custody. In handling evidentiary material, care must be taken not to disturb the viability of the material for later examination.[14] From the time it is collected and identified until it is presented at trial, physical evidence must at all times be accounted for and secured. This is accomplished by having anyone who handles the evidence provide the date, time, purpose of handling, and signature. Anyone who handles the evidence may be called to testify at trial to verify this information and again identify the evidence. This meticulous process ensures that the evidence has been maintained properly. It also ensures that only authorized personnel come in contact with the evidence and that the evidence has not been subject to tampering. This process is commonly referred to as the chain of custody. Any variance in the above can result in physical evidence's being inadmissible in court. This is an especially important consideration when reviewing a criminal case.

Forensic science is that which is applied to answering legal questions by examining, evaluating, and explaining evidence. It encompasses pathology, toxicology, biology, serology, chemistry, anthropology, odontology, and psychiatry, among other fields. One branch of forensic science is criminalistics, which deals with the study of physical evidence related to a crime. It encompasses firearms, questioned documents, tool mark comparison, fingerprints, photography, evidence collection kits, and trace elements, among other fields.[2] The reports generated by experts in the various forensic fields may play important roles in the presentation of evidence during a trial. LNCs interact with many of these experts in understanding and applying the specific field of science. This represents another aspect of their involvement in a criminal case.

Preliminary Hearing, Arraignment, Indictment

Once a suspect has been arrested and accused of a crime, the accused is entitled to a timely hearing to determine whether probable cause exists that a crime was committed and whether the accused committed it. The accused cannot be detained prior to trial unless this has occurred. The exact process will be determined by the seriousness of the crime and the jurisdiction in which the matter is pending. The accused is brought before a judge for an initial appearance, at which time he is told what charges are pending, advised of his rights, and given the date for a preliminary hearing. The information gathered during the initial investigation is presented to a judge in the form of a preliminary hearing or to a grand jury for review. In some jurisdictions and in some instances, preliminary hearings are not held.

If a grand jury determines that enough evidence exists to hold a defendant for trial, an indictment is returned charging the defendant with a crime or crimes. At the time of arraignment, the accused is given a copy of formal charges, is once again informed of his or her rights, and is asked to enter a plea. Criminal trials are usually held within a year of the indictment as opposed to civil cases in which several years may pass before a case reaches a trial calendar. This is because the defendant may be incarcerated during this period of time, depending on the seriousness of the crime, and has the constitutional right of an accused to a speedy trial.

Prosecution

The job of prosecuting criminals is within the purview of the prosecuting attorney's office. The prosecutor attempts to determine that the right person (the accused) has been identified, located, and apprehended, and that there is evidence sufficient to indict. If an indictment is not possible, then neither is a conviction. The burden of proof in a criminal case rests solely on the prosecution and is proof beyond a reasonable doubt. The verdict must be unanimous and is returned as guilty or not guilty. Since a crime by definition is against the state, the prosecution has the state's resources at its disposal in investigating and developing cases. This includes law enforcement agencies; the office of the medical examiner; the coroner; the state crime laboratory; and other state agencies, such as family and children's services, mental health, etc.

Defense

The job of the criminal defense attorney is to be an advocate for the client. This gives the attorney the responsibility of ensuring that the client's civil rights are respected. The Constitution guarantees everyone the right to a fair and speedy trial regardless of the evidence concerning guilt or innocence. The criminal defense attorney does not enjoy the same readily available access to the state's resources as the prosecution does, and at times must utilize private laboratories and forensic scientists in private practice for testing and consulting. The conclusions or test results provided by these private entities might challenge or refute conclusions or tests provided by the state. The conclusions or test results may also provide a sufficient basis on which to create a reasonable doubt for a jury concerning the state's case.

Civil proceedings have rules governing the disclosure of information (discovery) prior to trial, which are broad and entitle every party to relevant information. The same rules do not apply in criminal proceedings. The type and amount of information that is discoverable in a criminal case will vary from state to state. Therefore, the criminal defense attorney may or may not be privy to the state's case theory, depending upon the working relationship between the criminal defense attorney and the district attorney's office or the usual practices of the municipality. The criminal defense attorney will need to become an expert on any anticipated theory that the state may utilize. The LNC can assist the defense attorney in developing case theories and strategies. For example, if the state is pursuing DNA evidence, it would behoove defense counsel to know as much as possible about DNA in order to present testimony or additional evidence that could create reasonable doubt about the evidence. The LNC can produce medical literature on the topic. The LNC can also locate, identify, retain, and work with experts in the field as part of case development.

The LNC's Role

The LNC's analysis of the facts of the case will be the same regardless of which side of a criminal case one might be working. The scope of the LNC's duties may include one or more of the following. (*Note*: The following list is not intended to be all-inclusive, as the actions of the LNC will be determined by the type of case and the LNC's work environment.)

The LNC may be involved in the analysis of:

1. Medical or forensic reports to assess the extent of injuries and determine whether injuries could be consistent with the time frame and history given. Other factors to consider would be old injuries (in the case of domestic violence or child abuse) or whether an underlying medical condition or disease could be present.
2. Autopsy reports to:
   - Assess the extent of injuries.
   - Determine whether injuries match history (victim strangled, then house set on fire to make the death appear accidental).
   - Determine whether previous untreated injuries exist (especially in domestic violence cases).
   - Determine whether gunshot wounds are entrance or exit wounds (to substantiate claims of self-defense when victim is shot at a distance from behind).
   - Identify the type of weapon used (blunt instrument, tire iron, rock, knife, electrical cord) from wounds in, on, and through the body; cause and manner of death; whether the body had been moved, mutilated, or further injured postmortem; and the approximate time of death.
   - Determine whether the death was an accident, suicide, or homicide.
   - Identify how much time elapsed between the fatal injury and the time of death, etc.
3. Police reports to assess the initial crime scene (from measurements, photographs, drawings, and descriptions contained in the report), to identify witnesses, to determine persons and objects removed from the scene and their destination (by the police, hospital, morgue), and to determine the investigating officer and who made the initial call to police.
4. Supplemental investigative reports, including reports of police detectives, fire, emergency medical services, or investigations from the prosecuting

attorney's office or private investigators working for the criminal defense attorney. These reports may provide additional information concerning witnesses and witness statements and the additional gathering of evidence by the investigators involved in the case.

5. Sexual assault reports to assess the presence or absence of injuries. The presence or lack of injuries in sexual assault cases is related to the history and time frame. One cannot determine from injuries only whether the sexual contact was consensual or nonconsensual. The findings or lack of findings will be based on the history and time frame as stated in the report. The sexual assault report is only one piece of the evidence in a large investigation that must be evaluated.

6. Psychological testing/reports to evaluate the competency of the accused to stand trial, to assess the state of mind of both the perpetrator and the victim at the time of the crime, to evaluate the effect of the crime on the victim, to determine whether the accused had a history of mental illness (diagnosis, treatment, medications, compliance), to assess recommendations made by health care professionals, and to assess psychological profiles in the case of serial offenders.

7. Forensic science reports to determine whether the accused can be linked to the scene by trace evidence, fingerprints, blood, semen, DNA; to determine whether illicit or prescription drugs or alcohol were involved; to determine whether bite marks on victim match the accused's bite; to determine the sex and race of skeletal remains; to assess the evidence gathered during a sexual assault exam (semen in body orifice or on the body, pubic hair not belonging to the victim); and to determine whether the weapon (if located) is consistent with the type of weapon used in the commission of the crime.

In addition to analyzing reports, the LNC may be involved in:

1. Interviewing clients, witnesses, and potential experts to gather information about the crime from clients and witnesses and to determine whether the information supports or refutes physical evidence. If differences do exist, the task is to determine how to reconcile the differences and to provide information to experts regarding the case.

2. Assisting in obtaining experts and acting as liaison between expert and attorney, which may involve researching the literature, to determine experts in a given science and then contacting the experts to determine whether they are willing to review the case. LNCs may also be involved in providing information to experts regarding the case, determining whether their conclusions or findings support or refute issues of the case, and learning as much as possible about a particular issue from the experts.

3. Performing medical research as indicated. This could involve searches through medical literature, forensic science literature, and law enforcement literature. Research could also include interviews, telephone calls, and correspondence.

4. Providing information regarding case development based on the above and to assess and evaluate the ongoing development of issues of the case.

5. Preparing transcription of medical records and chronologies of events.

Examples of Types of Criminal Case Analyses Performed by the LNC

Child Abuse

In the case of alleged child abuse, it is important to consider the concept of the differential diagnosis to ensure that premature decisions about a diagnosis are avoided.[14] The best approach to child abuse is utilizing a multidisciplinary center that provides services in the local community.[15] The evaluation of the child is multifaceted when components include the medical history past and current, physical examination with diagnostic and forensic testing, and referrals. Most children who are being abused do not report the incident in a timely fashion (72 hours or less). The perpetrators of this crime usually know and have access to the child.

Example 19.1: Patty, a 5-year-old, disclosed to her mother that "Uncle John" had touched her bottom. Her mother notified the sheriff, and the child was interviewed. Patty was a poor historian and could only state that this had happened 10–15 times when Uncle John was her babysitter. The medical examination revealed no findings.

The LNC can help the attorney by knowing how to locate child abuse experts in this arena. The LNC will also be able to pull together all multidisciplinary reports and help in the analysis for the prosecution or defense.

Other variables that the LNC would need to consider:

- The medical history of the child, both past and present, must be assessed. Also, are there medical problems that mimic sexual abuse?
- Does the child have acute injuries, such as bruises or bite marks? Are any of an accidental nature?
- Did the child have a forensic interview?
- Is there a family history with child protective services (CPS)? Has the child been removed from the family before?
- Who are the childcare providers?
- Are the school records and school history available?
- Are there changes in the child's behavior?

It is frightening for a child to testify and confront the adult in court. Many children do not make good witnesses. In many incidents of child abuse, the LNC can be utilized in the record reviews for civil suits after the criminal case has closed.

Elder Abuse

Adult protective services (APS) serves adults age 18 or older who are mentally or physically incapacitated to the extent that they cannot provide self-care or manage their own affairs. Medical personnel, law enforcement, government agencies, and care custodians are mandated reporters of elder abuse, neglect by others, financial abuse, and self-neglect. There continues to be an increase in reporting these cases as people are living longer due to advances in medicine.[19]

If the LNC is involved in interviewing the person who was allegedly abused, the LNC should investigate these concerns:

- What is the state of the person's nutrition?

- Is there evidence of lack of food or inappropriate food in the house (e.g., candy, fast food)?
- Is the person malnourished?
- Are the utilities working?
- Is the person receiving in-home assistance, housecleaning, and personal care?

The LNC should make these observations or look for this type of documentation:

- Is the person unkempt or malodorous?
- Is the person inappropriately dressed?
- Is the person agitated?
- Are there bruises, cuts, scrapes, or evidence of poor health?
- Is the person confused or afraid?
- Was there a delay in seeking care?

Elder and dependent victims may be embarrassed, fearful, reluctant to be a nuisance, and unwilling or unable to go to court. A multidisciplinary team approach from the district attorney's office to APS provides the best approach for care, complete services with comprehensive follow-up, secondary assessments, and documentation.[16] APS has an 800 hotline in each state. In long-term care facilities, there is an ombudsman for advocacy for residents.

The LNC can help attorneys in the record review for these elder abuse cases. Multiple volumes of records exist because of the long medical histories of the elder.

Domestic Violence

The trend in the USA today is that domestic violence emergency response teams (DVERT) are forming to deal with domestic violence in a timely manner. This team consists of law enforcement, advocates, social workers, and medical personnel. All of these team members generate documentation and reports.

In a case of alleged domestic violence, the LNC should ask whether this is the first such incident. If not, are there previous police reports, arrests, or convictions? If this was not the first incident of abuse, what steps had been taken (if any) by the victim to remove herself from the perpetrator or have the perpetrator removed? Had any previous protective orders or warrants been served on the perpetrator? If so, what was the response of the perpetrator? Had previous charges been dropped by the victim? If so, why? Had the victim ever sought refuge in a shelter? If so, what happened? Had the couple undergone any type of counseling or therapy? If so, what were the conclusions? What was the victim's account of the incidents?

There are also other questions the LNC should ask:

- What is the medical history of the victim? What is the medical history of the perpetrator?
- Are there children involved? If so, what is the medical history of the children?
- Have the children been removed from the home? If so, how many times?

- Was CPS involved?
- Are the children in foster care or in the care of other family members?
- Who is the caseworker?
- Was there any evidence or indication of physical or sexual abuse of the children?
- If the victim was examined by a medical professional, what were the findings?
- Were physical injuries photographed?
- Was evidence obtained? If so, where is the evidence?
- What diagnostic tests were performed, and what were the results?
- Were statements made to medical professionals documented?
- What was the psychological/emotional state of the victim at the time of exam?
- How much time elapsed from the time of the physical abuse to the time treatment was sought?
- If rape occurred, was it reported?
- Was a sexual assault examination performed? If so, what were the findings?

Variables for the LNC to consider in the record review of the perpetrator of this crime include:

- Is there a previous criminal history?
- What does the police report say?
- Are the officers who took the report available to discuss the report?
- What is the medical history of the perpetrator? Does he use drugs and alcohol? Does he have a history of psychological or mental problems?
- Has there been an evaluation by a mental health provider?

The LNC's role in this area would be to assist with the record review and analysis.

Sexual Assault

Sexual assault or rape is defined as the act of forced penetration, meaning vulvar, anal, or oral penetration by a penis, object, or body part without consent.[17] This crime is a violent act motivated by a desire for power and control. Sex is the mechanism. A female is sexually assaulted every 6 minutes in the USA, but 80–90% of the cases are never reported.[17] Sexual Assault Nurse Examiners (SANEs) are forensic nurses who have received special training,[18] and demonstrate competency in performing sexual assault examinations. The role of the SANE is to collect evidence, document evidence collected, and testify in court.[21]

Example 19.2: Crystal and Rick were drinking at a party. Crystal passed out on a bed in the back of the house. When she woke up, Rick was on top of her. She told him to get off, but he had intercourse with her. She told a friend and then called the sheriff and consented to a sexual assault response team (SART) examination. There was an investigation and arrest, and now the LNC is helping prepare for the defense or prosecution of the case.

Variables and issues for the LNC to consider in assisting with this case include:

- Review of all documentation should occur from the 911 calls through the history and investigation.[20]
- Alcohol was involved, so the crime lab reports would provide the results of this information.
- Did the crime lab analyze the evidence collection kit?
- Can the chain of evidence be followed and documented?
- Were the SART examination findings positive or negative?
- Were there findings on the suspect examination?
- A health history should be present.[21]

There are only two defenses in sexual assault:

1. I did not do this.
2. There was consent.

Driving Under the Influence

The presence or absence of drugs or alcohol in a person's body and whether the subject was under the influence of a drug are important issues in traffic investigations, in cases of driving under the influence, in the legal defense of diminished capacity, and in public intoxication cases.

The majority of states in the United States set 0.10% as the blood alcohol level at which a person is presumed to be under the influence of alcohol such that the driver is unable to operate a motor vehicle in a safe and prudent manner. The amount of alcohol necessary to reach a level of 0.10% varies from one individual to another.

Law enforcement agencies across the country have routine procedures for analyzing blood, breath, and urine for blood alcohol levels. Blood and urine samples should be collected in a medically approved manner. Breath tests are conducted by technicians/officers who have been certified in the use of breath intoxylizers.

The LNC's analysis of this type of case should include searching for answers to questions. In the case of someone driving under the influence and causing a motor vehicle accident, does the driver have a previous history of driving under the influence (DUI)? Has the driver's license ever been revoked or suspended? If so, why? What is the driving history of the driver? What facts are documented on the police report concerning driving conditions, road conditions, speed at the time of impact, skid marks, time of day, appearance and behavior of driver, etc.? If injuries occurred, how serious were the injuries? Was emergency assistance required? Was anyone removed from the scene by ambulance? If so, to which facility was the person taken? What was the driver's condition at the scene and at the time of arrival at the emergency room? What treatment was required? What were the findings? If drug or alcohol tests were performed, were they blood or urine or both? What were the results? How much time had elapsed since the time of ingestion of drug and alcohol and the time of the accident and also the time that the drug or alcohol tests were performed? Were any narcotics administered in the emergency department before the urine or blood was tested for substances?

The LNC should consider the following factors when evaluating a DUI case:

- Physical makeup of the individual
- Existing and preexisting medical conditions
- Use of central nervous system depressants
- Proper evidence collection and preservation of physical evidence
- Use of nonprescription drugs that may elevate blood alcohol levels

Death Investigations

Of all criminal cases, death investigation is the most difficult and requires the greatest effort on the part of law enforcement. In sudden and violent death investigations it is important to determine as quickly as possible whether the deceased died from an accident, suicide, or the act of another person. The finding of a body is the starting point and initial focus of any death investigation. The first officer on the scene is responsible for determining whether the victim is dead or alive and maintaining the integrity of the crime scene. Determination of suspicious death at this point is critical. In many cases, the first officer to arrive at the scene has erred and pronounced the death to be of natural cause, only to learn at a later time that the actual cause of death was the result of an unnoticed bullet wound. Care and attention to detail are critical in this type of case. In order to conduct an efficient and effective investigation, the investigator must concentrate on the mechanical aspects of the death (i.e., motives and methods; wound structures; autopsy; crime scene reconstruction; the cause, manner, and time of death; and the other factors that provide clues to the dynamics of the event).

From an investigative point of view, it is imperative that an LNC have a practical understanding of the manner, means, and mode of several kinds of death:

- Gunshot and firearm wounds
- Cutting wounds
- Stabbing wounds
- Blunt force injuries
- Poisoning
- Asphyxia deaths
- Autoerotic deaths
- Arson and fire deaths

Example 19.3: A female body was reported in a shallow riverbed. The story given to police investigators was that the victim fell off an overpass and into the river. Attempts to rescue the victim by a male friend were in vain. There were noticeable cuts and bruises on the body, which would corroborate the story. After the autopsy, it was determined that many of the injuries did not match the description of the incident. Upon further investigation, it was determined that the person who attempted the rescue had recently taken out an insurance policy on the victim.

Was there a history of domestic violence with this couple? What interpersonal characteristics did this couple display prior to this event? What were the toxicology findings of the autopsy? Was anything found at the scene that would be consistent with the types of blunt injury wounds to the victim's head? Were there any findings at the time of autopsy to indicate that the head trauma was the fatal injury? Were there any findings consistent with drowning? What was the affect and response of the rescuer at the time police arrived on the scene? Who reported the incident? What was the financial situation of the couple? What was the work history of the rescuer? Was anyone else with the couple? If so, what was their relationship to the victim, etc.?

Death investigation requires a team effort. The actions and responsibilities of each person involved in this type of case are highly scrutinized during litigation. The successful solution to any death case relies on a professional, thorough, and intelligent investigation.

Summary

As is true in any case analysis, the processes of assessment, planning, implementation, and evaluation are ongoing as new information becomes available. The LNC who pursues this area of practice will benefit from objectivity, thoroughness, and inductive and deductive reasoning.

Acknowledgments

The authors wish to thank the following individuals for their time and contributions:

W.D. Bruckner, Chief Investigator, Office of the District Attorney, DeKalb County, GA

G. Gowitt, Medical Examiner, DeKalb County, GA

B. Harvey, Criminal Defense Attorney

S. Roberts, Special Agent, Georgia Bureau of Investigation

J.M. Shockley, Director, Office of the Medical Examiner, DeKalb County, GA

References

1. Neubauer, D.W., *America's Courts and the Criminal Justice System*, 5th ed., Wadsworth Publishing, Belmont, CA, 1996.
2. Swanson, C.R., Chamelin, N.C., and Territo, L., *Criminal Investigation*, 7th ed., McGraw-Hill, New York, 1999.
3. *Strickland v. Washington*, 466 U.S. 668 (1984).
4. *U.S. v. Cronic*, 466 U.S. 648 (1983).
5. *Miranda v. Arizona*, 384 U.S. 436 (1966).
6. *State v. Cressey*, 137 NH 402, 628 A.2d 696, 698 (1993).
7. *Daubert v. Merrell Dow Pharmaceuticals, Inc.*, 509 U.S. 579 (1993).
8. *Frye v. United States*, 54 App. DC 46, 293 F. 1013 (1923).
9. *United States v. Jackboots*, 955 F.2d 786 (2d Cir. 1992).
10. *Hayes v. State*, 660 So. 2d 257 (Fla. 1995).
11. *Commonwealth v. Rodgers*, 413 Pa.Super.Ct. 498, 605 A.2d 1228 (1992).
12. *Trimboli v. State*, 817 S.W.2d 785 (Tex. App. Waco 1991), *aff'd*, 826 S.W.2d 953 (Tex. Crim. App. 1992).
13. *Caldwell v. State*, 260 Ga. 278, 393 S.E.2d 436 (1990).
14. Reece, R.M., *Child Abuse: Medical Diagnosis and Management*, Lea & Febiger, Philadelphia, 1994.

15. Monteleone, J., *Physical Examination in Sexual Abuse, Child Maltreatment*, 2nd ed., GW Medical, St. Louis, 1998.

16. Grey, H., Elder Abuse, handout outline, San Diego, CA, January 12, 2001.

17. Satin, A. et al., Sexual assault during pregnancy, *Obstetrics and Gynecology*, 77(5), 710, 1995.

18. International Association of Forensic Nurses, Sexual Assault Nurse Examiner Standards of Practice.

19. Phillips, R., The laws protecting elders and dependent adults, *Law Enforcement Quarterly*, 5–13, May–July 1996.

20. Girardin, B. et al., *The Color Atlas of Sexual Assault*, C.V. Mosby, St. Louis, 1977, 5.

21. International Association of Forensic Nurses, Sexual Assault Nurse Examiner Educational Guidelines, 1998.

22. Knight, B., *Forensic Pathology*, 2nd ed., Oxford University Press, New York, 1996.

Test Questions

1. In order to be found guilty of a crime, the defendant must be
   A. Proven guilty by a preponderance of the evidence
   B. Proven guilty by 51% of the evidence
   C. Required to testify
   D. Proven guilty beyond a reasonable doubt

2. All of the following are types of evidence that can be relied upon EXCEPT:
   A. Scientific
   B. Physical
   C. Testimonial
   D. Circumstantial

3. The chain of custody refers to
   A. Ankle chains
   B. The reporting hierarchy in health care
   C. Handling of evidence
   D. Disputes between separated parents regarding custody of the child

4. Which of the following is the LNC least likely to analyze in a criminal case?
   A. Emergency room record
   B. Psychological testing results
   C. Autopsy report
   D. Auto body shop reports

5. Which of the following statements is NOT true?
   A. A felony is a crime punishable by imprisonment up to a year.
   B. An incident may give rise to both a criminal and civil suit.
   C. Criminal laws may vary from state to state.
   D. Violations of criminal law generally require some level of intent.

Answers: 1. D, 2. D, 3. C, 4. D, 5. A

Chapter 20

ERISA AND HMO LITIGATION

Cynthia Dangerfield, RN, CPN, and William J. Scott, Esq.

CONTENTS

Objectives

After review of this chapter, the legal nurse consultant (LNC) will be able to:

- Discuss different types of managed care products
- Define terms related to the Employee Retirement Income Security Act, health maintenance organizations, health insurance coverage, and litigation issues involving these topics

- Identify how the Employee Retirement Income Security Act has affected health maintenance organization litigation cases in the past and how legislative changes will impact future cases
- Assist in the development of cases involving health maintenance organizations covered under the Employee Retirement Income Security Act

Introduction to ERISA and HMO Litigation Issues

The Employee Retirement Income Security Act (ERISA) is a law enacted by Congress in 1974 as a way of ensuring that employees of companies that provide retirement and pension benefits receive the provided benefits. ERISA's main focus is to provide the framework through which the benefit plans are administered. Over time, the law encompassed health care plans, or "welfare plans," as well. This includes health maintenance organizations (HMOs).

As was common practice in the early 1980s, many companies looked to HMOs as a type of "health care reform," a financially manageable way to help cover the expense of providing health care coverage for their employees. HMOs and various other forms of managed care were viewed as the panacea to spiraling health care costs and mismanagement.

Millions of Americans belong to HMOs and other types of managed health plans. According to recently released managed care national statistics, 80.9 million Americans were enrolled in HMOs as of early 2000.[1] HMOs equip many employers with an affordable method of providing health care coverage to their employees.

As the growth of the managed care industry developed, so have the issues that were associated with this model of health care delivery, such as utilization review decisions that appeared to be acts of limitation by the HMO. The fear among health care providers and the public, who were unfamiliar with guidelines and "critical pathways" for treatment of the more common diseases, was that managed care arbitrarily withheld health care and followed some secret code of denial. Another example of HMO "strategy" that quickly fell under the light of suspicion was the belief that HMOs offered financial incentives to the physicians and health care providers who contracted with them. The latter seemed very unethical. Some of these incentives were limitations of referrals to specialists. It was felt that any competent internist or general practitioner could treat almost every illness with the exception of the most dire and complicated. Referrals to specialists were no longer the norm for treatment of conditions. The money that was saved by "withholding" care was distributed to the physicians.

Historically, ERISA's effect on HMO malpractice litigation was well known in that these suits were covered under the preemption doctrine and impervious to large civil and state settlements. Early into its development, the managed care industry became concerned that it would never be able to get a fair hearing in medical malpractice and negligence suits. With the advent of ERISA, however, the employer-provided HMOs were not subject to suit in state court for injuries as a result of negligence and medical malpractice because of the doctrine of preemption. This doctrine provided that employer-funded HMOs could be sued in federal court only for violations of ERISA, which offered very limited relief to HMO members.

As a result of recent congressional action, ERISA is no longer the safe harbor for the managed care industry. Today, with the advent of patients' rights, patient's bill of rights documents, and the focus on risk management and compliance programs, HMOs must take responsibility for their design and administration of benefits. Also, HMOs are responsible for the appropriateness of their utilization decisions, structuring of health care options under the practice of case management or disease management programs, and coverage decisions. These issues must be handled within the new framework of rising health care costs and less legal protection under the law.

Overview of ERISA

As described in the introduction, Title 1 of ERISA was developed to provide the minimum standards and the framework by which voluntary employee benefit plans would be administered. Employee benefit plans are generally established and offered by an employer, an employee organization (such as some types of unions), or a combination of both. Different types of employee benefit plans include pension plans; retirement income deferral plans; and "welfare" plans, such as health, disability, and some forms of life insurance. Historically, ERISA has applied to most private-sector employee benefit plans, but has not covered plans created or maintained by government bodies, churches, and benefit plans, which exist for the sole purpose of complying with workers' compensation, disability, and unemployment laws. In addition, ERISA does not apply to benefit plans that are maintained outside of the continental United States, regardless of the plan type.

ERISA essentially ensures that employee benefit plans are established and maintained in a financially sound manner. It mandates that once established, the employer is obligated not only to provide promised benefits but to do so according to ERISA guidelines. These guidelines are as follows:

- The plans are provided for the exclusive benefit of plan participants (employees) and their dependents/beneficiaries.
- The plan managers discharge their duties in "a prudent manner," while avoiding transactions that can appear to be a conflict of interest.
- The plan management complies with limitations in employer investments in securities and property.
- The plan funds benefits according to legal requirements and plan rules.
- The plan discloses information on benefits, management, and the financial condition of the plan to the appropriate government entities and plan participants (e.g., financial reports and summary plan descriptions [SPDs]).
- The plan provides documents required by government regulations to validate compliance with ERISA guidelines.[2]

The government agency with primary jurisdiction over Title 1 of ERISA and the entity that administers and controls benefit plans is the United States Department of Labor, along with the Pension and Welfare Benefits Administration and the Internal Revenue Service.

In addition, the Consolidated Omnibus Budget Reconciliation Act of 1985 was codified in Title 1 of ERISA to broaden the force of the regulation. This means that the benefit plan participant can retain the right to maintain continuous health care coverage, at his own expense, at a discounted rate or at the same group rate charged while the participant was still employed by the original issuer of the benefit plan. These statutes can be viewed in the November 21, 2000 edition of the *Federal Register*.[3] The rules and regulations for the administration, enforcement, claims procedures, SPD regulations, and any amendments are included in these sections.

ERISA was amended by the enactment of the Health Insurance Portability and Accountability Act of 1996. The act improved the portability and continuity of health care benefits coverage provided by an employer.

To summarize ERISA's impact on medical malpractice and negligence litigation, ERISA and its amendments basically supersede state and local laws that may be applied to an employee benefit plan and generally prohibit loss of pension benefits. This has historically been interpreted to apply to HMOs as well. HMOs were exempt from civil legal action related to medical malpractice, personal injury, and negligence, because with ERISA-regulated plans, any legal action would be removed to federal court under the preemption doctrine where legal remedies were very limited. Recent changes in congressional law have altered this school of thought, and ERISA may no longer apply to HMOs.

Overview of HMOs

In order to understand how litigation in an HMO case can be affected by ERISA, it is helpful to understand the structure of the different managed care plans. Managed care organizations (MCOs) provide active coordination of, arrangement for, and delivery of health care within a network of contracted providers (physicians, nurse practitioners, physician assistants, and other health care professionals) who receive monetary compensation for agreeing to provide services for patients that are enrolled in the plan. Often contracting providers will lower their usual fee substantially in exchange for the assurance of a consistent patient population, creating a steady income. Providers may contract with several plans at once, or may contract with only a select few. In some situations, providers work only for one HMO and do not see private, or nonmember, patients.

Managed care operates on three basic principles: (1) oversight of medical care given (utilization review); (2) contracts with care providers and organizations; and (3) benefits furnished by the plan, which can vary from employer to employer or even member to member (SPD). Among the types of managed care are HMOs, preferred provider organizations (PPOs), exclusive provider organizations (EPOs), physician-hospital organizations, and independent practice associations.

The most common model in managed care is the HMO. Some HMOs are known as "staff model" HMOs; the plan, or HMO, actually employs the physicians and ancillary health care providers for the sole purpose of providing care to its members. A "group model" HMO involves contracts with physicians in a group or professional association or a professional corporation. The health plan pays the group, and the group manages compensation of the individual provider group members by arranging contracts with hospitals and other health care providers, such as home health agencies and durable medical equipment (DME) companies, to provide these services to the patients assigned to the group.

Managed care plans also include PPOs and EPOs. Authorizations and referrals are generally not required for these two types of organizations as long as the member utilizes contracted providers for services. In addition, the members' costs and financial responsibilities will increase if they utilize extracontractual providers. This also applies if patients require the services of specific disciplines that are not provided by the PPO or EPO because they have failed to or were unable to contract with that type of provider. Monetary compensation for contracted providers may take the form of capitation, a per-member/per-month payment, or a flat fee for contracting with the plan.

Other forms of remuneration include bonuses, which were previously based on the lack of referrals to specialists, reduced inpatient hospital care, low pharmacy utilization, and other similar scenarios. The physician was financially rewarded when utilization of these services was low, but was financially penalized when usage was high. This is often referred to as an "incentive." Currently, the focus has shifted in the industry to rewarding physicians for high levels of patient satisfaction and quality service.

HMOs have been a source of health care benefit management since the early 1980s, and some pioneer forms of HMOs existed prior to that time. The general premise behind the HMO was prevention of illness and catastrophic health conditions. A person's health could be maintained through preventive services, rather than caring for conditions that resulted from physical neglect and lack of appropriate medical attention in advance of the illness.

These preventive services took the shape of programs, such as vaccinations for infants and children, influenza and pneumonia vaccination programs for the elderly and at-risk populations, prenatal care and "well baby" visits, smoking cessation programs, and community health fairs. Over time, the HMOs observed that few members availed themselves of these "added-value" benefits. What became evident was that on average, participants in HMOs experienced illness, injury, and chronic medical conditions as much as the participants in other types of managed care and traditional insurance plans.

In order for HMOs to remain competitive in the health care marketplace, the savings that HMO models promised their administrators, members, and employers had to be found elsewhere in the plan. Utilization review and case management seemed to be the answer to this dilemma.

Cost Control for the HMO

The main focus of utilization management is to monitor and control several aspects of a patient's care. Some plans focus on utilization from a quality-driven perspective: care is monitored to ensure that patients receive everything they need to recover, as expeditiously as possible, with the intent that maximum care would provide the fastest results. This would save money by reducing the length of hospitalization or recurrent illnesses. This is a rarity since few plans have the capital to offer this approach and remain competitive in the insurance market.

Most utilization plans are opposite in nature: only the most necessary procedures, supplies, and days in the hospital are "authorized," or approved, by the plan's utilization review department. Decisions for benefit denial, or nonauthorization of medical care, are generally initiated by a nurse who is employed by the plan and reviews the patient's records to determine whether or not evidence of "medical necessity" for the procedure, service, hospital stay, or supply is evident.

These decisions are then reviewed by a medical authority, usually a physician or the plan's medical director, and final disposition is determined. Not only does this process apply to hospitalization and utilization of expensive equipment and supplies, but it also applies to referrals to specialists, home health care, and customized equipment and supplies.

In standard HMO models, the money that is paid to the plan from member premiums is "pooled" after administrative expenses and plan costs are removed. The pool may then be equally divided among the contracted providers or left in one unit. For any "extra" care that is provided to a member outside of routine office visits, such as an emergency room visit or a referral to and treatment by a specialist, the value of the pool is diminished. For the provider who has his own pool, the incentive would be to preserve the balance in order to receive the money in the pool.

Although the incentives appear to motivate providers to refuse referrals to specialists, deny emergency room treatment, and discharge patients prematurely from hospitals in order to retain their pools, the original impetus to providers was to eliminate any unnecessary or extraneous referrals and services. The intent was to avoid prolonged hospitalizations, for example, or situations such as referring a patient to an otolaryngologist for treatment of a sore throat when the patient's physician (who may be a pediatrician or internal medicine physician) was quite capable of treating the condition.

Example 20.1: The following is an illustration of a prolonged hospital stay scenario: A patient is admitted to the hospital for surgery. The physician and patient agree to a hospitalization of 6 days. The intensity of service/severity of illness criteria utilized by the HMO indicate that the average hospital stay for this particular type of surgery, barring any severe complications, is 3 days, and that is what is "prior authorized" by the plan. Unless there was a medical reason for the patient to remain in the hospital after the approved 3-day stay, the patient would be financially responsible for any additional days over the initial 3 days covered by the plan. Also, the physician would more than likely be responsible for the "overutilization" of inpatient days and penalized by the plan.

When a joint pool is shared by many providers, it was felt that the providers may have attempted to influence each other by recommending the authorization of fewer referrals and services, creating a larger balance to share. This concept is known as "risk sharing." One of the benefits of a shared pool applies to doctors who are in the same group practice together, or professional organizations or partnerships. In this situation, patients could be referred to different specialists within the group practice, thereby controlling extraneous referrals and maintaining the pool money within the group. All of these incentives and health care delivery models are a type of utilization management.

Another type of utilization management is performed by a case manager. A case manager is usually a nurse or social worker, employed by the HMO, who is experienced in a variety of medical conditions. This person can anticipate most of the patient's needs and treatment requirements, making cost-effective arrangements for delivery of these services by providers within the HMO network. The case manager is usually familiar with clinical pathways, or usual and predictable courses of treatment for a given condition. Based on the criteria set, medical necessity is determined and care and services authorized and delivered in a controlled, closely monitored environment.

This model of utilization management falls short of delivering promised savings when the patient's medical condition does not follow the normal course of resolution. In addition, not all HMOs are capable of contracting every type of provider that a patient may potentially require, and in these situations, the case manager must consider extracontractual arrangements while still attempting to provide a savings to the plan.

Currently, the trend in case management is progressing to "care management," a sort of hybridized or refined case management program of coordinating the patient's care from a proactive viewpoint. There is more of a partnership with both the provider and the patient, and the care manager not only is a liaison for the health plan, but may also perform patient advocacy and physician/service coordination. This type of case management is usually restricted to specific and often common disease processes. Chapter 22, The Legal Nurse Consultant as a Case Manager, provides more information on case/care management.

It was once assumed that benefit denial decisions were arbitrarily determined by HMO accountants and financial officers as well as nonmedical clerical staff based solely on cost. In fact, most ethical and prudent HMOs leave the decision-making power to the medical staff, which usually includes nurses, social workers, physicians, and a committee of a variety of health care workers as a backup system.

Medical decisions are generated by a comparison of the patient's symptoms and physical condition to a national data set, or utilization guidelines, often referred to as *intensity of service/severity of illness* criteria. Two of the more popular sources of this information are InterQual Criteria[4] and Milliman and Robertson Length of Stay Index.[5] Both of these criteria sets and others like them give general guidelines for lengths of stay, the appropriate time during the progression of an illness to perform diagnostic tests or decide which ones are needed. The criteria that a patient must meet in order to be considered appropriate for discharge from care are also considered.

Decisions independent of these guidelines are made when a patient appears to progress at a faster rate than outlined in the criteria and when treatment may end sooner than expected. On rare occasions, making an accelerated decision turns out to be disastrous for both the patient and the plan. Early discharges sometimes result in a relapse of the condition, or unseen complications that may have been evident had the patient remained hospitalized under a watchful clinical eye or undergone more diagnostic studies.

Some data published in the *Journal of the American College of Cardiology* reported that compared to other types of health benefit plans, HMOs historically authorize fewer procedures, but report longer hospital stays for acute myocardial infarction admissions.[6] This could be due, in part, to lack of access to the appropriate facilities, providers, or specialists, and even diagnostic equipment and procedures within the HMO's network. In some situations, this policy results in a cost savings to the HMO. In other situations, the cost of patient care is significantly higher because the patient was denied access to necessary and needed care.

With the advent of the patients' rights movement, plans are turning to compliance and quality programs. One of the more popular "watchdog groups" to review plan activity according to higher industry standards is the National Committee for Quality Assurance. This is a not-for-profit organization independent of other insurance organizations and health care plans whose main function is to monitor various types of plans in order to ensure quality of services. This is done through member surveys, strict credentialing guidelines, and monitoring of Health Plan Employer Data and Information Set Data, a "report card" that indicates how a plan is performing compared to its peer group.

Organizations of this type generally will accredit or certify a plan after a rigorous on-site review of administrative and clinical practice processes and verification of contracting practices. Member surveys generally focus on such issues as access to care, customer service, and the members' expectations of the plan.[7] Organizations of this type and others like it are holding the current standard of health plans at a more patient-friendly level. Although meticulous and painstaking to undertake, successful accreditation or certification reviews also serve the plan by increasing its marketability and credibility as a quality health plan.

HMO management has been dissected and reevaluated in many superior court cases. With each case the opportunity has presented itself for the public to understand how an HMO is administered as well as how to maneuver within the managed care system. In addition, HMOs may be evolving into a more user-friendly, cost-effective answer to coverage of health care benefits.

Role of the LNC in HMO Litigation

Previously, the plaintiff, during litigation, could expect to recover an amount equal to the denied benefit, receive authorization to utilize the benefit, or obtain the requested medical care (when it was not originally a covered benefit). The plaintiff also had the opportunity to potentially recover attorneys' fees as long as the administrator of the plan was found to have made the denial in bad faith, or to have breached a duty to the plan participant.

Recent changes to the law have provided incentives for HMO members to seek assistance from the courts. When approached to review records and apply medical expertise, the LNC should be alert to potential issues involving HMOs. The primary issue will be to determine whether or not the client is covered by an ERISA plan. This is generally confirmed by the attorney prior to the case or medical record review, but the LNC should be familiar with how this is determined.

Some basic questions would include whether the employer contributes to the participant's benefit plan, and if so, this may be an ERISA plan. Determine whether the plan is voluntary or mandatory, and whether the premium, co-payments, and deductibles that may apply are covered independently by the client. The plan generally would not fall under ERISA if it is completely voluntary, or if the client is the sole payer for plan coverage. One exception to this rule is in situations where the employer actively promotes the availability of and actively encourages enrollment into the plan, even when the client is solely responsible for the premiums and other financial responsibilities. In addition, the common misconception that a "contracted" individual is not considered an employee, and is therefore not eligible for coverage under the plan, is currently being evaluated in the courts.

All ERISA plans allow for internal or corporate processes that must be followed in order for a claim denial review to occur. When an administrator denies a claimant's request for benefit coverage, the steps for requesting and obtaining a review are prescribed and must be followed. In order for this process to be appropriately initiated, the claimant must have knowledge of this process. ERISA requires that the plan provide notice of the denial in writing, and clearly delineate the steps that must be followed for a review. The claimant must also have enough time for the claim review. In other words, the plan should not delay the review for such an extended period of time that the claimant suffers ill effects simply because of the delay in the review.

Plans are permitted under law to administer their own benefits structure. A conflict-of-interest situation is innate in this arrangement. However, the law also clearly defines how the fiduciary (responsible plan administrator) must conduct business for the exclusive purpose of providing benefits to the plan participants. The law also states that the fiduciary must save the plan any superfluous expenses, while exercising "care, skill, prudence and diligence under the circumstances that a prudent man, acting in a like capacity and familiar with such matters, would use in the conduct of an enterprise of a like character and with like aims."[8]

The LNC Checklist

The primary role of the LNC involved in assisting with HMO litigation cases is to determine whether the HMO delivered promised health care benefits to the claimant. The attorney will most likely have ascertained the nature of the administrative issues associated with the case, such as scope of benefit coverage and the type of benefits selected by the claimant. It is helpful for the LNC to be familiar with some of the legal nuances that make this type of litigation distinct. The following is a checklist of helpful issues for the LNC and attorney to investigate:

1. Request the certificate of insurance, SPD (summary plan description), explanation of benefits, or the actual contract signed by the HMO member when the plan was elected. Familiarity with the benefits selected by the member (known as election of benefits) will help to determine whether the denied benefit was elected by the member and should be a covered benefit to which the client is entitled. Good sources to review for this type of information also include any pharmacy benefit plans, formularies, and DME coverage plans. This information should be available either in the contract or as an addendum to the contract.

2. When an exception to the contracted benefit plan has been requested by the HMO member and denied by the plan, it is then necessary to determine whether or not the benefit is an industry standard. This is something that is routinely provided by comparable HMOs and managed care organizations. Many national and well-noted HMOs will provide access to their benefit plans on a Web site's home page or even make them available upon request. The Internet may also provide a veritable gold mine of information related to standards of care through the managed care association, medical association, and insurance association Web sites.

3. Determine whether or not the SPD information is decisive and clearly understood by the reader. Although this can be a subjective judgment, it should be stated that a medical procedure/service/supply is covered. Language demonstrating this would be similar to "is considered experimental and therefore not a covered benefit," or "is not a covered benefit

under this plan due to the lack of medical evidence that this is a required procedure." Consider for whom the information is written. For example, if the HMO member speaks Spanish, the information should be available in Spanish. The plan should contain language that specifically grants the plan administrator the discretionary right to interpret benefits. If this is not present, then the case could be held to a different standard of review in court. If this language is included in the plan, then there is the possibility of a conflict-of-interest argument.

4. When changes occur to the client's plan, the member normally should have been notified in a timely manner, such that the impact of the change could be evaluated in time for the member to possibly choose another plan or make other arrangements for coverage. A stipulated timeline is usually established and documented in the plan with language and amendments describing the time limitation. As a general rule, these changes occur and are presented immediately prior to the annual enrollment period.

5. Inquire whether the member has exhausted all remedies, such as an appeal, hearing, or grievance procedure, that the plan advocates for settling claim disputes.

6. If any of the HMO's internal remedies listed in section 5 above have not been pursued, it would be in the member's best interest to do so prior to moving forward with a legal action. Many courts are currently leaning toward this being a mandatory step, even though pursuing these avenues appears optional and not required under ERISA. The LNC and attorney should be aware that fairly rigid timelines may be associated with the steps necessary to comply with an appeal process or grievance hearing.

7. Determine whether or not the request for a denial reversal is an emergency request. If the procedure or treatment is urgently needed or necessary before all plan remedies can be exhausted, a suit may be filed in order to seek emergency relief until all of the HMO's internal procedures can be followed. Additionally, the patient could potentially be responsible for payment for the procedure or service should it ultimately be denied.

8. Obtain a copy of the document outlining the denial and any supporting information. It will be necessary to understand and be familiar with what criteria (such as InterQual criteria) or plan policies are the basis for the denial. If the denial appears to be based upon language that is clearly stated in the SPD, a copy of the full and complete contract of coverage, in addition to any amendments, should be requested. If the member has a copy of the denial letter, it must include specific information as cited under ERISA: the reason for denial, notification to the client on the specific steps that can be taken in order to have the request reviewed, and a list of any information that the member may be able to submit that supports the appeal and claim.

9. Obtain a copy of an authoritative source for the standards of care related to the member's condition and benefit request. These can include managed care, nursing and medical standards, and standards for specialty fields that some specialists (physicians and nurses) are held to above and beyond the more common standards of general medical and nursing practice. Ask whether the standards were adhered to in this situation. Supporting infor-

mation can also be obtained from governmental or authoritative agencies such as the Food and Drug Administration (FDA), the National Institutes of Health (NIH), and the Centers for Disease Control. In some cases, the HMO member may never receive a letter, or the letter may be deficient or vague in the information required by ERISA. A referral to the specific area of the health care plan language that applies to this denial should be addressed and cited in the denial letter. When there are differences between the language in the SPD or benefits coverage information that the client received and actual plan or contract language, the plan or contract should carry the greater weight. Alternatively, if the SPD appears to be conferring benefits that are not included in the plan, the SPD usually prevails. Assessment skills and knowledge of medical terms and procedures equip the LNC with the ability to notice the subtle differences in the contract language. Attorneys will find the LNC's knowledge base helpful.

10. Gather any and all documents, sources, and information possible to support or refute the member's claim. When the information is submitted to the plan for the reconsideration of the denial, the aim is to provide enough information for the plan administrator to make an informed, well-supported, and well-substantiated decision. Close attention must be paid to procedural errors, conflicting or questionable language in the documents, and "arbitrary or capricious" behavior in the administration of the plan benefits.

11. The opinions of the treating physician are generally allowed significant weight by the court, particularly when the recommendations of this physician conflict with those of a plan medical director who has not examined the member. It would be prudent to determine the treating physician's preferences and how important the denial reversal is to the member's overall treatment plan. The value of a face-to-face meeting with the treating physician cannot be overestimated. It is in this situation that the LNC can bring the most value to case development; two medical professionals will communicate with each other in a fashion very different from the attorney-physician interaction.

12. Many resources are available via the Internet. Also, medical and legal libraries provide examples of forms that can be used for requesting information from HMOs, physicians, and medical facilities. These provide details of items that will assist the LNC and attorney in gathering necessary documentation in order to support or refute a case. In addition, networking with other LNCs and professionals will provide some of the support necessary to understand this complex situation.

13. Most importantly, the LNC must determine whether a medical decision was made by the HMO, as opposed to offering a less expensive alternative. Understanding the distinction between making a medical decision versus an administrative decision is key to this determination. An example of medical decision-making by the HMO could be denying necessary medical treatment or refusing to provide needed medical devices. If this is the case, it must be determined whether or not the member suffered any harm as a result. And if this determination is made, the attorney must decide whether the HMO has made a medical decision and, in effect, is practicing medicine as opposed to administering medical benefits.

Evaluating HMO Liability

In analyzing a managed care case, a number of preliminary questions must be addressed to determine what remedies are available to the client and how the attorney must plead the remedies. Three fundamental questions must be addressed by the legal team:

1. Is it a case involving significant injuries?
2. Does the case involve an ERISA plan, or is the HMO coverage/insurance coverage provided by a non-ERISA entity or an ERISA-exempt entity? The answer to this question in most cases controls the causes of action that the client may bring as well as what remedies are available.
3. Is the managed care entity an HMO, PPO, traditional indemnity insurance, or point of service contract?

Medical Malpractice

A medical malpractice claim must be investigated in order to identify duty, liability, damages, and proximate cause. The LNC should obtain a copy of or have access to authoritative sources or standards of care related to the member's condition and benefit request. These can include managed care standards, nursing and medical standards, or standards that some specialist physicians are held to above and beyond the more common standards of general medical practice. Ascertain that the standards were or were not adhered to in this situation. Supporting information can also be obtained from such entities as the FDA and NIH. See Chapter 12, Evaluating Professional Negligence Cases, and Chapter 13, Elements of Triage: Effective Case Screening of Medical Malpractice Claims, for more information about the evaluation of medical malpractice cases.

Significant Injury

The first step in the analysis is to determine whether the client has suffered significant injuries because of the managed care plan's actions. Cases involving managed care plans have many varied legal issues that will invariably result in lengthy appeals. Consequently, only those cases involving serious long-term injuries or potentially significant long-term consequences resulting from the denial of care justify the considerable financial expense and substantial time commitment required to pursue or defend the claim.

ERISA and HMO Coverage

In general, if the managed care plan is provided as part of a person's employment benefits package, then ERISA applies. ERISA does not apply when the client's claim is governed by state law. The potential causes of action to consider against an insurance/PPO company not involving an ERISA plan include breach of contract, medical malpractice, fraud in the inducement, intentional infliction of emotional distress, breach of fiduciary duty, common law negligence, and insurance bad faith.

HMOs are generally not subject to state insurance bad faith laws because they are not considered health insurance carriers. Consequently, the potential causes of action against an HMO include breach of contract, medical malpractice, breach of fiduciary duty, common law negligence, fraud in the inducement, intentional infliction of emotional distress, and state statutory causes of action. They may also include claims for vicarious liability as well as agency theories against the HMO for the actions of its doctors.

If the managed care claim involves an ERISA plan, then the client has no right to personal injury damages. The only right available to the client who has an ERISA-based plan is the option of an administrative remedy (i.e., an in-house review by the insurance carrier or the HMO). If the client disagrees with the findings of the in-house review, then an appeal to federal court can be made, arguing that the in-house review was arbitrary and capricious. The only remedy to be obtained from an appeal to federal court is payment of the benefit being sought or an interpretation of the contract.

When a client's claim arises from an ERISA-based plan, the potential causes of action against a managed care provider must be analyzed by the attorney and are beyond the scope of the LNC's analysis. It would be appropriate for the LNC to alert the attorney that the managed care plan may be employer-provided, and thus invoke ERISA.

Type of Entity

The final question to be determined is whether the managed care entity is an HMO, PPO, traditional insurance, point of service contract, or other such insurance plan. If the coverage is provided by an insurance carrier such as a PPO, point of service, or traditional health insurance contract, then the claim is a basic "denial of coverage" dispute. If the managed care plan is an HMO, then other standards will also apply.

Conclusion

HMOs are generally subject to statutory and regulatory duties. The LNC can assist the attorney by identifying the type of managed care provider at issue. If the managed care provider is an HMO, then the attorney will determine what statutes and regulations apply. The LNC can be an invaluable asset to the legal team when determining potential injuries, long-term effects of the denied benefit, and the ultimate effects on the client's life.

References

1. *The InterStudy Competitive Edge: HMO Industry Report 10.2*, figures as of January 1, 2000, InterStudy Publications, St. Paul, MN, 2000.
2. Subtitle B of Title I of the Employee Retirement Income Security Act of 1974.

3. *Federal Register, 29 CFR*, Parts VII and VIII, under Parts 2509, 2520, 2560.
4. InterQual Length of Stay Criteria©, InterQual Products Group, McKesson Corp., San Francisco, CA.
5. Milliman and Robertson Length of Stay Index©, Milliman, Seattle, WA.
6. Every, N. et al., Resource utilization in treatment of acute MI: staff model HMO versus fee-for-service hospitals, *Journal of the American College of Cardiology*, 26, 1995, 401–406.
7. National Committee for Quality Assurance, Health Plan Report Card, http://hprc.ncqa.org/index/asp, 2001.
8. 29 USC §1104, Fiduciary Duties, 2002.

Additional Reading and Resources

Baumberger, C., Vicarious liability claims against HMOs, *Trial*, May 1998.
Connette, E., Challenging insurance coverage denials under ERISA, *Trial*, May 1998.
Kongstvedt, P., *The Managed Care Handbook*, 3rd ed., Aspen Publishers, New York, 1996.

Web sites: The following Web sites can offer more information on the subject of managed care:

http://my.abcnews.go.com
http://www.atla.org
http://www.benefitsnext.com
http://www.dol.gov/dol/allcfr
http://www.harp.org
http://www.hcfa.org
http://www.hiaa.org
http://www.hprc.ncqa.org
http://www.managedcaremag.com
http://www.mcareol.com
http://www.medicalsocieties.org/hmo.htm
http://www.senate.state.mo.us/mancare
http://www.truemanlaw.com

Test Questions

1. The following are examples of managed care organizations:
   A. HMO, PPO, and SSA
   B. IPA, PPO, and EPO
   C. NCQA, SSI, and POS
   D. IRS, SDP, and PWAB

2. ERISA is a law that
   A. Describes how to perform utilization management
   B. Stipulates that lawsuits involving HMOs are to be argued in federal court
   C. Denies benefits when they are too costly
   D. Governs the administration of certain employee benefits plans

3. Utilization management is a form of
   A. Health care cost containment
   B. Torture
   C. Penalty for using services
   D. Micromanagement

4. When a health care provider is paid by the health plan to administer health care services to a group of members, it is known as
   A. Capitation
   B. Per member/per month
   C. IS/SI (intensity of service/severity of illness)
   D. Per capita

5. "SPD" is an acronym for
   A. A sexually transmitted disease
   B. A summary of the benefits offered by a health care plan
   C. Save Professional Doctors
   D. Sorry, Payment Denied

Answers: 1. B, 2. D, 3. A, 4. A, 5. B

Chapter 21

Complex Litigation

Betsy Isherwood Katz, BSN, RN, LNCC, and
Adella Toepel Getsch, BSN, RN, LNCC

CONTENTS

Objectives

- To define "complex litigation" and related concepts that require judicial management
- To describe the tools of complex litigation (class action and multidistrict litigation) established by the courts to deal with multiple claimants
- To identify the differences and parallels between toxic tort and product liability

0-8493-1418-6/03/$0.00+$1.50
© 2003 by AALNC

- To define "toxic tort"
- To define the concept of strict liability as it relates to product liability
- To describe the role of the legal nurse consultant (LNC) in complex litigation
- To describe the use of technology in the courtroom
- To explain expert guidelines in complex litigation
- To describe the use of technology in complex litigation
- To define "voir dire"

Introduction

One of the defining characteristics of complex litigation is the need for judicial management. Complex litigation usually involves many parties in numerous related cases, often in different jurisdictions, involving large numbers of witnesses, documents, and extensive discovery. The term *complex litigation* refers as much to the need for management by the court as to the resolution of difficult or challenging questions of law. The purpose of judicial management is to bring about the just, speedy, and inexpensive determination of the litigation.[1]

Role of the Court in Complex Litigation

Complex litigation frequently involves two or more related cases that involve the same defendant and different plaintiffs. All related cases pending or that will be filed in the same court will generally be assigned to the same judge. Counsel informs the assigned judge of any pending related cases, and the judge attempts to ascertain whether related cases are pending. This is to improve efficiency and coordination in the consolidation of related cases. Consolidation may be possible even when cases are filed in different courts. Cases from other districts may be transferred under 28 U.S.C. §1404(a) or 1406 to the consolidation court, and cases brought in state court may be removed (moved from state) to the federal court and transferred or refiled in the consolidating district court.[1]

The federal court system is more limited in size and purpose than the state courts. Federal courts have jurisdiction over five basic kinds of cases. They hear (1) cases in which the United States is a party, and (2) cases involving foreign officials. In civil matters, if more than $10,000 is involved, they may also hear (3) cases with parties from different states, and (4) cases involving the U.S. Constitution and federal laws. Federal courts also hear (5) "federal specialties," cases involving patents, copyrights, or bankruptcies. State courts share jurisdiction with federal courts in categories (3) and (4), and they exercise sole, or exclusive, jurisdiction in all other cases, mainly those involving state law. Only those state court decisions that involve the U.S. Constitution and federal law may be appealed to the federal courts. Counsel accomplishes coordination of proceedings with appropriate communication to the judge.

The earliest filed consolidated case will be designated as the lead case for administrative control and case management purposes. Rulings in lead cases may apply to other consolidated cases. The transfer of cases to the consolidating court is for case management purposes. Case management, as it applies here, refers to the fact that one judge handles the coordination of the litigation. Effective management requires the judge to be active, to have substantive involvement, to make timely dispute decisions, to monitor the progress of the litigation continually, to be fair and firm on time limits and other controls, and to be carefully prepared.[1] The attorneys play a significant part in developing the litigation plan and its execution, because they may be more familiar than the judge with the facts and issues in the case. Often cases with multiple plaintiffs, where there is common law and fact, are assigned a class action status or multidistrict litigation status (MDL). Multidistrict litigation is explained below.

Class Actions

Class action suits are brought by a group of people on behalf of themselves and others who have similar claims. An example of a class action lawsuit is the one involving silicone breast implants with plaintiffs filing the same complaint. To file and maintain a class action, a plaintiff or plaintiffs must file a motion for class certification. Federal Rule of Civil Procedure (FRCP) 23(a) states that the following requirements must be met for a class to be certified (certification is announcement of the official court definition of who the plaintiffs are in a class action lawsuit):

One or more members of a class may sue or be sued as representative parties on behalf of all, only if (1) the class is so numerous that joinder [the uniting of several causes of action or parties in one civil lawsuit] of all members is impracticable, (2) there are questions of law or fact common to the class, (3) the claims or defenses of the representative parties are typical of the claims or defenses of the class, and (4) the representative parties will fairly and adequately protect the interests of the class.[2]

The court reviews the motion for class action and other documents filed in support of and in opposition to the motion using relevant case law and the legal and factual issues raised by the class action complaints. After a class is certified, the court typically sets a deadline as to when one may opt not to participate in the class (opt out). Plaintiffs will opt out on the advice of an attorney, usually because their damages merit an individual lawsuit. After that date passes, the plaintiffs who have not opted out will be bound by the decisions of the court and class counsel.[1] Litigation in which claims are made by or against a class tends to be complex and will require judicial management (complex litigation). It calls for closer judicial oversight than other types of litigation because it imposes unique responsibilities on the court and on counsel. Once class allegations are made, various otherwise routine decisions are no longer within the individual litigant's control. The counsel representing the class incurs all the costs of the case, and reimbursement of those costs is sought from the court after a recovery has been made for the class. Class members and class representatives do not pay these costs. The court bears responsibility to protect the interests of the class members, for which FRCP 23(d) gives the court administrative powers.[1]

In the breast implant class action, claimants were classified according to the severity of their disease. LNCs were very helpful in reading medical records and helping to determine the options of the claimants.

Multidistrict Litigation

MDL is another tool established by the court to deal with multiple claimants who have at least one significant issue in common but have filed separate lawsuits. The goal of MDL case management is to bring about just, speedy, and inexpensive determinations, avoiding unnecessary and unproductive activity in litigation that may involve large numbers of witnesses and documents and extensive discovery. The certification of an MDL by the federal court allows for judicial management of complex cases where the litigation involves many parties in numerous related cases, especially if pending in different jurisdictions. Related cases pending in different federal courts may be consolidated in a single district and assigned to one federal judge by a transfer of venue. (Consolidation may be done in state court on a more informal basis, depending on the state rules of court.) The Federal Judicial Panel of Multidistrict Litigation is authorized to transfer civil actions pending in one or more than one federal district, involving one or more common questions of fact, for coordinated or consolidated pretrial proceedings.

No single factor determines the selection of the district to which the actions are transferred. The following are considered in the selection of the district: numbers of cases pending, where discovery has occurred, the site of occurrence of common facts, and the district where cost and inconvenience would be minimized. The panel will also consider the experience and skill of the available judges. Based on its consideration of these factors, the panel will designate a judge to whom the cases are transferred for pretrial proceedings.

Counsel in various cases may agree with the judge to try a lead case. Rulings in lead cases may be the basis for opinions or rulings, although not conclusive, in other courts. The power of the court enables the judge to exercise extensive supervision and control of the litigation under the federal rules, particularly FRCP 16, 26, 37, 42, and 83. FRCP 16(c) (12) specifically addresses complex litigation, authorizing the judge to adopt special procedures for managing difficult or protracted actions that involve complex issues, multiple parties, difficult legal questions, or unusual proof problems.[1] Such management allows the judge to use judicial time wisely and efficiently, especially early in the litigation. Therefore, pretrial conferences are held even if some parties have not yet appeared or even been served. The assignment of a single judge serves to satisfy these special judicial needs throughout, and the judge's role is crucial in developing and monitoring an effective plan for orderly conduct in pretrial and trial proceedings. The judge may decide to refer pretrial control to a magistrate judge or may appoint a special master (for limited purposes that require special expertise) and must order what is being referred to the magistrate or special master. The *Manual for Complex Litigation*,[1] last published by the Federal Judicial Center in 1995, is an important reference for the management of complex litigation.

An MDL is not a class action, although a class can be included in an MDL, along with other similar claims. The common issues could involve facts regarding:

- Product liability
- Negligence
- Breach of warranty or implied warranty (a breach by a seller of the terms of a warranty, as by the failure of the goods to conform to the seller's description or by a defect in title)
- Fraud
- Adequate warning
- Whether the product was defective

These claims may arise from the same event, product, or course of conduct and are based on the same general legal theories. The resolution of common issues in separate suits reduces considerable expense by avoiding redundant evidence in endless repetition of those common issues at individual trials. The courts have used trial techniques that include not only deciding common liability issues, but also determining compensatory and punitive damages. The court may try to identify common issues and reserve remaining issues, such as proximate (individual) causation and damages for individual suits based on medical history, general health, and extent of injury. For example, in mass tort actions, there are many separate issues relating to individual claimants, such as proof of injury, proximate causation, and damages. Certain issues may not be common to all who have filed a claim but are predicated on the defendant's liability for injuries from the same product or the same course of conduct by the manufacturer with respect to testing, research, manufacture, promotion, and marketing.

Mass Torts

Courts have recognized the need for special procedures in litigation involving multiple tort claims arising from a mass disaster, such as a plane crash of a commercial airliner, hotel fire, or chemical explosion. These injuries occur at a single site and usually manifest themselves immediately. In mass toxic tort or defective product litigation, injuries may occur in numerous, widely dispersed locations at different times, and the full impact of injury may remain hidden for years. All three types of litigation (class action, MDL, and mass tort) require courts to deal with multiple personal injury and damage claims, but management of mass toxic tort and defective product litigation is significantly more complex and demanding.[1] Many factors and falls in the realm of complex litigation can complicate management of mass tort litigation. Related cases may be filed in different courts, both federal and state, often with multiple plaintiffs and defendants. Cases may be governed by different state laws regarding issues of liability, the measure of compensatory damages, the standards for punitive damages, the statute of limitations, and insurance coverage. Conflicts among defendants may arise and third-party complaints may be filed, resulting in numerous additional parties. Highly technical expert testimony is usually needed, and sometimes its admissibility is disputed. This requires the judge to play the role of gatekeeper in reviewing novel scientific evidence. The judge may also need to assume the role of managing the litigation because of the sheer number of cases.

Consolidation of cases in a single court for joint trial may not be feasible because of individualized causation and damage issues. If MDL treatment of the federal cases and if consolidation treatment in a single court is not possible, state and federal judges may try to coordinate proceedings and will preside at joint hearings and conduct other court proceedings. Coordination between state and federal courts reduces duplicate efforts, aids in scheduling discovery plans, appoints special masters and lead counsel, and creates document depositories. Special masters are often appointed to carry out overall management of the case in its pretrial stage and to advise judges on scientific and technical issues. In some complex suits, judges have needed expert and technical assistance not to understand the subject matter of the suit or issues of causation, but to handle massive amounts of nontechnical information.

Recently, courts have made this mediation function more explicit and have appointed special masters expressly to achieve settlements in complex litigation, especially mass tort cases. At the post-liability stage, masters are also appointed to develop statistically sound, technically complex means of evaluating the damages of thousands of claimants from a limited pool of funds.[3] Some states have developed comprehensive legislation to deal with product liability cases, while other states have statutes that are issue-specific, such as statutes of limitations, strict liability, evidence, limitations of liability of nonmanufacturers, and defenses. The U.S. Department of Commerce has developed a Model Uniform Product Liability Act for voluntary use by the states in an effort to stabilize product liability law. It was published in the *Federal Register* on October 31, 1979.

In 1993, almost 9,000 individuals filed lawsuits against Dow Corning, claiming medical injury from their silicone breast implants. By May 1995, the company faced more than 20,000 individual suits. In addition, since early 1992, Dow Corning had faced a class action lawsuit brought by more than 100,000 claimants that hoped to compensate those injured by the implants more quickly. Dow Corning saw the number of claimants in this suit rise above 400,000 and then filed for Chapter 11 bankruptcy. This means that the company saw that its assets could not cover the liabilities it expected from the suit. The bankruptcy proceedings halted the litigation; it did not stop Dow Corning from continuing its other business activities.

Toxic Torts

"Toxic torts" are defined as civil actions asserting a demand for recovery of damages where there was exposure to a chemical substance, emission, or product that allegedly resulted in physical and psychological harm. In a toxic tort case, the defining event is exposure to the toxin. The defining consequence is some adverse health effect on the individuals, such as illness or reproductive problems. The typical toxic tort case involves a plaintiff with cancer suing for damages against an industrial site allegedly responsible for chemical releases, runoffs, or ground seepage that has affected the plaintiff's residence. The parties in toxic torts often know each other, and this familiarity can breed hostility because of personal outrage along with a serious illness. Often a toxic tort case involves multiple parties or could involve an employee in the absence of workers' compensation, or in addition to workers' compensation, where a third party has manufactured and released the toxic substance.

A familiar subset of plaintiffs in toxic tort litigation is older male blue-collar workers with lung disease from asbestos exposure. Another example of a subset of plaintiffs includes those with concerns and fears about future illness from exposure to cancer-causing materials. The defense counsel may be experienced with chemical and environmental defenses and will represent insurers or companies. Typically, the plaintiff's attorney will be working on a contingency-fee basis. The litigation is considered expensive, and expert witnesses and pretrial proceeding costs are so high that they are usually borne by experienced plaintiff lawyers in large firms. Some key terms in toxic tort cases include *acute risks*, which arise immediately from a brief contact with a chemical substance, and *air toxics*, which is the general name for chemicals released into the air as vapor, smoke, or airborne chemicals. The federal air pollution regulations determine what chemicals are toxic and what levels of exposure over a period of sustained contact are believed to have effects harmful to humans. There can be rare, sudden explosions, such as the Bhopal tragedy in India, which occurred at midnight on December 23, 1984. Over 40 tons of highly poisonous methyl isocyanate gas leaked out of the pesticide factory of Union Carbide in Bhopal. Thousands died in the immediate aftermath. At least 10,000 have died in the years that have passed, and 10 more are dying every month due to exposure-related diseases.

Typically, long-term releases causing chronic health effects are the usual sources of toxic tort litigation. *Air pollution* is a broader term and includes visible elements such as haze, smoke, and smog. *Carcinogenicity* is the scientifically demonstrated potential of a chemical to cause cancer (e.g., tobacco smoke, radiation). *Chemical substances* is a generic term that covers basic elements and complex chemical compounds. *Chronic risks* arise from repeated contact with a chemical substance over a sustained period. *Citizen suits* are statutory actions brought by persons other than a federal agency against defendants to enforce the penalty provisions of federal environmental laws. *Environmental releases* are liquids, solids, or gases that exit into a facility's external environment (e.g., sewers, landfills, bodies of water, etc.).[4] Except for asbestos and Agent Orange, toxic tort cases lack specific statistics kept in one national database. The tort system classifies toxic torts as a subset of complex litigation. The litigants generate considerable pretrial motions and maneuvers, often with an overlay of government environmental enforcement action. This assists with streamlining the case before trial commences. The cases are often highly publicized, which can generate considerable pressure on the court as the case is being administered.

A good example of a toxic tort is the asbestos litigation claiming that several companies had knowledge of the damage asbestos caused, but still kept it on the market. Asbestos causes mesothelioma, so a direct causation is easier to establish with these cases. Timelines are of great importance in cases like this because of the timing between exposure and disease manifestation. Chapter 18, Case Analysis: Evaluating Toxic Tort Cases, provides more information about toxic torts.

Product Liability

The term *product liability* applies to the liability of a manufacturer, nonmanufacturer seller, or processor to a buyer or third party for injury caused by a product that has been sold. Product liability includes negligence and claims, such as breach of implied warranties and breach of express warranties. Previously, such matters were dealt with under the legal classification of negligence or sales. However, product liability became a legal heading in its own right with the development of the doctrine of strict liability in tort. Within the strict liability formula, the one who sells any product in a defective condition deemed unsafe to users or consumers or to their property is subject to liability for physical harm or property damage. To support a strict liability cause of action, the plaintiff must prove that the product was in a condition not contemplated by the ultimate consumer, which would make the product unreasonably dangerous (refer to Chapter 17, Evaluating Product Liability Cases).

Theories of product liability had their origins in tort and contract law. For years, the most common ground for recovery for personal injury or other damages was negligence. Recovery for product-caused injury was also sought under the theory of breach of warranty. This caused difficulty for the injured party who had no direct dealing with the manufacturer. Beginning in 1963, a new basis for liability emerged — the principle of strict liability in tort. This is embodied in the Restatement (Second) of Torts and was first clearly applied by the California Supreme Court. Product liability, including strict liability, grew out of a public policy that people needed more protection against dangerous products than was currently afforded by the law of warranty. However, various theories of liability may apply to product cases, including breach of express or implied warranty, negligence, fraud, strict liability, alternative remedies, or other theories. It should be kept in mind that product liability cases share the basic characteristics of other lawsuits, and many legal techniques in litigating other kinds of cases may apply in litigating a product liability case.

The product may be defective because of a manufacturing flaw, a defective design, or a failure to warn of dangers in the use of the product within the meaning of the Restatement of Torts provision. The Restatement formula requires proof that the product is both unreasonably dangerous and defective. Some jurisdictions do not require proof that the product was unreasonably dangerous to permit the plaintiff to recover damages under the strict liability theory. Some jurisdictions, under the Restatement provision, substitute the term *not reasonably safe*. The consumer-expectation test, adopted by the courts for determining whether or not a product is in an unreasonably dangerous condition, is that the product sold must be dangerous to the extent beyond which the ordinary consumer who purchased it would have contemplated, with ordinary knowledge, common to a community, the characteristics of the product. To establish that an allegedly defective product was unreasonably unsafe, the plaintiff must prove that the product was more dangerous than the ordinary consumer might expect when the product was used as it was intended or used in a foreseeable manner. Proving that the product was defective generally requires showing not just that the product was defective for its intended use, but also that the product was so dangerous that a prudent manufacturer would not market the product knowing the product's condition. Similarly, the ordinary users or consumers of a product may have reasonable, widely accepted minimum expectations about the circumstances under which it should perform safely. Consumers govern their own conduct by these expectations, and products on the market should conform to them.

When the consumer-expectation test is inapplicable because the ordinary consumer would not form an expectation as to the safety of a product, the courts often apply risk/benefit factor analysis, meaning the utility of the product measured against the danger that is associated with its use. A product is not unreasonably dangerous or defective if it is inherently and obviously dangerous, or if its defect is one of which the user should be aware. Some products are incapable of being safe for their intended and ordinary use, but if properly prepared with proper instruction and warning, they are neither defective nor unreasonably dangerous. Such cases may involve prescription drugs, vaccines, blood, and medical devices, and are provided for under the Restatement (Second) of Torts Section 402A, Comment K. Comment K provides that two classifications of drugs are exempt from the doctrine of strict liability — drugs with a known but reasonable risk of injury and new and experimental drugs with an unknown risk. The manufacturer bears the burden of proving that its product is unavoidably unsafe.

Product liability does not include action against one's employer for injury covered by workers' compensation. However, an employer may be held liable in product liability contexts if the employer is also the manufacturer or seller of a defective product causing injury to the employee. Such an action would fall under the so-called *dual capacity doctrine* (provides an exception to the exclusive remedy of workers' compensation by allowing an employee to sue his employer when the injury caused by the employer to the employee is unrelated to the employee's capacity as an employee). The more common experience is that a third-party manufacturer is sued, although the injury occurred in the workplace. Common issues are present in every product liability case, regardless of the theory on which it is brought. The plaintiff must prove that he suffered injury or loss because the product was defective, and must prove that the defect was the proximate cause of such injury or loss. It is also necessary for the plaintiff to show that the product was defective when it left the control of the manufacturer or seller who is being sued, not merely that a defect existed at the time of injury. This is where it becomes very important for the plaintiff to provide experts who can testify to a design defect or other problem to show that the product was not altered by the plaintiff. The burden of proof remains with the plaintiff even where the action is grounded on a theory such as breach of warranty or strict liability in tort, which negates the need for proving a specific act of negligence or breach of duty on the part of the defendant.[5]

Parallels between Product Liability and Toxic Tort

The product liability system intersects with the law of toxic tort cases to the extent that some exposures can best be remedied under strict liability in tort. Although a toxic tort typically involves exposures to potentially hazardous chemicals, it can look like a product liability action. Some of the chemical exposures occur through products with which the plaintiff has worked or to which he has had exposure at work. Product liability theories include traditional remedies of negligence and warranty, as well as the recent concept of manufacturer strict liability. Under strict liability, plaintiffs need not prove fault or intent of the manufacturer, but they must prove that there was a defect that made the product unreasonably dangerous, that the defect was present when the product left the manufacturer's control, and that the injury was proximately caused by the defect.[4]

An example of this is a case that was filed against Medtronic. In 1987, Lora Lohr was implanted with a Medtronic pacemaker equipped with one of the company's Model 4011 pacemaker leads. On December 30, 1990, the pacemaker failed, allegedly resulting in a "complete heart block" that required emergency surgery. According to her physician, a defect in the lead was the likely cause of the failure. In 1993, Lohr and her husband filed this action in a Florida state court. Their complaint contained both a negligence count and a strict liability count. The negligence count alleged a breach of Medtronic's "duty to use reasonable care in the design, manufacture, assembly, and sale of the subject pacemaker" in several respects, including the use of defective materials in the lead and a failure to warn or properly instruct the plaintiff or her physicians of the tendency of the pacemaker to fail, despite knowledge of other earlier failures. The strict liability count alleged that the device was in a defective condition and unreasonably dangerous to foreseeable users at the time of its sale.

Role of the LNC

LNCs are a valuable and necessary asset in complex litigation requiring medical knowledge. They must be cognizant of all aspects of the case and coordinate the information and its dissemination. LNCs can function as case managers, freeing up the attorneys to litigate the case.

The statutes regarding the type of case must always be the first consideration when beginning work on a case. Timelines should be immediately drafted and research done regarding the defendant or plaintiff. The LNC needs to be sure that all defendants are named in the claim, so as not to miss a contributing party. When naming defendants in a case, all people who may have contributed to the damages must be considered because a defendant can name a nonparty. A designated nonparty is someone who shares a percentage of the blame, but was not named in the suit. If a named defendant is found liable for 50% of the blame and a designated nonparty is assigned 50% of the blame, the client receives only 50% of the judgment.

An expert witness must confirm negligence issues, and a causal relationship must be established between the negligence and the damages that occurred. Damages should be carefully considered by the LNC assisting plaintiff attorneys, as the clients end up paying all litigation expenses and it must be worth their while to pursue. It is not a desirable situation when plaintiffs win, but end up paying out more in expenses than they are awarded.

Conversely, the LNC assisting defense would want to point out that the plaintiffs have a weak case with limited damages. Complex litigation involves huge numbers of documents, tables, photos, etc. It would be nearly impossible for a single LNC to gather and organize all that is necessary. One very useful tool is to scan documents and keep them on CD-ROM. This makes it easier to disseminate the information to all parties and to store and index documents. All medical research is also stored this way. When experts need information or the attorney is preparing for trial, it is much smoother to pull it up from discs and send to a computer presentation.

The in-house LNC will have support staff and most likely will be working with other firms on these cases. All records pertaining to the case need to be filed, with individual claimants' records kept separate by indexing. Hard copies should be kept indexed and filed in notebooks, even if a computer presentation is used.

Chronologies and timelines must be made and can be done manually or by using one of the software programs that were developed for this.

It also helps to work with the other team (either plaintiff or defense) as much as possible to prevent everyone from doing double work. Parties often share information and documents with each other when it benefits both of them. All information should be dealt with as it comes in or important information may be missed. These cases typically last years and are difficult to put together.

Independent LNCs are likely to subcontract to other LNCs and general office help to gather, scan, index, research, and assist with trial prep. The lead LNC should establish how work will be handled by subcontractors. The subcontractors should be given specific instructions on what to look for in the medical records and how to format the reports. Providing the subcontractors with a sample format for reports is essential. The lead LNC should have contingency plans for handling cases that are improperly prepared by the subcontractor or, worse, not done at all. Giving the LNC feedback on the quality of work and what needs to be done differently on the next case is also helpful. The lead LNC should also have a general estimation of the amount of time it will take to complete the case, and should give the subcontractor a number of hours that should not be exceeded without getting approval from the lead LNC.

An independent LNC should be aware that to take on this kind of case is a full-time commitment, unless the LNC hires more subcontractors for outside work. The downside to this is that the lead LNC may lose some control over the quality of work that is being done. The LNC's regular clients may feel neglected if deadlines for their cases are not met. A large volume of cases can create high income, but also high stress.

Billing can be done ahead of supplying the work product and is a useful way to make sure that the attorney does not get behind. For those who want the work product first, bill when the work product is supplied and stay on top of a regular billing cycle. Another option is to get a large retainer up front for estimated expenses.

Experts/*Daubert* Issues

When retaining expert witnesses for a case, the Federal Rules of Evidence (FRE) must be followed. These rules lay out the qualifications that experts must have and what kinds of data they are relying on to form their opinions. *Daubert v. Merrell Dow* was the case that laid the foundation in 1993 for the current rules and their amendments. The rules governing experts are FRE 401, 701, 702, and 703. As the person who retains the experts, the LNC is best suited in assisting the experts in obtaining literature and exhibits that uphold the standards set forth by the federal rules. In complex litigation, this requires copious amounts of information, which must be made easily interpretable by a jury of laypeople.

Use of Technology

The impact of multimedia in our society is enormous, and attorneys are using this to their advantage in the courtroom. The LNC can be instrumental in orchestrating case presentation and, in doing so, affect the success of the trial. Using visuals without skipping a beat can bolster an attorney's opening statements, and appropriate exhibits can accompany closing argument and expert testimony. In any complex litigation, the smoother the dissemination of information, the easier it will be for a jury to understand the complexities of the case. It is a major feat to present a complex case in such a way that a jury can spend time deliberating over the points of law, rather than interpreting the medical aspects of the case. One of the most effective ways to present a case is with a computer presentation, with a screen for the jury. Illustrations and graphics can be as simple or as sophisticated as you choose. Many Internet sites have illustrations that may be downloaded for the presentation at a nominal fee. This can keep costs down as well as provide the case with strong demonstrative evidence.

Voir Dire/Juror Notebooks

Some attorneys will have the LNC accompany them to trial and assist with jury selection. It is the judge's decision in federal court whether or not to allow attorneys to conduct *voir dire* and to what extent they may carry it out, so this must be ascertained early on. The process can be started before trial by formulating questions for potential jurors that may assist in assessing whether they are the best jurors for this particular case. For instance, it would be pertinent to know whether a potential juror had any knowledge of the concept of "fail safe" (when a product fails to function as it was made to do, but causes no harm) for a product liability case based on that premise. A case can be greatly helped by the selection of the best jury for that case. Most nurses have the advanced communication skills necessary to participate in this important part of trial.

If the judge allows, notebooks can be made for each juror before trial with exhibits, glossaries, copies of documents, and any other information agreed upon by both attorneys and the judge.

As technology improves and medical issues become more complex, the LNC fills a necessary role on the medical litigation team. The LNC is able to assess, educate, and organize data, act on data that have been gathered, research issues, and formulate a plan of action. All the while, the LNC is communicating and acting as a liaison between clients, attorneys, and expert witnesses. If this role sounds familiar, it should. These are skills that LNCs have honed over their years in nursing and that transfer easily to the legal arena.

References

1. Federal Judicial Center, Ed., Part II: Management of complex litigation and Part III: Class actions, *Manual for Complex Litigation*, 3rd ed., Aspen Law & Business, Englewood Cliffs, NJ, 1995, 3–32, 211–246.
2. *Federal Civil Judicial Procedure and Rules*, 1996.
3. Federal Judicial Center, Ed., *Reference Manual on Scientific Evidence*, 2nd ed., 2000.
4. O'Reilly, J., *Defining Toxic Torts: Toxic Torts Practice Guide*, 2nd ed., McGraw-Hill, New York, 1992.
5. Travers, T., Ed., *American Law of Products Liability*, 3rd ed., Part I, The Lawyers Co-Operative Publishing Co., Bancroft-Whitney Co., Rochester, NY, 1987, chap. 1, 5D106.

Additional Reading

American Trial Lawyers Association Reference Materials, Vol. I, 1998 Annual Convention, ATLA Press, Washington, D.C., 1998.

Test Questions

1. Voir dire is best explained as
   A. The defendant's expert testimony
   B. Motions filed prior to trial
   C. The questioning of prospective jurors
   D. Combining suits into a class action

2. Which of the following statements is true?
   A. Complex litigation usually involves many parties, in numerous related cases, often in different jurisdictions, involving large numbers of documents, witnesses, and extensive discovery.
   B. Special masters are judges who know one area of law especially well.
   C. Product liability cases may involve products that were altered after purchase.
   D. A designated nonparty is someone named in a suit, but not being blamed for any damages.

3. The *Daubert v. Merrell Dow* case was important because
   A. It set a precedent for auto accident cases.
   B. It laid the foundation for the current federal rules regarding experts.
   C. It teaches us how to set up class action cases.
   D. It clarifies the doctrine of strict liability.

4. Which of the following statements is NOT true?
   A. Voir dire can be conducted by attorneys and judges.
   B. A plaintiff may opt out of a class action at any time.
   C. A designated nonparty may be assigned a percentage of the damages.
   D. The LNC is a valuable component of the litigation team.

5. Which of the following statements is true?
   A. Lawsuits involving asbestos damages are an example of a toxic tort.
   B. Product liability involves action against one's employer for injury covered by workers' compensation.
   C. Case management, from the legal perspective, refers to helping clients with their medical problems.
   D. Complex litigation is easily handled by an independent LNC, without other assistance.

Answers: 1. C, 2. A, 3. B, 4. B, 5. A

Chapter 22

The Legal Nurse Consultant as a Case Manager

Doreen Casuto, BSN, RN, MRA, CRRN, CCM, CLCP, F-ABDA, and Valerie V. Parisi, RN, CCM, CRRN

CONTENTS

Objectives

- To identify several different arenas for case management
- To understand the process of case management
- To understand issues facing the nurse case manager
- To identify the various roles and functions of the nurse case manager
- To identify professional organizations with which a nurse case manager may be affiliated
- To define some of the available credentials that are beneficial to the nurse case manager

Introduction

Some legal nurse consultants (LNCs) have diversified their practices to include case management, and many case managers have incorporated legal nurse consulting as part of their roles. The knowledge base and experience that LNCs possess is an asset in the various areas where case management is practiced.

The practice of case management requires the LNC to have a thorough understanding of the different arenas where case management is practiced and the scope and role of a case manager. Each area of practice has certain guidelines and restrictions that affect the way in which the case managers can function. Knowledge of these guidelines will improve the case managers' abilities and impact the role that they will have on the overall outcome of the case.

Definition of "Case Management"

The Case Management Society of America (CMSA) approved and published a definition of "case management" in 1995. That definition states: "Case management is a collaborative process which assesses, plans, implements, coordinates, monitors and evaluates options and services to meet an individual's health care needs through communication and available resources to promote quality cost-effective outcome."[1]

Case management strives to ensure that care needs are met in a timely and cost-effective manner. It is essential that case managers understand their roles and responsibilities. The case management model developed by CMSA illustrated in Figure 22.1 clearly indicates the pivotal relationship among the case manager, client, payor, and provider. This model illustrates the steps of the nursing process and additional key components required for success.[1] They are:

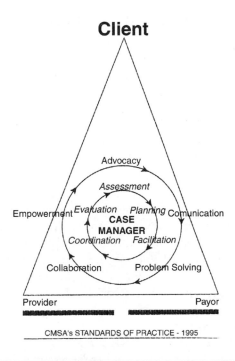

Figure 22.1 Case Management Model (Reprinted from the Case Management Society of America, Little Rock, AZ, 1995 [http://www.cmsa.org]. With permission.)

■ Collaboration
■ Advocacy
■ Empowerment

These elements enable the case manager to focus on achieving the maximum outcomes, while enabling clients to assume increased responsibility for their care and improving their quality of life.

Standards of Care for Case Management

The Standards of Care and Performance are delineated by the CMSA Standards of Practice. They identify the steps of the nursing process within case management and the measurement criteria that can be used to evaluate how case management is practiced. One area not typically included in the nursing process that has been incorporated in case management is "outcomes." The case manager identifies and coordinates changes in practice patterns and treatment plans to bring about appropriate care and cost-effective outcomes.[1]

Being *outcome-oriented* focuses the case managers' efforts and communicates what the expectations are for both the client and family. This outcome-directed process enables clients to delineate what their needs are and what obstacles might prevent them from achieving the outcome. When everyone, including the client and family, is working on the same goals and with the same timeline in mind, the chance of achieving and maintaining the outcome is more probable.

Arenas for Case Management Practice

Workers' Compensation

Workers' compensation is an arena where nursing case management is used extensively. "Workers' compensation" refers to medical and wage benefits that are provided when a worker is injured in the course of employment. Each state has its own workers' compensation act that governs how the benefits are administered. The federal government also has its own set of workers' compensation laws.

The goal of nursing case management in the workers' compensation arena is twofold. The first objective is to coordinate an appropriate and cost-effective treatment plan that will maximize the client's recovery and functional status. The second is to facilitate a return-to-work plan, which includes working with the employer and physician to provide modified-duty options while the client is recovering from his work-related injury. Catastrophic work-related injuries, such as spinal cord or traumatic brain injuries, require long-term case management. This type of case management is often provided by field case managers who visit patients, providers, and employers on site. They act as liaisons, providing a link among all involved parties.

Example 22.1: A 30-year-old male sustained a traumatic brain injury after a work-related fall from a forklift. The neurosurgeon who evaluated the patient at the hospital diagnosed a concussion, but was concerned about the amount of retrograde amnesia the patient was experiencing. Neuropsychological testing was done, and the patient continued with deficits in attention and concentration as well as dizziness and headaches. The carrier referred the case to medical case management. The nurse case manager referred the patient to a model brain injury setting for a series of evaluations, and a multidisciplinary rehabilitation program was established. The case manager evaluated the availability of light duty with the employer and visited on site to perform a job analysis of this light-duty job. The patient returned to work in a part-time sedentary capacity with job coaching provided by the rehabilitation team. Positive outcomes were achieved by prompt referral to an effective rehabilitation program and return to transitional employment.

Example 22.2: A 38-year-old male factory worker was found to have right carpal tunnel syndrome on electromyogram. Carpal tunnel surgery was recommended. The carrier referred the patient for medical case management. The nurse case manager referred the patient to a specialist in hand surgery. Modified lifting restrictions were obtained on a temporary basis. The patient was given a celestone injection with relief and was able to return to full duty. The patient was able to avoid surgery by referral to the appropriate specialist.

Accident and Health

Health insurers, especially managed care organizations, utilize nursing case management services to monitor the quality and cost of health care for the purpose of optimizing outcomes. Often they can also be involved in the process of precertification of procedures and tests, as well as in concurrent utilization review of care being provided in the hospital and other health care settings. Case management in this arena is often telephonic and involves contact with clients and providers. This type of insurance is usually purchased by an employer group. Coverage limits are dictated by the type of insurance that is purchased. This includes limits, caps, maximum coverage, and whether preexisting conditions or certain illnesses are covered. In the case of accident insurance, a causal link must be established between the accident and the alleged injuries.

Employers that have purchased health insurance plans will selectively use on-site case managers in catastrophic injury cases in which there is concern about their potential exposure or the risk of paying a large amount of money in claims or settlement payments. These cases usually involve clients who are young or have had injuries that require case managers with specialized skills. In these cases, the case manager will be asked to make an on-site assessment of the client, review the plan of treatment developed by the providers, and identify local community resources that can be utilized in augmenting the plan's coverage.

Example 22.3: An 11-year-old girl sustained a brain injury secondary to an automobile accident. The carrier requested the services of a private case manager to assist in assessing the child, reviewing and critiquing the treatment team's plan of care, and providing recommendations. The case manager evaluated the child at the patient's rehabilitation center and evaluated the family home for accessibility issues, communicated with the school district, reviewed the status of referrals to state and governmental entitlement programs, and met with both the family and rehabilitation team. As a result, the case manager was able to assist the team and family in refocusing their outcomes necessary for discharge, initiate referrals to appropriate community providers, and identify and access additional benefits from the insurance company that were not typically granted. The case manager's specialized rehabilitation skills and knowledge of legal issues ensured a more timely and effective result for the family and child.

Automobile and General Liability

As in the arena of workers' compensation insurance, the role of medical case management may depend on the state laws governing coverage for drivers. For example, in no-fault states such as New Jersey, which provide for a generous personal injury protection cap of $250,000, medical case management is used extensively to monitor the treatment plan for effectiveness from both a cost and quality standpoint. In states such as Pennsylvania, where drivers are required to purchase only $5,000 of medical coverage, the coverage is often exhausted before medical case management can be utilized, and referrals are made only in cases of catastrophic injury where extended medical benefits have been purchased. Case managers can also be used in general liability cases to monitor for cost-effectiveness and accident-relatedness of care. The case manager can provide medical cost projections at the outset of the case for the purpose of setting reserves, or putting aside money for the client's potential medical expenses for the case.

Example 22.4: A 16-year-old was involved in a head-on collision. He sustained multiple orthopaedic trauma with fractures of both femurs, the right ankle, and the left wrist. He also suffered a renal contusion, and had an external fixation device on the right leg and a cast on the left. The patient was referred by medical case management to the appropriate pediatric rehabilitation facility. After discharge, he received home care services for Lovenox injections and home physical therapy. He was eventually referred for outpatient physical therapy and was able to return to school. The medical case manager followed the case from hospitalization through the continuum of care and expedited appropriate referrals to the next level of care to enhance the patient's rehabilitation outcome and to preserve and stretch his reserve dollars.

Private Case Management

Case managers may be hired privately by patients or their families. Irrespective of who hires the case managers, their responsibilities and roles will be similar. Those hiring case managers seek individuals with experience and specialized knowledge in assessing care needs, identifying resources, and accessing services. This is coupled with the ability to maximize benefits from insurance providers and governmental entitlement programs. It is important for case managers to be knowledgeable of the legal rights of the client and the responsibilities of insurance companies and governmental agencies. The LNC, who is also a case manager, experienced in litigation is helpful in identifying potential pitfalls. In situations where an attorney may be necessary, the LNC would obtain additional necessary services.

Probate System

The probate court is the department within the county's superior court system that deals with issues such as conservatorships, guardianships, and estates of people who have died. The probate court has the responsibility for making decisions to protect a minor or conservatee's life and property if he is deemed in jeopardy. The court protects individuals who are mentally ill, have head injuries, are developmentally disabled, are seniors, and are under 18 years of age. A guardian (for a child up to the age of 18) or a conservator (for an incompetent adult) will be assigned or recognized by the probate court. The guardian or conservator may be responsible for the physical well-being of the person, his finances, or both, depending upon the decision of the court.[2]

Either the probate court judge or a fiduciary serving as a guardian or conservator may enlist the services of a case manager to assist in evaluating or meeting the care needs of the client. If a life care plan was prepared during a lawsuit, the services of a case manager may have been included. Based on these recommendations, a case manager will be called upon to explain the needs of the individual and what the associated costs will be on an ongoing basis.

Elder Care

The National Association of Professional Geriatric Care Managers identifies a geriatric care manager as one who is "committed to maximizing the independence and autonomy of elders while striving to ensure that the highest quality and most cost-effective health and human services are used where and when appropriate." The role of the case or care manager will vary depending upon the needs of the client who initiated the request and other involved parties.[3] At times, this may mean working with families with whom the client lives or families who are not in the same city. If the client is living with his family, it is important for the care manager to be mindful of the entire family and the manner in which they interact. It should not be presumed that clients living with family will not require outside assistance in order to fulfill their varied needs. When the family is in another state, the care manager often will serve as the family's "eyes and ears," for the purpose of alerting them to potential problems or when situations arise. Such a situation requires the care manager to anticipate potential problems far enough in advance to alert families and allow them to intervene successfully.

Process of Case Management

The process of case management is essentially the same as the nursing process and consists of the following steps as defined by CMSA: assessment, planning, implementation, coordination, monitoring, and evaluation.

Assessment is usually performed during an initial interview with the client. This can be done face to face or over the telephone and should include the following activities:

- Obtaining updated information about the client's medical status, including significant medical history
- Evaluating functional status or ability to perform activities of daily living
- Evaluating psychosocial status, including information about the client's social support system
- Evaluating vocational status, including a detailed work history in cases of workers' compensation

Consideration should be given to cultural factors and potential obstacles to recovery, such as preexisting and coexisting conditions, socioeconomic factors, and educational barriers. This information serves as a database from which an individualized case management plan can be formulated. The assessment phase, in workers' compensation case management, also includes contact with the physician and other health care providers and the employer. After the client has signed a release, appropriate medical records should be obtained and a job description should be obtained from the employer. An on-site job analysis by the nurse case manager, when possible, is an important aspect of this assessment process in workers' compensation cases.

The planning phase involves setting realistic and attainable short and long-term goals with the client. These goals must be achievable and measurable, and the client must be involved in setting them. The treatment and rehabilitation team should be consulted prior to goal-setting. Meetings or contacts with these providers should take place as part of the assessment phase, as should contact with the employer in workers' compensation cases. Strategies to meet these goals must be developed by the case manager.

Implementation of the plan involves maintaining contact with the client and treatment providers. In the beginning of a workers' compensation or automobile accident case, there is usually intense activity as a treatment plan is still being formulated. The client may be in the hospital and coordination is needed for either transfer to an appropriate post-acute facility or referral to home care services. Durable medical equipment and supplies may need to be ordered. The client may require referrals to a specialist for a second opinion or specialty care. The case manager must be aware of resources both in the client's community and nationally. Included in this chapter are some online resources that the LNC may find helpful when implementing a case management plan.

Case managers must stay in constant contact with the client and treatment providers, so that effective coordination of the case is achieved. Between field visits to the client, telephone contact must be maintained. Their role is often an extension of the traditional patient teaching role of nursing. Instruction in medications and disease process as well as signs and symptoms to report to the physician can decrease the potential for complications. Case managers must also be aware of the usual course of recovery from the injury or illness, so that they can be proactive in preventing or minimizing complications. This is especially true in catastrophic cases, such as spinal cord injury and traumatic brain injury. The case must always be moving forward toward resolution. Case management reports should be filed with the referral source in a timely manner and must reflect a case management plan that is moving toward a positive outcome.

Evaluation of the case management plan should be ongoing. Goals should evolve as needed to meet the needs of the client. The client and providers must be part of this evaluation process to make sure that the plan is still moving toward recovery. It can be challenging for the case manager with long-term case management files to stay proactive, especially as the client might be stable as a result of an effective case management plan. Contact must still be maintained so that the case manager does not have to go into "crisis mode" later if complications should arise. The case manager must be able to demonstrate to the referral source that goals have been achieved and positive outcomes have been reached.

Case Management Issues

Confidentiality

Confidentiality of patient information is an issue that has an impact on case management practice. The Health Insurance Portability and Accountability Act of 1996 (HIPAA)[4] has changed how health care organizations handle confidential information. Agencies have had to adopt policies and procedures to protect the privacy of health information and develop standards regarding electronic exchange of patient data. More information about standards and laws regarding HIPAA can be obtained through the Centers for Medicare and Medicaid Services, formerly known as the Health Care Finance Administration.

The Commission for Case Management Certification has a code of professional conduct for case managers that includes confidentiality issues. Case managers must be knowledgeable and act in accordance with federal, state, and local laws and procedures related to the scope of their practices regarding client consent, confidentiality, and the release of information. The case manager must also inform the client at the outset of the relationship that any information obtained through the relationship may be disclosed to third parties. Disclosure is limited to what is necessary and relevant. The case manager must also reveal to appropriate authorities information to prevent the client from causing harm to himself and others or committing criminal, illegal, or fraudulent acts.[5]

Professional Experience

Clinical experience is key for the nurse case manager. A recent survey conducted by American Health Consultants, publisher of the *Case Management Advisor*, found that approximately 80% of surveyed nurse case managers have 10 or more years of nursing experience.[6] Lack of clinical experience can result in poor outcomes or even unsafe situations.

Ideally, the case manager has achieved certified case manager (CCM) or other relevant certifications and is experienced in case management before functioning independently as a case manager. This chapter will discuss certifications for case managers in a later section.

The Code of Professional Conduct for Case Managers dictates that case managers practice only within the boundaries of their competence, based on their education, training, appropriate professional experience, and other professional credentials.[5]

Dual Relationships

Nurse case managers really have two "clients." There is the client who is in need of case management services through illness or injury and the client who is the payor source. The nurse case manager's duty is to the first client and not the payor source. Cost-effectiveness and resolution of a claim should never trump quality care as the prime concern of the case manager. Case managers who provide services at the request of a third party must disclose the nature of their dual relationship at the outset of the relationship by describing their roles and responsibilities to parties who have the right to know.[5]

Dual relationships can also exist when the client is a friend, relative, or co-worker of the case manager. The case manager should not enter into this type of dual relationship and should refer the case to another nurse case manager. Conflicts of interest, actual or potential, should also be disclosed to all parties. If any party raises an objection, the case manager should remove himself or herself from the case.

A life care planner may be asked to act as the client's case manager. This is no longer a dual relationship once the case has resolved. The life care planner is in an ideal position to implement the life care plan, which is a road map of care, for the best possible case management outcomes.

Case Mix and Acuity

The number of cases that a case manager can effectively manage is dependent not only on numbers, but on acuity. Some cases, such as catastrophic cases, are complex and long term and require more case management time. According to a 2001 study published by American Health Consultants, the average caseload is 16–30 cases, though telephonic case managers may have as many as 75.[6] Case managers must be sure that they can adequately manage their caseloads and refer out as needed so that quality standards can be maintained.

The Role of the LNC as a Case Manager

Nursing case management is in many ways a natural role for LNCs, who have expertise in functioning in the legal and insurance arenas. LNCs bring to nursing case management expertise in reviewing medical records and bills as well as finely honed analytical skills. The American Association of Legal Nurse Consultants recognizes case management as a function of the LNC.

As described in the previous sections, nursing case management can take place in many arenas. Case managers can also work as independent contractors, just as LNCs do. Many LNCs also function as nurse case managers in their private practices.

The Case Manager in the Litigation Process

A case manager may be hired to assist the attorney and the client during the litigation process of a personal injury or medical malpractice case. During this phase, the case manager primarily coordinates evaluations, monitors care, identifies resources within the community, and plans and assists in the implementation of services. This role is important in facilitating the valuation of future care needs and the development of a life care plan. Having a nurse skilled in case management who knows about litigation helps the attorney to anticipate and identify issues that can affect the outcome of the case.

Workers' compensation cases often go into litigation when there is a dispute about the work-relatedness of the alleged injury. In most states this involves a hearing in front of the workers' compensation commission or a judge. A worker who is permanently injured and unable to return to work may try to settle the lawsuit. Sometimes the injured worker may have a third-party suit if, for example, the injury was caused by a defective piece of equipment. Once the injured worker is represented by counsel, the case manager must work with the client through his attorney. Sometimes the client's attorney may prohibit direct contact with the client. In this case, the case manager can maintain contact with the treating providers and contact with the client through his attorney.

In both workers' compensation and automobile or general liability arenas, the nurse case manager may be asked to set up an independent medical examination (IME). Choosing a physician for an IME is very much like choosing any other expert. This physician may well end up testifying in the case. The case manager is the appropriate person to know which specialty should be chosen and may help in locating a well-credentialed, objective physician for this evaluation. The case manager is often asked to send the medical records with a query letter including questions for the IME physician to answer, such as relationship of the client's complaints to the alleged injury, appropriate treatment plan, further length of disability, and permanency of the client's injuries. The case manager may also be asked to attend the examination and can ask many of these questions. This is a distinctly different type of role from that of the LNC who is asked to attend an IME in order to observe the examination. In contrast to the role of the LNC, who will remain silent during the examination, the case manager takes an active role at the IME. The case manager will also review the report once it is received to ensure that the questions have been answered.

The Role of the Case Manager after Litigation

After litigation, a case manager may be retained to fulfill a specific assignment or assist for a longer time frame. The case manager's role will often depend upon whether the family has been prepared for their role as both parent and care coordinator. If the family has worked with an LNC experienced in case management or a case manager during the litigation process, they may have the necessary information and skills to assume these new responsibilities. Parents will often require temporary assistance to understand how to implement the life care plan while meeting budgetary limitations. Families are frequently so overwhelmed by the litigation process that they find it difficult to cope with the results of the suit and to realize that their lives must move forward. At this point, the case manager has a significant responsibility to calm and educate the family, assist in setting priorities, plan for care needs, and implement the life care plan. It is the role of the case manager to help the family and client accept increasing responsibilities in the implementation of the life care plan. The ultimate goal is to train the family to assume increased responsibilities for care coordination.

If the family is able to assume more responsibilities in implementing the life care plan, the case manager may act as an adviser to the family, attorney, or court. In this role, the case manager periodically reassesses the patient's needs, reviews the life care plan, identifies what the costs will be for the coming period, and provides the necessary medical or functional documentation for the annual budget, which is then presented to the court.

Private Case Management

When a case manager is hired privately by a family, it is important that the case manager understand his or her role and responsibility, the desired outcome, and the duration of the activity. Case managers, who are involved with long-term case management, need to involve the family with planning and coordinating future care. In order to avoid a misunderstanding, it is better to prepare the family to assume this role. The family then has the necessary understanding about their role and can then take on the responsibility themselves or delegate it to others. Proper preparation will provide the family with the knowledge to assume many of the roles that the case manager previously performed if the case manager is no longer available or if the family moves to an area where there is no one with the necessary skills.

Example 22.5: An 18-month-old boy sustained a facial injury, which was treated, but misdiagnosed. As a result, the youngster developed a brain abscess, seizures, blindness, and a resultant right hemiparesis. Due to the increasing complexity of the child's medical needs during the trial, the life care planner was asked by the family to assume a case management role immediately after the case ended.

Having identified that the mother had the interest and necessary skills, the case manager worked with her to assume many of the roles and responsibilities ordinarily performed by a case manager.

While maintaining the responsibility for evaluation and planning, the case manager gave the mother education and support in assuming her new role. Frequently, this entailed preparing the mother for appointments, role modeling behaviors, and reviewing outcomes after appointments. The case manager gradually relinquished responsibilities for attending meetings with selected providers, routine physician visits, etc. The mother initially called frequently to review issues and needs, but gradually gained more confidence in her skills. The case manager assisted her with identifying obstacles and reviewing strategies and techniques for advocating for her child's care needs. During the process, both the case manager and the mother identified certain times when the mother did not feel that she could handle her new role and required the assistance of the case manager. These instances included new physician appointments, meetings with specialists, appointments prior to surgery and subsequent hospitalizations, and school meetings.

At times, a case manager may be retained to assist only with a specific activity that the family feels that it cannot handle. It is important that the case manager understand the family's expectations, and conflicts or differences of opinions should be discussed prior to initiation of an activity. At other times, the case manager may feel that additional assistance or consultants may be needed to better communicate the child's needs during an appointment or meeting.

Example 22.6: A case manager who is managing a brain-injured child attends all the individualized educational plan meetings at school to ensure that the child and family are receiving needed and timely services from the school district. When the school district stops providing appropriate and recommended services, the case manager identifies the need for an attorney with specialized skills in dealing with school systems. The attorney meets with the case manager and school district officials to discuss the family's concerns and the child's needs. The case manager provides the necessary medical and therapeutic documentation to support the request, and the attorney uses his legal knowledge and experience with the Individuals with Disabilities Education Act to advocate for the child's care needs with the school.

Example 22.7: A case manager is asked to assist a family in communicating their disabled child's needs to the court for access to funds from an account. The family had been awarded additional funds to provide for the specialized needs of their child, but they are unaware of how to communicate these needs to the court. The child requires the modification of an existing bathroom to allow for wheelchair access. The case manager assesses the child, evaluates the family's plan, and reviews the contractor's proposal. The case manager then obtains two additional bids. When agreement with the family is reached on the type of needed modification, the case manager writes a report to the court. The report details the nature of the child's disability and the care needs and explains the process used in obtaining the bids along with supporting documentation. When the court reviews the request, it is beneficial if the case manager is present. Clear and complete documentation assists the judge in determining the appropriateness of the request, allowing the judge to release funds for the necessary modifications.

Workers' Compensation

In the workers' compensation arena, the injured worker may settle the portion of his claim that compensates for lost wages, but the claim may remain open for medical expenses. The nurse case manager will then continue to work with the injured worker. The nurse case manager will refer these cases, when possible, to vocational rehabilitation. These cases involve permanent and often catastrophic injuries that require long-term case management to prevent and monitor for complications. In the case of traumatic brain injury, the nurse case manager may be attending team meetings and may work closely with the family in determining which type of care facility may be needed, especially as the client ages.

Automobile/General Liability

In some states there are no-fault auto policies, which may be unlimited or have generous limits. Long-term case management is required in these cases, which can involve such conditions as spinal cord injury, traumatic brain injury, amputations, orthopaedic trauma, and chronic pain conditions (e.g., complex regional pain syndrome).

Role of the Case Manager in Setting Reserves for Insurance Companies

The nurse case manager may be asked to provide a medical cost projection, especially in cases of catastrophic injury. The purpose of this medical cost projection is for the insurance company to set reserves for the client. This medical cost projection, unlike a life care plan, is a snapshot in time and is continually updated as client needs change. The medical cost projection includes such items as hospitalization, physician's fees, rehabilitation costs, home care costs, durable medical equipment, and supplies. The nurse case manager is in constant communication with facility case managers and treating providers to obtain updated information about the treatment plan. The nurse case manager may also make on-site visits to the hospital or rehabilitation facility to meet with the client, providers, and facility case manager or social worker.

Role of the Case Manager with the Probate Court

There are differences in the way each probate court functions depending upon the county or state and whether a judge or commissioner heads the program. The resources available to the court enable the judge to make rational decisions to support the needs of the individual. Some judges feel strongly about their responsibility to protect the mentally and physically disabled. Many judges are mindful of the needs of families for respite when caring for the disabled, yet are cognizant of budgetary constraints. They feel that the individual should have appropriate care, services, and quality of life. Families who provide 24-hour care need respite and help, but judges do not believe that these funds should in any way negate parents' primary responsibilities. In other words, funds should not be used for basic care needs, which are normally a part of every parent's responsibilities.

At times the probate court or a fiduciary acting as guardian or conservator will request that a case manager be brought in to assist in the identification of needs and costs and also to determine whether finances have been appropriately spent. A case manager with legal nurse consulting experience is helpful in identifying the relevant issues, the medical needs, community resources available, and knowledge of the court system.

Example 22.8: A case manager was asked to evaluate a teenager who had athetoid cerebral palsy, was disabled at birth, and had received a substantial award after suing for a birth injury 18 years prior. After the lawsuit, the parents applied for and were deemed ineligible for the bond (to protect the funds) by the insurance company. The judge waived the bond requirement and allowed the family to manage the child's money. Eighteen years later, the court requested that an assessment be conducted to ensure the future financial stability of the young adult.

The case manager's assessment revealed that the young woman had spastic quadriplegia and was dependent on others both for her self-care activities and for her mobility. The young woman had a manual wheelchair, which she was unable to propel independently. In addition, while having the manual dexterity to control a joystick on a power wheelchair, she had not been provided with one. She was living with her parents, several aunts, and an uncle in a 2-story home, with the young woman's bedroom and the kitchen on the main level. The dining room, family room, and bathroom were a level below, and all additional bedrooms and bathrooms were on the second floor. There was a large non-gated pool in the backyard, which neither was wheelchair-accessible nor had a lift. The family's 3-year-old Plymouth Voyager did not have a ramp or a lift. The young woman had to be lifted into the van while her wheelchair was stowed in the back. There was no method of securing the wheelchair in the back of the van, and the seat belt did not include a shoulder strap that was adequate for her positioning and safety needs. This was the third home that the family had purchased in 18 years. The young woman had completed her schooling, but had not been integrated into any community activities. Her estate awarded a monthly annuity and balloon payments every 7 years to the account controlled by her parents. The court became concerned that the past level of spending would not provide sufficient funds to meet her current or future needs.

The case manager's experience enabled the court to document the young woman's current and future needs and identify the parents' liabilities to repay the child's estate. The court was also successful in obtaining an outside fiduciary to manage the estate and protect the young woman's assets while providing her access to needed equipment and services.

Role of the Case Manager in Elder Care

The case manager with a legal nurse consulting background is an asset when assisting the elderly. Although many key elements of case management are similar, the elderly usually require assistance with eligibility, legal, and insurance issues.

The knowledge to assess an elderly person's functional ability, support network "client system," and available financial resources may mean the difference between the client's being able to stay in his own home or having to go to a retirement complex or residential facility. Meeting with all the individuals in the "client system" will assist in identifying potential resources. It may also provide information regarding individuals within the client's network who have different motivations for their involvement. The ability to identify conflicting needs may prevent potentially harmful situations. For example, a caregiver may be attempting to alienate an elderly person from his friends in order to control and guarantee the relationship or employment. Although care managers may identify this type of issue, it is their responsibility to assist elderly clients to fully understand the issues so that they can assume the ultimate decision-making role. At times, the individual may not be able to handle the situation, and certain safeguards, such as bank controls, may need to be implemented.

Credentials

An understanding of the credentials that case managers can earn will help the LNC identify the background and accomplishments of case managers.

CRRN (critical care registered nurse): This is the credential for certified rehabilitation nurses and is earned by nurses who care for people with physical disability or chronic illness. Case management is an arena of practice for the rehabilitation nurse. To be eligible for this certification, the nurse must have a current, unrestricted registered nurse (RN) license; at least 2 years of practice as a rehabilitation nurse in the last 5 years; or 1 year of experience and 1 year of advanced study in nursing. This experience must be verified by 2 professional colleagues, one of whom must be a CRRN or immediate supervisor.

CDMS (certified disability management specialist): This credential indicates the certified disability management specialists, who provide services to ill or injured workers to minimize the cost of disabilities and absences for employers. A nurse may sit for this examination if the nurse has a current license as an RN and 24 months' employment in the field of disability management or 12 months under the supervision of a CDMS or CRC (certified rehabilitation counselor).

CCM (certified case manager): This credential identifies the individual as "possessing the education, skills and experience required to render appropriate services based on sound principles of practice."[5] It further identifies the individual as having advanced practice skills and licensure or certification to perform the essential activities of case management within the core components across the continuum of care. The individual must have 24 months of full-time experience as a case manager, 12 months of full-time experience under the supervision of a CCM, or 12 months as a supervisor of individuals providing direct case management services. Nurses who apply to take the examination must provide the necessary documentation (job descriptions and supervisor documentation) to validate the type and applicability of their experience. To achieve certification, a nurse must obtain a passing score on the examination. Certification renewals require 80 clock hours of acceptable education during a 5-year period without re-examination.

Professional Associations and Organizations

Professional organizations enhance the practices of case managers by providing educational and networking opportunities. CMSA is the premier organization for case managers and there are many benefits of membership, including various case management publications, online services and educational programs, and such products as the Standards of Practice for Case Management. The Association of Rehabilitation Nurses also provides many educational opportunities for its members.

Conclusion

The nurse case manager practices in many different arenas. The nurse case manager has many different roles throughout the litigation process and has interaction with clients, physicians and other health care providers, insurance carriers, and attorneys. These multifaceted roles require the services of a nurse who is committed to obtaining the proper certifications, has a strong knowledge base, and is experienced in the clinical arena. Case management demands the similar critical analytical thinking skills that are also essential in providing legal nurse consulting services. The nurse case manager must be a self-starter who can work independently and collaboratively with all team players to ensure optimal rehabilitation outcomes.

References

1. Case Management Society of America, Standards of Practice for Case Managers, Little Rock, AZ, 1995.
2. Judicial Council of California, *Handbook for Conservators*, San Francisco, 1992.
3. National Association of Professional Geriatric Managers, http://www.caremanager.org.
4. Health Insurance Compliance Insider, HIPAA Fact Sheet, March 2001.
5. Commission for Case Management Certification, Code of Professional Conduct for Case Managers, Rolling Meadows, IL, 2000.
6. Case Management Caseload Data: Results of National Survey, American Health Consultants, *Case Management Insider*, March 2000.

Additional Reading

Cesta, T., Tahan, H., and Fink, L., *The Case Management Survival Guide*, C.V. Mosby, St. Louis, 1998.

Chan, F. et al., Foundational knowledge and major practice domains of case management, *Journal of Care Management*, 5, 10, 1999.

Cohen, E. and Cesta, T., *Nursing Case Management from Concept to Evaluation*, 2nd ed., C.V. Mosby, St. Louis, 1997.

Huber, D. and Oerman, M., New horizons, *Outcomes Management for Nursing Practice*, 1, 1, 1999.

Huston, C., Outcomes measurement in healthcare: new imperatives for professional nursing practice, *Nursing Case Management*, 4, 188, 1999.

Liquire, R. and Houston, S., Outcomes management: getting started, *Outcomes Management for Nursing Practice*, 1, 5, 1997.

Marek, K., Measuring the effectiveness of nursing care, *Outcomes Management for Nursing Practice*, 1, 8, 1997.

Mass, S. and Johnson, B, Case management and clinical guidelines, *Journal of Care Management*, special ed., 18, 1998.

McPheeters, M. and Lohr, K., Evidence based practice and nursing: commentary, *Outcomes Management for Nursing Practice*, 3, 99, 1999.

Mullahy, C., *The Case Manager's Handbook*, Aspen, Gaithersburg, MD, 1998.

Murer, C. and Brick, L., *The Case Management Source Book: A Guide to Designing and Implementing a Centralized Case Management System*, McGraw-Hill, New York, 1997.

Stolte, C., Crisis in case management: the graying of America, *Case Manager*, 11, 57, 2000.

Tahan, H., Clarifying case management: what is in a label?, *Nursing Case Management*, 4, 268, 1999.

Toran, M.R., Geriatric case manager, *Case Manager*, 6, 97, 1995.

Internet Resources for Case Managers

1. Abledata— (assistive technology resources) — http://www.abledata.com
2. American Hospital Directory (medical costs and hospital data) — http://www.ahd.com
3. Association of Rehabilitation Nurses — http://www.rehabnurse.org
4. Brain Injury Association of USA — http://www.biausa.org
5. Case Management Society of America — http://www.cmsa.org
6. Case Manager's Resource Guide — http://www.cmrg.com
7. Commission for Disability Management Specialists — http://www.cmds.org
8. HealthMart (medical costs) — http://www.health-mart.net
9. MedMarket (medical supplies) — http://www.medmarket.com
10. National Spinal Cord Injury Association — http://www.spinalcord.org
11. Oncolink — http://www.oncolink.upenn.edu

Test Questions

1. Standards of Practice and Performance for Case Management are
   A. Defined by the nursing process
   B. The same thing as outcomes
   C. Delineated by CMSA Standards of Practice
   D. Determined by each state's nurse practice act

2. Workers' compensation laws
   A. Are the same nationwide
   B. Are determined by the state's workers' compensation act
   C. Provide for payment of medical benefits only
   D. Provide for tort action against the employer

3. What does a private case manager do?
   A. Provides for the needs of the family members of the catastrophically injured
   B. Assesses care needs, identifies resources, accesses services, and maximizes benefits from sources, such as insurance programs and government entitlement programs
   C. Selects private duty home health options for chronically ill or disabled individuals
   D. Helps the injured parties manage their finances

4. The process for case management
   A. Consists of assessment, planning, implementation, coordination, monitoring, and evaluation
   B. Should be implemented only by a certified case manager
   C. Acts as a guideline for providing medical case management services
   D. Is determined by the Case Management Society of America

5. An example of a dual relationship would be
   A. When a case manager provides services for a client for whom he has written a life care plan after the case is settled.
   B. When a client is a friend, relative, or coworker of the case manager.
   C. When the case manager provides vital case information to the physician and the insurance carrier.
   D. When the case manager also works clinically as a nurse in an acute care setting.

Answers: 1. C, 2. B, 3. B, 4. A, 5. B

ROLES OF THE LEGAL NURSE CONSULTANT IV

Chapter 23

Legal Nurse Consultant Practice within a Law Firm

Phyllis ZaiKaner Miller, RN, and Elizabeth K. Zorn, BSN, RN

CONTENTS

0-8493-1418-6/03/$0.00+$1.50
© 2003 by AALNC

Objectives

- To describe the variable structure of law firms, including size, types of legal services provided, management, and task delegation
- To describe the possible personnel in a law firm and their roles in carrying out the mission and work of the firm
- To describe the variable culture and politics of law firms as they relate to the role of an in-house legal nurse consultant
- To explain by example the fees, costs, and productivity measurements in plaintiff and defense firms and how they impact the role of the in-house LNC
- To identify in detail the role of the in-house LNC in the delivery of high-quality legal services at defense and plaintiff firms
- To identify the essential skills and personality traits of successful in-house LNCs
- To discuss compensation and benefits packages for in-house LNCs

Introduction

The role of a legal nurse consultant (LNC) in a law firm may vary considerably, depending upon the location and size of the firm, the nature of the work that is done, whether the firm does primarily defense or plaintiff work, and whether the firm has had prior experience working with an LNC. In most areas of the country, the responsibilities of the LNC in a law firm have evolved significantly over the past 15 to 20 years. Now, most LNCs not only participate in the organization, review, and summary of medical records, but also play an integral role in more complex and sophisticated activities, such as the analysis of liability, determination of proximate cause, assessment of damages, and identification of medical experts. This chapter discusses these roles and provides a general orientation to the law firm environment.

Structure of the Law Firm Personnel

The categories of personnel in a law firm depend upon the size of the firm. Small firms (fewer than 25 attorneys) typically have partners, associate attorneys, LNCs, paralegals (also known as legal assistants), secretaries, a receptionist, and a bookkeeper. Large firms (75 attorneys or more) typically have an array of additional support staff and services, such as librarians; word processors; private investigators; messengers; process servers; large-volume copying departments; audiovisual personnel; computer technicians; document coders and data entry persons; human resource, payroll, and benefits departments; continuing legal education and special-events coordinators; a business manager; marketing and public-relations staff; and office-supply and kitchen staff. In addition to LNCs, large firms may also have other nonattorney professionals, such as certified public accountants and environmental engineers. Generally speaking, the larger the firm, the more support persons and services are in-house. Many firms, especially small and medium-sized firms, contract with outside vendors for support services. The purpose of employing ancillary staff is to support the attorneys, paralegals, and nonattorney professionals in the delivery of client services and in the underlying business operation of the firm.

Among the lawyers there are distinctions in rank depending on the size, structure, and economics of the firm. Generally speaking, the lawyers are either partners or associates. Partners are more experienced in the practice of law, may have voting rights in the running of the firm depending on how the partnership is structured, and have a monetary compensation formula different from associates. Partners typically have practiced law for at least six to ten years. Lawyers are invited into the partnership of a given firm once they have proven their worth to the firm. This generally requires bringing in new business and demonstrating legal skill by managing cases effectively. In large firms there may be different levels of partnership, such as senior and junior partners or voting and nonvoting partners. Some partners are recruited from outside the firm if the firm is looking for someone with a particular area of expertise. This is known as a lateral move. Another type of experienced attorney is one who is "of counsel" to a firm. This means that the attorney is associated with the firm, but is not a member of the firm. Examples are a retired attorney who still consults with the firm and an attorney who has a mutual referral relationship with a firm. There may or may not be a business arrangement of some sort between the firm and this type of attorney.

Associates are nonpartner attorneys. They range in experience from recent law-school graduates to attorneys with six or more years of experience on the verge of becoming partners. It is useful to compare associates to medical-school graduates. First-year associates are much like new interns. They are rarely in a position to bring in new business and generally have no prior legal experience, other than possibly summer internships at a law firm during law school or prior work as a paralegal before attending law school. Most new associates spend a large proportion of their time doing legal research. They also work on specific case projects under the close supervision of a more senior associate or partner. Although they may be gradually permitted to take depositions in cases, associates are not often asked to handle trials by themselves until they have gained considerable experience. New associates in the larger full-service firms may rotate through the different practice groups to help them decide which area of the law they wish to pursue. Once they have completed their rotation, they typically become part of one particular practice group, working under the supervision of the partners in that practice group.

With time and experience, many associates move up the ladder toward partnership, just as the medical intern eventually moves to senior resident, fellow, and attending physician. As the associates advance, they have more responsibility for the overall management and outcome of the cases assigned to them. They also have increasing responsibility to engage in direct client contact and to bring in new clients to the firm. The structure of some firms is such that associates have the option to pursue a nonpartner track. An example of this is an associate in a litigation firm who is involved in the preparation of cases for trial, but does not actually try cases in the courtroom.

Paralegals work under the supervision of an attorney or nonattorney professional. They typically have a two- or four-year college degree and multiple job responsibilities that vary greatly with the particular practice group to which they are assigned and their level of experience. Often their responsibilities deal with organization and review of large numbers of nonmedical and medical documents, entry of case information into a computer database, preparation of draft legal pleadings for the attorney, investigative research, summarizing depositions, interviewing prospective clients with the attorney, preparing exhibits and computerized presentations for trial, sending out correspondence, and organizing files. Some firms even utilize paralegals to do legal research. Many paralegals eventually go on to attend law school. Others become career paralegals, sometimes periodically changing their area of practice or taking on a supervisory role as a paralegal manager or coordinator.

Although nurses who historically worked in law firms were often called nurse paralegals, it is increasingly common for LNCs to be considered nonattorney professionals and to receive commensurate respect, pay, and benefits. Some larger firms may be more hierarchical than smaller firms in their formal structure and in the distinctions they make between the status of attorneys and nonattorneys. The contributions of the competent LNC as a valued member of the team are increasingly recognized. Most attorneys who become accustomed to working with experienced LNCs are cognizant of the important role the LNCs play in assisting the attorney to provide high-quality client services in a cost-effective manner. The LNC has a large body of knowledge about anatomy, physiology, and medical and nursing practice that the attorney may not have. This allows the LNC to function as an educator, especially for less-experienced attorneys.

Delegation

Task delegation in a law firm varies with the size and structure of the firm. Generally, partners can delegate tasks to any (nonpartner) employee of the firm. If a partner is the chairperson of a department or practice group, he or she may even delegate responsibilities to another partner in the same practice group. Large firms are also likely to have committees that delegate tasks to all categories of personnel in the firm.

Most firms, regardless of size, have a hierarchical order of task delegation. Typically, a partner or senior associate delegates tasks to those people with whom he or she directly works. For a given case, this would likely include a junior associate, paralegal, LNC, and secretary. Associates delegate work to paralegals, secretaries, and LNCs. LNCs delegate work to paralegals and secretaries. Paralegals delegate tasks to their secretaries. Paralegals and secretaries typically delegate tasks to in-house or outside ancillary support personnel, although anyone else higher in the hierarchy could also do this if appropriate. An effective partner or senior associate responsible for a given case will periodically confer with the team working on the case to make sure that assigned tasks are getting done in a proper and timely manner.

Although task delegation usually follows a predictable order, the nature of work in most law firms is such that during intensely busy times or when an important deadline is looming, roles overlap, the usual hierarchical order is temporarily disbanded, and everyone on the team does whatever he or she can to complete the job.

As in all businesses, rank distinctions among the employees and partners of a firm do exist and are generally related to title, longevity, compensation and benefits packages, productivity, and responsibilities within the firm. In a well-functioning law firm, all personnel understand the importance of teamwork and have a common goal of providing quality services to their clients. This is most likely to occur in firms that value the role that each person plays in the delivery of client services.

Management of a Law Firm

The management of a law firm has traditionally been a function of the partnership, which votes on all significant personnel and operational decisions at regular partnership meetings. Most firms appoint a managing partner to handle the many administrative tasks that must be dealt with on a day-to-day basis. Typically, the managing partner will set the agenda for the partner meetings and make administrative decisions that do not require a formal vote by the partnership. Larger firms may also hire a business manager to coordinate the financial operation of the firm. Typically this person's compensation package is tied to the financial success of the firm during a given year.

Mission and Work of the Law Firm

The fundamental mission of any law firm is to act in the best interest of its clients in the provision of high-quality, ethical legal services. The type of work done at a law firm depends upon the particular work generated by that firm's clients. The practice of law is as diversified as the practice of medicine. Medium and large firms offer a wide range of legal services, with separate practice groups for different areas of the law. These may include litigation, intellectual-property matters, real-estate transactions, environmental law, estate law, commercial law, bankruptcy law, family law, and employment-discrimination matters, among others. Some firms may have satellite offices in different parts of the state, country, or world. Most firms that hire LNCs either are engaged solely in personal injury litigation or have a litigation practice group. Typically, litigation firms specialize in either plaintiff or defense work.

Plaintiff personal injury firms or practice groups represent individuals who have been injured and wish to commence medical malpractice, personal injury, toxic tort, product liability, workers' compensation, or Social Security disability claims. Defense firms represent the individuals or entities being sued. For example, in medical malpractice cases, defense firms represent the defendant physician, health care facility, nurse, or other health care provider (chiropractor, dentist, podiatrist, physician's assistant, nurse practitioner, etc.). Defense firms may also represent physicians or other health care providers who are being investigated by a state health department or involved in credentialing disputes with the hospital where they practice. In product liability cases, defense firms represent the manufacturer, distributor, or designer of a particular product, drug, or medical device. In a motor vehicle accident case, the defense represents the individual allegedly at fault for the accident. In toxic tort cases, the defense represents those entities allegedly responsible for environmental contamination or illness resulting from exposure to toxic substances.

Most defendants in personal injury actions carry liability insurance, and thus working for the defense usually means being retained by an insurance company to represent the interests of the health care provider or other insured. Claims agents at the insurance company assign cases that are in litigation to one of a number of defense firms, monitor the work and billing of the assigned defense firm, and give authority for settlement of claims. Some defense firms represent individuals directly, including those involved in criminal matters.

Culture and Politics of the Law Firm

Like most business cultures, law firm culture can vary tremendously from firm to firm. Generally, large established firms are more formal, structured, and hierarchical. In these firms, decisions about pending issues may take a long time due to the need to pass through several layers of approval. The larger the firm, the more likely it is that politics plays a role in the decision-making process. The relationships among partners and employees may be more informal in small firms. For example, it is not unusual for all employees in a small firm to have access to the managing partner when an issue arises. Medium-sized firms may fit anywhere along this continuum. A practice group within a large firm may have its own distinct culture. As in other sectors of the business world, there has been a trend toward less-formal attire in most law firms.

The best way to get a sense of the culture of a particular firm or practice group is to speak with past or current employees of the firm. Information about the culture and politics of a firm can also be obtained through the interview process. Typically, a prospective LNC interviews with one or more partners, associates, and LNCs already employed at the firm. Of particular interest to the LNC is the extent to which the LNC role and work are valued by the partners, associates, and clients. This includes whether LNCs have adequate secretarial support, especially in firms where LNCs have fairly heavy caseloads. LNCs currently employed at the firm are the best source of this information. For LNCs applying for the first LNC position at a firm, developing a new role in the firm can be exciting and very rewarding. It can also be quite challenging, especially if the LNC has not had any prior experience in the legal field. Networking with other nurses who work at law firms is especially important in this situation. A prospective LNC employed by firms with other LNCs derives great benefit from the orientation and ongoing mentoring of other LNCs familiar with the expectations at that firm.

Economics of the Law Firm

For the in-house LNC, a reasonable understanding of the economics of the firm is vital to any understanding of productivity measures. A law firm is a for-profit enterprise that brings in gross annual revenue, out of which overhead expenses, capital improvement expenses, and salaries are paid. The remaining profits are distributed among the partners according to the partnership agreement. The salaries, bonuses, benefits, and hourly rates of employees are determined by the partnership based upon position in the firm, longevity, and performance. LNCs are evaluated by the associates and partners with whom they work. Partners evaluate associate attorneys. All attorneys and nonattorney professionals evaluate their staffs, including secretaries and paralegals.

The economics of a law firm varies with its size and whether or not it is primarily a defense firm or plaintiff firm. Large firms have more complicated economic structures than small firms. Defense firms are usually paid on an hourly basis or sometimes have a flat-fee arrangement for certain legal work. Plaintiff firms usually generate income on a contingency-fee basis. This means that they generate legal fees only when they settle a case or obtain a favorable jury verdict for their clients.

The economic success of all firms depends upon satisfying and keeping existing clients, as well as bringing in new clients. Many insurance carriers and self-insured businesses utilize a number of defense firms to handle their litigation claims. Thus, defense firms may compete for a proportion of business from a particular client. Many firms engage in practice development, such as networking and advertising activities, in order to bring in new business. For most firms, a certain percentage of their business comes from referral-based sources, such as other attorneys and existing clients. Learning to network and having one's own clients may be part of the equation when associates are considered for partnership. Attorneys with the ability to bring in new profitable business consistently, often referred to as "rainmakers," are very valuable to a firm.

The LNC can contribute to the economic success of a firm by providing the attorneys with high-quality work product and educating them about the medical issues in their cases. The LNC can enhance client satisfaction by regular contact with clients to update them about the status and progress of their cases. This is especially true in plaintiff firms, where LNCs typically have a great deal of contact with clients. The LNC can also assist the attorney to nurture and satisfy relationships with referring attorneys by keeping them updated on the status of cases that they have referred to the firm. Finally, the LNC can bring new business into the firm directly by networking with other LNCs and attorneys and joining professional groups and committees in his or her legal community.

Fees and Costs in Litigation

At the most basic level, attorneys are paid a fee for their services in one of two ways: contingency, meaning a percentage of any recovery, or hourly. Plaintiff attorneys most often work on a contingency-fee basis, and defense firms work on an hourly basis. Legal fees cover the time and expertise of the lawyers and nonattorney professionals, the support staff's time, and the overhead of the firm. They do not cover costs or disbursements, which are out-of-pocket expenses that the firm incurs in the prosecution or defense of a case. Examples of disbursements are expert fees, copying charges, court-reporter and transcript charges related to depositions, and travel expenses. Ultimately, payment of disbursements is the responsibility of the client, whether a case is won or lost. Some plaintiff firms advance payment of disbursements until the conclusion of a case. Other firms bill clients for disbursements on a monthly or quarterly basis. Disbursements in personal injury matters, especially medical malpractice claims, can be sizable. Thus, plaintiff attorneys and their LNCs must consider whether or not the potential economic recovery substantially outweighs the likely cost of prosecuting the claim.

Fees and Productivity Measurements in Defense Firms

Defense firms are paid for their time, regardless of the outcome of the case. Most defense firms bill their clients by the hour for time spent on a case by all timekeepers. Attorneys, LNCs, and paralegals, with few exceptions, generate billable hours that translate into revenue for the firm. Secretaries, copy clerks, and other support personnel do not generate billable-hour revenue for the firm. Each category of billable personnel has an assigned billing rate for each single hour of time or part thereof. For example, a partner's time might be billed at $250 per hour or more, an associate between $125 and $250 per hour, and the LNC between $75 and $125 an hour. Billing rates are dependent upon the title, expertise, and experience of the timekeeper, and on what a particular client is willing to pay. Thus, the billing rate of a timekeeper may vary from client to client or among different types of cases for the same client. Generally, large established firms in metropolitan areas have higher billing rates than their counterparts in smaller cities or outlying areas. Some clients negotiate flat-fee arrangements for a portion of their legal services. For example, an insurance carrier might pay a set fee in malpractice cases for time spent from inception of the case through the conclusion of depositions.

Timekeeping by all billable personnel is documented on a daily time sheet, customarily in blocks of a tenth of an hour (0.1- or 6-minute increments) or sometimes a quarter of an hour (0.25- or 15-minute increments). The particular requirements for timekeeping records, including how much time must be accounted for each day, vary from firm to firm. The client may have specific requirements regarding the descriptive nature of time-sheet entries. Time sheets also provide a basis for measuring the productivity of the timekeeper. Typically, there are certain minimum monthly or annual billable-hour expectations for each timekeeper. If the firm has an annual bonus program, the bonus may in part reflect billable hours in excess of the minimum requirement. Nonbillable hours are also accounted for each day. Nonbillable time might include time spent attending educational seminars, participating in department meetings, or organizing medical-research files. (See Table 23.1.)

Defense firm clients often scrutinize their bills carefully when it comes to time records and may dispute certain entries or refuse payment for others. For example, the client may feel that he was billed for a task that should have been done by ancillary personnel. Or the client may dispute the amount of time billed for a

Table 23.1 Sample Time Sheet

Client/Case Name	File Number	Billable Hours	Nonbillable Hours	Description
Johnson, Clyde	12345	0.4		Telephone conference w/client
General Office	99999		1.25	Label medical library shelves
Henderson, Charlene	67890	5.3		Research preeclampsia
Anderson, James	34567	0.2		Prepare correspondence to client

particular project or task. It is critical that all timekeepers, including LNCs, generate accurate time sheets that reflect the exact nature of the work done. If it is allowed, being more descriptive in time entries may help explain why a particular task took as long as it did. Typically each client has an assigned billing attorney who reviews the bills for content and accuracy before they are sent to the client. The billing attorney knows the specific billing requirements of a particular client and should relay this information to all timekeepers. The billing attorney also has the authority to "write off" time before the bill is sent to the client or reduce billable time if a dispute ensues after the client receives the bill. Unfortunately, time that is written off translates into lost revenue for the firm. A firm that utilizes time efficiently to generate high-quality services will ensure profits, as well as future business from the client.

Most defense firm clients are insurance companies, self-insured hospitals, or other businesses. Instead of working with one firm exclusively, each client typically has an approved list of several defense firms with which it works. This allows the client to utilize the expertise of a particular attorney for a given case, manage conflicts that may arise (e.g., between co-defendants), and reap the benefits of competition among defense firms. Like any consumers, defense clients want high-quality service at reasonable rates.

Most clients recognize the value of having the LNC as an integral part of the legal team. LNCs possess a body of medical knowledge based upon their education and clinical experience. They also have the ability to research medical issues and communicate effectively with medical experts. In many firms, LNCs perform work formerly done by attorneys at higher rates. This is cost-effective for the client and allows the attorney more time to engage in activities that only attorneys can conduct. Timelines, medical research, and other work product generated by the LNC enhance the attorney's knowledge and organization of the medical issues in a case. This assists the attorney in providing high-quality legal work for the client and increases the chances for a favorable outcome for the client.

In a well-run, successful defense firm, the fees generated by the billable personnel are more than sufficient to cover overhead of the firm, including employee salaries, rent, supplies, computer expenses, and capital improvements. Any income generated in excess of the firm's overhead is profit for the partnership.

Fees and Productivity Measurements in Plaintiff Firms

Most personal injury firms take cases on a contingency-fee basis. This means that the firm is entitled to a percentage of any verdict or settlement. The percentage varies from state to state and sometimes with type of case. For example, the New

York State statute requires a sliding-scale contingency fee in medical malpractice cases that reduces the percentage of the attorney fee initially and again in incremental amounts for all awards in excess of $250,000 (30% of the first $250,000, 25% of the next $250,000, 20% of the next $500,000, 15% of the next $250,000, and 10% of everything above $1,250,000). In addition to legal fees for time spent on a case, plaintiff firms are also entitled to recover any disbursements not already paid by the client. Many firms deduct these costs from the total award and then calculate their percentage on the remaining amount. Other firms deduct their fee from the total amount of the award and then deduct their costs. The client collects the remaining amount of the award, assuming that there are no liens on the recovery, such as Medicare, Medicaid, or workers' compensation. If a lien is involved, the attorney has to consider this in any settlement negotiations. The attorney may also be able to negotiate a reduction in the lien, especially if settlement of a case is economically beneficial to the lienholder.

Example 23.1: A case has settled prior to trial for the sum of $100,000. The plaintiff's lawyer has a contingency agreement with the client for 40% and has spent $15,000 in out-of-pocket costs. $100,000 minus $40,000 (the attorney fee) minus $15,000 leaves the client with $45,000. If costs are first deducted, $100,000 minus $15,000 leaves $85,000, minus 40% equals $34,000 for the attorney's fee, leaving the client with $51,000. Some cases involve a split-fee arrangement with the referring attorney. While this reduces the fee of the attorney handling the case, it does not affect the amount of money that the client collects.

Unlike defense firms that are paid for their time whether they win or lose a case, plaintiff firms doing contingency work generate revenue only when they settle a case or obtain a favorable jury verdict. The amount of revenue generated from these cases depends upon the amount of the award and the costs associated with prosecuting the case. Keys to profitability in a plaintiff firm include maintaining continual sources of new clients, effectively screening cases, properly managing costs, and moving cases toward resolution in an effective and timely manner.

Many plaintiff firms do not utilize timekeeping records to track productivity of attorneys, LNCs, and paralegals. They use a number of other ways to measure productivity. Assessment of partner productivity and related compensation is complex and varies greatly among firms. Typically, partner compensation is based upon preset percentages or agreed-upon criteria (effort, cases resolved, and responsibilities) for allocation of profits as defined in the partnership agreement. Productivity of associate attorneys is based upon criteria set by the partners and is reflected in the associate's annual performance evaluation. Criteria may include number of cases resolved, new cases brought into the firm, quality of written work, and perceived effort. Associate salaries and bonuses are determined by the partners and are typically based upon seniority and performance. Likewise, LNC productivity is usually measured by the extent to which the associates and partners value the contribution of the LNC, as reflected in annual performance evaluations. A more detailed discussion of effective LNC performance in the context of key factors impacting plaintiff firm profitability follows.

Client Base

Plaintiff firms depend upon the continual referral of new cases. LNCs who network in the legal community by joining bar-association committees, speaking at medical–legal seminars, publishing relevant articles, or joining professional LNC groups may generate referral of cases to their firms. Existing clients are likely to refer friends and family members to a firm if their satisfaction is enhanced by regular contact with the LNC. LNCs who assist the attorney in nurturing referring-attorney relationships help ensure continual referral of cases from that attorney.

Screening Cases

Effective screening of potential cases is critical to the profitability of a plaintiff firm and thus is discussed in detail later in this chapter. Many plaintiff attorneys rely heavily on the knowledge, research, and advice of their LNCs when screening cases involving medical issues, especially medical malpractice cases. While ultimately it is the attorney's decision whether to accept or reject a case, the in-house LNC may be in the best position to help weed out claims that are nonmeritorious or economically nonviable. An effective LNC is able to assist the attorney to reject nonviable cases expeditiously. Discovering a major obstacle or a series of small ones at the outset results in less time spent on unprofitable cases. The productive LNC in the contingency setting recognizes how much information must be obtained to make a fair assessment of the merits of a case.

Cost Containment

Disbursements are associated with the pursuit of virtually all personal injury claims. Typical costs include those for copies of medical records, deposition transcripts, private investigator fees, and expert fees. These costs are especially high in medical malpractice cases, which may require the services of several experts and multiple depositions. A profitable firm must contain costs in proportion to the anticipated economic recovery; otherwise, expenses will consume a disproportionate share of either the client's recovery or the attorney's fee. The LNC can assist the attorney to achieve this balance by first providing a thorough assessment of the client's damages, including physical or emotional pain and suffering, functional limitations, lost income, and loss of services related to derivative claims. This allows the attorney to determine the likely settlement and verdict range in the venue for each case. Second, the LNC can assist the attorney in deciding whether a particular expense is necessary to litigate the case properly, whether or not it is reasonable in light of the expenses that have already been incurred, and whether or not the timing of a particular expense is appropriate. For example, if a particular case moves toward settlement negotiations at the conclusion of depositions, it may be prudent to cease incurring additional costs unless settlement talks fail. Ultimately, the management decisions of a case rest with the attorney. However, a knowledgeable LNC can guide the attorney to make prudent economic decisions that benefit both the firm and its clients.

Timely Resolution of Cases

Firms that accept cases on a contingency-fee basis do not generate revenue from those cases until they negotiate a settlement or achieve a favorable jury verdict. The gross revenue of a firm is directly related to the number and value of cases that it successfully resolves annually. Productive LNCs accept responsibility for assisting the attorneys in moving their cases toward resolution at each phase of litigation, much like a case manager. A competent LNC has all the tools to fulfill this role. This means providing the attorneys with timely work product at key points of the process and trying to stay one step ahead of the attorneys so that they always have the information they need to move the case to the next phase. This may involve maintaining a chart that tracks the progress of an attorney's cases and setting up regular conference times with the attorney to discuss cases that need attention.

The Role of an In-House LNC

Legal nurse consulting is a relatively nascent profession. The role of the in-house LNC is still evolving at most law firms. In many firms, the LNC performs much of the medical analysis traditionally done by the attorney. The roles may vary greatly among firms depending upon the firm's prior experience working with LNCs and the locality, culture, and size of the firm. The role of the LNC at plaintiff and defense firms is very similar, with the exception that LNCs at plaintiff firms are usually involved in the initial screening of cases, especially medical malpractice cases. The role of a plaintiff LNC in screening cases is a very important one, given that the economic success of a plaintiff's firm, which almost always takes cases on a contingency-fee basis, is directly related to making good choices about the cases they accept. The following section is devoted to this topic, along with a discussion of the roles that both plaintiff and defense LNCs play once a case is in suit.

LNCs at plaintiff firms are usually very involved in the initial screening and investigation of potential medical malpractice cases. The screening process begins when a client or the client's representative (friend, family member, or referring attorney) contacts the firm about a potential case. While the actual screening process may vary from firm to firm, typically a paralegal or LNC obtains the initial intake information on the phone and records it on an intake sheet. Sometimes a client or client's representative calls the attorney directly. The LNC then consults with an attorney about the disposition of that claim. The goal at this phase of the screening process is to obtain enough information to either reject the case right away or accept it for preliminary investigation. It is common for plaintiff firms to reject many more cases than they accept, due to lack of merit, conflicts, expired statutes of limitations, insufficient damages, or facts that make it unlikely that the attorney will prevail on the liability issues. For cases that are rejected, the LNC may draft a "reject" letter for the attorney's signature.

If the attorney decides to pursue an investigation of a potential claim, the LNC (and sometimes the attorney) typically interviews the client or representative to gather more in-depth information about the facts of the case and the nature of the alleged injuries, including current medical status and prognosis. It is also important to obtain a complete medical history and a list of all prior and current health care providers and hospitalizations. The LNC should also obtain information about potential liens. In death cases, it is important to inquire whether an autopsy was done. It is also helpful to request the client and family members to prepare a written narrative of their recollection of key events, because over time memories become less clear. On occasion, clients or their family members may already have prepared a journal of events as they unfolded or a diary related to the client's injuries and functional limitations.

The next step in the investigation of a potential medical malpractice claim is to request the relevant medical records. The LNC identifies all records needed for the firm and a medical expert to render an opinion about the merits of the case. Typically the LNC's secretary or a paralegal sends out correspondence requesting the medical records that have been identified by the LNC. It is important to have a tickler system, a manual or computerized reminder system, in place so that records are received in a timely manner. If the case involves a lengthy hospitalization and hence significant expense to obtain the records, the LNC may decide to review the entire chart at the hospital, selecting only those portions of the record needed for the initial investigation.

Once all the medical records are received, the LNC organizes and reviews them to form an initial impression about the merits of the case. The LNC is in a unique position to readily extract and analyze the relevant information in the medical records pertaining to liability, proximate cause, and damages. Sometimes the end result of the LNC's review is a recommendation not to proceed any further with the case if the claim lacks merit or if the potential economic recovery does not justify the great time and expense involved in pursuing a medical malpractice claim. In this situation, the LNC may prepare a brief summary of his or her rationale for rejecting the case to use when conferring with the attorney about the case. The attorney decides whether to accept the LNC's recommendation to reject the case.

If the case appears to have merit, the LNC may prepare a summary of the relevant documentation in the medical records. The format of the summary depends upon the nature of the case. It may be a narrative in paragraph form, a medical chronology of a sequence of events, or a multicolumn chart with very detailed information from a hospitalization. In addition to preparing a summary of the medical documentation, the LNC conducts a preliminary medical literature review, focusing on the medical conditions, signs and symptoms, and treatment options as they relate to the applicable standard-of-care issues relevant to the case. Once this process is complete, the LNC discusses his or her findings, including an analysis of the strengths and weaknesses of the case, with the assigned attorney. This includes an evaluation of the plaintiff's credibility, contributory negligence, and failure to mitigate damages, and of how the plaintiff is likely to be perceived by a jury. It also includes an evaluation of whether or not the plaintiff's injuries meet the firm's damage threshold. Armed with a thorough workup by the LNC, the attorney either rejects the case at this point or decides to send it out for review by a medical expert.

The expert medical review is the last phase in screening potential medical malpractice cases. If the attorney decides to proceed with one or more expert reviews, the LNC plays an important role in this phase of the investigation by identifying the appropriate specialty and individual physician or nurse to review the case. The LNC also consults with the attorney about whether or not more than one expert is necessary to address both the liability and causation issues. Once the LNC identifies an appropriate expert who is willing to review the case, it is the LNC's responsibility to prepare a package of materials for the expert. This includes an organized copy of the medical records, a summary of the facts, a list of questions or issues for the expert to consider, and usually a retainer check. It may also include photographs or other documents, if applicable. Attention to a detailed, organized package for the expert cannot be overemphasized. This facilitates a thorough review by the expert, whose primary job is to provide the attorney and LNC with an objective opinion about the merits of the case, including all strengths and weaknesses. The expert's time is very expensive and should not be spent on organizing medical records.

Once the expert has completed his or her review, the attorney and the LNC confer with the expert about the merits of the case. Based on the expert review, the case will be either rejected or pursued. In some cases, the expert may recommend review by an additional expert if some issue in the case is not within his or her area of expertise. If the expert feels that the case is meritorious, it is essential that the expert have a sound basis for his or her conclusions that will hold up under intense cross-examination. An effective LNC is able to discuss the medical issues in detail with the expert and serve as a liaison between the expert and the attorney. For cases that are put into suit, the LNC may confer with the attorney about which health care providers to name in the lawsuit.

Before putting a meritorious case into suit, the attorney may decide to approach the defendant's insurance carrier to see whether it is interested in discussing settlement prior to suit. If so, the LNC may draft a demand letter for the attorney, summarizing the facts, liability, and damages issues. Or the attorney may use the LNC's work product to prepare the letter himself.

The LNC at a plaintiff firm plays a prominent role in the overall management of medical malpractice cases under investigation. The goal in such cases is to conduct a thorough investigation in a timely manner well before the statute of limitations expires. This means that the LNC must have a system for tracking cases that are under investigation to make sure that progress is made in the timely disposition of each case, including regular conferences with the assigned attorney. The LNC may also have frequent contact with the client to keep him or her informed about progress in the investigation of the case.

Once a plaintiff attorney commences a personal injury claim by the filing and serving of a summons and complaint, the insurance carrier assigns a defense firm to represent the interests of its insured. Depending upon the number of defendants, more than one defense firm may be involved in a given case. LNCs who work in defense firms that handle medical malpractice cases usually become involved in these cases as soon as the firm receives them. Both plaintiff and defense LNCs may assist attorneys with portions of the initial legal pleadings that are exchanged. For example, defense LNCs may draft the initial responsive pleadings, such as the answer, interrogatories (in states where there is a demand for a bill of particulars), and other discovery demands. The plaintiff LNC may draft portions of the bill of particulars or interrogatories that articulate specific claims of negligence and injuries resulting from the alleged malpractice. The attorney may also confer with the plaintiff LNC about which nonparty witnesses should be deposed.

As soon as the plaintiff provides medical authorizations and a list of health care providers to the defendant, the defense LNC goes through the same process conducted by a plaintiff LNC who is investigating a potential claim. The LNC requests, organizes, and summarizes the medical records; confers with the attorney about the relevant medical issues in the case; and does some preliminary research about the relevant medical conditions and applicable standard of care. The defense

LNC also helps the attorney to identify experts and prepares a package of materials for the expert's review.

Following the initial exchange of legal pleadings in medical malpractice cases, the role of the LNC in both plaintiff and defense firms is much the same. The LNC often helps the attorney prepare for depositions. For example, the plaintiff LNC may help the attorney prepare for the deposition of the defendant health care provider or providers by educating the attorney about the medical issues in the case. This might include the relevant anatomy and physiology, a detailed explanation of a particular surgical procedure, or medical research about the applicable standard of care. The plaintiff LNC may also attend the deposition of the defendant health care provider to assist the attorney with unanticipated medical issues that may arise during the course of the deposition. This is especially helpful for those attorneys who are less experienced in dealing with the complex medical issues that often exist in medical malpractice cases. The defense LNC may help the attorney prepare for the plaintiff's deposition by reviewing all past and current medical records and informing the defense attorney about any factors that might impact the liability, causation, damages, or contributory-negligence issues in the case. Once depositions are completed, the LNC may provide transcripts of the depositions to the experts, after which the LNC and attorney reconfer with the experts to discuss any significant new information that was obtained during depositions.

Throughout the discovery phase of a medical malpractice claim, LNCs at both plaintiff and defense firms regularly update the client's medical records, conduct more in-depth research about the standard of care, identify and communicate with experts, and regularly confer with the attorney about the strengths and weaknesses of the case.

In addition to conferring with the attorney about the liability issues in the case, the LNC may provide a detailed assessment of the proximate cause and damages issues in the case based upon information contained in the medical records, the expert's review, and information obtained from the client at depositions. This may include an assessment of:

- The nature of the injuries (both physical and emotional)
- Which injuries are likely to be permanent
- Whether or not there has been aggravation of a preexisting injury
- The nature of any functional impairment
- Whether or not the plaintiff is partly responsible for his or her injuries
- Whether the plaintiff has failed to mitigate his or her damages
- Contributing causes for the plaintiff's alleged injuries
- Apportionment of liability when there is more than one defendant

Settlement negotiations may ensue at any time during the course of a personal injury lawsuit. If this happens, the attorney may ask the LNC and colleagues for their opinions about a good settlement range for a particular case. Many factors are considered when valuing a case, including physical and emotional pain and suffering, functional limitations, the age of the injured party, lost wages, previous awards for similar injuries in the same venue, and how a particular plaintiff or defendant is likely to be perceived by a jury.

For cases that go to trial, the LNC plays an important role in assisting the attorney in preparing for trial. This may include identifying medical exhibits, preparing additional medical charts or summaries, conducting further medical research, and obtaining and reviewing updated medical records. It may also include analysis and research related to the opposing side's expert medical opinions, testimonial history, publications, and disciplinary actions. During a trial, the LNC may attend trial to help evaluate the testimony of key witnesses or evaluate the jury's reaction to certain witnesses. The LNC may also assist the attorney with medical projects or issues that arise unexpectedly during the course of trial.

In other personal injury actions (auto, toxic tort, workers' compensation, slip and fall, etc.), the LNC's role is much the same as in medical malpractice actions except that, typically, the LNC may not focus much on nonmedical liability issues, but focuses instead on the proximate cause and damages issues. In personal injury claims, plaintiff LNCs often accompany their clients to defense medical exams arranged by the defendant. The purpose is to provide emotional support to the client and to provide the attorney with a summary of the doctor's exam. This includes the time spent on each aspect of the exam, the history elicited by the doctor from the client, and the exact nature of the physical examination. Such information is very useful if the examining doctor's report is inconsistent with what actually occurred during the IME. See Chapter 29 for additional information.

Market Expectations for LNC Salaries and Benefits

Prior to considering or interviewing for an in-house position, the prospective LNC should network with other LNCs in the area to get a feel for local benefits and salary packages. They may vary significantly from firm to firm, even in the same region. Most in-house LNCs are now salaried employees. LNC salary and benefits packages differ greatly with the size and locality of the firm, whether it is a defense or plaintiff firm, and the extent to which the partnership values the LNC role. Firms that have worked with competent LNCs typically offer higher salaries than firms hiring an LNC for the first time. Full-time LNCs often work in excess of 40 hours, but usually have the flexibility to work evenings, weekends, or at home and take time off during the week when necessary. Many successful plaintiff and defense firms realize that an LNC can do the work of an associate and more, and are willing to offer a salary in the range of an associate attorney, assuming that the LNC is experienced, competent, and takes an active management role in the firm's cases. In this setting, the average annual salary range is $45,000 to $75,000 in many parts of the country, with some firms offering salaries outside this range. In 1999, the American Association of Legal Nurse Consultants (AALNC) conducted a compensation survey. A total of 834 LNCs completed the survey, of which 615 indicated that they were compensated on a salary basis. Of the LNCs who were compensated by salary, 36.1% reported a base annual salary of less than $30,000, 36.3% reported a salary between $31,000 and $50,000, and 23% reported a salary between $51,000 and $80,000. Less than 5% of LNCs responding to the survey reported a salary of $81,000 or more.[1]

Some firms have bonus programs. A bonus is a portion of the firm's profits that is awarded to some or all employees. Calculation of bonus awards varies greatly from firm to firm. Typically bonuses are utilized to reward superior performance or productivity. However, they may also be awarded solely on the basis of seniority, be a percentage of salary, or be equal for different categories of employees.

Most salaried LNCs receive paid vacation and sick time. Additional benefits may include health and dental insurance, life insurance, retirement or pension plans, profit sharing, and flexible compensation plans. Some firms also pay the LNC's costs for RN state licensure renewals, AALNC national and local chapter dues, professional liability insurance, continuing legal or nursing education seminars, and membership in nursing specialty organizations.

Prior to accepting an offer, the prospective LNC should obtain detailed information about the firm's LNC salary, benefits, and bonus programs. It is also important to request an overview of the process for evaluating performance and productivity and how it impacts compensation.

Skills of the Successful In-House LNC

At the most basic level, job security for the in-house LNC depends upon the firm's maintaining an adequate volume of cases with medical issues. Beyond this, job security is directly related to performance. The LNC who develops the knowledge and experience to become a valuable and indispensable asset to attorneys in the delivery of high-quality legal services is most likely to enjoy long-lasting job security and a favorable compensation package. Although the skills required of the successful in-house LNC vary somewhat depending on the types of work done at the firm and the nature of the LNC role that exists at a given firm, the following are the basic skills of all highly effective LNCs.

Writing

LNCs and attorneys spend a large portion of their time researching and writing. The LNC's ability to prepare well-written documents in a timely fashion is a key component of successful performance. Having the skill to draft succinct medical-record summaries, informative research summaries, properly constructed correspondence, comprehensive interrogatories or bills of particulars, and persuasive summaries regarding the merits of a case is a tremendous asset to the attorney in the delivery of high-quality legal services. For example, the attorney can use a detailed, accurate, and updated medical summary or timeline that contains the relevant documentation from the medical records at key points throughout the life of the case, such as during preparation of pleadings, deposition outlines, and demand letters, and at trial.

The quality of written documents submitted to clients, judges, experts, and opposing counsel is a reflection of the depth of analysis and competence of its author and of the firm. Written documents should be well reasoned, factually accurate, and carefully proofread for spelling and grammatical errors. These include documents that are drafted by the LNC for the attorney to send out as his or her work product. The fewer revisions required of the attorney, the more valuable the work of the LNC. Learning and adopting the writing style of the attorney who will sign the ultimate product is also very helpful. LNCs who feel that they need to improve their writing skills should consider engaging the help of a mentor or enrolling in a writing course. Several books designed to improve writing skills may be useful references for the LNC. See Chapters 30 and 33 for more information about legal writing.

Medical Research

All personal injury attorneys rely heavily on the medical research done by LNCs to prepare their cases. Medical malpractice matters in particular often require that the attorney have an in-depth understanding of the anatomy, physiology, clinical presentation, treatment options, and prognosis for a given medical condition. The LNC must develop the means to gather this information from sources such as peer-reviewed medical journals, medical textbooks, and clinical guidelines promulgated by professional organizations. In recent years, the Internet has become an invaluable means for readily obtaining much of this information. The LNC must learn to conduct effective medical literature searches online and navigate the wealth of other professional medical information that is available on the Internet. Helpful Web sites relating to different medical topics should be categorized and saved for future use. Joining legal and medical listservs on the Internet is another way to gather medical information by networking with LNCs, physicians, and attorneys nationwide. See Chapter 32 for more information.

Teaching

Once the LNC gathers relevant information, he or she must decide how best to convey it to the attorney. The LNC may prepare a notebook with the relevant literature highlighted and organized by topic for the attorney to review, or prepare a written summary of the research results. The LNC must be prepared to teach the attorney any aspect of medicine that he or she does not fully understand. Teaching aids such as anatomical drawings, charts, and models may sometimes be helpful. The degree of instruction that is necessary will vary greatly with the experience of the attorney and the particular medical issues encountered. A young associate may need a lesson in basic anatomy and physiology before he or she can even understand the medical literature, whereas a senior partner may need explanations regarding only very esoteric or complicated medical issues. The LNC's role in educating the attorney about all the relevant medicine is critical. Personal injury attorneys must be able to interact effectively with their own medical experts, depose and cross-examine the opposing side's medical experts, and make persuasive oral arguments to a judge or jury about the medical issues in the case. Medical experts also play a role in educating the attorney, but generally their availability to the attorney is somewhat limited (and expensive), whereas the attorney typically has frequent contact with the LNC.

Analytical Skill

Evaluation of medical issues in the context of applicable legal standards is the essence of the work done at both plaintiff and defense personal injury firms.

Effectively analyzing the liability, proximate cause, and damages issues in a personal injury case is a very high-level skill that can be acquired only over time. To learn this skill, the LNC can engage in discussions with the attorney about the applicable legal standards throughout the life of a case. This allows the LNC to differentiate more effectively between the relevant and irrelevant information contained in the medical records or literature. It also allows an LNC working on behalf of the plaintiff to prepare a draft demand letter to an insurance carrier, or an LNC helping to defend a case to draft a case status report for the client. See Chapter 31 for more information about medical records analyses.

Organization

The LNC in a personal injury firm must keep track of tremendous amounts of information and large volumes of medical records. Most firms have a system for recording new information, maintaining files, and organizing documents. Some litigation firms utilize computer databases in addition to hard copy files to maintain case information. It is essential that the LNC adhere to the organizational system in place at the firm so that information and documents are readily available when needed. It is very helpful to organize medical records chronologically into notebooks, with tabs and dividers for each care provider. A large hospital record can be subdivided with preprinted medical index tabs for the different categories of records. Organized medical records are essential to an effective analysis of their contents by both the LNC and the medical and nursing experts. Personal injury firms request large volumes of medical records. Thus, it is essential that the LNC have a tickler system in place so that requested medical records are received in a timely manner. This can be a system maintained by the LNC, the secretary, or a records-acquisition service. See Chapter 2 for more information about obtaining medical records.

Prioritizing

An effective LNC must have the ability to balance multiple tasks on a daily basis. The LNC at a thriving personal injury firm typically has responsibility for a large volume of existing cases and new claims, resulting in dozens of tasks and attorney requests competing for the LNC's time on a daily and weekly basis. Balancing these tasks requires that the LNC develop a system for keeping track of and prioritizing the projects that need to be done. First, the LNC must maintain a current "to do" list of all pending tasks and projects. One way to accomplish this is to keep all cases in a database. Reports can be printed out weekly and reviewed for deadlines and tasks that need to be accomplished. This system can also incorporate case notes that keep track of the status of the case. It is also helpful to categorize projects in some way, such as by type of task (medical summary, literature research, organization of records, etc.) or amount of time required to complete the task (small vs. large projects). Some LNCs prefer to create a comprehensive case list that includes the assigned attorney, procedural status, and pending projects. Whatever the form of the list, it must be updated whenever the LNC identifies or is assigned new cases or projects. It should also be updated to reflect those projects that have been completed.

Second, it is critical that the LNC have a system for prioritizing the numerous pending projects and tasks. All cases being evaluated or managed in a litigation firm have statutory, procedural, or court-ordered deadlines. Failure to meet some of these deadlines may result in dismissal of a claim, sanctions, or even a legal malpractice action. All litigation firms have a system for tracking deadlines, and ultimately it is the responsibility of the managing attorney to meet them. However, the LNC must also be aware of deadlines and procedural dates (of depositions and trials) so that he or she can complete any projects needed by the attorney well in advance of the deadline. This maximizes the value of the work product to the attorney. Also, an LNC working in a plaintiff firm must consult with the attorney about the applicable statute of limitations in cases under investigation. Some medical malpractice cases require review of certain medical records before the applicable statute of limitations can be determined. Projects with these types of deadlines have priority over all other projects. Projects without specific or impending deadlines should be completed in as timely a manner as possible and roughly in the order in which the projects were received. This promotes a sense of fairness when the LNC takes direction from multiple attorneys.

Other Attributes of the Successful In-House LNC

Personality Traits

Highly successful LNCs possess the personality traits that one would expect in lawyers, physicians, and other professionals. This includes a strong work ethic, dedication to the mission of the work that is done at the firm, and a willingness to accept responsibility for seeing projects through to their conclusion. Litigation practice may involve the need to do research or produce a work product unexpectedly within a short time period, particularly when a case is at trial. This requires flexibility, including the willingness to work additional hours and reprioritize work projects during a crisis. Attorneys value the LNC who is independent, takes initiative to be aware of the procedural status of a case, anticipates work that needs to be done to move the case forward, and suggests ways to improve the management of cases. They also value LNCs who take the initiative to learn applicable legal standards and strategy.

LNCs spend a good deal of time communicating with many different people, including clients, medical experts, attorneys and LNCs outside the firm, and many personnel within the firm. Good interpersonal, conflict-resolution, and communication skills are essential. The LNC who supports and engages the staff that he or she supervises is likely to enhance its productivity. The plaintiff LNC must communicate empathetically with the injured client and their family members. The LNC in a defense firm has to be cognizant of the toll of litigation on the defendant health care providers.

LNCs serve in a consulting capacity and thus must have the ability to express ideas and thoughts logically and coherently. LNCs must also possess enough self-confidence and assertiveness to express their views and debate issues with highly educated attorneys and physicians. Sometimes the LNC is most valuable when playing devil's advocate or analyzing the case from the opposing side's viewpoint. Attorneys need as much information about the weaknesses of their cases as they do about their strengths. This is a high-level skill that can be acquired only over time through frequent discussions with the attorney about all aspects of a case.

Prior Clinical Practice

Most registered nurses with at least three years of prior clinical practice can learn to function effectively as LNCs. Because case analysis in personal injury firms requires evaluation of a wide range of medical conditions, in-depth knowledge of anatomy and physiology is essential. It is also helpful to have a clinical background in specialties requiring knowledge of many body systems and processes, such as critical care and emergency room nursing. Firms with several LNCs may prefer to employ nurses with different areas of clinical expertise, including obstetrics and orthopedics.

Summary

In-house LNC practice is associated with both advantages and challenges. The in-house LNC benefits from frequent contact with the attorneys in the firm. Regular discussions between the LNC and the attorneys regarding the procedural status of cases, strategy, and the applicable legal standards allow the LNC to gradually develop the skills and knowledge necessary to analyze medical issues in the context of legal standards. This is an evolving process that takes time. A prospective LNC joining a firm with other LNCs has the advantage of being mentored by other LNCs familiar with the role in that firm. With more than one LNC on staff, cases can be distributed more flexibly to prevent one LNC from being overburdened.

The in-house LNC benefits from a steady income, with job security dependent upon the LNC's performance and ability of the firm to maintain an adequate caseload of personal injury cases. The first LNC at a firm has the challenge of developing a new role that will be valued by the partnership. It can be a very rewarding and satisfying experience. Successful LNCs at all firms must continually strive to function at higher levels, including suggesting ways to enhance the firm's delivery of high-quality services to their clients. The prospective in-house LNC should consider all the variables of in-house work at a particular firm, including plaintiff versus defense work, size and culture of the firm, types of cases, and compensation and benefits packages, in selecting an environment most compatible with the LNC's goals, philosophy, and expectations.

Reference

1. American Association of Legal Nurse Consultants, *Compensation Survey*, American Association of Legal Nurse Consultants, Glenview, IL, 1999.

Test Questions

1. In-house LNCs working for the plaintiff represent
   A. The insured
   B. The physician
   C. The hospital
   D. The injured person

2. In a defense firm, all the following personnel generate billable hour income for the firm EXCEPT:
   A. Paralegals
   B. Secretaries
   C. Legal nurse consultants
   D. Associate attorneys

3. In a plaintiff firm, clients are usually retained on what basis?
   A. Hourly
   B. Contingency fee
   C. Cost
   D. Tentative

4. When prioritizing work projects, the LNC should give the least priority to
   A. Procedural deadlines
   B. Statutory deadlines
   C. Date the request was made
   D. Court-ordered deadlines

5. Elements of damages include all of the following EXCEPT:
   A. Functional impairment
   B. Pain and suffering
   C. Liability
   D. Permanency of injuries

Answers: 1. D, 2. B, 3. B, 4. C, 5. C

Appendix 23.1
Legal Nurse Consultant Position Description*

Legal Nurse Consultant
Position Description

Position: Legal Nurse Consultant (LNC)   **Revised:** July 1, 1996

Department: Mass Tort/Medical Malpractice/Personal Injury

Reports To: Supervising Attorney and Legal Assistant Manager

FLSA Status: Non-exempt

POSITION PURPOSE:

The role of the LNC is to provide the attorney with management of all assigned cases and substantive input on medical and legal issues of each case.

ESSENTIAL FUNCTIONS:

The Legal Nurse Consultant's responsibilities are to be carried out with minimal supervision by an attorney. Those responsibilities include, but are not limited to the following, dependent upon the speciality of the department:

- Triage: Make recommendations to the attorney regarding each potential claim's merit through an analysis of liability, causation, damage, economics, conflicts and applicable statute of limitations. Prepare appropriate correspondence after each such analysis and maintain records of each call through the firm's Litigation Support Department (LCS).

- Determine medical records, x-rays and other data necessary for each review and arrange for same, while being mindful of the economics of each case.

- Organize and then analyze medical records and other pertinent data to define issues of liability, causation, damages, conflicts, identification of parties, and advise responsible attorney of conclusions and recommendations

---

* Courtesy of Robins, Kaplan, Miller, Ciresi, LLP.

Appendix 23.1
Legal Nurse Consultant Position Description (*Continued*)

- Conduct medical research as deemed necessary based on the issues identified in the case analysis.

- Determine tentative statute of limitations for each case and present to attorney for approval.

- Determine type of experts testimony for aspects of liability, causation and damages. Locate necessary experts, prepare and send materials needed for expert's review, including a summary of records and facts and secure expert's opinion.

- Locate treating physicians and other fact witnesses and interview same.

- Maintain contact with all clients on a frequent basis.

- Perform client, witness and expert interviews.

- Maintain a written records of all file activity including; conversations, conclusions, recommendations, analyses, research and medical record summations.

- Assist with preparation for depositions of clients, medical experts, and medical defendants and attend those depositions.

- Identify, design and coordinate demonstrative evidence assuring relevance and accuracy.

- Educate members of the legal team on the substantive medical issues of each case.

- Prepare for and attend trial.

- Draft correspondence, pleadings and other documents.

- Utilize computerized information systems.

- Maintain monthly case status report.

- Organize, maintain and utilize a comprehensive medical library.

- Maintain medical expert/consultant databank.

- Attend and participate in departmental meetings.

- Prioritize workload daily based on applicable legal deadlines for each case and other factors.

- Maintain knowledge of current medicine and evolving standards of care, treatment and prognosis through regular review of medical and nursing journals.

Appendix 23.1
Legal Nurse Consultant Position Description (*Continued*)

TARGET BILLABLE HOURS ANNUALLY:

● 1700 (145 month)

EDUCATIONAL REQUIREMENTS:

● Four year B.A. or B.S. degree

● Current registered nursing license in the state of Minnesota

● Compliance with continuing education as required by the State of Minnesota to maintain nursing license.

PRIOR EXPERIENCE:

● Significant clinical nursing experience. Medical specialities may be relevant when hiring for specific matters of litigation.

SPECIAL KNOWLEDGE OR SKILLS:

● Working knowledge of the laws and rules applicable to medical malpractice, personal injury and/or product liability.

● Ability to apply medical knowledge to the legal process.

● Keen analytical, research and investigative ability.

● Ability to exercise accurate professional and legal judgment, and to understand and apply ethical standards required by the American Bar Association, the American Nurses Association and the American Association of Legal Nurse Consultants.

● Proficiency in computerized medical research.

● Strong oral, interpersonal and written communication skills.

● Strong problem solving skills and ability to exercise creativity in the process.

● Ability to work independently, with little supervision or direction.

Chapter 24

Communication with Plaintiff Clients

Sherri Reed, BSN, RN, LNCC

CONTENTS

Objectives

- To describe two purposes of plaintiff client interviews in a legal setting
- To describe three components of interviewing skills that nurses acquire through their practice and education
- To identify three skills that legal nurse consultants possess as interviewers that give them an advantage over in-house office staff specializing in plaintiff litigation
- To identify three potential barriers to communication with clients

Introduction

This chapter addresses the role of the in-house legal nurse consultant (LNC) during the initial plaintiff client interview as well as ongoing communication with plaintiff clients in civil tort litigation. The chapter provides information about the advantages of utilizing an LNC as a responsible and proficient communicator, with broad health care education and experience, to help the attorney litigate the plaintiff's claim effectively and successfully.

The nursing process, as described below, provides a systematic means for the nurse to demonstrate accountability and responsibility to the law firm's clients during the litigation process. Responsible communication conveys to clients that their feelings are respected, which leads to the clients' commitment and compliance. Commitment and compliance lead to successful implementation of strategies in a legal case.

"Communication" Defined

Webster's Dictionary defines "communication" as "a sending, giving, or exchanging of information, ideas, etc."[1] The primary purpose of communication is the conveyance of information. Interviewing is "a meeting of a person face to face especially for formal discussion or to meet with someone to examine his qualifications or to get information from him."[1] Communication through interviewing is a fundamental component of the LNC-and-client relationship. Interviews are always goal-directed.[2] They may be formal or informal, in person or over the phone. In order for the litigation team to represent the plaintiff effectively, there must be full, open, and honest communication. Common purposes of client communications are explained in detail below. (See Table 24.1.)

Communication in the Context of a Legal Case

The objective of the attorney/plaintiff relationship is a mutually satisfactory resolution of the business that the plaintiff brings to the attorney. The objective is a comfortable working relationship between the attorney and the plaintiff. The legal problem is evaluated in terms of whether or not the plaintiff will follow the course of action agreed upon in collaboration with the attorney and other members of the legal team. The plaintiff's actions and attitude depend in part on how the plaintiff feels about the attorney and support staff. The LNC plays a key role in the communication process as the one person on the legal team with both health care and legal experience. For this reason, a special bond is often forged between

Table 24.1   Purposes of Plaintiff Communication

- Establish and maintain rapport
- Collect data
- Educate plaintiff
- Support plaintiff

the LNC and the plaintiff. The LNC becomes a resource for the plaintiff and a liaison with other members of the litigation team.

The essence of an interviewing and counseling relationship is movement toward choice. To this end, there must be a proper balance of information and freedom.[3] Freedom means giving the plaintiff options from which to choose and allowing the plaintiff to make informed decisions. Information helps the plaintiff understand the risks and benefits of all options presented. Ultimately, the attorney needs to ensure that the plaintiff makes decisions only after the plaintiff has been informed of relevant considerations. It is often desirable for an attorney to point out factors that may lead to a decision that is morally just as well as legally permissible. The plaintiff's desires in the matter have to be carefully elicited and choices made with adequate legal information.

Often, the plaintiff's decisions in litigation proceed more from emotional factors (love, hate, fear, and anger) than the attorney's decisions do. Plaintiffs who have been injured or who have lost a loved one often seek financial retribution, and may also seek a public admission of fault from the defendant. Plaintiffs may be unable to see the facts of the case beyond the injuries sustained. It may be inconceivable to them that the defendant may not have been negligent or that the negligence may not have caused the injuries. Or they may be shocked to discover that even if the defendant is found negligent, his or her license to practice may not be at risk. The plaintiff's goals must be accurately identified. Education and emotional support can then be appropriately directed at those goals. It is crucial for the LNC to obtain the facts from an objective perspective in order to help the plaintiff and to assist the plaintiff in helping himself or herself.

Purpose of Plaintiff Interview in a Legal Setting

Establishing and Maintaining Rapport through Effective Communication

The rapport established between the plaintiff and the attorney or the LNC at the initial interview may have far-reaching consequences in terms of the accuracy and completeness of information obtained. It might also affect the attorney's ability to counsel the plaintiff effectively when alternative courses of action arise.[4] Inquiry call forms, such as the Personal Injury Inquiry Telephone Screening Form in Appendix 24.1, can be used to collect information when screening initial calls from potential plaintiff clients. The LNC is often the key person assigned to screen phone calls and collect information from potential plaintiffs.

The initial interview usually creates lasting impressions for both the plaintiff and the litigation team. Throughout a lengthy litigation process, the plaintiff will frequently deal with the legal support staff, such as the LNC, paralegal, and secretary, more than with the attorney. The fact-gathering process can be easily sidetracked or blocked if the plaintiff is suspicious of the attorney, resents the attorney as an authority figure, or for any other reason does not have a good rapport with the attorney or other members of the litigation team.

Nurses learn communication and interviewing strategies as part of their basic interpersonal and assessment skills. The skill of active listening means that the interviewer becomes engaged in the plaintiff's thought processes. It requires considerable energy on the part of the nurse interviewer. Nurses are trained to attend carefully to a patient's conversational flow and analyze it as the patient is speaking. The nurse then directs the patient into appropriate problem-solving modes based on the assessment. The same process is used during the initial interview between the potential plaintiff and the LNC.

Successful interviewing skills include a balance of verbal and nonverbal behavior, empathy, assertive responses, and client-centered techniques, each chosen specifically to promote trust.[5] In turn, these skills assist in preparing the plaintiff for deposition testimony or the negotiation process. A trusting plaintiff will be open and receptive to ideas and take the LNC and attorney seriously when discussing these areas. Successful interviewing solicits and provides pertinent information, influences the plaintiff to effect some change or to respond appropriately to a request for medical care compliance, and encourages attitudes that allow the plaintiff to consider settlement alternatives.

Many plaintiff interactions take place over the course of several years of litigation. The LNC is the appropriate contact person for the plaintiff, since these contacts often include obtaining updated medical information, answering medically related questions, or discussing the medical aspects of the case. Plaintiffs will remain more cooperative and receptive to advice or counsel if they feel that they have been attentively listened to. Plaintiffs need to believe that the attorney and the support staff are advocates, working on their behalf, in order to maintain a trusting and amenable relationship throughout the litigation process.

The LNC can assist in initiating a working relationship with the plaintiff in an open, reflective, and supportive atmosphere in the law office, on the telephone, or in the plaintiff's home. Electronic mailing has become another mode of communication with plaintiffs; however, it should never be a substitute for periodic verbal communication on the part of the attorney or LNC. Communication by electronic mailing can also be a useful and time-saving way for the plaintiff to update the LNC or attorney on his or her medical care. The LNC should always be cognizant of the fact that people can sometimes misinterpret the "tone" of an electronic communication. The LNC realizes that strategies such as active listening, empathic regard for the plaintiff's feelings, and acceptance are sometimes not interpretable via electronic mailing.

Data Collection

With every plaintiff, the attorney must gather sufficient facts to conduct the appropriate research and factual investigation, and enough information about the plaintiff's attitude toward those facts to guide the plaintiff in choosing an appropriate course of action. The initial stage of the interviewing and counseling process should conclude with a clear understanding between attorney and plaintiff of the future course of action, including what steps will be taken, when, and by whom. The attorney should be comfortable with the facts presented as accurate and complete, including preexisting medical conditions, in order to determine what, if any, role those conditions may play in the liability or causation issues.

The nursing process guides the LNC by providing a systematic means of collecting and assessing health care data accurately and thoroughly. LNCs apply their knowledge and expertise during the assessment to elicit a detailed, accurate clinical health history from the plaintiff. They identify damages resulting from the alleged negligence of the defendant and identify information concerning influences of past medical history and care (preexisting conditions). The LNC might be able to identify other medical conditions the plaintiff may have, based upon medications the plaintiff is taking. A plaintiff may not recognize the importance of this information. LNCs also identify factors that will influence compliance with future medical therapy. They anticipate the need for future medical care or evaluations related causally to the incident, such as coagulation studies for monitoring anti-coagulation or periodic abdominal series for gastrointestinal conditions (see Appendix 24.2). This information can then be added to the damage profile. When collecting data in obstetrical and neonatal cases, it is imperative for the LNC to include the infant's medical history, the family history, and any genetic history.

The assessment process enables the nurse to determine factors in the client's life that promote healthy behaviors and wellness. By eliciting information from the plaintiff regarding social and cultural background, support systems, value systems, or health perceptions, the LNC demonstrates the importance of focusing on the whole person rather than just the signs and symptoms of the medical problem at issue. These additional elements contribute significantly to the pursuit of a successful lawsuit. Such assessments might include understanding why the potential plaintiffs desirous of pursuing a medical negligence claim regarding the care for their fourth child's delivery did not seek medical care for the pregnancy until the time of delivery. Or it could clarify how the choice not to give an infant a recommended or ordered blood transfusion because of religious beliefs might affect the outcome of the claim.

The LNC is aware that a loss can include loss of body parts, functions, independence, or any other type of physical, emotional, or intellectual loss, whether real or perceived. Assessment of the plaintiff's reaction to loss can help the LNC evaluate the plaintiff's psychological status. Identification of the plaintiff's coping skills contributes to an understanding of how the plaintiff will deal with the stress of a lengthy lawsuit. The plaintiff may need to be referred to a psychologist or other mental health professional for help in dealing with unresolved issues related to loss. These needs are a significant part of the damages in a plaintiff's claim. They also may affect the plaintiff's ability to withstand the rigors of a stressful legal process. The LNC uses assessment skills to collect data about a case and formulates diagnoses of the major issues. The attorney and LNC can then formulate a strategic plan of action. The plan directs the work performed by the LNC, whereas the creation of work product can be compared to the implementation of the nursing process. The LNC (and others) evaluates the effectiveness of the plan of action and quality of the work product prepared. The plan is altered accordingly as new information about the case is obtained. The new information begins the cycle again.

The Initial Interview

The initial plaintiff interview may take place over the telephone, in the attorney's office, at the plaintiff's home, or in a health care facility. The purpose of the initial interview is to introduce the plaintiff to the LNC as a member of the litigation team, obtain background and factual information relating to the events and damages, and ascertain whether a working relationship is possible between the plaintiff and the members of the litigation team.

The LNC should begin the plaintiff interview with introductions and an elucidation of the LNC's role on the litigation team. The plaintiff is asked to explain briefly what happened or why the plaintiff is calling the law firm and what he or she thinks the health care provider did wrong. It may be clear early on that the plaintiff does not have a valid case. He may be angry because his call light continually went unanswered, but he has no injury. The LNC may provide a brief explanation to the plaintiff, but should avoid telling the plaintiff that the case does not have merit. If the LNC comments on the case's merit, the LNC might be providing information outside his or her professional realm. Instead, the LNC should tell the plaintiff that the information obtained will be provided to the attorney, who will make a decision about the merits of the case.

During the interview, the LNC should obtain the plaintiff's full name, addresses, and phone numbers, and those of the plaintiff's close relatives. The LNC should ask what prompted the plaintiff to contact the attorney and what the plaintiff wishes to accomplish by filing a lawsuit. The LNC may discover that the plaintiff does not necessarily want to file a lawsuit, but only wants to know what happened to cause an injury. The plaintiff may want financial compensation or to "prevent this from happening to someone else."

Early in the interview, it is important for the LNC to identify any conflicts of interest that would prohibit involvement in the case. Names of all potential health care defendants should be solicited. The LNC should also inquire about any previous involvement with the legal system and obtain the names of the attorneys and defendants involved. If it is determined that a conflict exists, the interview may need to be terminated until the conflict is resolved, if possible.

If no conflict is evident, the interview should proceed to solicit more detailed information again by asking the open-ended question "What happened to you?" Most plaintiffs are eager to tell their story to a nurse who understands the medical issues of their claim. The LNC must direct the interview efficiently to sort relevant information from irrelevant information by guiding the story with specific questions or requests for additional details. The LNC should allow the plaintiff to tell the story in his or her own words, listen carefully to the plaintiff, and not allow previous experience with similar cases to color the plaintiff's story. The LNC's notes should include, but not be limited to:

- Dates, times, and location of events described
- Names of all potential defendants or fact witnesses
- Any police or other reports
- Existence of logs or diaries of the events in question
- Documents such as discharge instructions or other written instructions from medical personnel, and the plaintiff's compliance with such instructions

If preliminary review of the case indicates that there may be merit, the LNC should refer the case to the attorney for determination of the statute of limitations. After the plaintiff has explained the concerns, the LNC and the plaintiff should discuss the impact of the injury on health, lifestyle, or job — i.e., identify the damages. The complete health history covering all body systems is elicited and reviewed to determine preexisting conditions. Specific questions about current medical problems caused by the injury and the effect of the injury on the

---

Table 24.2   Key Elements of Initial Interviews with Plaintiffs

- Listen carefully to the plaintiff
- Allow the plaintiff to tell the story in his or her own words
- Be empathetic
- Identify date of injury
- Obtain names, addresses, and phone numbers of the plaintiff and close relatives
- Determine conflicts of interest
- Identify the plaintiff's goals and objectives
- Obtain accurate and complete medical information using assessment tool
- Obtain names, addresses, and phone numbers of current and past treating health care providers
- Describe current compared with previous lifestyle
- Solicit brief occupational history and effects of injury
- Estimate medical expenses
- Estimate lost wages
- Introduce key office staff
- Provide the plaintiff with office phone numbers
- Identify potential future health care providers

---

preexisting medical problems are included. The LNC also gathers available data relative to medical expenses and wage loss. It is important to obtain names, addresses, and phone numbers of all past and current treating physicians or other health care providers and caregivers who may provide information about future medical problems and care related to the injury. It is vital to obtain prescription information and the names and addresses of all pharmacies that the plaintiff might have used. Depending on the age of the plaintiff, it may be essential to obtain work or school records. The LNC should determine whether a third-party provider paid the medical bills. If a third-party provider is involved, the name and address of the company should be obtained. The LNC should also determine whether the initial injury was work-related and whether a workers' compensation case has been initiated.

The interview should conclude with a brief explanation of the next step of the litigation process and a reminder to the plaintiff to notify the LNC or attorney of any change in his or her medical condition. The plaintiff should also be cautioned not to discuss the lawsuit with anyone outside his or her family. Key office staff may be introduced to the plaintiff and contact phone numbers provided. See Table 24.2 for elements of initial interviews with plaintiff clients.

In ongoing contacts with the plaintiff, the LNC must obtain updated medical information and records in order to evaluate and maintain an updated profile of damages. Once a lawsuit has been filed, the updated profile will supplement information to defense counsel. These contacts also serve to evaluate the plaintiff's compliance with subsequent medical treatment recommendations and provide ongoing support to the plaintiff. The LNC, as an educator, understands that assessment through interviewing and questioning is an ongoing process lasting as long as the claim lasts and that this process should clearly identify strengths and weaknesses in the plaintiff's case. The LNC working for the plaintiff in civil tort litigation is uniquely qualified to interview plaintiffs initially and perform any subsequent interviews.

Table 24.3   Educate the Plaintiff Regarding Legal Issues

- Elements of proof required for successful case outcome
  - Liability
  - Proximate cause
  - Damages
- Process of litigation
  - Interaction with defendant and insurance carrier
  - Medical releases
  - Expert case review
  - Petition/complaint
  - Discovery
    - Interrogatories
    - Requests for production
    - Depositions
  - Arbitration, mediation, medical review panel process, settlement
  - Trial
- Potential length of process
- Importance of compliance with current medical treatment
- Future course of action related to litigation
- Potential outcomes
  - Monetary damages
  - No loss of license or public admission of wrongdoing
  - Confidentiality clauses in settlement agreement

Education of the Plaintiff Client

Legal Issues

In addition to establishing rapport and collecting data, a third purpose of communication with plaintiffs is education. Often, the plaintiff's perception of the legal problem differs from that of the attorney, particularly in a medical malpractice action. For example, the plaintiff should understand that the defendant health care provider's license may not be suspended or revoked in the event of a successful outcome. Loss of monetary compensation may be the only effect suffered by the defendant health care provider. The attorney and LNC may use the initial and ongoing interviews with the plaintiff to educate him or her about the legal process. The LNC may prepare educational materials such as a booklet that can be provided to all plaintiffs. Plaintiffs should be instructed that their role in the litigation process is an active one and that they must respond to requests for subsequent information promptly and fully. Plaintiffs need to understand the possible length of the proceeding and the importance of avoiding discouragement by seemingly endless postponements and continuances (see Table 24.3).

Medical Issues

Plaintiffs often view the LNC as a resource person who can answer questions about their injuries, ongoing medical problems, and care. They want to know what caused their injuries and why. The LNC plays a vital role in educating the

Table 24.4   Potential Barriers to Communication with the Plaintiff

- Language
- Age
- Socioeconomic status
- Ethnic background
- Educational background
- Religion
- Plaintiff's previous experience with the legal system
- Legal team's previous experience with similar cases or plaintiffs

plaintiff about the reasons for continuing therapies and the importance of compliance with the medical plan of care.

Barriers to Communication

It is important to recognize the numerous potential barriers to effective communication between plaintiff and attorney or LNC (see Table 24.4). Such barriers are unique to each situation. They may include, but are not limited to, language, age, ethnic background, educational background, socioeconomic status, and religion. The plaintiff's prior legal experience, as well as the attorney's and LNC's previous experience with similar plaintiffs and cases, may also present barriers. Some examples of barriers that an LNC might encounter include a plaintiff who has suffered a stroke and can no longer speak, a plaintiff who does not speak English, or someone who practices a religion that does not allow blood transfusions and cannot understand how that issue might interfere with the prosecution of the case.

The natural tendency to judge, evaluate, approve, or disapprove of a plaintiff's statement based on one's own value system or preconceived ideas can be a major barrier to interpersonal communication. Once perceived by the plaintiff, this potential barrier may inhibit the plaintiff's freedom to provide information, place the plaintiff on the defensive, or force the plaintiff to make choices inappropriate to his or her situation and value system. It may also become a source of dissatisfaction with legal representation if the outcome of the case is unsuccessful or not what the plaintiff expected. An accepting, nonjudgmental attitude on the part of the attorney and LNC is essential to an effective relationship with the plaintiff.

Conclusion

LNCs, as plaintiff educators and skillful communicators, are critical to the litigation process. Their health-assessment skills assist them in obtaining data that describes a person's responses to potential or actual health problems. This assessment enables the LNC to determine factors in the client's life that promote healthy behaviors and wellness. Since the LNC's assessment focuses on the whole person rather than just the signs and symptoms of disease or injury, the LNC elicits information about social and cultural background, support systems, values, and health care perceptions. In turn, this information enables the attorney either to build a solid and complete case or to decide that it is not a case that should be taken on.

The LNC working for the attorney who represents a plaintiff in civil tort litigation is uniquely qualified by virtue of specialized communication and interviewing skills, data-collection and organizational skills, and knowledge of the nursing process to assist the attorney in the initial interview and subsequent plaintiff communication. Effective communication is important during advocacy for plaintiffs and one of the LNC's most effective tools for assisting persons to adapt to life changes and the ongoing stress of litigation. Beyond the nurse/plaintiff relationship, learned and familiar communication skills can be used with other health care providers (subsequent treating physicians and medical experts) and the public (attorneys and employers) to litigate a plaintiff's claim successfully.[4]

References

1. Cayne, B.S., Ed., *The New Lexicon Webster's Dictionary of the English Language*, Lexicon Publications, New York, 1995.
2. Balzer-Riley, J.W., *Communications in Nursing*, 3rd ed., C.V. Mosby-Year Book, St. Louis, 1996.
3. Shafer, T.L. and Elkins, J.R., *Legal Interviewing and Counseling in a Nutshell*, 3rd ed., West Publishing Company, College and School Division, St. Paul, MN, 1997.
4. Nelken, M.L. and Schoenfield, M.K., *Problems and Cases in Interviewing, Counseling and Negotiation*, National Institute for Trial Advocacy, St. Paul, MN, 1986.
5. Lindberg, J.B., Hunter, M.L., and Kruszewski, A.Z., *Introduction to Nursing Concepts, Issues, and Opportunities*, 2nd ed., Lippincott, Philadelphia, 1994.

Additional Reading

Chay, A. and Smith, J., *Legal Interviewing in Practice,* Law Book Company, Sydney, Australia, 1996.

Iyer, P., Taptich, B., and Bernocchi-Losey, D., *Nursing Process and Nursing Diagnosis*, 3rd ed., W.B. Saunders, Philadelphia, 1995.

Smith, L., Medical paradigms for counseling: giving clients bad news, *Clinical Law Review*, 4, 391, 1998.

Test Questions

1. Which of the following statements is NOT true?
   A. A legal nurse consultant plays a key role in the communication process as the one person on the legal team with health care and legal experience.
   B. A plaintiff's attitude and actions depend in part on how the plaintiff feels about the attorney and support staff.
   C. The plaintiff can often see the facts of the case beyond the injuries sustained.
   D. The plaintiff's goals must be accurately identified.

2. Which of the following statements is NOT true?
   A. The initial client interview often creates lasting impressions for both plaintiff and legal team.
   B. To use active listening skillfully, an interviewer needs to become actively engaged in the client's thought process.
   C. The legal nurse consultant should use electronic mailing instead of oral communication with clients.
   D. Successful interviewing skills can assist in preparing the client for deposition testimony or the negotiation process.

3. Identify the most essential component of data collection in a client interview.
   A. A clear understanding between attorney and client of the future course of action
   B. Identification of factors that influence compliance with future medical therapy
   C. Obtaining updated medical information
   D. Talking to family members every few weeks for additional information

4. Which of the following statements is true?
   A. Legal nurse consultants are not skilled educators.
   B. A legal nurse consultant's health-assessment skills help him or her obtain data that describes a person's responses to potential or actual health problems.
   C. Effective communication is not important to being an advocate for the plaintiff client.
   D. Legal nurse consultants' communication skills cannot be used with other health care professionals.

5. Which of the following statements is true?
   A. It is important to determine whether a conflict of interest exists.
   B. If the client has retained other counsel but does not wish to continue that relationship and meets with a new attorney, it is not considered to be a conflict of interest.

    C. If the LNC determines that a conflict of interest exists at the beginning of the meeting with a potential client, the LNC should always terminate the interview.

    D. During the initial interview, it is not the role of the LNC to determine whether a conflict of interest exists.

Answers: 1. C, 2. C, 3. A, 4. B, 5. A

Appendix 24.1
Personal Injury Inquiry Telephone Screening Form

PERSONAL INJURY INQUIRY CALLS

Name of Caller: _____

Address: _____
        Street

        City, State, Zip Code

Telephone: _____ (home)
             _____ (work)

Was call for a specific attorney? If so, name the attorney.

_____

Was the caller referred by another person? If so, name and address of person.

_____

Is caller currently represented by an attorney? If so, name and address of attorney.

_____

Date of incident giving rise to injury.

_____

Place of incident.

_____

Brief summary description of incident.

_____
_____
_____
_____
_____

Brief description of injury.

_____
_____
_____
_____
_____

Approximate amount of medical, hospital, and related expenses incurred.

Medical and hospital bills _____
Insurance Carrier _____
Wage loss _____
Date: _____ Person receiving call_____

Appendix 24.2
Medical Malpractice Questionnaire

Name: M ____. _____ ___. _____

Address: _____

City/State: _____

Home Ph: (____)_____-_____ Wk: (____)_____-_____ Alt: (____)_____-_____

Date of Injury/Occurrence _____/_____/_____ Statute Problem _____ (Y/N)
Suspected Statute of Limitation _____/_____/_____ REJECT ____ ACCEPT ____

LED's OFFICE ONLY

Date started ___/___/___ First knowledge ___/___/___ Surgery ___/___/___

Problem_____
_____
_____
_____
_____

Family Medical History _____
_____
_____
_____
_____

Person Medical History_____
_____
_____
_____
_____

Personal Surgical History _____
_____
_____
_____
_____

Medications (Past and Present)

From	To	Dosage	Medication Name
___/___/___ :	___/___/___ :	_____	_____
___/___/___ :	___/___/___ :	_____	_____

___/___/___: ___/___/___ : _____ _____
___/___/___: ___/___/___ : _____ _____
___/___/___: ___/___/___ : _____ _____
___/___/___: ___/___/___ : _____ _____
___/___/___: ___/___/___ : _____ _____
___/___/___: ___/___/___ : _____ _____
___/___/___: ___/___/___ : _____ _____
___/___/___: ___/___/___ : _____ _____
___/___/___: ___/___/___ : _____ _____
___/___/___: ___/___/___ : _____ _____

List all doctors seen concerning condition   Hospital (if any)
____ _____ _____ ph (~~~) ~~~~~~: _____
____ _____ _____ ph (~~~) ~~~~~~: _____
____ _____ _____ ph (~~~) ~~~~~~: _____
____ _____ _____ ph (~~~) ~~~~~~: _____
____ _____ _____ ph (~~~) ~~~~~~: _____
____ _____ _____ ph (~~~) ~~~~~~: _____
____ _____ _____ ph (~~~) ~~~~~~: _____
____ _____ _____ ph (~~~) ~~~~~~: _____
____ _____ _____ ph (~~~) ~~~~~~: _____
____ _____ _____ ph (~~~) ~~~~~~: _____

Name, ph # of other med care   Type (RN, Phy. Ther.)
____ _____ _____ ph (~~~) ~~~~~~: _____
____ _____ _____ ph (~~~) ~~~~~~: _____
____ _____ _____ ph (~~~) ~~~~~~: _____
____ _____ _____ ph (~~~) ~~~~~~: _____
____ _____ _____ ph (~~~) ~~~~~~: _____
____ _____ _____ ph (~~~) ~~~~~~: _____
____ _____ _____ ph (~~~) ~~~~~~: _____
____ _____ _____ ph (~~~) ~~~~~~: _____
____ _____ _____ ph (~~~) ~~~~~~: _____

Chronological list of events leading to present condition
___/___/___: ___/___/___ : _____ _____
___/___/___: ___/___/___ : _____ _____
___/___/___: ___/___/___ : _____ _____
___/___/___: ___/___/___ : _____ _____
___/___/___: ___/___/___ : _____ _____
___/___/___: ___/___/___ : _____ _____
___/___/___: ___/___/___ : _____ _____
___/___/___: ___/___/___ : _____ _____
___/___/___: ___/___/___ : _____ _____
___/___/___: ___/___/___ : _____ _____
___/___/___: ___/___/___ : _____ _____
___/___/___: ___/___/___ : _____ _____
___/___/___: ___/___/___ : _____ _____
___/___/___: ___/___/___ : _____ _____

___/___/___: ___/___/___ : _____ _____
___/___/___: ___/___/___ : _____ _____
___/___/___: ___/___/___ : _____ _____
___/___/___: ___/___/___ : _____ _____

Sign any releases _____ Explain_____
_____
_____
_____

Reason for procedure _____
_____
_____
_____

Complications/risks prewarned of _____
_____
_____
_____

Complications/risks existing that you were not warned of _____
_____
_____
_____

Suspected negligence _____
_____
_____
_____

Types experts needed _____
_____
_____
_____

Items brought _____
_____
_____
_____
_____

List all places where medical records need to be obtained

1 _____   6_____
2 _____   7_____
3 _____   8_____
4 _____   9_____
5 _____   10_____

Possible Defendants

Def 1 _____ Ph (____)_____- _____
Addr _____ City _____
Action _____

Def 2 _____ Ph (___)____- _____
Addr _____ City _____
Action _____

Def 3 _____ Ph (___)____- _____
Addr _____ City _____
Action _____

Def 4 _____ Ph (___)____- _____
Addr _____ City _____
Action _____

Def 5 _____ Ph (___)____- _____
Addr _____ City _____
Action _____

MALPRACTICE INFORMATION SHEET

INJURED OR DECEASED PERSON

Name _____ Date of Birth _____
         Last   First   Middle   Maiden   Month / Day / Year

Address _____
        Street   Apt. No.   City   State   Zip

Home Telephone _____ Social Security No. _____
            Please Include Area Code

Work Telephone _____ Occupation _____
            Please Include Area Code

Employer _____ How Long at this job _____

Is this injury related to a Workman's Compensation Claim _____ _____
                                            Yes   No

Estimated time lost from job as a result of this injury _____

Estimated total loss of earnings as a result of this injury __$_____

PERSON COMPLETING FORM (If Different)

Name _____ Date of Birth _____
         Last   First   Middle   Month / Day / Year

Address _____
        Street   Apt. No.   City   State   Zip

Home Telephone _____ Social Security No. _____
            Please Include Area Code

Work Telephone _____ Relationship _____
            Please Include Area Code

If Injured Person Is Deceased _____
                    Date of Death   Place of Death - City, County, State

Cause of Death _____

Was Autopsy Performed _____ _____ Where _____
                        Yes   No

Person with Power of Attorney/Executor/Executrix _____
                                  Attach Copy of Document Denoting Legal Representative

---

Referring Attorney _____
                 Name   Address

Date of Alleged Injury/Malpractice _____

Date you Suspected Malpractice _____

Alleged Defendant Physician(s) _____

Hospital Where Malpractice Occurred _____
                        Name of Hospital   City   State

MEDICAL HISTORY OF INJURED/DECEASED PERSON

	Yes / No	Detail Positive Remarks Include Date and Treatment		Yes / No	Detail Positive Remarks Include Date and Treatment
Diabetes			History of Transfusion		
Hypertension			HIV (AIDS)		
Heart Disease			Street Drugs		
Rheumatic Fever			Tuberculosis		
Kidney Disease/UTI			Asthma		
Nervous and Mental			Anes. Complications		
Epilepsy			Drug Allergies		
Seizures			Cancer		
Hepatitis/Liver Disease			Major Accident		
Varicosities/Phlebitis			Other		
Thyroid Dysfunction			Other		

Use of Tobacco	_____ # Cigs/Day _____ Age Began Smoking _____ Age Stopped Smoking	Use of Alcohol	_____ # Drinks/Wk _____ Age Began Drinking Alcohol _____ Do Not Drink Alcohol

Height _____   Weight _____ lbs.   Weight change in the last year _____ lbs.

Name of Family Physician _____

Address of Family Physician _____

Please list all hospitalizations **before** the injury occurred, including all surgical procedures

Date	Hospital	Reason for Admission
_____	_____	_____
_____	_____	_____
_____	_____	_____
_____	_____	_____
_____	_____	_____

FAMILY HISTORY OF INJURED/DECEASED PERSON
Includes Injured/Deceased's Mother, Father, Siblings (Brothers or Sisters)

	Yes	No		Yes	No
Cancer			Diabetes		
Hypertension			Heart Disease		
Seizures/Epilepsy/Neurological Problem			HIV (AIDS)		
Genetic or Chromosomal Disease			Other		
Other			Other		
Comments					

PLEASE ANSWER THE FOLLOWING QUESTIONS WITH RESPECT TO THE INCIDENT INVOLVING THE ALLEGED MALPRACTICE AND THE INJURED PERSON'S SUBSEQUENT CARE

List **ALL** medications you (the injured person) are taking routinely, including all pain medications

Medication	Date Prescribed	Doctor	Condition	Pharmacy (Drug Store)

List **ALL** physicians and therapists who are treating or have treated you (the injured person) <u>since</u> the date of injury

Name & Location of Health Care Provider	Date(s) Treated	Condition

List **ALL** hospitals that you (the injured person) have been treated at <u>since</u> the time of the injury

Name & Location of Hospital	Physician	Date	Condition

What is your (the injured person's) current condition _____

_____

What physical and/or mental problems do you (the injured person) believe were directly caused by the injury

_____

_____

Are you (the injured person) currently using any braces, canes, crutches, or other devices _____ _____
                                                                                             Yes   No

    If yes, please describe _____

Are you (the injured person) currently able to work _____ _____ Date returned to work _____
                                                       Yes   No

If you (the injured person) are working, are there any limitations _____ _____ Describe _____
                                                                    Yes   No

Give an <u>estimate</u> of the medical expenses you have incurred since the date of injury ___$_____
          (Please include all expenses paid by insurance, Medicare and/or Medicaid)

_____

Have you been involved in any previous lawsuits or claims _____ _____
                                                            Yes   No

If yes, please explain _____

_____

_____

THIS PORTION OF THE FORM MUST BE COMPLETED TO FAIRLY EVALUATE YOUR CLAIM

IN YOUR OWN WORDS, PLEASE GIVE A DESCRIPTION OF THE EVENTS THAT TOOK PLACE BEFORE, DURING, AND AFTER THE ALLEGED INJURY/MALPRACTICE, DETAILING THE INCIDENTS OR EVENTS, THE PERSONS INVOLVED, AND WHAT YOU OR YOUR FAMILY WERE TOLD REGARDING THE ALLEGED INJURY/MALPRACTICE. CONTINUE ON THE BACK OF THIS PAGE OR ATTACH A SEPARATE SHEET.

OBSTETRICAL INFORMATION SHEET

MOTHER   Name _____   Date of Birth _____
                Last   First   Middle   Maiden   Month / Day / Year

                Address _____
                        Street   Apt. No.   City   State   Zip

                Home Telephone _____   Social Security No. _____
                                 Please Include Area Code

                Work Telephone _____   Occupation _____
                                 Please Include Area Code

FATHER   Name _____   Date of Birth _____
                Last   First   Middle   Month / Day / Year

                Address _____
                        Street   Apt. No.   City   State   Zip

                Home Telephone _____   Social Security No. _____
                                 Please Include Area Code

                Work Telephone _____   Occupation _____
                                 Please Include Area Code

CHILD   Name _____   Date of Birth _____
                Last   First   Middle   Month / Day / Year

                Address _____
                        Street   Apt. No.   City   State   Zip

                Home Telephone _____   Social Security No. _____
                                 Please Include Area Code

If Injured Person Is Deceased _____
                                 Date of Death   Place of Death - City, County, State

                        Cause of Death _____

                        Was Autopsy Performed _____ _____   Where _____
                                       Yes   No

                        Name of Person with Power of Attorney _____
                                                Attach Copy of Document Denoting Legal Representative

Referring Attorney _____ _____
                               Name   Address

Date of Alleged Injury/Malpractice _____

Date You Suspected Malpractice _____

Alleged Defendant Physician(s) _____

Hospital Where Malpractice Occurred _____
                                        Name of Hospital   City   State

MOTHER'S MEDICAL HISTORY

Total Times Pregnant	Full Term Deliveries	Premature Deliveries	Abortions Induced	Abortions Spontaneous	Ectopic Pregnancies	Multiple Births	No. of Living Children

PAST PREGNANCIES

Date of Delivery	Weeks of Gestation	Length of Labor	Birth Weight	Type of Delivery	Anesthesia Used	Place of Delivery	Child Living Yes / No	Treatment for Preterm Labor Yes / No

PAST MEDICAL HISTORY

	Yes / No	Detail Positive Remarks Include Date and Treatment		Yes / No	Detail Positive Remarks Include Date and Treatment
Diabetes			RH Sensitized		
Hypertension			Tuberculosis		
Heart Disease			Asthma		
Rheumatic Fever			Drug Allergies		
Mitral Valve Prolapse			GYN Surgery		
Kidney Disease/UTI			Operations		
Nervous and Mental			Hospitalizations		
Epilepsy			Anes. Complications		
Hepatitis/Liver Disease			Abnormal Pap		
Varicosities/Phlebitis			Uterine Abnormality		
Thyroid Dysfunction			Infertility		
Major Accidents			DES Exposure		
History of Transfusion			Street Drugs		
HIV (AIDS)			Hepatitis B		
Genital Herpes			Rash/Virus Since LMP		
Chlamydia/Syphilis			Other		

Use of Tobacco	_____ # Cigs/Day Prior to Preg. _____ # Cigs/Day During Preg. _____ Age Began Smoking	Use of Alcohol	_____ # Drinks/Wk Prior to Preg. _____ # Drinks/Wk During Preg. _____ Age Began Drinking Alcohol

SCREENING STUDIES

Includes Baby's Mother, Baby's Father, Siblings (Brothers or Sisters), or Anyone in Either Family

	Yes	No		Yes	No
Mothers Age Greater Than 35?			Neural Tube Defect		
Downs Syndrome (Mongolism)			Tay Sach's Disease		
Sickle Cell Disease or Trait			Hemophilia		
Muscular Dystrophy			Cystic Fibrosis		
Huntington Chorea			Mental Retardation		
Other Genetic or Chromosomal Disease			More than 3 Spontaneous Abortions		
History of Stillbirth			HIV (AIDS)		
Learning Disability			Hydrocephalus (Water on the Brain)		
Seizures/Epilepsy/Neurological Problem			Cerebral Palsy		
Heart Defects			Other Birth Defects		
Comments					

PLEASE ANSWER THE FOLLOWING QUESTIONS WITH RESPECT TO THE PREGNANCY INVOLVING THE ALLEGED MALPRACTICE

	Yes/No	Detail Positive Remarks Include Date and Treatment		Yes/No	Detail Positive Remarks Include Date and Treatment
Vaginal Bleeding			Vaginal Discharge		
Nausea/Vomiting			Constipation		
Headaches			Abdominal Pain		
Urinary Complaints			Fever		
Exposure to Chemicals			Anemia		
Prenatal Vitamins			Diabetes		
Hypertension			Epilepsy/Seizures		
Swelling of Hands/Feet			Supplemental Iron		
Colds/Flu			Any Type of Infection		
Exposure to X-rays			Blurred Vision		

Was a Home Pregnancy Test Done _____ _____ Date _____ Result _____
Yes   No

Were Birth Control Pills Being Used at the Time of Conception _____ _____ Brand _____
Yes   No

Before Pregnancy Weight _____ lbs. Height _____ Weight at the Time of Delivery _____

Last Menstrual Period _____ Definite _____ Approximate _____ Unknown _____

Date of First Prenatal Examination _____ Pregnancy Confirmed by Physician _____ _____
                                                                                        Yes   No

Name of Doctor _____ Address _____

Did you continue to see this doctor for the entire pregnancy _____ _____
                                                                Yes   No

If other doctors were seen, please list them _____

What was the original estimated date of confinement (due date) established by the physician _____

If the due date changed during the pregnancy, please list here _____

Did you work at any time during this pregnancy _____ _____ Type of work _____
                                                   Yes   No

Date you stopped working _____ Were you exposed to chemicals/toxic substances _____ _____
                                                                                     Yes   No

When did you first feel the baby move _____ Was the baby active during pregnancy _____ _____
                                                                                        Yes   No

How often did you see the physician for prenatal visits _____

List **ANY** medications, including prescription, non prescription, or street drugs taken during this pregnancy

Medication	Date Prescribed	Doctor	Condition
_____	_____	_____	_____
_____	_____	_____	_____
_____	_____	_____	_____
_____	_____	_____	_____

Was an ultrasound done during the pregnancy _____ _____ Date _____
                                                Yes   No

Who performed the ultrasound _____ Result _____

If subsequent ultrasound done, list date performed and who performed _____

Was an amniocentesis done during the pregnancy _____ _____ Date _____
                                                   Yes   No

Who performed the amniocentesis _____ _____ Result _____

Was a glucose tolerance test (GTT) done during the pregnancy _____ _____ Date _____
                                                                Yes   No

Who performed the GTT _____ Result _____

Describe any problems the physician anticipated during the pregnancy or with the birth of the baby

_____

_____

Were you ever admitted to the hospital or seen in the emergency room during this pregnancy _____ _____
                                                                                            Yes   No

Hospital	Date	Doctor	Condition
_____	_____	_____	_____
_____	_____	_____	_____
_____	_____	_____	_____

Did you attend childbirth classes _____ _____ Where _____
                                    Yes   No

Date labor began _____ Time _____ a.m./p.m.

What were the first symptoms of your labor _____

When did the membranes (bag of water) rupture (break) _____

Did your membranes rupture spontaneously _____ _____ Was the fluid clear in color _____ _____
                                            Yes   No   Yes   No

Did the physician rupture the membranes _____ _____ Was the fluid clear in color _____ _____
                                         Yes   No   Yes   No

If the fluid was not clear in color, please describe _____

Was there any bleeding at the time the labor   _____ _____ If yes, when did it start _____
                                                     Yes   No

How long did the bleeding last _____ Was it spotty, mild, moderate, or severe _____

What time was the physician notified you were in labor _____ Physician's name _____

What were his instructions _____

Were his instructions followed _____ _____ If not, why _____
                                Yes   No

What time did the mother go to the hospital _____ Hospital name _____

Was an electronic fetal monitor used at the hospital _____ _____
                                                      Yes   No

How long was the labor _____ Did the mother receive any medication for pain _____ _____
                                                                                      Yes   No

Did the mother receive any medication to increase contractions (labor pains) _____ _____
                                                                              Yes   No

Did the mother receive epidural anesthesia _____ _____ What time _____
                                            Yes   No

BIRTH OF THE INJURED INFANT

What time was the baby born _____ a.m./p.m. What physician delivered the infant _____

Was the baby born by vaginal delivery or cesarean section _____

If a cesarean section was performed, what were you told as the reason _____

Was the father in the delivery room _____ _____ What was the baby's weight _____ lbs. _____ oz.
                                     Yes   No

Does the mother or father remember hearing the baby cry in the delivery room _____ _____
                                                                              Yes   No

Did the mother or father see the baby in the delivery room _____ _____
                                                            Yes   No

What was the baby's color _____ Was the baby moving _____ _____
                                                                        Yes   No

Name of the baby's pediatrician _____ Was the pediatrician at the delivery _____ _____
                                                                                    Yes   No

When did you first learn there was a problem with the baby _____

Who told you there was a problem _____

What were you told _____

_____

Was the baby treated in the Intensive Care Nursery _____ _____ How long _____

Yes   No

Was the baby on a ventilator (machine to assist the baby's breathing) _____ _____

Yes   No

Did the baby have problems sucking _____ _____   Did the baby have seizures _____ _____

Yes   No   Yes   No

How long was the baby in the hospital _____   Discharge date _____

Was the baby transferred to another hospital _____ _____   Date of transfer _____

Yes   No

Name and address of hospital _____

Why was the baby transferred _____

Primary physician caring for baby at the second hospital _____

Please list ALL physicians caring for the baby at the time of birth or at the hospital the baby was transferred to

_____ _____

_____ _____

_____ _____

_____ _____

What have you been told is the diagnosis of the child's condition _____

_____

_____

What have you been told caused this child's condition and who informed you of this _____

_____

_____

CHILD'S PRESENT CONDITION

What is the child's age today _____ Who is the child's general pediatrician _____

Please check the items that apply to your child at the present time

_____ Able to move his/her arms and legs normally

_____ Able to speak normally

_____ Recognizes Mommy

_____ Recognizes Daddy

_____ Problem with seizures

_____ Blind   Right eye _____ Left eye _____ Both eyes _____

_____ Hearing problem   Right ear _____ Left ear _____ Both ears _____

_____ Heart problem

_____ Microcephaly

_____ Hydrocephalus   Does the child have a shunt: Yes _____ No _____

_____ Feeds himself

_____ Sits without assistance

_____ Walks

_____ Attends school   Name of school: _____

_____ Allergies _____

Please list the names of the hospitals that the child has been treated at <u>since</u> the time of birth

Name & Location of Hospital	Physician	Date	Condition

List the names of <u>all</u> physicians, dentists, and therapists who are treating or have treated the child <u>since</u> birth

Name & Location of Health Care Provider	Date(s) Treated	Condition

Has the child had any psychological testing _____ _____ When _____
                                          Yes   No

Who performed the psychological testing _____
                                                        Name and Address

Has the child had any genetic testing _____ _____ When _____
                                       Yes   No

Who performed the genetic testing _____.
                                                   Name and Address

List all medications the child is currently taking

Medication	Date Prescribed	Doctor	Condition

Does the child use any type of braces or special equipment _____ _____ Describe _____
                                                                    Yes   No

Is the child cared for at home or at a special facility _____

Name and address of the special facility _____

_____

Have you initiated any previous lawsuits or claims _____ _____
                                                   Yes   No

If yes, please explain _____

_____

THIS PORTION OF THE FORM MUST BE COMPLETED TO FAIRLY EVALUATE YOUR CLAIM

IN YOUR OWN WORDS, PLEASE GIVE A DESCRIPTION OF THE EVENTS THAT TOOK PLACE BEFORE, DURING, AND AFTER THE BIRTH OF THIS CHILD DETAILING THE INCIDENTS OR EVENTS YOU BELIEVE ARE A BASIS FOR THE ALLEGED INJURY/MALPRACTICE. CONTINUE ON THE BACK OF THIS PAGE OR ATTACH A SEPARATE SHEET.

Chapter 25

Interacting with Defense Clients

Karen Fox, BSN, RN, LNCC, and
Margo Reed Conklin, MSN, RN, LNCC

CONTENTS

Objectives

Upon completion of this chapter, the reader will be able:

0-8493-1418-6/03/$0.00+$1.50
© 2003 by AALNC

- To state three roles in which the legal nurse consultant may interface with health care provider defendants
- To describe the role of the legal nurse consultant in interviews with health care provider defendants
- To describe how to participate as a defense team member
- To identify three duties and responsibilities of the legal nurse consultant when working with defense clients
- To explain the importance of understanding the philosophy of the company insuring the health care provider or health care system

Introduction

Legal nurse consultants (LNCs) play a vital role in the defense of professional negligence cases and other litigation involving health care issues. Today, many professional liability insurance carriers have integrated LNCs into their companies in roles such as claim specialists, adjusters, health care consultants, or loss-prevention and risk-management consultants. Insurance carriers or self-insured companies retain defense law firms to represent health care providers and health care systems, such as large health maintenance organizations (HMOs). These defense law firms also utilize LNCs, either as in-house employees or in a contractual capacity. In the defense arena, the health care provider defendant (HCPD) is often referred to as the client, particularly in the context of a law firm setting. However, LNCs currently find themselves in more expansive roles with their defense clients, including attorneys, insurance companies, third-party administrators (persons or companies hired to oversee and resolve claims), and self-insured companies. Although many of the principles are similar, there are some additional considerations for the LNC working within the context of a larger defense system, rather than with an individual HCPD. This chapter will look at defense clients in several contexts and at some of the roles that the LNC may fill in working with these clients.

The Health Care Provider as a Defense Client

The LNC as a Liaison

In the defense arena, one of the LNC's most important roles is that of liaison between the HCPDs and their attorneys and liability insurance carriers. Many HCPDs find the prospect of litigation very daunting; the concepts of law and the process of discovery and trial are as foreign to them as the practice of health care is to most attorneys. Fortunately, the LNC provides the bridge between these two disciplines by offering health-care and health-science education to attorneys and insurance professionals, and legal-process education to health care providers. On a daily basis, the LNC assists with many aspects of the litigation process, including processing or composing complaints, responding to allegations, preparing answers, composing or responding to discovery requests, preparing or responding to interrogatories, scheduling and preparing for depositions, seeking and retaining medical experts, and performing other aspects of discovery. Most of these terms and processes are unfamiliar and anxiety-producing to HCPDs who may be exposed to them for the first time.[1] Explaining legal jargon is a crucial part of assisting the HCPD through the legal process. Describing the expected time frames for the process also helps to prepare the HCPD who is used to a faster course of events. Explaining from the outset that the wheels of justice grind slowly, with the average medical malpractice case taking three to five years to resolve, may help change unrealistic expectations and decrease the HCPD's apprehension.

The LNC as a Facilitator

LNCs are knowledgeable about health care issues and are most often perceived as nonthreatening by HCPDs. Thus, another role that the LNC performs is that of facilitator for the HCPD in the legal process. Lawyers, even those on the defense team, are often viewed as threatening simply because of the adversarial nature of our justice system.[2] The pairing of an LNC with a lawyer for initial client interviews provides countless rewards for the defense team. During the initial interview, the LNC has the opportunity to facilitate for HCPDs at times when they may not be able to express an opinion or ask a question adequately. An LNC is usually intuitively aware of difficult issues for the HCPD and may be able to intervene with therapeutic communication techniques. The LNC can also be useful in identifying areas that need further clarification for either the HCPD or the attorney. Thus, the LNC serves as translator between the two, asking questions for clarification to be certain that the meanings of words are clearly understood and comprehended by all.

The LNC as a Support Person for the HCPD

HCPD anxiety can be dramatically reduced by the presence of another health care provider, someone who speaks the HCPD's language. Sharing commonalities is a highly effective stress-reducing, team-building technique. The LNC's involvement in the initial interview can build trust between the defense team and the HCPD. The LNC can initiate this connection by sharing stories about previous successful outcomes. The LNC can explain the defense team's role, including a general timeline of case development and a description of what will be expected of the HCPD. When the HCPD views the LNC as an advocate, initial apprehension is eased. Most health care providers who are calm, appropriately assertive, and equipped with knowledge of the legal process can participate fully and effectively in their own defense. Those who are paralyzed with fear or who are suffering damaged self-esteem because of the allegations against them create an extra burden for the defense. Just as providing explanations and information to patients helps decrease anxiety and improves self-care, providing information and guidance to HCPDs can be equally effective. Helping HCPDs see their role in the context of the litigation process while helping them persevere despite the inherent stress of that process will improve their ability to be highly functioning defense team members.

Additional intervention by a trial consultant who has psychological or communication expertise may be beneficial to help assess and prepare the HCPD witness. If the status of the HCPD warrants it, the assistance of a mental health professional may be necessary.

Example 25.1: A physician defendant whose wife died shortly before the malpractice action began found a therapist very helpful in separating his grief over the loss of his wife from the anger and anxiety produced by the malpractice allegations. The physician was able to participate more fully in his own defense once his mental health issues were addressed.

The LNC as Educator and Researcher

The LNC is also an educator and researcher. Videotapes describing the litigation process are frequently available from the HCPD's insurance carrier or from the medical–legal or risk management department of the health care organization. State and local medical and nursing associations are also good resources for state-specific legal information for health care providers. Discovery rules vary considerably from state to state. The LNC must be familiar with the rules in the state where the litigation is filed in order to accurately explain the rules to the HCPD. A simple chart of the legal process, as it relates to a medical malpractice lawsuit, can also be a helpful teaching tool.[1] The LNC may recommend role-playing or suggest videotaping a mock interview or deposition of the HCPD. By employing these tools, the HCPD can watch the testimony in a relaxed atmosphere, critique the performance, and ultimately develop confidence when testifying. Providing a list of available resources early in the litigation process helps HCPDs recognize and anticipate their own needs, thereby making it easier for them to request assistance.

HCPDs are often valuable resources for pertinent medical information related to the medical or nursing care issues in the case. They may have extensive literature collections, including bibliographies, articles, or monographs, on subjects pertinent to the litigation. They may have diagrams or anatomic models that can serve as cost-effective trial exhibits. They are often knowledgeable about the local and national experts who will be needed for evaluation of the standard of care and, potentially, for testimony. They may also direct the LNC to pertinent standards published by professional associations. Such information is readily accessible and serves as an avenue for the HCPD to participate in his or her own defense.

The Initial Interview with the HCPD

To evaluate the HCPD's background and effectiveness as a witness, the LNC should begin the interview process by focusing on questions about education, work experience, certifications, and publications. Most people feel comfortable talking about themselves, and in this way, the interview process starts out in a nonthreatening manner. The LNC and attorney (if present) can use this opportunity to observe and evaluate the HCPD's demeanor, communication style, credibility, and jury appeal.[3]

Depending on the practice setting, an LNC may perform the initial interview alone or may work, through a team approach, with the defense attorney or an insurance professional. If conducting the interview alone, an LNC must take detailed notes in order to prepare a memorandum to the defense attorney summarizing findings and recommendations. Providing such documentation is important to keep all the defense team members apprised of the status of the work in progress and to avoid duplication of effort and increased defense costs. To ensure a productive interview, it is important for the LNC to ask that all plaintiff's medical records in the possession of the client be brought to the interview. Physician HCPDs may have office records, billing records, and radiology films regarding the care of the plaintiff. Imaging films are particularly important if the allegations are radiological in nature.

In preparation for the initial interview with an HCPD, the LNC should prepare a list of questions covering such areas as:

- Clarification of the HCPD's charting
- Independent recollection of the issues
- Chronology of events
- Meetings and discussions with others
- Names of other witnesses
- Additional documents needed
- Theories and ideas for the defense
- Suggestions for experts
- Billing practices and procedures

Having the health care provider go over each chart note helps interpret handwriting and idiosyncratic abbreviations. This review helps refresh the HCPD's memory about the case. It is also an opportune time to seek information about routine care that may have been provided, but not charted; specific independent recollections about care can also be elicited. If the medical record is too extensive for interpretation during the initial interview, it is often useful to have the HCPD dictate the office notes (or other notes) verbatim for transcription. This can also be helpful when opposing counsel asks for clarification of the medical record and can save time later during the deposition of the HCPD. The LNC should arrive at the interview with a prepared chronological summary of the chart with annotated page numbers. This material will assist in expediting the interview and targeting information needed to complete any unreadable portions of the chart. A list of page number citations specific to the individual HCPD's chart entries will also help guide and speed the interview process. During the initial interview, the LNC assists the HCPD in identifying pertinent documents not in the chart or office record, which will be important to the case. Considerations may include:

- Any additional medical records in the defendant's possession
- Case-specific hospital or office policies and procedures
- Hospital credentialing materials
- Handwritten personal notes made at the time of incident, but not included in the medical record
- Curriculum vitae of all health care defendants
- Diaries, calendars, logs, or appointment books
- Telephone logs and message books
- Prescription records separate from the office chart
- Transcripts of previous deposition or trial testimony given in other cases

During this initial interview with the HCPD, it is important to obtain information about the HCPD's professional background and history. Has the HCPD been involved in litigation prior to this matter? Has the HCPD had any problems with licensure, suspension, or certifications? Is the HCPD board-certified in his or her specialty? If so, how many times did the HCPD take the certification board before passing? If the HCPD is not board-certified, elicit the reason why. It is important to ascertain this information before opposing counsel does so. Nothing is more embarrassing than having opposing counsel advise defense counsel that the HCPD's history includes a medical license suspension for a period prior to the allegations in the case at hand.

Throughout the case, the LNC serves as the HCPD's medical–legal case manager of sorts, the conveyer of case status reports, and a reservoir of resources and legal-process information. The LNC's practice setting and working relationship with the other members of the defense team are important factors to consider when planning the participation of various team members. As an example, an LNC employed in a law firm may be expected to call the HCPD as soon as he or she receives a verbal report from an expert witness. The LNC may find it necessary to consult with the involved attorney and convey the meaning of the expert review to the HCPD in the context of the case development. Independent LNCs usually provide a summary of expert witness conclusions to their attorney clients, but often the independent LNC does not have the opportunity to interact with the HCPD.

The principles discussed here are useful for all subsequent interactions with HCPDs, such as preparation of interrogatories, deposition preparation, trial preparation, assistance at trial, and coping with the outcome of the case.

The Attorney, Insurance Company, Third-Party Administrator, and Self-Insured Company as Defense Clients

Depending on the practice setting of the LNC, the term *defense client*, rather than referring to the HCPD, may refer to the defense attorney, an insurance company, a third-party administrator, or a self-insured company. It is crucial that the LNC understand the various relationships and coverage issues, as well as the timing and context of his or her role, when working with such clients (see Figure 25.1). Clearly defining performance expectations and identifying the parameters of desired involvement are key elements in creating a successful working relationship.[4]

Understanding the Defense Philosophy of the Client

Experienced LNCs frequently develop their own defense philosophies that they may erroneously believe are representative of those of all defense clients. Numerous considerations contribute to the defense philosophy of the party (e.g., the insurance company, the third-party administrator, or the claims-resolution committee of a physician-owned company) who controls the funds spent on the defense of a case or any settlement or award. Past loss experience, economic influences, ethical considerations, religious affiliations, and health care provider ownership are just a few of the variables influencing the overall defense philos-

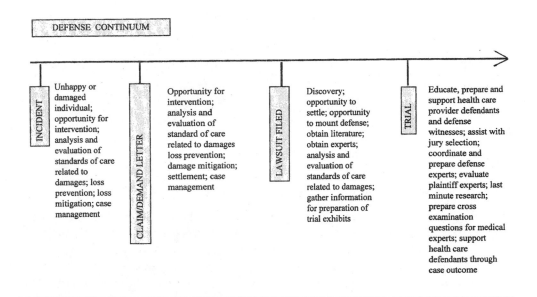

Figure 25.1   Defense Continuum

ophy of a health care organization or an insurance carrier. An LNC must have respect for these factors in order to understand the client and offer services appropriately within the greater defense context.

A self-insured HMO may choose to spend limited funds on early intervention and loss prevention, while applying the greater share of its defense budget to claims containing dollar demands and filed litigation. Another health care organization with a religious affiliation may have a mission to undertake early analysis and intervention in any untoward patient outcome, instituting loss prevention measures and case management for damage mitigation, even in the absence of medical negligence. It is paramount that the LNC understand and accept the differences in these defense approaches. Tailoring one's work product to the client's philosophies and goals is probably the most important and challenging task that an LNC must undertake.

Defense philosophies may be elicited during a tactful interview with the client before work is ever undertaken. The LNC's personal philosophies must be identified, isolated, and separated from those of the client for successful meshing of work styles and goals. Attending to the client's needs rather than personal preferences or beliefs is client-centered service at its best.[5]

Economic considerations are always important to defense clients. Identifying priorities with the client will help with cost containment. Spending hours on projects that the client does not perceive as important or valuable is pointless, even though the projects may be relevant to the case as a whole. Preparation of a detailed timeline chart may be appropriate prior to trial for use as an exhibit, but an insurance carrier may not consider it valuable or cost-effective during the preliminary stages of claim evaluation.

Another consideration to discuss with the defense client is the degree of detail or depth that is expected on a project. Some clients may want every medical word in a report defined parenthetically. Others may be medically sophisticated and request only an explanation of new procedures or treatments. Some clients want extensive medical research with copies of all pertinent articles reviewed and highlighted. Others want the results of medical research simply summarized in memorandum format until trial preparation begins. It is imperative for the LNC who is in doubt about the parameters of a project to clarify the client's expectations prior to undertaking the work. With some clients it may be necessary to do this in writing; other clients may prefer a spoken agreement. Learning to ask the right questions of the client before undertaking the work is a very important part of successful LNC practice.[6]

Defense Perspectives

Chapter 12 presents a detailed discussion of the evaluation of professional negligence cases. The following discussion assumes familiarity with the elements of negligence and evaluating professional negligence cases and focuses on the perspectives that LNCs encounter when working with defense clients.

When beginning the evaluation of a case for a defense client, it is critical to clearly identify the insured or self-insured party for whom the LNC is working. Many incidents, claims, and lawsuits involve a myriad of health care providers, and the professional liability coverage for the providers may stem from a variety of sources. In a staff-model HMO, physicians, nurses, and all other HMO employees are most often covered by the same insurance carrier or self-insured program. The defense of such a case may take on a more unified approach because defense costs and any potential settlement or trial award will come from one source regardless of the specific health care provider found liable for any deviation in the standard of care resulting in damages. For more information, refer to the discussion of HMO liability in Chapter 20.

In many health care systems, the nurses and other hospital employees are covered by the hospital's professional liability insurance plan, but each physician has his or her own professional liability coverage. A variety of liability insurance carriers may provide professional liability insurance to different physicians working in the same hospital. Even when several physicians are involved in one case and have the same insurance carrier, each physician will usually be assigned a separate claim representative and separate attorney to work on his or her behalf.

Though evaluation of any case should be thorough and complete, encompassing all involved providers, it is important to understand the economic interests of the LNC's client. If the LNC discovers that the party for whom he or she is working has little involvement in the case, the LNC should call this to the attention of the client before undertaking extensive workup of the case. Additionally, if another health care provider is responsible or partially responsible for an injury, and that healthcare provider has not been named in the lawsuit, the defense client will want to be made aware of that fact. All involved health care providers should be identified for the defense client. Another party may be responsible for sharing settlement costs, if appropriate. Careful attention to providing appropriately targeted, valuable, and fiscally important information throughout the case will strengthen the LNC's relationship with the defense client.

Some states have contributory negligence or comparative negligence laws that mandate evaluation of any act or omission by the plaintiff. In states where the doctrine of contributory negligence is recognized, any blame assigned to the plaintiff will preclude recovery of damages. Even if the plaintiff is found liable for only 1% of the injury and subsequent damages, the plaintiff is barred from any recovery.

When the doctrine of comparative negligence is recognized, the plaintiff's contribution to injury will be compared to any act or omission by any named defendant. Any jury award will be decreased by the percentage of the plaintiff's comparative fault. In some states, recovery is barred if the plaintiff's contribution to injury is deemed greater than 50%. The LNC should be aware of the specific laws governing the state(s) in which he or she practices.

Example 25.2: A jury award of $100,000 made to a plaintiff who was found to have comparative fault of 40% for the injury would result in an actual award of $60,000 to the plaintiff.

LNCs may become involved in the defense of cases at a variety of points on the defense continuum. At each stage, defense clients are interested in determining whether they have responsibility or liability for any injury that has occurred. This determination will help the client decide whether the case should be settled expediently or vigorously defended through trial if necessary. An early evaluation of the standard of care provided by the insured or self-insured health care provider and determination of the cause of any injury will assist in that determination. Upon careful evaluation, some injuries will be determined to be inherent to the claimant or plaintiff's disease process or to be a result of an expected medical complication, rather than due to an act of professional negligence. If injuries are documented and causally linked to deviations in the standard of care, liability is established. LNCs often provide data from the medical record that helps to determine whether the standard of care was met. This data includes evidence of the health care provider's thought process, monitoring, and response to changes in patient condition. Researching published standards of care as well as identifying and retaining appropriate clinical experts for standard-of-care reviews are additional services that LNCs often provide to defense clients.

Early evaluation of an incident may allow for intervention to minimize claimant or plaintiff damages. The provision of an expedient settlement may decrease the overall cost of the case to the defendants, minimize harm to their reputation in the community from adverse publicity, and improve the claimant or plaintiff's overall outcome.

Example 25.3: One health care system used a nurse case manager and pre-payment for a rehabilitation facility for a patient who broke a hip in a fall from a cardiac catheterization table. Clear liability was identified soon after the incident occurred. Early intervention resulted in an improved patient outcome and made litigation unnecessary.

Many cases in which standard-of-care deviations are causal to patient injury are settled at an early point in the defense continuum before a lawsuit is filed, and defense attorneys' fees and trial costs are completely avoided.

When liability has been firmly established, defense clients will be interested in all potential ways of mitigating and minimizing damages. LNCs may find important data during their review of the medical records that will help with this endeavor. Preexisting illnesses or injuries are important pieces of information to glean from the record. A claimant or plaintiff with a preexisting chronic illness that will shorten his or her life span will likely also have a decreased number of working years. Thus, economic damages in this case may be lower than for a patient with a normal life expectancy.

Attention to the size and potential value of any case is important when working with a defense client. Regardless of the merits of the case, a case involving an infant with a poor outcome will almost always require a more extensive workup than a case involving a 70-year-old with a heel ulcer. Seeking specific preauthorization for any work performed is appropriate for all cases. An LNC must be sensitive to the potential monetary value that each case may represent to the client.

Example 25.4: Social issues identified in the medical records are often important in the defense of cases. The total settlement value of a case involving the death of a 29-year-old mother of four was decreased by an LNC's important discovery in the medical records. The records showed that prior to her death, the mother lost custody of all four children and was not providing any financial support for them. This information made the settlement value of this particular case less than one in which a mother of 4 was caring for her children in the home and working to support them.

Identifying factors that may make a claimant or plaintiff more or less appealing to a jury is also an important LNC function that is valuable to defense clients. Medical-record documentation that describes the claimant or plaintiff's appearance, employment, family structure, and involvement in civic activities is important to point out to the defense client. It is also important to note whether or not the plaintiff missed or canceled appointments or was noncompliant with the prescribed course of care. This information will be utilized as part of the overall assessment of the case. Similar information about the health care defendants that appears in the medical record or is otherwise known to the LNC is also important to share with the defense client.

Job Duties and Responsibilities

This section defines the duties of the LNC once the complaint has been received. After the initial client interview, one of the first jobs for the LNC is to compare the allegations and facts in the complaint with the medical records. A chart may be used to assist with this comparison (see Figure 25.2).

In addition to assessing the complaint for veracity, the LNC should review the documents for the names of any possible witnesses, other defendants, and health care providers. Additional sources of medical records may also be identified.

Interrogatories or questions and requests for production of documents are usually the first set of discovery documents initiated by either plaintiff or defense in the litigation process. Often, the defense attorney will have prestructured interrogatories prepared. It is important for the LNC to review the prestructured interrogatories and the medical records to identify additional pertinent questions that need to be presented to the plaintiff. The LNC also needs to identify questions in the prestructured interrogatories that are not appropriate to the issues in the case at hand. Different interrogatories will be sent to the obstetric plaintiff as compared to the pediatric plaintiff or oncology plaintiff. It is often necessary to insert specific dates, times, names, and facts to develop succinct interrogatories. Most jurisdictions

Plaintiff v. Defendant(s)			
Chronology of Complaint Compared to Medical Records			
Date/Time	*Complaint/Allegation*	*Medical Records*	*Possible Answer*
05/07/97 Paragraph 19	Coronary Artery Bypass Graft x3 by Dr. Doe	OPERATIVE NOTE ■ Coronary artery bypass graft x3 with LIMA (left internal mammary artery) and right SVG (saphenous vein graft). NURSING ■ Capillary refill brisk all extremities ■ Edema – generalized	Admit
05/16/97 Paragraph 24	Right foot blister larger Second smaller blister forming on outer right foot	Records unavailable for review	Insufficient information and knowledge to admit or deny allegations
05/19/97 Paragraph 27	Examined by Dr. Doe Determined by Dr. Doe that right foot was ischemic and gangrenous	HISTORY ■ Excellent Doppler signals at both the dorsalis pedis & posterior tibial pulses. ■ Impression: Severe cellulitis. DISCHARGE SUMMARY ■ 1. DIC ■ 2. Gangrene secondary to DIC. No evidence of significant ischemia.	Deny
05/19/97 Paragraph 28	Transferred to extended care facility		Admit

Figure 25.2 Plaintiff v. Defendant(s) Chronology of Complaint Compared to Medical Records

have a limit on the number of interrogatories that can be presented to the plaintiff. Some interrogatories might be asked as complex questions.

Example 25.5: The interrogatory may state, "Identify all health care providers who saw you following your injury. For each provider identified, state the reason for the visit." Depending on the rapport between defense and plaintiff counsel, this interrogatory could be interpreted as one or two questions. It is important to be exact and specific. The objective is to obtain the most information possible through asking the fewest number of questions.

Requests for production of documents are often filed in conjunction with the interrogatories. In addition to the obvious medical records, it might be important to request records from previous and subsequent treating physicians and health care providers. Employment and school records may provide valuable information. School records can be important regardless of whether the plaintiff is an adult or a child. The plaintiff's counsel may object to the production of these records. If such an objection is made, a judge will direct the decision about production.

In addition to interrogatories and requests for production of documents, the LNC might also have the responsibility to draft subpoenas. If this role is delegated to the paralegal or legal secretary, the LNC should identify any and all sources for record and document requests. In addition to the obvious medical, radiological, and billing records, the following may need to be considered:

- Cardiac catheterization films, videotapes, and compact discs
- Fetal monitoring strips
- Prescriptions and pharmacy records
- Autopsy report and pathology slides
- School and employment records

It is common for the LNC to go to the medical-record department of the health care facility to examine the plaintiff's original medical records and compare them to the copies received. This is particularly true in the case of missing medical records. The LNC may need to meet with the pathologist. On occasion, the LNC may have the opportunity to discuss autopsy findings and review pathology slides, especially in complex litigation and cases with complicated medical issues. When the defense attorney's office has received demonstrative evidence such as original pathology slides and radiological films, it is crucial to secure these materials. The chain of custody must be carefully documented. All documents utilized to obtain the slides and films are retained. Any original slides or films must be stored in a safe manner.

Another important responsibility that the defense attorney or insurance company may assign to the LNC is researching, interviewing, and working with defense experts. Depending on location, defense experts might be readily available or difficult to locate. One way to encourage open communication with the HCPD is to ask this client for expert recommendations. If this is not possible, a review of scientific literature (or, more important, literature published contemporaneously with the time of the allegations) might be necessary to identify experts in the medical specialty at issue. Regardless of how the expert is identified and retained, it is often the LNC's responsibility to prepare some or all of the applicable medical records, discuss the case issues with the expert, and draft a summary of the expert's statements and opinions. Reports or comments written by the expert are considered discoverable and may be obtained by other counsel (including opposing counsel) involved in the case. For this reason, written reports are not requested of the experts unless required by state law. Any correspondence sent to the expert may be discoverable as well. Keeping this information in mind, the LNC should orally communicate all case theories, strategies, and analyses.

The LNC might also be asked to research medical literature for authoritative texts or peer-reviewed journal articles that might relate to the issues in the litigation. MEDLINE, PubMed, and MD Consult are useful Internet research tools. Research tools are discussed further in Chapter 32.

Throughout the litigation process, the LNC should be watchful for records and demonstrative evidence that might be useful exhibits. Professional anatomical drawings can be costly, and other materials may be identified in the medical literature. It is important to obtain permission to use copyrighted materials for exhibit purposes. See Chapter 40 for more information on the preparation of demonstrative evidence.

Depositions can be taken at any point in the litigation process. The deposition of an individual (plaintiff, defendant, or fact or expert witness) involves all parties' gathering, and one party's predominantly asking questions of the deponent. The inquiring party is usually the opposing counsel, although in the case of multiple defendants, co-counsel may also question the deponent. The tasks of the LNC with regard to depositions are varied and might include the following:

- Assisting the attorney in preparing to depose the plaintiff and plaintiff's experts
- Preparing the defendant and defense experts (although usually done by the attorney)
- Assisting the attorney in the preparation of deposition questions specific for the deponent
- Reviewing the plaintiff's deposition transcript for factual inconsistencies when compared to the medical record and other deposition transcripts
- Obtaining prior depositions of plaintiff's experts and comparing factual information for inconsistencies

Trial is usually the final stage of the litigation process. This topic is covered in Chapters 41 and 42.

In review, some of the duties and responsibilities of the LNC when working with defense clients include:

- Evaluating the complaint together with the medical records
- Drafting the initial response to plaintiff's interrogatories and other discovery documents
- Drafting interrogatories and other discovery documents
- Retaining, tracking, and communicating with experts
- Researching medical literature
- Assisting in the identification of demonstrative exhibits
- Assisting with depositions
- Assisting at trial

Summary

The LNC's application of this chapter will vary according to the practice setting, the timing of the work related to the defense continuum, the relationship with the other defense team members, and the defense philosophy of the health care organization or insurance carrier. Whether working with individual health care providers, defense law firms, insurance companies, third-party administrators, or self-insured health care systems, the LNC will find that his or her health science education and clinical experience serves as a firm foundation for broadened roles as liaison, facilitator, support person, educator, researcher, and legal case manager.

References

1. Carroll, R., Ed., *Risk Management Handbook for Health Care Organizations*, 3rd ed., Josey-Bass, San Francisco, 2001.
2. Louisell, D.W. and Williams, H., *Medical Malpractice*, Matthew Bender, New York, 1994.
3. Harney, D.M., *Medical Malpractice*, 3rd ed., Michie Law Publishers, Charlottesville, VA, 1993, Cumulative Suppl. 1996.
4. Katzenbach, J.R. and Smith, D.K., *The Wisdom of Teams*, HarperCollins, New York, 1993.
5. Spector, R. and McCarthy, P., *The Nordstrom Way*, John Wiley & Sons, New York, 1995.
6. Browne, M.K. and Keeley, S., *Asking the Right Questions: A Guide to Critical Thinking*, Prentice-Hall, Englewood Cliffs, NJ, 1994.

Additional Reading

Fiesta, J., *The Law and Liability: A Guide for Nurses*, 2nd ed., Delmar, New York, 1998.

Guido, G., *Legal and Ethical Issues in Nursing*, 3rd ed., Prentice-Hall, Englewood Cliffs, NJ, 2001.

Matthias, R., *Mothers Work*, Random House, New York, 1999.

Oregon State Bar Continuing Legal Education, *Torts*, Oregon State Bar, Portland, OR, 1992, Suppl. 2000.

Ries, A. and Trout, J., *The 22 Immutable Laws of Marketing*, HarperCollins, New York, 1994.

Test Questions

1. An LNC working for the defense of a medical malpractice case may work for all of the following EXCEPT:
   A. A self-insured hospital
   B. A third-party administrator
   C. A defense law firm
   D. An injured patient

2. Which of the following findings from the medical records would be helpful in mitigating damages in a case of clear liability?
   A. The plaintiff was a college graduate.
   B. The plaintiff was the sole support for a family of four.
   C. The plaintiff was a third-grade graduate.
   D. The plaintiff had sole custody of his children.

3. What factor has the most impact on the depth of evaluation that a defense client will request an LNC to perform on a given case?
   A. Liability
   B. Damages
   C. Defense philosophy

4. What is the primary economic advantage to the defense client in performing early evaluations of patients' complaints and claims?
   A. To complete the risk management data base
   B. To identify appropriate cases for early settlement to avoid defense fees and trial costs
   C. To ensure positive patient and community relationships
   D. To ensure positive health provider publicity

5. After a patient fall resulting in a broken hip, an example of an early intervention that may help avoid a claim or lawsuit is
   A. Completing an incident report to document the details of the fall
   B. Nurse case management to improve communication and patient outcome
   C. Notifying the insurance carrier to set adequate reserves for settlement
   D. Conducting a conversation with the facility risk manager

Answers: 1. D, 2. C, 3. B, 4. B, 5. B

Chapter 26

The Role of the Legal Nurse Consultant in the Insurance Industry

Melanie Eve Longenhagen, MBA, MSN, RN, CCM,
Patricia A. Jenkins-Barnard, RN, and
Melanie Osley, MBA, RN, CPHRM

CONTENTS

0-8493-1418-6/03/$0.00+$1.50
© 2003 by AALNC

Objectives

- To identify the different types of insurance products
- To understand the different types of employment roles in the insurance industry for the legal nurse consultant
- To identify professional organizations with which a legal nurse consultant working in the insurance industry may be affiliated
- To understand the various functions of the legal nurse consultant in the insurance industry
- To define credentials available to the legal nurse consultant working in the insurance industry

Introduction to Insurance Categories

Insurance is a contract in which the insurer (an entity) promises to pay a sum of money or give something of value to another (the insured or the beneficiary) if the insured is injured, dies, or sustains damage or loss as a result of a particular stated contingency. Insurance is protection for such an occurrence, loss, or event resulting from direct or indirect actions by another party or entity arising from a variety of circumstances or behaviors deemed as negligence, unlawful conduct, or misconduct. There is also the legislated allocation of responsibility of a party to a claimant — such as workers' compensation — in which employers are mandated to provide for their employees under certain conditions.

Legal nurse consultants (LNCs) practice in many types of insurance companies. This chapter will focus on those that most commonly sponsor, and benefit from, the LNC's contributions. Particular functions of the LNC depicted are not specific to any one type of insurance product or practice and are often interchangeable. The type of insurance, organizational structure, market, and administrative requirements of each product determine the LNC's job function and role. Nonmedical personnel in the insurance field are often intimidated and easily overwhelmed by the high degree of scientific complexity of the health care rendered by various modalities and specialties. They are also not as well versed in the flow and processes of the health care delivery system. The clinical and nursing background of the LNC often lends itself to a particular area of practice most commonly found in the insurance industry. For example, given that most work-related injuries are orthopedic or traumatic in nature, an LNC with a background in orthopedics, trauma, emergency room, critical care, or rehabilitation is commonly sought for consultation in workers' compensation cases. The following is a brief overview of the major categories of insurance products requiring LNC services.

Accident and Health Insurance

Traditionally the categories of accident insurance and health insurance are referred to together within the industry. This type of coverage provides the policyholder with medical benefits for illness and injury as described in the contract at the time of purchase. The insured is the policyholder and can be either a group or an individual. Frequently, the insurer contracts with a group (as is often the case with health coverage); the insurer's main duty is to the group, not the individual employee who is a member of the group. Each policy varies according to the amount of the deductible, maximum coverage, and types of illness and injuries excluded from coverage. These policies set benefit limits or caps, and certain criteria or conditions must be met before benefits are paid.

In the case of an accident policy, the LNC works to establish or refute a causal relationship between the occurrence and the injury. It must be proven that the occurrence was, in fact, an accident before any benefits are paid. It must also be determined whether the injuries sustained, and the benefits for those injuries, are specifically covered under the claimant's policy. In the case of health coverage, certain conditions may be excluded, or benefits may be denied if the required preauthorizations, medical clearances, or pretreatment reviews are not first obtained by the responsible parties as identified by the carrier in the terms and conditions of the insurance contract. This is a healthy market for the LNC, given the litigious climate of the managed-care marketplace. The emphasis on cost containment, quality assurance of services rendered, and cost-effective management of benefits is greater than ever. Addressing these issues requires a sound understanding of the health care delivery system, how it functions, and how charges and contracts are recognized. The LNC provides invaluable insight and expertise in these areas when evaluating loss with respect to coverage, benefits, the insurer's and claimant's responsibilities, and diagnoses of the treating providers within the overall episode of care.

Workers' Compensation Insurance

The defining premise of workers' compensation insurance is its direct application to the employee within the course, scope, and function of employment. It is a state-mandated insurance program defining covered services and payments imposed on employers to pay benefits and furnish care to injured employees, and to pay benefits to dependents of employees killed in the course of or arising from their employment. With few exceptions, depending on state law, employer size, and type of worker, employers must provide workers' compensation coverage. The coverage pays medical and wage benefits to the worker injured in the course and scope of his or her employment. This is a no-fault system of benefits, wherein the employer is held liable for occupational injuries or disease suffered by workers regardless of who is determined to be at fault for the untoward events and resulting injuries. When an employee is injured on the job, the case falls under the jurisdiction of the workers' compensation statute of the state in which the injured employee resides.

In many states, catastrophic injuries such as spinal cord or head injuries, severe burns, amputations, or loss of sight require the injured person to have lifetime medical care and ongoing management of that care. This alone makes workers' compensation an important insurance arena for the LNC and one of the most common current areas of practice. Often, the LNC works in tandem with a financial or employment consultant regarding the calculation of lost wages, projection of future expenses, and lifetime reserves as they pertain to the workers' compensation insurer.

State laws differ in this area of practice, and LNCs need to know and understand the laws for the state or states in which they practice. Information about the specific benefits available under a state's workers' compensation act can be obtained by contacting the workers' compensation commission for that state. The National Chamber of Commerce also prints a brief overview of the statutes. Each state, as well as the federal government, has its own workers' compensation system. The most common elements of any work-related compensatory program occur in the following steps:

- A job-related injury or illness occurs.
- The employee reports the injury or illness to the employer, who notifies the company's claim department or insurance representative.
- The claims representative determines whether the situation reported is compensable under the law, notifies all parties of the status of compensability, and adjudicates the claim.
- The claim is monitored and bills are paid.

Disagreements often occur between the injured worker and the insurance company about how much the insurance carrier should pay. When this happens, a formal document requesting a hearing is filed with the industrial commission or industrial board that has jurisdiction over the decision. The commissioner is the state-appointed official who reviews every workers' compensation claim to determine validity. A commissioner presides at a hearing and makes a ruling after the evidence from both parties is submitted. Once the claim has been accepted as a work-related injury or illness, all parties involved in the case, such as lawyers, physicians, and other health care providers, must file reports to keep the commission informed of progress or lack of progress on the case. The file can be closed when the injured worker returns to work, the benefits end, or a settlement is reached. Clinical expertise in such areas as orthopedics, trauma, rehabilitation, and restorative care is essential to the LNC, who provides medical review and ongoing monitoring of the injured worker's condition as it relate to the claim.

Automobile Insurance

An automobile insurance policy covers accidents and losses that arise out of the ownership, maintenance, or use of cars, trucks, and other motor vehicles. This type of insurance may be issued to a private person (personal auto policy) or to a business (business auto, garage liability, truckers' policy, etc.). Automobile coverage in part deals with property damage to the insured's vehicles and to other vehicles damaged in the accident. The remainder of the automobile policy deals with damage or liability that results in personal injuries or property damage from the operation of an automobile. The LNC is most likely to be involved in the investigation of bodily injury claims against the insurance company.

The two categories of motor vehicle coverage are collision and comprehensive. Collision insurance provides for coverage in the event of damage resulting from vehicular impact. Comprehensive insurance covers losses, damage, and destruction by fire, vandalism, theft, and acts of God (hail, hurricanes, falling trees, etc.). Automobile policies may also provide for the coverage of accidental death benefits, medical payment coverage, or other-driver coverage (also known as an omnibus clause), which protects the vehicle's owner if a second or third party drives the car with permission of the owner. Uninsured or underinsured motorist covers losses to the insured and other eligible persons when they are involved in an accident with someone who has no insurance or has inadequate insurance to compensate for the injuries sustained. Personal injury protection (PIP) or medical expense coverage provides for payment of medical expenses to the insured or eligible persons. PIP and medical expense coverage are the predominant areas in which the LNC is needed to oversee and coordinate the medical aspects of the claims process.

General Liability Insurance

General liability policies cover accidents and losses that do not involve motor vehicles. Examples of events considered under general liability are injury of a bystander at a construction site, injury as a result of a slip and fall on a sidewalk or stairs, injury due to negligent security, food poisoning, and injury due to a defective product in the stream of commerce. A general liability policy can be issued to a private person (typically a homeowner's policy) or to a business (commercial general liability policy). When the insurance company's claim office receives a claim, it assigns it to an insurance adjuster, who will evaluate all aspects of the claim, including the liability (is the insured to blame and does the insurer have to pay the claim?) and the damages (what are the injuries, are they causally related, are they serious, are they permanent, are they preexisting, etc.?). Evaluating damages is an area in which the LNC can have the most impact. Adjusters may have a great deal of experience in dealing with injuries and reading medical reports, but they rarely have any formal medical training or experience.

The LNC can provide practical support to the adjuster (and to counsel) in many ways:

- Reviewing medical records to determine causal relationships, legitimacy of alleged injuries, preexisting and unrelated conditions, and potential medical outcomes
- Determining what medical records are missing and what additional records are needed to complete the review
- Evaluating whether treatment provided was appropriate or excessive
- Providing factual evidence to defense counsel for use in limiting damages
- Recommending appropriate medical experts, peer reviews, etc.
- Researching unusual injuries and medical conditions that may impact recovery

The LNC is often called upon to determine the relationship of the accident to the injury and to assist in evaluating the severity and permanency of the injury in preparation for settlement or trial defense. To determine whether a plausible causal connection exists between the injury and the events associated with the accident, the LNC may be asked to research the medical literature to answer such questions as:

- Can new-onset diabetes occur because of abdominal trauma?
- Can trauma aggravate preexisting spinal column degenerative changes?
- How long does it take a disc to herniate after trauma?
- Can a preexisting cardiac arrhythmia worsen from steering wheel impact?
- Can first-trimester pregnancy loss occur as a result of a slip and fall?
- Can panic disorder result in a mitral valve prolapse?
- Can a closed head injury occur when only minor damage to a car exists?

The LNC working for an insurance company participates in resolution of claims in a variety of ways: joining roundtable discussions in the claim office; developing and delivering training sessions for adjusters; clarifying medical issues at arbitration or mediation; providing a thorough and objective analysis of available literature; and assisting defense counsel in preparation of deposition questions. The LNC contributes a thorough and objective analysis of the medical information in order to help the insurance carrier to reach a fair and equitable resolution of the claim involved, and to deny and defend cases with questionable or overreaching injuries. Inadvertent payment of fraudulent or questionable claims increases insurance costs for all insureds.

Disability Insurance

A disability insurance policy generally provides benefits for a covered member who is wholly and continuously disabled from performing an occupation that he or she might ordinarily be capable of performing. A disability can be either a physical or a mental impairment that limits one or more major life activities of an individual. It may be partially disabling, whereby the result of an illness or injury prevents an insured from performing one or more of the functions of a job, or totally disabling, whereby the individual can no longer work. Benefits are not withheld from individuals who are able to perform some job tasks or tasks of another type of job.

Disability insurance policies stipulate that the insured's activity must be related to the occupation ordinarily performed. Often the insured must be disabled in such a way that he or she is confined to his or her immediate premises (substantial, not permanent, confinement). Policies specify the types of disabilities covered and not covered. Limits for coverage are set initially, and coverage is generally capped at the set limits.

Malpractice (Professional Liability) Insurance

Malpractice insurance is coverage against liability claims resulting from alleged malpractice in the rendering of professional services. This insurance protects policyholders from malpractice claims brought against them by their patients or clients. Any professional who is licensed to practice often requires this type of insurance coverage. Dentists, physicians, nurses, attorneys, architects, real estate appraisers, title agents, and engineers frequently obtain malpractice insurance.

LNCs are vital in assisting the carrier of this type of insurance in determining whether or not a deviation of a standard of care has occurred or whether or not performance outside of the licensed scope of practice occurred. Detailed information on the roles of the LNC in malpractice cases, including screening cases for liability and assisting with the litigation process as a consultant or expert witness, is provided elsewhere in this text.

Business Organization and Structure

Employee Requirements

LNCs working in the insurance industry represent a wide variety of clinical nursing specialties. Specialty in clinical areas such as neonatal, psychiatric, home health, emergency, rehabilitation, and critical care provides excellent training and resources for insurance work. In the workers' compensation field, it is common to find rehabilitation, neurology, or orthopedic nurses, because a majority of workers' compensation injuries fall into these categories. Nurses from such specialties as operating room nursing, infectious disease, oncology, and gerontology are in increasing demand because of social and demographic shifts in the population that generate an increasing number of issues and claims in those areas. Nurses with managerial experience or a broad experiential background are also effective LNCs in this setting; the ability to interpret a wide range of policies and procedures is a useful skill for insurance work. Nurses use their clinical backgrounds as resources for understanding, identifying, and addressing a particular condition or situation, and often provide immediate interpretation and analysis of complex medical information.

Creative problem-solving skills are essential. The LNC should be a self-starter who is capable of working with little supervision. Analytical detective skills are useful in sifting through the medical facts of a case. LNCs with specific backgrounds are highly sought after because of specialty areas that the carrier may frequently cover or insure. Health insurance carriers may have case-management programs in place to identify, monitor, and review treatment for a specific patient population with a given diagnosis. Currently, the most prevalent types of disease-management programs are in the areas of orthopedics (hip and knee replacements), infectious disease (AIDS), cardiopulmonary disorders (asthma and congestive heart failure), and endocrine disorders (diabetes). Clinical-specialty certifications in a given field are not essential for positions. It is generally considered sufficient to have several years of practice experience working with the target population. Continuing education in the specialty is viewed favorably and adds to the LNC's professionalism and expertise. Some LNCs are employed to provide basic medical interpretation and summarize occurrences. Most are utilized more effectively to perform detailed audits, analyses, and client-management functions.

In addition to the clinical expertise required for a position, a minimum of two to five years of experience in that field may be specified as a requirement, particularly if the type of insurance product is specialized. The LNC requires a current license for the state in which the insurance company's office is located but not in other states in which a case is reviewed. Often the LNC will review a course of medical treatment or consider a request for coverage or services in cases or events not geographically matched to his or her clinical license. The vast majority of policy, liability, and insurance-coverage issues can be addressed without a need for the LNC to be licensed as a registered nurse in the state in which the incident occurred, unless licensure is required by a regulating entity or at the request of the carrier for whom the LNC works.

The Roles of the LNC

The LNC has emerged as a vital contributor in a wide variety of insurance management and administration settings. The current focus on managed care demands a thorough understanding of multiple health care delivery systems. LNCs possess a unique knowledge base that helps them provide services for this growing market. Acquired skills of interpretation, analysis, and management of the processes of establishing liability, coverage, appropriateness, standardization, and accountability of the medical community provide numerous arenas in which the LNC can practice.

Claims Consultant/Adjuster

Many claims consultants/adjusters have business backgrounds but little or no medical background or experience. As a claims consultant/adjuster, the LNC utilizes a diverse nursing and business knowledge base for evaluating, investigating, and negotiating claims. The LNC functions as evaluator, mediator, consultant, and technical analyst. The process includes anticipating potential claims, reviewing actual claims, negotiating settlements directly with claimant or attorney, and participating in mediation on behalf of the client. The LNC may also audit files for claim activity, assist defense counsel in discovery responses, and monitor trial proceedings.

The LNC's role as a claim consultant/adjuster is to investigate and evaluate claims to determine their worth or merit in relationship to a specific illness or injury episode. The potential financial exposure must be planned for and communicated to key rating and marketing contacts so that an appropriate monetary reserve can be established. Often the LNC claims consultant/adjuster provides findings to and works directly with attorneys and legal representatives in the preparation of an appropriate settlement package. The LNC also monitors total case costs by tracking activities of the attorneys involved to make sure that payment amounts are not exceeded. Depending on the state, the LNC claim adjuster may be required to pass an examination to obtain a license with periodic renewal and, in some states, may be subject to continuing education requirements to maintain standing.

Example 26.1: An LNC employed as a claims consultant/adjuster (CCA) for a major not-for-profit health care insurance company has been asked to handle a loss claim. A 27-year-old male sustained second- and third-degree burns over 10% of his body as a result of careless smoking. The request for authorization of ambulance transportation was the first indication of the accident. The injured party was treated and stabilized at a local hospital and required transportation to a university-based hospital for further treatment. He was admitted to an intensive-care burn unit and scheduled for a series of skin grafts. The CCA/LNC begins to work the case by contacting the admitting facility to determine whether he was a patient there. She then speaks with a family member of the client to obtain consent to release the necessary medical records and to inform the family member that she will be assisting in the processing of the bills.

Having established consent, the CCA/LNC contacts the attending plastic surgeon to determine the extent of injury and the plan of care and documents the conversation appropriately. According to corporate policy, the case manager assigned to the hospital is contacted and informed of the situation. Together they work to ensure that the care the client received was medically appropriate and covered by the policy. The CCA/LNC verifies eligibility and documents this on the file. During the time of admission, the CCA/LNC identifies potential claims and notifies all appropriate parties, such as rating and underwriting members, so that appropriate reserves (money for additional claims) can be set aside. After the client is discharged, the CCA/LNC obtains the bills for services rendered and reviews them for covered charges. She then adjudicates or finalizes the claims for payment. Should any care rendered be noncontracted, the CCA/LNC will begin the process of determining of medical appropriateness through the case manager. Once the process is completed and services are deemed medically appropriate, the CCA/LNC may negotiate rates for the services according to company policy utilizing usual, reasonable, and customary (URC) fee data or schedules for comparing charges. Once the last claims are adjudicated, the CCA/LNC closes the file, maintaining the records for at least seven years or a time frame required by the company's policy.

Case Manager

"Case management," as defined by the Case Management Organization Standards of the Utilization Review Accreditation Committee (URAC), is a collaborative process that assesses, plans, implements, coordinates, monitors, and evaluates options and services to meet a client's health needs through communication and provision of available resources to promote quality, cost-effective outcomes. The LNC case manager working for the insurance company assumes responsibility for identifying needs, planning and arranging service delivery, and monitoring service provision and outcomes. The LNC evaluates the nature of the client's clinical condition and may inspect the condition of the home or other care setting in preparation for initiation of services to ensure that accommodations are adequate. The LNC also directly monitors and evaluates the client's progress. Communication with health care providers such as physicians, home care companies, nursing agencies, and medical equipment or infusion companies may be required. If a client requires placement in a facility, the LNC as case manager may advise, authorize, coordinate, and monitor any episode of care rendered.

The LNC case manager is a role that has developed from the establishment of managed care insurance. Case management by the LNC directly affects case outcomes. Cost analysis, reimbursement directives, coverage provisions, and client satisfaction are constantly addressed by the LNC in this role. These activities are driven by the need for insurance companies to maximize the benefit of dollars spent on clients while keeping overall health care costs to a minimum — the fundamental principle behind managed care. The LNC in this role requires an in-depth knowledge of the health care delivery system. The position also requires the ability to match needs to available resources and delivery settings, and a thorough understanding of the levels of care and intensities of service of different providers. Insurance companies generally seek nurses with several years of clinical experience in a hospital setting in addition to recent experience in home care, home infusion, durable medical equipment (DME) management, discharge planning, or skilled-facility or subacute care. A minimum of three to five years of clinical nursing experience and a certification in case management (CCM) is the prevailing requirement of insurance employers.

Example 26.2: A case manager/LNC (CM/LNC) has been assigned to follow a pediatric "catastrophic loss" case. A premature female infant born at 28 weeks' gestation is admitted to a specialized children's hospital with the diagnoses of extreme prematurity, bronchopulmonary dysplasia, transposition of the great vessels, and respiratory failure. The CM/LNC assesses the case by verifying the infant's eligibility under her mother's policy. Once coverage is established, the CM/LNC contacts the mother and obtains consent for case management. The CM/LNC speaks with the attending physician and outlines the plan of care. As a final step, she establishes contact with the facility-based CM or designated social worker following the infant's progress. Based on the information received, the CM/LNC develops a care plan outlining the medical, social, and community-based needs of the infant. Referrals are made to community-based programs such as Easter Seals, early intervention programs, Special Kids Network, and Model Waiver Program, through the home state. The CM/LNC completes a cost–benefit analysis focused on projected future care, whether at home or in a long-term facility. This information is then communicated to all participating parties.

During the infant's hospitalization, the CM/LNC monitors utilization review notes and prepares for discharge disposition. The attending physician and parents agree that the child would thrive in the home setting. Upon obtaining the physician's orders, the CM/LNC begins to contact contracted vendors to supply the necessary DME and nursing support that home care will entail. Any required, medically appropriate items are negotiated and all necessary contracts drafted and sent for signature. Once the infant is set up at home, the CM/LNC continues to closely monitor and evaluate the transitional period. Specifically, she determines that all private-duty nursing (PDN) staff is in attendance as contracted; that needed DME is available and functional; and that the caregivers are receiving the support they required. Throughout the next weeks and months, the CM/LNC maintains close contact with all parties involved and updates the care plan and cost–benefit analysis accordingly. She continues to follow the case to closure, at which time the child is successfully decannulated and no longer requires respiratory support.

Benefits Coordinator

The position of benefits coordinator involves understanding, interpreting, analyzing, and calculating an insured's benefits and ensuring (particularly in the case of a catastrophic illness or injury) that the needs match the resources (benefits) available. This position investigates the origins of, conditions for, and risks associated with coverage for a group of individuals (most commonly employer groups). The LNC interfaces with the rating, underwriting, and marketing departments to establish the performance reliability and stability of an insured group. When a clinical condition of a group member is being evaluated, the LNC may seek out a medical management area or physician (usually employed either full time or as a consultant to the insurance company) for interpretation of a medical provision written into the benefit. While this position is similar to that of a case manager in matching needs to resources, it differs in that the primary focus is availability of applicable benefits rather than the clinical condition of the patient.

The LNC as benefits coordinator gives consideration to the nature of the insurance product or policy held by the insured person or entity, the type of employer group (large or small group), and how the group is rated. Rating is a factor derived directly from quantifying a group's or individual's direct exposure, or the history of dollars spent and benefit units utilized within a given time frame (usually for the term of the current policy), and indirectly from the likelihood of exposure or risk based on the group's demographics. Premiums are calculated on the basis of rating. In the case of a costly or catastrophic occurrence, the designated authority or representative for the group is contacted and informed of the nature of the occurrence and its potential impact on the premiums. The group may then request that some type of extension or exception to the policy benefits be made in order to accommodate the member's needs while providing an acceptable exposure outcome to the group. It is then up to the LNC benefits coordinator to identify or create a cost-effective alternative, determine the financial impact or cost (in premium dollars) to the group, and obtain the carrier's approval in the form of an additional contract or addendum to the original policy. The permission of the policyholder (member) may also need to be obtained in order to implement the proposed plan. Any discrepancies between the group, the policyholder, and the carrier are explored and negotiated by the LNC and other carrier designees.

Once the group has agreed to the alternative plan, the LNC benefits coordinator ensures that contracts defining the plan are developed and kept current and accurate for the duration of the case. Frequent interaction and communication with the attending physician, health care providers, client, and family is customary in this type of situation. The LNC benefits coordinator also provides direction to the claims-processing area in order to ensure that charges are appropriately addressed, applied, and covered. At times, this position is incorporated into case management, or a designated claims area within the insurance company structure may handle it. A background in clinical services, contract development and support, claims services, or case management is often required for the position of benefits coordinator. No special license or designated certification is required for this position.

Example 26.3: The benefits coordinator/LNC (BC/LNC) has received a referral for a client who has been diagnosed with end-stage amyotrophic lateral sclerosis (ALS). The family of the client has requested to take the client home with PDN. The attending physician has ordered tube feedings, supportive respiratory care including suctioning and oxygen, and 10 hours of PDN daily. The review of available benefits shows that the member is eligible for 240 hours of PDN, has 80% coverage of all DME (based on contracted allowed amounts), and has a hospice-at-home benefit.

The BC/LNC first reviews the hospice benefit, which carries a cap of $5000. He determines that the hospice benefit does not cover care other than intermittent skilled nursing, a daily certified nursing assistant visit, and hospice medications, primarily for pain management and comfort. This benefit would not allow for the cost of enteral formula, DME, or PDN shift nursing. Turning to the PDN benefit, the BC/LNC calculates that at 10 hours a day, the PDN would provide only 24 days of coverage. Although the client has been declared terminal, there is no conclusive method to determine the length of need. According to company medical policy the criteria are met to utilize this benefit. DME benefits of 80% of the contracted allowed amounts could be used with the PDN benefit to cover the cost of all medically appropriate enteral feeds and supplies, respiratory equipment, and tracheostomy care supplies. There is a $500,000 cap on these items.

The BC/LNC documents alternative options through a benefit exception. An example of a benefit exception in this case would be to fund continued PDN hours after the initial 240 hours are exhausted through the medical portion of the contract. He calculates the cost of this exception and prepares a cost–benefit analysis. The BC/LNC may be able to show cost savings in comparison to the costs of continued hospitalization of the client. The benefit exception would require the agreement of the group that holds the coverage, the medical directors panel (consisting of rating and underwriting members), claims representatives, marketing associates, and senior health care management members. Other viable sources of funding are state and federal programs that would take over the care once the PDN benefits are exhausted. The BC/LNC summarizes his findings and forwards them to the group for first-level approval. The BC/LNC is careful to closely estimate the financial exposure (or cost) to the group and provides all detailed documentation for their review.

The group decides to approve the benefit exception. The CM prepares the drafts of the contracts for the group to endorse. It is important for the BC/LNC to include time frames for renewal of the benefit exception, and medical criteria that must be met prior to continuation of the exception. This includes the need for preauthorization by the contracted vendors for all services and verification of the client's continued eligibility for coverage under the group's policy. It becomes the family's responsibility to handle Consolidated Omnibus Budget Reconciliation Act (COBRA) continuation should the need arise. After the contracts are finalized and the client has been returned home, it becomes the responsibility of the BC/LNC to remain informed about the client's status through the CM, to verify continued eligibility for services, and to maintain all documentation. The BC/LNC must also address billing, so that the claims may be directed to him for auditing and processing. Because a benefit exception was made, the claims are often handled outside of the "normal" claims-processing process.

Workers' Compensation Manager

The LNC as workers' compensation manager (WCM) closely parallels the role of the case manager. The objective of this position is to coordinate, implement, and evaluate care and outcomes to ensure that the claimant's needs are met and goals are achieved in the most cost-effective manner possible. The goal of the LNC in the workers' compensation realm is to return the injured worker to the workforce. Insurance companies seek LNCs with experience in negotiating rates for services rendered and claim analysis, and a working understanding of the workers' compensation system. The LNC functioning as WCM may perform on-site audits of providers to ensure that services billed for were in fact rendered. An audit of providers may be performed by surveying the medical records, including progress notes, therapy-session notes, and attending physician documents, and comparing them to the bills that have been submitted for payment. Preparing rate evaluations based on geographic pricing norms, negotiating claim reimbursements, and attending defense medical examinations with the injured employee are some of the more common activities for the LNC in this field.

The LNC may be called to a jobsite to compile an ergonomic evaluation of the work setting. The structural makeup of the worksite, job functions, and physical requirements are evaluated to determine if and when the client can return to work, and what if any accommodations or restrictions must be made when he or she returns. Many employers are required to have a detailed job analysis on file in their human resource offices that specifies the amount of physical effort required to perform the job being evaluated. The LNC must understand the implications of this information and communicate it to the attending physicians and treating therapists in order to define appropriate work goals. The LNC is then responsible for conveying this information to the employer and ensuring that the worksite or job function is modified in such a way that the client can return to work. During this process, the LNC may work closely with a vocational rehabilitation specialist who is licensed and educated to provide direction on job suitability and on retraining should it be determined that the client is unable to return to the former work position.

Some of the injuries and conditions dealt with in workers' compensation are difficult to manage because they focus on subjective complaints such as pain and restriction of movement. Workers' compensation law and rules that guide this coverage are very strict and succinct. The benefits are mandatory and defined by law, leaving less room for interpretation and possible misinterpretation. The focus is always on safety as well as minimization or management of a disability. In workers' compensation, the employer has virtually no financial obligation to a claim (no copayment, no deductible, no premium sharing), which does not provide incentive for cost containment. Employer premiums are based on specific job class code insurance rates and on three years of loss-experience information for that position. Traditionally, workers' compensation providers are reimbursed on a fee-for-service basis. History has shown that fee schedules are relatively easy to circumvent. Workers' compensation is a challenging field that has long been fraught with abuse and fraud. Many individuals have falsified claims in order to be paid while not working. With the advent of managed care in workers' compensation, this type of activity has diminished. There are now far too many checks and balances in the managed care system to allow for unjustified appropriation of health care resources.

It is possible to obtain an entry-level position as an analyst or auditor with some prior managed care experience and little or no workers' compensation background. This area of practice requires a solid understanding of federal statutes and regulations such as COBRA, the Family and Medical Leave Act, and the Americans with Disabilities Act.

Example 26.4: A WCM/LNC has been assigned the case of a 43-year old laborer who sustained a fractured tibia and fibula while on duty. The client requires open reduction internal fixation (ORIF) surgery and a case manager. The workers' compensation (WC) insurer has forwarded the statement of compensability documenting that the injury has been accepted as WC-related. The WCM/LNC begins the process of handling the claim by contacting the client and treating physician to determine an exact plan of care. The orthopedic surgeon forwards documentation of her findings and treatment plan to perform the ORIF surgery on the injured leg at a local hospital. The WCM/LNC then gathers information related to the costs associated with the surgery by contacting the hospital for room-and-board charges, operative costs, medications, and supplies and estimates the charges as closely as possible. The WCM/LNC may negotiate with the facility for a reduction in the overall cost by offering a percentage discount on total charges. All negotiations must be followed by contract documentation.

According to WC law in the state in which the client resides, the WCM/LNC arranges for a physical therapy vendor and negotiates rates as needed. Some states have a listing of preferred providers, while others may direct the use of a particular therapist or group. After consulting the standard of care (such as AHRQ — the Agency for Healthcare Research and Quality, a division of the U.S. Public Health Service), the WCM/LNC determines an appropriate length of therapy to be 6 to 8 weeks. She then prepares a cost analysis for the basis of reporting to the insurer. The WCM/LNC arranges for the operative admissions, discharge needs, and therapy sessions, and plans to attend the sessions to follow the client's progress and recovery closely. Interaction between the WCM/LNC, the client, and the therapist are key to containing the cost of the case. Throughout the process, the WCM/LNC obtains and forwards all related claims to the insurer's claims department. The WCM/LNC attends the treating physician's appointments with the client in an effort to evaluate the current plan of care. This further ensures that an appropriate period of therapy and recovery are established and maintained. The WCM/LNC handles all necessary forms required to ensure that the client continues to receive his wages during lost time, and provide periodic updates to the employer regarding an expected return-to-work date.

Once the physician and the therapist agree that the client is nearing readiness to return to work, the WCM/LNC obtains a job analysis. This analysis details the amount of physical strength and ability that is required to meet the demands of the job. The physical therapist then tests the client in a series of functional assessments that closely match the job-analysis requirements to determine the injured client's ability to return to the preinjury position. If the client passes all functional requirements in the examination, the WCM/LNC arranges for a return-to-work date with the employer and notifies all parties in writing. To close the case, the WCM/LNC closely follows the client as he returns to work and ensures that the transition is completed satisfactorily. Should the client not meet the functional requirements, the WCM/LNC may consult with a vocational rehabilitation specialist educated in the redirection of skills for other less physically demanding positions. All parties must be in agreement that this is the course to follow. The requirement for vocational rehabilitation intervention for the client with permanent restrictions varies by state. In the instance of disagreement, the WCM/LNC arranges for a WC mediator or arbitrator to assist with the resolution of placement and permanency of injury. See Chapter 22 for more information.

Medical Policy Coordinator

The LNC may function as a medical policy coordinator (MPC), an individual who creates new medical policies or evaluates and revises existing policies periodically, as needed, or upon request of the insurance company. Requests may come from a variety of sources, including medical staff, claims or underwriting staff, policy-holders, or groups wanting clarification of coverage issues. The MPC assists in maintaining the policy manual for the division or company.

In this position, the LNC functions primarily in a research and investigative role to define the guidelines used for establishing what is or is not covered under a policy. The LNC may contact the FDA directly to obtain the newest guidelines or research clinical study groups to obtain information about studies in progress or recently attained outcomes. Other sources of information include the NIH (National Institutes of Health) and AHRQ. The LNC conducts medical literature searches frequently to obtain current information on a particular service, treatment, or medication. As an MPC, the LNC is exposed to diverse information about the care and services rendered under an insured's benefit or coverage, including whether:

- A certain operative procedure is a covered service
- A procedure is performed for medical or for cosmetic reasons
- To provide payment for non-FDA-approved items
- The cost of certain equipment is covered
- Costs of certain products and services are covered

The LNC working as an MPC frequently becomes part of a team that may consist of:

- A benefits coordinator or marketing representative
- A medical director or physician adviser who addresses application of clinical issues
- An attorney who ensures that policies accord with the product or company guidelines for operation

The role of the MPC incorporates knowledge of benefits and coverage, clinical indications, the ability to compile and interpret medical data and guidelines, and basic research and writing skills. No specialized license or standard certification exists for this type of position.

Example 26.5: The MPC has received a request for a review of the administration of Flolan for the treatment of pulmonary hypertension. After consulting the company's medical policy, he finds that there is no statement of coverage. The MPC begins his investigation of the drug by contacting the FDA through its Web site and reviews all available indications, usage, dosage, duration, and cost of the medication. The MPC submits his findings to the medical policy panel for discussion. The panel defines the diagnoses covered for the drug's use and documents a statement of coverage. The panel pays special attention to the cost of the drug, and the criteria for administration are discussed and documented. The MPC documents this interaction for policy construction. The MPC may make contacts with the providers within their service area to determine whether any of them provide this service, and to expedite the contracting of services should they not exist. The MPC compiles all the information received and drafts a policy clearly documenting the medical and provider criteria for the administration of Flolan, and submits the draft for final review and sign-off by the panel. Periodically, the MPC reviews all new and existing medical policies to ensure that they remain current and reflective of the constantly changing standard of care.

Utilization Review Coordinator

The utilization review coordinator (URC) analyzes the medical need for and appropriateness of individual members' benefit use. The URC's primary responsibility is to ensure that the applicable benefit policies and clinical guidelines employed by the carrier are being followed. The LNC reviewer deals primarily with the provider who is scheduling delivery of services. Reviews may be on site (in the hospital or office setting) or over the phone. As a nurse, the URC consults as an advocate on behalf of the recipient of services as permitted by the guidelines of the carrier and client's coverage. Because this process may involve the inability to approve payment for services, the LNC in this role must be diplomatic in handling confrontation and scrutiny. The LNC must think clearly, analyze well, and apply criteria and guidelines through interpretation and review. If an unfavorable determination is rendered, the LNC will likely be asked to defend the decision. The LNC's decisions should always be carefully considered and based on a clear understanding of all the elements of a case.

During the review process, decision criteria are applied and the reviewer makes a determination of medical appropriateness and whether or not to approve a service, item, or procedure. Established references to principles and clinical guidelines are utilized in the evaluation and decision-making process. Standardized clinical criteria programs such as InterQual® (McKesson Health Solutions, Marlborough, MA) and Optimed® (SHPS, Lexington, MA) are sometimes used. These types of products provide clinical decision-making algorithms (questions) and guidelines for analyzing medical qualifications present for requested procedures or services. In the case of patients who need to be hospitalized, a length of stay is assigned with each review. For example, a patient undergoing a knee or hip replacement may be authorized for a three-day hospital stay with a follow-up or concurrent review needed on the third hospital day. The reviewer would then perform subsequent review until the patient is discharged or the stay (in part or whole) is denied for lack of medical appropriateness. This process usually provides for a right to appeal on the part of the provider. Often a medical panel or director is available to address exceptions. Currently, no license or certification is required for the position of URC. Insurance companies usually seek registered nurses with at least two to three years of current hospital experience and prefer a nurse with additional background in either insurance or hospital utilization. This position frequently interfaces with the insurance company's medical staff, the patient's physician, or other health care providers.

Example 26.6: A patient undergoing a total hip replacement has been entered into the utilization review system. The system, by compiling demographic, medical, and intensity-of-service data, approves three days for an inpatient stay. This authorization is communicated by the URC/LNC to the admitting facility. The admitting hospital is informed that any additional days required are subject to concurrent (day-to-day) review. The URC/LNC monitors the case and on the fourth day contacts the facility to determine whether the client has been discharged as planned. Should the client require additional days, a full review of the current stay and medical appropriateness is determined through the URC and system criteria. If the client is ready for discharge but requires an alternate level of care such as acute inpatient rehabilitation or skilled therapy, the URC coordinates this or makes referral to an orthopedic CM.

Risk Manager

The insurance company risk manager focuses on loss prevention and minimizing claim damages through creation of loss-prevention initiatives, education, and counseling of insured health care professionals on how to prevent occurrences. The role of the LNC risk management representative involves such duties as counseling, public speaking, performing practice assessments and telephone consultations with licensed medical professionals, and consulting with claim representatives or underwriters. The LNC risk manager may also develop educational programs or assist in the publication of educational literature. The risk manager role has a strong preventive and proactive focus.

This position requires a thorough understanding of the body of law relevant to the type of carrier (professional, health, or employment). Risk managers sometimes specialize. Some focus on hospital risk management, while others concentrate on specific groups of professionals. In this position, the LNC works as researcher, educator, and clinical analyst. Many nurse consultants in this position have dual degrees (J.D., M.S., or M.D.). Most companies require a higher level of education, as well as strong clinical and risk management experience. Chapter 27 provides detailed information on the role of the LNC as health care risk manager.

Medical Malpractice/Liability Consultant

The field of medical liability is one of the largest in which an LNC may practice within the insurance industry. Most of the medical malpractice cases that LNCs handle involve one or more of the following issues:

- Delay in treatment or diagnosis
- Failure to treat properly
- Improper medical or surgical procedures
- Medication error or side effect

Within the malpractice insurance area, the LNC works with claims-processing personnel, with physician reviewers, and often directly with the legal department. With a new case, the initial goal is to ascertain as quickly and as cost-effectively as possible whether or not the case is defensible. The LNC is often involved from the very beginning of a case, assisting the insurance carrier or attorney with any or all of the following activities:

- Requesting review or client interview
- Completing a medical history
- Obtaining necessary medical records
- Organizing, reviewing, and analyzing medical records
- Relaying results to the attorney (written or oral report)

- Assisting with identification of expert witnesses
- Assisting with any required clinical research

The services of the LNC are invaluable during the initial case-screening process. A committee or similar entity within the insurance company, usually composed of claims, legal, underwriting, and executive staff, reviews cases and determines whether to settle or defend the case. The decision is often based substantially on the analysis and recommendation of the LNC. If a case is correctly determined not to be worth defending, both time and money are saved in the short and long term for the insurance carrier, attorney, and any other parties involved. With experience, the LNC becomes proficient in case screening and thereby more valuable to the insurance company and legal staff.

If a case is deemed worth defending, the LNC continues to perform any or all of the above-listed services as assigned, but in much more depth and detail. The LNC may prepare defendant employees for the deposition process, provide the attorney with information and items to address, and attend depositions. The LNC's expertise helps the attorney focus on what is technically and medically pertinent to a case and avoid spending time on useless or irrelevant information. In addition to casework on medical malpractice cases, the LNC may work directly with the carrier's medical review board or medical performance panel in the investigation phase of a claim. The LNC may be asked to research similar cases and obtain and prepare the medical record and other documents related to the case issues. While no specific training or certification is required to function in this line of work, the attorney or carrier most often seeks a person with solid clinical expertise and the ability to analyze and organize material thoroughly, effectively, and efficiently. The LNC must possess excellent organizational skills and be very detail-oriented.

Example 26.7: The medical malpractice liability consultant (MMLC) has been assigned the case of a 70-year-old woman who, while under the care of a cardiologist, died of cardiac arrest after being treated for uncontrolled atrial fibrillation. The family of the client has filed a wrongful death suit. The MMLC sends for the medical records and begins to gather information related to the client's premorbid state. She conducts an interview with the client's family to gain insight into the client's overall health and understanding of medication self-administration and compliance. Once the medical record is received, the MMLC carefully reviews the documentation, paying close attention to the medication orders and the administration-of-medication document. She notes that the client had been digitalized one year prior to admission, and that during an admission interview the client had stated that she "took her medication regularly." An order for Digoxin 0.25 mg daily is noted on the medication-administration document. No documentation of an order for a Digoxin level is found.

The MMLC then sends for medical records from the attending physician's office and those of the client's family doctor. She reviews the records in detail to determine the last Digoxin level obtained and its result. The MMLC researches articles on the effects of Digoxin levels and cardiac arrest and summarizes the information in layperson's terms. The MMLC then presents her findings to the attorney and suggests the possibility of a breach in the standard of care. To further support this finding, she thoroughly researches the American Medical Association's standards of care for the cardiac patient. Based on the attorney's direction, the

MMLC arranges for an outside cardiac consultant to review and comment on the findings. The case is settled out of court for an undisclosed amount.

Business Practices and Professional Relationships

Since many insurance carriers do business nationally, LNCs working within an insurance company may be based in a regional local or corporate office, or they may work with an attorney who does insurance work. They may function primarily as health care professionals, claim specialists, case managers, or benefit analysts, or in a position that combines any or all of these positions. The common denominator of all these roles is the overall goal to maximize the outcome and reduce the risk to the insurance carrier.

The LNC's first responsibility is to be ethical and objective. The LNC is obligated to investigate and evaluate the claim properly and to inform the carrier fully of the pros and cons of each case. The insurance company's responsibility is to compensate claimants and insureds for damages covered by an insured event. The LNC working in the insurance industry may support a claimant's position in one case and come to the defense of the insurance company in another. Most often, the LNC must mediate and negotiate among the claimant or patient, the health care provider, and the policyholder or group purchasing the insurance coverage. The focus of the LNC's work is to provide objective clinical analysis, interpretation, and education.

LNCs in the insurance industry often work directly with more nonclinical persons than medical or peer professionals. Terminology and attitudes common to the medical setting may not be (and often are not) appropriate for the insurance company setting. Complex clinical information and medical terminology must be translated into layperson's terms so that the information can be understood by those who need it. LNCs may go through an adjustment upon entering the unfamiliar business setting with few, if any, LNC colleagues. It is helpful to recognize that the insurance company, like health care settings, consists of teams of individuals. The LNC must learn the roles of the team members and their individual responsibilities. The other members of the team must identify how the LNC can contribute to the work and goals of the team.

The LNC may work with different product lines within the same company, because many insurance companies have a mixed book of business. This means that they sell and administer more than one type of insurance product at the same office location. Frequently, the offices are separated, or the office layout at a given site is structured by product line or department. Each product has its own requirements and restrictions. In a large insurance company, several LNCs may be hired for each product line, and the LNC may work in only one particular department or product division. If a company is small or has limited resources, the LNC's role is usually more universal and less product-specific.

Assignments may come from any number of sources:

- The office manager who oversees the claim workflow
- The insurance adjuster for the case
- In-house counsel
- An independent case-management firm

Assignments may vary in length and intensity. The level of knowledge of the individuals making the assignments may also vary. The effective LNC educates the individuals about the role of the LNC, anticipates the needs of the case, and provides consistent follow-through.

Credentials and Certifications

Several credentials are available to the LNC who works in the insurance field. While none is required, obtaining specialty certification demonstrates mastery of pertinent bodies of knowledge. The more seasoned LNC working in the insurance industry has obtained some or all of the following common credentials and certifications during the course of his or her work experience:

- CDMS (Certified Disability Management Specialist; formerly CIRS, Certified Insurance Rehabilitation Specialist). This is a nonprofessional certificate obtained by passing an examination. Two years of experience working with the disabled population within the disability-compensation system is an eligibility requirement for taking the exam. The CDMS credential is available to many professional disciplines.
- CRRN (Certified Registered Rehabilitation Nurse). This is a professional certification offered only to registered nurses by the Association of Rehabilitation Nurses. The certificate is obtained by demonstrating two years of experience working in rehabilitation and passing an examination.
- CRC (Certified Rehabilitation Counselor). This is a professional certificate obtained by demonstrating work experience and passing an examination. The certificate is available to master's-prepared rehabilitation counselors.
- CCM (Certified Case Manager). This is a professional certification obtained by validating two or more years' experience in case management in any number of settings (insurance, hospital, home care, etc.). Several groups of professionals, such as registered nurses, rehabilitation therapists, and social workers, are eligible for this certification.

Professional Associations and Resources

The organizations listed below provide additional resources for information about the insurance environment. They are some of the more common groups to which LNCs working in the insurance industry may belong. The LNC may also join local and state claim associations. Attending association meetings offers excellent opportunities for the LNC to learn more about the different job possibilities within the insurance industry and to network with individuals employed in that industry.

> National Association of Insurance Commissioners (NAIC), 2301 McGee Street, Suite 800, Kansas City, MO 64108–2604. http://www.naic.org
> International Association of Rehabilitation Professionals (IARP), Rio Del Mar Boulevard, Suite 61, Aptos, CA 95003. http://www.rehabpro.org

Association of Rehabilitation Nurses (ARN), 4700 West Lake Avenue, Glenview, IL 60025–1485. E-mail: info@rehabnurse.org. (This organization has local chapters by state.)

Case Management Society of America (CMSA), 8201 Cantrell Road, Suite 230, Little Rock, AR 72227. E-mail: cmsa@cmsa.org. (This organization has local chapters by state.)

Risk and Insurance Management Society, Inc. (RIMS), 655 Third Avenue, New York, NY 10017. http://www.rims.org. (The organization is composed of risk managers for thousands of self-insured and insured companies.)

Workers' compensation resources: http://www.dol.gov/dol/esa/public/regs/statutes/owcp/stwclaw/stwclaw/htm

Summary

The insurance industry provides the LNC with many opportunities for professional practice, growth, and development. While some of the more highly specialized areas such as workers' compensation and risk management are a bit more difficult for the novice LNC, other areas such as utilization review, case management, and claims adjustment provide excellent entry-level opportunities for the LNC who wants to work within the insurance industry. This field of work exposes the LNC to many areas of medical practice and medical–legal analysis with significant impact on the parties served. The nature of the work forces LNCs to broaden their scope of practice and think beyond the traditional nurse/patient relationship. The critical thinking and problem-solving process required in the nursing profession provides a natural foundation for practice within the insurance industry.

Test Questions

1. Which of the following is the underlying principle of workers' compensation coverage?
   A. To be covered, an illness or injury must be job-related.
   B. It is a type of liability of coverage obtained by professionals for work-related claims.
   C. It provides benefits for a member who is usually wholly and continuously disabled.
   D. All employers are required to offer the benefit to employees.

2. "Insurance" is defined as
   A. A contract for the provision of coverage for services, injuries, or damages as set forth in the contract
   B. A request to the carrier for payment of benefits
   C. The quantifying of an insured's or group's activity
   D. A contract for payment of injuries

3. "Experience" refers to
   A. The type of coverage that an insurer may sell or handle
   B. The past performance history of injuries or accidents
   C. The analysis done for accepting risk
   D. The age of the adjuster

4. The LNC insurance role that most frequently deals with review of clinical activities for medical necessity and appropriateness is
   A. Case management
   B. Risk management
   C. Claim adjusting
   D. Utilization review

5. The type of data for comparison of charges is referred to as
   A. Usual, reasonable, and customary
   B. Rating
   C. Utilization review
   D. Likeness rating

Answers: 1. A, 2. A, 3. B, 4. D, 5. A

Chapter 27

The Legal Nurse Consultant's Role in Health Care Risk Management

Thomas B. Méndez, MSN, RN, ANP

CONTENTS

0-8493-1418-6/03/$0.00+$1.50
© 2003 by AALNC

Objectives

Upon completion of this chapter, the reader will be able to:

- Define and apply the risk management process
- Identify risk management techniques for loss control and loss prevention
- Identify at least four examples of adverse events that must be reported
- Develop a tool for use in the monitoring of a claim or potential claim
- List contributions that the legal nurse consultant can make to the area of risk management

Introduction

An interesting and challenging role for the legal nurse consultant (LNC) is providing services in the area of health care risk management. In this arena, LNCs can apply skills and knowledge they have gained from clinical practice, as well as knowledge and experience from management and administrative roles. Experience with accreditation and licensing issues, as well as knowledge of legal processes and the legal system, is of tremendous benefit when entering into risk management.

The role of the LNC in risk management varies according to credentials and experience. An LNC may be employed as a health care organization's in-house risk manager, or act as an outside consultant to the organization. Tasks performed may range from taking responsibility for risk management activities for an entire facility to educating staff and physicians about risk and compliance issues, accreditation, and licensing requirements. The LNC risk manager may also perform claims management. The risk manager's role in health care is not limited to hospitals. Other appropriate venues for the LNC health care risk manager include ambulatory care centers, physician groups, managed care organizations, insurance brokers, insurance companies, legal practices, home health care agencies, and long-term care facilities.

As health care is redefined and becomes more competitive, all health care providers are charged with managing costs of care, including care that affects exposure to liability. Patient satisfaction, provider productivity, and quality management are critical to successful cost containment; therefore, health care entities must explore new ways to reduce direct and indirect liability exposure and cost. Liability exposure increases the cost of health care in an industry that is already overburdened with financial constraints. The most obvious costs are those related to the litigation and resolution of lawsuits. These costs may also substantially impact premium payments charged by insurance organizations. The costs associated with patient dissatisfaction and defensive medicine are difficult to quantify but have had significant impact on health care facility operating costs. Additional expenses incurred to manage preventable complications are more easily identified. A proactive risk management program can serve to reduce these costs.

Changes to the Joint Commission on Accreditation of Healthcare Organizations (JCAHO) accreditation standards that went into effect July 21, 2001 dictate disclosure of unanticipated outcomes to patients and family members.[1] Patient and family response to these disclosures has increased public awareness of medical errors and has had an impact on health care organizations' liability exposure. Publications from the National Patient Safety Foundation and reports from the Institute of Medicine have provided insights into quality and risk issues within the health care industry.[2-4]

Several factors shape a successful risk management program. Visibility and accessibility of the risk management department staff, and risk management guidelines that are easy to follow, can greatly increase the likelihood that a program will succeed.[5] The level of expertise of the individual charged with risk management responsibilities and the availability of resources such as staff and computer support will also affect the program's success. Often, the individual charged with risk management is given additional areas of responsibility, such as corporate compliance, quality assurance, patient safety, and professional staff credentialing. This decreases the staff involvement with true risk management. When this occurs, the LNC can be of great benefit to a health care organization by providing consultative services, performing risk assessments, and developing educational programs for the risk manager's use.

Principles of Risk Management

The principles of risk management and the nursing process are quite similar. In both disciplines, situations are assessed, changes are made as necessary, and the outcomes of those changes are evaluated for effectiveness. Ultimately, the goal is to protect patients, their visitors, and the staff from harm. Levick identifies four basic steps in the risk management process:

- Identification of the sources from which losses may arise
- Evaluation of the financial risk involved in each exposure in terms of expected frequency, severity, and impact
- Management of risks by elimination, reduction, or control of risk factors, transfer of responsibility for risk to other parties, and funding through the operation of a coordinated and effective program
- Continuous and systematic monitoring of risks[6]

Although the terminology is somewhat different, the basic steps of risk management are similar to the steps of the nursing process: APIE — assessment, plan, intervention, and evaluation.

Identifying Sources of Risk (Assessment)

Identification of potential and actual areas of risk is similar to the assessment phase of the nursing process. The identification of risk can be informal, such as information obtained through the "grapevine," or it can involve more formal processes, such as reviews of incident or occurrence reports, attendance at committee meetings, direct patient or family complaints, review of patient satisfaction surveys, or receipt of a notice of intent to sue or of a summons and complaint. A review of relevant statutory and case law pertaining to the specific type of health care organization in which the LNC is employed may identify current risks that require attention. Risks may also be identified through:

- Receipt of complaints from physicians or staff
- Review of compliance with accreditation bodies, such as JCAHO, the National Committee on Performance Improvement (NCQA), and the Commission on Accreditation of Rehabilitation Facilities (CARF)
- Investigation by state or federal agencies such as the Department of Health or Occupational Safety and Health Administration (OSHA)
- Monitoring of industry trends such as development of or involvement with managed care organizations, professional organization standards, or guidelines
- Analysis of community events reflected in the media
- Reviews of policies and procedures
- Reviews of quality screens, clinical pathways, or care maps

Education about the process of risk identification should be a component of new employee orientation and readily available to all staff on an ongoing basis. Risk identification should be the responsibility of all staff and management. Confidentiality is an important part of the risk identification process if the risk manager wants staff support and cooperation. Any information provided to the risk management department should be protected from discoverability and verified as such with legal counsel. Information received should be labeled "attorney work product, prepared at the request of counsel in anticipation of litigation." However, this tactic may not protect the information from discovery by a plaintiff's attorney.

Creating a Risk Management Plan

The planning component of the risk management process includes an overall plan for general risk management and a plan of action for compensable events. A well-written risk management plan is a very important part of the risk management program because it defines the risk management process. As part of this process, roles and responsibilities are assigned and authority is delineated. The plan describes the facility's risk management activities, such as tracking, trending, and analyzing risk management data; conducting investigations of incidents; providing educational programs; reviewing risk financing; transferring risk; claims management; and monitoring defense counsel.

A plan of action should be developed as part of the risk management process to address specific issues or events. As with any plan of action, activities to be performed, responsibility and authority for those activities, time limitations, and reassessment plan should be clearly outlined. Plans of action should be reviewed frequently for appropriateness and compliance, and revised as necessary.

Implementing the Risk Plan

One method for implementing a risk management program is the application of controls, either to reduce the frequency of incidents, such as falls, or to minimize the severity of incidents when they occur. Patient falls are common and very expensive liability problems. For example, a health care entity has determined that falls constitute less than 5% of patient injuries per quarter. Through the process of risk identification, it was determined that the ratio of falls to patient injuries was well above the established threshold of acceptability during the first six months of data collection. Data collected through quality assessment, safety, and risk management was then analyzed concerning the number of falls, and a plan of action was developed as a means to reduce the frequency of adverse events. The development and implementation of a fall-prevention program might be indicated. As part of the process, early identification of individuals with a potential for falling would be a major component. Providing a fall-prevention education program for the staff should be an element in the plan for reduction of falls.

Another method of application of controls is to address the severity of certain occurrences. One example is application of controls to patient burns that result from faulty electrical equipment. The plan of action would include involvement with nursing, bioengineering, plant safety, risk management, and performance improvement to determine what actions should be implemented to control burns caused by electrical equipment. Establishing a preventive maintenance (PM) program for the equipment would be one important factor. The plan of action should also include ongoing review of the PM program, maintenance of records for all equipment in question, education of staff in the proper use of the equipment, and ongoing review of the PM program's effectiveness.

Evaluating Effectiveness of the Risk Management Process

The evaluation portion of the risk management program should include not only monitoring specific outcomes, but also an ongoing review of the program as a whole. Education is a valuable and effective component of any risk management program. A study in Maryland hospitals demonstrated significantly better claims experience in hospitals with certain risk management policies and activities such as education.[7] Closed case studies and sharing of trending information should be used to provide staff education. In one example, sharing the trending information on the problem of clotted specimens in an ongoing educational forum led to a decrease in the problem. This situation reduced the frequency of blood redraws and decreased the associated risks for and dissatisfaction of the patient.

Management of Losses

Loss Control

Two essential components of an effective risk management program are loss control and loss prevention. Loss control is the application of techniques designed to minimize loss in a cost-effective manner. Components of loss control are described below.

Risk Avoidance

One of the most common techniques is risk avoidance. In risk avoidance, known high-risk or problem-prone areas are avoided. Generally, obstetrical services are considered high risk or problem prone. An example of risk avoidance is a hospital's decision not to provide obstetrical services.

Risk Transfer

Risk transfer is another means of loss control. The three basic elements of risk transfer are purchase of insurance, contractual transfer, and segregation of risk exposures.

Purchase of Insurance

The first element of risk transfer involves purchasing insurance to cover identified risks. A hospital has an economic responsibility in the event of an injury to a patient, visitor, or employee. To transfer a portion of that responsibility, the facility should purchase insurance such as general liability insurance from an insurance company, which would then assume some or all of the risk in return for an amount to be paid (premium) by the facility.

Contractual Transfer

The second element of risk transfer is known as a noninsurance transfer of risk or a contractual transfer. With this technique, the transfer of risk is affected by a contract, other than insurance, in which one party transfers to another party legal responsibility for losses. One of the most common examples is the use of contractors who subcontract to perform certain functions. In this scenario, the subcontractors hire their own employees. The contract contains a hold-harmless clause releasing the contractor of any responsibility in the event of a loss. As a result, responsibility for the employees, by contract, transfers to the subcontractors, who then assume responsibility and are obligated to pay for any losses arising from their services.

A more complex contractual risk-transfer situation may include a "crossover." An example of a noninsurance or contractual risk transfer occurs in many emergency departments. Often, physicians staffing emergency departments are contract physicians and not hospital employees. Traditionally, in a noninsurance or contractual risk transfer, the contractor assumes liability. However, because the physicians are providing direct care to patients of the hospital, some percentage of the liability is transferred back to the facility due to vicarious liability — hence the term "crossover." In most states, "vicarious liability" laws impute professional liability to the health care entity even though the individual providing the care is not a direct employee of the entity. The entity has a duty to protect the patients, visitors, and employees from harm or injury. This issue can become very complex, and a thorough understanding of laws and regulations dealing with such issues is necessary. A close review of insurance policies and contracts is essential, since there is no margin for error when questioning exposure and coverage in these situations. Further, this issue has not yet been settled in the managed care arena, specifically for independent practice associations (IPAs). It is critical that close attention be given to precedents now being established in this area.[8]

Segregation of Risk Exposures

A third element of risk transfer involves the segregation of risk exposures. With this technique, risks are identified and are divided into separate areas or entities. An example is the separation of one entity into two distinct entities or corporations. Each entity or corporation is then responsible for its respective liabilities. This technique is frequently seen with acquisitions and mergers.

Risk Retention

A third type of loss control is risk retention. Risk retention is accomplished through establishment of self-insured retention (SIR). The majority of large medical centers are self-insured to a certain level and then transfer a portion of the risk to the insurance carrier in an umbrella coverage plan. The management of this type of fund provides much more autonomy and role independence for the risk manager.

Loss Prevention

Loss prevention is the proactive use of programs or activities to reduce or eliminate the chance of loss or to decrease the severity of a loss. One pivotal activity for the risk manager is focus on regular formal education programs to teach physicians and nurses about risk management and the role of the risk manager.[7] Employee orientation is an excellent example of an educational loss-prevention mechanism. In theory, providing employees with guidelines, policies, and procedures makes them aware of their responsibility for loss control, as well as the responsibility of the organization.

A proactive safety program is also an excellent loss-prevention technique. Such a program should include active participation by the safety officer or designee in the employee orientation program. The orientation should include:

- Identification of the individual responsible for safety
- Review of pertinent safety and security policies and procedures, with emphasis on electrical and fire safety
- Review of the PM program for all equipment, including furniture
- Disaster preparedness
- Location of the material safety data sheet (MSDS) manual
- Identification of the employee's role in the safety program
- Review of the method for reporting safety or security concerns

Ongoing education should include frequent walking rounds or site visits and annual risk management in-service employee education.

Practicing Collaborative Risk Management

Communication between the risk manager and other departments of the health care facility is critical to the success of any risk management program. This is particularly true with performance improvement, patient safety, security, administration, nursing management, and human resources. The wealth of information obtained by all areas should be shared. Data collected from patient complaints or satisfaction surveys by performance improvement may be invaluable in the prevention of losses. This also holds true for information compiled by safety and security, such as product recalls, waste management, and walking rounds, as well as reports from facility and ground inspections.

The risk manager should communicate regularly with the facility's professional staff, including physicians, midlevel practitioners (such as advanced nurse practitioners, physician assistants, and psychologists), nurses, and other support staff. A collaborative relationship encourages the early reporting of potentially compensable events (PCEs) by staff and serves to identify types of preventive risk management educational programs needed. Other sources of information include medical staff credentialing files, minutes from committee meetings such as pharmacy and therapeutics, and surgical case review minutes. Employee-related data, such as employee health reports and workers' compensation reports, are also beneficial.

Regardless of how information within departments is maintained, such data should be shared and communicated only on an "as needed" basis. Information must also be shared with those in administrative roles within the health care facility administration. Application of proactive mechanisms and programs will not eliminate all risks; however, it can have a substantial positive impact on frequency and severity of occurrences, as well as improve patient care and satisfaction within an institution.

Claims Management

One of the primary objectives in a claims management program is to reduce the overall number and cost of claims. This process works in tandem with the risk management process, because the management of claims involves both prevention and resolution. Like the risk management program, a claims management program should be a formalized process. Development of policies and procedures is important because they delineate actions to be taken and assign responsibility as well as accountability.

Most important is the identification of the incidents and information that should be reported. A general guideline should be that any event that has the potential to result in injury or any event that results in an injury to a patient, visitor, or staff member should be reported. Any event that is an unexpected outcome of the patient's stay in the facility should be reported. Examples of what should be reported include, but are not limited to:

- Unanticipated or unexpected cardiopulmonary or respiratory arrest with unsuccessful resuscitation
- Suicides
- Any type of unexpected deaths (non-CPR or suicide)

- Birth-related injuries, including maternal or fetal death, low APGAR scores at 5 and 10 minutes, infant resuscitations, fractures, dislocations, or decreased movements of any infant extremity after birth
- Any anesthesia-related injuries
- Unanticipated neurological or sensory deficits, such as brain damage, permanent paralysis including paraplegia and quadriplegia, and partial or complete loss of sight or hearing functions
- Unanticipated body-system failures, such as renal failure; or unexplained disease processes, such as coagulopathies or sepsis
- Burns from electrical, chemical, thermal, or radiological sources
- Any iatrogenic injuries to internal organs or major blood vessels
- Retention of a foreign body
- In-hospital injuries that limit activities of daily living, such as sprains, fractures, amputation, or disfigurement
- In-hospital drug–drug or food–drug reactions or unexplained allergic reactions
- Medication errors
- Leaving without being seen or leaving against medical advice
- Wrong-site surgery
- Allegations of in-hospital sexual assault

The instances listed above constitute major events. Reporting should also include minor events, such as slips and falls and injuries in elevators, pneumatic doors, or parking lots. Staff injuries such as needle sticks or cuts should be reported. Patient or staff injuries resulting from physical altercations are also reportable events.

A format and process should be established for the reporting of events. The form for reporting may be known as an incident report, occurrence report, or quality monitoring report. Ideally, the reporting mechanism should be a component of the performance improvement process. Upon receipt of the reporting form, a thorough investigation of the event and an evaluation as to its potential for a claim should take place. In the event of concern that a claim will be filed, the risk manager should begin an investigation. Hospital administration and hospital defense counsel should be notified about significant events. If the facility utilizes the services of an outside agency or third-party administrator (TPA) for some of its claims management, then that entity should be put on notice as well. Generally, a letter of assignment and any pertinent documents are forwarded to the defense counsel or outside claims investigator. Upon receipt, the defense counsel or outside investigator sends a letter of acknowledgment to the facility. The timely notification of the defense counsel is of utmost importance because it helps establish attorney–client privilege. In the investigation process, the risk manager generally functions as coordinator of all investigation activity, including arranging employee interviews and securing evidence.

Upon completion of the investigation, the defense counsel or TPA provides a report of the statement of the events to date, as well as any recommendations for further investigation or disposition of the claim. If additional investigation is required, periodic reports of the investigation should be provided to the facility by the defense counsel or TPA until the investigation is deemed to be completed. Again, any written report must be protected from discoverability. Disposition of the claim may include either offering a settlement to the claimant or proceeding to trial. In the event of a settlement, settlement authority should be defined in the risk management plan.

The facility's insurance carrier should be included in the process of notification. In most instances, the initial indemnity reserve is established; however, the reserve amount should be adjusted periodically to reflect findings during the investigation or discovery process. Most insurance carriers have specific reporting requirements. These requirements may include an initial evaluation of the case as well as determination of liability, damages, and settlement value. Reporting timelines associated with the various types and levels of insurance coverage are also of great importance. Improper or inadequate reporting can have an adverse impact on the coverage provided. Reporting requirements are found in the policy language and should be reviewed accordingly. The claim or potential claim should be monitored carefully.

Monitoring of an incident or claim can be very time-consuming. The use of a form is helpful in this process. Many varieties of forms are available; the preferences of the user and the needs of the institution determine which one to select. Such tools can be found in any basic risk management text.[5,8] Table 27.1 shows one example.

Education, Certification, and Credentials for Risk Managers

The LNC interested in the role of risk manager should become well acquainted with licensing and certification requirements. Generally, the state board of insurance regulates licensing requirements for individuals functioning in the role of risk manager or risk management consultant. Qualification is usually obtained by examination. However, there is no consistency from state to state, and some states have no requirements for licensing or certification. Some states require an individual to be licensed as a consultant or adviser and, in some instances, as an insurance agent or broker. A few states do not allow an individual to hold both an insurance agent or broker's license and an insurance adviser's license. LNCs wishing to provide these services should become familiar with licensing requirements in the states in which they wish to consult.

Several avenues for certification in risk management are available. Some insurance carriers have programs that provide courses in risk management; however, these programs are not generally endorsed or recognized by any national risk management professional organization. Upon completion, the participant is certified to have completed a course of study. The American Society for Health Care Risk Management of the American Hospital Association (ASHRM) offers a series of modules that, upon successful completion, provide the recipient with a certification that he or she has completed the course. Completion of the course can then be applied toward diplomat or fellow status. ASHRM also offers a certification program for risk management professionals who meet certain strict eligibility requirements. ASHRM confers the CPHRM (Certified Professional in Health Care Risk Management) on risk management professionals who have met the eligibility criteria and successfully completed the qualifying examination.[9] The Insurance Institute of America confers an Associate in Risk Management certification on students who successfully complete three required modules and three examinations.[10]

Table 27.1   Claims Management Tool

Patient or Claimant Information	*Comments*
Name:	
Address:	
Telephone number:	
Age:	
Social Security number:	
Occupation:	
Employment status:	
Marital status:	
Name of spouse:	
Number, name(s), and age(s) of dependents:	

Incident Information

Date of loss or date of report:
Description of loss or claim:
Name(s), address(es), and phone number(s) of all personnel involved in claim:

Indemnity Information	
Name, address, phone, fax, and e-mail of insurance company:	
Contact person (there may be one for policy issues and another for claims issues):	
Policy number:	
Policy period:	
Policy limits:	
Deductible:	
Type of policy (occurrence or claims made):	

Claim Information

Claim number (facility and insurance carriers if different):
Codefendant(s):
Codefendant(s) policy information:
Defense counsel(s):
Defense attorney(s):
Address, phone, fax, and e-mail:
Primary investigator:
Address, phone, fax, and e-mail:
Date assigned:
Plaintiff counsel(s):
Plaintiff attorney(s):
Address, phone, fax, and e-mail:

Table 27.1   Claims Management Tool *(Continued)*

Indemnity Information
Date of suit:
Court number:
Indemnity reserve:
Expense(s) (attorney costs):
Date reserve established:
Documentation of any changes to reserves, the amount, date, and reason for adjustments:
Payment schedule by date, amount, and category (display running totals):
Claims status — open or closed (if closed, by dismissal, settlement, or trial with verdict):

Role of the LNC in Risk Management

The LNC may offer a variety of services to risk managers, including consultation. In facilities that do not have a designated risk manager, the LNC may perform risk management duties directly. The LNC may also act as the claims manager in conjunction with the facility risk manager.

Risk Assessment Consultation

The performance of risk assessments is one opportunity for the LNC in risk management. Risk assessments may be clinical in nature and focus on certain areas, or they may include the assessment of property and casualty (P&C) as well as directors' and officers' (D&O) risks, depending on the expertise of the consultant. A clinical risk assessment is usually performed as part of an on-site visit. Generally, the assessment is of high-risk, problem-prone, and high-volume areas such as perioperative, perinatal, emergency, and behavioral medicine services. The process includes:

- One-on-one interview of key personnel
- Review of documentation, including a sampling of charts
- Committee minutes and plans from such areas as safety, risk management, performance improvement, and credentialing
- A walk-through of the high-risk areas

It is prudent for LNCs to be aware of the laws governing discovery in the state in which they are working. Knowledge of restrictions, such as those established by the Health Insurance Portability and Accountability Act (HIPAA) of 1996,[11] in the review of patient documents and the collection and use of data is imperative.

Risk assessments may be global, in which a survey or an overview of the facility or entity is performed. Or risk assessments may be focus assessments that are more intense in nature. Focus assessments may be performed on one department or service. System analysis is another form of risk assessment. The assessment may be done on one or more systems, such as quality management or the laboratory or radiology reporting systems.

Many consulting firms and insurance companies have tools with which to conduct the assessment. Tools are constructed from knowledge of case law, accreditation and licensing standards, and professional standards. Opportunities exist for the LNC to create tools to be used in nontraditional settings, such as physician group practices, substance abuse centers, and mental health clinics.

Risk Education

Staff development and education is a prime area of opportunity for the LNC. Educational needs may be the result of an event, an identified need from a risk assessment, or part of the monitoring and evaluation process. Many health care entities have reduced costs by the elimination of attendance at outside seminars or, in some instances, elimination of an education department.

Qualitative Claims Analysis

Services that the LNC provides in the area of claims analysis vary depending on the needs of the client. One service is the review of claims for frequency, severity, and impact. Another service may be the investigation of the claim itself. This involves reviewing the medical records and interviewing all pertinent employees, visitors, patients, and family members. The decision for future management of the claim is determined after analysis of the findings. Total claims management service involves the management of a claim from the evaluation phase to final resolution of the case. This may involve communicating with the defense counsel and insurance carrier, monitoring expenses, establishing reserves, and monitoring the evolution of the case.

Report Preparation

Many consultative firms and insurance companies have specific guidelines for report-writing. Initially, the report should identify potential or actual areas for improvement, as well as areas that are being performed well. Recommendations or suggestions for implementing changes to improve performance are generally included as part of the process. Documentation or references that support recommendations or suggestions are required.

Reports should be as concise as possible, be completed in a timely manner, and not contain language unfamiliar to the reader. It is essential for the organization's risk management consultant to follow up on the incident within a reasonable time after the report is completed.

A report should always contain a caveat explaining the position of the individual preparing the report. Most caveats include language that releases the writer of any liability as a result of the report. If possible, reports should flow through the facility's legal counsel or be a component of the peer-review or quality process to limit the potential for discovery of the document. An LNC in the role of outside consultant should work closely with the facility risk manager or legal counsel to determine the most appropriate method of communicating findings.

Summary

Many opportunities are available to the LNC who is interested in the area of risk management. They range from being an employee of an institution or organization to being an independent consultant to health care risk management departments. Because the health care industry is in a constant state of change, the LNC should stay abreast of current trends in case law, professional standards, and accreditation and licensing requirements and guidelines.

References

1. Joint Commission on Accreditation of Healthcare Organizations, *Proposed Revisions to Joint Commission Behavioral Health Care Standards in Support of Safety of Individuals Served and Health Care or Service Error Reduction*, Joint Commission on Accreditation of Healthcare Organizations, Oakbrook Terrace, IL, 2001.
2. National Patient Safety Foundation, *Statement of Principle: Talking to Patients about Health Care Injury*, National Patient Safety Foundation, Chicago, 2000.
3. Committee on Quality of Health Care in America, Institute of Medicine, *To Err is Human: Building a Safer Health System*, National Academy Press, Washington, D.C., 2000.
4. Committee on Quality of Health Care in America, Institute of Medicine, *Crossing the Quality Chasm: A New Health System for the 21st Century*, National Academy Press, Washington, D.C., 2001.
5. Youngberg, B., *The Risk Manager's Desk Reference*, Aspen Publications, Gaithersburg, MD, 1994.
6. Levick, D.E., *Risk Management and Insurance Audit Techniques*, 3rd ed., Standard Publishing Corporation, Boston, 2002.
7. Kavaler, F. and Spiegel, A., *Risk Management in Health Care Institutions: A Strategic Approach*, Jones and Bartlett Publishers, Sudbury, MA, 1997.
8. Carroll, R., Ed., *Risk Management Handbook for Health Care Organizations*, 3rd ed., Jossey-Bass/John Wiley, San Francisco, 2001.
9. American Society for Healthcare Risk Management of the American Hospital Association, One North Franklin Street, Chicago, IL 60606, (312) 422–3980, fax (312) 422–4580, http://www.hospitalconnect.com.ashrm.
10. Insurance Institute of America, 720 Providence Road, P.O. Box 3016, Malvern, PA 19355–0716.
11. Health Care Financing Administration, The Health Insurance Portability and Accountability Act of 1996 (HIPAA), U.S. Department of Health and Human Services, Rockville, MD, 2002, http://cms.hhs.gov/hipaa/.

Additional Reading

Agency for Healthcare Research and Quality, *Making Health Care Safer: A Critical Analysis of Patient Safety Practices*, U.S. Department of Health and Human Services, Rockville, MD, 2001.

American Society for Healthcare Risk Management, *Perspectives on Disclosure of Unanticipated Outcome Information*, American Hospital Publishing, Chicago, 2001.

Suggested Internet Sites

AIS Managed Care News: http://www.aishealth.com/AISManagedCare
Risk Management and Insurance Information Resource: http://www.irmi.com

Online Periodicals

American Association of Health Plans Online: http://www.aahp.org

Trade Journals

American Healthline: http://www.americanhealthline.com
American Hospital Association News: http://www.ahanews.com
Hospitals and Health Networks: http://www.hhnmag.com
Managed Healthcare: http://www.managedhealthcarenews.com
Modern Health Care: http://www.modernhealthcare.com

Government and Regulatory Agencies

Agency for Healthcare Research and Quality: http://www.ahcpr.gov
Centers for Disease Control: http://www.cdc.gov
Centers for Medicare and Medicaid Services (formerly Health Care Financing Administration): http://cms.hhs.gov
Food and Drug Administration: http://www.fda.gov
Health Resources and Services Administration: http://www.hrsa.gov/
National Center for Health Statistics: http://www.cdc.gov/nchs
National Clinical Guidelines Clearinghouse: http://www.guidelines.gov
National Institutes of Health: http://www.nih.gov
National Practitioner Databank: http://www.npdb.com/
Office of the Inspector General: http://oig.hhs.gov
U.S. Department of Health and Human Services: http://www.hhs.gov

Professional Associations

American College of Health Care Administrators: http://www.achca.org
American College of Healthcare Executives: http://www.ache.org

American Hospital Association: http://www.aha.org
American Medical Association: http://www.ama-assn.org
American Society for Healthcare Risk Management: http://www.hospitalconnect.com/ashrm
Integrated Healthcare Association: http://www.iha.org
Risk and Insurance Management Society, Inc.: http://www.rims.org

Licensure, Certification, and Board Specialty

American Health Information Management Association: http://www.ahima.org/certification
American Society for Healthcare Risk Management: http://www.hospitalconnect.com/ashrm

Test Questions

1. It is prudent for the LNC to be aware of costs when acting in the risk management role. In the event of a lawsuit, the highest costs are those associated with
   A. Investigating the lawsuit
   B. Defense and settlement of the lawsuit
   C. Obtaining expert witnesses

2. Identification of a risk through the "grapevine" is considered
   A. Formal
   B. Informal
   C. Both

3. Which of the following statements is NOT true?
   A. Contractual transfer is a form of noninsurance risk transfer technique.
   B. Knowledge of case law can be used in the development of an assessment tool.
   C. Education of staff or providers is not the function of the LNC in the area of risk management.
   D. Insurance policies contain language regarding reporting requirements.

4. All of the following are to be included in a report prepared as an outside or independent consultant EXCEPT:
   A. The name of the individual(s) who requested the report
   B. The date on which the report was written
   C. A caveat explaining the position of the person preparing the report
   D. The reviewer's personal opinions

5. Which of the following is NOT generally included in the clinical risk assessment process?
   A. Interview of key personnel
   B. Review of financial records
   C. Review of committee minutes

Answers: 1. B, 2. B, 3. C, 4. D, 5. B

Chapter 28

Health Care Claims Analysis

Agnes Grogan, BSN, RN

CONTENTS

Objectives

Upon completion of this chapter, the reader will be able to:

- Describe the differences between hospital and nonhospital claim review processes
- Define the clinical and educational qualifications necessary to perform claim audits
- List the essential tools for properly conducting claim review
- Identify indicators of potential fraud
- Discuss the value of claim review in litigation

Introduction

Claims review is an area relatively unexplored by the majority of legal nurse consultants (LNCs), yet a definite need and broad application for this expertise exist. Through this activity, the LNC's value to attorney clients increases, whether in the plaintiff or defense milieu. This chapter discusses the auditing process and its application in the legal arena, educational preparation, necessary tools for the task, benefits of claim review, and opportunities for the application of this skill. LNCs use claim review skills for the following purposes:

- To examine charts and claims submitted for inpatient and outpatient health care services as professional reviewers employed by insurance companies under an umbrella of titles ranging from claims analyst to health insurance specialist
- To be defense or revenue auditors in the hospital setting
- To participate as part of the routine liability and damages evaluation in a wide variety of cases for attorneys

Medical billings are an often overlooked rich source of evidence that can serve to support, mitigate, or even dismiss medical costs.

"Claims Review" Defined

Medical claims review cannot be defined simply as the verification of services billed or a determination that the total charges are accurate. The process involves many other components that apply to hospital claims; claims submitted by various medical providers, such as physical therapists, chiropractors, physicians, laboratories, and radiology facilities; review of medical records; determination of patient eligibility and provider qualifications; and application of knowledge of federal and local laws. The method by which the audit process is performed also depends on where, why, and when the review is performed. The audit process can also hinge on whether the charges are reimbursed by CMS (Centers for Medicare and Medicaid Services) on the assignment of a DRG (diagnosis-related group), or whether it is a skilled nursing facility receiving payment under a PPS (prospective payment system) that depends on assignment of a RUG (resource utilization group).

Hospital Billing and Claims Review

Hospital claims are reviewed and adjusted by comparing the itemized bill to the complete medical record. Hospitals generally have specific in-house audit policies relating to claim audits. The audit usually must be performed on site, and findings must then be reviewed by qualified hospital personnel before an adjustment is accepted and a payment is agreed upon. Some negotiation may take place between auditor and hospital personnel. However, audits can be performed off site in a procedure fittingly called a "desk audit." The disadvantage to performing an audit away from the facility is that the insurance auditor does not have hospital resource personnel available to explain or verify questionable items on the bill. Lacking appropriate explanation, the reviewer may make reductions on the bill. However, with proper documentation, billable services can be explained and the task can be accomplished without undue difficulty, leading to a higher reimbursement.

Briefly, the services or items listed on a hospital bill must be ordered or documented by a physician or other qualified health care provider in the medical chart or record; provided during a procedure ordered or performed by a physician; in accordance with a hospital compliance policy and procedure (a written policy and procedure must be available for examination if requested); and received by the patient.

In addition to accepting and disallowing charges, the LNC who reviews claims associated with personal injury cases must be cognizant of charges that are related to preexisting medical conditions and those associated with the accident or injury. The auditor must also identify charges that would not have been incurred had not a particular incident occurred, such as alleged negligence on the part of medical personnel. Detailed analysis of hospital bills can help support or refute claims of negligence.

Example 28.1: A central line has become infected, leading to a patient's sepsis and death. The procedure of proper equipment changes (dressings, tubings, and filters) is an issue. Hospital policy and procedures and medical records are carefully scrutinized, and tables are constructed demonstrating that documented care met standards. However, careful examination and comparison of hospital charges (more tables) reveal discrepancies. Necessary supplies for dressing and tubing changes obtainable only through a controlled delivery system were not removed on days when medical records showed that they were used.

At the present time, there is no published database of charges relating to the usual cost of items for which hospitals charge. Such a reference may be available in the future. Information relative to this issue can be obtained from state medical auditor associations. Publications are available that provide an average cost of a hospital stay given a particular diagnosis.

Another facet of hospital claim review relates to insurance coverage applied incorrectly by the facility. This review is primarily concerned with negotiated contracts of PPOs (preferred provider organizations) and HMOs (health maintenance organizations). The criteria for payment are determined by contract with regard to the eligibility of the patient, the care and treatment being provided, and the benefits available under the contract. In this context, the auditor must be able to interpret the maximum reimbursement by the third-party payer and compare this amount to the charges billed by the hospital.

Nonhospital Claims Review

Review of claims submitted by providers other than hospitals requires special expertise. The auditor must be aware of the physician's treatment of each patient, whether or not the patient carries medical insurance. The contract for care and treatment is between the physician and the patient, and the patient is financially responsible for the charges for services rendered. The one exception to the contract for care is workers' compensation.

The reviewer must possess expertise and familiarity with current procedural terminology (CPT) codes (described in detail later) and protocols for their application. The reviewer should also be knowledgeable about usual and customary fees, also referred to as U & C in the insurance adjuster world. The usual and customary fee is defined as the charge for health care that is consistent with the average rate or charge for identical or similar services in a certain geographic area. To determine the usual and customary fee for a specific medical procedure or service in a given geographic area, insurers often analyze statistics from a national study of fees charged by medical providers, such as the database profile set up by the Health Insurance Association of America (HIAA). Some insurers compile data using their own claim information. These statistics are used to chart a range of fees for each geographic area in which services are provided and are displayed according to a percentile. For example, an 80th percentile means that 80% of the providers charge a given amount or less. Software programs and publications that provide the fee ranges, updated annually, are available for purchase by the LNC reviewer.

In U & C reviews, the medical records are reviewed (if available) and compared with submitted charges to determine whether the services were in accordance with the specific medical description or CPT code listed. If not, the charges may be adjusted or rejected by the reviewer to reflect the documented service provided. The physician's documentation should support the codes submitted for payment. Most physicians do not "upcode," but "underdocument" for various reasons. Upcoding is the process of assigning a code that represents a more complex or involved service, which receives a higher reimbursement, than the one actually provided.

Example 28.2: An audit conducted at the request of a nephrology group finds a 76% error rate in billing for office visits. Of the 76% of bills found to be in error, 3% should have been billed at a higher level. More important, 73% of the bills had insufficient documentation to support the CPT code billed.[1]

Commonly, physicians do not use a form that encourages documentation of the required elements for billing a certain level of care. One physician stated that he had been instructed simply to code on the basis of time spent with the patient or according to the level of complexity of the visit. He was told, "Most office visits are a level three. If you do more during a particular encounter, then code a level-four visit. If you do less, code a level two." As for documentation, he was told simply to "document *everything*."[1]

Often, recommendations will be made to disallow charges associated with undocumented services, unnecessary services, unbundled services, or services excluded by the insurance policy. The reviewer must also distinguish charges related to treatment of preexisting medical conditions, those that are work-related, and those that have maximum limitations that should be disallowed in the determination of an insurer's responsibilities.

Hospital and Nonhospital Auditing — Specialized Review

Medicare: Acute Care Facility

Hospital Medicare reimbursement involves DRG, a patient classification scheme that categorizes the patient's medical diagnosis and treatment.[2] The facility assigns a DRG code used to bill for reimbursement, planning, budgeting, and utilization of services. The hospital receives payment according to assigned DRG, which is further modified by age, complications, coexisting conditions, and the discharge status. Since the purpose of the DRG-based scheme of Medicare reimbursement is to hold down health care costs, reviewers may be requested to evaluate the medical record to verify the six variables responsible for the DRG classification:

- Principal diagnosis
- Secondary diagnosis
- Surgical procedures
- Co-morbidity and complications
- Age and sex
- Discharge status

If the DRG is incorrect, there may be an overpayment or an underpayment. Computer programs that assign DRGs do not abstract all the information in the inpatient data profile. Proper documentation is critical, and the LNC's knowledge of International Classification of Diseases and Clinical Modification (ICD-9-CM) coding is essential to the correct DRG assignment.[2] The LNC may be requested to review records to determine whether a pattern of miscoding exists or a physician's documentation is inadequate. Several publishers offer DRG guides and ICD-9-CM materials, updated yearly, to assist the LNC in this critical review process.[2,3]

Example 28.3: A Colorado hospital paid $1,250,261 to settle allegations that it had submitted claims for inpatient treatment of pneumonia using diagnosis codes for more serious illnesses than those that the hospital actually treated, as reported by the U.S. Attorney for Colorado. The subpoenaed records in this case involved claims that St. Mary's Hospital and Medical Center of Grand Junction had designated a principal diagnosis by using the code corresponding to "pneumonia due to other specified bacteria," allowing it to obtain reimbursement under DRG 079. Coding for DRG 079 versus DRG 089 ("simple pneumonia") pays about $2,700 more per patient, said the U.S. Attorney. The settlement between St. Mary's

Hospital and the government is one of a series of cases that the Department of Justice and the Office of Inspector General investigated as part of a national initiative to address upcoding of pneumonia claims by hospitals. The settlement resolved the dispute with no admission of liability from St. Mary's Hospital.[4] Billing fraud related to pneumonia was uncovered by a physician who used data to recognize the pattern. A *qui tam* (false claims) action was filed against more than 100 hospitals.

Medicare: Skilled Nursing Facility

On July 1, 1998, skilled nursing facilities (SNFs) began implementation of a PPS for Medicare recipients. This new payment system has affected all areas of operation both clinically and financially, from increased demands on the minimum data set (MDS) process to implementation of a consolidated billing for Medicare part A and B services. The reimbursement system, known as RUG-III (Resource Utilization Groups — Version III), uses the MDS, a federally mandated standardized clinical assessment, to classify residents into 1 of 44 payment categories. Chapter 14 gives a detailed explanation of the MDS.

The 44 groups in RUG-III fall into a hierarchy of seven major resident types: rehabilitation, extensive services, special care, clinically complex, impaired cognition, behavioral problems, and reduced physical function. Each of these resident types contains different classifications based on the amount of activity of daily living (ADL) assistance required and other resident problems or services provided, such as depression, nursing rehabilitation, and number of treatments. Not all ADLs impact the resident class. Only bed mobility, transfer, toilet use, and eating are evaluated to determine the ADL score. The total per diem reimbursement for each resident is the sum of the applicable nursing and therapy rates for the RUG-III class into which the resident was classified. Grouping a resident into 1 of the 44 classifications is fairly complex. Computerized grouper software is utilized to check which criteria the resident has met and to calculate the resident's RUG class. Each of the 44 groups has a value or weight known as a case-mix index (CMI). The CMI is adjusted by wage and salary information per state. The Centers for Medicare and Medicaid Services (formerly Health Care Financing Administration [HCFA]) has made available basic MDS and RUG grouper software free of charge to facilities. The program, known as RAVEN, can be ordered on the CMS Web site at http://cms.hhs.gov.

In this setting, the nurse reviewer's familiarity with medical necessity of services is essential in determining whether or not the MDS is a valid reflection of the resident's needs and abilities. Incorrect and inconsistent RUG classifications can be costly for the facility. If the assigned RUG fails to take into account all the resident's services needed and provided, the facility's reimbursement will be less than deserved. On the other hand, if the resident's needs are overstated, the facility will be submitting claims for services not required or rendered. A pattern of such activity can be viewed as potentially fraudulent. Since the categories differ based on the amount of care a resident needs and the time it takes to provide that care, more skilled care needed equates with a higher reimbursement.

Example 28.4: Marking the largest-ever settlement in a nursing home case, Beverly Enterprises, one of the nation's biggest nursing home operators, paid $175 million to the federal government to settle charges that it had defrauded

Medicare out of $460 million between 1992 and 1998. The Department of Justice alleged that Beverly had routinely exaggerated the amount of time that nurses were devoting to Medicare patients.[5]

Medicare Compliance: Physician Bills

Many health-law attorneys and their physician clients prefer to be proactive through review of their billing practices prior to Medicare's scrutiny. The Office of Inspector General (OIG) of the Department of Health and Human Services (DHHS) has issued voluntary-compliance program guidelines focused on several areas and aspects of the health care industry. Hospitals, clinical laboratories, home health care agencies, durable medical equipment suppliers, third-party medical billing companies, and hospice organizations are some of the areas addressed. There are also voluntary compliance guidelines for individual and small group physician practices. All of the guidance is available on the OIG Web site at http://www.hhs.gov/oig in the Electronic Reading Room or by calling the OIG Public Affairs Office at (202) 619–1343.

The OIG believes that, for the most part, the majority of physicians are honest and share in the goal of protecting the integrity of Medicare and other federal health care programs. All health care providers have a duty to make certain that the claims they submit for reimbursement are true and accurate. The development and active application of an effective compliance program is a proactive measure that can help protect the physician's practice against the potential of erroneous or fraudulent conduct.

The OIG maintains that an effective compliance program should attempt to address all the applicable elements listed below, which arc based on the seven elements set forth in the Federal Sentencing Guidelines.[6] The Federal Sentencing Guidelines are detailed policies and practices for the federal criminal justice system that prescribe the appropriate sanctions for offenders convicted of federal crimes. The seven elements of an effective compliance program are:

- Establishing compliance standards through the development of a code of conduct and written policies and procedures
- Assigning compliance-monitoring efforts to a designated compliance officer or contact
- Conducting comprehensive training and education on practice ethics and policies and procedures
- Conducting internal monitoring and auditing, focusing on high-risk billing and coding issues through performance of periodic audits
- Developing accessible lines of communication, such as discussions at staff meetings regarding fraudulent or erroneous conduct issues and community bulletin boards, to keep practice employees updated regarding compliance activities
- Enforcing disciplinary standards by making it clear or ensuring that employees are aware that compliance is treated seriously and that violations will be dealt with consistently and uniformly
- Responding appropriately to detected violations through the investigation of allegations and the disclosure of incidents to appropriate government entities

When performing a review of the physician's billing practices, the LNC reviewer evaluates a representative sampling of the physician's office records and compares them with Medicare billing guidelines as well as the fiscal intermediary's specific criteria. The LNC may also be requested to provide education to physicians and their staffs regarding documentation, collection of copayments, and determination of correct and current ICD and CPT codes used in the billing process.

Physicians' Current Procedural Terminology (CPT)

The American Medical Association (AMA) publishes the CPT manual annually.[7,8] The manual includes five-digit numeric codes and descriptors for procedures and services performed by providers. These codes are a trademark of the AMA. In 1983, CPT was adopted as part of the Health Care Financing Administration's (now CMS) Common Procedure Coding System (HCPCS) to report services for Part B of the Medicare program.[9] In October 1986, HCFA also required state Medicaid agencies to use HCPCS in the Medicaid Management Information System. In July 1987, as part of the Omnibus Budget Reconciliation Act (OBRA), HCFA mandated the use of CPT for reporting outpatient hospital surgical procedures. Today, in addition to use in federal programs (Medicare and Medicaid), CPT is used extensively throughout the U.S. as the preferred system of coding to describe health care services. Medical care providers are expected to bill insurers using current codes, but they often become complacent and use outdated codes. It is recommended that the LNC reviewer keep at least three years of CPT books on hand: current year and two previous years. In many instances, when the reviewer finds discrepancies in coding, the code is adjusted to reflect the services as documented.

ICD-9-CM Codes

ICD-9-CM lists diagnoses equated with a three-digit number that may or may not be modified further for accuracy and specificity.[10] It is used to code and classify morbidity (disease) data from inpatient and outpatient records, physician office records, and most statistical surveys. In 1988, the Medicare Catastrophic Coverage Act mandated the reporting of ICD-9-CM diagnosis codes on Medicare claims. Private insurance carriers adopted similar diagnosis coding requirements. In 1992, the World Health Organization (WHO) completed work on the tenth revision, which has a new title, "The International Statistical Classification of Diseases and Related Health Problems," and a new alphanumeric coding system. It is expected that the change from ICD-9-CM to the National Center for Health Statistics (NCHS)-developed ICD-10-CM and the HCFA-developed ICD-10-PCS (Procedural Coding System) will be mandated for 2003 or later.

The medical coder's role is to translate written diagnoses into numeric and alphanumeric codes. CMS provides specific guidelines to aid in standardizing coding practices across the U.S. Many times a claim is disallowed when a CMS-1500 form (previously known as HCFA-1500 form), which is used to submit Medicare Part B claims, has an ICD-9 code that refers to a diagnosis that is not applicable and for which there should be no financial obligation. Further, if the CPT codes on the CMS-1500 form relate to services not usually associated with the ICD-9-CM diagnosis, the claim may be denied or payment delayed pending additional documentation. Two of the coding abbreviations often confused by coders and reviewers are NOS and NEC. NOS is defined as "not otherwise specified" and indicates that the code is unspecified and that, if possible, the coder should continue looking for a more specific code. This abbreviation is used only in Volume 1, the tabular list of diseases. NEC is the abbreviation for "not elsewhere classifiable" and identifies codes and terms to be used only when the coder lacks the information necessary to code the diagnosis to a more specific category. This abbreviation is used only in Volume 2, the alphabetic index.[3]

Suspect Nonhospital Billing

An LNC who is skilled in billing and claims review can identify suspect fraud and abuse. Numerous flags of fraud go unrecognized by a novice reviewer. Familiarity with the use and intent of CPT coding, correct billing protocols, treatment standards, and diagnostic codes is essential in this arena. Some examples of suspicious billing include:

- Misrepresentation of diagnosis codes
- Diagnosis codes that are inconsistent with treatment codes
- Incorrect E/M (evaluation/management) codes
- Lack of itemization
- No interim billing
- Unbundling (billing for individual items instead of one code encompassing all items)
- Procedure creep (also called upcoding; billing for a service with a higher reimbursement than the service actually performed)
- Pattern of inadequate documentation to support CPT codes billed
- Excessive frequency of services
- No decrease or change in therapy (therapy should reflect improvement or lack of improvement)
- Sudden cessation of therapy when no improvement documented
- Extended duration of treatment with no apparent reason

The LNC reviewer must be cognizant of the possibility of abusive billing to HMO, by the medical provider. Examples of fraudulent activity include:

- Inflation of the patient visits and costs in order to obtain higher capitation (fixed per-member/per-month payments) rates in subsequent years
- Inflation of bills to reach an agreed amount, after which the HMO pays on a fee-for-service basis (often called the stop-loss limit)
- Sending a high-cost member to a teaching hospital to shift the cost to the HMO
- Referring patients for noncapitated services
- Denying patients needed care, thus forcing them to leave the plan
- Claiming procedures that are not discounted under the negotiated contract (e.g., billing toenail-cutting as "surgery")

Qualifications

The LNC who embarks on medical claims review activity, whatever the context, should possess certain clinical and educational qualifications to perform the task in a competent and efficient manner.

Clinical Experience

The LNC reviewer should be an experienced nurse with recent clinical experience. Clinical experience provides the knowledge of equipment and medical procedures necessary to evaluate the appropriateness of items listed on a bill related to a wide variety of procedures. The nursing background most helpful for hospital bill audits is critical care or operative nursing, because those areas usually generate the most costly and therefore most questioned charges. However, lack of such experience does not disqualify the LNC from claims review. A willingness to ask questions about unfamiliar items and to analyze the information critically to determine the appropriateness of the billing is more important. In contrast to the seasoned reviewer, the inexperienced reviewer will ask many more questions and therefore take longer to complete an audit, but the results should be comparable.

Knowledge of current treatment, expected outcomes of care, and the rehabilitative process is extremely beneficial when reviewing orthopedic and neurological injury claims. These areas are frequently subject to close scrutiny by the insurance industry because of the increasing incidence of inflated, questionable, and fraudulent claims.

Familiarity with case management and utilization review protocols is extremely beneficial in reviewing billing for HMO issues. Taking courses and becoming certified in coding and in health care compliance along with updating knowledge annually is highly recommended as medical technology increases and regulatory guidelines frequently change.

A background in rehabilitation needs and proper completion of MDS in the skilled nursing facility setting helps the LNC to evaluate nursing home claims.

Auditing Experience

Nurses new to auditing are often amazed to discover the quantity of items listed on an itemized bill for a single procedure, such as an angiogram. Familiarity with the usual billing protocols of hospitals and other health care providers (chiropractors, physical therapists, acupuncturists, etc.) assists the nurse in determining whether or not particular charges are unusual or excessive. For the uninitiated, billing protocols or procedures direct the acceptable or usual format in which services are billed.

Example 28.5: Hospitals that bill for daily setup of overhead trapeze equipment or bill for individual items from an operating room pack are clearly unconventional. Another illustration of improper billing occurs when a surgeon who has performed an arthroscopy bills for both a diagnostic and surgical procedure because a surgical arthroscopy always includes a diagnostic arthroscopy. The physician is billing twice for the same procedure.

Acquiring Bill Auditing Knowledge and Experience

How does one obtain education and become experienced in bill auditing? Several possible avenues are available:

- Ask medical bill reviewers where they obtained their training
- Ask local (and respected) physician's office personnel about the availability of coding classes they attended
- Contact local colleges for coding courses
- Attend seminars targeting this topic
- Purchase coding instruction books and begin a self-taught course of study
- Volunteer to assist a local hospital's bill reviewer
- Consider employment in a cost-containment, auditing, or insurance firm

The LNC is advised to refrain from claims review in a formalized setting until he or she is comfortable with the process and possesses the necessary knowledge related to charges, regulatory guidelines, insurance coverage issues, and care guidelines.

Essential Tools

Certain tools and resources make the medical claims-auditing task much easier and provide credibility and validity to the audit. The resources most essential are briefly described below.

Coding References

In addition to using CPT and ICD references, the LNC should consult these manuals:

- DRG. A diagnosis-related group manual lists the diagnoses that hospitals must use to submit claims to Medicare for inpatient stays.[2]
- HCPCS. HCFA Common Procedure Coding System consists of three levels: (1) current procedural terminology; (2) national codes, commonly referred to as HCPCS codes, that are published by HCFA (now CMS) and include five-digit alphanumeric codes for procedures, services, and supplies not classified in CPT; and (3) local codes that are developed by local insurance companies and include five-digit alphanumeric codes for procedures, services, and supplies that are also not classified in CPT. (CMS plans to phase out local codes.)[9]
- Coding Instruction. *Principles of ICD-9-CM Coding* and *Principles of CPT Coding*, published by the American Medical Association, cover basic to intermediate concepts of CPT and ICD-9-CM coding.[8,10] Certification for professional coders can be obtained through the American Academy of Professional Coders. Coding guidelines such as *Code It Right, Coder's Desk Reference, Coding Tutor*, and *Coding Companions* are helpful publications for coders.[11-14] They provide definitions, guidelines, coding examples, and terminology.

Pharmacy References

- *Physician's Desk Reference (PDR)*.[15] The familiar *PDR*, published yearly, provides a drug's indications for use and the forms in which it is supplied, but does not provide pricing information.
- *Drug Topics Red Book*.[16] Better known as the Red Book, this text is relatively inexpensive and updated yearly. It lists medications by manufacturer, the forms and quantities supplied, the average wholesale pricing, etc. This can be helpful in determining the extent of markup on a particular pharmaceutical.
- *Physician's GenRX*.[17] This book is a combination of the information found in the *PDR* and Red Book and is published yearly. Unlike the *PDR* and Red Book, it is not available at most medical bookstores, but can be ordered by mail. In addition to all the necessary medical data, the *Physician's GenRX* contains essential pricing information and the conditions for which FDA approves use of drugs, when approval was granted, and other bits of useful information. The text is available in book form, on CD-ROM, and in disk format, which increases its usefulness.

Medical, Nursing, and Procedure Texts

Medical, nursing, and procedure texts are useful in acquainting the LNC reviewer with unfamiliar procedures and assist in defining the equipment and supplies generated when such procedures are ordered and performed. Texts devoted to radiological and surgical procedures are particularly helpful for the bill reviewer.

Chiropractic and Physical Therapy Texts/Manuals

Chiropractic and physical therapy texts and manuals are especially useful to the LNC reviewer who reviews billings for orthopedic and soft-tissue injuries. The reviewer should seek references that discuss indications for procedures, duration of treatment, and standards of care.

State Regulations

Many states have regulations pertinent to care delivered by medical providers, such as physical therapy and chiropractic treatment, that affect reimbursement. If care was not provided in accordance with these regulations, then such charges may be legally disallowed. To obtain these regulations, contact the state agency responsible for licensing the particular provider and request a copy. State regulations can be found in the local law library. It is suggested that the regulations be checked yearly because new laws may make certain sections obsolete.

Federal Regulations

The federal government has specific criteria relating to services rendered to Medicare patients. Regulations can be purchased from book publishers or obtained from the CMS Web site, http://cms.hhs.gov.

Fee Schedules

Medicare RBRVS: The Physician's Guide accesses relative values by CPT code, geographic practice, and cost indices, explains of payment rules for surgical packages and appropriate use of new modifiers, and provides a summary and history of payment reform.[18] Information that this publication provides is applicable only to Medicare reimbursement; excessive charges billed to other payers can be identified and decreased through application of other fee and coding reference books or software. It is important that the product used provide a geographically specific index for pricing of health care services relative to national average prices. Books are relatively inexpensive, but statistically reliable computer database software is beyond the budget of most reviewers, with costs ranging from $2,500 to $25,000 yearly for a national database. Both books and software are updated yearly.

Internet Resources

The Internet provides a wealth of information for the reviewer. Pharmaceutical information is available through medical sites and other sites that are direct links to the manufacturer or pharmacy information Web sites. Other sites contain up-to-date information on procedures, equipment, and medical abbreviations. Extensive familiarity with search techniques is not required; typing the item desired into an effective search engine should yield the desired information.

Computers, Software, and Forms

The reviewer who attempts to perform bill reviews without a computer will add unnecessary time to the task. With the proper software, worksheets can be devised with built-in formulas for calculations to replace the error-prone manual calculator. Not only can mathematical functions be accomplished with ease, but a professional-looking report can be easily generated for the client. Attempting a bill review without a methodical approach through use of a worksheet will not only prolong the task, but increase the risk of errors (see Figures 28.1 and 28.2).

Calendars can be generated showing frequency, duration, and patterns of care (see Figure 28.3). Such a visual aid depicts visits to medical providers much better than words. A user-friendly word-processing program can help the reviewer prepare explanatory narrative reports that describe in detail the rationale for decisions made in the bill review process. A printer with adequate memory is needed to print the audit results. A laser or ink-jet printer is preferable to a letter-quality dot matrix printer. A simple calculator with the basic arithmetic functions and memory features is useful for small tasks.

Value of Claims Review

The LNC brings analytical skills and the ability to perceive and communicate the legal implications of the information gleaned from the billings and medical records. This information may be viewed differently depending on the purpose of the audit since results may validate, increase, or mitigate economic damages in a lawsuit. Further, the LNC with claims review experience is in a unique position to assist

Date	Description	CPT Billed	$ Amount Billed	CPT Adjusted	U & C 80th Per-centile	Total $ Reduction	Total $ Amount Allowed	Rationale
1/23/96	O.V. New patient	99203	$200.00		$121.48	$78.52	$121.48	
1/23/96	Hot/cold packs	97010	$200.00		$29.27	$170.73	$29.27	CPT 96 states hot packs to one or more areas. MD charging for 5.
1/23/96	Elect. Stimulation	97032	$150.00		$22.05	$127.95	$22.05	CPT 96 states hot packs to one or more areas. MD charging for 3.
1/23/96	Ultrasound-15 min.	97035	$250.00		$15.35	$234.65	$15.35	CPT 96 states hot packs to one or more areas. MD charging for 5.
1/26/96	Hot/cold packs	97010	$200.00		$29.27	$170.73	$29.27	
1/26/96	Elect. Stimulation	97032	$150.00		$22.05	$127.95	$22.05	
1/26/96	Ultrasound-15 min.	97035	$250.00		$15.35	$234.65	$15.35	
1/28/96	Hot/cold packs	97010	$200.00		$29.27	$170.73	$29.27	Sunday: Not open per MD's office
1/28/96	Elect. Stimulation	97032	$150.00		$22.05	$127.95	$22.05	Sunday: Not open per MD's office
1/28/96	Ultrasound-15 min.	97035	$250.00		$15.35	$234.65	$15.35	Sunday: Not open per MD's office
1/29/96		99211	$80.00		$27.66	$52.34	$27.66	
1/29/96	Hot/cold packs	97010	$200.00		$29.27	$170.73	$29.27	
1/29/96	Elect. Stimulation	97032	$150.00		$22.05	$127.95	$22.05	
1/29/96	Ultrasound-15 min.	97035	$250.00		$15.35	$234.65	$15.35	
1/31/96	Hot/cold packs	97010	$200.00		$29.27	$170.73	$29.27	
1/31/96	Elect. Stimulation	97032	$150.00		$22.05	$127.95	$22.05	
1/31/96	Ultrasound-15 min.	97035	$250.00		$15.35	$234.65	$15.35	
2/2/96	Hot/cold packs	97010	$200.00		$29.27	$170.73	$29.27	Saturday: Not open per MD's office
2/2/96	Elect. Stimulation	97032	$150.00		$22.05	$127.95	$22.05	Saturday: Not open per MD's office
2/2/96	Ultrasound-15 min.	97035	$250.00		$15.35	$234.65	$15.35	Saturday: Not open per MD's office
2/3/96	Hot/cold packs	97010	$200.00		$29.27	$170.73	$29.27	
2/3/96	Elect. Stimulation	97032	$150.00		$22.05	$127.95	$22.05	
2/3/96	Ultrasound-15 min.	97035	$250.00		$15.35	$234.65	$15.35	
2/5/96	Hot/cold packs	97010	$200.00		$29.27	$170.73	$29.27	
2/5/96	Elect. Stimulation	97032	$150.00		$22.05	$127.95	$22.05	
2/5/96	Ultrasound-15 min.	97035	$250.00		$15.35	$234.65	$15.35	
2/7/96	Hot/cold packs	97010	$200.00		$29.27	$170.73	$29.27	
2/7/96	Elect. Stimulation	97032	$150.00		$22.05	$127.95	$22.05	
2/7/96	Ultrasound-15 min.	97035	$250.00		$15.35	$234.65	$15.35	
2/9/96	Hot/cold packs	97010	$200.00		$29.27	$170.73	$29.27	
2/9/96	Elect. Stimulation	97032	$150.00		$22.05	$127.95	$22.05	
2/9/96	Ultrasound-15 min.	97035	$250.00		$15.35	$234.65	$15.35	
2/12/96	Hot/cold packs	97010	$200.00		$29.27	$170.73	$29.27	
2/12/96	Elect. Stimulation	97032	$150.00		$22.05	$127.95	$22.05	
2/12/96	Ultrasound-15 min.	97035	$250.00		$15.35	$234.65	$15.35	
2/14/96	Hot/cold packs	97010	$200.00		$29.27	$170.73	$29.27	
2/14/96	Elect. Stimulation	97032	$150.00		$22.05	$127.95	$22.05	
2/14/96	Ultrasound-15 min.	97035	$250.00		$15.35	$234.65	$15.35	
2/15/96	Hot/cold packs	97010	$200.00		$29.27	$170.73	$29.27	
2/15/96	Elect. Stimulation	97032	$150.00		$22.05	$127.95	$22.05	
2/15/96	Ultrasound-15 min.	97035	$250.00		$15.35	$234.65	$15.35	
2/16/96	Hot/cold packs	97010	$200.00		$29.27	$170.73	$29.27	
2/16/96	Elect. Stimulation	97032	$150.00		$22.05	$127.95	$22.05	
2/16/96	Ultrasound-15 min.	97035	$250.00		$15.35	$234.65	$15.35	
2/19/96	Hot/cold packs	97010	$200.00		$29.27	$170.73	$29.27	
2/19/96	Elect. Stimulation	97032	$150.00		$22.05	$127.95	$22.05	
2/19/96	Ultrasound-15 min.	97035	$250.00		$15.35	$234.65	$15.35	
2/21/96	Hot/cold packs	97010	$200.00		$29.27	$170.73	$29.27	
2/21/96	Elect. Stimulation	97032	$150.00		$22.05	$127.95	$22.05	
2/21/96	Ultrasound-15 min.	97035	$250.00		$15.35	$234.65	$15.35	

Figure 28.1 Bill Review, Patient John Smith

in the investigation, prosecution, and defense of potential fraudulent billing activity. Since approximately one of every three dollars recovered through *qui tam* cases relate to health care fraud against the Medicare and Medicaid programs, the LNC can make a valuable contribution in the fight against health care fraud.

Value for the Plaintiff

Some benefits that bill review offers for different employers of the LNC reviewer are:

■ Verifies claims for damages

Dept.	Item Description	Price Ea.	Qty. Billed	Qty. Doc.	Qty. Allowed	Plus or Minus	Overcharge	Undercharge	Rationale
						0	$0.00	$0.00	
						0	$0.00	$0.00	
						0	$0.00	$0.00	
						0	$0.00	$0.00	
						0	$0.00	$0.00	
						0	$0.00	$0.00	
						0	$0.00	$0.00	
						0	$0.00	$0.00	
						0	$0.00	$0.00	
						0	$0.00	$0.00	
						0	$0.00	$0.00	
						0	$0.00	$0.00	
						0	$0.00	$0.00	
						0	$0.00	$0.00	
						0	$0.00	$0.00	
						0	$0.00	$0.00	
						0	$0.00	$0.00	
						0	$0.00	$0.00	
						0	$0.00	$0.00	
						0	$0.00	$0.00	
						0	$0.00	$0.00	
						0	$0.00	$0.00	
						0	$0.00	$0.00	
						0	$0.00	$0.00	
						0	$0.00	$0.00	
						0	$0.00	$0.00	

Figure 28.2 Hospital Bill Review

Calendar of Treatments, Procedures, and Office Visits
John Smith   File No. xxxxx

	Evaluations by Baraque and PT.
	Received PT, reevaluated by Baraque, then seen by Cabrera.
	ROM, nerve, and lift testing with Cabrera.
	Neurological consultation with Martinez.
	Received PT and went for EEG and neurological follow-up

Figure 28.3   Calendar of Treatments, Procedures, and Office Visits for Patient John Smith

- Establishes medical damages when care was provided by nonbilling institutions, such as Veterans' hospitals, National Institutes of Health, or managed care organizations
- Determines whether all provider records are present
- Identifies the billing issues upon which defense may focus, such as lengthy or excessive treatment, excessively high fees charged by physicians, etc.
- Identifies the impact of preexisting conditions on billings
- Corroborates the plaintiff's allegations of malpractice
- Provides basis for lien or settlement negotiation
- Validates physician charges for Medicare billing compliance

Value for the Defendant

- Verifies medical damages
- Decreases damages by disallowing charges
- Identifies services relating to preexisting conditions
- Identifies services not provided to patient
- Identifies services provided, but not in accordance with regulations
- Identifies services provided, but not medically appropriate or necessary

- Decreases damages by adjustment of CPT coding to reflect actual provided services and through utilization of U & C database application of U & C treatment schedule in absence of substantiating medical records from provider
- Disputes the plaintiff's allegations of medical malpractice
- Determines whether all provider records are present
- Points out red flags indicating possible fraud
- Provides a basis for settlement negotiation
- Validates physician charges for Medicare billing compliance

In conjunction with the bill review, the LNC prepares an understandable and defensible report for the client, whether the client is an attorney, insurance adjuster, investigator, or other person. Clear explanations for decisions made during the audit process relative to charges, legal issues, missing records, and possible suspicious activity should be presented. Regulatory citations and other references should be included when applicable.

Claim Review Testimony

When the LNC reviewer functions as a testifying expert, he or she is expected to have the necessary credentials to perform in this role: credible experience, the ability to present the issues in understandable language, and proper courtroom demeanor. Prior to accepting an audit assignment, the LNC should inquire about the likelihood that testimony will be involved.

Many plaintiff attorneys utilize an LNC reviewer to introduce medical costs at trial, both past and projected. Defense counsel utilizes the reviewer's findings to counter the plaintiff's contentions regarding the medical expenses. The LNC is in an excellent position to execute this aspect of case management. He or she can evaluate the bills and discuss whether the charges were reasonable, accurate, and within the expected range of fees for the hospital or outpatient care. When preparing future medical costs, the LNC has the skills necessary to interview the physician regarding the proposed surgery and expected postoperative therapy. The reviewer should also possess the proficiency for communicating with the appropriate hospital departments and medical personnel to obtain the information needed to provide a valid and defensible report.

Opportunities for Health Care Claims Auditing for the LNC

Numerous opportunities exist for the LNC who desires either to augment services offered to clients or employers or to seek new arenas of practice. Examples of areas in which the LNC's claim review experience can be exercised include:

- Case management organizations
- Insurance firms
- Hospitals: risk management; defense and revenue auditing

- Law offices: plaintiff and defense
- Private investigative agencies performing investigations of medical fraud
- Office of Inspector General for a number of federal departments: Health and Human Services, U.S. Postal Service, U.S. Department of Labor, U.S. Department of Justice
- Independent LNC practice

The addition of claim review to the LNC's practice can be rewarding, both financially and in terms of task satisfaction. Although the initial investment in time and the proper tools may be costly, the end results will more than compensate. Entrepreneurial LNCs who do not have the time, budget, or inclination to perform claim review can affiliate with an accomplished LNC reviewer.

References

1. Grogan, A., Personal communication, 2001.
2. *DRG Guide*, Ingenix Publishing Group, 2002.
3. *International Classification of Diseases — Clinical Modification*, Ingenix Publishing Group, 2002.
4. U.S. Attorney's Office, District of Colorado, "St. Mary's Hospital and Medical Center Settle Medicare False Claims Allegations," http://www.du.edu/usaoco/011702, January 17, 2002.
5. Legal News Network, "Nursing Home Chain Hit with Record Medicare Fraud Fine. Whistle-Blower Costs Beverly Enterprises $175 Million and 10 Homes," http://www.uslaw.com/library/article/lnnNursingHome, 2000.
6. U.S. Sentencing Commission, *2001 Federal Sentencing Guideline Manual*, U.S. Government Printing Office, Washington, D.C., 2001.
7. American Medical Association, *Current Procedural Terminology*, American Medical Association, Chicago, 2002.
8. American Medical Association, *Principles of CPT Coding*, American Medical Association, Chicago, 2002.
9. *HCFA Common Procedures Coding System (HCPCS)*, St. Anthony's Publishing & Medicode, Washington, D.C., 2002.
10. American Medical Association, *Principles of ICD-9-CM Coding*, American Medical Association, Chicago, 2002.
11. *Code It Right*, Ingenix Publishing Group, Washington, D.C., 2002.
12. *Coder's Desk Reference*, Ingenix Publishing Group, Washington, D.C., 2002.
13. *Coding Tutor*, Ingenix Publishing Group, Washington, D.C., 2002.
14. *Coding Companions — Comprehensive Illustrated Guides to Coding and Reimbursement*, Ingenix Publishing Group, Washington, D.C., 2002.
15. *Physician's Desk Reference*, Medical Economics Data, Montvale, NJ, 2002.
16. *Drug Topics Red Book*, Medical Economics Data, Montvale, NJ, 2002.
17. *Physician's GenRX*, Mosby-Year Book, St. Louis, MO, 2002.
18. American Medical Association, *Medicare RBRVS: The Physician's Guide*, American Medical Association, Chicago, 2002.

Additional Reading

CP Teach, MedBooks, Dallas, 1994.

Federal Register, Vol. 65, No. 194, Thursday, October 5, 2000, 59434–59452.

Fee Facts, Data Management Ventures, Inc., Woodstock, GA, 2002.

Guidelines for Chiropractic Quality Assurance and Practice Parameters, Aspen Publishers, Gaithersburg, MD, 1993.

Insurance Handbook for the Medical Office, 5th ed., W.B. Saunders, Philadelphia, 1997, updated annually.

Medicare Billing Guide 2002, Ingenix Publishing Group, Washington, D.C., 2002.

Medicare Payment Systems: http://cms.hhs.gov/hcprofessionals/payment.asp.

National Fee Analyzer, Ingenix Publishing Group, Washington, D.C., 2002.

Physician Fees, PMIC, Los Angeles, 2002.

Procedural Coding Crosswalk, Ingenix Publishing Group, Washington, D.C., 2002.

Procedural/Utilization Facts, 5th ed., Data Management Ventures, Inc., Woodstock, GA, 1995.

RBRVS EZ-Fees, Wasserman Medical Publishers, 2002.

Test Questions

1. Which of the following is the primary purpose of a hospital bill review for legal purposes?
   A. Identification of charges relating to preexisting medical conditions
   B. Refutation of negligence claims
   C. Determination of negotiated contract benefits

2. A hospital bill payable by Medicare differs from other insurance coverage in that
   A. The hospital receives payment according to a preset amount
   B. The hospital receives payment according to a DRG assigned by the hospital
   C. The hospital receives payment according to a DRG assigned by Medicare
   D. The DRG is not subject to review

3. All of the following are examples of possible fraudulent billing EXCEPT:
   A. Sending a patient needing expensive treatment to a teaching hospital to shift costs
   B. Misrepresentation of a diagnosis code
   C. Itemization of charges
   D. Excessive frequency of service

4. CPT codes are
   A. Alphabetic codes for reporting diagnoses
   B. Numeric codes for reporting services and procedures
   C. Published twice yearly
   D. Not required by Medicare

5. ICD-9 codes on a claim
   A. Establish medical necessity
   B. Have no bearing on CPT codes
   C. Are not required on Medicare claims
   D. Have no effect on timely reimbursement

Answers: 1. A, 2. C, 3. D, 4. B, 5. A

Chapter 29

Defense Medical Examinations

Karen L. Wetther, BSN, RN, and
Lorraine E. Buchanan, MSN, RN, CRRN

CONTENTS

Objectives

Upon completion of the chapter, the reader will be able to:

0-8493-1418-6/03/$0.00+$1.50
© 2003 by AALNC

- State the purpose of a defense medical examination
- Realize the importance of clarifying with the client the stipulations relating to defense medical examinations that apply to the state in which the client's case was filed
- List two reasons why a plaintiff's attorney might request the presence of a legal nurse consultant at the client's defense medical examination
- Describe the legal nurse consultant's recourse if the examiner will not permit his or her attendance at a defense medical examination
- State two documents that are helpful for the legal nurse consultant to have at a defense medical examination
- List two things that the legal nurse consultant should do to prepare for the examination

Introduction

During the discovery phase of litigation, the opposing parties often disagree about the physical or mental health claims. The defense may be unwilling to offer a settlement. The plaintiff may be unwilling to accept the settlement offered by the defense, while the defense is unwilling to offer a greater amount, frequently based on the belief that the claims of the plaintiff or the medical opinions of the plaintiff's treating physicians or experts are erroneous or exaggerated. The law allows the defense to have the plaintiff undergo a medical examination and, under certain circumstances, a mental examination by a health care practitioner of its choice, generally referred to as a defense medical examination (DME) or independent medical examination (IME).

Plaintiff attorneys rarely use the term "independent medical examination" because they often feel that it is a misnomer. The examination is not really independent or necessarily unbiased, because it is performed by a health care practitioner whom the defense selects and pays. Plaintiff attorneys generally refer to such examinations as DMEs. The term "independent" is used to designate the examination as independent of the plaintiff's case.[1] For those who prefer the term "IME," perhaps a better definition would be "insurance medical evaluation."

The term "independent medical examination" is used to describe the examination performed in the context of workers' compensation claims. In some instances, the term used to describe the exam is "agreed medical examination," but it is a misnomer because typically the reason for the exam is not "agreed upon." In general, plaintiff and defense counsels "agree" upon the examiner chosen for the worker's evaluation. The defense counsel reserves the right to choose the examiner to evaluate the injured worker.

Workers' compensation cases are governed by different, though similar, rules and vary from state to state. Examinations may also be done in the context of Social Security Disability claims, which are governed by federal guidelines. This chapter is limited to a discussion of DMEs.

A legal nurse consultant (LNC) may be asked by plaintiff counsel to attend and observe the DME as the attorney's representative. This chapter will discuss some of the legal requirements relating to these examinations and the role of the LNC who attends DMEs. Rule 35 of the Federal Rules of Civil Procedure governs the use of DMEs in federal cases; therefore, in federal cases, the DMEs are consistent from state to state. In cases filed in state court, statutes governing DMEs vary by state. The LNC retained to attend a DME is responsible for clarifying with the attorney his or her role at the examination.

Purpose of a Defense Medical Examination

A physical or mental examination of an opposing party is an accepted method of evaluating claims of injury, illness, or incapacity by that party. It provides the defendants in personal injury cases the opportunity to select a physician or physicians to examine the plaintiff and to evaluate the injury or injuries claimed.

Major Advantages and Disadvantages of the DME from the Defense Perspective

The following points are advantages of the DME from the defense perspective:

- May have the opposing party examined by a physician of its choosing
- May provide defense counsel access to reports that might otherwise be protected from discovery (Discovery rules vary from state to state.)
- May provide an opportunity for the defense to initiate surveillance of a plaintiff who has been difficult to locate
- May detect lack of any physical injury or symptoms in a plaintiff

Disadvantages of the DME from the defense perspective include:

- Costs, such as the examiner's fees for reviewing medical records, performing the examination, and preparing a report
- Necessity to obtain cooperation from plaintiff's counsel with regard to obtaining medical records and x-rays prior to the examination
- Necessary reliance on examiner to review medical records and x-rays prior to the examination
- The examination may have a reverse effect, e.g., the risk that the examiner's findings and report may support or even magnify the patient's claims. Therefore, the examiner's testimony in court may weaken the defendant's case.

Legal Requirements

A DME may be ordered or initiated in one of the following ways: stipulation or consent; demand or court order. Regulations governing DMEs may vary from state to state. This chapter includes regulations from California civil procedure. The LNC involved in observing DMEs should seek information about the specific regulations of his or her state.

Examinations by Stipulation

Most DMEs are arranged by a written stipulation between counsels. The stipulation should clearly define the conditions of the examination (date, time, location, examiner, who may be present, etc.) and should identify the scope of the examination as well as each test or procedure that may be performed.

Examination by Demand

A defendant or cross-defendant (i.e., a party who is brought into the case by a defendant who feels that that party shares some or all liability and therefore files a cross-complaint against that party) in a personal injury case is allowed one physical examination of the plaintiff by simply serving a written demand on the plaintiff or cross-complainants.[2] Conditions and limitations on examinations by demand include the following:

- Only a physical examination of a personal injury plaintiff is allowed by demand.[3] If the plaintiff claims psychological damages, a mental examination may not be obtained by demand, although it may be ordered by the court, unless the plaintiff limits the specific claims and evidence of mental suffering that will be made.
- The physical examination is limited to the specific injury or condition that is in controversy, i.e., that which is the subject of litigation.[4] The defense is limited to one examination only, even if multiple injuries are claimed. Should the defendant feel that additional examinations are necessary, a court order may be needed to authorize the additional evaluations.
- The examination of the plaintiff is not to include any diagnostic test or procedure that is painful, protracted, or intrusive.[3] A court order may authorize such tests or procedures, although this rarely happens because few physicians will perform them without the patient's express consent.
- The demand in most cases must specify the date, time, and place of examination; the identity and specialty of the examiner; and the manner, conditions, scope, and nature of the examination.[3]
- Statute may require that the examination be conducted within a specific number of miles of the examinee's residence.[3]
- In most states, the examination must be conducted by a licensed physician or other appropriate licensed health care practitioner.[5]

Although it may not be expressly stated in the statute, it may be permissible for the examination to be performed by persons working under the general direction of a licensed physician or other health care practitioner. This would apply in cases where the examination is performed by the retained examiner but x-rays and laboratory tests, if allowed, are done by someone under the examiner's direction.[6] Even though the statute may not specifically stipulate the conditions of the examination, the demand should be as specific as possible to avoid unpleasant surprises or refusals by the plaintiff, e.g., observers who will be present (such as an LNC), the examiner's intent to photograph or audiotape the examination, and the types of tests and procedures that may be utilized during the exam.[3] The plaintiff may state any objections to the demand in writing and may refuse to be examined, forcing the defendants to obtain a court order if they wish to proceed.

Examination upon Court Order

A court order for physical or mental examination must be based on a showing of "good cause," which in most cases requires that the examination have relevancy to the subject matter and that specific facts be presented that justify discovery, such as a need for information sought and lack of means for otherwise obtaining it.[7,8] Good cause may be found if the plaintiff claims additional injuries, if his or her injuries have worsened, if tests or procedures are requested, or if there has been a lapse of time since the initial examination. If the plaintiff's injuries are complex, several examinations with various specialists may be necessary and may be allowed by the court if the defense is successful in showing good cause.[9] The purpose of requiring a court order in specific DME situations is to protect the privacy of the examinee by preventing "fact-finding missions" by the opposing party who speculates that something of interest might surface.[10]

Mental Examinations

If there is a showing of good cause, a mental examination may be performed by either a licensed physician or a licensed clinical psychologist with a doctoral degree and at least five years of experience diagnosing mental and emotional disorders.[5]

Site of Examination

When the examination is pursuant to court order, the person to be examined may be required to travel to wherever the examiner is located. However, if a patient is required to travel more than a reasonable distance (specifically defined in some states), the court's order must be based on a finding of good cause for the travel involved and be dependent on the moving party paying the examinee's reasonable travel costs.[7]

Limit on X-Rays

Because of public concern regarding excessive exposure to x-rays, the Discovery Act allows an examinee to avoid submitting to x-ray examinations for purposes of a DME, but provides the examiner access to the plaintiff's existing x-rays of the same site to be examined. No additional x-rays may be taken without the consent of the plaintiff or on court order for good cause shown.[11]

Who May Attend the DME?

State courts permit certain other persons to attend a DME conducted for discovery purposes. The plaintiff's attorney may observe and record an examination in person or through a representative designated in writing.[11] The attorney or representative is permitted to observe every phase of the examination to ensure that the examination is restricted to the scope ordered by the court and to prevent improper questioning by the examining physician.[12] An LNC often attends as the attorney's designated representative.

The plaintiff's attorney is entitled to record (stenographically or by audiotape) any words spoken to or by the patient during any phase of the examination to ensure an objective record, thereby avoiding disputes between the attorney and the examiner. Videotaping of the examination is generally not permitted — unless it is agreed to in advance by all parties. Any additional person's presence is at the discretion of the court and with the permission of the examinee.

Some examiners have the patient's history taken by a staff member and may also have a staff member record the findings of the examination according to the examiner's instructions. A male examiner may also choose to have a female staff member from his office present during the examination of a female as a matter of practice. In this situation, the LNC should obtain the name of that staff member and include in the report the time when the staff member entered and exited the examination room and how attentive he or she was during the examination. In some states, the staff members who assist the examiner are not allowed to take notes, and the defense is not entitled to have an observer present.

Use of an Interpreter

Some states may require that an interpreter be present during any medical examination requested by the defendant or by an insurance company if the examinee does not speak or understand English proficiently.[13]

Controls on Abuse

If the attorney or designated representative disrupts the examination (e.g., by instructing the examinee how to answer questions), the examiner may suspend the examination. The party who ordered the examination may move for a protective order and for a monetary sanction.[11] Conversely, if the examiner becomes abusive to the examinee or attempts to perform unauthorized tests or procedures, plaintiff's counsel or designated representative may also suspend the examination and move for a protective order and monetary sanctions against the party who ordered the examination.[11]

Deposition of the Examiner

If the plaintiff's counsel is concerned about the accuracy of the examiner's report or conclusions, he or she may depose the examiner, inspect the notes and records from the examination, and introduce contradictory evidence at trial.[14]

Exchange of Medical Reports

Regardless of how the DME is obtained (by stipulation, demand, or court order), the plaintiff may demand in writing a copy of the examiner's report. Additionally, the plaintiff may demand copies of all earlier examinations of his or her condition made by the DME examiner or any other examiner.[15] Earlier examinations may include candid reports that may have been generated when the claim was being investigated by the insurance carrier, some of which may be devastating to the defense and may provide information about the weaknesses of its case. Consideration must be given to this possibility by defense counsel prior to ordering a DME.

The Role of the LNC

Once the LNC understands the legal requirements relating to DMEs, the role of the LNC "designated observer" should become clear. However, attorneys and clients may not always specify what they expect of the LNC. It is the responsibility of the LNC to determine the expectations of the client for each examination observed.

Guidelines

The following suggestions and guidelines may help to prepare the LNC who is asked to attend and observe a DME.

The details of the case may be discussed with the plaintiff's attorney so that the LNC is familiar with the site of the body to be examined, the date of loss, prior treatment, whether the plaintiff can complete any paperwork at the request of the examining physician or the physician's staff, etc. A copy of the response to the stipulation, demand, or court order may be taken to the DME. It is also helpful to have a copy of the appropriate statute or case law that permits the LNC's attendance at the examination if the physician examiner refuses to allow the LNC in the room during the examination. (Many physicians who perform these examinations are not aware of the laws governing DMEs.)

Prior to the examination, the LNC should clarify the plaintiff attorney's expectations for his or her participation in the DME, since expectations may differ among attorneys. He or she should clarify in advance with the attorney and client whether an additional report is required, other than the detailed account of events and the audiotape. If so, the LNC should submit all requested work product and the audiotape with the billing statement.

The LNC should have a clear understanding of the type of examination appropriate for the body site to be examined and the injury that will be evaluated during the DME. If unsure, the LNC should research in advance specific examination techniques and evaluative methods likely to be employed.

Establish a set time to meet the plaintiff at the examiner's office prior to the examination. The LNC should plan to arrive at the examiner's office before the plaintiff arrives; generally, 15 minutes prior to the examination time is sufficient. The LNC should ask the plaintiff's attorney to instruct his or her client not to agree to enter an examination room prior to the arrival of the LNC (if the plaintiff arrives at the examiner's office prior to the established meeting time).

The plaintiff and the LNC should converse briefly outside the examiner's office and make introductions if this is their initial meeting. The case should not be discussed. The attorney should have told the plaintiff that a registered nurse would attend and observe the examination as the attorney's representative.

The examiner is generally limited to the injury in question, and prior medical history is usually off limits. The plaintiff should be made aware of this so that prior medical history is not offered inadvertently. The physician is not expected to ask questions about how the accident occurred, such as "how fast were you going," which would reflect on liability issues in question.

Although the plaintiff should be prepared for the DME by the attorney (some use pamphlets or videotapes), the LNC should remind the plaintiff that the insurance carrier has retained the doctor to find a lack of injury or full recovery, if at all possible. The LNC should remind the patient that if any part of the examination hurts, he or she should say so aloud and not assume that the doctor is watching for facial expressions or other nonverbal signs of discomfort. The LNC and plaintiff should be aware that the office receptionist may have been asked by the physician to observe the plaintiff's actions and behavior in the reception area to determine whether they are different from those observed in the examining room. The office staff may have been asked to observe the plaintiff's gait, ability to open doors or utilize waiting-room reading material, and demeanor upon entering the office, while waiting, and when leaving the examination site.

In most cases, the LNC will be asked to keep a detailed written account and time log of what occurs from the time the plaintiff arrives until he or she leaves the office. This should include any time spent filling out forms in the waiting room prior to the examination (not allowed by most plaintiff attorneys), sitting in the waiting room, having x-rays taken or blood drawn (if authorized), being escorted to the examining room, and waiting in the examining room; time that the examiner or any staff members enter or exit the examining room; a detailed account of what transpires in the examining room; and anything that happens once the examination is completed prior to leaving the office. If the examiner exits the room for any reason, exit and reentry times should also be recorded. The times of commencement and completion of the examination are of specific importance to the attorney. When the examiner enters the room, the LNC should politely introduce himself or herself as a representative of the attorney who retained his or her services. Family members who have accompanied the plaintiff to the examination may be invited into the examination room by the patient. They should be instructed not to interfere or participate in the examination unless they are consulted directly. An exception to this rule may be made if the family member is needed to translate.

If the examiner has any dispute concerning the LNC's presence during the examination, what is disallowed in that particular case (such as intrusive tests or x-rays), or audiotaping — and the LNC does not have a copy of the response to the stipulation, demand, or court order — the prudent way to handle such a situation is to call the plaintiff's attorney and to suggest that the examiner contact the defense counsel who retained the examiner's services. In most cases, the problem is simply a lack of communication or knowledge of the law that can be clarified with a telephone call, if necessary.

If the examiner will not conduct the examination with the LNC present, the LNC should suspend the examination and call the plaintiff's attorney directly for instructions as to how to proceed. The LNC should not leave the patient and the examiner alone in the examining room to make the phone call. Physicians have been known to proceed with their examinations in the absence of the LNC, regardless of agreement to wait for response from the attorney. The plaintiff's attorney will often instruct the LNC to terminate the examination and to leave the examination site with the plaintiff immediately.

The LNC should be unobtrusive during the examination. The observer is generally not permitted to interfere with the examination unless the examiner is abusive to the patient, examines sites that are not a subject of the litigation, causes the patient unnecessary pain, or follows a line of questioning that is not permitted. If any of these occurs, the LNC may bring this to the examiner's attention and may be permitted to suspend the examination and leave with the plaintiff. The plaintiff's attorney should be notified immediately.

Observations

Depending on the type of examination, observations may include:

The Patient

- Use of any assistive devices (crutches, cane, walker, wheelchair)
- Gait (slow, antalgic, limp)
- Limitation of movements
- Ability to tolerate sitting (duration without position changes)
- Position changes (frequency)
- Grimacing or verbal responses during examination
- Degree of effort expended during active range of motion, resistance testing, pushes and pulls, and other active portions of the exam
- Clothing worn
- Visible scars in area of injury

The Examiner

- Interaction with patient
- Examination technique (gentle, moderate, or forceful palpation)
- Components of examination
- Use of examination tools (reflex hammer, pinwheel, dynamometer, etc.)
- Presence of medical records or x-rays in the examination room (does the examiner indicate whether they were reviewed prior to the exam?)

"I Couldn't See a Thing!" and Other Pitfalls

The LNC may encounter numerous pitfalls when accompanying a patient to a DME. The physician may not let the LNC attend the examination at all, or he or she may make every effort to block the LNC's view of the patient during the physical examination. In the worst case, the LNC may need to contact the attorney and terminate the examination. At best, the report of the evaluation should reflect the examiner's efforts to be obstructive.

A hostile doctor is generally not a new phenomenon for a professional nurse. A hostile patient may be more problematic. A patient who curses at the doctor may need the LNC to intercede and strongly suggest alternative behavior. Ideally, issues of anger, hostility, and decorum are addressed with the plaintiff by the attorney client and LNC observer prior to the actual examination.

More anticipated difficulties relate to the initial problems of taking notes, checking the time, listening, writing, and observing simultaneously. If a battery-powered tape recorder is used, the clarity of the recording should be checked before leaving the LNC's office to be sure that the batteries are strong. Bringing extra tapes and batteries to the examination is a good idea.

Given time, the professional nurse will develop her own style, and the facility of multitasking improves considerably with experience. The community of physicians who perform DMEs is relatively small, and over time, each one's style will be apparent to the LNC. With familiarity, the LNC will become more proficient.

Report Preparation

The LNC should not be expected to be a stenographer who takes verbatim notes throughout the examination. However, with practice, the LNC should be able to record contemporaneous notes that reflect the substance of the history portion of the examination and the elements of the physical examination, along with a time log of events as they take place. One way to record notes is to take several pages of blank paper on a clipboard to the exam. The history can be recorded on a page divided from top to bottom by a line. The LNC notes the physician's question in the left column and the patient's response on the right, making sure to number the pages. It is highly advisable to write the report of the examination the same day as it takes place in order to ensure that recall can assist in deciphering notes taken during the examination.

The format of the report should be consistent from one DME to the next. This ensures that the attorney client will understand what to expect of the report when he or she retains an LNC to accompany the client to a medical examination. The report should be arranged chronologically, reflecting the notes as they were taken. See Appendix 29.1 for a sample report. If the examination was audiotaped, the tapes should be submitted with the written report. The attorney's secretary is more likely to be proficient at transcription, so the LNC should not spend time or the attorney's money attempting to transcribe the audiotape verbatim.

Billing Considerations

The LNC may charge either an hourly fee for services rendered or a flat fee. Fees should allow for travel time, waiting time, observing the examination, and report preparation. A policy regarding "no-shows" and "same-day cancellations" must also be considered. The fee schedule and terms of payment should be clarified with the attorney client prior to the examination. Formal written contracts between the attorney and the LNC and retainer requirements are discretionary.

It is courteous, and good business, to clarify with the plaintiff's attorney in advance how the LNC should handle excessive waiting time at the examiner's office. If the attorney does not provide time parameters, it is courteous to call the attorney after waiting more than 30 minutes beyond the scheduled appointment time. The LNC's time is the client's money. Openly acknowledging that fact helps to ensure goodwill and future business.

Benefits of Using an LNC

Traditionally, plaintiff attorneys have attended DMEs themselves or sent a paralegal or secretary to observe the examination. In order to market this service effectively, the LNC should be prepared to explain the advantages of using a nurse. The LNC should emphasize that the plaintiff is apt to be more comfortable with a nurse than with a nonmedical person. A nurse can assist the plaintiff with changing into an examination gown and redressing without embarrassment.

A nurse is considerably more familiar with a medical environment than a nonmedical observer and often creates rapport that may not occur between medical and legal professionals. More important, a nurse is knowledgeable about what should be included in the examination of various body parts and may therefore be able to alert plaintiff's counsel (verbally) to important omissions in the examination. The nurse may also be able to detect whether or not a particular part of the examination is performed correctly.

An example of an important observation by a nurse that may not have been noticed by a nonmedical person occurred in a case in which the physician examiner repeatedly asked his office nurse for a Jamar dynamometer to test a patient's grip strength. When he was unable to find the device he sought, he used a bulb dynamometer instead. The LNC was able to note the use of the alternative device in her report — and to testify later as to the specific device used, even though the physician had documented that he made his measurements with a Jamar dynamometer.

An independent LNC may testify at trial regarding the report generated from the examination and about any discrepancies between his or her report and that of the examiner. Because the LNC's compensation is not dependent upon the outcome of the litigation, his or her report and testimony are more credible.

Court Testimony Relating to DMEs

When testifying about observations at a DME, the role of the LNC is to serve as a fact witness, not an expert witness. The testimony must relate to specific observations contained in the original report, unless the specific examination at issue is clearly recalled. The LNC may be asked specific questions regarding the length of the examination or particular observations made during the physical examination. Sometimes, the LNC is asked to read his or her report into the record verbatim. The LNC is expected to describe the events that took place, not to judge the examination. During testimony, the LNC will often be told what the examiner reported that conflicted with the LNC's report. Argument is the purview of the attorneys. It is the LNC's job to report only what he or she saw and heard.

Conclusion

The goal of a DME should be to obtain objective, accurate information about the patient's physical or mental status at the time of the examination relating to the subject injury that can be used to effect a fair settlement or verdict. Regrettably, some examiners' reports reflect some bias. For this reason, many attorneys now retain LNCs to assess, observe, monitor, and report detailed objective information to facilitate the accurate disposition of a case.

References

1. *Mercury Gas. Co. v. Sup. Ct. (Garcia)*, supra, 179 CA3d at 1033, 225 CR at 103, 1985.
2. CCP Section 2032(c)(1)(2).
3. CCP Section 2032(c)(2).
4. CCP Section 2032(a).
5. CCP Section 2032(b).
6. *Reuter v. Sup. Ct.*, 98 CA3d 610, 615, 159 CR 669, 672, 1979.
7. CCP Section 2032(d).
8. *Vinson v. Sup. Ct. (Peralta Comm. College Dist.)*, 43 C3d 833, 840, 239, CR 292, 297, 1987.
9. *Shapira v. Sup. Ct. (Sylvestri)*, 224 CA3d 1249, 1255, 274 CR 516, 5169, 1990.
10. *Vinson v. Sup. Ct. (Peralta Comm. College Dist.)*, supra, 43 C3d at 840, 239 CR at 298, 1987.
11. CCP Section 2032(g)(1).
12. *Sharff v. Sup. Ct.*, 44 C2d 508, 510, 282 P2d 896, 897, 1955.
13. Ev.C. Section 755.5(a).
14. *Edwards v. Sup. Ct.*, supra.
15. CCP Section 2032(h).

Additional Reading

Iyer, P., The malingering plaintiff, *Journal of Legal Nurse Consulting*, 11, 3, 2000.

Pollock, D.A., The LNC's vital role in a defense medical examination, *Journal of Legal Nurse Consulting*, 11, 8, 2000.

Seidel, H.M. et al., *Mosby's Guide to Physical Examination*, Mosby-Year Book, Inc., St. Louis, 1998.

Skidmore-Roth Publishing, *Expert 10-Minute Physical Examinations,* 1st ed., Mosby-Yea Book, Inc., St. Louis, July 1997.

Swartz, M.H., *Textbook of Physical Diagnosis: History and Examination*, W.B. Saunders, Philadelphia, 2001.

Wood, B.A., Legal and ethical considerations of patient/provider communications, *Journal of Legal Nurse Consulting*, 12, 10, 2001.

Test Questions

1. The purpose of a DME is
   A. To give the defense an opportunity to evaluate the plaintiff's claims of injury, illness, or incapacity
   B. To determine the impact of preexisting illnesses of injuries on the subject complaints and claims
   C. To allow the plaintiff to prove that he or she is injured
   D. To show the client that his or her attorney is earning his fee

2. Which of the following is not part of the LNC's role at a DME?
   A. To determine whether an adequate exam is performed
   B. To ensure that the examiner does not abuse the client
   C. To ensure that no x-rays of diagnostic tests are performed unless they have been agreed to previously
   D. To determine the opinion of the examiner with regard to the plaintiff's diagnosis and treatment

3. Which of the following would an LNC NOT be allowed to do at a DME?
   A. Audiotape the exam
   B. Videotape the exam
   C. Question the examiner about omissions in the examination performed
   D. Assist the patient with removing his or her shoes and socks

4. A potential disadvantage to the defense attorney who orders a DME is that
   A. The examination may be videotaped by the opposing party
   B. The examiner's findings and report may be detrimental to the defense of the case
   C. The patient may divulge the circumstances of the injury
   D. The LNC is considered to be an expert witness for the plaintiff

5. If the physician refuses to have the LNC observe the examination, the LNC should
   A. Leave the office without the plaintiff
   B. Call the defense attorney to explain why the LNC is allowed to be present
   C. Cancel the examination and leave with the plaintiff
   D. Call the plaintiff attorney from the examining room to explain the resistance that is being encountered

Answers: 1. A, 2. D, 3. C, 4. B, 5. D

Appendix 29.1
Orthopaedic "DME" Sample Report

12/21/01

John Doe, Esquire
123 Main Street
Anytown, New York 12345

RE: John Smith

Dear Mr. Doe:

On December 21, 2001, I accompanied your client, John Smith, to his scheduled 1:00 p.m. defense medical evaluation with James Jones, M.D., at General Hospital Medical Arts Building, Rm. 110, 100 E. First Avenue, Your Town, NY. The following is a report of the evaluation.

Mr. Smith was present in the waiting room when I arrived at 12:30 p.m. He was called to the examination room by the office receptionist at 1:16 p.m. Dr. Jones arrived at 1:18 p.m., introduced himself, and commenced the history portion of the evaluation immediately.

Mr. Smith confirmed his age of 73 years and that he is right-handed. Mr. Smith said that he is a retired postal worker. In response to Dr. Jones' question, Mr. Smith said that he was injured on 02/15/00, when he fell on a patch of ice. Mr. Smith said that he hurt his right wrist and the left side of his back, and that he cut his head. Mr. Smith confirmed being unemployed at the time of the accident. Mr. Smith said that he went to the emergency room at General Hospital.

When asked about his treatment, Mr. Smith said that Dr. Williams was his treating physician and that he was discharged from his care in July 2001. He said that Dr. Williams inserted an internal fixator into his right arm. Mr. Smith said that he was also referred to General Hospital from ABC Rehabilitation Center regarding the dermatitis on his right forearm. He said that he was also treated at General Hospital for varicose veins.

Mr. Smith related that he had broken his right arm as a child and is hyperglycemic, but not diabetic. He said that he is otherwise in good health, takes no medications, does not smoke, and has had no other accidents or surgeries. In response to Dr. Jones' questions, Mr. Smith said that he is 5 feet, 11 inches tall and weighs 180 pounds.

When questioned about current symptoms, Mr. Smith said that he has trouble rotating his right wrist and closing his right hand completely. He said that the strength in his right wrist is decreased; and although the pain in his shoulder has greatly improved, he still experiences difficulty in raising his right arm completely. Mr. Smith said that he cannot bear weight on his right arm or wrist, and he offered the example of lifting himself out of bed. Mr. Smith said that his back has healed completely, and the dermatitis, resulting from the use of the machines from ABC Rehabilitation Center, healed when therapy was completed. Mr. Smith responded affirmatively when asked whether he currently does home exercises.

Dr. Jones concluded the history portion of the evaluation at 1:30 p.m. and instructed Mr. Smith to remove his outer shirt and T-shirt. Dr. Jones returned at 1:32 p.m. and commenced the physical examination immediately.

Dr. Jones measured both forearms without comment. He tested tip-to-tip prehension by asking Mr. Smith to bring his right thumb into opposition with the other five fingers. Mr. Smith performed this maneuver without difficulty. Dr. Jones tested the grips of both hands using three widths without comment.

Cervical range of motion was assessed and appeared to be full and painless in flexion, extension, and rotation. The foramina compression test was performed with Mr. Smith bending his head to both sides and applying pressure. Mr. Smith denied pain bilaterally with this maneuver. Lumbosacral flexion was performed and appeared full and painless.

Manual muscle testing of the deltoids, biceps, triceps, and fingers was performed. The right arm appeared noticeably weaker with testing. Mr. Smith complained of soreness with testing of the right deltoid. With Mr. Smith's hands in supination, Dr. Jones asked that he abduct and adduct his wrists bilaterally. Mr. Smith exhibited difficulty with abduction and adduction of his right wrist. The Phalen's, Reverse Phalen's, and Tinel's tests were performed bilaterally with negative results.

With Mr. Smith seated on the edge of the examination table, knee extension was performed with no apparent gross weakness noted and no complaints offered. Mr. Smith was wearing TED stockings to control his varicosities. Shoulder range of motion was assessed and appeared full and painless in overhead extension and elevation through forward flexion. Dr. Jones assessed medial rotation and adduction and lateral rotation and abduction by requesting that Mr. Smith touch his hands behind his head and to his lower back. Range of motion in these areas was limited. Mr. Smith complained of pain with both of these maneuvers. Mr. Smith was asked to draw circles in the air with both arms, which he did without difficulty. Mr. Smith was then asked to touch his hands to his shoulders bilaterally. He seemed to experience difficulty touching his right hand to his right shoulder.

The deep tendon reflexes of the upper extremities (biceps, triceps) were tested with positive results. Dr. Jones checked the radial pulses without comment. Mr. Smith denied pain with palpation of both wrists.

Dr. Jones measured the distance between the thumbs and forefingers bilaterally without comment. Dr. Jones also measured the angles of the fingers bilaterally when at rest and when bent at the joints and knuckles. Dr. Jones assessed movements of the fingers by asking Mr. Smith to open and close his fingers and to cross his fingers. Mr. Smith complained of soreness in his right fingers with these movements.

Dr. Jones concluded the physical examination at 1:52 p.m. and left the examination room. Mr. Smith redressed, and he and I left the doctor's office together at 2:00 p.m.

Thank you for using the services of LNC DME, Inc.

Very truly yours,

Mary Smythe, RN, LNCC
Legal Nurse Consultant

RESPONSIBILITIES OF THE LEGAL NURSE CONSULTANT

Chapter 30

Legal Writing

Kevin Dubose, JD

CONTENTS

Objectives

- To describe the philosophical reasons for clearer, crisper writing
- To give four principles of clearer, crisper writing
- To write more clearly and concisely
- To provide clients with a more valuable work product

Why "Legal Writing" Is a Misnomer

The label "legal writing" suggests that writing by and for lawyers is different from other writing, and that it comes with its own rules, stylistic conventions, and expectations. Approaching legal writing with a different mind-set undoubtedly contributes to the stilted, convoluted, jargon-laden prose that we have come to recognize as legalese.

Legal writing does not have to be different from any other writing. The only thing that distinguishes legal writing from other writing is the subject matter, not the style. Writers who assume a different and unnatural voice in an attempt to "sound like a lawyer" rarely write with clarity and grace. The writer should strive to communicate clearly and concisely, not to sound like a lawyer.

Writers Should Consider Their Audience and Their Purpose

The sole goal of writing is communication. Communication is not a self-indulgent process in which writers merely disgorge information. Rather, communication must include both transmission and reception. Writing without regard for the audience is like shooting an arrow into the air and hoping that someone will run underneath it with a bull's-eye. Good communicators always present information with the audience and the purpose of the communication firmly in mind.

Potential Audiences for LNCs

Legal nurse consultants (LNCs) should pay particular attention to the sophistication of their audience in two areas: law and medicine. Some audiences have expertise in both law and medicine. This category includes attorneys who handle health law claims, expert witnesses with experience in the legal system, J.D.-M.D.s, J.D.-R.N.s, and other LNCs. Other audiences are familiar with the legal system but ignorant about medical matters. That group includes judges, attorneys, and legal assistants without experience in health law claims. Other audiences are well versed in medical matters, but inexperienced in legal proceedings. That group includes doctors and nurses without experience in the legal system. Finally, some audiences lack knowledge and sophistication in both law and medicine. This category includes nonmedical clients (usually plaintiffs), family members, and other nonmedical fact witnesses. Table 30.1 summarizes the potential audiences for LNCs' legal writing.

The writing style appropriate for these audiences varies considerably. The writer must assess the audience, and write on a level that is understandable to the audience, without talking down to it.

Potential Purposes for Writings by LNCs

Writers also must consider the purpose of the writing. Writing about legal matters serves one of four purposes:

- *Informative* writing transmits information to the reader. For LNCs, informative writing includes reports, memoranda, chart analyses, literature summaries, and reports evaluating the standard of care.

Table 30.1 Legal Nurse Consultant Writing Audiences

Type of Expertise	Audience
Expertise in law and medicine	Attorneys experienced in health care claims
	Expert witnesses with legal experience
	J.D.-M.D.s
	R.N.-J.D.s
Expertise in law, not medicine	Judges
	Attorneys without health care claim experience
	Legal assistants without health care claim experience
Expertise in medicine, not law	Doctors, nurses without legal experience
No expertise in law or medicine	Nonmedical clients
	Family members
	Nonmedical fact witnesses

- *Commemorative* writing records events. Medical chart notations and memoranda to document conversations are commemorative writings, as are summaries of client intake interviews and conferences with potential experts.
- *Inquisitive* writing poses questions. Inquisitive writings include interrogatories and requests for production.
- *Persuasive* writing tries to persuade. In litigation, persuasive writings include briefs, motions, and correspondence intended to induce settlement.

Table 30.2 provides examples of the four purposes of legal writing.

Writing style and substance vary tremendously depending on the purpose. For example, informative writing should be an objective, fair presentation of both sides; persuasive writing should be slanted in favor of the writer's position. Persuasive writing should be brief; inquisitive writing should be extremely thorough so that unasked questions do not result in withholding critical information.

No single method of writing is universally preferable. Rather, writers should be mindful of both audience and purpose, and choose a writing style that is appropriate for the circumstances.

For All Audiences and All Purposes, Writers Should Strive for Reader-Friendly Writing

Regardless of the purpose of the writing, the purpose cannot be achieved unless writers communicate to their readers. Communication is a difficult and uncertain art. However, writers greatly enhance the chance of communication when they make the reader's job easier.

Reasons for Reader-Friendly Writing

All readers engage in two activities: deciphering and comprehending. The deciphering function consists of determining what is being said and how it can be structured in a logical, absorbable framework. The comprehension function

Table 30.2   Purposes of Legal Writing

Purpose	Examples of LNC Legal Writings
Informative	Chart analysis, literature summary, compilation of injuries caused by a defective product
Commemorative	Client intake interview, conference with expert
Inquisitive	Interrogatories, requests for documents
Persuasive	Settlement brochures

consists of digesting what has been deciphered and responding to it. Readers have a fixed amount of time and energy. More time and energy spent on one activity reduces the time and energy available for other activities. Writers should want readers to spend their time and energy on comprehension. Accordingly, the goal of writers should be to minimize the time and energy required for deciphering, so that more time and energy can be devoted to the comprehension function.

Practically speaking, writers want to make a good impression on their readers, whether they are employers, expert witnesses, judges, or opposing counsel. Positive impressions are more likely if the reader does not have to spend time trying to glean the meaning of the writing. Readers who have to work hard are not favorably disposed to writers who place that burden on them. Accordingly, the goal of writers should be to make the reader's job easier.

Attributes of Reader-Friendly Writing

Brevity

Most readers would rather do something other than read legal writing. Judges, lawyers, doctors, and LNCs are all human beings with busy schedules, short attention spans, and limited tolerance for boredom. Readers appreciate writers who reduce the time required for reading. Necessary information should not be sacrificed for brevity. But unnecessary and redundant information should be ruthlessly trimmed so that the product is as short as possible.

Use short words, short sentences, and short paragraphs, and omit unnecessary words. Not only should the entire product be brief, but so should each of its components.

Short Words

Writing as if you have a thesaurus in one hand and a dictionary in the other is counterproductive. If writers use words that are unfamiliar to their readers, the readers must look them up in the dictionary (creating more work for readers), guess about their meaning (perhaps incorrectly), or just skip them without understanding them. Each of those consequences is unfavorable. Although the medical and legal professions are full of long, unfamiliar words that have no short, familiar substitute, writers should use shorter words when possible.

Short Sentences

Although it is possible to write clear sentences that happen to be lengthy, the possibilities for confusion and awkwardness increase when sentences get longer. Reading a sentence creates dynamic tension between writer and reader; if the tension is sustained for too long, the reader becomes uncomfortable and the ending is often disappointing. Sentences that exceed three or four lines should be carefully examined.

Short Paragraphs

Dynamic tension also applies to reading paragraphs. People like to receive information with an end in sight. When we read a book, we check to see how many pages it has. When we watch a television show, we check to see how long it lasts. When we read a paragraph, our eyes scan the left margin for the next indentation. Readers are disheartened when they see an entire page without paragraph breaks. Long paragraphs abuse the reader's patience and dissipate dynamic tension. Generally, shorter paragraphs are preferable.

Omit Unnecessary Words

Avoid expressions such as "ordered, adjudged, and decreed"; "if and when"; "null and void"; "save and except"; "each and every"; "aid and abet"; and "part and parcel." Do not use several words when one will do. Replace "in the event that" with "if"; replace "on or about" with "on"; replace "prior to" with "before"; replace "subsequent to" with "after"; and replace "for the reason that" with "because." Avoid two-word expressions when one word necessarily implies the other — e.g., "past history," "reason why," "mutual agreement," and "sum total."

Avoid meaningless modifiers, including adverbs used for effect that add nothing to the sentence's meaning. This list includes "actually," "basically," "essentially," and "generally." These words can be used meaningfully, but often are not.

Statements of Personal Belief

Be wary of beginning sentences with phrases such as "I believe ...," "it is my feeling that ...," and "it is our position that ..." These phrases should always be avoided in persuasive writing. First, it goes without saying that these statements are the writer's belief, feeling, or position. Second, the prefatory phrases weaken the statements that follow, making them sound tentative and uncertain. If writers are sure about their statements, they should make them directly, not qualify them or water them down by statements of personal belief. On the other hand, in informative and commemorative writing, LNCs sometimes are asked to provide personal impressions. In those situations, using a qualification of personal belief is appropriate. Nevertheless, statements of personal belief are overused and should be scrutinized to determine whether they are necessary and appropriate.

Clarity

Written communication is a miraculous process, even in the best of circumstances. Writers formulate initial ideas and then attempt to give form and expression to these amorphous concepts. Words are assembled and arranged on paper. Readers read those words and form their own ideas. The writer's goal should be for his or her original idea to be as close as possible to the idea ultimately formed in the mind of the reader. Most words in the English language have more than one meaning; when words are used in combination, the possible meanings increase geometrically. The fact that writers' ideas and readers' perceptions ever coincide is phenomenal.

Similarity between beginning and ending ideas is most likely to occur when writers communicate ideas as clearly as possible. Writers should strive to eliminate the potential for multiple meanings, misleading impressions, and confusion. Style and elegance should be sacrificed in favor of clarity.

Most writers are poor judges of the clarity of their own writing. They cannot fairly judge the mental impressions that their words generate in others because they are unavoidably reminded of their original ideas. The best way to evaluate the clarity of a piece of writing is to ask someone else to read it. Putting the work aside for a few days helps somewhat, but there is no substitute for a fresh pair of eyes brought to a writing effort.

Simplicity

Although simplicity is often related to clarity, the two are not synonymous. Complex ideas may be communicated clearly, and simple thoughts may be communicated in a manner that is unclear. As a general proposition, however, simple is more likely to be clear, and vice versa.

Complex and sophisticated concepts have no value if they cannot be communicated clearly to the most simpleminded member of the potential audience. At best, they are a waste of time. At worst, unfathomable concepts may frustrate and alienate the audience and be counterproductive. Complex writing makes the reader's job more difficult by making the reader spend more time and energy on deciphering, leaving less time and energy for comprehension. Writing should be so simple that the reader can read it once, put it down, and be able to explain what the writing was about. There are no stupid readers; there are only foolish writers who are unable or unwilling to communicate appropriately with their audience.

Structure

The human mind is incapable of processing and retaining unstructured information. If writers do not provide a structure that makes the information accessible, readers must do the work required to structure the information. Readers who do that extra work are resentful of the writer, and the opportunity to make a good impression has been squandered. Readers who are unwilling to do the work necessary to process the information allow it to pass quickly through their minds without perceiving or retaining it. The worst thing that a writer can do to a reader

Table 30.3 Attributes of Reader-Friendly Writing

Brevity	Use short words, sentences, paragraphs
	Omit unnecessary words
Clarity	Communicate the information clearly
Simplicity	Keep it simple
Structure	Prepare detailed outline
	Use headings, subheadings of outline in text

is to wander off in a rambling stream of consciousness, with no structure, order, or direction.

Effective structure requires two steps. First, writers should prepare a detailed outline before beginning to write. An outline forces writers to organize thoughts; it is probably a more important step in the creative process than translating those thoughts into prose. Although modifications may be necessary during the writing process, some form of structure must be maintained rigorously.

The second step to effectively structured writing is communicating the outline to the reader. There is no reason to be subtle or secretive about the outline. It should be communicated to the reader with headings, subheadings, boldfaced type, underscoring, enumeration, and any other type-style conventions to enhance the visual accessibility of the outline.

Table 30.3 summarizes the attributes of reader-friendly writing.

Reader-Friendly Writing Requires Rigorous Editing

Most writers do not write with brevity, clarity, simplicity, and structure in a first draft. These qualities are developed through rigorous editing, by primary writers and by others. Every paragraph, sentence, phrase, and word should be scrutinized to determine whether it is necessary, whether it is clear, and whether it could be stated more concisely. The timing of drafts and deadlines should allow ample time for editing, with as much time devoted to editing as the writer spent on the first draft. Good editing is hard work that takes a long time. It can make the difference between tolerable writing and great writing.

Reader-Friendly Writing Has Been Endorsed by the Bar

Suggestions for more user-friendly legal writing are not the pipe dreams of a few eccentric legal scholars who have fallen under the spell of the plain-language movement. Organized bar associations have endorsed these concepts. For example, the board of directors of the State Bar of Texas unanimously passed a resolution urging the members of that state to follow a "Charter for Plain Legal Writing," which contained the following suggestions:

- ■ Write simply. Never use a long word when a short one will do. Never use a Latin or French word when an English one will do. Avoid legal jargon and technical terms unless they are necessary.

- Omit needless words.
- Provide clear transitions from one idea to another.
- Generally, write sentences with an average of fewer than 20 words. Include only one main idea in a sentence.
- Prefer the active voice; that is, make sure that the subject of the sentence performs the action of the verb.
- Use concrete, specific words instead of abstract, general words.
- Make sure that each paragraph has a clear purpose, progresses logically, and contains one main thought.
- Use headings, lists, bullets, and ample spacing for appeal and clarity.
- Make sure that your documents are well organized, logical, accurate, and immediately comprehensible to the intended reader.
- Break a rule rather than say something silly.

Similarly, the Canadian Bar Association and the Canadian Banker's Association have drafted "The Ten Commandments for Plain Language Drafting":

- Consider your reader and write with that reader's viewpoint in mind.
- Write short sentences.
- Say what you have to say, and no more.
- Use the active voice.
- Use simple, "everyday" words.
- Use words consistently.
- Avoid strings of synonyms.
- Avoid unnecessary formality.
- Organize your text:
  - In a logical sequence;
  - With informative headings; and
  - With a table of contents for long documents.
- Make the document attractive and designed for easy reading.

These rules provide specific suggestions for achieving the qualities of reader-friendly writing articulated in this chapter: simplicity, clarity, brevity, and structure. Writing with those qualities in mind, and with an awareness of the audience and purpose, will make the product more reader-friendly and increase the likelihood of communication.

Additional Reading

Bouchoux, D.E., *Legal Research and Writing for Paralegals*, Aspen Publishers, Gaithersburg, MD, 1998.

Garner, B.A., *A Dictionary of Modern Legal Usage,* 2nd ed., Oxford University Press, New York, 1995.

Johns, M.Z., *Professional Writing for Lawyers*, Carolina Academic Press, Durham, NC, 1998.

LeClercq, T., *Guide to Legal Writing Style*, 2nd ed., Aspen Publishers, Gaithersburg, MD, 2000.

Stark, S.D., *Writing to Win: The Legal Writer*, Doubleday, New York, 1999.

Strunk, W., Jr., White, E.B., Osgood, C., and Angell, R., *The Elements of Style*, 4th ed., Macmillan, New York, 2000.

Test Questions

1. The most important goal of legal writing is
   A. To provide as much information as possible to the reader
   B. To entertain the reader with colorful language and imaginative prose
   C. To make the product easy for the reader to read and understand
   D. To provide tangible evidence of the work you've done

2. Which of the following phrases does not contain needless repetition?
   A. Each and every
   B. Dilation and curettage
   C. Aid and abet
   D. Past history

3. Which of the following statements accurately describes the relationship between the purpose of a piece of writing and the appropriate writing style?
   A. Informative writing should provide an objective, fair presentation of both sides.
   B. Commemorative writing should be as brief as possible.
   C. Inquisitive writing should be careful not to offend by asking for too much
   D. Persuasive writing should be lengthy and thorough to cover every possible angle.

4. Effective legal writing always requires
   A. A complex structure subtly embedded in the prose
   B. A liberal sprinkling of legal jargon so that it sounds like a lawyer
   C. Long words, long sentences, and long paragraphs
   D. Rigorous editing

5. Effective communication
   A. Depends on a reader's willingness to work hard to catch up with the writer's level of knowledge and experience
   B. Is impossible when the legal and medical fields intersect
   C. Depends on the writer's ability to express ideas in a manner appropriate and understandable to the audience.
   D. Is highly overrated.

Answers: 1. C, 2. B, 3. A, 4. D, 5. C

Chapter 31

Medical Record Analysis

Deborah D. D'Andrea, BSN, BA, RN,
Colleen D'Amico, BS, RN, and
Shirley Cantwell Davis, BSN, RN, LNCC

CONTENTS

0-8493-1418-6/03/$0.00+$1.50
© 2003 by AALNC

Objectives

- To list three types of medical records that may not be produced in response to a request for complete medical records and discuss why this may occur
- To outline the key points to be assessed in a complete review of an operative record
- To identify two types of altered records and five ways whereby the legal nurse consultant can detect alterations
- To discuss the various kinds of medical record summaries that a legal nurse consultant can perform and the advantages of each type of summary
- To describe two examples of common pitfalls in medical record analysis

Introduction

The American Association of Legal Nurse Consultants (AALNC) has defined the primary role of the legal nurse consultant (LNC) to be the evaluation, analysis, and rendering of informed opinions on the delivery of health care and the resulting outcomes. This is accomplished in part by reviewing, summarizing, and analyzing medical records and other pertinent health care and legal documents and comparing them to and correlating them with the allegations of the complaint.[1] Medical record analysis has been the foundation of legal nurse consulting practice since the profession first emerged.

Attorneys have no formal training regarding medical record analysis and rely heavily on LNCs to review and interpret medical records. Because of the complexity of medically related litigation today, it is essential that thorough medical record analysis be accomplished by all LNCs. Small but highly significant details can be overlooked, with potentially disastrous results during discovery and at trial.

Compilation of Complete Medical Records

Determine Allegations of Case and Disputed Medical-Legal Issues

The *AALNC Standards of Legal Nurse Consulting Practice* state that assessment of the issues is the first step in approaching any medical-legal case. The LNC collects data to support the systematic assessment of health care issues related to a case or claim.[2]

It is essential, before he or she begins to collect data and review any medical records, that the LNC understand the plaintiff's complaints regarding the subject injuries and the plaintiff's perception of how a particular injury occurred. If the case is in litigation, it is important to understand the specific allegations of the complaint.

Example 31.1: In reviewing the case of potential brain damage, caused by beta streptococcal disease, to a preterm infant, an LNC may ascertain the plaintiff's allegations to be that:

1. The physician negligently failed to admit the mother without signs of labor despite the fact that the membranes had ruptured;
2. The physician negligently failed to respond to fetal distress in a timely manner; and
3. The nurses negligently failed to interpret the fetal heart monitor strips appropriately and notify a physician in a timely manner.

Once the medical-legal issues have been determined, it will become clear which medical records are needed to make a thorough and complete evaluation of the case.

The LNC, at a minimum, would then collect the medical records related to the birth of the baby, including the obstetrical records of the pregnancy; all hospital records related to all hospital admissions for preterm complications and the actual labor and delivery; all fetal monitor strips (including nonstress and stress tests) for all admissions; records of the initial hospitalization of the baby; any emergency medical services (EMS) transport records of the baby to a tertiary institution; and the hospital records of the tertiary institution together with the office records of the baby's pediatrician, pediatric neurologist, and rehabilitation practitioners. An additional interview with the mother may reveal that several phone calls were made to the obstetrician that were not returned, that the mother had a history of positive beta Streptococcus cultures at 26 weeks, and that she had preterm labor with her previous children. This would prompt the LNC to follow up by obtaining the medical records from the obstetricians and hospitals concerning her previous deliveries. Once litigation is pending, the LNC would advise the attorney to serve a request for production of documents to include copies of the logs of the physician's phone-answering service.

Compile Complete Medical Records

The medical record must be complete, accurate, and authenticated before it can be introduced into evidence in most instances. All states have statutes regarding medical record maintenance, and failure to comply can be grounds for loss of hospital accreditation. Civil liability may also be found against a hospital for breach of duty to maintain accurate records.[3] The Joint Commission on Accreditation of Healthcare Organizations (JCAHO) regulations require prompt completion of records not to exceed 30 days after the discharge of patients. This time period is spelled out in the medical staff rules and regulations.[4] Persistent failure to complete records by hospital staff members may be used as a basis for suspension of those staff members.[3]

When requesting medical records, it is always wise to ask for a certified copy of each medical record. Hospitals and other health care organizations ideally should have a health information management administrator who is licensed by the American Health Information Management Association as a registered record administrator (RRA) in charge of the medical records.[3] The RRA will certify the accuracy and completeness of the copies of the original records. Often, the LNC will have to supply a physician or other health care provider with a fill-in-the-blank certification when requesting medical records, since many health care providers do not have an official records administrator and are not used to certifying copies of their medical records. See Appendix 31.1.

Note that although the health care organization has certified that the record is a true and complete copy of the original document, the LNC should never assume that this is true. Two-sided forms may not have been completely copied. Portions of the record may have been removed or not included at the time of the copy request. An index of suspicion should be maintained, particularly in the LNC's analysis of medical malpractice claims.

Records That May Not Be Produced as Part of the Medical Records

A number of additional types of medical records may or may not be included in a response to a request for medical records. The LNC should specifically request the following types of records by name to ensure their production.

Fetal Heart Monitor Strips

Fetal heart monitor strips are electronic transcriptions of medical information and are considered to be part of the medical record of the mother of the fetus. Failure of a health care provider to produce fetal heart monitor strips can be considered spoliation of evidence.

The LNC should specifically request fetal heart monitor strips for all admissions in obstetrical cases because their bulky configuration and odd size necessitate that they often be stored separately from the medical records. This is particularly true of antepartum testing strips, which usually remain in the labor and delivery suite for comparison when the patient returns for delivery at a later date.

Radiographic Films

When evaluating any case involving critical radiographic films, the LNC should always obtain copies of those films early in the litigation, preferably prior to litigation in a plaintiff's case, in case original copies are misplaced or lost. Loss of original films does not always imply that there was harmful intent to cover up or obscure evidence. Many types of radiographic films, such as CT, MRI, and PET scans, are stored on computer disks. Real-time echocardiograms, angiograms, and ultrasounds are also kept on tape, and copies can be obtained.

The LNC will often find that radiograph copies are of insufficient quality to provide an accurate interpretation by an outside radiologist. Health care facilities may provide original x-rays to patients if certain conditions are met, but infrequently to LNCs and attorneys. If a case is in litigation, original films may be produced by agreement of counsel or by subpoena. It is essential that the LNC have a precise way of tracking the receipt, storage, and transmittal of original films and other evidence. Loss of a film has profoundly affected more than one medical malpractice case.

Sometimes medical records generated by a radiological procedure that may be very helpful in determining facts about a patient's care are kept separate from the permanent medical record. A good example is the history and physical (H&P) exam done by a radiologist or radiology technician during a breast exam. The LNC will have to specifically request copies of this information directly from the radiology department.

Radiographic file folders that are normally used to store films may be another frequently overlooked source of important information. In addition to demographic information, such as the patient's name and address, these file jackets may also contain the patient's complaints, the date and time that the films were taken, and the radiology technician's name.

Videotapes or Photographic Documentation of Surgical Procedures or Deliveries

It is important to look for evidence in the medical records that suggests that videotaping was done or photographs were taken. If the case is in litigation, specific questions can be asked in the interrogatories about taping or photographs. Frequently the surgeon, not the hospital, keeps these photos or videotapes. The plaintiff may possess such documentation — e.g., a videotape of an exploratory laparoscopy — even though there is no written evidence that videotapes or photographs exist. Cardiopulmonary bypass monitoring records and flowsheets may not automatically become part of the medical record. If a cardiopulmonary bypass procedure was performed, these records may require a special request to the cardiac or radiology department.

Videotapes of surgical procedures are considered part of the patient's medical record. The health care organization is obligated to retain these tapes. However, the LNC should be alert to the fact that the surgeon may ask the operating room staff to turn off the video camera when difficulties are encountered. The surgical expert witness retained by the attorney may be able to spot the omitted segment. Videotapes of deliveries may be retained by the parents and can be useful in determining what occurred during key moments of the delivery.

EMS Transport Records

In many states the law requires that a health care facility release only records generated as a result of the care and treatment rendered at that particular facility. Thus, records from a previous treating facility and emergency-transport or ambulance records may not be released as part of the hospital medical record and have to be requested separately from the specific facility or EMS. The LNC should identify whether both a first aid or basic life support (BLS) squad and a mobile intensive care unit (MICU) treated the patient. Each record should be obtained. In a motor vehicle accident, or other instances in which the police are involved, the police report should be obtained because it may contain valuable information about the patient.

Autopsy Records

Even if a patient has died during a hospitalization, the hospital record may be considered complete by the medical records department without the autopsy results. This is especially true if the autopsy was performed outside the hospital at the medical examiner's or coroner's office. If the death is unexplained or occurs within 24 hours of admission, it may automatically become a "coroner's case." The LNC should request the original microscopic slides or recuts of the originals for outside pathological interpretation when the cause of death is in question, or if the patient had recent surgery. It can take several months to obtain the autopsy report, particularly when specimens are sent to special laboratories for analysis or are examined for toxicology results.

Billing Records

Billing records are helpful in determining the type of equipment used in a patient's care, what medications were given, and many other details of the care and treatment. Billing records can be of extreme importance, especially when the LNC suspects that an unfavorable laboratory result has been removed from the medical record. The LNC should check the billing records to determine whether the charge for laboratory testing was ever billed to the patient.

Example 31.2: In one case, the allegation was that the nurse had punctured the rectum during the negligent insertion of a rectal tube. After the insertion of the rectal tube the plaintiff developed peritonitis and sepsis and ultimately expired. Upon review of the medical records there was no indication in the physician's orders, physician's notes, or nursing notes that a rectal tube had been recommended and ordered by the physician or placed by the nursing staff. The hospital denied that this procedure had even been ordered or carried out. However, the itemized hospital billing record revealed that the plaintiff had been charged for the rectal tube and drainage bag on the date that the family stated that this procedure had been performed.

Records from Reference Laboratories

Occasionally a specimen is sent to an outside laboratory for testing, and the test result is sent back to the hospital after the patient is discharged. As a consequence, the results may not be contained in the chart.

Drugstore Pharmaceutical Records

Most drugstores that sell pharmaceuticals to the public keep track of all medication records by computer. These records, which are usually generated in chronological order, are invaluable when drug history is an essential part of a case (such as a pharmaceutical product liability case), or when there are allegations that the plaintiff was seeking drugs as part of a substance-abuse problem.

The following information, though not specifically a part of the medical record, is part of the hospital or health care documentation; it is available to plaintiffs or third-party defendants only by request for production of documents after a case is in litigation. Defense attorneys exhibit great resistance to supplying these logs, primarily because of concerns about confidentiality of the other patients involved. Understandably, the hospital or institution may insist that the names of the other patients be omitted for patient confidentiality prior to the release of the various logs to the plaintiff or the defendant.

Operating Room Logs

Operating room (OR) logs often include vital information concerning not only the plaintiff, but also other types of operations that occurred simultaneously in the OR suite during the plaintiff's operation. They may also contain clues to the availability of staff. For instance, if the plaintiff alleges that an anesthesiologist was overseeing too many operations during the subject time period, the OR logs may be able to clarify the situation for both sides.

Emergency Room Logs

Emergency room (ER) logs are very similar to OR logs. Such information as the time patients come into and are discharged from the ER is recorded. Like OR logs, ER logs can provide vital information regarding the plaintiff and the other types of patients and their diagnoses on the date in question. For example, in a case in which the plaintiff alleges damages due to delay in treatment by the emergency department staff, the hospital defense team may be able to use the ER log to prove the existence of an unusual patient acuity situation, e.g., several trauma patients or full cardiopulmonary arrests during the time period in question.

Laboratory Logs

Most laboratories use computers to monitor when certain tests were run and when the results were available to the health care providers. Laboratory logs often include information regarding nonroutine test results that may not be contained in the medical records because the results were not available prior to the printing of the final cumulative laboratory summary results. Sometimes when the results become available, the cumulative summary is not reprinted or an updated report is not sent to medical records. The pathology department personnel often maintain notebooks and autopsy photographs. Radiotherapy departments may also keep separate log-in records and information about medication dosage charts for their cancer patients.

Hospital Pharmaceutical Records

Hospital pharmacies are required by law to keep records of controlled substances. In cases involving narcotic administration, when there is a dispute over amounts of drugs given, copies of the records reflecting distribution of a controlled substance should be kept by hospital pharmacies.

Records of HIV Testing

The physician's order for an HIV test and the result of the testing itself are confidential and cannot be obtained with a standard medical release (see Chapter 2).

Monitor Tapes

Most electrocardiogram (EKG) monitor strips are retained within the medical records, although some hospitals may keep the monitor strips in other departments, such as cardiology and respiratory therapy departments. In a case in which the plaintiff alleges damages due to an unrecognized and untreated or inappropriately treated cardiac event, the EKG strips can be instrumental in the case determination. Efforts should be made to obtain legible copies of these printouts.

Specialty Procedures Reports and Films

During specialty procedures (usually performed in the cardiac catheterization laboratory or in the invasive radiology department) — such as cardiac catheterization, angioplasty, echocardiography, intracardiac electrophysiology, arterial or venous angiograms and arteriograms, and arterial stent placement — dictated reports as well as films or tapes are generated. Frequently the films and tapes are maintained not by the medical records department but by the cardiology department or radiology department. Requests for such documents or films must be made directly to the appropriate department.

Neonatal Transfer Reports

When testing procedures are performed on a critical newborn, the test results are frequently not available at the time of the transfer to a tertiary-care center. The test results may require a special request that states specifically that the tests were completed immediately prior to the transfer. A second request for production of medical records may be necessary in order to obtain a complete record.

Specialty Testing

Specialty testing that may not be contained within the normal medical records includes neuropsychology testing, audiology testing, and speech and language testing. The reports and testing results can be requested from the individual departments.

Biomedical Equipment Records and Logs

In cases that involve medical equipment, hospital records often identify the equipment involved. Hospitals maintain equipment information, such as the model number, serial number, and the manufacturer's name, address, and phone number. Equipment-repair log sheets or maintenance records may reflect that a specific piece of equipment had a history of problems. These records are usually maintained by the biomedical or engineering department.

Example 31.3: In one case, the claim was based on the nurse's failure to adequately monitor a patient who was injured by the malfunction of a mechanized bed. The records of the biomedical department reflected that the day before the alleged injury, the bed had been removed from one unit for repairs. How and why this specific bed ended up in another unit the next day and was involved in a patient injury remains a mystery, according to defense counsel.

Medical Records Dictation Logs

Most hospital medical records departments have a telephone dictation system or outside dictation service. In these systems, the time and date are automatically recorded at the time of the dictation. If the dictation does not go through a telephone system but is placed onto individual tapes that are dropped off in the medical record transcription department, these tapes are listed on a log sheet indicating the date and time received. These logs also contain information pertaining to the date and time of the transcription and the identification of the transcriptionist.

If there is a discrepancy between the injuries documented on an autopsy report and the type and extent of injuries documented on the emergency room physician's report and/or discharge summary, the log in the medical record department can confirm whether the dictation took place.

Example 31.4: A 51-year-old woman was admitted to the emergency department with complaints of sudden onset of left-sided chest pain that had been occurring for approximately two hours prior to the admission. She also related experiencing a fall three days prior to the admission. She was discharged home with a diagnosis of chest wall pain. Approximately ten hours later she was readmitted in full cardiac arrest and was pronounced dead. The medical records that were sent to the local medical examiner's (coroner's) office along with the body contained a very short note written by the emergency department physician. This note did not contain a description of a cardiac history and did not reflect that a cardiac examination had been performed. The autopsy revealed a left main coronary artery occlusion of 100% that was determined to be the primary cause of death, as well as a large area of bruising, abrasion, and ecchymosis on the left chest wall that was attributed to the previous fall. Once litigation was started and the medical records were obtained from the hospital, it was noted that the chart contained a dictated, transcribed, and detailed progress note that reflected a normal cardiac examination and history and chest examination that revealed normal findings with only one point of tenderness. Examination of the medical record department's dictation log revealed that the additional note had been dictated two days after the patient's death.

Miscellaneous Medical Records

Other specialty records that need careful scrutiny may require a special request. These include resuscitation records or "code blue" records, critical care flow sheets, and hemodialysis records.

Other Types of Medical Records

Visiting Nurse or Home Care

Home care has expanded rapidly in the wake of managed care, and home-care records have become more sophisticated. Home-care records encompass specific plans for treatment and documentation of those plans, patient assessments, and outcomes. The plaintiff or defense, in cases involving long-term outpatient care between acute hospitalizations or following hospitalization, should not overlook these records.

Mental Health or Substance Abuse

Because of the confidential nature of their contents, records pertaining to mental health or substance abuse usually require specialized consent forms. In most cases, legal counsel has to prove that the records are essential to the case before a judge will allow access.

Nursing Home Records

As part of the Omnibus Budget Reconciliation Act (OBRA) of 1987,[5] Congress passed the Nursing Home Quality Reform Act requiring substantial changes in nursing-home care with more vigorous and more punitive regulatory enforcement.[6] As a result of OBRA, awareness of negligence in nursing homes is increasing. Nursing home records should be obtained and inspected carefully for noncompliance with OBRA and for other general negligence issues. More information on this subject is found in Chapter 14.

Outpatient Therapy or Rehabilitation Records

The LNC should not disregard physical, occupational, and speech therapy records in either the prosecution or defense of medical malpractice, personal injury, or workers' compensation cases. They may include statements by the plaintiff or observations by the therapists that would not appear in the physician's records and could be damaging to or supportive of the plaintiff's case. The therapist's observations are usually detailed, precise, and legible. The therapists themselves can be excellent witnesses when deposed and at trial.

In medical negligence cases involving inpatient admissions, the therapist's assessments of a patient's behavior and clinical well-being can be compared and contrasted effectively with the nurse's and physician's observations of the patient during the same period of time. Comparing records from different disciplines often provides clues about what may have gone wrong.

Example 31.5: The plaintiff alleged that he had fallen out of bed while being cared for by the visiting nurse. He claimed that he had not been closely monitored prior to the fall and was not adequately evaluated by the nurse after the fall. The plaintiff alleged that the physician had not been notified of the fall or of the possibility of a problem. The visiting nurse's notes reflected that the "patient was alert and oriented with no complaints." The physical therapist's notes contradicted this statement. The physical therapist documented, on the same day, during the same shift, that the patient's left leg was externally rotated and that the patient complained of severe hip and upper thigh pain. The physical therapist's documentation also reflected verbalizations by the patient that described the fall and the nurse's actions.

Computerized Medical Records

Increasingly, health care facilities are moving toward greater use of computerized medical records. Most hospitals have computerized laboratory, pharmacy, radiology, EKG, and EEG reporting as well as computerized invasive monitoring in the intensive care unit (ICU) and electronic fetal monitoring in the obstetrical unit. Computerized medication records are being used more frequently because they diminish the possibility of medication transcription and administration error. In many areas of the country, operating rooms are experimenting with computerized anesthetic records.

Computerized nurses' notes and physician order transcriptions are often voluminous when they are printed. The LNC may also find computerized information to be difficult to access. However, with a computerized record the LNC is much more likely to be able to determine exactly when a physician ordered medications or tests and when the order was transcribed than he or she is able to with many standard physician's order sheets.

Benefits of Computerized Medical Record Systems

Technology

Computerized medical record systems can provide record-formatting consistency and the ability to record and store medical information. (E.g., CT scan images can be inserted into the patient's record and dictation machines can be attached directly to computers.)

Audit Trails

Computer medical record systems can be programmed to have audit trails that identify who entered or altered data, and in which field the information was located. The system puts a date and time stamp on each entry, making it easy to identify who entered, altered, removed, or deleted any data within a record. This helps reduce tampering with the medical record.

Interfacing

Many computer medical record systems have the ability to interface or communicate with other computerized systems, such as scheduling and billing systems. This makes communications between departments more effective and timely, because information entered into one system seamlessly flows from one system to another.

Legibility

Because computerized medical record systems use standard formatting for data entry, legible handwriting is no longer an issue in interpretation.

Backup and Recovery

In order to avoid loss of records, computerized medical record systems are backed up and recovered nightly. In case of a disaster (extended power loss, hurricane, etc.), all records can be transmitted to paper format at a designated location and shipped to the affected areas, based on a disaster backup and recovery plan.

Security and Confidentiality

To safeguard confidentiality, computerized medical record systems require access with a user ID and password. Most systems require each user to "secure" the screen after data entry so that unauthorized individuals cannot see the information on the screen. Policies and procedures should be developed at each institution to clearly identify confidentiality standards and consequences if policies and procedures are not followed.

In order to prevent inappropriate access, security levels are built into computerized medical record systems. For example, a nursing assistant should have access to view what medications a patient is on, but not have access to order prescription medications. A physician would need access to view the medication history as well as to order new medications.

Data Gathering

Reports can be run for statistical purposes or for tracking certain populations. Examples include reports that identify patients with a certain diagnosis, patients currently taking a certain type of medication, and patients who received a certain immunization. This information could prove invaluable if a medication were to be taken off the market or a vial of injectable medications were recalled by the pharmaceutical company. Reports could quickly identify the patient population that is affected.

Demographic Grouping

In order to target certain populations for educational purposes, computerized medical record systems can identify demographic populations and create mailing lists. For example, a list could be developed of females in the system age 35 or over who have not already had a mammogram. A computer-generated letter could then be mailed to those that fall into the targeted population.

Negative Aspects of Computerized Medical Record Systems

Entry into the Wrong Patient's File

A user can enter data on the wrong patient. If that occurs, two records are affected: the one with the erroneous information and the one that should have been modified. Because most systems will not allow for "erasing" of any data, usually a note has to be entered into the system to indicate that an error was made and that the erroneous information should be ignored for the patient in that record. As with paper charting, users should always confirm the patient's name on the record before documenting.

Access with Someone Else's ID

If a user fails to secure the screen before leaving the computer or someone "shares" his or her ID with another person, all data entry thereafter will appear to have been completed by the individual who logged in initially. Because security levels are determined by access IDs, the ability to access certain fields and screens may also be altered. By following their institution's confidentiality and compliance policies, users can decrease the likelihood that this will occur.

Voluminous Printed Records

When records need to be transmitted to paper format (e.g., during a disaster, after the closure of an office, or per legal request), the records may be voluminous.

Complexity

Some providers feel that computer technology is too complex for their needs. They are often more comfortable with handwritten data entry and dictation.

Nonspecific Documentation

For the sake of convenience, users may often select "generic" wording or terms that the computerized medical record system offers, rather than take the time to individualize the patient's specific concerns or conditions.

Corruption of Files

Computer systems require safeguards to prevent corruption of files and maintenance of data integrity. Since this technology can be very expensive to install and maintain, many institutions may unwisely decide to limit the amount of protection chosen.

The Law and Computerized Medical Record Systems

Laws that are relevant to electronic communication include the Electronic Communications Privacy Act of 1986 (ECPA).[7] This sets out the provisions for access, use, disclosure, interception, and privacy protections of electronic communications. The law covers various forms of wire and electronic communications. The U.S. Code defines "electronic communications" as "any transfer of signs, signals, writing, images, sounds, data, or intelligence of any nature transmitted in whole or in part by a wire, radio, electromagnetic, photo electronic or photo optical system that affects interstate or foreign commerce." ECPA prohibits unlawful access and certain disclosures of communication contents. The law also prevents government entities from requiring disclosure of electronic communications from a provider without proper procedure.

The proposed Medical Privacy Regulations drafted by the Department of Health and Human Services (HHS) may have an impact on medical record privacy. These regulations, which are the first federal protections for medical information, apply to both paper and electronic health records. Congress recognized the need for national patient record privacy standards in 1996 when it enacted the Health Insurance Portability and Accountability Act of 1996 (HIPAA).[8] HIPAA included provisions designed to save money for health care businesses by encouraging electronic transactions, and it also required new safeguards to protect the security and confidentiality of that information. The law gave Congress until August 21, 1999, to pass comprehensive health privacy legislation. When Congress did not enact such legislation after three years, the law required HHS to craft such protections by regulation.

Under the final rule, patients will have significant new rights to understand and control how their health information is used:

- Providers and health plans will be required to give patients a clear written explanation of how the covered entity may use and disclose their health information.
- Patients will be able to see and get copies of their records and request amendments. A history of nonroutine disclosures must be made accessible to patients.
- Health care providers who see patients will be required to obtain patient consent before sharing their information for treatment, payment, and health care operations. In addition, separate patient authorization must be obtained for nonroutine disclosures and most non–health-care purposes. Patients will have the right to request restrictions on the uses and disclosures of their information.
- People will have the right to file a formal complaint with a covered provider or health plan, or with HHS, about violations of the provisions of this rule or the policies and procedures of the covered entity.
- With few exceptions, such as appropriate law enforcement needs, an individual's health information may be used only for health purposes.
- Health information covered by the rule generally may not be used for purposes not related to health care — such as disclosures to employers or financial institutions — without explicit authorization from the individual.
- In general, disclosures of information will be limited to the minimum necessary for the purpose of the disclosure. However, this provision does not apply to the disclosure of medical records for treatment purposes because physicians, specialists, and other providers need access to the full record to provide quality care.

Incomplete Medical Records

The usual reason for receiving what appears to be an incomplete medical record from a hospital or other health care facility is that the page or pages in question are not in the expected chronological or sequential order in the chart. Therefore, it is important to organize the medical records properly before further action is taken. Often an LNC finds the critical "missing" consultation in the middle of the physician's progress notes or some other unlikely place. Sometimes the records are released from the health care facility prior to completion by the attending physicians or before final laboratory compilations have been forwarded to the medical records department. This may happen when records are requested soon after the discharge or death of a patient.

It is usually safe to assume that the medical record department is not deliberately trying to thwart the LNC's efforts to get a complete record. Sometimes, records are missing as the result of an error by the copy technician. Often a letter to the medical records administrator outlining the exact missing records will be all that it takes to procure them. If the hospital denies the existence of portions of the record that, in the LNC's opinion, should exist, the medical record administrator should be asked to document, in writing, that those portions of the record are absent and do not exist.

In some circumstances, the LNC may be permitted to view the original record to look for missing pages and forms. This action requires approval of the attorney who retained the LNC, and a document, usually a letter, that permits the LNC to view the record on behalf of the attorney. It is not unusual for the LNC to be observed by the risk manager or medical records department personnel to ensure that no documents are removed from the file.

When dealing with a health care practitioner's office, the LNC may find that the custodian of the medical records is often not a trained medical records administrator. Accordingly, the records may be missing because the person responding to the medical record request did not understand the specifics of the request. The correspondence or laboratory and radiology reports may be left out entirely because the custodian assumed that they were not necessary to comply with the request. When dealing with a health care practitioner's office, the prudent LNC will specifically delineate all portions of the medical record contemplated by the request. A typical physician's office record consists of handwritten or dictated notes of each visit; correspondence; diagnostic test results; copies of hospital records; copies of consultations or referrals by other physicians; billing records; records of phone calls; insurance forms; copies of prescriptions for drugs, therapy, appliances, or equipment; and return-to-work or work-restriction forms. The LNC should specifically request all handwritten notes, memos, billing records, and telephone conference notes. Most health care providers will not send copies of records received from other treating physicians unless specifically asked; some states have laws that prevent this under all circumstances. Once the records are received, the LNC should make certain that the handwritten database or medical history form that the patient filled out on the first visit has been included.

The LNC should be aware whether the law of the state in which the case is being litigated permits an adverse inference to be drawn against a person or facility that is unable to produce a document or study, whether it has been innocuously lost or not, since this may have great impact on the status of a case with incomplete records of any kind.[9]

In all cases of missing records, the LNC should advise the attorney of the specific records that are missing as soon as possible and the reason why collection of those records is essential for thorough case review. Many LNCs working for attorneys in law firms have ongoing authority to request whatever records are necessary; LNCs working outside an attorney's office either advise the attorney regarding which records to obtain or obtain them with a consent form that identifies the LNC as working on behalf of the attorney. Obviously, it is impossible for the LNC to analyze the medical records thoroughly and accurately and evaluate a particular case if complete medical records are not available.

Organization of the Medical Records

In order to review medical records in the most complete manner possible, it is essential to organize the records into an easily comprehensible format. LNCs have a more comprehensive understanding of medical records than any other litigation professional, so it is critical that LNCs oversee the organization of medical records. Most often this consists of organizing all records into chronological order and a logical order for ease in review. For the purposes of litigation, it is wise to apply this philosophy to all medical records. If, however, the task at hand is to review a potential case involving the possible fracture of a Bjork-Shiley heart valve, and a simple review of the final hospitalization and autopsy reveals that the patient died of a ruptured abdominal aortic aneurysm instead, it may well be a waste of the LNC's time, and the client's money, to organize ten different hospitalizations in chronological order. The attorney should make the decision about whether or not more work should be done with the medical records, since detailed organization of the medical records may be necessary for conferences, hearings, or other situations involving the client. In a potential plaintiff's case, it is possible that other issues may have been overlooked, such as a timely diagnosis and treatment of the abdominal aortic aneurysm in the above example.

Several logical sequences of various types of hospital records are suggested in Appendix 31.2. Health maintenance organization (HMO) and physicians' records encompass different types of information from hospital records and require a different organization. A logical sequence for these types of records is also suggested in Appendix 31.2. Often the records are released in a progression that facilitates ease of patient care, but not medical-legal review. A common presentation is to make the physician's orders section one of the first parts of the chart. Although critical in a few cases, the physician's orders are generally not of importance for the majority of medical-legal cases and may be placed farther back in the indexed chart. There is no "right" way to organize and sequence medical records. The type of case may suggest the most logical sequence for ease of review, or the LNC or attorney may have a specific format that suits his or her practice style. It is imperative, however, that all persons on the same side of the litigation team have medical records that are indexed in the same manner.

When the LNC has an abundance of medical records that are not critical to the investigation or litigation of a case — e.g., long-term nursing care due to brain damage resulting from an anesthesia accident — he or she may want to divide the "excess" records into file folders and label them so that the information can be easily retrieved and accessed whenever necessary.

Copies of fetal heart-monitoring strips can be difficult to interpret correctly on multiple separate sheets of paper. The LNC may want to take the extra time to meticulously line up and tape together all the pieces of the fetal heart monitor strips so that the panel numbers correlate chronologically. The same principle applies to ICU flow records when the original encompasses several folding sheets, so that the times for all the data match and can be easily read and interpreted. One technique that works particularly well is to use a colored sheet to divide and label each 24-hour flow sheet. Once the pattern of how the pages are organized is discernible, the LNC can quickly identify which pages are missing. The LNC should spend time doing this only in a case in which the ICU flow sheets are of central importance to the alleged negligence.

Indexing and Paginating Medical Records

Once they are complete, all medical records should be placed in a loose-leaf binder for ease of review, with subsections of each record tabbed and labeled "Progress Notes," "Medications," etc. Formulation of an index, such the one in Appendix 31.3, can be a valuable and time-saving aid. An index identifies the exact nature of the medical record contents, including the dates of treatment and the types of physicians who have treated the patient. Not only is the index helpful to the LNC in his or her continuous dealings with the medical records; it also helps the attorney to obtain a comprehensive assessment of the records at any time during discovery. When medical records are sent to expert witnesses, an index gives a concise record of exactly what information the expert has received and reviewed in order to arrive at his or her opinion. The LNC updates the index as further medical records are collected during the course of case evaluation or litigation. Use of preprinted indexes, purchased from a medical supply company, facilitates the organization of records.

If the medical records are extensive but complete and certified, pagination may be tremendously helpful in later discovery and at trial. Copies of the entire certified, paginated records can be used as invaluable "working copies" during discovery with the advantage of knowing that all the attorneys, experts, and LNCs are referring to exactly the same information. Complete, certified, and paginated records ensure expeditious review of medical records by expert witnesses, which in turn keeps client costs to a minimum. The LNC should not paginate records that are not complete and not certified, since the numbering system will only cause confusion once the remainder of the records are incorporated. Alternatively, if paginated medical records arrive from another law firm or a copy service, the records may be stamped a second time with a different type of pagination system that perhaps incorporates letters with the numbers, e.g., A001, A002, etc.

Medical Record Analysis

The AALNC *Standards of Legal Nurse Consulting Practice* states that once the appropriate data (medical records) have been collected, the LNC must analyze the data and identify the health care issues related to the case or claim.[2]

A quick assessment of the medical records should be done during the initial record organization. This assessment can provide an overview of the issues of the case and a mental note of who treated the plaintiff when and where. More important, the overview helps the LNC to determine whether any records are missing.

Example 31.6: In a case involving alleged failure to diagnose an ascending aortic aneurysm during an emergency visit, the LNC should make sure that the reports of the chest x-ray and CT scan that were ordered by the ER physician were in the chart and that copies of those films were complete when ordered from the radiology department.

Example 31.7: In a product liability case involving a prescription for the drug Prozac, a review of all pharmaceutical (drugstore) records would be essential to determining accurately all the drugs that the plaintiff was taking during the time of the alleged negligence, since it is common for physicians not to detail in their office records, on the occasion of each visit, the complete list of all the medications that the patient takes on an ongoing basis.

The LNC may find it helpful in complicated cases to make an outline of important events during the initial review of the medical records. The outline can be used as a guide for a more in-depth and systematic review of the medical records.

Systematic Review of Hospital Medical Records

Face Sheet and DRGs

The medical record's face sheet provides valuable information about the time that the patient was admitted to the hospital. This can be important in a case involving an alleged delay in an admission. The face sheet may list the date of a previous admission, which alerts the LNC to a potentially missing record. Diagnosis-related groups (DRGs) are the basis for HHS's prospective payment system (contained in the 1983 Social Security Amendments) for reimbursing inpatient hospital costs for Medicare beneficiaries. The key source of information for determining the course of treatment of each patient and the proper DRG assignment is the medical record.[3]

The most comprehensive overview of DRGs is *St. Anthony's DRG Guidebook*,[10] which provides an easy way to look up DRG groupings, relative weights, and mean length of stay statistics. The book can be found in most medical libraries and bookstores. Additional DRG sources are listed in the references and additional reading sections at the end of this chapter.[4,11]

Consent Forms

The LNC should be familiar with state statutes regarding the specific informed-consent laws for the state in which the case rests. The consent should be properly witnessed, dated, and signed by the patient and the physician. It should also delineate the expected usual, unusual, and rare adverse consequences of the operation or procedure and the risks of nonperformance of the procedure, including the need for, risk of, and alternatives to blood products.[4] The alternative treatment options that are available to the patient in the event of nonperformance of the procedure should be listed.[4] The consent form must also list the names of the surgeons who will perform the procedure. The consent form must be completed before the patient is given preoperative medication, which could impair his or her ability to give competent consent.[9] The LNC should determine whether the patient or his or her representative agreed to the particular operation or procedure performed and whether any exceptions to that consent were noted.

Example 31.8: A 42-year-old woman who underwent an exploratory laparoscopy for pelvic pain signed a consent form for the laparoscopy and also for laparotomy and hysterectomy, with the caveat that her uterus was to be removed only if the surgeon determined there was cancer or severe endometriosis. The surgeon found an ovarian cyst and a few other mild abnormalities but removed the uterus anyway. The woman sued the surgeon for battery due to lack of consent and for negligence.

Autopsy

The LNC should ascertain whether (1) the autopsy report is a complete protocol or reflects only the preliminary results, (2) all the microscopic examinations have been performed, and (3) the results of any toxicology tests or special consultations to outside agencies have been received. Autopsy evidence can be critical not only in confirming a diagnosis causing death, but also in disproving certain diagnoses.

Example 31.9: In a case alleging that the plaintiff died of a myocardial infarction shortly after being seen for chest pain in the ER, the autopsy may not be critical in proving the existence of an acute myocardial infarction, since it takes many hours for microscopic and gross evidence of myocardial infarction to manifest itself; however, it will be invaluable in ruling out other causes of death, such as stroke, aneurysm rupture, etc.

Discharge Summary and Instructions

Th discharge summary and instructions can be reviewed as an overview of the hospitalization: the dates of the hospitalization, reason for admission, complaints upon admission, course of treatment and significant findings, response to procedures and treatment, any complications that occurred, the status of the patient at discharge, and the instructions to the patient and family, if any.[4] The LNC should look carefully for details such as when the discharge summary was dictated, since it can have bearing on the subjectivity of the summary's content. The LNC should determine whether there are handwritten additions, deletions, or changes to the original document; when those changes were made; and their relevance to the subject of the lawsuit.

Nursing discharge summaries may provide comprehensive documentation reviewing the entire hospital stay. They may also contain information about patient and family education as well as specific discharge instructions pertaining to activity levels, dressing changes, medications, and follow-up appointments with physicians or other health care providers.

Example 31.10: A 35-year-old woman came to the hospital emergency department with complaints of feeling excessively nervous, being under a great deal of stress, and having a "funny" feeling in her chest. Emergency lab values reflected possible pneumonia as noted on the chest x-ray and an elevated white-blood count with a slight shift to the left. She was admitted with a diagnosis of anxiety disorder and an acute infection, probably pneumonia. The following day she was discharged home with a prescription for Xanax® and instructions to make an appointment with her private physician and at the local mental health clinic and to return to the ER if her symptoms became worse. Twelve hours after she was discharged, the patient returned to the emergency department with severe chest pain. The cardiac enzymes were found to be elevated, and an EKG was indicative of an old anterior wall myocardial infarction and a new inferior wall myocardial infarction. She was admitted to the ICU for observation and treatment. The discharge summary for the initial hospitalization was dictated several days after the second admission. Close examination of the discharge summary of the first hospitalization would be in order because the admitting physician may have downplayed the severity of the patient's symptoms prior to the first discharge after he learned of the patient's subsequent problems.

The discharge summary can also be used as a barometer against which the effects of any treatments that occurred during the admission can be measured. This is important in terms of damages, because it can indicate whether the patient suffered harm or injuries, to what extent he or she was injured, and how permanent the injuries are.

Emergency Medical Services

The LNC should compare the patient's admission status with the emergency-transport records. This may be important in cases in which the patient's condition prior to arrival or resuscitation efforts and response prior to admission are critical elements of the case.[9] The LNC should note how the rescue squad documented the patient's condition at the scene of the accident, e.g., whether the patient was dazed or lost consciousness, and look for descriptions of injuries to the vehicle in order to correlate them with the patient's injuries. For example, a squad member may have seen a "star" pattern of broken glass on a windshield resulting from impact with the patient's skull or made comments about the vehicle being "T-boned" (hit broadside) with intrusion of the side of the car into the passenger compartment. This may correlate with injuries to the side of the patient's body. The LNC should look for evidence of dashboard damage if the patient complained of a knee injury from hitting the dashboard and note any documentation of broken seat belts or seats, indicating that great force was exerted against the car. The LNC should note whether the "Jaws of Life" were needed to extract the patient from a crushed car.

Example 31.11: A 38-week-gestational-age baby was delivered precipitously at a rural hospital without a neonatal ICU. The infant immediately began to manifest respiratory difficulties and had severe hypoglycemia. The baby was intubated, but oxygen saturation levels indicated continued hypoxemia. Sepsis was suspected. An emergency medical transport team transported the baby to a tertiary-care institution and the baby died shortly after admission. Suit was brought against the rural hospital and the pediatrician for failure to transport the baby in a timely manner. The pediatrician claimed that he had called the tertiary-level hospital immediately after the baby was born; however, the EMS records indicated that the transfer was not requested until the baby was 8 hours old.

Emergency Department

Common problems resulting in litigation in the ER include (1) not seeing patients in a timely manner, (2) failing to diagnose the real cause of the plaintiff's problems as a result of inadequate assessment and testing, and (3) discharging patients who should be admitted for further observation and treatment. Knowing this, the LNC should:

- Review the time that the patient was admitted, the presenting complaints, and vital signs
- Look at the assessment made by the triage nurse and determine whether the appropriate triage classification was made
- Determine at what time the physician first saw the patient
- Compare the nurse's assessment of the patient with that of the emergency physician to determine whether the physician ordered the appropriate diagnostic studies and whether the diagnostic studies were performed in a timely manner
- Note any evidence that the plaintiff was under the influence of any alcohol or drugs
- Ascertain whether the patient responded to the treatment rendered

If a patient receives emergency, urgent, or immediate care, and leaves against medical advice, the health care providers are required to make a note of this.[4] The LNC should find out whether the patient signed a form to that effect. Some health care facilities consider the records generated in the emergency department as outpatient records, so they may need to be specifically requested.

If a case involves failure to diagnose or premature discharge from the emergency department, the LNC should search for discharge instructions. If a misdiagnosis has been made, the advice and instructions provided on the discharge instruction forms could be critical to evaluating this type of case.

In personal injury, workers' compensation, and criminal cases, the LNC should:

- Look for documentation that contains information or declarations by the patient about how the accident or injuries occurred
- Note whether the patient described having a loss of consciousness, and correlate this information with the rescue squad records
- Note the patient's complaints and correlate this information with the history recorded by subsequent treating doctor's office records
- Look for discrepancies between the initial symptoms of the patient as recorded in the emergency room records and subsequent records
- Note whether the emergency department health care providers recorded information about alcohol consumption (alcohol on breath [AOB] or ETOH [smell])
- Look for entries that refer to the use or the nonuse of a seat belt in a motor vehicle accident

History and Physical Examination

JCAHO requires that a patient's H&P examination, nursing assessment, and other screening assessments be completed within 24 hours of admission as an inpatient.[4] A physician may elect to document his or her H&P examination findings in writing or by dictation. The LNC should determine the date that the typed history was dictated. The information in a history dictated several days after an admission with complications may be suspect. The name of the person dictating the H&P examination may also have significance. If the H&P examination is performed by a nurse practitioner (NP) or a physician's assistant (PA), the LNC should be aware of state laws and hospital policy pertaining to documentation. Unlike an experienced physician, an NP, PA, or resident may not have the knowledge base or the clinical expertise to detect or follow up on subtle test findings. Because the NP works collaboratively with the physician and the PA works under the supervision of the physician, the physician retains legal responsibility for their actions. Likewise, a physician covering for a patient's regular physician may not know the patient well enough to be able to evaluate the patient's current situation in the light of a complex medical history.

History

The LNC should look at the patient's chief complaint and past history, searching for clues to the present illness. The LNC should evaluate the patient's complaints for validity, for the patient's perception of his or her own illness, and for the prior treatment the patient has received.[9] Sometimes patients give histories that are slightly or radically different during separate admissions. The LNC should compare the histories from all hospitalizations and those from physicians' records, checking for consistency. Often an error in a history becomes a self-perpetuating "fact" as each subsequent consulting physician obtains the history information from the chart instead of the patient. The LNC should be aware of this and look carefully for the origin of all information. He or she should look for historical information regarding medications, drug allergies, and drug and alcohol problems. The history of prior surgeries, illnesses, and injuries can be of extreme importance to the current picture. Failure of a physician to ask questions necessary to elicit an adequate history may constitute negligence.[9]

Physical Examination

A physical examination record can be important as much for what is omitted from the documentation as it is for the positive and negative (nonexistent) findings about the patient's presenting clinical situation.

Example 31.12: A 34-year-old woman presented to her family practice physician with a complaint of finding a breast mass on a recent self-examination. This physician documented the "possibility of a very small breast mass" and referred her to her gynecologist. The gynecologist stated that he could not find a mass on palpation and suggested that she return in six months. There was no documentation of her complaints of a breast mass or of the physical examination findings. During the next gynecologic visit, the NP located a mass, referred the patient for a mammogram to evaluate the mass, and told the patient to return one month after the mammogram. The patient returned to the physician's office. The physician performed a breast examination and told her that he did not palpate a lump. He also told the patient that the mammogram report was negative, although the radiologist reported a suspicious mass and recommended follow-up monitoring. There was no documentation of a breast examination during this office visit. Relying upon the recommendations of the physician, this woman did not return for any follow-up examinations for one year. After a year, when she presented for her annual pap and physical examination, she told the physician that she had continued to feel the lump in her breast. A repeat mammogram was performed, and it revealed a large breast mass. A biopsy confirmed the suspicion of breast carcinoma. The plaintiff brought suit against the NP and physician for failure to perform a complete physical examination, failure to perform a biopsy, and failure to refer to a surgeon, alleging that a surgeon would have performed a biopsy to determine the nature of the mass if an appropriate physical examination had revealed its presence.

The physician may often respond: "If I didn't write anything about it, then it must not have been a problem."[9] But the corollary to this is: "If I didn't write it down, then I did not examine or address the area or problem." Credibility in this type of situation is left for the jury to decide at trial and may depend on the remainder of the physician's examination and the physician's other charting practices, or simply on whether the physician is a believable witness on his or her own behalf. The LNC should compare the physical examination findings with those noted by the nurses or physical therapists or other members of the health care team. The physician's observations are dependent upon patient cooperation and patient reactions, which may be entirely spurious and misleading.[9]

Provisional Diagnosis

Since the provisional diagnosis reflects the physician's preliminary opinions regarding the patient's condition and is the basis for initial treatment, the LNC should look closely at the physician's conclusions to determine whether they are appropriate, whether the treatment plan encompasses an appropriate diagnostic workup, and whether the workup is specific to the diagnoses made.

Operative Records

Operative records consist of numerous types of documentation, including consent forms; preoperative and intraoperative nursing records; preoperative, intraoperative, and postoperative anesthesia records; surgical notes; pathology reports; and postanesthesia care unit records.

Preoperative Nursing Records

Preoperative nursing records are important in determining whether the appropriate preoperative preparation of the patient took place. Documentation of the patient's vital signs, preoperative testing, last food or drink, and signing of the consent form may have important implications for a case. For example, there may be serious implications if the patient aspirated during intubation and the preoperative documentation failed to note that the patient was mistakenly given breakfast, a fact that was clearly documented by the floor nurse.

Intraoperative Nursing Records

Nursing notes can be invaluable in documenting exactly who participated in a surgical procedure and the times that those persons were in the operating room, as well as when the procedure began and ended. The LNC should look for information regarding the skin preparation, the type of preoperative or intraoperative positioning of the patient, and the location of the electrosurgical ground pad. The nurse's operative record will contain specifics regarding any devices implanted during the procedure and, often, specialized types of equipment used by the surgeon. The notes will also include information not found elsewhere regarding drains, sponges, surgical packing, and catheters. Often the nursing portion of the operative record will include clues to what happened during the operative procedure that will not be contained in the anesthesia charting or the surgeon's operative note.

Anesthesia Preoperative Assessment

The anesthesia preoperative workup should be complete and include a history of the patient's response to previous anesthetics, potential problems involving the airway, and current medical illnesses and medications. An assessment of the degree of the patient's illness and his or her risk for anesthetic complications is determined by utilizing the Physical Status Classification System of the American Society of Anesthesiologists (ASA).[12] This assessment process assigns a category based upon the ASA scale of P1 (Class 1), which indicates "a normally healthy patient," through P6 (Class 6), the category used to define "a declared brain-dead patient whose organs are being removed for donor purposes." The ASA classification can be used as a barometer to judge whether the appropriate intensity of intraoperative monitoring of the patient occurred. For example, a Class III patient with diabetic neuropathy and cardiovascular disease should have more intense monitoring than a Class I patient with no systemic disease. At the conclusion of the preoperative workup, the anesthesiologist should determine an operative plan for the person giving anesthesia that includes the preoperative medication, the type of induction, and the type of anesthesia to be administered.

Anesthesia Records

The LNC should ascertain whether an anesthesiologist, a nurse anesthetist, or a PA (often titled anesthesiologist assistant) trained in anesthesia delivered the anesthetic agents and find out who monitored the patient. Often the induction is performed by an anesthetist with an anesthesiologist present, but the anesthesiologist subsequently leaves the OR suite to oversee another anesthetist. It is important to ascertain who actually administered the anesthesia. Depending on the degree of legibility, the actual anesthesia graphic charting and narrative records may be difficult to comprehend. In cases involving intraoperative events, the LNC should look at the types of inhalation agents (gases) and drugs used for induction, the time of intubation, whether there was any difficulty with the intubation, the number of times it took to intubate the patient, and the patient's vital signs in response to these events. Patient positioning can also have significance in cases involving intraoperative complications or postoperative findings such as neuropathies. Events will often be numbered on the graphic record and correspond to the narrative record. The LNC should determine the type of intraoperative monitoring used. An end tidal CO_2 monitor and an oxygen saturation monitor are essential, as recommended by the ASA.[12] The LNC should look closely at the patient's vital signs and the anesthetist's response to changes in them. It is important to determine whether the patient's condition is due to the effect of the anesthesia or the surgery being performed. The LNC should note the length of time that the patient was under anesthetic care and the time it took to perform the operation. These times should be compared with those on the intraoperative nurse's notes.

Operative Reports

The surgeon is required by JCAHO to dictate or write the operative report immediately after surgery, recording the name of the primary surgeon and assistants, findings, technical procedures used, specimens removed, and postoperative diagnosis. If the operative report is not placed in the medical record immediately after surgery, a progress note should be entered immediately.[4]

The preoperative diagnosis is sometimes contained in the operative report. In cases where the necessity of the operation is in question, the LNC should compare all the preoperative diagnoses, the operative findings, and the postoperative diagnosis with the H&P examination and the discharge summary for consistency. The LNC should be alert for operative reports that are brief and nonspecific, especially in commonly performed surgeries such as hysterectomies. He or she should note the date on which the operative report was dictated and look for a delay in dictation in cases that involve unrecognized surgical complications.

A good operative report also contains information about the types and locations of drains placed, estimated blood loss, detailed operative findings, and complications encountered during the procedure. The LNC should determine the names of any surgical assistants and types of specialized equipment used by the surgeon. He or she should pay close attention to the manner in which foreign bodies, such as hip and knee replacements, are described as being inserted, noting if the surgeon encountered any unusual bleeding that is not accounted for or if distorted or "difficult" anatomy is mentioned. This is especially important in cases where structures have been encroached upon improperly.

Example 31.13: A 45-year-old morbidly obese, diabetic woman elected to have a gastroplasty, roux loop. During the surgical procedure excessive bleeding was noted. Multiple interventions, including pressure and hemoclip application, were unsuccessful in controlling the bleeding, and consequently a splenectomy had been performed. The plaintiff alleged that the splenectomy was unnecessary and had been performed due to a surgical technical error. The operative report contained a complete patient history and explained the procedure and surgical findings. The medical expert related that occasionally excessive bleeding may be encountered that is not due to surgical error and, in this case, that the surgeon had exercised all appropriate options in an attempt to control the bleeding and that a splenectomy was an appropriate medical intervention. The case settled for an undisclosed amount of money.

Surgical Pathology

In cases where biopsies are being done, the LNC should look at the frozen section diagnosis and compare it with the surgical treatment performed, the follow-up treatment, and the final pathology diagnosis. Sometimes the frozen section diagnosis differs from the final pathology diagnosis. Obviously, there are serious implications if a misreading of the frozen section results in unnecessary removal of tissue or body parts. If surgery is being done to remove cancer, the LNC should note that the specimens removed have margins clear of tumor and note the size of each specimen removed. The LNC should determine whether the pathological diagnosis is consistent with the surgical diagnosis or the reason the surgery was being performed in the first place. It is important to be familiar with the standard of care in such situations. The LNC should consider the importance of adequate specimens for laboratory examinations.

Example 31.14: In a case involving breast surgery, a frozen section of the patient's tissue revealed carcinoma of the breast. Upon receiving the pathology results, the surgeon performed a mastectomy. Upon subsequent review of the paraffin section, the pathologist determined that this was a noncancerous condition. The plaintiff alleged negligence on the part of the pathologist and surgeon for unnecessary surgery. The case was dismissed after experts testified that frozen sections are uncertain and inconclusive, which is why paraffin sections are made and viewed, and that this did not necessarily mean that the surgeon had performed an unnecessary operation.

Postanesthesia Recovery

Postanesthesia recovery records are of vital importance in cases involving immediate postoperative complications that are usually respiratory or cardiac in nature. The LNC should look for trends in vital signs, mental and neurological status, and the timeliness of the nursing staff's response to those changes.

Postoperative Anesthesia

The anesthesia staff, either an anesthesiologist or a nurse anesthetist, will see the patient postoperatively, usually on the day after surgery, and note the patient's response to the anesthetic delivered. In the case of epidural anesthesia, the anesthesiologist or nurse anesthetist will see the patient at least once daily and be available to respond to any complications with the epidural until the catheter has been removed and a determination has been made that the patient has not sustained any complications. In cases in which the patient received postoperative anesthesia, the LNC should review the progress notes of the anesthesia staff and the flowcharts corresponding to the anesthesia in question. The anesthesiologist is usually involved in monitoring the status of a patient on a PCA analgesia pump. Some larger facilities may use an anesthesia pain service for this purpose.

Consultations

The LNC should determine whether the appropriate medical specialty consultations were ordered in a timely manner by looking at the date that the consultant was asked to see the patient and the consultant's response. The consultant should consider all the necessary patient history to draw conclusions. After the consultant has determined a course of treatment for the patient, the consultant should then follow the patient with the attending physician until the problem for which he or she was consulted is resolved. If the attending physician is a family practice physician, the consultant may become the physician in charge of the patient's care while the acute condition is being resolved. The LNC should:

- Look for the time relationships among consultants' examinations, the reports of diagnostic testing, and the entries on the order sheets.
- Pay close attention to the number of consultants being used in complicated medical and surgical cases.
- Determine whether one physician was looking at the patient as a whole or whether each consulting physician was looking at only an individual system, e.g., the respiratory system. Failing to put the entire clinical picture together in a complicated case can result in disastrous consequences for the patient.
- Consult the hospital medical staff bylaws to determine whether they govern how the responsibility for total patient care is to be shared or transferred between primary physicians and consultants.

Physician Progress Notes

Progress notes should contain reference to the patient's test results and response to treatment and therapy, and should document objective and subjective signs and symptoms.[9] The LNC should look at how often the physician charted. Lack of an entry in the progress notes does not necessarily mean that the patient was not seen. When there is no daily note written, the LNC should check the physician's orders, the nurses' notes, and the notes of other health care providers for clues that the physician actually did examine the patient on a particular day. The LNC should determine whether the physician's notes acknowledge other physicians' and health care providers' findings as well as the patient's complaint; check the narrative parts of the medical record, looking at the time (if written) and date of all notes, for logical sequencing and progression; look for notes that may not have been written contemporaneously; and note if the entry ends abruptly or looks as if it was continued on the next page to detect potentially missing records. The LNC should determine whether each page has the patient's hospital stamp plate on the corner and whether notes were written with lines drawn through the blank portion of the page so that no one else would write on that particular page. The LNC should analyze all notes written immediately after an incident, such as an unexpected cardiac arrest, with close scrutiny.

Radiology Reports

As with laboratory reports, the LNC should compare the times and dates that the x-rays were ordered with the time that the actual films were taken. Many health care facilities do not list this on the radiology report, but the LNC may be able to piece the information together by looking at the remainder of the record, especially the nursing notes. The LNC should determine whether the x-rays (or any diagnostic tests) were accomplished in a reasonable and timely manner or in the time frame contemplated by the physician when ordering the test. He or she should find out whether relevant clinical information was provided with the request, as is required for x-ray and clinical interpretation.[4] The LNC should compare successive radiology reports looking for differences in the findings. (Are there reports of air in the abdomen in a postoperative patient? Are accumulations of fluid noted? Does the report comply with the American College of Radiology (ACR) Standard for Communication: Diagnostic Radiology?[13]) The ACR Standard for Communication: Diagnostic Radiology states: "An official interpretation (final written report) shall be provided with all radiologic studies regardless of the site of performance (hospital, imaging center, physician office, mobile, etc.)." These standards go on to define the minimum items needed for a diagnostic radiology report and the type of written communication and direct communication that should be transmitted to the ordering physician as a result of such a diagnostic examination. If the technique of the radiology examination is in question, such as in diagnostic mammography, the LNC should compare the examination with that recommended by the ACR Standard for Diagnostic Mammography.[13]

Laboratory Records

The LNC should determine whether the appropriate laboratory tests were done for the patient's clinical diagnosis and treatment or as a preoperative workup. Laboratory results can be very meaningful evidence when a physician or other health care provider fails to follow up on abnormal test results. In cases where laboratory results are of importance, the LNC should ascertain whether or not all the laboratory results are in the chart. A final computerized summary of all the laboratory results gives the best assurance that this is so. The LNC should determine the time that the laboratory tests were ordered, the time the samples were obtained, and the time that the results were available to the health care providers. He or she should correlate the physician's progress notes and orders regarding specialized tests sent to outside laboratories and make sure that those results are on the chart. In cases involving extremes in laboratory values, such as hyperkalemia and hypoxemia, the LNC should look for "critical" or "panic" values in the laboratory results and the documentation as to who was called regarding those values (usually the nursing staff) and the response to those critical values. Various health care facilities use different normal parameters for various laboratory tests, but the results are always calibrated to that normal range.

The LNC should search for trends in laboratory results. He or she should:

- Look at the hemoglobin and hematocrit in a surgical case involving postoperative bleeding
- Ascertain the specifics of the white blood cell count and the differential in a case involving unrecognized infection
- Determine the result times and trends in cardiac enzymes for a case involving failure to diagnose myocardial infarction
- Pay close attention to the arterial blood gas results in cases where there are progressive respiratory difficulties or respiratory arrest
- Look at the culture and sensitivity results for a determination of timely and appropriate management of systemic or local infections

Transfusion Records

In cases involving transfusion reactions, the LNC should note the patient's and donor's ABO and Rh blood type, cross-matching tests, and antibody screening. He or she should establish the events surrounding the blood transfusion, including the time the blood product was started and stopped, the amount given, and the documentation of the transfusion reaction. Complete typing and cross-matching may not have been done due to the acute need for blood transfusion; however, technical errors account for most transfusion accidents in nonemergency situations. Improper patient and donor identification remains the leading cause of transfusion errors.[9]

Physician's Orders

Physician's orders often provide invaluable clues about communication between the physician and the nurses caring for a patient and the care being rendered. For example, there may be a telephone order for pain medication in the order section of the chart but no mention anywhere else of a communication between the physician and the nurse. It is sometimes important to distinguish between orders written directly by a physician, verbal orders, and telephone orders in order to establish the whereabouts of a physician at a certain time. Additionally, the time that orders were written and the time that the orders were taken off and countersigned by the nurse should be noted carefully, as well as whether or not the orders were transcribed correctly. The LNC should see whether the resident's or intern's orders were countersigned by the attending physician and pay particular attention to how orders were written in a case involving a medication error. The LNC should examine the record for orders such as "notify me of ...," and determine whether the nurses followed through.

Example 31.15: A 55-year-old man who had a history of falling developed a headache and several hours later developed decerebrate posturing and was minimally responsive to stimulation. The physician ordered a number of STAT electrolyte tests and STAT ABGs as well as a CT scan. The order for the CT scan was entered as a routine order by the unit secretary and signed off by the nurse in charge of the patient. As a result of this (and several other unrelated delays), the CT scan was not done until 8 hours after the original order, by which time the patient was having apneic spells and one of his pupils was dilated and fixed. The CT scan showed a subdural hematoma, which was subsequently emergently evacuated.

The physician's orders must be carried out, and failure to do so can mean a deviation in the standard of care, with only rare exceptions. Standing orders mandate certain actions when specific situations arise, e.g., "O_2 2 liters/by nasal cannula for O_2 saturation <93%." Did the health care providers follow these orders? The LNC should check the physician's orders for items such as the frequency of vital signs, the patient's prescribed activity level, and other types of required monitoring. Often these are the basis for judging nursing actions in negligence cases. (Did the nursing staff monitor the patient with sufficient frequency as contemplated by the physician? For example, did the patient fall while going to the bathroom when he was supposed to be on bed rest?)

Medication Records

Medication records give the LNC a complete picture of the types of medications being given to the patient and when they were given. JCAHO requires that medication effects on patients be continually monitored.[4] The LNC should look for evidence of the patient's reactions to medications and the nursing response to those reactions. A delay between the writing of a drug order and the administration of the first dosage can be very important to a case. The patient's medication allergies should be prominently noted. With computerization of medication records, the pharmacy staff will enter allergies in the computer and the computer will alert the pharmacist if a drug is ordered that has cross-sensitivity with a drug that the patient is allergic to, such as antibiotics. This important safety feature may be negated when one-time medications, such as narcotics, are ordered; e.g., administering Tylenol® #3 even when the patient is allergic to codeine because the nurse has access to this drug without going through the pharmacy. The "prn" medications are of great importance because they will occasionally not be mentioned in the nursing documentation. The LNC should compare the medications given and the doses of those medications with the physician's orders for discrepancies. He or she should note whether the site of administration of injection was recorded. This is important in nursing malpractice cases involving allegations of injuries due to injections.

Pharmacy bills can be helpful when the plaintiff alleges that a drug was not given, or given and not documented. Other sources of information for checking on the administration of narcotics include the pharmacy narcotic control slips, the pharmacy central narcotic record, and the pharmacy charge slips.[9]

Graphics and Flow Sheets

Graphics and flow sheets, such as neurological check sheets and diabetic urine and blood testing, are important in cases in which trends in a patient's condition are not recognized and no follow-up action taken. The intake and output sheets may show a progressive positive fluid balance with diminishing urinary output in a patient who has congestive heart failure. Intake and output sheets may be of critical importance in cases involving infants and geriatric patients who are easily subject to dehydration. The vital signs on the graphics sheets may be used as additional evidence to support the plaintiff's contention that shock was developing and was not recognized in a timely manner. Graphics and flow sheets may be of critical importance to the plaintiff especially when the information required on the graphics and flow sheets has not been completely documented.

Nurses' Notes

As LNCs know, the nurses' notes are often the most valuable portion of the medical record, substantiating or contradicting evidence found elsewhere in the patient's hospital chart.

Admission History and Physical

The nursing admission assessment, while not a complete medical history and physical, does assess important considerations for nursing care during the patient's hospitalization. The LNC can determine the patient's physical limitations and functional status assessment when warranted by the patient's needs or conditions,[4] mental status, understanding of his or her situation, special feeding problems, and allergies. Often, the admitting nurse will have ascertained and documented the most complete list of current medications. The LNC should compare the information in the physician's history with that written by the nurses for differences or contradictions that may have an impact on the case.

Nursing Care Plan

The nursing care plan is the basis for administering care to the patient and should be appropriate for the types of problems the patient is experiencing. The nursing care plan can be used in the legal setting as a barometer of the nurses' understanding of the type of care to be rendered to the patient and a standard by which that care is to be measured.

Example 31.16: A 79-year-old woman with a history of diabetes mellitus, congestive heart failure, and dementia who was being cared for at home by agency nurses was admitted to the hospital dirty and covered with extensive decubitus ulcers. Evidence showed that the agency employees did not reposition the client every two hours and did not keep her body clean. The agency employees kept very scanty records of their patient care activities, and documentation did not reflect the nursing care plan. The nursing care plan stated that this woman would be monitored closely and interventions would be instituted for the prevention of the development of decubitus ulcers. The plaintiff's family alleged that the agency failed to train and supervise their employees properly. In this case the nursing care plan was successfully used against the nurses to show multiple deviations from the standard of care.

Ongoing Documentation

LNCs know that the nurses' notes represent an ongoing account of patient complaints, signs, and symptoms and the nursing responses to these matters. A determination of the status of the patient before and after diagnostic and surgical procedures can be made, as well as the patient's response to blood products, IVs, and medications. This documentation can be of utmost importance in some medical-legal cases. The nurses' notes may be the definitive clue to the timing of certain events, such as physician visits and adverse reactions, patient injuries, or respiratory or cardiac arrest. The LNC should look specifically to see whether the nurses have followed through with their plan for nursing care of the patient and used appropriate judgment in complying with the standing orders. The LNC should look for trends in vital signs, wound problems, pain, and other patient complaints. (Did the nurses assess the patient adequately, and was the physician notified of adverse conditions and circumstances in a timely manner?) The nurses' notes may be invaluable for what they do not include as much as for what they do include.

Example 31.17: Several months postoperatively, a patient alleged that he suffered a stroke as a result of anesthesia administered during a thoracotomy. The anesthesia records did indicate that he experienced a prolonged period of hypotension during the surgical procedure. However, the patient was hospitalized for several days postoperatively, and there was no mention of any cognitive deficits or neurological signs and symptoms during this period of time in the extremely detailed and comprehensive documentation by the nursing staff.

The nurse is expected to document the clinically pertinent information about the patient. Various nursing documentation systems differ in the format and detail that is expected. Comparing the nursing documentation with the facility's policies on charting can reveal discrepancies that may be significant in a particular case.

Discharge Instructions

JCAHO requires that hospitals make it clear to patients and their families what their responsibilities are regarding the patient's ongoing health care needs and gives them the knowledge and skills they need to carry out their responsibilities.[4] The LNC should review these instructions for appropriateness when a posthospital complication is in contention, determine whether they are reasonable instructions applicable to the patient's diagnosis and treatment, and find out whether the patient complied with the instructions. For liability purposes, many health care facilities now require that the discharge instructions given to a patient by the nursing staff be documented and signed by the patient and the nurse discharging the patient.

Obstetrical Records

The LNC who does not possess expertise in the field of obstetrical nursing can be at a distinct disadvantage in reviewing obstetrical records. However, certain preliminary information can be determined easily. It may behoove the LNC to review the American College of Obstetrics and Gynecology's Educational Bulletins and Committee Opinions[14-17] regarding the subject at hand prior to reading obstetrical records.

Prenatal Records

Prenatal records are of extreme importance in cases involving progressive problems such as gestational diabetes and other medical conditions that become apparent or more serious at the time of delivery. The prenatal records should include a good medical history of the mother, including any prior pregnancies, family history of systemic diseases such as hypertension or genetic problems, an assessment of pelvic capacity, and progressive monitoring and management of the fetus throughout pregnancy. When the gestational age of the baby is in contention, the LNC should check the dates of the last menstrual period against the fundal height measurements and any ultrasound testing for size performed during the pregnancy. In cases involving complications from ecampsia, he or she should look for trends in blood pressure, urine protein, and edema and how these problems were managed. (Was the patient screened between 24 and 28 weeks for gestational diabetes?[15]) The LNC should look for Group B beta streptococcal screening between 35 and 37 weeks in suspected neonatal sepsis cases. (Was the patient seen frequently enough, especially in the last trimester, and if not, was this due to patient noncompliance?) He or she should determine whether any problems became apparent after the record was faxed or sent to the hospital labor and delivery suite and, if so, whether the hospital nurses were apprised of those problems.

Labor Records

Labor records contain graphic flow sheets that chart the numerous variables monitored during labor as well as narrative nurses' notes documenting the progress of labor and the patient's and fetus's response to it. The LNC should:

- Determine whether vital signs were taken with sufficient frequency, especially in cases involving fetal sepsis and preeclampsia.
- Look at the assessments of uterine contractions, frequency, and quality in cases involving placental abruption and uterine rupture.
- Assess the manner in which any oxytocin was administered. (Was it given in a judicial dose and turned off in a timely manner?)
- Judge whether the monitoring of the labor matches the fetal heart monitor strips, looking to see whether the nurses made accurate assessments of the type of fetal heart rate patterns that they were interpreting.
- Check the progress of labor on the Friedman curve. (Did the station of the fetus and the dilation of the cervix move along the curve at a reasonable rate for a primigravida or multiparous patient? Was the physician or nurse midwife informed of abnormalities in the labor progress in a timely manner? Given the situation, did the physician or nurse midwife respond appropriately?)

Fetal Heart Monitor Strips

Fetal heart monitor strips can be the definitive documentation in an obstetrical case that proves or disproves the plaintiff's case. Interpreting these strips correctly requires special expertise and is almost a science unto itself; LNCs are encouraged to educate themselves about the techniques involved before attempting independent interpretation. In cases in which the labor records themselves reflect a relatively normal delivery without evidence of negligence, the health care providers may have interpreted the fetal heart monitor strips erroneously. The initial fetal heart rate pattern should be carefully evaluated for the presence or absence of accelerations, decelerations, and abnormalities of the baseline. The presence of variability or variation of successive beats in the fetal heart rate is a useful indicator of fetal CNS integrity and may serve as an indicator of fetal response to hypoxia in the absence of maternal sedation or extreme prematurity. Prolonged decelerations of at least 60 to 90 seconds are always of concern and may be caused by virtually any mechanism that can lead to fetal hypoxia. When late decelerations become persistent, they are considered a nonreassuring pattern, regardless of the depth of the deceleration. Only when variable decelerations become persistent, progressively deeper, and longer lasting are they considered nonreassuring. A true sinusoidal (regular oscillation of the baseline resembling a sine wave) is always nonreassuring.[16] Fetal tachycardia may be an early indicator of maternal fever, or it may be an early response to hypoxia.

Delivery Records

Delivery records are especially important in cases in which the plaintiff alleges untimely or delayed delivery resulting in an asphyxiated baby or in cases involving birth trauma, such as Erb's palsy. The LNC should determine the exact amount of time that passed between the recognition or appearance of fetal distress and the time of delivery, whether cesarean or vaginal. (Was this time period and method of delivery reasonable given the presenting problems?) In cases involving cephalopelvic disproportion and birth trauma, he or she should determine whether the correct sequence of maneuvers was carried out to effect vaginal delivery and ascertain the type of personnel present at the delivery and their role in the care of the patient and infant. In cases in which a compromised infant is suspected, a neonatal nurse and a pediatrician are often necessary. (Was the baby resuscitated properly and by whom?) It is important to determine who made the Apgar assessment and whether or not the assessment was made at 1, 5, and 10 minutes of age. In a case where hypoxic ischemic encephalopathy is alleged, the LNC should keep in mind that causation in such a case cannot be proved solely on the basis of Apgar results. The American Academy of Obstetrics and Gynecologists (ACOG) and the American Academy of Pediatrics (AAP) have determined that profound metabolic or mixed acidemia (pH < 7.00); Apgar score of 0 to 3 for longer than 5 minutes; neonatal neurological manifestations such as seizures, coma, or hypotonia; and multisystem organ dysfunction are all demonstrated in the neonate who has had asphyxia, severe enough to result in acute neurological injury, proximate to delivery.[18] (Was the baby resuscitated appropriately and by whom?)

Dietary Records

The LNC should examine dietary records to:

- Check ideal body weight recommendations versus the documented actual body weight
- Check monitoring of albumin levels in a patient who develops pressure ulcers
- See whether the physician has followed the dietician's recommendations concerning tube-feeding solutions, rate of administration, etc.

Physical Therapy, Occupational Therapy, and Speech and Language Therapy Records

The LNC should examine physical therapy records to see whether the physical therapy staff is documenting the amount of assistance needed by the patient, and if this correlates with the nursing notes. LNCs should compare the outcomes and recommendations noted by the occupational therapy documentation with the nursing notes to determine whether they correlate. Speech and language therapy is responsible for providing swallowing evaluations, which are important for patients at risk for aspiration. The LNC should find out whether the health care providers followed these recommendations.

Review of Other Medical Records

Physicians' Office Records

Physicians' office records vary greatly from specialty to specialty. An internist who has seen a patient for many years may have extensively documented medical records, whereas an ophthalmologist may keep small index cards full of terms and acronyms unfamiliar to anyone without ophthalmology training. For maximum information to be extracted from these records, they should be placed in chronological order and logically sequenced.

The LNC should begin a review by determining how and why the patient came to see the particular physician. Was there a referral by another physician, and what problems were specifically to be addressed? Did the physician complete a reasonable H&P examination given the nature of the problem? Were the appropriate diagnostic studies ordered? Did the physician communicate effectively with other health care providers concerning previous treatment regimens or proposed treatment regimens? Were consultations with other specialists obtained in a timely manner and were the recommendations of those specialists followed? The LNC should look for evidence of compliance on the part of the patient with the treatment regimen prescribed and analyze the types of drugs prescribed for the patient as well as the amounts, duration, and possible interactions of those drugs.

Many clues regarding the patient's lifestyle, not evident in hospital records, can often be obtained from physicians' records, e.g., drug abuse, psychiatric problems, stressful family situations, and aberrant social behavior such as domestic violence. The LNC should not overlook this type of information because of its potential impact on damages for the plaintiff.

HMO Records

The LNC should review HMO records in the same manner as physicians' records, because HMO records usually consist of a primary care physician's care and treatment of a patient with consultations obtained either "in-house" or outside the HMO or health care network. Given the incentive of HMOs to cut costs in health care delivery, the LNC should pay particular attention to the manner in which consultations are managed, i.e., whether it appears that a consultation was obtained in a reasonable period of time, whether appropriate diagnostic and health maintenance tests (e.g., mammograms) were ordered, and whether abnormal diagnostic test results were investigated or followed. Since some HMOs require that their providers limit the types of treatment for certain diagnoses, the LNC should determine whether the plaintiff was given all reasonable options or choices for treatment currently available for the patient's diagnosis. See Chapter 20 for more information.

Comparison of Allegations with the Medical Records

After systematically reviewing the medical records, the LNC should compare the complaints of the plaintiff (before a suit is filed) or the allegations of the lawsuit to the medical records to determine consistency and to detect discrepancies from the medical records. Many well-meaning but ill-informed plaintiffs have drawn the wrong conclusions from their care and treatment experiences, and the medical records may substantiate this. If the complaint has been filed, the defense LNC should use the medical records to assist in determining the validity of the plaintiff's case. Review of the medical records may indicate that the plaintiff's allegations do not parallel the actual medical negligence that occurred or that the allegations are not even focused on the proper potential defendant.

The LNC working for either the plaintiff or the defendant also identifies all alternative or potential causation theories and investigates the medical records for substantiation of these theories, in order to determine whether a case should be pursued by the plaintiff or, alternatively, vigorously defended or settled by the defendant.

Example 31.18: In the case of a plaintiff who alleges that her infant was brain-damaged due to undiagnosed and untreated Group B beta streptococcal infection, the LNC would review the medical records for other causes of the infant's condition. The LNC would look for common causes of brain injury, such as prematurity, genetic or developmental abnormalities, and even other infections such as those caused by the TORCH (toxoplasmosis, other viruses, rubella, cytomegalovirus, and herpes simplex virus) organisms.

Re-Review of the Medical Records

After the initial review of the medical records and comparison with the allegations, especially in a complicated case, the central issues of the case will become clearer to the LNC. It is often helpful at this point to clarify some issues with the client, such as the timing of a certain symptom or the effect that a surgical complication has had on the client's life. A physician defendant could be asked why certain notes were made and about their meaning. A preliminary medical literature review may also be helpful in clarifying natural history and pathogenesis of a disease or outlining information necessary to prove causation. In order to conduct a thorough medical record analysis, however, it is often necessary to review the medical records a second time, taking note of specific facts relevant to the case. The LNC should use these specifics to generate a written report as detailed later in this chapter.

Altered Medical Records

The plaintiff can use altered medical records to establish liability based upon the defendant's conscious wrongdoing. Juries do not respond favorably to intentional record alteration, and exposing such actions frequently leads to an award of punitive damages. Falsification of medical records can be the basis for both criminal indictment and civil liability for damages suffered.[3] If the plaintiff can prove that the defendant altered the medical records, most insurance companies will strongly negotiate to settle the case.

Numerous types of alterations can be made to medical records. The LNC should be suspicious of any alteration and alert the attorney to the suspected nature and validity of the alterations.

Late Entries

The most common alteration is the late entry. Hospitals usually have policies and procedures for entering later entries into the record. If the case is in litigation, and if a late entry exists, the LNC should obtain a copy of that policy. Ideally, the entry should clearly state the time and date when the late entry was written and the time and date to which the late entry refers. It is up to the LNC to determine the validity of the entry based on the context.

Example 31.19: Late entries are commonly seen on code sheets or narratives concerning codes. A late entry written one hour after the fact concerning the administration of several drugs during the course of a code can be considered a legitimate late entry. The LNC should raise questions about an entry that occurs several hours or days later and has extreme detail about the patient being monitored closely prior to the cardiac arrest, or when there are other reports in the chart, such as that the patient was cyanotic when found with the pulse oximeter turned off.

Falsified Entries

Falsification of records is rarely done, but when done, it is illegal, and physicians and nurses can be indicted and criminally prosecuted for such activity. Falsified entries include those that are backdated or changed at a later date. Detecting falsified entries demands a high level of attention by the LNC and requires that the entire record be heavily scrutinized for supporting information if the falsified entries are to be proven.

Example 31.20: A registered nurse mistakenly transfused the wrong blood to a 23-year-old who had recently undergone hip surgery due to a fracture caused by a motor vehicle accident. The nurse administered the wrong unit of blood and then took several steps to conceal the transfusion error. Upon discovering her error, she stopped the transfusion, but approximately 220 cc of blood had been transfused. The nurse failed to inform the physician and her immediate supervisor at the time she noticed the error. She disposed of the remaining blood and bag and changed her documentation on the chart pertaining to blood pressure and temperature to mask the effects of the transfusion reaction. The patient developed congestive heart failure, renal failure, and DIC and expired 7 days after the transfusion. Very shortly afterwards the case was filed and the discovery process was started. Both the hospital and the individual nurse settled for an undisclosed amount of money.

Fabricated Medical Records

Fabrication of medical records can be as damaging as falsifying entries. Fabrication occurs when a physician or other health care provider invents a set of circumstances, usually in retrospect, in order to justify the outcome of some of his or her actions.

Example 31.21: In a case involving an unnecessary hysterectomy in a perimenopausal woman, the physician's dictation in the hospital chart included a history of hypermenorrhea and dysmenorrhea that had been increasing over a period of many months and had been unresponsive to hormone therapy. This history, with varying degrees of severity, was found in several areas of the hospital chart. The physician's diagnosis was severe endometriosis and adenomyosis. However, the referring physician's records revealed that the patient had experienced no menstrual periods for several months and had been referred for left lower abdominal pain. No conservative therapy was even entertained, and the patient was taken to the operating room for hysterectomy two days after the initial consultation. The operative report and the pathology report showed no evidence of endometriosis or adenomyosis, and the uterus was of normal size. The case was settled due to the obvious fabrication of the medical records indicating the necessity for the operation.

Fabrication of the medical records also includes rewriting and replacing notes in the chart. Physicians' office records are the easiest to fabricate. New sheets can be added to the chart or copied over. The dictated notes may be inserted to replace handwritten ones that are then discarded. A whole new chart can be started and the original destroyed. Liquid correction fluid can be used on undesirable content and then the original photocopied. A common fabricated condition in the medical record is that of adhesions. A bowel or bladder perforation will be diagnosed postoperatively and the surgeon will then begin the second operative note discussing the numerous severe adhesions that were present during the first operation (which are not identified in the first operative note) and how the adhesions made the first surgery difficult.

Rewriting and replacing hospital progress notes or other health care provider notes is most commonly seen in catastrophic situations such as cardiac arrests and acute situations in a hospital that lead to a patient's untimely death due to acute and severe unrecognized postoperative surgical bleeding or progressive respiratory problems after anesthesia.

Destroyed Records or Medical Evidence

Each state has statutes or laws that address health care facilities' responsibility to maintain and protect patient records. These statutes impose a clear duty on these institutions not to lose or destroy records or medical evidence, such as radiology films or pathology specimens, within a specific time frame. Usually this time frame corresponds with the individual state's statute of limitations for medical negligence. Destruction of medical records or evidence includes loss and concealment of relevant x-rays, laboratory tests, and other evidence such as pathology slides and operative videotapes. The loss, concealment, or destruction may occur at the time of a potentially legally damaging incident or injury or at some later point when the health care provider anticipates becoming a defendant.

Omissions

Intentionally omitting a true entry or preventing one from being made, while not a written act, does constitute altering a record because the record fails to accurately reflect the care given to, and the response of, the patient.

Illegible Entries

Although illegible entries rarely constitute negligence per se, the interpretation of illegible entries may contribute to negligence by others.

Example 31.22: A 5-year-old child was given ten times the dose of a chemotherapy drug because the physician wrote the chemotherapy orders haphazardly. The pharmacist who filled the prescription and the nurses who administered the chemotherapy did not check the mathematics for the appropriate dose per kilogram of that drug prior to administering it. The child suffered an overwhelming bone marrow depression and died of the consequences.

How to Identify Altered Records

Identification of altered records requires a high degree of attention and a fair amount of skepticism on the part of the LNC. Recognition of the following findings can be the first step in proving record alteration:

- Long defensive narrations of facts that do not appear to be in sequence with the remainder of the medical record
- Pages that are written without the patient's stamp plate in one of the corners
- Notes that are written with the wrong date or time and may not correlate with the remainder of the chart
- Additions to the notes, orders, or dictated summaries that are on the edge of the page
- Laboratory records reflecting tests not done when orders and physician notes reflect that the tests were ordered
- Notes that are handwritten on top of a previous entry
- A series of separate notes by any health care practitioner that encompass a long period of time but are written one after the other with times in sequence in a seemingly homogeneous handwriting pattern, or unusual neatness or consistency in the writing
- Medical bill charges for diagnostic or laboratory tests, medications, or equipment not referenced or seen in the chart
- Fresh condition of the piece of paper compared to the general state of the medical record
- Unusual spacing of words or sentences or excessive blank spaces on a page
- References to events that occurred after the purported date of the entry
- Pathology or diagnostic findings that do not correlate with the H&P or stated need for a surgical or diagnostic procedure

Minimizing Medical Record Alteration, Loss, or Concealment

When LNCs evaluate cases from a plaintiff's perspective, it is often wise to obtain the critical evidence or copies of the same at the earliest time possible by having the plaintiff obtain a copy of his or her own medical records (as opposed to having an attorney officially write for them). This may reduce the possibility of alteration, loss, or concealment of potentially important evidence. The evidence should be conveyed in the safest manner possible, such as hand-delivery by courier or another method whereby the package can be tracked.

If the LNC suspects medical record alteration or tampering, he or she should recommend that the attorney hire a document examiner. Document examiners use a myriad of techniques that can determine, among many things, whether all writing on a page was made at the same time and whether handwriting and pen inks match. Even when the client has supplied copies of the medical record to the attorney, the attorney will submit a request for the medical record. The client's copies of the records are compared to the attorney's copies to detect any alterations. Some attorneys send a second request for the medical record after the suit has been filed, and the two copies are compared for discrepancies that are due to alterations.

Summary of the Medical Records

Determine Analysis Format Necessary to Summarize Medical Records

The *AALNC Standards of Legal Nurse Consulting Practice* require that the LNC identify the desired outcome of his or her work product as it relates to the health care issues of a case or claim.[2] When performing medical record analysis, the LNC should identify the type of analysis necessary to convey the most accurate and complete summary of the medical records that the case requires.

Chronologies of Events

A chronology should refer the reader to the exact location in the medical records of all the information presented. This can be accomplished by referring to the date and type of entry, or by page number of the entry if the records are paginated. An overwhelming amount of information can be simplified into a manageable sequence of events. Chronologies can be extremely useful in outlining a minimum of events to assist an attorney in understanding a sequence of events in a patient's history.

Alternatively, a chronology can encompass a myriad of details concerning the patient's medical history and treatment (see Appendix 31.4) and can be a very useful tool throughout discovery and even in the trial. However, during the course of discovery, additional facts concerning the plaintiff's medical history may become known or additional theories of liability developed that the original chronology does not address. It is wise to date the chronology and update it from time to time as additional facts become known. Appendix 31.4 illustrates the medical history of a baby with complex respiratory problems who was being weaned from paralyzing drugs after a tracheotomy and suffered a respiratory and cardiac arrest.

In cases in which the medical records are sketchy on details, yet there is an abundance of deposition testimony reflecting timing (such as in anesthesia-related cases) or dates, the LNC can take a chronology and incorporate only the information gleaned from the medical records into information obtained from the depositions.

Chronologies such as these, if done correctly, prove extremely useful during discovery and at trial in clarifying and delineating sequences of events and actions. The LNC and the attorney, or any other legal professional, should be cautioned not to rely on chronologies in place of the medical record itself, since a chronology is useful only to the extent that it includes *all* relevant information regarding the plaintiff's medical records.

Charts and Graphs

In some cases, the most effective summary of medical information is a chart or timeline that communicates important facts of the case immediately. A chart or graph may be as simple as an inventory of laboratory results, or it may consist of more complicated graphic representations of certain facts. Figure 31.1 involves a woman with familial hyperlipidemia who was given subcutaneous estrogen pellets after a hysterectomy and oophorectomy. Her physician then gave her a prescription for Estrace to be taken in addition to the estrogen pellets, which the plaintiff alleged to have caused extreme hypertriglyceridemia resulting in severe acute hemorrhagic pancreatitis. Charts like Figure 31.1 can be used to incorporate a modicum of relevant events and actions and illustrate alleged cause and effect on some aspect of the patient's well-being.

Summaries

A short summary or outline of the facts of a case may be all that is necessary or desirable for an attorney, especially in a relatively simple medical malpractice or personal injury case. A plaintiff's attorney who is screening a case to decide whether to pursue it further will most likely want a brief summary that he or she can use to make decisions regarding the next step. The LNC's recommendations regarding the merits of the case should accompany this summary and will be useful to the attorney in the screening process. Personal injury attorneys usually have a large number of less complex cases and need the basics of who, what, when, where, and how from the medical records instead of meticulous physiological and standard-of-care detail. Their interest is the effects of an accident or event on the client compared to the client's preexisting condition.

A defense attorney may want to use a short narrative type of summary when planning how to approach a case initially or when communicating with the insurance carrier, but will want an extensive timeline or chronology once the case is well in progress. Medical negligence cases usually require more extensive detail because the focus is on medical or nursing judgment and whether or not the professionals involved complied with the standard of care.

Alternatively, the attorney may have a good understanding of the facts of the case but want the LNC's input in determining discrepancies or problem points in the medical record (see Appendix 31.5). In this situation, the LNC may want to provide an objective summary that discusses the facts of the case but adds the LNC's subjective comments, always in parentheses, to assist the attorney in understanding the context of the medical record findings and follow-up recommendations. Appendix 31.5 is an example of such a summary of a case involving a young man who was hospitalized in a small rural hospital after a motor vehicle

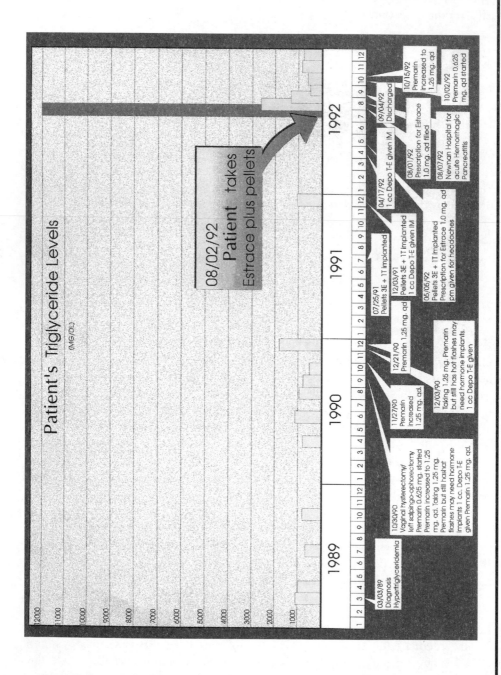

Figure 31.1   Graph Illustrating an Alleged Effect of Estrogen on Triglyceride Levels

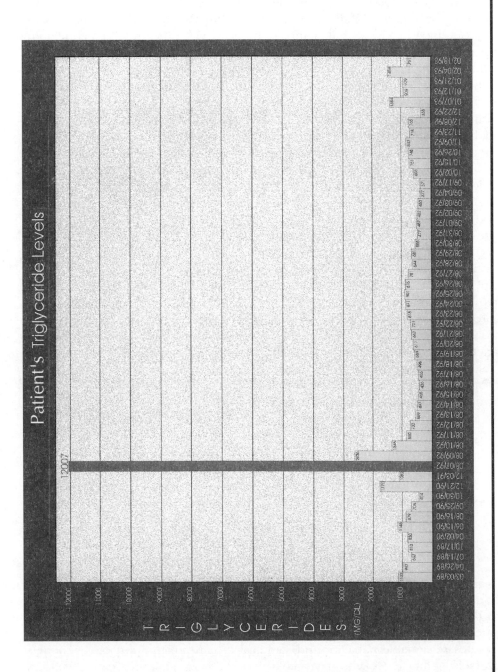

Figure 31.1 Graph Illustrating an Alleged Effect of Estrogen on Triglyceride Levels (*Continued*)

accident. He was admitted with abdominal pain for observation. Less than 12 hours later, he developed severe septic shock from a ruptured stomach and died the following day.

While there are many different LNC approaches and attorney preferences to medical record summaries, most attorneys want to read an analysis that not only gives a concise overview of the facts and issues, but also helps them to understand the bottom line quickly. With this approach, the LNC can begin with a concluding paragraph followed by substantiation of those facts and opinions. This could include review of the medical records in relation to the issues in contention in the case, as well as the standard of care (in a medical or nursing malpractice case) and the current medical literature on the subject.

Some summaries require total adherence to chronological order to be under-standable. In such cases, the date and time of the care provided are of great importance. Other types of cases require that each health care provider's care be summarized chronologically and separately so that the attorney can see exactly what kind of treatment each provider rendered to the plaintiff. Yet another type of summary can be done in cases with multiple injuries or trauma. The records can be very briefly summarized by injury so that the attorney can quickly see the progress of each injury from the acute event through rehabilitation and final outcome. Each health care provider's records are reviewed specifically for the portion that addresses the specific injury or diagnosis.

An in-depth summary of the medical records may be best accomplished in narrative style that puts together all the records from various health care providers in chronological order or summarizes each separately. The most comprehensive approach to a medical record summary is a formulation that not only encompasses the facts of the case as reflected in the various medical records, but also provides an objective analysis of the implications for the attorney and the client and, in a medical malpractice or even a product liability case, an analysis of the standard-of-care issues involved (see Appendix 31.6).

Whenever an LNC provides subjective commentary in any type of medical record summary, he or she should label the summary as "confidential attorney work product specifically requested by (the attorney in question)" to minimize the possibility for discovery in an adverse situation. The LNC should also be knowledgeable about discovery rules and recent court rulings regarding LNC work product in his or her state.

Pitfalls in Medical Record Analysis

LNCs must provide professional services with objectivity, free of personal prejudice and conflict of interest.[1] It may be difficult to set aside personal bias in providing analysis of medical records. LNCs who have always participated in litigation from the plaintiff's side may lose their objectivity regarding what constitutes reasonable behavior and standard of care on the part of defendants. Conversely, many LNCs who have never worked on a plaintiff's case develop a pervasive feeling that plaintiffs are "in it for the money" and are not really badly injured. These biases must be overcome in order to provide a professional and objective work product.

As the LNC gains experience, bias should become less of a problem. An LNC working for a plaintiff's attorney should always look for the defense of the case as he or she is evaluating the facts supporting the plaintiff's case, even if the negligence is obvious. Were there coexisting factors that contributed to the injury? Did the plaintiff contribute to the injury (important in some states where contributory negligence affects jury awards)? Was the injury a known risk of the procedure? When reviewing a defense case, the LNC should review the allegations and determine whether there is substantiation for them in the medical record and other evidence. (Is the defendant's documentation complete and professional? Were all the mandated policies followed?) The LNC should always look for defenses in a plaintiff's case and for facts supporting the plaintiff in a defense case, and should apprise the attorney of all the known strengths and weaknesses of the case that are evident in the medical record.

The LNC should not purport to be competent in matters in which he or she has limited knowledge or experience.[1] This is of great importance in medical record analysis. When analyzing medical records in a case involving complications from a relatively new surgical or diagnostic procedure, the LNC may not have the expertise to evaluate the complications properly, even after consulting standard texts and the medical literature. In such cases the LNC must consult a medical specialist in the relevant field prior to rendering an opinion, or inform the attorney of his or her limitations in that area. Providing inaccurate or inadequate medical analysis yields an inferior work product that will ultimately affect the LNC's professional reputation negatively.

Of paramount importance in medical record analysis is the ability to address the central issue of the case in a quick and decisive manner. An LNC may use information collected from the plaintiff or defendant for this purpose. This basic step will prevent the LNC from focusing on issues not central to the reason for the review, which wastes the LNC's time and the client's money and may even lead to incorrect conclusions. If a case is in litigation, it is always advisable for the LNC working for either the plaintiff or the defendant to review the allegations of the complaint. The LNC working for the plaintiff may be able to advise the attorney that a major point of the case was not included in the allegations. An LNC working for the defense may review the medical records based on the allegations of the complaint and immediately determine that the plaintiffs have no basis for a case at all.

One of the biggest mistakes that an LNC can make is to fail to review the entire record to get a complete overview for causation, liability, or damages. It takes practice to know how much review is necessary to be thorough. The LNC may feel constrained by the negative reaction of an attorney or insurance company to excessive time billed for such a review, yet missing critical details will not benefit the attorney's workup and resolution of the case, not to mention the LNC's reputation.

When a medical record is illegible, the LNC should not make guesses regarding its content. It is advisable to leave a blank or a question mark in the summary so that the author can be questioned further regarding the entry during a deposition. If the handwriting is legible but the copy is of extremely poor quality, insist that the health care provider or attorney provide a legible copy or permit review of the original medical record. As the case progresses, the lawyer can submit the records to the physician in an interrogatory request and request that the physician translate and transcribe the records, or, during the deposition of this physician, the deponent can be asked to read the illegible writing. If deponents are unable to read their own writing, this fact can be emphasized to the trial jury.

Overlooking missing or fraudulent records is another pitfall in medical record analysis. The fraud may be very skillfully accomplished and difficult to determine. The LNC must entertain a high degree of suspicion to make such determinations.

Reviewing the records too hastily will also prevent a superior work product by potentially missing important points in the record. Again, independent consultants being paid by the hour, and those who bill insurance companies for their work, may feel pressure to get through the material. Ethical principles require that LNCs perform their work with the highest degree of integrity,[2] and one must learn to balance the outside financial constraints with the pursuit of a superior work product.

Finally, LNCs must overcome the temptation to tell the attorney/client what he or she wants to hear. Not only would this be unethical and dishonest, but it would do undeserved harm to other parties. Instead, a thorough and competent medical record analysis will list the strengths and weaknesses of the client's position. The medical record summary and analysis should always be followed with conclusions and recommendations to assist the attorney in determining how he or she wishes to proceed.

Summary

Medical record analysis is the cornerstone of LNC practice. The successful and effective LNC approaches the compilation, organization, review, and analysis of medical records with complete objectivity, providing his or her clients with analyses that are thorough and pertinent.

References

1. American Association of Legal Nurse Consultants, *AALNC Scope of Practice for the Legal Nurse Consultant*, American Association of Legal Nurse Consultants, Glenview, IL, 1995.
2. American Association of Legal Nurse Consultants, *AALNC Standards of Legal Nurse Consulting Practice*, American Association of Legal Nurse Consultants, Glenview, IL, 1995.
3. Pozgar, G.D., Information management and health care records, in *Legal Aspects of Health Care Administration,* 7th ed., Aspen Publishers, Gaithersburg, MD, 1999.
4. Joint Commission on Accreditation of Healthcare Organizations, *2002 Hospital Accreditation Standards*, Joint Commission on Accreditation of Healthcare Organizations, Oakbrook Terrace, IL, 2001.
5. Omnibus Budget Reconciliation Act of 1987, Health Care Financing of the Department of Health and Human Services (OMBRA), 1987.
6. Sartwelle, T.P., Malpractice in nursing homes, in *AALNC Fifth Annual Conference Syllabus*, American Association of Legal Nurse Consultants, Chicago, 1994.
7. Electronic Communications Privacy Act of 1986 (ECPA).
8. Health Insurance Portability and Accountability Act of 1996 (HIPAA).

9. Janulis, D.M., Medical records, in Louisell, D.W. & Williams, H., Eds., *Medical Malpractice*, Matthew Bender, New York, 2001, 35.1–35.100.

10. St. Anthony, *St. Anthony's DRG Expert 2002: A Comprehensive Reference to the DRG Classification System*, Ingenix Publishers, Salt Lake City, 2001.

11. St. Anthony, *St. Anthony's DRG Guidebook (Diagnosis Related Groups)*, Ingenix Publishers, Salt Lake City, 2000.

12. American Society of Anesthesiologists, *Standards, Guidelines and Statements,* American Society of Anesthesiologists, Park Ridge, IL, 2001.

13. American College of Radiology, *Standards*, American College of Radiology, Reston, VA, 2001.

14. American College of Obstetrics and Gynecology, Diabetes and pregnancy, *ACOG Educational Bulletins*, 200, 1–8, 1994.

15. American College of Obstetrics and Gynecology, Fetal heart rate patterns: monitoring, interpretation and management, *ACOG Educational Bulletins*, 207, 1–9, 1995.

16. American College of Obstetrics and Gynecology, Prevention of early-onset group B streptococcal disease in newborns, *ACOG Committee Opinion*, 173, 1–8, 1996.

17. American College of Obstetrics and Gynecology, Use and abuse of Apgar score, *ACOG Committee Opinion*, 174, 1–3, 1996.

18. American Association of Legal Nurse Consultants, *AALNC Code of Professional and Ethical Conduct*, American Association of Legal Nurse Consultants, Glenview, IL, 1995.

19. Garner, B.A., Ed., *Black's Law Dictionary*, 7th ed., West Group, St. Paul, MN, 1999.

Additional Reading

Becker, S., Medical information and confidentiality, in *Health Care Law: A Practical Guide*, Lexis Publishing, 2000.

Buckner, F., Medical records and disclosure about patients, in *Legal Medicine,* 5th ed., Mosby-Year Book, St. Louis, MO, 2001.

Dewitt, R.E., Patient information and confidentiality, in *Treatise on Health Care Law*, Matthew Bender, New York, 2001, 1–131.

Roach, W., Jr., *Medical Records and the Law*, 3rd ed., Aspen Publishers, Gaithersburg, MD, 1998.

Test Questions

1. Which of the following statements is NOT true?
   A. Upon receiving a request for medical records, the facility copies and sends the entire medical record.
   B. Although records of HIV testing are considered confidential, they are routinely contained within the standard medical record release.
   C. Upon receiving a request for the release of medical records, the facility routinely sends copies of all typed reports.
   D. When maternal and fetal records are ordered, fetal heart monitoring strips require a separate request form.

2. Which of the following statements is true?
   A. The LNC should identify the type of medical record analysis necessary that will reflect the most accurate and complete summary of the medical records.
   B. A comprehensive chronology of events is necessary in every medical record review.
   C. Graphs and charts are always complex representations of the important facts of a case.
   D. In-depth summaries are necessary for the medical record review of all cases.

3. Which of the following statements is true?
   A. The attorney usually knows the strengths and weaknesses of the case that are evident in the medical record prior to the LNC review.
   B. Personal bias is not a concern when LNCs provide medical record analysis.
   C. It is important that the LNC have the ability to address the central issue of a case in a quick and decisive manner.
   D. It is not necessary to review the entire medical record to get a complete overview for accusations, liability, or damages.

4. Which of the following statements is NOT true concerning audit trails?
   A. Audit trails help reduce chances of tampering with the medical record as deletions are easily identified.
   B. Most computer systems put a date and time stamp on each entry, making it easy to identify who entered information.
   C. It is difficult to determine who altered data in a computerized medical record system because the final product will only show who last entered data.
   D. Computer medical record systems have the ability to generate audit trails that identify who entered or altered data, and in which field the information was located.

5. Which of the following statements is NOT true?
   A. In order to target certain populations for educational purposes, computerized medical record systems can identify demographic populations and create mailing lists.

B. In order to provide flexible access, it is not necessary to build security levels into computerized medical record systems.

C. Because computerized medical record systems use standard formatting for data entry, eligible handwriting is no longer an issue in interpreting what an individual has written.

D. Computerized medical record systems can provide record-formatting consistency as well as the ability to record and store medical information, such as CT scans and EKGs.

Answers: 1. B, 2. A, 3. C, 4. C, 5. B

Appendix 31.1
Certification

I hereby certify that the attached is a true and complete copy of the medical records pertaining to _____ (patient) kept in the office of _____ (health care practitioner) in my custody and that I am the custodian and keeper of said records.

I further certify that said records were made in the regular course of business of this office and that it was in the regular course of business for such records to be made at the time of events, transactions, or occurrences to which they refer or within a reasonable time thereafter.

Signed this _____ day of _____, 200___.

_____
CUSTODIAN OF MEDICAL RECORDS

Sworn and subscribed to before me on this
the ___ day of _____, 200___.

_____
NOTARY PUBLIC
My commission expires: _____

Appendix 31.2
Sequences of Records

Hospital Records

Adult	Pregnancy	Baby
Face sheet	Face sheet	Face sheet
Consents	Consents	Consents
Autopsy	Autopsy	Autopsy
Death summary	Death summary	Death summary

Adult	Pregnancy	Baby
Discharge summary	Discharge summary	Discharge summary
Emergency medical services	Emergency record	Labor summary
History and physical	Prenatal record	Resuscitation record
Consultations	Labor admission H&P	Emergency record
M.D. progress notes	Labor record	History and physical
Code sheets	Obstetrical anesthesia record	Consultations
Anesthesia reports	Delivery record	Operative reports
Operative reports	Obstetrical operative report	M.D. progress notes
Radiology	Consultations	Radiology
EEGs	M.D. progress notes	EEGs
EKGs	Code sheets	EKGs
Laboratory	Anesthesia records	Laboratory
ABGs	Operative reports	ABGs
M.D. orders	Radiology	M.D. orders
Respiratory therapy	EEGs	Respiratory therapy
Physical therapy	EKGs	Physical therapy
Occupational therapy	Laboratory	Occupational therapy
Speech therapy	ABGs	Speech therapy
Social worker notes	M.D. orders	Social worker notes
Dialysis	Respiratory therapy	Graphics
Graphics	Physical therapy	Medications
Medications	Occupational therapy	IV fluids/medications
IV fluids/medications	Speech therapy	Nursing assessment
Nursing assessment	Social worker notes	Nursing care plans
Nursing care plans	Dialysis	I.C.U. notes
I.C.U. notes	Graphics	R.N. notes
R.N. notes	Medications	Nursing discharge planning
Nursing discharge planning	IV fluids/medications	Nursing discharge summary
Nursing discharge summary	Nursing assessment	
	Nursing care plans	
	I.C.U. notes	
	R.N. notes	
	Nursing discharge planning	
	Nursing discharge summary	

Physician or HMO Records

Office Notes	Hospital Records
Consultations	Consents
Radiology	General correspondence
Laboratory	Financial records
Other diagnostic tests	

Appendix 31.3
Sample Index

HARRIET SMITH
MEDICAL RECORDS
VOLUME I OF II

Appendix 31.4
Medical Records Chronology

Memorandum

TO: William A. Todd, Esq.

FROM: Sally H. Davidson, RN, BSN
        Legal Nurse Consultant

DATE: July 21, 2002

RE: MASON v. COATES et al.

As you requested, I am enclosing a chronology of the medical records concerning the events on 11/19/01, pertaining to the weaning of Baby Mason from a ventilator, after receiving paralyzing agents post-tracheotomy.

Date/Time	Location (in Records)	Narrative
0536	ABG	pH 7.45, pCO_2 36, pO_2 51, BE 2.3, O_2 sat 87%
0536	x-ray	CXR
		Left lower lobe basilar atelectasis persists with no significant clearing compared to 11/18/00. No significant change in the appearance of the chest.
0800	Vent Flow Sht	RR 19, HR 140
		Work of breathing easy, breath sounds coarse, chest rise good, color pink
		FIO_2 0.33, Peep +4, IMV 17
		Pulse oximeter 97%, end tidal CO_2 38
		R. Guenther, RRT
1000	M.D. Notes	Pulmonary:
		Respiratory stable–pediatric #1 trach
		On IMV 17, FIO_2 0.33, IMV mode; T 96.4, HR 120–127, RR 17
		Good chest excursion, clear breath sounds
		O_2 sat 96–97%, pO_2 51–56, pCO_2 36–38, pH 7.44–7.45
		CXR — diffuse atelectasis left lower lobe
		Assess: Subglottic/laryngeal obstruction, new tracheostomy
		Plan: Will lift paralysis following radiological evaluation of femoral catheter. Discussed with Drs. Wilson and Myers.
		Coates, M.D.
1000	Vent Flow Sht	RR 18, HR 124; Pulse oximeter 97%; aerosol treatment
		R. Guenther, RRT
1006	ABG	pH 7.38, pCO_2 45, pO_2 71, BE 1.4, O_2 sat 93.5%
1010	MD Orders	1. Stat AP and lateral view of abdomen — take film directly to Dr. Abre
		2. To fluoro as needed to establish location of catheter tip
		3. D/C Norcuron when position of catheter tip confirmed
		4. When paralysis lifts, change vent to SIMV, pre____ support, use 10 cm psv level
		Coates, M.D.
1135	Vent Flow Sht	Pulse oximeter 93%; FIO_2 increased to 0.35
		R. Guenther, RRT
1145	ICU Notes	Dr. Sink paged per Dr. Coates
		G. Lillian, RN
1200	ICU Flow Sht	Fentanyl 8 mcg/ml @ 1 cc/hr
		Norcuron 1 mg/ml @ 1 cc/hr
1230	Vent Flow Sht	RR 20, HR 128; FIO_2 0.35
		R. Guenther, RRT
1245	ICU Notes	Dr. Sink here
1300	ICU Flow Sht	Fentanyl 8 mcg/ml @ 1 cc/hr

Date/Time	Location (in Records)	Narrative
		Norcuron 1 mg/ml @ 1 cc/hr
1305	ABG	pH 7.44, pCO$_2$ 38, pO$_2$ 56, BE 2.4, O$_2$ sat 95%
1400	MD Orders	Isovue dye study of central venous catheter position in x-ray department (done)
		Sink, M.D.
1400	ICU Flow Sht	Fentanyl 8 mcg/ml @ 1 cc/hr
		Norcuron 1 mg/ml @ 1 cc/hr
1430	ICU Notes	Patient transferred back to ICU. Vital signs stable.
1430	MD Notes	Pediatric Surgery:
		Left femoral venous catheter is in left common femoral vein by Isovue contrast study via catheter proximal and distal ports suitable for medications and dilute HAF.
		Sink, M.D.
1500	ICU Flow Sht	T 96.2 ax, HR 124, RR 19, BP 94/52, Mean 66, pulses 3+, <2 sec capillary refill
		Respiratory effort — IMV only; Breath sounds equal and coarse
		Color pink, warm and dry skin
		Activity — None; Norc ___ d/c'cd; Glasgow coma scale 10/15
		Position — Supine, 2 upper extremity restraints
		FIO$_2$ 33% via trach, tidal volume 115, 4 cm. PEEP, IMV 17/minute, pulse ox 99%
1500	ICU Flow Sht	Fentanyl 8 mcg/ml @ 1 cc/hr
		Norcuron 1 mg/ml @ 1 cc/hr
1500	ICU Notes	Report given to C. Hauten, RN. Pt left attended.
		G. Lillian, RN
1500	ICU Notes	Patient received. __ 9 mo old baby — baby in open crib with sides up. Upper extremities restrained on ____ ___ via trach settings per flow sheet. On cardiac/ resp. monitor and pulse oximeter with alarms set. Central venous line in left groin with maintenance fluids at 33 cc/hour. Other ports clamped. Fentanyl drip at 0.5 cc/hr via peripheral IV (PIV) in right foot. Site without redness or swelling. Scalp PIV intact, clamped. Baby remains sedated at this time. No spontaneous respirations riding vent — Foley patent to bedside bag. Nasogastric to LIS. Parents at bedside.
		C. Hauten, RNC
1526	MD Orders	Decrease Fentanyl to 0.5 cc/hr
		T.O. Dr. Coates/L. March, RN
1532	ABG	pII 7.48, pCO$_2$ 33, pO$_2$ 65, BE 2.7, O$_2$ sat 94%
1600	Vent Flow Sht	FIO$_2$ decreased to 0.30
		R. Guenther, RRT
1600	ICU Flow Sht	HR 122, RR 21/minute, BP 119/80, mean 96, pulses 3+, respiratory effort spontaneous, breath sounds very coarse and rhonchous

Date/Time	Location (in Records)	Narrative
		Skin pink and warm and dry; Glasgow coma scale 10/15
		Position — Supine with 2 upper extremity restraints
		FIO_2 decreased to 30%, TV 115 with PEEP 4 cm.
		IMV at 17/minute, O_2 saturation 98%
		Suctioned via ETT tube
		C. Hauten, RNC
1600	ICU Flow Sht	Fentanyl 8 mcg/ml decreased to 0.5 cc/hr
		Norcuron 1 mg/ml turned OFF
1600	ICU Notes	Baby moving, opening eyes, fussy. IMV decreased to 15 and FIO_2 decreased to 30%. See flow sheet for P.E. C. Hauten, RNC
1630	Vent Flow Sht	RR 22, HR 124
		Work of breathing easy, breath sounds coarse, chest rise good, color pink
		FIO_2 0.30; IMV decreased to 15/minute
		Pulse oximeter 99%, end tidal CO_2 36
		R. Guenther, RRT
1700	ICU Flow Sht	Temp 97.2 ax, HR 122
		IMV decreased to 15/minute
1700	ICU Flow Sht	Fentanyl 8 mcg/ml @ 0.5 cc/hr
		Norcuron — OFF
1800	ICU Flow Sht	Temp 98.4 ax, HR 155, RR 22
		Skin pink and warm and dry
		Activity ++ 15 (??); Glasgow coma scale 10/15
		Pupils are equal and reactive to light
		Patient supine with 2 upper extremity restraints
		FIO_2 0.30, TV 115 with 4 cm. PEEP. IMV 15/minute
		C. Hauten, RNC
1800	ICU Flow Sht	Fentanyl 8 mcg/ml @ 0.5 cc/hr
		Norcuron — OFF
1800	ICU Notes	In process of doing vital signs, respiratory therapist doing respiratory therapy. Baby became extremely agitated. Thrashing head, crying, flailing arms, legs. Sats 88–92 — bagging but no chest rise with manual bagging, unable to auscultate bagged breath sounds. Dr. Coates here, made aware of baby's agitation. Before able to place on trach collar per Dr. Coates, baby began to desat, color became mottled, unable to ventilate; baby became very stiff, dusky to blue. 1810 Dr. Coates in unit — called to bedside; attempted to reinsert trach, then to intubate; 2.5 ETT placed per Dr. Coates, but unable to get chest rise. HR decreased, sats 0. At this time, 1815, other MDs here and other nursing staff and RTs at bedside and CPR begun. Refer to code blue sheet for remainder of code. C. Hauten, RNC
1815	Code Sheet	Medication nurse Sallie Wentworth, RN

Date/Time	Location (in Records)	Narrative
		Physician in charge Dr.
		Recorder Lisa Pento, RN
		Also attending code: Drs. Peters, Sink, and Coates
		HR 0, BP 0; Pulse strength 0/4
		4 cc. Epinephrine; CPR in progress
1815	Disch Sum	The child was maintained sedated and paralyzed. He was stable until 11/19/00. At that time, while emerging from the sedation and paralysis, the child had a cardiac arrest and there was a question of displacement of the tracheostomy tube. Other considerations were that the child had a pneumothorax, after severe bronchospasm. The exact etiology of this event never was entirely clear. The child was resuscitated and chest tubes were placed. Sedgewick, M.D.
1815	Consultation	(Scallion — 11/28/00) At that time, shortly after Norcuron had worn off, the child self-removed the airway. Cardiopulmonary arrest resulted, and the child was without heart rate for some 15 minutes

Appendix 31.5
Sample Review 1

Preliminary Merit Review — Plaintiff

MEMORANDUM

CONFIDENTIAL ATTORNEY WORK PRODUCT

TO: Joseph Black, Esq.

FROM: Susan D. Johnston, RN, BSN
        Legal Nurse Consultant

DATE: June 13, 2002

RE: CHRIS SMITH, deceased
        Review of the medical records from Wender County Hospital and Northside Medical Center

---

The ER TRIAGE Assessment (6:10 p.m. on 2/18/01) reflects the abdomen to be tender, soft, and nondistended. Chris was noted to be diaphoretic and complaining of chest and abdominal pain and was using a lot of profanity. The pain was described as sharp and constant and nonradiating.

Dr. Sigelman (ER physician) notes that the abdomen was extremely tender but with no rebound or actual guarding, yet he found voluntary guarding upon deep palpation over the bladder. The bowel sounds were minimally diminished. There were two areas of induration on the lower abdomen (probably where Chris gave himself insulin shots). Sigelman felt that something had given Chris a real bash on the abdomen. Despite these observations, no abdominal flat plate x-ray was ordered, nor was any further investigation of the abdominal pain done even though Dr. Sigelman decided to admit Chris because of the amount of pain that he was in. Chris requested morphine sulfate, but Sigelman would give him only Toradol so that Dr. Collins would be able to follow the abdomen without masking. (In other words, all his thoughts were on acute abdomen, though he really did not try very hard to make the diagnosis himself.)

Sigelman ordered that Collins be notified of the admission because Chris "will need to have abdomen rechecked fairly often." (This sentence may have been added by Sigelman at a later time. It would appear that Collins was notified of the admission by the nurses sometime prior to 7:30 p.m. because he gave the orders for morphine and the first dose was given at 7:30 p.m. The question is: what was he told?)

Orders by Sigelman on admission are for "routine vitals including O$_2$ sat q1h × 8, then q4h × 2, then q shift." There is no indication in the records that this was done by the nurses as ordered. Chris was transferred to the floor at 6:55 p.m. The admission BP on the floor was 124/70. The BP was not taken again until 12:00 midnight when it had dropped to 88/70 and then not again until 4:00 a.m. when it was 82/50. There is no indication that the 88/70 was called to the attention of Sigelman or Collins. The respiratory rate was 20/min at 4 p.m., 24 at 8 p.m., 28 at 12 midnight, and 48 at 4 a.m. The rise in respiratory rate was also not called to the attention of any physician.

Collins ordered morphine sulfate 10 mg IVP q3h. (This is a *huge* dose, especially to someone who is being "observed." What can one possibly observe if you knock the patient out?)

The nurses noted the laceration to the left chest/abdomen on their initial assessment sheet. Nurse Mary Jones, RN (7a–7p) found the abdomen to be tender, firm, and rounded with positive bowel sounds in all four quadrants. She notes in the narrative notes that "patient guards entire abdomen and screams with pain upon palpation." Neither Collins nor Sigelman was notified of these findings even though they are different from the ER assessment.

Nurse Belinda Winston, RN (11–7) found the abdomen to be tender, firm, and *distended* with positive bowel sounds in all but the LLQ (questionable if you look at markings on page). She also notes in the narrative notes that Chris was complaining of pain in chest and knees and difficult respiration at 12:10 a.m. Neither Sigelman nor Collins was notified of this change in condition, and furthermore, Nurse Jenkins gave Chris an additional 10 mg of morphine IVP at 12:10 a.m. (*after* the documented hypotension).

The graphics for the 3–11 shift show that Chris voided 725 cc of urine but was incontinent of urine and bowel movement (very unusual in a patient who does not have something extremely wrong with him) one time apiece (no note as to whether this occurred simultaneously). Neither Sigelman nor Collins was notified of this event. The 11–7 "checklist" filled out by Nurse Winston reflects O_2 saturation levels of 80% down to 60%. (This is hard to believe!)

Nurse Jenkins recorded all the notes between 12:30 a.m. and 3:30 a.m. They all appear to have been written at the same time — or at least the notes from 2:15 to 3:30 a.m. The notes do not address abdominal pain specifically at all, i.e., no follow-up assessment by the nurses.

The patient was found by Nurse Winston at 4:05 a.m. to be diaphoretic with no palpable pulses and no recordable blood pressure. Sigelman was notified at 4:10 a.m. and arrived on the scene, and then Dr. Collins was notified at 4:30 a.m. Sigelman thought that the abdominal exam had changed markedly from the time of admission. There was marked involuntary guarding, guarding in the upper part of the abdomen, as well as lower and absent bowel sounds. Chris could not respond satisfactorily in order to assess for rebound tenderness.

ABG on admission to Northside Medical Center at 0635 was pH 7.09, pCO_2 40, pO_2 80, and B.E. 17.6 on 100% O_2. This shows severe metabolic acidosis (must have been present for quite some time — probably began when the respiratory rate was increasing as a compensatory mechanism). The admission PT and PTT were 14.1 and 34.4, indicating that a clotting disorder was present (probably early DIC). The admission CBC shows 23% bands (immature neutrophils) and 22% segmented neutrophils. (This is highly abnormal and indicative of bacterial infection that had been present for quite some time.) The hemoglobin and hematocrit on admission were 8.5 and 26.0 (one would expect them to be lower, but the hypovolemia, hypotension, and shock were probably sepsis-related and not entirely from loss of blood).

The operative report by Robert D. Vasco, M.D., notes gross contamination of the peritoneal cavity with gastric contents from the laceration of the stomach and only mild active bleeding from the upper left quadrant. The actual repair of the stomach laceration and spleen removal appears to have been relatively easy to accomplish. Chris died at 4:15 p.m. on 2/19/01, approximately 24 hours after the accident.

As you requested, I will obtain a certified copy of the Wender County Hospital and Northside Medical Center records as soon as the client returns the medical authorizations (not in the file as of 6/13/01). You indicated that you already have the x-rays from Wender County. It would appear that there is a good chance of proving negligence in this case. I will be happy to assist you in having this case reviewed by a medical surgical nurse as well as an emergency physician for standard-of-care issues and by a general surgeon for causation. We also need to look at the possible effect of Chris's severe brittle diabetes on his life expectancy in order to make an accurate assessment of damages.

Appendix 31.6
Sample Review 2

Preliminary Merit Review

MEMORANDUM

CONFIDENTIAL ATTORNEY WORK PRODUCT

TO: Martha Ann Bulow, Esq.

FROM: Lauren H. Griffin, RN, MSN
          Legal Nurse Consultant

DATE: February 22, 2002

RE: BISSON v. SOUTHERN MEDICAL CENTER
          Suzie Bisson, deceased
          Review of the medical records from Southern Medical Center

---

Facts of the Case:

Ms. Suzie Bisson was 66 years old when she was admitted to Southern Medical Center (SMC) by Dr. John Tucker on 8/11/01 for an anemia workup. It was determined that the most probable cause for her anemia was gastrointestinal (GI) loss of blood since Ms. Bisson had a positive hemoccult test. A series of GI tests were ordered, including an esophagogastroduodenoscopy (EGD) and a colonoscopy.

Initial laboratory tests showed abnormalities of the prothrombin time (but not the PTT) as well as the hemoglobin and hematocrit, and Dr. C. Suarez (presumably a gastroenterologist) was called to consult with Ms. Bisson. He wanted to do an EGD but thought he would wait until Vitamin K had been given for several days because of the coagulopathy that was evident. Additionally, several units of packed red blood cells were transfused to treat the anemia.

On 8/12/01, a potassium (K+) level was noted to be low at 3.2 mEq/L (normal 3.5–5.3 mEq/L). The IV fluids were changed from D5 ½ NS to D5 ½ NS with 20 mEq KCl/liter by Dr. Tucker. The IV was to infuse at KVO or at a minimal rate to keep the vein open. A second IV was started for the purpose of delivering Zantac (to decrease gastric acid secretion) at 10 cc/hr. The first low K+ level was treated with an order by Dr. Tucker for three separate doses of 20 mEq KCl to be given 1 hour apart. This was done during the early hours of 8/13/01, and a follow-up K+ level at 0630 was 4.0. A CT scan of the abdomen later that day showed a 6 cm abdominal aortic aneurysm (AAA) with no signs of leaking or rupture.

On 8/14/01 (Saturday), the K+ level was 3.4 (low again), but no attempt was made to increase the level by medications. On 8/15/01, an order for two doses of K-Lor 20 mEq to be given 1 hour apart was given by Dr. Suarez (?? can't read writing) at 1900. The K+ level was to be checked again the next morning.

At 0552 on 8/16/01 (Monday), the K+ level was still low at 3.2 despite the supplementation the previous day. An order was written at 0925 for an additional 20 mEq of KCl to be given *IV over 2 hours stat* (which indicates concern) by Dr. Suarez (?? can't read writing). The EGD was performed by Dr. Suarez that morning and showed no active bleeding from the stomach — only distended veins in the esophageal and cardia areas. The diet order by Dr. Suarez after the EGD was for clear liquids only. At this time he scheduled a colonoscopy to be done the following day, 8/17/01. An order was written for Ms. Bisson to receive nothing by mouth after midnight in anticipation of this. At 1700, a Go-Lytely GI prep was started (this involves drinking a powder that is mixed with 4 liters of fluid, which is intended to clear out the GI tract) for the colonoscopy. The last order for a K+ level was ordered by Dr. Tucker as a stat SMA-7 on 8/16/01 at approximately 2030. He ordered that a K-rider of 20 mEq be given over 1 hour if the K+ was <3.5. The result, reported at 2045, was 3.6 (low normal), which did not prompt additional K+ administration according to the orders by Dr. Tucker.

At 0830 on 8/17/01 (Tuesday), the PT results were again abnormal and called by the nurse to the attention of Dr. Suarez. As a consequence, he canceled the colonoscopy (presumably he was worried about bleeding as a complication due to the coagulopathy) and returned Ms. Bisson to a clear liquid diet. Two Dulcolax suppositories were ordered for later that day in anticipation of the rescheduled colonoscopy to be performed on 8/18/01. Another order was written for Ms. Bisson to receive nothing by mouth after midnight. Additionally, 3 units of fresh frozen plasma (FFP) were ordered (presumably due to the continued abnormal clotting factors). The infusion was stopped after the second unit because of sudden abdominal pain and worries about possible leaking from the AAA. The IV fluids of D5 ½ NS were continued at KVO.

At 0430 on 8/18/01 (Wednesday), one of the nurses called Dr. Suarez regarding continuing abnormal PT results. No mention is made of anything relating to the K+ level from 8/16/01 even though the nurse was anticipating giving Ms. Bisson a tap water enema at 0600 that morning. The IV fluids of D5 ½ NS were continued at KVO. At 0930, Dr. Suarez canceled the colonoscopy for the second time. A CT scan was done to reevaluate the AAA but no changes were found. An EKG, which appears to have been performed sometime that morning (there is no date and time on any of the EKGs), shows ST depression. Orders were written by Dr. Suarez for Ms. Bisson to receive another two Dulcolax tablets that evening and another tap water enema on the morning of 8/19/01 in anticipation of the re-rescheduled colonoscopy. An additional 5 units of FFP were to be given and an additional order was written by Dr. Suarez for 20 mg Lasix (powerful diuretic) to be given IV before the first unit and after the third unit. The first dose of Lasix was given at 2220 on 8/18/01 by Baldwin, LPN (?spelling).

At 0030 on 8/19/01 (Thursday), the nurses' notes written by Y. Pillets, LPN (the initial assessment sheet either was not done or is missing from the record) reflect that Ms. Bisson's heart rate was 120/minute (normally it was 70–84/minute) and that she was restless and trying to sit up in the bed. There is also a note to the effect that she was in a posey and some other kind of restraint device, which leads me to believe that she was disoriented and possibly agitated. The second dose of Lasix was given by Nurse Pillets at 0050 on 8/19/01.

At 0205, Nurse Pillets notes that Ms. Bisson went into ventricular tachycardia but at 0212 the patient was defibrillated for the first of four times (indicating that there must have been ventricular fibrillation). CPR was begun immediately, and a sinus tachycardia rhythm returned at 0220. Initial ABGs at 0223 reflect a pH of 7.293, pCO_2 of 34, and pO_2 of 196 on 100% oxygen and a base excess of -9.5. An SMA-7 was done at 0345 and showed a K+ level of 2.3 (drastically low). At 0615, an order was written by Dr. C. Lee for a K-rider of 40 mEq to be given IV in 100 cc of normal saline IV over 3 hours and 20 mEq KCl to be added to the regular IV fluids of normal saline infusing at 100 cc/hour. A repeat K+ at 1635 was 4.5.

Pillets' notes appear to have been written in retrospect because of their neatness and the fact that no assessment was done (the notes and the assessment are usually, or should be, started together soon after the beginning of the shift). Additionally, since there are no rhythm strips in the medical records documenting the arrhythmia causing the code, I suspect that the ventricular tachycardia actually occurred prior to 0205 and/or not very effective or timely CPR was employed because the patient sustained hypoxic encephalopathy. It may be, however, that the patient's emphysematous disease prevented effective oxygenation in a CPR situation.

Dr. Mission, a cardiologist, was consulted and concluded that the low K+ level probably caused Ms. Bisson to go into ventricular tachycardia. As a result of the cardiac arrest and code, Ms. Bisson's clinical condition deteriorated. She developed hypertension, which was treated in the ICU with Nipride. It soon became evident that she had suffered hypoxic encephalopathy during the arrest. Ms. Bisson had a second cardiac arrest in the early hours of 8/21/01 and was noted to have blood in her endotracheal tube and a rock-hard abdomen during the code. She was not successfully resuscitated. There is no autopsy contained in these records, but it would appear that Dr. Tucker felt as though she died due to a ruptured AAA.

Analysis of the Issues of the Case:

This is not an uncomplicated case in terms of the medical issues involved. Ms. Bisson was obviously a sick woman with a variety of medical illnesses that had to be addressed and evaluated at the same time. She obviously had a large AAA that needed repair, but the vascular surgeon felt that this was stable and that it was more important to determine the cause of her underlying medical problems causing the anemia, elevated PTs, etc., prior to operating. There was some question whether or not Ms. Bisson had multiple myeloma, but this was never proven. The underlying medical problem (whatever it is determined or guessed to be) will be used as the defense in this case to question causation and to minimize life expectancy.

It is clear from the beginning of the hospitalization that Ms. Bisson was having problems maintaining a normal K+ level. She had been on Vasoretic (Vasotec and hydrochlorothiazide, a diuretic) prior to hospitalization, but once she was hospitalized, she was not given much in the way of food (most of the time she was on a clear liquid diet or NPO) or regular substantial K+ supplementation in her IV fluids. Obviously 20 mEq KCl/liter of IV fluids was not enough to maintain Ms. Bisson's K+ level given that she was receiving her IVs at only a KVO rate. KVO rates are left to the discretion of the nurses and it would appear that she did not receive any more than 50 cc/hour (and most times less) while she was hospitalized. It is difficult to tell how much IV and oral fluid she was receiving because the intake and output records are not complete. At the same time, from 8/16/01 through the time of the arrest on 8/19/01, Ms. Bisson was being prepared for, or undergoing, GI evaluation. In addition to limited fluids by mouth, she was given two Dulcolax tablets on 8/17/01, a tap water enema, two more Dulcolax tablets, and 20 mg of IV Lasix on 8/18/01, and shortly before the arrest on 8/19/01, she was given an additional 20 mg of IV Lasix. The reason for the Lasix was to minimize fluid overload in the face of receiving 5 units of FFP (about 1000 cc of fluid) to correct abnormal clotting factors.

The problem here is that no one, physicians and nurses alike, bothered to remember or check the laboratory studies regarding the previous K+ problems. As a result, Ms. Bisson was allowed to go for nearly 3 days *after* a borderline low normal K+ level on the evening of 8/16/01 without an additional K+ level being checked in the face of minimal K+ supplementation and numerous medications and procedures known to decrease K+ levels. As an additional physician concern, it would appear that the last EKG taken before the arrest showed ST depression, which is typical for hypokalemia. The nurses' notes also show tachycardia and restlessness and possible confusion, which are also signs of hypokalemia. It is not reasonable for the nurses to have determined that Ms. Bisson was indeed hypokalemic, but it is reasonable for them to have suspected that it might be a problem and communicated all abnormal findings to a physician.

Finally, the cardiologist, Dr. Macheski, concluded that the cause of the arrest (which subsequently caused the hypoxic encephalopathy, hypertensive events, and apparent AAA rupture) was a low K+ level (and he would be considered an expert regarding this), probably because there was minimal evidence for another cardiovascular or pulmonary cause. The only downside to this is the fact that the patient converted to a sinus rhythm rather easily after CPR was started and that the K+ was not supplemented after the arrest until approximately 5 hours later, during which time there appear to be minimal problems with the cardiac rhythm. This may be explained by the use of IV Lidocaine during the arrest, which numbs the heart and increases the threshold for arrhythmias. Additionally, often during CPR, K+ will be released from the cells into the plasma due to the inherent injury caused by the act of performing CPR.

Deviations from the Standard of Nursing Care:

It is my opinion that the nurses employed by SMC were negligent in the following actions or omissions to act in the nursing care and treatment of Suzie Bisson:

a. In administering medications including Dulcolax and Lasix and a tap water enema to Suzie Bisson on 8/17/01, 8/18/01, and 8/19/01. The nurses employed at SMC administered two Dulcolax tablets on 8/17/01; two Dulcolax tablets, a tap water enema, and 20 mg Lasix IV on 8/18/01; and an additional 20 mg of IV Lasix on 8/19/01 to Ms. Bisson without ever questioning her K+ level. They knew or should have known that such medications and a tap water enema can cause a decrease in the K+ level; that Ms. Bisson had had minimal amounts of potassium administered in her IV fluids during the previous 48 hours; and that the last measured K+ level on 8/16/01 was 3.6 mEq/liter. They also knew or should have known that Ms. Bisson had had nothing more than a clear liquid diet during this same period of time.

b. In failing to report changes in Ms. Bisson's clinical condition to a physician during the early morning hours of 8/19/01. The nurses employed at SMC failed to report changes in Ms. Bisson's clinical condition, including sinus tachycardia, restlessness, probable confusion, and the need for restraints, to a physician during the early morning hours of 8/19/01 when they knew or should have known that Ms. Bisson had a history of hypokalemia, had received a number of medications and a tap water enema that could potentially lower her K+ level to a dangerous level, and had had only minimal amounts of K+ administered in her IV fluids, and that the last measured K+ level on 8/16/01 was 3.6 mEq/liter.

It is my opinion, to a reasonable degree of nursing certainty, that had the nurses employed by SMC appropriately evaluated and provided nursing care for Suzie Bisson, she would not have developed a dangerously low K+ level.

Chapter 32

Literature Research

Karen L. Wetther, BSN, MS, RN, and Maureen A. Cregan, RN

CONTENTS

0-8493-1418-6/03/$0.00+$1.50
© 2003 by AALNC

Objectives

- To identify the steps in a database search
- To list two ways to access information from the National Library of Medicine
- To list five National Library of Medicine databases other than MEDLINE® that can be helpful in accessing information on specific topics
- To state one drawback of using information from the Internet
- To identify two Internet sites that might be beneficial in researching information for a case involving alternative medicine
- To identify three sources for finding expert witnesses
- To list two sources that can be used to research a physician's credentials
- To state two ways to determine the validity of published information
- To list two sources for locating standards of care or clinical practice guidelines
- To state one method of doing a docket search

Introduction

One of the valuable services that a legal nurse consultant (LNC) can offer clients is the ability to identify and locate biomedical information specific to issues in their cases. Most nurses are relatively comfortable doing research in health sciences libraries and have had considerable experience in retrieving information from medical and scientific textbooks and journals. They may not perform online literature searches with the same amount of ease.

We live in an information society, and much of the information is not available in textbooks. Because of time constraints in the publication process, textbooks cannot have the most recent information. They do contain a wealth of information, and their detailed, in-depth material is invaluable for many research projects. Because the LNC often needs to locate information relating to medical conditions, procedures, standards, and practice guidelines that were relevant at the time of the subject incident or accident, textbooks are often very pertinent and helpful.

The most current information can be accessed on the Internet, which links minds worldwide. The Internet has revolutionized the way that LNCs perform their research projects. While online information on certain topics and at different sites may still be somewhat limited, the volume of information on the Internet is rapidly expanding and becoming more sophisticated. The information explosion is exciting but can also be daunting to the LNC who needs to expeditiously find the needle in the proverbial haystack.

The goals of this chapter are to help the LNC develop the art of identifying and locating information appropriate to clients' needs; to increase awareness of the many resources available; and, perhaps most important, to help the LNC analyze the information obtained for its validity and credibility in the medical and scientific literature.

Research Sources

The LNC can consult a variety of sources to identify the best available evidence on a medical topic or to research a medical professional's credentials:

- Consultation with a professional in the appropriate specialty
- Textbook research
- Professional specialty organizations (e.g., American Association of Critical Care Nurses [AACN] and American College of Obstetrics and Gynecology [ACOG])
- Governmental agencies (e.g., Food and Drug Administration [FDA], Centers for Disease Control [CDC], National Institutes of Health [NIH])
- Nonprofit organizations (e.g., American Cancer Society and National Kidney Foundation)
- Directories (e.g., the *Official ABMS Directory of Board Certified Medical Specialists* and the *Health Care Standards Directory*)
- Computerized literature searches using a bibliographic database such as MEDLINE
- The Internet (which can provide access to all of the above-listed resources)

Overview of the Research Process

The nursing process serves LNCs well when they conduct research. Each element of that process is critical to a research strategy that delivers the best results.

Assessment

This initial step in the process involves assessing what information is needed from the client in order to conduct a valid search. Failure to collect the important data at the outset may result in delays and may not provide complete information specific to the client's case. In addition to knowing the topic that should be researched, the LNC should understand the issues involved in the case: the date of loss (i.e., the date when the incident or accident occurred); the age and gender of the plaintiff; ethnicity; concurrent medical conditions; medications taken; whether the client has a preference for textbook information or medical or nursing journals; how far back in years the search should extend; and the date of the subject incident. An easily retrievable form is helpful in prompting the LNC to solicit the necessary information (see Figure 32.1).

Analysis and Issue Identification

The LNC must use analytical and critical thinking skills to sort out the primary issues to be addressed. The client may have identified one issue that he or she

Client _____ Date _____
Firm _____ Due date _____
Address _____ Date of loss _____
_____ E-mail _____

_____   _____
Phone _____ Fax _____
Case Name _____ File # _____
Client represents _____Plaintiff _____Defendant
Type of case _____Med Mal _____PI _____Products Liability
          Other _____

Issue(s): _____
_____
_____

Topic(s)/Author(s) to be searched (be specific): _____
_____

Gender: _____Female _____Male   Age: _____
Ethnicity _____
Diagnoses (primary and secondary) _____
_____

How far back should search extend? _____

Limit search to (circle letters): a b c d e f
a Medical journals   b Nursing journals   c English language
d Medical text books   e Nursing textbooks   f Other_____

_____

Figure 32.1   Literature Search or Medical Research Request (Modified from Wetther, K.L., ***The Nuts and Bolts of Legal Nurse Consulting,*** **2nd ed., Medical Legal Resources, Carlsbad, CA, 2001. With permission.)**

considers to be the key issue, whereas the LNC may have a different opinion once the initial data is solicited and the situation is analyzed.

Example 32.1: An attorney reports to the LNC that his client is a woman who has asked him to file a wrongful death suit against a hospital due to the death of her husband. Subsequent to undergoing coronary bypass surgery, her husband became increasingly depressed and agitated. He presented to the emergency department (ED), accompanied by his wife, and she told the triage nurse that she felt he needed medication to treat worsening depression and agitation because he no longer had any interest in anything and refused to eat. His primary physician was paged but was on vacation, the house M.D. was paged but said he could not authorize treatment because he was not one of the patient's HMO providers, and a third physician was paged who was an HMO provider, but he failed to respond. After waiting in the ED for four hours, the patient left and, later that afternoon, committed suicide by shooting himself in the head.

The attorney tells the LNC that he needs to know what the standard of care is for a triage nurse in the ED when a patient offers complaints of depression and agitation. The LNC agrees that this is a key issue but also feels that, since the nurse did attempt to reach three physicians but was unable to obtain authorization for treatment, perhaps the larger issue is the protocol that the hospital and HMO have in place for authorizing treatment when psychological complaints are observed, and for obtaining treatment for a patient whose primary physician is unavailable.

Outcome Identification

After collecting the initial data from the client, analyzing it, and identifying the primary issues, the LNC must identify the desired outcome of the literature search. The LNC should consider these questions:

- What does the client need to prove?
- Are the key issues controversial?
- Does the client want the full articles or are article abstracts or synopses sufficient?
- How soon is the material needed?

Planning

For this chapter's purposes, planning involves determining which types of textbooks to research (if textbook research is required); researching standards of practice or a physician's credentials; or, in the case of a computerized search for journal articles, selecting the most relevant medical subject heading (MeSH) for the MEDLINE search and appropriate *limits* in order to retrieve the most relevant articles. Planning expedites and focuses computerized literature searches.

Example 32.2: An LNC is asked by an attorney to research abdominal rhabdomyosarcoma because she has a potential client who believes that a delay in the diagnosis of her 14-year-old daughter's condition resulted in her death in September 2000. The LNC may decide to look for pertinent information in pediatric oncology textbooks and to perform a computerized literature search for medical journal articles relating to this issue. The LNC accesses PubMed® or MEDLINEplus® on the Internet via the National Library of Medicine Web site (http://www.nlm.nih.gov), enters the MeSH term "'Rhabdomyosarcoma'" in the query box, and clicks on the word *GO*, resulting in a search that yields 7327 citations. In order to expedite the search and retrieve only the articles most relevant to this potential case, the LNC clicks on the word *Limits* just below the query box to limit the search according to the options presented. By limiting the search to the *Adolescent (13–18 years)* age group, *English language* articles only, *Human* studies only, and the publication years *1995 to 2000,* the number of citations decreases to 378. Noting that many of the articles (citations) retrieved pertain to rhabdomyosarcoma at various sites of the body, the LNC limits the citations retrieved to retroperitoneal rhabdomyosarcoma by adding two words in the query box after the word *Rhabdomyosarcoma* — the Boolean operator *AND* followed by the word *peritoneal.* Keeping the same limits selected previously, she clicks on *GO* and notes that the search decreased the number of citations to only 9, but they are more pertinent to the primary issue than the 378 citations retrieved previously. She decides to go back 10 years rather than just 5, so clicks onto *Limits*, changes the range of publication dates to *1990 to 2000,* and retrieves 19 citations.

It is also possible to click on *Abstracts only* when limiting a search, since an abstract is not available for some articles. This would retrieve only those articles that have abstracts, but some relevant citations may be missed if this option is chosen. The LNC can always obtain the articles that do not have abstracts if the titles appear to indicate that the articles may be relevant to the topic being searched.

Implementation

Implementation is the act of following through with the established plan. In Example 32.2, the LNC chose the appropriate MeSH term and limited the search to fit the parameters of her client's case. This decreased the number of citations from 7327 to 19, a reasonable number to review. Each case is different, and the LNC must use critical thinking skills to determine whether the resulting number of citations, once limits have been selected, is too small. Limits may be deselected, which results in a larger number of citations, but many of the articles may not be pertinent to the primary issues. Also, if the search is limited to *Review articles*, most likely fewer citations will be retrieved — but Review articles provide an overview of the medical literature on a specific issue or topic, so the author has done some of the LNC's work.

To implement the plan, the LNC viewed the 19 citations and their abstracts and selected 10 of those that appeared to relate to the client's case. The next implementation step is to print out the citations and abstracts selected. In some cases, the articles can be ordered (see discussion of Loansome Doc® below), or the LNC may retrieve the 10 journal articles from the library shelves. For LNCs who are employed by a hospital or medical center, the medical librarian often retrieves and copies articles free of charge. Some LNCs with easy access to a large medical library offer document-retrieval services to other LNCs and will retrieve and send (or fax) full-text articles for a fee.

Evaluation

Before copying textbook information and articles for the client, the LNC should review them to evaluate whether or not the information is relevant to the client's case and needs. The client may need broad information on a medical topic or issue for his or her own education before accepting a case or deposing medical professionals, or specific information to support his or her position. The client's needs, of course, should have been determined early in the process by asking the client and can then be evaluated by the LNC once the information is retrieved.

The LNC must be able to answer the question: "Will this information meet my client's needs for this particular case?" If not, "Plan B" must be formulated, followed by implementation of the plan and subsequent evaluation. If the first four steps of the process (assessment, analysis and issue idnetification, outcome identification, and planning) are completed thoughtfully, implementation and evaluation should be successful.

Textbook Research

The LNC should not find textbook research particularly challenging as long as access to a health science library is available. The LNC's personal library is helpful for immediate access to information but may not be extensive enough to rely on for many research projects.

The following pointers will help to safeguard the LNC who relies on printed information to support a position relating to a medical issue or topic:

- Use grandfather texts, i.e., authoritative textbooks, that are widely accepted in the general medical and scientific community. Grandfather texts are generally those used as textbooks in medical and nursing schools. (Examples are *Harrison's Principles of Internal Medicine*,[3] *Williams' Obstetrics*,[4] Ashcraft and Holder's *Pediatric Surgery*,[5] and *Nelson Textbook of Pediatrics*.[6]) A good source of authoritative textbooks and journals is the Brandon/Hill list, which is published annually in the *Bulletin of the Medical Library Association* (medical and nursing literature listed in alternate years). The list can be obtained at medical libraries by asking the librarian. It is helpful to make a personal file copy.

- Make sure that the book is time-appropriate to the case, especially when attempting to locate standards of care or clinical practice guidelines. If the LNC is researching an issue related to an incident in 2001 that is the subject of a medical malpractice lawsuit, the books consulted should have been published in, or prior to, 2001. Any information relating to standards or guidelines would have to have been available to the treating health care practitioners at the time of the subject incident.

- Refer to a minimum of three authoritative sources to confirm that there is general agreement or controversy among the experts regarding the issues in question.

- Prior to submitting printed materials (from textbooks and journals) to a client, highlight the pertinent information to expedite review of the materials. In some cases, a client may want the LNC to prepare a synopsis of each article submitted.

References and bibliographies at the ends of textbook chapters may direct the reader to additional information on the subject. Also, editors and authors of authoritative texts may be potential expert witnesses because they are considered experts in their specialties or subspecialties.

Professional Specialty Organizations, Governmental Agencies, and Nonprofit Organizations

The *Encyclopedia of Medical Organizations & Agencies*[7] provides a subject guide to more than 11,000 associations, foundations, federal and state government agencies, research centers, and medical and allied health schools. The table of contents lists medical organizations and agencies by subject, e.g., birth defects, child abuse and family violence, emergency medicine, chiropractic, and nursing.

The reader is then directed to the pages that include listings and a brief description about the organizations that relate to the topic being researched.

For example, the section on obstetrics and gynecology lists 61 national and international associations, including the ACOG, the American College of Nurse-Midwives (ACNM), the American Society for Colposcopy and Cervical Pathology (ASCCP), the International Society for Twin Studies (ISTS), the National Perinatal Association (NPA), and the Society for the Study of Breast Disease. Many of the organizations are excellent sources of information.

An LNC who has difficulty reading and understanding chiropractic records or who needs to locate recognized standards for chiropractors might benefit from consulting the section on chiropractics in *Encyclopedia of Medical Organizations & Agencies*.[7] The listing for the Commission on Accreditation of the Council of Chiropractic Education includes addresses and phone numbers as well as the chiropractic schools, listed by state, that are approved by the commission.

Another source of valuable information for the LNC is nonprofit organizations such as the American Cancer Society, the Arthritis Foundation, and the National Kidney Foundation, to name a few. They can often provide statistics, other resources relating to the condition being researched, prospective medical experts, and other valuable information. Many of their brochures are published in lay language and include simple drawings or diagrams that may help to educate the client.

Governmental agencies such as the CDC, FDA, and NIH are also invaluable resources. These may all be located through the *Encyclopedia of Medical Organizations & Agencies*[7] or on the Internet.

The *Health Care Standards Directory*[2] can help direct the LNC to health care standards, guidelines, and recommended practices, which are often difficult to locate. It includes listings for standards issued by medical societies, professional associations, government agencies, and other health-related organizations. The directory includes:

- Complete citations to standards, legislation, and referenced articles.
- An alphabetical listing of organizations that have issued standards related to health care (Listings include the full name, address, and telephone number of each organization as well as the title of each standard issued by the organization and information relating to price or how to order the standards.)
- An alphabetical listing of federal and state agencies that have issued health-related regulations or guidelines; includes the name, address, and phone number of each agency
- A quality-of-care bibliography that lists significant articles relating to assessing and providing quality health care

Computerized (Online) Literature Searches

In this information society, numerous sources of information are available on the Internet. Awareness of that information and quick access to it can significantly enhance the LNC's value to his or her clients. Online information retrieval is the process of identifying desired information by direct interactive communication with a computer.[1]

The National Network of Libraries of Medicine

A nationwide network of regional health-sciences and biomedical libraries — the National Network of Libraries of Medicine (NN/LM) — provides the nation with access to the most comprehensive collection of biomedical information in the world.

The NN/LM is based in Bethesda, Maryland. The National Library of Medicine (NLM) serves as the overall coordinator and as a backup resource for all other libraries in the network. The NLM, which is part of NIH, is the largest and most prestigious medical library in the world. MEDLINE searches tap the vast resources of the NLM.

Online Access to the NLM (MEDLINE)

The Medical Literature Analysis and Retrieval System (MEDLARS®) includes numerous databases. MEDLINE — *MEDlars onLINE* — is a database of more than 7 million references and abstracts of articles contained in more than 4000 journals published since 1966.[2] It includes three printed indexes:

- Index Medicus
- International Nursing Index
- Index to Dental Literature

Other NLM databases that, with MEDLINE, make up MEDLARS include citations and factual information about specific diseases and medical conditions, chemical compounds, health planning and administration, ethics, and toxicology, as well as a listing of books (CATLINE) and audiovisual materials (AVLINE)[2] (see Table 32.1). Further information on these databases is available from the NLM by phone or through its Web site (see Resources).

NLM Gateway

The NLM Gateway was developed primarily as a one-stop shopping site for the Internet user who accesses the NLM Web site but is unaware how best to search for information. It is user-friendly, presents a single interface that allows users to search in multiple retrieval systems, and offers value-added capabilities that the user may not know to request. It offers citations, full text, video, audio, and images.

The user enters one query (such as a MeSH term) that is automatically sent to multiple retrieval systems. The NLM Gateway currently searches:

- MEDLINE/PubMed (which retrieves citations of journal articles)
- OLDMEDLINE
- LOCATOR*plus* (catalog information for books, serial titles, and audiovisuals)
- MEDLINEplus (which includes consumer information on health topics; drug information; a medical dictionary; directories for locating physicians and dentists and checking their credentials; and access to organizations, international medical Web sites, and more)
- DIRLINE® (directory of health organizations)

Table 32.1 Selected Databases for the Health Sciences

Database/Producer	Description
AIDSDRUGS/NLM	Dictionary of chemical and biological agents being evaluated in the AIDS clinical trials
AIDSLINE/NLM	AIDS information hotline
AIDSTRIALS/NLM	AIDS clinical trials
Birth Defects Information (BDIS)/Center for Birth Defects Information Services	Full text of articles and monographs, differential diagnosis system for birth defects
CANCERLIT/U.S. National Cancer Institute	Cancer literature contained in journals, monographs, reports, dissertations, and meeting papers
CATLINE/NLM (CATalog onLINE)	Catalogued titles (books) in the NLM
CHEMLINE/NLM	Factual information on chemical substances and properties
DIOGENES: Washington News Document Retrieval Network/FOI Services	Full-text *Federal Register* notices and reports, FDA approvals, Washington Business Information publications, and Medical Device Reports
DIRLINE (DIRectory of Information Resources onLINE/NLM)	Directory of organizations providing information services
DRUG INFO/University of Minnesota	Drug information published in journals, books, and other print formats
Hazardous Substances Data Bank (HSDB)/NLM Toxicology Information Program (TIP)	Full-text information on potentially hazardous chemicals
Health Device Alerts/Emergency Care Research Institute (ECRI)	Full-text problem-reporting network for medical equipment and supplies industry
MEDLINE/NLM (MEDlars online)	Journals contained in the NLM
MeSH Vocabulary File/NLM	Dictionary of current biomedical subject headings for MEDLINE and other NLM databases
NIOSH/U.S. National Institute for Occupational Safety and Health	Published and unpublished technical material, NIOSH reports, and conference proceedings
Nursing and Allied Health Database (CINAHL)/CINAHL Information Systems	Journals, ANA and NLM publications, dissertations, books, and popular literature
PsychINFO/American Psychological Association (APA)	Periodicals, reports, and dissertations on psychology topics
TOXLINE/NLM	Journals, monographs, reports, theses, meetings, papers, and abstracts relating to environmental toxins

- AIDS meeting abstracts
- Health services research meeting abstracts
- Space life sciences meeting abstracts
- HSRProj (health services research projects)

The Gateway also provides document delivery via Loansome Doc (see "Retrieving or Ordering Articles" below).

Steps to Performing an Online Search

A MEDLINE search can be performed by accessing the NLM Web site directly (http://www.nlm.nih.gov) and clicking on *PubMed* or by accessing MEDLINE from a number of different medical Web sites. Either way, the following steps should expedite and focus the search to achieve the best results.

1. Collect adequate information from the client to formulate a focused search strategy.
2. Formulate the overall search strategy.
3. Input the MeSH term(s), author, or journal that is the focus of the search in the Search or Query Box (see the sections on Author Searches and Journal Searches below).
4. Limit the search, if desired.
5. Click *GO* or *Search* to retrieve the results of the search.
6. View the citations and click on relevant citations to view the abstracts (if available).
7. Print out search results (list of citations and relevant abstracts).
8. Locate or order articles.

MeSH Term Searches

A MeSH term search is the most common type of search and involves entering one or more MeSH terms in the Query (Search) Box. Either a single term or multiple terms can be entered; multiple terms can ensure a more focused search. If additional terms are entered, Boolean operators (AND, OR, NOT) should be inserted in capital letters between the terms. (PubMed now automatically adds the Boolean operator "AND" between multiple terms when retrieving citations.)

Example 32.3: An LNC is asked to do research on malignant melanoma for a case in which the primary issue involves the failure of the defendant physician to diagnose melanoma and treat the condition or refer the patient to a dermatologist in a timely manner. If the LNC performed a search using the single term *Melanoma* in the Query Box, thousands of citations would be retrieved and many would probably be irrelevant to this case. In order to focus the search, keeping the primary issue in mind, the LNC enters "*melanoma* AND *diagnosis*," because the most important articles are those that relate to early diagnosis of melanoma.

Limiting the Search

MEDLINE allows the searcher to limit searches in order to decrease the number of citations retrieved and, more important, to retrieve only the most relevant articles. In PubMed, click on the word *Limits* beneath the Query Box after entering the MeSH terms; when the new screen appears, the user selects the limits determined to be appropriate for the search. The search can be limited to a specific age group and gender, human studies or animal studies, a particular language, a range of years, type of article, a specific journal, etc. The user then clicks on *GO* or *Search*, and the search results appear in seconds.

Author Searches

Author searches are often used when an attorney wants to review published works of opposing experts or even his or her own experts. The search is usually simple and straightforward, and no search strategy or analysis is required. The searcher need only enter the author's last name and one or two initials (first and middle names) and then click *GO* or *Search*. If the author's middle initial is not known, it is sufficient to enter the last name and first initial. This calls up all authors with that name and initial. Entering the middle initial helps to narrow the search, especially if the last name is common. If the physician's last name might be mistaken for a MeSH term, the searcher can clarify an author search by entering the physician's last name and two initials followed by [au], which designates *author,* e.g., SMITH JS [au].

The total number of citations retrieved will appear at the top of the first page. It is important to print out the *entire* list of citations; usually only 20 citations appear on each page.

The LNC may be asked to analyze or prepare a synopsis of the author's articles once they have been located and retrieved, or to review the expert's deposition transcript (if the deposition has been taken) followed by a review of the expert's publications for any discrepancies that might provide a basis for impeachment.

Journal Searches

Limiting a search to one particular journal is time-efficient in certain situations. For instance, an attorney may learn by an opposing expert's deposition that an article that related to a particular issue in the case was recently published in the *Journal of the American Medical Association.* However, he or she is unsure of the issue's publication date or the article's title. The attorney may relay this to the LNC so that the article can be retrieved. To perform this type of search, the LNC should enter the name of the desired journal or the abbreviated title in the Query Box (Search Box) instead of or in combination with a MeSH term or author's name. A health sciences reference librarian can provide a list of accepted journal abbreviations.

Retrieving or Ordering Articles

Loansome Doc is the document retrieval system offered by the NLM. It allows users to order full-text copies of articles located on MEDLINE from a medical library. The user must register with the NLM to use the service. The NLM Web site walks the user through the registration and ordering processes. An agreement must first be established with a local library that uses DOCLINE®. If unsure about which library to contact, the user can call 1–800–338–7657 on weekdays between 8:30 a.m. and 5:00 p.m. (all time zones) to connect with the appropriate NLM Regional Medical Library. *Loansome Doc* service charges a fee.

If access to a local medical library is available, obtain the articles needed and copy them at the library for a nominal fee or, if employed at a hospital or medical center, order the articles from the medical librarian at no charge.

Internet Access to Biomedical Information

The Internet may be described as a vast conglomeration of computers connected in a variety of ways to form a worldwide network.[8] The amount of information available on the Internet is staggering, and the Internet is doubling in size and traffic every two months.[9]

Benefits and Drawbacks to Accessing Information via the Internet

The primary benefits of using the Internet to access information of any type are speed and volume. Current technology enables rapid transmission of large files, including those with color images, sound, and even motion pictures. With regard to volume, vast numbers of computer users can simultaneously send mail and take part in electronic bulletin board discussions.

The major drawbacks to accessing information on the Internet are the volume of information (also a benefit), the fact that most of the information is relatively current (a drawback if information is needed for cases that involve incidents that occurred several years earlier), and the difficulty in determining the authenticity and reliability of information available on the Internet.

Authenticity and Reliability of Information on the Internet

Anyone who uses information obtained via the Internet should be cautious about the source of the information. Anyone can publish information on the Internet, resulting in a wealth of unsupported as well as supported online information. It is the responsibility of the user to determine what information can be relied on.

The Internet has no single owner and is not subject to the laws of any one nation. The Internet Society develops protocols used to transmit information, but many aspects have developed by consensus, adaptation, and the free exchange of information and programs.[8]

No standards, review committees, or authorizing organizations monitor or control new information that makes its way onto the Internet daily, so ensuring the authenticity of much of that information is impossible. Even sites that may seem credible may simply contain information copied from some other site.

When the LNC finds an article that seems relevant to a case, it is important that it be a peer-reviewed article. Many medical sites do have articles from peer-reviewed journals, so it may be prudent to confine journal article searches to those. The guidelines are much the same as those used when retrieving articles from a health sciences library (also see Assessing the Validity of Medical Literature later in this chapter).

It is important to determine who is publishing the material. Sites from major universities, governmental agencies, and major medical centers can usually be considered to publish high-quality, well-supported information. Many medical-related Web sites abide by the Health on the Net (HON) code, which gives them greater credibility. (The HON logo should be displayed on the home page.) The HON code is available at http://www.hon.ch.

The LNC should also try to determine the credentials of the authors, including their titles and affiliations. Some sites offer more information than others regarding authors' credentials. He or she should also try to determine whether the sponsor of the site has a conflict of interest. Some sites are sponsored by individual medical or dental practitioners who may want the users to purchase products they have developed or in which they have a financial interest. They may publish articles online primarily for the purpose of gaining business from the user.

Confidentiality

The guidelines for maintaining confidentiality on the Internet are much the same as those that any clinical nurse or LNC should follow. A patient or the details of a case should never be discussed in public. (The Internet is the epitome of "public" because anyone may be online.) The LNC must use utmost caution when using the Internet — including e-mail, listservs, and talklists — to discuss anything relating to a case. All comments should be confined to general statements that cannot be specifically related to the case.

Assessing the Validity of Medical Literature

It is often said that "you can prove anything you really want to prove." All published information is not valid; the LNC should be mindful of this fact when selecting journal articles for clients or using information to support a position while filling the role of a nurse expert.

LNCs learn to develop critical-thinking skills to analyze the facts of their cases critically. This skill should extend into the area of analyzing medical literature, whether it is obtained in the library or from an online source.

Textbook research should be confined primarily to grandfather texts, e.g., authoritative texts. Clues to their validity can be found by looking at the publishers, editors, and contributors. The LNC can usually feel safe using texts published by well-known publishers of medical textbooks (examples include but are not limited to Mosby, W.B. Saunders, Lippincott, Williams & Wilkens, and Appleton & Lange), texts that have been published in several editions, and texts in which the editors and contributors are associated with reputable and well-known medical centers. However, it is always a good practice to use at least three reputable texts to be sure that there is general agreement or controversy regarding the issues being researched. Many texts published by publishers who are not well known may also contain valid information.

To help physicians review journal articles critically and to determine whether or not results of published clinical studies are valid, the Evidence-Based Medicine Working Group has published a series of articles entitled "Users' Guides to the Medical Literature."[13] LNCs may find these resources helpful. They suggest that the following questions be answered:

- Are the results of the study valid?
- Primary guides
    Was the assignment of patients to treatments randomized?
    Were all patients who entered the trial properly accounted for and attributed at its conclusion?
    Was follow-up complete?
    Were patients analyzed in the groups to which they were randomized?
- Secondary guides
    Were patients, health workers, and study personnel "blind" to treatment?

Were the groups similar at the start of the trial?

Aside from the experimental intervention, were the groups treated equally?

What were the results?

How large was the treatment effect?

How precise was the estimate of the treatment effect?

Will the results help me in caring for my patients (or, in the case of LNCs, will the results help me with my case)?

Can the results be applied to my patient care (i.e., the LNC's case)?

Were all clinically important outcomes considered?

Are the likely treatment benefits worth the potential harms and costs? (This may not be applicable to the LNC depending on the issues of the case.[13])

It is a good practice to use information primarily from refereed (i.e., peer-reviewed) journals. A statement within the first few pages of a refereed journal should identify it as such. The medical and scientific community generally views peer-reviewed journals as more credible and authoritative than those that have not been peer-reviewed. Throwaway journals may publish some interesting articles that relate to cases in litigation, but the LNC should not rely only on them. Likewise, there is much controversy over "junk science" and its place, if any, in the courtroom. "Junk science" refers to purportedly scientific information that is not widely accepted in the medical and scientific community, but that has an aura of validity. Since every article that an LNC presents to an attorney may potentially be relied on in a court of law, this must be taken into serious consideration.

In summary, the researcher should ask the following questions to help evaluate the validity of the information found in journal articles and books:

- What qualifies the author to publish on this topic?
- What is his or her reputation and affiliation?
- Did the author refer to other relevant literature on this topic?
- What is the reputation of the journal (if it is an article in a medical or scientific journal)?
- Is the article in a refereed (peer-reviewed) journal?
- If referring to a book, who is the publisher?

Biomedical Resources Available via the Internet

A comprehensive list of specific resources that an LNC might wish to access on the Internet would be too extensive to provide in this chapter. Table 32.2 is an annotated list of medical specialty sites (many of which link to other sites relating to that specialty); Table 32.3 lists resources for nursing and other health-related fields (such as chiropractic and alternative medicine); and Table 32.4 provides a small sampling of medical journals on the Internet. (Keep in mind that Web addresses change from time to time. The addresses in the tables were current at the time of publication but may have since changed or been discontinued.) A number of the medical specialty sites also provide access to many of the mainstream peer-reviewed medical journals.

Table 32.2 Medical Specialty Sites on the Internet

Specialty	List or Site	Description	Address
AIDS	HIV Insite	A project of the University of California, San Francisco (UCSF), AIDS Research Institute; UCSF AIDS Program at S.F. General Hospital; Center for AIDS Prevention Studies; and the Henry J. Kaiser Family Foundation	http://hivinsite.ucsf.edu
	JAMA HIV/AIDS Information Center	News reports, treatment guidelines, resources for patients and professionals, prevention facts and policy reviews	http://www.ama-assn.org/special/hiv
Alternative medicine	Complementary and Alternative Medicine Homepage	Oregon Health & Science University site	http://www.ohsu.edu/ohmig/camlinks.html
	Alternative Medicine AltMed Web	Falk Library of the Health Sciences site, University of Pittsburgh; has links to other sites	http://www.pitt.edu
		An international directory of alternative medicine practitioners	http://www.teleport.com/~mattlmt
Anesthesiology	GASNet (Global Anesthesia Network)	Excellent anesthesia resource from Yale University; links to other sites	http://gasnet.med.yale.edu
	American Association of Nurse Anesthetists	Patient, professional, and member resources	http://www.aana.com
Cardiology	American Heart Association	Sections include: Clinical Practice Guidelines, Warning signs, What's your risk?, Heart and Stroke A–Z Guide, Family Health	http://www.americanheart.org
	Cardiothoracic Surgery Network	Sections include: Outcomes and Databases, Clinical Trials, Surgeons, Organizations, Journals, Clinical Resources	http://www.ctsnet.org
Critical care	EKG File Room	Interesting EKGs with analysis and explanation	http://www.embbs.com/ekg/fileroom.html
	Archives of the Critical Care mailing list	Full text of articles related to critical care medicine; information on code status, drug therapy, medical and nursing management, resource management	http://www.pitt.edu/~crippen/index.html

Diet and nutrition	American Dietetic Association	Meta-site with links to consumer-education and public-policy sites; dietetic associations; dietetic practice groups; food, foodservice and culinary organizations; medical and health professionals; and journals	http://www.eatright.org
	Cyberdiet	Sections include: Nutritional Profile, Daily Food Planner, Assessment Tools, Food Facts	http://www.cyberdiet.com
Drugs	Drug InfoNet	Sections include: Drug Information, Ask the Experts, Pharmaceutical Manufacturer Information, Hospitals and Medical School On-Line	http://www.druginfonet.com
	RxList	Drugs currently on the U.S. market or close to approval, keyword search, RXList, Top 200 Prescriptions	http://www.rxlist.com
Endocrinology and diabetes	American Diabetes Association	Detailed information on diabetes	http://www.diabetes.org
	National Institute of Diabetes and Digestive and Kidney Disease	A part of NIH	http://www.niddk.nih.gov
Evaluation	HON Code	Code of conduct for medical and health sites	http://www.hon.ch
Experts	Expert Witness Network	Attempts to link attorneys and expert witnesses	http://www.witness.net
	IDEX	Defense-oriented services; national network consisting of more than 2000 insurance companies, defense-oriented law firms, corporations, and government entities	http://www.idex.com
	PaLAWnet	Pennsylvania attorneys' online guide to expert witnesses and consultants	http://legalcom.com
	Noble Directory	Expert witnesses, corporate consultants, speakers	http://www.experts.com
	Online Directory of Expert Witnesses	National directory of expert witnesses, continually updated; hundreds of experts and consultants; more than 400 categories of technical, scientific, and medical expertise	http://www.claims.com/online.html

Table 32.2 Medical Specialty Sites on the Internet (*Continued*)

Specialty	List or Site	Description	Address
Family medicine	Family Medicine Resources	Links to other sites that relate to this specialty	http://www.uwo.ca/fammed/resource.html
Fitness and exercise	Shape Up America	Sections include: Cyberkitchen, Body Mass Index Center, Health and Fitness, Media Center	http://www.shapeup.org
Gastroenterology	Gastroenterology Web	Links to other sites that relate to this specialty; extensive information on liver disease	http://cpmcnet.columbia.edu/dept/gi/
General medicine	ChronicIllNet	Devoted to chronic illness, information about AIDS/HIV, autoimmune disease, cancer, chronic fatigue syndrome, heart disease, Gulf War syndrome, neurological diseases, and vaccine safety	http://www.chronicillnet.org
	Doctor's Guide to the Internet	Medical news, new medical sites, new drugs, medical conferences, Internet medical resources	http://docguide.com
	HealthWeb	Provides access to evaluated noncommercial, health-related, Internet-accessible resources	http://healthweb.org
	American Academy of Family Physicians	Sections include: The Body, Common Conditions/Diseases/Disorders, Treatments, Healthy Living, Herbal and Alternative Remedies, Dictionary, Daily Health Tip	http://familydoctor.org
	Martindale's Health Science Guide — the Virtual Medical Center	Health-decision guides; huge listing of diseases and conditions organized by medical specialty; first aid	http://www-sci.lib.ud.edu/HSGuide.html
Geriatrics	Alzheimer's Web	Links to the Alzheimer Foundation; articles, books, conferences, research sites, mailing lists	http://werple.mira.net.au/~dhs/ad.html
Government	CDC/NCHS	Search feature; data and statistics; publications and products (e.g., *HIV/AIDS Surveillance Report*; *Morbidity and Mortality Weekly Report*) available in PDF (portable document format)	http://www.cdc.gov
	Food and Drug Administration	FDA consumer magazine, press releases, MedWatch	http://fda.gov

Infectious disease	HCFA Homepage	Statistics, data research, demonstration publications, forms, technical publications in PDF	http://www.hcfa.gov
	National Center for Health Statistics	FASTATS (fast statistics); Data Warehouse of published and unpublished tables; FEDSTATS (statistics compiled by more than 70 federal agencies)	http://cc.gov/nchswww
	MMWR (Morbidity and Mortality Weekly Report)	Published by the CDC; full text of the reports with searchable index; charts and tables available in PDF	http://www.cdc.gov/mmwr
Internal medicine	Yahoo: Internal Medicine	Links to relevant sites	http://www.yahoo.com/Health/Medicine/Internal_Medicine/
Journals	*Journal of the American Medical Association (JAMA)*	Web edition of *JAMA* back issues from July 1995 (volume 274) to present	http://ama-assn.org/journal/standing/jam
	New England Journal of Medicine (NEJM)	Web edition of *NEJM*; current week's journal, archives from 1990 to present	http://www.nejm.org
Malpractice	Lectric Law Library's Lawcopedia on Medicine & Law Malpractice	Topics relating to errors to avoid when handling medical malpractice cases; medical malpractice statutes; checklists for direct examination of medical experts	http://www.lectlaw.com
	Summary of United States Malpractice Laws	MC&L publications include a summary of malpractice laws organized by state and a state chart on the insurability of punitive damages	http://www.mcandl.com
Managed care	Health Administration Responsibility Project	Links to pertinent sections of the federal and California codes; relevant cases; information on ERISA; mandatory arbitration; torts, contracts, and fiduciary breach	http://www.harp.org
	Joint Commission on Accreditation of Healthcare Organizations	Information for the general public, health care organizations, professionals, purchasers, employers, and unions	http://www.jcaho.org
	National Quality Assurance Association	The accreditation body for HMOs	http://www.ncqa.org
Medical records	Medical Records Institute	Conferences, seminars, publications	http://www.medrecinet.com

Table 32.2 Medical Specialty Sites on the Internet (*Continued*)

Specialty	List or Site	Description	Address
Medicine	Medical Records Privacy	Sections include: Hot Topics, Medical Privacy Law and Policy, Consumer Advice	http://www.epic.org/privacy/medical
	American Medical Association	Links to peer-reviewed journals on the Internet; full text of *JAMA*; archived abstracts of back issues of *JAMA*; directory of medical societies in most states	http://www.ama-assn.org/
MEDLINE	MeSH Medical Subject Headings	MeSH files available for download; tree structures browser	http://www.nim.nih.gov
	PubMed	Access to the 9 million citations in Medline; basic and advanced search options	http://www.ncbi.nim.nih.gov/PubMed
Nephrology	National Institute of Diabetes and Digestive and Kidney Disease	Information on diabetes and on kidney, urologic, and endocrine diseases	http://www.niddk.nih.gov/
Neurology	Neurology	Links to other pages; information presented at the medical student, intern level; includes neuropsychological information	http://www.neuro.mcg.edu/
	Neuroland	Excellent site for any neurological information	http://www.neuroland.com
	Neurosciences on the Internet	Links to sites with information on neurology and neuroscience	http://www.lm.com/~nab
Obstetrics and gynecology	Breast Cancer Information Center	Extensive index, medical information, toll-free numbers, listservs, and regional groups	http://nysernet.org/bcic
	Gynecology Handbook	Designed for house staff; short, practical	http://indy.radiology.uiowa.edu/Providers/ClinRef/FPHandbook/07.html
Oncology	American Cancer Society	Sections include: Tobacco settlement; About the ACS; The local ACS; Finding answers; Search; In the news; WWW directory	http://www.cancer.org
	Cancer Care, Inc.	Multiple links for the cancer patient and caregivers: immediate help; online assistance; support groups and workshops for professionals	http://www.cancercareinc.org
	CancerNet	National Cancer Institute; multiple links to NIH sites relating to cancer	http:cancernet.nci.nih.gov

	Name	Description	URL
	CancerWeb	Multiple links to cancer sites	http://www.graylab.ac.uk/cancerweb.html
	Medicine Online	Cancer forums, HIV news and links, cancer links, search	http://www.meds.com
	Michigan Cancer Center	List of active protocols	http://www.cancer.med.umich.edu
	OncoLink, University of Pennsylvania Cancer Resource	Excellent site for the layperson or professional for cancer information	http://cancer.med.upenn.edu
Orthopedics	Southern California Orthopedic Institute	Good site for reviewing information on anatomy, basic orthopedics, arthroscopies, etc.	http://www.scoi.com
Pathology	PathPics	High-quality education page; excellent graphics; links to other pathology sites	http://amber.medlib.arizona.edu/pathpics.html
Pediatrics	Kids Health	American Medical Association	http://ama-assn.org/insight/h_focus/neumours
	Pediatric Neurosurgery	Information on a number of pediatric conditions requiring neurosurgical intervention or expertise	http://cpmcnet.columbia.edu/dept/nsg/PNS
Pharmacology	PharmWeb	Annotated listing of publications, electronic products, and journals related to pharmacology; links to pharmacy-related sites, including pharmaceutical companies	http://www.mcc.ac.uk/pharmacy
Physician information	American Board of Medical Specialties	Physician board certification verification	http://www.abms.org
	American Medical Association	Reviewed medical sites, medical society directory, database of over 650,000 physicians	http://www.ama-assn.org
Radiology		Radiology news; practice guidelines; practice directory; nuclear medicine teaching files; links	http://www.auntminnie.com
	Human Anatomy Online	Fun, interactive, and educational views of the human body	http://www.innerbody.com
	Mediclip	Electronic art and images to preview, purchase, and download	http://www.mediclip.com
	Merck Manual of Diagnosis and Therapy	Searchable; includes symptoms, common clinical procedures, laboratory tests	http://www.merck.com/pubs/mmanual
	OneLook Dictionaries	Links to more than 482 dictionaries, including more than two dozen medical dictionaries and glossaries	http://www.onelook.com

Table 32.2 Medical Specialty Sites on the Internet (*Continued*)

Specialty	List or Site	Description	Address
Reference	Health Square	Full text of *PDR Family Guide to Prescription Drugs, PDR Family Guide to Women's Health, PDR Family Guide to Encyclopedia of Medical Care*	http://www.healthsquare.healthology.com
Search tools	Achoo	Links to human health and disease directory; links to business and finance of health organizations and sources; links to journals, periodicals, and statistical information	http://www.achoo.com
	Hardin Meta Directory of Internet Health Sources	Directory of medical topics, conditions	http://www.llb.uiowa.edu/hardin/md
	HealthAtoZ	Current health topics in the news; BMI calculator, due-date calculator, growth calculator, target heart rate	http://www.Healthatoz.com
Sleep disorders	SleepNet	"Everything you wanted to know about sleep disorders but were too tired to ask"	http://www.sleepnet.com
Surgery	TransWeb	Organ transplant information for patients and health care professionals	http://www.med.umich.edu:80/trans/transweb
Surgery (Plastic)	Plink, the Plastic Surgery Link	Links to sites relating to plastic surgery	http://www.IAEhv.nl/users/ivheij/plink.html
Toxicology	National Library of Medicine Tox Page	Links to government toxicology resources	http://tamas.nlm.nih.gov/~boyda/htdocs/
Women's health	Menopause Online	Up-do-date information on menopause	http://www.menopause-online.com
	Resolve	Nonprofit organization assisting people in resolving infertility	http://resolve.org

Table 32.3 Nursing and Other Health-Related Fields

Subject	Site	Description	Address
Alternative medicine	Alternative Medicine Home Page	Annotated links to other sites related to this topic	http://www.pitt.edu/~cbw/altm.html
Child abuse	National Data Archive on Child Abuse and Neglect	Disseminates information on child abuse and neglect; provides training and technical support for analysis of the data	gopher://gopher.ndacan.cornell.edu
Chiropractics	Chiropractic Page	Links to other chiropractic and alternative-medicine sites	http://www.mbnet.mb.ca/~jwiens/chiro.html#soft
Home health	Belson/Hanwright Video, Inc.	Links to home health equipment vendors; home health videos	http://www.earthlink.net/~bhv/
Nursing	American Journal of Nursing Company	Selected articles from *American Journal of Nursing (AJN)* and *Maternal Child Nursing (MCN)*; AJN Network in progress provides instruction, databases, news, access to consultants, bulletin board, ANA annual conference information, CEUs, career guide	http://www.ajn.org
	Chronic Wound Healing	Extensive graphics; instruction in proper wound care; good teaching tool for students and attorneys	http://coninfo.nursing.UIOWA.EDU/www/nursing/virtnurs/chronwnd/!int.htm
	NURSE	British site (University of Warwick, England); attempts to organize all nursing-related sites on the Internet	gopher://nurse.csv.warwick.ac.uk:70/11/
	NurseNet	Forum for discussion of nursing issues; archive of the NurseNet listserv group	gopher://vm.utcc.utoronto.ca:70/11/LISTSERV/nursenet
	NurseWeb at UCSF	From the University of California, San Francisco; links to other nursing Web pages	http://nurseweb.ucsf.edu/www/ucsfson.htm
	Nursing Index	Well-annotated links to sites; information regarding clinical topics, educational programs, research, organizations, and more	http://www.lib.umich.edu/tml/nursing.html

Table 32.3   Nursing and Other Health-Related Fields (*Continued*)

Subject	Site	Description	Address
Nursing AIDS	National Institute of Allergy and Infectious Diseases	From the National Institute of Allergy and Infectious Diseases (part of the NIH); information, including teaching handouts, regarding nursing practice related to AIDS patients, assessment, alternative treatments, etc.	gopher:odie.niaid.nih.gov/11/aids/nursing
Nutrition and wellness	Electronic Sources of Food and Nutrition Information	Good source for descriptions and guide to nutrition databases from a number of organizations and agencies	gopher://una.hh.lib.umich.edu/00/inetdirsstacks/food nut%3abussmann
	The Internet Doctor	Send questions and physicians who operate the service answer them; there is a moderate charge for their services	http://www.montrealnet.ca/netdoctor/index.html
Osteopathic medicine	Osteopathic Medicine	An introduction to this field; some abstracts and bibliographies from the online journal (*The Osteopath*)	http://www.demon.co.uk/osteopath/index.html
Physician assistants	Physician Assistant training	Information about P.A. training at Duke University	http://dmi-www.mc.duke.edu/cfm/pap/
Public health	Hazardous Substances & Public Health	An online journal from the CDC	http://atsdrl.atsdr.cdc.gov:8080/HEC/hsphhome.html
	Health Services and Public Health Sites on the Internet	Annotated index of sites, primarily governmental	http://weber.u.washington.edu/~larsson/hsic94/resource/hsr-ph.html
	National Center for Health Statistics (CDC)	Publications may be downloaded or are available on CD-ROM, diskette, or paper	http://www.cdc.gov/nchswww/nchshome.htm
	National Health Information Center	Has extensive listings and links; provides referrals to appropriate organizations	http://nhic-nt.health.org/odphp.htm

Table 32.4 Medical Journals and Other Publications on the Internet: A Sampling

Publication	Description	Address
CNN Food and Health News	Source for locating media coverage of health and medicine; provides short abstracts on current stories, with links to full text	http://www.cnn.com/HEALTH/index.html
Essential Medical Resources	Links to a list of peer-reviewed journals; compiled by the AMA	http://www.aladdin.co.uk/biopages
International Health News	Abstracts and articles from mainstream medical journals (*JAMA, Lancet*, etc.); monthly online newsletter	http://www.perspective.com/health/index.html
Journal of the American Medical Association (JAMA)	Full text of *JAMA* and archived abstracts (back issues)	http://www.ama-assn.org
Journal of NIH Research	News, research, NIH resources, funding, clinical trials, legal and ethical issues; some articles available online from each issue; information about research and science policy in the biomedical field	gopher.enews.com/11/magazines/alphabetic/all/nih
MedWeb: Electronic Newsletters and Journals	Provides a comprehensive listing of medical and nursing journals, newsletters, and tables of contents that are available online; publications are primarily mainstream medical and nursing journals	http://www.cc.emory.edu/WHSCL/medweb.ejs.html
MMWR	Text of the *Morbidity and Mortality Weekly Report*; free reader software available to print the publication verbatim	gopher://cwis.usc.edu/11/The_Health_Sciences_Campus/Periodicals/mmwr

Even if a specific URL (Web address) is unknown, the LNC can do a general search by typing a subject in the Search Box and pressing the Enter key. Search engines and Web crawlers are becoming increasingly more efficient and usually bring up numerous sites that have information on the search subject.

The LNC should view a computer as a window through which he or she can explore the world from thousands of miles away in a matter of minutes. While it may take some time to learn to navigate the information superhighway, experience and patience will lead to more expedient searches and uncover new resources. The LNC should be aware of the types of information available on the Internet that may enhance his or her practice. The following are a few of the possibilities:

- Search the medical and scientific literature and other databases from the NLM and other information providers
- Receive concise, current synopses of diseases and treatment
- Send and receive still or animated medical images
- Obtain standards of care from professional medical, nursing, dental, and scientific organizations
- Obtain pharmaceutical databases

- Receive detailed information on medical devices and products
- Send and receive electronic mail (e-mail) with colleagues anywhere in the world in a matter of seconds
- Read and post notes to electronic bulletin boards that are accessed by thousands of people with similar interests
- Stay abreast of current medical news from newspapers and news services
- Access regulations and other information from governmental agencies such as the CDC, FDA, NIH, and the Occupational Safety and Health Administration (OSHA)
- Obtain research reports, practice guidelines, medical protocols, and digests of conferences and meetings
- Locate experts

Locating Standards of Care and Clinical Practice Guidelines

LNCs who are new to the field often expect to find lists of standards of care in books that they can easily refer to when they need to compare a health care professional's conduct to the standard of care that should be followed. Unfortunately, it is usually not that simple. The following resources can be consulted when standards of care or clinical practice guidelines are needed:

- *Health Care Standards Directory* (in the reference section at a medical library)
- MD Consult (http://www.mdconsult.com) — requires a subscription
- The Cochrane Library (http://www.update-software.com/cochrane) — abstracts of extensive literature reviews may be browsed free of charge, but a subscription is required for full-text reviews
- Agency for Healthcare Research and Quality (http://www.ahrq.gov)
- Professional organizations
- Medical and nursing textbooks
- Nursing care plans and critical or clinical pathways
- In-house protocols and policies

Suggested Ways to Perform Witness and Expert Witness Searches

LNCs may be called upon to locate current or background information about treating physicians or a potential physician expert witness. Before the LNC begins the search, it is important to clarify with the attorney what type of information he or she requires and how detailed it should be. The budget for a particular search is also a consideration. Searches can be very costly and labor-intensive, especially when done in depth. The LNC should include in the budgeted amount the cost of time spent performing, analyzing, and organizing the results of the search, as well as the costs incurred in the search. An extensive search can cost from $500 to more than $1000. Much less costly searches that are still quite informative can also be done.

Simple Search

Is there an in-house database of witnesses or experts? Has an individual attorney, LNC, or paralegal maintained a file of curriculum vitae (CV)? Does the attorney want general information that may be found on the Internet, prior testimony, or more details such as license status, board certifications, involvement in malpractice or any other types of suits and the outcomes, and positive or negative media coverage?

A search may be as simple as searching the Internet for the known person's name to determine what data is available or calling the state licensing board to determine issues of licensure. (What are the dates of current licensure and renewal date? Has there ever been or is there currently pending any disciplinary action?) The LNC can call the individual state medical society or board to request any information that might be available in its files concerning a particular physician. Call 1–800–CALLABMS or check the Web site (http://www.abms.org) of the American Board of Medical Specialists (ABMS) to verify board certifications, to inquire whether renewal of certification is necessary, and to learn the date on which recertification is to be required. More information can often be found in the *ABMS Directory* at a medical library than on the Web, but time constraints may prevent making a trip to the library. Check the American Medical Association's Web site (http://www.ama-assn.org) for details on the physician's medical school and subsequent internship, residencies, and fellowships. Often the location and phone number of the practice, the type of practice, and whether the practice is inactive will be listed. MEDLINE searches will determine any articles that may have been published during the time period that the database covers. Obtaining the above information should not incur any charges or fees.

Public Citizen (http://www.citizen.org) is a watchdog group that has published rather detailed information on physicians who have been disciplined or who have had their licenses suspended or revoked, in which states, and for what reasons.

Another resource that conducts searches of physicians' backgrounds is http://www.SearchPointe.com. A cursory search to verify licensure and certification is free of charge. To determine whether there have been sanctions, revocations, or any adverse information from the FDA (e.g., falsifying information while conducting clinical trials), the person who is inquiring must register with a password and pay a small fee.

Lexis-Nexis® and Westlaw® may also be used for a witness search. These companies will be discussed in more detail under the section called Extensive Searches.

An LNC searching for an expert witness has several avenues to explore. Again, the budget will help determine how much will be spent on the search and on the expert's fee. Possible resources for the search within the workplace include an in-house expert databank, an LNC, paralegal, or attorney who maintains his or her own expert file and is willing to share information, and a colleague who might be familiar with an expert. Some AALNC chapters have listservs or talklists that can be utilized when an expert is needed. Medical textbooks and medical journals in the library may reveal an expert working at a nearby facility.

The local bar association or trial lawyers association can be contacted for plaintiff experts. The LNC may be able to find a defense expert through IDEX or the Defense Research Institute (DRI) — companies specializing in collection of defense testimony — if the law firm subscribes to one of them. LNCs can search http://www.mdconsult.com for the names of authors of authoritative textbooks and articles who may be nearby, and can search the faculties of nearby medical centers and universities. Anyone can put a CV on the Internet and claim to be an expert; it is always prudent to verify all credentials, no matter where the name of the potential expert was found.

Extensive Searches

When very detailed information is needed, it will be necessary to use Lexis-Nexis or Westlaw. These companies have extensive databases. Although the databases are quite comprehensive, neither company has access to all public records in all 50 states. Information may exist that cannot be accessed through either of these companies.

There are many reasons to search these databases. The LNC is looking for both positive information and negative information that might be utilized to impeach or tarnish experts and their credibility. An example is executing a search of newspapers, periodicals, and news. (Has an expert recently received an award by the faculty and students at his or her institution or been the recipient of a large grant from NIH? Has he or she been convicted of a DUI or possibly involved in fraudulent billing?)

Searches utilizing Lexis-Nexis and Westlaw can incur high costs. It is important to know how to do the most effective search for the least amount of money. Several people can be searched for in a database at one time. This will incur a single fee rather than individual fees for each person researched. This can be accomplished by entering a string like *(Nancy/3 Nurse) or (Doctor/3 Cardiologist) or (John/3 Doe) or (Jane/3 Doe)* to search for Nancy Nurse, Doctor Cardiologist, John Doe, and Jane Doe. This should result in multiple documents. By clicking on the "focus" at the top of the screen and entering one person's name, e.g., Nancy/3 Nurse, any documents relating to this individual can then be reviewed, printed, and e-mailed. Clicking on "focus" again lets the user repeat the process for each name until all the individual searches have been completed.

Depending on the type of litigation and whether the case has been filed in federal or state court, data relating to the following topics may be available in databases that the LNC utilizes in Lexis-Nexis and Westlaw to assist in searches: United States Material; State Material; Experts Jury Verdicts, Settlement Summaries, and Multistate Public Records include databases for Locating People; Professional Licenses; Liens and Judgments; Lawsuit Records; Executive Affiliations; Business and Corporate Information, Legal News, Notable Trials; Topical Materials by Areas of Practice.

IDEX (http://idex.com) and DRI (http://www.dri.org) maintain multiple databases of information. They include Testimonial History Search, containing hundreds of thousands of documents with monthly additions. Additional databases contain Depositions, Transcripts, CVs, Discipline Search, Articles Naming the Expert, Articles Authored by the Expert, Similar Case Search, and Scientific or Medical Literature.

Docket Searches

At times it may be necessary to search court dockets to determine pertinent information related to a particular case or cases. The docket will contain information including the case number, case caption, filing date, particular court, location, whether or not a jury trial has been requested, the type of case, the case status, any related cases, case event schedule, case parties (i.e., name of the plaintiff[s]), name and address of plaintiff's attorney, names and addresses of the defendant(s) and defendant's attorney(s), and all subsequent docket entries that follow the initial case filing. The docket entries will enter the date and time of a filing, the docket type, the docket entry, the party filing, and the disposition amount.

If the LNC does not know the court's Web site address, the process of accessing the court on the Internet starts with entering the court name into a Web search engine (e.g., Yahoo). For example:

1. Enter "Philadelphia Courts."
2. Click on "*Search*."
3. A hypertext link to the Web site that contains information relating to "Philadelphia Courts" will appear.
4. Click on "Philadelphia Courts" to connect to the court home page.
5. In the box that is designated "Fast Access to" click on the triangle on the right.
6. Highlight and click on "Enter the Civil Docket Access."
7. Click on "Search by person name or company name."
8. A disclaimer will need to be accepted or rejected. Clicking on "Accept" will then bring up the search page.
9. Enter information in the box for names.
10. Click on the "Search" button.
11. Results will indicate whether or not the party is listed in any dockets.
12. If there are dockets available, a list of all cases will be on the screen.
13. Click on the hypertext link to open the docket.

Web Sites

One of the benefits of accessing Web sites is that most of them have links to other related sites. In addition, some are referred to as value-added sites because they also provide information, such as full-text books, journal abstracts, and graphics (see Tables 32.2, 32.3, and 32.4).

Because of the amount of traffic on the Internet, it is sometimes difficult to connect to a site. If this occurs, the following strategies may help:

- Attempt to connect at a later time or even on another day; sites may be busy or may even go down completely at times.
- Try to connect directly to the site computer, rather than to the actual document. For example, in Table 32.2, the AltMed Web address is http://www.teleport.com/~mattlmt. Try connecting to http://www.teleport.com rather than using the entire address, which includes a subdirectory and the type of document. To put it simply, omit everything other than the part of the address between http:// and the next slash (/). This will connect to the host computer for the organization, and a search of the listings for the specific document can be conducted.
- Try one of the index sites for the specialty.
- Try a general subject listing.

American Psychological Association (APA) style is the accepted format to use when referencing sources of information. The following are examples of the proper APA style for citing Internet sources. The APA Web site offers examples and other information at http://www.apastyle.org/elecref.html.

- Online periodical:
    Writer, A.B., Writer, C.D., Writer, E.F., (year). Title of article. *Title of Periodical*, xx, xxx-xxx. Retrieved month day, year, from source
- Online document:
    Writer, B.B. (year). Title of work. Retrieved month day, year, from source
- Article in an Internet-only journal:
    Writer, N.L., (year, month day). Name of the article with only the first word capitalized. Name of journal, volume, article number, retrieved month day, year, from (insert the entire Web site address)
- Electronic of a journal article, three to five authors, retrieved from database:
    Writer, A.B., Writer, C.D., Writer, E.F., Writer, G.H., (year). Name of the article. Name of the journal. Volume, page numbers. Retrieved month day, year, from (the name of the database)
- Daily newspaper article, electronic version:
    Writer, J.P. (year, month day). Name of article. Name of the newspaper. Retrieved month day, year, from (complete Web site address)
- U.S. Government report available on government agency Web site, without publication date:
    Name of the Agency (n.d. [no date]). Name of the report. Retrieved month day, year, from (complete Web site address)
- E-mail:
    A.A. Person (personal communication, month day, year)

Literature Citation Tips

Proper citation of references of authors either directly quoted or paraphrased is imperative. These tips are based on the format in the *Publication Manual of the American Psychological Association*.[12]

- Citations
    When citing a source in a paper, write the author in the reference page. One work by one author — if the name is part of the narrative, cite only the year in parentheses. Example: Adams (1994) found in a recent study. Otherwise, name and year are put in parentheses. Example: In a recent study of nursing students (Adams, 1994)
    One work by multiple authors
    – Two authors — cite both names every time
    – Three, four, or five authors — cite all authors the first time the reference occurs. In future citations include only the name of the first author followed by "et al." and the year if it is the first citation of the reference within a paragraph.

Example: One, Two, Three, Four, Five, and Six (1996) noted the
… ; then One et al. (1996) found that; then One et al. found that
  – Six or more authors — cite only the first author followed by "et al."
  and the year. In the reference list provide the initial and surnames
  of the first six authors and shorten remaining authors to "et al."
■ Direct quotes — give the author, year, and page number.
  Example: "Nursing students learn to role model caring behaviors from
  faculty."
■ Quotes
  Short (fewer than 40 words) quotes should be incorporated into the
  text and enclosed with double quotation marks ("/").
  – Example: Smith (1998) found that "nursing students learn to role
  model caring behaviors from faculty" (p. 52).
  Long (40 or more words) quotes should be displayed in a double-
  spaced block of typewritten lines with no quotation marks. Indent five
  to seven spaces from the left margin. Include the citation at the end
  of the quote.
  – Example: Leininger predicts that all professional nurses in the world
  must be prepared in transcultural nursing and demonstrate compe-
  tencies in transcultural nursing. Transcultural nursing must become
  an integral part of education and practice for nurses to be relevant
  in the twenty-first century.
■ Frequently utilized references:
  Journal article, one author:
  – Surname, Z.Z. (year). Title of article (capitalize only the initial word).
  Name of publication. Volume, page numbers
  Journal article, two authors, publication paginated by issue:
  – Writer, A.B., Writer, C.D. (year). Title. (*Journal Name*), 17(3), 44–54.
  (Any line below the author's name will be indented as below)
  Journal article, three to six authors:
  – Writer, A.B., Writer, C.D., Writer, E.F. (year). Title (capitalize only
  the initial word) *Name of Publication, volume*, page numbers.
  Journal article, more than six authors:
  – One, Z.V., Two, A.B., Three, M.M., Four, C.C., Five, I.O., Six, K.M.,
  et al. (year). Title of the article. *Name of Journal*, volume, page
  numbers.
  Daily newspaper article, without author's name:
  – The title of the article. (year, month day). *The name of the newspaper*,
  p. C17. (Any line below the author's name will be indented as above)
  Reference to an entire book:
  – Writer, Z.Z., Writer, X.X. (year). Name of book with the first word
  capitalized (edition). City, State: Name of Publisher. For a well-
  known city (e.g., New York), the state is not necessary. State
  abbreviations should be in a two-letter format.
  Chapter in an edited book:
  – Author of chapter, C.J. (year). Chapter title with only the first word
  capitalized, in K.K. Author, C.K. (Eds.), *Name of the book with the
  first word capitalized* (pp. x-x). City, State: Name of Publisher.

Book, no author or editor:

– Name of book (edition). (year). City, State two-letter Abbreviation: Publisher.

Examples: *Diagnostic and Statistical Manual of Mental Disorders*: American Psychiatric Association. (year). *Diagnostic and statistical manual of mental disorders* (4th ed.) Washington, D.C.: Author.
DSM-III (1980) third edition
DSM-III-R (1987) third edition, revised
DSM-IV (1994) fourth edition
DSM-IV-TR (2000) text revision

Ethics

The Medical Library Association (MLA) Code of Ethics offers several guidelines that are applicable to any researcher who acts as an intermediary between a client and the information, whether the information is obtained from textbooks or by computer. The following guidelines that directly apply to LNCs have been adapted from the MLA Code of Ethics.[1]

■ Use interview techniques to clarify the client's needs before doing research on any case.
■ Maintain awareness of the range of information resources to advise the client fairly and impartially.
■ Maintain a reasonable skill level in the systems available if performing online searches.
■ Avoid bias in the selection of appropriate databases and systems when performing online searches.
■ Maintain alertness with regard to information that might be detrimental to the client's case.
■ Maintain confidentiality.

Conclusion

Research is an art that develops with experience. It can be fun, challenging, and frustrating, but it is also very rewarding, especially when it contributes to the success of clients' cases.

References

1. *The Official ABMS Directory of Board Certified Medical Specialists*, American Board of Medical Specialties (order from http://www.marquiswhoswho.com).
2. *Health Care Standards Directory Online*, ECRI (http://www.ecri.org or 610-825-600).
3. Fauci, A. (ed.), *Harrison's Principles of Internal Medicine*, 14th ed., McGraw-Hill, New York, 1998.

4. Cunningham, F. (ed.), *Williams' Obstetrics*, 20th ed., Appleton & Lange, Stamford, CT, 1999.

5. Ashcraft, K. and Holder, T. (eds.), *Pediatric Surgery*, 3rd ed., W.B. Saunders, Philadelphia, 1999.

6. Behrman, E. (ed.), *Nelson Textbook of Pediatrics*, 15th ed., W.B. Saunders, Philadelphia, 1999.

7. *Encyclopedia of Medical Organizations & Agencies*, 7th ed., Gale Group, 1998.

8. Hogarth, M. and Hutchinson, D., *An Internet Guide for the Health Professional*, 2nd ed., New Wind Publishing, Sacramento, CA, 1996.

9. Shortliffe, E.H. and Perreault, L.E., *Medical Informatics: Computer Applications in Health Care*, Addison-Wesley, Reading, MA, 1990.

10. Comer, D. and Angell, D., *The Internet Book*, Prentice Hall, New York, 1994.

11. Rosenfeld, L., Janes, J., and Vander Kolk, M., *The Internet Compendium: Subject Guides to Health and Science Resources*, Neal-Schuman Publishers, New York, 1995.

12. *Publication Manual of the American Psychological Association*, 5th ed., Washington, D.C., 2001.

13. Bunting, A., *Current Practice in Health Sciences Librarianship*, Vol. 1: *Reference and Information Services in Health Sciences Libraries*, Medical Library Association and The Scarecrow Press, Metuchen, NJ, 1994.

14. Blonde, L.,McKibbon, K.A., Zaroukian, M., and Guthrie, R., Jr., Medical literature management, in *Computers in Clinical Practice: Managing Patients, Information, and Communication*, Osheroff, J., Ed., American College of Physicians, Philadelphia, 1995, 37–57.

Additional Reading

Anderson, P., How to get started with computer literature searches, *American Journal of Hospital Pharmacy*, 51(18), 2303, 2304, 2307, 1994.

Begg, C. and Berlin, J., Publication bias: a problem in interpreting medical data, *Journal of the Royal Statistical Societ*, 151, 445-463, 1988.

Department of Clinical Epidemiology and Biostatistics, McMaster University, How to read clinical journals. I. Why to read them and how to start reading them critically, *Canadian Medical Association Journal*, 124, 555-558, 1982.

Easterbrook, P., Berlin, J., Gopalin, R., and Matthews, D., Publication bias in clinical research, *Lancet*, 337, 864-872, 1991.

Familette, K., personal communication, January 30, 2002.

Free access to electronic AIDS information (news), *MCN-American Journal of Maternal Child Nursing*, 20(2), 118, 1995.

Guyatt, G., Sackett, D., and Cook, D., Users' guide to the medical literature: II. How to use an article about therapy or prevention. Are the results of the study valid?, *JAMA*, 270, 2598–2601, 1993.

Hancock, L., *Physicians' Guide to the Internet*, Lippincott-Raven Publishers, Philadelphia, 1996.

Haynes, R., McKibbon, K., Fitzgerald, D., Guyatt, G., Walker, C., and Sackett, D., How to keep up with the medical literature. V. Access by personal computer to the medical literature, *Annals of Internal Medicine*, 105, 810-814, 1986.

Jacschke, R., Guyatt, G., and Sackett, D., Users' guide to the medical literature. III. How to use an article about a diagnostic test. A. Are the results of the study valid? *JAMA*, 271(5), 389-391, 1994.

Kilby, S., Database searching made easy, *Nursing Education Microworld*, 5(3), 18, 1991.

Kleeberg, P. and Masys, D., Telecommunications, in *Computers in Clinical Practice: Managing Patients, Information and Communication*, Osheroff, J., Ed., American College of Physicians, Philadelphia, 1995, 127–148.

Nicoll, L., The practical computer:keeping abreast of the literature electronically, *Nursing Reasearch*, 42(5), 315-317, 1993.

Nolan, J.R. and Nolan-Haley, J.M., *Black's Law Dictionary*, 6th ed., West Publishing, St. Paul, 1990.

Oxman, A. and Guyatt, G., Guidelines for reading literature reviews, *Canadian Medical Association Journal*, 138, 697-703, 1988.

Oxman, A., Sackett, D., and Guyatt, G. (for the Evidence-Based Medicine Working Group), Users' guides to the medical literature. I. How to get started, *JAMA*, 270(17), 2093-2095, 1993.

Oxman, A., Cook, D., and Guyatt, G., Users' guide to the medical literature. VI. How to use an overview, *JAMA*, 272(17), 1367-1371, 1994.

Rogers, G., Innovative informatics: nurses and the Internet, *Journal of Emergency Nursing*, 21(2), 160-162, 1995.

Silverman, C.R., personal communication, January 29, 2002.

Smith, C. and Ayers, M., Medical resources on the Internet, in *Medical Resources on the Internet Symposium* conducted at seminar on Medical Resources on the Internet, Philadelphia, June 1999.

The Internet Handbook: The Introductory Guide for Health Professionals, Biomed General Corporation, 1997.

Wetther, K., *The Nuts and Bolts of Legal Nurse Consulting*, 2nd ed., Medical Legal Resources, Carlsbad, CA, 2001 (http://www.medicallegalresources.com).

Resources

National Network of Libraries of Medicine (NN/LM)
National Library of Medicine (NLM)
8600 Rockville Pike
Bldg. 38, Room B1-E03
Bethesda, MD 20894
(301) 496–4777
www.nlm.nih.gov
For regional services and information, call (800) 338–7657

Test Questions

1. The document retrieval system available through the National Library of Medicine is
   A. PubMed
   B. Loansome Doc
   C. MEDLINEplus
   D. MEDLINE

2. Which of the following words is NOT a Boolean operator?
   A. OR
   B. NOT
   C. BUT
   D. AND

3. Which of the following is NOT a National Library of Medicine database?
   A. CHEMLINE
   B. IDEX
   C. CATLINE
   D. CANCERLIT

4. Which is the only one of the following that is used to perform an extensive expert witness search?
   A. The Official ABMS Directory of Board Certified Medical Specialists
   B. www.SearchPointe.com
   C. Public Citizen
   D. Lexis-Nexis®

5. Which is the only one of the following options that will NOT be found in a docket?
   A. Case number
   B. Type of case
   C. Address of the plaintiff
   D. Name and address of the plaintiff's attorney

Answers: 1. B, 2. C, 3. B, 4. D, 5. C

Chapter 33

Report Preparation

Patricia Raya, BS, RNC

CONTENTS

Objectives

- To define the three parts of communication
- To describe three different types of reports

0-8493-1418-6/03/$0.00+$1.50
© 2003 by AALNC

Introduction

Communicating thoughts, ideas, and recommendations in a case analysis in a concise and effective manner is important. The legal nurse consultant (LNC) should develop writing skills to create effective memos, letters, correspondence, and written reports that the attorney can use to develop and substantiate his or her case.

Written Communication

Communication is a three-part process. The message is put into words, or written; the message is delivered to the reader (letter, memo, report); and finally, the reader understands the proposed message. Having clear ideas and goals, and an understanding of the audience's needs, is essential. A writer should consider the audience's knowledge of, attitude toward, and need for information on the topic.

Unfortunately, there are chances for that message to be misinterpreted. Garver-Mastrian and Birdsall[1] note that "noise" such as bad grammar, misspellings, poor organization, and sloppy thinking can hinder communication. Such "noise" is within the control of the writer. If the reader is tired or distracted, does not like the topic, or has skimmed the report, the communication process will be ineffective. The writer must guide the reader toward the intended message; this can be done effectively only when the topic, purpose, and audience's need for information are considered.

Topic

Before starting to write, the LNC should discuss the issues of concern to the attorney: What does the attorney need to know about this subject? How familiar is he or she with the subject? Does he or she have preconceived ideas about the topic? What does he or she hope to obtain through use of the report?

Purpose of the Written Report

A written report may be requested following the LNC's completion of the medical record review, research, analysis, and conclusion. He or she should determine the purpose for writing the report: Is the purpose to educate, to inform, or to persuade the reader? What is the message to be conveyed? Whether the objective of the report is to create a chronology of events, or to inform or educate the attorney about the adherences to or deviations from standards of care, the message should be clearly and concisely conveyed to the reader. A report may also be written for the purpose of persuasion or to offer an alternative viewpoint. Knowing the need of the audience can help the writer present the information in a more effective manner.

Developing the Document

The document plan should be brief and to the point. The LNC should review the purpose of the report, e.g., to determine whether a case is meritorious or to prepare an analysis with references to standards of care. He or she should develop a theory and define the objectives or purpose of the report. For example, is the intent to convey a deviation from acceptable standards of care, to explain the injuries sustained by the plaintiff, or to present a chronology of medical events?

The LNC should determine the attorney's deadlines or budgetary limitations before beginning to write a report, and work efficiently and effectively. Once the purpose of the report is determined, the LNC should organize the available information and then expand on it through research. He or she should allocate approximately 30% of the document preparation time to researching the topic, 40% to composing the message, and the remaining 30% to editing and refining the final report.

Research

A review of the medical record will provide a guide to the topics that need to be researched. If the attorney has not gotten the medical records, it may be necessary for the LNC to write to the institution or physician's office to obtain a certified true copy of the records. Before releasing the records, the institution will require an authorization letter stating that the plaintiff authorizes the facility or physician to release the medical records to the agent acting on his or her behalf. If the medical records are to be turned over to the LNC, the request should state that the LNC is affiliated with the attorney, and a certified copy of any and all medical records, x-rays, test results, fetal heart monitoring strips, etc., is to be given to the LNC. Usually a fee is charged for the records and must be paid before the records are forwarded. The sample letter follows:

> Dear Dr. Brown:
>
> Please provide a complete and certified copy of any and all medical records, chart notes, x-ray results, memos, etc., regarding any and all treatment rendered to John Smith by you. We are in dire need of these medical records and request that you forward them to our office as soon as possible. Enclosed you will find a fully executed authorization for the release of this information to our office.
>
> If there is a fee for the copying of this material to our office, kindly send an invoice along with the requested materials and we will gladly send you a check.
>
> Thank you for your prompt attention to this most important matter.
>
> Very truly yours,

Once the medical records are received, the LNC should use research time effectively. Before starting the research, he or she should determine the purpose and the best source for obtaining the needed information: Is the purpose to establish or get new information, to locate a specific article or text, or to locate names and addresses of potential witnesses? An extensive selection of textbooks and journals and Internet access may be available at a local hospital or university library. If a specific journal article is not available, it can often be obtained, for a fee, through interlibrary loan. The reference librarian may be able to offer assistance in further defining and implementing the research process. If the university or library is not accessible or has limited resources, the LNC should consider database vending services. (See Chapter 32 for more information.) Other sources of information include professional organizations, the board of nursing, and other LNCs.

Revising

With the findings of the research and other new information, the document outline will need to be revised. Fine-tuning the outline will help the writer reassess and, if appropriate, change the initial premise of the report. The writer should constantly be asking whether the initial assumptions were correct and consciously looking to see whether the new information requires that these assumptions be changed. When satisfied that research has revealed sufficient information to draw a conclusion, the LNC should rewrite a formal outline.[2]

Report Format

The way in which information, facts, and ideas are organized can influence a reader's comprehension. When writing a report, albeit a memo, analysis, chronology, or expert report, the LNC should set aside a sufficient uninterrupted block of time to accomplish as much as possible. He or she should:

- Begin by organizing a framework to assist the reader, i.e., an introduction, body, and conclusion
- Develop a theme and support it with facts, leaving out irrelevant information
- Present facts in a format that is clear and concise
- Clearly identify and back up personal opinions, using professional literature and published standards
- Draw a conclusion based on scientific evidence and professional standards of care

If "writer's block" occurs, the LNC should take the time to refocus. Reorganization of thoughts and ideas may be needed to be more effective. If satisfied with the format and contents, the LNC should rewrite the report, using a recognized publication manual as a guide for presenting the final report (see Chapter 32).

The American Psychological Association (APA) provides a guide for documenting text citations.[3] Sources should be acknowledged in the text of the paper itself and in an alphabetical list at the end of the text. A parenthetical citation should contain the author's last name, the date of publication, and often the page number from which material is borrowed. Numerous textbooks and guides on the APA style are available in local libraries and bookstores.

The final report should look neat and professional. It should use a font and type size that is easy to read and allows the attorney to jot down notes right on the report if needed. Before submitting the report, the LNC should proofread and edit it, preferably several times, and if possible have a colleague review it before sending it to the attorney.

Audience

It is important to know who will be reading the report. Garver-Mastrian and Birdsall[1] encourage the writer to consider whether the reader is:

- Interested or uninterested in the topic
- Likely to be pleased or displeased
- Knowledgeable about or ignorant of the subject
- Sympathetic or hostile toward the writer or topic

Keeping in mind that a report may be read by multiple audiences with different education and skills, the LNC should be sensitive to who the audience is and how it will use the document. Readers may need to:

- Understand
- Locate information
- Act immediately (put something together, use a new procedure)
- Answer questions to fill out a form

An attorney, paralegal, client, and expert witnesses may review and incorporate the report into their aspects of the case.

Discoverable and Nondiscoverable Reports

A report that is written by the testifying LNC or expert witness is considered discoverable. The attorney and his or her experts, as well as opposing counsel and his or her experts, will read the report, and the report may be referenced in another expert's work. Work is usually nondiscoverable if it is the result of "working behind the scenes" rather than as a testifying expert. The LNC should check jurisdictional laws and rules or ask the attorney whether the report will be discoverable. A nondiscoverable work-product report may contain opinions that a nursing expert witness could not express, such as the negligence of other health care providers, or suggestions for strategy. It is important to write the words "attorney work product" on the report so that it does not inadvertently get identified as a discoverable document.

Types of Reports

Memo

The word "memo" is short for "memorandum"; it is perhaps the most frequently used form of communication in any institution.[1] Memos are usually used to communicate to people within the agency or institution and follow the basic format of:

DATE:
TO:
FROM:
SUBJECT:

The memo is a very basic piece of communication. It is usually shorter than a letter and quickly summarizes the message in an introduction, body (discussion), and conclusion. To be effective, it should be concise, clear, interesting, and "user-friendly."

Informal Report

The informal report is essentially a three- to four-page piece of information. It does not need a title page, table of contents, etc. It does include the three basic components: introduction, body, and conclusion. The goal is to educate the readers or try to persuade them into agreeing with the written opinion.

Formal Report

Medical Research

Often an attorney will ask the LNC to summarize a piece of medical literature. It is the job of the LNC to put the article into language that is easy to understand by the attorney and other laypersons. It may be necessary for the paralegal, the client, or other persons less knowledgeable about medical terminology to understand a medical issue, so the summarization must be in "user-friendly" prose.

Chronology

A chronology is a sequential listing of pertinent events related to the incident in question. The chronology may be day by day, week by week, or even as intense as minute by minute. The LNC should determine what time frame is appropriate for the chronology and then list in order the medical incidents. The chronology must be objective, listing just the facts. When completed the chronology should be like a road map, leading from one medical fact to another.

Chart Analysis

Chart analysis provides the attorney with a complete account of the events, alleged potential malpractice, and an evaluation of the significance of those events in relation to the injury.[4] These facts are then presented in an organized, logical manner in a written report. The report should "tell the story" in chronological order so that the attorney can use the information to construct a fact pattern relative to the occurrence and injury.

The report should review and address the central issues of a case; these issues should be evident to the reader. Include direct quotes or citations from the medical record. The first page of the report should include:

- Date of report
- Patient's name
- Name of the attorney for whom the report was written
- File number given to the case by the attorney
- Treatment dates

■ Listing of medical records, expert reports, depositions, and interrogatories that were reviewed for the analysis

The LNC should prepare an objective and factual chronology or summary of medical records that includes all material that is relevant to the case (e.g., nurses' notes about an incident). Abnormal findings are especially important to include. The analysis should present facts of the case, followed by comments and recommendations, identifying any relevant missing records.

Expert Report

The expert report provides an analysis of the alleged malpractice. It attempts to prove or disprove deviations in acceptable standards of care. The expert report addresses only facts relating to the expert's area of expertise. The nurse expert comments on issues within the scope of nursing. Medical issues are addressed by physician experts. The expert report should contain a brief summary or chronology of the event, a discussion regarding the standards of care, and a professional opinion and thoughts on whether or not a deviation from acceptable standards of care occurred.

Summary of Independent Medical Examination

The Independent or Insurance Medical Examination (IME) provides an overview of a client's history and a detailed evaluation of his or her treatment and recovery. It is generally requested by the defense to determine the actual extent of the plaintiff's injuries. An IME may also be requested by a plaintiff attorney, insurance company, employer, or the court. The IME is conducted by an impartial physician to prevent undue influence by the interested parties. (See Chapter 29 for more information.)

The defense may require that the plaintiff submit to a physical or mental examination by a physician chosen by the defense. The plaintiff has the right to refuse an IME, but refusal may be viewed unfavorably by the court. The examining physician reports on the extent and possible causes of the injuries and may render an opinion as to the merits of the plaintiff's allegations.[4] If asked to accompany the plaintiff to the IME, the LNC should be prepared to write notes and, if allowed, audiotape the examination. The LNC should note when the examination began and ended. He or she should note the physician's and plaintiff's gestures and body language. For example, if the doctor asked the plaintiff to bend over and touch his toes, did the plaintiff grimace in pain when doing so, was it an easy maneuver, or did the plaintiff do it hesitantly? The LNC should write down things not picked up on tape. Did the doctor appear to lead the plaintiff to answer "yes" or "no" by his or her facial expression? After the IME, the LNC needs to prepare a written "transcript" of the examination. Incorporate notes into a detailed chronology and report of the assessment.

Client Intake Interview

An LNC may be asked to conduct an initial client interview to gather facts from the client about what happened and the issues involved. The LNC should:

- Note the date of the interview, and the interviewee's name, address, and phone number.
- Obtain the interviewee's recollection of the event and his or her role in it.
- Ask the interviewee to recall any significant dates and times of incidents: Were any contributing factors involved? Does he or she remember the physician's orders, lab work, treatments, or physical therapy that was done? Did the health care provider say anything to a family member regarding the care or treatment?

After gathering the information, the LNC should prepare a written report objectively documenting the facts that the interviewee revealed. The report should also include the date and time of the interview, and whether it was conducted in person or by phone. It should note whether the interviewee "recalled," "confirmed," or "speculated" about different issues when relating the incident.

Conference with Potential Expert

Both the plaintiff and defense are entitled to have a physician review the medical records and prepare an opinion as to the allegations regarding standards of care. The physician expert should be board-certified and have experience in the area of medicine under review. The LNC should review the physician's curriculum vitae, noting any published articles, speaking presentations, involvement in academics, and attendance at seminars in the expert's area of expertise. The expert should be current in his or her field, render an opinion as to the standards of care provided, and note and discuss any deviations. A verbal report is usually undiscoverable unless the opinion is to be used in court. A written report is discoverable. Therefore, it is important for the attorney to meet with the physician expert, if feasible, so that the medical and legal portions of the case can be discussed and reviewed.

Interrogatories

Interrogatories are written questions from one party to the other. Written interrogatories are generally used to obtain information not readily available during oral depositions. The LNC may be utilized to help the attorney formulate questions to be posed. After the responses are received, the LNC may be asked to write a summary of the responses, as well as to explain complex medical issues. (See Chapter 3 for more information.)

Conclusion

LNCs write numerous reports, chronologies, summaries, memos, and other types of correspondence. Effective communication requires that the LNC consider the scope of the topic, the purpose or objective of the communication, and the audience's need for information. The final product should be clear, concise, and professional.

References

1. Garver-Mastrian, K. and Birdsall, E., *Writing on the Job: A Guide for Nurse Managers*. John Wiley & Sons, New York, 1986.
2. Goldstein, T. and Lieberman, J., *The Lawyer's Guide to Writing Well*, University of California Press, Los Angeles, 1989.
3. *Publication Manual of the American Psychological Association*, 5th ed., Washington, D.C., 2001.
4. Acerbo-Avalone, N. and Kremer, K., *Medical Malpractice Claims Investigation: A Step-by-Step Approach*, Aspen Publishers, Gaitherburg, MD, 1997.

Additional Reading

Aaron, J.E., *The Little, Brown Compact Handbook*, Pearson Custom Publishing, Reading, MA, 2000.

Garner, B.A., *Legal Writing in Plain English: A Text with Exercises*, University of Chicago Press, Chicago, 2001.

Poirrer, G., *Writing to Learn: Curricular Strategies for Nursing and Other Disciplines*, NLN Press, New York, 1997.

Shelton, J.H., *Handbook for Technical Writing*, NTC Business Books, Chicago, 1994.

Zilm, G., *The Smart Way: An Introduction to Writing for Nurses*, Harcourt Brace, Orlando, 1998.

Test Questions

1. "Noise" that can interfere with effective written communication includes
   A. Thoughtlessness
   B. Misspellings
   C. Television
   D. Current newspaper articles

2. A writer should be sensitive to the audience reading the document. Readers may need to read to
   A. Locate information
   B. Order supplies
   C. Review additional literature
   D. Set up an interview with the attorney

3. A common style guide that provides ways of documenting text citations is
   A. PAR
   B. SKR
   C. APA
   D. KFC

4. The nurse attending an IME will present an audiotape, as well as prepare a written report that includes
   A. Body language and gestures of the nurse recording the IME
   B. Comments made by the receptionist
   C. Body language and gestures of the physician or the plaintiff
   D. Fee charged by physician to conduct IME

5. In the client intake interview, the LNC should NOT include
   A. Interviewee's recollection of the event
   B. Interviewee's recollection of contributing factors
   C. Interviewee's recollection of the physician's orders
   D. What the plaintiff had for lunch before arriving at the IME

Answers: 1. B, 2. A, 3. C, 4. C, 5. D

Chapter 34

Locating and Working with Expert Witnesses

Patricia A. Fyler, BS, RN, CEN,
and Eileen Croke, EdD, MSN, RN, LNCC

CONTENTS

0-8493-1418-6/03/$0.00+$1.50
© 2003 by AALNC

Objectives

- To describe the role of the expert witness in medically related civil litigation
- To differentiate the types of expert witnesses
- To identify the qualifications of the expert witness
- To describe the characteristics of an effective expert witness
- To provide an effective approach to locating an appropriate expert witness
- To provide guidance in the support of the expert witness
- To familiarize the reader with key legal decisions affecting expert witnesses

Introduction

Today's health care delivery system is replete with specialized knowledge not understood by the ordinary layperson. Most jurisdictions require the use of an expert witness during the litigation process to educate the triers of fact (i.e., judge and jury) about specialized knowledge. An expert witness is an individual who is qualified by his or her experience, training, or education to opine about a specific subject, such as standards of practice.[1] This chapter addresses the selection and support of medical, nursing, ancillary, and related expert witnesses. Discussion will be directed toward:

- Qualifications and characteristics of the ideal expert witness
- Resources for locating and qualifying experts
- Support requirements involved in working with experts
- Legal rulings affecting the expert witness and admissibility of expert testimony

Role of the Legal Nurse Consultant

The legal nurse consultant (LNC) may serve as the expert witness or may be put in charge of finding, selecting, and supporting experts, whether they be nurses, physicians, ancillary personnel, or support staff such as human-resource managers. To succeed at the task, it is essential that the LNC have a thorough understanding of the liability and damages involved, the expertise and qualifications of the opposition experts (if known), and the theme of the case. It is also essential to know the laws relating to expert witnesses in the state in which the case is to be tried.

The LNC may be asked to consult on a case involving the need for expert witnesses. The consultant is not expected to testify in the case. The consultant LNC works behind the scenes for either a plaintiff or a defense attorney. In a confidential process, the LNC may interview potential clients; review medical records; educate the attorney regarding medical terms, procedures, and issues in the case; identify missing or required documents or policies and procedures; prepare or locate visual aids and exhibits; and assist in determining which medical, nursing, or associated experts will be needed and locate or assist in locating them. These consultants are sometimes asked to help prepare an expert witness who has precisely the clinical expertise the case requires but who may lack testifying experience.

The consulting LNC's name and work product are usually nondiscoverable because, by law, they are considered "attorney work product." If a testifying expert relies on the work product of the consultant to formulate an opinion, the consultant LNC's work product may be discoverable (only on request) by the opposing party. In several states (e.g., Arizona and Texas), the attorney is required by law to consult an expert before a case is filed.

Types of Expert Witnesses

The role of expert witnesses is one of the most crucial in civil litigation. Their main function is education of attorneys and triers of fact. Without the benefit of education on the relevant medical and nursing issues by professional experts, many jurors would find it very difficult to render informed verdicts.[2] The main types of experts working as members of today's litigation team include testifying and fact witnesses. Each type of expert is educated, trained, and experienced in one or more specialty practice areas.

Testifying Expert

The expert witness is involved in litigation to teach — to explain issues that are not common knowledge. Ideally, the expert has the ability to explain complex or specialized issues in language that will be easily understood by all jury members, arbitrators, and judges. If the expert's opinion supports the attorney's perspective, the expert may be asked to become a testifying expert. In this case, the expert's work product becomes discoverable. For this reason the attorney's decision either to request written reports or analyses or to keep all communications verbal must be made at the time the expert is engaged. The testifying expert testifies at trial, establishing standards that were in force at the time the alleged event took place, and explains how the defendant did or did not adhere to those standards. The expert, when qualified to do so, may be asked to testify whether a deviation from the standard caused the injury.

Because experts are relied upon to educate the triers of fact on the standards of care as applicable to a given case, care must be:

> exercised that such expert testimony does not narrowly reflect the
> expert's views about applicable standards to the exclusion of other

Table 34.1   Expert Qualifications

Current professional licensure*
Clinical expertise*
Current clinical practice
Concurrent clinical practice in the specialty (usually)
Specialty certification
Graduate degrees
Professional refereed publications and research

* Indicates minimal legal requirements.

acceptable and perhaps more realistic choices. … Truthfulness is essential and misrepresentation or exaggeration of clinical facts or opinion to establish an absolute right or wrong may be harmful, both to the individual parties involved and to the profession as a whole.[3]

Expert Fact Witness

The role of the expert fact witness is strictly instructive, which excludes rendering an opinion on the applicable standard of care. A fact witness may be retained by an attorney or appointed by the court. The expert fact witness reviews and summarizes the medical records and relevant professional literature, then provides the trier of fact with relevant factual information using layperson's terminology. See Chapter 36 for more information about this role.

Qualifications of the Expert Witness

Rule 702 of the Federal Rules of Evidence states that if specialized knowledge (e.g., medical, nursing, or technical) will assist the trier of fact to comprehend the evidence on facts at issue in a case, then an individual who is qualified as an expert by knowledge, skill, experience, training, or education may provide testimony in the form of an opinion.[1]

Minimal legal credentials for a health care expert include a current professional license and clinical expertise in the area at issue. Professional credibility is enhanced by other credentials, such as graduate degrees, refereed journal publications, research, and certification in the specialty. These professional credentials speak to the highest level of expertise and knowledge of the appropriate standard of care.[4] (See Table 34.1.) Professional credibility is damaged by a past history of any type of disciplinary action against the expert by the licensing board.

Selection and Location of the Nurse Expert Witness

Qualifications

While some courts have held that the only requisite qualification to testify as an expert witness is knowledge that is greater than that found in the general community, other courts have disallowed testimony by nurses and others they have deemed to be inadequately qualified. The most common criterion for acceptance of an appropriately educated or experienced expert is current and relevant clinical practice. Occasionally courts have allowed testimony by people who no longer practice in the specialty or perhaps never did actual clinical practice but restricted their practice to teaching, research, or similar activities. More commonly, such a person would be disallowed as an expert witness. For example, in one case a nurse who had worked in a law firm office for several years was listed as an expert witness regarding nursing practice about which she felt absolutely qualified to testify. The judge refused to qualify her as an expert, citing her lack of current clinical practice in the issue under litigation and her lack of clinical practice at the time of the alleged incident, which left the attorney without an expert witness in the matter.

The LNC is usually conversant with the numerous specialties and subspecialties of physicians. Similarly, there are many specialties within nursing. Table 34.2 is a partial listing of nursing specialties to help in identifying the nurse specialist who will be required in a given case. For example, the LNC should be aware that not all emergency nurses deal with trauma; that the prehospital-care medication and treatment guidelines are different not only from state to state, but also from county to county; and that care in a tertiary teaching center may be significantly different from that in a community hospital, which affects not only the level of medical care provided but even the qualifications of the person doing triage. When a children's hospital is available in the area, most general emergency departments rarely care for a child with a complex chronic illness or a life-threatening illness or injury, but will usually do stabilization and transfer procedures. These usually require written agreements and protocols. It would be impossible to identify the subsets of knowledge for every specialty; it is essential for the LNC to be aware that they exist.

The expert witness must have at least the educational background of the person whose practice is under review. In practice, the greater the educational preparation of the expert, the greater his or her perceived credibility. In nursing, a registered nurse (R.N.) with a bachelor of science in nursing has greater credibility with a jury than an R.N. with an associate of science in nursing degree. A master's degree in nursing, particularly with preparation as an advanced practice nurse, will have great impact. A doctorate confers a special luster of advanced preparation, whether it be in nursing, education, or a related discipline.

Certifications that demonstrate a certain level of competency in the specialty are great assets. Certification that was obtained by examination but not renewed, common among C.C.R.N.s, provides more credibility than never having taken the certification exam. The authors have seen curricula vitae (CVs) in which the nurses have listed as certifications the hospital in-service requirements of their employers. While this will tend to support the premise that the nurse is well prepared for her nursing tasks, attendance at such required developmental programs and educational seminars should be clearly described and not appear to be an attempt to "puff up" the CV for deceptive purposes.

The expert witness with publications, particularly in refereed journals, has additional credibility, particularly when the subject matter relates to the case under scrutiny. A caveat is that these publications are available to the opposing counsel, who, the expert witness can be sure, will obtain and carefully review them for evidence of a conflicting opinion to that which the expert now professes.

Table 34.2 Nursing Specialty Areas

Abortion
AIDS, AIDS-related complex
Alzheimer's
Anesthesia
Angioplasty
Assisted living

Behavioral disorders
Bill auditing
Board and care homes
Bone marrow transplant
Burns

Cardiac care
Cardiac rehabilitation
Cardiac special procedures
Case management
Chemical dependency
Chemotherapy
Claim management
Clinical specialist
Clinics
Coagulation disorders
Complex home care
Convalescent care
Critical care (all types)
Critical care transport

Defense medical exam (DME/IME)
Diabetes
Diabetes education
Dialysis (hemo- and peritoneal types)
Discharge planning

Emergency (including prehospital)
Endoscopy
Enterostomal therapy
Epidemiology
Ethical issues
Evidence location and preparation
Eye surgery

Genetic counseling
Geriatrics

Hemophilia
HMOs
Home health care
Hospice
Hospital regulations and standards

Infection control
IV insertion and monitoring

Laparascopic surgery
Life care planning (adult and pediatric)
Long-term care

Managed care
Med/surg (medical and surgical)
MICN (mobile intensive care nurse)

Neonatal (including NICU)
Nephrology
Neurology
Nurse practitioner (all specialties)
Nursing administration
Nursing standards of care

Obstetrics (labor and delivery, postpartum)
Oncology
Orthopedics

Pain management
Paramedic care
Pediatrics
Physician Assistant
Plasmapheresis
Psychiatric nursing
Pulmonary care

Quality improvement

Radiology (including special procedures)
Recovery (post anesthesia)
Rehabilitation
Research
Resuscitation
Risk management

School nursing
Sexual assault
Shunts
Skilled nursing facilities
Surgery (all types)
Surgicenter

Toxic exposures
Transplants
Trauma
Urgent care
Ventilators

Refereed journals publish materials that have undergone a peer-review process by eminent consultants with diverse professional backgrounds. Examples of refereed journals include the *American Journal of Nursing (AJN)* and the *Journal of Legal Nurse Consulting.*

Characteristics of the Desirable Expert Witness

In addition to legally required licensure and practice requirements, advanced education, certification, teaching and publication activities, and personal characteristics may be of great importance. The expert witness should be poised, articulate, and able to explain complex concepts or procedures in simple language. Physical attractiveness is a plus; a warm personality and sincere, believable affect are desirable. The expert witness should be able to absorb hostile questioning without taking offense. An excellent memory will enable the expert to identify misquotations of testimony and to correct them in a timely fashion.

The following are key characteristics for successful working relationships.

Compatibility

Attorneys who hire nurse expert witnesses will be working closely with them, so it is important for the attorney and the expert to have a comfortable working relationship. It is safe to assume that if the attorney does not like the expert, it is entirely possible that one or more of the triers of fact will have the same reaction. If the LNC has the key role of locating the expert, the impressions the LNC forms while interacting with the expert are important. The courteous, responsive expert who readily provides information in the initial contact is likely to have an edge over the expert who does not react in this manner.

Presentation Skills

Although most nurses are expert at presenting complex medical issues in language understandable to a person functioning at eighth grade level — a skill essential to the testifying expert — occasionally an LNC may encounter a nurse who cannot easily make the transition from professional language to common language. Asking the nurse expert to explain a medical issue that the LNC "doesn't understand" can test this. A tendency to use medical terms or graduate school-level vocabulary is not enough to disqualify the nurse, but it does signal a need for significant preparation time.

Specific Knowledge

The nurse expert witness must have current knowledge of the illness, injury, procedure, or equipment at issue in the case. It is possible to work in the operating room, for example, but have no experience with open-heart surgery, or to work in pediatrics but never to have encountered the illness from which a client has suffered. To believe that any nurse can testify to virtually all nursing issues is a recipe for disaster.

Example 34.1: In a case involving the sudden and unexpected death of a young oncology patient, the plaintiff nurse expert had never worked in oncology and had, in fact, been working in chemical dependency for the previous five years. At a deposition she testified to causation, blaming the chemotherapy that had been administered, apparently because *Drug Facts and Comparisons* indicated that the drug was nephrotoxic, and ignoring that the reference also stated that symptoms of toxicity appear approximately three weeks after treatment. She not only lacked specific knowledge, but also exceeded her scope of practice in testifying to medical causation. She left the deposition in tears, and the attorney was left to attempt to find a qualified witness immediately. She was absolutely unqualified to testify in the case. The plaintiff attorney said that she had "held herself out to be qualified," which may have left her vulnerable to a charge of malpractice.

Practical Experience

The expert should have absolute command of the clinical area. A nurse who has worked in a specialty area for 20 years but now works only part time in that area is an entirely satisfactory witness. A nurse who has worked in the specialty area part time for the past three years may lack the requisite command of the specialty.

Experience as an expert witness is desirable because testimony experience in deposition, arbitration, or trial improves the likelihood that the person will be an effective witness. Some attorneys actually prefer the novice expert witness, believing that people who have no history of providing expert testimony are somewhat immunized against characterization as "hired guns" (experts who do extensive testifying, particularly representing only plaintiff or only defense, and from which they derive the bulk of their income).

Honors

Honors awarded to the expert can cause the jury to be predisposed to like or accept the nurse expert. If the nurse expert was named outstanding nurse educator, for example, or employee of the quarter or a nominee for the excellence award at the employing hospital, it adds to credibility.

Balance

Although in the past it was common for an expert to work exclusively for either defense firms or plaintiff firms, such one-sidedness is now considered a negative. The more closely the expert's work is evenly divided between plaintiff and defense, the more objective the expert will appear to be, and in all probability, the more objective the expert will be.

Resources

To ensure that an appropriate expert is identified, it is advisable for the LNC to have an intake format that addresses all requisite information (see Figure 34.1). The elements should include the issues in the case; the case caption or name; the facility, nurses, and doctors involved; the attorney's name and any other contact at the law firm or insurance company; the firm name, address, and telephone and fax numbers; whether plaintiff, defense, personal injury, or other; important dates; materials to be mailed or faxed; expert or consultant assigned; date and time the information was sent; and the source of the referral and the date.

Issues: _____

_____

Case Name: _____

Facility/Personnel Involved: _____

Attorney: _____

Contact: _____

Firm Name: _____

Address: _____

Telephone: (___) _____ Fax: (___) _____

Plaintiff, Defense, PI, Other: _____

Important Dates: _____

Specialty Required: _____

Potential Expert: _____

Materials to Be Mailed or Faxed: _____

Date & Time Information Sent: _____

Source of Referral: _____

Comments: _____

_____

Date: _____ Signature: _____

Figure 34.1   Sample Intake Format

While some elements of the intake format form are self-explanatory, others are best explained. Issues in the case should be as comprehensive as is necessary to enable the LNC to determine the appropriate expert for the case. Elements should include the allegations of negligence; the alleged damage from that negligence; the locale in which the event or events took place (acute hospital, skilled nursing facility, board and care facility, surgicenter, psychiatric facility, or other); and the department within the facility in which the alleged negligence occurred.

Identification of the facility and personnel involved enables the LNC to screen for conflicts with the potential expert witness. This information is not always available at intake, but every effort should be made to obtain it.

While it would be preferable to review all cases while unaware of whether the attorney represents the plaintiff or defense, in the real world this is usually not possible. Some physicians, nursing administrators, and ancillary personnel will testify only for the defense. At some point the expert must know the litigation orientation of the attorney to be able to offer advice regarding liability and to advise how best to develop or defend the case.

The form includes a space for important dates, which may include dates on which the attorney must name his experts, depositions are planned, and reports are due, and dates that have been set for arbitration or trial. The potential expert should be apprised of these dates to ensure his or her availability.

The source of the referral is important. This section should include information in response to a question such as "How did you hear of our services?" The names of clients who have referred colleagues, or the location of advertising or other marketing performed by the LNC's company, represent valuable information. The date of intake is important because it identifies the date of first contact, a common question at deposition.

Site Locations

Finding an effective and appropriately qualified expert can be a daunting task. Here, networking skills are invaluable. The local American Association of Legal Nurse Consultants (AALNC) chapter is a rich source of nurses of varied clinical backgrounds. The in-house nurse at a large medical malpractice or malpractice defense firm may be an excellent source of highly recommended experts. If the LNC is clinically active, many qualified experts can be identified through the LNC's place of employment. Some LNCs prefer not to draw attention to their work with attorneys and therefore do not recruit experts at their employment sites.

The local bar association may publish a directory of experts and consultants, including nurses, particularly in heavily populated areas. The AALNC membership data may lead the LNC to precisely the required nursing expert. When an exceptionally well-qualified nurse is required, the best resource may be a nurse expert at one of the major university centers. Often this person can refer you to others in his or her network. Online registry sources such as http://www.ExpertPages.com, nursefinders.com, and the state board of registered nursing (BRN) can also be accessed. An expert witness screening form (see Figure 34.2) can be utilized when making contact with an expert to elicit details about experience and fees.

Support for the Nurse Expert

Even the most experienced expert witness needs some support. The relative newcomer to this function requires a great deal of support. At minimum, the LNC should be certain that the expert is confident in the following areas:

- Elements of liability
- Understanding the litigation process
- Standards of care
- Community standards

Elements of Liability

The elements of liability are as follows:

- There must be a duty to provide care. (Good Samaritans, for example, have no such duty.)
- There must be an act or failure to act that falls below applicable standards of care.

Expert name: _____ Date: _____

Specialty: _____

Office address: Mailing address: where to send records

_____   _____

_____   _____

_____   _____

_____   _____

Phone #: _____   Fax #: _____

Best time to call: _____
(day or evening)

Name of office contact: _____

Current CV on file: yes or no   Entered into database: yes or no

Signed contract: yes or no   Date of contract: _____

Rate for review: _____   Typed fee schedule: yes or no

Rate for deposition: _____

Rate for trial: _____

Cancellation fee: _____

Time cancellation fee will be effective: _____

Retainer required: yes or no   Amount of retainer: _____

Number of cases reviewed per year: _____

Number of times testified at deposition: _____

Number of times testified at trial: _____

Number of plaintiff cases _____ # vs. defense cases _____#

Percentage of plaintiff cases _____ % vs. defense cases _____%

Comments: _____

Figure 34.2 Expert Witness Screening Form

- There must be damages.
- The breach of the standard of care must have caused or contributed to the damages.

It is possible to provide nursing care that is substandard but that will incur no liability because the poor nursing neither caused nor contributed to the damages, if any, suffered by the plaintiff.

Understanding the Litigation Process

The nurse must understand that the litigation proceeds in a standardized format. Occasionally, an expert witness will be directed to turn in the entire file relating to a case, including notes on the outside, Post-its®, notes regarding conversations with the attorney, and anything else that was written. The novice expert may innocently write both the favorable and unfavorable impressions that he or she derived from reviewing the medical record, depositions, policies, and procedures. The more experienced expert knows that all impressions should be communicated to the attorney, but that all written work is potentially discoverable, so will limit negatives to verbal communications.

The LNC should proofread written reports several times; avoid criticisms of other personnel and submit reports in a timely fashion. Figure 34.3 provides one example of format guidelines.

An expert witness may be called to give a deposition if the case is proceeding toward arbitration or trial. Some states (e.g., Pennsylvania and New York) do not require depositions. Occasionally an attorney will choose not to depose an expert, to save on costs.

The novice expert witness should receive some preparation for the deposition experience. The process should be explained, with emphasis on the fact that this is not an environment in which the nurse is a teacher. Rather, each question, and only that question, should be answered. The response should be fairly concise and should not include information that the attorney has not requested. In this venue the opposition is the "enemy," who may attempt to lead the expert to express opinions either that the expert does not hold or that conflict with previous testimony.

The nurse should know that a break may be requested at any time. The expert should pause before answering any question to give the retaining attorney time to object. The expert may declare that a question is not clear, and may ask that complex questions be broken down into their elements. Any misquotation on the part of the opposing attorney should be corrected. The nurse must be conscious of the limitations of his or her expertise and must not exceed them, for example, by testifying to medical causation.

When the deposition has been transcribed, the expert witness should request a copy of it to review and sign. This is the time to make any corrections that are necessary, but the expert should be aware that a change of opinion will damage credibility.

Many publications address the deposition process. It is advisable to refer the novice expert witness to one of them or even to supply the desired material. Chapter 35 explores the process in greater depth.

Preparation of the Expert for Trial

The LNC who prepares an expert for trial must take an organized approach to the task. He or she should:

- Review the testimony experience of the expert witness. The thoroughly experienced expert will need little preparation; the novice will require intensive preparation and guidance regarding:
  Attire
  Arrival time, place, and parking
  Documents or exhibits that the expert is expected to bring
  Material that should not be brought to court

DATE:

TO: (claim adjuster, attorney, contact person)

FROM: (your name, title, degrees, certifications)

SUBJECT: Medical Record Review

FILE NO.: (Insurance company or law firm file number)

CASE CAPTION: (Case name: Fyler v. St. Agatha Medical Center)

CO. FILE NO.: (your personal filing system)

NURSING MEDICAL RECORD REVIEW

[Brief statement:] At your request I have reviewed the ... records of ... to ascertain ...

RECORDS REVIEWED

[Listing of each segment of each chart:]
    Office Records Dr. Walsh, 4/16/75 to 6/6/00
    Paramedic Report 1/3/99
    Prehospital Report, Mission Hospital 1/3/99
    University of California Irvine Medical Center 1/3/99 to 3/1/99
        Emergency Department Record, 1/3/99
        Radiology Reports
        Laboratory Reports
        Intensive Care Nursing Record
        Interdisciplinary Progress Record
        Physical Therapy Evaluation, 1/5/99
        Occupational Therapy Evaluation, 1/5/99
            etc. Give dates, when multiple.

SUMMARY OF FINDINGS

Mrs. Williams is a 45-year-old lady who was struck by a car while crossing Harbor Blvd. in Costa Mesa at 1700 on January 3, 1999. She was treated at the scene by Orange County Paramedics, Unit 59, and taken to UCIMC where she was treated in the Emergency Department by the trauma team, headed by Dr. ..., and found to have ... injuries. Following surgery she was admitted to the Trauma Intensive Care Unit. She made good progress, and was transferred to the orthopedic unit on ... date. Physical therapy and occupational therapy were started on ... date. She has continued to make good progress. However, she has ... injuries, which can be expected to require treatment for some time and which may cause permanent disability.

CHRONOLOGY

[This should provide a chronological record of relevant data. It is not always required, but when it would be valuable to the attorney or claims representative it should be included. It is wise to obtain permission before providing a chronology because it can be time-consuming (and thus expensive). It is most often needed in complex cases and long-term care but may prove invaluable as a minute-to-minute record of an emergent episode.

    Data might include: day of injury or illness, x-ray findings, abnormal laboratory or cardiology results, significant progress notes, physical therapy notes — anything that should be identified, noting its place in the progression of care.]

Continued.

Figure 34.3 Sample Report Format

DISCUSSION

There is a concern that ... diagnosis was not made until ... Additionally, there are numerous nursing notations describing the patient as "uncooperative," "resistant," "demanding," and "distraught." Nursing care appears to have met most standards of care. There were missed medications [describe medicine, date, and time], failure to document output [times, dates], and an incomplete day of admission assessment. None of these deviations would have caused or contributed to a less than satisfactory outcome in this case. [OR: the failure to monitor and record circulation in the right leg may have contributed to ...]

CONCLUSIONS

[It is very important that you come to some conclusions and state clearly if there is or is not any consequential deviation from the standard of care. These should include both general and specific deviations and associated damage. Cite the standards, specifics of your opinion that it was not met, and the harm that did result or may have resulted from this deviation from the standard of care. It is important to cite official standards of care (nursing specialty organization, AHRQ [Agency for Healthcare Research and Quality], or hospital policy and procedure relating to the issue of care). Your opinion must be as honest and objective as you can possibly make it. If you cannot support a plaintiff attorney's case, tell him so, and why this is so. This is equally important in a defense case. The insurance company or defense attorney must be informed of the significant issues that are likely to be addressed by the opposition.]

Important: Do not write a report for either the attorney or the insurance company until you have discussed your findings and opinions and have determined that a written report is desired.]

RECOMMENDATIONS

[Identify missing records that should be obtained.
Identify relevant policies and procedures that should be obtained.]

REFERENCES

[Appropriate standard or standards
Books or magazines reviewed, noting edition and pages
Copies of articles]

DEFINITIONS

[If few in number, terms can be defined in the body of the text. If many, do a definition (glossary) page. Keep the vocabulary simple. Some attorneys and claims representatives are quite sophisticated. Some know virtually no medical terminology. Err on the side of caution.]

THANK YOU

[A simple statement of thanks for providing you the opportunity to review this interesting case (or whatever fits).]

Figure 34.3   Sample Report Format (*Continued*)

■ Ask the expert witness to express, briefly, the facts and the testimony that he or she intends to provide. If these vary in any way from the attorney's theme, this must be discussed with the attorney.

Evaluate the effectiveness of the presentation.

Work with the expert witness to present more effectively, if needed.

Emphasize the need to answer only the question that is asked.

Remind the expert to pause before answering to give the attorney time to object.

Review the expert witness's right to ask to have a question repeated if it is unclear, and to ask to have complex, multiple-focus questions broken into their components.

■ Practice responses.

Develop sample questions of the type that the opposing attorney may ask.

Ask the expert witness to respond to the questions.

Ask, "Is that really what you want to say?" if the response is off target.

Emphasize honesty. Questions are often asked in several forms.

When the answers are always honest, there should be no inconsistency.

Watch for distracting mannerisms such as finger tapping, knee jiggling, or eyebrow raising and work with the expert to eliminate them.

Remind the expert witness that most answers should be addressed to the jury, but that the response can be to the attorney when it seems more appropriate.

■ Warn the expert witness about attorney tactics, such as:

Attack on the expert witness's qualifications

Attack on the expert's testimony by using amazement, sarcasm, or disbelief

The "best friend" approach

Misstating the expert witness's previous testimony

■ Videotape a practice testimony, if possible. This is very beneficial because the expert witness can view it to critique his or her responses and mannerisms.

■ View a mock trial video such as those produced by Creative Education Unlimited.[5]

Standards of Care

Standards of care can be national, local, community-based, or specific to an agency. National standards are found in nursing textbooks, laws, journal articles, and pharmacology books (e.g., the *Physicians' Desk Reference* or *Drug Facts and Comparisons*). Nursing specialty organizations as well as the American Nurses Association have published comprehensive standards of care. The standards that have been established by the U.S. Department of Health and Human Services in the Agency for Healthcare Research and Quality (AHRQ) are excellent sources. The Joint Commission on Accreditation of Healthcare Organizations (JCAHO) has established standards in the Accreditation Manual for Hospitals that are used to evaluate and monitor the clinical and organizational performance of health care facilities. Local standards are found in the facility's policy-and-procedure manuals and internal instructional documents. Those will be discovered only if requested by the attorney, and the expert witness should identify to the retaining attorney any of these that will be needed to support the proposed testimony.

Community Standards

The concept of "community standards" is controversial. In nursing it is generally believed that the standards are the same throughout the nation, because nurses use the same textbooks, read the same journals, and attend the same symposia. Even within the nursing community it is unrealistic and improper to expect the nurse at a rural facility to recognize and intervene in an obscure neurological syndrome that might be commonplace for the nurse in the neurological intensive care unit at a tertiary center. This is less a "community" standard than it is a standard relating to the practice of a reasonably prudent nurse with similar education and experience.

In law, however, the principle of community standard is still applied in some states and jurisdictions. Some states have a requirement that the expert witness must practice in the state where the incident occurred or in an adjacent state, an apparent application of the "community standard" rule. State laws are a source of community standards (e.g., Title 22 in California). The potential expert witness should be prepared to describe how the witness knows the community standard, particularly if he or she has been employed at one facility for many years.

Resources

This text provides guidance on many issues that confront the expert witness. The American Nurses Association publishes comprehensive standards for clinical nursing, which serve as a template for specialty standards and standards for nursing administration. Every nursing specialty organization publishes standards of care as they relate to that specialty. All states will provide a copy of their Nurse Practice Act on request. A useful book for preparing a nurse expert for trial is *Presentation of Evidence, A Survival Guide for Nurse Witnesses*.[6] There are LNC listservs on the Internet that enable the nurse to obtain input from many LNCs.

Legal Rulings on Nurse Expert Testimony

In nursing malpractice litigation, negligence is established through expert testimony as to the applicable standard of care for the specific circumstance at issue, a deviation from that standard, and an injury proximately caused by that deviation. Standards are referenced to demonstrate that the nurse did or did not breach the duty of care owed to the client. If the nurse failed to meet the standard of care and breached his or her duty, by definition the nurse is negligent.[7]

Before 1980, physicians served as the expert witnesses at trials regarding nursing standards of care. In 1980, two landmark court cases, *Avret v. McCormick*[8] and *Malony v. Wake Hospital Systems*,[9] set the stage for acceptance by the court system of nurse experts, defining roles and standards of care for nursing practice. In *Avret v. McCormick*, a trial court excluded a nurse expert from rendering an opinion as to standards of care in keeping sterile a needle used to draw blood from a client. At trial, the physician against whom the medical malpractice suit was brought testified that blood drawing is not a procedure exclusively limited to professional skills of physicians. The Georgia Supreme Court held that the nurse was qualified as an expert witness in that a "nurse duly graduated from school of nursing and licensed in this state and who has drawn blood and given intravenous injections in numbers exceeding two thousand, is qualified to testify as an expert witness."

A similar ruling was made in *Malony v. Wake Hospital Systems*. The North Carolina Court of Appeals held that the trial court had erred in disqualifying a nurse expert who was certified in intravenous therapy from stating an opinion as to the cause of a physical injury. The plaintiff suffered burns on her hand due to an intravenous administration of undiluted potassium chloride into the tissues. The appellate court held that "an expert witness is not disqualified from giving an expert opinion as to the cause of a physical injury simply because she is not a medical doctor. ... Her expertise is different from, but no less exalted than that of a physician."

Judicial decisions have restricted the scope of nursing expert testimony relative to causation on injury issues and medical diagnosis issues. In *Dikeou v. Osborne*[10] and *Kent v. Pioneer Valley Hospital,*[11] the Utah appellate court concluded that a nurse expert could opine on the nursing standards but was not qualified to opine on proximate causation of injury. In *Stryczek v. Methodist,*[12] the Indiana Court of Appeals held that the nurse expert could render an opinion as to the standard of care for administering cardiotoxic medications by nurses, but not to medical diagnosis because nurses do not have the same education, training, and experience as physicians. Similar rulings were found in *Chadwick v. Nielson*[13] and *Taplin v. Lupin.*[14]

With the emergence of advanced nursing practice, judicial decisions traditionally held the duty of care owed by the advanced practice nurses to the medical (physician) standard.[15,16] More recent court findings have disagreed with the preceding case rulings and have found that advanced practice nurses are not subject to the same standards as physicians.

In *Ewing v. Aubert*[17] and *Fein v. Permanente Medical Group,*[18] the courts found that the nurse practitioner was held to the standard of care for an advanced nurse practitioner in diagnosis and treatment and not to the physician standard of diagnosis and treatment. Court decisions have also allowed advanced practice nurses to testify as expert witnesses against physicians when the services provided by the physician were the same as those that could legally be provided by an advanced practice nurse.[19] In courts the breach in the standard of care is proven through the expert witness testimony, and generally nurses are held to standards applicable to their specialty practice area and level of qualifications.[20]

Selection and Location of the Medical Expert Witness

The medical expert may be an M.D., chiropractor, podiatrist, dentist, psychologist, or other who practices medicine in some form and who is addressed as "Doctor." See Table 34.1 for a list of qualifications for medical experts. Desirable characteristics include:

- Board certification in the specialty
- History of achievement in the specialty (e.g., fellowships, awards, and recognition)
- Medical school teaching appointments
- Publications in refereed journals
- Staff privileges at prestigious hospitals

■ Experience as an expert witness (preferably reviewing cases for both plaintiff and defense attorneys)
■ A sincere, believable affect
■ The ability to explain complex medical issues in lay terms

Resources

Resources for finding medical experts are much like those that can be used to find nursing experts. Expert and consultant directories published by the local bar association are rich sources of qualified individuals. Other directories are frequently included in the annual membership guide of the local bar association. Some directories are published by legal organizations such as Martindale-Hubbell and publications that report jury verdicts (e.g., *Legal Expert Pages*). Both directories of experts and specialty membership lists can be found online. Characterization of the expert witness as a "hired gun" is a risk when the expert is found in these publications.

Personal contacts are valuable resources. A physician whom the LNC has utilized as an expert witness in the past may be able to provide a referral to a colleague. Many physicians who are associated with medical schools will do medical–legal work. One can find them by accessing the physician referral service. If the contacted specialist does not testify, he or she can usually refer you to a colleague who does.

The local medical association will refer callers to an appropriately specialized physician who may or may not be willing to do medical–legal work, but most specialty organizations are somewhat close-knit groups, so the contacted specialist will usually be a source of a good referral. The clinically active LNC who works with an appropriate specialist can ask whether he or she does this kind of work. The LNC should be aware of agency policies and avoid drawing attention to part-time work with attorneys if the employing agency frowns on it.

It is important to look for specialists in the right places. The pediatric neuro-radiologist will probably be found at a children's hospital. The chiropractor can be found at the chiropractic college. The physiatrist who specializes in physical rehabilitation will be found as the director of a hospital rehabilitation department, or as one of many physiatrists at a rehabilitation (not convalescent) hospital.

Online registry sources include:

http://www.expertpages.com
http://www.chiropractor-finder.com
http://www.dentist.com
http://www.locateadoc.com

Support

Like all other expert witnesses, the medical expert witness must be familiar with the elements of liability; sources of practice standards; local, state, and national legislation that governs practice in the specialty under litigation; community standards; and legal rulings on the admissibility of expert testimony (e.g., *Frye v.*

United States;[21] Federal Rule of Evidence 702;[1] *Daubert v. Merrell Dow Pharmaceuticals, Inc.*;[22] and *Kumho Tire Company, Ltd. v. Carmichael*[23]).

Preparation for trial or deposition should follow a carefully orchestrated scenario similar to that described in this chapter regarding nurse expert witnesses. The physician may need extra coaching to avoid an affect that will be perceived as either arrogant or "thin-skinned." The physician, like the nurse, will be well served by viewing himself or herself in a practice testimony session and by watching a tape of a mock trial.

Physicians have been allowed to testify to nursing standards of practice. While this is now much less commonly allowed than in the past, if the LNC finds himself or herself working with a physician who is expected to do so, some very comprehensive preparation will be required. Most physicians know nothing of nursing standards; they just know what they want the nurses to do, which is not at all the same thing. Preparation for physician testimony regarding nursing practice will require considerable education in the sources of nursing standards, the laws that direct nursing practice in that locale, and the existence of policies and procedures that may govern the nurse's action.

Legal Rulings on Medical Expert Testimony

Frye v. United States[21] established the "general acceptance" standard for opinion testimony. In *Frye v. United States*, trial counsel for the defendant offered as an expert witness a scientist who had conducted a blood pressure deception test on the defendant. The court disallowed the testimony, holding that

> the systolic blood pressure deception test has not yet gained such standing and scientific recognition among physiological and psychological authorities as would justify the courts in admitting expert testimony deduced from the discovery development and experiments thus far made.

A more liberal thrust to opinion testimony was made by the courts with the adoption of Federal Rule of Evidence 702 in 1975. The federal rule of expert testimony was void of any reference to the "general acceptance" standard and was applicable to all disciplines. Rule 702, Testimony by Experts, states:

> If scientific, technical, or other specialized knowledge will assist the trier of fact to understand the evidence or to determine a fact at issue a witness qualified as an expert by knowledge, skill, experience, training or education, may testify thereto in the form of an opinion or otherwise.

Daubert v. Merrell Dow Pharmaceuticals, Inc.[22] involved two children and their parents as petitioners who alleged that the children's birth defects had been caused by the mothers' prenatal ingestion of a prescription drug for nausea (Bendectin) marketed by Merrell Dow Pharmaceuticals. The trial court determined, and appeals court held, that the evidence presented by the petitioners' experts did not meet the "general acceptance" test. The Supreme Court reversed the decision, holding that the "general acceptance" standard was superseded by the 1975 adoption of the Federal Rules of Evidence. Intending to liberalize the admissibility of expert testimony, the Court levied the task of managing admission of evidence on the trial judge. The trial judge assumed the role of "gatekeeper," allowing the admission of reliable scientific evidence and excluding less reliable evidence. The Court articulated four nonexclusive criteria that were to be considered when evaluating expert testimony:

- Whether the theory is tested
- Whether the theory or technique has been subjected to peer review and publication
- The potential error rate
- The existence and maintenance of standards controlling the technique's operation[24]

Three subsequent Court rulings have attempted to clarify the *Daubert* ruling. In *General Electric Company v. Joiner*,[25] the Court ruled that appellate review of admitted expert testimony is limited to an "abuse of discretion" standard rather than the "particularly stringent" standard.

In *Kumho Tire Company, Ltd. v. Carmichael*,[23] the plaintiff expert intended to testify that by virtue of his experience he knew that a tire had failed because of a manufacturing defect. He based his opinion on the absence of certain criteria that he believed would be present if the tire had failed due to abuse. His testimony was disallowed because the Court held that the admissibility criteria of *Daubert* and Rule 702 apply to all experts providing testimony at trial, not just to novel scientific theories, and that the proposed testimony did not meet those criteria.

The Court, in *Weisgram v. Marley Company*,[26] determined that under Federal Rule of Civil Procedure 50(a), "appellate courts have the power to direct a district court to enter judgment notwithstanding the verdict against a winning plaintiff if the appellate court determines that admitted testimony was unreliable and inadmissible under *Daubert*."[24]

The advisory committee for the Federal Rules of Evidence deemed it necessary to amend Rule 702 on the basis of the Court's recent decisions on expert testimony and the disparate treatment of Rule 702 by the district courts.[24] The new rule adds that expert testimony is admissible "if (1) the testimony is based on sufficient facts or data, (2) the testimony is the product of reliable principles and methods, and (3) the witness has applied the principles and methods reliably to the facts of the case."[27]

In *Chambers v. Dr. Ludlow*,[28] the Indiana Court of Appeals reversed a summary judgment against the plaintiff, holding that (1) every element of a prima facie case of medical malpractice need not be satisfied by a single expert opinion, and (2) a genuine issue of material fact existed regarding every element of a prima facie case. Generally, in order to establish a claim of medical malpractice, the plaintiff must establish by means of expert medical testimony the applicable standard of care; the manner in which the defendant doctor breached that standard of care; and that the breach in the defendant doctor's standard of care was the proximate cause of the injuries noted in the complaint.

The evidence code as applied also states that for a witness to qualify as an "expert," the subject of opinion or implication must be so related to the profession, trade, business, or occupation as to be beyond the understanding of the layperson, and the witness must have sufficient skill, experience, or knowledge in that field to make it appear that his or her opinion or inference will aid the trier of fact in arriving at a just conclusion.

In *Broders v. Heise*,[29] the Supreme Court of Texas held that the witness proffered by the plaintiff was not qualified as "expert" on the issue of cause in fact. The case involved failure to diagnose a head injury in the emergency department, and the disqualified witness was an emergency physician. The court held that the mere fact that the witness was a medical doctor did not qualify him as "expert" in a medical malpractice action against other doctors. The fact that the witness proffered as an "expert" possesses knowledge and skill not possessed by people generally does not in and of itself mean that such expertise will assist the trier of fact (Rule 702).

In *O'Conner v. Commonwealth Edison Company*,[30] the district court held that the physician was not qualified to render an expert opinion that radiation cataracts are pathognomic or that the plaintiff's cataracts could be caused only by exposure to radiation. The physician was a board-certified ophthalmologist who specialized in contact lenses and had no experience in the field of radiation-induced cataracts, nor had he studied published literature on the subject.

Selection and Location of the Ancillary Expert

The ancillary expert category encompasses all medically related disciplines that do not fall under medicine or registered nursing. These include pharmacologists, x-ray technologists (including CT, MRI, and radiation-therapy technicians), laboratory technicians (including blood bank technologists), licensed practical nurses (LPN/LVN), human resources administrators, biomedical engineers, and more. Their qualifications and characteristics mirror those of nursing and medical experts, and they require the same support.

These specialists can often be found among the clinically active LNC's co-workers. Their specialty organizations can usually be found online. As for nursing and medical experts, a contact at a major medical malpractice firm, whether plaintiff or defense, may be able to direct the LNC to an appropriate expert and provide an assessment of that person's work as an expert witness. Less often, they can be found in the expert and consultant directories that are published in print or online.

Compensation

The independent LNC should be compensated for locating an expert. The most common methods of billing are to charge a flat fee for the expert location service, to charge for time spent, or to add an hourly rate to the expert's charges.

Flat Fee

The advantage to a flat fee charge is that it is readily understood by the attorney, as long as this charge is clearly identified prior to service and does not lead to a conflict regarding billing. One disadvantage is that the LNC must make certain that the expert located is actually utilized in the case, because attorneys usually refuse to pay for the location of an expert who they believe is not the best choice for the case. The expert can be asked to notify the LNC when the engagement is finalized or rejected, but often they fail to do so. The attorney can be asked to notify the LNC of the final decision, but this, too, is often omitted. The result may be a denial of charges when the work is invoiced by the LNC.

The LNC who chooses to charge a flat fee for expert location must be aware of any laws governing this activity. California law forbids charges that exceed the actual time spent in locating the expert.

Charge by Time Spent

The advantage to charging only the time spent for expert location is that, usually, it will be viewed as fair and as a charge that is easily justified to the client. One disadvantage is the same that applies to charging a flat fee — the LNC must be advised that the potential expert has been engaged. If the LNC has a large base of potential experts, this method may limit the return to an hour or less of time charged, despite the extensive time and resources that were expended to develop the expert base. If extensive time and money are required, for example when unusual expertise or credentials are needed, the attorney may dispute the charges. In such situations the LNC should notify the attorney if the search is taking more than 2 hours and obtain permission to continue.

Add-On Fees

Some LNCs obtain compensation by adding a fee to each hour of activity billed by the expert. On average, this provides a more appropriate level of compensation than charging either a flat or hourly location fee. Disadvantages to this approach are that it requires a contractual relationship with the expert and that it slows the collection time and payment to the expert because the expert bills the LNC, who then bills the attorney. Payment is made to the LNC, who then pays the consultant.

It is legal in California to add a fee to each hour the expert bills, as long as the client is aware that this is the method by which the LNC will be compensated. Fees obtained by this method are generally adequate to provide for marketing activities, to compensate the LNC for expert-finding activities that do not result in an engagement, and to provide a fair return for services rendered.

Regardless of the method chosen, the LNC should inform the attorney at the time expert search is requested that there will be a charge for this service, and should provide a clear explanation of the manner in which it will be done. Failure to inform the attorney can lead to inappropriate expectations and a conflict over fees.

Idiosyncratic State Laws on Expert Testimony

All LNCs must be knowledgeable about the nurse practice act in their states, legal opinions that have been issued, and legislation regarding testimony that may affect the ability of the chosen expert to testify. A few examples follow.

In Texas, a deposition may not last longer than six hours.

In California, it is illegal for anyone to be called "nurse" who is not licensed as an R.N. or L.V.N.

In California, the attorney general issued an opinion that a nurse may not take orders from a physician assistant (PA). The PA may transmit orders from the physician but may not, himself or herself, institute such orders.[31]

In several states, the expert must have been practicing in the identified clinical environment in the year in which the incident occurred. In one case a cardiovascular perfusion nurse with over 20 years of experience, both before and after the alleged incident, was not allowed to testify because she had not worked during the year of the alleged malpractice.

In California, there is a requirement that to qualify to testify in an emergency physician malpractice case, the physician must have been in full-time emergency practice for at least 5 years or have comparable qualifications as demonstrated by board certification. This was promoted by the California chapter of the American College of Emergency Physicians (Cal-ACEP) to eliminate the practice of specialists such as neurosurgeons and orthopedists testifying to standards that would be appropriate for a fellow specialist, but were believed to be inappropriate as a standard for the emergency physician.

Other states have their own idiosyncratic laws. It is not sufficient to assume that the attorney will know all laws governing nursing practice in the state in which he or she practices. The LNC should study the Nurse Practice Act in his or her own state, and should regularly access any source of legal rulings affecting nursing practice in that state. It would be unreasonable to expect that the LNC should have legal responsibility for knowing each idiosyncrasy of the law in his or her state, and the attorney bears the final responsibility in this matter, but the more in-depth knowledge the LNC brings to the table, the greater his or her value to the attorney.

Conclusion

Finding, selecting, and supporting expert witnesses is one of the more challenging aspects of the LNC's chosen field. The LNC who approaches the task in an organized fashion, maintaining a database of useful contacts and sources, will succeed in this endeavor. However, it is not enough to locate a qualified expert if that expert is unfamiliar with the legal process or is a novice at testifying. In that case, the LNC can apply skills that he or she developed as a clinical nurse to support the expert witness and achieve a successful outcome.

References

1. Testimony by Experts, Federal Rule of Evidence 702, 1998.
2. Bogart, J., Ed., *Legal Nurse Consulting: Principles and Practice*, CRC Press, Boca Raton, FL, 1996.
3. American Academy of Pediatrics, Policy statement guidelines for expert witness testimony in medical malpractice litigation, *Pediatrics*, 109(5), 974–979, 2002.
4. Guido, G., *Legal and Ethical Issues in Nursing,* Prentice-Hall, New York, 2000.

5. *Medical Legal Adventures*, Creative Education Unlimited, Los Angeles, 1999.
6. Salovesh, C., *Presentation of Evidence: A Survival Guide for Nurses*, West Haven University, Cypress, CA, 2000.
7. Aiken, T. and Catalano, J., *Legal, Ethical and Political Issues in Nursing*, F.A. Davis, Philadelphia, 1994.
8. *Avret v. McCormick*, 271 S.E.2d 832 (Ga. 1980).
9. *Maloney v. Wake Hospital Systems*, 262 S.E.2d 680 (N.C. Ct. App. 1980).
10. *Dikeou v. Osborne*, 881 P.2d 943 (Utah Ct. App. 1994).
11. *Kent v. Pioneer Valley Hospital*, 930 P.2d 904 (Utah Ct. App. 1997).
12. *Stryczek v. Methodist Hospital, Inc.*, 694 N.E.2d 1186 (Ind. Ct. App. 1998).
13. *Chadwick v. Nielson*, 763 P.2d 817 (Utah Ct. App. 1988).
14. *Taplin v. Lupin,* 700 So. 2d 1160 (La. Ct. App. 1997).
15. *Harris v. State through Huey P. Long Hospital*, 371 So. 2d 1221 (La. 1979).
16. *Hendry v. United States*, 418 F.2d 744 (2d Cir. 1969).
17. *Ewing v. Aubert*, 532 So. 2d 876 (La. Ct. App. 1988).
18. *Fein v. Permanente Medical Group*, 38 Cal. 3d 137 (1985).
19. *Samii v. Baystate Medical Center*, 395 N.E.2d 455 (Mass. 1979).
20. O'Keefe, M., *Nursing Malpractice and the Law: Avoiding Malpractice and Other Legal Risks*, F.A. Davis, Philadelphia, 2001.
21. *Frye v. United States*, 293 F. 1013 (D.C. Cir. 1923).
22. *Daubert v. Merrell Dow Pharmaceuticals, Inc.*, 509 U.S. 579 (1993).
23. *Kumho Tire Company, Ltd. v. Carmichael*, 526 U.S. 137 (1999).
24. Leesfield, I. and Sylvester, M., *Admissibility of Expert Testimony, What's Next*, http://expertpages.com/news/admissibility/testimony.htm, 2000.
25. *General Electric Company v. Joiner*, 522 U.S. 136 (1997).
26. *Weisgram v. Marley*, 528 U.S. 440 1001 (2000).
27. Report of the Advisory Committee on Evidence Rules (1999), in *Federal Rule Changes 2000 part B: Rules 701–703*.
28. *Chambers v. Ludlow*, 598 N.E.2d 1111 (Ind. Ct. App. 1992).
29. *Broders v. Heise*, 924 S.W.2d 148 (Tex. 1996).
30. *O'Connor v. Commonwealth Edison Company*, 807 F. Supp. 1376 (C.D. Ill. 1992).
31. Anderson, R., *Legal Boundaries of California Nursing Practice*, Sacramento, CA, 1997.

Additional Reading

Babitsky, B. and Mangraviti, J., *How to Excel During Cross-Exmination: Techniques for Experts That Work*, Seak, Inc., MA, 1997.
Drug Facts and Comparisons, St. Louis, 1991.
Federal Rule Changes 2000 Part B: Rules 701–703. Opinion Testimony, http://www.depo.com/Evidence2000.htm.
Iyer, P., Working with expert witnesses, in *Nursing Malpractice*, 2nd ed., P. Iyer, Ed., Lawyers & Judges Publishing Company, Tucson, AZ, 2001.
Pierson, E., Ed., *Wiley Expert Witness Update: New Developments in Personal Injury Litigation*, Aspen Law & Business, New York, 2000.
Purver, J., Ed., *Expert Witness Update: New Developments in Personal Injury Litigation*, Aspen Law & Business, New York, 2002.
Smith, J., *Hospital Liability*, Law Journal Seminars Press, New York, 2000.
Stedman's Medical Dictionary, 26th ed., Williams & Wilkins, MD, 1995.
Testimony by Experts, Federal Rule of Evidence 702, 1998.
Weber, E., *Pediatric Asthma: An Expert Witness Perspective*, AALNC, 2001.

West's Legal Thesaurus/Dictionary, West Publishing Company, New York, 1985.
Writing and Defending Your Expert Report, Seak, Inc., MA, 2001.

Online Resources

Code of Federal Regulations: Title 22, http://lula.law.cornell.edu/cfr/cfr.php?title=22
http://dir.yahoo.com/government/law/journals
http://www.alllaw.com/journals_and_periodicals/legal
http://www.legalexpertpages.com

Test Questions

1. Which of the following statements is NOT true?
   A. Current licensure is requisite for an R.N. expert witness.
   B. Clinical expertise in the specialty is usually required.
   C. Old disciplinary action by the B.R.N. is of no significance.
   D. Certification in the specialty is desirable.

2. Place the following actions in the best sequence when locating an expert.
   A. Notify the attorney of the potential expert and send a copy of his or her CV.
   B. Identify one or more potential experts.
   C. Obtain comprehensive information about the issues in the case.
   D. Contact the potential experts to determine availability and conflicts.

3. Which of the following statements is NOT true? Criteria for admission of evidence according to *Daubert* include
   A. Whether the theory or technique has been subjected to peer review and publication
   B. The potential error rate
   C. Whether the theory is tested
   D. Whether the theory meets the "general acceptance" test

4. Which of the following statements is true?
   A. An R.N. without advanced practice credentials may opine as to physician standard of practice.
   B. The R.N. credential, in and of itself, qualifies the nurse to opine as to nursing standards of care in any department.
   C. It is unnecessary to know the laws restricting nursing practice in the expert's state. The attorney is expected to know them and advise the expert.
   D. It is important to know the sources of nursing standards.

5. Which of the following statements is NOT true?
   A. Once an individual has been qualified as an expert by a trial court, he or she may give opinion testimony in any jurisdiction.
   B. The "general acceptance" test establishes admissibility based on scientific evidence.
   C. An in-house LNC at a medical malpractice firm may provide a good referral to an appropriately qualified expert witness.
   D. An effective expert witness will have good personal as well as professional characteristics.

Answers: 1. C, 2. CBDA, 3. D, 4. D, 5. A

THE LEGAL NURSE CONSULTANT AS EXPERT WITNESS

Chapter 35

The Liability Nurse Expert Witness

Elizabeth Edel, MN, RN,
Deborah Dlugose, BA, BS, RN, CCRN, CRNA,
Patricia W. Iyer, MSN, RN, LNCC, and
Janet G. Foster, MSN, RN, CCRN

CONTENTS

0-8493-1418-6/03/$0.00+$1.50
© 2003 by AALNC

Objectives

At the conclusion of this chapter, the reader will be able to:

- Discuss the foundation for nurses serving as liability expert witnesses
- Describe routes by which nurses may assume the role of liability expert witness
- List steps for record review and analysis by liability expert witnesses
- Delineate expectations for communications by liability nurse experts
- Relate the legal definition of "standard of care" to the clinical definition
- Explain the liability nurse expert's role in deposition and trial

Introduction

Providing expert testimony as a liability nurse expert witness is a challenging and rewarding experience that is critical to resolution of legal disputes associated with patient care. An expert witness is an individual who is qualified by education, training, and experience to provide an opinion about specific subject matter, such as nursing standards of care. The liability nurse expert witness should be prepared in the same specialty as the nurses involved in the case, with knowledge and experience in similar clinical scenarios. In professional-negligence actions, plaintiffs' attorneys provide the court with expert testimony supporting the case allegations, and defendant health care providers' attorneys offer opinions that rebut the allegations. In this context, experts testify to assist triers of fact (judge or jury) to make a decision by providing scientific and technical information that is more than common knowledge. As a member of the nursing profession, the liability nurse expert witness identifies standards of care for nursing aspects of the case and objectively describes the details of whether or not standards were breached. This role provides an opportunity for nurses to synthesize professional education and knowledge with experience from clinical, administrative, educational, and research settings and apply them to situations in the legal domain.

The role of liability nurse expert witness must be understood to include commitment to testimony at deposition and trial. Nurses who prefer to work behind the scenes should clarify their intentions to serve as screening legal nurse consultants (LNCs) or nontestifying consultants. T§F#1

Nurse experts are now commonly involved in litigation. Because legal qualifications for testimony as an expert witness may vary from state to state, nurses should discuss their qualifications very carefully with retaining attorneys. Croke and Fyler review this topic in detail.[1] The major responsibilities of the nursing expert have been summarized by Iyer and Banes-Gerritzen.[2] These include:

1. Offering opinions based on the standards of care, not on the morals, motivations, or scruples of any party
2. Rendering an opinion based on his or her knowledge, abilities, and training and the information reviewed
3. Basing an opinion on "a reasonable degree of nursing certainty" for each alleged act of negligence demonstrating a deviation (major or minor) from the acceptable standard of care

4. Avoiding offering opinions on causation, since physicians must testify to the question of causation: "if not for (the negligent act) the injuries would not have occurred."

This chapter describes the milieu of this niche of professional nursing; its principles apply to nurse experts retained by either plaintiff or defense attorneys. The role of liability expert witness is a serious undertaking. Several areas of long-term responsibility are required, including time allotment, schedule flexibility, well-organized records management, and sound business principles. Professional accountability, integrity, objectivity, demeanor, and communication are essential.

Legal Culture versus Health Care Culture

The legal arena is a venue that differs from health care culture in many ways. Nurses who propose to work as liability expert witnesses may find it helpful to visit the law library to peruse the textbooks and journals that attorneys use as they prepare cases. Practice-oriented journals for attorneys such as *Trial* and *For the Defense* describe specific communication techniques and strategies. Books such as *Theater Tips and Strategies for Jury Trials*[3] delineate drama and communication techniques for legal practice. As members of a profession that is highly regarded by the public, nurses who pride themselves on their missions of caring, kindness, and integrity may be shocked at the communication rules and adversarial style of the legal world. Experienced nurses are familiar and comfortable with indirect communication with physicians, such as querying potentially deleterious orders in a manner that preserves the physician's ego and role in the health care hierarchy.[2] Direct, powerful communication from attorneys may feel uncomfortable to nursing professionals. The liability nurse expert witness should not be intimidated by unfamiliar communication rules. Educational and professional preparation in critical thinking, and experience in clinical crises, provide a firm foundation for nurses to adapt to the foreign territory of the legal arena. Resources written specifically for expert witnesses in other specialties and professions are also available (see Additional Reading).

Obtaining Cases for Review

Professional reputation, clinical expertise, and communication skills are the most significant factors sought in nurse expert witnesses. Attorneys look for professionals with characteristics such as these:[4]

- Strong teaching skills that can be adapted to the courtroom's unique environment
- An open, pleasant personality with relaxed manner and appropriate sense of humor
- Ability to explain rather than advocate (despite nursing's self-defined commitment to patient advocacy, legal advocacy in the courtroom belongs to the attorneys)

- Ability to offer and defend concise, clear, and objective opinions
- Honesty, integrity, professional responsibility, and ethical conviction

Professional authenticity and confidence are also essential for liability nurse expert witnesses. In some situations, novice nurse experts may have more credibility with juries than experts with long experience in testifying. Ability to meet the requirements of the liability nurse expert role is more important than being experienced in the role.

Multiple sources exist for obtaining cases for review. Nursing colleagues may provide an expert's name to a particular attorney. Liability nurse expert witnesses experienced in case review may be asked to provide referrals of other nursing experts. Some legal nurse consulting firms provide names of registered nurses (RNs) to requesting attorneys or claims adjusters who seek assistance for case review. The RN interested in expert witness review may refer colleagues to legal nurse consulting firms or may interview with a firm directly. LNCs who prefer to function as nontestifying experts may provide referrals. Attorneys may also contact potential nurse expert witnesses directly.

Membership in the American Association of Legal Nurse Consultants (AALNC) is a valuable resource for obtaining cases to review. A listing on the LNC Locator, a service provided on the AALNC Web site (http://www.aalnc.org), may result in a case coming to the expert. Attending local and national AALNC meetings, networking with colleagues and speakers, and distributing business cards are marketing options. Demonstration of professional expertise and strong communication skills by speaking at local and national meetings or publishing in journals and books is a reliable method for increasing the nurse's visibility to other professionals who seek such expertise.

Commercial advertising for case solicitation is not recommended, because the liability nurse expert witness is an expert clinician serving as case reviewer and analyst. Marketing this clinical expertise as a business reduces credibility and objectivity. "Hired gun" is a common term used to describe experts whose opinions are for sale. The liability nurse expert witness bases case review and analysis fees strictly on time expended on the matter; although time-based bills are created, opinions cannot be bought. It is unethical to contract with attorneys on the basis of the outcome of the case. Business principles for testifying experts are discussed in Chapter 38.

Accepting the Case

The attorney typically provides some case details about the patient, events, reason for choosing the expert, and instructions for the nurse expert's role. Acceptance by the nurse expert should be based on the appropriateness of background, education, research, publications, and experience in the clinical scenario described by the attorney. Matching the expert's qualifications and abilities to the case's situation is an important goal. Before accepting a case, the expert should be clear that experience and professional credentials are appropriate. If doubt exists, the issue should be discussed in detail with the attorney, perhaps including a referral to a more qualified colleague. Maintaining a network of other qualified nursing and medical experts is a sign of professional involvement. Such referrals define the expert's integrity and set the stage for future contact from the same attorney.

It is also essential for the nurse expert to be sure that the attorney's intent is evaluation of *nursing* care. Although nursing experience includes abundant knowledge about many other health care providers and specialties, it is not appropriate for nurses to define standards for other professions. Follow-up correspondence to thank the attorney for consideration in a specific case is always appropriate, even if the nurse expert does not accept the assignment.

Although a case may be accepted for initial review by telephone, the nurse expert should immediately write to the attorney to confirm details of the arrangement, fee structure, deadlines, and destination and format of the first report. Fee schedules should always reflect that the expert is charging for time expended. The expert's commitment to objective evaluation should be apparent in conversation and correspondence. No opinions should be offered until the records and other supporting documents have been reviewed and analyzed.

Liability nurse experts must also confirm that there can be no potential for bias, impropriety, or conflict of interest. Personal experience with individuals or institutions should be discussed with the retaining attorney; if any doubt exists about conflict of interest, the nurse expert should refer the case to a colleague.

Case acceptance should be accompanied by a clear understanding of deadlines, which are important in the legal arena. The nurse should not accept the case unless there is time to review and analyze the materials appropriately. Communication channels should be clearly delineated to the attorney to avoid awkward situations for the nurse, such as receiving phone calls at clinical jobs or at home.

Case Review

The liability nurse expert witness must base testimony on the legal standard of care. Understanding this definition is essential. The legal standard of care is the degree of competence and skill exercised by a reasonable and average practitioner in similar circumstances.

Many nurses set their own personal standards of care that may be considerably higher than the legal definition. This is a pattern commonly seen in inexperienced expert witnesses. It is important to remember that the standard of care is based on the reasonable average practitioner and not the expert clinician. While those higher standards certainly may benefit patient care, it is inappropriate to apply them in the context of legal case review.

The definition of "standard of care" must also be matched to the date of the event associated with the injury to the patient. Rapid advances in technology create changes in standard of care from year to year. The nursing expert must be able to delineate standard of care for the case's time period; thus, the expert must be familiar with standards of care at that time, including educational and clinical involvement in similar care. With long statutes of limitations associated with obstetric and pediatric cases, it may be challenging for attorneys to find an expert who practiced in the prior era associated with the clinical event. Changes in institutional policies and procedures, state statutes and regulations, national professional standards, certification criteria, and academic curricula must all be considered as the expert researches these sources to aid in opinion formulation.

The definition of "standard of care" was historically linked to the geographical community in which the event happened. However, lower local standards of care are no longer justified for current clinical practice, which now includes advanced communications, standardized educational curricula, widely distributed professional publications, and standards promulgated by professional organizations.

All applicable records must be present to allow the nurse expert to develop coherent and complete opinions. Clinicians are aware of the variety of records that are created in any patient care situation, with notes and documents from a variety of physicians, nurses, and allied health personnel. Although attorneys sometimes write to experts describing allegations and central issues of the matter, the nurse expert and attorney should discuss which records would be essential, because the expert's opinion cannot be based on the attorney's summary.

The nurse expert's first scan of the package should focus on identification of potential missing records. Ideally, a complete set of all medical records associated with the event will be provided. These records should be organized by the expert in a logical manner that will allow opinions to be developed as well as provide easily retrievable data for discussion with the attorney. It is common for legal office staff to create a master set of records automatically Bates-stamped, to minimize confusion when pages are identified. While the nurse expert may choose to create page order that is logical for review, the ability to refer to the original page numbers is essential. This point is particularly important because the record packages are likely to be created by legal office staff who have no medical background. If only abstracts or selected pages from a record are provided for the expert's initial overview, the opinion rendered should clearly express that it is based on limited information and thus subject to change if more information is provided. The nurse expert should ask whether all pages of the record have been sent, or it may be apparent from review of the Bates-stamping that some pages are missing, either accidentally or intentionally. In some situations, the nurse expert may decline to provide an opinion until appropriate documents are received and analyzed.

Determining the Standard of Care

The nursing process defines each patient as unique, requiring individual assessment, diagnosis, planning, interventions, and ongoing evaluation. Although many professional commonalities are involved in meeting standards of patient care, the expert must define standards for the patients and clinical scenarios presented for review. Written standards are developed by several sources:

- State and federal statutes and regulations, including nurse practice acts and interpretive statements
- Academic curricula
- National nursing associations, including specialties
- Professional literature, particularly peer-reviewed publications
- Institutional policies and procedures
- Regulatory agencies such as the Joint Commission on Accreditation of Healthcare Organizations

Use of published standards reduces subjectivity of opinion in judgments of whether the standard of care was met. However, many documents accepted as standards contain disclaimers that point to the use as guidelines that are neither comprehensive nor limiting. In some ways, these disclaimers may seem to dilute the strength of the information as published; however, such disclaimers also refer to the importance of tailoring care to individual patient circumstances and to the fact that professional responsibility requires a "thinking cook," as the American Heart Association describes in its discussion of application of algorithms to clinical care.[5] If patient care could be reduced to a set of objective "cookbook" requirements, there would be no need for analysis by nurse expert witnesses.

Record Review and Analysis

After ensuring that appropriate medical records are present and organized, the nurse expert carefully reviews the documents to extrapolate key information related to the case. Review style and tools vary. Some experts prefer to make notes on temporary stickers such as Post-it® notes; some may create detailed notes, outlines, and chronologies; and others may prefer to read the material and formulate opinions without creating written materials of any kind. Since all written materials created by expert witnesses are subject to discovery, the expert should discuss the creation of written materials with the attorney at the time the case is accepted. Many attorneys prefer that no documents be created.

Familiarity with medical records provides a firm foundation for the nurse expert's review. Applicable sections of the record are examined in detail, with the framework of the nursing process and standards of care kept in mind to ensure objective evaluation. Time frames, nursing care (including all the elements of the nursing process), patient responses, and continuity of care are significant elements for meeting the standard of care. Validation of data from other health care providers (such as physicians, pharmacists, and other ancillary departments) is essential. Documentation from other providers that may support or diminish the nurse's initial opinion must be considered as case analysis progresses. In order to be as unbiased as possible, opinion formulation should be based on findings in the medical record, perhaps supported by information from published sources of standards of care.

Witness Statements

At times, attorneys obtain written statements from the plaintiff or witnesses to an incident. These statements do not constitute sworn testimony and do not carry the same weight. The expert witness may review these prior to the taking of depositions.

Depositions

Depositions constitute sworn testimony. A court reporter creates a record of the questions and answers. The court reporter's transcript is utilized by the expert to evaluate the case. The expert witness should note pertinent information in the transcript with Post-it notes or other methods of flagging pertinent information. It is not recommended that highlighting be applied to documents, as these passages may have to be explained, one by one, in the expert's deposition.

Depositions typically begin with an explanation of the process. The attorney may instruct the witness to keep responses verbal and to not interrupt the attorney's questions. The witness is asked to request clarification of unclear questions. Once the question is answered, it is assumed that the witness understood the question. The witness is often instructed that breaks are permitted, and that the goal of the deposition is to obtain information.

The plaintiff may be the injured patient or a family member who filed a suit on behalf of a deceased or incompetent patient. The plaintiff's deposition often begins with background questions, such as address, number of children, and so on. Next, the plaintiff is asked questions about the medical care leading up to the incident or care in question. Details concerning the incident are solicited. The last part of the deposition typically consists of questions to determine the nature of the injuries and their impact on the plaintiff's life. The pattern of the deposition may vary from one attorney to the next. Sometimes more than one deposition of the plaintiff is taken if all the questioning cannot be accomplished in one sitting.

The nurses involved in the suit may be deposed. Their depositions often begin with questions about their backgrounds. Details regarding education, employment history, and experience are found in the transcript. The plaintiff attorney will follow with questions about the care of the plaintiff. The recollections (if any) of the witness will be explored. The medical records are often referred to in the deposition. Key pages of the records or the institution's policies and procedures may be identified as exhibits. If the exhibits are not provided with the transcript, the expert may request the attorney client's office to supply them. The nurses' transcripts should be reviewed for discrepancies with the plaintiff's testimony. The expert evaluates the nurses' descriptions of the care or incident and knowledge of the standard of care. The expert looks for admissions of mistakes, lapses in judgment, and lack of knowledge of the facility's policies.

A nurse hired by the defense may have received the plaintiff nursing expert's report and deposition transcript before the defense expert is expected to write a report. The opposing nursing expert witness's deposition testimony often begins with an exploration of the expert's background (education and clinical experience). The expert may be questioned about experience reviewing cases and testifying. The next part of the deposition explores the expert's opinions as contained in the report. The expert is given an opportunity to add any additional opinions based on new material reviewed after authoring the report.

Acquisition of other information from depositions or opposing experts' reports may support the expert's opinion or may serve as foundation for reanalysis of the records. Receipt of more medical records may also affect the expert's initial opinion. Thus, it should be clear at all times that the nurse's opinion is based on currently received information and is potentially subject to change. If this possibility arises, it is the expert's responsibility to contact the attorney immediately to discuss the matter.

Initial Report to Attorney

After initial review, a telephone or personal conference with the attorney provides the expert with an opportunity to discuss opinions and ask questions. The nurse expert's clinical experience and education should be apparent in this conversation as elements of the nursing care are reviewed with the attorney to support opinions about whether or not the standard of care was breached. The expert's initial verbal report also provides more details of record analysis to assist the attorney, including suggestions for additional document requests, advice about other areas to investigate in the patient's care, and provision of literature that is pertinent to the case.

If the expert hired by a plaintiff's attorney believes that no breach occurred, or the expert retained by the defense attorney believes that breach of standards occurred, those opinions should be substantiated in order to allow the attorney to make decisions about continuing with the case, reformulating the case strategy, or halting the case. No matter which side retains the nurse expert, opinions should reflect knowledge and understanding of the standards of care and how the medical record defines nursing actions as appropriate or not.

The nurse expert must show personal and professional integrity at all times. Most attorneys appreciate frank discussion of case merits and disadvantages, even if it means that the nurse feels unable to continue as an expert witness.

A discussion with an attorney detailing the reasons why the expert cannot support the attorney's case is always needed before writing a report. The attorney may not want a written report that is unfavorable to his or her position, because the report may have to be supplied to the opposing attorney if the case is in suit. If a plaintiff attorney has not yet filed suit, a written report may be a welcome method of proving to the plaintiff that a nursing standard of care evaluation has been completed. This helps the attorney establish with his or her client that the attorney has taken the appropriate steps. The nursing expert is advised always to speak to the attorney before writing a report.

If the expert's opinion is not strong, with firm ground in experience, education, literature, and clinical practice, it is inappropriate to continue. Weak opinions are a disservice to all involved in the matter.

The liability nurse expert may encounter barriers that interfere with timely analysis and report preparation.[2] These issues include being overwhelmed by the size of the records package, inadequate time-management skills, ambivalence about case issues, difficult case issues that require extensive research, unanticipated demands on the expert's time (including personal emergencies), and missing documents. Vigilance for the development of such problems will allow the nurse expert to work with the attorney's deadlines in a professional manner.

Written Reports

A report should not be written unless it is specifically requested by the attorney. If a report is requested, its format and style should be described by the attorney, although the professional content must be defined by the expert's own opinion.[6] It may be helpful to look at similar reports from other cases supplied by the attorney for writing and format techniques, but the final result must not be tainted by the attorney's input. Individual states may promulgate specific rules for expert reports that the attorney should clearly explain to the nurse expert.

Most expert reports include a list of documents that were reviewed, a description of the events that led up to the injury, a definition of the standard of care, and the actual opinion about whether the standard of care was met or breached. Such opinions must be supported with specific nursing behaviors identified for each area of concern, and explanation of the standard of care's relationship to the activity.

Reports should be concise, carefully organized, and clear. Rambling writing dilutes and muddles opinions. Using the five elements of the nursing process provides a simple framework that allows a variety of nursing activities, events, and outcomes to be described cogently. If more than one breach of the standard of care is identified, each element discussed should follow the same written format.

References to professional literature should be carefully considered before they are included in written reports. Although the nurse expert may examine such documents as part of opinion formulation, the expert's background, education, and experience in similar clinical situations constitute the strongest foundation for opinions. The dynamics of rapid change in health care may outdate some information by the time it is printed, and published material may not exactly fit the individual patient scenario of the case.

Case development can go on for several years. The nurse expert must create an organized filing system to maintain records safely and completely. As in clinical practice, these records are confidential. Filing systems need not be elaborate; their main functions are safekeeping of documents and rapid retrieval of information. Inability to follow good business practices reflects poorly on the expert's professionalism. Chapter 38 provides more detail about business practices for expert witnesses.

The Deposition Process

Formality and strict rules of deposition create an environment that may be intimidating to the new nurse expert who is comfortable with clinical expertise, patient care, and health care culture and communication. Prior to the deposition, the retaining attorney should spend time with the nurse expert to prepare for understanding the manner in which it will proceed and the rules that are followed. However, rules of discovery require that attorneys should not coach witnesses or obstruct information. The nurse expert must be able to explain opinions clearly, defending them in the face of a variety of questioning strategies from the opposing attorney. Above all, the expert must focus on the goal of this event: to clearly state and defend opinions about the standard of care for the particular case. Ability to meet this goal is enhanced by strong professional background, personal confidence, calm demeanor, and careful attention to every word heard and spoken. The court reporter's transcription of the deposition creates a permanent record that may be used at trial.

Predeposition planning includes careful review of the documents and a conference with the retaining attorney. Conservative business attire and accessories should be selected. Having a good night's rest, a healthy breakfast, and generous travel times is wise. Retaining counsel should be consulted about personal and professional items to be brought to deposition, in view of the fact that everything in the expert's file is discoverable. It is common to bring a copy of an updated curriculum vitae. The court reporter appreciates receiving a nurse expert's business card to verify identifying information that is part of the deposition. The nurse expert should mentally rehearse good posture, pleasant facial expressions, and positive body language. Electronic devices such as cell phones and pagers should be disabled. The nurse expert should exhibit professional demeanor from the moment of arrival at the deposition, because attorneys from both sides will evaluate potential for strong courtroom appearance and testimony.

Questioning

Opposing counsel conducts the deposition to discover information about the case and to develop the case for trial. Nurse experts should not minimize the importance of discovery and case development. Opposing attorneys craft specific strategies to discredit testimony or individuals. The expert is expected to take an oath or make an affirmation about the truthfulness of the upcoming testimony, because the deposition's transcript is an official record of the court. The nurse expert may expect to have any elements of professional practice queried, often in a negative style designed to reduce the expert's credibility: education, clinical experience, research, publications, and fees are often brought up. Careful consideration of the exact question asked and formulation of an answer that is responsive to the question are essential. A responsive answer provides only the information requested by the single question. Rambling explanations should be avoided because they may provide points for reducing credibility. Familiarity with attorney questioning strategies[7] described in legal practice literature can be very helpful for nurses entering the legal arena. Nurse expert witnesses have also written about strategies for deposition preparation.[2]

The nurse expert should be careful to keep testimony focused on nursing practice without venturing into practice areas of other health care providers. If opposing counsel asks hypothetical questions, the expert should provide hypothetical answers. Hypothetical questions sometimes lead to complicated lines of questioning and potential for confusion. It is always appropriate to request that the question be repeated or clarified, especially with regard to being hypothetical rather than for the patient involved in the case. Questions about authoritative literature must also be carefully considered, in light of the multiple factors that create the standard of care and the fact that no author's every word is completely authoritative. All answers should be visualized in their future black-and-white transcript format; playful quips or humorous remarks are likely to diminish the expert's credibility when the opposing attorney reads them aloud later in the courtroom. Fine distinctions of language and meaning that are minimized in daily life become paramount in the legal system.

Other attorneys who are present at the deposition may object to certain questions or answers. The nurse expert should have been prepared for this eventuality with instructions from the retaining attorney in the predeposition meeting. Objections constitute a legal procedure for the record; they may be distracting to the expert, who may request that the question be reread by the court reporter; an objection does not negate the need to answer the question.

The nurse expert or any of the attorneys may request a break at any time. The deposition ends when all the attorneys, including the retaining attorney, are finished with their questions. The retaining attorney may choose to withhold questions or may ask questions that further clarify the expert's opinions.

The deposition may be videotaped, especially if the expert may not be available for trial. While the presence of the camera may be intimidating at first, the nurse expert should consider that the film will preserve verbal testimony as well as calm demeanor and professional presentation of information. Especially in the face of negative or badgering behavior by opposing counsel, videotaped testimony creates a positive record of the nurse's opinions and communication skills.

Reviewing the Transcript

The transcription of the deposition will be sent to the nurse expert for review. It should be closely checked for accuracy with any changes noted on the form that is attached, with rationale for each change (such as spelling error, typographical error, or obvious omission of a word). Such errors may be corrected, but the substantial nature of the content must not be changed by this process. If the nurse expert believes that a change in the substance of the testimony must be made, the retaining attorney should be contacted immediately.

Trial Testimony

Most cases are settled by the attorneys prior to trial. If the case proceeds to trial, the nurse expert's testimony is required. Since a long time lapse between deposition and trial is common, the expert must prepare with another review of all the case materials as well as consultation with the retaining attorney. Well-organized files simplify this process.

Personal and professional preparation for trial follows the same rules as for deposition, with even more emphasis on appearance, demeanor, communication, and strong testimony. The nurse expert must be prepared for the content of testimony as well as for trial-scheduling uncertainties, anxiety that may be associated with the unfamiliar environment of the courthouse, and development of techniques to enhance communication with the jury.

The Witness Stand

The witness starts testimony with swearing or affirming to tell the truth. The retaining attorney does initial questioning, starting with credentials and curriculum vitae to establish credibility as an expert, as discussed by Croke and Fyler.[1] This supporting data is then offered to the court to accept the nurse as an expert who is qualified to testify at trial. Opposing counsel may question credentials at this time or wait until cross-examination.

After the judge accepts the nurse as a qualified expert, the retaining attorney asks specific questions about the circumstances relevant to the alleged malpractice. The nurse expert's testimony then addresses standards of care and specific issues that are in question for the jury. At this point, the nurse expert may feel quite comfortable in the teaching role, which is an inherent part of nursing care, as explanations are made to allow the jury of laymen to help them understand the intricacies of health care and patient outcomes. The opposing attorney then questions the nurse in cross-examination, which is often focused to elicit information that discredits the nurse expert. At this point, the nurse expert must display an extremely calm demeanor, focus on the elements of the case, and communicate clearly in the face of hostility. Although cross-examination is not comfortable to endure, it gives the well-prepared expert an opportunity to show true professionalism to the jury. The retaining attorney then has the chance to redirect, questioning answers or ideas that need to be emphasized to the jury. Finally, the opposing attorney has the opportunity for recross-examination. Appendix 35.1 provides information about common cross-examination strategies.

In *Theater Tips and Strategies for Jury Trials*, attorney David Ball discusses how witnesses can look good and sound good for the jury.[3] Confident eye contact, word delivery, and body language make witnesses look good; talking into space or down to the floor or shirt fronts reduces communication. Vocal support with full, relaxed breathing techniques as well as clear and strong speech articulation and volume enhance communication. Speech volume should not fade at the end of sentences. Ball recommends practicing these techniques, with the warning that "practice" does not mean "memorize." The expert should become comfortable with expressing the substance of testimony in a variety of wording.

Demonstrative evidence and visual aids may be helpful to the judge and jury, because they provide emphasis, concreteness, and memorialization of evidence. The nurse expert may play an important role in developing this evidence, which may be as simple as an enlargement of a medical-record page or as complicated as computer-generated graphics that demonstrate physiology or mechanism of injury. Pieces of medical equipment may also be shown in action. Part of the nurse expert's testimony may include teaching the jury about the role of these pieces of evidence in the case. Visual aids should follow rules of simplicity, readability, and easy comprehension.

Summary

Professionals set their own standards of care. The courts use expert testimony to define and examine these standards as they relate to specific clinical events. Nurses are well prepared to assume the role of liability expert witnesses, with appropriate consideration of the demands and challenges of the role. Education of the judge and jury about the standard of care and how it was breached or not breached allows the plaintiff's counsel to build a case and the defense counsel to rebut allegations. This role in the legal arena is a natural extension of the professional responsibility of nurses to support standards of care.

References

1. Croke, E. and Fyler, P., Nurse experts: contributing members of today's litigation team, *Journal of Legal Nurse Consulting*, 13(1), 8–12, 2002.

2. Iyer, P. and Banes-Gerritsen, C., Working with nursing expert witnesses, in Iyer, P., Ed., *Nursing Malpractice*, 2nd ed., Lawyers and Judges Publishing Company, Tucson, AZ, 2001.

3. Ball, D., *Theater Tips and Strategies for Jury Trials*, 2nd ed., National Institute for Trial Advocacy, Notre Dame, IN, 1997.

4. Ross, J., How jurors perceive expert witnesses, *Trial*, 51–57, June 2000.

5. American Heart Association, *Circulation*, 102 (Suppl. 1), 140–141, 2000.

6. Carter, B., Drawing the line: attorney involvement in preparing expert reports, *For The Defense*, 15–19, 86, August 2001.

7. Morris, C., Effective communication with deposition witnesses, *Trial*, 70–75, July 2000.

Additional Reading

Brodsky, S.L., *The Expert Witness: More Guidelines and Maxims for Testifying in Court*, American Psychological Association, 1999.

Test Questions

1. Marketing liability nurse expert witness services is best achieved by
   A. Commercial advertising in legal journals
   B. Networking with LNC colleagues
   C. Paying attorneys for referrals to their colleagues
   D. Purchasing listings in commercial expert witness directories

2. Fees for expert witness work should
   A. Depend on the outcome of the case
   B. Include a bonus for the nurse expert if the retaining attorney wins the case
   C. Be negotiable depending on the potential award amount
   D. Be completely time-based

3. Which is true about deposition testimony?
   A. It is an opportunity for opposing counsel to discover the liability nurse expert's opinions.
   B. It is considered unimportant except as a partial rehearsal for trial.
   C. It may not be admitted into the evidence at trial.
   D. The retaining attorney conducts the deposition to allow the nurse expert witness to clarify opinions.

4. Record review and analysis by the liability nurse expert witness should include
   A. Detailed note-taking and outlining of all case elements in a timeline
   B. Colored highlighting of critical elements of the original medical record
   C. Ensuring that all appropriate pages of the record are present
   D. Advising the attorney that a detailed written report is essential

5. The liability nurse expert witness's case analysis should hold nursing actions to which standard?
   A. Actions expected of a reasonably prudent nurse in similar circumstances
   B. Actions expected of advanced-practice clinicians in the same specialty
   C. The universal standards for all health care providers
   D. The highest possible standards in order to improve patient care

Answers: 1. B, 2. D, 3. A, 4. C, 5. A

Appendix 35.1
Cross-Examination Techniques

The expert witness will encounter a number of strategies used by attorneys in cross-examination. This appendix provides an overview of some of the more common techniques. The expert can become more skilled at identifying and reacting to these techniques by anticipating them and knowing effective ways of responding. Each strategy is briefly explained, followed by sample dialogue. "A" stands for "Attorney" and "E" stands for "Expert." Comments in italics are provided by the authors.

1. Expect detailed probing into the expert's background, fee structure, and experience as an expert. The expert should calmly and nondefensively provide the answers to these questions.
   A: Nurse __, where did you go to nursing school?
   E: University of Louisiana.
   A: Do you have any advanced degrees in nursing?
   E: Yes, I have a master's of science in nursing.
   A: You don't have a doctorate in nursing?
   E: No.
   A: And yet you feel qualified to be an expert in this case?
   E: Yes, I do, based on my experience as a nurse and my education. *(A doctorate in nursing is not the entry-level degree for expert witness review.)*
   A: Where have you worked as a staff nurse?
   E: Baton Rouge Medical Center and University of Alabama Hospital.
   A: You realize that the nurses who were sued in this case worked in Denver?
   E: Yes.
   A: And yet you have never worked in Denver, have you?
   E: I have not.
   A: Why do you feel qualified to comment on the standard of care for nurses who work in Denver?
   E: I believe the standard of care is a national one. The nurses in Denver are expected to adhere to the same standards as do the nurses in the state in which I work.
   A: How much do you charge per hour to review a case?
   E: $175 per hour.
   A: How much? (shocked)
   E: $175 per hour. (repeats answer calmly)
   A: Do you know how much nurses earn who work in hospitals in Denver?
   E: Not precisely.
   A: Why are your fees so much higher?
   E: They reflect my education, training, and expertise.
   A: How much are you being paid for your testimony today?
   E: I am being paid for my time at the rate of $175 per hour. *(The expert should be clear that his or opinion is not being bought, but rather his or her time.)*
   A: How many cases have you reviewed as an expert?
   E: Twenty.

A: So, you are really a novice at this work, aren't you? *(This question is an effort to intimidate the expert.)*

E: I have reviewed a fair number of cases.

A: How much money did you earn last year doing expert witness work? *(The courts generally permit the expert to provide a percentage of income rather than have to reveal the expert's income.)*

E: My expert witness earnings represented about 15 percent of my income.

A: Are you going to be paid a percentage of the recovery that plaintiff hopes to get in this case?

E: No. *(It is illegal for experts to work on contingency.)*

2. Asking questions in no obvious order — this is designed to prevent the expert from seeing a pattern in the questions. The expert should answer each question as clearly as possible.

A: Let's talk about your opinions in this case, all right?

E: All right.

A: What is your understanding about the responsibilities of the nurse for keeping the doctor informed of changes in the patient's condition?

E: The nurse should report significant changes in the patient's condition.

A: What is the purpose of giving insulin to diabetics?

E: It is to provide a medication that will control blood sugar.

A: What is a patient acuity system?

E: It is designed to help determine how to staff a nursing unit.

3. Deliberate mispronunciation of words — the attorney is trying to present an uneducated air so that the expert's guard will be let down. The expert should ignore the mispronunciations.

A: Nurse___, this case is about a patient who had hypertrophy of the ventricles. (Mispronounces words) Is that right?

E: Yes. The patient's echocardiogram showed that the patient had hypertrophy of the left ventricle. (Pronounces it correctly)

A: What is that?

E: *(The expert gives an explanation of this term.)*

4. Flattery — the opposing attorney acts impressed with the expert's credentials in order to lower the expert's guard. The expert should politely acknowledge the flattery and wait for the next question.

A: You went to nursing school, right?

E: Yes, I did.

A: You went to one of the finest nursing schools in the country to get your degrees, didn't you?

E: Yes.

A: You have written a number of articles that have been published in prestigious journals, correct?

E: Yes.

A: Why, I bet you know more than about 99 percent of the nurses in this country, don't you?

E: I don't know about that, but I do know the standard of care and how it applies to this case.

5. Goading the expert — the attorney is hoping the expert will lose his or her temper or respond in a flippant way. The expert should remain calm.

A: Did you speak to any of the nurses who were sued in this case? *(This is a misleading question to ask in front of a jury, because it implies that the nursing expert was not being fair to the defendants by not allowing them to tell the expert their side of the story.)*

E: I did not, as it is my understanding that I am not permitted to contact the defendants.

A: Did you think it was important to know what they had to say about how this incident occurred?

E: I did, and that is why I read their deposition transcripts.

A: Have you heard the expression that hindsight is 20/20?

E: Yes.

A: Wouldn't you agree that the nurses taking care of the patient did not have the benefit of hindsight?

E: I agree with that statement, but it is my position that the nurses should have followed the standard of care.

A: You have testified that it is your opinion that the nurses did not follow the standard of care, isn't that right?

E: Yes, I have.

A: This is only your *opinion*, isn't it?

E: It is my opinion based on my education, training, and knowledge of the standards of care.

A: You are telling this jury that these dedicated nurses, who work day in and day out, made a mistake, aren't you?

E: Yes, they deviated from the standard of care.

A: You want the jury to believe that these nurses were negligent, don't you? *(This is a blatant effort to attack the nursing expert. The expert must remain firm in his or her convictions.)*

E: Yes, I do.

6. Using body language to intimidate — pointing fingers, shouting, and leaning into the expert's space are often tactics that the attorney who retained the expert can bring to a halt by objecting.

7. Asking questions in a rapid manner — the attorney may be hoping that the expert will mimic the pace of questioning and give a careless answer in haste. The expert should think through the answer to each question and establish a pace that is comfortable for the expert, remembering that a pause does not show up on a transcript.

8. Asking repetitive questions — the expert should provide consistent answers to the same question asked several times.

A: Now, let me be sure I have this right. You are saying that you don't think the nurses did anything wrong with respect to the care that was provided to my client, right?

E: Yes, I am.

A: And you believe, in your professional opinion, that the standards of care were met?

E: Yes, I do.

A: There was nothing that should have been done differently, is that right?

E: That is true.

A: You are very sure about that?

E: Yes.

9. Asking vague or complex, convoluted questions — whether on purpose or because of difficulty framing questions, the attorney should be asked to rephrase the question so that it is clear.

   A: What is nursing all about?

   E: I don't understand your question.

   A: What do you do as a nurse?

   E: In what context?

10. Questioning the expert about details in the medical record to test the expert's memory — the expert is allowed to refer to the materials that were reviewed and does not have to answer questions based on memory alone.

11. Use of silence — the attorney may pause after the expert's answer, hoping the expert will elaborate on the answer. The expert should answer the question and wait for the next one.

12. Asking about nursing literature to identify "authoritative texts" — the attorney should prepare the expert to answer these questions based on the jurisdiction's case law.

    A: Nurse ___, what texts do you have in your library?

    E: *Luckmann and Sorenson Medical Surgical Nursing, Barker's Neuroscience Nursing.*

    A: What texts do you believe are authoritative in the field of medical surgical nursing?

    E: I find several to be generally reliable.

    A: Do you rely on those texts for information?

    E: Yes, but no text is completely up to date because of the lag time from sending it to the publishers and getting it into print.

13. Hypothetical questions — the expert needs to be sure that the details included in the hypothetical question match the case issues.

    A: Now, Nurse ___, I'd like you to assume that the following is true. The patient has been admitted to the hospital for a breast reduction. She tells the nurses that she has numbness and tingling in her legs after surgery. She complains each shift to each nurse. What is the standard of care regarding notifying the physician of these changes?

    E: I am having difficulty with your hypothetical because it is not based on the facts of this case. My review of the medical record and the depositions of the nurses shows that the patient complained on only two shifts.

    A: You are aware of my client's testimony that she complained to each nurse who took care of her?

    E: I read her testimony to that effect, but it is contradicted by the nurse's testimony.

    A: Can you answer my question?

    E: If I accept the facts of your hypothetical, I would want to know how often her physicians were visiting her and what they were documenting about her legs.

    A: Nurse ___, I am not asking you about what the doctors were doing. I am asking you about the nursing standard of care. Do you understand that?

    E: Yes.

    A: Now can you answer my question?

E: I would have to say, if I accepted your hypothetical, that I would expect the nurses to report this finding to the doctor if it was a new one, but I understand from the testimony of the nurse that the patient said this was not new.

14. Failing to bring materials to the deposition will make it more difficult for the expert to answer questions. This dialogue illustrates the difficulties in not bringing the materials.

A: Do you have with you the copies of materials that were provided to you for review in this case?

E: I do not have a copy with me, but Ms. Wilson does have the materials that you reviewed in order to supply this expert report.

A: When you say Ms. Wilson has copies of those materials, did you bring your copies with you today?

E: Ms. Wilson has a copy of my nurse expert report and she has copies of all of the material that was sent to me from her office that I reviewed in compiling the report.

A: I realize that she has copies of those materials, but does she have your copies of the materials?

E: No, my copies are at home.

15. Making derogatory remarks on the material that was reviewed is *not advisable*. The attorney has the right to look at anything in the expert's file.

A: Did you make any notations or marks of any kind on the materials you reviewed?

E: Yes, I did.

A: May I see your file? (Looks at materials.) Why did you highlight this sentence in Nurse Perry's deposition?

E: I thought it was significant.

A: What was significant about it?

E: It was in conflict with what the doctor said happened.

A: I see a comment in the margin of the report that was prepared by Nurse Watson, who is the expert for the plaintiff. What does this mean: "She should stick to obstetrics where she belongs and not review this case"?

E: I thought the expert was not qualified to review this case.

A: What does this comment mean: "What a jerk"?

E: I thought his conclusion was not correct.

16. Failing to read and consider all information — the expert should ask for pertinent documents, depositions, and other records needed to obtain an opinion.

A: When you undertook this assignment, did you want to render a fair opinion? The following dialogue illustrates the problems that can occur.

E: Yes, I did.

A: And in order to render a fair opinion, did you think it was important to know as much as you could about the facts of this case?

E: Yes.

A: Did you read the depositions of the nurses?

E: No, I did not.

A: Why did you not read them?

E: They were not sent to me.

A: Did you ask the attorney for them?

E: No. *(This question is designed to make the expert look unfair. The expert is placed in an awkward position if the attorney does not provide him or her with the depositions. The expert can prevent this type of trap by asking the attorney for all relevant material.)*

17. Failing to listen to the question and failing to stay focused are shown below.

A: Could you explain to the jury why Mrs. Queen was admitted to the hospital?

E: She stayed in the hospital after her fractured hip because they were trying to find a nursing home bed.

A: I asked you why she was admitted. What caused her to be hospitalized?

E: She was unsteady on her feet and falling frequently.

A: Can we agree that there does not appear to be an order for taking these compression stockings off this patient?

E: No.

A: No, we can't agree or —

E: We can agree.

18. Failing to be responsive, especially giving more explanation or more information than is asked for, is *not* recommended.

A: Did the job as an instructor involve teaching emergency nursing to students?

E: Yes, I took the students into the emergency room for one semester. They were assigned to observe the triage nurse and to perform simple treatments. At times, they would observe cardiac arrests, of course always standing in the back of the room where they would not be in the way. Many of them found this to be the most traumatic experience they had as students, although I did have one student one time who fainted when the doctor started suturing a head laceration on a child. *(This was a yes-or-no question.)*

19. Failing to stand behind the expert report is ill-advised.

A: It says in your report that Nurse Williams did not deviate from the standard of care when she administered morphine to my client.

E: Yes, that is what it says.

A: Do you hold that opinion today?

E: Actually, I have changed that opinion.

A: What have you changed about your opinion?

E: I now believe that she should not have given 35 mg of morphine at one time, when the doctor ordered 10 mg. *(This expert should have come to this realization long before the deposition.)*

20. Going too far out on a limb — not being flexible — creates problems for the expert.

A: How often does the tube-feeding bag need to be changed?

E: It should be changed every 24 hours.

A: What is the purpose of changing the tube-feeding bag?

E: It is to keep the bag sanitary.

A: You have heard testimony that Mrs. Viglione's family saw fungus growing on the inside of the tube-feeding bag, correct?

E: Yes, but that does not really matter.

A: Why is that?

E: The stomach is not sterile, so fungus will not hurt it.

A: Would you eat bread that has mold growing on it?

E: No.

A: Why is that?

E: (long pause) I would not want to get sick.

A: If a fly flew into the tube-feeding solution, would you feed the fly to the patient?

E: Yes, I would, because the stomach is not sterile. *(This is actual testimony by a nursing expert.)*

21. Testifying to issues outside his or her expertise is inappropriate.

A: Do you have an opinion as to whether or not Dr. White should have prescribed Keflex® to this patient?

E: Yes, I do.

A: And your opinion is?

E: My opinion is that he should not have prescribed the Keflex, even though I am not an orthopedic surgeon, based on the fact that the patient herself had requested that she not be given this drug.

   Defense attorney #1: Can we just take a two-minute break? I want to talk to her outside.

   Defense attorney #2: I object to any break.

A: Are you through with your response?

E: Based on those two things I still believe that Dr. White should have, based on his medical judgment, not given Keflex to the patient.

   (Attorney #1 puts his hand on expert's arm, whispers in her ear, and forces her to stand up.)

   Defense attorney #2: Let the record reflect that the attorney is coaching the expert during this deposition. His witness did not ask to speak to counsel. Counsel has asked to speak to his expert. The expert and her attorney are leaving the room.

   Defense attorney #1: I object to the use of the word "coach" in terms of characterizing because I want to speak to my expert witness. I just want to talk to my expert in private with regard to the scope of her testimony that we will hope to use at the time of trial. I would like to clarify with her, and I don't consider that coaching at all with regard to anything. We will be back in a few minutes after I have had that opportunity to talk with her.

   Defense attorney #2: "Coaching" is a good word, and I stand by my description of what you are doing here, Counsel.

A: Before you leave, are you able to put on the record the scope of this witness's intended testimony?

   Defense attorney #1: I intend to do that when I come back.

A: You can't do that beforehand?

   Defense attorney #1: I will come back and do it.

   Defense attorney #2: That's after he coaches her.

   (Expert and defense attorney #1 leave room for a minute, then return.)

   Defense attorney #1: Before we begin, I would like to put a statement on the record with regard to my conversation with the witness.

A: Which the record should reflect was three minutes.

Defense attorney #1: I have had the opportunity to discuss with the expert the scope of her review. I was concerned that she might have some questions about her role. She is being offered as a nursing expert who will address the standards of care for the nurse. At the end of her report, she has a paragraph that seems to conclude that Dr. White prescribing Keflex may have been a cause of the problems.

A: Let me ask you this.

Defense attorney #1: Go for it.

A: Will this witness be testifying about causation? In other words, what damages, if any, were caused by administering Keflex?

Defense attorney #1: We are offering her as an expert witness as to the standard of care of the nurse. We are going to limit her testimony to the duty of the nurse.

Defense attorney #2: Exactly! *(The nursing expert may not testify about the physician standards of care.)*

22. Failing to know the topic is problematic.

A: What is the nursing process?

E: It is the process by which we give nursing care.

A: Can you be more specific?

E: No, I can't.

A: Can you list any of the steps of the nursing process?

E: No.

23. Using terms such as "always" and "never" can be too sweeping and trap the nurse.

A: Does a nurse read the entire medical record before she takes care of a patient?

E: Yes, nurses always read the chart.

A: So, without exception, nurses always read about the patient before they take care of him, is that correct?

E: Yes.

A: The standard of care requires the nurse to always read the medical record, is that what you are saying?

E: Yes, it is.

A: Can you give me a reference to an article or textbook that says that the nurse should always read the medical record before taking care of the patient?

E: No, I can't.

A: So this is your opinion on what the nurse should do?

E: Yes, it is.

A: In your practice as a nurse, have you seen nurses sit down before taking care of the patient and read the entire medical record?

E: No, I have not. But they should do it. *(It is difficult to maintain that this is the standard of care if the expert cannot support her opinion with a text or common practice.)*

24. Trying to be a lawyer is not advisable. The nursing expert should avoid adopting legal language.

A: Do you believe that the patient did anything wrong?

E: Yes, I believe she was contributorily negligent.

25. Being biased or an advocate is to be avoided. The expert's role is to be objective and an educator about the standard of care.
    A: Nurse __, you have been retained to be an expert in this case, isn't that correct?
    E: Yes, I was hired to defend the nurses.
    A: I'm confused; isn't Ms. Corner the defense attorney?
    E: Yes, she is.
    A: What do you see as your role?
    E: My role is to make sure that these nurses don't have to pay for something that was not their fault. It was not their fault that the patient did not follow instructions. There would be far fewer lawsuits if patients just did what they were told!

26. Being argumentative, evasive, aggressive, or too clever is not recommended. The expert often comes out on the losing end of this type of tactic.
    A: It is your opinion that the nurses at Major Hospital did nothing wrong, is that right?
    E: Yes, it is. I think the nursing care was perfectly fine.
    A: Do you have an opinion about whether this order sheet existed?
    E: (Smiling) I have an opinion that will remain private.
    A: Why?
    E: I find it interesting that this order sheet was supposed to be in the chart, and it is the most crucial document in this case and it is missing. I find it unusual that it is missing because it should be there. I mean, I have never seen this type of patient being cared for in the hospital without that type of order sheet in place.
    A: I don't think you have answered my question as to what your belief is as to whether that order sheet ever existed.
    E: I cannot testify with any certainty that the document existed because I was not there to see it. Based on my review of the deposition of the nurse and her answers to interrogatories, I question that a possibility does exist that this order sheet was there, and then destroyed.
    A: When I asked you the question originally, and I know that the reporter can't take this down, but you gave a little smile as to indicate that perhaps you did have an opinion as to whether or not this existed. What is your opinion about whether or not it really existed?
    E: I think anything is possible at this point since we have so many pieces of paper involved in this case.
    A: Yes or no, do you believe is it more likely than not in your opinion that the paper existed?
    E: I would say no, that it probably did not exist. It is a possibility either way, 50/50. *(This response is completely ambiguous and not helpful.)*

27. Answering two-part questions with one answer — each part of the question should be answered separately or the attorney should be asked to rephrase the question.
    A: Do they read the whole chart or just portions of the chart?
    E: Yes.

28. Speculating about the actions of others is dangerous.
    A: What is the purpose of the medical record?
    E: It is to document the significant aspects of patient care.

A: Would you expect the physician to document significant observations about the patient?

E: Yes, I would.

A: You are aware that the house doctor recorded that there was a strong pulse in the patient's right leg at 10:00 a.m.?

E: Yes, I read that.

A: You are also aware that the vascular surgeon came in at 10:45 a.m. and recorded that the patient had compartment syndrome in the right leg?

E: Yes.

A: Is it possible that the patient had a strong pulse in the right leg at 10:00 a.m.?

E: Anything is possible. *(The expert may find it more useful to say that it is highly unlikely.)*

A: Do you believe that it was likely that the patient had a strong pulse at 10:00 a.m.?

E: No, I do not.

A: Why do you believe the house physician documented the presence of a strong pulse?

E: Sometimes when there is a bad outcome there is a cover-up. *(This may be viewed as an inflammatory statement.)*

29. The attorney may ask the expert to speculate. The expert has to analyze information provided to him and should not speculate.

A: Do you know how long the nurse was with this patient?

E: I don't know for a fact, no.

A: Do you have an opinion as to when the nurse saw this patient?

E: I have an opinion that she saw her at the end of the evening shift rather than at the beginning of the evening shift, based on her testimony at the deposition.

A: Is there anything in the medical record to indicate that valuables had been taken from the patient?

E: I did not find anything to that effect.

A: If valuables are taken from a patient, does that usually include jewelry?

E: Not necessarily.

A: What does that usually include?

E: It depends on what the patient has.

A: Could that include rings, necklaces, and money?

E: It depends on what the patient comes into the hospital with.

A: In a situation when a patient comes in with a drug overdose, when a hospital will take valuables from a patient, what does that generally include? *(The expert is being asked to speculate.)*

E: I can't answer that question.

A: Why not?

E: Because I don't know what the patient had. Patients come into the hospital with all kinds of things.

A: You have no understanding what general hospital procedure would be in terms of removing a patient's valuables under those circumstances?

E: No. The definition of "valuables" is highly variable.

30. Do not charge fees that are difficult to justify to the jury.

A: What do you charge to come to court for the day?

E: My trial fee is $5000 per day.

A: Do you know how much nurses make at General Hospital?

E: The nurse working in a hospital makes between $22 and $35 per hour.

A: So, that is $176 per day if we use $22 per hour and $320 per day if we use $35 per hour, right?

E: Yes.

A: And you charge $5000 per day, correct?

E: Yes, I do.

31. Explain medical terms in the language of laypersons to avoid talking over the heads of the jury. Avoid doing what this expert did:

A: Could you explain to the jury what type of surgery Mrs. Wilson had?

E: She had a bilateral salpingo-oophorectomy and a vaginal hysterectomy with fulgeration of areas of endometriosis. *(The jury will have no idea what she just said.)*

32. Avoid talking down to the jury.

A: Could you explain to the jury what type of surgery Mrs. Wilson had?

E: Every woman has a uterus, ovaries, and tubes. The eggs are made in the ovaries. The male seeds are called sperm. The male seeds meet the egg in the tube and the egg travels down the tube to the uterus or womb. The fertilized egg stays in the uterus until the baby is ready to be born. The baby comes out the birth canal or vagina. The patient had removal of her ovaries and tubes. Her womb was removed from her vagina. She had areas of endometriosis, which are made up of cells from the uterus that travel outside of the uterus. Each month when a woman has her monthly, these cells swell and this causes pain. The doctor used electricity to burn these cells.

33. Avoid making statements that defy the common sense of jurors.

A: Do you accept as true everything that the nurse said happened?

E: Yes, I do. I believe in her honesty.

A: So if I told you that she testified yesterday that she took care of the patient on February 30, would you believe her testimony was true?

E: Yes, I would.

34. Referring to the insurance company is to be avoided.

A: Have your bills been paid by my firm?

E: No, I have gotten my checks directly from the insurance company. *(The jury is not supposed to know that an insurance company is involved in the case.)*

35. Being able to cite sources of information makes the expert's testimony stronger.

A: What do you base your opinion on that restraints may not have been mandated on the evening shift?

E: I based that opinion on the testimony of the plaintiff and on the medical record, which states that the patient was cooperative and awake, alert, and oriented, and the testimony of the patient's mother and her friend.

36. The attorney may ask questions of the expert to trap the expert into admitting that she has committed malpractice.

A: Have you ever been a staff nurse assigned to a patient who was in restraints of any nature where the patient sustained an injury?

E: No.

A: Have you ever been a staff nurse assigned to a patient where the patient was not restrained and sustained an injury as a result of not being restrained?

E: No.

A: Have you ever been a staff nurse assigned to a patient who sustained an injury in a hospital?

E: Yes.

A: Tell me about those circumstances. First of all, on how many occasions?

E: Do you mean when I was caring for the patient?

A: Yes.

E: I can recall taking care of an elderly person with frail skin. I inadvertently applied pressure to the skin and the skin tore. I recall that situation. Other than that I don't recall other situations.

A: Okay. Have you ever cared for a patient where a patient fell out of bed?

E: No.

A: Have you ever committed malpractice?

E: Not that I know of.

A: Have you ever been sued for malpractice?

E: No.

37. The expert should avoid being backed into a corner.

A: Is it your opinion that any time the patient sustains an injury while in four-point restraints, malpractice has occurred?

E: I would be hard pressed to agree to a blanket statement like that. I would have to know the circumstances.

A: Have you cared for patients who were in four-point restraints because they were being abusive, combative, and at risk to themselves or others if they were not restrained?

E: Yes.

A: And in those situations is it possible that the patient can sustain an injury while in four-point restraints in the absence of nursing malpractice?

E: I personally have not seen it happen. I've seen many efforts to try to avoid friction, irritation, tightness, and problems with circulation. It's my opinion that if the standard of care is followed, the probabilities of the patient sustaining injury are greatly reduced.

A: So, would that allow for the possibility that even if the appropriate standards of care are followed for monitoring a patient in four-point restraints, an injury may happen in any event?

E: It would be a very remote possibility.

A: Is it possible that a combative patient in restraints can create a friction burn?

E: Yes, it is possible, if she is continuously pulling.

A: Okay. So even if they are being monitored to make sure that the restraints are not too tight, and they are being released from them periodically as the protocol requires, that could occur?

E: The answer to that question is not that simple because when a nurse observes that type of continuous friction and pulling against the restraint, the nurse is obligated to consider alternatives to avoid the friction. These could include putting padding under the restraint to prevent the abrasion to considering the fact that the very act of restraining the patient can cause combativeness. The combativeness can be independent of the underlying medical reason that the combative behavior might have existed. There must be some efforts at problem-solving with respect to how to avoid damage to the skin. So, your question was can it cause abrasion? Yes, it can, but there are multiple interventions to avoid that outcome, and I do not see that those were taken in this situation.

38. The attorney may question the knowledge of the expert or realize that he has just laid a trap for himself.

A: Your criticism that Ms. Winters failed to release the restraints is based on the patient's testimony, correct?

E: Well, Ms. Winters also testified that she did not release the restraints.

A: That's your recollection? Let's strike that.

E: Would you like me to show her testimony to you?

A: No.

Chapter 36

The Expert Fact Witness: Noneconomic Damages Testimony

Patricia W. Iyer, MSN, RN, LNCC, and
Jenny Beerman, RN, LNCC

CONTENTS

0-8493-1418-6/03/$0.00+$1.50
© 2003 by AALNC

Objectives

- To describe the role and purpose of an expert fact witness
- To discuss foundation issues for the role
- To describe the approach to organization and presentation of medical records to a jury
- To identify steps in preparing to testify as an expert fact witness

Introduction

Most laypersons have little understanding of what occurs within the health care system. The triers of fact (judges, mediators, and jurors) as well as attorneys need to understand the injuries, treatment, and responses of the patient. Medical records used as evidence during a trial are often incomprehensible to the average juror, since abbreviations and symbols used by health care providers are often meaningless to laypersons. To overcome this obstacle, attorneys have attempted to educate the triers of fact by using treating physicians to explain medical treatment to the jury. Although a treating doctor may have an understanding of care provided to the patient, it is rare that this doctor will have read all the medical records from beginning to end. Even if requested to do so, few practicing physicians have time to read a medical record thoroughly and prepare a detailed report. The cost of having a physician do so would be beyond the resources of many plaintiff attorneys.

At trial, family members may describe what they observed during the patient's treatment, but these persons typically have no medical training and cannot provide cogent medical explanations for the triers of fact. The nursing expert fact witness is the ideal person to present a comprehensive picture of the patient's injuries, treatment, and reactions. This chapter discusses the role of the nurse as an expert fact witness who conveys this information in a teaching role.

Definition of the Role

Legal nurse consultants (LNCs) have developed new testifying roles as "expert fact witnesses."[1] The expert fact witness is one who by virtue of special knowledge, skill, training, or experience is qualified to provide testimony to aid the fact-finder in matters that exceed the common knowledge of ordinary people, but does not offer opinions on the standard of care. The expert fact witness is not engaged to express opinions about the quality of care and treatment rendered but to educate the judge or jury about that care and the plaintiff's response to it. In this role, an LNC evaluates, summarizes, and explains contents of medical records. A report is submitted to the attorney who hired the LNC, and then provided to opposing counsel. The nurse may offer testimony at mediation or deposition. If the case proceeds to trial, the nurse's testimony aids in understanding the extent of a plaintiff's injuries, treatment, pain, and suffering.

The term "expert fact witness" does not yet appear in standard legal dictionaries. The *expert witness* has special knowledge, skill, training, or experience and is qualified to provide testimony to aid the fact-finder in matters that exceed the common knowledge of ordinary people. The role typically addresses liability or damages. A *liability expert witness* forms an opinion about the adherence to the standard of care. A nurse who acts in the role of a *damages expert witness* typically provides a life care plan that defines the expected cost for caring for the patient. A *fact witness* may be a nurse who is not a defendant but has knowledge of the events that occurred. A fact witness may also be a layperson who is not a defendant. As a witness to the events, the fact witness testifies about events.

The LNC's expertise is also helpful for detailed explanation of events from initial hospitalization following an injury through discharge and rehabilitation. Injuries, care, and related pain and suffering often represent substantial damages. This testimony is particularly useful in cases in which the plaintiff is unable to testify clearly due to cognitive impairment, language barrier, young age, or death.

At trial, the expert fact witness's presentation of medical record details bridges the gap in testimony between the liability for the accident or medical malpractice and the life care plan. The jury needs a clear, concise, and understandable accounting of events based on medical records. Frequently, this testimony concentrates on presenting facts in the medical records that support the allegation of the plaintiff's pain and suffering, which is a key component of damages important for judge or jury to understand. The expert fact witness may be retained by the defense to refute claims that the patient experienced extensive pain and suffering. By virtue of the plaintiff's need to prove that damages occurred, it is more common for plaintiffs' attorneys to hire nursing expert fact witnesses.

Federal Rules of Evidence

The Federal Rules of Evidence govern the conduct of cases tried in federal courts. Many state courts model their rules of evidence after the federal rules. Federal Rule of Evidence 702 states: "If scientific, technical, or other specialized knowledge will assist the trier of fact to understand the evidence or to determine a fact in issue, a witness qualified as an expert by knowledge, skill, experience, training, or education may testify thereto in the form of an opinion or otherwise, if (1) the testimony is based upon sufficient facts or data, (2) the testimony is the product of reliable principles and methods, and (3) the witness has applied the principles and methods reliably to the facts of the case."[2] The nurse with specialized knowledge, skill, experience, training, and education thus qualifies as an expert according to the Federal Rules of Evidence. The nurse has a greater understanding of medical details than do laypersons and thus is able to assist the trier of fact to understand what occurred to the patient.

A second Federal Rule of Evidence helps to support use of a nurse in this expert role. Federal Rule of Evidence 1006 states: "The contents of voluminous writings, recordings, or photographs which cannot conveniently be examined in court may be presented in the form of a chart, summary, or calculation. The originals, or duplicates, shall be made available for examination or copying, or both, by other parties at reasonable time and place. The court may order that they be produced in court."[2] The report prepared by the expert fact witness constitutes a summary of medical records. Although no precise definition of "voluminous records" exists, the records generated when the patient has sustained significant injuries would usually meet this definition.

Expert fact witness reports and testimony are based on the medical records. Medical records are considered business records, recorded contemporaneously with events, and as such are admissible as evidence. Though not a witness to the actual events, the expert fact witness is allowed to act as a conduit of medical record information to the judge or jury.

Expert Witness Qualifications for the Role

Several attributes strengthen the role of the expert fact witness. Above all, the expert fact witness must be an analytical thinker. The ability to interpret and analyze medical records is essential for the expert witness role. Analysis of medical records requires the ability to be extremely detail-oriented. The expert must be able to identify missing records, extract essential data from the records, and prepare a clear report that articulates the events and injuries. The ability to prepare clear, logically organized, and accurate reports is essential.

Although nurses without advanced degrees have been accepted by the courts as expert witnesses, the ideal expert fact witness has a master's degree or doctorate. The emphasis on writing integral to graduate studies is essential preparation for developing reports. An advanced degree enhances the expert's credibility and reduces reasons for opposing counsel to object to testimony of the expert fact witness.

The expert fact witness should be familiar with the clinical specialty relative to the patient's alleged injuries. It is not necessary for the expert to have experience in the exact type of nursing specialty, but an expert who has never worked in acute care, for example, may have difficulty explaining medical and nursing issues without some firsthand knowledge.

The expert fact witness must possess expertise to explain health care and medical records without providing opinions about the facts. The expert fact witness must have a thorough understanding of different types of medical records. In order to suspect missing records, inconsistencies, or tampering, the expert fact witness must know the elements typically found in each type of record.

Applicable Cases

The expert fact witness may be retained to review records, prepare a report, and testify about injuries and treatment associated with bodily injury, medical or nursing malpractice, product liability, domestic violence, and criminal cases. This role is appropriate whenever a person sustains significant injuries that are documented in medical records. Examples of the types of cases in which the authors have prepared expert fact witness reports include:

- Surgical errors
- Chemical and thermal burns
- Paralysis
- Closed head injury
- Major trauma from motor vehicle accidents, pedestrians hit by cars, or those with work injuries
- Worsened prognosis caused by delay in diagnosis of cancer

- Death or injuries from surgical or treatment errors
- Battering during domestic violence
- Death or permanent injuries caused by medication errors

Cases in which services of an expert fact witness would usually not be needed include those in which records are not voluminous, or injuries were insignificant or nonexistent. As a practical matter, many plaintiff attorneys who try cases with significant injuries but have great difficulty proving liability may not wish to incur the expense of retaining an expert fact witness.

Marketing the Role to Attorneys

Success of the expert fact witness depends on effective marketing of the role. Armed with an understanding of this specialized role, it may fall to the expert fact witness to convince an attorney to retain the nurse in this capacity. Attorneys may have little or no understanding of the advantages of using a nurse for this role. Common responses are "I'll have the treating doctor testify," or "I'll find the treating nurses and bring them to court." The expert fact witness may point out the expense of having a doctor prepare a detailed report. If the attorney has previously used a doctor to explain treatment, the expert fact witness may want to show the attorney an example of an expert fact witness report (with identifying information redacted) to explain differences in scope and content, which are valuable in case presentation. Another advantage of employing nurses as expert fact witnesses is that their reports are often broader in scope. Nurses have greater knowledge of the elements of pain and suffering as well as the intricacies of the health care system.

It is often impractical and expensive to use treating professionals to testify about the patient's ordeal. Treating health care professionals may be difficult to locate and unable to remember the patient, and they usually do not have the communication skills to testify. They may be intimidated by the legal system or even antagonistic to the plaintiff attorney.

When marketing the expert fact witness role, the expert should be prepared to answer questions about the likely cost of such a service. Attorneys often ask for an estimate of the cost for preparing a detailed report. Given the amount of information to be extracted, illustrated, and compiled, these reports are time-consuming and therefore usually expensive for the attorney. The wise expert attempts to determine in advance whether the attorney has the resources to pay for this service. Tailoring the report down to the bare bones may be needed when the attorney is unable to fund an extensive report. A signed fee agreement and a large retainer are recommended.

Record Organization and Report Preparation

The LNC starts by organizing the records. Medical records received from a variety of facilities and providers may span a considerable period of time. Use of indexes, medical record tabs, and binders help control the paper and enable the expert fact witness to locate information quickly. The LNC's familiarity with medical records allows early recognition of missing records. Since records are often delivered in a disorganized state, evaluation of completeness is essential. Missing records should be requested as soon as possible. The attorney may have unknowingly requested only the records that the client or family remembered, or believed that an abstract instead of the full certified copy of the medical record would suffice.

As with other expert witness work, writing on the records or using a highlighter is not recommended. Being able to refer to Post-it® notes on significant entries is helpful when writing the report. To save time while reviewing records and preparing the report, the expert may wish to use voice-activation software or to type the report as the records are being read.

When condensing and summarizing the records, the LNC should not alter the facts. The expert witness must not speculate about what the patient was thinking or feeling. For example, the report should not contain statements such as "She must have been scared to wake up in the emergency room with no recollection of the accident." Instead, the report might contain the statement: "The nurse described the patient as anxious, and asking, 'Where am I?'"

The LNC must differentiate preexisting conditions from those caused by the accident. At the same time, preexisting conditions exacerbated by the injuries should be noted. All damages or potential damages found by the expert fact witness should be listed and discussed with the attorney. Examples of damages that attorneys may not be aware of are cognitive delays in head-injured children that may require yearly psychological testing or a torn diaphragm that may have the potential to rupture repeatedly and require future surgeries. If permanent disabling injuries have resulted, a colleague may be recommended to formulate a life care plan. A treating or expert witness physician may be needed to testify about the permanency and prognosis related to damages.

The expert has an ethical obligation to tell the attorney about potentially damaging information that is found in the medical records, such as substance abuse or data that contradicts the attorney's theories of liability. This is particularly important if the patient did something that contributed to the accident or injury. The attorney is responsible for determining how to use this information in the process of litigating the case.

The expert fact witness should not lose sight of the fact that the report will be read by laypersons. This requires the ability to view the health care experience from the layperson's perspective. Foundation in patient education assists the expert fact witness in preparing the report. Concepts contained in the report should be explained in lay terms. Complex medical terms should be broken down to simple language, avoiding slang, abbreviations, and incomplete sentences.

The expert fact witness's report may be used as the basis for preparing demonstrative evidence. Timelines made from the narrative chronology are effective, serving as a representation of the chronology and a useful visual aid for the jury. Exhibits can also include lists, charts, or illustrations of medications, tests, operations, treatments, complications, damages, and health care providers. The report may be illustrated with images of normal anatomy, medical procedures, schematic drawings of pain medications, graphs, changes in laboratory values, or quotations from the medical record.

Opposition to the Expert Fact Witness Role

Even before the mediation or trial begins, the opposing counsel, usually the defense attorney, may object to the testimony of the expert fact witness. The opposing counsel may prepare a brief after the expert fact witness's report has been received. The expert fact witness should help the attorney who has requested the services of the expert to anticipate opposing counsel's strategies. The expert may assist the retaining attorney in responding to the brief by:

- With permission, supplying names of clients who have successfully used the expert fact witness in court
- With permission, supplying briefs written by attorneys who have defended the use of an expert fact witness (with the names of the patients redacted)
- Supplying the text of the Federal Rules of Evidence and applicable state law

As is required for the acceptance of other expert witnesses, the attorney must offer proof to the court that the nurse is qualified to testify in this role. Opposing counsel and judges may not understand that nurses are qualified to present medical record evidence by virtue of their specialized education and certification, familiarity with hospital procedures and processes, medical records, medical terminology, and clinical education and experience. As key members of the health care team, nurses spend more time with patients and medical records in the clinical setting than any other care provider. With the exception of advanced practice nurses, nurses do not make medical diagnoses or prescribe medical treatment. They do teach patients about health and diseases, medical terminology, diagnostic tests, procedures, and a wide variety of treatment modalities. Nurses are qualified to provide this same information to educate jurors. Ultimately, acceptance of the qualifications of the expert fact witness is at the judge's discretion after review of the brief, or after hearing a motion in limine at the time of trial.

Appendix 36.1 incorporates examples of the kinds of objections raised by opposing counsel. This material, based on briefs prepared by defense and plaintiff attorneys in an actual case, was presented at the 2001 American Association of Legal Nurse Consultants conference. The case settled before trial.

Deposition of the Expert Fact Witness

Depositions of expert fact witnesses are taken less frequently than depositions of liability expert witnesses. The purpose of taking the deposition of a liability expert witness is to evaluate the expert's ability to assert and defend opinions, and maintain composure under questioning. There should be little question about what the expert plans to say in the courtroom.

If depositions of the expert fact witness are scheduled, they are typically short. Attorneys who have not previously encountered the expert fact witness role may be initially puzzled by the report and the role. The expert fact witness's prior experience preparing such reports may be explored, and the outline of the testimony defined. Opposing counsel often need assurance that no liability opinions will be offered by the expert fact witness. Efforts to prevent the expert fact witness from being able to testify at trial may be instituted by opposing counsel after the deposition. Detailed reports explaining graphic injuries, treatment, and response to care may stir up the most resistance from opposing counsel. This reaction can be a measure of the report's success in conveying a vivid picture of the patient's injuries, treatment, pain, and suffering.

Trial Preparation

The expert fact witness should understand from the outset that the case may go to trial. The report may be used by the attorney to focus on key details and to prepare other witnesses for trial. After the report is submitted, the expert fact witness can provide further assistance to the attorney, as described below.

Drafts of Trial Exhibits and Demonstrative Aids

The jury remembers images, diagrams, and pictures long after an expert has left the stand. Collaboration with the attorney allows creative planning and development of effective exhibits. The attorney may have ideas from past trials or from colleagues. The LNC should know where to get equipment and demonstrative evidence. Exhibits must then be created, enlarged, and mounted for the courtroom; demonstrative aids are collected and prepared. See Iyer, Appelbaum, and Parisi[3] for more information on planning demonstrative evidence.

As computerized technology in the courtroom becomes increasingly accepted, use of presentation software with a laptop computer is becoming more common. Telling an effective story becomes even easier with this medium. Enlarged photographs, medical illustrations, pictures of medical equipment, and scanned pages from the medical record enhance the jurors' understanding. Exhibits that will be a part of the testimony may be printed out as slides and supplied to opposing counsel in advance of the trial as required by court rules. See Chapter 40 for more information.

The LNC reviews exhibits for correctness, simplicity, and readability at every stage of production. As the trial date draws near, all equipment should be checked for proper functioning. Extra supplies, such as colored markers, pointers, and easels to display the exhibits, should be gathered. Bulbs for projectors, extension cords, and other equipment needed for a laptop presentation should be available. Technical problems should be anticipated and backup plans formulated. See Chapters 41 and 42 for further information on trial preparation.

Practice of the Presentation

The expert fact witness is often consulted by the attorney prior to testifying at a mediation or trial. They discuss the content of the expert's testimony, plan visual aids, and attempt to anticipate cross-examination. The LNC and attorney should plan the presentation prior to trial. Strong, effective teaching in the courtroom derives from basic principles of patient education and does not differ greatly from bedside teaching for patient and family.

It is helpful to practice the final presentation in front of a layperson rather than an attorney, nurse, or doctor. Because testimony may have to be altered extemporaneously, the LNC should concentrate on the main events of the injury. Memorizing word-for-word texts is risky because the courtroom's climate may differ greatly from the privacy of rehearsal.

Supervision of Exhibit Setup

The LNC should arrive early at court to assist in exhibit arrangement in the courtroom. Sitting in the jury box and witness chair before anyone arrives, if possible, is recommended to help the LNC become familiar with the courtroom's layout. In the witness chair, note shelf space, microphone, and distance between the attorney and the jury. If the LNC uses exhibits mounted on Foamcor® board, each exhibit should be placed on the easel and viewed from several jurors' chairs to test readability. The LNC should verify delivery and setup of all equipment and safety of cords and wires.

Trial Testimony

A motion in limine may be made at the trial's start to prevent the expert fact witness from testifying. If the expert is accepted as qualified, the judge may either restrict testimony to strict and narrow boundaries or extend liberal boundaries for testimony. It is important to understand and abide by any limits imposed by the court. The goal is to present the facts of the medical record clearly and accurately.

At trial, the LNC may testify after the liability issues have been presented. The expert fact witness may be the first of the damages witnesses. This testimony lays the foundation for other health care professionals. The expert fact witness may be the only person who has read the medical records completely. After review of the nursing expert fact witness's report, treating physicians may be prepared by the attorney to highlight specific areas or events in the medical record. All experts must understand their specific roles in the outline of the medical testimony. For example, in a complicated trauma case, the nurse defines and explains anatomy of the injured areas, management of the patient in traction, the amount and frequency of pain medication, and weekly physical therapies. The trauma surgeon then explains the complicated surgery, elaborating on complications, causes, treatment, and long-lasting disabilities.

The expert fact witness serves to educate the court about the technical facts, issues, and events of the medical record. The first few minutes on the stand are critical to establishing rapport with the jury. As the attorney asks questions, the LNC should be attentive. Eye contact with each juror is vital. Testimony under oath requires accurate reporting without embellishment or deletion. Meticulous, accurate, and complete testimony is difficult for the defense to discredit.

The LNC should listen carefully to each question, answering only the question asked. However, some attorneys prefer a free flow of information as the expert teaches the jury. Descriptions of the timeline of events of the hospitalization or the patient's pain and suffering should be animated without boring the jury with too much detail. Exhibits and demonstrative evidence can keep the jury interested, as long as they can see demonstrations clearly. Everyday analogies, visual aids, and lay terminology are essential, with the main points of the case always in mind.

The opposing attorney may cross-examine the LNC. In contrast to the extensive cross-examination that the liability nurse expert has come to expect, this cross-examination may be brief. Accurate introduction of medical record evidence and clear explanations of treatment and medical terminology leave little room for questions. The opposing attorney may try to discredit or diminish the effectiveness of testimony by asking detailed questions regarding the expert's professional background to imply that the LNC may not be qualified. The LNC's pretrial preparation should include review of relevant clinical practice experience and professional positions to enhance such testimony.

Summary

LNCs who undertake to present medical record evidence testimony at trial should have an extensive background in clinical practice and teaching experience. While physicians tend to concentrate on explanations of specific medical treatments and procedures, LNCs are more likely to present a broader, more comprehensive view of the events described in the medical records to improve the court's understanding of the case.

Serving as an expert fact witness may be rewarding for nurses because it is not associated with the more adversarial, confrontational nature of nursing malpractice testimony. The testifying nurse provides the jury with an understanding of the pertinent issues in an organized, systematic, and memorable format. Opportunities for nurses to testify as expert fact witnesses are expanding as attorneys and judges are educated about financial, educational, and strategic advantages of this role.

References

1. Bogart, J. and Beerman, J., Expert fact witness: a testifying role for the legal nurse consultant, *Journal of Legal Nurse Consulting*, 6(4), 2–8, 1995.
2. http://www.2.law.cornell.edu.
3. Iyer, P., Appelbaum, S., and Parisi, J., Trial exhibits: types and uses in demonstrative evidence, in *Medical Legal Aspects of Pain and Suffering*, Iyer, P., Ed., Lawyers and Judges Publishing Company, Tucson, AZ, 2003.

Additional Reading

Iyer, P., Bogart, J., and Beerman, J., The legal process: a view from the expert witness's hot seat, *NeuroRehabilitation*, 7(137), 137–149, 1996.

Test Questions

1. Which of the following statements is NOT true?
   A. A judge may prevent a nurse from testifying as an expert fact witness.
   B. The expert fact witness presents opinions about the standard of care.
   C. A nurse who is not named as a defendant in a case may be a fact witness.
   D. An attorney may resist using a nurse to explain medical records.

2. Which of the following statements is true?
   A. Defense attorneys commonly hire an expert fact witness to explain the patient's pain and suffering.
   B. The term "expert fact witness" is widely understood by attorneys.
   C. The use of expert witnesses without advanced nursing degrees is often challenged by opposing counsel.
   D. Use of treating professionals to testify provides the same benefits as using an expert fact witness.

3. Which of the following statements is NOT true?
   A. The expert witness may write notes on medical records.
   B. The physician is the appropriate expert to testify about permanency of injuries.
   C. The expert fact witness's report may contain trial-appropriate exhibits.
   D. The expert fact witness is rarely deposed.

4. Which of the following statements is true?
   A. Few trials require demonstrative aids.
   B. Memorizing testimony is an effective way to prepare for testimony.
   C. Knowledge of patient education principles is useful when testifying as an expert fact witness.
   D. The expert fact witness should proofread demonstrative evidence thoroughly when arriving at the witness box.

5. Which is the *most* essential way to prepare for the role of the expert fact witness?
   A. Develop strong written and oral communication skills.
   B. Prepare a concise marketing package.
   C. Locate attorneys who handle personal injury cases.
   D. Visit local hospitals to view medical equipment.

Answers: 1. B, 2. C, 3. A, 4. C, 5. A

Appendix 36.1
Motion in Limine Regarding the Expert Fact Witness's Role

Opening Statement by Paul Pierson, Esq., Plaintiff Attorney

Ladies and gentlemen of the jury, thank you for your attention. The evidence will show that my client, Lisa Miller, was 34 years old on a beautiful day in June in 1997. Lisa was a star athlete who loved to participate in triathlons during her free time. She prided herself on her strength and fitness. Lisa worked at a children's center taking care of emotionally disturbed kids. Her job involved being on her feet all day, bending and lifting. She had to be able to respond quickly if the children needed holding or to prevent them from hurting each other.

Lisa is an only child. After going to college, Lisa moved into her own home, a mobile home. She was proud of her independence. Although she had a loving relationship with her parents, she enjoyed having a place of her own.

On June 10, 1997, Lisa was riding her bike on the shoulder of a country road. The evidence will show that the bus left the travel portion of the road surface. Lisa was hit from behind by a 30,000-pound bus that was traveling at 55 miles per hour. She was thrown 15 feet through the air and landed in a nearby field. The medical evidence that we will present will show that Lisa suffered devastating injuries to her pelvis, hip, and knee. She had multiple other broken bones. She underwent months of rehabilitation and physical therapy. You will hear testimony from Lisa that she was forced to move back with her parents when she first got out of the rehabilitation hospital. She had to give up her independence and become dependent on her parents for her most basic needs. She was unable to walk without the assistance of a walker, and then a cane. It took months before she was able to drive again and almost a year before she was able to get back on a bike.

The evidence will show that the bus driver, Richard Felton, did not see Lisa before he hit her. He has admitted that he was at fault. We are here to decide how Lisa should be compensated for the loss of her health, for her months of treatment, and for her permanent pain and limitations in her knee. Lisa would love to turn the clock back and have her fitness again. She would give anything to be able to alter the events and relive that day, and not be on that road at the time Richard Felton was driving down the road. However, Lisa cannot change what happened. She cannot turn back the clock.

You will hear her orthopedist, a world-famous doctor, testify that Lisa's injuries will get worse as she ages. She already has signs of posttraumatic arthritis, and can expect to have prosthetic knees and hips in the future. You will hear that Lisa had $125,000 in medical bills and had a wage loss of between $300,000 and $1.2 million. You will hear that she lost out on a promotion at work, and that there are limitations to what she can do now.

You have been asked to participate in helping Lisa resolve this accident. Lisa does not want your sympathy. You are the only people in the world who will hear the full story of what happened to Lisa after the accident. You are the only people who are in a position to compensate Lisa for what she has lost. This is Lisa's only chance to obtain compensation for her injuries. She won't be able to come back in 15 years when she requires her total knee replacement or her total hip surgeries. This case is about pain and suffering. It is about the destruction of bones by a bus. It is about months and years of pain. This case is simply entitled *Bus Versus Bike*. When a bus and a bike collide, the person on the bike always loses.

At the end of our testimony, we will ask you to make a decision about how Lisa will be compensated for her devastating injuries. It is my hope that you will be fair and generous in your decision-making. My client is entitled to recover for pain and suffering, embarrassment and humiliation, for her medical costs and lost income, and for everything else that she endured as a proximate result of the bus striking her.

Opening Statement by Diane Dunne, Esq., Defense Attorney

Ladies and gentlemen of the jury, I represent the bus driver. We are here today because of an unfortunate accident. Accidents are just that — accidents. My client did not get up that morning saying to himself, "Who can I hit today?" The very unfortunate accident was our fault. We admit that. We are here to decide what to do about Lisa. You will hear testimony that Lisa has made an excellent recovery. She rides her bike and drives her car. Lisa is very active today — perhaps more active than many people. She is not in a wheelchair, and she can work. I would ask that you keep that in mind when you complete your job on the jury.

Motion in Limine

Judge: Mr. Pierson, before you call your first witness, I understand that there is a motion to be heard. Jury, you may be excused. When you return to the jury room, remember my earlier instruction that you are not to discuss this case amongst you. Mrs. Dunne, I understand that you have filed a motion in limine to preclude the testimony of Nurse Iyer. You may present your position.

Diane Dunne: Your Honor, the defense objects to the use of Nurse Iyer as an expert in this trial. She was not involved in the plaintiff's treatment in any way. There are no nursing issues involved in this case. There are no claims of medical malpractice in the care of this patient. Since plaintiff intends to call her treating physicians as witnesses, Nurse Iyer's testimony is cumulative of the testimony of her doctors and the plaintiff herself. Nurse Iyer's report, exhibits, and slide show are highly prejudicial and inflammatory, and given the cumulative nature of the report, that prejudice far outweighs any marginal probative value.

Nurse Iyer's background and expertise are strictly in nursing. She lacks any specialized medical education or experience. The practice of professional nursing is defined as "diagnosing and treating human responses to actual or potential health problems through such services as case finding, health teaching, health counseling, and provision of care supportive to or restorative of life and well being, and executing medical regimens as prescribed by a licensed physician or dentist." Nurse Iyer lacks the skill, training, knowledge, or experience to summarize plaintiff's medical records. The medical records consist of medical diagnoses, treatments, and prognoses. A medical doctor, and not a nurse, is competent to provide analysis and summary of *medical* records. Nurse Iyer cannot provide such a summary. She is merely a nurse. Plaintiff's treating physicians are the appropriate personnel to explain the surgical procedures, diagnoses, and other purely medical details, as distinguished from nursing events. Nurse Iyer's mere familiarity with these matters does not qualify her to provide an appropriate, accurate, and reliable medical summary.

The primary purpose of expert testimony is to assist the trier of fact in understanding complicated matters, not simply to assist one party in winning their case. An examination of Nurse Iyer's report, exhibits, and slide show clearly demonstrates that she anticipates doing nothing more than selectively repeating the medical record without bringing any nursing expertise to bear upon issues pertinent to the fact-finder. Nowhere in the report does Nurse Iyer comment upon plaintiff's nursing regimen or any nursing-care-related issues. Plaintiff is perfectly capable of testifying about her course of treatment and symptoms.

Finally, Nurse Iyer's report and slide show contain photographs of the injuries of Lisa Miller. These photographs are highly prejudicial. Her report contains a diagram of Ms. Miller's fractured hip. This drawing is so rudimentary that it cannot properly be qualified or explained except by its author. Without the exhibit's caption, it is questionable whether anyone would know what it is.

Judge: Counsel, are you finished?

Diane Dunne: Yes, Your Honor.

Judge: Mr. Pierson, you may respond.

Paul Pierson: My esteemed adversary argued earlier that Nurse Iyer was not qualified to summarize medical records. As Ms. Dunne herself noted, the practice of nursing includes health teaching and the provision of care supportive to or restorative of life and well-being, and executing medical regimens as prescribed by a licensed physician. In order for Nurse Iyer to function as a nurse, she must be able to interpret and analyze medical records. Part of the role of the registered nurse is to be able to use and explain equipment such as Foley catheters, Hoyer lifts, Rotorest beds, nasogastric tubes, and the other equipment that is explained in her report. Patient education is a basic function of all nurses. Nurse Iyer will be applying her expertise in patient education to help the jury understand the medical and nursing details of Lisa Miller's care.

Nurse Iyer's testimony is permitted under Rule 702. It states: "If scientific, technical, or other specialized knowledge will assist the trier of fact to understand the evidence or to determine a fact in issue, a witness qualified as an expert by knowledge, skill, experience, training, or education may testify thereto in the form of an opinion or otherwise." As a registered nurse with 30 years of experience, Nurse Iyer has specialized knowledge beyond that possessed by the jury. She has expertise in understanding and interpreting medical records.

Your Honor, my adversary has argued that nowhere in Nurse Iyer's report does she comment on nursing-care-related issues. As you will note from reviewing her report, she comments on several nursing-care-related issues, including the symptoms my client experienced after she was run down by the bus driven by Mr. Felton.

Judge: Now, Mr. Pierson, let's stick to the arguments. Save the dramatics for the jury.

Paul Pierson: I'm sorry, Your Honor. Nurse Iyer's report describes the many sources of discomfort my client experienced, her difficulty eating, her emotional distress, her dependence on others, just to name a few. These are all issues that nurses are educated to treat as part of their role in providing care to patients such as my client. Further, my adversary has argued that my client, Lisa Miller, is capable of testifying about her medical treatment and symptoms. My client was sedated for part of her admission, although capable of feeling and reacting to her medical treatment. She lacks the specialized knowledge and training that Nurse Iyer has, and is unable to explain to the jury why certain treatments were performed on her. Nurse Iyer has the educational background to be able to explain the drawing of Miss Miller's fractured hip, one that my adversary objected to as rudimentary. Clearly Nurse Iyer was able to understand it, when my adversary could not! This is exactly why the jury needs Nurse Iyer to help them understand what happened to my client. It is unclear how the defense can assert that Ms. Iyer serves no useful purpose whatsoever when, in fact, she has just assisted the defense counsel to understand the nature of Ms. Miller's pelvic fractures.

Further, the defense has had five months to obtain a counter expert, and they have no one. There is not a single defense expert who in any way questions the accuracy, appropriateness, or reliability of the medical information in Ms. Iyer's report. The defense's orthopedic surgeon reviewed Ms. Iyer's report as part of his medical opinion. He does not, in any manner, criticize her report. I'd like to stress that the defense argues that the plaintiff can testify to her course of medical treatment. My client, who had just been struck by a 30,000-pound bus going 55 miles per hour, was in no condition to even think! In a case such as this, where the plaintiff was in the hospital for three weeks, there would be testimony from at least 25–30 different health care professionals, including doctors, nurses, and therapists, to accurately convey that which Ms. Iyer is conveying in the course of approximately one hour's worth of testimony. To request that photographs of the plaintiff's injuries not be utilized at the time of the trial under the guise that they are prejudicial is simply wrong. In fact, it would be prejudicial to the plaintiff to not be able to accurately display the full extent of her injuries to the jury. These are simply photographs of bruises. Simply because the bruises may be a foot in circumference does not make them more prejudicial to the defense.

I would also cite Rule of Evidence 1006, which states that the "contents of voluminous writings, recordings, or photographs which cannot conveniently be examined in court may be presented in the form of a chart, summary, or calculation." Nurse Iyer's report and testimony will assist the jury in understanding my client's voluminous medical records.

Judge: Are you finished?

Paul Pierson: Yes, Your Honor.

Judge: Mrs. Dunne, do you have anything further?

Diane Dunne: Yes, if the court please. I want to add that Nurse Iyer continually states her personal interpretation of plaintiff's medical treatments. She frequently comments on plaintiff's injuries, using such terms as "large amounts of bruising," "extensive bruising," "fortunately did not disrupt her elbow joint," "maximum assistance," "moderate assistance," and "minimal assistance." The subjective nature of Nurse Iyer's characterization of plaintiff's injuries demonstrates that the sole purpose of this testimony is to excite the passions of the jury rather than to provide an accurate, brief, and objective summary of the medical record, which is too voluminous for the jury to otherwise comprehend.

Judge: Are you now finished?

Diane Dunne: Yes, Your Honor.

Judge: Counsel, any response?

Paul Pierson: Yes, Your Honor. The comments that my esteemed colleague has just cited are taken directly from the medical records of my client. The terms are not Nurse Iyer's but those of the doctors, nurses, and therapists who attended my client. Why, if Mrs. Dunne would like to see, I can point out each term and where it is located in the medical record.

Judge: That will not be necessary, Mr. Pierson. I am satisfied that Nurse Iyer has performed a thorough review of the medical record. I agree that she possesses specialized skill, knowledge, experience, and training well beyond that of the average layperson. She is familiar with medical terminology and has worked with medical records in the course of her duties as a nurse. She has taken direction from medical professionals and implemented instructions and orders. I do not wish to spend excessive court time bringing in a parade of doctors and nurses to testify about the treatment they rendered to the plaintiff.

Furthermore, I agree that the medical records are voluminous in this case and filled with symbols, abbreviations, and terms not understood by the average layperson. I find that the medical records are difficult to interpret without Nurse Iyer's testimony. I do not believe that Lisa Miller's doctors are prepared to render such detailed and extensive testimony as Nurse Iyer will in this case. I find that the Pennsylvania Rules of Evidence permit this type of witness to testify. Further, I do not find the photographs of the plaintiff to be prejudicial. The images of normal anatomy are also acceptable, as they are intended to provide the jury with an understanding of the issues in this case. Her testimony is permitted, and I will allow the jury to hear her. Further, I will allow the jury to see the photographs of the plaintiff that are part of the slide presentation. Anything further, Mrs. Dunne?

Diane Dunne: Judge, Nurse Iyer's report does not constitute evidence in this case. We respectfully ask the court to prohibit Nurse Iyer's report from being entered into evidence or being placed with the jury while they deliberate.

Judge: I disagree. Nurse Iyer may testify, and her report will be placed into evidence. Mr. Pierson, you may call Nurse Iyer to the stand.

Chapter 37

The Life Care Planning Expert

Mona Yudkoff, BSN, MA, RN, MPH, CRRN, CCM, CLCP

CONTENTS

Objectives

- To utilize a life care plan in assessment of damages in a personal injury case
- To choose an appropriate and qualified life care planner
- To state the steps required to complete a life care plan
- To describe legal and ethical principles critical to effective use of life care planning in assessment of damages
- To understand the deposition process
- To prepare for deposition
- To understand the trial testimony process
- To prepare for trial testimony on damages
- To help prepare the life care planner for trial testimony

Case Preparation

Introduction

The unspoken question foremost in litigation is: "How much is this case worth?" In personal injury cases, including medical malpractice and product liability, damages are directly related to the injuries suffered by the plaintiff. These injuries may include bodily harm, psychological damage, loss of future earnings, and pain and suffering. A quantifiable estimate of future costs to the plaintiff resulting from the injury is critical to the assessment of the case's value. The life care plan is a time extension of the traditional nursing-care plan, designed to allocate resources for the injured person's lifetime. In the clinical setting, the completed plan is a comprehensive assessment of all of the patient's future needs over time. In litigation, a life care plan relates specifically to disability subsequent to the catastrophic illness or injury alleged to have been caused by the defendant. Costs of care that are related to the plaintiff's preexisting conditions are not included in future projections.

On April 12, 2000, more than 100 professionals who were experienced in preparing life care plans met to discuss the process. They agreed that a life care plan is:

- Individualized to reflect specific needs and promote optimal health, function, and autonomy
- Objective and consistent
- A lifelong and flexible document
- Comprehensive and based on multidisciplinary data[1]

Insurance companies and medical case managers were the first professionals to use systematic projection of future costs, usually to set reserves for high-cost cases. Deutsch[2] first described the forensic use of the life care plan in the early 1980s. Today, use of life care planners in personal injury litigation has become standard procedure to present future medical damages in cases involving catastrophic injuries or illnesses.

Use of the Life Care Plan in Assessment of Damages

The life care planner educates the parties concerned about the impact of the disability on quality of life. Detailed analysis of the injured person's medical, allied medical, and psychosocial needs presents a clear picture of dollar costs, as well as cost in noneconomic resources, such as time, relationships, and self-esteem.

The life care plan is "an indispensable tool of the plaintiff's attorney in catastrophic injury cases. A valid life care plan based on quantifiable data adds credibility to the plaintiff's proposal for settlement by providing a realistic picture of the plaintiff's future needs."[3] Money sought for settlement is therefore based on a factual description of need that is derived from firm and indisputable data.

In cases that go to trial, the life care plan assists the jury in understanding the need for the plaintiff's monetary demands. During this process, the jury also learns about physical and emotional resources required for the plaintiff's care.

Defense attorneys are responsible for mitigating damages if they fail to disprove liability. Life care planners are frequently retained by the defense to evaluate validity of the plaintiff's damages proposal. The defense attorney must present "reasonable" damages without offending the jury or appearing insensitive to the plight of the injured party. The life care planner may be retained by the defense counsel to develop strategies for cross-examination of the plaintiff's expert or to present an alternative strategy for meeting the injured party's needs in a more economical manner.[4]

Choosing an Appropriate and Qualified Life Care Planner

In most ways, choosing a life care plan expert is similar to choosing any medical expert. Credibility is the most important factor. This characteristic is determined by a combination of appropriate education, relevant experience, recognized credentials, communications skills, and professional appearance.

A life care planner should always be a rehabilitation professional. Significant hands-on experience in care of persons with chronic and catastrophic deficits is critical. In addition, the life care planner should have case management experience, a role that includes coordination of services to the catastrophically ill or injured. Familiarity with vendors and health care providers, as well as the ability to find these sources in various locales, is essential. The expert should have professional background, certification, and experience that are relevant to the diagnosis, age, and medical needs of the plaintiff.

> Nurses are often uniquely qualified to prepare life care plans. They have the medical training and experience to understand the needs of an injured person and to anticipate those needs or services which have not yet been addressed by health care providers. In addition, nurses traditionally have played a pivotal role in rehabilitation medicine as facilitators of the management of disabled patients. Nurses are well experienced in organizing plans of care and coordinating the recommendations of team members.[5]

Witness credibility depends greatly on credentials. Advanced academic preparation shows an enriched knowledge base with commitment to professionalism.

Attendance at professional meetings, conferences, and continuing-education courses demonstrates ongoing acquisition of current skills and knowledge.

Rehabilitation nurses can earn specialty certification to demonstrate peer recognition of experience and expertise. Valid certifications are offered by professional organizations, which should be independent of special interests. Certification may help the law firm to identify the rehabilitation nurse whose background best suits the individual case. Rehabilitation nurses who are also life care planners often have one or more of these specialty certifications:

- C.R.R.N. (Certified Registered Rehabilitation Nurse) — demonstrates experience in rehabilitation nursing and the strong knowledge base required to understand, address, and explain complex medical needs resulting from severe injuries or illnesses. This medical background may be especially important when the damages represent only a part of the total impairment, e.g., a case with a preexisting medical condition.
- C.C.M. (Certified Case Manager) — indicates multidisciplinary certification reflecting experience and expertise in coordinating and obtaining rehabilitation services.
- C.R.C. (Certified Rehabilitation Counselor) or C.D.M.S. (Certified Disability Management Specialist), which has replaced the CIRS (Certified Insurance Rehabilitation Specialist), may be the appropriate credential in a case in which significant damages are related to retooling of the plaintiff's vocational life.
- C.L.C.P. (Certified Life Care Planner) — indicates multidisciplinary certification reflecting experience and expertise in preparing life care plans.
- C.N.L.C.P. (Certified Nurse Life Care Planner) — a professional nursing certification reflecting experience and expertise in preparing life care plans.

Inclusion of the above certifications in this chapter does not imply validation by the American Association of Legal Nurse Consultants. The retaining attorney or the firm's legal nurse consultant (LNC) must evaluate the validity of certifications presented by a life care planner.

Steps Required to Complete a Life Care Plan

Assessment

The life care planning process begins with complete assessment of the injured person and his or her medical history. All records relevant to damages should be reviewed. Record packets prepared for experts in liability or causation cases are often irrelevant and incomplete for the purpose of determining damages. It may be necessary to request ongoing treatment records and additional assessments to build an adequate foundation for the opinions of the life care plan. In some cases, a literature search may be needed to define the expected course and treatment of a particular diagnosis.

A face-to-face meeting with the injured person is almost always beneficial. The injured person's home is usually the most productive environment for the gathering of information, because detailed descriptions are necessary when accessibility modifications are recommended. The assessment interview should include the primary caregiver. When the plaintiff has sustained cognitive injuries, is unable to communicate, or is a minor child, the caregiver is the primary source of information regarding daily care.

The injured person's health care providers should be solicited for input into future care. When future care is not discussed in the records, it is usually appropriate to seek information directly from the physician or other providers. It is always necessary to inform the plaintiff's attorney before contacting any parties regarding the plaintiff. In many cases, it is necessary to obtain release forms from the attorney's office. It is often more difficult to contact providers when working for the defense attorney. The defense attorney needs to provide assistance in obtaining necessary input.

Determining the Needs

Each recommendation in the life care plan must be supported by medical records and input from health care providers. Services and products must be available in reasonable proximity to the plaintiff's residence. The plan should provide the reader with a clear rationale for the relationship between recommended services and damages. It is critical to evaluate duration and frequency of recommended services and products, as well as to delineate changes in frequency, which could be due to growth, disease process, complications, aging, or other factors.

Cost of Services

Costs in the life care plan are always presented in today's dollars. The attorney usually retains an economist to interpret the numbers, incorporating inflation, interest rates, and other economic factors. These calculations are beyond the scope of expertise of most rehabilitation nurses. The economist must ensure that the final cost projection conforms to local jurisdiction rulings. Costs should reflect usual and customary rates in the geographic area proximate to the injured person's home. Whenever possible, the plaintiff's own treatment providers should be used as resources for development of cost estimates. If the injured person is not currently receiving the recommended service, a representative sample of appropriate providers should be referenced. The life care planner should use the middle range of costs as a reasonable estimate of the cost of future care, or show the entire range and let the jury determine appropriate allocation.

The Life Care Plan

The life care planner should always determine whether a written report is desired. In some cases, the attorney may request a verbal report before a written and discoverable document is prepared. This occurs more often when the plan has been prepared for the defense.

Although life care planners use a variety of formats, basic writing principles for expert reports apply. The ultimate goal is a clear picture of the injured person's needs, as well as the relationship of these requirements to the plaintiff's injury. Clarity and brevity are essential. A well-prepared life care plan projects damages in a defensible and organized report. Each plan is unique, reflecting the medical needs, family composition, values, cultural variants, and premorbid lifestyle of the plaintiff.

In most cases, the plan begins with a brief summary of the plaintiff's medical history, current status, and description of the injury's impact on daily life. In addition to the plaintiff's needs and associated costs, the report should also identify documents that were reviewed and cost sources that were utilized. See Appendix 37.1 for a sample life care plan.

The life care plan should project a fair and comprehensive assessment of the plaintiff's needs, relative to the damages in the case. All aspects of the plaintiff's care should be addressed, including medical care, therapeutic modalities, surveillance, preventive care, equipment, supplies, medications, diagnostic testing, hospital care, accessibility (housing), transportation, psychological support, case management, and attendant care. The goal of the life care plan is to allow the injured party to approximate as closely as possible the levels of independent function and quality of life that could have reasonably been expected if the injury had not occurred.

Medical care projections should incorporate costs of care by physicians, allied health professionals, and therapeutic modalities, as well as costs associated with diagnostic testing and anticipated hospitalizations and procedures. Surveillance or preventive care should be included to prevent or retard further complications. Costs of durable equipment should include replacement costs, length of expected service, and annual maintenance charges. Both unit cost and frequency of use should be described in lists of costs for medications and supplies. When housing modifications are needed to improve accessibility, the life care planner should provide a detailed assessment of the current home and specific modifications recommended. In most life care plans, the cost of attendant care or respite services is the most expensive item. It is important to be able to justify the level of home care personnel recommended (R.N., L.P.N., or aide). The frequency of service should also be clearly explained. Services should not be duplicated. If services are provided to prevent complications, then the cost of those complications should not be included.

Cost projections in the life care plan should be organized by modality and by the years (of age of the plaintiff) for which the service will be required. A summary table significantly facilitates the economist's work and also allows the jury to understand clearly that the life care plan is a fluid document. It should be apparent that the life care planner has taken into account any changes that the plaintiff is likely to undergo over the course of a lifetime. Table 37.1 shows a sample summary table from a completed life care plan. The columns represent the annual cost for each year in a particular age grouping. The first year includes one-time costs for housing modifications and for an initial period of intensive counseling. The break between ages 16 and 17 shows that when full skeletal growth is reached, equipment replacement periods lengthen and frequency of some physician follow-up decreases. Attendant care needs are increased at age 22 to relieve the parents of the need for ongoing around-the-clock supervision. This relates to the goal of restoring family members to the quality of life that they could have expected without the injury. Most parents are not responsible for the daily (and hourly) needs of their adult children. The column for facility-based care shows what would be needed if the family could no longer care for the injured person, due to aging of parents or other factors. The table should indicate costs that are included in

Table 37.1   Summary of Annual Costs by Age

	6 Years	7–16 Years	17–21 Years	22 Years–Life (Home)	22 Years–Life (Facility)
Medical care	$49,547	$49,547	$49,035	$49,035	$49,035
Equipment	$11,855	$11,855	$10,599	$10,599	$9,079
Rehabilitation	$1,184	$1,184	$1,184	$592	$0
Housing	$129,300	$1,500	$1,500	$1,500	$0
Transportation	$5,009	$5,009	$5,009	$5,009	$0
Supportive services	$6,200	$1,800	$1,800	$1,200	$0
Attendant care	$60,636	$60,636	$60,636	$271,560	$73,000
Total annual cost	$263,731	$131,531	$129,763	$339,495	$131,114

the facility's per diem charges. Some life care planners do not include pages with summaries or totals, and some use a "year-by-year" format. The life care planner should consult with the attorney and economist to choose a particular format.

Life Care Plan Reviews

The nurse life care planner may be retained by the defense attorney to provide commentary on the life care plan presented by the plaintiff. A life care plan review addresses only those issues presented in the plaintiff's plan. Each issue should be evaluated for appropriateness to the injury, relevance to the litigated damage, reasonableness of the cost, and availability of the service in an area that is geographically close to the plaintiff. The defense attorney may request an oral report before receiving the life care planner's written opinions. A face-to-face assessment of the plaintiff should always be requested, so that the plaintiff's attorney cannot utilize the absence of such a meeting to impeach credibility. In some cases, the defense attorney may request a complete life care plan, independent of the plaintiff's submission.

The nurse life care planner can assist the defense attorney in building his or her case. The attorney may be particularly interested in potential sources of investigation to delineate the premorbid condition. For example, examination of school records or work history may show premorbid cognitive deficits that mitigate some of the alleged damages.

Collateral sources such as government or private agencies may provide necessary services and equipment at a reduced fee. The admissibility of such collateral sources depends upon the local rules of evidence. When admissible, collateral sources show that the plaintiff would not go untreated if the litigation favored the defendant. Appendix 37.2 shows a sample life care plan review.

Legal and Ethical Principles in Effective Use of Life Care Planning in the Assessment of Damages

The life care plan should present a comprehensive and accurate representation of the plaintiff's needs. The life care planner's role is to *educate* attorneys and the jury about the disability sustained by the plaintiff. All services in the plan must be appropriate, reasonable, and necessary. The life care planner is not an advocate for the injured person. The opinions of the life care planner should not depend on whether he or she is retained by the attorney for the defense or for the plaintiff.

Quality of life is often an issue in determining needs. Proposed services should reflect an attempt to restore the plaintiff (or the plaintiff's family) to the approximate lifestyle that may have been realized if the disability had not occurred. This discussion is particularly relevant to resources intended to increase the plaintiff's independent function or to provide respite for the primary caregiver.

The life care plan should be a unique document that has been individualized to the circumstances of the plaintiff's injury and premorbid lifestyle. It is usually appropriate to consider cultural and sociological factors in determining needs. Costs included in overall projections should be relevant to the damages, addressing only incremental costs specific to the litigated injury. Costs associated with preexisting conditions should be clearly identified. Use of collateral funding sources as an offset for projected costs depends on the local jurisdiction of the case. In some states, collateral sources are allowed as evidence. The distinction between those needs that will possibly occur and those that are probable within a reasonable degree of professional certainty must be clearly noted. Vendors, health care providers, and projected costs should be clearly annotated. All sources should be local for the plaintiff.

The damages expert should not address liability, causation, or standard of care. It is critical that the life care planning expert remain within the life care planning field of expertise. The report should provide an appropriate foundation for all opinions, especially those related to future care from physicians, therapists, and other nonnursing health care providers. Opinions on life expectancy or economic considerations related to the life care plan, but not within the expert's scope of practice, should be clearly referenced. It is rarely appropriate for the life care planner to serve also as a liability expert on the same case. As is the case for all expert witnesses, compensation should never be dependent on the outcome of the case.

The Deposition Process

This discussion is specific to depositions taken to identify damages. See Chapter 1 and Chapter 35 for general instructions regarding preparing for a deposition.

File Review

Careful file review precedes the deposition. The deposition request may include a call for the expert's entire file. The opposing attorney is entitled to review all notes, drafts, resources, and records in the file. File maintenance should be a priority throughout all stages of consulting. The expert should bring an updated curriculum vitae to the deposition because counsel may want to explore the expert's background in great detail.

Before the deposition, the life care planner should review any current medical records that have been generated between completion of the report and date of deposition. The plaintiff's expert should contact the plaintiff or caregiver for an update if the deposition takes place several months (or more) after the completion of the report. The defense expert should request an update on the plaintiff's condition through the defending attorney's office. Depositions and reports of other expert witnesses should also be reviewed.

Preparation with the Attorney

The deposition is essentially a dress rehearsal for trial testimony. The opposing attorney uses the deposition to evaluate validity of testimony and quality of the presentation. "The expert can be challenged on each and every aspect of his review of the material, familiarity with it, the course and conduct of the examination and the opinions. The plaintiff attorney is there to test the knowledge of the witness and also to judge the relative effectiveness of the defense RHE's (Rehabilitation/Habilitation Expert) presentation versus his own."[2] Before the deposition, the attorney should review all areas of anticipated questioning with the life care planner.

Testimony

Deposition testimony differs from trial testimony in that the questioning begins with the opposing attorney. Most deposition time is allotted to the opposing attorney for cross-examination. The retaining attorney may elect to ask questions at the end of the deposition in order to get certain facts on the record before trial. Successful testimony in damages cases is dependent on consistency, credibility, and clarity, just as in all expert witness testimony. In some cases, the deposition may be videotaped and used at trial in place of live testimony from the expert.

Trial Testimony

File Review

This discussion is specific to trial testimony on damages. File review and update is the first step in preparing for trial testimony. With many months or years between preparation of the report and the trial date, an update of the file is required, even if no changes are made. Updated medical records must be obtained and reviewed. It may be helpful to speak with physicians, therapists, home health nurses, and vendors. The plaintiff or the plaintiff's caregiver should be contacted, and a new assessment interview is often appropriate. The life care planner should have a comfortable grasp of case details during testimony. Demonstrating knowledge of the plaintiff's condition without constant referral to files is most convincing.

Careful review of deposition testimony of the plaintiff, caregivers, other damages experts, and defendants provides critical information about the opposing attorney's theories in the case as well as the attorney's style of cross-examination.

It is also helpful to review one's own deposition testimony. The opposing lawyer may seek to elicit contradictions in prior testimony by reading sections of the deposition to the jury. Explanations for any changes in opinions between deposition and trial should be carefully considered.

Preparation with the Attorney

The retaining attorney should carefully review all aspects of trial testimony with the life care planner. Some attorneys prefer to rehearse direct examination, while others prefer more general discussions of the point to be covered. Preparation is most critical in regard to cross-examination questions. The attorney and life care planner must anticipate the strategy of the opposing attorney and prepare concise answers to expected areas of attack. Expert testimony involving damages is usually presented toward the end of trial, which provides opportunity to discuss previous testimony. It is helpful for the life care planner to know what the jury has already heard.

Testimony

Testimony focuses initially on the expert's qualifications. The witness must be able to present background information and credentials in a clear, confident, and impressive manner. The jury must regard the witness's testimony as credible and important to the verdict. The opposing attorney may attempt to disqualify all or part of the life care planner's opinions by arguing that a nurse may testify only about nursing issues. It is critical that the rehabilitation nurse's professional role in recommending participation of other health care disciplines be established during the presentation of the witness's credentials. It is helpful to have the life care planner qualified as an expert in rehabilitation or case management and not solely as an expert in nursing.

Recent legal decisions have affected the process of qualifying experts. Some jurisdictions demand more rigorous standards of proof of expertise. The nurse life care planner can utilize the state nurse practice act to show that the role of the nurse includes assessing patients, developing nursing diagnoses, devising plans of care, implementing plans of care, and evaluating the patient's response to the plan of care. All the steps involved in the preparation of the life care plan are clearly included in the scope of nursing practice. The nurse life care planner should discuss the issue of qualifications with the attorney prior to the trial in order to have a strong foundation.

The life care planner will be asked about remuneration, in the attempt to assign "hired-gun" status to testimony. It must be clear that fees are not related to the outcome of the case. It is usually helpful if the expert has testified in prior cases on behalf of both plaintiffs and defendants.

During direct examination, the opinions expressed by the life care planner are presented. The attorney usually leads up to specific recommendations with an introduction to the life care planning process itself. The opposing attorney attempts to prove that the life care planner's opinions are invalid. A well-written, defensible life care plan is the best preparation for cross-examination.

References

1. Weed, R. and Berens, M.S., Eds., *Life Care Planning Summit, Proceedings*, Elliot and Fitzpatrick, Inc., Athens, GA, 2000.
2. Deutsch, P.A., *Guide to Rehabilitation Testimony: The Expert's Role as an Educator*, PMD Press, Orlando, FL, 1990, 17.
3. Elliot, T., The plaintiff's view of the life care plan for the catastrophic case, *Natl. Assoc. Rehabil. Professionals Private Sector J.*, 9, 69, 1994.
4. Gunn, L.D., IV, Life care planning — a defense perspective, *Natl. Assoc. Rehabil. Professionals Private Sector J.*, 9, 63–77, 1994.
5. Yudkoff, M. and Iyer, P., The life care plan expert, in Iyer, P., Ed., *Nursing Malpractice*, 2nd ed., Lawyers and Judges Publishing Company, Tucson, AZ, 2001, 652.

Additional Reading

Barker, E., Life care planning, *RN*, 62(3), 58, 1999.

Casuto, D. and McCollum, P., Life care planning, in O'Keefe, M., Ed., *Nursing Practice and the Law*, F.A. Davis, Philadelphia, 2000, chap. 23.

Deutsch, P., *A Guide to Rehabilitation Testimony: The Expert's Role as an Educator*, PMD Press, Orlando, FL, 1990.

Deutsch, P., Life care planning: into the future, *Natl. Assoc. Rehabil. Professionals Private Sector J.*, 9, 79, 1994.

Deutsch, P. and Sawyer, H., *Guide to Rehabilitation*, Ahab Press, Purchase, NY, 1999.

Elliot, T., The plaintiff's view of the life care plan for the catastrophic case, *Natl. Assoc. Rehabil. Professionals Private Sector J.*, 9 69, 1994.

Gunn, L.D., IV, Life care planning — a defense perspective, *Natl. Assoc. Rehabil. Professionals Private Sector J.*, 9, 63, 1994.

McCollum, P., Life care planning, in Johnson, K., Ed., *Advanced Nursing Practice in Rehabilitation: A Core Curriculum*, ARN, Glenview, IL, 1997, 251–255.

Powers, A.S., Life care planning: the role of the legal nurse, *Natl. Assoc. Rehabil. Professionals Private Sector J.*, 9, 51, 1994.

Weed, R., *Life Care Planning and Case Management Handbook*, CRC Press, Boca Raton, FL, 1999.

Weed, R. and Berens, M.S., Eds., *Life Care Planning Summit, 2000, Proceedings*, Elliot and Fitzpatrick, Inc., Athens, GA, 2000.

Weed, R. and Field, T., *The Rehabilitation Consultant's Handbook*, Elliot and Fitzpatrick, Inc., Athens, GA, 1994.

Certifying Bodies

Certification of Disability Management Commission, 1835 Rohlwing Road, Suite E, Rolling Meadows, IL 60008; (847) 394–2106 (C.C.M., C.D.M.S., C.R.C.)

Commission on Disability Examiner Certification, 13325 Queensgate Road, Midlothian, VA; (804) 359–3563 (C.L.C.P.)

Professional Testing Corporation, 1350 Broadway, 17th Floor, New York, NY 10018; (212) 356–0660 (C.N.L.C.P.)

Rehabilitation Nursing Certification Board, Association of Rehabilitation Nurses, 4700 W. Lake Avenue, Glenview, IL 60025-1485; (800) 229–7530 (C.R.R.N.)

Test Questions

1. A life care planner should always have the following qualification:
   A. Extensive experience in all the stages of the rehabilitation process
   B. Training or education in the field of law
   C. At least a master's degree in his or her professional field
   D. Experience in public speaking

2. The life care plan in the litigation setting includes
   A. All the needs of the plaintiff, including food and housing
   B. All the medical needs of the plaintiff, including all physician treatment and medications
   C. Only the rehabilitation needs of the plaintiff
   D. Incremental needs of the plaintiff related to the injuries alleged in the action

3. The needs in the life care plan are not based on
   A. Input of the plaintiff's medical providers and medical records
   B. "Wish list" of the plaintiff
   C. Knowledge base of the life care planner
   D. Information gathered in the assessment

4. In reviewing a life care plan for the defense, the life care planner should NOT consider
   A. General needs of the plaintiff related to preexisting medical diagnoses
   B. Accuracy of the costs projected
   C. Relation of the recommendations to the injuries alleged in the action
   D. Appropriateness of the recommendations

5. Opinions of the life care planner should NOT be
   A. Clearly within the limits of his or her professional expertise
   B. An objective assessment of the needs related to the injuries in the action
   C. Dependent on the referral source (plaintiff or defense)
   D. Well supported by appropriate professional foundation

Answers: 1. A, 2. D, 3. B, 4. A, 5. C

Appendix 37.1
Sample Life Care Plan*

LIFE CARE PLAN
John Doe

Date of Birth   4/9/71
Date of Report   3/8/01

MONA GOLDMAN YUDKOFF, R.N., M.P.H.
C.R.R.N., Certified Rehabilitation Nurse
P.O. Box 745
Bala Cynwyd, PA 19004 (610) 664-8760

Contents

Introduction to the Life Care Plan for John Doe

John Doe is a 29-year-old male who was injured in a motor vehicle accident on February 2, 1998. After surgery to repair an aortic dissection, Mr. Doe was paralyzed in both legs. Prior to this injury, Mr. Doe led an active and independent lifestyle. He was employed at Home Depot while saving money to complete his bachelor's degree in psychology toward his goal of a clinical psychology career. Mr. Doe frequently played tennis and basketball, and he enjoyed participating in many sports on an informal basis. He was able to complete all his personal care without assistance and assisted with both indoor and outdoor maintenance on his family home. Mr. Doe was responsible for gardening, snow removal, and some house-cleaning. He helped to paint both the inside and the outside of the home.

Today, this gentleman requires assistance with all activities of daily living. He is unable to walk, has no control of his bowel or bladder, and is able to work only part-time. Mr. Doe must depend on friends and family for help with his most personal functions. He will always require assistance with personal care and home maintenance. Most painful to him is his diminished ability to form adult relationships and to play sports with his friends.

The purpose of this report is to outline necessary services and devices that Mr. Doe will require in the future as a result of his injuries. Medical care and therapy will ensure early detection of complications. An accessible home is recommended to increase independent function. Equipment is needed to maximize comfort, physiologic function, and independence. Psychological support may help Mr. Doe facilitate a healthy and productive adjustment to his chronic handicaps.

Mr. Doe was assessed on June 10, 2000 at his family home in Philadelphia. His mother, Jane Smith, and her husband, John Smith, were present for the assessment.

According to the physiatrist, Mr. Doe has a normal life expectancy with appropriate care. Life expectancy for a 29-year-old male is 45.9 additional years, based on Table 3, "Expectation of Life at Single Years of Age, by Race and Sex: United States, 1996," from *National Vital Statistics Reports*, National Center for Health Statistics, Hyattsville, Maryland, Volume 47, Number 13, December 24, 1998, Page 10.

All costs are based on today's dollars without regard for inflation, cost-of-living increases, or other economic considerations. This report may be amended or supplemented upon the receipt of additional medical records or evaluations. Opinions expressed in this report are held to a reasonable degree of professional certainty.

Mona Goldman Yudkoff, RN

Medical History

Prior to the motor vehicle accident on 2/2/98, John Doe was a healthy and physically active 26-year-old male. At the scene of the accident, he was reported to be conscious but unresponsive to stimuli, with garbled speech and severe pain. He was taken to the emergency room at Local Hospital, where he had gross blood in the Foley catheter. A CT scan of his abdomen showed a thoracic aortic dissection, mediastinal hematoma, rib fractures, renal contusion, bladder perforation, and right acetabular fracture. Mr. Doe was intubated and taken immediately to the operating room for the placement of a chest tube and suprapubic tube, as well as for repair of his bladder.

That same day, he was transferred to Major Hospital due to a diagnosis of aortic dissection and trauma to the distal aorta. The admitting physical examination note states that Mr. Doe moved all his extremities prior to having surgery for resection of the proximal descending aorta with the placement of a tube graft. He was unable to move his lower extremities following the procedure. On 2/6/98, he returned to the operating room for an open reduction and internal fixation of the right acetabulum. The discharge note for this admission states, "Pt. suffered an ischemic injury to T8-T10 vertebral levels during X-clamping of aorta."

Mr. Doe was transferred on 2/16/98 to Good Rehabilitation Hospital, where he remained until 3/18/98. The suprapubic tube remained unclamped throughout the night, and urine drained into a bag. He learned to do intermittent catheterizations during the day. At the time of discharge from Good Rehabilitation Hospital, Mr. Doe was independent with transfers and wheelchair mobility. He needed assistance with some activities of daily living, and all skin ulcers had healed.

Home care nurses visited 13 times. He also had four sessions of homebound occupational therapy and two sessions with the social worker. He received 1 month of daily outpatient therapy in August 1998. He was seen in follow-up at Good Rehabilitation Hospital by the physiatrist. Intermittent skin ulcers remained a persistent management problem.

Mr. Doe was admitted to Neighborhood Hospital on 7/9/98, where he remained until 7/16/98, due to a small bowel obstruction. He underwent surgery, in which approximately 20 centimeters of necrotic intestine was removed.

Mr. Doe reports that he was treated at least twice by the urologist for urinary tract infections.

Mr. Doe was seen twice by a psychologist. The sessions focused on Mr. Doe's grief regarding his altered physical capability.

He was seen in the emergency room at Neighborhood Hospital on 2/15/00 because of severe leg pain related to muscle cramping.

Current Status

Mr. Doe has a spinal cord injury at the lower thoracic level. He has reasonable head control and some trunk control, and his upper extremity function is within normal limits. He has no voluntary movement or sensation in his lower extremities. Swelling in both feet increases when he is sitting in his wheelchair. He complains of back and neck pain, and throbbing in both legs. Mr. Doe reports that contractures in his hips prevent him from standing to exercise. Muscle spasms cause mild to moderate discomfort.

Mr. Doe has both neurogenic bowel and bladder. He performs intermittent catheterizations for urine collection and wears a diaper most of the time to mask leakage. Bowel function is spontaneous and uncontrolled. Mr. Doe often has embarrassing fecal incontinence and/or flatulence. He has learned to manage his diet in an attempt to prevent diarrhea. He avoids dairy products and other foods that cause him to have gastric distress. Sexual function is impaired; Mr. Doe reports that he is unable to have an erection or to ejaculate. Skin care has been an ongoing management challenge. He currently has a large open area on his toes.

Mr. Doe uses a manual wheelchair. He is able to transfer independently. In a totally accessible environment, Mr. Doe can attend to his own personal needs. However, the process of bathing, dressing, and getting ready for the day takes more than 2 hours and is exhausting.

Cold weather causes increased leg pains. In hot weather, Mr. Doe has trouble regulating his body temperature and must remain in air-conditioned environments.

His social contacts and ability to access community activities have been significantly diminished. Mr. Doe is employed part-time as a receptionist.

Needs

Total Lifetime Costs for John Doe
(assumes a life expectancy of 45.9 additional years from next birthday)

$ 3,348,306

Summary of Annual Costs by Modality

	One-Time Cost	First Year (age 29)	Age 30–49	Age 50–65	66–Life
Primary Care	$ 0	$ 92	$ 92	$ 92	$ 92
Physiatry	$ 0	$ 785	$ 785	$ 785	$ 785
Urology	$ 0	$ 2,115	$ 2,115	$ 2,115	$ 2,115
Orthopedics	$ 0	$ 195	$ 195	$ 195	$ 195
Podiatry	$ 0	$ 600	$ 600	$ 600	$ 600
Therapeutic Modalities	$ 0	$ 1,232	$ 1,232	$ 1,232	$ 1,232
Counseling	$ 0	$ 4,250	$ 850	$ 850	$ 850
Case Management	$ 0	$ 2,304	$ 2,304	$ 2,304	$ 2,304
Hospital Care	$ 0	$ 8,552	$ 8,552	$ 8,552	$ 8,552
Equipment/Supplies/ Medication	$ 0	$ 13,370	$ 13,370	$ 13,370	$ 13,370
Transportation	$ 1,380	$ 5,953	$ 5,953	$ 5,953	$ 5,953
Attendant Care	$ 0	$ 17,575	$ 17,575	$ 35,150	$ 66,475
Housing	$ 167,200	$ 0	$ 0	$ 0	$ 0
Total Annual Costs	$ 167,200	$ 57,023	$ 53,623	$ 71,198	$ 102,523
Number of Years	once	1	20	16	8.9
Total Lifetime Costs	$ 167,200	$ 57,023	$ 1,072,460	$ 1,139,168	$ 912,455

Explanation of Costs

Primary Care

Clients with spinal cord injury require a comprehensive physical examination by their primary care physician at least annually, to monitor general health issues and to provide a baseline for the physician, so that deviations from normal health are clearly recognized. Dr. West expects to see Mr. Doe every 3–6 months. Therefore, an average of at least two visits/year, related specifically to issues resulting from the spinal cord injury, is included in this report.

    Cost: $ 46
    Annual Cost: **$ 92**

Physiatry

Mr. Doe is currently seen three to five times each year in the Spinal Cord Injury Clinic at Good Rehabilitation Hospital. Dr. Rehab states that this may diminish to an average of three times yearly. Mr. Doe is at risk for spinal curvatures, heterotopic ossification, and other orthopedic abnormalities. His upper extremity joints are subject to "overuse syndrome." Additional impairment to his arms would further diminish function. Home therapy to maintain strength and range of motion must be monitored and adjusted as needed. His functional level will be assessed in order to modify his home therapy program as necessary. Blood studies are required annually. Skin, bowel, and bladder protocols are monitored. Dr. Rehab states that Mr. Doe will require a CBC with differential, SMA 20, and PSA each year.

Cost:	$100–250 visit (average used)
	$ 29 CBC with differential
	$ 108 blood chemistry panel with lipids, liver function
	$ 123 PSA
Annual Cost:	$ **785 3 visits; blood tests annually**

Urology

Mr. Doe requires urologic consultations for genito-urinary and sexual dysfunction issues at least twice each year. Urinalysis and urine cultures will be needed, on average, at least four times each year. According to Dr. Waters, a cystometrogram, cystogram, and renal ultrasound will be done at least once each year, and an IVP will be needed periodically.

Cost:	$ 1VT 50 visit
	$ 10 urinalysis
	$ 100 culture and sensitivity screen
	$ 504 cystogram
	$ 685 renal ultrasound
	$ 220 cystometrogram
	$ 831 intravenous pyelogram (IVP)
Annual Cost:	$ **2,115 2 visits; U/A and culture 4x; IVP every 5 years; other studies annually**

Orthopedics

Mr. Doe has contractures in his hips that interfere with independent function. Persons with spinal cord injury are at increased risk of developing hip dislocations and scoliosis. Long-term orthopedic management will be required to follow the effects of spinal cord injury on physiologic function and on skills for independent living.

Cost:	$ 60 visit
	$ 365 x-rays, hips
	$ 310 x-rays, spine
Annual Cost:	$ **195 annual visit; x-rays every 5 years**

Podiatry

Mr. Doe has no sensation in his toes. He is at risk for serious foot infections. He should have his toenails clipped and his feet examined monthly by a professional podiatrist.

Cost:	$ 50 visit
Annual Cost:	$ **600**

Physical Therapy/Occupational Therapy

Mr. Doe should have a professional physical and occupational therapy evaluation at least once each year. The therapists will monitor independent function, implement and supervise a home therapy program, and prescribe appropriate daily living equipment. Mr. Doe is at risk for deconditioning and deterioration of function. He requires an average of 10–14 sessions each of outpatient occupational and physical therapy every 3–5 years.

Cost:	$	162 physical therapy evaluation/treatment session
	$	146 occupational therapy evaluation/treatment session
Annual Cost:	**$ 1,232**	**annual OT and PT evaluations; 3 sessions each OT and PT**

Functional Electronic Stimulation (FES)

Mr. Doe would benefit from aerobic conditioning with the para-step machine, which utilizes functional electronic stimulation to allow weight-bearing and aerobic exercise. The machine should be used daily. Initially, there should be several sessions of physical therapy involving training on proper use of the equipment. This should be followed by professional evaluations on a regular basis. The para-step machine should be replaced every 10 years.

Cost:	$	12,780 para-step machine
	$	14 set of 4 small electrodes, 12 sets/year
	$	19 set of 4 large electrodes, 24 sets/year
	$	7,164 initial training/physical therapy, 32 sessions
	$	149 PT session, 4 in first year, 2 in second year, then 1/year
	$	50 annual maintenance
One-Time Cost:	**$ 7,164**	**initial training/physical therapy**
	$ 596	**4 additional PT sessions during first 2 years**
Annual Cost:	**$ 2,101**	**machine, electrodes, maintenance, PT session**

Counseling

Mr. Doe must cope with major adjustments in his body image and ability to function as an independent individual. His relationships with friends and family members have changed significantly. One year of individual weekly therapy is recommended, followed by an average of at least ten weekly sessions per year for maintenance.

Cost:	$	85 session
Annual Cost:	**$ 4,250**	**50 sessions, 1st year (includes family members)**
	$ 850	**10 sessions/year thereafter**

Case Management

A rehabilitation case manager is necessary to assist Mr. Doe to coordinate all his medical and therapy needs and to access agencies that can provide needed services. An average of 8 hours of case management services will be required quarterly.

Cost: $ 72 hour
Annual Cost: $ 2,304

Hospital Care

Mr. Doe's decreased mobility and his muscle spasms put him at risk for pneumonia and other respiratory conditions, skin breakdown, muscle contractures, skeletal deformities, depression, and urinary and bowel dysfunction. Frequency of hospitalization will increase as he ages. While it is impossible to predict actual costs for these problems, it is conservative to estimate that he will have, on average, one 6-day hospitalization every 3 years.

Cost: $ 4,076 day: hospital charges, therapies, medications
                          $ 200 day: physicians' fees
Annual Cost: $ 8,552 2 days/year (average)

Note: these charges do not include surgical procedures, surgeons' fees, and operating time.

Equipment/Supplies/Medications

Equipment was selected to allow Mr. Doe to achieve his maximum level of independence. Emphasis is put on mobility, maintaining physiologic alignment, and providing a safe environment.

	Unit Cost	Replacement/ Usage	Annual Maintenance	Annual Cost
Equipment				
Manual Wheelchair, Invacare Action	$ 1,350	5 years	$ 150	$ 420
Jay Active Cushion	$ 320	2 years	–	$ 160
Power Wheelchair, Jazzy 1120v	$ 4,695	5 years	$ 500	$ 1,439
Jay Active Cushion	$ 320	2 years	–	$ 160
Stand-Aid, Model 1503 Lift & Drive	$ 7,895	5 years	$ 800	$ 2,379
Adaptive Equipment for ADL	$ 250	1 year	–	$ 250
Air Pressure Pump and Pad	$ 198	2 years	–	$ 99
Para-Gym	$ 2,617	10 years	$ 250	$ 512
Roll-In Shower Chair, Invacare 6492	$ 1,010	5 years	$ 100	$ 302
Hospital Bed, Rails, Invacare	$ 2,045	10 years	$ 150	$ 355
Computer	$ 2,500	5 years	–	$ 500
Supplies				
Collagenase Santyl, 30-gram tube	$ 55.00	2/month	–	$ 1,320

	Unit Cost	Replacement/ Usage	Annual Maintenance	Annual Cost
Supplies				
Bactroban Ointment, 15-gram tube	$ 22.65	2/year	–	$ 45
14 French Catheters, each	$ 1.00	150/month	–	$ 1,800
KY Jelly, surgilube, 2 oz	$ 2.75	18/year	–	$ 50
Urinal, plastic, each	$ 3.00	2/month	–	$ 72
Duoderm, 4 x 4, 20 sheets	$ 125.00	15/month	–	$ 1,125
Depends, large, 18	$ 18.75	105/month	–	$ 1,312
Wipes, 40	$ 6.75	40/week	–	$ 351
Gloves, 100	$ 8.00	6/day	–	$ 175
Creams and Lotions	$ 200.00	1 year	–	$ 200
Bed Pads, 72	$ 57.60	15/month	–	$ 144
Allowance for extra cleaning, wear & tear on clothing	$ 200.00	1 year	–	$ 200
Total Annual Cost				$ 13,370

Transportation

To facilitate mobility and foster increased independence, Mr. Doe needs a van outfitted with a raised roof and doors, dropped floor, semiautomatic power lift, hand controls, and power wheelchair tie-downs. Prior to the injury, Mr. Doe did not drive. He used public transportation and, therefore, an offset of $50/week ($2,600/year) is used against the purchase price of a van. The van will be replaced every 7 years. Mr. Doe will require a driving evaluation and driving lessons, to learn to operate the special controls.

Cost:	$ 24,400	purchase price of van
	$ 14,270	conversion, adaptations to van
	($ 2,600)	offset for normal transportation costs
	$ 800	annual maintenance on adaptations
	$ 180	driving evaluation
	$ 120	hour, driving lesson
Annual Cost:	**$ 5,953**	
Once Only:	**$ 1,380**	**driving evaluation, 10 lessons**

Attendant Care

In a properly designed home, with a power wheelchair and modified van, Mr. Doe could be independent in many areas of daily living. However, he would require assistance with some personal care, daily therapy exercises, bowel and bladder care, housekeeping, and some shopping and errands.

Mr. Doe requires an average of at least 2–4 hours a day of assistance. This will relieve his parents, who are providing much of his care, and also preserve his energy for more fulfilling activities. As he ages, his need for assistance will increase. A live-in attendant is the most economical way to provide around-the-clock coverage.

Cost:	$	175	day, live-in Home Health Aide (HHA)
	$	50	week, food and utilities for the live-in HHA
	$	16.05	hour, HHA
Annual Cost:	**$**	**17,575**	**3 hours/day, to age 49 years**
	$	**35,150**	**6 hours/day, age 50–65 years**
	$	**66,475**	**live-in attendant, age 66 years–life**

Housing

Mr. Doe and his family live in a three-bedroom semidetached home in Philadelphia. Both the front and back entrances have a full flight of steep steps to the main living areas of the home. Mr. and Mrs. Smith have converted their basement into a studio apartment for Mr. Doe, allowing him to enter and leave through the basement door, directly at ground level. Mr. Doe rarely goes upstairs. In order for him to sit in the living room or dining room with family members, someone must carry both Mr. Doe and his wheelchair up and down the steps. The house is not amenable to accessibility modifications due to its size and configuration.

An accessible home will facilitate independence in activities of daily living. Doorways should be wide enough to permit the wheelchair to pass safely. The home should have a fully accessible bathroom, with roll-in shower and an accessible sink and commode. The kitchen should have table-height counters that are accessible with modified storage, full-suspension drawers, and accessible appliances. Flooring must be wheelchair-friendly. The house may need ramps at the entryways. The bedroom should have an emergency exit. Parking must be accessible to the house and covered, to allow for use in inclement weather. Bedroom storage should be modified to allow independent access. Light switches should be lowered and outlets raised.

The Does purchased their three-bedroom home for $98,000 in 1998. The purchase price of this home is typical of the type of home that Mr. Doe could have lived in if he had not been injured. Therefore, the purchase price of the accessible ranch-style home has been reduced by $98,000 in consideration of the normal costs for housing.

Details of the housing modification costs may be found in the Addendum following this report.

Cost:	$ 184,900	ranch home (purchase price)
	(-$98,000)	offset for normal housing expenditure
	$ 13,000	closing and relocation costs
	$ 99,900	net price of home
	$ 6,200	front entrance modification
	$ 2,400	garage modification
	$ 4,200	rear entrance modification
	$ 20,000	accessible bathroom and bedroom
	$ 5,600	bedroom exit
	$ 1,200	doorways and openings
	$ 3,800	flooring
	$ 3,200	electrical and mechanical
	$ 13,000	kitchen

$ 3,200 laundry
$ 4,500 finishes, miscellaneous
Total Cost: **$167,200 net purchase with modifications**

Sources of Costing Estimates for This Life Care Plan

(*) Based on previously incurred expense
(**) Based on local facilities, vendors
(***) Based on national facilities, vendors

Primary Care

(*) A. West, M.D., Neighborhood Hospital Family Practice, Philadelphia, PA

Physiatry

(*) B. Rehab, M.D., Good Rehabilitation Hospital, Philadelphia, PA

Urology

(*) C. Waters, M.D., Philadelphia, PA
(*) Major Hospital, Department of Radiology, Philadelphia, PA
(*) Major Hospital, Department of Nuclear Medicine, Philadelphia, PA

Orthopedics

(*) D. Bone, M.D., University Hospital, Philadelphia, PA
(*) University Hospital, Department of Radiology, Philadelphia, PA

Podiatry

(*) J. Foot, D.P.M., Philadelphia, PA

Physical/Occupational Therapy

(**) Good Rehabilitation Hospital, Philadelphia, PA

Counseling

(*) H. Head, M.A., Philadelphia, PA

Case Management

(**) Good Rehabilitation Hospital, Philadelphia, PA

Hospital Care

(***) *Current Trends in Health Care and Dental Costs and Utilization*, Mutual of Omaha, 1998 Edition

Equipment/Supplies/Medications

(***) GPK Incorporated, Carlsbad, CA
(***) Invacare Corporation, Elyria, OH
(***) Stand-Aid of Iowa, Sheldon, IA
(***) Sammons Preston, Incorporated, Catalogue, Bolingbrook, IL
(**) Medical, Philadelphia, PA
(**) Medical Supply, Philadelphia, PA
(**) Pharmacy, Philadelphia, PA

Transportation

(**) Handi-Van, Incorporated, Philadelphia, PA
(**) Good Rehab Hospital, Philadelphia, PA

Attendant Care

(**) Health Services, Philadelphia, PA
(**) Baywatch Nurses, Philadelphia, PA

Housing

(**) Adaptive Design Associates, Swarthmore, PA

Documents Reviewed for This Life Care Plan

A. West, M.D.	records	4/21/98–6/25/98
	correspondence	6/9/00
Local Hospital	discharge summary	2/2/98–2/2/98
	records	2/2/98
Major Hospital	discharge summary	2/2/98–2/16/98
	admission, records	2/2/98–2/16/98
Good Rehabilitation Hospital	discharge summary	2/13/98–3/18/98
	admission, records	2/13/98–3/18/98
Neighborhood Hospital	admission, records	7/9/98–7/16/98
	ER admission, records	2/15/00
More Rehab	progress notes	5/22/90; 7/6/90
B. Rehab, M.D.	correspondence	6/9/00
	record of visit	7/20/00
H. Head, M.S.	treatment report	7/21/00
C. Waters, M.D.	records	6/22/98–7/8/98
Miscellaneous Invoices		

Appendix 37.2
Sample Life Care Plan Review*

JOHN "JACK" DOE

Date of Birth   4/15/96
Date of Report   3/15/00

MONA GOLDMAN YUDKOFF, R.N., M.P.H., C.R.R.N.
Certified Rehabilitation Nurse
P.O. Box 745
Bala Cynwyd, PA 19004 (610) 664–8760

Review of the Life Care Plan for John Doe

This report has been prepared as a response to the life care plan for John "Jack" Doe, a 47-month-old male with cerebral palsy, prepared by Susan Nurse, R.N. on July 30, 1999. To simplify comparison, the sections in the table on the next page follow the outline used in the life care plan presented by SN, RN and detail the cost projections by modality.

Mrs. Doe was interviewed in her attorney's office on March 6, 2000. Jack Doe was present during this assessment. Mrs. Doe noted that Jack has had ongoing medical follow-up. Specifically, he was seen by the pulmonologist and gastroenterologist in November 1999, the physiatrist in February 2000, and the ophthalmologist in September 1999. This report may be amended upon review of the medical records associated with those visits.

All costs are based on today's dollars without regard for inflation, cost-of-living increases, or other economic considerations. This report may be amended or supplemented upon the receipt of additional medical records or evaluations. Opinions expressed in this report are held to a reasonable degree of professional certainty.

_____
Mona Goldman Yudkoff, RN

The following records were reviewed for the preparation of this report:

Susan Nurse, RN	life care plan	7/30/99
Sam Black, M.D.	report	3/8/99
L. Hospital	admission, discharge summary	4/13/96–7/18/96
H. Medical Center	PT evaluation, progress report	5/26/98, 11/8/99
	OT notes	6/98, 1/99, 6/99
	initial evaluation	5/19/97
	ER record	6/21/97
	admission record	2/4/98–2/6/98
S.T. M.S.,		
John Doe, M.D.	genetic testing results	2/23/98

M Memorial Hospital	admission, discharge summary	10/4/96–10/6/96
	admission, discharge summary	10/15/96–11/1/96
	admission, discharge summary	12/26/96–1/1/97
	operative report	10/28/96
John Doe, M.D.	pediatric gastroenterology report	11/18/96
John Doe, M.D.	pediatric ophthalmology reports	3/7/97, 9/15/97
John Doe, M.D.	pediatric neurology report	1/22/97
Special Follow-Up Program	evaluations	4/9/97, 7/9/97
John Doe, R.N.C., John Doe, M.D.	report	12/5/96
Respiratory Center	apnea interpretation	10/28/96–11/27/96
	home apnea interpretation	11/27/96–1/6/97
John Doe, M.D.,	swallow study referral	undated
P & A Associates, P.A.	reports	7/19/96, 10/15/96, 11/12/96,
John Doe, M.D.,		
C S Hospital	evaluations	9/22/97, 12/22/97, 3/2/98, 3/3/99
John Doe	Botox injection	2/3/98
	deposition (relevant portions)	3/2/99

Total Lifetime Costs

(Using life expectancy of 70.7 additional years as provided
by SN for comparison only)

| S. Nurse | **$2,628,948** (corrected for math errors as noted below) |
| Yudkoff | **$1,284,240** |

Costs by Modality

Nurse	Yudkoff	Annual Costs		Total Lifetime Costs	
		SN	MGY	SN	MGY
Pediatrician, $50/yr	Pediatric care is for normal health issues; however, it is not unreasonable to allow one extra visit per year for specific issues.	$ 50	$ 50	$ 3,535	$ 3,535
Pulmonologist, $100, 4x/yr	Reasonable for several years, although likely to decrease in frequency over time.	$ 400	$ 400	$ 28,280	$ 28,280
Gastroenter. $100/yr	OK to age 12. Likely to be off of the feeding supplements by age 12.	$ 100 to 12	$ 100 to 12	$ 7,070	$ 900
Physiatrist, $100, 2x/yr	OK	$ 200	$ 200	$ 14,140	$ 14,140
Opthalmolog., $95/yr	OK	$ 95	$ 95	$ 6,717	$ 6,717

Nurse	Yudkoff	Annual Costs		Total Lifetime Costs	
		SN	MGY	SN	MGY
Hospital, $2,750/ day, 3 days/yr	Has decreasing respiratory compromise. Hospitalization related to his injuries is more likely to be orthopedic in nature. Looking at the entire lifespan it is reasonable to assume one hospitalization every 5 years on average.	$ 8,250	$ 1,650	$ 583,275	$ 116,655
Respite Care, $100, 28x/yr	OK	$ 2,800	$ 2,800	$ 197,960	$ 197,960
Psychological Support Jack $100, 12x/year	OK	$ 1,200	$ 1,200	$ 84,840	$ 84,840
Mother, $100, 12x/yr, 18 yrs	OK as written in text; Calculation	$ 21,600 once	$ 21,600 once	$ 21,600	$ 21,600
Sister, $100, 12x/yr, 18 yrs	error; 12/yr for 18 years totals 216 times in total, not annually	$ 21,600 once	$ 21,600 once	$ 21,600	$ 21,600
Case Manager $80/hr, 12 hrs/yr	OK	$ 960	$ 960	$ 67,872	$ 67,872
Accessible Van $45,000/8.33 years	Current auto is a 1999 Toyota 4-Runner—which is in the same price range as a van. Allow for modifications only—$15,000 every 8.33 years.	$ 5,400	$ 1,801	$ 381,780	$ 127,331
Housing, $250,000/once	Current rental is $825/month. Assume $200/month allowance toward taxes and insurance, leaving $625 for mortgage payments. At 8% over 30 years, $625 will purchase $85,177 in mortgage funds. Use this amount to offset cost of new home, representing the cost of normal housing for this family.	$250,000 once	$ 164,823 once	$ 250,000	$ 164,823
Bath Chair, $350 2 times		$ 700 once	$ 700 once	$ 700	$ 700
Power Chair, $7,500/4 yrs		$ 1,875	$ 1,875	$ 132,563	$ 132,563
Batt. Charger, $300/4 years	OK	$ 75	$ 75	$ 5,303	$ 5,303
Battery $150, 2x/yr		$ 300	$ 300	$ 21,210	$ 21,210
Wheelchair, $3,500/4 yrs		$ 875	$ 875	$ 61,863	$ 61,863
Cushion, $395/year		$ 395	$ 395	$ 27,927	$ 27,927
Lift/Sling, $1,100/4 yrs	Not needed; he is able to stand to transfer	$ 275	$ 0	$ 19,443	$ 0
Shower chair, $800/4 years	OK	$ 200	$ 200	$ 14,140	$ 14,140

Nurse	Yudkoff	Annual Costs		Total Lifetime Costs	
		SN	MGY	SN	MGY
Hospital Bed, $1,100/10 yrs	OK	$ 110	$ 110	$ 7,777	$ 7,777
Diapers, $50/month	Starting to toilet train, OK for 5 years	$ 600	$ 600 to 8	$ 42,420	$ 3,000
Braces, $500/6 mnths	OK	$ 1,000	$ 1,000	$ 70,700	$ 70,700
Nebulizer, $180/4 years	OK	$ 45	$ 45	$ 3,182	$ 3,182
Pulse Ox, $4,160/4 yrs	No longer needed	$ 1,040	$ 0	$ 73,528	$ 0
Oxygen Tank, $75, 6/year	No longer needed	$ 450	$ 0	$ 31,815	$ 0
Walker/ Crutches, $75, 2/year	OK	$ 150	$ 150	$ 10,605	$ 10,605
Mic Key Kits, $158, 12/year	OK to age 12	$ 1,896	$ 1,896 to 12	$ 134,047	$ 17,064
Syringes, $0.50, 1/day	1 feed/day, change 1–2/wk to age 12	$ 182.50	$ 38 to 12	$ 12,903	$ 342
PediaSure, $342/month	Is now receiving 8 oz/day to supplement calories. PediaSure costs less than $2.00/8 oz. can. May require oral supplements, even after the G-tube is discontinued.	$ 4,104	$ 730	$ 290,153	$ 51,611
Total				$ 2,628,948	$ 1,284,240

Chapter 38

Business Principles for the Nurse Expert Witness

Renee Miller, MSN, RN,
Karen Cepero, MSN, RN, CCRN, CEN, CS,
Julie B. Pike, MN, RN, LNCC, CPHRM, and
Kathleen Martin, MSN, MPA, CCRN, CS

CONTENTS

0-8493-1418-6/03/$0.00+$1.50
© 2003 by AALNC

Objectives

- To discuss the elements and responsibilities of contracting with attorneys and serving as a nurse expert witness
- To describe key issues related to contracting to provide expert services
- To discuss marketing techniques
- To discuss factors pertinent to determining fee structure and retainers
- To delineate practical aspects of office organization and business practices

Introduction

A testifying nurse expert working as an independent contractor must be aware of the practical issues and decisions involved in conducting business. The expert witness nurse must carefully guard his or her credibility and integrity in professional clinical practice and testimony, as well as in business practices. Details of both areas are discoverable and will be included in questions at deposition and trial. The nurse who considers working as an expert witness must deliberately plan ethical, defensible, practical, and legally sound business practices. Business principles for the independent contractor are described in another chapter. This chapter examines issues unique to the role of expert witness, including marketing, contracting directly with attorneys, fees and collections issues, disclosure of financial information, contracting with a broker service, and other business issues. Examples of relevant documents included in this chapter are intended only as guidelines.

Marketing

Expert services can be marketed in several ways. The nurse expert must first determine the most cost-effective marketing techniques as well as consider the consequences of marketing. In deposition, opposing attorneys will ask if the nurse expert advertises services in an attempt to make the expert look as if the only goal of testifying is financial, thus decreasing credibility of the testimony.

The nurse expert can advertise services in legal publications; by direct mailing of brochures, newsletters, and letters; or through a Web site. The expert should be aware that any written material can and will be used at cross-examination. Direct calls to attorneys and listings in expert directories, in catalogs, or on Web sites may also be used. Some companies or associations with expert directories, catalogs, and Web sites function as advertisers, listing experts in different areas. One example is the LNC Locator[SM] provided by the American Association of Legal Nurse Consultants (AALNC). Each group collects a fee for its services from the expert or the attorney. The expert pays an annual membership fee for a listing in a directory or Web site. The company advertises and may sell the expert's name or directory to interested attorneys. The company does not screen experts who pay to be listed or attorneys who buy the listings, remaining uninvolved in the relationship between attorney and expert. The expert is not required to sign a contract to be included in the directory.

Generally, the most productive ways to obtain cases for review include publishing an article, giving a presentation to a community group or group of lawyers, or being referred by other attorneys, legal nurse consultants (LNCs), or nurse colleagues. Many attorneys and LNCs review the literature to obtain names of potential experts who have written about the subject of their case. They may also note nurse experts who have given presentations to community groups and local groups of lawyers. The best method of obtaining work is by direct referral from attorneys, LNCs, and nurse colleagues. After attorneys and other LNCs identify a nurse expert as reliable and knowledgeable, they may be willing to refer the expert for other cases. Nurse colleagues who know the expert's clinical expertise may also make referrals.

The nurse expert should keep a database of all attorneys who have contracted for services as well as the addresses of opposing plaintiff or defense attorneys who have requested the expert's testimony during deposition or trial. Sending holiday greeting cards with an enclosed business card to current or potential clients is a friendly reminder that services are available. Changes in address, phone number, or e-mail address should always be communicated to attorneys with whom you have contracted to ensure accessibility and availability.

Brokers, Agents, Advertisers, and Contracts

Many companies and independent LNCs broker experts for attorneys. They compile names of experts or locate experts on request and provide those names to attorneys for a fee. Brokers or agents use different methods to collect fees for their services. Some broker services collect their fee from the attorney by adding a per-hour charge or a percentage charge to the base rate of the expert's hourly rate. Such broker services require the expert to submit hours of work to the broker for invoicing rather than send an invoice directly to the attorney. The advantage of this arrangement is that the expert does not become involved in the collection process.

A broker may require the expert to sign a contract binding him or her to certain rules and restrictions of the broker service. Some contracts contain a "noncircumvent" clause to prevent the expert from working directly for the attorney on another case. This clause may say that if the broker refers the expert to an attorney, the expert must work on any subsequent cases from that attorney or firm through the broker service, even if the attorney directly contacts the expert.

The nurse expert should read the entire contract carefully and consult a business or contract attorney for education and advice before signing. The contract is legally binding, and the broker may vigorously seek recompense for violations. Although violations of such contracts are difficult to discover and enforce, the LNC is ethically bound to adhere to any signed contract. The wise LNC should ask for references from other nurses who work through the broker and inquire about the amount of work referred and payment practices.

Other broker services and LNCs who provide this service collect a flat fee from the attorney at the time the expert's name is provided. The fee may represent a basic rate for finding an expert or may reflect actual time and expenses of the search. The rate may also vary depending on the expert's specialty, educational preparation, or unique qualifications. After the expert is provided to the attorney, the service is no longer involved unless assistance is requested by attorney or expert.

Contracting with the Attorney

Many nurse experts contract with attorneys to review cases or serve as expert witnesses without a formal written contract. The attorney calls and interviews the expert by telephone or makes an appointment for a personal interview. Medical records are sent to the nurse, who reviews them, reports findings, and then sends a bill for time spent on the case. Most attorneys pay their bills to experts on time. However, almost every expert has had at least one difficult experience collecting payment. Such unfortunate instances have prompted some experts to require signed contracts or large retainers, especially with new clients or previous clients who have not been prompt in their payments. A contract will prevent misunderstandings regarding the services to be provided, fees for services, and payment schedule. The contract may be formal or informal, as in a letter of agreement.

During initial contact with an attorney, the nurse expert provides a brief review of his or her qualifications and pertinent clinical experience. An expert is expected to provide an academically oriented curriculum vitae (CV) with lists of presentations, publications, professional associations, and continuing education. During initial discussion, the attorney usually asks about other cases for which the nurse has served as an expert and may request a list of other attorneys for whom the expert has reviewed cases. Learning how the attorney obtained the expert's name helps the expert track marketing successes and thank the referring person. The nurse expert should also obtain information about the parties involved in the litigation and their attorneys to check for conflict of interest. Basic fees, retainer, and terms and conditions of payment should also be discussed. The fee schedule delineates hourly rates; list of expenses to be paid by the attorney, such as travel costs; and terms of payment. The terms of payment should be repeated on each invoice. See Figure 38.1 for a fee schedule and Figure 38.2 for a fee agreement.

Following the phone conversation or receipt of medical records, the nurse expert should send a letter to the attorney, confirming the conversation in general terms and enclosing the requested CV and a fee schedule if these have not yet been sent. All correspondence with the attorney is discoverable if the LNC agrees to serve as an expert in the case. Correspondence should be brief and factual, with direct, professional, articulate, and firm communication.

Receipt of medical records should be acknowledged. Delay in record receipt should trigger a query to the attorney. If the requested retainer does not accompany medical records, the LNC should notify the attorney and delay review until it is received. After the client attorney sends review materials, with a retainer check if requested, a contract is understood to be in existence between the two parties: The attorney has agreed to the fee schedule provided verbally and in writing. The LNC has agreed to review and render an opinion in the case within a certain time period, which is essential to honor. If the expert's opinion is not helpful to the case, the attorney will need time to find another expert.

If the nurse expert's opinions are helpful to the attorney's case, and if the nurse agrees to serve as testifying expert, the attorney may then disclose the

YOUR LETTERHEAD

EXAMPLE FEE SCHEDULE
(Effective Date)

Retainer	$500
	Cost per Hour
Reviewing Records/Depositions	$100
Preparing a Summary	$100
Research	$100
Travel	$100
Testimony Time	$150
Rush Fee	$150

Payment is due within 30 days of receipt.

Figure 38.1   Example Fee Schedule (Reprinted from Blevins, N., Miller, R., Pugh, J., and Riggs, E., *Developing an Independent Legal Nurse Consulting Practice*, AALNC, Glenview, IL, 2001.)

expert's name and opinions to the opposing attorney(s). An unfortunate, improper, and unethical abuse of the process occasionally occurs if an attorney names the expert without the expert's knowledge or consent. If discovered, the nurse is advised to insist on withdrawal of his or her name from the case. The nurse is also justified in invoicing the attorney for the unauthorized disclosure, because the opposing attorney was thereby prevented from contacting the expert to review the case. Disclosure may have served the attorney's purpose, but the nurse expert's association with an implied (and possibly contrary) opinion may damage the nurse expert's credibility. In that case, compensation may not be an adequate remedy, and the nurse expert should consult an attorney to discuss further appropriate actions.

Financial Issues

Rates

Abraham Lincoln said, "A lawyer's time and advice are his stock-in-trade." This also holds true for the nurse expert witness. The fee or hourly rate charged by the nurse expert should reflect his or her educational background and the value of years of expertise achieved through clinical experience, specialty certifications, and experience as a nurse expert witness. To determine an appropriate fee, the LNC can survey nurse colleagues in the same geographical area who have served as experts, as well as other professionals with similar education and years of practice in their field. Another source is attorneys or in-house LNCs who routinely engage nurse experts to review cases. The nurse expert should avoid charging a fee that is substantially higher or lower than the fees of other nurse experts.

Expert Witness
Professional Services and Fee Schedule Agreement

Charges

Charges are made in quarter (1/4) hour increments and include time spent for clients during office consultations, review of medical records and other material, research, preparation of reports, telephone consultations, testifying at depositions, hearings and trials, and travel time to and from the office. The expert cannot predict or guarantee total fees. Billing will depend on the amount of time spent on the case and other expenses.

Fees

- The expert's time to review case materials, preparation for deposition, hearings, arbitration and/or trial, office consultation, travel time .... $XXX/hr
- The expert's time for testifying at deposition .... $XXX/hr
- The expert's fee for testifying at hearings, arbitrations, or trial .... $XXX/hr
  (plus preparation and travel time)

Rates are subject to change. Charges are based upon the prevailing fee schedule when the work is performed.

Payment of Testifying Fees

Payment of the court appearance fee is due in full seven days prior to the trial appearance date. Any balance owed will be billed following the trial. Payment of any remaining unpaid invoices and expenses, plus the court appearance fee, is to be received in full seven days prior to the expert's court appearance. An invoice for court appearance expenses (such as mileage, parking, and meals) will be sent following the appearance at the trial. In the event that the case settles before the expert leaves for court, the testifying fee will be refunded.

Invoices

Invoices will be sent periodically to clients, and are due immediately upon receipt. Failure to make payment of invoices shall constitute a default of our agreement. Any questions pertaining to the billing must be put in writing and postmarked no more than ten business days after the date of such billing, after which time the billing will be considered correct and payable as billed. Outstanding balances over 30 days are subject to an interest charge of 1.5% per month each month until paid. The expert, without liability, may withhold delivery of reports, and may suspend performance of his/her obligation to a client pending full payment of all charges.

Retainers

For all matters, a $XXXX retainer fee and a signed fee schedule and/or a retaining letter are required. Billing will be charged against the retainer. It should be noted that we reserve the right, at its discretion, to require a retainer from its clients for any anticipated or requested work beyond the work covered by the initial retainer fee. We reserve the right to modify the amount of the retainer. Please make check payable to _____ and forward directly to our office.

Figure 38.2   Example Fee Agreement (Courtesy of Patricia Iyer.)

Responsibility for Payment

Billing is **not** contingent upon the findings and/or conclusions reached. Responsibility for payment is that of the client (law firm) engaging the expert's services and is not contingent upon client's contractual agreement(s) with plaintiff/defendant/insurance company and/or case status. The client is responsible for paying the fees even if the outcome of the case is not favorable. As a convenience, we may agree to prepare separate invoices for testifying at a deposition. Responsibility for payment of any fees associated with the deposition remains that of the client. Responsibility for the notification of settlement of a matter is that of the engaging client. All charges incurred to the time of notification will be billed. Lack of notification will not obviate charges incurred even when disbursements related to this matter have been made. Failure to include a billable item in an invoice shall not constitute a waiver of the right to add the charge to a subsequent billing.

In the event that it becomes necessary for _____ to retain an attorney or collection agency for collecting outstanding fees or any other breach of this agreement, the client agrees to pay _____'s reasonable attorney fees and costs incurred in enforcing his/her rights under this agreement. A 30% surcharge will be added to the outstanding balance if a collection agency becomes involved in the collections process.

Expenses

Including, but not limited to:

- Travel: Automobile expenses are billed at $0.40 per mile plus tolls and parking charges. Airfare, train fare, lodging, etc. are to be paid in full seven days in advance. Meals are billed as incurred, when time away from office exceeds four hours.
- Telephone, Document Reproduction, Supplies, and Delivery Costs (Federal Express, courier, and other expenses): As incurred.

Modifications to the Agreement

All modifications must be agreed to and confirmed in writing.

I have read the **Expert Witness Professional Services and Fee Schedule Agreement**. I understand and agree to the terms contained therein.

Date: _____
Signed: _____
Firm: _____
Case name:

Please sign this page and return the original agreement to _____ accompanied by the retainer after copying for your files.

Figure 38.2   Example Fee Agreement (*Continued*)

When setting fees, the LNC can also give consideration to the cost of doing business, such as office expenses, costs of marketing and billing, taxes on income, and maintaining professional knowledge through continuing education. It is recommended that the nurse expert consider factoring expenses into the base hourly rate when setting fees. Using a simple hourly rate structure that includes expenses, rather than billing for time and each expense, simplifies record keeping and invoicing.

Establishing a flat rate for a case is not recommended. A quote for review of a medical record may seem reasonable at first, but unforeseen circumstances may occur. The issues may not be as simple as the attorney has described, or the medical record may double in size by the time missing records are collected. Variations in the legibility of the records and the amount of technical information they include make it impossible to predict how much time may be required for any given case.

It is also customary to establish one base rate for all time spent to review records, research and review appropriate literature, generate a report or affidavit if requested, review depositions, and discuss the case by phone or in person. However, some experts charge a higher rate for deposition and trial time because of the amount of physical and emotional preparation that it entails. For example, a nurse expert may charge a base hourly rate of $150 for record review and consultation services and an hourly rate of $175 to $250 for testimony time either in deposition or at trial. Another nurse expert may charge $125 to $200 for each hour spent on the case regardless of the activity.

Retainers

During initial discussions with the attorney, the LNC should to request a retainer before record review and opinion formulation. A retainer is an advance payment for future work. Most attorneys require retainers in their own practices before beginning work. The retainer formalizes the agreement and ensures payment for work. Some experts apply the retainer to the final payment. Some ask for another advance payment when the first is exhausted, particularly if they anticipate investing an extensive amount of time in a case. Other experts request payment after certain portions of work on the case are completed. A retainer becomes particularly helpful in cases in which a favorable opinion cannot be provided and payment for services becomes difficult to obtain. For cash flow purposes, the expert is advised always to ask for a retainer. The retainer's amount should cover the estimated initial review of the case, depending on the size of the medical records, or a flat fee for the time, typically ranging from 5 to 10 hours. Figures 38.3 and 38.4 are examples of invoices.

Payment for Deposition or Trial Testimony Time

Attorneys pay nurse experts for the time they spend on cases. The exception to this arrangement is time spent in deposition. Because the opposing attorney requests that the expert appear and testify at the deposition to discover the expert's opinions, opposing counsel is usually responsible for paying for the expert's time at deposition. Time spent preparing for testimony or traveling to the deposition

Company Address

1234 Medical Road
City, State 19000
Phone Number   Fax Number

Invoice

BILL TO
Robert Taylor Jones Attorney at Law Law Office 5555 Street Road City, State 10000

DATE	INVOICE NO.
4/15/2002	**22222**

ATTORNEY	CLIENT NAME/NO.	TERMS
Robert Taylor	William Green	7 days

DESCRIPTION	HOURS/QTY	RATE	AMOUNT
3/30/01–4/4/02 Review of records, depositions, phone call with attorney, report preparation.	9.25	$175	$1618.75
Retainer			−$1000

	Total	$618.75
An outstanding balance over 30 days is subject to an interest charge of 1.5% per month until the balance is paid. E.I.N. 33–333333		

Figure 38.3   Sample Invoice (Courtesy of Patricia Iyer.)

may be paid by either side as stipulated by state statutes or mutual agreement. Prior to the deposition, the nurse expert should inquire about who is responsible for paying for travel time and the deposition. The expert witness contract with the client should specify that the client is responsible for payment of all fees associated with the deposition, even if the opposing counsel is obligated to pay for that portion of the expert's time. Consideration may be given to requesting payment in advance, or at the time of deposition and trial. A deposition at the expense of the defense attorney, who must submit the expert's invoice to an insurance company, may relegate the expert to waiting for payment for a longer period of time. If no advance request is made, the nurse expert submits an invoice

YOUR LETTERHEAD
Tax ID Number

INVOICE

Date

Client Name

Case Name

	Hours	Rate/Hr.	Fee
Review of Depositions And other Material	20	$75	$1500
Deposition/Trial Time	2	$125	$250
Total Due			$1750

Figure 38.4   Sample Invoice (Reprinted from Blevins, N., Miller, R., Pugh, J., and Riggs, E., *Developing an Independent Legal Nurse Consulting Practice,* **AALNC, Glenview, IL, 2001.)**

after the deposition and collects payment from the attorney who took the deposition, either directly or through the sponsoring attorney.

Months or weeks ahead of a scheduled trial, the expert is given the date on the court's docket. Several cases are scheduled for the same dates because most cases settle prior to trial. Thus, all but one of the remaining trials must be rescheduled to a later date. Because the expert must keep the calendar clear for the trial date, the expert may charge a fee if the case settles at the last minute or if trial is rescheduled to a later date. If the case proceeds, the expert may be "on call" waiting to testify, usually charging for this time at the base rate or at an "on call" rate. Many experts charge a flat half-day or full-day fee for trial testimony that is based on their hourly testimony rate.

Attorney Payment Methods

Most plaintiff attorneys pay expenses for experts directly. The expert submits an invoice to the attorney, and it is usually paid in a short period of time. By agreement, however, some attorneys submit invoices for expenses to their plaintiff clients for payment, which may delay payment to the expert. The nurse expert has contracted with the attorney, who is responsible for payment of invoices, rather than with the client.

Defense attorneys must submit invoices to insurance companies for payment. Unless the defense attorney pays the invoice directly and awaits reimbursement from the insurance company, payment from defense attorneys via an insurance company may take longer simply because another (rather complex) entity is involved.

Regardless of whether they are directed to plaintiff or defense attorneys, invoices should reflect consistent policy and procedure that is clearly stated on invoices and fee schedules.

Time for Out-of-Town Travel

Out-of-town travel time (other than time for deposition or trial) is generally figured by adding time from portal to portal minus sleep time, personal time, and time working on other matters. For example, an expert leaves home one afternoon to fly to another city, meeting with the attorney for one hour that evening. The expert rises early the next morning to review material before the deposition or trial. The deposition or trial testimony lasts 2 hours. The expert returns to the airport after testifying, reviews depositions from another case while waiting to return home and on the flight, and arrives home that afternoon. The expert may invoice a base rate for the elapsed time from leaving home until returning home, excluding sleeping and personal time, and the return trip when he or she reviewed material for another case. To avoid tracking these hours, some experts simply set a flat daily or one-day rate for this time. The invoice for time reserved for this matter may be sent if cancellation does not occur at least 48 hours prior to departure.

Expenses for Out-of-Town Travel

It is standard to charge the client attorney for expenses incurred for case review and appearance at deposition and trial. All travel expenses are billed for such items as meals, car rental, parking, and ground transportation. The nurse expert or a representative from the attorney's office may determine the most convenient flight and purchase the ticket. The attorney should also arrange and pay for the expert's hotel accommodations. If deposition or trial testimony is scheduled for the morning, several hours from home, the nurse expert should arrive the previous night. Although this entails hotel expense for the attorney, it is important for the case that the nurse expert have a good night's sleep before testimony. If the expert drives a personal car out of town for testimony, the attorney is billed at the current IRS mileage-allowance rate, for the duration of the drive.

Time Logs

LNCs who keep good time records earn more than those who keep poor time records. Those who estimate time tend to underestimate the actual time spent. A timer may be used to assist in tracking time. Several methods are available for recording time, including computer programs and paper logs. See Figure 38.5 for a sample time log. Whatever system is chosen, it should be readily accessible and easy to use. The nurse expert must time all case-related activity and enter it into the log as soon as possible, or it will be forgotten or inaccurate when reconstructed. Time logs are essential for accurate billing and to satisfy the client who wants to see the exact services for which he or she is paying. The log should include the date; the work performed, such as medical record and deposition review, literature review, and conferences with the attorney; and the amount of time spent on each. Any time spent for which the expert does not charge should be listed on the

Nurse Billing Sheet

Your Name ___Sara Smith___   Rate/hr ___$175/hr___   Page ___1___ of ___1___

Firm/Attorney/Client: ___Jones/Taylor/Green___

| Date | Time Tracking | | Subtotal Time | Total for Day | Staff Initial | Billing Code/Description (other) |
	Start	Stop				
3/30	7:30	9:00	1.5	1.5	SS	Review of records
4/1	9:00	11:00	2			Review of depositions
	1:00	4:00	3	5	SS	Review of depositions
4/2	4:00	4:15	.25	.25	SS	Phone call with attorney
4/4	1:00	3:30	2.5	2.5	SS	Report preparation

Figure 38.5   Nurse Expert Witness Billing Sheet (Courtesy of Patricia Iyer.)

invoice as a "no-charge" item rather than left off the invoice. If the expert chooses to charge for expenses rather than factor them in an hourly charge, they should be documented with receipts, such as those for parking fees, fees for professional literature searches, and photocopy charges. Defense experts should note that insurance companies might restrict expenses for which they will reimburse. The nurse expert should ask the defense attorney at the beginning of the case about the insurance company's expense policy and quote an hourly rate to accommodate those anticipated out-of-pocket expenses.

Cases can progress for several years without correspondence from the attorney. It is good practice to communicate with the attorney at least every six months about the status of the case and to inquire whether there are any more documents or records to review. The expert is advised to invoice clients on a routine basis rather than allowing long periods of time between the time spent and the creation of the invoice. When a case has been settled, the expert should promptly review all time logs and invoices to determine that all fees have been paid. The expert's fee agreement should specify that any outstanding fees should be paid, even if the case is resolved, or payment may be difficult to obtain after an attorney "closes the books" on the case. Inefficient business practices by nurse experts may cloud the attorney's overall assessment of the expert's value.

Fee Collections

Collecting payment for services is a necessary part of expert work. Most attorneys value their experts and pay invoices promptly. Invoices should be sent monthly or after each substantial portion of work is done. They should include the date of service, type of service rendered, hourly rate, terms of payment, and the expert's taxpayer I.D. number or Social Security number. Most attorneys prefer more frequent smaller bills rather than large bills at the end of a case. Because cases may go on for years, the expert should not wait until settlement for payment. If the attorney is slow to pay, a letter or personal phone call is appropriate, with interest charged after a designated period of unpaid time. With that policy, the attorney client should receive monthly notice of the balance due and interest charged. The nurse expert should remember that charging interest is discretionary and can be waived in certain situations. To avoid a large loss, the expert should not continue working on a case until payment is received. If the attorney declines to pay or does not respond to requests for payment, the expert should send a notice by certified mail describing impending actions that will be taken to collect the fee, and attach a copy of the invoice. See Figures 38.6, 38.7, and 38.8 for sample collection letters. If a deposition is requested with an invoice outstanding, the expert can politely decline to appear until the invoice is paid. This notification usually prompts immediate payment. If the expert is not paid after several attempts, other impending actions may include filing a case in small claims court or hiring a collection agency or attorney to pursue payment. The expert should proceed with the most reasonable and cost-effective action to collect the payment due.

XYZ Consulting Corporation
12345 This Street
Anytown, CA 00000
Tel: 555/123/4567
Fax: 555/123/4568
XYZ@net.com

(Date)

(Client Name)
(Client Address)
(Client City, State, Zip)

In RE: (Case Name/Style)

Dear (Client Name):

Thank you for using (Your Company Name) for LNC services. You are a valued client. We appreciate your business and know that you want to keep your account current with us.

On (Date of Services), we provided (List of Services) for you in the above-listed case. Your payment of (amount) is now overdue.

In the agreement you signed, you agreed to pay for our services upon invoice. That invoice was sent to you on (Date Invoice Sent).

Failure to pay on time will affect your ability to obtain our services in the future and may lead to additional action on our part. Thank you for your prompt attention to this matter.

You may call me at (Your Phone Number) if you have any questions or concerns. Your continued business is important to us.

Sincerely,

(Your Name)(Your Title)

Figure 38.6   Sample Collection Letter (Reprinted from Blevins, N., Miller, R., Pugh, J., and Riggs, E., *Developing an Independent Legal Nurse Consulting Practice*, AALNC, Glenview, IL, 2001.)

Disclosure of Financial Income and Previous Cases

At deposition, the nurse expert is usually asked about compensation rates and the amount of money paid to date on the current case. Many times the expert will be asked how much has been billed for his or her opinion. The best answer includes the phrase "for the time spent reviewing the documents and formulating my opinion." The expert is usually also asked about the number of cases that he or she has reviewed, whether plaintiff or defense, as well as the number of depositions and the number of trials. Another area of questioning that frequently arises during deposition is the percentage of annual salary that is derived from nursing expert review and testimony. Such questions usually take the form of requesting an estimate of the percentage of time and income spent on case review and testimony as an expert as compared with clinical practice. From a statutory

Date

Law Offices of Ellen Landau
Ellen Landau, Esq.
1521 City Street
10th Floor
Winston, PA 19102

Dear Ms. Landau,

Re: Riji, Krishna

This is just a friendly reminder that you have 1 overdue invoice, with an overdue balance of $262.50. If you have any questions about the amount you owe, please give us a call and we'll be happy to discuss it. If you've already sent your payment, please disregard this reminder.

We appreciate your continuing business, and we look forward to hearing from you shortly.

Sincerely,

Your name

Figure 38.7   Sample Collection Letter (Courtesy of Patricia Iyer.)

perspective, this is relevant in states that mandate that experts spend a certain percentage of their professional time practicing in the clinical area about which they offer expert opinions. From a practical perspective, if the expert does not spend a majority of time in the clinical area, the opposing attorney may use that fact to try to undermine current knowledge and experience of the expert. If the nurse expert makes a substantial amount of income from case review and testifying, the opposing attorney may try to label the expert as a "hired gun" to decrease credibility. The expert does not usually have to disclose total income or the total money earned as an expert.

Prior to deposition, the nurse expert should ask the sponsoring attorney what financial information is and is not required to be disclosed in the state in which the case was filed. The nurse expert should also rely on the sponsoring attorney to object to questions that are not allowed by state statute. If unsure how to respond to questions asked during the deposition regarding income, the expert may request a break to discuss the issue with the sponsoring or personal attorney.

The expert may be asked to identify cases in which he or she testified, and to produce depositions or billing records. Prior to deposition, the nurse expert should discuss with the sponsoring attorney what information of that type is expected to be produced in the court in which the case was filed. According to the Federal Rules of Civil Procedure, an expert testifying in federal court must produce a signed written report that contains "the qualifications of the witness, including a list of all publications authored by the witness within the preceding ten years; the compensation to be paid for the study and testimony; and a listing of any other cases in which the witness has testified as an expert at trial or by deposition within the preceding four years."[1] If the opposing attorney asks the expert for any such documents, the LNC may agree to do so but should request

SENT VIA FAX AND BY FIRST-CLASS AND REGISTERED MAIL

July 30, 2002

James Lenny, Esquire
James Lenny Law Offices
235 Main Street
White Lake, NV 98877

RE: Lott vs. White Lake Medical Center

Dear Mr. Lenny,

We have made several attempts to collect the payment owed for the final services provided on this case. Calls were placed to your office on May 17 at 11:00, June 6 at 9:15, June 21 at 4:00, June 28 at 1:00, and July 12 at 3:00. Each time I was told that you were unavailable and that your bookkeeper was on an extended leave of absence. I left messages for you at the time of each call, requesting a return phone call. I have not heard from you.

Enclosed are two invoices totaling $2000. Please give these your prompt attention. I would like to receive payment on these as quickly as possible and appreciate your attention to the matter. If I do not receive payment on these invoices by August 15, I will be left no choice but to refer this matter to our collection agency. As per our fee agreement, a copy of which is enclosed, a 30% surcharge will be added to the amount that you owe. This will bring the amount that you owe to $2600. Prompt payment is necessary to avoid having to pay the surcharge.

Very truly yours,

Name

Enclosure

Figure 38.8   Sample Collection Letter (Courtesy of Patricia Iyer.)

that the attorney pay for time and expense to search through files and copy, compile, and submit the information. The request and the attorney's agreement to pay should be made on the deposition record. It is a good practice when a case settles or is completed to destroy or safely store all records associated with the case to maintain confidentiality. It is recommended that expert witness reports be kept at least 4 years. After these documents are destroyed, the expert cannot be compelled to compile or produce nonexistent documents.

As with all aspects of testimony, information given regarding income and hours of clinical experience should be consistent with previous depositions. All legal documents of a case that has been filed, including depositions and trial testimony, are a matter of public record and can be obtained by the opposing attorney. Any discrepancy may be used to discredit the expert.

Tax Returns

An attorney may request tax returns by interrogatory or at deposition to verify income derived from testimony. For most LNCs, tax returns do not yield that information because consulting income on nontestifying cases is also included in business income. If tax returns are subpoenaed, the expert can take certain actions to avoid producing them or to limit exposure of private information. Through the sponsoring attorney, the expert may file a motion to quash or a protective order to modify or limit disclosure. These must show that the request is unduly burdensome, fails to allow reasonable time for compliance, or requires the expert to disclose some privileged or otherwise protected material. In some cases, a subpoena may be difficult to quash because the court may find the information relevant to the subject matter. If an expert refuses to comply with the court's decision, the court may find the expert in contempt.

Attorneys will not usually pursue detailed information about an expert's finances that is not pertinent to the case issues or credibility. Prior to deposition or trial, the LNC should ask the sponsoring attorney about the boundaries of such information in the state of the testimony.

Terminating a Contract to Serve as Expert

A contract to serve as expert witness, whether a formal contract or mutual acceptance of terms in letters of agreement, ethically commits the expert to complete the service through case conclusion by settlement or trial. The decision to terminate a contract is a serious matter. On occasion, there are compelling reasons for which the nurse expert may and should withdraw from a case with a previous commitment. If new information causes a change in opinion, the expert must discuss the changed opinion with the attorney and possibly withdraw from the case. Also, if the expert recognizes a conflict of interest through new information, that must also be discussed with the attorney, followed by withdrawal from the case. See Chapter 46 for more information on ethical issues. Another obvious reason for withdrawal could be development of serious illness or impairment. In such cases, the expert should fully discuss the circumstances with the sponsoring attorney.

The expert might also wish to withdraw from a case if the attorney fails to pay for the expert's work, displays behavior that the expert believes is unprofessional or unethical, or is abusive to the expert. It is rare for attorneys to behave abusively toward experts, especially those whom they retain. However, disrespect, dishonesty, harassment, or undue or inappropriate pressure to alter opinions are examples of conduct that should not be tolerated. It is difficult to state firmly opinions in which the expert does not fervently believe, and it can endanger any future as a testifying expert. Such abuse may cause bias and interfere with the expert's ability to represent opinions enthusiastically on behalf of the attorney's client. As the case progresses, withdrawal may be increasingly detrimental to the case. If the expert has given a deposition, more problems are created by withdrawal than if withdrawal occurs before deposition. Regardless of the reason, it is wise for the expert to seek counsel from a personal attorney before deciding to resign from a case because of problems with the case attorney.

To terminate the contract in this type of situation, the nurse expert should package all medical records, copies of depositions, and other material and return them to the attorney with a letter informing the attorney of the inability to continue with the case. Although an explanation can be provided, it is not necessary, just as an attorney can dismiss the expert from a case without disclosing the reason. If unprofessional conduct is the reason, it may be better left unsaid, or the written description should be reviewed by the expert's personal attorney before mailing. The package should be sent by some method that requires signature as proof of delivery. When the material is received by the attorney, the nurse expert may expect to receive a call or correspondence from a disappointed or irate attorney who will have to locate, hire, and pay another expert to review the case. Anticipating that the attorney will ask for a refund of fees paid, the expert should develop a plan to respond to this demand. The case may be jeopardized if it is late in the process or the expert has been deposed and legal deadlines are approaching.

The nurse expert who terminates an expert contract must keep in mind that the attorney may still subpoena appearance at trial. This is unlikely because the nurse might be considered a hostile witness who may damage the case. Opposing counsel may also subpoena the nurse expert.

Withdrawing from a case should be undertaken with very serious consideration of potential consequences to the case, the attorney's client, and the nurse's reputation as an expert. At times it is unavoidable. If necessary, withdrawal from the case should be done as early as possible.

Malpractice Insurance for the Expert Witness

The nurse expert should consider carrying individual professional malpractice insurance, which includes errors and omissions coverage. The liability insurance policy carried by the nurse's clinical practice employer does not provide coverage for work performed off the employer's premises or outside the scope of practice defined by the nurse's job description. A personal liability policy for clinical nursing practice does not include errors and omissions coverage.

A remote possibility always exists that a nurse could be sued for negligence in the performance of work as a testifying expert. This is unlikely if the nurse adheres to codes of ethics and standards of practice for LNCs, does not misrepresent credentials, and shows meticulous work, careful consideration, and commitment to truth in opinions. However, the possibility should not be discounted, considering that the expert's clients are skilled attorney litigators with professional negligence cases that often represent years of work and large amounts of money at risk. For example, a malpractice lawsuit could be triggered if the nurse expert were to give an opinion that jeopardized the case without substantial evidence in medical or nursing literature. Professional malpractice insurance for independent LNCs and testifying experts may be available through insurance agents or brokers specializing in health care. Some of the larger medical professional insurers include The St. Paul Companies, CNA, Seabury & Smith, Nurses Service Organization, and the Chicago Insurance Company.

The Expert's Commitment

Serving as nurse expert in a legal case is a serious responsibility that carries an ethical commitment to see the case through to the end, barring unforeseeable circumstances, even if the case ends several years after initial contact with the attorney. The nurse who wishes to serve as an expert can seek mentors with years of testifying experience for advice on how to handle the myriad of business decisions and dilemmas that may arise during the process. Adherence to business principles prevents misunderstandings and reduces the possibility of difficulties related to financial aspects of being an expert.

Reference

1. Rule 26(a)(2)(B), *Federal Civil Judicial Procedures and Rules*, West Group, St. Paul, MN, 2001.

Additional Reading

AALNC Greater Detroit Chapter, Collecting payments, *Journal of Legal Nurse Consulting*, 8(1), 23, 1997.

Developing an Independent Legal Nurse Consulting Practice, AALNC, Glenview, IL, 2001.

Larig, S., The basic principles of consulting, *Journal of Legal Nurse Consulting*, 10(3), 18, 1999.

Vermeer, M., A billing system that works, *Journal of Legal Nurse Consulting*, 7(3), 21, 1996.

Test Questions

1. After agreeing to review a case, the nurse expert should
   A. Send a letter of agreement to the attorney
   B. Not contact the attorney until the records are reviewed
   C. Review the records at leisure
   D. Call the attorney when time permits

2. The most ineffective marketing technique is
   A. Sending brochures and newsletters to attorneys
   B. Listing one's services in expert witness directories
   C. Speaking to a local group of attorneys
   D. Not following up with previous contacts

3. The purpose of a retainer is to
   A. Ensure that payment will be received for services rendered
   B. Prevent the need for a contract with the attorney
   C. Immediately increase one's income
   D. Have the capital with which to work

4. Which statement regarding time logs is NOT correct?
   A. LNCs who keep good time records earn more money.
   B. Immediate entries into the time log will ensure accurate information in the time log.
   C. The time log should include the date, work performed, and length of time spent.
   D. Time that is nonbillable should not be entered into the log.

5. The most important item to consider when setting fees is
   A. The cost of doing business
   B. Years of clinical experience
   C. The cost of one's specialty certification
   D. Financial needs at the time

Answers: 1. A, 2. D, 3. A, 4. D, 5. A

MEDIATION, SETTLEMENT, AND TRIAL

Chapter 39

Alternative Dispute Resolution: Settlement, Arbitration, and Mediation

Nancy Wilson-Soga, BS, MS, RN,
Tracey Chovanec, BSN, RN,
Barbara J. Levin, BSN, RN, ONC, LNCC, and
Janet Kremser, BS, RN, C-SN, CDON/LTC

CONTENTS

Objectives

- To define "alternative dispute resolution"
- To define "arbitration" and compare and contrast the processes of binding arbitration and nonbinding arbitration
- To discuss the role of the legal nurse consultant in the arbitration process
- To define "mediation"
- To identify the steps in the mediation process
- To discuss the role of the legal nurse consultant in the mediation process
- To review the steps used in the preparation of a settlement brochure to be used at mediation
- To discuss other settlement methods

Introduction

Alternative dispute resolution (ADR) has become an increasingly popular process within our justice system and is a method used to aid in resolving lawsuits outside of the courtroom. The United States Code[1] defines "alternative dispute resolution" as any procedure that is used, in lieu of adjudication, to resolve issues in controversy. This includes but is not limited to settlement negotiations, conciliation, facilitation, mediation, fact-finding, minitrials, and arbitration, or any combination thereof. While ADR may be used in cases involving many types of issues, it is perhaps most useful in those cases involving personal injuries, medical malpractice, employment issues, and contract disputes. With court dockets becoming more and more overcrowded, judges are ordering the participants in lawsuits to attempt to resolve their disputes through ADR.

The advantages to ADR are that both sides avoid the cost of continuing litigation and that it allows a claim or dispute to be resolved in a timely fashion and without a lengthy and expensive trial. This chapter focuses on two types of ADR that have gained the most in popularity nationwide — arbitration and mediation — and the legal nurse consultant's (LNC's) role in the process.

Arbitration

Arbitration is an arrangement for abiding by the judgment of selected persons in some disputed matter, instead of carrying the dispute to established tribunals of justice. The intention is to avoid the formalities, delay, expense, and vexation of ordinary litigation.[2]

There are two categories of arbitration — binding arbitration and nonbinding arbitration — each of which can be either mandatory or voluntary. Mandatory arbitration involves cases in which contractual relations are present, such as labor–management disputes; insurance claims (personal injury); and auto accident injury cases in no-fault states such as New York, New Jersey, Minnesota, Hawaii, and Oregon. Trade associations and professional insurance liability carriers utilize arbitration to resolve conflict. Voluntary arbitration occurs when both parties agree to resolve the dispute by a third party chosen by the plaintiff and defense.

Binding Arbitration

In binding arbitration, the parties submit the dispute to one or more impartial arbitrators who have both expertise and knowledge of the case as well as a substantive basis for rendering informed decisions and awards. Once the arbitration decision is rendered, this leads to finality, in which the award is contractually based and imposed. Some states allow hospitals to place arbitration clauses in hospital admission agreements, thus the LNC should inspect all signed hospital admission forms to determine whether they include such clauses. Binding arbitration is an agreement between the parties in advance to abide by an arbitrator's decision. The process usually takes place when a contractual agreement states that the conflicts will be resolved by binding arbitration.

Because there is a finality to decisions under binding arbitration, the process is generally covered by state statutes that outline specific guidelines and require explicit warnings to the participants about the consequences of entering into arbitration. In Texas, for example, *Vernon's Annotated Statutes*, Article 4590i, Sec. 15.01(a) states:

> No physician, professional association, or health care provider shall request or require a patient or prospective patient to execute an agreement to arbitrate health care liability claims unless the form of agreement delivered to the patient contains a written notice in 10-point bold-face type clearly and conspicuously stating: UNDER TEXAS LAW, THIS AGREEMENT IS INVALID AND OF NO LEGAL EFFECT UNLESS IT IS ALSO SIGNED BY AN ATTORNEY OF YOUR OWN CHOOSING. THIS AGREEMENT CONTAINS A WAIVER OF IMPORTANT LEGAL RIGHTS, INCLUDING YOUR RIGHT TO A JURY. YOU SHOULD NOT SIGN THIS AGREEMENT WITHOUT FIRST CONSULTING WITH AN ATTORNEY.

The Texas statute also states that violations of the above section by a physician or professional association of physicians constitute violations of the Medical Malpractice Act. This action would be subject to enforcement provisions and sanctions.

The binding arbitration process usually involves submitting a contested matter to a 3-member panel. Appeals to the binding arbitration decision are very limited. As a result, this process is the least desirable in personal injury or medical malpractice cases. Binding arbitration is more commonly used in contract disputes.

Nonbinding Arbitration

Nonbinding arbitration usually involves one arbitrator, yet the decision is not final. If either the plaintiff or the defendant is dissatisfied with the arbitrator's decision, the case remains on the court's docket. The nonbinding arbitration process is often preferred over the binding arbitration process because the nonbinding type is less final. An individual can still have his or her day in court if arbitration does not produce any resolution.

The Arbitration Process

The American Arbitration Association (AAA) provides procedural guides to dispute resolution as a method to resolve claims in an inexpensive manner. Examples of types of claims submitted to the AAA include slip-and-fall cases that are in suit for several years, auto accidents, swimming-pool accidents, false arrests, and medical malpractice. Often the role of the LNC employed at a law firm is to initiate the process of preparing the submission to an arbitration board. This can be easily carried out by:

1. Logging on to http://www.adr.org, the Web site for the AAA, and determining where a local state office can be found.
2. Submitting names and addresses of the insurer, claimant, and their attorney or representative, along with contact phone numbers.
3. Completing case, claim, or docket numbers.
4. Providing a brief synopsis of the claim along with the dollar amount involved in the case.
5. Adding any additional information that may assist the AAA in arranging the case for arbitration or mediation. Here it should be stipulated whether the decision will be binding or nonbinding.

The AAA office then contacts all parties to gain approval for submission to arbitrate (binding) or mediate (nonbinding). Once agreement to arbitrate is unanimously established, the AAA appoints an experienced arbitrator from its panel of neutral attorneys. A biographical sketch of the arbitrator is sent to all parties to review and, if necessary, to object if a conflict of interest is identified.

Following the appointment of an arbitrator a hearing is scheduled in a convenient location. The LNC assists in preparing medical documentation of the case as well as gathering evidentiary material such as x-ray reports, highlighted medical documents, photographs of the injured area, and anatomical charts. These materials serve to educate the arbitrator. Under most states' arbitration laws, arbitrators have the right to subpoena witnesses and documents. Attorneys may choose to have witnesses and experts interviewed prior to the arbitration hearing to make certain that these individuals understand the format of arbitration and the importance of their testimony.

Although the arbitration hearing is less formal than court trials, the process is as important to the parties as a trial. Hearings are conducted in a manner that affords a fair presentation of the case by both parties. Opening statements are made to describe the case and to detail what each party is seeking. This aids the arbitrator in understanding the relevance of the testimony that will be presented and the decision being sought. The arbitrator decides what evidence or testimony is relevant in understanding the issues and can reject evidence that he or she does not deem useful. The claiming party customarily presents first, then each party states its position, trying to convince the arbitrator of the correctness of his or her position. This is not the strict "burden of proof" that would have to be outlined in a civil court trial. Witnesses are utilized to clarify issues and identify documents and exhibits. Cross-examination is permitted. Closing statements include a summary of the facts and arguments as well as refutation of points made by the opposing party.

The arbitrator closes the hearing and has 30 days to review all the evidence and testimony in order to determine an appropriate decision and award. The award is a brief statement detailing which party will be providing a specific relief. This decision must be adhered to in a binding arbitration.

The Mediation Process

By far, the preferred process for most litigants considering ADR is mediation. "Mediation" is defined as the act of a third person in inter-mediating between two contending parties with a view to persuading them to adjust or settle their dispute.[2] In this forum, the plaintiff and defendant agree for an impartial third party known as a mediator to conduct a settlement conference. The case needs to have reached a mature status — exhibits having been collected and discovery nearing completion — to be ready for mediation.

Retired judges and lawyers with special expertise and training offer services as mediators. In some states, nonattorneys with training in mediation proceedings and expertise in a specific field of practice (e.g., physicians, nurses, psychologists, educators) make excellent mediators. The mediator's fee is agreed upon in advance by all parties. Average daily mediation fees vary, ranging from approximately $600 to $1500 per party. Sometimes mediators charge fees on an hourly basis.

Mediations occur when courts order parties to mediate or when either side approaches the other informally to inquire whether mediation is desirable. Both sides must agree upon the selection of a mediator and the date on which the settlement conference will be held.

Although the mediator is an impartial third party, it is important to educate and inform him or her about the issues of the case prior to the settlement conference. One tool frequently used by the plaintiff is a settlement brochure, which is discussed in depth later in this chapter. The mediator can study the brochure and then develop an opinion that is likely to reflect the potential outcome in the courtroom. The plaintiff naturally hopes to convince the mediator of the possibility of a large jury verdict. The defense wishes to convince the mediator of the opposite. The ideal result of mediation is for the mediator to persuade both sides to meet somewhere on middle ground and resolve the claim without a jury trial.

During mediation, the settlement conference itself often has a friendly atmosphere. At the beginning of the settlement conference, all parties meet together with the mediator, and counsel for each side presents a brief oral synopsis of the case. The parties then proceed to separate conference rooms. Privately with each party, the mediator strives to influence each party to adjust expectations, pointing out strengths and weaknesses of each side's case. The ultimate goal is to resolve the differences between the parties and reach a settlement that is satisfactory to both sides. The mediation process requires that all parties have representatives present who have the authority to finalize settlement agreements.

The LNC's Role in Mediation

LNCs often play a very visible role in mediation, both before and during the settlement conference. In a medical malpractice case, for example, an LNC could be employed by either plaintiff or defense side to audit the presentation during mediation, with the aim of detecting discrepancies or inaccurate information. The LNC would, of course, privately relay such information to the employing attorney. The LNC can also serve as an informed educator at the mediation forum. When complex medical issues are introduced, the mediator sometimes needs more information on the standard of care or the medical issues in dispute, or explanations of medical terminology. The LNC can be a resource liaison to the mediator.

An LNC can offer valuable assistance in mediations as an educator about the medical aspects of a medical malpractice or personal injury case. The following is a mediation presentation outline of the medical aspects of a case:

1. Overview of the case
2. Health history of the plaintiff
3. Injuries sustained and definitions
4. Long-term and short-term rehabilitation goals
5. Questions and clarifications

Figure 39.1 describes the vital role that an LNC played in the successful outcome of a mediation in a personal injury case. The mediator and parties were able to gain a comprehensive understanding of the medical issues and damages, which helped move the case to settlement.

Production of a Settlement Brochure

Prior to the settlement conference, the LNC is a major contributor to the production of a settlement brochure. The term "brochure" is somewhat of a misnomer. Brochures, as the term is typically used, are often simple trifold documents. A brochure used as a settlement tool is several inches thick and is bound with dividers. The settlement brochure can vary in size depending on the issues and evidence to be presented. Both plaintiff and defense sides prepare brochures, although the plaintiff's is usually more extensive. A settlement brochure serves three purposes:

1. It aids the trial team in focusing on specific medical issues that may later be used for trial of the case in the courtroom.

Mrs. Smith, a 41-year-old married woman with two children, was in a motor vehicle accident on a snowy February 1, 1995 at 2:30 p.m. While Mrs. Smith was driving north, Mr. Jones' car was driving south and crossed over the median strip and hit Mrs. Smith's car head-on at 30 mph.

Mrs. Smith's injuries included a left open grade 3B tibia fracture, a left shoulder dislocation, and a 4-inch laceration to the parietal area of the head. She required emergent open reduction internal fixation (ORIF) surgery to stabilize the tibia fracture, and 20 sutures to the left parietal area. A week later, she underwent a Bankart procedure to stabilize the left shoulder.

Approximately 8 months after the surgery, a nonunion of the tibia was diagnosed on x-ray. A second ORIF with right iliac crest bone graft was performed. A month later, the hardware in the tibia fractured due to the nonunion of bone. Another surgical procedure was required to replace it.

Mrs. Smith's health history included a history of smoking 2 packs per day for 20 years and adult-onset diabetes mellitus treated with insulin, both of which contributed to ineffective healing. At approximately 7 months after the accident, Mrs. Smith showed signs of osteomyelitis. Intravenous and oral antibiotics were administered. Within 5 months and following multiple irrigation and debridements, she required a left below-the-knee amputation.

Three long-term goals for Mrs. Smith were identified and presented:

1. Return to previous level of function
2. Bipedal ambulation utilizing a prosthesis
3. Return to her job as a corporate secretary

During the presentation, the LNC provided detailed information regarding the grade of the fracture, surgeries, effects of diabetes and smoking on the healing process, and definitions of medical terminology, such as osteomyelitis and the Bankart procedure.

Figure 39.1   A Successful Outcome of a Mediation in a Personal Injury Case (Courtesy of Barbara Levin.)

2. It educates the mediator as to the strengths and weaknesses of the medical aspects of the case.
3. It presents evidence that the parties are prepared for trial.

The Plaintiff's Brochure

A number of formats are used in preparing an effective brochure from the plaintiff's perspective. Appendix 39.1 provides a sample of a portion of an LNC's contribution to a settlement brochure. Also, the guidelines below can be incorporated into a brochure format. The LNC should begin by dividing the document into six sections titled Table of Contents, Brief Statement of the Case, Detailed Discussion of Medical Management Issues, Damages and Injuries, Negligence, and Exhibits.

1. The table of contents refers the reader to the pages where specified information is located.
2. The brief statement of the case is a precise statement of position. An example is: "John Doe collapsed and died from cardiac arrest while waiting to be attended to at ABC Hospital." Avoid conveying a description of the case in the statement. The theme of the case can sometimes be used in the brief statement.

3. The detailed statement of medical management issues should be prepared by the LNC in consultation with the attorney. An in-depth study of medical records and medical references enables the LNC to prepare a detailed synopsis of the medical issues.

4. The LNC may also have input into the section on damages and injuries. The one purpose of this section is to humanize the plaintiff, showing the impact of the injuries on the plaintiff and his or her family — what they can and cannot do anymore. An example is John Doe, whose left leg was amputated. An avid skier, he and his two daughters used to take yearly vacations to Colorado at Christmastime to ski, snowboard, and cross-country ski. The reader is referred to photographs of last year's vacation in Tahoe. Poetic license is often used to dramatize the plaintiff's injuries and damages. The damage section should include an itemized accounting of the economic losses (i.e., medical expenses, lost earnings, property damage, etc.). An offer of settlement is also noted.

5. Negligence or gross negligence can also be addressed by the LNC. Violations of standards of care or deviations from policies and procedures fall within the area of the LNC's expertise. Expert reports and experts' curricula vitae are also presented in this section. Authoritative papers, guidelines, and standards written by specialty or other organizations should also be included.

6. The section for exhibits consists of pertinent medical records (appropriately highlighted), medical expense invoices, funeral and burial expense invoices, photographs, greeting cards, letters, school records, employment records, certificates, graphs, charts, etc. This section contains references to supporting data for the brochure. These exhibits are numbered and may be referred to in the narrative of the brochure by number.

The Defendant's Brochure

A defense brochure can be divided into five similar sections:

1. The brief statement of the case from the defendant's viewpoint.

2. The detailed statement of medical management issues may or may not be addressed by the defense; in its place, the defense may wish to insert the defendant doctor's qualifications, experience, and a listing of professional and community services.

3. The section for damages and injuries could be used by the defense to address any mitigating factors.

4. The negligence or gross negligence issue may be addressed by the defense by discussing the defense expert's opinions about the standard of care or any contributing negligence of the plaintiff.

5. The exhibits section may or may not be applicable for defense brochures.

In general, a settlement brochure may present any factor or aspect of a case on which either side wishes to focus. There are no rules or requirements. This is a place where the evidence can be presented creatively for effect.

Other Settlement Modalities

Minitrials

Other settlement tactics that go a step beyond ADR have been created. For example, minitrials have been used in personal injury and medical malpractice cases. The plaintiff's attorney invites the defense attorney, insurance representatives, risk managers, and all pertinent parties to attend a formal preview of the plaintiff side's version of how the trial will proceed. The attorney presents an introduction, summary of the issues, and theories of liability. He or she anticipates the defense theories and offers rebuttals. A verdict form detailing monetary amounts being requested for damages is presented. There may be a discussion of punitive damages, if applicable, with supporting case law. Audiovisuals and exhibits are displayed. The goal is to entice a reluctant defendant to a settlement. Minitrials usually contain only the plaintiff's presentations, with a set time limit after presentation for a defense response to the plaintiff's settlement offer.

Trial Consultants

A variety of consultants aid trial attorneys in developing the themes of a case, sometimes using mock jury presentations or focus groups before entering into settlement discussions or going to trial. Mock juries and focus groups can give the trial team valuable information about what a disinterested third party feels about the facts of a case, the plaintiffs, the defendants, and the experts. This information can be crucial to the strategic planning and development of the case. Such sources of information can help to determine the overall chances of obtaining a satisfactory verdict or judgment. This impartial information can assist the LNC in evaluating complex medical issues in the case to see whether additional explanations or evidence are necessary.

Some LNCs have developed a specialty practice providing jury consulting. Mock jury trials are usually used in cases that involve either large dollar demand or multiple parties, such as class action suits. The LNC specializing in organizing mock jury trials or focus groups works with marketing firms that gather a sample of 50 to 80 persons representative of the demographic area where the trial is to be held. These individuals, who may be randomly selected, receive payment for spending 1 or 2 days listening to and observing a "mock trial." During the mock trial, opening statements as well as witness testimony and demonstrative evidence are introduced to determine or analyze the "jurors'" impressions of what they are hearing and seeing. The jurors may record their responses on a computerized handheld device and the information is entered into a database for future statistical analysis by the trial team. Often members of the trial team sit behind one-way mirrors to determine how the "jurors" discuss the testimony. The LNC may be involved with the statistical analysis of the material or may role-play the expert witness to the jury. After the closing arguments, the mock jury breaks into smaller groups for deliberation. Each group renders a decision (verdict). The verdicts are important because they provide a representation of what an actual jury may render at trial. If all deliberating groups render a higher dollar amount than the defense firm is requesting, then the insurance company will likely be compelled to settle the case.

Jury Research

It is extremely important for a legal team member to adequately research jury verdicts on similar case scenarios prior to the offer of settlement. Reference sources include databases kept by insurance companies, the Association of Trial Lawyers of America, and special reports that are usually compiled by private sources that work through the local courthouse records of verdicts rendered.

The Medical Review Panel

Many states have adopted variations on the medical review panel to provide for resolution of medical malpractice cases outside of a formal trial. Goals of such panels are to reduce the court's caseload, reduce the costs of medical malpractice litigation, and provide a better means of resolving cases. The panel's evaluation of a case provides an objective expert view for both plaintiff and defense counsel. The panel's decision may induce a settlement or convince a plaintiff to reconsider filing a lawsuit. Expensive litigation in court is thus avoided. Louisiana's medical review panel system is one example. Figure 39.2 describes Louisiana's panel system.

The LNC contributes to preparation of the case for presentation to the panel in the same way that he or she prepares for mediated settlement conferences or

---

Louisiana permits its health care providers to become qualified. The advantage of being a qualified health care provider is that all medical malpractice claims must go through a medical review panel prior to filing suit. To become qualified, the participant health care provider must pay an annual premium that supplements the malpractice insurance premium paid to the patients compensation fund.

Once the provider is qualified, there is a cap on the amount awarded in a malpractice claim. The health care provider, or its insurer, is responsible for the first $100,000. The maximum amount awarded by the patient's compensation fund is $400,000, for a total award of $500,000 plus medical costs.

Prior to filing a lawsuit, a case is reviewed by a medical review panel. This panel consists of an attorney chairman and three health care providers, usually physicians: one chosen by the plaintiff, one chosen by the defendant(s), and one chosen by the two selected health care providers.

All parties involved submit evidence to support their positions to the members of the medical review panel. After reviewing the information, the medical review panel attorney chairman convenes a meeting to discuss the information. The panel delivers one of three decisions:

1. The evidence supports the conclusion that the defendant or defendants failed to comply with the appropriate standard of care as charged in the complaint.
2. The evidence does not support the conclusion that the defendant or defendants failed to meet the applicable standard of care as charged in the complaint.
3. There is a material issue of fact, not requiring expert opinion, bearing on liability for consideration by the court.

In rendering an opinion, the panel provides typed reasons to support its decision. The plaintiff has a specified period of time following the panel decision in which to file a lawsuit.

Figure 39.2   Louisiana's Panel System (Courtesy of Janet Kremser.)

for trial. The LNC attends the panel presentations and plays a vital support role for the attorney in helping to detect errors in the opposition's case presentation and analyzing the strengths and weaknesses of the case. The LNC may also serve as a panel member in nursing malpractice cases.

Strengths and Weaknesses of ADR

ADR is considered in its infancy state, and research continues to be conducted to test the efficacy of its use in the private or court system. According to David Sellinger, a Washington, D.C. attorney and mediation proponent, "Litigators in today's economic environment have to think about ADR in most every case they handle."[3] Choosing to utilize one of the various methods of ADR can be a matter of achieving the right results for all parties economically, thereby creating a win–win outcome. Lawyers must decide with their clients how best to proceed with a case, while at the same time evaluate their clients' satisfaction with the desire to create solutions and to participate in the ADR process.

Some persons are concerned that ADR forces certain individuals to give up or lose some rights to which they are entitled in litigation. When parties do not possess equal power and resources, and the informal process of ADR lacks procedural protection, ill-informed decisions can result. Critics of ADR focus their concerns on family law, particularly cases involving domestic disputes. Divorce mediation works well for the entire family unit when both parties control equal positions and work to agree on solutions; when a power imbalance is evident, traditional trial litigation may be the better method of adjudication.

The LNC together with the attorney can provide the best representation for the client. Working to achieve a win–win outcome can be a rewarding experience for a nurse preparing a case to be presented before an alternative forum of adjudication.

References

1. 5 USC § 571(3) (Suppl. 1993).
2. Garner, B.A., Ed., *Blacks Law Dictionary*, 7th ed., West Group, St. Paul, MN, 1999.
3. Hoffman, E., The impact of the ADR Act of 1998, *Trial*, June 1999, 30.

Additional Reading

Craver, C., Mediation: a trial lawyer's guide, *Trial Negotiation and Settlement*, June 1999.

Emery, J., Edwards, L., and Edwards, J., *Civil Procedure and Litigation*, West Legal Studies, New York, 2000.

Hechler, D., ADR finds true believers, *New Jersey Law Journal Business and Law,* July 9, 2001.

Meek, S., *Alternative Dispute Resolution*, Lawyers and Judges Publishers Inc., Tucson, AZ, 1996.

Tex. Rev. Civ. Stat. Ann. art. 4590i, § 15.01.

Test Questions

1. What is the most widely used format of ADR that issues a binding decision?
    A. Mediation
    B. Arbitration
    C. Negotiations
    D. Minitrials

2. An LNC's role in arbitration may include all of the following EXCEPT:
    A. Preparing evidentiary material
    B. Interviewing experts
    C. Educating the litigation team and arbitrator about medical issues
    D. Discussing the facts of the case with the arbitrator after the hearing ends and before the award is rendered

3. Components of a settlement brochure include
    A. Brief statement of the incident
    B. Facts of the dispute
    C. Damages
    D. Demand

4. During mediation, what role does the LNC carry out?
    A. Negotiates the mediator's fee
    B. Is a resource liaison to the mediator
    C. Prepares written negotiated agreement
    D. Develops questions for cross-examination

5. A decision rendered by an arbitrator or a tribunal of arbitrators is referred to as
    A. Award
    B. Decision
    C. Verdict
    D. Memorandum of understanding

Answers: 1. B, 2. D, 3. D, 4. B, 5. A

Appendix 39.1
Components of a Settlement Demand Letter Outlining a Personal Injury Case

(Courtesy of Patrick J. McGroder, JD, and Marlene Vermeer, RN)
United Public Gas Company
RE: Robert Smith
D/L: 4/5/99
Policy #: TX123490

Dear (insurance adjuster):

As you know, I represent Bob Smith in connection with his claim against United Public Gas Company arising from a gas explosion and fire that occurred on April 5, 1999 at approximately 7:50 a.m.

On the day of the explosion, my client had arrived early to work. He remembers well turning on a switch to start a machine. There was a sudden explosion and fire. He was trapped in this flash fire explosion with his body being subjected to flame temperatures of 1500° to 2000° for approximately 1 minute. What he has lived through since the explosion is nearly incomprehensible. His burn scars today are so hideous and disfiguring that both adults and children stare at him wherever he goes. He describes himself as a mutant form of who he formerly was. Whatever he does involves pain; activities are not gauged by whether they cause pain, but rather by how much pain he thinks he can endure in order to do them. For the next 5 years, my client has to look forward to two to three major reconstructive surgeries each year and, as his reconstructive surgeon, Dr. Williams, related, "a tremendous amount of pain from surgery and intense hand therapy postoperatively." While my client visualized working again some day, he has no idea when that day will be or what it is he will do. And he is yet only 29 years old.

Biographical Profile

Bob is the son of James and Karen Smith, ranchers near Hanna, Wyoming. James and Karen were married in January 1967. Just a year later, a phone call came to Karen that her husband had been seriously injured in a trucking accident on icy roads. He was hospitalized nearly 2 months, then laid up for a year from his injuries. It was these memories James had upon seeing his own son injured, knowing the agony of pain and patience his son would endure, if he even survived. On 1/5/70 Karen gave birth to their first and only child, Bob. Karen was 28, James almost 40, and because of James's age they decided to have only Bob.

Bob has meant everything to James and Karen. Later, when Karen learned that her only son was about to be taken from her, she agonized that he was all she had. She remembers 4/5/99 and thinking and praying, "Oh, dear God, he is the only one I've got. Let me get to him before he dies." Karen and James delighted in raising their son. While there seemed always the demands of work, they nonetheless frequently hunted and fished. As a child, Bob would catch wild cats around the barn and tame them. He would ride the countryside on his bike, encountering wolves and getting chased by them. He and his friends hunted up skunks, they were too often "on the south end of a northbound skunk." His mom would then have him in a tomato juice bath before she even allowed him back into the house. But Bob's energy did not stop in his youth with the work on the farm, wrestling, or music. When he was in the seventh grade, he befriended Mary, an elderly German woman whose husband had been killed in a farming accident. Mary was not an easy individual to get along with. However, Bob saw beneath her rough exterior and often performed chores for her. When Bob was in high school, Mary fell and broke her hip, and upon her return home, Bob remained at her bedside as she was afraid to be alone. Bob's mom remembers that when Mary died, he grieved her death greatly.

Bob chose not to attend college after high school. He played in the band and did odd jobs, including construction and farm work. He really did not know what he wanted to do with his life. It was then that Bob's good friend, Tim Krkosa, who lived in Dallas, came home to Wyoming for Christmas in 1996. He spoke glowingly of Dallas, and Bob became more and more curious about the city. When Tim suggested to Bob that he return to Dallas with him, Bob quickly decided that he was "ready for a change." They left Wyoming in the middle of a bad snowstorm, and by 3:00 a.m. the next day, Bob was already on the phone to his dad and mom. "Mom, you ought to see the lights and scenery here in Dallas." Karen still cherishes that phone call — it exemplifies their relationship with their son and how they have shared their lives.

When he got to Dallas, Bob answered an advertisement in the newspaper and was employed at One Stop Printing with Sam Dobson. He learned the business, and when it merged with TriCity Printer in June of 1997, he went there to work. Bob began to change his mind about school. His goals and attitudes expanded. He wanted an education, and he chose electronics technology at Hi-Tech Institute. By the time he was injured, he was enrolled in his fourth term and making good progress. He planned to graduate, but that is now over. His condition does not allow him to concentrate, and he must be totally focused on surgeries and therapies. The time to learn is now gone indefinitely, or at least for years to come.

It was just 2 or 3 weeks before the accident that Bob met his girlfriend Beth. She did not know of the accident, and finally a friend of Bob's told her of the explosion. Beth then called her mom in Wyoming and told her of the situation, wondering whether or not it was appropriate for her to even show up at the hospital, as she barely even knew Bob. Her mom encouraged her to go see Bob "for the sake of his parents. They will appreciate that you went to be with him." Beth was thus with Bob often at the hospital, and upon his discharge, their friendship deepened. Several months ago they moved in together. Beth continues to attend school full time and work part time. She and Bob see each other in the evenings.

Explosion

On the morning of the accident, Bob Smith arrived for work earlier than his usual time. He remembers where everyone in the shop was standing when he turned on a switch to start a machine. He was standing in the middle of the shop. He felt a pressure in the room, then an explosion like a fireball came out of the wall and threw him back 15 feet, where he landed on his back and neck. He got up to run away, ran about 5 feet, when the ceiling collapsed on him. He got up again and continued running out toward the back of the shop. No one was with him at that time. The whole shop collapsed.

As Bob came outdoors he felt more shock than pain. There had been no time to think. He had a sense of feeling confused, and by then the building was on fire. Bob had no idea he had been burned. When he looked down at his arms, they looked bright white like leather, almost like a mask, and they stung a little. Along with the others, he walked to a nearby lawn. One of the guys from the paint store next door took off the rest of Bob's clothing that had not been ripped away in the explosion, except for his underwear, because the clothes were still smoldering. He then just stood and waited and walked around with the others until the paramedics came and rushed him into an ambulance. Bob's co-worker Danny had to be transported with him, so there was a wait for Bob to be ready to be transported. By then, he was beginning to feel pain, but if he did not move too much, it was not too bad.

Bob remembers his good friend Danny being in the ambulance with him. They were both conscious. He talked to Danny on the way to the hospital, recalling since then that he was the last person Danny knew who talked to him before Danny died. They were in adjoining rooms in the Burn Unit, but he never saw his friend again.

Upon Bob's arrival at the emergency room, he was extremely agitated, to the point where he jumped out of the ambulance, ran to the doorway, and stood confused. The nurses immediately placed him on a gurney and wheeled him into a room. He remembers everyone running around and the nurse telling him, "I am going to give you something for the pain." Then he was out, and that is really the last thing he remembered of his 6-week stay at the Burn Unit at Texas Medical Center. He says he knows he saw his dad there, but he can't really remember the experience. What he does know for certain is that there has been so much pain since then that he is really not able to focus on that experience separate from the rest.

Medical Records Report

Paramedics at the scene noted "second and third degree burns over the entire body," with "severe skin sloughing" of the upper and lower extremities and back. According to the Texas Medical Center records, Bob arrived at the Burn Unit at 0813. Initial nurses' notes indicate the following: "Slipping epidermis on face and all four extremities. Hands degloved. Intact tissue appears leathery white to head and face, arms and hands, and upper thighs to ankles circumferential. Back approximately 58% moist pink, partial thickness burned. All facial hair burned with small patch in back of head left intact. Eyes appear opaque."

Twelve minutes later, at 0825, Bob was given morphine 10 mg IV, a potent narcotic for pain. Four minutes later, he was given another 10 mg of morphine and 5 mg of Versed® (a short acting muscle relaxant and also an effective amnesiac — although patients may declare pain while on Versed, they afterwards tend not to remember the painful experience). At 0836 Bob received not only another 10 mg of morphine but also 10 mg of Norcuron® (a drug that totally paralyzes the body, including the ability to breathe, but does not inhibit consciousness, the will to breathe, or the experience of pain). It was obvious that not only was the Versed not sedating Bob enough, but also the 10 mg morphine increments were inadequate; he was subsequently given 15 mg increments during his resuscitation. Over the next $1^1/_2$ hours, as aggressive treatment was initiated and continued, Bob received a total of 215 mg of morphine, 10 mg of Versed, and 40 mg of Norcuron. During this time, the following was undertaken:

1. An arterial line, which involves an invasive procedure into an artery, was placed for blood pressure monitoring.
2. SwanGanz line was inserted through a vein near the neck, with a catheter tube threaded through the heart and into the lungs, to monitor pressures that guided fluid resuscitation.
3. Bob was intubated secondary not only due to concern regarding burns to his airway and toxic inhalation injury, but also because of receiving paralyzing medications — morphine, Versed, and Norcuron. Note the anesthesia entry:
   0820. "Responded to call regarding burn patient. Arrival at Burn Unit. Upon arrival patient excited, agitated, requesting pain medication." The anesthesiologist administered Norcuron and then performed intubation.
4. Escharotomies[1] of both legs and escharotomies/fasciotomies[2] of both arms, including the hands and fingers, were done.

Burn Chief notes: Following loss of pulses to the lower extremities, "escharotomy quickly performed using Bovie electrocautery (a hot knife that coagulates blood and tissue as it cuts) on both lower extremities. Pulses returned."

Hand surgeon notes: "No radial or ulna pulses (wrist). No capillary refill in nail beds (fingertips). Emergency escharotomy/fasciotomy of bilateral upper extremities done with electrocautery and scalpel as needed, including two upper arm, forearms, carpal tunnel (wrist), thenar and hypothenar areas (palms of hands), and interosseus (between the bones in the hands and fingers). Subcutaneous tissue and muscle underneath visible, though almost no bleeding noted from the fingers (secondary to no blood supply to them)."

Upon admission it was determined that Bob had sustained 65% TBSA (total burn surface area) burns, of which 50% were 3rd degree.[3] Note the Burn Chief's notes: "Burns covering entire face including forehead, eyelids, nose with singed

---

[1] Escharotomy is done in an effort to save limbs secondary to the massive swelling that occurs with severe burns. When tissue is burned, there is an exodus to and leaking of fluid to the burned areas. Meanwhile, the burned skin is tough and nonpliable and does not stretch to accommodate this swelling. In confined spaces, such as limbs and digits, this fluid builds up such high internal pressures as to compress nerves and cut off blood supply. Left untreated, the limb quickly dies, and if the patient is still alive, the limb is eventually amputated.

[2] When burns are so severe that escharotomy does not satisfactorily relieve the burn pressures, then one proceeds to the more radical emergency fasciotomy. This involves incising the eschar and continuing down into the muscle belly compartments. While escharotomy may not be exceedingly painful (nerve endings in eschar tend to be coagulated by the burn injury), such is not the case for fasciotomy, where visible tissue and nerves are transected. It is noted that in Bob's hands and fingers burn injuries were severe. There was barely any bleeding when the cautery dissection was undertaken.

[3] Dr. Williams later corrected these percentages. In his report of 11/6/94, he has noted that Bob "sustained 80% total burn surface area and 60% full thickness burns to his body."

nasal hairs, lips, ears, neck, bilateral circumferential burns from mid biceps to fingertips, bilateral circumferential legs from above the knees to ankles, posterior thighs and entire back."

Besides the skin burns, there was massive inhalation lung injury. With intubation, his vocal cords were noted to be edematous and his glottis erythematous; lung sounds were "coarse to raw."

Shortly after admission, a call was made by the Burn Chief to Bob's parents in Wyoming. Mrs. Smith was informed of the gravity of the situation and traveled to Dallas as soon as she could. She arrived in Dallas at 4:45 p.m. and went directly to the Burn Unit at Texas Medical Center. By then, Bob's condition had been momentarily stabilized. CT scans of his head and cervical spine x-ray were reported negative, and despite the abnormal breath sounds and suspected inhalation injury, chest x-ray did not show pulmonary infiltrates, pleural effusion, or pneumothorax. (Chest x-rays in burn victims are often normal and must not give false reassurance to the status of the respiratory system.)

Twenty-four hours after Bob's burn, his problems began to compound and his condition deteriorate. By 0200 on 4/6/93, his platelet counts were beginning to plummet, at 117,000 (N = 140,000–440,000). Six hours later, the count was down to 74,000, then 65,000 at 3:45 p.m. that day. While his blood was initially concentrated after the burns (hemoglobin and hematocrit were elevated at 18.1 and 52.8, a normal reaction to burn injury), due to massive fluid exodus from the blood vessels while leaving the red cells behind, the counts were stable on day 2, 4/6/99. The fasciotomies done on Bob's arms 24 hours earlier failed, with increased pressures, requiring again deep incisions into the fascia and muscle bellies of the arms to allow for pressure release.

The pain following these procedures was excruciating, and Bob began to talk with the nurses about his fear of dying during this time:

4/7/99   Progress Note: "Patient with extreme agitation last night unresponsive to Morphine, Versed, Ativan® and finally resolved with Haldol®" [a powerful antipsychotic]."
         Nurse's Note: "Agitated at times, anxious, 'Am I dying.'"
4/8/99   Nurse's Note: "Able to communicate by whispering words. Asked if he is dying." "Patient mouthed the word, 'Why?,' patient calmed with talking."
4/12/99 Nurse's Note: "Increasing agitation. Wants dressing off of hands, informed can't get those off until Monday. Patient mad and held hands against rails. Respiration up to 30–40 … heart rate up." "When asked again what he was upset about he kept shaking his hands."
5/21/99 Nurse's Note: "Patient crying. States terrified to leave here."

On 4/15/99, Bob learned his friend Danny had been killed. Support from the Burn Unit psychologist is noted in the records: "Bob's friend informed me that they have informed Bob of his friend's death. Although tearful, Bob appears to be coping well."

Bob was ready for discharge from the Burn Unit on 5/21/99. By then the chest tubes had been removed, as had the tracheotomy tube from his lung. His Foley catheter was taken from his bladder, and despite drainage of blood from his penis upon its removal, he was able to void independently. The tubes that had been placed through his nose into the stomach (the nasogastric tube for suctioning his stomach, the duodenum tube for high-protein administration directly into his intestines) were removed, and Bob was allowed to eat. Dr. Hampton's discharge notes of 5/21/99 have succinctly summarized what happened to Bob during his hospital stay:

> Final diagnosis: 60% total body surface area burns, 2nd and 3rd degree, to face, arms, legs, and back, including hands and feet. Showed evidence of mild inhalation injury. Escharotomies were performed immediately on his lower legs and then upper arms and hands.... Will be discharged to Avery's for rehabilitation.

Discussion with Mr. and Mrs. Smith

Mr. and Mrs. Smith have discussed with us at length their experiences with their son at the Burn Unit. They recalled the events of that day, starting with the phone call received from the Sheriff's office. Mrs. Smith immediately contacted her husband and then placed a call to Texas Medical Center. However, the surgeon was operating on Bob and would return the call as soon as surgery ended. Meanwhile, Karen Smith sat by the phone and waited. Dr. Hampton phoned informing her of Bob's condition, stating, "I don't know how much longer I can keep him alive." He told her that they should come right away to Dallas. They were on the next flight to Dallas, and the airlines subsequently held the plane waiting for them due to the gravity of the situation.

Mrs. Smith recalled the time that Bob was informed of Danny's death after the explosion. While she was out of the room, a friend of Bob's (Ray) informed Bob of their friend's death. Bob was devastated, became very emotional, and cried and cried while they held him.

On 7/20/99, Dr. Williams did his next surgery on Bob. He performed full facial dermabrasion and then further surgery on his face and all the extremities — further release of oral commissures, right elbow and hand, and left hand contractures. Bob has noted improved use of his hands since the surgery was done, to the extent that he can now drive. However, he still has no dexterity in those hands. Now, another surgery is planned for later this month, with further reconstruction of his facial scars and his right upper extremity, with split thickness grafts to all open areas on the right hand.

Dr. Williams has recently prepared a report and is willing to testify regarding his care for Bob to date as well as his projected treatments over the next 5 or more years. In that report he commented that essentially the only part of Bob's body that is not scarred is his upper thighs. As you are aware, however, Dr. Williams has used even Bob's groins to get grafts. He projects that Bob will need at least 2, possibly 3, operations per year for the next 5 years, "in order to take care of the majority of his functional and visible problems." These surgeries will total at least 15, making it approximately 40 surgeries that Bob will then have had for his burn injuries. Despite all of his surgeries, Bob will always have visible deformities from at least 30 feet away. There will always be scars around his cheeks and mouth, and his lips will always be enlarged and swollen. Even though he has regained some function of his hands, they will always be visibly full of scars and according to Dr. Williams "will always look terrible." Kids will see him, turn away, and ask their mothers, "Why does that man look that way?"

Dr. Williams says that Bob will always have contractures; however, if Bob experiences a good outcome from the surgeries, and if he is as persistent with therapy in the years to come as he is today, he will at best have a 25% loss of function in his upper extremities. Dr. Williams does add that Bob may also realistically have a "50% loss of functioning" and no matter what, his skin grafts will always be unstable. A minor trauma of a bump against a wall could be a major trauma for Bob as he would need to go back to surgery for a repeat skin graft.

Dr. Williams also discussed with Bob the plan for treating the terrible scarring on Bob's legs. "His legs are of lowest priority," not that he does not require surgical attention, but in Bob's case there is no available skin to work with. A two- or three-stage dermabrasion to soften the texture of the skin may be attempted. However, the deformities will always remain. Bob will continue to require hand therapy three to five times per week over the next several years. He will also need to continue wearing Jobst garments over that time. Dr. Williams further describes Bob as a person and as a patient:

> "I think, in spite of this major reconstructive effort in this most coop-
> erative and stoic patient, the patient is in for a tremendous amount of
> pain from surgery, and from intense postoperative hand therapy. The
> patient, now, has major functional deficits of both upper extremities
> with minimal flexion and extension of the elbows, and minimal use of
> his hands. He cannot hold things, and he easily drops things. The scars
> on both his face and both upper extremities are very unstable. Repetitive
> friction on the hands, and just the act of shaving on the face, causes
> skin to literally come off. Hopefully, this will improve as well as we
> replace the burn tissue on his face and hands with more durable slab
> and skin graft tissue. I would predict that the patient, if we are lucky,
> would, after 5 years of multiple operations per year and intense hand
> therapy, have perhaps 60% maximum function of his elbows, wrists,
> and hands. As far as visible scars, the patient will always have marked
> scarring of both lower extremities and both upper extremities, and his
> face will continue to be obviously scarred. This psychologically devas-
> tates this young man, who was very active physically and socially prior
> to the burn. I have noticed after taking care of this patient, now, for
> 7 months that he is in dire need of emotional support. He frequently
> stops by the office to talk to my office staff, who have been very
> supportive to him; he is basically looking for a friend to talk to, and
> to give him positive reinforcement. A fair amount of time is spent at
> each office visit, encouraging the patient that he will over time improve
> his appearance, and that we are desperately trying to get him to a point
> where he can go out in public without people staring at him and young
> children being scared by his appearance."

Functional Limitations

Dr. Williams stated that Bob will always need a job in a cool environment, due to his inability to lose heat — his sweat glands, according to Dr. Williams, "were cooked in the fire." And if he works outdoors, he will always have to be covered, as he can have absolutely no sun exposure. For Bob vocational retraining cannot even be entertained until his surgeries and therapies are finished, and by then he will have been out of the work force a minimum of 7 years. He will return not only "out of touch" as a worker, but also as a newcomer in a new vocation, applying for a job as a physically disfigured worker.

Bob states that he is able to keep up his apartment. He can vacuum, but he must manipulate the vacuum hose, for instance, so that it does not get away from his contracted and immobile hands. He cooks, but this too is a creative endeavor, as Bob cannot open a sealed jar. According to Bob, "Nothing is fluid, everything is clumsy and slow." Dr. Williams has told us that Bob will always have tactile and sensation problems with his hands. He says that if Bob can't lift a glass of water now without clumsily adjusting it (which Dr. Williams knows to be true), then that will never change — Bob will never be able to even lift a glass of water normally.

Before the accident, Bob wore contacts. Now he can't get them into his eyes with his injured hands, so he wears glasses. Regarding his hands, he thinks the sensation is there, but he can't grab with or bend them. Not only were the pads of his fingertips burned away, but also he has only smooth thin grafted skin on his fingers and fingertips. Therefore, there is no friction, and everything just slides out of his hands, and he can't hold on to anything without somehow manipulating what he is holding.

He has also attempted to return to school. Even Bob believes, however, the strength of his mind was compromised by the trauma, the medication, and what he has since gone through. Dr. McNully has commented on this as well:

> "His attempts to reinstitute more control over his life and his functioning are often thwarted by the reality of his physical limitation. He would like to have returned to DeVry but was unable to pass the necessary prerequisites to do so and declined a one-class-at-a-time schedule. The traumatic injury and burns and the multiple surgeries and the lengthy drug-induced stuporous condition in the hospital likely impacted his attention span and short memory function."

Finally, the psychological pain that Bob has endured has been immense and already discussed in this correspondence. Bob describes himself as a mutant. He said on June 10, 2000 to psychologist Rick McNully, Ph.D., "I haven't gotten used to my appearance. This is not me. This is a mutant form of me, and I will never be the same." When he is with people he knows, he is safe, and no one stares. When out in public, especially alone, the stares are painful and hard. Children stare the hardest. When Dr. McNully saw Bob on three different visits between 6/10/00 and 6/21/00, he administered neuropsychological and personality tests.

Summary

The above describes a young man who is hard pressed to find anything in life to anticipate other than more pain. He will remain grossly disfigured and will stand out as scarred and distorted wherever he goes. Whether he will ever be able to work, at least in a position that suits his mental capacities and interests, is indeed questionable. What does a man — disfigured, his mind numbed with torturous pain and events of past years, with fragile skin grafts everywhere, and who has been out of the work force for years — find for gainful and satisfying employment? We already know that not even TriCity Printer would take him back. He and Beth are young. What if their relationship is not for the long term? Dr. McNully has described Bob's desperation to keep Beth for fear no other woman would have him. Bob plays pool every day — few other recreational pursuits are reasonably available to him. And the future mental toll is impossible to calculate — Bob already struggles dreadfully emotionally. What if he can't hold it together? Dr. McNully has even mentioned future psychiatric hospitalization as a possibility.

What about Bob's parents and their agony? Every day their minds are with their only son. What had their wishes been for his future? They were delighted to hear he had found employment he liked and was getting an education after he went to Dallas. And will they assume some of his physical care in the future too, not to mention the emotional sustenance they have provided and will continue to provide him?

Bob Smith was a fun-loving, ambitious kid from Wyoming. He had a promising future. There is nothing left to offer him at this time other than generous and expeditious compensation.

[Reader's note: The remainder of the settlement demand letter was authored by the client's attorney and included economic damages, legal theories, etc. Pre- and postinjury photos were also presented. This case resulted in a multimillion-dollar nonlitigated settlement for Bob and his parents.]

Chapter 40

The Role of the Legal Nurse Consultant in Preparation of Technical Demonstrative Evidence

Rosie Oldham, BS, RN, LNCC, and
Patricia Karalow, BA, RN, LNCC

CONTENTS

0-8493-1418-6/03/$0.00+$1.50
© 2003 by AALNC

Objectives

- To describe the role of the legal nurse consultant in preparation and presentation of demonstrative evidence
- To discuss preparation of digital exhibits and successful presentation of case issues
- To review the admissibility and use of technical demonstrative evidence in the courts

Introduction

The courts are quickly adapting to the 21st century through the use of available technology, with more than 100 federal courtrooms across the country prewired for paperless trials. Hampered by lack of skill in the use of technology, many trial lawyers still present demonstrative evidence to jurors by holding up exhibits, handing documents to jurors, and using foam board blow-ups and easels that the jurors cannot easily see.

Legal nurse consultants (LNCs) possessing technical skills and legal nurse consulting experience can provide a winning edge to their attorney clients through the technical presentation·of evidence. The LNC can do this by taking advantage of the recent technological advances. The best way to present evidence, particularly in document-intensive cases, is to use readily available equipment such as a laptop computer and a portable projector. The next section of this chapter discusses the skill requirements and the equipment that LNCs need to incorporate into their practices. This information is critical to presenting evidence at conferences and trial by electronic methods.

Skill Requirements for the LNC

Advanced Technical Skills and Use of Software, Hardware, and Equipment

A "technical nurse consultant" is an LNC who has advanced expertise in the use of technical equipment and assists the attorney client in presenting the demonstrative evidence. It is essential for technical nurse consultants to be very familiar with hardware and software integration, aware of potential conflicts that may exist in coordinating the resources of the computer to match or exceed the software requirements, and able to troubleshoot these systems independently.

The LNC must be able to problem-solve, remove, or replace hardware and software components that may stop functioning during a presentation. A local backup technician should be identified and prepared in advance to repair or replace the equipment on site if the LNC is not able to do so. It is recommended that additional equipment be available on site to use as an alternate plan in case the LNC is unable to restore the malfunctioning system. Backup equipment is a virtual necessity because postponement of the presentation during a trial will likely interrupt the flow of the trial, frustrate the client and judge, and compromise the LNC's relationship with the client attorney.

The equipment needed for technical presentation of a case minimally includes a laptop computer (with dual monitor capability), appropriate trial presentation and graphics software, and a projector. A desktop computer can be used if a laptop computer is not available. The main drawback to the desktop computer is its size and weight, which make it cumbersome to move.

Presentation software runs the gamut in cost and functionality from basic presentation programs, such as Microsoft PowerPoint®, to programs designed to organize thousands of courtroom exhibits such as documents, graphs, illustrations, video- and audiotapes, video depositions, and photographs. Individual software programs need to be closely analyzed for functionality in the specific environment.

Exploring a program requires time to evaluate its trial version (the test version) before deciding to purchase. If the maker does not offer a trial version, then an in-depth brochure about the software should be available, although it is difficult to determine a program's applicability from only a description.

The software purchase creates a foundation for other computer purchasing decisions. Software requirements dictate how much memory and disk space the laptop computer requires. The hard drive must have the capacity (20 to 60 gigabytes) to accommodate large volumes of digitized documents; no size is too big. Some Internet sites that can help the LNC begin investigating equipment and software are http://www.indatacorp.com, http://www.trialvis.com, http://www.projectorcentral.com, http://www.microsoft.com, and http://www.projectus.com. Their mention here is not to be construed as an endorsement of any particular product. A simple search engine, such as http://www.google.com, is beneficial in locating current Internet sites for medical graphics software.

The projector's quality is measured in lumens and resolution. The choice of projector depends on the presentation venue. Larger rooms require higher lumens. It is recommended that the native resolution of the projector match the screen resolution the computer uses.

A projector stand, a screen, sound equipment, and a surge protector are also probable needs. A surge protector is recommended because the building's electrical system may have variances that can cause damage to the equipment. Some manufacturers of surge protectors provide insurance for the equipment if the surge protector fails to protect it. A prudent technical nurse consultant also considers purchasing additional insurance on the equipment to cover theft, damage, and loss.

A digital video camera can also be set up on a tripod and connected to the projector to project three-dimensional exhibits onto the screen, allowing everyone to see the exhibits simultaneously. This method is used primarily with three-dimensional exhibits that have not been digitized (scanned) previously or that will be handled in the courtroom.

Technical presentations can be complex, and attorneys may have difficulty understanding the labor-intensive process of developing demonstrative evidence. It is practical to give clients a terms-of-engagement document that outlines issues related to use of technology in the courtroom. A good business attorney can assist in the development of this document.

Presentation Style

The LNC who chooses to enter the realm of technical nurse consulting or expert fact witnessing (many provide both services) must possess excellent skills to evaluate, analyze, and present information in a visual manner that enables jurors and judges to understand the case issues. Chapter 36 presents more information on this topic. A minimum of 2 years' experience as an LNC is crucial because reviewing and analyzing medical records prepares the nurse to develop technical presentation skills based on knowledge of case facts.

The LNC should possess highly sophisticated technical skills to assist the attorney with presenting the case by utilizing graphics that clearly reflect relevant issues. The LNC must pay attention to scale, color, and contrast. Taking a basic art class may assist the LNC in developing these creative skills. Colors are especially meaningful, and the judicious use of color in demonstrative evidence can communicate ideas beyond printed words. High contrast at a distance improves readability. For example, blue text on a green background would detract from the message.

Not only must the LNC's dress and demeanor be professional, but his or her ability to appear calm and confident is vital. Taking a speech class or joining a Toastmasters group can assist the LNC with building confidence in making presentations. Attending classes that provide preparation for using software to present a story can also be useful.

Knowledge of Resources, Utilization of Graphics and Anatomical Exhibits, and Digitization of Exhibits

Authoritative Internet sites, textbooks, and journals can be used as resources for preparation of information to be used as demonstrative evidence. Exhibits can be purchased from any medical organization with a Web site that is considered to be an authoritative body, or from standard-of-care resources (e.g., http://www.americanheart.org). Some sites may require subscription activation to access information and exhibits. Authoritative textbooks and journals are mainstay resources for potential exhibits.

Graphics and anatomical exhibits can be obtained by outsourcing to a medical exhibit company such as http://www.doereport.com or http://www.vesalius.com, or the exhibits can be scanned from authoritative medical textbooks, with adherence to the appropriate copyright regulations. Most often the price of exhibits purchased from medical exhibit companies includes the copyright fee, and the companies give instructions on how their copyright restrictions apply.

Advantages of digitizing (scanning) exhibits and using an electronic presentation method include the following:

- This technology provides easy on-screen annotation during presentation, including zooming in on and enlarging a particular portion of the exhibit.
- Annotated exhibits can be saved for later use without having to take an actual exhibit out of the courtroom for copying.
- Video depositions and other video files can be played onto the projector from the computer. Videos can be displayed side by side with the syn-

chronized transcript. Using special deposition software, other exhibits can be displayed simultaneously on the screen to correlate to the video segment. The exhibit can be "attached" to a certain segment of the transcript in advance in order to appear automatically in the open field on the screen, and the video can be paused while the exhibit is discussed.

■ Significant segments of the audio or video can be made into clips and instantly retrieved and played at just the critical moment.

■ Computer-animated accident reenactments can easily be presented.

■ Poor-quality audio or video can be enhanced for clarity by linking with the transcript of a particular tape, such as a "911" audiotape that may be difficult to hear. A simultaneous transcript can be cued for synchronous play to allow visual clarity of the content.

■ Trial-presentation programs can often support multimedia file formats such as RealAudio™ and RealVideo™, and tools such as Microsoft PowerPoint, Adobe Acrobat™, Internet Explorer™, Microsoft Word™, and QuickTime Player™.

■ File formats supported often include, but are not limited to, AVI, WAV, MPEG1, Word, ASCII, PowerPoint, HTML, PDF, JPG, TIFF, and BMP.

■ Digital exhibits can be prepared in a thumbnail format (minimized picture of the image) in a trial notebook for easy reference, with an associated bar code next to the thumbnail image for retrieval and display.

■ Digital exhibits can be sent over the Internet to facilitate discussion by the legal team of the applicability of the particular exhibit for a particular witness or segment of the trial. Graphics and presentations can be uploaded to a password-secured Web site for viewing by the trial team.

■ Digital exhibits make it possible to have all demonstrative evidence on hand in the courtroom.

Case documents and other exhibits are digitized and stored on CD-ROM discs. Digitization for a large number of exhibits is best outsourced to a production company that has equipment to scan and digitize large numbers of exhibits quickly. The production company scans each exhibit and assigns a file name and Bates number or bar code to each document. The original exhibits are returned along with one or more CD-ROMs on which the digitized documents are stored. The software program will dictate the file format for the exhibits. If fewer than 10 to 20 exhibits are to be used, they can be digitized with an office scanner.

A digital exhibit file can be located by various methods, the simplest method being the bar code that was assigned to that document. The bar code technology is extremely beneficial for long trials in which document retrieval is often time-consuming. Other methods of file retrieval are dependent upon the particular presentation software that is used.

Example 40.1: Use of technical demonstrative evidence helped result in an $18 million verdict in *Guerrero v. Republic Silver State Disposal*, Department 19, District Court of Las Vegas, NV in November 2001. Graphics showing evidence of the defendant's liability (the driver of the disposal truck) were reflected by using a "scrolling" timeline depicting multiple safety citations. Accident photos in which sections were enlarged while projected on the screen showed the damage to the plaintiff's crushed car. Pictures of the plaintiff before and after the accident were critical in showing the damage to the client. The use of the technology enhanced the jurors' understanding of the brain damage that the plaintiff had incurred in the accident.

Role of the LNC

Identify Critical Time Frames and Coordinate Evidence with Facts

As part of a legal team, the LNC uses clinical expertise to assist attorneys with the medical records review and analysis of case evidence where law and medicine are intertwined. The LNC may work as a technical nurse consultant or expert fact witness with the legal team on cases in the arenas of medical malpractice, product liability, personal injury, and other medical issues. Through clinical experience, education, and research, the LNC identifies significant medical facts of the case and educates the legal team about the health care issues and what evidence would best be presented in the courtroom.

Through review of relevant medical records, the LNC is able to develop an analysis of case evidence. The LNC must summarize and analyze pertinent medical information and correlate this with the allegations relevant to each case. Providing literature research, the LNC identifies pertinent standards of care, guidelines, and regulatory requirements. The LNC may be needed to define and identify issues of liability, negligence, or inconsistencies in deposition testimony, and interpret complex information in the medical records. Simplifying complex information in a graphic chart will help the judge and jurors understand the issue represented. For example, in a case in which unexpected postoperative bleeding is indicated by abnormal vital signs as seen in the anesthesia record, a graphic of the vital signs can be produced that indicates the approximate time the bleeding began. If the bleeding was recognized, the anesthesiologist may have documented this on the record. The vital sign graphic and the digitized record by the anesthesiologist can be presented side by side to assist the jurors with understanding the proximity of vital sign changes in the patient to the actual time the bleeding began.

It is important during production of evidence to identify critical time frames and their correlation with the facts of the case. Once these issues are identified, collaboration with the LNC allows the litigation team to focus on the key points.

Issue and Focal Point Identification

Evidence obtained through the LNC's review of medical records and other relevant documents is frequently used as demonstrative evidence. This evidence, which is usually gathered during the discovery phase of a case, can be illustrated through the use of technology. Technologically generated images can emphasize key points in the legal team's arguments. As part of the litigation team, the LNC must understand the key points of the case and determine how the attorneys want those points presented to the jury. Communication between the LNC and the legal team is critical to a successful strategy for presenting the demonstrative evidence.

Conference with the Legal Team to Develop Case Strategy

Demonstrative evidence is a powerful tool and one that needs to be fine-tuned. Brainstorming sessions help in the development of powerful and cost-effective courtroom graphics, animations, and illustrations. The brainstorming process reduces cost by fine-tuning what will actually be useful in the presentation of the evidence. The ideal situation allows the LNC to plan ahead 3 to 5 months before trial. The initial meeting focuses only on the technical strategies of demonstrative evidence and how it will be illustrated, generated, and presented to the jury. It is important that all members of the litigation team be present.

The brainstorming process begins with the development of ideas. This leads to the details for each idea and an evaluation to determine which are relevant. For example, in a case in which a lung was perforated by placement of a nasogastric tube, the details of the graphics included an animation of the tube being advanced correctly into the stomach. A second presentation for this case included animation of the tube placement through the lung with the addition of blood at the site of perforation. During the planning process, the LNC needs to assess who will use the graphic in testimony or whether it will be a part of the opening statement or closing argument. It is important that the source of the evidence or data be documented and disclosed to the court.

Final Review

Once the litigation team has decided on the demonstrative evidence and how it will be presented, a step back must be taken to ensure the illustration's merit to the case. The LNC should evaluate the flow and quality of the evidence. It is imperative after completion of the project to have a last review of the evidence with the litigation team and others important to the final presentation of the evidence.[2]

The LNC is responsible for determining which exhibits should be digitized. The attorney gives final authorization that is based on consideration of costs and deadlines. Adherence to deadlines prior to trial or settlement conferences is mandatory.

Preparation of Demonstrative Evidence

Legal Team Review of Admissibility of Evidence in Presentation Format and Rules of Procedure

Countless hours can be spent generating demonstrative evidence that the technical nurse consultant or fact witness will present. It is the attorney's responsibility to obtain the court's approval of the use of the technical nurse consultant or expert fact witness. The technical nurse consultant and the expert fact witness roles may be intertwined but also may be separate. The technical nurse consultant may present the information in the courtroom using a laptop computer without ever taking the witness stand. The expert fact witness may never utilize a computer, but present testimony with or without demonstrative aids. Attorneys are recognizing the value of the expert fact witness capable of presenting information from the medical record using demonstrative evidence.

The attorney must follow certain preliminary steps, such as authentication and accuracy. This is known as "laying the foundation" and is mandatory whenever any scientific expertise is forthcoming. Foundational requirements (other than those dealing with the expertise of the person) usually involve:

- Authentication. The demonstrative evidence should convey what it is meant to convey.
- Representational accuracy. The demonstrative evidence should depict the scale, dimensions, and contours of the underlying evidence fairly.
- Identification. The demonstrative evidence must be an exact match to the underlying evidence or the testimony illustrated.[3]

The U.S. Supreme Court decided in *Daubert v. Merrell Dow Pharmaceuticals* (1993) that the role of the judge is to be the gatekeeper who evaluates the methodology, reliability, and relevance of expert opinions. If the judge decides that expert opinions are not founded on valid scientific methodology, then the expert's opinions are not admitted into evidence for consideration by the jury.[4] The LNC needs to be aware of the principles of the *Daubert* decision and the impact that decision has made on the admissibility of evidence. The sources used for the presentation must reflect scientific knowledge and accuracy. Several of the Federal Rules of Evidence (FRE) were amended on the basis of the *Daubert* case. It is important for the LNC to understand these rules and to be aware of state requirements regarding evidence admissibility.

FRE 104 refers to the preliminary questions. This rule states:

(a) Preliminary questions concerning the qualification of a person to be a witness, the existence of a privilege, or the admissibility of evidence shall be determined by the court, subject to the provisions of subdivision (b). In making its determination it is not bound by the rules of evidence except those with respect to privileges.

(b) When the relevancy of evidence depends upon the fulfillment of a condition of fact, the court shall admit it upon, or subject to, the introduction of evidence sufficient to support a finding of the fulfillment of the condition.

LNCs must be prepared to answer questions regarding nursing education and clinical experiences. A copy of the LNC's curriculum vitae should have already been provided to the attorney.

FRE 401 refers to the definition of "relevant evidence." This rules states:

"Relevant evidence" means evidence having any tendency to make the existence of any fact that is of consequence to the determination of the action more probable or less probable than it would be without the evidence.

The evidence must correspond to the information in the medical records that is to be presented and must be pertinent to the facts of the case. It must help educate the trier of fact about the medical issues of the case.

FRE 402 refers to the admissibility of relevant evidence. This rule states:

> All relevant evidence is admissible, except as otherwise provided by the Constitution of the United States, by Act of Congress, by these rules, or by other rules prescribed by the Supreme Court pursuant to statutory authority. Evidence which is not relevant is not admissible.

The LNC must make sure that all information presented refers to the specific medical issues of the case and keep the information clear and concise. It is important to stick to the facts of the case.

FRE 403 refers to the exclusion of relevant evidence. This rule states:

> Although relevant, evidence may be excluded if its probative value is substantially outweighed by the danger of unfair prejudice, confusion of the issues, or misleading the jury, or by considerations of undue delay, waste of time, or needless presentation of cumulative evidence.

Again, the judge might choose, on the basis of pretrial motions, to exclude some information that could be presented. The LNC must keep abreast of changes by communicating directly with the attorney and insisting on motion updates that may impact the presentation, and be ready to make changes as necessary. The attorney needs to be aware of this responsibility and to advise the LNC of changes.

FRE 611 refers to the mode and order of interrogation and presentation. This rule states:

> (a) The court shall exercise reasonable control over the mode and order of interrogating witnesses and presenting evidence so as to (1) make the interrogation and presentation effective for the ascertainment of the truth, (2) avoid needless consumption of time, and (3) protect witnesses from harassment or undue embarrassment.
>
> (b) Cross-examination should be limited to the subject matter of the direct examination and matters affecting the credibility of the witness. The court may, in the exercise of discretion, permit inquiry into additional matters as if on direct examination.

Again, the judge has the final say in permitting the presentation by the LNC expert fact witness.

FRE 701 refers to the opinion testimony by lay witnesses. This rule states:

> If the witness is not testifying as an expert, the witness' testimony in the form of opinions or inferences is limited to those opinions or inferences which are (a) rationally based on the perception of the witness [and] (b) helpful to a clear understanding of the witness' testimony or the determination of a fact in issue ...

The expert fact witness does not provide any opinions regarding the issues. The LNC is to provide an educational presentation regarding the medical facts of the case.

FRE 702 refers to the testimony by experts. This rule states:

> If scientific, technical, or other specialized knowledge will assist the trier of fact to understand the evidence or to determine a fact in issue, a witness qualified as an expert by knowledge, skill, experience, training, or education, may testify thereto in the form of an opinion or otherwise, if (1) the testimony is based upon sufficient facts or data, (2) the testimony is the product of reliable principles and methods, and (3) the witness has applied the principles and methods reliably to the facts of the case.

The LNC must make sure that research is done from accurate and reliable sources. Anatomical pictures or diagrams must be from reliable, authoritative resources.
FRE 703 refers to the bases of opinion testimony by experts. This rule states:

> The facts or data in the particular case upon which an expert bases an opinion or inference may be those perceived by or made known to the expert at or before the hearing. If of a type reasonably relied upon by experts in the particular field in forming opinions or inferences upon the subject, the facts or data need not be admissible in evidence in order for the opinion or inference to be admitted. Facts or data that are otherwise inadmissible shall not be disclosed to the jury by the proponent of the opinion or inference unless the court determines that their probative value in assisting the jury to evaluate the expert's opinion substantially outweighs their prejudicial effect.

The LNC must make sure that the information presented is accurate.
FRE 1006 refers to summaries. This rule states:

> The contents of voluminous writings, recordings, or photographs which cannot conveniently be examined in court may be presented in the form of a chart, summary, or calculation. The originals, or duplicates, shall be made available for examination or copying, or both, by other parties at reasonable time and place. The court may order that they be produced in court.

Many times the LNC may use graphs or charts to reveal the sequence of the medical facts of the case. These must be accurate, reliable, and relevant to the issues of the case.
FRE 1008 refers to the functions of court and jury. This rule states:

> When the admissibility of other evidence of contents of writings, recordings, or photographs under these rules depends upon the fulfillment of a condition of fact, the question whether the condition has been fulfilled is ordinarily for the court to determine in accordance with the provisions of rule 104. However, when an issue is raised (a) whether the asserted writing ever existed, or (b) whether another writing, recording, or photograph produced at the trial is the original, or (c) whether other evidence of contents correctly reflects the contents, the issue is for the trier of fact to determine as in the case of other issues of fact.

The judge makes the final decision as to the admissibility of evidence. The attorney client working with the LNC will help the LNC understand the decisions. The LNC must expect that testimony will include a review of qualifications and nursing education because the LNC is presenting the demonstrative evidence as an expert fact witness. The LNC must be able to adapt smoothly to changes made during the legal proceedings.

Developing Evidence for Disclosure: Digitizing Medical Records and Pertinent Documents

Production companies usually take several days to a week to digitize trial exhibits. Once the LNC receives the files on disk, the LNC can organize the files into folders, i.e., opening statement, witness folders, closing arguments, etc. The software also allows the organization of the documents into categories for quick and easy retrieval, such as medical records, graphics, depositions, video, digital video transcripts, and OLE files such as PowerPoint presentations, Adobe files, etc.

Often last-minute exhibits require digitization. Sending them to the production company as they come in is recommended. This saves time and money by avoiding last-minute in-house scanning. The typical cost to have documents and graphics digitized at the production house is approximately $.17 to $.25 each. This is quite a savings over in-house scanning.

Exhibits that are frequently used throughout the development of the case include:

- Photographs
- Deposition testimony
- Policies and procedures
- Standards of care
- Research
- Regulatory-agency documents
- Diagnostic films
- Videos
- Audiotapes

Organization of these potential exhibits and authorization from the attorney client for their use and disclosure should ideally be planned well in advance of disclosure deadlines.

Many production companies also can convert video or audio into file formats such as MPEG and AVI. Synchronizing a transcript to the video will require a software program that supports the relevant file format and also converts the video and transcript into an editable format. Refer to http://www.indatacorp.com, http://www.trialpro.com, and http://www.trialtec.com for examples of such programs. This type of file is not easily produced at the LNC's office without extensive knowledge and an investment in highly specialized equipment. The typical rate for digitizing video- or audiotapes with a transcript is $150 to $200 per hour of tape. To digitize only the video- or audiotape without a synchronized transcript costs approximately $100 per hour of tape.

Presentation Delivery at Settlements, Arbitration and Mediation Hearings, and Trial

The LNC must be well prepared for the presentation of the demonstrative evidence. By the time the case is ready for any settlement conferences, arbitration or mediation hearings, or trial, the LNC must know the case details intimately. The LNC must be comfortable relating the medical and nursing issues of the case to the legal representatives, such as attorneys, mediators, judges, and jurors. It is important for the LNC to have practiced the presentation in order to provide the highest quality presentation possible. The LNC must allow for plenty of time to arrive at the hearing destination and set up the equipment in preparation for the presentation. The clerk of the court or the bailiff can be very helpful in providing information about the courtroom. It is strongly suggested that the LNC set up a time prior to trial to do an "equipment layout" visit to the courtroom.

The LNC should prepare a checklist of items and equipment that are necessary for the presentation. It should include extras of items such as batteries and light bulbs. Chapter 41 has additional information regarding the contents of the supply box and special items. With good organization and preparation, the presentation will be seen as professional and will be well received.

Conclusion

The use of technology by the LNC in presenting demonstrative evidence can be very rewarding. A lot of preparation time is involved. A thorough knowledge of the technology and commitment to learning new software programs are absolute necessities. Only imagination limits the use of presentation methods today.

References

1. Federal Judicial Center Advisory Committee, *Effective Use of Courtroom Technology: A Judge's Guide to Pretrial and Trial*, National Institute for Trial Advocacy, Notre Dame, IN, 2001, xiv–xv.
2. Krehel, G., Think first, draw second: planning better visuals, *Trial*, April, 58, 2000.
3. Connor, T., Demonstrative evidence, MegaLinks in Criminal Justice, http://faculty.ncwc.edu/toconnor/, 2001.
4. Oldknow, P., Daubert, the scientific method, and the legal nurse consultant, *Journal of Legal Nurse Consulting*, 12(4), 2001.

Additional Reading

Beerman, J., The expert fact witness: noneconomic damages testimony, in Bogart, J.B., Ed., *Legal Nurse Consulting: Principles and Practices*, CRC Press, Boca Raton, FL, 1998, 687–693.

Federal Rules of Evidence, 2000.

Gudgell, K., Access to medical records, in Bogart, J.B., Ed., *Legal Nurse Consulting: Principles and Practices*, CRC Press, Boca Raton, FL, 1998, 119–137.

Heninger, S., Persuasive proof, *Trial*, April, 55, 2000.

Joye, M., Avoiding 10 pitfalls of demonstrative evidence, *Trial*, November, 94, 2000.

Perry, C., What evidence works, *Trial*, December, 66, 1999.

Rouda, R. and Bailey, R., Multiple benefits of multimedia, *Trial*, April, 53, 2000.

Watts, S., Technology creates winning visual evidence, *Trial*, September, 68, 2000.

Webopedia: http://www.pcwebopedia.com.

Woods, W., Electronic exhibits trump trial boards in cost, convenience, *Maricopa Lawyer*, August, 12, 2001.

Test Questions

1. What court decision was instrumental in changing the ways that evidence was reviewed?
   A. *Smith v. Jones*
   B. *Daubert v. Merrell Dow Pharmaceuticals*
   C. *Webster v. Merriam*
   D. *Darrell v. Clarke Enterprises*

2. The main points to remember regarding the admissibility of evidence for legal proceedings are
   A. Length and subject
   B. Content and readability
   C. Reliability and relevancy
   D. Color and style

3. Which of the following is not an important aspect of the presentation style and use of graphics?
   A. Color
   B. Contrast
   C. Scale
   D. Age

4. Which of the following is the simplest way to locate a digital exhibit file while in the courtroom?
   A. Bar code
   B. Order from the exhibit company
   C. Obtain from Internet site
   D. Check out from library

5. Which of the following federal rules refers to the definition of "relevant evidence"?
   A. FRE 104
   B. FRE 611
   C. FRE 401
   D. FRE 1008

Answers: 1. B, 2. C, 3. D, 4. A, 5. C

Chapter 41

Trial Preparation

Jane Barone, BS, RN, LNCC, and Judy Ringholz, BSN, RN

CONTENTS

Objectives

Upon reading this chapter, the legal nurse consultant will be able to:

0-8493-1418-6/03/$0.00+$1.50
© 2003 by AALNC

- Describe the purpose of well-organized trial and witness notebooks and identify eight to ten items to include in each
- Explain the difference between admissible and inadmissible medical records
- State one issue to be concerned with when preparing each type of evidence — deposition testimony, documents, and physical evidence — for trial
- List three examples of demonstrative evidence
- Identify three points to keep in mind with regard to how a witness may feel about testifying, and the purpose of preparing for trial testimony
- Identify one way to put a witness more at ease

Introduction

The role of the legal nurse consultant (LNC) may vary during trial preparation, as well as during the trial itself, depending on the needs of the attorney. Variations in the role of the LNC can occur in different areas of the country and even within a law firm. The LNC who combines nursing expertise with creative, independent thinking soon becomes an essential member of the litigation team. The LNC's role is different from that of the attorney, so the LNC should not expect the attorney to teach the LNC what he or she needs to know in order to accomplish a particular task. An experienced LNC is the new LNC's best resource. The LNC may be expected to assume responsibility for tasks that a paralegal performs routinely in this type of situation. An experienced litigation paralegal can also be an invaluable resource. If the LNC is working on a litigation team that includes both paralegals or legal assistants and LNCs, a clear division of responsibilities must be established. All members of the team must be aware of which person is responsible for each task. This will eliminate duplication of efforts, as well as prevent an important task from being overlooked. On the other hand, the trial team must display the true meaning of the word "team." A cooperative effort is necessary in order for things to run as smoothly as possible during trial.

Trial is the culmination of all the efforts put forth in developing a case. Depending on the nature of the case and its jurisdiction, the LNC and the trial team may have spent years working on a particular case. Thorough preparation is the key to a successful outcome. The attorney must be able to rely on the LNC to assist him or her in presenting the case in an organized fashion. The jury easily detects lack of preparedness in the trial team, and this will reflect on the team's competence. The ultimate outcome of the case will be influenced by how well, and in what manner, each side makes its presentation before the jury.

Trial Notebooks and Electronic Trial Notebooks

Trial notebooks are used to compile all the information that is needed at the time of trial in a convenient format. Today software packages can also be used for this purpose, such as Summation™ (http://www.summation.com) and Trial Director™ (http://www.indata.com). (See Chapter 40 for more information about the use of software and hardware in the courtroom.) The LNC should begin to prepare the trial notebook during the initial phases of developing the case and update it periodically as necessary. The trial notebook should be organized in a three-ring binder with tabs to include the necessary documents pertaining to each section of the notebook. Color-coding various sections may be helpful. The LNC should prepare a concise index and organize the notebook with enough detail to allow the attorney or anyone working at his or her side instant access to pertinent documents. Trial notebooks commonly contain pleading and discovery documents for both plaintiff and defense.

The LNC may also wish to incorporate some or all of the following elements into the trial notebook or have these documents available at trial in some other form:

- Motion in limine
- Proposed jury instructions
- Notes on voir dire examinations
- Notes on opening statement
- Notes on final argument
- Pretrial order
- Court's docket control order
- Designation of witnesses by plaintiff
- Designation of witnesses by defendant
- Order of proof (order in which witnesses will be called)
- Plaintiff's list of exhibits to be admitted at trial
- Defendant's list of exhibits to be admitted at trial
- Relevant portions of medical records at issue
- Summaries of medical records and medical chronologies
- Pertinent medical literature
- Definitions of pertinent medical terminology
- Relevant portions of other significant records (education, employment, etc.)
- Expert reports
- Opening statement
- Final argument

Witness Notebooks

In addition to a trial notebook, the attorney may require a separate notebook or file folder for each witness. The notebooks or folders should include:

- Contact information
- Copies of correspondence sent to or pertaining to the witness
- Notes taken during meetings with witness
- Any written item or statement prepared by witness
- Compressed transcript (miniscript) of deposition with concordance
- Errata sheet with revisions to deposition testimony and signature page
- Summary of deposition or line and page outline
- Outline of direct or cross-examination
- Copy of report (for experts)
- Copy of curriculum vitae and bibliography (for expert)
- Other pertinent document (e.g., medical literature authored, notes regarding significant entries made by witness in medical records)
- Pertinent investigative reports

Computer programs are available that store the transcripts of depositions. This allows deposition testimony to be easily accessible during trial from a laptop computer. Searches can be made by key word for information that may be needed. Some courtrooms have real-time court reporting, which allows attorneys and LNCs with laptop computers immediate access to transcripts during trial.

Burden of Proof

Chapter 1 discussed the concept of negligence. Recall that the burden is on the plaintiff to prove each of the four elements of negligence. Both sides prove their respective cases through the evidence that they present at trial. This proof is prepared by the plaintiff from the initial client intake, through discovery, and by experts.

Evidence

Status of Admissibility of Records

Evidence comes in many forms, including testimony of parties and witnesses as well as various types of records. In addition to preparing parties and witnesses for trial (which will be discussed later in this chapter), the LNC also plays a crucial role in obtaining, reviewing, and summarizing records, especially medical records (see Chapter 31). Medical records must be in admissible form in order to be introduced into evidence at trial. The LNC must understand what makes medical records admissible. Admissibility is determined by the method through which the records are obtained (see Chapter 2). In Texas, for example, medical records can be obtained in admissible form by subpoena or with an affidavit that is accompanied by a current medical authorization executed by the client. If records are obtained with affidavits, they are not admissible unless the affidavits are filed with the court at least 14 days before the trial begins. When records are obtained by subpoena, the ordering party receives the original or court copy of the records. If a co-defendant ordered records and settles before trial, the LNC must remember to obtain the court copies from that party. If the co-defendant obtained the records by affidavit with an authorization, the LNC must obtain proof that the affidavit was filed in a timely fashion.

Procedures for obtaining records vary from state to state. A reputable record-retrieval service should be able to explain the difference between admissible and inadmissible records. Imagine the potential result of not learning until after trial has begun that the most significant medical records are not admissible and, as a result, cannot be used as evidence or referred to during the trial. In New Jersey, for example, hospital records must be certified by the hospital as a complete copy of the records in order for them to be admissible. This information should be easily accessible and updated as additional medical records are received. There are computer databases that are designed for this purpose. The LNC may wish to design a database for specific needs with programs such as Word and Excel. Appendix 41.1 displays an example of how the information can be recorded in a computer database.

Deposition Testimony

For witnesses who are not called to the stand to testify live at trial, each side identifies the portions of the witness's deposition testimony that they wish to offer into evidence and the portions to which they object. These offers and objections are exchanged with opposing counsel prior to trial. Particularly if the witness is a health care professional, the LNC may be asked to review the transcript or videotape of the witness's deposition and to draft proposed offers and objections. In order to do this, the LNC must be aware of and note on the amendment page or errata sheet any revisions the witness makes to the deposition testimony, and indicate the page number and line number in the transcript where each section that is being offered or excluded by objection begins and ends. The reason for any objection must be indicated. The reason must be supported by the rules of court. Once the offers and objections have been exchanged and, if necessary, ruled on by the court, the videotape can be edited to include only the testimony that will actually be offered. If videotape is not available, the portions to be offered are read from the transcript at trial. The LNC may be asked to role-play the witness and read the responses contained in the deposition transcript of the witness from the witness stand. When role-playing, the LNC should keep in mind that the transcript needs to be read as objectively as possible with no vocal inflections.

Preparing Exhibits

The attorney must determine, in advance, which documents he or she intends to use as trial exhibits. The LNC should establish the order in which the attorney plans to use the exhibits and organize the documents accordingly. The LNC should:

- Create a separate folder for each exhibit.
- Mark the document as Plaintiff or Defense Exhibit _____ (the blank will be filled in by a letter or number according to the local court rules), and prepare a corresponding exhibit list. Familiarity with the local procedural rules will assist in marking the exhibits properly for identification during trial.
- Whenever possible, use the original document and have a copy available in the exhibit folder.
- Never mark, staple, or alter the original document in any way.
- If the original document is not available, insert a note in the folder regarding where it is kept and how it can be obtained.

In some jurisdictions, the actual exhibits are exchanged between the parties before trial begins. Some court clerks prefer that exhibit lists be submitted on computer disks so that they can input the data into their files. During the pretrial conference, as well as during the trial, it is necessary to keep the exhibit list (and the opposing party's exhibit list) available at all times, noting directly on the list when each exhibit is offered into evidence, objected to being admitted, or withdrawn. The attorney must be able to know at a glance which exhibits have been properly introduced into evidence and which have not. The LNC must also be aware of whether or not the attorney intends to introduce specific documents, records, or other exhibits into evidence through a particular witness by having that person authenticate them while under oath. If so, the LNC should be certain that the documents are organized before the witness takes the stand. If the LNC is coordinating the offering of exhibits with a co-defendant, he or she should be certain to determine ahead of time which party will be responsible for which exhibit. This prevents the submission of duplicate exhibits.

Physical Evidence

Physical evidence is any tangible item that may be used or displayed as an exhibit during trial. An example of physical evidence is a medical device (e.g., intravenous infusion pump or fetal monitor) that has been positively identified as the one used, or is representative of the one used, during a procedure at issue. The item must be appropriately marked and identified on the exhibit list.

Demonstrative Evidence

Demonstrative evidence allows the attorney to demonstrate certain issues to the jury in a way that helps them understand the concepts being presented. The LNC, as the person on the litigation team who is most familiar with the medical records, can be particularly helpful in identifying issues that can best be presented through demonstrative evidence. Issues can be demonstrated in the form of a chart, table, diagram, illustration, or animation. The LNC can blow up a document contained in the medical records that illustrates a specific point. Medical illustrations are often helpful in explaining an anatomical matter, and computer-generated animation can be used to reconstruct an accident. The LNC should consider what the attorney is trying to prove or disprove and how that information can best be presented. The LNC should then make certain to have the necessary equipment available in the courtroom for the presentation, calling the clerk ahead of time to determine what audiovisual equipment is available and what equipment needs to be brought to court. See Chapter 40 for more information.

Many companies can create medical illustrations, courtroom graphics, animation, etc. to be used as demonstrative exhibits. Some even provide the necessary equipment and assist with the actual presentation. The LNC should plan for the possibility that an outside vendor may take more time than anticipated to create a desired exhibit. The LNC may need to weigh the high cost of an elaborate exhibit against its benefit — i.e., successfully communicating his or her side's position to the jury. Experts need to approve any demonstrative evidence they will refer to during their testimony. This approval process is needed to authenticate the exhibit and eliminate any errors.

Example 41.1: Emily Smith, an elderly woman, aspirated a piece of solid food while eating lunch at home with her husband. As a result, her lower airway was partially obstructed. She was brought to Lakeside Hospital for treatment to remove the obstruction. Ms. Smith had been diagnosed with Parkinson's disease more than 10 years before this incident. Her family members alleged that her deteriorating condition was caused by delays in the treatment rendered by the defendants. The hospital, the emergency room physician, and the pulmonologist were sued. In this case the defendant hospital was being represented. The defendants claimed that Ms. Smith's condition was a result of the progression of her Parkinson's disease. Appendix 41.2 quotes excerpts from multiple medical records in an effort to establish the progression of her disease prior to the time of the incident in question. Appendix 41.2 displays the chronology of events that took place at the defendant hospital on the day of the incident in an effort to controvert the plaintiff's claims that there were extended periods of time during which Ms. Smith was not attended to by the hospital staff. Appendix 41.2 was enlarged to 30 × 40 in. for display at trial.

Medical Literature

Chapter 32 discusses medical literature research. The focus in this section is on organization of the research for purposes of trial preparation. A medical literature notebook, organized in a three-ring binder, can be useful, or these articles can be placed with a particular witness's information in the trial notebook. The LNC should begin to collect and organize medical literature during the early phases of case development. The literature may assist in the development of plaintiff or defense theories. Beginning early also makes the task more manageable. The LNC should include pertinent journal articles, articles from newspapers or periodicals, and chapters or excerpts from medical textbooks that support the theory of the case. The items can be organized chronologically, by topic, or by author. Each item should be tabbed to correspond with a concise index. The LNC should always include identifying information for each item, such as a copy of the title page with the date of publication.

Once the LNC has obtained and organized pertinent medical literature, it is just as important that he or she review it thoroughly. An article that includes statements that support the case may also say something that is quite damaging to the case. For that reason, the LNC may wish to consider the color-coded method for literature review: the LNC uses three differently colored highlighters, e.g., pink, yellow, and green, and associates each highlighter with a traffic signal. Information highlighted in pink (stop) signals the attorney that it may be damaging to the case. Statements highlighted in yellow (make note) are significant to the case in some way, but neutral in nature. Portions that are highlighted in green (go) are supportive of the theory of the case and potentially damaging to the other side. If the LNC chooses instead to highlight with only one color, he or she should bring potential damaging information to the attention of the attorney. The LNC should insert the highlighted copy in the notebook in order to help the attorney find the information that he or she needs, and also insert an unmarked copy. An unmarked copy is submitted to the court when applicable. The attorney may find it helpful to have a concise summary of the article to use as an easy reference.

When preparing medical literature to be used at trial, the LNC must be aware of the rules regarding admissibility. For example, in some jurisdictions it is permissible to refer to literature that speaks to issues pertaining to standard of care only if it was published prior to the date of the alleged incident. However, articles that speak to causation issues, and were published subsequent to the occurrence, may be allowed. The LNC should also be aware of major court decisions that have an effect on what may be submitted, such as *Daubert v. Merrell Dow*, which limits "junk science" (see Chapter 40).

Witness Preparation

Effective preparation of a witness before he or she gives testimony at trial is absolutely necessary. Preparation requires both time and patience. In most cases the witness has never seen the inside of a courtroom, and may be anxious or even frightened. The LNC should try to alleviate the witness's anxiety by helping him or her understand what will take place at trial. The LNC may be asked to assist the lawyer in, or to be solely responsible for, preliminary preparation of the witness.

The first step is to establish a rapport with the witness and to put the witness at ease. The LNC should not role-play the attorney for the opposite side and ask the tough questions initially; that would probably only increase the witness's anxiety and make the preparation more difficult. The purpose of preparing the witness is to make certain that the witness anticipates the questions or types of questions that he or she will be asked on the witness stand, as well as how the witness will answer those questions. The LNC should explain that the attorney will ask questions (direct examination) that may be followed by questions from opposing counsel (cross-examination), which may again be followed by redirect and recross-examination. The LNC should make certain that the witness clearly understands the theory of the case.

The LNC should tell the witness to:

- Maintain a demeanor that is polite and sincere. On cross-examination, the attorney may make an effort to make you angry or defensive. Do not lose your composure or be condescending.
- Be aware of body language. Maintain eye contact with the attorney when he or she is asking you a question. Shift your glance between the attorney and the jury when responding. Do not cross your arms. Do not put your hands over your mouth or near your face.
- Dress appropriately for the courtroom and make sure that any family members or friends who may accompany you dress appropriately as well.
- Be aware of the techniques that attorneys use in an effort to get you to answer the question in a certain way, such as hook, compound, and hypothetical questions. A hook question is one that incorporates or implies facts that, if not corrected by the witness prior to the time that he or she responds, will be assumed to be true by virtue of the witness's silence regarding the issue.

Example 41.2: Nurse Wilson, you testified that the nurse is not responsible for assessing blood pressure after surgery. Isn't it true that the nurse does not have to check the pulse either?

A compound question is one that incorporates two or three questions into one. If the witness responds, the same answer may be assumed to apply to each component of the question.

Example 41.3: Is it true that the Post Anesthesia Care Unit nurse does not have to check the blood pressure every 15 minutes and to observe for airway obstruction?

A hypothetical question usually begins with, "Assume with me…"

Example 41.4: Nurse Webster, I'd like you to assume for the purposes of this question that the following are true.

- It is most important to listen very carefully to the question and answer only what is directly being asked. Do not offer additional information.
- Never answer a question that you do not understand. Ask the attorney to repeat it or rephrase it. Do this as many times as is necessary until you understand the question.
- If you perceive that the attorney is asking a question that you have answered previously, but he or she is wording it differently, give the same answer that you gave earlier.
- Always be certain that the attorney has finished asking the question before you begin to answer. Pause for a moment. This allows you time to reflect on your response. It also allows the opposing attorneys time to object if they choose to do so. Do not attempt to answer if an objection is made. Wait for the judge's ruling and respond accordingly.
- Speak clearly and slowly. Speak loudly enough for each juror to hear your answers without straining.
- Use your own words. Do not adopt the attorney's language. If you disagree with a portion of the question or would phrase it differently, do so before you answer.
- If the attorney references a specific document in the question (e.g., a medical record or journal article), request a copy of the document and read it carefully before responding.
- If instructed to answer the question "yes" or "no" and cannot limit the answer this way, state that you cannot provide an accurate answer using only yes or no.
- If you do not know the answer to the question being asked or you do not recall, say so. Never guess or speculate.
- Always tell the truth based on your personal knowledge. Give brief and concise answers.
- After practicing repeatedly, you will begin to memorize the answers to anticipated questions. Do not let your responses sound as though they were rehearsed.

The LNC should adequately review with the witness any materials that could be used for impeachment purposes. These include prior deposition testimony, answers to interrogatories, answers to requests for admission, and any oral or written statements that were made previously. Explain the process of impeachment.

Example 41.5: Nurse Freedman, you have just testified that the nurse is expected to check blood pressure every 15 minutes while in the recovery room. Yet in your deposition you stated that every 30 minutes was an acceptable time frame. Which statement would you like the jury to believe?

Discuss the probable testimony of other witnesses in order to ascertain whether or not there is a potential for inconsistencies in testimony at trial. The LNC should advise the attorney of any such inconsistencies as soon as possible. The LNC should review and discuss any exhibits that the attorney has determined that he or she will prove or authenticate through the witness.

An attorney may prefer on some occasions to have a deposition videotaped or videoconferenced rather than take a live deposition. Videoconferencing is done in real time as opposed to taped, and interaction takes place between the parties and the witness. This may be done when the witness is unable to be present at the time of trial. Videoconferencing may be used to prepare a witness for testimony or for a deposition, or at the time of trial. The witness should be prepared as previously described and also be made aware that videoconferencing equipment will be present in the room.

Even if all parties are in agreement about who will appear at trial, it may be necessary in a particular jurisdiction, or the attorney may prefer, that all witnesses and parties be served with a subpoena or notice to appear at trial. The LNC should determine what local rules require and discuss with the attorney what his or her wishes are. If the attorney plans to serve a subpoena on a friendly witness (one who agrees to testify and is supportive of the theory of the case), the LNC should discuss the matter with the witness ahead of time, explaining the rationale for issuing a subpoena even though the witness has agreed to testify. The LNC should also alert the witness's office staff, if applicable, so that they are not surprised when the process server arrives.

Supply Box

Maternal-child health nurses and those who have children may relate to the analogy of the new parents who were preparing to take their infant to their first family outing. The parents created a list of every item that they might possibly need while away from home. Then they carefully packed the supply bag. Unfortunately, when the time came to leave, they were so excited and concerned about whether or not the baby was dressed appropriately for the weather and secured properly in her safety seat that they left the supply bag behind. After an LNC has spent years assisting with the development of a case, it is likely that he or she will feel as though it is the LNC's baby. The LNC organizes the case materials, boxes them securely, and sees that the box is safely transported to the courthouse. The baby analogy will perhaps serve as a reminder not to leave supply boxes behind.

Items for the supply box include:

- Various types of pens and pencils
- Easel
- Colored markers (for easel)
- Thick black permanent marker
- Highlighters
- Legal pads
- Extra folders
- Two-hole and three-hole punch
- Post-it® notes and tabs in various sizes
- Correction fluid and correction tape
- Transparent tape
- Stapler and staples
- Paper clips and binder clips
- Ruler

- Pointer
- Exhibit stickers
- Envelopes
- Business cards (attorney's and LNC's)
- Rolls of quarters (for pay phones and copy machines)
- List of phone numbers of people the LNC will need to contact
- Medical dictionary and relevant medical textbooks
- Copy of the rules of civil procedure and rules of evidence that apply in your jurisdiction
- Acetaminophen, ibuprofen, and aspirin
- Antacids
- Adhesive bandages
- Facial tissues
- Energy snacks
- Extension cords
- Luggage cart
- Cellular phone
- Umbrella

Packing Up and Heading Out

Numbering each box (i.e., 1 of 25, 2 of 25, etc.) will benefit the LNC greatly in the trial if he or she takes the time to do it with precision while packing. Then, he or she should list the contents of each box. This will prevent the LNC from having to rummage through boxes and appear disorganized during trial. The LNC should remember that he or she is being observed and monitored by the jury and others from the moment that he or she walks into the courtroom until the trial ends.

Conclusion

Assisting at trial can be challenging and stressful, but it can also be exciting and rewarding. An LNC who has done everything possible to assist the attorney in presenting a case effectively will have a feeling of ownership in the trial's outcome and will enjoy a feeling of personal satisfaction (not to mention job security).

Reference

1. Mauet, T. and Maeroweitz, M., *Fundamentals of Litigation for Paralegals*, 2nd ed., Little, Brown, Boston, 1996.

Test Questions

1. All of the following may be contained in the trial notebook EXCEPT:
   A. Pleadings and discovery
   B. Trial exhibits
   C. Medical bills
   D. Judge's rulings on admissibility of evidence

2. Which of the following is NOT true of admissible records?
   A. Records must be in admissible form in order to be introduced into evidence.
   B. The definition of admissibility of records varies from state to state.
   C. Records that do not follow the format for admissibility will not be admitted for trial.
   D. The LNC does not need to know what constitutes admissibility of records.

3. Which of the following is NOT correct regarding preparation of exhibits for trial?
   A. The attorney will determine which documents he or she intends to use at trial.
   B. The LNC may prepare a trial exhibit list.
   C. When preparing an exhibit list, one does not need to know the local court rules.
   D. Physical evidence may be used as a trial exhibit.

4. The LNC can assist in preparing demonstrative evidence for trial by
   A. Advising the attorney on legal strategies
   B. Preparing charts, tables, or graphs of pertinent information
   C. Drawing anatomical diagrams
   D. Signing off on the exhibit for the expert

5. Which is NOT true concerning witness preparation?
   A. The LNC cannot become involved in witness preparation.
   B. Part of preparing a witness for testimony is educating the witness about what to expect, in order to decrease his or her anxiety.
   C. The witness should be instructed in how to dress appropriately for the courtroom.
   D. The witness should be instructed to listen closely to the questions that he or she is asked.

Answers: 1. D, 2. D, 3. C, 4. A, 5. A

Appendix 41.1
Excerpts from Medical Records Pertaining to Emily Smith

Date	Doctor	Page	Entry
11/14/80	Brown	17	(History and Physical from Lakeside Hospital) Hospitalized in January of 1980 with arthritis
11/17/80	Brown	14	(Discharge summary from Lakeside Hospital) Ms. Smith is a 63-year-old lady who has a history of arthritis, but over the past year has had difficulty with her mobility and noticed that she has had some tremor in her right hand. She has difficulty initiating movement, but denies any specific paralysis. Her neurological exam was suggestive of probable Parkinson's disease. She was admitted to work up other possible problems. Final Diagnosis: Probable Parkinson's disease The patient will be discharged on Sinemet 10/100 mg.
01/18/83	Stevenson	1	Has had arthritis of the back for the past 3 years. She complains of low back pain, upper back pain, and neck pain, some decreased strength in her hands, but no real peripheral arthritis.
02/18/85	Brown	9	Complains of slowness of movement
02/10/86	Brown	10	Very upset...depressed
05/28/86	Brown	11	Exam: Speech much slower; slurs; shuffles more
07/16/86	White	41	(History and Physical from Lakeside Hospital) The patient has become very stiff, immobile like there is a heavy weight pulling her down to the ground. She has Parkinson's disease. This morning she had an unusually severe episode of this, associated with severe, excruciating, unbearable back pain. The patient is stiff and rigid, almost statue-like, very immobile, has to be helped to do anything. Impression: Parkinson's disease with off-on phenomenon Severe back pain
07/16/86	White	36	(EEG Report) Interpretation: Abnormal EEG indicating diffuse cerebral dysfunction. The record is abnormal by virtue of increased amounts of slow activity consistent with a mild diffuse encephalopathy.
07/31/86	Feldman	50–52	(Initial Neurological Evaluation) She has noted increasing difficulties with her gait, which has become slow and shuffling, and she has difficulties turning. She has difficulties arising from a chair and, in fact, occasionally has to get down on her fours in order to get up from a chair. She occasionally spills liquids when she brings them to her mouth. She had noted some insomnia, which she attributes to generalized body discomfort during the night. In fact, she sleeps on the floor. Has a 7-year history of slowly progressive Parkinson's disease. Amitriptyline will be substituted. This latter medication should improve her insomnia as well as mild depression.

09/23/87	Feldman	46	She also occasionally stammers and has increased forgetfulness. According to her husband, she is less alert and has occasional visual hallucinations. Most recently, a month ago, she saw mice in her bed.
07/27/88	Feldman	43	There has been some deterioration in her symptoms since her last visit. She seems to stutter more and is frequently mixed up, occasionally having hallucinations. Her balance also has deteriorated and she has fallen on two occasions…possibly developing into PSP (progressive supranuclear palsy).
04/24/89	(General)	10–12	Intermittent bouts of confusion and irrational pain for approximately 6 months. These spells are described as forgetting her surroundings, believes she is in different places with different people. These spells have been increasing in intensity and duration occasionally lasting an entire day. There is question of a stroke 8 years ago, although husband refutes this.
04/25/89	(General)	63	(EEG Report) Impression: This is an abnormal record, characterized by the following: (1) Diffuse slowing of the background activity, indicating a diffuse disturbance in brain function. (2) A focus of very slow (Delta) activity in the left temporal region, indicating the presence of a lesion involving that region.
04/27/89	(General)	57	(Magnetic Resonance Images (MRI) of the brain) Impression: Mild to moderate age-related and/or atrophic changes as described with periventricular white matter ischemic change.
08/15/89	Benton	21	(History and Physical form Lakeside Hospital) Initially had a little tightness in the chest. Then later on she began to notice a fluttering in the chest. Impression: Ventricular tachycardia; parkinsonism; degenerative arthritis.
08/18/89	Stevenson	5	Her arthritis is stable. Her parkinsonism is progressing.
09/27/89	Feldman	32	During the last month her condition clearly has deteriorated. She has developed more dyskinesias, particularly after 11 a.m., and this interferes with her eating. She also has become more nervous and depressed and has had period of palpitations lasting 5 to 10 minutes, associated with a smothering feeling. She continues to have some anxiety and phobias, particularly phobias of crowds.
08/14/90	Benton	6	47-pound weight loss over 2 years. Now 100 pounds. Parkinson's.
12/17/90	(General)	256	(EEG Report) Impression: As compared to the previous EEG of 4/25/89, there continues to be diffuse slowing of background activity, indicative of a diffuse disturbance in cerebral function
12/18/90	(General)	255	(MRI of the brain) Impression: (1) Small focal ischemic insults (2) The ischemic changes have appeared since the last study dated 4/27/89.

12/20/90	Feldman (General)	23–26 (235–238)	(Discharge Summary from General Hospital) Discharge Diagnosis: 1. Right subcortical stroke. 2. Parkinson's disease…evidence of a left nasolabial droop with drooling from the left corner of the mouth, wide-eyed stare with decreased blinking and hypermetric. The patient's stance was stooped. EEG was done on the patient and compared to the previous EEG done in April 1989. There continued to be diffuse slowing in the background and activity indicative of a diffuse disturbance in cerebral function. The patient also had an MRI scan done that showed small focal ischemic insults. The ischemic changes were not seen on the last MRI done in April of 1989.
12/26/90	Feldman	27	Ms. Smith has recently been discharged from the hospital after suffering a mild stroke that gave her swallowing difficulties. At this time, she is very frozen and has difficulty moving about. This improves after taking Sinemet, but she becomes quite confused and begins hallucinating.
04/12/91	Feldman	21	According to the patient and her husband, she is clearly worse. She has more fluctuations.

Appendix 41.2
Demonstrative Exhibit

June 17, 1999

3:00 p.m.	Ms. Smith arrives in emergency room and is assessed by Carol Jones, RN. Cardiac monitor applied. Dynamap applied and oxygen begun by Ms. Jones.
3:05 p.m.	Examination by Dr. Green. Order received by Ms. Jones. IV started, arterial blood gases obtained, and pulse oximeter applied by Ms. Jones.
3:08 p.m.	Dr. Benton notified. Portable chest x-ray obtained. Dr. Ross notified by Dr. Green.
3:30 p.m.	Blood gases redrawn and oxygen changed to 100% per face mask.
3:45 p.m.	Ms. Smith continuously monitored by Nurse Jones, who describes respirations as easy and nonlabored. Dr. Green speaks with Dr. Ross.
4:05 p.m.	Nurse Jones speaks to Dr. Ross. Orders received. Consent signed for bronchoscopy.
4:25 p.m.	EKG obtained.
4:30 p.m.	Ms. Smith is transferred to pre-op holding area on continuous monitors accompanied by orderly and Carol Jones RN and received by Susan Lewis RN and report given and continuous monitors exchanged.
4:40 p.m.	History and assessment by John Carter, CRNA. Preoperative assessment by Nurse Lewis.
5:00 p.m.	Ms. Smith is continuously monitored by Nurse Lewis, who notifies Dr. Ross that she is ready for bronchoscopy.
5:45 p.m.	Dr. Ross arrives to OR holding area. Receives report from Susan Lewis.
6:00 p.m.	Ms. Smith is transferred to MICU. Continuous monitors are exchanged. Report received by head nurse who admits Ms. Smith to unit.
6:30 p.m.	Amanda Parker, RN receives report from head nurse and assumes care of Ms. Smith. Dr. Ross and respiratory therapist at bedside upon her arrival. Assessment performed by Nurse Parker. Flexible bronchoscopy initiated.

Chapter 42

The Trial Process

Lucille Evangelista, BS, RN, Patricia Raya, BS, RNC, and
Barbara Loecker, MSEd, BSN, RN

CONTENTS

0-8493-1418-6/03/$0.00+$1.50
© 2003 by AALNC

Objectives

- To name and describe the major portions of a civil trial
- To identify the role of the legal nurse consultant during jury selection and presentation of testimony
- To discuss the important issues involved in determining the verdict
- To discuss jury awards, including comparative and contributory negligence and punitive damages
- To evaluate posttrial activities
- To discuss ethical considerations at trial

Introduction

The role of the legal nurse consultant (LNC) in a trial is as varied as the practice settings and specializations of nurses in the field. The common theme is anticipation — anticipation of testimony from witnesses for both the plaintiff and the defense. The LNC must be familiar with trial procedure and should be comfortable in the courtroom. This applies to all LNCs who have a role in the courtroom, whether as an expert witness or as a member of the trial team.

Preparation for the LNC's role in the courtroom begins well before the trial. It begins during the discovery phase of the case. Trial strategy, testimony, and exhibits are developed during discovery in anticipation of the trial. The trial is the showcase for the case, and barring appeals, it is the culmination of years of work for all the parties involved. Meticulous preparation and presentation are vital for success in the courtroom. Juries do not decide cases on the merit of the claim alone. Cases are often won or lost by the presentation from the attorney and the experts. An attorney who fumbles for exhibits, forgets key information, and backtracks when presenting testimony is not viewed as a winner and is not successful in the courtroom. The presentation must be a well-orchestrated work of art.

The LNC is a key member of the litigation team in a medical case. The LNC participates in the development of the trial strategy and testimony and in the preparation of the trial exhibits. Having the testimony and exhibits organized is essential. The trial is the opportunity for the plaintiff and defense to tell the story. The party who convinces the jury will prevail. The LNC's role is to develop the medical side of the story while the attorney concentrates on the legal side, with constant communication between the two. Neither develops one part of the case in isolation from the other.

The LNC may share responsibilities with a legal assistant or a paralegal in case preparation. Although a legal assistant or paralegal frequently attends the trial and takes notes during the voir dire and testimony, the LNC is uniquely qualified to appraise the medical testimony. LNCs become the ideal nonlawyer members of the team to attend the trial because they can perform necessary routine duties as well as the analysis of the medical testimony, the role for which their attendance is essential. The LNC at trial must therefore be prepared to perform a wide variety of tasks as the lone assistant to the attorney.

The key elements of a trial include motions in limine, voir dire, opening statements, presentation of testimony by witnesses through direct and cross-examination, rebuttal, closing arguments, and finally the verdict. Exhibits are used to enhance testimony from witnesses. Instructions are given to the jury to outline the law and are usually prepared by the attorney and approved by the trial judge.

This chapter will present the key elements of a trial and the preparation necessary for each of the key elements, as well as the conduct of the trial.

Ethical Propriety

The conduct of attorneys applicable during the trial process is governed by the Code of Professional Responsibility, also referred to as the Canon of Ethics. Although these are mandated for attorneys, LNCs are bound by the same ethical code. These rules and disciplinary guidelines concern expected professional conduct, integrity, and competency; compensation practices; prohibition of unauthorized practice of law by nonlawyers; exercise of competent professional judgment; preservation of the client/lawyer relationship; conflict of interest; communication restraints; trial publicity; avoidance of even the appearance of impropriety; and contact between parties, witnesses, and jurors during an ongoing trial.

Initial Trial Proceedings

Motions in Limine

A motion in limine is a written statement that is usually made before or after the beginning of a jury trial for a protective order against prejudicial questions and statements. The purpose of such a motion is to avoid injection into the trial of matters that are irrelevant (immaterial), inadmissible (evidence that according to law cannot be entered, evidence that was illegally seized, and certain types of hearsay), and prejudicial (a preconceived opinion). Should a motion in limine be granted, then records need to be revisited and exhibits need to be altered or information removed from the records. The assisting LNC performs this function in order to be in compliance with the judge's ruling. Failure to adhere to the motion in limine may result in sanctions (punitive measures) or a mistrial.

Voir Dire — Jury Selection

The Sixth Amendment of the U.S. Constitution guarantees the right of an individual to a public trial. Rule 47 of the Federal Rules of Civil Procedure provides for the selection of jurors. Cases may be tried before the court (bench trial) or before a jury. Most malpractice suits are presented to a jury. The rationale behind this is the belief that the jury will be more sympathetic to the injured party (the plaintiff) and provide a substantial verdict award.

Prospective jurors are randomly chosen from voter registration lists, driver's license lists, or a combination of the two. The jury selection process has become a science, with a host of trial and jury consultants available to the trial team. Jury consultants use jury focus groups and trial simulations to identify jurors' attitudes toward trial issues.

Jurors are questioned to ascertain prejudice and bias. This questioning — voir dire (which means "to speak the truth") — is an important element of selecting a jury. The oral examination of prospective jury members is performed by the judge or by the plaintiff's and defendant's attorneys. In addition, a "silent voir dire" may be employed in which written questions are answered by the juror and then analyzed. The voir dire process varies widely depending on whether the case is being tried in federal or in state court. The attorney's search for the ideal juror, one who will openly listen to testimony and render an impartial judgment, can take different avenues.

Disqualification for Cause

The preliminary voir dire is conducted by the judge, who shares some general information relating to the case with the jurors. Having done this, the judge may ask the jurors as a whole if they are unable to render a fair and impartial verdict. Those responding positively are often excused. Following this a judge and/or the attorneys might ask specific questions of the individual jurors. The questions posed vary widely depending on the case but may include the prospective juror's connection to any one of the parties or legal counsel, any financial interest in the case or outcome, or any prejudicial or biased belief on the prospective juror's part.

Disqualification of a prospective juror for cause is referred to as a causal strike. There is no limit on the number of causal strikes allowed.

Peremptory Challenges

The initial voir dire is directed toward elimination of prospective jurors for cause. Following this, each side's attorney is entitled to strike additional jurors in order to secure a jury more harmonious to his or her side. The trial team reviews the notes of the voir dire and ranks the jurors in order of compatibility with the juror profile previously obtained. These peremptory challenges are limited to three strikes for each side, and the attorneys are not obligated to offer any reason for invoking these privileges.

Detailed notes by the assisting LNC are crucial to this process. The note-taking method must be accurate and detailed. The note-taking system should allow space for identification and separation of responses that do and do not fit the jury profile. One system that has been effectively used lists demographic information followed by the attorney's questions with sections for responses perceived as positive or negative (see Table 42.1).

In addition to taking notes during the voir dire, the LNC may draft questions beforehand and should observe the questioning as well as the jurors' reactions to the questions.

Opening Statements

According to Polchinski,[1] the opening statement is an argument to the jury within the rules of evidence and professional ethics. It is not an outline, preview, or inventory of evidence. The purpose of the opening statement is to advise the jury of facts relied upon and of issues involved, and to give the jury a general picture

Table 42.1 Sample Jury Voir Dire

NAME _____

ADDRESS _____

AGE _____ OCCUPATION _____

MARITAL STATUS _____ CHILDREN_____

GENDER _____ DESCRIPTION _____

PREVIOUS EXPERIENCE WITH LAW _____

Questions	Positive	Negative
1. Education		Engineering degree
2. Belief in lawsuits for injury		No
3. Negative experience with medical treatment	Yes	

of the facts so that the jury will be able to understand the evidence. The opening statements are made by the plaintiff's attorney at the beginning of the trial just before the presentation of the first witness. The defense counsel may give his or her opening statement following the plaintiff's statement or may elect to wait until the opening of the defense portion of the case.

The opening statement of a medical malpractice case is extremely important. The opening statement is not evidence; it familiarizes the jury with the essential facts that each side expects to prove. The lawyers inform the jury of the facts they expect to prove and of the witnesses they expect to call to make such proof.[2]

It is the job of the LNC to take notes of the opening remarks and be able to discuss them with the attorney. The LNC should be able to analyze the opposing counsel's remarks and see whether any new theories may require a change in trial strategy, emphasis, or additional follow-up.

Order of Proof

Presentation of Witnesses

Witnesses take center stage in a trial; through their testimony, a story is told to the jury. Two types of witnesses testify in a civil trial: expert witnesses and fact or lay witnesses. An expert witness is one who by reason of education or specialized experience possesses superior knowledge about a subject about which jurors have no particular training and would be incapable of forming an accurate opinion or deducing correct conclusions without the expert's testimony. An expert witness is a witness who has been qualified as an expert and who is thereby allowed (through his or her answers to questions posed) to assist the jury in understanding complicated and technical subjects not within the understanding of the average lay juror.

In a professional-negligence trial, the role of expert witnesses is to explain the medical facts of the case to the jury. Plaintiff experts describe deviations from accepted standards of care and the care that should have been provided to the plaintiff. Plaintiff damage experts describe the injuries to the plaintiff and project the impact on his or her life in the future. These witnesses describe the financial, emotional, and physiological changes that the plaintiff can expect. Defense witnesses testify in the same areas but are supportive of the care provided by the defendant physician. Defense damage experts present a different evaluation or refute the testimony regarding financial, emotional, and physiological impact on the plaintiff.

Medical expert witnesses also testify in other types of personal injury cases not involving professional negligence as cause of the injury. These experts do not testify about standard-of-care issues, but do explain the plaintiff's injuries, treatment, and projected impact of the injuries in the future. Defense expert witnesses present another view of the impact of the plaintiff's injuries, and highlight other possible causes of the injuries.

Fact witnesses may present testimony about the mechanism and impact of the injury. In a professional-negligence case, these witnesses are often family members or close friends who have observed the care provided to the plaintiff and witnessed the impact of his or her injuries on the plaintiff's lifestyle. They may also include employers or coworkers, ministers, etc. Fact witnesses in other personal injury cases may also be witnesses to the event that caused the injury. The role of the expert fact witness in summarizing medical records is explained in Chapter 36.

The LNC's Role

The LNC is usually responsible for ensuring that the witness is available when called for testimony. This may mean meeting an expert at the airport and transporting him or her to the hotel or courtroom. The attorney may ask the LNC to summarize previous testimony and review anticipated testimony with the witness (see Table 42.2). This transportation time is an opportunity to discuss testimony and consult with the expert about issues that have arisen in the course of the trial. The LNC may have to coordinate local transportation for a fact witness or simply greet the witness as he or she arrives outside the courtroom. Many witnesses are nervous about testifying before a jury and are not familiar with courtroom etiquette or appropriate attire. It is the responsibility of the LNC to explain courtroom procedures and etiquette, and provide reassurance and information to the witness. The witness should always be reminded not to discuss any aspect of the trial while in the halls or restrooms of the courthouse. The witness should also be reminded never to speak to the jurors outside of the courtroom.

At the conclusion of the testimony, the LNC may be responsible for transporting the expert witness to the hotel or airport or coordinating transportation for local witnesses. She or he may be asked to correspond with expert witnesses regarding

Table 42.2 Sample Notes for Witness Testimony

Examination	Follow-Up
1. Board certification	How many times taken?
2. Hospital privileges	Any revoked?
3. Informed consent	Plaintiff given any narcotics before discussion of risks?

their testimony or the outcome of the trial. If the case settles prior to the witness testimony, it may be the responsibility of the LNC to notify the witness of this and to provide other information as allowed in the settlement agreement.

Examination of Witnesses

Following opening statements, the judge instructs the plaintiff's attorney to begin the presentation of his or her case. It is the responsibility of the plaintiff to prove his or her case to the jury. The case is proved by examination of expert and fact witnesses and the introduction of exhibits that assist the witnesses in telling their story to the judge or jury.

After the plaintiff has presented his or her case to the jury, the defense has the opportunity to present a case to disprove the plaintiff's case. The defense does not have to disprove the plaintiff's case but generally presents witnesses to do so.

Although the plaintiff's case and the defendant's case are presented separately, examination of each witness is performed by both parties. Examination of witnesses has three primary phases: direct examination, cross-examination, and rebuttal. Redirect and recross-examination may also be warranted. In summary, presentation of testimony occurs in the following order: direct examination, cross-examination, redirect examination, recross-examination, and rebuttal.

Direct Examination

Direct examination is conducted by the party who calls the witness. Leading questions are generally not allowed. A leading question gives the witness clues about the response expected by the attorney. An example is: "Tell the jury what you did when you approached the intersection and saw the red light." Direct questions may be open-ended to allow the witness to elaborate on an answer or may be close-ended and require a brief response. A direct examination question may ask, "What happened when you approached the intersection?" Close-ended questions are used often for adverse or hostile witnesses from whom a simple answer without elaboration or explanation is desired. An example of a direct close-ended question is: "Did you step on the brake when you saw the red light?"

Cross-Examination

Cross-examination is conducted by the adverse party at the conclusion of direct testimony. Examination is limited to the subject matter of the direct examination. Cross-examination focuses on proper questions so that the elicited testimony and evidence are accurate and simple for the jury to understand. At the same time the cross-examination attempts to undermine or discredit the witness. The tone of the questioning is often intentionally adversarial. Questions may be leading, such as "You did not step on the brake, correct?" Through counsel's aggressive questioning, witnesses may become intimidated, angered, and confused. The jury may perceive this response in a negative light and decide in favor of the adverse party. Therefore, the jury's perception during cross-examination is relevant to the case. An effective cross-examination can make or break the case, especially in medical malpractice trials in which large sums of money are involved.

Redirect and Recross-Examination

Cross-examination may be followed by redirect examination. The attorney uses this examination to clarify or reinforce previous testimony. This questioning may be followed by recross-examination. Again, this testimony is used to clarify or emphasize specific testimony. New subjects cannot be introduced during redirect or recross-examination.

Rebuttal

Rebuttal testimony is offered after the close of the defendant's case. The plaintiff may wish to call additional witnesses to contradict or dispute testimony given by a defense expert witness. The same rules for direct and cross-examination of witnesses are in effect for rebuttal witnesses. Rebuttal testimony provides an opportunity to respond to testimony of the defendant's witnesses other than through cross-examination.

The LNC's Role

The LNC follows the planned testimony as the attorney questions each witness, making detailed notes of the witnesses' responses and noting additional areas for examination by the attorney. Detailed and accurate notes are imperative. Trial transcripts are not generally available on a daily basis unless the attorney pays for them. The trial team may need to rely on only memory and notes for its review of testimony and planning for additional witnesses. However, modern technology allows access to real-time court reporting via the Web. Since the O.J. Simpson trial in 1994, remote access to transcripts has been possible; transcripts can be researched, indexed, and managed immediately. The attorney often consults with the LNC in the courtroom before concluding his or her examination of the witness. At that time, the LNC must be prepared to suggest specific questions, or further areas of questioning, or point out inconsistencies in previous testimony. If an expert has quoted from an article or textbook, the LNC must be prepared to advise the attorney if the testimony is incorrect or incomplete. The LNC should also be very familiar with the relevant medical records and can point out inaccuracies in testimony regarding the records. The LNC may need to provide this information in written form if the court discourages verbal conferences in the courtroom.

Throughout the trial, the LNC should listen to each witness's testimony to analyze its impact on the case as a whole. Trial strategy is dynamic and may change during the trial. The LNC must observe the jurors as the case is presented and note their responses to witnesses and exhibits. These observations and the notes of the testimony will assist the trial team in evaluating the progress and potential for success of their case. Alterations in demeanor, emphasis on a particular point of testimony, or presentation of an exhibit can be made during the presentation of the case. The LNC as a member of the trial team must always be cognizant of the fact that this is a one-time opportunity for the plaintiff or the defendant to tell the story. Critique and discussion of the testimony and exhibits following the trial does not help win the case. Inconsistencies in testimony must be noted immediately for effective impeachment. If jurors do not appear to be listening to specific testimony or do not appear to understand testimony, alterations in questions or demeanor of the attorney or witness must be made immediately.

Each LNC will develop his or her own method of note-taking. A legal pad with a vertical line dividing the page in half allows notes for testimony on one side and areas for follow-up on the other side. Notes to be handed to the attorney in the courtroom should be written legibly on a small note card. The cards should be unobtrusive and written clearly to avoid lengthy discussions in the courtroom while the jury is present. Alternatively, a notebook or laptop computer can also be used for note-taking and provides ability to store and retrieve information.

Trial testimony can be frustrating for the LNC who is primarily an observer to the process. Witnesses may not respond as planned, and new theories may be considered by the opposing party. The LNC may need to conduct additional literature searches on specific topics during the trial to develop new theories or expand on earlier ones. New theories need to be communicated by the attorney to witnesses in preparation for their testimony.

Trials can be exhausting and invigorating at the same time. Long hours may be necessary to ensure that the client's case is presented as clearly and convincingly as possible. It can be rewarding to see the years of work by the trial team and the client come together to tell the complete story to the jury.

Evidentiary Issues

Chain of Custody

The Federal Rules of Evidence regulate how the facts may be proved at trial. This is applicable in all civil and criminal cases in federal court. In order for real evidence (physical, documentary and demonstrative evidence) to be properly submitted into the trial proceeding, it is imperative that it be accountable from the discovery phase through the trial phase. The object's whereabouts as well as the names of individuals to whom its care has been entrusted are paramount. This is referred to as the chain of custody and cannot be broken. The condition of the item at trial must be in the same condition as at the time of the incident.

Exhibits

Trial exhibits are used to help the attorney tell the story to the jury. An exhibit is a document, model, or computer presentation exhibited to the court during the trial to present proof of facts. After being accepted and marked for identification, the exhibit is made a part of the case. Exhibits may be admitted as evidence and sent with the jury for deliberation. Exhibits that are not admitted are used for demonstrative purposes only and are not viewed by the jury during deliberations. In this case, witnesses use the exhibits to demonstrate a point of their testimony. Medical records are generally admitted as evidence, but enlargements of specific

Table 42.3   Sample List of Exhibits

No.	Exhibit	Date	Introduced	Offered	Accepted
1	ER report	1/1/98	11/4/98	11/4/98	11/4/98
5	Consent	1/2/98	11/4/98	11/5/98	11/5/98
8	Consent	1/10/98	11/5/98	11/5/98	11/5/98
15	Death certificate	2/1/98	11/4/98	—	—

portions of the record may be used as demonstrative evidence. Anatomical models or scale replicas of equipment may be used as demonstrative evidence to assist the jury in understanding an expert's technical testimony. Scale drawings of an accident site, or photographs of the site or equipment, can help the jury to "see" the event.

Exhibits help the jury to understand and retain key elements of the testimony. Often jurors become tired and distracted when technical testimony is presented without the visual element offered by exhibits. Exhibits are used to enhance the memory of witnesses for details of complex records. The LNC may be responsible for transporting exhibits to the courtroom and for securing them at the close of each trial day. The LNC may have to coordinate audiovisual equipment, such as overhead projectors, slide projectors, computer projection equipment, and easels for charts or enlargements. The LNC should keep a record of each trial exhibit so that it is easily recoverable by the attorney (see Table 42.3). Also, most courts require each piece of the trial exhibits to be marked prior to the trial. The LNC can assist with that task.

The LNC can assist the attorney in preparing trial exhibits and presentations of evidence. The following demonstrates several evidentiary issues with which the LNC can become involved.

Medical Literature

Medical journal articles are not admissible in court as evidence. The same is true for the use of a *Physicians' Desk Reference* to establish the standard of care in relation to the administration of medication. In one case in which a defendant physician based his expert opinion that he had not been negligent upon medical literature, the appellate court refused to admit the articles as evidence.[3]

Medical Bills

The plaintiff has to prove that the damages occurred as a result of the negligence. Hence the burden of proof lies on the plaintiff. A plaintiff must be able to prove what medical bills are related to the malpractice incident. For example, an Illinois case alleged failure to diagnose a postsurgical complication. The plaintiff failed to introduce testimony explaining what portion of the medical bills were incurred as a result of malpractice. Thus there was no way to distinguish which charges were the result of negligence and which charges were incurred regardless of any negligence. Therefore, it was determined that the medical bills should not have been admitted as evidence.[3]

Hospital Policy and Procedure

Hospitals, clinics, nursing homes, and other health care facilities have policies and procedures for surgical, emergency, and routine activities. Failure to abide by the facility's policies and procedures may be evidence of a lack of ordinary and prudent care.

Hearsay Rule

There are exclusionary rules of evidence. Among the most noted is hearsay. This form of evidence is ordinarily inadmissible in court unless one of the exception rules prevails (refer to Federal Rules of Evidence 803 and 804). According to Fisher,[4] hearsay is a statement made outside the courtroom to establish the veracity of matter contained in the statement. It is considered secondhand information by the declarant, the person making the statement. It may be oral or written. Not all out-of-court statements by nonwitnesses are hearsay. Some examples of exceptions to the hearsay rule include statements for purposes of medical diagnosis or treatment, public records, and reports and statements made under belief of impending death.

Summation

Closing Arguments

Closing arguments are the summation of the testimony by the attorney for each party. These final statements are made by attorneys to the jury or court to summarize the evidence they think they have established and the evidence they think the other side has failed to establish. These statements are the final words from the attorneys before the judge's charge to the jury. The arguments by the attorney do not constitute evidence and may be limited in time by the court. The LNC should note any areas for rebuttal or areas that require further clarification by his or her party. Generally, each party may allot a brief time for rebuttal.

Jury Instructions and Deliberations

Jury instructions are written explanations of the laws that jury members must follow when determining the outcome of the case. Proposed jury instructions are presented to the judge by each party before the start of the trial. At some point before or during the trial, the attorneys and the judge discuss the proposed instructions. The judge determines which instructions will ultimately be presented to the jury. At the conclusion of closing arguments, the judge reads the instructions to the jury and provides any necessary explanations or clarifications.

In most civil trials, the jurors are not sequestered; that is, they are allowed to go home each evening during the presentation of evidence and during deliberations. The jury is escorted to the jury room by the bailiff and deliberates during the hours established by the judge. During deliberations, the jury may request clarification of the jury instructions by the judge or may request that portions of the transcript be read to them.

Negligence

The burden of proof for civil trials is different from that for criminal trials. In civil trials, the plaintiff must prove his or her case by a preponderance of the evidence. Some states now use "clear and convincing evidence" as the standard for civil trials. That is, the scales must tip only slightly toward one party or the other for the jury to find in favor of that party. In many jurisdictions, the jury may find the defendant negligent but also find the plaintiff to have been negligent.

Under comparative negligence statutes or doctrines, negligence is measured in terms of percentage, and any damages allowed should be diminished in proportion to the amount of negligence attributable to the person for whose injury, damage, or death recovery is sought. Many states have replaced contributory negligence acts or doctrines with comparative negligence. Where negligence by both parties is concurrent and contributes to injury, recovery is not barred under such a doctrine, but the plaintiff's damages are diminished proportionately, provided that the plaintiff's fault is less than the defendant's and that, by exercise of normal care, the plaintiff could not have avoided consequences of the defendant's negligence after it was or should have been apparent.

Contributory negligence is the act or omission by the plaintiff that, along with the defendant's negligence, was the proximate cause of the plaintiff's injury. Most jurisdictions allow the jury to find either comparative or contributory negligence by the plaintiff.

A querulous or contentious plaintiff can lose a case. A plaintiff who the jury concludes was exaggerating or lying can lose a case. The best position for the plaintiff to be in is that of a litigant who describes the same course of events as is recorded in the medical records, avoids controversy, and isolates himself or herself from being the focus of the case.[4] The defense counsel will make every effort to shift the focus of the trial from the conduct of the defendant to the conduct of the plaintiff.

Jury Ballot

A ballot is prepared by the plaintiff's attorney and submitted to the jury. The ballot requires several questions to be answered by the jury before deliberations are completed. The first question requires the jury to determine whether the plaintiff has proved negligence by one or more of the defendants. The next question asks the jury to determine the percent of negligence attributed to each defendant. In jurisdictions with comparative or contributory negligence, the jury must then determine what percent, if any, the plaintiff was negligent.

Damages

In order for monetary damages to be recovered, a victim must prove that some specific injury has occurred. This financial reparation for a tortious act may be awarded as a consequence of the harm — loss of body parts or function, lost wages, inability to continue in an occupation, emotional impairment, and related damages. The jury may also award damages for pain and suffering, although these awards may have statutory limits in some jurisdictions. In negligence cases, compensatory damages are common (i.e., out-of-pocket costs including medical expenses, lost wages, and mental anguish).

Punitive or exemplary damages, as the name implies, are awarded over and above compensatory damages. These are granted to punish or make an example of the defendant. Punitive damages are often requested in product liability cases. When punitive damages are demanded, the trial may be bifurcated, that is, divided into two separate phases of liability and damages.

The jury hears testimony on liability and causation, then deliberates on these issues. If it finds negligence by the defendants and that the negligence caused the plaintiff's injuries, the damage phase of the trial begins. Evidence is presented to prove damages as well as the economic worth of the defendant.

Punitive damages are almost nonexistent in negligence cases, although they are awarded in gross negligence cases in which willful and wanton disregard for the standard practices is proven.

In wrongful death cases, the statutes allow the surviving family members of the deceased to recover damages for projected income. Computation is based on insurance actuarial tables and takes into consideration the victim's life expectancy with adjustments for projected living expenses.

In cases (wrongful death, medical malpractice, etc.) in which a judgment is anticipated to be excessive, a high–low agreement may be considered as an alternative. The high–low agreement is similar to a typical settlement agreement, with some added features. The theory behind the agreement is that the plaintiff and the defendant insure the other against an excessive verdict. The plaintiff and defendant agree that the outcome of the case will be no less than X dollars (the low) and no more than Y dollars (the high). If the verdict is in favor of the plaintiff, and exceeds Y dollars, the plaintiff gets Y dollars. If the verdict is in favor of the defendant, and lower than X dollars, the plaintiff gets X dollars.[5]

Verdict

After receiving instructions from the judge, the jury retires. In all cases, jury deliberations are secret. In both state and federal courts, jurors must reach a unanimous decision. However, previously arranged agreements may preclude a unanimous verdict and make a vote of the majority of jurors acceptable. Some state courts permit a majority vote after six hours of deliberations. The time a jury takes to reach a verdict depends on the case. Three to six hours is considered average time, but great variances can occur.

When a verdict has been reached, it may be given to the parties by the judge by telephone, but in most instances the jurors will reenter the courtroom. The foreperson then reads the verdict. The different sides may request a polling of each juror's verdict. If the judge suspects an error, the jury may be retired to deliberate again, or a mistrial may be declared.

Judgment is the verdict of the case signed by the judge. The prevailing party can prepare this, or it may be in a form document. It will usually state a monetary amount. The judge has the authority to accept the verdict as presented, to set it aside, or to reduce the amount of money awarded to the plaintiff. Unless sealed by a judge, this information is public record.

Posttrial Activities

Jury Interviews

The LNC may be assigned the task of interviewing the jurors after the trial is concluded. The jurors are under no obligation to talk to any party but are free to do so provided that state laws are not violated. Valuable information for future trials may be gained from juror interviews. Questions regarding the presentation by the attorney, including demeanor, the exhibits, or the witnesses, may yield areas for change or improvement in the attorney's next trial. The opposing party's attorney should question the jurors about the presentation as well.

Bill of Costs

Most jurisdictions allow the prevailing party to be reimbursed for court costs by the opposing party. This is referred to as the Bill of Costs. The items in which relief can be sought vary between federal and state courts. The usual court costs include filing fees, fees for service of process, printing and copying expenses, and costs associated with subpoenaed witnesses. In federal court an affidavit attesting to the accuracy and necessity of the costs is required. The deadline for filing the Bill of Costs is usually 10 to 30 days from judgment. A copy of the bill must be served on all other parties. The LNC may be asked to calculate the amounts of the medically related costs, such as expert witness fees, medical exhibit fees, and time spent on case presentation by the LNC.

Motion for a New Trial, J.M.O.L., or Appeal

The jury's verdict can be set aside through the process of posttrial motions. The most common is a motion for a new trial or a motion for judgment as a matter of law after trial (J.M.O.L.). The trial court judge who heard the case usually decides posttrial motions. The judge grants a J.M.O.L. when it is believed that the jury rendered a wrong decision as a matter of law. In situations in which the J.M.O.L. is granted, the original verdict is overturned with a new judgment in favor of the other party.

Motions for a new trial are based on the principle that a prejudicial error occurred at trial that ultimately affected the outcome. These motions are not granted lightly.

Another venue for relief of the verdict is the appeal. An appeal is made to a higher court to review the lower court's decision. Different codes and rules are applicable during the appeal process.

Throughout the posttrial period, the LNC assists with researching and drafting posttrial motions or assists in preparation of an appeal.

Conclusion

Meticulous preparation and presentations are vital for the LNC who prepares the discovery phase of a case or engages in strategic legal analysis (with the attorney) prior to entering trial. Cases are won or lost by the presentation set forth by attorneys and expert fact witnesses; those who fumble for exhibits or key pieces of information are not seen as winners, and their success in the courtroom may be limited. The LNC's role, whether for the plaintiff or defense, should be a work of art providing an opportunity for the attorney to tell a story that will convince the jury which party should prevail.

References

1. Polchinski, P.D., *Elements of Trial Practice*, Lawyers & Judges Publishing Company, Inc., Tucson, AZ, 2000.
2. Corley, R.N. and Reed, O.L., *The Legal and Regulatory Environment of Business*, Irwin McGraw-Hill, Boston, 1999.
3. Shandell, R.E. and Smith, P., *The Preparation and Trial of Medical Malpractice Cases*, Law Journal Seminars-Press, New York, 1996.
4. Fisher, K., *The Process of Civil Litigation with Contract and Tort Law*, Vol. 2, The National Center for Paralegal Training, Atlanta, 1994.
5. Connelly, Roberts, and McGivney, *High-Low Agreements: A Viable Settlement Alternative*, http://library.lp.findlaw.com, 1999.

Additional Reading

Anderson, J. et al., *Legal Medicine*, 3rd ed., Mosby-Year Book, Inc., St. Louis, 1995.

Andrews, S., The changing face of court reporting, *Internet Newsletter for Lawyers*, http://www.venables.co.uk, March/April 2001.

Parke, A., Planning cross-examination, *For the Defense*, 43(9), 20, 2001.

Scheeman, A., *Paralegals in American Law*, Delmar Publishers, Inc., Albany, NY, 1995.

Singer, A., Trial consulting: a much-in-demand, highly effective, and nicely profitable professional subspecialty for legal nurse consultants, *Journal of Legal Nurse Consulting*, 7(2), 2, 1996.

Statsky, W., *Introduction to Paralegalism,* 5th ed., West Publishing Company, St. Paul, MN, 1997.

Weishepple, C., *Introduction to Legal Nurse Consulting*, West Thompson Learning, Albany, 2001.

Test Questions

1. Motions in limine are used to
   A. Highlight the key points of the trial strategy
   B. Prohibit introduction of certain testimony into trial
   C. Determine the order of witnesses
   D. Object to the other party's witnesses

2. An attorney may use a peremptory challenge to
   A. Dismiss a potential juror without specific cause
   B. Object to a question by the opposing attorney
   C. Question the qualifications of an expert witness
   D. Attempt to remove a judge from the case

3. Demonstrative evidence is
   A. Evidence used by the jury to show how they reached a verdict
   B. Evidence used to assist a witness in explaining his or her testimony
   C. Sent to the jury room with the jurors for deliberation
   D. Evidence used only in opening statements or closing arguments

4. Cross-examination
   A. Reinforces the credibility of the witness
   B. Is a process by which leading questions are not permitted
   C. May appear to be theatrical
   D. Is of little consequence to the outcome of the trial process

5. When a plaintiff is assessed with comparative negligence, it means that his or her
   A. Award is compared with other awards for similar injuries
   B. Negligence is compared with the defendant's and his or her award reduced proportionately
   C. Injuries are compared to those of individuals in similar cases
   D. Negligence is compared to the defendant's but his or her award is not changed

Answers: 1. B, 2. A, 3. B, 4. C, 5. B

BUSINESS PRINCIPLES

Chapter 43

Starting a Business: Legal and Business Principles

Deborah D. D'Andrea, BSN, BA, RN,
Adrienne Randle Bond, JD, BA, and
Doreen James Wise, EdD, MSN, RN, C-P/MH

CONTENTS

Objectives

- To determine the pros and cons of business ownership
- To discuss the major legal components of establishing a business
- To discuss the steps necessary in choosing legal counsel for the business
- To identify and discuss the three types of business structures
- To outline the key points necessary to complete a business plan
- To identify the legal requirements pertaining to owning a business
- To discuss the key start-up decisions necessary to owning a business
- To discuss the key financial issues necessary for maintaining a successful business

Introduction

Consulting business is risky business, more likely to fail than to succeed. Understanding the problems and having the solutions will maximize the opportunity for success. Creating a business from nothing, and then succeeding at it, requires motivation and perseverance beyond imagination. Nurses who develop their own thriving businesses reduce their success to several core elements and a few basic rules. The core elements encompass legal, business-planning, financial, and marketing issues. The basic rules of successful entrepreneurship include: (1) developing a business plan, (2) knowing business goals and philosophy, and (3) seeking professional consultation in legal, insurance, financial, and accounting issues.

Legal Principles

Many legal nurse consultants (LNCs) start their businesses as sole proprietors and often do not seek the help of a legal professional. Although this basic business form may not require a legal professional, it does call for some knowledge of legal principles in meeting state and local requirements. When an LNC decides to incorporate or to set up a partnership, whether at the beginning of the business or at a later stage, consulting with a legal professional is a crucial step. This section guides the LNC in selecting a legal professional and determining the right legal entity for the business, and outlines the steps to getting the business off to a good start with respect to legal issues.

Choosing the Right Legal Professional

In a new business, the first function of an attorney is to separate personal and business matters, legally and financially protecting the business and the individual client. Given the potential for businesses to fail, the right attorney can assist in protecting personal assets from creditors of a (potentially failed) business. Despite one's optimism (and maybe in support of it), finding appropriate legal counsel early is essential. Experienced legal counsel can offer prevention of and protection from problems. As nurses often tell patients, preventive maintenance is far less expensive than treating a serious problem; the same advice is true for preventing legal problems.

The Search Process

The process of finding counsel for a new business, like any other major financial commitment, requires careful research and interviewing. Seeking and engaging a specialist in corporate law who has a subspecialty in business start-ups is ideal. It is wise to avoid the attorney friend or relative whose specialty is in an unrelated area of the law. Larger firms have senior practitioners, with proportionately senior fees, and may also have less experienced attorneys working under close supervision who can carry out more routine portions of the work at a lower billable rate. For some LNC entrepreneurs, these younger attorneys mature with the business owner, making for a successful career-long affiliation. Smaller specialty or "boutique" firms that concentrate their work in the business start-up arena are an attractive alternative. The LNC may find quite competent and experienced attorneys offering a more client-centered approach than the institutional approach of larger firms.

Although costs for services vary from one area to another, the LNC should look beyond the billable hourly rates. A $250-per-hour specialist may spend half the time and do a better job than a $175-per-hour general-practice attorney. The LNC should ask potential lawyers for a fee schedule and for an estimate of billable hours and fees for each job requested. He or she should pursue references from clients with actual experiences with the attorney's time and billing.

To research and find the proper professional, it makes sense to consult a legal directory, such as Martindale-Hubbell; this and similar directories can be found at any public or law library and most business libraries. Legal directories include biographical information about attorneys and a brief description of legal practice and experience. Frequently, the attorney's representative clients are listed; the LNC entrepreneur should look for other professional service companies as examples of clientele served.

Generally, there are two basic specializations in legal practice: office practice and trial practice. Although the trial attorney may be familiar to most LNCs, the office practitioner is more likely the desirable professional for structuring the business start-up.

It is advisable to consult with LNC colleagues and friends, asking whom they have retained and whether they can recommend that attorney or another. LNCs can call the state bar for a list of expert speakers at continuing legal education seminars on emerging business. The bar may also send membership rosters for business law or related committees within its ranks. Once the LNC has identified some practitioners in this area, it might be smart to learn the names of their most serious competitors as well. Eventually, the same names and firms will be recommended repeatedly.

The next step is examination of the attorney's credentials. Not all law schools are created equal, nor are all law students; both are regularly ranked from the outside and from within. One should examine the attorney's work record: Has there been a logical progression from a large, well-established firm with business specialty departments to partnership therein? Alternatively, has the attorney ventured from the larger firm into a private practice specializing in business law? In addition, there are many opportunities to review, write, teach, and speak within the legal profession; participation in these activities may indicate acknowledged expertise in a given area of practice, and savvy attorneys will have reported such participation in legal-directory publications.

Once the realm of possibilities is narrowed to a short list, perhaps three to six, the next step is to arrange for personal interviews. At the interview the LNC should inquire what the attorney provides for and needs from new clients and what fee arrangements are to be made. It is smart to ask how services are delivered and in what ways that lawyer differs from the others on the short list. The wise LNC next asks for personal references, calling each and discussing the attorney's strengths and weaknesses.

Some LNCs then call attorney friends and clients to ask about the targeted professionals. The final appraisal calls for some personal inquiry beyond professional qualifications. The LNC must ask: Does this person seem trustworthy? Will this attorney give truthful advice, even if it is painful? Will this lawyer litigate aggressively when called for, but not recommend that course unless absolutely necessary? Each LNC has questions of this nature, which must be answered satisfactorily for a successful long-term relationship.

Choosing the Right Legal Entity

Once counsel is selected, it is imperative for the LNC to educate himself or herself about the tasks to be undertaken, because several critical decisions must be made. The single most important function for an attorney at this stage is to separate the client's personal assets from business assets. This is accomplished by establishing a legal entity, such as a corporation, separate from the LNC starting the business. The basic tasks are to: (1) set up a separate legal entity that minimizes the owner's personal liability; (2) ensure that the new entity has the legal rights necessary to conduct its proposed business; and (3) make certain that the new business entity pays its federal, state, and local taxes as required by law.

Establishing a Clean and Separate Legal Structure

The business needs to be established from inception with a clean legal structure. The entity needs absolute clarity about its ownership and the limitations on the owner's liability to the fullest legal extent possible. The choices include incorporation, limited partnership, limited liability partnership (a general partnership with an election to create limited liability), and a limited liability company (LLC). Selecting from among these is determined depending on:

- The number of owners — partnerships and LLCs require two or more persons
- The tax effects of formation

- Choices about day-to-day management
- The type of assets placed in the entity
- Pension and insurance concerns
- Projected plans to sell or terminate the business
- State regulation and taxation

The business's attorney needs to provide concise analyses for each relevant issue and to identify the choices appropriate to the LNC's personal situation and state laws. Any will work, but the best choice for each LNC depends on his or her unique situation and preferences.

Most independent LNCs start as sole proprietors. This means that the individual LNC personally is in business and has no separate legal identity. The LNC is the only owner and may be the only employee. To undertake this approach, the LNC visits the county courthouse, filing a "DBA" ("doing business as") or assumed-name certificate. The name is then registered within that county, assuring the LNC of being the only business entity with that name. For example, the person Florence N. Gale could do business as "LNC Enterprises." For legal purposes, the LNC is the responsible individual whose personal assets are unprotected legally as separate from the business. Personal tax returns report the LNC owner's income generated from all professional activities, including the sole proprietorship.

Many LNCs have begun to incorporate their business endeavors. Corporations are relatively easy to form and operate and, absent permission from the IRS to the contrary, are taxed separately from the individual owner. This means that the owner faces double taxation on income earned in the corporation, once on the corporate level and again as an individual "shareholder." It is possible to avoid such double taxation through a federal tax election as a subchapter S corporation. An S corporation is a regular corporation under state law that qualifies and affirmatively files a written election to be taxed similarly to a partnership. There are strict qualifying requirements for an S corporation about which an attorney can advise.

Some LNCs prefer to venture with a friend or colleague, forming partnerships. Partnerships and their close cousins, LLCs, are more difficult to form. Regular general partnerships do not shield the owners (partners) from personal liability, although limited liability is offered through a limited partnership, a limited liability partnership, or an LLC. Day-to-day business affairs in a limited partnership, a limited liability partnership, or an LLC also require some forethought and education. The law governing partnerships is less easily understood than the law governing corporations. Despite these drawbacks, these entities provide the benefit of "pass-through" taxation: if properly formed and operated, neither entity pays federal income tax. Other crucial considerations include state tax, the number of owners, and how the assets of the new business, if any, are to be contributed to the new entity.

Many new business corporations may qualify for the S election with the IRS, allowing taxation similar to that of the partnership and avoiding double taxation. Corporations are generally more cost-effective because: (1) the cost of filing fees is lower, (2) standardization of forms for incorporation lowers the setup costs, and (3) because of standardization, business owners are ordinarily more familiar with standard day-to-day operations that lower costs. The S election, if available, offers the benefit of partnership or pass-through taxation, with the cost-effectiveness of the corporate form.

Example 43.1 (this example is representative of standard formation of an S corporation; each business situation must be individually assessed): The entire start-up budget for Florence N. Gale, an LNC, is $2000, so cost considerations are important. Although the LLC is an option, this LNC opts for an S corporation as the best type of entity for her planned operations and also the best bargain. This LNC entrepreneur lives and works in Texas, where corporate filing fees are $300. The attorney's time spent in document creation for Ms. Gale's practice is one-quarter of that required to prepare a limited partnership agreement. (This is because corporate forms are fixed by the state, and can be "boilerplated," while partnership forms require more extensive, individualized drafting.) Because of service in her American Association of Legal Nurse Consultants (AALNC) chapter, Ms. Gale has working knowledge of such corporate terms as "president," "bylaws," and "board of directors." The attorney advised against a partnership, partly because of costs but also because understanding partnership rules is very difficult.

Florence N. Gale's attorney warned that there are certain disadvantages to the S corporation: There are tax limitations on the type and number of shareholders; S corporations are limited to one class of stock, and therefore, it is almost impossible to separate ownership control from profit sharing, which is perhaps necessary for raising outside capital; and an S corporation may not be able to take advantage of deductions available to regular corporations for many employee benefit programs.

Checklist of Required Documents

The first document required to form a new corporation is the articles of incorporation, or certificate of incorporation; state law mostly dictates the document's contents. It is filed, as a matter of public record, with the secretary of state in the same state in which the entity is formed. Bylaws, usually relatively standardized, and minutes of an organizational meeting of the board of directors are created next. The minutes should record election of officers, the issuing of shares, and any other business matters related to the corporation's formation. If there is more than one shareholder, it is advisable to commit, in writing, to an agreement about voting the shares and selling the shares. It is imperative that this shareholders agreement clearly delineate what will happen upon the divorce or death of the shareholders, and whether or not a shareholder may use shares as loan collateral. Because of community property laws in many states, and the rights of spouses to equity interests in the business, the death or divorce of an owner can give unintended rights to the spouse. In community property states, a simple shareholders agreement concerning rights upon death and divorce is necessary. Once again, lack of clear equity ownership can create havoc in times of life change, so good records are essential. It is recommended that the issue of transfer of shares to spouse or children as a means of estate planning be addressed directly. In small entities, in which the same people who manage the business also share ownership, it is advisable to set and keep strict boundaries on what is permitted under law. Many prosperous businesses (and long-term friendships) have been demolished because decisions regarding the business were not made in advance of crisis. Further, the most frequent cause for failure of an existing business is the death or divorce of an owner. Forethought about such matters can make all the difference.

For an LLC, the documents are substantially the same but bear different names and serve slightly different functions. For example, one files "articles of organization" with the Secretary of State and executes "regulations" (rather than bylaws). Although the forms are similar, they are *not* dictated by state statute and must take into account tax matters that are applicable to partnerships (but not corporations). Regulations in an LLC also serve the same function as a shareholders agreement (transfers of interest, death, divorce).

If the entity selected is a limited partnership, two documents are involved. The first is a certificate of limited partnership, which in many states is a one-page notice of filing of the name and address of the partnership. The second document is an agreement of limited partnership, a document containing all features of organizational content, bylaws, and shareholders agreement.

Whatever form is undertaken, the LNC should clarify in advance with the attorney what documentation is recommended, how long the work will take, what the work will cost, and what alternative approaches might be available. If the LNC business owner experiences start-up jitters that the attorney has caused, a second opinion is recommended. Starting a business is difficult work, and working with an attorney in whom one has confidence can make a significant and positive difference.

Keeping Clean Legal Records

Once the business entity is formed, using it correctly is the next critical step. Bearing in mind the purpose of the entity — separating personal from business assets — the LNC must be scrupulous about making proper use of its advantages. At a minimum, this implies the creation and preservation of careful legal records. Two critical tasks flow from this commitment. The first task is to make sure that the ownership is absolutely clear, and the second is to make sure that the property, particularly the technology or other intellectual-property rights used by the business, is properly owned by the business entity. Although there are other tasks of importance in forming a business, these two tend to be the ones that commonly create trouble if not handled correctly. The attorney can advise about other issues that may arise in the unique contractual situation.

Clarity of Technology Rights

On start-up, and prior to hiring, it is essential to explore whether employees of the new company are contractually free: (1) to work in the job for which they are being hired and (2) to bring processes and devices — i.e., the technology — they have developed in other employ. Any legal obligations of a prospective employee to current or former employers should be carefully considered. The business attorney should review and analyze any preexisting agreements held by intended employees or associates. The existence of an employment agreement probably implies a noncompete, nonpiracy, or confidentiality agreement. If any of these is in effect, it must be honored; it is extremely risky to ignore such agreements. Many companies seriously enforce such agreements for reasons of principle, pursuing violators on an individual basis at great expense in order to make a point. It falls to the business attorney to ensure that all owners and personnel of the start-up business have the right to engage in the new occupation, and under what limitations.

The new business must also have the right to use its technology. Technologies, devices, or processes developed while in the employ of another may belong exclusively to the former employer. Any technology rights must be properly assigned to the new entity, through direct ownership or license. Because that technology can be key to the new business, the attorney must be sure that the rights are properly held.

Example 43.2: An LNC seeking to work with Florence N. Gale was interviewed, in part, because she had created innovative software for a chronological medical records summary. On review of the LNC's employment agreement with her former company, Ms. Gale's attorney found that all devices and technology that the LNC had developed while in its employ remained its property. The LNC was not free to use the summary format once she had left its employ to join Ms. Gale's company.

It is also highly advisable to ensure that the new business has licenses for all the software used by its employees. Unauthorized use of software copyrights can result in fines of up to $100,000.

Avoiding Devastating Personal Liability

It is a difficult, but unavoidable, fact that a significant number of new businesses fail. With this in mind, the attorney for a business start-up focuses on minimizing the LNC's personal risk from inception.

Using the Limited Liability Vehicle Properly

The S corporation, or other limited-liability entity holding the business, offers important protection for the individual LNC owner. Once the entity is formed, however, the LNC owner must operate the legal entity properly to maintain its protective effect. The attorney should provide clear written instructions for operating the entity. This will allow the LNC to avoid errors that may defeat the protective liability limitations. For example, an LNC choosing a separate entity should be counseled to establish separate personal and business bank accounts. All communication from and about the entity should indicate its legal designation ("Inc.," "LP," "LLC," etc.). This includes answering the phone, preparing wording for signs in an exhibit booth, printing letterhead, etc. Each and every use of the company name should include the legal assignation.

The business should have a separate telephone line and listing, office space (even if it is a home office) delineated as such, and, if the LNC owns several businesses, separate office areas marked accordingly. Personnel must be paid and accounted for through the new entity, and items such as leases, equipment contracts, and other operational agreements need to be in the name of the new entity, not the owner's name. Instead, the owner executes such documents as an officer of the company, in a representative capacity on behalf of the company. All signatures must contain a designation for the office held on behalf of the entity, lest the individual signing be considered executing individually and thus be personally liable.

It is smart to negotiate all business agreements as an officer of the company. However, new business owners may be requested or even required to give a personal guarantee for business obligations such as equipment or office leases, at least at first. Practically speaking, most landlords and equipment lessors usually look to the business for repayment rather than to the individual owner, or accept a limited guarantee from the individual owners. For example, limits for personal guarantees, even if required, can be in time (the first 2 years of operation) or amount (fixed number or percentage). Even bankers will consider guarantees that are limited to the percentage of the business that the individual owns. Therefore, it may be worth fighting to limit personal guarantees, and renegotiating as soon as possible any that are demanded.

Example 43.3: Florence N. Gale will serve as president of the new entity, an S corporation to be called LNC, Inc. She has leased office space in her capacity as president, signing the lease as such. Newly designed letterhead reads "LNC, Inc.," as do the business cards. The new receptionist is trained to answer the telephone, "Good morning. Thank you for calling LNC, Inc. How can I help you?"

Buying Insurance

It is wise to arrange for casualty, property, and umbrella liability insurance, in an amount sufficient to settle a serious lawsuit. It is smart to shop around for insurance carriers, investigating and comparing the companies' coverage, exclusions, and claims-payment history. A cheaper quote on insurance may be false economy if the carrier fights all claims. For some partnerships or associations, so-called "key-man" insurance might be considered. This insures the life of the owner, to carry on the business, if the owner dies. If the business plan is critically dependent on one entrepreneur, key-man life insurance can prevent costly liabilities for the other players in the event of the owner's untimely death. Exotic insurance products such as product liability or officer and director insurance are not advisable for the LNC entity at the start-up phase. Long-term growth, however, may lead to the desirability of these products. The insurance professional can assist in setting up safety procedures and answering questions about premises liability; client-education materials are usually available from the carriers on this topic and on types of liability coverage. However, there is no substitute for careful reading of the policy and thoughtful inquiry about items not understood. As always, time spent preventively helps forestall the worst disasters. Prevention strategies can be set in place from the outset to avoid large claims later. Some insurance carriers for professional organizations offer member business owners policies at a competitive cost.

Paying Taxes

It is essential to file and pay all federal, state, and local taxes in a timely fashion. Both the federal and state governments have the right to assess individual officers of entities that have not filed and paid taxes on time. This includes income taxes for the entity and payment of amounts withheld for employee taxes. Not paying these obligations is the most expensive way to "borrow" money because not only subsequent interest payments but also significant penalties must be paid. The penalties are significant enough that it is advisable to borrow money from a bank or use a credit card to pay federal taxes rather than to delay filing and paying the federal government. States have enacted personal liability provisions so that individual executives are also personally liable for payment of state taxes, including income, franchise, and employment. Many jurisdictions require "licenses" to operate businesses, which serve as another source of revenue for those jurisdictions. A start-up strategy should include determining whether local licenses are required to commence business, and budgeting for them. It is important to understand that government entities have almost limitless powers to pursue collection of deficient tax and licensing fees. Compliance is absolutely mandatory.

Business Principles

For many individuals, starting a business is the culmination of a life's dream. Years of education and experience are brought to bear on what many regard as the ultimate financial freedom — the right to plan, pursue, and benefit from the direct results of one's own hard work. Nurses, predominantly female and traditionally employees of large corporations, have flocked to the concept, and many have succeeded. For some, it has meant the long-awaited opportunity to apply highest standards of patient care in a private clinical practice, unhampered by the political realities of today's corporate health systems. For others, starting and running a business means hope for financial independence. Still others start businesses in order to evolve from nursing to other professional interests. No matter their individual choices and circumstances, all entrepreneurs imprint their businesses with their talents, life experiences, and personal values. Each business is reflective of all that the unique entrepreneur has been, has achieved, and has dreamed of becoming.

Although nursing curricula traditionally have scant inclusion of business topics, more and more nursing programs are including courses that focus on business and management concepts. The systematic planning and decision-making process, the emphasis on "customer service," the creative utilization of limited resources, and the ideology of commitment to what is highest and best all translate from successful nursing practice to a thriving business. Each LNC seriously contemplating operating a small business should assess the advantages and disadvantages of doing so (see Appendix 43.1).

The Business Plan

Sound business practice flows from the same systematic approach as the nursing process. A business plan, not unlike a nursing-care plan, essentially drives the business decision-making process and orchestrates a systematic, goal-oriented approach. While many LNCs have successfully created viable consulting businesses without a formal business plan, it is suggested that those considering starting their own business develop a formal business plan that addresses growth, development, and goals. Samples of business plans are available in several of the books listed in the References section. Successful businesses uniformly have a plan, usually committed to writing. Keeping goals clearly in mind and in view can make a significant difference in the outcome of business efforts.

Purpose of the Business Plan

One traditional use for the business plan is to obtain financing; however, the true function is directing the business decision-making process. The main purpose of the business plan is to crystallize the year's goals. Those goals are accomplished through: (1) a marketing and sales activities plan and (2) a financial management plan consisting of cash flow and profit plans. Regardless of the ultimate use for business planning, whether orchestrating day-to-day operations or securing outside funding, the outcome is a goal-oriented, systematic enterprise. It is a process that is critical for both start-up and mature businesses.

Fundamentally, the business plan helps the would-be entrepreneur create and commit to a plan of action. It demands that outcomes be related to time and resources and literally provides the structure by which the new (or growing) business proceeds. Failing to commit to the concept of deliberate planning leads to disaster. Few successful business owners prosper without at least an informal plan of action from the inception of the business. The discipline of writing a plan, referring to it regularly through the year, and making responsive course corrections virtually ensures progress toward goals and the efficient use of resources.

Components of the Business Plan

The main components of a business plan include company background; key personnel; marketing concepts and analysis; and financial components, which include profit plan, cash-flow plan, and financial request for funding. Brief examples that demonstrate information that might be included in each component follow. The examples provided were prepared for the purpose of obtaining outside funding from an LNC's bank.

Company Background

Company background describes the nature and history of the business; it may give its location, facilities, and details of operation. It presents the basis of the business in understandable terms for the layperson.

Example 43.4: LNC, Inc. is a nurse-owned medical information service, established during the owner's graduate studies. LNC, Inc. provides medical/legal consulting services and products to clients involved in the litigation process. Clients traditionally served are defense attorneys in the medical malpractice arena and professional liability insurance carriers. Services include medical record and case analyses, medical literature research, and preparation for litigation.

Key Personnel

Key personnel gives a resume of the owner's education and experience, emphasizing aspects relevant to success in the particular enterprise. Managers and outside consultants with critical roles in the company are featured.

Example 43.5: The owner of LNC, Inc., Florence N. Gale, has master's degrees in nursing and business, as well as 30 years of critical care and trauma clinical nursing experience prior to founding LNC, Inc. Company staff includes equally skilled clinicians, with bedside and management expertise in obstetric and medical/surgical areas. A full-time office manager and secretary support these professionals. Established relationships with a CPA and business attorney augment the corporate structure and personnel.

Marketing Concepts

Marketing concepts describe special factors that make the company effective in the marketplace. The purpose is to define how the company has succeeded thus far, and the plan for continued future growth.

   Example 43.6: The owner of LNC, Inc., in addition to active participation in nursing professional organizations, participates in the planning committee for continuing legal education programs for the Defense Research Institute. Through that affiliation, LNC Inc. maintains collegial relations with its target clientele. In addition, because LNC, Inc. was the first such service in this community, and because it provides quality service and keeps pricing competitive, LNC, Inc. enjoys an established practice and continuing confidence of the defense bar. During the upcoming fiscal year, plans include expanding the client base to provide consultation and expert testimony to selected, credible plaintiff's attorneys in neighboring states.

Marketing Analysis

Marketing analysis presents information in more detail about clientele and prospects for sales. It provides detailed analyses of projected sales volume, growth trends, competitors, and other market factors.

   Example 43.7: Current clientele includes defense attorneys representing professional liability insurance carriers. In the coming fiscal year, an advertising campaign will tap the identified need for medical/legal services among plaintiff's attorney members of the Association of Trial Lawyers of America. By the end of the fiscal year, it is projected that income from services can be increased by 25% while maintaining fixed costs of doing business. A local medical student has initiated a medical/legal consulting business and offers the possible threat of competition. Her fees are lower, but her time is constrained by studies. This potential competitor has limited clinical experience that is dwarfed by the cumulative experience of nurses at LNC, Inc.

Sales Plan

Sales plan is the logical outcome of the preceding sections, projecting the monthly income from services for the upcoming year. Such projections are to be solidly based on past performance and current market conditions. Specific selling strategies are included. These will be evaluated at the close of the upcoming year.

   Example 43.8: The Company plans to continue its practice of careful selection of marketing and sales venues, in keeping with the values of the health professions. The bulk of new clients has traditionally come from word-of-mouth reference by satisfied clients and quality work. However, for the first time, a low-keyed display booth will be arranged at Trial Lawyers Association meetings in five nearby states.

A professional staff member will attend each meeting, and marketing materials will be sent by direct mail to targeted groups of attorneys in each of the five states. Customary marketing to local clients will continue, and, in addition, staff members will attend all bar association meetings. Each current staff member will increase annual billable hours by 500 for a total of 1500 hours, and a new staff member to be hired will produce an additional 500 hours as well.

Financial Components of the Plan: Financial Background

Financial components of the plan: financial background lays the foundation for financial projections and requests for outside funding. (For more information, see the section on Financial Issues.) Financial statements and tax returns from the prior 3 years and personal financial statements for the company's principals are generally required in requests for funding.

Profit Plan

Profit plan, which is the first portion of the financial plan, demonstrates the projected profitability of the planned enterprise. Critical assumptions on which the profit plan is based should be emphasized. This includes a percentage of revenues for service over the prior year, the ratio of gross profit to revenue, level of expenses contrasted to prior years, and comparisons to competitors' revenues if known.

Example 43.9 (narrative attached to financial statements): Current revenues are $255,000, or 1000 hours billed at $85 for each of the three nurses. Projected revenues of $340,000 are based on an increase in business through marketing and the addition of one nurse working 500 hours at $85/hour ($42,500) and an additional 500 hours to be accomplished by existing staff. In addition, selected expenses are planned for reduction: transfer to a lower-cost long-distance carrier, ending monthly payments on copier by using cash to pay it off, and replacing departing secretary with less costly staff will save 2000 hours at $5/hour ($10,000). Selling LNC, Inc.'s medical records collection service, the company's least profitable current activity, to a thriving competitor in the medical records business will also reduce costs.

All business owners informally do a cash-flow plan to predict the money needed to pay upcoming obligations. In this day-to-day operations approach, and in the more formal business plan, it is wise to address how and when money owed to the company, or accounts receivable, is to be collected. Cash-flow planning addresses work and invoicing schedules, scheduling of major purchases, and routine operating expenses paid on a regular basis, such as rent, telephone, and payroll. Addressing plans for collection of past-due accounts is advised, including reports of progress made. It is best to include information about seasonal fluctuations, if any.

The financing request formally addresses moneys requested from the bank or nonbank funding source. It should include the amount desired, plans for how it will be used, and repayment schedule. More detail is provided in the section on Financial Issues.

Example 43.10: Based on the information herein, LNC, Inc. requests a loan of $10,000 to create a local area network computer system, to add a new computer for a new employee, and to update existing machines with additional memory, fax modems, and electronic mail. Staff will be able to prepare, fax, or e-mail reports directly to clients, saving personnel costs, staying in better communication with clients and each other while making more productive use of their time. LNC, Inc. proposes to finance the loan over a 3-year period to reduce drain on current monthly cash flow, while utilizing the new equipment to generate income from new clients.

Establishing the Business: Key Start-Up Principles

Once legally in place, the business must be housed, staffed, equipped, and grown. The following start-up principles map out the steps necessary to start and grow a successful business.

Determining a Business Name

Choice of a business name is personal and subjective. Some prefer to keep the individual's name as the business name — e.g., Office of Florence N. Gale, R.N. — and others may wish to create a new name. The name of the business (e.g., Medical-Legal Consulting, Inc.) should project the LNC's image or identify the focus of services rendered. If incorporating the business, a lawyer may need to do a search to determine whether the business name chosen is already in use or whether it is acceptable.

Identification and Development of a Business Philosophy

Most LNCs have a clearly defined set of beliefs about nursing and nursing practice. Integrating a well-defined set of beliefs into the overall business philosophy can influence general business operations. This business philosophy generates vision and values for the business. This simple statement of beliefs and values serves as a guide for the practice that provides a basis for future decisions and actions. In some venues, this statement is often called a mission statement. LNCs who start a business with partners or employees realize that their philosophical approach affects the overall climate of the organization. This business philosophy should reflect the LNC's commitment to making sound business decisions that ensure the company's survival. There should be a clearly defined code of business ethics that will assist in helping the LNC resolve moral and ethical dilemmas that occur in the business world. Development of this code of business ethics and values increases the ability to deal with unexpected ethical dilemmas with confidence (see Chapter 46).

Identification of Business Goals

Goals should be developed in order to provide directions for the activities of the business. Business goals help determine the size of the company and help evaluate progress as the business grows.

Example 43.11: The following are sample goals developed by LNC, Inc. Six to nine months prior to the projected start-up date the following will be accomplished: start a marketing campaign, limiting the initial market to a specific geographical region. Design a company logo. Develop a marketing brochure. Develop a marketing and research plan. Develop employee job descriptions.

Marketing techniques are addressed in depth in Chapter 44.

Determining the Size of the Company

Although some may think that size just happens, it can be planned as surely as any other business aspect. Proponents of small and larger businesses advocate for the advantages of their own preference and are articulate about the disadvantages of the other model. For any business owner, thinking through one's preferences, and perhaps tolerances, early on is essential. This allows for change in the plan as one's business evolves over time, reflecting uniquely changing needs and preferences across a career.

Proponents of the keep-it-small approach state their preference for working alone or with a very few chosen co-workers. These entrepreneurs equate higher quality work and better managed workflow with limited size and volume. One way to accomplish this is to narrow efforts by serving a select group of desirable clients to a higher level of quality. Keeping things small is a way to limit expenses, especially fixed financial commitments. Everything from office space to payroll is likely to cost less.

One downside of small is less revenue. For most solo practitioners, revenue is limited to the number of billable hours that they themselves can produce in a given time frame. It may leave the LNC overdependent on a few clients; if even one client moves on, significant problems can result. A more numerous and diverse client mix is desirable for any business. For the LNC exquisitely aware of individual limits to knowledge and resources, narrowing of focus and client base may seem too confining. On the other hand, it may represent hands-on casework and rewarding collegial relationships with a few valued clients.

For individuals who want to nurture a growing business, the challenge of locating, training, and encouraging other professionals is attractive. The advantages are the possibility for more revenue, a more diverse client and product mix, the excitement of interprofessional synergy, and a chance to build an entity that will live beyond the founding individual. The LNC with a desire for revenues beyond one person's billable hours must also experience the headaches associated with managing staff and a larger business, and contend with the issue of dependence on co-workers.

For the LNC who swore on leaving the frustration of his or her last hospital management position that the largest organization she or he would ever manage again was a household, working as a solo act may seem like heaven. The less attractive elements could be viewed as the hassle of making and enforcing policies and procedures, dealing with complex governmental employment and interpersonal issues, finding ways to convince other people to work in the planned manner, and praying that expenses do not always outgrow revenue. Growth is expensive and must be closely orchestrated to result in profit. Chapter 45 discusses growing a business in more detail.

There may be a suitable midpoint between keeping a business small and allowing it to grow. Recent trends of workforce reductions, or "rightsizing" an industry, and refocus on working "smarter, not harder," offer provocative alternatives to the traditional small-versus-large arguments. By carefully planning the work, selecting and directing employees and consultants wisely, and making maximal use of technology, even the solo practitioner has the option to attract more clients, produce more work product, and generate more profit.

Creating the Business Image

Business image is an important aspect of developing a business and plays a significant role in the success of the business. The goal is to generate a positive response in prospective clients. The primary business image is reflected in the choice of stationery, logo, business cards, and brochures, and in the personal appearance presented to prospective clients. Other aspects of the business image are reflected in the choice of office location, furniture, and written correspondences or communications such as introductory letters and reports. When selecting the business cards, stationery, brochures, and other marketing tools, as well as office furnishings, the LNC should choose the best quality that is affordable and available. The savvy LNC recognizes the message to which clients respond favorably and develops the skills and style that project that message effectively and efficiently.

Every contact with clients should be carefully evaluated. The LNC should be aware that most attorneys are conservative in their business practice and that high quality is essential to all aspects of the enterprise, not just in the work product but in all the services provided.

Determining the Location of the Business

Selecting an office site reflects individual preferences, business goals, and unique circumstances. Some LNCs prefer establishing offices at home; others lease or purchase property in an office complex or free-standing building. The considerations usually involved in this decision include the image desired, initial costs that the LNC is willing to invest, general operating expenses, convenience, clientele, and special needs of the business relating to the LNC's individual strengths, weaknesses, and personal preferences. Each type of site has both benefits and drawbacks.

The Home-Based Office

Independent consulting particularly lends itself to the home-based office model. Available technology affords an entirely professional operation with the convenience of a home-based location. Since the legal nurse consulting process can be conducted largely through receipt, review, and evaluation of medical records and other written materials, it can be accomplished out of sight of the client. Face-to-face meetings can be scheduled in the client's office or a public building. Work product can be delivered, mailed, or faxed to the client, all readily initiated from the home office. In many instances, the client may want only verbal reports, which can be executed by telephone, by teleconference, or in person. Vast resources are available to support the home-based enterprise. Entire publications are devoted to setting up and operating successful home-office endeavors.

The benefits of a home office include reduced start-up and maintenance costs, such as overhead and no daily commute. There are specific tax benefit considerations, best made in consultation with a tax specialist during the start-up phase. In this way, solid business practices are established early. There is considerable flexibility in use of office hours as work can often be accomplished at any time, night or day, allowing for flexibility based upon project deadlines and family demands. Another benefit includes the possibility of achieving better balance between family/personal and business life. Those with young families (or aging parents) at home may wish to be available while working. Physical safety may be better ensured, and outside distraction by co-workers is reduced.

The disadvantages include working around the family's demands, or family members who do not consider the work to be important. Because the LNC is isolated from a peer group, no support system is readily available. Some entrepreneurs find working at home to be detrimental to family time because the work is always readily available. The home office may not project a positive business image to potential clients, who may view a home-based business as a lack of commitment or lack of professionalism. The wise LNC will investigate local zoning laws to determine whether they restrict the amount of space that may be devoted to a home office.

Those who prefer an outside office say that working at home can be lonely, and they miss the informal exchange of ideas. Others find the management and distraction of the home even more frustrating than the presence of and interruptions by co-workers. The LNC who chooses to work in a home-based office needs to plan a work space that reflects the degree to which he or she wants to separate home duties from work. Some home-based LNCs retain housekeepers and babysitters to provide services during regular business hours, just as they might do if they left home to work. Others find that, at home, they lack the same discipline imposed by outside office expectations for a dress code and work ethic. For these individuals, consciously planning and establishing businesslike routines and practices for the home office may be advised. Many home-based LNCs dress in business attire, mentally leaving home behind each day before walking into the office in the next room to go to work. They return "home" again at the end of each day.

Traditional Office

The traditional business office projects a positive business image to potential clients. This traditional office is less vulnerable to intrusion from nonbusiness sources, such as interruptions from family members, and specific business hours are routinely maintained. This formal business setting is conducive to hiring employees, such as a secretary. The major disadvantage to the formal business office is the cost of leasing or buying the space, as well as the daily commute.

Many LNCs begin their careers as employees of law firms and develop a preference for the office routines and setting. Some set up office space physically close to major clients or even lease space from them. Others prefer to find and set up an entirely separate office space. Leasing office space within a law firm may create a confusing impression that the LNC is an employee of the firm, and the LNC may experience frequent interruptions from attorneys from the firm who take advantage of his or her proximity.

Leasing or purchasing an office provides tax benefits. All rent or mortgage payments are deductible, as are many of the related expenses. The ability to lease or purchase space depends on a favorable credit history. Committing to the first lease or making the first purchase, and doing it responsibly, sets a positive foundation for all like transactions to follow. The first-time lessee likely will have to guarantee financially at least a portion of the lease both as an individual and as an agent of the business entity.

Advantages to working at an outside office include mental and physical separation of work and home. Establishing credit through leasing in one's own right can be seen as an advantage, even though typically it is considerably more expensive than maintaining a home office. If the LNC's goal is to grow a business to substantial size, an outside office is almost required. Hiring employees to come into a home office becomes very difficult and, in some instances, is a violation of local zoning laws. Some business owners wish to purchase an office property, viewing it as an investment and a way of arranging the office space to their preferences.

Another option under the outside office category is the use of an incubator organization. Incubator organizations allow the LNC to acquire office space on a month-to-month lease agreement, at usually greatly reduced rates compared to those of comparable conventional office suites. This office space usually comes with a variety of centralized services such as copy machines or secretarial support, at relatively low cost. Other incubator services may include computer support, billing, and small accounting services. Incubator organizations often provide specialized services, such as assistance with the development of a business plan or with market testing.

Determining What Services Need to Be Purchased

Start-up costs are dramatically affected by decisions about support services and required equipment. The LNC must decide whether it is more cost-effective to lease, rent, or purchase certain office equipment. Decisions about full-time or part-time support personnel need to be examined. (This is discussed in detail later in this chapter.) The LNC must decide whether an answering machine will be adequate for off-business-hour calls or whether an answering service will be required.

The LNC needs to decide whether specific services are necessary, such as computer support services or a graphic artist to design a corporate logoand perhaps assist in the development and printing of a marketing brochure. Once a logo has been developed, a printing service will be necessary for the brochures, business cards, letterhead paper, envelopes, and invoices.

The services of an accountant will be beneficial when addressing issues surrounding quarterly and year-end taxes. The accountant can render advice pertaining to the leasing of a business or corporate vehicle, how to set up and maintain an appropriate bookkeeping system, payroll deductions, and other financial-planning aspects of running a business.

Selecting Business Equipment

Equipping the office depends on the individual's planned work, intention for growth, space, and budget and will be determined by individual preferences. Basic essential office equipment will include a computer, telephone, and answering machine or service. Essential office furniture will include a desk, computer station, files, chairs, lamps, and bookcases.

A secretary or other support personnel requires a desk, computer, chair, lamp, and supplies. Decisions will need to be made concerning other office equipment, such as a copy machine, facsimile, printer, or scanner. Having proper office supplies such as letterhead paper, file folders, memo pads, pens, and pencils helps promote an efficient environment and directly influences the effectiveness of the work process.

For start-up businesses, financial caution is advised. It is incredibly easy to overbuy, committing the fledgling business to fixed expenses beyond its ready ability to pay. Costs of essential equipment and supplies can vary depending on locale and quantity. It is possible to create attractive, workable space without undoing financial stability. In most communities, recycled office furniture and equipment are available. Shopping the used-furniture stores can be helpful, and many companies recondition computers, offering them "loaded" and with warranties at bargain prices. Some entrepreneurs shop through catalogs with satisfactory results. Multiple resources are available with product information, financing. Other business owners in the community may have suggestions for best buys.

The LNC's local business banker may be more comfortable loaning money for capital expenditures such as computers and furniture than working capital for start-up expenses because the bank can repossess tangible property if the loan fails. Financing such purchases through the bank, even those that could be paid for easily with a credit card or cash, might be in the business's best interest. Longer payout periods can augment much-needed cash flow for day-to-day use and help build credit for future loans.

Employee Selection and Management Styles

Much has been written and said about hiring, firing, and managing employees. Perhaps not surprisingly, in general, it makes the most sense to follow the golden rule. Meeting and treating employees in a way that appealed to the owner while he or she was still an employee can help the owner minimize problems and make the workplace more humane. Moreover, the government has set some standards for this aspect of business; it is essential to know these requirements and to act in accordance with legal advice. The attorney who helped with the start-up may not be the best person to consult about employment issues, because this is a specialty area.

Key questions relating to employee selection and retention include:

- How do I know when to hire and under what guidelines?
- How do I know whom to hire? How do I keep the employee for the long term?

- How much do I pay? How else do I compensate and for what?
- How do I know if this employee is working out?
- What if the employee does not work out?
- What salary range is appropriate for secretarial services?
- What salary range is appropriate for the LNCs that I hire?

A good time to hire is before the business is shorthanded and the current staff is overworked; knowing when that time is may seem a mystery. The answer lies in setting objectives for company and individual employee productivity. The owner should set goals for the amount of work expected in a reasonable period of time. Clearly, for a new business such an appraisal will be an informed guess refined by experience over time. If there are goals for revenue, the owner calculates how many billable hours it would take to generate that amount of money at the hourly fees to be charged. If the owner cannot accomplish the task of meeting revenue goals alone, it is time to seek help. Help can come in the form of either employees or contract workers. IRS guidelines differentiate between the two and discuss small-business consultants (see Additional Reading).

Employees

Employees are paid either an hourly wage or a salary that reflects associated time and productivity expectations. They work in a place set, and do tasks designated, by the employer, using equipment and other resources that the employer provides. Even if there is a slowdown in work for the company, the employee is to be paid an agreed-upon wage or salary. In addition, the employer is responsible for a set portion of state and federal withholding, unemployment, and social security taxes. For employers of more than 15 employees, there are strict hiring, compensation, and firing guidelines.

Subcontractors

Subcontractors create their own offices and are dependent on more than one source of income. They set and schedule their work, provide their own supplies and equipment, and are responsible for all taxes. The employer is the contractor who requests services (and is held responsible only for wages) when work is needed. The employer determines whether or not the worker will be requested to work. The IRS continually challenges employers about who qualifies as a subcontractor. Accountants and nurses who work for temporary placement services frequently qualify as subcontractors. In general, W-2 forms reporting all compensation must be submitted annually for employees. The contracting company must submit 1099 forms in a timely manner to report income over $600 paid to subcontractors.

Appendices 43.2 and 43.5 are examples of noncompete agreements, and Appendix 43.3 is an example of a subcontractor's agreement.

For the beginning business, it may make the most sense to retain help through subcontractors. The variability of volume of work at first (and, frequently, on a continuing basis) makes committing to employees a daunting thought, whereas simply arranging for outside workers to do the "overflow" makes more sense to many. Advantages of using contract help therefore include avoiding financial and managerial commitments when the amount of work (and income) is unpredictable. Another advantage is a more extensive array of talent and expertise (such as diverse clinical specialties) without having to pay for additional work space, equipment, and supplies. Disadvantages to reliance on subcontractors may be less "control" over workers' time, their availability on short notice, and variable work quality. It is important to protect one's proprietary client base by insisting that all workers sign nonpiracy agreements. These constrain the worker from using the contractor's proprietary report formats for a reasonable period of time, usually 1 to 2 years. See Chapter 46 for ethical considerations related to not marketing to attorneys whom the subcontractor may meet while working for the contractor. Appendices 43.4 and 43.5 are examples of client retainer-fee and confidentiality agreements.

Selecting Staff

Selecting staff is an art, but can be approached systematically even by the novice. Starting with a job description — a list of tasks to be accomplished by the new staff member — the employer then develops a statement of attributes and experience necessary to achieve the tasks. Some small-business employers announce to friends and colleagues that hiring is in progress. Others prefer to call employment services specializing in professional staff placement. The agencies research each applicant's job history and references and conduct personal screening interviews before recommending applicants for placement. In addition, most agencies offer a guarantee if the employee does not work out well. One disadvantage is the agency fee, often a relatively large portion of the new employee's annual compensation. Other employers run advertisements in professional newsletters.

Experienced employers consult and follow government policies and guidelines before hiring. Potential applicants need to submit a summary of past education and job experience, with references included. It is essential that potential employers verify any licensee with state authorities and pursue each reference, no matter how frustrating the task. In this day of restrained communication, it may be all but impossible to determine accurately what the applicant's status was on leaving the last employment. Some references read, "Due to corporate policy, only dates of employment can be verified." One excellent approach is to give the potential LNC employee a "test case" to work, including medical records and other discovery. The would-be employee then prepares a written report as directed, accounting for time spent in preparation. This allows the employer to assess the LNC's analytic and writing abilities and to note how long the candidate takes to accomplish the project. It is also wise to verify that the applicant is able to proofread and possesses the computer skills needed for the job. The applicant should be asked to perform basic computer functions, such as copy, cut and paste, create headers, open more than one document or program at a time, and so forth. The few minutes spent testing skills may eliminate hours of trouble if the applicant has misrepresented his or her skills.

Compensation

Compensation should be planned prior to hiring an individual. Compensation is based on the pay scale in the hiring community for the relevant caliber of employee and experience. Ensuring that the company makes money enough to cover the cost of the employee's total compensation package (salary, all taxes, vacation, insurance, etc.) and some profit is rudimentary to a successful enterprise. One approach to paying hourly service employees is the so-called rule of threes. By this formula, the company pays one third of what will ultimately be charged for the employee's time. For example, if the employee is paid $25 per hour, following the rule of threes implies charging at least $75 for each hour of service provided. Most seasoned employers urge hiring for lower wages during a probationary period. Once the stability and viability of the employee as a positive contributor to the company's efforts is assessed, compensation can be increased accordingly. Compensation in its ideal state is a dynamic combination of components, including salary or hourly wages, bonus for productivity toward individual or company goals, and other benefits, such as vacation, insurance, retirement moneys, and so forth. In general, nurses and other employees tend to be most drawn by flexibility of scheduling and a sense of making a positive contribution to the company, given roughly equivalent dollar amounts of salary.

Employee Evaluation

Employee evaluation is another topic about which much has been written. A job description, coupled with an ongoing dialogue between supervisor and employee, allows for objective and constructive evaluation of performance. The focus of evaluation is ongoing employee learning. At its best, the evaluation should be mutually instructive, lead to a clearly stated plan for improvement based on both employee and company objectives, and leave both participants with a sense of understanding and even satisfaction. A goal-based employee evaluation makes it possible to set performance outcomes and to determine how closely they are being met. Ordinarily, employee goals should include documentation of statements pertaining to what is expected, to what degree of excellence, and in what time frame.

The intention of employee evaluation is development of a mutually satisfying relationship between a thriving business and a productive, adaptive employee. In situations in which the company goals and those of the employee do not mesh, it may become necessary to release the worker from service. Ideally, the termination will be a mutual decision, crafted over time and with the input of both parties. The evaluative process will have documented, over time, problems and recommendations for improvement in the employee's performance. When the employee is not progressing toward the preset goals, it is suggested that the employee be counseled to begin seeking work elsewhere. Some employers prefer a swift severance of the employment relationship. This limits the employee's opportunity to retaliate against the employer. Terminated employees have been known to misfile documents, format hard drives to erase data, and engage in other destructive activity. Once again, governmental rules may apply, and the LNC business owner is advised to know and comply with them. Many of these governmental rules and regulations can be obtained by going online to various federal agencies such as the U.S. Small Business Administration (SBA). In addition to gathering online information, the LNC is encouraged to discuss these governmental rules with a business attorney.

The employees are the most valuable assets of a business. This is especially true of professional-service businesses. Careful planning for successful identification, selection, and reward of one's employee colleagues can pay off in financial rewards for owner and worker alike.

Financial Issues

Prudent basic financial business practice calls for starting a company checking account. It is very important that personal and company moneys be kept as separate entities. A local banker can help select the type of checking account that best meets the company's current and future needs. Another important financial tool is a software accounting program, many of which are available on the market. The business's certified public accountant (CPA) may prefer that the client's financial software be compatible with the CPA's.

Selecting the Financial Institution

The financial institution, bank, or credit union that is used for personal accounts may not be the best fit for the business. The bank or financial institution chosen for the business may be different from the bank for the LNC's personal account. Banks offer a variety of special services specific to the needs of small businesses. These services may include different types of checking accounts, retirement plans such as SEPs, IRAs, and Keoghs, and a variety of business loans, lines of credit, and credit cards. Financial institutions that offer services directed toward a small business may also offer online banking services that can be used for cash transfers, payment of monthly bills, and tax deposits.

Selecting the Financial Consultant or Employee

CPAs receive extensive basic and continuing professional education and have one of the most formidable professional licensing examinations in existence. In addition to preparation in accounting principles, they receive instruction on client relations and are often skilled educators. Some accountants may have special interest and skill in small-business start-up and growth. It is wise to inquire regarding each of these qualities when searching for the accounting consultant. The integrity of the accounting professional is of special significance. This aspect must be closely investigated before a business owner can feel totally safe in hiring the financial consultant. Careful scrutiny of references, inquiry to licensing boards and such community resources as the Better Business Bureau, and recommendations from trusted friends and colleagues all are essential to selection of the financial consultant. Careful monitoring as the collaboration begins and proceeds remains important as well.

Once the business is underway, the owner's attention becomes focused on strategic planning, managing growth, and getting the work done. When the daily operations require more than one person to do the work, the accounting professional can take on a greater role. If an employee is hired to perform the financial functions of invoicing, collections, payments, and preparing financial statements, the accountant should consult in setting up the financial system. In addition, the accountant can educate that employee and can monitor performance of the company and the employee. The accountant can advise a system of "internal controls" — routine procedures for the office that add a layer of protection against theft. For example, one person may open the mail and remove checks, and another person deposits the checks in the bank. Ideally, the accounting professional will continue to consult as the business matures toward predictable developmental milestones and encounters the inevitable financial crises.

Financial Records and Reporting

Clear, accurate, and timely financial information is essential to the success of any business. It is the single source of data about how the business is actually doing. Critical elements for a start-up business include money owed to the business (accounts receivable), money owed to others (accounts payable), and the view of general financial health of the business found in profit-and-loss reports and the company balance sheet. This information is often referred to as internal reporting.

The same data that are useful to the internal running of the business can serve as foundation for reporting to outside authorities. This is frequently referred to as external reporting. The federal government has set regulations for reporting and payment of workers' income and taxes, and those for the business entity. Accurate and timely reporting and payment must be done or business, by law, can be brought to a halt. Other external reporting can include updated financial information required when funding is requested or received. Ordinarily, quarterly financial statements for the company are submitted to the loan source as a measure of progress and as a way to monitor appropriate use of loan money.

Financial Statements

Financial statements are the financial maps by which the business is run. Profit-and-loss reports lay out major sources of revenue and expenses. An accountant can help determine exact categories to list in the "chart of accounts," but typically they include the various sources of income to the business balanced with typical expenses, such as cost of outside consultants, salaries, rent, supplies and equipment, advertising, and so forth. The so-called bottom line of the business is revealed here. This report cites whether there is more income than expense. If the business is profitable, income exceeds expenses. If the business is not profitable, the expenditures exceed the income. The balance sheet lays out the exact financial status of the business — both assets and liabilities — and yields a statement of what exactly the owner has to show for all the work and risk taken; that is the owner's equity.

Start-up businesses tend to employ cash-basis accounting that reports money received by the business versus money actually paid out; this is a good tool for day-to-day cash management. The difference between money collected and money paid out is the number used to report earnings to the IRS for income-tax purposes. Cash-basis accounting has one serious flaw — it neglects to take into account moneys owed by the business but not yet disbursed. Cash in the bank has given false comfort to more than one unsophisticated business owner. What lurks in the accounts payable report can quickly undo that sense of comfort when the bills come due and available cash is not enough to pay them. Therefore, some entrepreneurs utilize accrual accounting for a more complete picture of exactly how profitable the business has become. The accrual statement includes additional information on revenues billed but not yet collected, as well as moneys owed and not yet paid out. Income-tax reporting is based on the difference between all the money paid and owed to the company and all the money the company paid or owed others, that is, the net profit. Consulting with a business accountant will result in the best approach for any individual business.

Financing a Business

As a first step to running a financially sound business, the LNC owner must plan and budget the movement of money through the business. Anticipating how much money will be needed, and having tight control over its movement in and out of the business, makes it possible to start and conservatively run a business. Continuing to employ the same responsible practices builds the good habits essential to every successful business. Even one-person, part-time businesses require a budget and cash management plan. Business consultants recommend that the budgeting should flow logically from the business plan. The plan should include projected work, the money needed to complete the work, and built-in evaluative measures to monitor and control for success.

Planning and Budgeting

An accountant is a key resource in developing a budget plan, but a beginner can develop a simple approach on his or her own. The first step is to plan the work to be accomplished on the basis of how many clients are in place and how much work each will require. The number of hours that will be billed as a result defines expected or desired revenue. The second step is to calculate how many hours the owner has available to work during a certain time period and determine what hourly billing rate is desirable and realistic for the community and, if there is more work than the owner can do, to determine how many additional hours must be done by outside help and for what cost. This information yields the costs of doing business, also known as direct expenses. The third step is to determine what materials, supplies, and equipment are needed to accomplish the work and get the money in the door. Answers to these and similar questions lead to the budget.

Cash-Flow Issues

The business owner's responsibility includes ensuring that there is enough money to pay the obligations of the company in a timely way. The budget lays out the plan, but the owner must make the plan happen. A process must be established for seeing that time spent and amount of work done are recorded and that bills are sent in a timely manner. It is critically important that provision be made for qualifying the clients' ability and intention to pay, and there must be a way to ensure that money is collected. Knowing what money is owed and making sure that it comes in time to be useful are part of the business owner's responsibility. All of this must be accomplished with a strict eye to the bottom line; the owner manages the company in order to make a profit.

Business owners must avoid the temptation to send invoices only when cash is needed to pay the company's bills. Establishing and maintaining invoicing as an orderly and predictable routine reduces the chance of "cash crunch" crises. Some owners establish a paper-and-pencil ledger system in which they record all time spent by case and send bills either monthly or at completion of the work. The other critical part of this process is getting the money in the door. It is highly recommended that LNC business owners require a retainer to begin each new project. Retainers are familiar to attorneys, who often collect them as part of their own office procedures. Smart business owners set collection procedures in place and adhere to them. A proven method includes these steps:

1. Clearly state, and repeat in writing, the exact payment procedures that the client is to follow. If the LNC's business policy includes remitting a $1000 retainer with the records, state such orally and in written correspondence. Some LNCs go so far as to have clients sign a contract indicating that the client understands and will commit to honoring the policies. Appendix 43.4 is a sample Client Retainer — Fee Agreement.

2. Always collect a retainer from every client for each matter. For established clients who may pay more slowly than 30 days, it is acceptable to require a larger retainer and to bill against it, replenishing it often.

3. Bill frequently, at the conclusion of each phase of work or monthly at the longest interval.

4. Make a point to inquire about, and then follow up on, the exact payment process followed in the client's office. Determine responsible employees, make note of their names, and stay in close touch with them. This can also make a significant difference in feeling reassured that someone will see that payment is made or in working out an amicable payment plan. Attorneys sometimes have their own cash-flow problems. Defense attorneys may be slow payers because their insurance-company clients reimburse their expenses. Sometimes the LNC's invoice is sent to the insurance company, which pays the LNC directly. The contracting law firm is still responsible for the payment, and the LNC contacts this law firm in case of a delay in payment. Plaintiff's attorneys have to win the case in order to collect any money. There may be times when working with a client over a longer payment cycle makes sense. However, more than one small entrepreneur's business has failed through slow payment practices by even well-meaning clients.

5. At 30 to 45 days after the bills go out, make a call to each client from whom payment has not been received in full. Politely inquire whether the bill was received, whether any questions or concerns can be answered, and when payment can be expected. Surprisingly, attorneys may not even know that the bill has been received or may have placed it out of the pay process to get questions answered, but were too busy to call. This simple call by the business owner or clerk can prevent many slow-payment

problems by staying in communication. This step often prevents having to take any of the following actions that may seem harsh to some LNCs.

6. At 45 to 60 days, fax a reminder letter with copy of the bill, stamped "PAYMENT OVERDUE." Some LNCs begin at this point to add 18% annual interest to the bill. The practice of adding interest needs to be included in all contracts, fee statements, and so forth, so that clients are forewarned.

7. At 60 to 75 days, send a letter on pink paper with a windowed envelope for all to see that the bill is overdue. The letter should state that all work on the matter will cease in 2 weeks unless payment in full is received. If the LNC is serving as, or is providing, an expert witness for the case, it is acceptable to indicate in the letter that if payment is not received immediately, the expert will be notified in writing to cease all work. Remember that all correspondence in the testifying expert's file is discoverable, so attorneys will pay to avoid the letters being sent.

8. If payment is still not received shortly thereafter, send letters to all experts contracted through the LNC service and have the business attorney take over the collections. It may also help to write to the state bar association complaining about the attorney's payment practices.

Taking a businesslike and proactive approach to billing and collections prevents or resolves many cash-flow issues and can make the difference in whether the business succeeds or fails.

Cash-Flow Management

Cash flow is considered a complex process, but it need not baffle the LNC business owner if procedures are worked out with an accountant and rigorously followed. Hours billed to the client create an account receivable, which becomes cash when payment is made. In the interim, the owner and other workers must be paid, and any rent, routine payments, bills for supplies, and other bills must be paid. Planning is required for good cash-flow management.

To control and manage cash, some LNCs create cash-flow projections to calculate the need for money on a scheduled basis. Long-range forecasting is generally seen as looking ahead for the next 12 months and projecting the moneys that will be needed. Then the LNC looks at the next three of those months, and finally at the current week and the week following. For each time period, he or she anticipates bills that must be paid, and what money is expected to come in and when. Plans for bill-paying are made accordingly with contingency plans created for any shortfalls. Although sometimes tedious, cash-flow planning is essential for small struggling businesses and, perhaps surprisingly, for thriving, growing, profitable enterprises as well.

Funding Sources and Issues

The following discussion is for those LNCs entertaining serious thoughts about alternative funding sources. One key reason why even apparently thriving businesses sometimes fail is that they have too little money when it is needed. Understandably, some LNC business owners take pride in paying cash for all purchases and relying totally on the business's own revenues to finance growth. However, there are times when it might make better business sense to borrow money in a responsible way. Building credit and allocating smaller routine payments during times when cash is needed elsewhere in the business can foster growth or, in more trying times, determine whether or not the business survives.

Business Financing

The smart entrepreneur recognizes that the bank's only true business is to make money by loaning it to its customers, including small-business owners. It is smart for the LNC owner to select a bank that specializes in small-business operations that resemble his or her own business. Each LNC owner should request a meeting with the officer assigned to the business's account to introduce the business and the owner's professional experience and plans. Presenting written information about the business, and even recent financial reports if the business is already active, can help impress the banker. Taking the time to know the bank, the services it offers, and the officers working with small-business accounts is in the owner's best interest.

There may be some truth to the stereotype that bankers make loans only to business owners who do not "need" the money. This may discourage the LNC who is venturing into a first business, even one who has sought a working relationship with the bank. However, there are steps to take to build that "past" that bankers seek. In addition to getting to know one's banker, taking an unemotional look at one's past personal financial asset management is an essential first step. Remedying any unpaid loans, overdrawn accounts, and the like is best done before starting the business. Requests for start-up or later financing will be met with demands to take these same steps, and bankers will be impressed if time has elapsed since any curative action took place. As indicated above, there will likely be insistence on personal guarantee by the individual owner for all debt incurred, even that secured with equipment or property. If so, asking the banker for a date when all personal-guarantee restrictions can be lifted is smart, as is determining all requirements needed to accomplish that goal.

The bank makes money when its customers borrow and repay loans. Rather than being shy about requesting loan money, it makes sense for the LNC owner to discuss frankly under what circumstances the business is "bankable" and then take steps in that direction. The LNC should find out what types of loans the bank makes and whether it is a certified lender with the federally funded SBA. In keeping with other such government programs, the SBA gives special consideration to minority business owners, including persons of color, females, disabled individuals, Native Americans, and Vietnam veterans. Most LNCs qualify on the basis of one or more of those considerations.

Other Funding Sources

Because bank loans may be scarce, some start-up businesses turn to family sources for funds. While not always advisable for a long-term financial approach, borrowing from family and supplemental income are the most frequently cited funding sources for start-up companies. These strategies may be the way to start and run the business until there is history enough to build the bank's confidence and to become bankable. However, borrowing from family members may create trouble within the family if the business owner is unable to repay the loan under the intended plan. Some owners supplement the business by working at a job and using paychecks to finance a business initially run part-time. Starting an LNC practice is ideal for such an approach, because the work can often be accomplished on one's own time and at reasonable expense.

Some entrepreneurs make a point of borrowing a small amount from a bank and then repaying the loan to build a track record of borrowing and timely repaying. A related strategy is to place an amount of money in savings at the desired bank, then borrowing that amount as a business loan, using the savings account as collateral. The cost of the interest in either approach is a legitimate business expense and is definitely worth the price to enable future loan opportunities. Although the concept seems counterintuitive, the more a business grows, the greater the possibility that a loan of some sort will be essential to survive and thrive in the growth. It is a lifeblood function for successful businesspeople to make and cultivate cordial, effective relationships with their bankers. Bankers look for qualities such as confidence and integrity. The banker seeks evidence that the business owner is competent to run the business, will maintain a satisfactory financial condition, and has a realistic set of goals. An owner who sets out to provide this evidence will speed the process of becoming established.

Conclusion

All LNC entrepreneurs can benefit from a well-thought-out view of the needs in the marketplace as they relate to the entrepreneur's special talents. Creating a market niche and positioning it deftly can be the beginning of a successful practice. Legal nurse consulting is a relatively new subspecialty of nursing. However, the same foundations on which one bases an effective nursing career also serve the founding and growth of a successful LNC independent practice. The basic rules of successful entrepreneurship are to: (1) develop a business plan; (2) know the business goals and philosophy; and (3) seek professional consultation in legal, insurance, financial, and accounting issues.

Additional Reading

Consulting

Block, P., *Flawless Consulting; A Guide to Getting Your Expertise Used*, 2nd ed., Jossey-Bass, San Francisco, 2000.

Holtz, H., *Concise Guide to Becoming an Independent Consultant*, John Wiley & Sons, New York, 1999.

Nelson, B. and Economy, P., *Consulting for Dummies*, Hungry Minds, Inc., New York, 1997.

Phillips, J., *The Consultant's Scorecard: Tracking Results and Bottom Line Impact of Consulting Projects*, McGraw-Hill, New York, 2000.

General Business

Adams, B., *Complete Business Plan*, Adams Media Corp., Holbrook, MA, 1998.

Allen, K., *Entrepreneurship for Dummies*, IDG Books Worldwide, Chicago, 2001.

Caplan, S., *Small Business Success Kit*, Adams Media Corp., Holbrook, MA, 2001.

The Entrepreneur Magazine's Small Business Advisor, 2nd ed., John Wiley & Sons, New York, 1999.

Hingston, P., *Starting Your Own Business*, Dorling Kindersley Book Co, New York, 2001.

Kraass, P., *The Book of Entrepreneur's Wisdom*, John Wiley & Sons, New York, 1999.

Lesonsky, R., *The Entrepreneur Magazine's Start Your Own Business*, 2nd ed., Entrepreneur Press, Irvine, CA, 2001.

Tyson, E. and Schell, J., *Small Business for Dummies*, IDG Books Worldwide, Inc., Chicago, 2001.

Government; Internal Revenue Service

Market Segment Specialization Program, *Business Consultants*, U.S. Department of Treasury Internal Revenue Service, Training 3123–012 (3–01) TPDS No. 86821N, 2001.

Venture Capital

Cardis, J. and Kirschner, S., *Venture Capital: The Definitive Guide for Entrepreneurs, Investors and Practitioners*, John Wiley & Sons, New York, 2001.

Gladstone, D., *Venture Capital Handbook; An Entrepreneur's Guide to Obtaining Capital to Start a Business, Buy a Business or Expand an Existing Business*, Prentice Hall, New York, 1998.

Test Questions

1. Which of the following statements is NOT true?
    A. As a sole proprietor, the LNC is the only owner and may be the only employee.
    B. As a sole proprietor, the LNC's personal assets are legally protected because they are separate from the business assets.
    C. Corporations are easy to form and operate, and taxation is done on a double basis — the individual as well as the corporate level.
    D. Double taxation can be avoided through the development of a sub-chapter S corporation.

2. Which of the following statements is true?
    A. Traditionally, a business plan is drafted in order to obtain either bank or venture capital funding.
    B. The LNC who is not interested in obtaining financial backing does not need to draft a formal business plan.
    C. Drafting a successful business plan requires professional assistance and should be completed by a professional business planner.
    D. Business plans do not always need to map out financial background or address cash-flow patterns to be successful and complete.

3. Which of the following statements is NOT true?
    A. A general business philosophy creates a vision and sets the values for the business.
    B. Business goals help direct the activity of the business.
    C. The goal of a successful business image is to generate a positive response in prospective clients.
    D. Once the business is housed, staffed, and equipped, it will grow naturally.

4. Which of the following statements is true?
    A. The LNC should identify requirements developed by the government pertaining to employees and contract workers.
    B. Finding competent LNC employees is an easy process for the LNC business owner.
    C. Yearly employee evaluations are necessary only in large corporations and are not generally seen as necessary in an independent LNC business.
    D. Hiring and firing practices come naturally to the LNC business owner, and careful selection of employees is not necessary because any nurse with a clinical background can function successfully as an LNC.

5. Which of the following statements is true?
    A. Personal and business finances can be intermingled throughout the year and then can be sorted out by the CPA at the end of the tax year.
    B. Retirement plans are not necessary for the LNC business owner.

C. It is important that the LNC's financial partner have intimate knowledge about the business.
D. While profit-and-loss reports map out major sources of revenue and expenses, they are time-consuming to develop and usually not necessary or required by the CPA.

Answers: 1. B, 2. A, 3. D, 4. A, 5. C

Appendix 43.1
Advantages and Disadvantages to Starting and Owning a Business

Characteristics	Advantages	Disadvantages
Freedom and flexibility	The LNC can choose the time and place to provide services. The LNC can balance a variety of roles more easily. The LNC can structure work and personal time.	The market for the specific services may eventually disappear. The workload varies as periods of high volume alternate with low-volume periods. The LNC may have difficulty in separating work and personal time. The LNC may experience a lack of support and understanding from significant others.
Independence	The LNC is free to structure the approach to any project or problem. The LNC assumes total responsibility for the quality and outcome of each project.	The client's needs, wants, and desires may override the LNC's. The LNC may experience self-doubt or loneliness due to isolation and lack of a structured peer group or team.
Control of reimbursement for services rendered	The LNC identifies and charges fees appropriate to personal skills, expertise, and location.	Nurses tend to underestimate the worth of their services. Cash flow, like workload, ebbs and flows.
Professional and personal growth and challenge	Each new project or opportunity stimulates growth and challenges the LNC both professionally and personally as he or she stretches to meet those goals.	New projects or requests for services may demand development of a new knowledge base and skills. Those with less creativity and self-confidence may not be able to meet the demands.

Appendix 43.2
Agreement Not to Compete during and after Engagement

This agreement is made as of this _____ day of _____, _____ by and between Medical-Legal Consulting, Inc., an Illinois corporation, and _____, hereinafter referred to as Subcontractor.

WHEREAS, Subcontractor desires to perform or continue to perform services for _____ and _____ desires to secure such services subject to the terms hereof,

NOW, THEREFORE, in consideration of the mutual covenants contained herein, and other good and valuable considerations, the receipt and adequacy of which is hereby acknowledged, _____ and Subcontractor agree as follows:

1. Subcontractor agrees that at no time during the term of Subcontractor's engagement with _____, or for a period of two years immediately following the termination of Subcontractor's engagement with _____, will Subcontractor, for Subcontractor or on behalf of any person or entity other than _____, engage in the nursing consulting business in conflict with or adverse to _____ and any of _____'s clients.
2. Subcontractor will not, directly or indirectly, solicit or attempt to solicit business or patronage of any of _____'s clients for the purpose of nursing consultation and such other business and service now engaged in by _____.
3. Subcontractor will not, during the term of Subcontractor's engagement, service contracts and clients with interests adverse to or in conflict with _____ or any of _____'s clients.

THE PARTIES ACKNOWLEDGE THAT THEY HAVE READ THIS AGREEMENT AND UNDERSTAND IT AND AGREE TO BE BOUND BY ITS TERMS AND CONDITIONS.

MEDICAL-LEGAL CONSULTING, INC., an Illinois corporation

Signature & Title: _____
Date: _____

SUBCONTRACTOR

Signature & Title:_____
Date: _____

Appendix 43.3
Subcontractor Services Agreement

This agreement is made as of this _____ day of _____, _____ by and between Medical-Legal Consulting, Inc., an Illinois corporation, hereinafter referred to as Company, and _____, hereinafter referred to as Subcontractor.

WHEREAS, Company desires to contract for certain Services of Subcontractor, as are hereinafter more particularly defined; and

WHEREAS, Subcontractor understands that Company does not practice medicine, nursing, or law, but is acting solely in the capacity of a purely consulting expert to attorneys in order to assist such attorneys in the preparation of medical and nursing malpractice cases and other cases involving medical, nursing, health care, or other related issues; and

WHEREAS, Subcontractor is licensed to practice nursing in the state of _____ and is competent and willing to provide the Services, as are hereinafter defined,

NOW, THEREFORE, in consideration of the mutual agreements, covenants, and conditions herein contained, the parties hereto covenant and agree as follows:

1. INDEPENDENT CONTRACTOR: The parties hereto agree that the Services rendered by Subcontractor in the fulfillment of the terms and obligations of this agreement shall be as an independent contractor. Subcontractor shall not be considered an employee of Company.
2. TERM: This agreement shall be effective until termination by either party hereto by tendering 30 days' advance written notice to the other party.
3. SERVICES: Subcontractor is willing and competent to provide the following Services, including but not limited to consulting with Company, evaluating medical and nursing malpractice cases and other cases involving medical, nursing, health care, or other related issues, and rendering written and verbal opinions or reports concerning such cases.
4. CONSULTATION: Subcontractor agrees to meet all deadlines, as agreed upon.
5. CONSIDERATION: Subcontractor shall invoice Company at an hourly rate of $_____ per hour for Subcontractor's Services hereunder. Subcontractor's invoice shall be in writing and shall contain Subcontractor's Social Security number and mailing address and shall reflect only reimbursable expenses. Subcontractor shall be reimbursed by Company for all reasonable expenses.
6. TAXES: Subcontractor assumes full responsibility for, and agrees to pay, all contributions and taxes payable under federal and state Social Security acts, workers' compensation laws, unemployment compensation laws, and income tax laws as to all the compensation received by Subcontractor from Company hereunder.
7. CONFIDENTIALITY: Subcontractor agrees not to disclose to any attorney, law firm, or any other entity, person, firm, or corporation: (a) information relating to the business of Medical-Legal Consulting, Inc. or any parent, subsidiary, or affiliate; (b) trade secrets; (c) information encompassed in all designs, written work product, attorney/client work product, work instructions, test data, research data, reports, recommendations, plans,

proposals, financial information, or customer or client lists; (d) legally related information; or (e) other documents of every description disclosed to and made available to Subcontractor by Comapny's clients and professional agents (including accountants and attorneys). Confidential information also includes: (a) information in Subcontractor's memory, in oral or written form, or contained in any form, relating to customers, clients, employers, representatives, or professional agents (such as attorneys and accountants); and (b) existing or proposed written work product.

8. TERMINATION FOR DEFAULT: Company may terminate this agreement for cause at any time by furnishing Subcontractor with 2-day advance written notice. If Subcontractor is unable to cure the default within 2 days, or any longer cure period agreed to in writing by the parties, the agreement shall terminate and Subcontractor shall be paid for all work and services satisfactorily performed and all materials delivered through and until the effective date of termination.

9. SURVIVAL: The representation and warranties and obligations of indemnity set forth in Article 13 of this agreement shall survive the agreement for a period of 2 years following the termination or expiration of this agreement.

MEDICAL-LEGAL CONSULTING, INC.

Name & Title: _____

Date: _____

SUBCONTRACTOR

Name & Title: _____

Date: _____

Appendix 43.4
Client Retainer — Fee Agreement

This agreement is made as of this _____ day of _____, _____ by and between Medical-Legal Consulting, Inc., an Illinois corporation, and _____, hereinafter referred to as Client.

Client hereby retains Medical-Legal Consulting, Inc. for the performance of consulting services on behalf of Client and agrees to pay Medical-Legal Consulting, Inc.

A $1000 retainer, covering 10 billable hours, for cases involving medical, nursing, or health care related issues, is payable upon execution of this agreement. The retainer shall be credited on a 30-day monthly basis.

Medical-Legal Consulting, Inc. shall invoice Client at an hourly rate of $100 per hour. The above hourly fees shall be for actual time spent performing and completing the designated services requested. Client is the attorney, and the attorney, not the attorney's client, is responsible for all charges regardless of the outcome of the case. Payment of fees or any portion thereof is not contingent upon the outcome of any case.

Client understands and agrees that all billings by Medical-Legal Consulting, Inc. will be made on a monthly basis, and are required to be paid by Client within 30 days from receipt. Client agrees to pay a monthly assessment of 2% of the unpaid balance of overdue charges. Medical-Legal Consulting, Inc. reserves the right to cease services for Client under this agreement when a bill is not paid within the required 30 days, and Client agrees to a cessation of activity.

If collection efforts are necessary by Medical-Legal Consulting, Inc., either directly or as an assignee of any debts incurred under this agreement, Client agrees to pay to Medical-Legal Consulting, Inc. reasonable attorney's fees and all costs incurred pertaining to such collection efforts together with all due amounts and interest.

Medical-Legal Consulting, Inc. may terminate this agreement for cause at any time by furnishing Client with 2 days' advance written notice. Medical-Legal Consulting, Inc. shall be paid for all work and services performed and all materials delivered through and until the effective date of termination.

This written agreement contains the sole and entire agreement between the parties pertaining to the subject matter herein. No modification or waiver of this agreement shall be binding unless executed in writing by both parties hereto.

MEDICAL-LEGAL CONSULTING, INC.

Signature & Title: _____
Date: _____

LAW FIRM/ATTORNEY

Signature & Title: _____
Date: _____

Appendix 43.5
Proprietary Information, Confidentiality, and Noncompetition Agreement

This agreement is entered into on the date set forth below by and between the undersigned ("Employee") and LNC, Inc.

Background

Employee has been offered employment by LNC, Inc. As a term and condition of Employee's employment by LNC, Inc., Employee has agreed to execute and be bound by the terms and conditions of this agreement.

Agreement

NOW, THEREFORE, in consideration of the foregoing Background and intending to be legally bound hereby, LNC, Inc. and Employee agree as follows:

1. *Confidentiality.*
    (a) Employee acknowledges and recognizes that during the term of Employee's employment by LNC, Inc., Employee may participate in the development of, or gain access to, oral and or written materials and information considered by LNC, Inc. to be of confidential or proprietary nature ("Confidential Information"), including, but not limited to:
        (i) *Proprietary Information.* Proprietary Information shall include, without limitation, information disclosed to Employee or known by Employee as a result of Employee's employment by LNC, Inc. about LNC, Inc.'s methods, processes, services, referral services, clients, customer lists, customers' wants, requirements, and preferences, and business practice, including, without limitation, research and development, purchasing, financing, financial information, data processing, marketing, marketing techniques, marketing areas, and potential marketing areas.
        (ii) *Company Procedures.* Company Procedures shall include, without limitation, information concerning the business affairs and internal policies and procedures of LNC, Inc., such as internal financial controls, compensation arrangements, direct and indirect costs, and similar items related to contracts and arrangements with clients.
    (b) Employee undertakes and agrees that during the term of Employee's employment by LNC, Inc. and after termination of Employee's employment by LNC, Inc. (regardless of the reason for or the party causing such termination), Employee will not disclose any such Confidential Information to any person, partnership, corporation, or business entity and will not utilize any such Confidential Information in any manner.
2. *Noncompetition.* Employee undertakes and agrees that during the term of Employee's employment by LNC, Inc. and for a period of two years after the termination of Employee's employment by LNC, Inc. (regardless of the

reason for or the party causing such termination), Employee will not, directly or indirectly:

(a) Contact, or otherwise act in any way to induce, any person, partnership, corporation, or entity that was a client or potential client of LNC, Inc. during the term of Employee's employment by LNC, Inc. for the purpose of soliciting the business of such customer. The term "potential clients" shall include a person, partnership, corporation, or entity contacted by any employee or agent of LNC, Inc. within the 90-day period preceding termination of Employee's employment by LNC, Inc.

(b) Participate or work, directly or indirectly, as an owner, shareholder, partner, employee, subcontractor, or agent in the Territory in any business, firm, or entity that markets, sells, or provides services that are or may be competitive with those services provided by LNC, Inc. The term "Territory" shall mean:

(i) the following locations in which LNC, Inc. is currently engaged in the business of providing consulting services: (specify geographic area); and

(ii) any other state in which, during the term of Employee's employment, LNC, Inc. establishes an office or provides consulting services.

(c) For purposes of this Section 2, Employee acknowledges that LNC, Inc. is in the business of providing consulting services, including, without limitation, screening for malpractice, providing expert witnesses, summarizing records, preparing questions for deposition or trial, and all phases of litigation support in connection therewith.

3. *Nonsolicitation.* Employee undertakes and agrees that during the term of Employee's employment with LNC, Inc. and for a period of two years after the termination of Employee's employment by LNC, Inc. (regardless of the reason for or the party causing such termination), Employee will not, directly or indirectly, induce, invite, solicit, or attempt to induce, invite, or solicit any person who shall have been an employee, subcontractor, or agent of LNC, Inc. as of the date of this agreement or the date of the termination of Employee's employment with LNC, Inc. or at any time in between these dates:

(a) to be interested in, work for, or in any way be connected with a business, firm, or entity that competes, directly or indirectly, with LNC, Inc.;

(b) to work for or in any way be connected with Employee or any business, firm, or entity in which Employee has an interest that competes, directly or indirectly, with LNC, Inc.; or

(c) to terminate such person's employment or other relationship with LNC, Inc.

4. *Return of Documents.* Employee agrees that upon termination of Employee's employment by LNC, Inc., Employee shall return to LNC, Inc. the originals and copies of all documents, books, papers, records, and other materials regarding LNC, Inc.'s business that had been delivered to or come into the possession of Employee, whether such documents, books, papers, records, and other materials contain Confidential Information, as defined above, or not.

5. *Remedies.* Employee acknowledges that LNC, Inc. will suffer immediate and irreparable injury upon Employee's failure to strictly obey and comply

with the terms of paragraphs 1, 2, and 3 of this agreement. Employee further acknowledges that the remedy at law for any breach of any of the aforementioned provisions of this agreement will be inadequate and that LNC, Inc. shall be entitled to injunctive relief without bond. Such injunctive relief shall not be exclusive, but shall be in addition to any other rights and remedies that LNC, Inc. might have for such breach. If Employee breaches any restriction set forth in paragraph 2 or 3, the time period of such restriction shall be extended for a time period equal to the time period of such breach.

6. *Independent Covenants.* The provisions of this agreement contain independent covenants of Employee. The failure of LNC, Inc. to comply with any term, covenant, or condition of this agreement shall not in any way affect, alter, or change Employee's obligations hereunder.

7. *Separability.* The invalidity or nonenforceability of any particular provision of this agreement shall not affect the other provisions hereof and the agreement shall be construed in all respects as though such invalid or unenforceable provision was omitted.

8. *Modifications by Court.* Should the duration, geographical area, or range of proscribed activities contained in this agreement be held unreasonable or unenforceable by any court of competent jurisdiction, then such duration, geographical area, or range of proscribed activities shall be modified by the court to such degree or extent as to make it or them reasonable and enforceable.

9. *Governing Law.* This agreement shall be interpreted in accordance with the laws of the State of _____.

10. *Choice of Forum.* Both parties agree that any litigation regarding in whole or in part the terms of this agreement or the validity or enforceability of the provisions of this agreement shall take place in the Superior Court of _____ in _____ County, _____, or the _____ circuit in federal district court in _____ (if subject matter jurisdiction exists).

11. *Successors and Assigns.* The rights, obligations, and duties of Employee and LNC, Inc. under this agreement shall inure to the benefit of and be binding upon Employee's personal representatives, heirs, and assigns and LNC, Inc.'s successors and assigns.

12. *Amendment.* This agreement may be amended at any time only by written instrument signed by both parties.

13. *Nonwaiver.* The failure of LNC, Inc. to demand strict compliance with any of the terms, covenants, or conditions hereof shall not be deemed a waiver of such terms, covenants, or conditions, nor shall any waiver or relinquishment by LNC, Inc. of any right or power hereunder at any time(s) be deemed a waiver or relinquishment of such right or power at any other time(s).

14. *Headings.* The headings in this agreement are inserted for convenience only. The headings shall not be referred to or used in any way in interpreting or construing the terms of this agreement.

15. *Entire Agreement.* This agreement sets forth the entire agreement between the parties with respect to the subject matter hereof and supersedes all prior arrangements, agreements, or understandings with respect to the subject matter thereof.

16. *Acknowledgment.* Employee acknowledges that Employee has read and understands the contents of this agreement and that Employee has been afforded the opportunity to consult with counsel prior to signing this agreement.

IN WITNESS WHEREOF, LNC, Inc. has caused this agreement to be executed by its duly authorized officers and Employee has read, agreed to, and signed this agreement on the date written below.

ATTEST:

Secretary   By:
                                                  President

{Corporate Seal}

Witness   Employee
                                             Dated:

Chapter 44

Successful Marketing for the Legal Nurse Consultant

Nancy R. Ellington, BS, RN,
Geraldine B. Johnson, BSN, RN, LNCC, and
Betty Joos, MEd, BSN, RN

CONTENTS

Objectives

- To discuss marketing concepts
- To describe the marketing process
- To assist with developing a marketing plan
- To identify marketing tools and techniques of the legal nurse consultant
- To evaluate marketing practices
- To discuss advanced marketing strategies

Introduction

Marketing is one of the keys to success for anyone choosing to start a legal nurse consulting business. Although the legal nurse consultant (LNC) has nursing knowledge and experience required for this business, most nurses lack the essential business and marketing skills necessary to become successful in this field. The LNC who desires a viable business must take responsibility for developing these marketing skills. This chapter provides fundamentals for marketing a legal nurse consulting business.

LNCs who plan to work for law firms or insurance companies, instead of starting a business, will find that understanding marketing concepts can also benefit them. There is usually more competition for LNC positions than for positions sought by nurses in health care settings. An understanding of the marketing concepts presented in this chapter can help the LNC obtain a desired position in a firm.

This chapter discusses marketing concepts, describes the marketing process, and gives specifics of implementing the marketing plan using marketing tools, strategies, and personal marketing practices of the LNC.

Marketing Concepts

The LNC must understand a few basic marketing principles in order to develop a useful marketing plan. The first issue is to understand what marketing encompasses. Marketing is often confused with selling or advertising; it is much more than that. Marketing includes all activities that attract and keep clients, from the inception of the business throughout its life. This section describes three basic concepts that have an effect on the marketing planning for the LNC: (1) marketing is about perception; (2) marketing pervades all aspects of the LNC business; and (3) marketing is a continuing process.

Marketing Is About Perception

The potential client must recognize a benefit from using an LNC's services. Clients do not buy goods and services; they buy expectations and benefits. Some clients may have knowledge about the benefits of using an LNC or may even have worked with an LNC; others may have no knowledge of the services that LNCs offer. Between these extremes are varying perceptions of the nurse as a consultant or expert witness within the legal arena. Whether planning to seek a position in a law firm or insurance company or set up an independent practice, for LNC must recognize that educating clients about the benefits that LNCs can provide is a part of marketing.

The LNC must help a potential client perceive the LNC as a valuable resource, whether as an expert witness or as a behind-the-scenes consultant, in cases with medical issues. The potential client can then decide whether the LNC's services can benefit his or her particular situation. The LNC must first be able to articulate the benefits for himself or herself in order to help the client understand them. The LNC in business must understand what the client needs and offer services that address those needs. Convincing potential clients that they need the LNC's services is part of marketing.

The business plan, which is referred to later in this chapter and covered in more detail in Chapter 43, is the appropriate place to develop what a specific LNC's business encompasses. Once the focus of the business is clear to the LNC, he or she is better equipped to prepare a marketing plan that is based on helping potential clients recognize the many ways an LNC can benefit the client in cases with medical issues.

Marketing Pervades All Aspects of the Business

Marketing is part of all aspects of the LNC's business. Obtaining new clients is only one goal of marketing; it is also important to keep clients. The LNC must present a professional appearance in person, in the materials that represent the business, in verbal communications with clients, and in any work product. Professionalism, or lack of it, influences the client's perception of the business. A business perceived as professional and dependable is more likely to engender trust, which is an important factor in promoting a long-term relationship with clients. Following up on issues and seeking evaluation of work product provide opportunities for the LNC to keep his or her name in the minds of clients in a positive way. This professionalism may influence the client to give the LNC repeat business or to agree to refer the LNC to other attorneys for additional work. The LNC in business should keep marketing concepts in mind in all client contacts.

Marketing Is a Continuing Process

Marketing is not done only once or only at the beginning of a business venture. The viable business must retain clients as well as expand by obtaining new clients. Developing relationships with clients is an important part of retaining clients. The LNC must set aside time for both attracting and retaining clients and must allocate part of the budget for the continuing marketing effort.

Development and printing of business cards, stationery, and brochures are initial marketing expenses, but these marketing devices may be changed or updated as the business grows and changes. Having a brochure or business card that has handwritten changes or marked-out portions does not meet the standards of a professional business. Continued assessment of these items is necessary to determine when changes and reprinting are necessary.

Other marketing strategies that can be useful throughout the life of the business include exhibiting at a meeting of attorneys, developing materials for advertising in legal journals or newspapers, and joining organizations or attending seminars and workshops for networking purposes. Each LNC must plan for a continuing method of keeping the business in the mind of clients and potential clients.

Although a marketing plan is a dynamic process and changes according to needs, the LNC must prepare a thorough plan from the start. Planning encourages goal-setting and identifies steps to accomplish those goals. Changes should occur because they move the business forward, not because the LNC does not like performing certain tasks set out in the plan. For example, actual contact with potential clients through letters or initial "cold" calls is often difficult for LNCs but is a necessary task that should continue for as long as the business seeks to grow.

The Marketing Process

The target market, the competition, and the available marketing budget influence the LNC's marketing process. The LNC's business begins by refining this information and the LNC's goals into an organized business plan, determining how to best implement that plan, and evaluating outcomes in order to make changes in the plan as needed. The LNC who decides to start an independent practice, rather than seek a position at a law firm or insurance company, must start with a well-thought-out business plan. The marketing plan is a subset of the business plan. The mission statement, or the reason for the business, is at the heart of the LNC's business plan and influences the marketing plan.

The Mission Statement

Each LNC must decide what particular services or products he or she wishes to offer in the business. This is the time to decide whether testifying as a nurse expert will be one of the services. If services as a testifying expert are planned, current and specific clinical expertise and ability to testify under pressure are necessary. LNCs may have specific skills or abilities from which to develop a niche specialty. Artistic skills may lead to offering medical-illustration services as part of the business. An LNC may use extraordinary computer skills to develop computer graphics to support case issues or use exceptional ability in doing medical research to develop that area of specialization. A mission statement helps the LNC focus and plan on the specific business services to offer and determine whether a niche specialty is appropriate.

In *The Complete Book of Consulting*,[1] Salmon and Rosenblatt point out that the mission statement involves asking the questions:

- What business am I in?
- How should it be conducted?
- What gives me a competitive advantage?
- What values guide my actions?

Each LNC should consider these questions and verbalize a response for the business planned. An LNC might convert these questions to relate specifically to his or her consulting business. The questions might then be:

- What services will the business offer to clients?
- What personal standards are important to the business and to the potential client?
- What special strengths and skills set this LNC business apart?
- What are the personal expectations of an independent consulting business, and how will this be recognized?

Example 44.1 is an example of a mission statement.

Example 44.1: Legal Nurse Consultants of America, Inc. (LNCA, Inc.) provides consulting services to defense law firms handling cases that have medical issues. LNCA, Inc. reviews medical records, locates and analyzes medical resources, provides appropriate medical literature resources, and prepares reports of the records and resources as the attorney requests. LNCA, Inc. also offers guidance in developing demonstrative evidence, preparing questions and resources for depositions, and other services as may be requested by the client and appropriate to the case. While LNCA, Inc. personally does not provide nursing expert testimony, expert witnesses in both the medical and nursing field will be located and provided as clients request such services. LNCA, Inc. seeks to understand the problems and needs of the client involved in a medical case and to provide solutions to those problems.

LNCA, Inc. abides by nursing ethics as well as the ethical canons of the legal profession and always seeks to provide a thorough and objective work product. It is the intention of LNCA, Inc. to develop long-term relationships with clients through integrity in dealings and an emphasis on professionalism.

Relationship of the Business Plan to the Marketing Plan

The business plan gives direction for the initiation and growth of the business. Forming a business plan requires that the LNC do a market analysis for the business, which helps identify the target market and the demographics of that market. Competitors are also identified and assessed for how long they have been in business, how successful they are, how they market their business, and what their specialty niche is, if any. In this way, the business plan addresses marketing issues at a high level and in a generalized fashion. The marketing plan, as a subset of the general business plan, deals with the fundamentals of what marketing is required for the specific LNC's business and defines the tasks necessary to accomplish it.

Every business venture requires a budget as part of the business planning. The LNC's business plan considers the budget in planning for computer hardware and software, office location, office supplies, phone service, and other required items along with costs of marketing. The budget includes pricing of services as well. This necessary feature has impact on the marketing plan. Decisions regarding what to charge for services in an independent LNC business are not easy. The LNC must be able to charge enough per hour to cover the cost of doing business, including taxes, direct expenses, and benefits such as health, disability, and malpractice insurance. Not knowing the local market may prevent the business from getting clients if rates are too high. Likewise, rates that are too low may not cover expenses and are difficult to raise to appropriate levels as the LNC's expertise increases. Experience and expertise are considered in determining rates and the types of services offered. Nursing experience of at least 8 to 10 years is important; however, it is the nurse with experience in the specialty of LNC work who can charge the higher fees. Rates are also different for behind-the-scenes consulting and for expert witnessing, with the expert witness charging a higher fee. The American Association of Legal Nurse Consultants (AALNC) has published a compensation survey[2] of LNCs across the U.S. This resource provides AALNC members with important information about fees and salaries.

The Marketing Plan

Once the LNC has the information about the services, target market, competitors, and financial projections, a marketing strategy or plan can be formulated. The LNC develops the marketing plan from knowledge of these factors, not from assumptions about them.[3]

The Target Market

Not every attorney is a good target for the LNC's marketing efforts. While the LNC may be able to help in any case with medical issues, even a probate case or a criminal case, it is more useful to target attorneys who have greater need for medical-legal information on an ongoing basis. This includes attorneys and firms that do personal injury, workers' compensation, product liability, toxic tort, and medical malpractice work. Analysis of the target market involves the LNC's identification of a niche area such as providing nurse expert testimony, or working only for defense or plaintiff firms, or specializing in workers' compensation issues. Joos and Joos, in *Marketing for the Legal Nurse Consultant*, discuss the issue of determining a niche for the LNC.[4] A niche, or specific focus, of the LNC's business venture can help set the business apart from others. Some LNCs feel that a niche limits them early in their business and choose to be generalists at first. Each LNC must make this decision at the beginning of the business but can change focus at any time under the right conditions.

If, like LNCA, Inc. in Example 44.1, the business indicates a niche of only defense firms, then the target market includes those specific firms. The LNC can identify and learn about those firms by researching the *Martindale-Hubbell Law Directory*[5] for his or her state, an annual publication that lists most law firms, each attorney within the firm, and his or her specific area of legal work. Defense firms list their representative clients and information about their firms. This gives the LNC better guidance regarding which firms, and which attorneys within a firm, to target.

LNCs who intend to offer services to both plaintiff and defense firms should also research potential clients. Although researching law firms in the telephone

Yellow Pages directory seems the simplest approach, this does not provide the kind of information that is available from Martindale-Hubbell. The Yellow Pages may list attorneys under specialties; however, they do not clearly distinguish plaintiff from defense firms, or attorneys within a firm, and it is not clear which are partners and which are associates within a given firm. It is preferable to send marketing information to a partner within a firm. Martindale-Hubbell distinguishes which attorneys in a firm are partners and indicates the specialties that each attorney practices. Knowing which partner specializes in cases with medical issue identifies a good target for marketing efforts within a firm. Both Martindale-Hubbell and the Yellow Pages can be used to avoid attorneys who practice only business, real estate, or other types of law that do not involve medical issues.

Research and knowledge about the target market can reduce the cost of marketing, since the LNC will not wish to spend funds marketing to firms that are not part of his or her identified market. This enables the best use of funds for the greater result. As the LNC business grows, there may be a time when it is appropriate to expand or reassess the target market.

Competitors

Knowing about one's competitors can be advantageous to the LNC. Joining the local AALNC chapter can help the LNC get to know the competitors. If there is no chapter in the area, it is still possible to identify potential local competitors through the national AALNC directory. Some law firms have LNCs on staff. These LNCs could be seen as competition, but they might also be helpful in identifying other LNCs who are in independent practice. The new LNC business may discover that identified competitors have a specialty niche of their own. This information can help new LNCs make decisions about how to approach the target market with their own unique business approach or niche. The new LNC can learn more about legal nurse consulting, as well as business practices and marketing, from getting to know other LNCs.

The Marketing Budget

The LNC must periodically assess the budget in relation to the marketing plan: Is the marketing strategy in line with the budget constraints? What can be done that costs little or no money? On which materials should the LNC spend the greatest amount of money?

Example 44.2: A new LNC business spent about $15,000 on a full-color, 4-page brochure to mail out to all attorneys in a broad geographic area. The partners in this business were convinced that they would recoup their brochure expenses in a very short time. While the brochure was attractive and the mailing list was extensive (though not researched and targeted), it is quite feasible that a much less expensive brochure with well-thought-out content mailed to a narrower, but researched, list of attorneys and firms would have better results on a percentage basis. The recovery of the costs incurred would also be quicker. Each LNC business must plan a personal marketing strategy that falls within his or her available budget and supports the overall business plan.

Implementing the Marketing Plan

Making Contacts

The marketing plan identifies the target market and the tasks necessary for contacting that market. Many LNCs start with a list of firms that includes specific attorneys to whom marketing materials will be sent, and mail out a brochure and business cards with a cover letter of introduction. Following this, the LNC calls the attorney to attempt to set up an appointment. If the LNC is able to obtain an appointment, or at least speak by telephone with an attorney, he or she must be prepared to communicate the services offered and how these can benefit the attorney. Thorough preparation should precede each contact. A poor first impression, through either written materials or personal contact, is difficult to overcome.

Calling the potential client after first making contact with a marketing package of a cover letter with brochure and other materials is not the same as "cold calling." A "cold call" occurs when no other contact has been made with the firm. Although it is better to send out a marketing package with an attention-getting cover letter before calling, there may be times when a cold call works. Whether the LNC uses a cold call or makes a follow-up call after mailing out a marketing package, he or she must be prepared to communicate what services and benefits the business offers and try to gain an appointment to present services more fully. A good way to be prepared for any telephone contact is to write out a script to follow (do not read it but have it ready to refer to) to be certain that nothing is forgotten. Smiling while talking on the phone can reduce the LNC's stress and make the call seem friendly to the recipient. Whether following up on a mailed marketing package or a placing a "cold call," the LNC must get past the gatekeeper — the person at the law firm who stands between the LNC and the attorney. The LNC should never lie in order to get to talk with the attorney. Implying that the call concerns a potential case for the attorney is not appropriate and sets the stage for loss of integrity for the LNC. If the attorney is available, it is quite likely that the LNC will have an opportunity to speak with him. Attorneys are often on the telephone, at depositions, at trial, or in meetings. The LNC should treat gatekeepers with civility and consideration; they may be the LNC's best contact within a firm. If, after several calls, there has still been no chance to speak with the attorney, the LNC can try calling at lunchtime or shortly after closing hours; attorneys often stay late at work, while paralegals and secretaries usually go home on time.[4]

The LNC should not be discouraged if he or she has made many calls without a response that might lead to potential work. Marketing is a "numbers game," and a 1 to 3% response rate is considered good. The LNC must also realize that not every attorney who might be interested in his or her services will have a case that needs those services at the time of the contact. A good impression through a phone call, marketing materials, or personal contact may be the stimulus for the attorney to call later when he or she does have a case.

Developing Materials for Marketing

After the LNC completes the business plan, the business will have established a name, phone number, and address. This information is used in developing marketing materials, including a brochure, business cards, and business stationery.

The LNC's initial marketing package for mailing includes the brochure, at least two business cards, and a one-page cover letter. Some LNCs include other items, such as a resume or curriculum vitae (CV), but this is usually not necessary; a well-written brochure covers the necessary marketing information about the LNC. Other marketing materials that the LNC must develop include a set of work-product samples.

Each LNC would do well to develop a portfolio to take to any personal meeting with a client. The portfolio would include brochures (in case other attorneys in the firm might desire one), business cards (having plastic covers that convert a business card into a form that fits into a rotary card file is a good idea), a resume or CV (important if the LNC does expert witness work), and work-product samples. Each of these materials, or tools, is discussed below.

Resumes and CVs

A CV is more detailed than a resume; it lists all presentations, publications, specialty education, and so forth, in detail. A resume covers this information in a more general form and is a shorter document. Both of these should be well prepared in form as well as content. The documents should be printed, preferably on a laser printer, and should not include handwritten additions or mark-outs. Neither document should "embellish" but should indicate skills and experience that support a background for LNC work. A resume is usually no more than two pages, while a CV may be many pages long to include all specifics. Many LNCs prefer to obtain professional help in developing their resumes or CVs.

Brochures

The successful brochure includes much the same information given in a well-done mission statement; however, brochure language must be more benefit-oriented than the mission statement. Clients buy expectations and benefits. The client does not want to know how the service is accomplished but how the services meet his or her business needs. The brochure should explain what the business does, tell the benefits of the services, describe the person or organization offering those services, and clearly indicate how to get in touch to find out more or use the services. A brochure is a representation of the business and must project professionalism. Brochure development and printing can be expensive, or it can be done inexpensively by the LNC with desktop-publishing software. A good-quality, heavy paper stock (at least 38-pound weight) is most appropriate for brochures. Many office-supply companies have specific paper for brochures that can be used with desktop publishing. The choice of a predesigned paper for a brochure must include consideration of professionalism; some brochure paper designs do not project a suitable image of the LNC's business. Some tips on form in the development of a brochure include:

- Use an easy-to-read font such as Times New Roman.
- Do not use all capitals in the material.
- Do not use jargon of any type.

- Use sufficient white space. (Do not cover every inch of space with print.)
- Print the business name and contact information where it can be easily located.[4]

A picture of the LNC personalizes the brochure; clients feel that they know whom they are dealing with when they can visualize the LNC. Several publications in the Reference and Additional Reading sections at the end of this chapter discuss the process of developing a brochure.

Business Cards

Purchase the most professional cards that the business can afford. These small advertisements are an indication of the LNC's professionalism. Professionals' business cards rarely use extreme design, color, or shape. New LNCs can collect cards from attorneys and other LNCs to get ideas. Simple and elegant style works best. The most professional-looking card is of heavy card stock of white, beige, gray, or ivory color; has an easily readable font of sufficient size to be read at an arm's length; is not cluttered with too much print; and includes all pertinent information for contacting the LNC business. A sentence or phrase describing the services is helpful if it does not clutter the card. Desktop publishing does not work well for making business cards. Cards should be printed on at least 80-pound card stock; paper stock offered for printing cards on desktop publishing is usually of insufficient weight and results in insubstantial cards. Cards can be ordered from most office-supply companies, which have a selection of styles and colors from which to choose; examining available samples can help in making a decision. These cards are affordable, good-quality products.

Work-Product Samples

Samples of work product help the potential client understand some of the benefits that an LNC can provide. Samples are a visual representation of the type of work product that the LNC can offer. The samples need not be the complete work product for a case; the LNC shows them for format and for the discussion of benefits of the LNC's knowledge of medical issues. The LNC can use the information on medical record evaluations found in other chapters in this text to develop samples. Work-product samples are an important part of the portfolio that the LNC uses in making contacts with potential clients.

Networking

Networking is a powerful tool for generating new business and for increasing the LNC's knowledge of legal nurse consulting. The LNC who attends meetings and joins organizations related to his or her consulting career can expect to develop a clientele more quickly than those who do not network. Most attorneys use the networking process to grow their own business, gaining clients by getting to know and be known by them.

Some see networking only as a sales opportunity. In fact, if the LNC makes a "sales pitch" to everyone he or she meets at an appropriate meeting or gathering, it is likely that the approach will backfire. The LNC makes best use of most meetings to introduce himself or herself; exchange business cards; find out about others and, if they are attorneys, what their needs are; and leave the meeting with a feeling of having learned something about potential clients or cohorts. In some networking situations the LNC can request to contact the potential client in person following the meeting; otherwise, the networking experience is followed up in other ways shortly after the meeting. For those with whom the LNC exchanged business cards, a personal follow-up call or letter is an excellent opportunity to further the relationship and possibly gain an appointment to present one's services.

An important point of networking is that a later contact (but not long after the meeting) will have the advantage of the fact that the potential client has met the LNC personally. One way for the LNC to remember items about people he or she meets at these gatherings is to make notes on the back of their business cards. The notes can include personal or business information that will bring back a memory of the meeting when the LNC refers to the information in a phone call or letter.

Not only does networking consist of attending gatherings and exchanging business cards; it also includes all the contacts made by phone, letters, thank-you notes, and other forms of developing relationships with clients or potential clients. Networking includes keeping in contact with LNC cohorts and interacting with them. These contacts offer opportunities for the LNC to grow in skills and knowledge and to give back to the LNC community in kind. Networking is a process that continues throughout the business and grows more meaningful with time.

Evaluating the Marketing Plan

Marketing can be a black hole for the budget of a small business. The LNC must continually evaluate the marketing plan and the strategies for achieving that plan. The original budget should include consideration for anticipated changes in marketing as the business grows — or if it does not grow as expected. The LNC must determine which strategies are working well and which are more drain than gain. Additional strategies might need to be considered. Whether the business is beginning to boom or there is little evidence of marketing results, evaluation of the situation is important.

Many LNCs become discouraged as time passes and they receive few or no cases. Instead of becoming discouraged too quickly, the LNC should assess what has been done and what is the continuing strategy in marketing the business:

- Are the marketing materials appropriate, and do they fulfill their purpose, or do they need changing to better present the business?
- Has the target market been appropriately identified and researched?
- Has the LNC dedicated time and effort to contacting the target market?
- What has been done, or can be done, to build better client relationships?
- Has the LNC followed up after each project received to determine whether the client was satisfied?

- If the client was satisfied, did the LNC ask for more work or request to use this client as a reference?
- If the client was not satisfied, what efforts did the LNC make to provide a solution to the problem?
- What skills does the LNC need to improve his or her services?

All of this is relevant information needed to determine the status of a business that is not growing as anticipated. Understanding where the weaknesses are in the strategies completed helps the LNC determine what better strategies might be put in place.

If the business develops well and the LNC has several clients that provide a maximum amount of work, he or she should assess what is being done to retain those clients:

- Is there a need to find and train subcontractors or hire other LNCs to help with the workload and keep the work product on time and of high quality?
- Is the business actively developing client relationships and assessing the client's needs for the future as well as the present?
- Is there a way to increase the amount of work from the client by increasing the services offered?
- Is there a need to update the marketing materials to better represent the growing business?

Some LNCs grow a business to the point that the owner, or partners, will be less involved in the day-to-day work-product development and more involved in client development and finding new clients. This requires changes in marketing strategies.

The LNC should document the marketing strategies used and consider what other strategies might be added. The LNC may build a database of prospects and clients. Keeping a database of all contacted firms and attorneys may appear initially to be too much work, but this kind of information provides an excellent record for future marketing strategies. When contacts become clients, the LNC should keep a special data file on the firm or attorney with information that includes name, address, phone, e-mail address, original contact date, the type of work the client does, the contact name for that office (such as a paralegal or legal secretary), and a list of the cases that have been provided to the LNC. This is the least amount of information that should be maintained on a client. When the client is better known, more specifics can be added, such as preferred type of report, whether research of issues is always welcomed, and preferences for binding of records.

Additional Marketing Strategies

There are many marketing strategies beyond the basics discussed above. These include developing a newsletter for clients, speaking and writing about the business, developing a business Web site, and exhibiting at legal meetings and associations.

Newsletters

LNCs often consider publishing a newsletter as a marketing technique for their businesses. Few newsletters are actually done, and even fewer are done well. Newsletters are a good method for both furthering relationships with existing clients and developing new clients. Publishing a newsletter requires consistent and dedicated effort. A newsletter should have a regular schedule rather than be a haphazard occurrence. The content must be of interest to the client and not just "advertising" for the LNC, suggesting benefits and solutions to which the client can relate. The content should be brief, timely, and in an easy-to-read format. The writing must be clear, organized, and free of spelling and grammatical errors. A poorly written newsletter is worse than no newsletter at all.

Speaking and Writing

Speaking and writing are useful opportunities for marketing. The LNC who speaks or writes on the topic of legal nurse consulting or an associated issue is seen as someone with expertise in that area. Speaking and writing articles are considered advanced strategies, since it is usually better for the LNC to postpone these activities until he or she has reached a certain level of experience in legal nurse consulting. However, each LNC must make that determination individually. LNCs can leverage a speech from having written an article and vice versa.

There are opportunities to speak to the local and state bar associations, the Chamber of Commerce, and other local business groups such as Rotary or Kiwanis. Some people find speaking to be stressful. If the LNC is too nervous to do a good job of speaking, it is best to wait until he or she can obtain some training to improve these skills and techniques. The LNC should consider the topic of any talk carefully, being cautious not to overstep and appear to offer legal advice. Preparation and practice are essential for a good speech. Brevity is also of some importance, since a talk that is too lengthy can leave listeners with a bad reaction to a good speech.

Writing articles or books is a method of marketing that can set the LNC apart from others. There are opportunities to write articles for nursing or legal publications and local newspapers. Newspaper articles may include a press release about the opening of the LNC business, or it could be a "special interest" story about how a nurse provides services to law firms. The usual caveat is to avoid making a piece of writing a sales pitch, unless it is intended to be a paid advertisement.

The LNC who wishes to publish in a newsletter, journal, or newspaper must polish his or her writing skills. Although these publications have editors who review and suggest improvement for submissions, a poorly written and grammatically challenged article may never make it to that stage. The LNC writer must know the style and requirements of the specific publication and have an understanding of the target market for the publication before submitting an article. The benefit of being a published writer is worth the investment of the time and energy involved in developing or improving writing skills.

Exhibiting at Legal Meetings

Exhibiting at a legal meeting or other appropriate gathering of attorneys can be an expensive venture. Renting a booth or table for exhibiting usually entails a large expense. The LNC should consider whether the cost is worth the potential marketing outcome. (Sponsors of the conference can often provide predictions of attendance.) A professional display setup requires additional expense. If the LNC concludes that the expense is worth the opportunity, then preparation is the key. Exhibits are usually open to meeting attendees at specified times. Someone must always staff the exhibit at these times. Leaving an exhibit unattended is a waste of money and opportunity.

An exhibit should include, at minimum, brochures, business cards, newsletters (if the LNC publishes one), and some item with the business name on it for a giveaway. Highlighters with the company name are popular giveaways; staple removers, mail openers, and luggage tags are also popular items. Having some item for a drawing is also important. LNCs often offer some service as the prize for drawing, such as a free case review or a specified number of hours on any one case. This allows the LNC to give away a worthwhile prize and to have an opportunity to show what services are available to a potential client. The most usual method for a drawing is to collect as many business cards as possible and draw from those. The drawing does not necessarily have to be a random one. The cards can be placed in a fishbowl, or other container, and the drawing should be held before the exhibits close for the session. The LNC should always follow up the other business cards in the bowl as well, even if just by sending a note to thank the card owner for stopping by the booth. Not to do so is to waste the money spent for the exhibit.

Experienced exhibitors never approach an attorney who is talking with another exhibitor. To do so violates etiquette and can create an annoyed attorney and fellow exhibitor. Getting to know the other exhibitors can be a profitable use of downtime in the exhibit area. Helpful alliances can be forged with other exhibitors that may lead to referrals of new clients. Some LNCs find it useful to attend personal injury or medical malpractice sessions at the meeting to improve their knowledge.

LNCs who develop their businesses by exhibiting their services at attorney conferences may be provided a list of attendees after the conference is over. This list is another source of potential clients. The LNC is typically asked to provide a sample of the marketing material that will be mailed out and to agree to use the list one time only. The list of attendees is often "seeded" with fictitious names in order to verify that the list is not used more than once. If an attorney on the list responds to the LNC to request more information, mailing to that person again does not violate the agreement.

Developing a Web Site

Increasingly, LNCs are setting up Web sites for their businesses. At this time, there are no studies to indicate that a Web site advances the business of an LNC. Not all Web sites are equal; some may certainly be a marketing advantage for a business, while others may languish and never bring in new clients. The difference depends on how well the Web site is developed, how well it is kept up to date, and what value it offers to those who visit it.

Many of the considerations for a newsletter are also appropriate to developing a Web site. It must be easy to navigate, have timely and interesting information, include brief but well-written articles, and be kept current on a regular basis.

Writing for the Web requires different styles and formats from writing for print media. Articles tend to be briefer and contain highlighted keywords (hyperlinks) that take the reader to definitions or additional information. Bulleted lists make scanning for key points much easier. Carroll[7] states that writing articles for online use requires not only consideration of the target market but also an understanding of how most readers of online material "scan" for content rather than read an item thoroughly. Web users are more likely to read nonlinearly; they may follow links and then return to the article. Carroll also notes that research shows that most users do not like long pages that require scrolling. It is important to consider how the users of Web materials are most likely to approach an article and then write a way that makes the most of that behavior.

Some Web sites are essentially a Web brochure — static and unchanging. While these may not be bad, they do not take advantage of the dynamic and valuable resource of the Internet. Even these brochure formats must be presented in a manner that will catch the attention of an Internet user; emphasis on the best effect and information, rather than a sales pitch, is the best approach.

LNCs who develop Web sites must consider whether they are making the most of this strategy. The LNC may find it worthwhile to pay an experienced Web site designer to design or improve a Web site or keep it current. At this time, only a small percentage of attorneys are active on the Internet, but that is changing. As the number of attorneys and paralegals online increases, there will be a better chance for the well-developed Web site to bring in new clients.

The Internet is here to stay, and LNCs are discovering listservs and making e-mail contacts. Many LNCs are active on these mail lists and appear to use them as part of a marketing strategy. This can be a viable technique, but the LNC must take care not to divulge too much information about any case in which he or she is involved. LNCs must also consider that they have not read the medical records associated with questions asked by others online. LNCs must reflect on this before responding with suggestions or agreements about a case unknown to them.

Summary

- The marketing plan is a subset of the business plan and is important in helping the LNC identify goals and state specific tasks to achieve those goals.
- Marketing requires a budget. The LNC must consider how much money is available for marketing and develop strategies within that budget.
- Marketing is about perception. LNCs must project professionalism in personal presentations, in materials used to represent their businesses, and in all aspects of their services.
- Clients buy with benefits and expectations in mind. LNCs must understand how they provide benefits before they can educate the attorney client about the value of their services. LNCs must remember this concept when they develop marketing materials also.
- Networking is a valuable tool for getting to know clients and becoming known by them. Networking extends beyond exchanging cards at a gathering; it involves an investment of time and interest to make the most of networking contacts.

- All marketing plans must be periodically evaluated and updated. Whether the business is growing well or languishing, evaluation of marketing outcomes can move the business forward through better strategies when there is recognition of weaknesses and strengths.
- Marketing takes dedication of time, effort, and money. The LNC business owner gets out of marketing what he or she puts into it.

References

1. Salmon, B. and Rosenblatt, N., *The Complete Book of Consulting*, Round Lake Publishing, Ridgefield, CT, 1995.
2. American Association of Legal Nurse Consultants, 1999 Compensation Survey, AALNC, Chicago, 1999.
3. Covello, J. and Hazelgren, B., *Your First Business Plan*, 2nd ed., Small Business Sourcebooks, Naperville, IL, 1995.
4. Joos, B. and Joos, J., *Marketing for the Legal Nurse Consultant: A Guide to Getting All the Clients You Can Handle Using Proven, Low-Cost Strategies*, Sky Lake Productions, Sautee, GA, 2000.
5. *Martindale-Hubbell Law Directory*, Martindale-Hubbell, New Providence, NJ, http://www.Martindale.com, 2002.
6. Harding, F., *Rain Making*, Bob Adams, Inc., Holbrook, MA, 1994.
7. Carroll, P., Writing for the Web: different style considerations, *Nurse Author & Editor*, Winter, 4, 2002.

Additional Reading

Davidson, J., *Marketing on a Shoestring: Low-cost Tips for Marketing Your Products or Services*, 2nd ed., John Wiley & Sons, New York, 1994.

Levinson, J.C., *Guerrilla Marketing: Secrets for Making Big Profits from Your Small Business*, Houghton Mifflin, Boston, 1993.

Martinent, J., *The Art of Mingling: Easy, Fun, Proven Techniques for Mastering Any Room*, St. Martin's Press, New York, 1992.

Ross, M., *Shameless Marketing for Brazen Hussies: 307 Awesome Money-Making Strategies for Savvy Entrepreneurs*, Communication Creativity, Buena Vista, CO, 2000.

Test Questions

1. The LNC must convince clients that he or she can be a valuable resource on medical issues, because the client buys
   A. Goods and services
   B. Marketing perceptions
   C. Expectations and benefits
   D. Education and looks

2. Acquiring and keeping clients depends on all but one of the following:
   A. Professionalism
   B. Having the lowest hourly rates
   C. Quality and timeliness of work
   D. Oral and written communication

3. Budgeting is an integral part of the business and marketing plan. What two things are most important when planning the marketing budget?
   A. Cost and recovery time
   B. Budget limits and geographic area
   C. Attention-getting business cards and brochures
   D. Type of clients and the "gatekeeper"

4. Networking can be an important way to increase business. Which of the following is NOT likely to work well at meetings or gatherings?
   A. Gathering information about potential clients
   B. Pitching your business to everyone at the gathering
   C. Interviewing your competition
   D. Introducing yourself to other LNCs

5. What must the LNC do periodically to ensure that the business is on track from a marketing perspective?
   A. Spend more money on marketing
   B. Hire additional LNCs to work in the business
   C. Do less of the work and more of the marketing
   D. Evaluate the success of the marketing strategy

Answers: 1. C, 2. B, 3. A, 4. B, 5. D

Chapter 45

Growing a Business

Rosie Oldham, BS, RN, LNCC, Paula Windler, MS, RN, LNCC, and Roxanne Bush, MHSA, BSN, BA, RN

CONTENTS

Objectives

- To describe the process of preparing to expand the size of a legal nurse consulting practice
- To review the steps of structuring business growth

- To define the role and development of leadership skills for the legal nurse consultant owner
- To discuss staff recruitment, training, and retention
- To evaluate ongoing quality improvement and response to future client needs and services

Introduction

Many legal nurse consultants (LNCs) who operate businesses reach a point at which they decide either to cease operating the business or to expand and grow. The infancy stage of a business calls for the owner to be entrepreneur, manager, and work producer. During the growing pains of an adolescent business, the owner attempts to balance all these roles to the point of exhaustion and burnout. At the burnout stage many LNC business owners seek to identify productive and predictable ways to grow their businesses successfully. Some LNCs decide to limit their practices to a select number of clients. Others walk away from their practices because they see no way of balancing all the roles. Many successful LNC practices in the U.S. are maturing as their owners realize the potential of owning a business without the business owning them.

Strategic Planning to Facilitate Business Growth

Many books about successful business growth advise owners to start with a mission statement for the business. The owner then identifies the purpose of the business and outlines goals and strategies. Many resources can assist the business owner with strategic planning (see Additional Reading at the end of the chapter). Multiple resources in local communities also give direction and mentoring at no charge. These include the Service Corps of Retired Executives (SCORE), chambers of commerce, community college adult education programs, and local small business administration agencies.

Imagine the Possibilities and Find the Opportunities

The LNC expanding his or her business must do creative strategic planning that identifies other products and services the business can provide and looks for opportunities to expand the role of the business into uncharted areas. Some legal nurse consulting firms contract risk managers into hospitals. One large LNC firm specializes in product liability and works nationally on thousands of cases; another LNC firm specializes in technical courtroom demonstrative evidence. These firms' owners realized that such opportunities existed and forged into exciting areas of LNC practice and business growth.

Evaluate Roles: Entrepreneurial, Managerial, or Service Provider

Each LNC business owner must decide what he or she does best and then strive for professional balance of key attributes and skills. The role of the entrepreneur is to produce creative ideas and methods for marketing and growing the business. The role of the LNC manager is to oversee and make the new ideas, products, and services "happen." The service provider, or producer of the work product, does the hands-on work. LNCs who are unable to assume the role of manager or entrepreneur are at high risk for failure. Most LNCs are in business because they can produce the work product. Many oppose change because they are unable to release control over a work product. These LNCs are resisting the very change that can free them up to grow and advance their businesses.

Evaluate Factors for Business Growth

The LNC should evaluate the following factors when determining his or her ability to grow the business:

- Reaction to change
- Creation of documentation of policies, procedures, and formats for producing the work product
- Use of resources to expand one's vision of the business
- Long-term commitment to business growth and to clients and employees

Reaction to Change

Is the LNC able to embrace change and uncertainty? Business growth can be demanding and yet very fulfilling. However, growth comes at a price. As the LNC business expands, many unexpected hardships are likely. Change is part of everyday life, and the LNC must acknowledge this aspect of growing a business. Can he or she be flexible in responding to daily challenges and the diverse personalities of the employees? The LNC business owner needs to be willing to adapt to the changes that occur daily and explore various business options and alternatives.

Creation of Documentation of Policies, Procedures, and Formats for Producing the Work Product

It is best to build a business that can function during any absence of the LNC. Setting up procedural manuals in order to provide the quality and consistent excellence in the work product that the firm produces can take a great deal of work. Procedural manuals should include the type and formatting of reports that the LNC has chosen to use, along with explanations and examples for completion. The written policy-and-procedure manual can then be used during staff training and development to ensure that each individual receives the same information. The LNC should also utilize a noncompete and nonpiracy clause in any separation agreement to cause ex-employees to think twice about duplicating the work product. The ideal LNC firm has all procedures in place, so that even if the firm were sold, the clients would not notice a change in the quality and consistency of the work. With all necessary steps documented, procedures are in place to allow a smooth change in direction when the business takes unexpected turns.

Use of Resources to Expand One's Vision of the Business

Leaders who look to the future and maintain a steady course in the present are more likely to succeed in the rapidly changing business environment. Joining organizations of business owners, attending seminars for motivation, evaluating other LNC Web sites, and reading the great resources listed at the end of this chapter can all assist with personal development as a visionary leader. Networking with other business owners who are growing their businesses is essential to success. A mentor can offer assistance and guidance.

Another method of seeking opportunities for growth is to survey the current client base for information on additional services that the LNC's business can provide. A survey should also ask clients about their satisfaction with current work products. Client surveys can assist with retention of clients as well as generate new business. The LNC should listen to clients and determine whether they need a service that would decrease their workload. The LNC should peruse the medical-legal environment and seek opportunities to provide services that clients may not even know they need.

Long-Term Commitment to Business Growth and to Clients and Employees

The LNC must make a long-term commitment to expand and grow the existing business. The LNC owes a continued and strong relationship to clients and employees. Maintaining relationships with clients can be accomplished by newsletters, holiday gift baskets, periodic quality-improvement surveys, meetings, lunches, and telephone calls. The LNC must continually strive to keep contacts with all clients and perform ongoing analysis of the work product. The LNC's vision of the business must be clear.

Maintaining relationships with employees can be accomplished by being fair, respectful, trustworthy, discreet, and compassionate. Employees also need support while the business is undergoing the growth process. They may be uneasy and unsure of the future during these times. The LNC owner needs to give them encouragement and feedback about the actions of the company. Providing truthful information and listening to the opinions of employees are methods for retaining and nurturing employee relationships during growth periods. The business owner must be mindful of the costs associated with turnover and recognize the need to choose and train employees carefully.

Preparation for Restructuring and Expansion

Financial Planning

One of the principles of running a small business is to recognize that many businesses fail not from lack of work but from lack of cash flow. Capital purchases, and increases in equipment and supplies and the number of staff, all require cash outlay. Good financial planning is an absolute must. The LNC may have large personal cash reserves that the business can use, but this is rare. The LNC can choose among several options to increase cash flow. The LNC should explore all advantages and disadvantages of each option and keep expenditures to an absolute minimum in the beginning. It may take 2 to 4 years before the business starts to show a profit after expansion.

Bank Loans

One option is to obtain a business loan from a commercial bank. Many banks will make financial arrangements to assist businesses. The bank officers will most likely want to see the business plan and future projections before they offer any money. Chapter 43 discusses the details of obtaining bank financing.

Independent Investors

Another option is an individual who is willing to loan money to the business. Again, a good strategic business plan that reflects goals and strategies can help forge a successful financial investment. Many times the investing individual wants to become part of the business.

Finance Companies

A third option for financial assistance is a finance company. Finance company loans are probably easier to obtain than bank loans, but they may involve high interest rates. Money borrowed from this source may need to be paid back in a short time frame.

Government Loans and Grants

A fourth option is the use of federal government loan programs, grants, or loan-guarantee programs. The U.S. Small Business Administration (SBA) can offer assistance in determining the requirements for obtaining government loans or grant money. Strict guidelines and many forms are involved. The SBA also offers a counseling program for assistance in how to obtain loans and handle other business-related difficulties. Local chambers of commerce may also have information about obtaining money from government sources.

Other Options

Other options include using credit cards, cashing in certificates of deposit, cashing in bonds, selling stocks, and so forth. The LNC should examine these options thoroughly before proceeding, because they can involve high interest rates, penalties, and loss of funds and security. It is wise to be cautious and seek advice from a financial counselor and accountant.

Office Space

Home Offices

As the business grows, it becomes necessary to move away from the kitchen table and boxes of medical records to a more permanent and suitable place to work. Some major decisions must be made. Space, finances, privacy, contacts, and suitability of office location require evaluation.

As employees are added, they too can have home offices. They must be able to connect with the main home office just as if it were an outside office. Each employee must have a good computer system and all the supplies and equipment to be able to perform job functions and provide the work product in a timely fashion. The employees may need assistance setting up their computer systems to best suit the needs of the company. One advantage to having employees working in their homes is that the LNC owner does not need the extra space and equipment in the office. The disadvantages are that the phone systems may need to be adjusted for a transfer of calls to the employee's phone, and the employer incurs shipping costs of transmitting medical records. Communication among the employees can be hampered by lack of face-to-face interaction. If the employees live at some distance from each other and from the employer, getting them together for a staff meeting at a central location may be difficult. Video-conferencing and other technological innovations may help overcome some of these difficulties.

Executive Offices

A popular option for office location is working in executive offices. Renting office space is useful in making the choice to grow a professional consulting business. If the LNC meets clients regularly, this may be the best choice because it is more professional and businesslike. It allows the office to function in a location that is suitable for clients. Renting office space can be very expensive, but many of the expenses are tax-deductible. The LNC must sign a lease, and this may prevent moving easily to a different location. Obtaining input from an accountant or business attorney would be wise in this decision process.

Office Sharing

Another option is office sharing with another business. With this option, two businesses can share the rent, operating expenses, and equipment purchase and usage. Support personnel, such as secretaries and receptionists, can also be shared. The LNC needs to be very cautious in choosing the type of business with which he or she will share space and resources. A similar option is to rent space in an executive office complex area. Many such complexes offer fee-for-service arrangements, such as conference-room rental for $20 to $30 per hour.

Purchase Office Space

A final option is purchasing office space, such as in an office condominium. A decision to purchase office space involves several considerations. First, the LNC should evaluate the other types of businesses in the complex. Appropriate fellow condominium owners are professionals such as attorneys, accountants, and psychologists. Nail salons, dry cleaners, or other retail establishments would not blend as well. Second, the LNC should consider the cost and amount of space available. The LNC business may need a significant amount of storage for medical records of ongoing cases, and supplies such as binders, stationery, printer toner, marketing materials, and exhibiting equipment. A library space is desirable for storage of medical and legal textbooks. If the office is large enough, it may be equipped with a conference room. Attorneys are comfortable doing business with LNCs at a conference table but much less so at a kitchen table. Third, the LNC should consider whether the office condominium's location is safe, secure, and convenient. The ability for the support staff to walk to lunch may seem like an insignificant issue until the owner recognizes the productivity that can be lost by being in an out-of-the-way location. A final consideration is to investigate the ability to obtain high-speed connectivity for computers in the office.

Retention and Ensuring Excellence in Services

Staff Recruitment

A growing business means that the LNC business owner needs to add employees or subcontractors to meet client demands. Expending energy to locate and train new employees is worthwhile for ensuring quality performance in the growing business. Bringing poor performers on board can hinder and slow the development of the business, as well as disappoint clients. Through networking relationships, the LNC is likely to be aware of other LNCs who are looking for new or different positions. Some nurses are eager to get into the field. Announcements can be made at networking functions regarding additional job openings.

It is fair practice to screen potential staff. Testing the candidate's knowledge of computers and the software necessary to produce LNC work product is prudent. The LNC owner should provide the most suitable candidates with a test case and see how the applicant is able to handle the review of the medical records and preparation of the report. Potential applicants should be given a specific time frame for completion of the review and report. If an applicant is unable to complete the task, the LNC business owner may have to think twice about the candidate's competency. The owner should do thorough background checks and ask pertinent questions about past work experiences and specific skills during the interview process. By law, certain questions may not be asked during the interview. It is best for the LNC owner to consult with a business and/or employment-law attorney for information regarding the laws governing the interview and hiring process.

Bringing the candidate on board as a subcontractor to start gives the LNC owner insight into performance. The subcontractor can complete the test case and, if the test results meet the owner's standards, can continue to work out of his or her home. This eliminates or delays bringing the candidate to the owner's location until the work product shows evidence of meeting or exceeding the LNC owner's expectations.

Staff Training

The LNC owner needs to train each new employee. Policy-and-procedure manuals are invaluable in this process. Each new worker needs detailed and guided training so that the work product can be of the highest quality. The manual needs to explain thoroughly the rationale and requirements of the process. Communication to and from each employee or subcontractor must be clear, and providing guidelines and deadlines is essential. A probationary period for initial review of the work standards is an absolute must.

Staff Development and Quality Improvement

Quality-improvement standards dictate that work product should be reviewed by a second reader to check for appropriateness of content and grammar. In the beginning phases of business expansion, this review falls to the LNC owner. As an LNC lead nurse role is developed, that nurse can assume the quality-review role.

The owner should provide ongoing constructive feedback and consistently let the staff know when they are doing a good job by:

- Providing written feedback when products need improvement
- Completing performance evaluations on a regular basis
- Providing employees with little "perks" such as movie tickets, coupons, and bonuses from time to time
- Conducting periodic personal meetings with employees and subcontractors for educational and social purposes

Ongoing Education, Compensation, and Recognition

Ongoing education and training must be provided to employees. The LNC business owner can pay annual dues for membership in the American Association of Legal Nurse Consultants (AALNC), cover liability-insurance costs, and encourage and financially assist each LNC to attend local and national conferences on legal nurse consulting. If the employee is unable to attend the annual AALNC conference, the business owner should consider purchasing audiotapes of the conference. Purchasing AALNC case studies, booklets, and other helpful materials can enhance the employees' growth. Owners should expect LNC staff to become certified in legal nurse consulting through the AALNC. The owners should provide a library of books on legal and ethical issues of nursing and medicine, reward employees for quality improvement, and recognize growth and certifications.

Use Professional Guidance

The business owner should consult an employment-law attorney for assistance with formulation of policies regarding vacation time, sick days, workers' compensation, and other employment issues. These employment issues must be clear, comprehensive, written, and uniformly applied. Chapter 43 discusses retaining professional legal help in more detail.

Contracts and Office Manuals

As more employees are hired, the LNC business work ethic and beliefs must be visible in the work product and business services. The LNC employee or subcontractor should continue to provide the recognized quality of work product that reflects the LNC business owner's design.

Employee Contracts

Whether the business owner uses LNC subcontractors or employees, having them sign a confidentiality agreement is in the owner's best interest. The agreement helps to protect the business's trade secrets, design products, concepts and ideas, finances, client listing, research data, proposals, and so forth.

Another contract that all employees should sign is an agreement not to compete during and after engagement. This prevents employees of the established business from going out on their own with the knowledge they have learned there. Chapter 43 discusses noncompeting and provides a sample contract. Typically, a noncompete contract indicates a time frame of 1 to 2 years, but it can vary from state to state. Obtaining attorney review of the agreement is prudent.

Employees are not to directly or indirectly solicit or attempt to obtain work from any of the business clients outside the scope of the employee's job. To do so would be a breach of the contract and a breach of ethics as a professional. Chapter 46 discusses the ethics of noncompeting. If a subcontractor is an expert witness, the LNC owner must remind the subcontractor of conflict-of-interest issues that may involve past or present work relations or personal conflicts that could hinder the expert's opinion. Chapter 10 and Chapter 46 discuss the ethics of conflicts of interest in more detail. Open communication between the LNC owner and the subcontractor is necessary.

Policy-and-Procedure Manual

A policy-and-procedure manual explains the policies and actions of the business. Much of the information in the policy manual can be taken from the business plan and rewritten so that employees can understand work expectations and work practices in order to perform their duties as required. Each LNC employee should receive a handbook that outlines business expectations and responsibilities. It should also include other employee-related matters such as dress, hours, equipment, and equal-opportunity issues, especially if there is an outside office. The procedure manual provides specific information about the requirements for completion of the work product, with detailed instructions and examples.

Subcontractors should not receive policy manuals because they are not actual employees. Subcontractors should be provided with a guideline to the type of report and information they should produce. This can be an abbreviated version of the policy manual that includes only the information that a subcontractor needs for completing the work product.

Again, it is best to consult with a business attorney for more detailed legal issues governing the differences between employees and subcontractors.

Positioning the Business for Continued Growth

Motivating the Motivator

Many books on motivation and leadership are published every year. They all have ideas that can show an LNC how to be a credible and successful business owner. These books discuss topics such as values, self-empowerment, goals, strategies, challenges, risks, and rewards. Motivation is the basis of all actions and is connected to the LNC owner's needs. Business decisions and actions reflect the desire to target a particular goal. The identification and selection of management ideas depend on the character of the business owner. Organizations change with time; they mature and develop a culture that, when led successfully, can navigate them through a difficult competitive marketplace.

Continued growth and advancement for the LNC business owner should incorporate the following key aspects:

- Possessing leadership skills
- Understanding the employee's perception of management
- Ongoing learning of leadership skills
- Managing stress
- Understanding quality improvement
- Benchmarking toward excellence

Possessing Leadership Skills

The owner of the LNC business needs to possess leadership skills in order to respond to the needs of the market. Reflective reaction and being proactive are necessary skills for an effective, credible business leader. Reflective reaction is a concept that incorporates thought and action with reflection, allowing the LNC owner to analyze actions with the goal of improving professional business practices. An example is having a specific goal in mind and then using past experiences to put that goal into a plan. The LNC owner in a management position must analyze the decisions made each day in order to improve business outcomes.

Understanding the Employee's Perception of Management

Obtaining feedback from employees is the best way to understand their perception of how they are being managed. The LNC business owner must keep open lines of communication with each employee and subcontractor. The LNC owner should be willing to accept the suggestions from employees and discuss them with the employees. The ultimate decision or action remains that of the LNC owner.

Ongoing Learning of Leadership Skills

A successful LNC owner continues education relative to leadership skills. Mentors can be helpful; workshops and books on leadership can supplement experience. Concepts, models, and theories can assist in acquiring leadership abilities, but time and effort will afford the experience needed to be a credible leader.

Managing Stress

Stress reduction is an attainable goal and should be a process that the entire LNC business organization uses. Growing an LNC business without the understanding of a need for balance can be very stressful. Anxiety management is best served by networking with other business owners who are expanding their businesses. LNC owners need to vent and be given support to reevaluate stressful issues such as attorney clients who do not pay invoices, loss prevention of critical data, virus protection software, and problem employees. The key is to know what is needed from a support network and to develop one. Stress management benefits the entire organization.

Understanding Quality Improvement

Quality improvement is the effort to improve performance. This principle is also called total quality improvement or continuous quality improvement. The basic premise is that for quality to improve, defects in the process must be eliminated. In order to do this, all systems involved must be analyzed and corrected to improve the outcome. The goal of quality work involves the path for excellence. Quality defects are costly whether related to productivity or inefficient work product. By developing tools for tracking and trending, defective processes can be discovered. Tracking indicates the monitoring of an idea or direction, while trending indicates maintaining a consistent way or direction. Through statistical tools, the LNC owner can identify desired performance levels and put into action strategies to implement processes that are more effective.

One example of quality improvement is development of a survey tool for analysis of satisfaction with the merit screen format from the attorney clients. Another example is to analyze the time spent on a particular type of work product and then strive to improve that work product and decrease the amount of time spent on it.

Benchmarking Toward Excellence

Excellence can be achieved through benchmarking. Benchmarking is a method of developing the organization's standards to the highest quality possible. Benchmarking involves analysis of the competition and assists in identifying areas for improvement. The LNC owner looks for new and unique aspects in operating a business and formulating professional ideas to utilize. Weinstein and Johnson[1] refer to Robert C. Camp's statement that benchmarking is a process of "consistently researching new ideas for methods, practices, and processes, either adopting the practices or adapting the good features, and implementing them to obtain the best of the best." This requires time, communication, and feedback from attorney clients regarding the work product. Continued analysis, review, and updating of the work product format are essential to producing quality work.

Looking to the Future with a Purpose

The LNC business owner should anticipate the value-added services that the business can provide in the future. Looking toward the future, the LNC owner must be ready to embrace the inevitable constant — change. The LNC owner must analyze and study the needs of the marketplace. Pioneering ideas, new technology, and customer demands should be seen as a motivating opportunity. This is the LNC owner's opportunity to create the momentum within the business. The business must be able to meet the needs of the marketplace in order to survive. The LNC owner must be able to steer the business organization and develop quality products on a consistent basis. The products should be created efficiently and with greater excellence than those of the competition. If an LNC business can accomplish this during expansion and growth, it will become one of the many LNC success stories.

A clear and concise vision statement that encompasses the LNC's business will attract the kind of employees needed to preserve ideas and goals. Once this workforce is in place, it will produce the consistent quality work that can enable the organization to mold its place in the market.

A successful LNC owner acknowledges that the people who make up the organization — not just finances and technology — enable long-term survival. In order for an organization to flourish under quality leadership, that leadership must recognize and embrace change, momentum, and uncertainty, as well as continue to value the diversity of its workforce.

Conclusion

The LNC owner who wants to grow his or her business seeks to attain a unique position in the marketplace. To achieve this, the firm needs to develop a strategy that fills a niche that few other LNC firms can fill. The business's products and services must meet the needs of the clients in an exceptional manner and not be easy to duplicate. The LNC owner must consider changes, resources, finances, personnel issues, and personal development of leadership skills in order to develop a successful, profitable, and growing business.

Reference

1. Weinstein, A. and Johnson, W., *Designing and Delivering Superior Customer Value: Concepts, Cases, and Applications*, St. Lucie Press, Delray Beach, FL, 1999, 40–42.

Additional Reading

Abbott, J. and Blostone, I., *Secrets of the "Energized" Business*, Lawyers and Judges, Tucson, AZ, 2001.

Alberti, R. and Emmons, M., *Your Perfect Right: A Guide to Assertive Living*, Impact Publishers, San Luis Obispo, CA, 1995.

Balch, R.B., *Brag Your Way to Success*, R.B. Balch & Associates, Glendale, AZ, 2001.

Bellman, G.M., *The Beauty of the Beast: Breathing New Life into Organizations*, Berrett-Koehler Publishers, San Francisco, 2000.

Cafferky, M.E., *Let Your Customers Do the Talking*, Upstart Publishing, Chicago, 1996.

Camp, R., *Benchmarking: The Search for Industry Best Practices That Lead to Superior Performance*, Productivity Press, Portland, OR, 1989.

Collins, C.J. and Porras, J.I., *Built to Last: Successful Habits of Visionary Companies*, Harper Business, New York, 1997.

Cunningham, R., Ten questions to ask before you sign a lease, Suppl. to *Inc. Magazine*, 1996.

Drucker, P.F., *Management Challenges for the 21st Century*, HarperCollins, New York, 1999.

Fairfield Poley, M., *A Winning Attitude: How to Develop Your Most Important Asset*, SkillPath Publications, Mission, KS, 1992.

Feder, M.E., *Taking Charge: A Personal Guide to Managing Projects and Priorities*, SkillPath Publications, Mission, KS, 1989.

Folland, S., Goodman, C.A., and Stano, M., *The Economics of Health and Health Care*, 2nd ed., Prentice-Hall, Upper Saddle River, NJ, 1997.

Forsyth, D., *Group Dynamics*, 2nd ed., Brooks/Cole Publishing, Pacific Grove, CA, 1990.

Fottler, M.D., Hernandez, S.R., and Joiner, C.L., *Strategic Management of Human Resources*, 2nd ed., Delmar Publishers, New York, 1994.

Gerber, M.E., *The E Myth Revisited: Why Most Small Businesses Don't Work and What To Do About It*, Harper Business, New York, 1995.

Godfrey, J., *Our Wildest Dreams: Women Entrepreneurs Making Money, Having Fun, Doing Good*, HarperCollins, New York, 1992.

Holtz, H., *How To Succeed as an Independent Consultant*, John Wiley & Sons, New York, 1993.

Imparato, N. and Harari, O., *Jumping the Curve: Innovation and Strategic Choice in an Age of Transition*, Jossey-Bass, San Francisco, 1996.

Johnson, M., *The Delivery of Quality Health Care*, Mosby Year Book, St. Louis, 1992.

McGraw, P.C., *Strategies: Doing What Works, Doing What Matters*, Hyperion, New York, 1999.

Orman, S., *The 9 Steps to Financial Freedom*, Crown Publishers, New York, 1997.

Puetz, B. and Shinn, L., *The Nurse Consultant's Handbook*, Springer, New York, 1997.

Richardson, C., *Life Makeovers*, Broadway Books, New York, 2000.

Robert, M. and Weiss, A., *The Innovation Formula*, Harper & Row, New York, 1988.

Rose, J., Getting the most from client surveys, *New Jersey Law Journal*, Morristown, NJ, 2001.

Salsbury, G., *The Art of the Fresh Start: How to Make and Keep Your New Year's Resolutions for a Lifetime*, Health Communications, Deerfield Beach, FL, 1995.

Sommer, R.B., *The Winning Spirit: Achieving Olympic Level Performance in Business and Personal Advancements*, Griffin Publishing, Glendale, CA, 1996.

Spence, G., *How To Argue and Win Every Time*, St. Martin's Press, New York, 1995.

Swift, S., *That Winning Feeling!*, Trafalgar Square Publishing, North Pomfret, VT, 1992.

Weiss, A., *Best-Laid Plans: Turning Strategy into Action Throughout Your Organization*, Las Brisas Research Press, Shakopee, MN, 1994.

Weiss, A., *Managing for Peak Performance: A Guide to the Power (and Pitfalls) of Personal Style*, Las Brisas Research Press, Shakopee, MN, 1989.

Weiss, A., *Million Dollar Consulting*, McGraw-Hill, New York, 1992.

Weiss, A., *Money Talks: How To Make a Million as a Speaker*, McGraw-Hill, New York, 1998.

Williams, J.S., *Contemporary Issues in Health Services*, Delmar Publishers, Albany, NY, 1993.

Williams, J.S. and Torrens, R.P., *Introduction to Health Services*, 4th ed., Delmar Publishers, Albany, NY, 1993.

Wise, D., Starting a business: legal and business principles, in *Legal Nurse Consulting: Principles and Practices*, Bogart, J.B., Ed., CRC Press, Boca Raton, FL, 1998, 573–608.

Zagury, C., *Nurse Entrepreneur: Building the Bridge of Opportunity*, Vista Publishing, Long Branch, NJ, 1993.

Ziglar, Z., *Over the Top*, Thomas Nelson, Nashville, TN, 1994.

Test Questions

1. Growing a business requires the LNC to review all of the following factors EXCEPT:
   A. Office location
   B. Business structure and finance planning
   C. Age of LNC business competitors
   D. Employee training and education

2. Which of the following is the least effective way in which the LNC business owner can develop leadership skills?
   A. Reading books on leadership and values
   B. Taking a leadership class at the local college
   C. Joining an LNC or business organization
   D. Accepting only suggestions that agree with his or her preconceived ideas

3. Quality improvement of the work product and services
   A. Is unnecessary and time-consuming
   B. Is an effective way to ensure continued growth of the business
   C. Causes newly hired LNCs difficulty in learning the work product
   D. Is not required if the clients are satisfied

4. Which of the following is a measure of success in growing a business?
   A. The LNC owner is so busy that he or she is burned out and tied to the business.
   B. The business is losing clients but has a large budget to cover the losses.
   C. The LNC owner is better than the competitors but unable to retain clients.
   D. The LNC owner has a unique business that offers a special service and shows a profit.

5. Which of the following is NOT necessary for continued growth and advancement of the LNC business?
   A. The business owner possesses leadership skills and runs the business while others provide the work product.
   B. The LNC business owner understands the importance of quality improvement.
   C. Once a niche is achieved, marketplace change can be discounted.
   D. Benchmarking is used to achieve excellence.

Answers: 1. C, 2. D, 3. B, 4. D, 5. C

Chapter 46

Business Practices and Ethics

Jo Anne Kuc, BSN, RN, LNCC, and Betty Joos, MEd, BSN, RN

CONTENTS

0-8493-1418-6/03/$0.00+$1.50
© 2003 by AALNC

Objectives

- To establish a business using ethics as guiding principles
- To identify ethical conflicts that can occur in a legal nurse consultant's business
- To clarify basic ethical conflicts faced by the legal nurse consultant
- To apply the principles of ethical conduct and professional codes to the business practice of the legal nurse consultant

Introduction

For most professions, ethical behavior is defined in a code that describes minimally acceptable conduct within that profession. The practice of the legal nurse consultant (LNC) acknowledges guidance from several professional codes of ethical conduct. These include the *Code of Ethics and Conduct of the American Association of Legal Nurse Consultants* (AALNC),[1] the American Nurses Association's (ANA's) *Code of Ethics for Nurses*,[2] and the *American Bar Association Compendium of Professional Responsibility Rules and Standards*.[3] The *Code of Ethics and Conduct of the American Association of Legal Nurse Consultants* is found in Chapter 6, and the ANA's *Code of Ethics for Nurses* is found in Chapter 10. Whether an employee or an independent contractor, the LNC maintains personal integrity and engenders trust by adhering to these codes.

The Code of Ethics for LNCs is a guideline for their ethical conduct, whereas attorneys are bound by the codes of ethics established by their state bar associations and state judicial systems. Some state statutes also govern attorneys' ethical behavior. Most states have adopted the model code of ethics or the model rules of professional conduct set out by the American Bar Association (ABA); however, the ABA is a voluntary organization and does not provide regulatory authority over attorneys. Attorneys can be disciplined for unethical behavior by their state bar disciplinary board. A client can bring a civil suit against an attorney for legal malpractice; attorneys can even be criminally prosecuted if state statutes are involved. The attorney is also accountable for any unethical behavior of nonlawyer employees. This provides additional reason for the LNC to become knowledgeable about basic ethical standards of the legal profession.

The LNC applies ethical principles to the practice of this specialty and must apply the same moral and ethical principles to related business practices. The LNC business owner who approaches moral dilemmas in business with knowledge and guidance from the codes of conduct for his or her profession is better able to prevent unintentional, as well as foreseeable, ethical improprieties. In the end, however, the ethics of the individual imbue the business with moral integrity. This chapter identifies and discusses some of the ethical issues faced by the LNC business owner (see Figure 46.1).

Ethics in Starting a Consulting Practice

Ethics and the Mission Statement

The LNC provides a service to attorneys and other clients. The independent LNC who offers this service through his or her own business not only provides the

I. The legal nurse consultant does not discriminate against any person based on race, creed, color, age, sex, national origin, social status, or disability and does not let personal attitudes interfere with professional performance.

II. The legal nurse consultant performs as a consultant or an expert with the highest degree of integrity.

III. The legal nurse consultant uses informed judgment, objectivity, and individual competence as criteria when accepting assignments.

IV. The legal nurse consultant maintains standards of personal conduct that reflect honorably upon the profession.

V. The legal nurse consultant provides professional services with objectivity.

VI. The legal nurse consultant protects client privilege and confidentiality.

VII. The legal nurse consultant is accountable for responsibilities accepted and actions performed.

VIII. The legal nurse consultant maintains professional nursing competence.

Figure 46.1   Code of Ethics and Conduct of the American Association of Legal Nurse Consultants

consulting service to clients but also must develop and maintain a business enterprise according to ethical guidelines. The LNC begins his or her business by developing a business plan that contains a mission statement outlining the LNC's overall business objectives or goals. The mission statement should articulate a customer service strategy and characterize the commitment to clients as well as the integrity of the business owner.

Among other considerations, the LNC's business-plan development is guided by the AALNC's Code of Ethics and Conduct, Code I, which states that the LNC "does not discriminate against any person based on race, creed, color, age, sex, national origin, social status, or disability and does not let personal attitudes interfere with professional performance." Additionally, Ethics Code V states that the LNC "provides professional services with objectivity." These two guidelines serve to emphasize that LNCs are to provide conscientious and nonprejudicial service to all clients.

The LNC business owner also considers the client's rights. The client has a right to expect that the relationship is valued and respected, and that the LNC performs the work with integrity and competency and provides the work product in a timely manner. The client also has a right to expect that the work product is kept confidential, the information is correct and appropriate to the case, and the comments and explanations are unbiased. The LNC's business practices include providing the client with a fair and informed billing process.

Example 46.1: Anne Newencee has just started her LNC business as a sole practitioner and has begun to market her services. She researched the *Martindale-Hubbell Law Directory* to locate the plaintiff attorneys in her area for her initial target market. A non-LNC friend asked her why she wanted to market to only plaintiff attorneys. Anne's response was that she did not like or trust defense attorneys, since she had been involved in a lawsuit as a plaintiff and had lost her case. Anne's feelings were that all defense attorneys were corrupt, because they represented the defendants and insurance companies against plaintiffs like her.

Discussion: Anne has a right to limit her target market to only plaintiff clients, so what is the ethical issue? Anne's personal experience as a plaintiff could make her more sensitive to plaintiffs' concerns and issues. However, Anne appears to have developed a personal prejudice against defense attorneys and insurance companies because she lost her case in court. How will her bias affect her work with all cases? Will her bias lead her to recommend that some cases are meritorious when they are not? Alternatively, will she overlook mitigating defense factors that should be brought to the plaintiff attorney's attention? Only through recognition of her bias and careful objectivity will Anne provide an unprejudiced work product.

Ethics and Accountability in Business

Business owners are accountable for the adverse effects of their actions on others. Professional malpractice suits are sometimes brought against those who are seen as liable for damages involving their services to a client. *Black's Law Dictionary*[4] describes malpractice as "any professional misconduct, unreasonable lack of skill or fidelity in professional or fiduciary duties, evil practice, or illegal or immoral conduct."

LNCs are accountable for presenting themselves knowledgeably and ethically to attorneys and others who seek their services. The *Code of Ethics and Conduct of the American Association of Legal Nurse Consultants* states in Code II that the LNC "performs as a consultant or an expert with the highest degree of integrity." Code III states that the LNC "uses informed judgment, objectivity, and individual competence as criteria when accepting assignments." The LNC business owner who keeps these aspects of the ethical code in mind will have a firm basis of integrity, objectivity, and competence for accountability in the business.

New LNCs often face a unique ethical dilemma in the first attempt to establish their businesses. How do new LNCs, with no experience in the litigation process or in preparing an effective work product, market themselves as knowledgeable? Although it may seem that one must prevaricate about some issues in order to get business, the ethical LNC acknowledges the importance of trustworthiness and integrity from the beginning. It is unethical for the novice LNC to present himself or herself as an experienced LNC; however, it is acceptable to emphasize the value of one's nursing experience in the performance of the fundamental services of legal nurse consulting.

The nurse expert witness who agrees to testify in a case for which he or she is not qualified presents another ethical challenge. Specific expertise in the area under litigation is required of the expert witness. Although LNCs may provide the consulting services of organizing, analyzing, and summarizing records in various types of medical cases, the nurse expert witness is held to a higher standard of specific knowledge and experience. It is essential for the LNC who practices as an expert witness to accept only cases for which his or her nursing experience is commensurate.

Example 46.2: Nancy Novice was trying to obtain new clients for her business. Nancy interviewed one potential client who was impressed with her and wanted her to testify in a nursing issue case already under litigation. Nancy was excited and wanted to do the case — until she discovered that it was an obstetric case. Nancy's experience was in intensive care. She refused the opportunity but offered to locate a nurse expert in obstetric nursing for the client.

Discussion: Nancy really needed this work in order to develop her business; however, she chose to refuse the case. Nancy's integrity did not permit her to claim that her intensive-care experience would be appropriate to act as an expert in an obstetric case. She located an experienced nurse as an expert for the client and impressed him with her adaptability as well as her integrity. She continues to receive work from this client, with whom she developed a trustworthy relationship from the outset.

Code VII of the *Code of Ethics and Conduct of the American Association of Legal Nurse Consultants* states that the LNC "is accountable for responsibilities accepted and actions performed." Examples of LNC accountability to the client include providing work product in a timely manner; providing an accounting of services, billable hours, and expenditures appropriate to the fees charged; and maintaining all information about a case in a confidential manner and in a safe location. Additionally, LNCs who act as expert witnesses are accountable for being prompt and prepared in regard to the case and for the integrity of their opinion. By federal law, LNC expert witnesses maintain a list of cases in which they have testified or been deposed in the last 4 years, as well as copies of reports prepared for those cases.

Example 46.3: Carol Ellencee accepted a case in which she testified at deposition regarding nursing care. The plaintiff attorney for whom she took the case asked Carol to testify that not only was the nursing behavior negligent but that it was also egregious enough to warrant punitive damages. Carol disagreed with this and stood by her opinion as she had stated it previously.

Discussion: Carol arrived at her expert opinion through review of the records, and she believed there was nursing negligence; however, Carol did not feel that the negligence was a flagrant disregard of standards that deserved punitive damages. She understood punitive damages to mean that the negligence involved malice or willful conduct on the part of the nurses in the conscious disregard of the needs of the patient. Carol refused to adapt her testimony simply because the attorney asked her to go along with him in his case strategy to achieve a larger judgment.

On occasion, an LNC may be asked to do something that he or she feels is potentially improper. For example, an attorney may ask the LNC to contact a plaintiff or defendant whom the attorney in question does not represent. Even with little experience in the legal arena, the LNC should be concerned about the propriety of such a request. In this and similar situations, the concerned LNC can seek input from LNCs who are more experienced or can use a formalized process of resolving ethical issues, such as the one in Chapter 10. LNCs must accept accountability for their behavior and not claim that they are unaware of what defines improper or unethical behavior. They may not disregard their responsibility by stating that they were told to do something by an attorney. Ultimately, each LNC must assess and resolve issues such as these; his or her own ethics are the foundation for these decisions.

Maintaining an Ethical Business Practice

The Unauthorized Practice of Law

The *AALNC Scope of Practice for the Legal Nurse Consultant*[5] clearly states that the LNC's role is that of a registered nurse who "performs a critical analysis of healthcare facts and issues and their outcomes for the legal professions, and others, as appropriate." The LNC does not engage in the practice of law. When serving behind the scenes as either a nurse consultant or a nurse expert witness, the LNC must avoid any appearance of making legal decisions. The LNC may indicate a breach in medical or nursing standards but does not decide whether the case has legal merit. It is also not the LNC's role to tell an individual that he or she has a legitimate case and should file a lawsuit. The attorney makes this legal determination, considering not only the medical issues but also other legal issues involved in the filing of a lawsuit.

LNCs must develop their business names and marketing materials with care to avoid misrepresenting their services and to avoid even the appearance of practicing law. LNCs offer services to the legal profession, not to the lay public. An often-espoused statement is that LNCs do not need education beyond nursing, since the basis of their practice is their nursing skill and knowledge. LNCs should keep this perspective in mind, considering that they do not have the background or knowledge (even if they have taken a paralegal course) to offer interpretations on the subject of legal issues; their knowledge lies in the health care arena.

Competing Ethically

The word "competition" is often associated with aggressive and antagonistic behaviors. However, competition does not have to be seen as negative; it can be healthy for the business market in that all participants must strive to offer a better quality of professional services. The incentive to improve services is a driver for growth and development in the LNC's business.

Competition becomes unethical when an LNC takes unfair advantage of others. Such unethical behavior includes improper or misleading advertising that embellishes his or her credentials or makes disparaging statements about other LNC competitors.

Using an ethical decision-making process can guide the LNC business owner in recognizing inappropriate competitive behaviors. The individual determines the most ethical course of action when faced with competitors and recognizes that collegiality is an important aspect of dealing with LNC peers.

Example 46.4: Susan Nuncee and her partner, Violet Alson, helped their local AALNC chapter staff an exhibit table at the trial lawyers' conference. The chapter reserved the exhibit table to share information about all LNCs and how their services could benefit attorneys. On several occasions, Susan and Violet were overheard discussing their own business rather than describing the local chapter and the role of the LNC in general.

Discussion: Susan and Violet were present at the exhibit table as representatives of all the LNCs in the chapter. They had chapter brochures and AALNC materials to hand out to attorneys for general information about LNCs. The local chapter paid the exhibit fee for the benefit of all chapter members. Susan and Violet engaged in unethical competition, since they had not paid for the privilege of marketing themselves and took advantage of the chapter's resources to do so.

Ethical Advertising

LNCs run advertisements in legal newspapers and journals and on the Internet as a way to attract clients. Advertising not only promotes the LNC's services, but

```
┌─────────────────────────────────────────────────────────────────┐
│                                                                   │
│                    XYZ CONSULTING SERVICES                        │
│                                                                   │
│   ▪ Case reviews/testimony by highly credentialed board-certified │
│     physicians and nurses                                         │
│   ▪ 24-hour turnaround-time on all cases                          │
│   ▪ Fees far lower than other consulting services                 │
│                                                                   │
│              CALL NOW TO GET YOUR NEEDS MET                        │
│                                                                   │
│                      888-888-8888                                 │
│                                                                   │
└─────────────────────────────────────────────────────────────────┘
```

Figure 46.2   Example of Misleading Advertising Copy

also is a way to educate attorneys and influence their decision-making processes when they choose LNCs. Because advertising is such a powerful tool, there must be truth in the advertising. It is unethical to run ads containing information known to be misleading or false. General rules of truth in advertising are summarized by Richard DeGeorge's statement in *Business Ethics*:[6] "It is immoral to lie, mislead, and deceive in advertising. It is not unethical to use a metaphor or other figures of speech if these can be interpreted as figurative use of language, nor is it immoral to persuade or inform." Consider the fictitious advertisement in Figure 46.2. Advertising case reviews and testimony by "highly credentialed board-certified physicians and nurses" may lead attorneys to believe that the LNC has immediate access to a database of experts that are qualified and willing to review records. It is not ethical for an LNC who does not possess immediate access to such individuals to make such a statement. Until such a database of potential experts is developed, the LNC should avoid misleading statements such as these.

Advertising a "24-hour turnaround time" may not be realistic and is misleading. Certain services, such as medical research, can be accomplished in 24 hours, but the majority of LNCs' services take time and skill. Promising work in 24 hours lures the potential client into believing that all services can be completed by the next day. A better alternative is "Efficient and prompt turnaround time."

Another ethical consideration in this ad is the message sent by advertising "fees for lower than other consulting services." Is the LNC planning to undercut all others in the area? To "undercut" fees of others, the LNC must know what all other competitors are charging. A better statement might be "reasonable rates." Setting fees is a complex and confusing issue for many LNCs. There is no "rule book" to go by, and the cost of running a business is often overlooked. Trying to undercut others' fees may give the appearance of "bargain-basement" work and inherently damages the professionalism of all LNCs.

Experienced LNCs can use their experience with high-profile cases and prestigious attorney clients as a powerful advertising strategy to attract additional clients. In order to do so, LNCs must obtain the clients' permission. Most clients will wish to review a draft of the marketing material for approval. The LNC can avoid legal action by obtaining this approval and allowing the review. Before using the names of firms and attorneys in promotional materials of any sort, the LNC should request permission.

Most experienced LNCs find that "advertising" is not the best use of money or marketing efforts. Preparing ad copy can be difficult; it is challenging to make important points in a few words. Advertising is also expensive, considering the typical lack of response it elicits. Marketing includes much more than advertising and requires thorough consideration to retain personal ethical standards in all aspects; this includes business cards, brochures, marketing letters, requests for referrals, and other methods. Information about the LNC's services and persuasion about the value of an LNC to the attorney must be truthful, precise, and carefully designed to convey appropriate and effective information.

Subcontracting Services

Often an experienced LNC subcontracts work to other LNCs. There are ethical and business expectations on both sides of this practice. The experienced LNC, who is the contractor, must be clear about what is expected of the subcontracted LNC. Information about the case issues, the form of the work product, and the subcontractor fees is required for the subcontractor. A written agreement is preferred because it clarifies the responsibilities and obligations of both parties. The client "belongs to" the contracting LNC; the subcontractor performs the work for the employing LNC. It is unethical for the LNC who has provided subcontractor services for another LNC firm to state that the other firm's clients are her own. LNCs who are employed by, or subcontract for, other LNCs compete unethically when they market to the employing LNC's clients or when they use the specific forms and formats from the employing LNC. The subcontractor may market to other attorneys or law firms. A case that is referred to an LNC differs, since there is nothing to prevent marketing to the referred client. These distinctions must be clear to LNCs who do subcontracting work.

LNCs involved in subcontracting are held to the same ethics of confidentiality, conflict of interest, and other LNC ethics related to the case involved and to the contracting LNC. All LNCs, whether contractors or subcontractors, should keep in mind their business ethics concerning expenses, fees, and hours billed.

The Duty of Confidentiality

Nurses are familiar with the duty of confidentiality of patient information. LNCs are privy to client communication, attorneys' strategies and thought processes, work product, and other privileged information, including patients' records. The duty of confidentiality, whether in the medical or legal arena, requires LNCs not to use or communicate confidential information.

Rule 1.6 of the *ABA Model Rules of Professional Conduct* states: "The principle of confidentiality is given effect in two related bodies of law, the attorney–client privilege (which includes the work product doctrine) in the laws of evidence and the rule of confidentiality established in professional ethics." The attorney–client privilege is a sacred trust that the information from the client will not be divulged in other than the presentation of the case. If the LNC is privy to this information, the LNC is held to this same privilege and confidentiality. The attorney–client privilege protects the work product of the contracted LNC. This work product is "safely confidential" as long as it is not divulged to those outside the case. The work product also loses this "privilege" when offered to testifying experts for their review.

Ethical LNCs hold all medical record and personal client information in strict confidence. LNCs should not discuss cases with personal acquaintances, at a professional meeting or seminar, or on Internet chat rooms, listservs, or bulletin boards in any way that would allow a case to be identified — whether by name, issues under suit, or a complete discussion of case issues. Although some nurses wish to gain additional perspectives to assist with a case, there is a risk of exposing confidential information and of jeopardizing the client's case.

Example 46.5: Mary Newsom casually discussed information about a case's litigation strategies, even though she did not mention the case name or client, with a group of individuals at an AALNC meeting. Unknown to Mary, the group included an LNC from the opposing side (Jane). Jane recognized the case and reported the overheard conversation to her attorney; this information resulted in an adverse case outcome for Mary's client.

Discussion: Mary showed a careless disregard for confidentiality in this case, and the result was adverse to her client. At the least, Mary's actions showed her to be untrustworthy, and at the worst, she was liable for divulging confidential work product information and could be liable for malpractice.

Other information that requires confidentiality is acquired information that is not linked to any particular case. This includes information that might be associated with individuals or items that the attorney uses to enhance his practice. Examples of acquired information are a database of medical experts and consultants that the attorney uses, referring attorneys from whom the attorney client receives work, and other materials that the LNC may have access to by working in the firm or by having access to its computer systems when working as a contractor for a firm. These databases are the property of the firm, and it is unethical for the LNC to use them for personal benefit. Other acquired information may be knowledge gained about an individual or entity through work as an expert witness or a consultant on another case. The LNC must assess such issues and, if it is a confidential matter, must not disclose this information even if it might help another client.

Example 46.6: June Bothered, an LNC expert witness, became aware of a physician's substance-abuse problems when she was involved in a case in which he was sued. She discovered that a new attorney client planned to hire this physician as an expert for one of his cases. June realized that the attorney was unaware of the potential expert's history of substance abuse, but she was concerned that she would divulge confidential information if she informed the attorney of this. June's dilemma was whether she could tell the new attorney client that this physician had a history of substance abuse or whether she would be divulging confidential information. June checked with the former attorney client for the case against the doctor about the confidentiality of the information and discovered that it could not be construed as confidential, since the story of the physician's problems had been front-page news in his area. June provided the information to the new attorney client and prevented a costly mistake in trial strategy.

Discussion: LNCs should assume that *all* information they receive from clients is confidential and should preserve that confidentiality at all times. The LNC is responsible for determining the appropriateness of disclosing information gained through her or his work with other cases.

If the LNC is required to dispose of records, it is best to shred them unless the attorney requests the LNC to do otherwise. Although the patient records lose confidentiality when the plaintiff files a lawsuit, the medical file contains information (such as Social Security number) unrelated to the lawsuit itself, and the client could claim damages if this information were made available. Although LNCs may keep, or in some cases are required to keep, reports of cases on file and in the computer after completion of a case, any reports that must be disposed of are best shredded. Although case outcomes are sometimes published after trial, the LNC should use discretion in any discussion of a case.

Conflict of Interest

The "General Rule of Conflict of Interest" in legal issues stated in Rule 1.7 of the *ABA Model Rules of Professional Conduct* is that no representation of a client should be undertaken if there is any issue or knowledge that would be "directly adverse to another client." Independent LNCs work with many clients and must always be cognizant of potential conflicts in cases. The LNC who leaves a position with a law firm in order to develop an independent practice — or vice versa — is admonished to identify clearly any areas that might present a conflict in his or her practice. Most independent LNCs maintain a list or a database of cases and clients so that they can avoid any conflicts.

Rule 1.9 of the *ABA Model Rules of Professional Conduct* states that a conflict of interest is that which might be "materially adverse to the interests of the former client unless the former client consents after consultation." For the LNC, the "former" client could be a hospital or other facility for which she or he worked in a position that gave access to information that was confidential, of sensitive nature, or specific to the case that the LNC is asked to review. Each nurse must consider this issue and must inform the attorney of the conflict involved. If an attorney requests the LNC to act as a testifying expert in such a situation, the opposing side could use this conflict issue to challenge or impeach the LNC, making any testimony ineffective or damaging to the case. The LNC should use personal discretion and should not agree to continue in a case in which a conflict of interest is apparent, even if the attorney client requests this.

Other examples of conflict of interest for the LNC are (1) working for both plaintiff and defense on the same case, or "switching" between the plaintiff and defense in the middle of a case; (2) cases involving doctors or nurses whom the LNC knows on a personal basis; and (3) cases in which the LNC personally knows or is related to any party in the case. In all cases of concern about the conflict-of-interest issue, the LNC should make the client fully aware of the situation. The LNC must first recognize these potential conflicts in order to avoid them.

Ethical Practices in Billing and Expenses

Independent LNCs and testifying experts should establish a fee schedule when they set up their businesses. The LNC needs to establish a working agreement with the attorney regarding fees and expenses during an initial interview or upon the first referral of a case. It is appropriate to expect reimbursement for reasonable out-of-pocket costs incurred in the course of a case assessment, but expense charges are not a way to increase the LNC's profit. The LNC's hourly rate should already include a portion to cover the "overhead" (such as taxes, FICA, and utilities) in doing business. Each LNC must decide what direct expenses are suitable to charge a client in a given case. For example, the LNC might charge for binders and indexes used to assemble case materials, but might decide not to charge for the cost of phone calls.

Some LNCs negotiate a lower hourly rate based on a predetermined agreement of a minimum number of billable hours from a single firm. The discounted rate makes good business sense, because the LNC does not have to market as much for additional work. Some consultants view fee customization as unprofessional, but it is not unethical and may be a logical option in lieu of working part-time for a firm. Each LNC must determine a fee schedule that is fair, ethical, and consistent with good business practices. Charging higher fees because the attorney or insurance client has "deep pockets" is unethical business practice.

Most attorneys will arrange for out-of-town travel and accommodations for expert witnesses. However, if the attorney requests the LNC to make travel arrangements, it is not appropriate to expect reimbursement for first-class air travel or expensive meals and hotels. The LNC can avoid most potential problems with reimbursement by clarifying all issues with the attorney before making any travel plans.

Consultants generally bill by increments of 6, 10, or 15 minutes. Testifying experts may bill using these increments or may bill a flat rate such as a half-day or entire day when travel to depositions or availability for trial is involved. Some LNCs charge a flat fee for finding an expert witness; others bill for the expert and add on a percentage of the expert's billing rate. However the LNC's billing process is set up, it should be consistent.

Many new LNCs have difficulty determining how much of the work on a "first" case is due to their learning curve and if that time should be billed to the client. While some LNCs and attorneys recommend billing all time spent on a case, even in the learning phase, most LNCs agree that this concept has some limits. A new LNC can benefit by discussing this issue with an experienced LNC, a mentor, or with the members of the local AALNC chapter. Subcontractors providing LNC services for other LNCs should inquire about the expected number of hours needed to complete a project and adhere to restrictions on the total number of hours.

Most LNCs require a retainer fee along with the records in a case. The retainer can be a flat rate determined by the LNC or can involve an estimated percent of the time anticipated to do the work in a given case. When the case requires less time than the retainer fee covers, any remaining retainer fee should be returned to the attorney client. It is unethical to keep retainer money that covers more hours than the LNC spent on the case.

Example 46.7: Frank Finder, an LNC for the defense, received a retainer from Attorney Jones, who worked for Big Law Firm, for the White case. The retainer was paid from the Big Law Firm account. Before Frank did any work on the White case, Attorney Jones left Big Law Firm to start his own practice. Attorney Jones took the White case with him and contacted Frank to begin work on the case, using the retainer money he had received from Big Law Firm. Frank was concerned about the ethics of using the retainer money when Attorney Jones was no longer a member of Big Law Firm. He contacted Big Law Firm to determine whether there was an agreement with Attorney Jones regarding expenses in the White case. Big Law Firm had not made any agreement about expenses in the White case. They confirmed to Frank that they wished to have the retainer returned to them, which he did. Frank then contacted Attorney Jones concerning the return of the retainer fee and told Attorney Jones that a retainer from him was required. Attorney Jones was not happy with the situation but did negotiate a retainer fee with Frank to begin work on the White case.

Discussion: When the identity of the client changes partway through a case, the LNC should determine who is paying the bills. Failing to raise this issue at the time of occurrence may result in an inequitable financial arrangement for the client or complications for payment of the LNC.

Sometimes new LNCs set their rates extremely low in order to get work. This practice is detrimental to all LNCs. Undercutting the fees of competitors is self-defeating in the end. As the LNC gains more experience, it is difficult to raise fees that were set too low at the beginning. LNCs, as professionals, should charge appropriately for all work, and they deserve to be paid accordingly. ABA Opinion 302, written in 1961, refers to compensation for attorneys but may be applicable to LNCs as well. Opinion 302 states: "When members of the Bar are induced to render legal services for inadequate compensation, as a consequence the quality of the service rendered may be lowered, the welfare of the profession injured, and the administration of justice made less efficient."[3]

LNCs provide unique services that should be adequately compensated. ABA Opinion 302 makes a point that what one individual does may have an impact on others in the profession. While fees vary from one area to another, it is incumbent on the LNC to establish fees that are consistent with other LNCs with similar experience.

Contingency Fees

Contingency fees are often an issue of concern when LNCs discuss fees and billing. Attorneys for the plaintiff usually work on a contingency basis — the plaintiff client pays only direct expenses (if able to do so), and the attorney and his or her staff do not receive payment until the case is settled or won in court, at which time they get a percentage of the settlement or judgment for the case. The attorney and staff are not paid for their time if there is no settlement before trial or if the case is decided in favor of the defendant.

Under their own code of ethics, attorneys are charged with representing their clients "zealously within the bounds of law" (Canon 7 of the ABA Model Code of Professional Behavior[3]). LNCs have a different obligation; the AALNC Code of Ethics and Conduct, Code V, specifies that they are to provide "professional services with objectivity." The LNC's explanation and information may or may not support the allegations of the case. Expert testimony should not change, regardless of which side the expert testifies for, but should state the facts truthfully as the nurse expert knows them. It is inappropriate and unethical for the LNC to accept a contingency fee, because doing so would suggest that the testimony the LNC provided was not objective. This can be damning for even the appearance of bias and could suggest that the testimony was influenced by the desire to have the case conclude in the client's favor to increase the LNC's fee from the transaction. The LNC may argue that his or her integrity is not at issue, but even the "appearance of impropriety" disallows the acceptance of contingency fees.

Honesty in billing is a vital part of an effective consultant/client relationship. Trust is the cornerstone of the client relationship and in other facets of the business relationship. The LNC should understand billing issues and prepare appropriate guidelines for billing clients in this work. Keeping precise records of time spent working on a case is an essential aspect of honest, ethical billing that can be crucial when a client raises questions about services that the LNC provided.

Business Ethics for the Employed LNC

While business ethics are necessary for the LNC in independent practice, they are also important for the LNC employed by a law firm, by an insurance company, or in other settings. The employed LNC is responsible for maintaining an ethical practice in a business setting. This begins with truthfulness in the resume and interview. The LNC employee is accountable for tracking his or her billable hours with integrity. Confidential and privileged information should be discussed only with the attorneys involved in the case, not the whole office. Neither cases nor office business should be discussed outside the firm.

LNCs are also accountable for personal behaviors in the office setting. As an employee, "taking" items such as office supplies for personal use is unethical. The ethical LNC does not demean any attorney or other staff within the firm or to others outside the firm. There should never be a question about the integrity of the employed LNC. Unethical behavior of the LNC can result in loss of job, damage to a client's case, sanctions for the attorney, and potential charges of malpractice against either the LNC or the attorney or both.

Summary

Performing Outside of One's Area of Expertise

It is unethical for the LNC to testify as an expert if he or she lacks the requisite knowledge and current experience. LNCs who perform consulting activities, such as review of medical records with a report, clearly distinguish between the role of expert and that of consultant. When not acting as an expert, the LNC informs the attorney client that the information provided is based upon general nursing knowledge and a medical literature search. The consulting LNC can recommend verification by the designated medical expert.

Unauthorized Practice of Law

The LNC should not engage in any actions that can be construed as practicing law or giving legal advice and should not become involved in any matters that require professional legal judgment.

Objectivity of Work and Work Product

The LNC does not discriminate against any person, and individual differences do not influence the LNC's professional performance and practice. The LNC does not discriminate against those who have different religious and social beliefs. The

LNC may work for either the plaintiff or the defense, because case assessment and written reports should be objective and unbiased. The LNC fulfills the ethical obligation of informing the attorney of negative aspects of a case, such as critical information in the medical record of which the attorney is unaware, as well as aspects that are positive for the client.

Conflict-of-Interest Issues

Only the LNC involved in a given situation can identify and act on conflict-of-interest issues. It is imperative that all LNCs in independent practice maintain records that help identify conflicts of interest. An LNC promptly withdraws from cases of known conflict regardless of pressure to continue on the case.

Confidentiality

The LNC carries a deep regard for confidentiality from former nursing experience and continues that regard in legal nurse consulting. The LNC should have a thorough knowledge of confidentiality related to legal issues as well as to medical issues.

Appropriate Fees and Billing

The LNC determines rates and fees before seeking out clients. LNCs do not accept contingency fees. The ethical LNC keeps meticulous records of time spent on cases and bills only for hours worked and for legitimate expenses. The LNC who does both consultant and expert witness work clearly states the fee schedule for each.

Integrity of the LNC

There should be no question of integrity in any dealings of the LNC, whether in business or personal behavior. Once integrity is under suspicion, there is often little chance to repair the damage. Integrity in small things is indicative of a person's integrity in all things.

References

1. American Association of Legal Nurse Consultants, *Code of Ethics and Conduct,* rev. ed., American Association of Legal Nurse Consultants, Chicago, 1999.
2. American Nurses Association, *Code of Ethics for Nurses with Interpretive Statements,* American Nurses Publishing, Washington, D.C., 2001.
3. American Bar Association, *ABA Compendium of Professional Responsibility Rules and Standards,* American Bar Association, Chicago, 1991.
4. Black, H.C., Nolan, J.R., and Nolan-Haley, J.M., *Black's Law Dictionary,* 6th ed., abridged, West Publishing Company, St. Paul, MN, 1991.

5. American Association of Legal Nurse Consultants, *AALNC Scope of Practice for the Legal Nurse Consultant*, American Association of Legal Nurse Consultants, Chicago, 1995.

6. DeGeorge, R.T., Will success spoil business ethics?, in *Business Ethics*, 4th ed., Freeman, E.E., Ed., Oxford University Press, New York, 1995.

Additional Reading

American Medical Association, *Code of Medical Ethics, 150th Anniversary Edition: Current Opinions with Annotations*, American Medical Association, Chicago, 1997.

Brown, M.T., *Working Ethics — Strategies for Decision Making and Organizational Responsibility*, Jossey-Bass, San Francisco, 1990.

Casperson, D.M., *Power Etiquette — What You Don't Know Can Kill Your Career*, American Management Association International, New York, 1999.

Freeman, R.E., *Business Ethics — State of the Art*, Oxford University Press, New York, 1991.

Kidder, R.M., *How Good People Make Tough Choices: Resolving the Dilemmas of Ethical Living*, Simon & Schuster, New York, 1996.

Seglin, J.L., *The Good, the Bad, and Your Business: Choosing Right When Ethical Dilemmas Pull You Apart*, John Wiley & Sons, New York, 2000.

Solomon, R.C., *A Better Way to Think About Business*, Oxford University Press, New York, 1999.

Test Questions

1. The *mission statement* in an LNC's business plan includes
   A. A customer service strategy
   B. An advertising strategy
   C. A personal profile
   D. A plan for contacting clients

2. Of the following, which describes ethical competition?
   A. Marketing the LNC business to plaintiff attorneys only
   B. Contacting the client for whom you have done only subcontracting work
   C. Pointing out at an interview that the LNC's competitor does not have a BS degree and has recently started in business as an LNC
   D. Advertising as an experienced LNC when one has 10 years of consulting experience

3. Contingency fees are acceptable
   A. When the LNC is clear that the work product is completely unbiased
   B. When the LNC is convinced that the client is in the absolute right
   C. When the attorney does not have the money to pay the LNC at the time the work is done
   D. Never

4. Which of the following best defines a *conflict of interest?*
   A. Reviewing a case involving a hospital where the LNC is not employed
   B. Working on a case in which the LNC knows the plaintiff personally
   C. Working on a case involving a hospital in which the LNC was employed 10 years before the events of the suit
   D. Providing research for the defendant attorney in a case in which the LNC knows of the defendant

5. It is ethical for the LNC who acts as expert witness to
   A. Review a case for a defense attorney after having reviewed and rejected the same case from a plaintiff attorney
   B. Use his or her general nursing knowledge to act as an expert in any case
   C. Refuse to act as an expert in a conflict-of-interest situation
   D. State his or her expert views according to the attorney's wishes

Answers: 1. A, 2. A, 3. D, 4. B, 5. C

Glossary

Compiled by Sherri Reed, BSN, RN, LNCC, and
Bruce Kehoe, JD

Access: Approach to electronic information through any storage medium. When used in relation to the term "online," it implies the availability of suitable telecommunications, plus user IDs and passwords for the online host system.

Account Balance: Difference between debit and credit sides of an account.

Account Debtor: Person who is obligated on an account, chattel paper, or general intangible.

Account Payable: A debt owed by an enterprise that arises in the normal course of business dealings and has not been replaced by a note payable of a debtor. A liability representing an amount owed to a creditor, usually arising from purchase of merchandise or materials and supplies, not necessarily due or past due.

Account Receivable: A debt owed to an enterprise that arises in the normal course of business dealings and is not supported by negotiable paper. A claim against a debtor usually arising from sales or services rendered, not necessarily due or past due.

Account Rendered: An account made out by the creditor and presented to the debtor for his examination and acceptance. When accepted, it becomes an account stated.

Account Settled: An agreed balance between parties to a settlement.

Account Stated: An account that accumulates additions to another account.

Accountant: Person who works in the field of accounting and is skilled in keeping books or accounts; in designing and controlling systems of account; in giving tax advice and preparing tax returns.

Accountability: An obligation of providing, or being prepared to provide, an account of one's actions.

ADL: Activities of daily living; includes bathing, dressing, toileting, feeding, and grooming.

0-8493-1418-6/03/$0.00+$1.50
© 2003 by AALNC

Address: (1) A label or number, which identifies a database disk location where information is stored in the computer; (2) may also refer to the location of a host computer on an online network.

Adverse Drug Reaction Reports: Summaries of adverse experiences with a specific product reported to the Food and Drug Administration.

Adverse Event (AE): Any untoward change in health or medical status, such as a new medical occurrence, or a change (such as an exacerbation) in a preexisting medical condition, that occurs during the course of a study from the signing of the informed consent by the study participant to the final study visit (study completion). The medical condition does not have to be considered as related to the study drug or device to be termed an "adverse event." The adverse event must be evaluated by the investigator (not the study coordinator) for relationship to the study drug and designated as possibly related, probably related, definitely related or definitely not related.

Affidavit: Sworn, voluntary statement of fact or declaration.

Affirmative Defense: A defense to a cause of action (claim) for which the defendant has the burden of proof. Comparative negligence is an example of an affirmative defense.

AHCPR: Agency for Health Care Policy and Research, established standards of practice for a variety of patient care issues.

AHRQ: Agency for Healthcare Research and Quality (formerly AHCPR).

Allegations: The claims, statements, or assertions made by a party to a legal action or a potential legal action. These assertions may be incorporated in the complaint or the answer.

ANA: American Nurses Association, national association of nurses.

Analysis and Issue Identification: As an LNC standard, analysis of data to identify the health care issues related to a case or claim.

Annotation: The process of highlighting, drawing circles, underlining, etc. on an exhibit.

Answer: The formal written statement made by a defendant in response to the complaint, setting forth the grounds of the defense.

APA 5 Format: The Publication Manual of the American Psychological Association (5th Ed). Used as a reference for manuscript citations.

Apportionment of Liability: Assigning a percentage of the total negligence to each culpable party (e.g., a jury could find that the plaintiff was 20% liable, one defendant was 30% liable, and another defendant was 50% liable).

Arbitration: Informal hearing held before a neutral third party who renders a decision and issues an award.

Arbitrator: Disinterested third party chosen by the parties or appointed by the court to render a decision.

Arraignment: The stage of the criminal process in which the defendant is formally informed of the charges and is allowed to enter a plea.

ASCII: Acronym for the American Standard Code for Information Interchange. Pronounced Askee (e.g., ASCII is a code for representing English characters as numbers, with each letter assigned a number from 0 to 127. For example, the ASCII code for uppercase M is 77.). Most computers use ASCII codes to represent text, which makes it possible to transfer data from one computer to another.

Assault: Unlawful, intentional inflicting, or attempted inflicting, of injury upon another.

Assessment: As an LNC standard, a collection of data to support the systematic assessment of health care issues related to a case or a claim. The first step of the nursing process, during which data are gathered and examined in preparation for the second step, diagnosis.

Assigned Risk: A risk underwriters do not wish to insure but, because of state law or otherwise, must be insured. The coverage is assigned through a pool of handlers, each taking turns.

Attorney–Client Privilege: The protection of communication between the attorney and the client which is made for furnishing or obtaining professional legal advice; the privilege which allows the client to refuse to disclose and to prevent any other person from disclosing confidential communications between the client and attorney.

Attorney Work Product: Materials that are protected from discovery. It includes materials prepared by an attorney in anticipation of litigation, including private memoranda, written statements of witnesses, and mental impressions of personal recollections prepared or formed by an attorney in anticipation of litigation or for trial.

Audit Trails: The capability to identify who entered or altered data in a computer system, and in which field the information was located, as well as the date and time.

Authorization: The process by which permission is granted by the plan for a member to receive a treatment or service by a health care provider.

Autonomy: The right to self-determination and independence. Autonomy pertains to decisions individuals make to serve their interests.

AVI: Short for Audio Video Interleave, the file format for Microsoft's *Video for Windows* standard.

Award: A decision rendered by an arbitrator or a panel of arbitrators. If the parties are satisfied with the arbitrator's award, a judgment is entered.

B & B: Bowel and Bladder, as in bowel and bladder incontinence or training.

Backup and Recovery: Sometimes referred to as DBAR (disaster backup and recovery) — the necessary computer programs written to ensure that data are not lost during nightly processing or any disaster that would prevent normal computer access and function.

Backfile: A portion of a database or directory that is separate from the original file. Used as a backup for information, which may somehow become lost or deleted.

Battery: The unlawful use of violence against another.

Benchmarking: Serving as a standard of reference or comparison.

Beneficence: The ethical view that the right action is to protect the patient and to provide treatment that promotes the good of the individual.

Beyond a Reasonable Doubt: The degree of certainty required for a juror to legally find a criminal defendant guilty. It means that the proof must be so conclusive and complete that all reasonable doubts of the fact are removed from the mind of the ordinary person.

Bias: Inclination; prejudice.

Bill of Particulars: A legal document in which the plaintiff sets forth the specific negligence and damage claims.

Billable Hours: Hours worked that have a direct relationship to the project at hand.

Biomechanics: Mechanics as applied to the body and encompasses the responses of the human body to various forces.

Bit: A binary digit, i.e., either 0 or 1. The smallest storage unit for data in a computer.

Blocked Account: Placement of a conservatee's money in a bank or other financial institution, which cannot be withdrawn without court approval.

BMP: The standard bit-mapped graphics format used in the Windows environment.

Bond: A judge will require that a conservator of the estate obtain a bond to guarantee that there will be no loss to the conservatorship estate if the money is mismanaged or taken by the conservator. The bonding agency will reimburse the estate for any loss, dishonesty, or negligence. The bonding company may then sue the conservator to repay the loss.

Book of Business: The specific type(s) of insurance products an insurance company might provide; for example, a company may have a book that is comprised of 50% automobile, 40% workers' compensation, and 10% group life and health.

Boolean Logic: Consists of logical "operators," also referred to as Boolean operators (AND, OR, and NOT), which allow a searcher to create logical search statements or sets that show relationships. (Example: Meperidine OR Demerol.)

Brief: A formal written presentation of an argument that sets forth the main points with supporting precedents and evidence.

Burden of Proof: The amount of proof required to prove an element of a cause of action or an affirmative defense. In civil cases, the amount of proof required is "a preponderance of the evidence."

Byte: A group of bits sufficient to define a character. Usually represents eight bits, but ten bits are used per character for online transmission.

Capitation: A specific dollar amount for the coverage of cost of health care delivered per person. It is usually a negotiated per-capita rate paid periodically, usually monthly, to a health care provider for the delivery of services to a covered member. In most situations, the provider receives a specific amount of money each month for every member who has selected that provider as his or her primary caregiver. The provider is paid the capitation rate for each assigned member, regardless of whether or not the member receives any services from the provider during the time period.

Carrier: The company that provides the insurance.

Catastrophic Injury: Injury or illness that permanently alters an individual's functional status.

Catastrophic Loss: Loss of an extraordinarily large value.

Cause of Action: A claim in a lawsuit with specific elements that must be proven. For example, to state a cause of action for negligence, there must be sufficient proof of the four elements of negligence. The plaintiff has the burden of proof regarding these elements.

Certify: (Of a court) to issue an order allowing a class of litigants to maintain a class action; to create (a class) for purposes of a class action.

CFR: Code of Federal Regulations, contains regulations that govern nursing homes.

Chronological Chart Summary: A written document that consists of a verbatim summary of pertinent information from medical records. The summary may include the date and the page number of the referenced information.

Citation: The bibliographic information (author, title, publication, volume, date, pages) in a complete reference. Often used synonymously with the term "reference."

Claim: Used in reference to insurance, a demand by an individual or corporation to recover, under a policy of insurance, for loss that may come within that policy.

Claimant: The individual petitioning for or receiving benefits.

Claims Consultant: Person designated to represent the insurance company in investigations and negotiations in order to reach an agreement on the amount of a loss or the insurer's liability.

Claims Management: A mechanism that can substantially reduce the overall cost of claims.

Claims Processor: Carrier's employee responsible for handling claims as they are received from patients and providers.

Claims Specialist/Adjuster: The independent agent or insurance company employee who investigates claims, sets insurance reserves, and settles claims against the insured.

Client: The purchaser of services.

Clinical Pathways: A precalculated plan of routine services usually required by a patient for a given disease, based on average medical recovery outcomes.

Clinical Trials: Premarketing evaluations of a drug or medical device performed by the manufacturer to determine the safety and effectiveness of the drug or device.

CMS: Center for Medicare and Medicaid Services (formerly HCFA).

CMS 1500 (HCFA 1500): A standard claim form for submission of charges.

CNA: Certified Nursing Assistant, has completed standardized training with the goal of becoming employed in a nursing home.

Code of Ethics: An explicit statement of the primary goals and values of a profession.

Coefficient of Friction: A measurement of friction (or the degree of slipperiness) of the floor or other surface. On ice, and on wet and oily surfaces, the co-efficient of friction is low (.10). Excellent traction is at a coefficient of friction of .40 to .50 or more. "Slip resistant" is defined as a coefficient of friction (COF) of .50.

Cold Calls: A sales and marketing term used for making contact with a potential client, usually by telephone, to solicit new business.

Collaboration: As it applies to the LNC, the LNC collaborates with legal professionals and health care professionals when necessary.

Collegiality: As it applies to the LNC, the LNC shares knowledge and contributes to the development of peers, colleagues, and others.

Command Language: Instructions entered by the searcher that tell the computer retrieval program to perform specific tasks or operations. The command languages vary by vendor system, and symbols may be utilized.

Common Law: In general a body of law that develops and derives through judicial decisions, as distinguished from legislative enhancements.

Communication: The transmission and reception of information.

Comparative Negligence: A proportional division of the damages between the plaintiff and the defendant in a tort action according to their respective share of fault contributing to the injury.

Competent: Duly qualified; answering all requirements; having sufficient capacity, ability, or authority; possessing the requisite physical, mental, natural, or legal qualifications; able, adequate, sufficient, capable, legally fit.

Complaint: The original or initial pleading by which an action is commenced under codes or Rules of Civil Procedure. It is the pleading that sets forth a claim for relief.

Complex Litigation: Usually involves many parties, in numerous related cases, often in different jurisdictions, involving large numbers of documents, witnesses, and extensive discovery that will require judicial management generally assigned to the same judge.

Concept: A term used to describe a phenomenon or group of phenomena.

Concept Analysis: The method for examining attributes and characteristics of a concept as a foundation for theory development.

Concept Derivation: A process in which a previously defined concept from a parent field is transposed to a new field, then redefined as a new concept in the new field.

Conceptual Framework: A categorization or classification of a mental image.

Conciliation: Adjustment and settlement of a dispute in a friendly, non-antagonistic manner.

Concordance: An index showing the context in which words occur.

Confidentiality: The duty to keep private all information provided by a client or acquired from other sources before, during, and after the course of the professional relationship. This includes information from the client's medical records.

Conflict of Interest: A situation where one person has information that may potentially be used to influence a case and cause harm, injury, or prejudice to the client.

Connect Time: The time between log-on to a database and/or termination. It is one of the primary components of online searching costs.

Conservatee: A person who a judge has deemed unable to care for himself or herself or to manage financial affairs and for whom a conservator is appointed.

Conservator: Either an organization or a person whom the court appoints to handle either the financial or personal affairs of an individual or both, as a result of the individual being deemed incompetent.

Conservator of the Estate: An organization or person whom the court appoints to handle the financial affairs of an individual, as a result of that individual (conservatee) having been deemed unable to do so.

Conservator of the Person: A person or organization whom the court appoints to handle the personal care and protection of a person whom a judge has decided is unable to do so (conservatee).

Consulting or Reviewing Expert: An expert offering an opinion on a particular subject, but not expected to testify at trial.

Consumer Expectation Test: Consumers of a product may have reasonable, widely accepted minimum expectations about the circumstances under which it should perform safely.

Contingency Fee: A fee arrangement in which the attorney receives a percentage of the plaintiff's settlement or verdict.

Contract: Voluntary agreement that creates legally binding responsibilities for the parties named in it to facilitate predetermined amount or type of service or work to be performed for a specific reason or period of time.

Contractor: One who contracts to perform a work for another party; the person who retains the control of the means, method, and manner of the project result.

Contributory Negligence: Negligent conduct by the plaintiff that contributed to his or her injury.

Controlled Vocabulary: An authorized listing of subject heading or descriptor strings used by indexers to assign subject terminology to items described in records in a database or in files. May also be referred to as a thesaurus. (An example is the extensive list of MeSH for MEDLINE.)

Co-Payment: A sharing in the cost of certain covered expenses on the part of the insured on a percentage basis.

Coverage: The assurance against losses provided under the terms of a policy of insurance. It is used synonymously with the term insurance or protection.

CPT (Current Procedural Terminology): A systematic listing of descriptive terms and corresponding 5-digit codes for reporting services and procedures performed by medical providers.

Credentialing: A process of review to approve a provider who applies for a contract with a health plan.

Credibility: Worthy of belief must be preceded by establishment of competency (legally fit to testify).

Crime: Performance of an act which is forbidden by law or the omission of an act required by law.

Criteria: Variables known to be relevant, measurable indicators of the standards of clinical nursing practice.

Cross-Jurisdictional Advocacy: An LNC who manages care interventions for clients in differing jurisdictions by bridging the paradigms of law and health care for the purpose of reducing conflict and producing change.

Culture Brokering: The act of bridging, linking, or mediating between groups or persons of differing cultural backgrounds for the purpose of reducing conflict or producing change.

Curriculum Vitae: A more formal, academically oriented resume that includes presentations, publications, professional associations, and continuing education, as well as work experience.

Damage Mitigation: Actions or steps that reduce or limit the damage resulting from an event.

Damages: A pecuniary compensation or indemnity, which may be recovered in the courts by any person who has suffered loss, detriment, or injury, whether to his person, property, or rights, through the unlawful act or omission or negligence of another. A sum of money awarded to a person injured by the tort of another.

Database: An organized collection of data in electronic form, generally related by subject, concept, or idea. (Examples: MEDLINE, TOXLINE, CHEMLINE.)

Declarant: A person who makes a declaration; one who makes a sworn statement.

Declaration of Helsinki: International guidelines for investigators conducting biomedical research involving human subjects. Recommendations include procedures to ensure subject safety in clinical trials. Adopted by the 18th World Medical Assembly, Helsinki, 1964.

Deductible: A pre-set amount which each insured must pay toward the cost of treatment before benefits go into effect.

Defective Design: A drug or device that is not reasonably safe for its intended use or a use that can be reasonably anticipated.

Defective Manufacture: A product that is not reasonably safe as a result of the manner in which it is manufactured and the defect existed when the product left the manufacturer's control.

Defendant: The person or entity against which a lawsuit is brought.

Defense Client: Any of the entities that may be referred to as the defense client of the LNC. The LNC may work with one or more entities in assisting the defense in a professional liability case. These entities may include the HCPD, the defense attorney, an insurance company, a third-party administrator, or a self-insured company.

Defense Team Member: The individuals working on behalf of the defense. The team may include the trial attorney, associate attorneys, LNCs, expert witnesses, and other consultants.

Delta V: Change in velocity; the delta v is the difference between the speed just prior to the impact, and the speed immediately after the impact. A low velocity motor vehicle crash is one with a delta v approximately 10 mph or less. The greater the delta v, the greater the forces, and the greater the likelihood of severe injury. An accident reconstructionist will calculate the delta v(s) in a collision.

Demand Letter: A letter to the insurance company by the plaintiff's attorney demanding settlement of the case.

Demonstrative Evidence: Evidence in the form of objects (as maps, diagrams, or models) that has in itself no probative value but is used to illustrate and clarify the factual matter at issue broadly.

Deposition: Pretrial sworn testimony of parties or other witnesses to elicit information about the claims and defenses. Deposition testimony may be used for various purposes at trial (e.g., to impeach a witness). Depositions are conducted outside of the courtroom, usually at a law firm.

Derivative Claim: The claim of an injured party's spouse, child, or parent for damages resulting to them which may include one or more of the following: loss of companionship, loss of services, and expenses incurred.

Descriptor: A word or phrase used to describe a subject, concept, or idea.

Designated Nonparty: A party deemed responsible for all or part of damages, which were not named in the suit.

Diagnosis: The second step of the nursing process, during which data are analyzed and pulled together for the purpose of identifying and describing health status (strengths, and actual and potential health problems).

Digitalization: The process of making a two-dimensional or three-dimensional exhibit into a computer file format that can then be stored and retrieved from a disk on a computer. This allows easy access, quick retrieval, and simplified method of transporting exhibits.

Disbursements: Attorney's out-of-pocket expenses incurred on behalf of a specific case (e.g., expert witness fees or copying charges for medical records).

Disclosure: Communication of information regarding the results of a diagnostic test, medical treatment, or surgical intervention.

Discoverable: That which can be brought into discovery, pre-trial acquisition of knowledge from opposing side.

Discovery: Pre-trial devices that can be used by one party to obtain facts and information about the case from the other party in order to assist the party's preparation for trial.

Disk: A circular plate coated with magnetic material used to store digital or machine-readable data. May be "hard" or "floppy."

Docket: A formal record, entered in brief, of the proceedings in a court of justice. A book containing an entry in brief of all the important acts done in court in the conduct of each case, from the inception to its conclusion.

Docket Control Order: Order from a judge outlining deadlines for discovery etc.

Domains: Territories that shape practice.

Do-Not-Resuscitate Order (DNR): An order by a physician(s), following discussion with and informed consent by a legally competent patient or the patient's legal representative, which orders health care providers NOT to perform resuscitation procedures on this patient when these procedures are necessary for sustaining the patient's life; a DNR order is frequently initiated by the patient's living will or the legal representative's medical power of attorney.

Dose–Response: The process of quantifying the relationship between the level of exposure and increased risk of adverse effects such as cancer.

Downloading: The practice of copying data in electronic form on a computer which may then be manipulated or stored permanently on a personal computer.

DRG (Diagnosis Related Group): A classification scheme whose patient types are defined by patient's diagnoses or procedures and, in some cases, by the patient's age or discharge status.

DRI: Defense Research Institute, a professional organization of attorneys primarily employed in the defense of claims.

Drug Formulary: A listing of medications that are preferred for use by the health plan. An "open" or "voluntary" formulary will cover both formulary and non-formulary drugs, and a "closed" formulary covers only those drugs in the formulary. The patient must pay for any drugs purchased by the patient not listed on a closed formulary, even if the ordering physician specifies the drug and even when no generic or alternative form exists.

Duty: An action or observation that is expected to occur once a relationship has been established between two people, such as health care provider and patient.

DVERT: Domestic Violence Emergency Response Team.

E/M (Evaluation and Management): CPT codes that represent services (e.g., office, emergency department, inpatient visits) that are the most frequently performed by medical providers.

Employee: One who is engaged in paid services for another.

Entrepreneur: One who organizes, manages, and assumes the risks of a business or enterprise.

EPO: Managed Care Organization known as the Exclusive Provider Organization. In this plan, the providers are exclusive to the plan and its membership.

ERISA: Employee Retirement Income Security Act of 1974, a law designed to protect the rights of employees who receive employer-provided benefits such as pensions, deferred retirement income, and health care benefits such as HMOs, long-term and short-term disability coverage.

Errata Sheet: A document that shows corrections to the text of the deposition.

Ethics: The systematic investigation of questions about right and wrong. Ethics involves critical analysis of different views of right and wrong, with particular attention paid to the underlying values of each view, its coherence and consistency, and its implications in actual situations. As it applies to the LNC, the ANA Code for Nurses with Interpretive Statements, and the AALNC Code of Ethics guide for the LNC.

Euthanasia: The act, by commission or omission, of painlessly ending the life of persons suffering from incurable and distressing disease as an act of mercy.

Evaluation: The fifth step of the nursing process, during which the extent of goal achievement is determined; each of the previous four steps is analyzed to identify factors that enhanced or hindered progress, and the plan of care is modified or terminated as indicated.

Excess (Insurance) Coverage: Insurance that provides coverage when damages reach a certain level. This is also the function of umbrella coverage. Excess coverage may involve an additional insurance carrier.

Exclusions: Noted services or conditions that the policy will not cover.

Exemplary Damages: Also known as punitive damages, an award made to the plaintiff for the purpose of punishing the defendant when oppressive, malicious, or fraudulent conduct is involved.

Exhibit: A document or object produced and identified in court as evidence; a document labeled with an identifying mark (as a number or letter) and appended to a writing (as a brief) to which it is relevant; something exhibited; an act or instance of exhibiting.

Expert: A person possessing the knowledge, skills, and expertise concerning a particular subject who is capable of rendering an opinion.

Expert Fact Witness: One who by virtue of special knowledge, skill, training, or experience is qualified to provide testimony to aid the fact finder in matters that exceed the common knowledge of ordinary people, but does not offer opinions on the standard of care.

Expert Witness: A witness (as a medical specialist) who by virtue of special knowledge, skill, training, or experience is qualified to provide testimony to aid the fact finder in matters that exceed the common knowledge of ordinary people.

Experience: The history of injuries or accidents, which is used for substantiating the setting of a current premium amount.

Exposure: The maximum amount of money that an insurer could spend on one claim (often coincided with the policy limit).

External Standards: Standards that stem from sources such as state nurse practice acts, state boards of nursing (federal organizations [e.g., Joint Commission for Accreditation of Healthcare Organizations, JCAHO], professional nursing organizations [e.g., American Nursing Association]), nursing literature, and continuing education programs.

Fabricate: To invent; to devise falsely.

Fact Witness: One who is not named as a defendant in a lawsuit who has knowledge of events that have occurred.

Federal Rules of Civil Procedure: Body of procedural rules that govern all civil actions in U.S. District Courts and after which most of the states have modeled their own rules of procedure.

Field: An area of a unit record used to store a defined category of data.

Field Case Management: Case management services provided face-to-face through visits with the client at home, in an inpatient setting, and at treatment provider's offices.

File: A collection of related records. The term is often used as a synonym for database. Sometimes used to refer to part of a database structure.

Five Cs of Communication: Five elements that represent effective communication skills: clear, concise, complete, cohesive, and courteous.

Floppy Disk: A thin, flexible disk with magnetic surfaces that is used to store computer programs and data.

Food and Drug Administration (FDA): United States government agency established for the provision of regulations and guidelines for compliance with the Food, Drug and Cosmetic Act.

Forensic Science: Science applied to answering legal questions by the examination, evaluation, and exploration of evidence.

Foreseeability: The implication that the damages must be the foreseeable, or reasonably anticipated, result of substandard practice of the defendant health care provider.

Free Text: A method by which a searcher may select the terms on which searching will be performed without the requirement of matching them to a controlled vocabulary list or thesaurus. Also referred to as "text words."

G: This is the unit of measurement of a load caused by acceleration or deceleration. One G is the "force" that holds us onto the Earth (the "force" of gravity, hence the "G"). A person on a roller coaster experiences more than one G. A jet pilot might experience as much as 6 Gs in a turn. Acceleration/deceleration in an accident subjects the occupants to increased Gs. The Gs in a motor vehicle collision are calculated by an accident reconstructionist.

Gatekeeper: The secretary, paralegal, or other personnel who take and screen calls for the professional.

General Acceptance Test: A standard for the admissibility of expert testimony. Expert testimony based on a scientific technique is inadmissible unless the relevant scientific community has accepted the technique as reliable.

General Damages: Also referred to as noneconomic damages. General damages are nonpecuniary damages recognized as compensable, but on which the law is unable to place a dollar amount. Examples of general damages are "pain and suffering" and "loss of consortium."

Gigabyte: The largest unit of mass storage used in common parlance. One gigabyte is equal to 1000 megabytes, 1 billion bytes, or 500,000 pages of information. Used in huge computer storage depots by major vendors of on-line databases.

Gopher: A service that provides a menu-like interface to voluminous amounts of information available on the Internet. The data in "Gopher space" may be efficiently browsed using a Gopher client.

Grand Jury: A body of people randomly selected in a manner similar to trial jurors whose purpose is to investigate and inform on crimes committed within its jurisdiction and to accuse (indict) persons of crimes when it has discovered sufficient evidence to warrant holding a person for trial.

Guardian: A person lawfully invested with the power, and charged with the duty, of taking care of and managing the property and rights of another person, who, for defect of age, understanding, or self-control, is considered incapable of administering his or her own affairs.

Guardianship: A court proceeding in which a judge appoints an individual to care for a person under the age of 18 and/or manage the estate.

Guidelines: A process of client care management that has the potential of improving the quality of clinical and consumer decision-making; includes assessment and diagnosis, planning, intervention, evaluation, and outcome.

Hard Disk: A rigid storage device coated with a magnetic surface on which computer programs and data may be stored.

Hardware: The equipment and computers used in data storage and processing systems.

HCFA: Health Care Finance Administration, involved in regulating nursing homes (now Centers for Medicare & Medicaid Services).

HCPCS (HCFA Common Procedural Coding System): A uniform method for health care providers and medical suppliers to report professional services, procedures, and supplies.

Health Care Provider Defendants: Any of the individuals involved in providing care for the plaintiff who are alleged to have fallen below the standard of care, resulting in the claimed damages. These defendants may include physicians, nurses, therapists, pharmacists, and similar care providers.

Health Maintenance Organization (HMO): Groups of participating health care providers (physicians, hospitals, clinics) that provide medical services to enrolled members of group health insurance plan.

HIPAA: The Health Insurance Portability and Accountability Act of 1996 establishes privacy and security standards to protect a patient's health care information. In December 2000, the Department of Health and Human Services issued final regulations governing privacy of this information under HIPPA.

Hired Gun: Per Webster, "a person hired to handle a difficult problem." In the legal arena, a person who may be perceived as someone who will provide any desired testimony for a price.

Hits: See Postings.

HMO: Health Maintenance Organization. This type plan is based on the premise of preventative medicine and management of dollars spent for the health care benefits of its members.

HTML: Short for HyperText Markup Language, the authoring language used to create documents on the World Wide Web. HTML defines the structure and layout of a Web document by using a variety of tags and attributes.

Hypermedia: Similar in concept to hypertext except that it also includes multimedia capabilities such as sounds and graphics related to the subject.

Hypertext: A hypertext document contains live links to related pieces of information (e.g., in a hypertext document about photography there may be a link or button from the word camera which, when pressed, sends the reader to another document that includes both terms and concepts).

ICD-9CM (International Classification of Diseases and Clinical Modification): Required by Medicare Part B, three-digit codes referring to a disease with additional number of up to two decimal places for specificity.

ID Code: A code issued by a vendor to individual users for identification.

IDEX: A company specializing in retrieving testimony of experts, available to the defense bar.

IDT: Interdisciplinary Team, consists of the nurse, physician, and therapists.

Impeachment: To call into question the veracity of the witness by presenting information which conflicts with testimony.

Implementation: As an LNC standard, implementation of the plan of action.

In Camera: To the judge only.

***In Vitro* Study:** "In glass;" a biologic or biochemical process occurring outside a living organism.

***In Vivo* Study:** "In life;" a biologic or biochemical process occurring within a living organism.

Incident: A broad term used to describe any occurrence that is not consistent with routine hospital activities.

Incompetency: A relative term which may be employed as meaning disqualification, inability, or incapacity, and it can refer to lack of legal qualifications or fitness to discharge the required duty and to show want of physical or intellectual or moral fitness.

Independent/Insurance Medical Examination: An examination requested by the carrier to determine appropriateness of medical care to date, causality of work/accident-related injury, length of disability, and work status.

Independent Contractor: Legal nurse consultant who works independently as a consultant or testifying expert, not as an employee.

Indictment: A formal accusation from a grand jury of a criminal offense made against a person.

Individual Retirement Account (IRA): Individuals with earned income are permitted, under certain circumstances, to set aside a limited amount of such income per year for a retirement account. The amount so set aside can be deducted by the taxpayer and is subject to income tax only upon withdrawal. The Internal Revenue Code limits the amount of this contribution that can be deducted for adjusted gross income depending upon (1) whether the taxpayer or spouse is an active participant in an employer-provided qualified retirement plan and (2) the magnitude of the taxpayer's adjusted gross income before the IRA contribution is considered. I.R.C. § 219.

Informed Consent: The process of disclosure of information, usually regarding proposed medical or surgical treatment, by health care professionals to a competent patient who is presumed to have the capacity to understand the information, and a decision by that patient based on the information received.

Informed Consent Form: A document that outlines and fully explains a research study that includes required elements. The form is to be approved, by the IRB designated for the particular jurisdiction of study location and investigator, prior to presentation to the potential study participant. The study subject is to read, sign, and date this form prior to performance of designated study procedures, to indicate acceptance to voluntarily participate in the study. The subject is considered as enrolled into a study at the time the consent form is signed and dated by the participant.

Inherent Risk: A risk of a complication or condition that is existent in and inseparable from the medical procedure or treatment.

Institutional Review Board (IRB): A committee that reviews clinical study protocols, informed consent documents, and other relevant study materials to evaluate that the protection of the rights and welfare of human study subjects is maintained.

Insurance: A contract for the provision of coverage for services, injuries, or damages as set forth in the conditions, types, and terms of the contract.

Insurer: The party agreeing to reimburse another party for loss by designated contingencies.

Integrity: The distinctive element of being honest; the soundness or moral principle and character, as shown by one person dealing with others in the making and performance of contracts and fidelity and honesty in the discharge of trusts. Firm adherence to a code, especially moral or artistic.

Intellectual Property: Refers to copyrights, trademarks, and patents.

Intensity of Service/Severity of Illness: Also referred to as IS/SI, this is a description of how sick a patient is and the level of health care services the patient requires.

Interfacing: The ability to send and/or receive information from one computer system to another.

Internal Standards: Institutional standards that stem from internal sources such as policies and procedures, professional job descriptions, or internal educational materials.

Interrogatories: A set or series of written questions about the case submitted by one party to the other party or witness. The answers to the interrogatories are usually given under oath, i.e., the person answering the questions signs a sworn statement that the answers are true.

Internet: The name given to the worldwide collection of data networks (an Internet or Internet work) which all speak the TCP/IP network protocol, or language.

Internet Work: A collection of two or more distinct networks joined together typically using a router to form a larger "network of networks."

Intrapreneur: A nurse who creates innovation within the health care organization through the introduction of a new product, a different service, or simply a new way of doing something.

IPA: Individual Practice Association. Physicians contract with one or more specific plans and provide services to patients for an agreed-upon rate, and bill the plan on a fee-for-service basis.

Job Analysis: Process of looking at a job to determine physical requirements needed to perform the essential functions of the job.

JPEG: Short for Joint Photographic Experts Group, and pronounced jay-peg, JPEG is a glossy data compression technique for color images. Although it can reduce file sizes to about 5% of their normal size, some detail is lost in the compression.

Justice: The principle of ethics that involves the obligation to be fair to all persons. Distributive justice is the allocation of a good as fairly as possible. The good of health care is distributed on the basis of need, which means that some people will get more than others because their needs are greater.

Kantianism: This view holds that consequences do not make an action right or wrong. The moral rightness of a person's actions is dependent upon whether or not those actions uphold a principle, regardless of outcome.

Keogh Plan: A designation for retirement plans available to self-employed tax-payers. Such plans extend to the self-employed tax benefits similar to those available to employees under qualified pension and profit sharing plans. Yearly contributions to the plan (up to a certain amount) are tax deductible.

Key Words: Single words or terms of importance in an article drawn from titles, abstracts, subject headings, or any part of a record which is used for indexing.

Kilobyte: The most common memory storage unit quoted. It is 1000 bytes, or approximately one half page of single-spaced, printed material.

Leadership: The office, position, or capacity of a leader who gives guidance and has the ability to lead or exert authority.

Learned Intermediary: The person with knowledge who prescribes the drug to the patient.

Learned Treatises: Documents that include standards, methods, and principles of care, typically textbooks.

Legal Causation: Causation in fact and foreseeability or the "but for" test. (See Proximate Cause.)

Legal Writing: Writing pertaining to, or intended to be used in, the legal process; in style and execution it need not differ from other writing.

Liability: Any legally enforceable obligation. In insurance, this usually is associated with a monetary value.

Liberty Interest: An interest recognized as protected by the due process clauses of state and federal constitutions.

Lien: A right or claim against an asset (e.g., Medicare may have a right to reimbursement of health care benefits it paid for treatment of the injury giving rise to the lawsuit from the damages recovered in that lawsuit).

Life-Sustaining Medical Treatment: Medical treatment which sustains a person's life functions, including respiratory and cardiopulmonary functions, preventing the person's body from reaching that state where it is declared legally dead.

Limits: The amount the payer covers.

Litigation: A lawsuit, legal action; includes all proceedings therein. Contest in a court of law for the purpose of enforcing a right or seeking a remedy. A judicial contest, a judicial controversy, a suit at law.

Living Will: A document executed by a competent person that governs the withholding or withdrawal of life-sustaining treatment from an individual in the event of an incurable or irreversible condition that will cause death within a relatively short time, and when such person is no longer able to make decisions regarding his or her medical treatment.

Logical Operators: Also called Boolean operators (see Boolean Logic).

Loss Control: An application of techniques that is designed to minimize loss in a cost-effective manner.

Loss of Chance: A theory of recovery in medical malpractice cases for a patient's loss of chance of survival or loss of chance of a better recovery. This theory applies where the patient is suffering from a preexisting injury or illness that is aggravated by the alleged negligence of the health care provider to the extent that (1) the patient dies, when without negligence there might have been a substantial chance of survival; or (2) the patient survives, but the actual recovery is substantially less than it might have been absent the alleged malpractice.

Loss of Consortium: A claim brought by the spouse of an injured party for loss of the benefits of companionship caused by the injuries suffered in the accident.

Loss Prevention: A program that seeks to reduce or eliminate the chance of loss or the potential severity of a loss.

Mainframe: A very large computer that has many megabytes in the central processing unit, or CPU. Because it can store many gigabytes of disk memory, it may act as a host computer, which controls searches from instructions or commands from many remote terminals.

Malpractice: Misconduct, negligence, or failure to properly perform duties according to professional standards of care.

Marginalization: Peripheralization, to be situated on the border or edge so that there are memberships in dual domains.

Markup: See Annotation.

Mass Tort: A civil wrong that injures many people. Examples include toxic emissions from a factory, the crash of a commercial airliner, and contamination from an industrial waste-disposal site.

Material Risk: A risk that, if the patient were informed about it, could influence his or her decision to consent to the proposed treatment or procedure.

MCO: Managed Care Organization such as an HMO, EPO, IPA, or PPO. All types of MCOs utilize health care cost containment methods such as providing care within a specific network of providers and facilities, utilization management, and case management.

MDS: Minimum Data Set, a national tool used to assess the resident's needs and to determine reimbursement.

Mediation: A problem-solving process involving a neutral third party who facilitates the parties in reaching a resolution but lacks authority to render a decision.

Mediator: A neutral third party who assists the parties in negotiating a compromise.

Medical Review Panel Process: Requires the submission of a medical malpractice claim to a medical review panel for its opinion prior to the institution of the judicial action.

Megabyte: One million bytes, 1000 kilobytes, or 500 pages of data.

Mentor: A wise legal advisor, trusted teacher, or guide.

Middle Range Theory: Theories that are more limited in scope, with less abstraction, and that reflect practice.

Mitigation of Damages: Claim that plaintiff has responsibility to minimize the adverse impact of his injury and, therefore, his failure to do so should reduce the amount awarded to him by the damages that would have been avoided had he done so. This claim is typically used in the context of a defendant's assertion that plaintiff's award should be reduced by a prior act/omission of plaintiff (e.g., failure to wear a seat belt) because it would have lessened the injury, or because a treatment (e.g., a medicine, physical therapy, or a surgical procedure) is available to cure plaintiff's condition or diminish the effects of it.

Model: A mental image, a conceptualization of phenomena.

Model Cases: The process of defining and identifying exemplars to illustrate a concept.

Modem: Acronym for Modulator–Demodulator. It is a device that allows a terminal to interface with the telecommunications network and converts the electrical or digital signals of a terminal.

Morality: Refers to the common societal conceptions of what is right and what is wrong. Our morality and morals are reflected in how we live, the decisions we make, and what we hold as valuable.

Motion: An application to a court or judge for the purpose of obtaining a rule or order direction for some act to be done in favor of the applicant.

Motion in Limine: A pretrial motion that requests the court to issue an interlocutory order which prevents an opposing party from introducing or referring to potentially irrelevant, prejudicial, or otherwise inadmissible evidence until the court has finally ruled on its admissibility.

MPEG1: Short for Moving Picture Experts Group, and pronounced m-peg, The term also refers to the family of digital video compression standards and file formats developed by the group. MPEG generally produces better-quality video than competing formats, such as *Video for Windows, Indeo,* and *Quick-Time.* MPEG files can be decoded by special hardware or by software.

NANDA: North American Nursing Diagnosis Association, an organization involved in developing and promoting the use of nursing diagnoses.

Native Resolution: In referring to a projector's resolution, it is common to refer to "true" or "native" resolution. If a projector's native resolution is 800 × 600, that means that the actual number of physical pixels on the display device is 800 × 600. The projector needs to match the resolution of the computer. Resolution is usually quoted in two numbers where the first number refers to the number of pixels from side to side across the screen and the second number refers to the number of pixels vertically from top to bottom.

Natural Language: A language that uses natural speech (words) rather than symbols.

NCQA: The National Committee for Quality Assurance. It is an independent, non-profit organization that evaluates health care coverage provided by insurers and managed care organizations by reviewing the clinical outcomes of its members, contracting practices, and member satisfaction surveys. Successful accreditation by the NCQA is considered a standard by which MCOs can be compared. Accreditation also implies a higher standard of service.

NEC (Not Elsewhere Classifiable): Indicates that the condition specified does not have a separate more specific listing. Used only in Volume 2 of the ICD-9.

Negligence: Negligence is a failure to act as an ordinary prudent person or "reasonable man" would do under similar circumstances. There are four elements of negligence that must be proved in order for there to be a viable medical malpractice claim.

1. A duty must be owed to the patient. This duty usually occurs when the health care provider accepts responsibility for the care and treatment of that patient.

2. The breach of duty or standard of care by the professional. The standard of care for that type of specialty and that particular type of treatment must be determined to see if there has been an act of omission or commission that has caused damage to the patient.

3. Proximate cause/or causal connection must be evident between the breach of duty and the harm or damages that have occurred to the patient/plaintiff.
4. Damages or injuries suffered by the plaintiff. Damages or injuries can take the form of any of the following, including but not limited to loss of love and affection; loss of nurturance, pain, and suffering; mental anguish; emotional distress; loss of chance of survival; disfigurement; past, present, and future medical expenses; past, present, and future loss of wages; premature death; and loss of enjoyment of life.

Netiquette: Etiquette (manners) on the Internet.

Network: A collection of computers linked together by a physical medium (wires, microwaves, etc.) for transmission of data between computers or "nodes" on the network.

Network Protocol: The set of rules or "language" used by computers on a network to communicate. (Examples: Novell IPX, Appletalk, and TCP/IP.)

Networking: Meeting and establishing a network of other like professionals to enhance information exchange and business relationships.

NIC: Nursing Interventions Classification, a method of placing interventions in taxonomy.

NOC: Nursing Outcomes Classification, a method of placing outcomes in a taxonomy.

Nonbillable Hours: Hours worked that do not directly relate to the client/customer's project; hours spent in administrative or other support areas of a business project.

Nonparty Witness: A witness who is not a plaintiff or defendant or employee or agent of a plaintiff or defendant.

NOS (Not Otherwise Specified): Used only when the available information does not permit assignment to a more specific code. Used only in Volume 1 of the ICD-9.

Notice of Intent: A document sent to a health care facility that puts that facility on notice that a party has initiated legal action against the facility.

NPA: Nursing Practice Act.

Nursing Process: An organized, systematic method of giving individualized nursing care that focuses on identifying and treating unique responses of individuals or groups to actual or potential alterations in health.

Objection (form, hearsay, privilege): Legal format for not allowing testimony into evidence based on various legal reasons such as form of question, hearsay, or privilege.

OBRA: Omnibus Budget Reconciliation Act of 1987, changed the standard of care in nursing homes by defining minimum standards.

Occupant Kinematics: The movement of the occupants of a vehicle due to the motor vehicle collision.

Off-Line Printing: Printed records generated at the mainframe after the user has logged off the computer system.

Off-Line Searching: Computer processing of a search after the user has entered the appropriate strategy and has logged off the system.

Ombudsman: An official or semiofficial office or person to which people may come with grievances connected with the government. The ombudsman represents the citizen before the government.

Online: The term describes the status of a searcher conversing with the host computer in the interactive mode.

Open Account: An account that has not been finally settled or closed, but is still running or open to future adjustment or liquidation. Open account, in legal as well as in ordinary language, means indebtedness subject to future adjustment, and which may be reduced or modified by proof.

Opt-Out: After a class action is certified, a deadline is set, typically by the court, as to when one may voluntarily decide to not participate in a class action; after the date passes, plaintiffs who have not opted-out will be bound by the decisions of the court.

Ostensible Authority: Ostensible authority is a doctrine of law whereby a hospital is liable for the negligence of an independent contractor if the patient has a rational basis to believe that the independent contractor is a hospital employee, for example, a physician in the emergency department.

Outcome: Result of medical treatment and medical case management services. These should be measurable.

Outcome Identification: As an LNC standard, the identification of desired activities as related to the health care issues of a case or claim.

Paradigm: The body of values, commitment, beliefs, and knowledge shared by members of a profession.

Paralegal: A person qualified by education, training, or work experience is employed by an attorney and performs specifically delegated substantive legal work for which a lawyer is responsible.

Partnership: A business owned by two or more persons that is not organized as a corporation. For income tax purposes, a partnership includes a syndicate, group, pool, or joint venture, as well as ordinary partnerships. Partnerships are treated as a conduit and are, therefore, not subject to taxation. The various items of partnership income, gains and losses, etc. flow through to the individual partners and are reported on their personal income tax returns.

Password: A unique set of characters assigned to a user for security purposes to grant access to specific databases.

Paternalism: An extension of beneficence. Paternalism is the view that the professional understand the patient's best interests better than the patient does and is entitled to act in behalf of the patient's well-being even when the patient does not agree.

Pathognomic: Characteristic or indicative of a disease.

Payroll Tax: A type of tax that is collected by deduction from an employee's wages. Federal, state, and half of the Social Security tax are paid by employees, with the Social Security tax matched by the employer.

PDF: Short for Portable Document Format, a file format developed by Adobe Systems. PDF captures formatting information from a variety of desktop publishing applications, making it possible to send formatted documents and have them appear on the recipient's monitor or printer as they were intended.

Peer-Reviewed: A process used by professions for monitoring and regulating member practice.

Percentile: Group of fees arranged in sequence from highest to lowest, which results in a range, that when containing 100% of the fees received, the 80th and 90th percentile fees would be the actual fees which are higher than (or equal to) 80 or 90% of all fees in the range, respectively.

Performance Appraisal: Evaluation of the practice of the LNC in relation to professional standards and relevant statutes and regulations.

Persistent Vegetative State: Denoting especially an enduring state of grossly impaired consciousness, as after severe head trauma or brain disease, in which an individual is incapable of voluntary or purposeful acts and only responds reflexively to painful stimuli.

PIP (Personal Injury Protection): Coverage by the client's own auto insurance carrier for medical expenses. Dictated by state auto law and amount of coverage purchased.

Plaintiff: A person who brings an action; the person who complains or sues in a civil action and is so named on the record. A person who seeks remedial relief for an injury to rights; it designates a complainant.

Planning: The third step of the nursing process. In this step, specific measures are identified to put into action based upon the initial assessment.

Pleadings: The formal allegations by the parties of their respective claims and defenses. Under rules of civil procedure, the pleadings consist of a complaint, an answer, a reply to counterclaim, and a third-party complaint and third-party answer.

PMPM: Per member per month. The formula by which utilization management calculates average utilization and cost for each member of the plan.

Postings: The number of citations or references retrieved as a result of a search. Synonymous with "hits."

Power of Attorney: An instrument in writing whereby one person, as principal, appoints another as his agent and confers authority to perform certain specified acts or kinds of acts on behalf of principal.

PowerPoint: A Microsoft slide presentation software program.

PPO: Preferred Provider Organization. Members of this type plan receive benefits at a discounted rate as long as they utilize only the providers who have a contract with the plan.

PPS (Prospective Payment System): A payment system, such as DRGs, that pays on historical data of case mix and regional differences.

Premium: The amount of money paid to an insurer in return for insurance coverage.

Preponderance of the Evidence: A standard of proof that is more probable than not; just over 50% of the evidence favors the party.

Principal Investigator (PI): An individual, usually a physician, with appropriate qualifications (eligibility usually evaluated and determined by an IRB and/or pharmaceutical sponsor) who is responsible for the research study trial conduct.

Probable Cause: Standard used to determine if a crime has been committed and if there is sufficient evidence to believe a specific individual committed it.

Probate Court: The department of each county's superior court that deals with probate: conservatorships, guardianships, and the estates of people who have died.

Procedure Creep: Billing for a higher level of service than provided; see Upcoding.

Procedures: A series of recommended actions for the completion of a specific task or function. Procedures may be either specific to an institution or applicable across settings.

Process Server: One who serves papers on parties.

Product Liability: Concept in the law holding a manufacturer responsible for the article placed on the market.

Professional Code of Ethics: Rules that govern the conduct of an organization and its members.

Profit and Loss: The gain or loss arising from goods bought or sold, or from carrying on any other business, the former of which, in bookkeeping, is placed on the creditor's side; the later on the debtor's side.

Properties of the Nursing Process: Purposeful, systematic, dynamic, interactive, and flexible.

Provider: The party providing services and supplies to the beneficiary.

Proximate Cause: An act or omission that was a substantial factor in bringing about or failing to prevent an injury.

Punitive Damages: Also known as exemplary damages. Punitive damages exceed the amount intended to make the plaintiff whole. Punitive damages are awarded with the intent to punish the defendant, to set an example, and to deter future behavior considered "outrageous." Most jurisdictions determine if punitive damages can be awarded and often set a cap on the amount of punitive damages that can be awarded.

Qualification: Quality or circumstance that is legally or inherently necessary to perform a function.

Qualities and Traits: Characteristics that personify the behaviors of an individual.

Quality Assurance: Ongoing program that objectively and systematically monitors and evaluates quality and resolves identified problems.

Quality Improvement: Focuses on processes or systems that contribute to or distract from outcomes.

Quality of Practice: Evaluation of the quality and effectiveness of practice.

RAI: Resident Assessment Instrument, consists of the MDS, RAPS, and the care plan.

RAP: Resident Assessment Protocol, defines the problems that were identified through the use of the MDS.

Rating: The quantifying of an insured or group's activity (experience).

Reader-Friendly Writing: Writing that is tailored to the audience and the purpose, that attempts to minimize the effort required by the reader; typically characterized by brevity, clarity, simplicity, and structure.

Records: Groups of related elements that, when handled as units, make up files.

Redaction: The act of deleting identifying information, as in "redacting the names of patients."

Refereed Journal: A professional journal that publishes material only after comprehensive review by the author's peers.

Referral: The process of sending a member to a second care provider for a consultation, second opinion, or further diagnosis and treatment of an existing condition.

Reflective Reaction: Incorporates thought and action with reflection to analyze actions.

Request for Admissions: Written statements of fact concerning the case that are submitted to an adverse party and which that party is required to admit or deny; those statements that are admitted will be treated by the court as having been established and need not be proven at trial.

Request for Production: A formal written request compelling a party to produce materials subject to discovery rules.

Reserves: Monies set aside by the insurance company for the future expenditures on a claim based on an educated projection.

Res Ipsa Loquitur: Latin for "the thing speaks for itself"; the mere facts provide information supporting negligence.

Resource Management: As it applies to the LNC, the LNC selects expert assistance on the needs of the case or the claim.

Respondeat Superior: Latin for "let the superior make answer"; employer liability for employee's wrongful actions within the scope of employment.

Restatement (Third) Tort Products Liability Section 6: A statement that reflects that a prescription drug or medical device is not reasonably safe due to defective design if the foreseeable risks of harm posed by the drug or medical device are sufficiently great in relation to its foreseeable therapeutic benefits that reasonable health care providers, knowing of such foreseeable risks and therapeutic benefits, would not prescribe the drug or medical device for any class of patients.

Retainer: The act of withholding what one has in one's own hands by virtue of some right. In the practice of law, when a client hires an attorney to represent him, the client is said to have retained the attorney. This act of employment is called the retainer.

Risk: A chance of loss. Risk is a variation in possible outcomes that exist in any given situation or event. Risk may include two categories: (1) objective variations that exist in nature and that are the same for all individuals facing the same situation and (2) subjective — an individual's estimation of the objective risk.

Risk Management: A process that identifies, evaluates, and takes corrective action against potential or actual risks to patients, visitors, employees, or property.

RUG (Resource Utilization Group): A federally mandated system of classifying residents into one of 44 payment categories.

Rule 702: A federal rule of evidence governing the admissibility of expert testimony.

RVS (Relative Value System): A procedure/service is assigned a value multiplied by cost factor.

S Corporation: A small business corporation with a statutorily limited number of shareholders that under certain conditions, has elected to have its taxable income, taxed to its shareholders at regular income tax rates. I.RC. § 1361 et. seg, Its major significance is the fact that S corporation status usually avoids the corporate income tax, and the shareholders can claim corporate losses. In terms of legal characteristics under state law, "S" Status Corporation is no different than any other regular corporation.

SART: Sexual Response Team.

Search Statement: A user-entered instruction that combines key terms and Boolean operators (which see) to retrieve a set of citations or records.

Search Strategy: The selection of an essential set of planned search statements.

Securing: The protection portion of a computer system which prevents access to sensitive material.

Self-Insured Companies: Companies or businesses that set aside a fund to cover potential business liability losses instead of insuring against such a loss through a separate insurance company.

Sick Building Syndrome: The term used to describe the cluster of symptoms found to occur in office environments, particularly in sealed buildings with centrally controlled mechanical ventilation.

Software: Computer program or sets of computer-readable messages/language that instruct a computer to perform specified tasks.

Sole Proprietorship: A form of business in which one person owns all the assets of the business in contrast to a partnership, trust, or corporation. The sole proprietor is solely liable for all the debts of the business.

Special Damages: Out-of-pocket expenses incurred by the plaintiff as a result of the negligence.

Standard of Care: The degree of care that a reasonably prudent person should exercise under the same or similar circumstances. In the case of a professional (e.g., nurse, doctor, lawyer), it is the degree of care that a reasonably prudent person in that profession should exercise under the same or similar circumstances.

Statute: A formal written enactment of a legislative body, whether federal, state, county, or city. A particular law enacted or established by the will of the legislative department of the government.

Statute of Limitations: Specific period of time between an occurrence and the filing of the lawsuit. In malpractice claims, this is usually when the party claiming injury first discovers or should have discovered the injury.

Statutory: Relating to a statute.

Stopword List: A list of terms that are ignored for online searching, such as articles and prepositions.

Strict Liability: Doctrine by which the one who sells any product in a defective condition deemed unsafe to the user or consumer or to property is subject to liability for physical harm or property damage; the plaintiff must prove the product was in a condition not contemplated by the ultimate consumer, which would make the product unreasonably dangerous.

Sub Rosa: A technique of investigation that uses videotape surveillance of a plaintiff or claimant; carried out by a private investigator for the defense.

Subcontract: An agreement between a party of the original contract and a third party.

Subcontractor: One who has entered into a contract, express or implied, for the performance of an act with the person who has already contracted for its performance. One who takes from the principal or prime contractor a specific part of the work undertaken by the principal contractor.

Subpoena: A command to appear at a certain time and place to give testimony upon a certain matter.

Subpoena Duces Tecum: A process by which the court commands a witness who has in his possession or control some document or paper that is pertinent to the issues of a pending controversy, to produce it at the trial.

Summary Judgment: The process by which a court decides, based on evidence presented by the defendant doctor, that there is no genuine issue of material fact for a jury to consider. Therefore, the court dismisses the case against the defendant as a matter of law and the case does not go to trial.

Summary Plan Description: An overview of the benefits elected by a plan member, detailing the expectations a member can expect covered by the plan. It is an overview of the benefits elected by a plan member, detailing what the member can expect to be covered by the plan, and possibly what is not covered. The structure and wording of SPDs are stipulated in ERISA.

Summons and Complaint (or Petition): A document that sets forth allegations against the defendant(s) that the plaintiff intends to prove. The document is formal notification and initiates the legal action against the facility. The method of instituting a legal proceeding and notification of such action to all concerned parties is regulated by the individual.

Tax: A charge by the government on the income of an individual, corporation, or trust, as well as the value of an estate or gift. The objective in assessing the tax is to generate revenue to be used for the needs of the public.

Technical Nurse Consultant: A nurse who has advanced skills and expertise in the use of computerized presentations for legal proceedings.

Telecommunications: Transmission of voice or data by means of telephone networks or carriers.

Telephonic Case Management: Coordination of services provided through telephone contact only.

Terminal: An electronic device for transmitting to and receiving signals from a computer.

Testifying Expert: An expert who is capable of rendering an opinion as a potential trial witness.

Testimony: Spoken or written evidence by a competent witness under oath.

Text Word: A single word that appears in the title or abstract of a citation, which may be used as a search tool rather than, or in addition to, the subject terms (such as MeSH terms) assigned by an indexer. Also, see Free Text.

Theory: A conceptualization of an aspect of reality for the purpose of describing phenomena, concepts that are interrelated in a coherent whole for some purpose.

Theory Development: The process or integrated approach by which theory is developed including the evolution of an idea, the concept analysis, the proposal of a framework and theoretical definition, substantiation through research, and critique of the theory.

Third-Party Administrator: A person or company hired to oversee and resolve claims and actions. Third-party administrators, known as TPAs, are often utilized by large self-insured companies such as a health maintenance organization or large health care conglomerates to handle claims against the company.

Third-Party Counterclaim: A separate cause of action that a defendant asserts against a third person or party.

TIF: Acronym for tagged image file format, one of the most widely supported file formats for storing bit-mapped images on personal computers. TIFF graphics can be any resolution, and they can be black and white, gray-scaled, or color.

Time Management: A method of efficiently using energy, space, and time to enhance task completion.

Tort: A civil wrong or injury other than breach of contract.

Total Quality Management: Process used to improve the ability to satisfy the customer; expectations; based on belief that quality is a positive strategy for growth and integrated into the business plan.

Toxic Tort: A civil wrong arising from exposure to a toxic substance, such as asbestos, radiation, or hazardous waste. A toxic tort can be remedied by a civil lawsuit (usually a class action) or by administrative action.

Tracking: Following and monitoring the awareness of a direction or idea.

Trending: Maintaining a consistent way or direction.

Trial Consultant: A consultant employed or hired to assist with trial preparation, typically through the preparation of witnesses and parties for testifying at trial. Trial consultants may also assist in jury selection, through the creation of a profile of desirable jurors. Trial consultants often have background education in psychology and/or communication.

Trier of Fact: Judge, arbitrator, or juror.

Truncation: A means of retrieving words that share a common root or stem.

Trustee: A person or an institution that manages the assets for the benefit of someone else, perhaps the conservatee.

U & C (Usual and Customary): A fee defined as the charge for health care that is consistent with the average rate or charge for identical or similar services in a certain geographical area.

UB-92 (Universal Bill 1992): The form used by hospital-based providers to bill for services.

Unbundling: Breaking a single service into its multiple components to increase total billing charges.

Underwriting: The analysis done for accepting insurance risk and determining the amount of insurance the company will write on each risk.

Upcoding: The process of assigning a code that represents a more complex or involved service than actually provided and thus receives a higher reimbursement.

Update Service: A periodic online search of a previously selected topic. The search strategy is stored and activated periodically (i.e., monthly or quarterly) to provide new citations. Also known as "Selective Dissemination of Information" or "SDI."

URC: Usual, customary, and reasonable. A method for determining benefits by comparing the charges of one provider to like charges of others in the same area and specialty.

Utilitarianism: The ethical view that the right action is that which promotes a greater balance of good over harm for everyone concerned in a situation.

Utilization Management: A method employed by the insurance and managed care industry to track and manage the use of medical benefits by covered beneficiaries. It is a formal assessment of medical necessity, efficiency, appropriateness of health care services, and treatment plans. This assessment can occur prior to, during, and after delivery of services.

Utilization Review: A process of evaluation of health care based on medical necessity and appropriateness. Utilization Review can include preadmission review, concurrent review, discharge planning, and retrospective review.

Vendor: A service company that stores databases electronically and makes them available, via telecommunications, to clients for a fee.

Venture Capital: Funding for new companies or others embarking on new or turnaround ventures that entails some investment risk but offers the potential for above-average profits. Venture capital is often provided by firms that specialize in financing new ventures with capital supplied by investors interested in speculative or high-risk investments.

Veracity: The principle of telling the truth without deception.

Vicarious Liability: Vicarious liability occurs when the law, in certain limited instances, imposes liability on a principal for the acts or omissions of an agent.

Vision Statement: Articulation of a view of a realistic, credible, attractive future for the organization.

Voir Dire: The questioning of prospective jurors by a judge and attorneys in court.

Warranty: An assurance by the manufacturer that the product is merchantable or fit for the purpose for which it was sold.

WAV: The format for storing sound in files developed jointly by Microsoft and IBM. Support for WAV files was built into Windows 95 making it the de facto standard for sound on PCs.

Welfare Plans: Benefit plans that include insurance or health care coverage, long- and short-term disability coverage, and life insurance benefits.

Word: When capitalized, short for Microsoft Word — a word-processing software.

Worker's Compensation: A Federal and State mandated insurance program that provides medical care and wage loss replacement for workers injured on the job.

World Wide Web (WWW): A collection of hypermedia documents that reside on computers (Web servers) located all over the Internet that is linked together in a "worldwide web" of information. A Web browser (such as Mosaic or Lynx) is needed to gain access to the World Wide Web.

Wrongful Death: Type of legal theory argued on behalf of a deceased person's beneficiaries that alleges that death was attributable to the willful or negligent act of another.

Wrongful Life: Refers to a type of medical malpractice claim brought on behalf of a child, alleging that the child would not have been born but for negligent advice to, or treatment of, the parents.

Index

A

AALNC, *See* American Association of Legal Nurse Consultants

Abuse
  child
    legal nurse consultant's role in, 248–249, 470
    sample, 248–249
  elder, 303–304, 470–471

Accident insurance, 600–601

Accident reconstructionist, 358–359, 373, 388

Accountability
  description of, 15, 228, 232
  ethics and, 1062–1063
  standards of practice as basis for, 184

Acquired immunodeficiency syndrome
  medical record information regarding, 43
  reporting requirements by state, 44

Active listening, 557–558

Acute care facility, 643–644

Adjuster, 606–607

Administrative law, 5–6

Admissibility
  demonstrative evidence, 945–949
  expert witness testimony, 425
  foundation requirements for, 53–54
  records, 956
  scientific evidence, 463–464

Admission of facts, request for, 25, 65, 73

Adult protective services, 470

Advance directives
  do-not-resuscitate order
    definition of, 113
    description of, 107
    guidelines for, 113
    health care provider's immunity for acting on, 114–115, 117–118
    out-of-hospital, 113–114

state statutes regarding, 113–115
    witness present during signing of, 115
    wrongful death actions, 133
  durable health care powers of attorney, 120–122
  falsification of, 118–119
  living wills
    definition of, 115
    state statutes, 115–120
    terminal condition provision, 116, 118
  patient transfer, 116–117
  physician refusal to honor, 116
  violations of, 118–119

Adverse drug reactions, 418, 422–423

Adverse effects
  clinical trials of pharmaceuticals to detect, 413–414
  reporting of, 415–416

Adverse witness, cross-examination of, 51

Advertising
  ethical, 1064–1066
  expert witness, 826, 896–897

Advocacy theory, 241–242, 252

Affirmative defenses, 347

Agency for Healthcare Policy and Research, 300

AHIMA, *See* American Health Information Management Association

Air pollution, 501

Airbags, 382–383

ALNCCB, *See* American Legal Nurse Consultant Certification Board

Alternative dispute resolution
  arbitration
    binding, 919
    definition of, 918
    demonstrative evidence presented at, 950
    mandatory, 919
    nonbinding, 920
    process of, 920–921